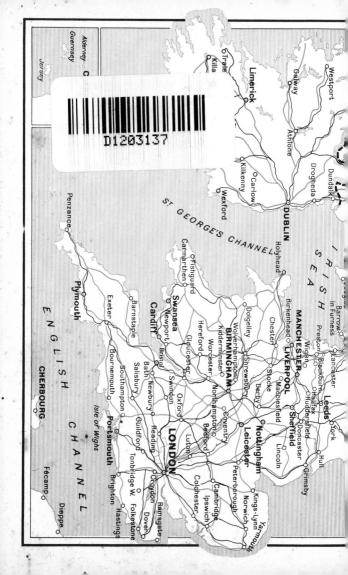

GREAT BRITAIN

NAGEL'S

ENCYCLOPEDIA - GUIDE

Awards
Rome, 1958   Paris, 1961   Vienna, 1968

GREAT BRITAIN

1296 pages
108 pages of plans in black and white
18 pages of plans in colour
1 map of the British Isles
Third edition, revised and corrected

NAGEL PUBLISHERS
GENEVA · PARIS · MUNICH

ISBN 2-8263-0760-6

HOW TO USE THIS GUIDE

In this Guide the whole of Britain has been divided into a number of **routes**, each carefully designed to cover an itinerary or region of particular interest. The main routes generally follow the shortest or easiest way between two points, but where a route offering greater pleasure of scene or interest of place is available without adding greatly to the distance this route has been selected. The alternative routes suggested often lead by minor roads to little known but interesting and beautiful places off the main route: they will frequently offer return routes after an excursion on one of the main routes.

For each town or village the Guide gives first the practical details which are of importance to the passing traveller — the mileage from the starting point, the population and the early closing day (E.C.) on which shops will be closed in the afternoon. The rest of the material given in the body of the Guide is of descriptive, historical or general sightseeing interest. All other information (e.g. about hotels and restaurants) is given in the section of PRACTICAL INFORMATION at the end of the volume.

To find the best route between two towns, look for the two towns on the index map. If you want to reach some small place not shown on the map, look it up in the Index, which will refer you to the appropriate route.

To plan a tour in any particular part of the country you should begin by consulting the introduction to the section of the Guide dealing with the region which interests you and then make a selection from the routes suggested.

PUBLISHER'S NOTE

Here, in one volume, is a guide to three countries — England, Wales and Scotland — containing detailed information on the towns, villages and places of scenic and historic interest in Britain. The object of the Guide is to meet the needs of all visitors to Britain, whether travelling by car or by public transport, whether cyclists or walkers: it seeks to be of service not only to holiday-makers and sightseers but also to students, sportsmen, businessmen or others with specialised interests. Accordingly this single volume brings together in convenient form and compass a wide range of information, making it not only a traveller's guide but a compact encyclopedia of Britain.

Relations between Britain and the Continent have always been close, and across the narrow stretch of water between Calais and Dover the mainstream of European culture has never ceased to flow. Thus Britain is, historically and culturally, an integral part of Europe: but at the same time it displays points of contrast and distinction that are constantly fascinating to the visitor. We have sought in this Guide to bring out these distinctive characteristics.

Following the usual plan of Nagel's Encyclopedia-Guides, the first section contains articles on the history, geography, economy and arts of Britain. The section of *Practical Information* at the end of the Guide deals with the practical details of travel and everyday life.

Mr *G.F. Lucas* compiled the considerable mass of material on which this volume is based, and Mr *Theo Lang*, author of many books on Britain, was responsible for editing the final version. The maps and plans were drawn by our own cartographic service. *The British Travel Association* and its local offices also provided much valuable material. To all who have contributed to the preparation of this Guide we should like to express our gratitude.

The Nagel Guides contain no advertising matter and can therefore be relied on to provide information which is completely objective and unbiassed.

NOTE TO THIRD EDITION

In this new edition Great Britain has been separated from Ireland, which is now dealt with in a separate Guide. The descriptive material has been carefully revised and updated to take account of changes within the last few years: the Practical Information has been brought up to date: and new plans have been included and older ones revised.

We are grateful to Mr *Lickorish*, Director of the British Travel Association, and his colleagues Mr *French-Hodges* and Mr *Barnes* for the ready helpfulness with which they have put their knowledge and experience at our disposal.

CONTENTS

How to use this Guide 5
Publisher's note 6

General Introduction

Geography 19
History 27
Government and administration 47
Population and economy 53
Literature and the arts 75
Museums 97
Art galleries 103
Castles, country houses and gardens 109

Description and Itineraries

I: LONDON

History 123
Aspects of London 129
    I. Royal and official London 138
    II. The West End 154
    III. The City 175
    IV. The South Bank 199
    V. Museums and galleries 203
    VI. The Port of London 228
    VII. Greater London 233

II: SOUTH-EASTERN ENGLAND

1. London to Dover via Canterbury 244
2. London to Maidstone and Folkestone 279
3. Folkestone to Hastings 285
4. London to Tunbridge Wells and Hastings 292
5. London to Eastbourne 305
6. London to Brighton 312

7. London to Worthing and Shoreham 319
8. London to Bognor Regis 324
9. London to Chichester and Portsmouth 328
10. London to Winchester and Southampton 341
The Isle of Wight 355
The Channel Islands 362

III: SOUTH-WEST ENGLAND

11. London to Salisbury and Bournemouth 373
12. Salisbury to Dorchester and Weymouth 390
13. Salisbury to Exeter 400
14. Exeter to Plymouth by the coast road 417
15. Exeter to Plymouth by the inland road 422
16. Exeter to Penzance 431
17. Exeter to Ilfracombe and Exmoor 444
18. Exeter to Dunster 450
19. The north Cornish coast: Barnstaple to Newquay 452
20. Exeter to Taunton 460
21. Taunton to Wells and Bristol 465
22. London to Bristol 477
23. Bristol to Bath and Salisbury 506

IV: EAST ANGLIA, CAMBRIDGESHIRE AND LINCOLNSHIRE

24. London to Southend 517
25. London to Great Yarmouth 521
26. The Norfolk coast from Great Yarmouth to King's Lynn 535
27. London to Cambridge, Ely and King's Lynn 541
28. London to Norwich 560
29. London to Lincoln 577
30. The Lincolnshire coast (via Boston and Skegness) 593

V: THE MIDLANDS

31. London Northampton 598
32. London to Leicester and Nottingham 604
33. Derbyshire and the Peak.................... 628
34. London to Shrewsbury 644
35. London to Birmingham 655
36. London to Oxford 674
37. Oxford to Birmingham via Stratford-upon-Avon 691
38. Oxford to Worcester 699
39. Oxford to Gloucester 710
40. The Welsh border, the Wye valley and the Forest of
    Dean 720
41. Gloucester to Reading (Cirencester) 732

VI: THE NORTH OF ENGLAND

42. The Great North Road to Scotland 738
43. York and the Yorkshire coast 765
44. Scarborough to Thirsk 783
45. The Yorkshire Dales 786
46. Manchester, Leeds and Sheffield 794
47. Liverpool and Chester 807
48. Manchester to Blackpool 823
49. The West Coast route to Scotland 827
50. The Lake District 835
The Isle of Man 845

VII: WALES

51. The South Wales coast (Chepstow to Carmarthen) ... 851
52. Monmouth to Fishguard 863
53. Worcester to Aberystwyth and Cardigan 871
54. Shrewsbury to Barmouth 876
55. Shrewsbury to Holyhead 879
56. Bangor to Barmouth via Caernarvon 885
57. The North Wales coast (Chester to Bangor) 891

VIII: THE LOWLANDS OF SCOTLAND AND THE BORDERS

58. Edinburgh 901
59. The Borders 930
60. Edinburgh to Stirling 943
61. Fife 949
62. Glasgow 957
63. Dumfries and Galloway and the Burns country 964
64. The Ayrshire coast and the Isle of Arran 972

IX: THE HIGHLANDS

65. Glasgow to Oban 983
66. The Hebrides 989
67. The Trossachs 996
68. Perth to Aberdeen 999
69. Pertht o Inverness 1015
70. Inverness to Aberdeen 1021
71. The Great Glen, the north-western Highlands and Glencoe 1027
72. The far north 1033
73. Orkney and Shetland 1043

Practical Information 1049

Welsh and Gaelic Glossaries 1114

Hotels 1119

Index 1257

MAPS AND PLANS

In Colour

Outline map	Front endpapers
General map	At end of Guide
Central London	Sheets II-V
Central Liverpool	VI and VII
Central Manchester	VIII and IX
Central Birmingham	X and XI
Glasgow	XII and XIII
Edinburgh	XIV and XV

In Black and White

London

Westminster	142-143
Westminster Abbey	145
Mayfair, Soho, Bloomsbury and Marylebone	156-157
Hyde Park and Kensington	168-169
Holborn and Fleet Street	177
St Paul's Cathedral	183
City of London	188-189
Tower of London	193

Rest of country

Aberdeen	1011
Aberystwyth	874
Ayr	978
Bath	509
Beverley	775
Bournemouth	389
Brighton	317
Bristol	497
Bristol Cathedral	501
Caernarvon Castle	886
Cambridge	543

Canterbury	259
Canterbury Cathedral	263
Cardiff	855
Carlisle	833
Chester	815
Chester Cathedral	819
Chichester	333
Colchester	525
Conwy	895
Coventry	663
Derby	629
Dover	277
Dryburgh Abbey	936
Dumfries	965
Dundee	1005
Dunfermline	951
Durham	753
Durham Cathedral	751
Edinburgh (St Giles)	909
Edinburgh (Centre)	914-915
Ely	555
Ely Cathedral	557
Exeter	407
Exeter Cathedral	409
Folkestone	283
Glasgow Cathedral	960
Gloucester	715
Gloucester Cathedral	713
Guernsey	365
Hereford	725
Hereford Cathedral	724
Holyhead	884
Hull	777
Inverness	1019
Jedburgh Abbey	940

Jersey	367
Kilmarnock	973
Leeds	801
Leicester	617
Lichfield Cathedral	647
Lincoln	583
Lincoln Cathedral	587
Liverpool Cathedral	811
Melrose Abbey	937
Monmouth	729
Newcastle-upon-Tyne	757
Newport	852
Northampton	599
Norwich	569
Norwich Cathedral	571
Nottingham	623
Oxford	683
Perth	1001
Peterborough Cathedral	591
Plymouth	427
Portsmouth	339
Ripon	790
Ripon Cathedral	791
Rochester	247
Rochester Cathedral	251
Salisbury	379
Salisbury Cathedral	381
Sheffield	805
Shrewsbury	653
Southampton	351
St Albans	606
St Albans Cathedral	609
St Andrews	955
Stirling	945
Stratford-upon-Avon	695

Swansea 859
Truro Cathedral 437
Wells 470
Wells Cathedral 472
Winchester 343
Winchester Cathedral 345
Windsor Castle 479
Worcester Cathedral 703
York 767
York Minster 769

General
Introduction

GEOGRAPHY

This Guide is concerned with the island of **Great Britain,** consisting of *England*, *Scotland* and *Wales*, with a total area of 89,000 sq. miles. Together with *Northern Ireland*, it forms the **United Kingdom** (area 94,000 sq. miles). With the whole of Ireland (Northern Ireland and the independent *Republic of Ireland*) it makes up the **British Isles** (area 121,000 sq. miles).

For Northern Ireland and the Irish Republic, see the Nagel Encyclopedia-Guide IRELAND.

By continental standards the British Isles are of small area. Look at them on the map of the world and they seem only a tiny group in the north-western corner of Europe. But in that modest space exists nearly type of landscape the world can offer — indeed practically every kind except glaciers and deserts. And to the beauty and variety of the scenery is added the advantage of easy access; a day's journey will take the visitor from the delightful wooded valleys of central England to the rugged mountains of Wales, from the quiet level countryside of East Anglia to the impressive cliffs of the north-east coast.

From the industrial towns of the Midlands there is easy access to the hills of the Welsh border and to the undulating country stretching across to the flatter scenery of East Anglia. Nearer London are pastoral Essex, the leafy corners of Hertfordshire, the beech-clad Chiltern Hills, the Thames valley and, southwards, the chalk hills of the North Downs, the wooded ridges of the Weald and the softly swelling South Downs.

In the north of England (the Lake District), in Scotland and in North Wales (the Snowdon region) the country is mountainous. In the east England is largely low-lying, and in parts, particularly where there are bulb-fields and wind-mills, strongly reminiscent of the Netherlands. In the south-west of England, and in the Scilly and Channel Islands, are the flowers and palm trees that denote a warm climate and a fertile soil. In the far north of Scotland, and in the islands of the Hebrides, the scenery has a bleak and rugged grandeur which has a very different, though equally strong, appeal.

The villages are the jewels of the British countryside, and the tourist who goes in search of them can be assured of reaching the true heart of the country. Each county has at least two or three villages which claim to be the prettiest in the kingdom. It is a safe claim, for who could decide finally between the mellow brick and tile of the south-east, the thatched roofs of East Anglia and the western counties, the black-and-white half-timber of the Midlands, the exquisite stone villages of hilly districts such as the Cotswolds and the Yorkshire Dales, or the remote villages set amid idyllic surroundings in the Highlands of Scotland?

Cities like York, Chester and Shrewsbury proclaim their ancient origin with the half-timbered frontages of mediaeval and Tudor days. For the classical architecture of the 18th century one should go, above all, to the spas, for it was in that highly civilised era that most of them established their fame, and to wander in the terraced streets of Bath, Cheltenham or Leamington, to name three examples, is to be transported back to the serenity of the Augustan age. Edinburgh too is rich in streets of this period.

The Coasts

The length of Great Britain from north to south is 600 miles, but its coast-line is so indented that it is nowhere possible to be more than 80 or 90 miles from the sea. This maximum is attained in the heart of the English Midlands: but for the greater part of the country the limit is 40 or 50 miles. Consequently, for the vast majority of British holidaymakers, a visit to the seaside inevitably forms part of the annual summer routine.

The character of Britain's long coastline varies as strikingly as does that of the inland countryside. To most visitors from the Continent its best-known feature is, of course, the rampart of white chalk cliffs which gleams a welcome to the cross-Channel steamers approaching Dover or Folkestone, but this is surpassed in magnificence by the cliffs of Beachy Head in Sussex, which rise nearly 600 feet sheer from the water's edge, and provide an impressive introduction to Britain for travellers on the Dieppe-Newhaven route.

The western coasts of Britain are notable for their magnificent fjords where the Atlantic has bitten deep into the mountains and glaciers in ancient times and carved out deep and noble valleys. In the south are the cliffs of Cornwall and, on the opposite side of the Bristol Channel, those of Pembrokeshire. In North Wales the mountains of Snowdonia rise almost out of the sea. In the north-west of Scotland the coast is seen at its most rugged, broken by innumerable islands and inlets of the sea.

On the eastern seaboard of Britain there are fewer cliffs and the formation of the land has encouraged the growth of seaside resorts to a greater extent than on the west coast. There are, however, long stretches of coastal scenery, particularly in Yorkshire and Berwickshire, which rival Cornwall in grandeur.

Southern England

To travellers accustomed to the impressive distances and the vast plains and forests of the Continent, the scale of the British countryside appears astonishingly small and compact. The fields are bounded by neat green hedges: the roads and lanes twist and turn over miniature hills and descend into valleys watered by streams which appear to be no more than silver ribbons. It is a charming and friendly landscape, in which everything — woods, bridges, villages, and even railway trains — fits into place and seeks to avoid dominating its neighbours.

North-west of London are the gracious, beech-clad Chilterns Farther west are the bare windswept Cotswolds of Oxfordshire and Gloucestershire, where can be found the most enchanting stone villages in Britain. Still farther west are the western counties of Devonshire and Cornwall, where there is hardly a square mile of level ground, and where lovely coasts are beaded with fascinating fishing villages.

Northern England

In the mountainous regions north and west of a line drawn from Scarborough on the Yorkshire coast to Gloucester at the head of the Severn estuary we find a very different country. Here there are vast tracts still untamed by man's husbandry. In the north-west is England's mountain country — the lovely and famed *Lake District*. Counting only the larger lakes, there are more than a dozen, each reflecting in its waters the graceful peaks of surrounding mountains; and there is some magic in the Lakeland air which makes it impossible to believe that these almost alpine-looking giants are only a few thousand feet high, and can be climbed quite easily between lunch and supper.

A favourite topic for discussion among visitors to the Lake District concerns the respective merits of the various lakes. Each exercises its own distinctive appeal. Windermere is the largest and, with its steam-yachts, perhaps the most civilised: Grasmere is associated closely with the poet Wordsworth, whose simple cottage almost on its banks is one of the most visited of Britain's literary shrines: and Derwentwater and Ullswater inevitably figure prominently in everybody's list. Wastwater is the wildest, deepest and most remote of the lakes.

The Lake District, for which the chief touring centres are Keswick, Ambleside and Kendal, might be regarded as the western extension of the long range of hills which stretches down the centre of England as far south as Derby. This is the Pennine Range — aptly described as the backbone of England — the steep-sided valleys and clean-cut hills of which are invaded at weekends by thousands of people from the great industrial towns of Lancashire and Yorkshire which lie on either side.

Some of the finest scenery is to be found in the extreme south of the range, in the *Peak District* of Derbyshire, of which the principal resort is the well-known spa of Buxton.

Scotland

Britain's main mountain mass is concentrated in the extreme north of the islands. In the *Highlands* of Scotland are found not only the highest mountains (Ben Nevis, 4418 ft) and the largest lakes (in Scotland, lochs), but also country as wild and untamed as any in Europe. One can travel for miles without coming across any sign of modern civilisation nor, indeed of any human habitation, save, at wide intervals, the cottages of the crofters and an occasional fishing inn, situated beside the waters of a mountain loch. There is no suggestion of the pretty pastoral landscapes of the south in the stark and sombre magnificence of the Highland scene.

And yet, for all their apparent remoteness, the Highlands are surprisingly accessible, and their hotels extend a warm and friendly welcome. Within an hour of leaving the crowded streets of Glasgow, one can be driving along the banks of Loch Lomond, the largest and possibly the most beautiful loch in the country, at the head of which one is in the heart of the

Highlands, the home of the red grouse, the wild deer and the golden eagle.

Linked by the road along Glenmore, the Great Glen, a remarkable chain of lochs extending from the North Sea to the Atlantic Ocean, are the two chief tourist centres of the district; Inverness, the capital of the Highlands, and Fort William, a cheerful place at the foot of Ben Nevis, the highest mountain in Britain.

The Highlands are bounded on the south by the plains of central Scotland, extending between the wide estuaries of the River Clyde on the west coast and the Forth and Tay on the east. This is a rich industrial area, and in it are to be found some of the most famous places in Scotland. Each of the three rivers has led to the growth of an important city — Edinburgh on the Forth, Glasgow on the Clyde and Dundee on the Tay.

South of Glasgow and Edinburgh the hills rise up again to form the *Southern Uplands*. Except in the south-west, however, this countryside has little of the rugged grandeur of the Highlands: its attraction lies in its sweeping vistas, its well-wooded river valleys, its domestic and ecclesiastical architecture, and its wealth of historical and literary memories.

Wales

West of England lies the principality of Wales, a land famous for its mountains, its lakes, its castles and its singing. The topmost peak of all, and the most shapely, is Snowdon, which boasts the only mountain railway in Britain. Among the most popular places from which to explore Snowdonia are Caernarvon, and Llanrwst and Betws-y-Coed, both beautifully situated in the valley of the river Conwy.

The borderland of England and Wales — rich, undulating farming country — is graced by the valleys of two important rivers — the Severn, which is the longest river in the country, exceeding the Thames by a few miles: and the Wye, which many regard as the loveliest. The lower reaches of the Wye are bordered by the Forest of Dean, one of Britain's ancient forests.

The Islands

This brief geographical survey may well end with a mention of the smaller islands — or rather of some of them, for they are too numerous even to catalogue.

The most southerly are the *Channel Islands*, nearer to France than to the mainland of Britain, and popular with holiday-makers from both countries.

The *Isle of Man*, situated in the exact centre of the Irish Sea, is a beautiful island, the home of ancient culture, and accommodates thousands of holiday-makers every summer.

Off the west coast of Scotland are the romantic *Hebrides* or Western Isles, of which the largest is Skye, dominated by the fantastic skyline of the Cuillin Hills, one of the most dramatic mountain ranges in Europe. In the far north are the *Orkneys* and the remote *Shetlands*, the latter famous for its breed of miniature ponies and for its hand-woven textiles.

Two of the most picturesque of Britain's islands are Holy Island off the coast of Northumberland, on which are the ruins of an ancient priory, and Iona, an islet at the western tip of the Scottish island of Mull, sacred to the memory of St Columba, who conducted from here his mission in Scotland.

There are countless other islands which provide a home only for sea-birds, and are seldom, if ever, visited by man.

Climate

The climate of Great Britain is of typically maritime character, reflecting its geographical situation. The range of temperature during the year is relatively small (from 10° to 15 °C), the rainfall fairly high, the weather often changeable. London has a mean temperature of 3.7° C in winter, 17° in July. The winter is generally mild, with little frost and only occasional snow: the summer tends to be cool, with really hot weather occurring rarely.

The most notable feature of the British climate, however, is its humidity. Rain falls throughout the year, brought by the west winds from the Atlantic: the rivers never dry up as in the Mediterranean countries. Mist and fog are frequent, although the famous London "pea soup" is less of a menace than it used to be, when the smoke from factories mingled with fog to produce the dreaded smog. The anti-pollution measures of recent years have much reduced the danger of smog.

A contrast can be observed between the western part of the country, exposed to the full force of the humid west winds, and the more sheltered plains in the east. The Highlands of Scotland receive more than 2000 mm of water a year, some of it in the form of snow. The acid soils of this region are covered with a moorland of heather and peat bogs: trees are found only in the more sheltered places where they can escape the buffeting of the winds. The plains in the east, on the other hand, with a rainfall of some 7500 mm, are cereal-growing country (wheat, particularly in East Anglia), where woodland (deciduous trees) can also flourish.

HISTORY

Roman Britain

The recorded history of Britain begins with the arrival of the Romans in the 1st century B.C.

When the Romans came to Britain the southern part of the country was occupied by the Britons, Celtic tribes related to the tribes of Gaul. In the west and in Ireland were the *Hibernians*, whom the Celts had driven back to these remoter areas.

The first Roman invasions, by *Julius Caesar* in 55 and 54 B.C., were unsuccessful, but in 47 A.D. *Aulus Plautius* conquered southern Britain, and for 400 years the country was under Roman rule. Numerous remains dating from this period are still to be seen.

According to legend Christianity was brought to England by Joseph of Arimathea, who built a church at Glastonbury. In 284 a soldier of the Roman garrison at Verulamium, *Alban*, became the first Christian to suffer martyrdom in Britain.

With the conversion of the Emperor Constantine to Christianity in 313, Roman rule in Britain began to decline, and it ceased altogether in the year 410, when the Roman legions were withdrawn to defend Rome against the Goths.

Saxon and Norman Invasions

As the Roman power waned Gaels from Ireland came to aid the Britons and Picts. One expedition was led by Niall of the Nine Hostages, who is reputed to have established Tara, central kingdom of Ireland. Then, taking advantage of Britain's undefended state, two Saxon chiefs from Jutland, *Hengist* and *Horsa*, landed at Ebbsfleet, near Ramsgate, in 449.

For the next 350 years England was a confusion of small kingdoms, some Christian and some pagan, at war with each other, but during this period — in 597 — St Augustine, agent of Pope Gregory, came to the island and spread Christianity from his monastery at Canterbury: and at Jarrow a school was founded by the *Venerable Bede*, the first English historian.

The first Danish invasions came towards the end of the 8th century. In 802 King Egbert, King of Wessex, became the first king of all England, although the invading Danes had established themselves in many parts of his kingdom. Indeed, the struggle against the Danes was to last for the next two hundred years.

The year 1013 saw the final defeat of the English, and Sweyn, first of the Danish kings of England, assumed the throne. In 1042 the Danes recalled a Saxon king, *Edward the Confessor*, who founded Westminster Abbey.

In 1066 William Duke of Normandy, crossed the Channel, and defeated Harold, Edward's successor, at the battle of Hastings — one of the great landmarks in English history. William the Conqueror was not only a courageous military leader but an excellent organiser. Before dividing up the country into baronial estates he took the precaution of having himself crowned both in Westminster Abbey and at Winchester, the ancient capital of England.

During the reigns of *William II* (1087-1100) and *Henry I* (1100-35) the barons became increasingly ambitious and hostile to the Crown. Henry left no heir, his son William having died in the shipwreck of the "White Ship" off Normandy.

The Plantagenets

Stephen, son of Matilda, William the Conqueror's daughter, was chosen as king by the people of London, but not by the barons and great dignitaries of the kingdom, and his succession was disputed by his cousin Matilda, herself a grand-daughter of William the Conqueror and wife of Geoffrey Plantagenet.

Although Matilda was unsuccessful in her bid for the throne, her son, owing to the fact that Stephen left no heir, became Henry II, first Plantagenet king of England (1154-89). By his marriage at the age of nineteen to Eleanor of Aquitaine, Henry added to his Norman and Anjou territories those of Aquitaine, Poitou, Limousin and Gascony. He ruled more than half of France as well as the whole of England, and Pope Adrian IV sanctioned his plan for the conquest of Ireland. The Anglo-Norman conquest of Ireland began in 1169, and in 1172 Henry II visited Ireland and established his overlordship.

In 1170, while holding court near Bayeux, Henry gave vent to his hatred of Thomas Becket, Archbishop of Canterbury; whereupon four knights, hoping to win favour with the king, crossed over into England and murdered Becket in the north-west transept of Canterbury Cathedral on the night of 29 December 1170.

Henry II's successor, *Richard I* (1189-99), known as the Lion-hearted, passes picturesquely, if rapidly, across the scene as a gallant knight who fought ineffectively in a series of expensive crusades against Saladin in the Holy Land.

King John (1199-1216), Richard's youngest brother, succeeded to the throne by murdering his nephew Arthur, Duke of Brittany. John has an almost undisputed claim to be the wickedest man ever to have sat upon the throne of England. His insolence, lust, cruelty and cynicism led to his excommunication and to the loss of all England's possessions in France. Finally at Runnymede, near Windsor, on 15 June 1215 the barons forced him to put his seal to the Great Charter, or Magna Carta, which defined the freedom and justice which should henceforth be an Englishman's by right. The barons later enlisted the help of France and made war on King John, who died at Newark, possibly from poisoning, during this campaign.

His son, *Henry III* (1216-72), made unsuccessful attempts to regain English territory in France. His lavish expenditure led to the Barons' War (1258-65), in which the barons were led by Simon de Montfort, a great soldier and a capable administrator. The king was forced to agree to the Provisions of Oxford, which called for the establishment of a Parliament composed of earls, barons and bishops; but de Montfort was killed at the battle of Evesham by Henry's son, who became *Edward I* (1272-1307).

The new king subjugated Wales and Scotland, and had his son Edward proclaimed the first Prince of Wales in Caernarvon Castle, one of the strongholds he had built in Wales. Edward Prince of Wales succeeded to the throne as *Edward II* (1307-27) and married Isabella of France. During his reign Scotland was reorganised under *Robert Bruce*, who defeated the English army at Bannockburn in 1314. Edward was deposed by the barons, led by Queen Isabella, and replaced by his son, *Edward III* (1327-77).

Edward III launched a series of campaigns against France, which developed into what was known later as the Hundred Years' War (1337-1453). The two most famous battles of Edward's reign were Crécy in 1345 and Poitiers in 1356.

The *Black Prince*, hero of Poitiers, died before his father, and the crown passed to Edward's grandson, *Richard II* (1379-99).

Richard was kind, timid and artistic, but the death in 1394 of his first wife, Anne of Bohemia, changed his character, and he became tyrannical, cruel and revengeful. Henry Bolingbroke,

Duke of Lancaster, son of John of Gaunt, led a revolt of the
barons and seized the king. Richard was never heard of again:
it is believed that he was starved to death in Pontefract Castle.
Henry Bolingbroke, as grandson of Edward III, assumed the
throne and became *Henry IV* (1399-1414), the first Lancastrian
king.

His son *Henry V* (1413-22) resumed the war against France
and landed at Harfleur in 1415. Like his predecessors, he fought
a brilliant rearguard action, but the only result of his victory at
Agincourt was to facilitate his retreat. He returned two years
later and was more successful, France then being involved in
civil war. The Burgundians recognised Henry as heir to the
French throne, and he married Katharine, eldest daughter of
the mad French king Charles VI, by whom he had a son, Henry.

Wars of the Roses

Henry VI (1422-61) was England's most unfortunate king.
He was only a baby when he came to the throne, and was
crowned in Paris at the age of ten. By the year 1451 the English,
having suffered heavy defeats at the hands of Joan of Arc and
a reunited France, had lost all their French possessions except
Calais. Two years later the Hundred Years' War came to an
end. But in 1455 began in England the civil war known as the
Wars of the Roses, which lasted for thirty years. This prolonged
and bloodthirsty struggle for the crown was a fight between
the descendants of Edward III's third son John of Gaunt, Duke
of Lancaster, whose device was a red rose, and the descendants
of Edward III's fourth son Edmund Langley, Duke of York,
whose device was a white rose.

The Lancastrians were defeated at Towton in 1461 by Henry
VI's third cousin, Edward, Duke of York, who thereupon
became *Edward IV* (1461-83). Henry was imprisoned in the
Tower of London, but his valiant wife, Margaret of Anjou,
made two attempts to regain the throne with French help. The
second attempt ended at the battle of Tewkesbury, when Margaret's son was killed in cold blood by the young Duke of
York. In the same month Henry was found dead in the Tower
of London, murdered by his cousin the Duke of Gloucester,
the future Richard III.

Edward left two sons; *Edward V* (1483), aged thirteen, and
Richard, aged eleven. Their uncle, Richard, Duke of Gloucester,
put the two princes in the Tower of London and had himself
crowned in Westminster Abbey as Richard III (1483-85). The

princes were never heard of again: but two centuries later the skeletons of two youths were found under a stone step in a staircase of the tower.

The Tudors

Richard III's crimes earned him such hatred that any contender for the throne was sure of public support: already making his plans was such a contender — *Henry Tudor*, grandson of Katharine of France, mother of Henry VI, who as a widow had married her Welsh servant, Owen Tudor. In 1485, Henry marched against Richard, whom he met at Bosworth, near Leicester. Richard was killed and Henry crowned himself on the field of battle as *Henry VII* (1485-1509). Thus the Wars of the Roses ended in the victory of a third party and the foundation of the Tudor dynasty.

Henry summoned Parliament only twice during his reign, drawing his revenues from fines imposed by the Star Chamber. In order to consolidate his position within England he married Elizabeth of York, daughter of [Edward IV: and to secure his northern frontier he married his daughter Margaret to James IV of Scotland, who was killed at the battle of Flodden in 1513 while invading England. For the sake of improving relations with Spain he married his son Arthur to Catherine of Aragon.

Arthur predeceased his father, and his brother Henry inherited both the throne and his brother's widow. As *Henry VIII* (1509-47) he was to become notorious for his matrimonial adventures and for his cruelty.

Catherine of Aragon gave birth to many stillborn sons and to one daughter, Mary, who later became queen. Despairing of a son, Henry turned his attention to Anne Boleyn, one of Catherine's ladies-in-waiting. There followed, during the courtship of Anne, protracted attempts to obtain a divorce from Catherine: but when these failed Henry broke with Rome and proclaimed himself Supreme Head of the Church of England. Then, having granted himself a divorce, he married Anne and began the spoliation of the Church known as the *Dissolution of the Monasteries*.

Anne produced one daughter, Elizabeth, who also became queen: but Anne was found guilty of misconduct, and was executed in the Tower of London. Henry married her lady-in-waiting, Jane Seymour, who died at Hampton Court in giving birth to the future Edward VI.

Henry's minister Thomas Cromwell arranged his master's marriage with Anne of Cleves, a German Protestant princess. When Henry saw the "Flanders mare" he repudiated the marriage and agreed to the execution of Cromwell, whose enemies were quick to take advantage of the king's displeasure. Catherine Howard, Henry's new wife, was found guilt of adultery and beheaded in the Tower. His last wife was Catherine Parr, an unassuming young woman who was a good wife and mother.

Edward VI (1547-53) was only ten years old when he became king. During his reign English forces invaded Scotland in order to enforce the marriage treaty arranged by Henry VIII between Edward and Mary Stuart. The Scots were defeated, but Mary fled to France, where she married the Dauphin.

Mary Tudor (1553-58) came to the throne with a determination to re-establish the Catholic religion. The Dukes of Northumberland and Suffolk attempted to dethrone her in favour of Lady Jane Grey, but were beheaded in the Tower of London. Mary's marriage to Philip of Spain in Winchester Cathedral was followed by Protestant riots, but, having effected a reconciliation with Rome, Mary set out to purge England of Protestantism.

The reign of her sister and successor, *Elizabeth I* (1558-1603), was the most colourful in English history. Noted for her intelligence, clearsightedness and courage, she inspired the same qualities in those who served her. She was faced by problems of extreme complexity, which she sought to solve, or at least to postpone, by holding out the prospect of her marriage with some foreign prince — French, or Spanish, or Austrian — which would have given her husband a dominant position in Europe.

The two most immediate dangers to the throne were the hostility of Spain, and the arrival in Scotland of Mary Stuart, who now became Mary Queen of Scots. The Spanish threat of invasion was removed by the destruction of the mighty Armada in 1588 by Howard of Effingham, Drake, Hawkins and Frobisher. Mary Queen of Scots took her own road to destruction. After a first marriage to her cousin Darnley, she married Bothwell, the man suspected of conniving in Darnley's murder. The Scottish nobles imprisoned Mary in Loch Leven Castle, from which she escaped and after defeat in battle fled into England and placed herself under the protection of Elizabeth. After a long period of captivity she was beheaded in Fotheringhay Castle (1587).

Elizabeth's chief ministers and servants were William Cecil, who became *Lord Burleigh*, his son Robert Cecil, her secretary Walsingham, who unmasked the plots in which Mary Stuart was involved, and Walter Raleigh, who colonised Virginia and introduced tobacco and the potato into England. Her favourites were Robert Dudley, Earl of Leicester, whom some believe she secretly married, and his stepson Robert, Earl of Essex, whom she deeply loved. Essex, a hot-headed and impetuous young man, sought to gain the crown for himself and was beheaded in the Tower.

Before dying at the age of 70 the queen designated James VI of Scotland, son of Mary Stuart and Darnley, as her successor. So ended the Tudor dynasty.

The Stuarts

The reign of *James I* (VI of Scotland) (1603-29), a stubborn and quick-tempered king, was marked by a constant struggle to wring money out of Parliament and by the marriage of James's daughter Elizabeth with the Elector Palatine Frederick, the origin of the later Hanoverian dynasty. James's reign also saw the colonisation of America by the persecuted Puritans.

Charles I (1625-49) inherited from his father the perennial problem of how to raise sufficient money without summoning and therefore conceding power to Parliament. Unsuccessful wars against both Spain and France, undertaken on the advice of the Duke of Buckingham, necessitated asking for grants from Parliament. Parliament replied with a demand for the dismissal of Buckingham, a Petition of Rights, and the withdrawal of the King's prerogative of imposing taxes. Parliament was dissolved. The threat contained in the large French fleet being built by Cardinal Richelieu, the invasion of the north of England by the Scottish army as a protest against the new Church service enforced by Archbishop Laud, and the outbreak of the Irish rebellion compelled Charles to summon Parliament. The Commons laid the Grand Remonstrance, defining Parliament's difficulties and dangers, before Parliament, and introduced a bill providing that Parliament should not be dissolved except at its own request.

Charles, flouting all constitutional law, entered the House of Commons with 300 of his followers and called for the surrender on a charge of treason of the five members — Hampden, Pym, Hollis, Strode and Haselrig — who had been the most active in opposing the royal will.

Charles then raised his standard at Nottingham and the civil war began. The better training and equipment of the Round-heads — as the Parliamentary troops were called — led by Oliver Cromwell, wore down the King's cavaliers led by Prince Rupert; and after some fruitless negotiations with the Scots, to whom he surrendered, Charles was handed over to Parliament and imprisoned. Thereafter the king was brought to trial in Westminster Hall. The trial lasted five days, during which Charles courageously contested the court's right to try him. Finally, however, he was condemned to death and beheaded at Whitehall on 30 January 1649.

The country now became a Commonwealth, governed by a committee of 14 members of the House of Commons. Meanwhile Cromwell continued to harry and massacre the royalists wherever he found them. The late king's eldest son, Charles, was proclaimed king in Scotland and marched south at the head of an army. This was routed at the battle of Worcester, and Charles fled to the Continent, embarking at Brighton.

After a period of makeshift Parliamentary rule (the Rump Parliament, followed by the Barebones Parliament) Cromwell expelled the members, and in 1654 had himself proclaimed Lord Protector and divided England into 12 areas, each in charge of a major-general. He died in 1659. His son Richard inherited his title, but lacked his father's qualities.

One of Oliver Cromwell's most capable generals, George Monk, to whom had been allotted the task of maintaining order in Scotland, had been intriguing with Charles on the Continent: and when he judged that the time was ripe he marched on London, seized power and sent word to Charles, who landed at Dover on 15 May 1660.

Charles II (1660-85) was by far the cleverest man of his time. He had married Catherine of Braganza, a Portuguese princess and a Catholic, but had numerous mistresses. He effected the Triple Alliance between England, Sweden and Holland and frustrated Louis XIV's ambitions in the Netherlands at the Peace of Aix-la-Chapelle. The ink was barely dry on the treaty when Charles accepted financial aid from the French king on the understanding that he would re-establish Catholicism in England — an objective which was very far from his intentions.

The Great Plague of 1665, of which 100,000 persons died, and the Great Fire of 1666, which destroyed the city of London, were two outstanding events of Charles's reign.

When the Duke of York became king as *James II* (1685-88) he had two wives: Anne Hyde, daughter of the Earl of Clarendon, by whom he had two daughters, Mary and Anne, and Mary of Modena, by whom he had a son, James, later known as the Old Pretender. James was a militant Roman Catholic. Regardless of the strong Protestant feeling of the country, he appointed Catholics to all positions of authority in the state, and made Roman Catholic worship public. The end was not long in coming. An invitation to occupy the throne of England was sent to William of Orange and his wife Mary, James II's daughter by his first wife. They landed at Torbay on 5 November 1688. Lord Churchill at the head of the regular army went ostensibly to resist their progress to London, but in reality to join forces with them. This revolution was the spark which set off fighting between Catholics and Protestants in Ireland.

William III and Mary (1689-1702) formed an unromantic and one-sided partnership. William, who refused to be merely a regent and insisted upon being crowned as king, was interested only in arresting Louis XIV's victorious progress on the Continent: and with this object in view he formed the Grand Alliance of Germany, Savoy, Spain, Holland and England and declared war on France, on the pretext that the French had helped the Jacobite rebels in Scotland and Ireland.

The war on the Continent achieved little or nothing and was brought to an end by the Treaty of Ryswick. So far as Britain was concerned its most important result was the establishment in 1694 of the Bank of England, which in return for a government guarantee lent them money and took responsibility for the National Debt. In the same year Queen Mary died.

No sooner had peace been negotiated with France than Europe became involved in the War of the Spanish Succession. Britain's participation became inevitable when, on the death of James II, Louis XIV recognised his son, James, afterwards known as the Old Pretender, as James III. In the midst of preparations for war, William had a fall when riding near Hampton Court, broke his collar-bone and died.

Queen Anne (1702-14), sister-in-law of William III, inherited the throne and with it the War of the Spanish Succession, which lasted throughout the whole of her reign. The reins of government were seized by John Churchill, Lord Marlborough. In the Netherlands Marlborough, who was made a duke in 1703, won a series of brilliant victories — Blenheim, Ramillies and Oudenarde — over the French, and, with a diplomacy as skilful as his generalship, kept together the heterogeneous collection of allies of the Grand Alliance.

After the defeat of his forces at Malplaquet Louis sued for peace. Public opinion in Britain was divided; the Whigs wanted to continue the war, while the Tories were anxious to end it.

Under the Treaty of Utrecht in 1713 Britain received Newfoundland, Nova Scotia, the Hudson Bay territories and Gibraltar. These acquisitions, and the union with Scotland in 1707, were the enduring achievements of Queen Anne's reign.

The Hanoverians

The question of the succession was a difficult one. The Tories favoured James, Anne's half-brother, on condition that he renounced the Catholic faith: but this he refused to do. The Privy Council thereupon declared the Elector of Hanover king under the name of *George I* (1714-27). The new king, however, knew nothing of British life or the English language, and the country was governed by a committee of the Privy Council.

The first Whig government, led by Lord Stanhope and the Earl of Sutherland, came to an end with the collapse of the South Sea Company (1721), which created financial panic. Sir Robert Walpole then became Prime Minister, with the task of restoring order and confidence, and occupied the post for 21 years.

George II (1717-60) was far more capable and ambitious than his father. France and Spain, jealous of Britain's rapid commercial development, made the Family Compact, and in the following year Britain became involved in the War of the Spanish Succession, following an appeal for help from Maria Theresa. The war began with a personal victory at Dettingen in 1743 for George II, the last British king to command troops in the field. But Britain was also involved in difficulties at home. In 1745 Prince Charles Edward, grandson of James II, landed in Scotland, rallied the Jacobite forces and won a victory at Prestonpans; he then advanced south to Derby, where, after a fatal hesitation, he was compelled to retreat. British troops were hastily recalled from the Continent, and in 1746 the Duke of Cumberland, the king's brother, defeated an army of Highlanders at Culloden.

The war of the Austrian Succession ended with the Treaty of Aix-la-Chapelle in 1748, but Britain and France remained as bitter rivals as they had been before, and were in fact openly fighting in India and Canada. When the Empress Maria Theresa formed an alliance with France and Russia against Frederick II, Frederick appealed to Britain for help and the Seven Years' War began.

Immediately Britain suffered a series of disasters. Minorca was lost, and Admiral Byng, held responsible for its loss, was executed. Montcalm, the French commander in Canada, inflicted heavy defeats on the British colonial forces. In India the loss of Calcutta was followed by the horrors of the Black Hole. When the incompetent Duke of Newcastle was replaced by William Pitt, however, the country's fortunes changed. Britain won naval victories at Lagos and Quiberon; Clive won a great victory at Plassey and conquered almost the whole of India; and in Canada General Wolfe captured the Heights of Abraham. The British flag now flew from the North Pole to the frontiers of Spanish America.

In the midst of these triumphs George II died. *George III* (1760-1820) was hard-working, obstinate and stupid, but by assuring himself of the unwavering support of a sufficient number of "king's friends" in the House of Commons by granting them pensions, he controlled Parliament.

The war with France was concluded by the Peace of Paris in 1763, by which Britain received Canada, the West Indies and large portions of America, but the mishandling of the American colonies by George and his Prime Minister, the Tory Lord North, led to the War of American Independence. War broke out in 1776. George Washington quickly proved himself a capable American leader, and in 1777 British troops were routed at Saratoga.

The difficulties which now faced Britain gave France, Spain and Holland an opportunity for declaring war in 1778. The country's position was extremely precarious; surrounded by enemies on all sides, it also had grave domestic troubles — the violent anti-Catholic demonstrations known as the Gordon Riots. Once again, however, the British navy saved the situation. Admiral Rodney defeated a French fleet in the West Indies, and Lord Howe drove off the French and Spanish ships which were blockading Gibraltar. These victories brought the war to an end. At the Treaty of Versailles (1783), however, Britain lost her colonies in America and the West Indies.

The treaty was followed by ten years of peace. Pitt, the second son of the great Chatham, became Prime Minister. He was helped in his task of restoring the depleted finances of the country by the immense growth of wealth resulting from the great industrial development which followed the mechanical inventions of such men as Watt and Arkwright.

In 1789, when Pitt was at the height of his power, the French Revolution shook Europe to its foundations. When the French executed their King and Queen, overran Belgium and established a naval base at Antwerp, Pitt protested. France declared war.

This war, which lasted, with one short breathing space, from 8 February 1793 until 7 July 1815, opened with Howe's naval victory on the "glorious 1st of June". The defeat of the Spanish fleet at Cape Saint Vincent by Admiral Jarvis and the destruction by Nelson, at the battle of the Nile, of the French ships which had taken General Bonaparte to Egypt lessened Britain's peril.

Napoleon's bid to conquer India by way of Egypt failed and he returned to Europe to inflict crushing defeats on Britain's subsidised allies, Russia and Austria, and imposed upon Russia, Sweden and Denmark a state of "armed neutrality" towards Britain. Nelson's answer was to sink the Danish fleet in the harbour of Copenhagen.

Britain and France signed the Peace of Amiens in 1802, but in 1803 Napoleon demanded that Britain should recognise officially his annexations in Italy and Switzerland. With her refusal to do this, Britain sent a declaration of war. During 1803-1805 Napoleon tried to invade Britain: but the combined fleets of France and Spain were defeated by Nelson at the battle of Trafalgar, in which he was killed.

From 1805 to 1808 Britain's involvement in the war was confined to financing her allies on the Continent. Napoleon, now master of Europe, signed the Berlin Decrees and took other measures to maintain the "Continental blockade". When in 1808 Portugal refused to join in the blockade Britain sent troops into the Peninsula in response to the French invasion of Portugal and Spain.

The destruction of Napoleon's army in the Russian winter of 1812 gave fresh hope to the Allies, who summoned what was left of their strength und gained victories at Leipzig and Laon, and then entered Paris in March 1814. Napoleon abdicated and retired to Elba.

The aged George III, after a series of illnesses, had finally gone mad in 1810, and his place was taken by his son as Prince Regent.

In February 1815 Napoleon escaped from Elba to France and made a triumphant and unopposed entry into Paris, but his last gamble failed in front of the thin red lines of British infantry on the field of Waterloo, where the Duke of Wellington gained one of the decisive victories of the world's history.

The 19th Century

On the death of Princess Charlotte, the Regent's only child, the question of the succession again arose. The old king died in 1820 and was succeeded by the Prince Regent, who now became *George IV* (1820-30). The advent of the new king made little difference to the conduct of affairs, though his ill-treatment of Queen Caroline brought him much unpopularity. On the death of George Canning the Duke of Wellington became Prime Minister, and during his tenure of office a Catholic Emancipation Act was passed, as a result of pressure by Daniel O'Connell, a leading Irish member. In 1830 the reform of the House of Commons was pressed for by the Whigs; feeling throughout the country ran high, and in the midst of the agitation George IV died.

The crown now passed to George's brother *William IV* (1830-37), an honest and constitutional monarch who tried to do his best.

With the beginning of the new reign, the Whigs introduced the Reform Bill. The bill was thrown out by the Tory Lords, and the rioting which followed reached such proportions that the king let it be known that he would create sufficient Whig peers to ensure the passage of the bill through the Upper House. The Tory peers then abstained from voting, and the bill was passed.

Daniel O'Connell, the Irish member, now raised two new agitations in the Commons; Home Rule for Ireland and the Tithe War, a crusade against the payment of tithes by Irish Roman Catholics to the established Church of Ireland. The first question was not to be settled before the passing of another century: the second was settled by compromise, but it caused another election and the resignation of Grey, the Whig leader. The Whigs were, however, returned to power with Melbourne at their head. It was at this time that the Tories, disorganised by their hostility towards the Reform Bill, began to form again under the name of Conservatives and the leadership of Sir Robert Peel.

William IV died in 1837 and was succeeded by his niece *Victoria* (1837-1901), whose reign was the most prosperous and glorious in Britain's history. Her government was conducted by a series of outstanding ministers, but the one to whom she owed most was probably Lord Melbourne. He was Prime Minister when she came to the throne, and until her marriage acted as a counsellor and mentor, teaching her the duties of a constitutional monarch. In 1840 she married her cousin *Prince Albert* of Saxe-Coburg, a man of great ability and energy.

In 1841 the Conservatives returned to power under Sir Robert Peel, who introduced income tax — a new impost which was intended to last for only five years. The Conservative government fell when Peel proposed the repeal of the Corn Laws as a means of helping Ireland, then threatened with famine as a result of a blight which had affected the country's potato crop. Leading Conservatives like Disraeli and Bentinck opposed the measure, and the party fell to pieces. William Ewart Gladstone, later to be Prime Minister, went over to the Whig camp, which was led by Lord John Russell. The Whig government brought forward another Reform Bill, but fell from power when the Foreign Secretary Lord Palmerston, a man of strong and independent mind, supported Napoleon III's coup d'état in France on his own authority and was dismissed by the Queen. There followed a period without any clear majority in the House of Commons or any stable government, until the Conservatives associated with Peel joined the Whigs to form the Liberal party. Lord Aberdeen now became Prime Minister and Palmerston Home Secretary.

As a result of Britain's failures and mismanagements in the Crimean War Aberdeen was forced to resign. It had been necessary to withdraw troops from India to take part in the war, and this weakening of British power led to the bloody Indian Mutiny of 1857-58. When order had been restored the old East India Company was dissolved and Britain took over the government of India. The first Viceroy was Lord Canning.

While these stirring events were taking place abroad an immense industrial development was taking place at home. Railways and canals now covered the country, extensive coalfields had been discovered and were being mined, manufacturing had developed in an infinity of different ways, and Britain was acquiring the vast wealth that was to stand her in such good stead during the dark days that lay in the future.

Palmerston died in 1865, and thereafter the political scene was dominated by two men, Benjamin Disraeli, Lord Beaconsfield, the great leader of the Conservatives, an imperialist, a great intellect and the man who made Queen Victoria an empress, and Gladstone, the leader of the Liberals, who introduced a Bill which became the Reform Act of 1884 and promised Home Rule to the Irish.

At the close of the 19th century English and Dutch settlers in South Africa — the former under the leadership of Cecil Rhodes who had founded the British South Africa Company — were contending for domination at the southern end of that continent. The trouble came to a head with the discovery of gold in the Transvaal. Lord Milner failed to come to any amicable settlement with President Kruger at the Bloemfontein Conference of 1899, and war was declared in the same year.

Before the Boer War had reached its long delayed but inevitable conclusion, Queen Victoria died. Under her rule Britain had reached heights previously unknown; under her rule the British Empire had been born and the Union Jack had encircled the world; under her rule Britain had become rich, powerful, experienced and just. Hers was the greatest reign in British history.

The 20th Century

The twentieth century ushered in a short period of lavish and extravagant frivolity which, under the reign of Victoria's son, *Edward VII* (1901-10), became known as the Edwardian age. The end of his reign saw increasing tension on the continent with the commercial and military strengthening of Germany and the increase of her territorial ambitions, and a period of great prosperity and peace was closed in 1914 with the outbreak of war. *George V* (1910-35) was then on the throne. Later in his reign Britain went through the years of economic depression following 1929, and a National Government was formed under the leadership of a Labour Prime Minister, Ramsay Macdonald. The Labour Party had gradually supplanted the old Liberal (Whig) party as one of the two great political parties in Britain.

After George V's death the country faced a major constitutional crisis. His eldest son *Edward VIII* (1935-36) abdicated after less than a year on the throne, putting his personal happiness above the duties of the throne, and took the title of Duke of

Windsor. He was succeeded by his brother *George VI* (1936-52), in whose reign Britain faced the perils of the second world war under the indomitable leadership of Winston Churchill.

Chronology of Main Events, 1945-80

1945 (8 May): end of second world war.
  (25 July): Labour victory in general election: Clement Attlee becomes Prime Minister and attends the Potsdam Conference.

1946 (January): nationalisation of coal.

1947 (February): nationalisation of electricity.
  (20 November): Princess Elizabeth marries Prince Philip, Duke of Edinburgh.

1948 (April): austerity budget introduced by Sir Stafford Cripps.

1949 (May): ratification of Atlantic Pact.
  (October): first flight of Comet jet aircraft.

1950 (23 February): Labour win election with reduced majority.

1951 (February): nationalisation of steel industry.
  (April): death of Ernest Bevin, a leading Labour minister.
  (25 October): Conservatives win election; Churchill again Prime Minister.

1952 (6 February): death of George VI and accession of Elizabeth II.
  (3 October): explosion of first British atomic bomb in Australia.

1953 (March): denationalisation of steel industry.
  (2 June): coronation of Elizabeth II.

1954 (July): end of food rationing, which had been in force since 1939.

1955 (April): Anthony Eden succeeds Churchill as Prime Minister.
  (26 May): Conservative success in general election.

1956 (October-November): Suez crisis.

1957 (January): Anthony Eden resigns as Prime Minister and is succeeded by Harold Macmillan.
  (May): explosion of British H bomb at Christmas Island in the Pacific.

1958 (December): partial return to convertibility of pound.

1960 (October): launching of first British atomic submarine.

1961 (August): Britain applies to join Common Market.

1963 (19 October): Macmillan resigns as Prime Minister and is succeeded by Sir Alec Douglas-Home.

1964 (15 October): narrow victory for Labour in general election; Harold Wilson Prime Minister.
(December): abolition of capital punishment.

1966 (31 March): Labour wins election with increased majority.

1967 (18 November): devaluation of pound.

1969 (July): inauguration of Prince Charles, the Queen's eldest son, as Prince of Wales.

1970-71: introduction of decimal currency.

1970 (18 June): Conservative victory in general election; Edward Heath becomes Prime Minister.

1973 (1 January): Britain enters Common Market.

1974 (7 March): Labour return to power as a minority government; Harold Wilson Prime Minister.
(10 October): in a further general election Labour are again returned with a narrow majority.

1975 (5 June): In a national referendum Britain votes 2:1 in favour of continued membership of Common Market.

1976 Harold Wilson resigns and is succeed as Prime Minister by James Callaghan.

1979 Conservative victory in a general election; Margaret Thatcher becomes the ffrst woman Prime Minister of Britain.

Kings and Queens of England, the United Kingdom and Scotland

England

Saxon and Danish kings

Egbert, 825-39.

Ethelwulf, 839-57.

Ethelbald, 857-60.

Ethelbert, 860-66.

Ethelred I, 866-71.

Alfred the Great, 871-901.

Edward I, 901-25.

Athelstan, 925-40.

Edmund I, 940-46.

Eadred, 946-55.

Edwig, 955-59.

Edgar, 959-75.

Edward II, the Martyr, 975-79.

Ethelred II, 979-1013 (deposed).

Swein Forkbeard (Danish), 1013-14.

Ethelred II (again), 1014-16.

Edmund II, 1016-17.

Canute the Great (Danish), 1017-35.

Harold I (Danish), 1035-39.

Canute II (Danish), 1039-42.

Edward III, the Confessor, 1042-66.

Harold II, 1066.

Norman kings

William the Conqueror, 1066-87.

William II, 1087-1100.

Henry I, 1100-35.

Stephen, 1135-54.

Plantagenets

Henry II, 1154-89.

Richard I, 1189-99.

John, 1199-1216.

Henry III, 1216-72.

Edward I, 1272-1307.

Edward II, 1307-27 (deposed and murdered).

Edward III, 1327-77.

Richard II, 1377-99 (deposed).

House of Lancaster

Henry IV, 1388-1413.

Henry V, 1413-22.

Henry VI, 1422-61 (deposed).

House of York

Edward IV, 1461-83.

Edward V, 1483 (deposed and murdered).
Richard III, 1483-85.

House of Tudor
Henry VII, 1485-1509.
Henry VIII, 1509-47.
Edward VI, 1547-53.
Lady Jane Grey, 1553 (deposed and beheaded).
Mary, 1553-58.
Elizabeth, 1558-1603.

United Kingdom

House of Stuart
James I, 1603-25.
Charles I, 1625-49 (deposed and beheaded).

Commonwealth, established 1649
Oliver Cromwell, Lord Protector, 1653-58.
Richard Cromwell, 1658-60.

House of Stuart, restored
Charles II, 1660-85.
James II, 1685-88 (deposed).
William III, 1689-1702, and Mary, 1689-95.
Anne, 1702-14.

House of Hanover
George I, 1714-27.
George II, 1727-60.
George III, 1760-1820.
George IV, 1820-30.
William IV, 1830-37.
Victoria, 1837-1901.
Edward VII, 1901-10.
George V, 1910-36.
Edward VIII, 1936 (abdicated).
George VI, 1936-52.
Elizabeth II, from 1952.

Scotland

Robert Bruce, 1306-29.
David Bruce, 1329-32 (deposed).
Edward Balliol, 1332-42.
David Bruce (again), 1342-46.

Interregnum, 1346-57.
David Bruce (again), 1357-71.
Robert II (Stuart), 1371-90.
Robert III, 1390-1406.
James I, 1406-37.
James II, 1437-60.
James III, 1460-88.
James IV, 1488-1513.
James V, 1513-42.
Mary, 1542-67 (abdicated).
James VI, 1567-1625.

GOVERNMENT AND ADMINISTRATION

Great Britain is part of the political entity called the United Kingdom of Great Britain and Northern Ireland. The first stage in the formation of the United Kingdom was the union of England with Scotland, and this was followed by the incorporation of Ireland in 1801. In 1922, however, Southern Ireland became independent, leaving only Northern Ireland within the United Kingdom.

Great Britain consists of England, Wales and Scotland, with a total area of 88,765 sq. miles and a population of 54,000,000. The areas and populations of the three countries are as follows;

England	50,335 sq. miles	45,870,000
Wales	8,016 sq. miles	2,724,000
Scotland	30,414 sq. miles	5,228,000

The Isle of Man and the Channel Islands are not strictly part of the United Kingdom but are dependencies of the Crown. Their areas and populations are small;

Isle of Man	227 sq. miles	50,000
Channel Islands	75 sq. miles	125,000

Political Institutions

Britain's political institutions are the result of a compromise between ancient traditions and a process of evolution which obviates the need for revolution (apart from the episode of the Commonwealth during the 17th century). "Great Britain", it has been said, "is still a country of mediaeval uniforms, of judges in wigs and of gentlemen wearing bowlers and carrying umbrellas who travel up to town every morning in their accustomed train; but it is also the country which first brought jet aircraft into commercial service and the first nation in Europe to become an atomic power." The spirit of British institutions lies in a deeply rooted attachment to freedom, to all the freedoms (of thought, of worship, of meeting, of association, of the press). As Montesquieu said in the "Spirit of Laws"; "There is one nation in the world which has political freedom as the direct object of its constitution."

Britain is unusual among nations in having no written constitution. The country is governed by an accumulation of laws
of very varying form and subject matter passed over a very
long period of time and never brought together into a coherent
whole, and by a complex of traditions and conventions which
are none the less powerful for being unwritten. The development
of British institutions has always been based on a pragmatic
approach. The *Great Charter* of 1215 was the first stage in the
process by which the people gained control over the actions
of those who governed them. Monarchs who sought to establish
an absolutist system paid for the attempt with their life (Charles I)
or the loss of their throne (James II). The *Declaration of Rights*
of 1689 firmly established the basis of British democracy and
of individual rights.   Parliament, originally representative of
the nobility and prosperous middle class, gradually developed
into a body representing the whole nation, with the final establishment of universal suffrage in 1918.

Parliament, sitting at Westminster, consists of the two traditional Chambers, Lords and Commons. In fact, however, the
House of Lords has been progressively divested of its powers.
It has no concern with financial matters, and its power to veto
other legislation was reduced by the Parliament Act of 1911
to a power to delay legislation for two years and by a further
Act in 1949 to a power of delay for one year. The original
members of the House of Lords were peers created by the
sovereign and their successors by hereditary right, but in recent
years the trend has been towards the creation of life peers who
do not transmit their title and their right to sit in the House
of Lords to their descendants. There are also the "Lords Spiritual" — the Archbishops of Canterbury and York, the Bishops
of London, Durham and Winchester, and 21 other bishops of
the Church of England according to seniority. In practice the
House of Commons has almost complete control of legislation
and of the government. It consists of 635 members elected for
a term of five years by the votes of all men and women over 18.
The method of voting, by the plurality system (i.e. with election
depending on a majority vote over the next candidate, not an
absolute majority) in single-member constituencies, may not
always produce an exact reflection of the state of opinion in
the country but makes it easier to achieve a stable government
majority. The deliberations of the Commons are presided over
by the Speaker. The responsibilities of the Opposition in ensuring
the effective functioning of the House are recognised in the

payment of a salary to the Leader of the Opposition as well as to government Ministers.

Executive power is in the hands of "Her Majesty's Government", led by the Prime Minister. The Prime Minister is appointed by the sovereign, who normally invites the leader of the party which has won a majority in a general election to form a government. Other Ministers are appointed by the sovereign on the nomination of the Prime Minister. A group of senior Ministers form the *Cabinet*, which controls and directs the government's general policy. One of the most influential members of the Cabinet is the Chancellor of the Exchequer, the Minister responsible for finance. Ministers are individually and collectively responsible to Parliament.

The Crown

The Crown remains the symbol of permanence and tradition, even though its powers have been steadily whittled away in the course of the centuries. The monarchy is hereditary on the basis of primogeniture (male heirs having precedence over female, so that a daughter succeeds only if there is no son). The sovereign is the personification of the state, the symbol of the Commonwealth; justice is dispensed in his name, and foreign ambassadors are accredited to him; he is head of the Church of England; it is the sovereign who summons and dissolves Parliament, gives assent to laws, declares war and signs treaties.

In fact, however, the sovereign — in a famous phrase — reigns but does not govern. The "speech from the throne" which opens each session of Parliament is drafted by the government and expresses their policy. The sovereign acts only on the advice of Ministers, and has no influence on policy. Even his power to appoint the Prime Minister after a general election is controlled by the strict convention that he must send for the leader of the majority party.

The Parties

The two-party system has long been solidly entrenched in British politics, although in very recent years the sharp division into two parties has been blurred by the attempts of the Liberals to establish themselves as a third party and by the rise of nationalist parties in Wales and Scotland. The two-party system has made possible a periodic alternation between the parties and enabled changes in policy to be carried through by a new govern-

ment without violence and in a spirit of at least relative tolerance
and fair play. In many respects, of course, the policies of the
two main parties have often been very close to one another, and
there have been occasions when the voters were clearly at a
loss to decide between them. Often enough reforms initiated
by one party have been brought to fruition by the other, and
it is not unheard of for a member of one party — following an
example set by Sir Winston Churchill — to "cross the floor"
and transfer his allegiance to the other. In recent years, too, it
has become increasingly common for individual members of a
party to rebel against party policy on a particular matter about
which they feel strongly, and this has on occasion led to unusual
cross-party alignments.

In the 19th and early 20th centuries the two great parties
were the Liberals and the Conservatives. The Liberals, or
Whigs (originally a nickname of Irish origin), found their
support among nonconformists and in the towns: their most
noted leaders were Mr Gladstone and Lloyd George. The
Conservatives, or *Tories* (a term originally applied in the 17th century to certain religious fanatics in Scotland), represented mainly
the aristocracy and their rural dependents and the High Church;
in Victorian times their outstanding leader was Disraeli. After
the first world war, however, there was a change; the Liberal
party almost disappeared, giving place to the Labour party as
the alternative to the Conservatives, whose policies also evolved
over the years and began to appeal to a wider spectrum of
voters. The Labour party, looking for its support to the working
classes and the less prosperous urban voters, established itself
as a governing party between the wars and went on to consolidate
its position after the second world war, under leaders like
Ramsay Macdonald between the wars, Clement Attlee in 1945
and, more recently, Harold Wilson.

The parties have connections with various pressure groups,
the links between the Labour party and the *Trades Union
Congress*, which represents some 8 million trade unionists,
having their counterpart in the close relationship between the
Conservatives and the *Confederation of British Industry*, which
speaks for 7500 employers. Although in British politics the
terms "left" and "right" cannot be applied in the same sense
as in some other European countries, it appears nevertheless
that the two main parties reflect certain well matched social
realities.

Local Government

Local government in Great Britain has been for some years in the throes of reorganisation. New administrative structures came into effect in England and Wales in 1974 and in Scotland in 1975: local government in Greater London had already been reorganised some years previously. This has involved changes in the size and frequently in the name of the local government units, and the old county boroughs have disappeared as separate administrative units (though many of them form the nucleus of new districts under their old names). It may be expected, however, that for some years to come familiar designations that have officially been superseded will remain in unofficial use.

Under the new structure England and Wales (outside Greater London) are divided into 53 *counties* and 369 smaller *districts* within these areas. In general the counties are responsible for the major local government services, the districts for the more local services; in certain densely populated "metropolitan counties", however, the districts are responsible for some of the major services also. Populations of non-metropolitan counties range from 280,000 to 1,300,000, of metropolitan counties from 1,200,000 to 2,800,000. The average district of a non-metropolitan county has a population between 75,000 and 100,000, although many fall outside this range; districts within metropolitan counties have populations ranging between 173,000 and 1,100,000.

Greater London is administered by the councils of the 32 London boroughs and the City of London, and by the Greater London Council.

The reorganisation of Scottish local government in 1975 was even more radical, the old county and town councils being replaced by nine new regional authorities responsible for certain major functions, 53 district authorities concerned with a wide range of other functions and three island authorities in the island groups of Orkney, Shetland and the Western Isles.

The affairs of these various authorities are run by councils of elected members with a four-year term.

Religion

In terms of religion Great Britain is predominantly a Protestant country.

The national church of England (the "established church")
is the Church of England, instituted by Henry VIII at the Reformation. The sovereign is head of the Church of England,
and archbishops, bishops and deans are appointed by the Crown
on the advice of the Prime Minister (a procedure which has
given rise to some criticism within the Church and is at present
being reviewed). There are two archbishops, the Archbishop
of Canterbury (Primate of All England) and the Archbishop of
York (Primate of England) and 43 episcopal dioceses. The
Church in Wales (which was "disestablished" in 1920) has
six dioceses.

In Scotland the established church is the Church of Scotland,
which is Presbyterian and non-hierarchical, with no bishops:
its General Assembly meets annually, presided over by a Mode-
rator who holds office for a year. There is also a Scottish Episcopalian Church, with 6 dioceses, which is in full communion
with the Church of England.

There are also various other Protestant denominations (in
England known as the "free churches" or "nonconformist
churches"), including Methodists, Baptists and many smaller
sects.

There are some 6 million Roman Catholics in Britain, with
seven archbishops and 20 bishops, and 400,000 Jews. In addition
there are Moslems, Orthodox, Buddhists, and a wide range of
other communities.

POPULATION AND ECONOMY

The Demographic Pattern

There is no British race in any valid sense, but there is a
British people, or perhaps more exactly a British nation, built
up over many centuries out of many different elements — the
Celts, followed by the Romans, the Angles, Jutes and Saxons,
the Vikings and finally the Normans in the 11th century. The
Norman Conquest was the last invasion of British soil, though
since then there has been a continuous infusion of new blood
by peaceful immigration right down to our own day. The
native Celtic inhabitants were driven back into the outlying
mountainous regions of the north (Scotland) and west (Wales,
Ireland), where they preserved their distinctive characteristics,
their traditions and, in varying measure, their language. Everywhere else the Anglo-Saxons formed the main basis of the
population, though subject during the Middle Ages to strong
French influences — first under the Normans and later under
the Plantagenet kings.

The result of this process has been described by a French
observer (V. Prévot) as follows:

"A distinctive character and temperament came into being.
The British are often thought of as slow thinkers: but their
great quality is their ability to adjust to reality, a consequence
of their practical commonsense, their enterprising and businesslike approach, their tenacity and matter-of-factness, an indivi-
dualism which recognises the need on occasion to accept col-
lective disciplines, a sense of national pride... The characteristic
British sense of humour has been neatly defined as 'an apprecia-
tion of the absurd'. The development of the British way of
life has been profoundly influenced by religion. The British
recognise the ambiguity of the world and recognise that not
all problems are capable of solution. They respect tradition
but are ready to accept new ideas. They cherish old stones,
trees, birds, green lawns; but above all they love freedom."

Although the term British is applied to the inhabitants of the
British Isles or of Great Britain, it is important to remember
that it covers three separate groups of people — the English,
the Welsh and the Scots — who still retain their own identities.
In particular, visitors should beware of offending Welsh or
Scottish susceptibilities by applying the terms England and

English to the whole of Britain. Although the language of the whole country is English — with Welsh as the everyday language of large numbers of people in Wales, and Gaelic, the "old language" of Scotland, still spoken in the remoter parts of the Highlands and Islands — it is spoken with different accents and with different turns of phrase in Wales and Scotland: and the consciousness of a different history and different traditions is still very much alive in these countries. In recent years, too, the economic difficulties which have particularly affected Wales and Scotland have led to the rise of nationalist movements seeking greater power to control their own affairs.

The population of Britain has increased from 10,000,000 in 1800 to 54,000,000 today; and this very considerable increase has been achieved in spite of large-scale emigration over the period. Emigration was not a new phenomenon in Britain — in earlier centuries many people left the country for religious reasons, like the Pilgrim Fathers in 1620 — but in the 19th century it took on considerable proportions for economic reasons, with large numbers of people emigrating to escape from unemployment and destitution at home. In this way Britain made a major contribution to the peopling of the Dominions of Canada, Australia and New Zealand and the United States of America. Without the safety valve provided by emigration the population of Britain might well have reached 90,000,000 by now.

The birth rate has fallen considerably over the last 180 years, from some 37 per 1000 in 1800 to 21.7 in 1921 and 16 today. The death rate has also fallen, until it is now little more than 11 per 1000: and infant mortality has been brought down to a low level (18 per 1000). Emigration has now almost stopped, and since the last war the movement has been very much in the reverse direction, with large influxes of immigrants from Central Europe (the "displaced persons" of the post-war period), the Mediterranean countries (mainly Italians) and, sometimes on a mass scale, from overseas (the West Indies, Guyana, India and Pakistan, East Africa). This immigration of coloured people from the former dominions and colonies gave rise to certain social problems, and steps were taken, notably in 1968, to control the flow of immigrants. In spite of this influx, largely of the younger age groups, the age pyramid of the population has still a relatively narrow base, with 30.4% under 20, 50.9% between 20 and 60, and 18.7% over 60.

Britain is a highly urbanised country, with under 15% of the population living in the country and 85% living in the towns.

This is an old-established tradition, since Roman civilisation in Britain was centred on the towns (York, Chester, Bath, etc.); but the period of substantial urban growth came with the industrial revolution of the 18th and 19th centuries. There are now 72 towns in Britain with a population of over 100,000, accounting for more than half the total population of the country. The average density of population is high (594 to the sq. mile), but very unevenly distributed; side by side with the giant industrial conurbations there are large empty areas like the Scottish Highlands and the moorlands of the Pennine chain. The continuing depopulation of these remoter areas has reduced Scotland's share of the total population from 20% at the time of the Union (1701) to something like 10% today.

Seven large conurbations account for two-fifths of the total population; Greater London (7,700,000), followed by Birmingham and Manchester (2,550,000 each), Leeds-Bradford-West Yorkshire (over 2,000,000) and Glasgow, Liverpool and Newcastle-Tyneside. The largest towns (on the basis of boundaries as they were before the recent reorganisation) are;

London (county)	3,200,000	Bristol	450,000
Birmingham	1,100,000	Coventry	330,000
Glasgow	1,050,000	Nottingham	315,000
Liverpool	750,000	Hull	300,000
Manchester	650,000	Cardiff	300,000
Leeds	510,000	Bradford	300,000
Sheffield	490,000	Leicester	300,000
Edinburgh	470,000		

Agriculture

Of Britain's 400,000 farms some are quite tiny, while at the other end of the scale there are some of as much as 10,000 acres. These extensive farms, or groups of farms, usually occur in districts where the fields are large and easy to cultivate, as in some parts of Hampshire, Wiltshire, Berkshire and East Anglia. Flat fields of 100 to 200 acres, and many of 30 to 50 acres, are characteristic of these countries and most suitable for the employment of machinery for mechanised corn growing. Wheat, barley and oats can be grown in these districts with yields rivalling those of farmers in any other part of the world.

To these same counties belong some of the biggest milk-producing farms, where 200-300 cows are milked under one ownership, or 800-1000 cows in the case of a privately owned group of farms. Large-scale milk production was developed in the 1920s and 1930s partly as the result of the invention of the "bail" system of milking, whereby cows are milked by a machine in a portable shed or "bail" which is kept out in the fields, has no floor and is moved to clean ground each day. In this way the cows live out in the open air all the year round, never coming into a house, and one man and a boy can do all the work, including the milking, for as many as 60 cows.

The proportion of the population engaged in agriculture is very small — only 3% of the total working population. Much of the country's land is still in large estates, following the enclosures which began in the 17th century. There are relatively few independent freeholders, on the pattern found in France and other European countries, the land being farmed by farmers who employ agricultural workers on a wage-earning basis. The standard of living enjoyed by the farmers is reasonably high, on a par with that of many town-dwellers — apart perhaps from the 12,000 "crofters" in the Scottish Highlands who own small holdings of fairly poor land.

The average size of farm holdings is about 75 acres. Some 60% are under 50 acres, 37% between 50 and 300 acres and 3% over 300 acres.

In the 19th century British agriculture declined considerably as a result of the ready availability of food supplies from overseas, so that by 1914 it produced only a quarter of the country's needs. The crisis situation produced by two world wars led successive governments to take steps to reverse this trend, and by 1945 Britain was producing half its food requirements. Post-war agricultural legislation (Acts of 1947 and 1957, a White Paper in 1965) provided protection for British agriculture by a system of guaranteed prices, subsidies for modernisation and advisory and information services. Farming is now carried on by modern scientific methods, almost on an industrial basis, with one tractor for every 30 acres of agricultural land. In consequence Britain now produces 100% of the milk and eggs it needs, 70% of its meat, 50% of its bacon and 25% of its cereals and sugar.

Although agriculture accounts for only some 2.8% to 3% of the gross national product, its output is, in absolute terms, very substantial — 1,300,000 tons of oats, 5,000,000 tons of wheat, 8,000,000 tons of barley, 7,000,000 tons of potatoes and 7,000,000 tons of sugar-beet. The preponderant element in British farming, however, is livestock. While 7,500,000 acres are under food crops, 40,000,000 acres are given up, either directly or indirectly, to livestock production. Britain has 13 million cattle, 26 million sheep and 9 million pigs, and produces annually 2,300,000 tons of meat and 13,000,000 tons of milk.

Fruit and vegetable production has become a very big industry during recent years. Fruit growing is carried on in many districts but chiefly in Kent, Cambridgeshire and East Anglia, Devon, Somerset, Hereford and Worcester, and Hampshire. Market gardening is mainly centred on suitable ground round the thickly populated areas.

Livestock

Cattle. British farmers have always been good livestock men. For centuries they have been improving their cattle by breeding from selected sires, by rejecting low-grade dams and by keeping pedigree records to establish the various strains and families. The *dairy shorthorn* as it is today was developed during the period between 1730 and 1850. The shorthorn is a dual purpose animal: it provides both milk and beef, and is to be found in all parts of the United Kingdom and indeed all over the English-speaking world and in some South American countries.

Other dual-purpose breeds are the *Red Poll*, the *Devon*, the *South Devon* and the *Welsh*. The first of these is encountered mainly in the eastern counties, but it is now to be seen in many other parts of the country, and in overseas countries as well; the remainder belong to their own home districts, though Devon and Welsh steers are known far and wide for their excellent beef characteristics.

On the exclusively dairy side, the leading breeds are the British *Friesians* and *Ayrshires*, and the English strains of the Channel Island breeds, the *Guernseys* and *Jerseys*. These four breeds are now making great headway, and are popular all over the country.

The beef breeds are led by the *shorthorn*, as distinct from the dairy shorthorn, the *Hereford*, *Aberdeen-Angus* and *Galloway*. An extensive export trade has been developed, and vast herds in the South American countries have been largely built up and maintained on the blood of sires bred in British herds.

Sheep. There are no fewer than 31 pedigree breeds of sheep in Great Britain, in addition to five or six pure-breeds and established crosses which do not rank as pedigree. This seemingly large number is due to differences in soil and climate which caused various districts, through the ages, to establish and fix the breed which throve best under their own local conditions. As a result there emerged a wide variety of breeds ranging from the *Blackface* of Scotland and the *Mountain Sheep* of Wales to the *Down* breeds of the south of England. The former will scratch a living out of the thin mountain grasses at 1500 to 2000 feet, and will withstand weather conditions that would prove fatal to less hardy breeds. Many visitors to Britain find it difficult to believe that, almost without exception, sheep in this country spend the whole of the winter out of doors.

The effect of climate and soil on sheep — and on all domestic livestock — is interesting in another way. While the various breeds will live and thrive continuously in their own home region, their descendants tend to lose some of their best characteristics when removed from their native soil. This tendency is perhaps more noticeable in some breeds than it is in others. It certainly explains why the big cattle breeders of South America come back year after year to Britain to buy sires to replenish their breeding stock.

Pigs. There are a dozen or more pedigree breeds of pig in the United Kingdom, of which some are fitted for the production of bacon and others for pork. The leading bacon breeds are *Large White*, *Tamworth*, *Wessex Saddleback*, *Essex* and *Large Black*, while the *Berkshires* and *Middle Whites* are the leading pork breeds. All these are flourishing breeds, and many animals are exported every year.

Horses. Owing to the rapid and drastic development of mechanisation working horses are far less numerous now than they were a few years ago. Nevertheless, there are four heavy horse societies, all of which publish a stud book to maintain the pedigree of their registered animals. The natural heavy horse of England is the *Shire*, big-bodied, heavy-boned and carrying a certain amount of hair or "feather" on his legs. The corresponding breed in Scotland is the *Clydesdale*, a little cleaner in the leg and a very active mover.

Percherons and *Suffolks* are also popular breeds, rather similar in conformation, with good deep bodies on short clean legs. The Percheron is a horse which very easily takes the eye. Dapple grey in colour, the breed is noted for its power, docility and intelligence. It was first introduced into this country in 1918 and is rapidly gaining in favour, particularly in Scotland. The Suffolks are found chiefly in the eastern counties. Both Percherons and Suffolks are equally suitable as plough-horses and as draught horses.

Fisheries

Britain's fisheries are an important industry, and the British are great fish-eaters, with an average annual consumption of over 40 lb of fish per head. Small-scale offshore fishing is still practised in some areas (e.g. Cornwall). The North Sea herring fisheries have declined considerably in importance (120,000 tons annually), giving place to white fish (sole, dab, plaice, turbot, etc.), but British trawlers still go off after cod and deep-sea fish in the waters round Iceland, Greenland, Norway and Spitzbergen. The total catch for all types of fishery is of the order of a million tons annually.

Some 20,000 men are regularly engaged in the sea fisheries. The main fishing fleet consists of between 500 and 600 large trawlers owned by individual large ship-owners or companies. The main fishing ports are on the North Sea — Grimsby, Hull, Yarmouth and Aberdeen. The only port of any size on the west coast is Fleetwood.

Industry: General

Britain played a pioneering role in the technological and industrial development of Europe and of the world. Here were evolved the great technical inventions (spinning and weaving machinery, Watt's steam engine) which paved the way for the machine age, the industrial revolution of the 19th century. Thanks to its abundance of raw materials (in particular iron and coal), the resources of manpower which flooded into the towns from the rural areas, the country's financial power, largely based on the profits of its world-wide trade, and its possession of the greatest colonial empire in the world and of an incomparable fleet, Britain was able to forge far ahead of other countries. The system of free trade in force from 1846 to 1932 also enabled it to bring in cheap food and raw materials from other countries and find ready markets for its manufactured goods. The squalor and poverty of the lower classes, reflected alike in Dickens and in Engels, was the basis of the prosperity of the Victorian middle class.

Britain's difficulties began at the end of the 19th century, with the emergence of competitors like the United States, Germany and later Japan. The equipment and machinery of British factories began to fall short of their rivals in up-to-dateness and efficiency, while coal lost its hitherto unchallenged pre-eminence to oil. The two world wars, together with the great depression of the 1930, aggravated a decline which had already begun; the City of London lost its position as the world's banker to Wall Street, and the pound sterling was supplanted by the all-conquering dollar. This led to a rise in the number of unemployed, the closing down of firms which had failed to adjust to modern conditions, a fall in exports and the flight of foreign capital from London banks. In spite of the abandonment of free trade at the Ottawa Conference in 1932, Britain seemed unable to find a way out of its crisis.

The need for government intervention, long repugnant to Britain's firmly established liberal tradition, was increased by the consequences of the second world war. Even before the war some measures of compulsory reorganisation had been carried through, like the reduction in the number of railway companies from 118 to 4; and after 1945 the newly elected Labour government embarked on a far-reaching policy of nationalising the main sectors of the economy (coal, gas and electricity, the railways, air transport, steel). At the same time a comprehensive but expensive programme of social security was established.

Policies on these lines have been continued by successive governments, though with some differences of approach and emphasis between Labour and Conservative administrations. Measures were introduced to help firms in difficulty, and in particular to aid the "depressed areas", those parts of the country which were particularly hard hit by the decline of the coal-based industries (the Scottish Lowlands, Northumberland, Cumberland, Lancashire and South Wales). At the same time efforts were made to establish industry in the traditionally rural areas of south-east England. The need to promote the development of the most advanced technologies was particularly acute, and a new Ministry of Technology was established for this purpose. More recently attempts have been made to introduce some measure of industrial planning, though on a more modest scale than the French planning system. Real progress was, however, made in the field of regional planning, and the "new towns" which now began to be established (see below, p. 72) were a notable achievement in this direction.

At the present time three main sectors can be distinguished in the British economy, and particularly in British industry. First there is the state or nationalised sector — the National Coal Board, the British Gas Corporation, the authorities responsible for the supply and distribution of electricity, British Rail, British Airways, the Atomic Energy Authority, etc. Secondly there is the cooperative sector, particularly strong in the northern half of the country, which is mainly active in retail trade, supported by the powerful Cooperative Wholesale Society, with 54,000 employees. Thirdly there is the private sector, still preponderant, and now concentrated to a considerable extent in huge national or multi-national companies like I.C.I. (Imperial Chemicals, employing 110,000 workers), Shell, Unilever, Courtaulds, and the Distillers Company. Of the total number of wage-earners a third are employed by firms with more than 1000 workers, 57% by firms with between 50 and 1000 workers, and only 10% by firms with a staff of under 50.

Energy

Coal still supplies some 40% of Britain's energy, but this proportion is steadily declining. The highest annual output was achieved in 1913 (287 million tons), but by 1973-74 the figure had fallen to 107 million tons. Many uneconomic pits were closed during the reorganisation which followed the 1929 depression and the even more radical reconstruction after the industry was nationalised in 1947. The number of pits being worked has been reduced to 260, grouped in twelve areas, and the labour force employed has fallen to some 240,000, less than half the number employed in the early 1960s. Britain's share of world coal production has fallen from 22% in 1913 to 7% today.

Production is now concentrated on the most productive mines and faces, particularly the rich Yorkshire coalfields, which account for almost half the total output. The Northumberland and Durham coalfield produces between 15% and 18% of the total, some of the seams being under the North Sea. Other coalfields are in decline — the Scottish Lowlands, South Wales (now almost worked out), Lancashire and Cumberland, the Midland coalfields, which now hardly justify their old name of the Black Country, and Kent. There is little export of coal, and it is a far cry from the days when British coal supplied the needs of steamships all round the world. The oil supply problems of the 1970s, however, have led to a revival of interest in the possibilities of coal, and there may also be the prospect of exports to other countries in the European Community; it may be, therefore, that the British coal industry has more of a future than seemed likely a few years ago. Nevertheless it remains the case that within Britain itself the use of coal by the railways, gas-works and private households continues to fall, only coke plants and thermo-electric power stations being still major consumers.

Oil and natural gas. The ground lost by coal has been made good by the hydrocarbons. There is no oil within Britain itself apart from a small field of negligible importance near Nottingham, but recent prospecting on the North Sea continental shelf has yielded very promising results. The British sector is the largest in this area, and indications have been encouraging; with more than 200 bores drilled by the end of 1974, proven oil reserves were estimated at over 1000 million tons, plus over 44 trillion cu. feet of gas. Concessions have been granted to a number of different companies, including Esso, B.P., Shell, Phillips, Petrofina and ENI. In the Irish Sea prospecting is being carried out by the Gulf and British Hydrocarbon companies.

Britain's refinery capacity is the fifth largest in the world (about 150 million tons in 1974). The main refineries are on the coast — at Fawley, near Southampton (Esso); Shellhaven (Shell), Grain (B.P.) and Cory (Mobil) in the Thames estuary; Grangemouth (B.P.) in the Firth of Forth; Stanlow (Shell) on the Mersey; Llandarcy (B.P.), Pembroke (Texaco) and Milford Haven (Esso) in Wales; Killingholme (Linsey), near Lincoln; Teesport (Shell); Ellesmere (Burmah), etc.

Electricity. Practically the whole of the 280,000 million kWh produced in 1974 came from thermo-electric stations burning coal, gas or oil, with a much smaller proportion coming from nuclear power stations. Hydroelectricity is of little importance in Britain except in the Scottish Highlands, where there are 53 hydroelectric stations operated by the North of Scotland Hydro-Electric Board (established 1943). The nuclear power stations produce some 7 % of total output (25,000 million kWh)— a much higher proportion than in France or Germany. In addition to the Atomic Energy Research Centre at Harwell, near Oxford, there are some 20 nuclear power stations in different parts of the country. The first of these was the one at Calder Hall, Cumberland, followed by others at Dounreay in the north of Scotland, Dungeness in Kent, Hinkley Point in Somerset and Hunterston in Ayrshire. The Atomic Energy Authority was set up in 1954 to be responsible for all problems concerning the use of nuclear power. All the uranium used has to be imported from Commonwealth countries: only slight traces of uranium have been located within Britain itself (e.g. in Scotland).

The Pattern of British Industry

Minerals. The British output of iron ore now takes a much more modest share of total world production than in the past — less than 0.8% (3 million tons), compared with half in 1870. Most of the lodes are worked out, and those that remain (Northampton) are phosphoric ores of low iron content. It is accordingly necessary to import considerable quantities of high-grade ore from Sweden, Spain, Labrador and Africa. The non-ferrous metals for which Britain was renowned in antiquity (lead, zinc, tin, Cornish copper) are now produced only in negligible quantities.

Metal manufacture. The working of iron is an old-established tradition in Britain. In the Middle Ages the country's forests were cut down to produce the charcoal required for working forges; in the 18th century charcoal was supplanted by coke; and in the 19th century the invention of new processes for the manufacture of steel (Bessemer, 1855; Thomas and Gilchrist, 1878) increased British pre-eminence in this field. By 1880 Britain was producing half the world's steel, but this proportion has now fallen to 4% (with a similar fall in the output of cast-iron), and Britain now comes after the United States, the Soviet Union, Japan and West Germany among the world's steel-producing nations. Production is now concentrated in 13 major publicly owned companies, controlled by the British Steel Corporation (established 1967), together with 200 privately owned firms which account for under 10% of total production. The production of copper, tin, zinc and lead is centred in South South Wales, while the refining of aluminium is shared between Scotland and the Isle of Anglesey.

Metal-using industries. This old-established branch of industry plays a major part in Britain's export trade (motor vehicles, railway rolling-stock, aircraft, electrical equipment, etc.). Ship-building has, however, declined in face of competition from Japan and Sweden; in spite of the considerable reputation of firms like John Brown's on the Clyde, no British shipyard ranks among the world's "top ten". The motor vehicle industry is mainly concentrated in four large groups — British Leyland (an amalgamation of such well-known makes as Austin, Morris, Riley, Wolseley and Leyland), Ford, Chrysler United Kingdom and Vauxhall (a subsidiary of General Motors), with one or two independents like Lotus and Rolls-Royce. With an annual output of 1,800,000 vehicles, Britain's automobile industry ranks fifth in the world. The aerospace industry has some outstanding achievements to its credit (the Comet, the BAC 111, the Trident and, more recently, Concorde, a joint venture with the French firm of Sud-Aviation). It is mainly concentrated in two firms, the British Aircraft Corporation and Hawker-Siddeley. Aero-engine manufacture has long been the almost exclusive province of Rolls-Royce, which has gone through a difficult period in recent years. Other fields in which British industry has made a name for itself are mechanical and electrical engineering.

Other industries. The list of Britain's other industries is a long one. The textile industries are old-established and have long been renowned — woollens since the Middle Ages, cotton since the 18th century: and although the export trade in textiles has fallen a long way below its earlier level the quality of British products has been fully maintained. The fall in the production of natural textiles, however, has been counterbalanced by a continuing expansion in the output of synthetic and artificial fibres. There has also been a vigorous growth of the chemical industry, and continuing development of a variety of other industries — foodstuffs (brewing, distilling, flour-milling, sugar-refining) and many more (tobacco, furniture, arts and crafts, etc.).

Industry in the Regions

(For *London*, see p. 132). (For *London*, see p. 132).

Lancashire. With the arrival of the machine age *Manchester* became the centre of an ever-widening ring of industrial towns engaged in spinning, weaving, dyeing, bleaching, calendering, printing, processing, finishing and merchanting. Accrington, Blackburn, Bolton, Bury, Lancaster, Preston and Wigan are among the many towns engaged chiefly in the cotton trade. Lancashire possesses, however, many additional industries of great importance: iron and steel works, engineering, smelting, refining, rolling, wire drawing, the manufacture of all kinds of textile and other machinery, locomotives, electrical equipment, power units, motor cars, paper, cardboard and other packing materials, foods and clothing. At *Port Sunlight* are the Unilever soap-works.

Liverpool has for generations been a famous port, and it receives and despatches the majority of the imports and exports of Lancashire and the Midlands. The city's principal industries are those which process and manufacture imported raw materials and re-export finished products. Flour-milling, sugar refining, oilcakes and soap manufacture, tobacco and rubber are industries of this type.

At *Macclesfield*, due south of Manchester in the neighbouring county of Cheshire, are centred all branches of the British silk industry.

Cumberland (Cumbria). Coal, haematite and iron and steel production have long been the chief industries, but latterly there have been a variety of new developments in the industrial area on the coast, where Whitehaven, Workington, Maryport and, a short distance inland, Cockermouth are the chief towns. These new developments include the manufacture of aluminium alloy components, transparent viscose paper and clothing. *Carlisle* is noted for the manufacture of textiles, carpets, tin boxes, cranes and biscuits. Barrow-in-Furness has large shipyards.

Tyneside. The more important towns are *Newcastle-upon-Tyne* and *Gateshead*. A centre of industry world-famous for its shipbuilding and ship-repairing yards. The light industries located in the district include electrical engineering, flour milling, food preserving and packing, and the manufacture of tobacco, glass-ware and clothing. To the south are the rich coal-fields of Durham and the iron and steel works of Middlesbrough. In Durham itself carpets, confectionery and printing are among trades that have recently been established. Wilton has become a centre of the chemical industry.

Teesside. On the lower banks of the river Tees, which forms the boundary between the counties of Durham and Yorkshire, is another area of intense industrial activity. Shipbuilding and the manufacture of chemicals are the chief industries at Billingham: iron and steel, bridging materials, railway equipment and clothing are manufactured at Guisborough, Eston, Skelton and Loftus.

3

Yorkshire.   From time immemorial Yorkshire has been associated with wool, and *Bradford, Halifax, Huddersfield, Leeds* and *Wakefield* are the giants of the wool trade.   In their vicinity is Brighouse, which manufactures machinery, silk, cotton, woollens and worsteds, iron and brass, chemicals, dyestuffs, wire, soap, clothing, carpets, fire-bricks and electrical appliances.   *Doncaster* has important railway locomotive and carriage works.   *Sheffield* is chiefly associated with the manufacture of special and alloy steels, railway materials and heavy engineering equipment, tools, cutlery, silverware and coal-mining.   *Hull* is the largest centre of the seed-crushing and oil-extracting industry in the world.   Among its products are acetates, boots and shoes, whale oil, paint, paper, polishes, rope, starch, tar products, varnishes, etc.

Birmingham.   The centre of a great metal-working region, *Birmingham* alone claims 1500 different industries.   The area is rich in coal, as is instanced by the mines around Wolverhampton, where also are such light industries as the manufacture of ball-bearings, clothing and jewellery.   *Shrewsbury*, to the west, is an important railway centre.   *Coventry* is renowned for its motor-cars, bicycles and electrical equipment.

North of Birmingham is the district known as the *Potteries*, with Stoke-on-Trent as its centre, which produces fine china as well as ordinary domestic ware and industrial ceramics, together with tyres and rubber goods.

West Midlands.   To the south of Birmingham is *Kidderminster*, famed for its carpets and rugs, but also a producer of car bodies and chemicals.   Farther south are Banbury, where agricultural implements and aluminium are made; *Witney*, which has produced blankets for the last seven hundred years; and *Oxford*, with one of the largest motor-car assembly plants in the world. *Gloucester* has given its name to many famous aircraft, but also has a variety of light industries; *Hereford*, which is embowered in orchards, makes cider, jams and canned fruits, as well as agricultural implements; and *Worcester* counts among its seventy-two industries Royal Worcester porcelain and Worcester sauce.   South of Gloucester is *Stroud*, headquarters of the West of England cloth industry.

Thames Estuary.   On the north bank of the Thames are Walthamstow, Stepney and West Ham, where the vast enterprises of the Port of London Authority may be seen at work; Dagenham, which is concerned chiefly with automobile manufacture

(Ford); and Thurrock, which includes cement, soap and cardboard amongst its products. On the south bank are Woolwich, famous for its Royal Dockyard and Ordnance Factory; Erith, with heavy engineering and oil-refineries; and Gravesend, noted for marine engineering. At Rochester aircraft and agricultural implements are manufactured.

Southampton. One of the chief ports on the south coast, linked to London by excellent road and rail communications. Among the outstanding achievements of Southampton's industries have been the building of the winning Schneider Trophy aeroplane, the first Spitfire, the world's largest helicopter and the Scott-Paine motor-boat.

Bradford-on-Avon. Now an important centre of the rubber industry.

Basingstoke, in Hampshire, is an industrial centre. Among its principal industries today are the manufacture of commercial vehicles, clothing, leather, precision instruments and pharmaceutical products.

Bristol. One of the oldest seaports in Britain. Bristol's industrial enterprises now number over 300, of which the principal are the manufacture of tobacco and cigarettes, chocolate and cocoa, aircraft and straw hats. Engineering, however, has become in recent years the city's biggest single industry.

East Midlands. Leicestershire is an important pig-iron producing district and at *Leicester* itself engineering, sewing-cotton, artificial silk, boots and shoes, hosiery and flour-milling are among the staple industries. Leicester is probably the greatest centre in the world of the knitwear industry.

Other large industrial centres in the East Midlands are *Derby*, long associated with heavy engineering, and with the construction of locomotives; *Burton* with brewing; *Nottingham* with a long list of such diverse products as bicycles, tobacco and lace; and *Rugby* (electronics).

In the Derbyshire town of *Chesterfield* coal is the main industry, but the town also manufactures cardboard, chemicals, furniture, iron and steel tubes, railway carriages and sugar.

Lincoln. The city's main industry is heavy engineering, and its principal manufactures are engines, crushers, rollers, boilers, dredgers, pumps and crankshafts. Scunthorpe, farther to the north, produces iron and steel. *Grimsby*, on the coast, is known for its extensive commercial docks which handle a busy trade in timber and coal.

The manufacture of boots and shoes is centred chiefly in *Northampton* and *Norwich*. Wisbech, another inland seaport, does a considerable trade in agricultural products.

Letchworth Garden City, the first garden city in Britain, produces machinery of almost every kind, scientific instruments, corsets and matches. A few miles to the west is *Dunstable*, close to the important industrial town of Luton: its industries include the manufacture of cars (Vauxhall), pumps, plastics and conveyors.

Wales

South Wales has the third largest coalfield in Britain and three notable ports: *Cardiff*, the centre of a busy and up-to-date industrial area; *Swansea*, which, in addition to its coal interests, manufactures sulphuric acid, metallic tin, copper and zinc, and has oil refineries; and *Newport* (Monmouthshire) which also engaged in the steel, engineering, aluminium and chemical industries. In North Wales there are chemical works as well as paper and artificial silk mills.

Scotland

The division between the urban industrial areas and the rural agricultural areas is strongly defined in Scotland. The industrial belt is an area only 33 miles wide stretching diagonally across the narrow waist of the country in the valleys of Clyde and Forth, with only one major industrial city — Aberdeen — outside it.

Features of Scottish industry in recent years have been the provision of modern factories on "industrial estates" by a government-sponsored body and the development of light industries like clothing, plastics, furniture and foodstuffs.

Glasgow. The great industrial metropolis of the country, famed for its steel-works and shipbuilding, but also engaged in a multiplicity of trades. The cotton industry which led to its tremendous development in the 19th century — in 50 years 134 mills were built — is even today one of its foremost industries. Its neighbour city of Paisley, home of the beautiful Paisley shawl, continues that tradition, and Glasgow's importance as a textile centre is increased by its production of hosiery, woollen goods and carpets. It is, however, for shipbuilding that Glasgow and the Clyde are most widely known. Here were built the giant liners "Queen Mary" and "Queen Elizabeth".

The area round Glasgow — the former counties of Lanarkshire and Renfrewshire, now part of the new Strathclyde region — contains Scotland's densest concentration of heavy industry. Only a few years ago Lanarkshire produced half the Scottish output of coal, but its pits are now almost worked out. The district is still highly industrialised, with large steelworks at Coatbridge and Motherwell.

In the middle of the industrial belt is *Falkirk* with its foundries. The 200 year old Carron ironworks are the largest of their kind in Britain. There are large oil refineries at *Grangemouth*, now Scotland's third largest port.

Edinburgh. At the eastern end of the industrial belt is Edinburgh, the capital, the second largest brewing centre in Great Britain and notable also for its whisky distilleries, including two of the largest in the world. Among Edinburgh's most noted industries are book-publishing — it was the home of the *Encyclopaedia Britannica* and *Who's Who* — and paper-making. Its other products include biscuits, furniture, glassware, leather goods, surgical instruments and toys.

The *Lothian* region, surrounding Edinburgh, is almost entirely agricultural in its eastern part, but there are mining areas in the central and western parts of the region.

Fife. *Dunfermline* is one of the centres of the Scottish linen industry: linen is the traditional fabric of Scotland and Scotland has been famous for its manufacture for 400 years. On the south coast of Fife, at *Kirkcaldy*, linoleum was invented, and still provides its major industry.

Dundee. Jute, jam and journalism have always been popularly listed as this Tayside port's chief industries. Local products also include "Dundee cake" and "Dundee marmalade".

Aberdeen is the "granite city", built of that stone and formerly a world-famous provider of it; but its traditional industry is shipbuilding. It was the home of the China clippers, and is still actively engaged in the industry. It has five paper mills, and along with Dundee it produces most of the woollen gloves made in Great Britain. Another of its industries is the weaving of plaids, and that characteristic Scottish craft is also carried on farther north at Inverness and Elgin.

The Highlands. The principal occupations of the Highlands are crofting (small-scale farming) and fishing, but the native craft of weaving tweeds and tartans is an industry of some importance. Efforts have been made in recent years to establish light industries in the Highlands, and hydroelectric development and forestry have also made great strides.

The Borders. This region is the home of the tweed industry, using wool from the local Cheviot sheep, the main towns being Galashiels, Selkirk and Hawick. Hawick and Dumfries, in the south-west, are noted for their hosiery industry.

Transport and Trade

The *roads* of Britain are good and well maintained, but many of the older roads, still following ancient land boundaries, have a rather winding course. Two-thirds of the country's freight traffic is carried by road. Since the last war the road network has been modernised and improved, with the building of motorways and major engineering works like the new tunnels under the Thames and the Mersey and giant new bridges over the Severn, the Forth and the Tay.

The *railways* were the earliest in the world and developed on a very considerable scale during the 19th century. For long the railway was the best means of getting about the country, but in the present century it has suffered increasingly from the competition of road and air travel. Attempts to make the railway system more economic by closing down little used lines (involving the loss of 5000 miles out of the original 20,000 miles over a period of ten years) and by modernisation (diesel traction, electrification) have met with only limited success.

The *canals* of Britain, built two centuries ago, are out of date and unsuited to the needs of modern traffic. *Coastal shipping*, particularly on the east coast, is still of some importance, accounting for 40% of the total traffic handled by British ports.

Britain's *merchant shipping fleet* was for long the largest in the world, and is still the third largest, coming after Liberia (much used as a flag of convenience) and Japan, with a total of 27,000,000 gross tons. Britain's 4000 vessels represent some 13% of the world total. The merchant fleet is managed by 270 companies and employs 140,000 seamen. The old "tramps", picking up cargoes as opportunity offers, play a less important part than in the 19th century, and regular cargo services by the various shipping lines have increased in relative importance.

There has been a particular development of oil tanker traffic and, more recently, of container traffic. Large passenger liners like the prestigious old "Queen Mary" and "Queen Elizabeth" are continuing to lose ground in face of competition from the airlines, though the renown of companies like Cunard, P. & O. and the Union Castle line remains legendary. Britain's largest port is London, with a turnover of 60,000,000 tons annually. Second place is taken by Milford Haven (40,000,000 tons), thanks to its oil traffic. Then come Southampton and Liverpool, with 28,000,000 tons each.

Civil aviation in Britain was born in 1924 with the establishment of Imperial Airways. Services to India began in 1929 and to Australia in 1943. In 1939 the British Overseas Airways Corporation (B.O.A.C.) was formed by the amalgamation of a number of existing airlines, and British European Airways (B.E.A.) came into being in 1946. Finally in 1972 B.O.A.C. and B.E.A. became divisions of the state-controlled *British Airways*. There are also a number of independent airlines like British Caledonian, mostly flying domestic services but with some international services. London Airport (Heathrow) is by far the largest airport in Britain, handling more than half the country's passenger traffic, and indeed the largest in Europe.

British *foreign trade* is the third largest in the world, coming after the United States and Federal Germany. In terms of value it represents about 10% of the world total — a considerably lower proportion than at the beginning of this century. Imports are mainly raw materials (oil, minerals, foodstuffs), exports mainly manufactured products. The trade deficit, of the order of 8% to 10% in terms of value, is offset to some extent by "invisible exports" — income from British capital invested abroad, insurance (particularly the celebrated "Lloyd's of London", with its monopoly of shipping insurance), the sale of patents, ship charters, etc. The tourist trade is a developing source of income, partly as a result of the excellent work done by the British Tourist Authority.

After a period during which Britain remained outside the European Economic Community and played a leading part in the European Free Trade Association, founded on its initiative as an alternative grouping for the non-E.E.C. countries, the British government applied to join the Community, and in 1973, under Mr Heath's Conservative administration, became a member, along with the Republic of Ireland and Denmark.

In 1975 Britain's terms of membership were renegotiated in some respects by Mr Wilson's Labour government.

New Towns and Regional Planning

Traditionally there has long been a contrast between two parts of Britain separated by a line running from north-east to south-west — a contrast between the north-western part of the country, hillier and less fertile but with supplies of coal which led to its earlier industrialisation, and the green and rural south-east. In the last thirty years, however, the situation has been reversed. The north-west, with 57% of the total area, has now no more than a third of the total population. From the 1930s onwards, with the continuing decline of the coalfield areas and the traditional industries (textiles, iron and steel, shipbuilding), men who could find no work in their home areas flocked to London and the south-east. In consequence this part of the country now contains two thirds of the population, and the country's largest conurbations (London, Birmingham) have developed here.

The extent of the problem was realised during the depression of the 1930s, and the first measures were taken to deal with it. Legislation passed in 1934 established four "special areas" (Scotland, the North-West, Merseyside, South Wales) which were to qualify for special government help. Then in 1937 the Barlow Commission, after a thorough examination of the problem, recommended measures for the proper planning of the larger cities, assistance towards the development of medium-sized and small towns, the establishment of "new towns" offering employment opportunities of their own, and the decentralisation of industry from London.

Legislation passed in 1945 provided aid for "depressed areas" (the Scottish Lowlands, Cumberland, Northumberland, South Wales) which had particularly acute economic problems. Acts of 1946 and 1947 provided the basis for the establishment of new towns, and the National Parks Act of 1949 made it possible to protect particular areas of natural beauty or interest. It was not, however, until 1963-64, which saw the first regional development plans (Scotland, north-eastern England, the south-east), and subsequent years that coordinated efforts really began to get under way. Three types of area were distinguished:

(a) the *development areas*, representing more than half the total area of the country (the whole of Scotland, Cumberland

and Northumberland, the whole of Wales, Devon and Cornwall, and Northern Ireland). A Highlands and Islands Development Board was set up to promote development in this part of Scotland.

(b) the *special development areas* (within development areas) requiring special measures of assistance. These were mainly the old coalfield and iron-working areas (Glasgow, Ayrshire, Fife, Cumberland, Northumberland, Swansea and the Merthyr Tydfil coalfield).

(c) *the intermediate areas* (Edinburgh, the area north of Manchester, the Leeds-Hull-Sheffield area, Cardiff and Plymouth).

In order to promote development in the areas of special need a whole battery of investment incentives, grants, subsidies and allowances was provided. At the same time the government tried to control the continuing expansion of London. Restrictions were imposed in 1947 on the building of new industrial and office premises in the capital. Government departments moved some of their staffs out of London, and private business was encouraged to do the same. Between 1963 and 1973 almost 1200 firms employing some 100,000 people left London. In consequence of these various measures there was a significant redistribution of industry; in the Scottish Lowlands, for example, 45,000 new jobs were created, particularly in electronics, petrochemicals, precision engineering, motor vehicle production and the aerospace industry.

One instrument for the relocation of industry was the establishment of industrial estates — groups of modern factory buildings with all necessary facilities and associated services. The estates might be provided by private enterprise, local authorities or the government. The government-owned industrial estates are now managed by three Industrial Estates Corporations, one each in England, Wales and Scotland.

The object of the *new towns* was to draw population and industry away from the rapidly growing conurbations, particularly London, with its concentration of 12,500,000 people within a radius of 40 miles. A wide green belt within which industrial development was not permitted was drawn round London and other large cities; and it was an essential part of the new town conception that each new town should have industrial employment for its inhabitants and should not merely be a kind of outer dormitory suburb for the big city.

The first new towns were established between 1946 and 1950, and there are now 23 in England and Wales and six in Scotland. Many of them involve the expansion of existing small towns. Eleven of the English new towns (Basildon, Bracknell, Crawley, Harlow, Hatfield, Hemel Hempstead, Milton Keynes, Northampton, Peterborough, Stevenage and Welwyn) are intended to relieve congestion in Greater London; the Scottish new towns are designed to draw population and industry from Glasgow.

The new towns have been an exciting experiment which has offered architects and planners the opportunity of planning attractive modern towns in which workers can live near their work but there is a clear separation between residential and industrial areas. The layouts of the towns vary according to the requirements of the site, the character of the town and the ideas of the architects and planners concerned, but in general they have been successful in providing good working and living conditions for their citizens. Experience has still to show whether they will succeed in establishing and preserving the corporate sense and atmosphere of an established community: but the omens are favourable, and the experiment has attracted interest and imitation in many other countries.

LITERATURE AND THE ARTS

By D.A. Young

This section contains a brief account of the local traditions of English literature and general summaries of the historical development of painting, architecture and the arts in Britain. Fuller information about works of art and architecture, art galleries and museums, concert halls and festivals will be found in the descriptive part of this Guide and in the Practical Information at the end.

LITERATURE

Of all the arts, it is through her literature that Britain has made her most precious gifts to the culture and civilisation of the western world. For an article on the arts in Britain to leave out any reference to English literature would be unthinkable: and yet to attempt to do justice to its infinite riches in the limited space of a section of this article would be as foolish as to hope to confine an appraisal of the wines of France to the bounds of a single paragraph.

The attempt, therefore, will not be made; and indeed the average visitor to Britain, to whom the treasures of her literature are so readily available and so long familiar, would find little use for a prosaic summary. He may not, however, be aware of the extent to which the literary influences of Britain's past make themselves felt as one travels from one end of the country to another. The great figures of literature are still felt as a living presence, and their spirit, in those parts of the country which they made particularly their own, is inescapable and sometimes almost tangible. The "Shakespeare country", the "Burns country", the "Hardy country": these are not the pious tributes of devotees to the memory of their idol, but are everyday expressions accepted naturally by ordinary men and women. In fact, it is true to say that such terms as "Shakespeare land" and the Scott Country have a vivid significance in the minds of many people to whom a reference to Warwickshire and Roxburghshire, though more precise geographically, would convey very little.

And so it is that as the traveller from the coast approaches Canterbury, with the three towers of the cathedral rising before him into the Kentish sky, he will see them not merely as a wonder of mediaeval architecture but as the goal of the Canterbury pilgrims, that happy band of story-tellers immortalised by *Geoffrey Chaucer*, the first and one of the greatest of English literary figures. At Rochester, a little farther on, his mind will be on *Dickens* and Mr Pickwick, and Dickens will spring to life again when he reaches London. Nor, if he has poetry in him, will he leave London without visiting the garden of that house at Hampstead, where *Keats* wrote of the nightingale.

On the Sussex Downs the literary voyager will enjoy the robust companionship of *Belloc*, and at Dorchester he will remember that he is in the "Casterbridge" of *Thomas Hardy*. In the east, which is also the country of the great painters, he will find *Tennyson* and *Swinburne* and *Cowper*, and amid the bleakness of the Yorkshire moors — the *Bronte Country* — he will walk in spirit with the three tragic sisters of a century ago. In the border hills, still redolent with memories of battles long ago, the landscape will be coloured for him by the mediaeval romances of *Walter Scott;* and in the fastnesses of the Highlands he will have *Stevenson* for his guide.

Returning by the western side of the island, the first literary giant to be encountered is *Robert Burns*, once a familiar figure in Ayr and Dumfries. In the Lake District it is *Wordsworth* who rules the scene, and the traveller will doubtless take the opportunity to pay court in that far from regal cottage at Grasmere; in Shropshire the presiding genius is *Mary Webb;* and then come the gentle meadows and leafy glades of Warwickshire, the forest of Arden, the land of **Shakespeare.** At Stratford, where he was born and lies buried, the plays are given on summer nights in the great modern theatre by the Avon, a stone's throw from the garden of the house where their author died.

But Shakespeare belongs not only to Stratford, but to London — where his spiritual home is the Old Vic Theatre, in a crowded quarter of the city south of the Thames — and indeed to the whole of Britain.

When we think of Shakespeare, we think of *George Bernard Shaw*, which is exactly what Shaw would have wished us to do. For his admirers there are two places of pilgrimage; Malvern, where his plays are performed during the Festival which he himself still attended in his eighties, and, nearer London, the little village of Ayot St Lawrence, where the house he lived in for almost fifty years can be visited.

PAINTING

In 1629 Rubens, the great Flemish painter, paid one of his frequent visits to England, where he enjoyed the high favour of that noted connoisseur of the arts King Charles I. He wrote to a friend: "This island seems to me worthy of the consideration of a man of taste, not only because of the charm of the countryside and the beauty of the people, not only because of the outward show which appears to me most choice and to announce a people rich and happy in the bosom of peace, but also by the incredible quantity of excellent pictures, statues and ancient inscriptions which are in this court."

If Rubens were to return to Britain today he would find that the royal treasures, now the richest private collection in the world, are even more "incredible" in quantity than in his day; but his admiration would not now be confined to the works of art in royal palaces. In our day treasures even more valuable than those reserved for the privileged eyes of Charles I and his court are freely available to be enjoyed by all who visit the museums and galleries of London and the other great cities of Britain.

During the two centuries after the Reformation, when some of Europe's greatest artists were at work, it would be difficult to cite a British painter of any quality. Practically the only pictures of any importance produced in Britain during this period were the work of the numerous foreign artists, mostly portrait-painters from Germany and the Netherlands, who enjoyed the favour of the court and the great families of the day, and some of whom settled in Britain. **Holbein,** for example, did most of his finest work at Henry VIII's court, and there are so many pictures by **van Dyck,** Charles I's favourite painter, in the palaces and museums of Britain that it is sometimes difficult to remember that he was not a native of the country. Similarly *Lely* and *Kneller,* two of van Dyck's most notable successors, who also settled in Britain and rose to the honour of knighthood, came respectively from the Netherlands and from Germany.

In the Middle Ages British decorative artists — illuminators of manuscripts and painters of frescoes — were renowned throughout Europe; but the destruction of their work at the Renaissance on religious grounds, combined with the over-enthusiastic restorations of the 19th century, has left us little of their work to admire today. There are a few outstanding

exceptions, like the Winchester Bible, the wall paintings in
the chapter house of Westminster Abbey and the chapel of
Eton College, and the Wilton Diptych in the National Gallery.
In general, however, it might be said that for the ordinary art
lover the mainstream of British painting begins with the 18th century and with the pioneer work of Hogarth.

William Hogarth (1697-1764), who can be seen to be an early
forerunner of the 19th century realists, brought into British art
qualities which it greatly needed. Realising that it was useless
to vie with the great foreign artists of the day for the favour
of the nobility, he sought to create a new style which should
appeal more directly to the ordinary people of his day. His
two great picture series, the "Rake's Progress" (Soane Museum,
London) and "Marriage à la Mode" (Tate Gallery, London),
can be read either as stories or as sermons. At the same time
they can be appreciated purely as art, for Hogarth's brushwork,
his use of colour and above all his grasp of character and grouping proclaim him a serious artists and no mere illustrator. The
"Rake in Bedlam", for example, is as carefully composed as
any Italian painting in the classical tradition, and the expressive
power and spontaneity of the "Shrimp Girl" (National Gallery)
makes this one of the finest portraits in 18th century European
art.

It was, however, only with the appearance of **Joshua Reynolds**
(1723-92), a generation after Hogarth, that fashionable society
gave full acceptance to a national painter. On the face of it
Reynolds was the very antithesis of Hogarth. He had been
in Italy, and his study of the Renaissance masters had given
him something of Raphael's sure draughtsmanship and Titian's
sense of colour; and throughout his career he followed their
principles, and indeed their style. Towards the end of his life
he was still anxious to paint the ambitious mythological pictures
dear to the classical school, but public taste was still faithful to
the style of Holbein and van Dyck, and accordingly he remained
almost exclusively a portrait-painter. The degree to which he
penetrated into the character of his sitters can be seen in the
charming "Age of Innocence" (National Gallery), "Miss Bow-
les" (Wallace Collection, London) and "Dr Johnson" (National
Gallery).

Nevertheless, for all their warmth and harmony, one is
conscious of a certain self-consciousness in many of Reynolds'
portraits. In this his work presents a marked contrast to that
of his great contemporary and rival **Thomas Gainsborough**

(1727-88), the attraction of whose paintings lies in their freshness and lack of sophistication and in their delicate refinement of tone and texture. For many art lovers the silvery tones and subtle artifice of Gainsborough's works hold a more powerful though less easily definable charm than the rich golden tones of his rival. Very typical of Gainsborough are "The Artist's Daughters" (National Gallery) and "Mrs Robinson" (Wallace Collection). But whenever he could escape from the tyranny of commissioned portraits Gainsborough liked to paint straightforward landscapes; and in spite of his immense reputation as a portrait-painter it is mainly in his landscapes that we can see his chief contribution to the development of British painting.

Other prominent portrait painters of the time who helped to restore British painters to the favour of the nobility included **George Romney,** whose mastery of charm and colour gave him, at one time, a reputation almost as great as that of the two established leaders; **Henry Raeburn,** a vigorous painter whose best work is displayed in the National Gallery at Edinburgh; and **Thomas Lawrence,** principal portrait painter to King George III, who in the months following Waterloo painted many of the leading figures of Europe.

There is another contemporary painter who should not be forgotten — the lonely and enigmatic figure of **William Blake** (1757-1827). He was a deeply religious man who lived in a mystical world, and it is only in the present century that the compelling qualities of his dream-like and fantastic representations of Biblical scenes have achieved the serious recognition that is their due.

The earliest of the great English masters of landscape painting was **Richard Wilson** (1714-81). He might be described as the Reynolds of the landscape artists, and at his best — as in "On the Wye" (National Gallery) and "Landscape with Bathers" (Leeds Art Gallery) — he achieves a serene grandeur of design and a glowing luminosity which place him in the foremost rank.

In Gainsborough's landscapes we discern the same impatience with the classical conventions that is so apparent in his portraits, showing that he was the successor, in spirit if not in form, to Hogarth. While Wilson was inspired by abstract grandeur, Gainsborough was moved by an essentially local and intimate conception of landscape. Realism of this kind, however, was not yet fashionable, and only his portraits enabled him to earn a living. Nevertheless his revolutionary way of treating landscape exercised a lasting influence on his East Anglian fellow-countryman.

It can hardly be merely by chance that East Anglia, that countryside of open fields, venerable trees and vast skies, a countryside which is filled with a particular light that can be found nowhere else in Britain, nurtured some of the greatest of England's landscape artists. One of the foremost of the East Anglians was **John Crome** (1768-1821), founder of the Norwich School which adopted and developed the realistic outlook of Gainsborough. "Even if your subject is a pigstye", declared Crome on his deathbed, "give it majesty".

This new freedom in the choice of subject was one of the harbingers of the Romantic movement which was just beginning to influence the art of Northern Europe. Hitherto painters who made their living by painting "views" had not been taken very seriously as artists, but when people of culture became aware that nature — in its natural state, if the expression may be used — was supremely romantic the prestige of the painters of rural scenes was greatly enhanced. But here too, as in portrait-painting, it was necessary to take account also of the classical and academic tradition.

The two greatest landscape painters of the age — **William Turner** (1775-1851) and **John Constable** (1776-1837) — tackled the problem from opposite angles. Turner had visions of a fantastic realm of dazzling harmonies and of striking and dramatic effects — a vast and insubstantial dream world which had, paradoxically, a firmly realistic, and often even prosaic, foundation. Thus his "Steamer in a Snowstorm" (Tate Gallery) shows a conception of nature at its most romantic and sublime, with an unexcelled mastery of the problems of luminosity. Conversely, a mythological subject, such as the superb "Garden of the Hesperides" (Tate Gallery), is made as convincing as fact. In his last works Turner became increasingly visionary, and can be seen as a prophet of the purely aesthetic school, of "art for art's sake", the chief representative of which was Whistletr.

Turner remains the subject of discussion, and his place as an artist has not been finally established. One need only consider Monet's "Gare St Lazare" (1877; Louvre, Paris), however, to realise the influence he had in Europe. He also played a conspicuous part in the development of watercolour painting, one of Britain's most notable contributions to European art, which had been pioneered by such men as *Cozens* and *Girtin*. Other prominent watercolourists were *Cox*, *Colman*, *Bonington* and *Birket Foster*.

Constable's task was simply to paint what he saw with his own eyes, and in this respect he continued where Gainsborough and Crome had left off. He went beyond them in his insistence on truth to life and his refusal to make a scene more impressive or more idyllic than it was in reality. He had an immense colour range, and got closer than any of his predecessors to the true green of the fields and the blue of the sky. His European reputation was established when his masterpiece "The Hay Wain" was exhibited at the Paris Salon in 1824. Delacroix is said to have re-painted the whole background of his "Massacres of Chio" after seeing this picture, and Constable's influence on Millet and the Barbizon group is well known.

About the middle of the 19th century a group of British painters, although sharing Constable's concern for sincerity and truth and his irritation with the rather theatrical pretensions of "official" art, struck out on a very different line from that opened up by the East Anglian masters. If art was to be re-formed, they declared, it was necessary to look back before Raphael, who had idealised nature and sought beauty at the expense of reality, to the time when artists were honest craftsmen who sought not earthly but celestial glory in the straightforward representation of the world in which they lived. In an attempt to return to the "age of faith", therefore, the **Pre-Raphaelite** group of painters was formed in 1848 under the leadership of **Dante Gabriel Rossetti** (1828-82), a Londoner born of Italian parents who had settled in Britain.

The principles of Pre-Raphaelitism are exemplified supremely well by Rossetti's "Ecce Ancilla Domini" (Tate Gallery). Here there is no Renaissance idealism; the story of the Annunciation is seen with a fresh mind, and achieves much of the simple, though effective, emotional force of the primitives. Equally successful are some of the works of the other Pre-Raphaelite leaders — **Ford Madox Brown's** "The Last of England" (Birmingham Art Gallery), **Holman Hunt's** "The Hireling Shepherd" (Manchester City Art Gallery) and **Edward Millais'** "Christ in the Home of His Parents" (Tate Gallery), in which the figure of Mary was bitterly attacked by Charles Dickens as being too commonplace. So far had the Pre-Raphaelites departed from the principles of Raphael ! It must be admitted, however, that their idea of becoming modern primitives was itself artificial and idealised. Whereas in France, with Millet, Courbet and Monet, the attempt to break free of all convention in the exploration of nature was extremely fruitful, the Pre-Raphaelites found themselves at the end of the day in the same dead end from which they had hoped to extricate the art of their period.

It is no longer fashionable to appreciate the Pre-Raphaelites, and it must be said that they delayed for some decades the assimilation by British artists of the new discoveries of the French Impressionists. Out of the mainstream though it may be, however, the Pre-Raphaelite movement is a fascinating study. One lasting effect of this curious artistic episode was the growth of the so-called arts and crafts movement, initiated by **William Morris** (1834-96), who sought — successfully, as it has turned out — to preserve the ancient hand crafts such as furniture and tapestry-making which were in danger of being lost for ever with the advance of machinery. Morris's influence led to the revival of a whole range of activities, from folk dancing to the making of musical instruments, which were apparently doomed to disappear but which still flourish on a scale that would have seemed inconceivable eighty years ago.

The mainstream of European art returned to Britain largely under the auspices of an American-born Londoner, **James Whistler** (1834-1903). Regarding the Pre-Raphaelites as reactionaries, he advocated a purely aesthetic theory of art, in an attempt to stem the flood of anecdotic pictures which was then invading the galleries (though in this field the works of **G.F. Watts** had genuine artistic value). Nature, maintained Whistler, provides all the elements of a picture, just as a piano provides all the notes of a sonata on its keyboard, but it is left to the artist to compose and interpret. And so, out of the unpromising material of a misty evening on the Thames, Whistler would compose such a masterpiece as "Battersea Bridge" (Tate Gallery); and under his leadership the riverside quarter of Chelsea became the artistic centre of London, a distinction to which it still manages to cling, in spite of the competing claims of Hampstead, Camden Town and even Kensington.

The 20th century has produced in Britain great artists in all branches of painting. Portraiture has been particularly strong. The leading figure before 1914 was **John Sargent**, whose richly toned portraits in the graceful aristocratic manner are well represented at the Tate Gallery: and there is character and distinction in those of his successor, **William Orpen.**

The leading figures in the new landscape school were **Graham Sutherland** and **John Piper**; but perhaps the most controversial name in British 20th century painting has been that of **Stanley Spencer**, whose vast "Resurrection" now occupies a place of honour in the central hall of the Tate Gallery, the champion of modern art, which is frequently at odds with the conservative Royal Academy. (Even today it is better not to pronounce the name of Sir Alfred Munnings, a former President of the Academy and a great opponent of modern art, within hearing of the Tate !).

Within recent years there has been a marked revival of sculpture in Britain, in which the periodic open-air exhibitions held in Battersea Park in London have played a not unimportant part. The two great names of modern British sculpture are *Jacob Epstein* and *Henry Moore.*

It is, of course, always dangerous to prophesy in matters concerning art, but it seems safe to predict that future historians will decide that the two outstanding British painters of the first half of the century are **Walter Sickert,** the greatest of the post-Impressionist followers of Whistler, and **Augustus John,** a draughtsman of unrivalled pungency, the acknowledged leader of the non-academic portraitists. With his flowing cape and no less flowing beard, John was one of the great picturesque figures of his day.

Since the end of the last war London has become one of the leading centres of contemporary art, attracting many artists from the Continent. The followers of **Ben Nicholson,** chief among them Victor Pasmore, have developed a form of nonfigurative art: and since the 1950 London has been the headquarters of *Pop Art*, which seeks to integrate all the elements of everyday life to create an art accessible to all (Paolozzi, Blake, Hamilton, Caulfield, Boshier, Kitaj, etc.).

Finally, the visitor should be reminded that many of the magnificent private houses throughout the country are frequently open to the public and that the art treasures which in the course of centuries have been amassed within their walls may be inspected as easily as those in the museums and galleries. In addition, a selection from the Royal Collection may be seen in the new Queen's Gallery at Buckingham Palace.

ARCHITECTURE

Prehistoric. No country in Europe is richer in prehistoric remains than Britain, particularly in the western counties which must have been thriving centres of human activity in the Stone and Early Bronze ages. The most impressive memorial of this period, about 1600 B.C., is *Stonehenge*, Wiltshire.

Roman.   Many evidences remain of the high degree of civilisation which the Romans imposed on the most northerly outpost
of their empire.   The Roman lighthouse on the cliffs at *Dover*,
Kent, c. 50 A.D., is believed to be the oldest standing masonry
in Britain.   At *Bath* in Somerset, still celebrated for its hot
springs, is a Roman bath, 82 feet long, with the original lead
lining still intact.   In the north, stretching for miles across the
empty hills of Northumberland, is the fortified wall erected
by the Emperor Hadrian.

Anglo-Saxon.   In the comparatively few surviving examples
of Anglo-Saxon work — mostly churches — can be traced the
tentative beginnings of the Romanesque style which was to
reach its full fruition in Britain under the Normans.   The plan
of a Saxon church is usually rectangular, with round-arched or
triangular-topped doors and windows and a massive tower at
the west end.   The pillars are short and squat, with capitals and
bases formed of undecorated blocks of stone.

Norman.   For a century following the Norman conquest
architecture in England and France followed roughly parallel
lines, and the features already prevalent in Normandy — the
rounded arches and windows; the massive circular piers; the
exuberant, if somewhat crude, decoration and carvings — were
transplanted intact in the receptive soil on the other side of the
Channel.   The impressive simplicity of Norman Romanesque is
seen in unspoilt perfection in the tiny St John's Chapel in the
White Tower of the *Tower of London*, but undoubtedly the
grandest example of the style is *Durham Cathedral*.

Visitors from the Continent may sometimes be surprised by
the contrasting styles to be found in many British cathedrals,
but for most visitors this is one of their most interesting characteristics, giving these great buildings a humanity which is
sometimes lacking in buildings belonging to a single style or a
single period.

Gothic.   The end of the 12th century marks the transition,
simultaneously in Britain and in France, from Romanesque to
the Gothic which, in all its changing phases, was to dominate
the ecclesiastical architecture of northern Europe throughout
the remaining centuries of the Middle Ages.   The round arch
gave place to the pointed arch, horizontal lines to vertical lines,
and the large windows gave the buildings of this period a new
lightness.   Of the exterior features of Gothic in Britain the most
striking is the importance given to the towers, of which there

are normally three, giving to such typically English cathedrals as *York*, *Lincoln* and *Canterbury* their impressive skyline. The cathedrals of *Winchester* and *St Albans* are the two longest Gothic churches in the world. Internally, the most notable feature is the treatment of the vaulting and the large stone-traceried windows, which in some cases take up the whole of the east end (normally square rather than rounded as in France).

The English cathedrals owe much of their charm to the fact that they do not stand in the narrow streets of the town but in a "close", with pleasant lawns round which stand the picturesque old houses of church dignitaries and sometimes the residence of the bishop himself. Surely nowhere else in the world can be found the same sense of tranquillity, in such a satisfying architectural setting, as in an English cathedral close.

Early English (c. 1190-1280). The 13th century was marked by a triumphant burst of church-building which produced some of the most beautiful achievements of mediaeval architecture. Early English is the purest and simplest form of Gothic: the decorative details are restrained and graceful, and the pointed-arch windows rely on grouping and proportion rather than elaborate tracery for their effect. The supreme example of the Early English style is *Salisbury Cathedral*.

Decorated (c. 1280-1380). The 14th century witnessed the development of Early English Gothic into the elaborate, flowing and infinitely expressive form known as Decorated. Pervading the Decorated style is a sense of freedom: the architect, throwing off restrictions and even restraint, concentrated on achieving an effect of spontaneity and spaciousness as well as of height. Windows expanded to hitherto unimagined proportions — the west window of *York* probably constitutes the greatest single area of mediaeval glass in existence, and the east window of *Carlisle* is almost as large, with an intricacy and beauty of tracery which is almost overwhelming. The same complexity is found in the pillars and vaulting, and the exterior is embellished with a profusion of pinnacles and other decorative features. The Gothic style now achieves its full stature, exemplified by the little three-towered cathedral of *Lichfield*, the nave and west front of *Exeter* and the magnificent Angel Choir at *Lincoln*.

Perpendicular (c. 1380-1550). In the 15th century English Gothic diverged even farther from the path followed by continental architects. While the cathedrals of northern Europe were blossoming out into the full-blown glories of Flamboyant,

England was developing a highly individual style which has no counterpart in any other country — the Perpendicular, so called because the decorative features were designed to emphasise height and the vertical line above all other features. In a sense this was a return to the original principles of Gothic, though the manner was very different. In the windows long vertical mullions took the place of the radiating tracery of the Decorated style, and the areas of glass became so large that in some cases they covered the whole wall. The most striking example of this is the great east window of *Gloucester*. This was also the golden age of tower-building: the central tower of *Canterbury Cathedral*, which dates from this period, is perhaps the finest in the country, but there are many small village churches, particularly in East Anglia, Somerset and Devon, whose towers can fitly take their place beside it. But undoubtedly the crowning glory of the Perpendicular style is the fan tracery which embellishes the roofs and vaulting of many of the most important buildings of the period. Fan tracery is an exclusively English creation, and all visitors interested in architecture will want to see some of the buildings in which it can be admired in all its delicate and impressive beauty. The classic examples are the cloisters at *Gloucester*, where the style is said to have originated; the chapels of *King's College*, *Cambridge*, and *Windsor Castle*, both masterpieces of Perpendicular art; and above all Henry VII's chapel in *Westminster Abbey*. The timber roofs of the 15th and 16th century are almost equally remarkable; particularly fine examples are to be seen in the corbel-roofed country churches of East Anglia, in *Hampton Court Palace* and in the halls of the *Oxford* and *Cambridge* colleges.

Castles. Many castles survive in all parts of the country, either preserved as private residences or existing in a state of romantic decay. Of the former class the most important is *Windsor*, the greatest fortress-palace in existence, for nearly 1000 years the principal home of the reigning monarch. Of the ruined castles probably the finest is *Caernarvon* in North Wales. It is appropriate that the fortresses in the two oldest of Britain's historic towns — the *Tower of London* and *Edinburgh Castle* — should still retain something of their military role through their occupation by at least token garrisons.

Abbeys. As a result of the dissolution of the monasteries which followed the Reformation, many of the abbeys erected in the Middle Ages are today in ruins. Yorkshire is particularly rich in abbeys, *Fountains* and *Rievaulx* being the finest; and other notable ruins are those of *Melrose* in the Scottish Borders and *Tintern* on the banks of the Wye in Monmouthshire. Of the numerous abbeys which are still in use as churches, *Westminster* is, of course, the most celebrated, and is a treasure-house of all periods of English Gothic.

Market crosses. Among the minor achievements of mediaeval architecture are the market crosses, often elaborately decorated, to be seen in some old towns. Two of the finest are at *Chichester* and *Salisbury*.

The Renaissance. The wealthy magnates of this period began to build palaces and colleges instead of churches and chantry chapels, and abbeys and castles gave place to magnificent country houses. For the first time since the Norman period British architecture was now exposed to a powerful wave of foreign influence. Travellers returning from the Continent brought with them the new ideas current in France and Italy. The most typical architecture of the new era is to be found in the great country houses erected by the newly enriched nobility under the Tudor and Stuart sovereigns, and more particularly under Elizabeth I (1558-1603) and James I (1603-25). The houses of the Elizabethan period in particular were a picturesque and romantic assemblage of Gothic mullions, turrets and pinnacles and features of the classical style, still not fully assimilated. But what a splendid picture is presented by these sumptuous forests of Tudor masonry standing, supremely self-confident, in their formal gardens — *Hampton Court Palace*, near London; *Wollaton Hall*, Nottinghamshire; *Hardwick Hall*, Derbyshire; *Burghley House*, Northamptonshire; and many others. In the Jacobean mansions, such as *Hatfield House*, Hertfordshire, and *Aston Hall*, Warwickshire, classicism is seen to be gaining ground, but the effect is still overwhelmingly romantic. "Jacobean" may be regarded as the final gesture of the hitherto unbroken Gothic tradition.

The 17th century. First of the great architects of the English Renaissance was *Inigo Jones*, whose prolonged studies in Italy of the works of Palladio left their mark on all his principal achievements, which include the *Banqueting Hall* of Whitehall Palace in London and the *Queen's House* at Greenwich. The fame of Inigo Jones tends to be eclipsed by that of his successor, *Sir Christopher Wren* (1632-1723), the most celebrated of all British architects, who went to Paris in 1665 while the Louvre was being built and was much influenced by it and the other Renaissance buildings he studied in the French capital. His

St Paul's Cathedral in London is the great masterpiece of the age; his secular works included the new wing at Hampton Court Palace and Greenwich Hospital. None of his secular work, not even at the royal palaces, approached the monumental magnificence of the great houses designed by the foremost of his followers, *Sir John Vanbrugh* (1664-1726) — notably *Castle Howard*, Yorkshire, and *Blenheim Palace*, Oxfordshire, the façade of which extends for nearly 1000 feet. These splendid residences of the powerful 18th century aristocracy gave the impulse to a fresh wave of country house building, so that an English landscape can now hardly be considered complete unless it includes a distant glimpse of a majestic portico appearing through the trees.

Georgian. By the 18th century the architecture of the Renaissance, following the period of Palladian exuberance, assumed in Britain a similar distinctive quality and became what is universally known today as "Georgian". The Georgian architects, working in stone or red brick and resolutely avoiding the heavy ornamentation of which the Palladians were often guilty, achieved their effects by a close regard for symmetry and proportion, and by an exquisite refinement of detail, the latter being seen at its best in the buildings designed by the *Adam brothers*. Some of the finest Georgian architecture is to be seen in the spas, favourite resorts of fashionable society in the 18th century, and especially at *Bath*, where the serene and impressive proportions of the buildings fit harmoniously into the hilly setting. The New Town of *Edinburgh* is another magnificent example of Georgian layout and architecture.

The Regency. Under the benevolent rule of the Prince Regent (1810-20) a new note of gaiety and extravagance was introduced into the orderly civilisation of Georgian Britain. The severe unornamented buildings of the 18th century were now enriched with mouldings and embellished with columns and cornices. Every town which was ambitious of securing the Prince Regent's favour now hastened to erect imposing white palaces, which were in fact merely rows of houses concealed behind impressive façades to which in any scheme of architectural logic they were not entitled. Since the last war the authorities have spent large sums of money in restoring Nash's beautiful classical terraces round *Regent's Park* in London to their former glory. *Carlton House Terrace*, fronting on to the great processional way leading to Buckingham Palace, is another outstanding example of Regency architecture in London; and outside the capital it can be seen at its best at *Brighton* in Sussex and *Cheltenham* in Gloucestershire.

Local styles. One of the great charms of a visit to Britain is to observe the variations in building styles from one part of the country to another. The local builders showed considerable skill in adapting their style to the materials available. In the Cotswolds, Gloucestershire and Oxfordshire, for example, the villages are built of soft limestone, easily workable by the masons; and even the humblest cottages, with their mullioned windows, their harmoniously proportioned gables and their groups of decorative chimneys, vie in elegance with the neighbouring great houses in their parks. Cotswold stone mellows into a warm honey-coloured tone, and the villages show an attractive uniformity of colouring in spite of the contrasts between Tudor, Georgian and later styles. There are also very attractive buildings in the stone villages of Northamptonshire and Somerset. In the wooded regions of Warwickshire, Herefordshire and Cheshire the local builders made much use of timber, and the "black and white" half-timbered cottages and manor-houses of these areas are among the most charming in England. In the larger towns like *Chester* and *Shrewsbury* the beams and gables are often embellished with splendid carving. In the well wooded counties of Kent, Essex and Sussex the old cottages are notable for their shingled or barge-boarded walls, painted in a variety of colours, contrasting with their tiled roofs.

In most of the southern counties of England the normal building material was red brick, which was much employed by the Georgian builders of the 18th century. In East Anglia the characteristic external finish was "pargeting", a plaster coating embellished with all manner of elaborate patterns. In the north of England the traditional building material was stone, and in Scotland stone remained the normal building material right up to the first world war.

Perhaps the most characteristic feature of English rural architecture, however, is the thatched roof, which is found in almost every part of the country. Even today the tradition remains alive, and skilled thatchers are rarely at a loss for employment, so great is still the demand for their services.

Victorian (1837-1901). During the long reign of Queen Victoria the models most favoured by architects and their patrons were drawn largely from classical Greek and mediaeval Gothic architecture. Between the protagonists of these two

diametrically opposed schools arose the celebrated "battle of
the styles", which provided the main architectural interest of
the century. After such early triumphs as the building of *St
George's Hall* in Liverpool, one of the most splendid examples
of Greek revival architecture in Europe, the classical style
began to yield place rapidly to the Gothic. This development
was promoted by the Romantic movement in literature, and
particularly by the interest in the Middle Ages aroused by the
works of writers like Scott. Not only churches but office buildings, private houses and even railway stations acquired the
pointed windows, the fretted pinnacles and the cloister walks
which had not been seen in British architectjre since Tudor
times. It was as if men sought reassurance by concealing the
ugliness and materialism of the new industrial age behind a
façade of mediaeval piety and mystery. It is the easiest thing
in the world to accuse Victorian architecture of blatant hypocrisy
and of a lack of original inspiration, but that is not to say that
the age did not produce some excellent buildings. Barry's
neo-Tudor *Houses of Parliament* are an imposing and completely
effective pile by any standard, and it already appears, as it was
meant to appear, as if it were built four hundred years ago.
Similarly, the Gothic churches of Augustus Pugin, both in
mass and detail, will bear comparison with any mediaeval original,
and Wyatt's *Ashridge House* in Hertfordshire might well be a
typical monastic building adapted for domestic use in the reign
of Henry VIII.

The tendency to squander the effect of Gothic by using it
for every kind of building, however, led to the decline of the
neo-Gothic style. The proliferation of turrets and pinnacles
on suburban roofs and the spectacle of provincial town
halls vying with one another in numbers of spires and finials
soon reached the point of absurdity; and Palmerston seems to
have realised this when he preferred a Renaissance-style building
for the new Foreign Office to the Gothic design proposed by
Sir George Gilbert Scott. It is said that Scott used his plan,
almost unchanged, for *St Pancras Station*, whose fantastic
silhouette enlivens an otherwise rather dull part of London;
but this official disapproval was nevertheless a heavy blow to
the supporters of the mediaeval style, and it was accepted by
the end of the century that Gothic should be reserved for religious buildings. For public buildings the Renaissance style
was favoured.

But of all the buildings erected during the 19th century none had a greater influence on the future course of architecture than the Crystal Palace, which, neither Gothic nor classical, was a vast structure of glass and iron set up in Hyde Park to house the Great Exhibition of 1851. Purely functional in design, the Crystal Palace was nearly a century in advance of its time: indeed, when it was finally destroyed by fire in 1936, its seeds were only just beginning to bear fruit.

The 20th century. Functionalism in architecture is now, of course, universally accepted, and it is already clear that in future histories of architecture this will be the style particularly associated with the 20th century. The application of the functional style can be observed, for example, in *Guildford Cathedral* in Surrey, completed in 1960, in the imposing new buildings of *London University* and in the *Royal Festival Hall* on the banks of the Thames in London, opened in 1951, the centenary year of the Crystal Palace.

Meanwhile the older styles continue to develop alongside the new. The largest church built in London in this century, the imposing *Westminster Cathedral*, draws its inspiration directly from Byzantium. *Liverpool Cathedral*, the largest in the country, is more traditional in style — a modern version of Gothic, interpreted with a freedom and an imagination absent from the resolutely mediaeval but unappealing churches of the 19th century. Other buildings are no less resolutely modern, like Sir Basil Spence's *Coventry Cathedral* (1962).

One imaginative feature of post-war architecture has been the work of the town planners responsible for the rebuilding of war-damaged towns like Plymouth and for the building of the "new towns" round London and other large cities (see p. 74).

MUSIC

British music is in process of gaining for itself an international renown such as it has not enjoyed since the golden age of the 15th and 16th centuries, when England was famed throughout Europe for its composers and instrumentalists.

No record of pouplar music survives before the 13th century, but about the year 1220 a monk of Reading Abbey composed a remarkable six-part choral piece — a spring song opening with the joyous announcement that "Summer is i-cumen in". What gives this song its particular value is that nothing compar-

rable appeared for the next 150 years either in England or
anywhere else. It is the first great monument of English popular
music, followed two centuries later by the noble "Song of
Agincourt", written in 1415 to celebrate the triumphant return
of Henry V.

The end of the Middle Ages was a fruitful period throughout
Europe for church music, composed according to the universal
tenets laid down by the music schools in Rome. National
differences counted for little, and the style and accomplishments
of Josquin des Prés, Orlandus Lassus, Palestrina and Vittoria
on the Continent were reflected in those of **Thomas Tallis** (1515-
85) and his pupil **William Byrd** (1542-1623) in England.

The music of Tallis, in particular his plainsong, and Byrd's
motets are still played in the services of the Church of England.
Byrd also wrote much secular music and was the founder of
the English madrigal, one of the glories of the Tudor and Jacobean periods. Nowhere else was the art of the madrigal developed to such an extent as in England, and composers vied
with one another in the intricacy and brilliance of their part-
writing. Besides Byrd, two other masters of this form were
John Dowland and **Orlando Gibbons.** Instrumental music,
particularly for the viol and the lute, was also fashionable, and
Dowland's compositions for the "consort of viols" to be found
in all the great houses of the day are a treasury of music which
is still played today. Shakespeare's plays are full of references
to music and musical instruments, and the action is frequently
interrupted by songs or madrigals. Music, indeed, was the
recreation of the whole people, from the agricultural labourer
to the cultured nobility, and even so down-to-earth a king as
Henry VIII was proud to be accounted — and not merely by
his flatterers — one of the foremost composers of his day.

The golden age was brought to an abrupt close in the 17th century by the rise of Puritanism and by the Civil War, which
disrupted the artistic energy of the country and left English
music of the time in much the same state as English painting —
dependent almost entirely on foreigners for its inspiration.
Nevertheless it was at this unpropitious moment that England
produced the man whom many still consider to be her greatest
composer — **Henry Purcell** (1658-95). In his short life Purcell
wrote much magnificent church music, but his genius displays
itself most unchallengeably in his operas, such as "Dido and
Aeneas", "King Arthur" and "The Fairy Queen". Purcell's

mastery of the recitative, as in the lovely "When I am laid in earth" from "Dido", has never been surpassed.

The early death of Purcell, coupled with the accession of the Hanoverian sovereigns, who in common with most Germans at the time were interested almost exclusively in Italian music, dealt another severe blow to the progress of the native art, although the enthusiastic reception of "The Gentle Shepherd" by **Allan Ramsay** in 1725 and "The Beggar's Opera" by **John Gay** three years later showed that British composers, even if spurned by the court and aristocracy, could still find favour among the populace. The first important operas of the century which were entirely original were those of **Thomas Arne** (1710-70), who is, however, far more famous today for the composition of "Rule, Britannia !" Even in these unassertive times, this rousing and reassuring song is still honoured almost as a second national anthem.

The greatest composer working in Britain in the 18th century was undoubtedly **George Frederick Handel** (1685-1759). Handel was by birth a German, but he became a naturalised Englishman and composed most of his greatest works for and in his adopted country. In this respect he is comparable with van Dyck, the painter, in the previous century, although his influence extended still more widely. After his death Handel festivals became important regular events in British musical life, and even today, 200 years after its first performance, the "Messiah" still features prominently in the repertoire of all the great choral societies.

The influence of Handel, reinforced by that of **Mendelssohn,** who paid frequent visits to Britain and wrote "Elijah" for the Birmingham festival, was pre-eminent during the first half of the 19th century. British composers wrote large numbers of oratorios and choral works, though without achieving any notable originality. The period was not, however, an unfruitful one, for many choral societies which still survive and flourish were established at this time and did a great deal to maintain the high traditions of British choral singing.

Of the early Victorian composers only a few are remembered today — **John Field,** whom the great Chopin acknowledged as the originator of the pianoforte nocturne; **Sterndale Bennett,** an accomplished, if somewhat academic, reflection of Mendelssohn; and **Michael Balfe** and **Henry Wallace,** whose most popular operas — "The Bohemian Girl" and "Maritana" respectively — are now performed mainly by amateur companies.

By the end of the century, however, the picture had undergone a remarkable transformation. The long and consistently successful series of light operas composed by **Arthue Sullivan** to the librettos of William Gilbert — "The Mikado", "The Gondoliers" and the rest — had opened the eyes of the British public to the fact that in this field they were not dependent on the works of Offenbach and Strauss. Moreover, the symphonic, choral and operatic works of men like **Charles Stanford, Hubert Parry** and **Edward German** seemed to presage the rise of a new and vital school of British composers, and, though it was hard to realise it after so long a period of mediocrity, it became quickly apparent that in **Edward Elgar** (1857-1934) Britian had at last produced a modern composer of international importance.

It is perhaps not surprising, therefore, that Elgar's genius had to be applauded on the Continent before being recognised in his own country. After the reception given abroad to his oratorio "The Dream of Gerontius" he became the outstanding figure in British music. His symphonies, choral works and above all his "Enigma Variations" and concertos for violin and cello — exquisite music reflecting a powerful inspiration — are among the finest work of the kind composed during this century. Although Richard Strauss, with whom he had considerable affinities, called him "the last great romantic", Elgar prepared the way for a group of contemporary composers who have fully restored the former prestige of British music.

Two other important composers died in the same year as Elgar — **Frederick Delius,** who developed the impressionist manner of Debussy, and **Gustav Holst,** whose mastery of orchestral colour is best appreciated in his symphonic suite "The Planets".

Elgar was succeeded as the doyen of British composers by the rugged figure of **Ralph Vaughan Williams,** whose fame will mainly rest on a noble series of symphonies. No. 6, in E minor, is a work of extraordinary power which has been accepted into the repertoire very much more quickly than any other comparable modern work. Vaughan Williams also wrote some fine choral works. His early compositions were strongly influenced by British folk music. Other composers of the same generation were **Arnold Bax, William Walton, John Ireland** and **Arthur Bliss.**

In the younger generation the names of **Michael Tippett, Alan Rawsthorne** and **Edmund Rubbra** stand out, and that of **Benjamin Britten** (1913-76) is pre-eminent. Britten's style, though essentially modern, is easily understood by the ordinary listener, as is shown by the success of his cantata "St Nicholas", his "Spring Symphony" and his "War Requiem". He is, however, mainly an operatic composer, and his first major success, "Peter Grimes" (1946), has been performed in all the world's leading opera houses. Britten was in the van of an unprecedented flowering of musical composition in Britain: it is centuries since British music showed so much vitality or held out so much promise for the future.

Centres of Musical Life in Britain

The musical geography of London is quickly assimilated, and any visitor who is acquainted with the whereabouts and functions of the five principal concert halls and opera houses — the Royal Albert Hall, the Royal Festival Hall, the Royal Opera House, Sadler's Wells Theatre and the Wigmore Hall — may regard himself as reasonably well equipped to move with confidence among the musical circles of the capital.

The senior of London's concert-halls is the *Royal Albert Hall*, which faces Kensington Gardens.

The *Royal Festival Hall*, overlooking the Thames on the south bank of the river, was built in connection with the Festival of Britain in 1951, and is as modern in atmosphere as the Albert Hall is Victorian. It has excellent acoustics and a high standard of comfort. Nearby is the smaller *Queen Elizabeth Hall*.

The Royal Festival Hall and the Albert Hall share between them the main series of symphony concerts given by the leading London orchestras. These are the Royal Philharmonic, founded by Sir Thomas Beecham; the London Philharmonic; the B.B.C. Symphony Orchestra; the Philharmonia; and the London Symphony Orchestra, the oldest of them all. The Royal Philharmonic usually plays at the concerts given by the Royal Philharmonic Society, which earned Beethoven's gratitude on his deathbed for the financial help it gave him during his last illness, and which is now concerned to promote the work of the younger composers.

One of London's most popular musical events is the annual series of "Promenade Concerts", held nightly from July to September, which offer a unique opportunity of hearing within a period of eight weeks all the leading items in the orchestral repertoire. The quality of the playing is high and the prices are very reasonable. The Promenade Concerts are given in the Albert Hall, the only place big enough to hold them. The

Royal Choral Society and other organisations also perform
oratorios and other choral works in the Albert Hall at frequent
intervals.

The *Royal Opera House* in Covent Garden is one of the finest
and most celebrated opera houses in Europe, and most of the
world's leading singers can be heard there. Covent Garden is
also the home of the world-famous *Royal Ballet*, formerly the
Sadler's Wells Ballet, whose performances alternate with those
of the opera company.

The *English National Opera Company*, formely the Sadler's
Wells Opera Company, is based in the Coliseum Theatre in St
Martin's Lane, just north of Trafalgar Square.

London's busiest concert hall is probably the *Wigmore Hall*,
in Wigmore St. This pleasant and intimate hall is always much
in demand for recitals, both by soloists and instrumental groups
of established reputation and by those who have still to make
their name.

Outside London, the chief scenes of musical activity are
Manchester, home of the *Halle Orchestra*, Liverpool, Edinburgh,
Glasgow, Swansea and Leeds.

MUSEUMS

Britain has a rich variety of museums; and although the country's chief treasures are to be seen in London there are many important museums in the rest of the country, some of them containing items of unique value and interest. The normal opening hours are from 10 to 5 on weekdays and on Sunday afternoons, but the latest information about hours for the various museums is given in the "Description and Itineraries" part of this Guide.

London

British Museum. The British Museum suffered damage during the last war, but this has been made good and much has been done to improve and modernise the galleries so that the exhibits are displayed to advantage. Rearrangement is still in progress, but the Museum now offers an incomparable display of treasures, though still only a selection from its vast holdings. Among items of particular interest are the "Elgin marbles" from the Parthenon, the Mildenhall Treasure, the Sutton Hoo ship burial, a note written by Nelson before the battle of Trafalgar, Shakespeare's signature, the Portland Vase, and a great range of Egyptian and Babylonian antiquities. The Museum's Greek, Roman, Assyrian and Egyptian collections are of outstanding importance and interest. The British Library housed in the Museum is one of the richest in the world, and among rare and valuable items on view are one of the four copies of Magna Carta, an unfinished letter from Nelson to Lady Hamilton written just before Trafalgar, autographs of all British sovereigns since Richard II and the First Folio of Shakespeare. A whole day is required to get even the most general idea of the riches displayed in the Museum.

Natural History Museum, South Kensington. This museum was originally an offshoot of the British Museum, and its official designation — the British Museum (Natural History) — may sometimes give rise to confusion. It has one of the most comprehensive collections of animals in the world, and is particularly notable for its display of birds nesting in Britain. On the ground floor are the remains of prehistoric creatures like the giant plesiosaurus and ichthyosaurus and a very fine collection of fossils, including one of a prehistoric lobster.

Science Museum, South Kensington. This museum contains a collection, of interest both to the general public and to students, of machines, scientific instruments and other apparatus. In the section devoted to aeronautics are the first powered aircraft, built by the Wright brothers in 1903, a model of the Vickers-Vimy which made the first crossing of the Atlantic in 1919, and many of the early flying machines, some of them laboriously constructed from feathers. Among other items of particular interest are "Puffing Billy", the world's first railway engine, the first brougham carriage, George Stephenson's "Rocket" and a collection of rockets and flying bombs from the last war.

Victoria and Albert Museum. This possesses one of the richest collections of applied and decorative art in the world, covering all periods and all styles. The collection is divided into eight sections — architecture and sculpture; ceramics, glass and enamels; the graphic arts; the printing and production of books; metal-working; painting; textiles; and woodwork (furniture) and leatherwork. The architectural items displayed range from a painted ceiling from Spain to an 18th century shop front from the City of London. The collections of costume of different periods, drawings and theatre bills are particularly popular.

Soane Museum, Lincoln's Inn Fields. Among items of particular interest in this collection, assembled by Sir John Soane, architect of the British Museum, and still displayed in his own house, are the splendid alabaster sarcophagus of Pharaoh Seti I, William Hogarth's famous "Rake's Progress", and much fine furniture of various periods.

Record Office Museum, Chancery Lane. Here can be seen the famous Domesday Book, a record of the whole country prepared for William the Conqueror in 1086. Other unique documents on show include a petition of 1685 from William Penn to James II; a map of New York in 1700; the "Olive Branch Petition" addressed to George III in 1775 by representatives of New Hampshire, Massachusetts, Rhode Island, Connecticut, New York, New Jersey, Pennsylvania, Maryland, Virginia and the two Carolinas, with the signatures of John Adams, Benjamin Franklin and Thomas Jefferson, who also signed the Declaration of Independence on 4 July 1776; a letter of 25 August 1795 from Washington to George III; a request from William Franklin of Boston to Cromwell, with Cromwell's comments and signature; and a manuscript map of Ohio drawn by Major George Washington in 1753.

National Maritime Museum, Greenwich. Among items of interest are personal relics of Nelson, including the uniform he was wearing when he was killed, ship models of all periods, rare charts and early navigational instruments.

Imperial War Museum, housed in the old Bethlehem Hospital. Here are displayed arms and equipment of all kinds used by modern land, sea and air forces, including relics of the Normandy landings of 1944 and the bombing of London, as well as a large collection of material relating to the first world war.

Madame Tussaud's, Marylebone Road. London's popular waxworks museum, with famous people of the past and present day. The exhibits are changed and brought up to date from time to time.

Outside London

The Universities of Oxford and Cambridge have a number of museums and collections of first-rate importance. At *Oxford* is the Ashmolean Museum, the country's first museum, which includes among its treasures the 9th century "Alfred Jewel" and a magnificent collection of Italian drawings. *Cambridge* has the Fitzwilliam Museum, with rich collections of prints and drawings, musical instruments and china. (See also under Art Galleries, below).

Stratford-on-Avon is the Mecca of Shakespeare-lovers, and few visitors will leave the town without seeing the charming Tudor house in which he was born and the New Place Museum, on the site of the house to which he retired in 1611.

Other specialised museums are to be found in *Plymouth*, associated with Drake and Hawkins, the great seamen of Elizabeth I's reign; *Portsmouth*, birthplace of Charles Dickens and the last berth of Nelson's "Victory"; *Grasmere* in the Lake District, where Wordsworth lived and wrote; and *Haworth* on the Yorkshire moors, the home of the Bronte family. It is difficult, indeed, to find any part of the country which has not some association with a famous man or woman.

There are an increasing number of museums open to the public in private houses, some of them containing priceless treasures. Among them are *Knole*, near Sevenoaks, home of the Sackville family, which is now owned by the National

Trust; *Temple Newsam*, near Leeds, birthplace of Lord Darnley, who married Mary Queen of Scots in 1565: and *Christchurch Mansion* in Ipswich, birthplace of Cardinal Wolsey. Many old castles are now also used as museums; *Norwich Castle*, for example, has a famous collection of paintings by local artists and a fine natural history section devoted to birds.

In *Bath* is the Holburne of Menstrie Museum, a beautiful classical mansion with a collection of silver, porcelain, miniatures and drawings. The Lady Lever Gallery at *Port Sunlight* contains sculpture, enamels, porcelain and articles in jasper as well as its large collection of pictures. The Bowes Museum at *Barnard Castle* contains fine French furniture, important tapestries and numerous objets d'art.

Roman antiquities are to be seen all over the country. Among local museums with interesting collections of Roman material are those at *Bath*, *Caerleon*, *Canterbury*, *Cirencester*, *Colchester*, *Dorchester*, *Gloucester*, *Hull*, *Leicester*, *Newcastle*, *Ribchester*, *St Albans* and *York*, as well as *Chesters* and other Roman stations on or near Hadrian's Wall.

There are also many important and interesting municipal museums at *Liverpool*, *Manchester*, *Leeds*, *Sheffield*, *Leicester*, *Shrewsbury* and *Colchester*. *Birmingham* has what is perhaps the finest collection of applied art outside London. *Bristol* has much material illustrating the history of the West Country as well as the important Schiller Collection of Chinese ce mics. At *Stoke-on-Trent* the development of British pottery ca be studied. The Bolling Hall Museum in *Bradford* has an interesting collection devoted to the history of weaving. The old port of *Hull* is almost a museum in itself, but it also has a well known natural history museum and a museum of fishing and seamanship, with a unique collection of ship models and equipment. There are other noted provincial museums at *Huddersfield* (the Tolson Museum); *Newcastle-upon-Tyne* (the history and industry of Northumbria); *Winchester* (Arthurian and mediaeval); and *Dorchester* (associations with the local poet William Barnes and with Thomas Hardy, the novelist of Wessex).

Among smaller museums may be mentioned the Educational Museum in the charming little Surrey village of *Haslemere*, which includes a natural history collection as well as a display of country arts and crafts.

In **Scotland,** *Edinburgh* has a number of museums of outstanding interest. The Royal Scottish Museum in Chambers St has important collections of material in the fields of art, ethnography, technology and geology. The National Museum of Antiquities in Queen St includes among items of particular interest the "Traprain Treasure", a hoard of Roman silver, and relics of Mary Queen of Scots. *Glasgow* has the Kelvingrove Museum, which covers a wide range but has particularly good sections on natural history and navigation; the People's Palace, principally devoted to local history and art; and other important collections, including particularly the University's zoological collection. At *Dumfries* is Burns's house, a shrine for all Burns lovers; and the mansion of *Abbotsford*, in the Borders, attracts admirers of Sir Walter Scott.

In **Wales** the leading museum is the National Museum of Wales in *Cardiff*, with large collections of archaeology, metalworking and Welsh domestic crafts. At *Swansea* is the Royal Institute of South Wales, and at *Bangor* the Museum of Welsh Antiquities

ART GALLERIES

Britain possesses in its National Gallery in London what is probably the most comprehensive and best displayed collection of classic paintings in the world, and its representation of all European schools (particularly the Italian and Dutch schools) is without equal. Other collections of first-rate importance in London are to be seen at the Tate Gallery, Hertford House (the Wallace Collection) and Ken Wood (the Iveagh Bequest)

From the days when Henry VIII persuaded Holbein to become his court painter and create the wonderful series of portraits which are now treasured in galleries throughout the world the British have been renowned as art collectors, and it was the growing consciousness of the immense artistic wealth collected in the country which led to the foundation in 1824 of the National Gallery and, during the whole of the 19th century the founding of galleries in the principal cities and towns, including the National Gallery of Scotland in Edinburgh. But wherever the art lover goes he may be confident that he will find something of interest, something that he has not seen before. It may be that he will find a surprisingly fine collection of works by purely local artists, as at Exeter, where a gallery is set aside for the paintings of early Devon artists; or he may come upon a wholly unexpected treasure like the superb Brangwyn decorations for the House of Lords, which may be seen at Swansea; or again he may discover that, of all unlikely places, the charming little village of Compton, near Guildford, has an art gallery devoted to the work of G.F. Watts. To the art lover, Great Britain is a land of great occasions and of continual discovery.

London

Pride of place is of course due to the National Gallery, the country's leading storehouse of art treasures. Every school of painting is represented here by masterpieces of its leading representatives. All the paintings are hung at eye level and are allowed sufficient space to be enjoyed individually, without disturbance from their neighbours. It is difficult to make a selection out of the abundance of riches on display, but among the items which must be seen on even the briefest visit are Michelangelo's "Entombment", Raphael's "Ansidei Madonna" and "St Catherine", Leonardo da Vinci's "Virgin of the Rocks", Titian's "Bacchus and Ariadne", van Eyck's "Jan Arnolfini

and his Wife", Rubens's "Straw Hat", Holbein's "Duchess
of Milan" and the Vermeers. Among paintings of the English
and Scottish schools are immortal works by Reynolds, Gainsborough, Romney and Raeburn. In the entrance hall the
visitor will be struck by the mosaic floor with representations
of some contemporary notabilities.

Tate Gallery. Originally concerned only with British art, the
Tate Gallery is particularly notable for its paintings of the
English 18th and 19th century schools (including Hogarth's
"Marriage à la Mode" series) and its large collection of works
by contemporary artists. In recent years it has also acquired
works by modern French and Dutch artists, particularly Monet,
Manet, Degas, Cézanne, van Gogh, Gauguin, Seurat, Matthijs
and Jacobus Maris, Mauve, Forain, Renoir, Matisse, Sisley
and Utrillo. The magnificent Turner Wing, presented by Sir Joseph Duveen, contains a large number of paintings and sketches
by Turner. There is also an important collection of sculpture.
Special exhibitions are held from time to time.

Wallace Collection, Hertford House. This is one of London's
least conventional and most charming museums, where fine
examples of 18th century French art can be seen in an appropriate
setting, with furniture, sculpture and porcelain of the period.
There are also numerous works by old masters, including
Titian's "Perseus and Andromeda", Ruben's "Crucifixion",
Velazquez's "Lady with a Fan", Frans Hals's famous "Laughing
Cavalier", Reynolds's "Mrs Hoare and her Son", and masterpieces by Metsys, Terborch and Rembrandt.

The *National Portrait Gallery* is of more interest to the historian
than the art-lover, but it is notable for its fine series of portraits,
a genre in which British painters have excelled.

Victoria and Albert Museum. Although this museum is
mainly concerned with the applied arts (see p. 98), it contains
a fine series of 19th century paintings, being particularly rich
in works by Constable, as well as English drawings of all periods.
Here too can be seen Raphael's cartoons, the "Acts of the
Apostles", outstanding works of the Italian Renaissance.

The *British Museum* (see p. 97) has one of the richest collections
in Europe of woodcuts and engravings by old masters, displayed
in the Department of Prints and Drawings.

The *Soane Museum* (see p. 98) contains two masterpieces by
Hogarth and also his series, "The Rake's Progress".

The *Imperial War Museum* (see p. 99) has a small collection of modern British painting.

Royal Academy, Burlington House, Piccadilly. The Academy holds an annual exhibition of works by living British artists (oils, watercolours, sculpture) from May to August, and frequently has special exhibitions earlier in the year (devoted in recent years to French, Dutch, Chinese, Italian and Greek art). The Academy also possesses a fine cartoon by Leonardo da Vinci.

Hampton Court Palace (see p. 236) houses important works belonging to the royal collections. In the Orangery is Mantegna's "Triumph of Caesar", the finest surviving series of decorative paintings of the Italian Renaissance, and the Palace itself contains works by Holbein, Giorgione and Tintoretto, as well as Lely's famous series of "Windsor Beauties", the ladies of Charles II's court.

Windsor Castle (see p. 238). The royal apartments (open to the public when the royal family is not in residence) contain important works by Rubens, van Dyck, Canaletto and other artists.

National Maritime Museum. Although primarily concerned with naval history, this museum contains some very fine 18th century portraits (Reynolds, Gainsborough) and sea pictures by van de Velde and other Dutch artists.

Greenwich Naval College. The paintings by Thornhill in the great hall are among the few Baroque decorative paintings to be seen in Britain.

Dulwich College Picture Gallery (see p. 234) contains works by old masters, particularly Poussin, Gainsborough and the Dutch and Flemish schools (Rubens, van Dyck, Rembrandt).

Outside London

The university towns of Oxford and Cambridge, which will be included in the programme of every visitor to Britain, both have notable art collections. In *Oxford* the Ashmolean Museum has an excellent collection of works by old masters of all schools, particularly works by Italian primitives (including Uccello's "Hunt in a Forest") and a unique series of drawings by Michelangelo and Raphael (the remains of a magnificent collection formed by the portrait-painter Thomas Lawrence). The library of Christ Church College has a number of Italian works and old drawings bequeathed to the college in the 18th century, with some later acquisitions. In *Cambridge* the Fitzwilliam Museum has a collection of over 1000 pictures, including important works by Simone Martini, Domenico Veneziano and other Italian primitives, Titian's "Rape of Lucretia", fine works by Rubens, Rembrandt, Reynolds, Gainsborough and Hogarth, and also modern works.

Birmingham's Art Gallery is famous for its collection of Pre-Raphaelite works, including Millais' "Blind Girl", Ford Madox Brown's "The Last of England" and Holman Hunt's "The Finding of Christ in the Temple", and also has a very comprehensive series of works by the watercolourist David Cox. The Barber Institute of Fine Arts, belonging to Birmingham University, has a fine collection of old masters of all schools.

In *Nottingham* the 17th century Castle contains some interesting pictures, including family portraits of the Dukes of New-castle, as well as various paintings deposited on indefinite loan.

The Walker Art Gallery in *Liverpool* contains an outstanding collection of Italian and Flemish primitives assembled by Thomas Roscoe, a famous city banker noted for his studies of two great art patrons of the Italian Renaissance, Lorenzo the Magnificent and Pope Leo X. The collection also contains Pre-Raphaelite and modern works. Recently a small number of important 16th, 17th and 18th century works have been added. The nearby *Port Sunlight* has an art gallery founded by Lord Leverhulme for the benefit of the employees of his soap-works, which contains some fine portraits, including two works by Reynolds, "The Hon. Mrs Peter Beckford" and "The Misses Paine", together with a collection of English furniture which forms an appropriate setting.

The City Art Gallery in *Manchester* contains works of the English school, including characteristic portraits by Reynolds, Romney, Gainsborough and Hogarth and landscapes by Wilson, Turner, Constable and other artists. The Pre-Raphaelites are also well represented, with Holman Hunt's "Hireling Shepherd" and "Scapegoat" and works by Ford Madox Brown.

The *Leeds* City Art Gallery has a collection of modern British paintings, but the average visitor may be more interested in the collection of old masters, furniture and objets d'art in the splendid 17th century mansion of *Temple Newsam*, in the city suburbs, which was acquired from Lord Halifax in 1922.

The Graves Art Gallery in *Sheffield* has a "Virgin and Child" attributed to Verrocchio, drawings by Turner, Ruskin and others, and some interesting illuminated manuscripts. For those who can spare the time there are also interesting galleries at *Hull*, *York* and *Wakefield*. Farther north, at *Barnard Castle*, is the Bowes Museum, with a rich collection of French paintings and important works of the Spanish school, including in particular Goya's "Portrait of my Brother" and El Greco's "St Peter".

At *Lincoln* there is a very comprehensive display of works by the leading local painter, Peter de Wint. At *Norwich* the Castle contains the largest collection in existence of works by landscape painters of the Norwich school: it is particularly rich in pictures by Crome, Cotman and Stark.

Bath has two art galleries. The municipal collection in the Victoria Art Gallery consists mainly of works by local artists, while the Holburne of Menstrie Art Museum has some fine 18th century English portraits, miniatures, period furniture, etc.

The City Art Gallery in *Bristol*, although founded only at the beginning of this century, contains an interesting collection of old masters, including important works by Jordaens and Antonio da Solario, and a recently acquired and very interesting collection of miniatures by Italian and Flemish painters.

In Scotland, Edinburgh and Glasgow have collections second in importance only to the national collections in London.

Among the treasures of the National Gallery in *Edinburgh* are one of Vermeer's religious paintings, "Jesus in the House of Martha and Mary", Rembrandt's "Hendrickje Stoffels", Tiepolo's "Moses saved from the Water", Gainsborough's "Hon. Mrs Graham" and a particularly charming group of 18th century French pictures, including Watteau's "Fête Champêtre" and one of Boucher's most celebrated portraits of Madame de Pompadour. There is also a good representation of Scottish art, including in particular Sir Henry Raeburn. The Scottish National Portrait Gallery, in Queen St, contains portraits by Scottish artists like Jamestone, Raeburn and Geddes.

Glasgow Art Gallery has a fine collection covering all the main schools, with Rembrandt's "Man in Armour", "St Victor and a Donor" by the Master of Moulins and Giorgione's "Woman taken in Adultery" among its chief attractions.

In **Wales,** the National Museum in *Cardiff* has an important series of landscapes by Richard Wilson, the most notable Welsh artist, together with interesting 18th century works and some modern paintings. The Library of the University of Wales, in *Aberystwyth*, has a charming collection of watercolours, mostly on Welsh subjects, by Rowlandson and other artists.

CASTLES, COUNTRY HOUSES AND GARDENS

Castles

Wherever the traveller goes in Britain he will find himself near some castle dating back to the turbulent days of the Middle Ages. Many of them are still occupied by the families who have lived in them for centuries, like *Arundel* (seat of the Duke of Norfolk, Britain's premier duke), *Warwick* (Earl of Warwick) and *Alnwick* (Duke of Northumberland). The castles of Britain are a fascinating study. In them the development of the castle can be traced through its various stages from the first Norman strongholds built on "mottes" (artificial mounds) in the reign of William the Conqueror to the artillery forts constructed by Henry VIII round the coasts. Sometimes, as at Windsor or Arundel, several phases of development can be seen in the same building: elsewhere, as at Harlech, Bodiam and Tattershall, the whole structure dates from a single period.

The finest motte in the country is the great mound at *Thetford*, on which the original timber palisades were never replaced by stone ramparts. The castle which stands near the railway at *Berkhamsted* is an excellent example of a motte originally defended by palisades. At *Warkworth* in Northumberland, a stronghold of the Percy family, the mound is topped by a 15th century cruciform keep. The well-known Round Tower of *Windsor* Castle is an example of a keep surrounded by stone walls replacing earlier timber defences. Other examples in the south of England are *Farnham*, *Arundel* and *Carisbrooke*, and there is a group of very well preserved castles of this type in the south-west — at *Totnes* in South Devon and *Trematon*, *Launceston* and *Restormel* in Cornwall.

The typical Norman keep was a large square tower three or four storeys high. One of the largest and oldest, completed in the reign of William Rufus, is the White Tower in the *Tower of London*. Most of these keeps, however, date from the reign of Henry II (1154-89): e.g. *Portchester*, *Dover*, *Orford*, *Scarborough* and *Bamburgh*. Other fine examples can be seen at *Colchester* and *Hedingham* in Essex, *Castle Rising* in Norfolk, *Appleby* in Cumbria and *Newcastle upon Tyne*. The finest of all, however, is probably the gigantic keep which looms over *Richmond* in North Yorkshire. Departures from the usual square plan are found at *Pembroke* in South Wales and *Conisbrough* in South Yorkshire, where the keeps are round, and at *Orford* (Suffolk) and *Chilham* (Kent), where they are polygonal.

Some castles, like *Kidwelly* (Dyfed, South Wales) and *Beaumaris* (Anglesey) had both outer and inner defences. Beaumaris was the last and the most advanced of the castles built by Edward I in North Wales to watch over the territory he had conquered. The military engineering of the day reached its highest point in the six castles built for Edward I by his engineer and architect James de St George at *Flint, Rhuddlan, Conwy, Caernarvon, Harlech* and *Beaumaris*. The powerful castle of *Caerphilly* (Mid Glamorgan), built by Gilbert de Clare, Earl of Gloucester, between 1267 and 1272, was protected by an artificial lake. *Kenilworth* in Warwickshire was similarly protected by an artificial lake. *Kenilworth* in Warwickshire was similarly protected, but the lake — on which the Earl of Leicester mounted a great spectacle for the entertainment of Queen Elizabeth I — has long since dried up. Many castles were defended by moats, and some of these remain highly impressive, whether ruined like *Bodiam* in Sussex or still inhabited like *Maxstoke* (Warwickshire) and *Shirburn* (Oxfordshire). Castles of this type are often rectangular in plan with a round tower at each corner.

Henry VIII built a chain of forts along the south coast of England as a defence against invasion. Steamers sailing up the Solent pass four of these Tudor castles, at *Hurst, East Cowes, West Cowes* and *Calshot;* and of the four strongholds built to "guard the dunes" three still remain at *Deal, Walmer* and *Sandgate.*

Castle-building followed a different pattern of development in Scotland, where the keep or tower house retained its function as a fortified residence until the 17th century. From 1400 onwards it increased in size and height. Three fine 15th century examples have been preserved at *Comlongon* (Dumfries and Galloway) and *Elphinstone* and *Borthwick* (Lothian). In the 16th century the typical Scottish castle acquired the crowstep gables and corbelled pepperpot turrets at the corners which were to become the hallmarks of the "Scottish baronial" style. *Glamis*, seat of the Earls of Strathmore, is the finest example of this style in its last phase. Scottish architecture of this period is often more similar to contemporary French than to English architecture, and this is no less true of castles than of other buildings.

Many Scottish castles are impressively situated. *Dunnottar*, the last stronghold to surrender to Cromwell, stands on a rugged headland reaching out into the North Sea. *Culzean* (18th c.) rears its imposing bulk on a sheer crag rising out of the sea on the Ayrshire coast: a suite in this castle, which is National Trust property, was presented to Gen. Eisenhower for life in token of the gratitude of the British people. Other notable Scottish castles are *Dunollie*, near Oban; *Dunvegan*, the stronghold of the Macleods on the island of Skye; *Loch an Eilean*, an island fortress in the Rothiemurchus forest, south of Inverness; and *Kilchurn*, on Loch Awe. The royal castles of *Edinburgh* and *Stirling* are both impressively situated on rocky crags high above the surrounding area. *Balmoral*, the Queen's Highland home, is a 19th century mansion in Scottish baronial style in the beautiful Dee valley. A short distance away is *Braemar*, a small but perfect example of a Scottish castle.

Most of these castles can be visited either free of charge or on payment of a modest admission charge. Many are now national property or belong to local authorities, but many too are privately owned, and some are still occupied. The outstanding example of an ancient castle which is still used as a residence is *Windsor*, most of which, including St George's Chapel, is open to the public daily; other parts, including the royal apartments, can be visited only when the royal family are not in residence. Other privately owned castles which are open to the public at fixed times are *Alnwick*, *Arundel*, *Glamis*, *Warwick*, *Berkeley*, *Saltwood* and the moated castle of *Leeds* in Kent. *Durham* Castle is now occupied by the University, and other castles, like *Nottingham* and *Norwich*, house museums and art galleries. The magnificent castle at *Lancaster* is now occupied by law courts. The *Tower of London* and *Edinburgh Castle* have token garrisons, but the most interesting parts are open to the public.

Country Houses and Manor-Houses

Many of the famous country houses of Britain are regularly open to visitors. Much of the country's history is written on their mellow walls, and much of its characteristic beauty, in architecture and gardens, and no less in the surrounding landscape of parks, farms and woodland, has been brought into being round such historic mansions as *Knole* and *Penshurst*, *Haddon Hall* and *Longleat*. Since these houses were built centuries of Britain's greatest achievements have added the stately homes of Queen Anne's reign, the classical splendours of the 18th century and the romantic imaginings of the Victorian age. With their accumulated contents of furniture and works of art these great houses, set amid haunts of ancient peace, are unique treasure-houses of the art of living. Rarely so magnificent as the palaces of Italy or so ostentatious as some of the French châteaux, they are above all homes — that peculiarly British conception — of the men and women whose first love went to their ancestral acres. This continuity of loyalty and living persists, preserving and still enriching homes which have sometimes been occupied continuously for five hundred years or more by the same family.

The brief survey that follows can give no more than a general impression of the number and variety of the country houses and manor-houses which visitors can see as they go about the country. Even before the 15th century there were manor-houses of some size, buildings of a type to be distinguished from the castles of the period. They were stone built, or more commonly half-timbered, defended against possible attack by a moat, an enclosed inner courtyard and a gatehouse. The smaller ones were often built over an undercroft, and could be closed against intruders by removing the external staircase or ladder by which they were entered. Surviving examples of this type are *Boothby Pagnell* (12th c.) in Lincolnshire, *Old Soar Manor* (13th c.) in Kent and *Little Wenham Hall* (14th c.) in Suffolk, one of the oldest brick-built structures in the country. The commonest type, however, was the "hall house", with a gabled wing at each end of the central hall. *Horton Court* in Gloucestershire is a surviving example of a Norman hall house, and *Compton Wynyates* in Warwickshire is a magnificent 15th century example.

Penshurst Place in Kent, which dates from about 1350, has the finest surviving example of a mediaeval great hall as its nucleus. The fireplace is still in the centre, with a lantern in the open timber roof structure to enable the smoke to escape. At one end is a carved wooden screen concealing the door to the kitchen and domestic offices, with a musicians' gallery above it. At the other end, on a dais, is the table used by the family, while the retainers sat at tables ranged round the walls. This layout, still to be seen in the dining halls of the Oxford and Cambridge colleges, remained the rule into Jacobean times, and fine surviving examples can still be seen at *Great Chalfield* in Wiltshire and *Lytes Cary* in Somerset (both dating from about 1450 and still intact), *Rufford Old Hall* in Lancashire and *Ightham Mote* in Kent. *Cotehele* in Cornwall and *Haddon Hall* in Derbyshire are among the finest surviving examples of old manor-houses, with their courtyard, guard-room, chapel and panelled rooms added in later centuries. The great hall at Cotehele, with its armour and banners, still preserves all the atmosphere of the Middle Ages. Haddon Hall, the scene of Dorothy Vernon's elopement with an ancestor of the present owner, the Duke of Rutland, is perhaps the most attractive country house in England, perched above rocky terraces, its rooms hung with tapestries.

Many old yeomen's houses survive in Kent, particularly at *Sole Street*, *Stoneacre* and *Loose*. *Paycockes* (1500), in Essex, was the home of a wealthy wool merchant. These houses are timber-framed, with a brick or plaster infill: a form of construction (the "black and white" house) which remained in vogue until the 17th century, particularly in north-western England, where some fine examples have survived. Perhaps the finest of all are *Little Moreton Hall* in Cheshire, a tall house with projecting upper storeys, surrounded by a moat, and *Speke Hall* near Liverpool, a low rambling house with a courtyard surrounded by ditches and shaded by old yews.

The 16th century saw major changes which led to the emergence of a new type of country house. After the dissolution of the monasteries many of the old monastic houses came into the hands of newly rich henchmen of Henry VIII, who converted them into stately residences. *Forde Abbey* in Dorset and *Lacock Abbey* in Wiltshire are fine surviving examples of such conversions, still preserving many of the monastic buildings adapted to meet the needs of the Tudor and later periods. *St Michael's Mount* in Cornwall, originally a small monastery, is an interesting combination of fortress, church and manor-house situated on a precipitous little offshore island.

The Renaissance brought Italian and French art to Britain, matching the greater refinement and elegance of life in this period. The houses now built had more and larger windows, the old towers gave place to turrets and pinnacles, colonnades and vaulting replaced the massive piers of earlier days, and there was a proliferation of sculptured decoration. Among the great Elizabethan mansions of the new type are *Longleat* (1547-80) in Wiltshire; *Burghley House* in Lincolnshire, built between 1550 and 1570 by Robert Cecil, Elizabeth I's great minister; *Wollaton Hall* in Nottinghamshire; *Longford Castle* in Wiltshire, built on an unusual triangular plan; and *Kirby Hall* in Northamptonshire, built by Sir Christopher Hatton, now in ruins but still impressive. Elsewhere the tradition of the gabled manor-house was maintained but combined with the new style, as at *Sutton-at-Hone* in Kent and *Barrington Court* and *Montacute* in Somerset. The early 17th century saw the development of the characteristic Jacobean style, of which *Hatfield House* (Hertfordshire), *Blickling Hall* (Norfolk), *Audley End* (Essex) and *Castle Ashby* (Northamptonshire) are magnificent examples, with beautiful carved wainscoting, elaborate mouldings, tapestries and needlework decoration. The finest example of a Jacobean interior is to be seen at *Knole* in Kent, a mediaeval house which was enlarged and embellished by successive generations of the Sackville family, reaching its present form in the 17th century. Among other fine houses of this period are *Chastleton House* (Oxfordshire), which contains many relics of the past; *East Riddlesden Hall*, a typical Yorkshire house; *Kiplin Hall*, also in Yorkshire, the home of the Lord Baltimore who founded Baltimore in the United States, with family portraits; *Hinchingbrooke* (Cambridgeshire), which has associations with Cromwell and Pepys; *Batemans* (Sussex), a 17th century ironmaster's house which was later occupied by Rudyard Kipling; and *Quebec House* (Kent), the home of Gen. Wolfe. All these Jacobean mansions are extraordinarily picturesque, whether they are built of Cotswold limestone, the pink bricks of East Anglia, the flint and plaster of Wiltshire or the oak timber of the forested regions. *Winton House* (Lothian) is a very beautiful late 17th century Scottish house showing both English and French influence.

In the years before the Civil War Inigo Jones built the classical-style *Wilton House* (Wiltshire), which has associations with Sir Philip Sidney. The finest example of this first phase of the classical style is the *Queen's House* at Greenwich, built by Inigo Jones for Charles I's queen. The tradition continued after the Restoration, following an interruption during the Commonwealth. *Ham House* (Surrey), *Drayton* (Northamptonshire) and *Lyme* (Cheshire) are typical of Charles II's reign, both in their magnificent interior decoration and in their transitional style. Soon, however, the Baroque style came into its own, its principal exponent being Sir Christopher Wren, who built the splendid mansion of *Chatsworth* in Derbyshire, seat of the Duke of Devonshire, a world-famed treasurehouse of art. In the reign of Queen Anne squires and yeomen built themselves plain dignified houses like *Upton House* (Warwickshire), which has a large collection of English sporting pictures; *Wallington* (Northumberland), which contains a collection of Pre-Raphaelite paintings; *Gunby Hall* (Lincolnshire); and *Owletts* (Kent), with beautiful moulded ceilings, a fine example of a Kentish yeoman's house of the reign of Queen Anne.

At the beginning of the 18th century a severe classical style came into fashion for the great houses built by Whig noblemen in settings of Arcadian beauty. Excellent examples, still preserving period decoration and furnishings, are to be seen at *Stourhead* (Wiltshire), with fine Chippendale furniture; *Holkham* (Norfolk), designed by William Kent; *Stoneleigh Abbey* (Warwickshire); and *West Wycombe Park* (Buckinghamshire). In the second half of the century the classical style reached its purest expression in the work of the Adam brothers, prefiguring the Empire style which prevailed on the Continent in Napoleonic times. Two of the finest Adam houses are *Syon House* and *Osterley Park*, on the outskirts of London. The Adam brothers were also responsible, in whole or in part, for *Harewood House* in Yorkshire (in collaboration with John Carr of York): *Kedleston* in Derbyshire (with James Paine); *Hatchlands* in Surrey; and *Ken Wood*, Hampstead. Most of these houses have fine Chippendale furniture. *Blair Castle* (Tayside region) is notable for its splendid 18th century furniture. *Attingham* (Shropshire) and *Heaton* (Lancashire) are fine examples of the classical style of late Georgian times.

In the early 19th century the Romantic movement exerted its influence on architecture. An example of this style is *Hughenden* in Buckinghamshire, the home of Disraeli, novelist and statesman of the Victorian age. In the field of painting Romanticism produced Turner, whose finest works are to be seen at *Petworth* in Kent, a large 17th century mansion in the Baroque style belonging to the Percys, Dukes of Northumberland, and Constable, who painted the countryside round Flatford Mill in Suffolk (now the property of the National Trust). The Romantic movement led to a better understanding of earlier styles, in particular the old "black and white" half-timbered house. An example of this style built between 1887 and 1893 is *Wightwick Manor* in Staffordshire, which contains an unrivalled collection of Pre-Raphaelite works.

Since the beginning of this century it has become increasingly difficult and costly to maintain these historic old houses. Increasingly, therefore, they have been coming into public hands, many of them becoming the property of the National Trusts in England and Scotland, sometimes retaining accommodation for occupation by the original owners. Many other houses are now open to the public, whose admission charges help towards the maintenance and running costs.

Gardens

It is commonplace that the visitor to Britain, on seeing the patchwork of fields and hedges that is the British countryside, declares that Britain is a garden; and later, when he is confronted with a veritable British garden, he has no words with which to describe his astonishment and his delight.

It is only by a visit that any idea of the serenity, the atmosphere and the peace of a British garden can be gained. The soft, rich, green velvet that is an English lawn tended through the centuries by loving hands and watered by the soft rains of the south-west wind; lilies sitting, like translucent cups lined with gold, upon the surface of a moat that laps the walls of some ancient castle; borders ablaze with all the colours of an English June and reflected in the mullioned windows of a Tudor manor; sombre walls and yet more sombre yews that were already venerable trees when they gave their branches to be fashioned into the long bows that fought upon the field of Agincourt; roses that unfold their petals to reveal enchanted depths of carmine, pink and apricot, and want only to scatter their perfume on the evening air: all these await the visitor who passes through the gate of a British garden. In no country in the world have climate, soils and the national character combined to produce so many and so varied gardens, large and small, traditional or specialised, as in Britain. Centuries of democracy and voyaging have combined with the gentle climate and the ideal of the "Englishman's home" to make gardening an almost universal occupation, a national folk art. Every cottage has its gay front garden, a tradition which persists vigorously in the newer town suburbs. The visitor in search of gardens need do no more than wander in summer through country villages, especially in the south, or even through London's outer suburbs, to find endless variety and garden pride.

This universal interest in gardening, and today in some cases perhaps also high taxation, has led to arrangements whereby many of the finest private gardens, from those of the Queen to the gardens of individual enthusiasts, often quite small, are thrown open to the public at times when they can be seen at their best.

Originally the garden was merely an enclosed space attached to a monastery or castle in which vegetables and fruit, medicinal plants and a few flowers were grown. There is still a garden of this type at *Edzell* (Angus, Scotland). At *Eltham* (Kent) and *Dartington Hall* (Devon) there are remains of the lists in which tournaments were held, which were included within some of the larger mediaeval gardens. Many old houses have preserved their moats, now incorporated in their gardens. After 1500, when times were more settled, regularly planned gardens were added to the manor-houses, with flowers, vegetables and fruit, neat paths and clipped hedges. Gardens of this kind have been laid out on the old model at *Hampton Court*, at Shakespeare's house in *Stratford-on-Avon* (containing only plants mentioned in his works) and at *Cawdor Castle* (Nairn, Scotland), the legendary home of Macbeth. The great age of the botanists, who described the many new flowers brought back from the Indies and the New World, produced the first botanic garden in Britain, at *Oxford* (1632). Private gardens which have preserved a layout dating from the first half of the 17th century can be seen at *Cranbourne* (Wiltshire), *Canons Ashby* (Northamptonshire) and *Rhual* (Clwyd, Wales). There are splendid gardens of clipped yew at *Levens Hall* and *Hutton John* (Cumbria), *Packwood* (Warwickshire), *Chilham* (Kent), *Chastleton* (Oxfordshire) and *Rous Lench* (Worcestershire), and in the terraced gardens at *Haddon Hall* (Derbyshire) and *Penshurst Place* and *Northbourne* (Kent). The character of these Jacobean gardens can also be appreciated at *Montacute* (Somerset), with its splendid Elizabethan pavilions, *Sudeley Castle* (Gloucestershire), at Shakespeare's birthplace and New Place in *Stratford-on-Avon* and at *Earlshall* in Fife.

In the latter part of the 17th century French and Italian influence led to the laying out of magnificent formally planned gardens with radiating avenues, canals and fountains. The accession to the throne of William of Orange popularised the growing of tulips, irises and other bulbs from Holland. *Hampton Court* gardens were laid out for William about 1700, and one of his courtiers created the magnificent terraced gardens of *Powis Castle* (Salop). There are other famous gardens of this period at *Chatsworth* (Derbyshire); *Drayton House* (Northamptonshire); *Hall Barn* (Buckinghamshire), laid out by the

poet Edmund Waller about 1670; *Albury* (Surrey), the garden
of John Evelyn, the diarist; and *Bicton Park* (Devon).

In the 18th century poets and art-lovers discovered the beauties
of English scenery and, as one of them wrote, saw all nature as
a garden. This was the great age of the carefully landscaped
"natural garden", the leading exponent of which was Lancelot
Brown (1716-83), known as "Capability" Brown from his
practice of assessing the "capabilities" of a landscape. There
are fine examples of landscaped gardens at *Rousham Park*
(Oxfordshire); *Stourhead* (Wiltshire), with temples, trees and
flowering shrubs picturesquely disposed round a lake; *Longleat*
(Wiltshire); and *Studley Royal* and *Duncombe Park* (Yorkshire),
the former incorporating Fountains Abbey and the latter
Rievaulx Abbey. The great royal gardens at *Kew*, now a world-
famed botanic garden, were originally laid out on this pattern
by Frederick Prince of Wales. Every country house also had
to have a walled garden, the finest example being on the royal
estate at *Sandringham*. There are some particularly fine gardens
of this period in Scotland, for example at *Crathes Castle* (Kincardine and Deeside), *Mellerstain* in the Borders, *Ravelston*
(Edinburgh) and *Newbyth* (Lothian).

The finest gardens of the Victorian period are difficult to
distinguish from those of the 17th century: e.g. *Harewood
House* (Yorkshire), *Drummond Castle* (Perth and Kinross) and
Blickling Hall (Norfolk). The tradition has been maintained
in some splendid modern gardens attached to old houses, like
those at *Blenheim* (Oxfordshire), *Sissinghurst Castle* (Kent),
Ammerdown Park (Somerset), *The Courts* (Holt, Wiltshire) and
Julians (Hertfordshire).

Between 1880 and 1900 there was a reaction against formal
planning and a preference for putting plants in their natural
setting and by this means creating picturesque effects. The
modern trend can be seen at its best in the national botanic
gardens at *Kew* and *Edinburgh*, in the gardens of the Royal
Horticultural Society at *Wisley* (Surrey), and at *Bodnant* (Gwynedd, Wales), the Arboretum at *Westonbirt* (Gloucestershire),
Dawick in the Scottish Borders, and the astonishing gardens
on the Scottish west coast, at *Pollok Park* (Glasgow), *Inverewe*
(Ross and Cromarty) and *Lochinch* and *Logan* (Merrick). There
are magnificent displays of rhododendrons and azaleas in the
new gardens in *Windsor Great Park*, at *Waddesden* (Buckinghamshire), *Exbury* and *Pylewell* (Hampshire), *Riverhill* (Kent),
Wakehurst and *Leonardslee* (Sussex) and *Devonhall* (Perth and

Kinross), and in many gardens in Cornwall. There are also unusual gardens like the marvellous garden laid out in a limestone quarry at *Highdown* (Sussex) or the one on *St Michael's Mount* (Cornwall), on a rocky crag. Finally for beauty, general attractiveness and horticultural interest the gardens at *Hidcote Manor* (Gloucestershire), *Sutton Courtenay* (Berkshire), *Hascombe* (Surrey), *North Mymms* (Hertfordshire), *Old Wisley* (Kent) and *Crathes Castle* (Kincardine and Deeside) might be selected to conclude this enumeration.

Description
and
Itineraries

Note. — The local government structure of England, Wales and Scotland was reorganised in 1974 and 1975 (see p. 51), involving changes in local government areas and sometimes in the names of local government authorities. So far as possible this Guide takes account of these changes. Where population figures are given, however, they relate to the old authorities.

I: LONDON

London *is not only the capital of the United Kingdom and the
centre of the Commonwealth: it is also one of the largest cities
in the world, with a distinctive personality of its own — a personality which may sometimes puzzle or disconcert the visitor from
abroad. The stereotypes of London are well known — the bowler
hats of the City, the rolled umbrellas of Whitehall, the cheerfully
irreverent repartee of the Cockney (the native Londoner), the
helmeted policemen, the double-decker buses. The reality is much
more complex, and nowadays increasingly cosmopolitan; for
London is an international city as well as the national capital.
But one thing is cetain: whether they come on business or pleasure,
for shopping or sightseeing, visitors to London need never be
bored. Dr Johnson's remark is even truer today than it was two
hundred years ago: "When a man is tired of London he is tired
of life; for there is in London all that life can afford."*

History

Roman London. The Thames, rising in the Cotswolds, is for
much of its course a pleasant inland stream, flowing through
a green and park-like landscape. Below Richmond, however,
it begins to feel the influence of the tides, and soon afterwards
opens out to form a wide estuary. The first human settlement
in this area was established at the exact point where river-borne
traffic meets sea-borne traffic, where the river is tidal but still
conveniently narrow; and this first settlement determined the
site of the town and city which were to develop here.

North of the river extended large areas of marshland and the
dense forest of Epping, providing protection on that side. At
low tide the Thames could be crossed by the Westminster ford,
and the river was not too wide to be bridged. The first bridge
was probably built at the position of the present-day London
Bridge — *the* bridge of London. The name of London seems
likely to have come from the name of the Celtic village which
grew up at this spot — *Llyn-din*, "the fort on the lake", which
gave the Roman name *Londinium*.

The Romans invaded Britain in 43 A.D. and after completing
the conquest of the English lowland areas established a thriving
city at Londinium, on the main road from Dover to Chester.
In spite of the ravages caused by Boadicea's rebellion in 61 A.D.

the town grew to become one of the leading cities of the island. Seven of the fifteen roads described in the Antonine Itinerary led to Londinium: the city was granted the style of *Augusta*, and the Emperor Theodosius honoured it with a visit. Even today some of the streets in the City of London follow the line of old Roman roads, and some of the city gates, like Newgate and Bishopsgate, were on the position of the Roman gates.

Londinium enjoyed a high standard of civilisation, as is shown by the numerous objects recovered by excavation — mosaics, pottery, rings, coins and much more besides. Statuettes like the little bronze archer of Cheapside have been found at depths of some 15 to 20 feet, and the Thames yielded a colossal bronze head of the Emperor Hadrian (now in the British Museum). Stretches of the Roman town walls and the foundations of temples (including particularly a temple to Jupiter found in 1953) and other buildings have been located in many places; and the venerable London Stone in Cannon St is a Roman milestone, the point from which distances along the roads from London were reckoned.

Mediaeval London. After the departure of the legions and the fall of the Roman Empire London fell into the hands of Saxon and later of Danish invaders. The Saxons made it the capital of Essex, the kingdom of the East Saxons; and when they became converted to Christianity about the year 600 London became one of England's three episcopal sees (the others being York and Lincoln). King Alfred rebuilt the Roman walls in 886 and successfully held the town against the Danish Vikings.

The Danes, however, returned to the attack, burning and plundering the outlying districts of the town. The names of some of London's streets and buildings still recall these violent times. The Strand bears a Danish name, and in it stands the church of St Clement Danes: and three other London churches are dedicated to St Olaf. Finally the Danish king Knud or Canute was recognised as king of England in the 11th century, and thereafter the town benefited from royal patronage. Canute's successor Edward the Confessor promoted the establishment of religious houses, and in particular founded Westminster Abbey. The new foundation soon acquired considerable prestige, and William the Conqueror had himself crowned in the Abbey after his victory at Hastings in 1066.

At the time of the Norman Conquest London consisted of three distinct settlements, which are still readily identifiable today: the area of the present city, the borough of Westminster, and Southwark, on the south bank of the Thames near the port. Like all mediaeval towns, London was a maze of narrow lanes, lined by timber houses with overhanging roofs which almost met across the street. London Bridge, the only bridge over the river, was likewise lined with houses, shops and chapels. It remained the only bridge until 1750: accordingly a multitude of boats plied to and fro across the river, and the boatmen of London were a flourishing community.

William the Conqueror maintained the town's privileges, as set out in a charter still preserved in the Guildhall, but at the same time built the first Tower of London to keep a watch on the city. In 1189 Richard Cœur-de-Lion granted the city's chief officer the style of mayor, a dignity which was raised to Lord Mayor in the 15th century. The leading citizens played their part in administering the city's affairs as sheriffs or aldermen, and down the centuries the power of the city companies or guilds steadily increased. The various religious orders also flourished, so that by 1250 two thirds of the city was said to be occupied by churches and religious houses. The main orders were the Dominicans (Black Friars), the Franciscans (Grey Friars) and the Carmelites (White Friars), who still feature in many London place-names.

London was now asserting its status as capital. It was at Runnymede, near London, that King John granted the Great Charter, the basis of British freedom, in 1215: and it was the support of the London townspeople that gave Richard II the crown.

The Reformation and the modern period. The 16th century saw bitter religious conflicts which ended in the victory of Protestantism; the monasteries were dissolved and for many years to come the "Papists" were persecuted. The "merry England" of the Elizabethan age, the age of Shakespeare and his friends, gave place in the 17th century to an austerer England, the country of Puritanism and of Cromwell. In spite of all political and religious difficulties, however — the Civil War, the execution of Charles I in Whitehall (1649), the Revolution of 1688 — London continued to increase in size and importance. Its port became one of the largest in the world, trading with the Indies, America, Scandinavia and the Levant, and its warehouses were filled with exotic goods from far-off countries. The growth of the port enriched the whole city, and the Royal Exchange, which had been established in the second half of the 16th century, provided a meeting place for London's prosperous merchants. When England was threatened with invasion by the Spanish Armada London supplied 38 ships and 20,000 seamen for the defence of the country.

During this period the port was extending eastward towards the sea, and Greenwich and Gravesend were growing up near the position of the docks constructed in later centuries. The town itself extended westward. The Strand, lined with handsome palaces, already provided a link between the City and Westminster, but Piccadilly and Oxford Street were still tree-lined country roads and Covent Garden was still a garden. The court was in Whitehall, Parliament at Westminster; but aristocratic mansions were also being built in the surrounding area, in what is now the West End. William III, finding the smoke of the city bad for his health, took up residence near the little hamlet of Kensington. The different parts of London were already taking on the distinctive functions which they have largely retained ever since — the residential West End, at a safe distance from the dust and soot carried by the east winds; the business centre in the City; and the East End, the area round the port, a district of poor houses frequented by some of London's less desirable citizens.

The extension of London outside its original bounds gave the country's rulers cause for concern, and in 1580 Elizabeth I ordered that no further new houses should be built within a radius of 3 miles round the city. The ban was repeated in 1602 and again in 1630, but seems to have had little effect. Fortunately the growth of London left many open spaces in the parks and gardens which are still such a characteristic feature of the city — large parks like Hyde Park and Regent's Park and the smaller enclosed gardens in so many of London's squares.

During the 17th century London — which now had a population of 200,000 or 300,000 — suffered a series of misfortunes. Plague wrought havoc on a number of occasions — in 1603, in 1625 and in the Great Plague of 1665. Deaths were counted in tens of thousands, and the toll of the Great Plague is estimated at 100,000. And in this labyrinth of thatched wooden houses there were frequent disastrous fires, culminating in the Great Fire of 1666.

The fire started in a baker's shop in Pudding Lane at 1 o'clock on the morning of 2 September 1666 and spread with terrifying speed. After burning for four days it came to an end at Pie Corner. (The coincidence of names, incidentally, led a preacher of the day to declare that the fire was "occasioned by the sin of gluttony"). The destruction was enormous; 13,000 houses, 400 streets and 89 churches were burned out, and six months later the ruins were still smoking. The city was rebuilt in brick, in the style which was to give London its particular stamp, but the rebuilding was carried out in a piecemeal and unplanned way, in spite of proposals put forward by Sir Christopher Wren and other architects for laying out new and wider streets and building embakments along the Thames. Later generations, suffering from the traffic jams of modern times, have had cause to regret this failure to take advantage of the opportunity offered by the fire. It can at least be claimed for the Great Fire, however, that it eradicated for ever the menace of plague.

The 19th and 20th centuries. Until 1832 London still consisted of its three mediaeval elements, the City and the boroughs of Westminster and Southwark, now overflowing into the parishes on the outskirts of the town. In that year the expansion of the built-up area was recognised by the establishment of four new boroughs — Marylebone, Finsbury, Tower Hamlets and Lambeth. Half a century later, in 1888, a more logical structure was introduced by the creation of the County of London with 29 constituent boroughs.

As the city increased in size it was also modernised. The 19th century saw the erection of numerous public buildings in the rather lifeless neo-classical style of the Victorian era, together with many office buildings, clubs, shops, hotels and theatres. New bridges were built over the Thames to relieve the pressure on the ancient London Bridge, which was no longer adequate for the traffic across the river. New streets were driven through the older parts of the town, and London began to acquire its numerous railway stations, beginning with the one opened in 1836 for the new London-Greenwich line. A network of sewers was constructed, proper street lighting was introduced, and public bus services were started. London now developed into a modern city.

Until the first world war London was the unchallenged metropolis of world trade: of its port, which contributed largely to this status, more will be said below. Many international diplomatic conferences met in London, from the conference which established Greek independence in 1832 and the one which guaranteed Belgian neutrality in 1839 to the conference in 1913 which ended the Balkan war. International exhibitions held in London drew huge crowds, beginning with the Great Exhibition of 1851, which left London with one of its most noted landmarks, the Crystal Palace (destroyed by fire just before the second world war).

The first world war left its mark on London in the form of isolated raids by aircraft or zeppelins; but this was nothing to the havoc wrought by the air raids of the second world war. London was exposed throughout the war to enemy bombing, but there were two main periods of intense attack — during the autumn of 1940 and winter of 1940-41 and in the summer of 1944. The first of these periods was the "blitz", when bombs rained down on the city and the docks, causing gigantic conflagrations. The City was devastated, the British Museum damaged and the House of Commons destroyed, and 30,000 people were killed. In the summer of 1944 London suffered attack by a new type of weapon, the flying bombs (V 1s), which spread death and destruction aimlessly and at random in every part of the city. They were followed by the terrible V 2s, which swooped down silently at speeds greater than that of sound. In all London was the target of more than 1000 flying bombs or rockets, which killed some 3000 people. But "London could take it", and the people of London never flinched in the face of their ordeal.

While the war was still in progress, in 1943, the government produced a plan for the rebuilding and replanning of London. Westminster was to remain the centre of political life, while the devastated City was to be opened up and modernised, leaving space to set off the historic buildings which had hitherto been lost in the tangle of commercial development; the south bank of the river was to be attractively laid out, with museums and concert halls — an appropriate use for a part of the town in which Shakespeare's Globe Theatre had once stood.

Since the war, in addition to the rebuilding of the war-damaged areas, attempts have been made to relieve the crowded outer districts of London. The continued extension of the city's tentacles has been halted by the designation of a green belt round London in which no building is permitted. More positively, new towns have been established round London to draw population and industry away from the city to new centres where both employment and housing are available. It is hoped by these means to find a solution to the endemic 20th century problem of the remorseless expansion of large cities. Following the pioneering Abercrombie Plan of 1945, a far-reaching plan was produced in 1967 by the South-East Economic Planning Council covering the development of the whole metropolitan area until the year 2000.

Aspects of London

It is difficult to define the extent of London with any precision. There are a number of different Londons, and it is necessary to be clear in each case which one we are talking about — whether inner London, or Greater London, or the whole "metropolitan area" which lies within the orbit of London. In this section we consider successively the City, London proper (corresponding to the old county of London) and Greater London as it now exists.

The City, now covering an area of 678 acres, originated as a small settlement on a ridge of limestone rising out of the marshes on the banks of the Thames. The mediaeval city, still enclosed within its Roman walls, extended from the Tower in the east to beyond Ludgate in the west, its extreme limit being marked by the river Fleet, from which Fleet St takes its name. At the end of Fleet St is Temple Bar (although the actual gate called Temple Bar is no longer there), where the Lord Mayor greets the sovereign on the Monday following the second Saturday in November and hands over the keys of the City.

The administration of the City still preserves some old-world features. The Lord Mayor presides over a Common Council of 26 aldermen and 159 councillors, and is elected annually by the city companies (guilds) assembled in "Common Hall". Within the City he takes precedence over all other subjects of the Crown, including royal princes. His official residence is the Mansion House. Among his privileges is the right to be informed every three months of the password of the Tower of London.

The City is still the business centre of London, but it no longer enjoys the monopoly it had before 1914. The large companies and corporations have increasingly tended to build their offices in the adjoining districts of London; thus Shell and I.C.I. have their headquarters farther upstream on the left bank. The City still, however, has the Bank of England, the Stock Exchange, Lloyd's of London and of course the Guildhall.

5

The bombing of the last war cut great swathes of destruction through the closely packed huddle of buildings in the City, but fortunately St Paul's Cathedral survived with relatively minor damage.

The unique feature of the City is that very few people actually live in it, although during the day it is crowded with people who travel in every morning and return home in the evening. The daytime population is estimated at 500,000 or 600,000 people, but there are only some 5000 permanent residents, mostly caretakers and night-watchmen. On Sundays the City is silent and deserted, offering a striking contrast to its normal weekday appearance.

London proper. For most of this century London, as officially defined, was the county of London, administered by the London County Council, which was established in 1888 at the expense of the surrounding counties (Middlesex, Essex, etc.). This administrative unit, with an area of 120 sq. miles and a population of 3,225,000, disappeared in 1963 with the establishment of the Greater London Council (see below). It consisted of the cities of London and Westminster and 27 other metropolitan boroughs, each a separately identifiable part of the town (Chelsea, Fulham, Kensington, Lambeth, Marylebone, St Pancras, Stepney, etc.). Each borough was governed by a mayor, aldermen and councillors, who were responsible for local services; services of major importance were the responsibility of the London County Council.

London within the old L.C.C. area is conventionally divided into two very different parts, the *East End* and the *West End*, together with the outlying areas. The East End includes the poorer parts of the town (Whitechapel, Stepney, Poplar, etc.), the industrial districts round the docks. In spite of much post-war rebuilding there are still many of the old narrow and squalid streets left, extending endlessly in monotonous rows of identical little houses. In the evening the streets swarm with activity, and the cafés, fish and chip shops and pubs are crowded with customers. Many foreigners live in this part of the town, and London has its own Chinatown in Limehouse.

Very different is the aspect of the **West End**. Most of the official buildings — government departments, Parliament, Buckingham Palace — are in Westminster; the great museums and scientific institutes are in Kensington; Mayfair is the fashionable residential district; Bloomsbury is a centre of scholarly activity. Everywhere there are shady parks and quiet squares and gardens to provide oases of peace and coolness in the stuffy atmosphere of London in summer. The shops of the West End, in and around Piccadilly and Regent St, are world-renowned. Here too are the celebrated London clubs, still largely a male preserve; and not far away is Soho, a continental enclave in the heart of London, crowded with little foreign restaurants and other more dubious forms of entertainment.

To the north of the West End and on the south bank of the Thames are the business districts, with the main railway stations (Paddington, St Pancras, Waterloo, etc.), and beyond these again extend the outer districts of London, merging imperceptibly into the suburbs and the wider commuting area. These other parts of London have little to offer the tourist in comparison with the City and Westminster, although Southwark, on the south bank, is worth a visit.

Greater London. This new administrative unit, set up in 1963, takes in the old counties of London and Middlesex together with parts of the neighbouring counties of Essex, Hertfordshire, Surrey and Kent. It extends for a distance of some 15 miles from Charing Cross, its geographical centre, and has a population of some 8 million living within an area of 730 sq. miles. A population comparable with that of Greece is thus crowded together on a territory one-75th of the size of Greece. There are twice as many Londoners as there are Norwegians, one and a half times as many Londoners as there are citizens of Switzerland.

The people of London have long shown a preference for living on the outskirts of the town, with their own house and garden, and the crowded central districts have increasingly been abandoned. The life of the city therefore depends on the existence of a complex system of transport facilities, consisting of the network of bus and underground services now coordinated under the management of London Transport together with the suburban railway services provided by British Rail.

The old boroughs on the outskirts of London have been swallowed up by the constant expansion of the built-up area along the main roads leading out of the city, and places like Croydon, Epsom, Kingston, Twickenham, formerly independent, are now merely part of London's interminable suburban sprawl. In some of these districts, particularly the Staines-Slough-

Ealing area in the west, light industries have been established (the H.M.V. factory, the Lyons bakeries, breweries, etc.). These relatively clean modern industries contrast with the smoke-belching heavy industries below London Bridge — cement works, oil refineries, pulp mills, chemical plants, etc.

London's sphere of influence is reaching steadily farther out beyond the bounds of Greater London. Brighton, Folkestone and Dover, an hour's train journey away, are now involved in the life of the great city, and the commuting area extends as far afield as Southampton, Oxford and Cambridge. The whole of southern England contributes to supplying the needs of the metropolis, which now contains a sixth of the country's population; significantly, the five neighbouring counties are known as the "home counties". London, like ancient Rome, is pre-eminently *the* City, the centre of the nation's life.

The economy of London. London provides employment for some 3 million people — 500,000 in commerce, 445,000 in transport, about the same number in metal-working (considerably more than in Birmingham), 180,000 in the clothing trade (more than in Leeds), 160,000 in printing and publishing, 140,000 in the foodstuffs industries, 85,000 in woodworking, 70,000 in the chemical industry, etc. London is by far Britain's largest centre of the processing industries.

This primacy is due to a number of factors — the huge market for consumption goods, the availability of large supplies of manpower, the existence of areas of good building land with easy access, and the excellent facilities for bringing in supplies by sea or by rail. The lack of coal in the area, however — there is only one small coalfield in the London area, in Kent — has discouraged the development of heavy industry, which is mainly in the north and east of the country, where the coalfields are. London has mainly light industries producing consumption goods.

The main industrial districts are in the East End, near the Thames. A third of London's workers are employed here, in engineering, the clothing trade, leather-working and woodworking, printing and cigarette manufacture. The shipbuilding yards of the past have given place to car factories (Ford's, Dagenham) and the production of television and radio sets, plastics, etc. A few old-established workshops have survived from mediaeval times, like the Stepney bell foundry.

The Lea valley, to the north of London, specialises in market gardening and flower growing, carried on in innumerable glass-houses. The West End has only a few activities concerned with luxury products (the fashion trade, jewellery and other valuables). To the west and north-west, however, there has been a remarkable development of industry since the first world war, mainly the production of electrical equipment and foodstuffs, in such districts as Wembley, Hendon, Acton, Willesden and Hayes. The Wembley stadium was also the scene of the 1948 Olympic Games: and a short distance away is Heathrow Airport. The south bank of the Thames has little in the way of industry.

The feeding of a large city like London is a major problem in itself. There is no single market like the old Halles in Paris, but a series of specialised markets. London's fruit and vegetable market was established in Covent Garden, off the Strand, in 1670, and although inadequate for modern requirements remained in use for 300 years before being replaced by a new market at Nine Elms. The country's main fruit and vegetable market is at Spitalfields, in the East End, while the King's Cross market, near King's Cross station, handles the produce of the market gardens in the Fens and Lincolnshire. Smithfield market has been the main market for meat, eggs and dairy products since the reign of Edward III (1327-77). Finally Billingsgate market, on the north bank of the Thames, is the fish market, nowadays drawing its main supplies from Yarmouth and Grimsby rather than from the Thames. The vigorous and uninhibited language of the fish porters has made "billingsgate" a synonym for ribald and abusive talk.

The face of London. Perhaps the most striking impression a foreign visitor will take away from London is the monotony of the townscape, resulting from the long rows and terraces of precisely similar houses. "In England", wrote a Frenchman at the end of the 18th century, "all the houses are the same. It is as if, after expelling the monks from their island, the English made it into one large monastery with cells of the most relentless uniformity. In this country it would be all to easy to mistake your neighbour's house for your own".

As a result of the Englishman's preference for living in a house of his own there are relatively few blocks of flats in London, and those mostly of fairly recent construction. When the town was rebuilt after the Great Fire of 1666 the houses were built on the old foundations, using brick instead of the timber which had previously been the normal building material:

this had the advantage of offering more protection against
fire, and at the same time of being a quicker and cheaper form
of construction than stone.   The soot-blackened bricks of
London's older houses create a rather depressing effect, and
even stone turns a dingy black under the influence of the soot
and the fog, only the side facing the rain-bringing west winds
remaining clean and white.

The London fog — much less formidable than it used to be —
has a certain atmosphere of its own.   The banks of the river,
seen on a misty day with a wan sun attempting to find a way
through the haze, have the intimate and unemphatic charm
of a picture by Turner.   On a day like this, with the ships'
sirens sounding down river and St Paul's looming mistily
above the City, London reveals its distinctive atmosphere more
authentically than under an Italian sky.   Lacking the easy
charm of a Mediterranean city, London conveys an impression
of power, of sovereignty, which is not to be found in every
European capital.

The absence of embankments on the south bank of the
Thames gives it a less attractive aspect than the other side of
the river (which itself only began to acquire its embankments
about 1860).   There is a striking contrast between the opposite
banks — the one with its huddle of warehouses, factories and
docks, the other with its government offices and the Palace of
Westminster.

London has developed in this rather haphazard way as a
result of the matter-of-fact and businesslike attitude of its
citizens.   "Time is money", objected the City merchants when
Wren put forward his plan for the methodical rebuilding of
the fire-devastated city, and they proceeded to rebuild it after
their own fashion without further ado.   Little attention was
paid to the artistic aspect of the rebuilding — reflecting the
same kind of philistine and utilitarian approach as had led
to so much destruction at the Reformation.   And a severe critic
might also point to the nondescript character of so much later
building in London, whether the style is Gothic Revival or
neo-classical; indeed it is often difficult to put a date on a
particular building, which might have been erected at any
time between, say, 1670 and 1830.

The people of London.   Unlike their neighbours across the
Channel in Paris, the people of London have not — at any
rate in recent centuries — had any experience of revolution,

and have clung to tradition and continuity. They have rebuilt their city but retained the old-established street names. The old entrances to the city are still known as gates, even though the gates themselves have long since disappeared: and Lud, the legendary founder of London, still has his memorial in Ludgate. There may not be a single Shakespeare Street in London, but the George Streets are counted by the dozen.

Londoners are also traditionalists in their respect for the liberty of other people. The right of *habeas corpus* (which prevents arbitrary detention for more than 24 hours) was granted in response to their demands. The newspaper reports of court cases are, by the standards of some other countries, astonishingly restrained: in this country the accused person is presumed innocent until he is shown to be guilty. At Speakers' Corner in Hyde Park everyone is free to express his own opinion and to seek to persuade others, regardless of the other speakers maintaining a directly contrary view only a few yards away. And the word "Sorry" is perhaps the one most frequently heard in passing contacts between strangers on the pavements of London.

The Londoners showed their spirit of discipline during the blitz in the second world war, and the same imperturbability is displayed in the everyday business of life. The traffic waits patiently for the lights to change, and pedestrians can cross safely at the marked crossings. In general, indeed, the Londoners are a law-abiding race, and even during war-time rationing there was very little in the way of a black market.

Getting about London. Although the traffic is well disciplined, getting about London can sometimes present problems to foreign visitors unused to driving on the left. This practice is perhaps another reflection of the British attachment to tradition. It is said that the habit of keeping to the left began in the Middle Ages, when a horseman travelling the unsafe roads of the time had to be ready to take action against a possible assailant; and it was easier to draw his sword quickly if he rode on the left-hand side. The "keep left" signs of the present day may thus have a long history behind them.

Another, more recent, tradition of the London streets is the London policeman, recognisable from a distance by the high-crowned helmet which the Metropolitan Police have retained long after other British police forces have adopted the less formal flat cap. With all his reputation for friendliness and helpfulness, particularly to visitors, the London policeman is a stern disciplinarian when controlling London's traffic, and his directions are instantly obeyed. He is familiarly known as a "bobby" (after Sir Robert Peel, founder of the modern police), but this term is better not used to his face.

Visitors may sometimes be disconcerted by the numbering of London streets. The numbers may be arranged with even numbers on one side and odd on the other, but often enough the numbering is based on obscure rules which defy logic. It may run in sequence along one side of a street, or it may zigzag about from one side to the other. This may result, for example, in having No. 18 on one side of the street facing No. 306 on the other. In these circumstances only experience and patience will serve.

The names of the streets themselves show a corresponding lack of system. London has no fewer than 13 King Streets and 23 High Streets. Moreover similarity of name does not mean geographical propinquity; if you are looking for Grosvenor Street and find yourself in Grosvenor Road, do not think you are nearly there. One is in Chelsea and the other in Mayfair, with a good hour's walking between — and with Grosvenor Place and Grosvenor Square somewhere between the two. Sometimes, on the other hand, the same names continue with minor variations for a very long way — Kennington Road, Kennington Park Road, Kennington Lane, Kennington Oval, and so on. And the logically minded visitor may also find it disconcerting that so many terms are retained which no longer reflect any topographical reality — for example "mews" (originally stables), "gate", "terrace", "gardens" and so on are now often no more than ordinary streets. It is perhaps worth reminding visitors from the Continent that the "place" they may be looking for is not an open square but another ordinary city street.

London traditions. Reference has already been made to some of the respects in which Londoners, like their fellow-countrymen elsewhere in the British Isles, remain attached to the traditions of the past. Wherever they go in London visitors will come across evidence of this — the traditional decor of the pubs, the full wigs of the judges, the standard bowler hat and rolled umbrella of the City businessman — but there are a number of more spectacular features which delight tourists. There are the mounted sentries in full-dress uniform who stand guard in front of the Horse Guards in Whitehall and attract large crowds to the daily changing of the guard; the equally picturesque Beefeaters at the Tower of London, in their Tudor uniforms; the splendid royal procession when the Queen drives in the state coach, with an escort of cavalry, to open Parliament; the almost equally splendid Lord Mayor's procession which is an annual event in the life of the City. Other traditional ceremonies are less public, like the search which is carried out annually in the cellars of the Houses of Parliament to anticipate any repetition of the Gunpowder Plot of 1605 (an event still commemorated all over the country by the bonfires on Guy Fawkes Day, 5 November). Indeed the whole proceedings of Parliament are governed — and sometimes considerably delayed ! — by ceremonies and practices which have come down from earlier days. But the inconveniences of tradition are not matters that need concern the visitor; he can enjoy the more picturesque survivals from the past, remembering at the same time that they reflect a sense of continuity and stability which is one of the great qualities of the British way of life.

I. ROYAL AND OFFICIAL LONDON

The centre of London for millions of people is **Buckingham Palace,** the residence of British sovereigns since 1837, when Queen Victoria took up residence there. To the great expanse of road and lawns around the *Queen Victoria Memorial* (1911) opposite the Palace tens of thousands flock on the occasion of any great national event and, from a centrally situated balcony on the façade of the palace, the royal family respond to their people's greeting.

The original palace was built by the Duke of Buckingham in 1703 and bought by George III in 1762. Changes were subsequently made to the façade, but the front in its present form was added in 1913 by Aston Webb. The royal standard flies from the mast-head when the Queen is in residence, and the Guard before the gates is changed every day at 11.30 a.m.

In Buckingham Palace Road, which runs along the left-hand side of the Palace, are the *Queen's Gallery* and the *Royal Mews*.

In the Queen's Gallery (open 10 to 5, except Sundays mornings and Monday afternoons) are displayed works of art from the royal collection. In the **Royal Mews** (open Wednesdays and Thursdays in summer, Wednesdays only during the rest of the year, 2 to 4) can be seen the State coaches.

From the Queen Victoria Monument a broad processional way, the **Mall,** leads to Admiralty Arch and, beyond, Trafalgar Square. The Mall is always the beginning and the ending of every state procession — the opening of Parliament, the visit of a foreign head of state or any other great occasion.

Along the south side of the Mall is **St James's Park** (95 acres), formerly a marshy area, drained in the 17th century.

Charles II tried to acclimatise mulberry trees here, and also had a menagerie and an aviary in the park; from the latter comes the name of *Birdcage Walk*, which runs along the south side of the park from Buckingham Palace to Westminster. The park was laid out in its present form by the architect John Nash in 1829. From the bridge over the lake, rebuilt in 1957, there is a fine view of Buckingham Palace.

On the south side of Birdcage Walk are *Wellington Barracks*, occupied by the Grenadier Guards, with the Guards' Chapel (rebuilt after bomb damage during the last war).

To the south of the Palace is the area round **Victoria Station** (services to Dover and the Continent), with the Roman Catholic *Westminster Cathedral* (neo-Byzantine, 1903, with marble, mosaics and replicas of Byzantine capitals) and the ultra-modern tower blocks of *Portland House* (30 storeys) and *Westminster City Hall* (20 storeys).

Along the north side of the Mall are *Lancaster House*, *Clarence House*, *St James's Palace* and *Marlborough House* (p. 152). In front of Carlton Gardens (where Gen. de Gaulle lived from 1940 to 1944) is a statue of George VI by W. McMillan (1955).

At the east end of the Mall is the **Admiralty Arch,** built by Aston Webb in 1911. To the south of this is the *Admiralty* (the Old Admiralty to the east, the New Admiralty to the west).

From here we turn round the south side of **Trafalgar Square** (see below, p. 150) into **Whitehall,** a wide street lined by government offices.

On the west (right-hand) side is the **Horse Guards** building, in front of which two mounted troopers stand guard throughout the day (changing of the guard at 11 and 4, on Sundays at 10). To the rear of the building is a spacious parade ground, used in the time of Henry VIII and Elizabeth I for tournaments, on which the ceremony of "Trooping the Colour" takes place annually on the Queen's Birthday. The building itself dates from the mid 18th century.

Opposite the Horse Guards, Horse Guards Avenue runs east off Whitehall, with the old *War Office* on the left and the **Banqueting House** on the right.

The Banqueting House, built by Inigo Jones in 1622, was part of the old Whitehall Palace, destroyed by fire in 1697. It has a panelled ceiling with paintings by *Rubens*. From the Banqueting House Charles I walked on to the scaffold in 1649.

Returning to the west side of Whitehall, we pass *Dover House*, an 18th century mansion now occupied by the Scottish Office, the *Treasury* and, beyond Downing St, the *Foreign Office*.

Downing Street, a short and narrow street, was built in 1670 by Sir George Downing, Secretary of the Treasury in the reign of Charles II. No. 10 is the official residence of the Prime Minister, No. 11 of the Chancellor of the Exchequer.

On the opposite side of Whitehall is a huge modern block, with neo-classical pretensions, occupied by the Ministry of Defence. Beyond this point Whitehall runs into Parliament St.

In the centre of the street, opposite the Home Office, is the *Cenotaph*, designed by Sir Edwin Lutyens, erected to commemorate those who fell in the first world war. A commemorative ceremony is held at the Cenotaph every year on 11 November, the anniversary of the 1918 Armistice, when wreaths are laid at the foot of the Cenotaph: the poppies laid here and in Parliament Square ("Flanders poppies") are made by ex-servicemen. In 1946 a new inscription commemorating the dead of the second world war was added to the Cenotaph.

Beyond more government offices, Parliament St opens into Parliament Square, over whose green lawns tower on the left the Houses of Parliament and on the right Westminster Abbey and St Margaret's Church.

The **Houses of Parliament,** still known officially as the **Palace of Westminster,** occupy the site of the original palace of Edward the Confessor (1042-66); it was the royal residence until Henry VIII transferred his palace to Whitehall. The old buildings were destroyed by fire in 1834; Westminster Hall and the crypt and cloisters of St Stephen's Chapel remained and were incorporated into new buildings erected between 1840-50 by Sir Charles Barry. They cover over eight acres, contain over 1000 rooms and 100 staircases and have more than 500 statues in or around them.

The new buildings form a rectangle. At the north end is the *Clock Tower* (326 ft), next to Westminster Bridge. The B.B.C. have made known the world over the chimes of *Big Ben*, the bell (one of the largest known, 13½ tons) which tolls the hours. The *Central Spire* serves as a ventilation shaft. At the south-west corner is the *Victoria Tower*, the tallest (336 ft): in this is the *Archive Room*, in which voting papers are kept for a year after a general election.

On the eve of the State opening of Parliament the Yeomen of the Guard in their picturesque Tudor uniforms still formally search the cellars below the Commons Chamber. This is a survival of the *"Gunpowder Plot"* when a group of Roman Catholics planned to blow up Parliament during the official opening address of James I on 5 November 1605. The conspiracy was revealed and during a search of the cellars on 4 November Guy Fawkes was caught hiding among barrels of gunpowder. All over the country on the night of 5 November children celebrate this event by firework displays and by burning effigies of Guy Fawkes.

From the west front projects **Westminster Hall,** to which the modern building is joined, and which divides *New Palace Yard* from *Old Palace Yard*. William Rufus built the original palace in 1097, but this was almost completely burnt out in 1291. In 1398 Richard II built the new palace of which this Hall remains. Charles I was tried and condemned to death here. During the 18th century and until 1883 the Hall was used as the chief Court of Justice. In 1910 Edward VII lay in state here after his death. (Open Saturdays 10 to 3.30. On other days visitors must be accompanied by a Member of Parliament). During the second world war the Chamber occupied by the Commons was destroyed during air raids, and damage was

WESTMINSTER

0   500 m

also caused to the magnificent 70 feet wide roof of Westminster Hall.

When Parliament is sitting a flag flies during the day from the Victoria Tower and a light burns at night in the lantern over the Clock Tower. The Houses of Parliament can be visited free by the public on Saturdays from 10 to 3.30 or at any time when invited by a Member. Admission to the gallery to hear debates after 4.15 p.m. (11.30 a.m. on Fridays) is obtainable on application to the Admission Order Office in St Stephen's Hall.

On the sunk lawn outside Westminster Hall is a bronze statue of *Oliver Cromwell* (1599-1668) by Sir Hamo Thornycroft. In Old Palace Yard, beyond Westminster Hall, is a statue of Richard Cœur-de-Lion.

A copy of Rodin's "Burghers of Calais" stands in the gardens to the south of the Houses of Parliament, on a site selected by the sculptor himself.

In **Parliament Square** are many statues of British statesmen, including one of Sir Winston Churchill (1973), as well as a figure of Abraham Lincoln.

Opposite the Houses of Parliament, to the west, is **Westminster Abbey**, in which all sovereigns have been crowned since Harold, who seized the crown after the death of Edward the Confessor in 1066.

No documentary records prove the existence of any church on this site before the Benedictine abbey of St Peter's was erected about 740, but it is generally believed that Sebert, first Christian Saxon king, built on the marshy Thorney Isle (the original name of the district) a church which was consecrated in 616 by Mellitus, first bishop of London. Edward the Confessor (1042-66), whose palace stood a little to the east, rebuilt the church, but the existing building, one of the most splendid examples of the Early English style, dates mostly from 1269. Open 8 a.m. to 6 p.m. (8 p.m. on Wednesdays).

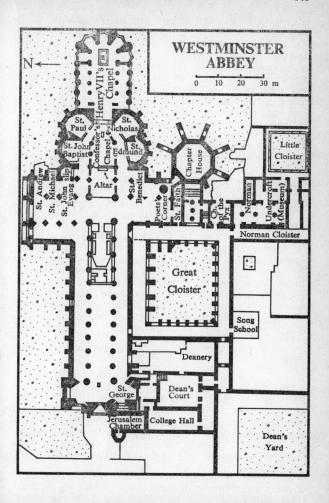

WESTMINSTER
ABBEY

0   10   20   30 m

N ←

Henry VII's Chapel

St. Paul

St. Nicholas

St. John Baptist

Confessor's Chapel

St. Edmund

St. Andrew

St. Michael

St. John slip Evang

Altar

St. Benedict

Chapter House

Little Cloister

Poets Corner

St. Faith

Ch. of the Pyx

Norman Undercroft (Museum)

Norman Cloister

Great Cloister

Song School

Deanery

St. George

Dean's Court

Jerusalem Chamber

College Hall

Dean's Yard

Henry VII's Chapel (Perpendicular style) was added at the beginning of the 16th century, and Wren and later Hawksmoor designed the towers. The plan of the building is a Latin cross, and Henry VII's Chapel continues the line of the apse to the east (facing Old Palace Yard of the Houses of Parliament), making the total length 515 feet. Westminster Abbey is the traditional setting for historical ceremonies such as royal marriages, and it is the scene of the lying-in-state of monarchs and important personages. It is above all a national shrine and contains the tombs or commemorative monuments of the illustrious of the land. Among them are William Pitt, Bacon, Charles Darwin, Newton, Wordsworth, Livingstone, Walter Scott, Goldsmith, Shakespeare, Dickens, Robert Browning, Tennyson, Longfellow, Henry VIII's wives Anne of Cleves and Jane Seymour, Mary Queen of Scots, the Duke of Buckingham and Queen Elizabeth I. A black marble slab let into the floor of the west end of the nave marks the last resting-place of the *Unknown Warrior* (1914-1918 war). In the apse are the tombs of the mediaeval sovereigns of England, with the Coronation Chair (beneath the seat is a recess for the Stone of Scone, the Scotitsh coronation stone, captured in 1297 by Edward I, which was stolen by Scottish nationalists in 1950 and recovered the following year) and the sword and shield of Edward III, during whose reign the greater part of the abbey was built. The south transept is known as **Poets' Corner**, a name originally acquired by the interment there of Chaucer and Spenser. Many famous poets, authors, musicians and actors are either buried here or commemorated by monuments.

Note the 14th century wall-paintings on the wall of the south transept.

King Henry VII's Chapel was erected over the tomb of Henry VII (1485-1509) and his Queen, Elizabeth of York, whose marriage after the Wars of the Roses had united not only the Houses of York and Lancaster but England itself. Note the beautiful bronze doors and the exquisite fan vaulting of the ceiling. The oriel windows in the apse contain some fine examples of modern stained glass (R.A.F. Memorial Chapel).

The Abbey has a small *museum* containing the funeral effigies of kings and queens of England, among which are Elizabeth (1558-1603) and Charles II (1660-85) and William and Mary (1688-1702).

Other features of interest. *Chapter House*, in which the House of Commons met from the 13th to the 16th century. *Cloister* (11th and 12th c.), with tombs of Norman abbots. *Jerusalem Chapel*, formerly used by the Knights of St John of Jerusalem. *Chamber of the Pyx*, a gloomy vaulted room (11th c.) which until 1303 housed the royal Treasury. Later it contained the pyx (chest) in which the gold and silver standards were kept; this is now preserved in the *Mint*, near the Tower of London.

St Margaret's Church (Westminster parish church), adjacent to the north façade of the abbey, is a good example of the Perpendicular style, although it has undergone repairs and alterations from the time of Edward I (1272-1307) onwards.

There is a splendid east window made for Henry VII (1485-1509). Since 1916 it has been dedicated to the British overseas Dominions, and for several centuries has been the official church of the House of Commons. See the Speaker's pew in the front; *the tomb of Walter Raleigh* and the window erected by American subscriptions to his memory in 1882; and the tombs of Caxton and of Milton's second wife and child. Samuel Pepys the diarist was married here in 1655.

From the great west door of the Abbey we see on the left a Victorian Gothic façade through which is the arched gateway to *Dean's Yard*.

Within Dean's Yard part of *Westminster School* buildings can be seen on the left (entrance in Little Dean's Yard). The ancient foundation was attached to the monastery as early as 1339, but the present school dates from the time of Elizabeth (1560). Air raids in the last war caused severe damage to the school buildings, particularly the old monks' dormitory and the Great Hall.

From the Abbey **Victoria Street** runs west, passing the *Board of Trade* on the left and the new *Scotland Yard* (police headquarters) on the right. It then passes close to *Westminster Cathedral* and comes to *Victoria Station* (above, p. 139).

Half a mile south of Westminster, on the river (Millbank), is the **Tate Gallery** (p. 147).

From the north-east corner of the Houses of Parliament (Clock Tower) **Westminster Bridge** crosses to the south bank of the Thames, with views of *St Thomas's Hospital* to the right and *London County Hall* to the left. Below the statue of Boadicea in her chariot (by Thomas Thornycroft, 1902) at the Westminster end of the bridge is the pier for motor launch trips on the river.

From this point too the **Victoria Embankment** runs north along the left bank of the Thames to Blackfriars Bridge.

The embankment was built in 1870. On the right is the *R.A.F. Memorial* (bronze eagle by Sir W. Reid Dick). Just beyond this is Hungerford Bridge (foot-bridge and, above it, the suburban lines into Charing Cross station), and then, in a public garden, the old York Water Gate, the river approach to York House before the embankment was built. Towards the far end of the gardens, on the embankment, stands the pink granite obelisk called *Cleopatra's Needle*. It is 70 feet high and weighs more than 180 tons; it dates from about 1500 B.C. and comes from Heliopolis, Egypt. It was erected in its present position in 1878.

Fine view over the river to two new concert halls, the *Royal Festival Hall* and the *Queen Elizabeth Hall* (p. 199).

To the north, beyond the gardens, are the large modern blocks of *Shell-Mex House* and the *Savoy Hotel*.

On the far side of **Waterloo Bridge** is moored the "*Discovery*", used by Scott in his polar expeditions (open to visitors 1 to 4.30), and beyond it are three other ships, the "Wellington", the "Chrysanthemum" and the "President". A short distance beyond this is the City (Route III).

Turning up to the left, we come into the **Strand,** a main thoroughfare between Westminster and the City. On the south side, facing on to the river, is **Somerset House** (government offices, particularly the Registrar-General of Births, Deaths and Marriages).

The present Georgian building (William Chambers, 1776) occupies the site of an earlier mansion begun by Lord Protector Somerset in the mid 16th century. The main front on the Thames is nearly 600 feet long and still has its old water gate, which gave access to the river before the embankment was built. To the east is the new building (1972) of King's College (London University).

On an island site in the middle of the road opposite King's College is the church of *St Mary-le-Strand* (James Gibbs, 1717), built to replace the former church, which was demolished during the building of Somerset House. Thomas Becket was rector of the parish in 1147. Interesting chapel of King Charles the Martyr. In Strand Lane, opposite the church, is the so-called Roman Bath (probably not in fact Roman).

Also in the Strand, a short distance farther east, is **St Clement Danes,** a Wren church restored after its destruction by fire in an air raid in 1940. The steeple, added by Gibbs in 1719, survived the fire, but the famous bells were cracked.

The name of the church is said to refer to the Danish settlement which existed here before the Norman conquest. This may also explain the name of *Aldwych* ("old settlement"), a wide street (laid out after slum clearance at the end of the 19th century) which branches off the Strand on the north opposite St Clement Danes and curves round to rejoin it at its intersection with Wellington St. Between the Strand and Aldwych is a massive group of modern buildings *(Bush House, India House* and *Australia House).*

Kingsway runs north from Aldwych to High Holborn, while the Strand continues to Charing Cross and Trafalgar Square, passing on the left the area called the Adelphi. The district was laid out towards the end of the 18th century by the Adam brothers, who have given their name to the Adam style of architecture and interior decoration. Adelphi Terrace was demolished at the beginning of this century to make way for a group of modern buildings, but there are still many Adam houses in the narrow little streets round about.

A short distance north of the Strand is **Covent Garden Opera House** (Barry, 1858), home of the Royal Opera and Ballet. Here too until 1974 was the Covent Garden Market, now transferred to Nine Elms. Nearby are the historic *Drury Lane Theatre*, with its memories of Restoration London and Nell Gwynn (now famous for its Christmas pantomimes), the *Lyceum Theatre*, where the famous actor Sir Henry Irving used to appear, and **St Paul's Church** (Inigo Jones, 1638: rebuilt 1795), containing memorials of many famous actors and actresses and others connected with the theatre.

The *Strand* is a scene of lively activity all day long, crowded with people and with traffic, holding out a great variety of attractions, with its shops of all kinds, its restaurants and pubs, and its nearness to so many other public buildings, theatres and other features of interest.

Charing Cross, at the west end of the Strand, is named after the cross erected by Edward I in 1291 at the point where the cortege bearing the body of Queen Eleanor halted for the last time on its way to Westminster Abbey.

The Strand runs into **Trafalgar Square,** a spacious and well proportioned open space much used for public meetings and demonstrations.

The square was laid out between 1829 and 1841. Its name commemorates the battle (1805) in which Nelson defeated the French fleet. In the centre is the *Nelson Column*, 150 feet high, bearing a 17 foot statue of Nelson: at the foot are the famous Landseer lions (1867). Two new statues, commemorating Admirals Beatty and Jellicoe, were unveiled in 1949, when reconstruction work was also carried out on the square and the fountains (which are supplied by artesian wells). On the south side of the square is a fine 17th century *statue of Charles I.* Two massive round lamps come from Nelson's flagship at Trafalgar, the "Victory": under one of them is a police box with narrow slit windows, with room for only one policeman.

At the north-east corner of the square is the church of **St Martin in the Fields,** whose name is a reminder of the rural character of the area in earlier times. It is the royal family's parish church, with a special royal pew. The B.B.C.'s religious services are broadcast from here. The church was built by James Gibbs in 1726.

Along the north side of the square is the **National Gallery,** with one of the finest collections of paintings in the world. The pictures are arranged according to schools, which makes it easier for visitors to see what particularly interests them.

The National Gallery was founded only in 1824, but the collection was considerably increased during the 19th century by gifts and purchases, including Sir Robert Peel's collection. For a guide to its contents, see p. 209.

The façade, in classical style, extends for 450 feet on a terrace standing above the square. In front of it are statues of *James II* (Grinling Gibbons) and *George Washington* (after the original marble by Houdon).

To the rear of the National Gallery is the **National Portrait Gallery** (1896, with later additions). Parts of the building suffered war damage. Although the gallery contains many works by well-known masters, its main interest is historical rather than artistic. See p. 216.

From the north side of Trafalgar Square **Pall Mall** runs west.

A short distance along Pall Mall East, **Haymarket** (named after a market which was held here until 1830) goes off on the right. In this street are the tower block of *New Zealand House* (1963), a number of leading theatres and (near the top, on right) the *Design Centre*, a permanent exhibition of British design.

Pall Mall is notable for the number of well-known clubs to be found along its length. Its name (French *pail-mail*) comes from a game played there by the nobility in the 16th century.

Pall Mall intersects with *Waterloo Place*, with numerous banks and insurance offices and a variety of statues (soldiers, explorers, etc.). At the south end is the *Duke of York's Column*, 124 feet high, erected in 1834.

A number of the clubs occupy very fine buildings: *United Services Club* (John Nash, 1826), *Athenaeum* (Burton, 1830), *Travellers'* and *Reform* (Charles Barry, 1840). The style is that of the Italian *palazzo*. In addition to their other amenities, the clubs are noted for the excellence of their cuisine and their cellars.

Pall Mall runs into the **Mall** (p. 138), near the far end of which is **Marlborough House,** built by Wren in 1710 for the Duke of Marlborough. George V was born here in 1865 and lived in the house until 1910, when he came to the throne. His widow, Queen Mary, lived in Marlborough House until her death in 1953. It is now occupied by the Commonwealth Secretariat.

Beyond Marlborough House is **St James's Palace,** the sovereign's London residence until the accession of Queen Victoria in 1837.

Many English or British kings, including Charles II and George IV, were born in this picturesque red brick palace, and Mary Tudor died here. At least as early as the late 12th century the site was occupied by a leper-house. In 1532 it was acquired by Henry VIII, who wished to build a palace for Anne Boleyn: but Henry was persuaded by Cardinal Wolsey, anxious to regain his favour, to move his court to Whitehall. When Whitehall was burned down at the end of the 17th century William and Mary brought the court back to St James's. In 1809 the east wing was destroyed by fire, but the **Chapel Royal** (visitors admitted to certain services), part of the Presence Chamber and some rooms of lesser importance still survive from the original Tudor building. During the second world war a bomb fell close to the palace, destroying the new buildings but leaving the Tudor buildings and gatehouse standing, though damaged. The palace is not open to visitors.

From here **St James's Street** runs north, another street notable for its clubs: *White's* (Nos. 37-38), the oldest in London, founded in 1697 and now occupying premises built in 1788; *Brooks's* (No. 60); the *Devonshire* (No. 50); the *Carlton* (No. 69). There are some handsome 18th century houses in the neighbouring streets (King St, St James's Square, etc.).

Farther west are a number of fine old mansions: *Clarence House* (Nash, 1825), adjoining St James's Palace, the residence of Queen Elizabeth the Queen Mother; to the north of it *Bridgewater House* (1849); and just beyond it **Lancaster House** (Wyatt, 1827), restored after war damage and now occupied by government offices (open on Saturdays and Sundays in summer, 2 to 6).

From here we cross *Green Park* to return to our starting point at **Buckingham Palace.**

II. THE WEST END

The term **West End** cannot be exactly defined, but would be generally understood as covering an area extending between the City in the east and Chelsea in the west, including the best residential, shopping and commercial districts. Its boundaries have become increasingly difficult to draw as business has pushed steadily westward into what were formerly fashionable and aristocratic parts of the city. Berkeley Square, which once possessed some of the largest and most sumptuously appointed mansions in London, has now become the centre of big business. Nevertheless this area of London, ill defined and variegated though it may be, has more to offer the visitor than is generally thought.

Of the wide area covered by the term, the most easterly part is difficult to consider apart from the City which it adjoins, and is therefore dealt with in section III (p. 175). The remainder of the West End is described in this section in two parts: the area between Piccadilly and Regent's Park, including Mayfair, Soho, Bloomsbury and Marylebone, and the area to the west (south of Hyde Park) which takes in Kensington, Brompton and Chelsea.

A. Between Piccadilly and Regent's Park

Piccadilly and the adjoining streets form London's most fashionable shopping district. Here are to be seen enticing displays of fine furs, jewellery and high-quality fabrics, and here too are the salons of the great couturiers, the temples of high fashion, art galleries to tempt the wealthy collector, shops and agencies catering for every need.

It has been said that to become a Londoner you must learn to find your way about Piccadilly. In this area you can find anything you want—and perhaps, if you wait long enough, meet anyone you want to meet. The street is always throbbing with traffic, the pavements crowded with people.

Piccadilly starts from **Piccadilly Circus**, one of the busiest traffic intersections of central London, and

runs west. In the centre of the Circus, which after
dark is a blaze of coloured neon signs, is the famous
statue of *Eros* on his fountain, erected to commemorate the Earl of Shaftesbury (d. 1885), after whom
the adjacent Shaftesbury Avenue is named. The area
round the statue, hemmed in by the ceaseless traffic,
was traditionally the pitch of flower-sellers but is
now a favourite haunt of young people with time
on their hands.

The name Piccadilly is said to go back to the 16th century,
when there was a house of entertainment known as Piccadilla
House ("house of peccadilloes"). The name "pickadil" was
given to a kind of collar or ruff, the manufacturer of which
called his shop Pickadilly Hall. Hence — according to this
theory — the present name.

MAYFAIR

Mayfair takes its name from a large fair once held here in
spring; and *Shepherd's Market* is perhaps another relic of
that time. Since then, however, the district has undergone a
change, and is now the most fashionable and elegant district in
London. In this part of the city are the leading hotels (the
Ritz, Claridge's, the Hilton, the Dorchester), the most exclusive
restaurants, the best clubs. Here the world of fashion and
society has its centre. *Park Lane*, the wide avenue which runs
down the side of *Hyde Park*, is usually regarded as the "best"
address in the country.

Starting from Piccadilly Circus, **Piccadilly** runs
west for roughly a mile to the south-east corner of
Hyde Park, from which point it is continued by
Knightsbridge (p. 170) and the Great West Road.

At the beginning of Piccadilly, standing slightly
back from the street on the left-hand side, is **St James's
Church**(Wren, 1676-84), now restored after war damage.
Behind it in St James's Square is *Norfolk House*,
which was Gen. Eisenhower's headquarters in 1944.

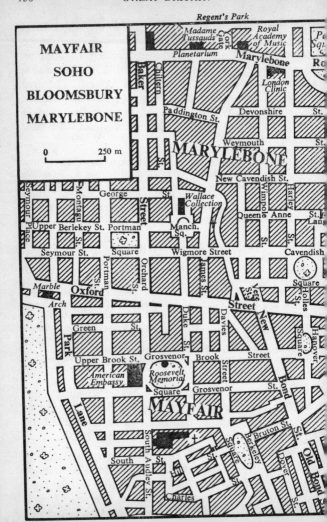

MAYFAIR
SOHO
BLOOMSBURY
MARYLEBONE

0   250 m

Regent's Park

Madame Tussauds
York Gate
Royal Academy of Music
Planetarium
Marylebone

Baker
Chiltern

London Clinic

Paddington St.
Devonshire   St.

Weymouth
MARYLEBONE   St.

New Cavendish St.

George   St.
Wallace Collection
Wimpole
Harley

Montagu
Queen Anne   St. J
Lan

Upper Berkeley St.   Portman
Seymour Place

Manch.
Sq.

Seymour St.   Square   Wigmore Street   Cavendish

Portman

Marble
Oxford   Orchard   James St.   Vere
Holles
Square

Arch   St.   St.   Street
New   Hanover

Green   St.   Duke
Davies St.

Park   Upper Brook St.   Grosvenor   Brook   Street   Bond
Grosvenor   Berkeley   St.

American Embassy
Roosevelt Memorial   St.
Square   Grosvenor

Lane   MAYFAIR   Bruton St.
Old Bon

South Audley St.   Square   Berkeley   Dover
St.

South   St.
Charles   St.

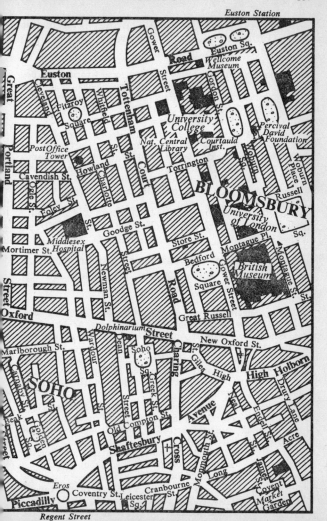

Euston Station

Gower

Road

Street

Euston Sq.

Wellcome
Museum

Great

Crescent

Euston

Portland

Fitzroy
Square

Whitfield

Tottenham

Gordon St.

University
College

Percival
David
Foundation

Post Office
Tower

Howland

Charlotte

St.

Court

Nat. Central
Library

Courtauld
Inst.

Torrington

Woburn
Place

Cavendish St.

BLOOMSBURY

Orie St.

Foley

St.

Goodge St.

University
of London

Russell

Sq.

Mortimer St.

Middlesex
Hospital

Newman St.

Store St.

Montague Pl.

Montague St.

Street

Bedford
Square

Gower Street

British
Museum

Oxford

Street

Road

Great Russell

Dolphinarium

Street

New Oxford St.

Marlborough St.

Warour

Dean

Soho
Sq.

Greek St.

Charing

St. Giles

High

High Holborn

Carnaby St.

SOHO

Golden Square

Street

Cross

Drury Lane

Endell

Beak

Street

Old Compton

Avenue

Monmouth

Shaftesbury

Cross

Long

James St.

Acre

Eros

Coventry St.

Cranbourne

Leicester
Sq.

Covent
Market
Garden

Piccadilly

Farther along, on the right-hand side, is **Burlington House** (17th-18th c.), with a massive façade in Italian Renaissance style built in 1872.

In Burlington House are the headquarters of various learned societies and the **Royal Academy of Arts,** which holds two annual exhibitions: contemporary artists, May-August, and a loan exhibition devoted to the art of the past, September-March. Open weekdays 10 to 6, Sundays 2 to 6.

Along the west side is the *Burlington Arcade* (luxury shops, open weekdays 9 to 5). This leads to *Burlington Gardens,* in which (No. 6) is the **Museum of Mankind,** the British Musem's department of ethnography (15 rooms, with changing displays of the Museum's finest pieces — Benin bronzes, turquoise mosaics from Mexico, etc.); open 10 to 5, Sundays 2.30 to 6.

Beyond this, on the right, is the fashionable shopping street known successively as *Old* and *New Bond Street,* in the heart of aristocratic **Mayfair.**

In this district of busy streets and fashionable shops a quieter note is introduced by two shady squares, *Berkeley Square* and *Grosvenor Square.*

Berkeley Square suffered in the air raids of the last war, and few 17th or 18th century houses are left. At No. 46 is *Lansdowne House* (Robert Adam, 1768). No. 45 was occupied by Clive, the conqueror of India, who committed suicide in the house in 1774. Some years later a maid and a young man living at No. 50 are said to have died of fright on seeing a ghost — perhaps, it was suggested, the ghost of Clive returning to haunt his old home.

North-west of Berkeley Square is **Grosvenor Square,** which has so many American associations that it is sometimes called "Little America". At the corner of Duke St and Brook St is the house occupied by John Adams, first American Minister to Great Britain, 1785-88, afterwards second President of the United States. A tablet commemorating John Adams was placed on the front of the house in 1933.

The *American Embassy* is on the west side of the square. In the gardens of Grosvenor Square on 12 April 1948, Mrs Roosevelt unveiled, in the presence of the King and Queen, the memorial to her husband, *President Franklin Roosevelt*, on the third anniversary of his death.

No. 25 Brook St was occupied by *Handel* for more than thirty years, and in this house he composed many of his works, including the "Messiah".

In north-eastern Mayfair, near Regent St, is *Hanover Square*, in which is a statue of William Pitt (1831). On the south side is *St George's Church* (John James, 1724), with 16th century Flemish stained glass in the apse.

Regent Street brings us back to Piccadilly Circus. It was originally built by Nash in 1818 to link Regent's Park with Carlton House, the residence of the Prince Regent (in Waterloo Place: p. 152). The curved part at the foot which runs into Piccadilly Circus is known as the Quadrant. The whole of Nash's street was pulled down and rebuilt in the first half of this century.

SOHO

The colourful district of **Soho** lies to the north of Piccadilly Circus, between Regent St in the west and Charing Cross Road in the east.

Although adjoining Mayfair, Soho is totally different from it. It is a cosmopolitan area in which Greek, Italian, Hungarian and French restaurants line the narrow streets, along with places of entertainment of very varying quality. The name of the district comes from a hunting call used to summon the hounds. French Huguenots expelled by France in the 17th century, followed by further French refugees during the Revolution, played a major part in giving this part of London its foreign stamp, but Soho is now an area in which people of all nationalities rub shoulders, forming a kind of Latin quarter in which Londoners can find something of the "vie de Bohême".

Soho is also a centre of avant-garde intellectual activity, an area frequented by film people from Wardour St and theatre people from the many theatres round about. It was while staying in Soho that Mozart composed his London Symphony at the age of 8. There are many bookshops well stocked with

Continental books, newspapers and periodicals. Soho has also
a claim to fame in the world of fashion; it was from *Carnaby
Street*, a little street just east of Regent St and parallel to it,
that the mini-skirt set out on its triumphant career in the 1960s.

Soho is thus totally different from any other part of London,
a separate little world with a life of its own.

From Piccadilly Circus *Coventry Street* runs a
short distance east into **Leicester Square,** in the
17th century an area of open country to which the
gentlemen of the day resorted to fight duels. In the
centre is a small garden with a statue of Shakespeare.

On the north side of the square is the church of *Notre-Dame
de France*, a circular building destroyed during the last war
and completely rebuilt in 1955 (Aubusson tapestry above the
altar: frescoes by Jean Cocteau, 1960, in one of the chapels).

Going north by way of *Shaftesbury Avenue* with
its theatres and either *Dean Street* (*St Anne's Church*,
1685, with a red brick steeple and a clock of 1806)
or *Frith Street* (at No. 20 of which Mozart stayed
as a child), we come to **Soho Square.**

In the centre is a statue of Charles II, who had the square
laid out in 1681. On the south side is *Barnabas House* (1750),
on the east side the Roman Catholic church of St Patrick, on
the north side a French Protestant church.

Immediately north of Soho Square is **Oxford Street.**
Turning right into this street and its continuation *New
Oxford Street*, we come to the district of Bloomsbury.

BLOOMSBURY

Bloomsbury is a quiet residential district of 18th
and early 19th century houses, generally of uniform
type, with plain well-proportioned façades, laid out
in terraced streets or round squares with gardens
(sometimes private) in the centre. The whole area

is a fine example of 18th century town planning; particularly fine is *Bedford Square* with its Adam houses. Many of the houses are now used as offices, and many are private hotels and guest-houses. In this area are many cultural, academic and scientific institutions, in particular the **British Museum** (main entrance in Great Russell St).

The **British Museum** is one of the glories of London and of Britain, with a worldwide and well-earned reputation. It has long been famous for its Library, nom separately organised as the British Library, which receives a copy of every book or other publication produced in the country. Among the library's particular treasures are a parchment copy of the Great Charter, a 4th century manuscript of the Gospels, a Gutenberg Bible and Leonardo da Vinci's notebooks. The museum is famous for its unique collections of Egyptian, Assyrian, Greek and Roman antiquities.

The building, in the Greek classical style in favour at the beginning of the 19th century, has a façade 400 feet long, with a central portico and two projecting wings; Ionic colonnade. Some of the galleries were badly damaged during the blitz, but the most important items had been removed to places of safety.

Detailed description; p. 203.

To the south of the British Museum is *St George's Church* (1724). To the south-east is *Bloomsbury Square*, laid out in 1665 (statue of the 18th century statesman Charles James Fox).

To the north of the British Museum are the various buildings of **London University** (Charles Holden, 1933), dominated by the 210 foot high tower containing the Library. The University of London, founded in 1836, comprises 33 departments and 10 institutes, with 50,000 students and a professorial and teaching staff of 1700.

East of the University is *Russell Square*, with a statue of the fifth Duke of Bedford (Westmacott, 1806). On the far side of the square is Guilford St, which leads to *Coram's Fields* (on left), where there was formerly a Foundling Hospital established by the 18th century philanthropist Thomas Coram. At No. 40 in the adjoining Brunswick Square are the headquarters of the **Coram Foundation for Children,** with works by *Hogarth, Gainsborough, Kneller* and other artists, together with mementoes of *Handel* (open Mondays and Fridays 10 to 12 and 2 to 4). Farther along Guilford St, on the right, is Doughty St, at No. 48 of which is **Dickens House,** where Dickens lived in 1837-39 (small museum; open weekdays 10 to 5).

Immediately north-west of Russell Square, on the west side of Woburn Square, are the **Courtauld Institute Galleries,** attached to the University of London (open weekdays 10 to 5, Sundays 2 to 5).

A very fine collection of paintings, largely assembled by Samuel Courtauld (d. 1949), particularly notable for its **Impressionist and Post-Impressionist works:** *Degas, Sisley, Cézanne* ("Card-Players", "Montagne Sainte-Victoire"), *Manet* ("Bar at the Folies-Bergère"), *Renoir* ("La Loge"), *Pissarro, Claude Monet, Seurat, Vuillard, van Gogh* ("Peach-trees", "Self-Portrait with Bandaged Ear"), *Bonnard, Utrillo, Dufy, Gauguin, Toulouse-Lautrec, Modigliani,* etc.   Other important features are the Gambier-Parry Collection (mediaeval and Renaissance art), paintings by **Italian primitives** and 15th and 16th century masters *(Botticelli, Simone Martini, Giorgione, Filippino Lippi)* and works by *Goya, Rubens, Gainsborough, Velazquez, van Dyck* and others.

At 53 Gordon Square, immediately north of Woburn Square, is the *Percival David Foundation of Chinese Art*, also attached to the University.

A collection of Chinese ceramics and a library left to the University in 1950 by Sir Percival David. Open Mondays 2 to 5, Tuesday-Friday 10.30 to 5, Saturdays 10.30 to 1.

From here *Gordon Street* runs north to *Euston Road.*

On the far side of Euston Road is *Euston Station* (west coast route to Scotland, the Lake District, Wales, boat services to Ireland, Liverpool and the industrial Midlands). To the east is *St Pancras Station* (midland route to industrial Yorkshire and Lancashire), and beyond this is *King's Cross Station* (east coast route to Scotland, the eastern Midlands, the seaside resorts on the east and north-east coasts and industrial Humberside).

A little way last *Gower Street* runs south from Euston Road. A short distance down this street is **University College.**

Founded 1828, incorporated in London University in 1900. Museums of anatomy and zoology (open to qualified students) and interesting *Egyptian collections* (open weekdays except Saturdays 10 to 5). Just beyond University College is the *National Central Library* (1933).

Gower Street continues south into **Bedford Square,** a magnificent example of late 18th century town planning in the neo-classical style (Adam).

MARYLEBONE AND REGENT'S PARK

The sights of Marylebone, which are few in number and fairly far apart, are best seen by car.

To the east, in Howland St, is the 620 foot high **Post Office Tower,** built in 1965 at a cost of £1,250,000, with television and radio-telephony transmitters. Revolving restaurant with wide views.

In Portland Place, at the north end of Regent St, is the headquarters of the B.B.C., **Broadcasting House,** shaped like the prow of some immense ship. Beside it is *All Souls Church* (Nash, 1824). Going down Regent St to the busy junction of **Oxford Circus,** we pass on the left the *Polytechnic Institute* (1911).

Turning right, we continue west along **Oxford Street.**

Holles St, on the north side of Oxford St, runs into *Cavendish Square*, laid out in 1717. At the north-west corner of the square is *Harley Street*, the great centre of medical consultant practice.

Beyond this, just north of Oxford St, is *St Peter's Church* (Gibbs, 1824), and beyond this again are *Stratford Place* (a cul-de-sac of late 18th century houses) and *Duke Street.*

Duke St leads north into *Manchester Square*, in which is the famous **Wallace Collection**, in *Hertford House*, built in 1788 for the Duke of Manchester.

The collection was formed by the third Marquess of Hertford, who figures in Thackeray's "Vanity Fair" as Lord Steyne, and his son the fourth Marquess, who lived mainly in Paris. The fourth Marquess bequeathed it to his natural son Sir Richard Wallace, after whose death his widow offered the collection to the city of Paris and, when the offer was refused, bequeathed it to the nation in 1897. The collection must be among the most valuable private collections ever assembled.

For the collection itself, see p. 219.

Oxford St leads to **Marble Arch** (originally intended as a monument to Nelson), formerly erected in 1828 by John Nash in front of Buckingham Palace; but as it proved to be too small for the state coach to pass beneath it, it was moved to its present position in 1851.

In its new position the arch formed the entrance to Hyde Park. The busy traffic at this important intersection (Oxford St, Bayswater Road, Park Lane and Edgware Road), however, made it necessary to carry out street widening, and in 1908 the north-east corner of Hyde Park was cut off, leaving the arch in its present isolated position. It is modelled on the Arch of Constantine in Rome.

Until 1759 *Tyburn gallows* ("Tyburn Tree") stood at the junction of Bayswater Road and Edgware Road. London's last public execution (a practice abolished through the influence of Dickens) took place in 1868. Just inside the Marble Arch entrance to Hyde Park is "Speakers' Corner", where speakers on behalf of every variety of cause compete with one another on Sunday afternoons to attract an audience. For **Hyde Park**, see p. 166.

From the north-west corner of the junction *Edgware Road* branches off, following the line of an old Roman road. To the west is the rather characterless district of Paddington, with *Paddington Station* (main lines to Devon, Cornwall, Somerset, Wales, boat services to Ireland and the industrial West Midlands).

Bayswater Road runs west from Marble Arch to Notting Hill Gate through the district of Bayswater. Thereafter, with several changes of name, it continues to Shepherd's Bush, Kew and Richmond. To the north of Notting Hill Gate is Portobello Road, with a colourful fruit and vegetable market on weekdays and a "flea market" on Saturdays.

Returning along Oxford St, we turn north into *Baker Street*, noted for its association with Sherlock Holmes. This runs into *Marylebone Road*, an important east-west thoroughfare. To the right, on the north side of the street, are the **London Planetarium** and **Madame Tussaud's Waxworks** (open 10 to 7: single admission ticket for both).

Madame Tussaud's was founded by a Madame Tussaud who fled from France after the French Revolution. The display includes noted people from all over the world, of either enduring or merely temporary fame, and a "Chamber of Horrors".

Farther along Marylebone Road, on the south side, is the church of *St Marylebone* (Hardwick, 1813). Just opposite the church is *York Gate*, which leads into **Regent's Park.**

Regent's Park (470 acres), once a royal hunting ground, was laid out by *John Nash* in 1812 for the Prince Regent, the future George IV. It was opened to the public on the accession of Queen Victoria in 1837. To the left of the entrance are the modern buildings of *Bedford College* (University of London), and beyond this is **Queen Mary's Garden,** belonging to the Royal Botanic Society (rose garden; Mermaid Fountain, by McMillan, 1950; open air theatre).

The splendid terraced houses round the park were damaged by bombing during the last war but have been restored. Particularly fine are Nash's neo-classical mansions to the north-west.

In the northern part of the park is the **Zoo** (open 9 to 7), established in 1828, with its *Reptile House, Lion House, Aquarium, Children's Zoo, Small Mammal House* and *Chimpanzee House*.

B. Hyde Park, Kensington and Chelsea

The itinerary suggested is long, and best done by car.

Hyde Park.   No account of London would be complete without some reference to its parks, the lungs of the city, which bring a little light and air into its crowded streets.   There are parks all over London; some of them relieve the monotony of the East End and the southern districts of the city, but the principal parks are in the West End, extending from Whitehall to Regent's Park and Kensington Gardens.

Most of the parks are either former royal hunting grounds — as late as the 17th century deer were still hunted in Hyde Park — or church lands confiscated at the Reformation.   For the most part they were laid out as parks in the 19th century.   Some of them have lakes, like the famous *Serpentine* in Hyde Park, which offers boating in summer and skating in winter.

From *St James's Park* to *Kensington Gardens* there is a continuous stretch of open space over 3 miles long.   With their trees and grass, their beds of flowers, their innumerable birds, the swans and other wildfowl on the lakes, they create all the atmosphere of the country within the city.   Even St James's Park seems many miles away from Westminster, only a stone's throw away.   And perhaps what may impress some foreign visitors most is that they are allowed to walk at will on the grass.

Hyde Park (350 acres) has entrances at Marble Arch to the north and Hyde Park Corner to the south.   For Marble Arch, see p. 164.   Adjoining Hyde Park Corner is *Apsley House*, home of the Duke of Wellington.   *Rotten Row* (said to be derived from the French "route des rois") is a sandy track reserved for riding.

Until the time of James I this was still a deer park, as it had been since the time of Henry VIII.   Charles I laid out the Ring, which became a fashionable promenade.   Later the park became a favoured venue for duels.   During the reign of George II, however, Queen Caroline created the delightful park which we know today. The *Serpentine* was formed in 1733; the lake covers an area of 40 acres and has a bathing lido (open in summer) on the south side.

In 1851 the first great international exhibition, the Great Exhibition, was held in Hyde Park, in an immense structure of iron and glass, later known as the *Crystal Palace*, an outstanding piece of engineering by Sir Joseph Paxton. The Crystal Palace was later transferred to Sydenham, south of the Thames, but was destroyed by fire in 1936. The towers remained standing, but were demolished during the last war for the sake of the metal they contained.

In Hyde Park is the most controversial of London's 350 statues, Epstein's "Rima", commemorating the naturalist and writer W.H. Hudson.

Kensington Gardens (270 acres) adjoin Hyde Park to the west, and convey the impression of being deep in the country. Admirers of Sir James Barrie will wish to visit the statue of *Peter Pan* (George Frampton) on the west bank of the Long Water (as the upper part of the Serpentine is known). In the south of the park, the *Dutch Garden* provides a blaze of colours with its ever fresh herbaceous borders.

Cars are not allowed into Kensington Gardens, and this gives it a particular tranquillity, while the fine trees give it something of an aristocratic air. It is a favourite playground for children, particularly round the statue of Peter Pan. On the west side of the Gardens is **Kensington Palace** (entrance in Broad Walk). The south front, north-west wing and orangery were built by Wren; but the building as he designed it was never completed, and the interior was finished by William Kent in the reign of George I. The palace was a royal residence until 1760. The future Queen Victoria was born here, and lived in the palace until her accession in 1837. It is now the home of Princess Margaret. Some rooms in the palace are open to visitors.

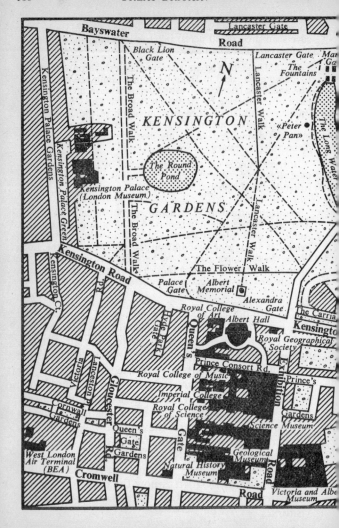

HYDE PARK & KENSINGTON

0   500 m

Apsley House, at the west end of Piccadilly and the south-east entrance to Hyde Park, is a neo-classical mansion built by Robert Adam in 1778 and completed by Wyatt (Corinthian porticoes) in 1829. It was the residence of the great *Duke of Wellington* until his death in 1852. Since 1952 it has been a *Wellington Museum* (open weekdays 10 to 4, Sundays 2.30 to 6).

Decorations, trophies and other mementoes of the Duke. Statue of Napoleon by *Canova*. Many objets d'art; Meissen, Vienna and Sèvres china; paintings by famous masters, including *Vermeer*, the elder *Brueghel*, *Teniers*, *17th century Dutch masters*, *Ribera*, *Velazquez*, *Rubens*, *Murillo*, *Correggio*, *Vernet*, *van Dyck*, *Reynolds*, *Lawrence* and *Goya* (portrait of the Duke on horseback).

In front of Apsley House is a *statue of Wellington* (1888).

On the east side of the busy traffic intersection of *Hyde Park Corner* is the **Wellington Arch,** erected in 1825 by Decimus Burton (quadriga by Adrian Jones, 1912). To the west is St *George's Hospital*, with a classical façade (1827). At the entrance to Hyde Park, to the left of Apsley House, is a triumphal arch (Burton, 1825), with reproductions of the Parthenon frieze.

From Hyde Park Corner the important thoroughfare of **Knightsbridge** runs west: it is the route to Heathrow Airport. At its intersection with Sloane St (on left) is *Bowater House* (1960), with Epstein's last piece of sculpture, "Pan". From the same junction *Brompton Road*, a great shopping and business street (with the well-known department store, *Harrods*, on the south side) runs south-west, with many shops and foreign restaurants in the adjoining streets. From here we continue west along the south side of Hyde Park.

Alternatively it is possible to go through Hyde Park from Hyde Park Corner on Serpentine Road, turning left over the Serpentine Bridge to join Kensington Road, the continuation of Knightsbridge.

On the south side of Kensington Road, at its junction with Exhibition Road, is the *Royal Geographical Society*, with statues of the explorers Shackleton and Livingstone. Beyond this is the huge bulk of the **Royal Albert Hall** (1871), in Italian Renaissance style, a concert hall which can accommodate an audience of 10,000, and beyond this again is the *Royal College of Art* (1961).

Opposite, on the edge of Kensington Gardens, is the *Albert Memorial* (1872), a not very successful essay in the neo-Gothic style, erected by Queen Victoria to commemorate the Prince Consort.

In Hyde Park Gate, a short street on the south side of Kensington Road just beyond the Albert Hall, is the house in which Sir Winston Churchill died in 1965.

Between the Albert Hall and Cromwell Road, to the south, is a whole group of important **museums and scientific institutions.** The architecture of these buildings is dignified and rather cold, but entirely appropriate to their function.

The **Imperial College of Science and Technology,** part of the University of London, was completed in 1963 (architects, Norman and Dawbarn). It incorporates the older *Queen's Tower* (1893), 220 feet high, with a carillon presented by an Australian donor.

The **Science Museum** (entrance in Exhibition Road; open weekdays 10 to 6, Sundays 2.30 to 6) is concerned with the history of science and technology. Among its exhibits are the first railway engine (Stephenson's "Rocket"), ship models, early motor cars and aircraft, and a wide range of machinery and scientific equipment.

The **Natural History Museum** (entrance in Cromwell Road; same opening hours as Science Museum), originally part of the British Museum, contains the most comprehensive palaeontological collection in the world. Among its exhibits are the famous *Piltdown skull*, believed to date from the Pleistocene

period but shown in 1953 to be a fake, the skeleton of a whale
80 feet long and a life-size model, 88 feet long, of an American
diplodocus.

The **Geological Museum** (entrance in Exhibition Road; same
opening hours) has a comprehensive collection, including an
extensive range of gems and semi-precious stones.

To the east of these museums, in Cromwell Road,
is the Italian Renaissance façade (Aston Webb, 1910)
of the **Victoria and Albert Museum,** devoted to applied
and decorative art.

The collection includes paintings (Constable, Holbein) and
sculpture (Houdon) as well as metalwork, furniture, silver and
tapestries, in a varied range which takes in an 18th century
shop front no less readily than a painted ceiling from Spain.
See p. 221.

Immediately east of the Victoria and Albert Museum
is the **Brompton Oratory,** a Roman Catholic church in
Italian Renaissance style (Gribble, 1844), with a very
beautiful *altar* from Brescia (1693) in the Lady Chapel
and twelve statues of Apostles from Siena Cathedral
(1690). The church is served by the Oratorians.

Holland Park

To the west of Kensington Gardens is *Campden Hill*, a district
once the resort of poets, writers, scholars and statesmen. In
this area is *Queen Elizabeth College* (University of London), a
women's college (domestic and social science) built in 1915.
Beyond this is **Holland Park,** a pleasant oasis of greenery and
flowers, in the centre of which is the *King George VI Memorial
Youth Hostel* (1958), incorporating the remains of *Holland
House* (1607), destroyed by bombing in 1941.

On the south side of Holland Park, in the wide Kensington
High St, is the curious modern building occupied by the **Commonwealth Institute** (architects Matthew and Johnson-Marshall),
with collections of material on the Commonwealth countries
(open weekdays 10 to 5.30, Sundays 2.30 to 6): occasional
special exhibitions.

A short distance west, in Holland Park Road, is **Leighton House** (open 11 to 5), home of the noted Victorian painter Lord Leighton (Arab Hall with Oriental ceramic tiles and Syrian windows from Damascus, mosaic frieze by Walter Crane, works by Leighton). Adjoining is the *British Theatre Museum* (open Tuesdays, Thursdays and Saturdays 11 to 5), with material illustrating the history of the theatre in Britain.

To the west and south-west, in the West Kensington-Earl's Court area, are the large *Olympia* and *Earl's Court* exhibition halls.

Chelsea

Chelsea lies south of the districts just described, on the banks of the Thames. In earlier days it was a quiet little village much favoured by royalty and the nobility; Henry VIII married Jane Seymour here, Erasmus lived for a time in Chelsea, and Charles II found it a convenient place to pursue his amours. In the 18th century the Chelsea china manufactory rivalled Sèvres and Meissen. Something of the atmosphere of the past is still preserved by Chelsea's attractive old red brick houses, sheltered behind wrought-iron railings.

Later, however, Chelsea became the resort of artists and developed into a kind of London equivalent of Paris's Montparnasse. It was first made fashionable by 19th century artists like Turner, Rossetti and Whistler, some of whose works can be seen in the *Tate Gallery* (p. 217). *Thomas Carlyle* lived from 1834 until his death (1881) in 24 Cheyne Row (small museum, open Wednesday-Saturday 11 to 1 and 2 to 6, Sundays 2 to 6). *James McNeill Whistler*, the great American painter, lived in a number of different Chelsea houses and died at 74 Cheyne Walk (destroyed by a bomb during the last war). Another American artist, *John Singer Sargent*, died at 31 Tite St (plaque on house) in 1925. *Henry James*, the famous American writer who became a naturalised British citizen in 1915, died at 21 Carlyle Mansions in 1916.

Near Carlyle's House, at the corner of Cheyne Walk and Old Church St, is **Chelsea Old Church**, a 12th century Gothic church altered in the 15th and 16th centuries and completely restored after war damage. It contains numerous monuments, including one to *Sir Thomas More*. In the churchyard are buried the poet *Thomas Shadwell* (d. 1692) and *Sir Hans Sloane* (d. 1753). Farther west, at the corner of Danvers St, is **Crosby Hall**, transferred from Bishopgate in 1910, with a magnificent great hall dating from 1466 (open 10 to 12 and 2 to 5, except Sunday mornings). At 20A Danvers St *Sir Alexander Fleming*, discoverer of penicillin, died in 1955.

Returning east along *Chelsea Embankment*, we come to the **Royal Hospital, Chelsea**, commonly known as Chelsea Hospital (Wren, 1702). It consists of a central block surmounted by a tower and cupola, containing the *Great Hall* and *Chapel*, flanked by two wings. From the inner courtyard there is a good view of the building with its handsome white stonework, its mellow red brickwork, its columns, well-proportioned pediment and arcades, with green lawns running down to the river. In the Centre Court is a statue of the founder, Charles II, by Grinling Gibbons. The Hospital is occupied by old soldiers with long service, the "Chelsea pensioners". It was severely damaged by air raids and flying bombs, but the main building is intact (open weekdays 10 to 12 and 2 to 4: services in the chapel on Sundays at 11 and 6.30). To the east of the Hospital are Ranelagh Gardens, where the *Chelsea Flower Show* is held annually in May.

III. THE CITY

The **City of London** is a fascinating place, a hive of activity during the week and an oasis of solitude and quiet on Sunday. The visitor who wants to get a proper impression of this part of London ought, therefore, to see it twice — once on a weekday and once on a Sunday. On Sundays the best way to explore the City is on foot; on weekdays a convenient way of seeing the sights is from a front seat on the upper deck of a bus.

A. Fleet Street to Holborn

Holborn is now the name of a street connecting the West End with the City, but in earlier times it was a separate borough, now swallowed up in the expansion of London. Its massive brick buildings mostly date from Victorian times, apart from a few picturesque remains of Tudor architecture like *Staple Inn* with its half-timbered façade. *Lincoln's Inn* and *Gray's Inn* are quiet and peaceful retreats. *Sir John Soane's Museum* has good pictures by Canaletto and Hogarth.

Coming from Trafalgar Square along the **Strand** and past *Somerset House* (p. 148), or taking the underground to *Aldwych* station, we pass *St Clement Danes* (p. 149) and come into **Fleet Street,** which continues the line of the Strand to Ludgate Circus and St Paul's Cathedral.

The name of Fleet St, the centre of the newspaper industry, comes from the river Fleet, a tributary of the Thames now carried in a conduit. There are many memories of the past in the streets round about Fleet St: *Gough Square*, with Dr Johnson's house, *St Bride's Church* in which Samuel Richardson is buried, *Mitre Court*, the *Cock Tavern* where Pepys spent a pleasant evening with the charming Mrs Knipps, other inns and coffee-houses where Goldsmith, Johnson and Boswell were accustomed to meet, and the *Devil Tavern* in which Ben Jonson founded London's first club, the Apollo Club. In Wine Office Court is the *Cheshire Cheese Tavern*, still justly proud of its cheese.

The church of **St Dunstan in the West** (John Shaw, 1833) has a slender Gothic tower modelled on the graceful "Boston Stump" in Lincolnshire (p. 594). Although it stands on the site of a church in which William Tyndale, the translator of the Bible, used to preach it is the newest of the City's churches. Over the east porch is a statue of Queen Elizabeth I, brought here in 1763 when the Ludgate, at the foot of Ludgate Hill, was demolished. The clock, with figures of giants which strike the hours (1671), belonged to the original church. The Great Fire of London reached to within a short distance of the church. The roof suffered slight damage during the raids of the last war.

At the end of Fleet St is **Temple Bar.** Today only the *Temple Bar Memorial* (the City griffin; statues of Queen Victoria and Edward VII as Prince of Wales) remains in the centre of the road to mark the site.

In 1672 Christopher Wren built a finely proportioned triple gateway to replace the wooden gate of 1502 which was destroyed in the Great Fire. In 1878 this was removed to leave more room for traffic, and was later re-erected at Waltham Cross as an entrance gateway to Theobalds Park, where James I once had a manor. Near Temple Bar was a pillory in which Daniel Defoe, author of "Robinson Crusoe", was condemned to stand.

Just to the south is the **Temple,** which stretches from Fleet St to the river. It comprises the *Inner Temple* and *Middle Temple*, two of the four "Inns of Court" which alone have the right of preparing and permitting a person to set up practice as a barrister in England. The name dates back to the English lodge of the Knights Templar, founded in about 1118 in Jerusalem, and its connection with the law to the 14th century. It is now the centre of the legal profession, and many leading lawyers have their chambers here.

With the delightful *Temple Gardens* extending down to the river, this is an area of quiet on the very verge of the noisy City. The buildings suffered severe damage during the last war, and the magnificent Elizabethan Middle Temple Hall had

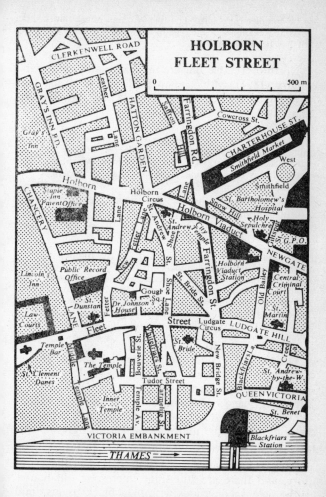

HOLBORN
FLEET STREET

0   500 m

CLERKENWELL ROAD

Leather

GRAY'S INN RD.

Saffron

Farringdon Rd.

HATTON GARDEN

Cowcross St.

CHARTERHOUSE ST.

Gray's Inn

Smithfield Market

West

CHANCERY

Holborn

Staple Inn
Patent Office

Holborn
Circus

Lane

Smithfield

Holborn Viaduct

St. Bartholomew's
Hospital

Snow Hill

Holy
Sepulchre

Snow Hill

G.P.O.

NEWGATE

Lincoln's
Inn

Public Record
Office

New Fetter Lane

St. Andrew

St. Andrew

Shoe Lane

City Temple

Farringdon St.

Holborn
Viaduct
Station

Central
Criminal
Court

Old Bailey

St.
Dunstan

Fetter

Gough
Sq.

Dr. Johnson's
House

Shoe Lane

St. Bride St.

St.
Martin

Law
Courts

Fleet

Street

Ludgate
Circus

LUDGATE HILL

Temple
Bar

Middle Temple Lane

The Temple

Whitefriars St.

Bouverie St.

St.
Bride

New Bridge St.

Blackfriars La.

Creed

St. Andrew-
by-the-W.

St. Clement
Danes

Inner
Temple

Tudor Street

Temple Av.

Carmelite St.

QUEEN VICTORIA

St. Benet

VICTORIA EMBANKMENT

Blackfriars
Station

← THAMES →

to be completely rebuilt. The fine Norman **round church,** one
of the few examples of the type in England, was badly damaged
but has been restored.

North of Temple Bar are the Victorian Gothic *Law
Courts* (1871), with a main front 500 feet long and
covering an area of over 5 acres. They contain more
than 1000 rooms.

When the courts are in session visitors are admitted to the
public galleries, and can watch the law in action, with the
judges wearing their wigs and ermine-trimmed robes. The
Great Hall is 138 feet long, 38 feet wide and 80 feet high.

Lincoln's Inn, to the north of Fleet St, can be entered
by the magnificent old Henry VIII Gateway in Chancery Lane, in which is the *Public Record Office.*

This Inn, the third of the Inns of Court, comprises a hall
and chapel, offices and chambers, mainly of Tudor and Georgian
date. The hall and chapel, however, were largely reconstructed
in the last and the present century. An atmosphere of peace
and quiet reigns amongst these old buildings whose rose-tinted
façades and variegated brickwork blend agreeably, and presents
a startling contrast to the activity of Kingsway (to the west)
and Chancery Lane (to the east).

On the north side of the extensive square known
as *Lincoln's Inn Fields* (laid out as gardens, with a
refreshment pavilion and tennis courts) stands (No. 13).
Sir John Soane's Museum, once the private residence
of the architect of the Bank of England, who was
responsible for the unusual and surprisingly modern
façade (early 19th century). See p. 216.

The Holborn area was not destroyed in the Great
Fire, and there are still some interesting old houses
to be seen, incongruous with their black beams amid
their more modern neighbours.

Staple Inn (early 16th century), on the right beyond
Chancery Lane, one of the Inns of Chancery since
the 18th century, received a direct hit from a flying
bomb during the last war. The old Tudor projecting
façade with latticed and mullioned windows remains,
but the hall, which stood at the far side of the courtyard behind the building, was totally destroyed and
had to be rebuilt.

On the north side of the wide thoroughfare of High
Holborn, at No. 23, is **Gray's Inn,** the fourth of the
Inns of Court.

The Inn was founded in 1370. At the end of the 16th century
Francis Bacon was its Treasurer. Wartime bomb damage has
now been made good, and visitors can see the Chapel, the *Hall*
(1560, rebuilt 1951), the Chancery (1723) and the magnificent
Gardens. *Sun Yat-Sen* lived for some time in a small house
in Gray's Inn.

In the side streets off Holborn are many Georgian houses.
The whole area used to be residential, and many of Dickens's
characters had houses here.

Clerkenwell to the City

Beyond *Holborn Viaduct* (built in 1869 to relieve traffic
congestion) is a large area which was destroyed by wartime
bombing. *Smithfield Market*, London's wholesale meat market,
stands on the site where many Protestants perished at the
stake during the reign of Mary Tudor, and where in Elizabeth I's
reign Roman Catholics suffered the same fate. Beyond the
market is the rather drab district of **Clerkenwell,** now the centre
of the watch and clock industry.

In St John's Lane, north of Smithfield, are the remains of
the *Priory of St John of Jerusalem*. Of the building erected in
1188 by Heraclius, Patriarch of Jerusalem, who offered Henry II
the crown of Jerusalem, there remains only the gate known as
St John's Gate or Clerkenwell Gateway. It was burned down
during Wat Tyler's rebellion in 1381 and restored in the early
16th century. The present buildings are now used only for
the ceremonies of the Order of St John.

Clerkenwell Road runs past the buildings of **Charterhouse School.** Before the war there were still some remains of the original Tudor building, but the most interesting parts were destroyed during the bombing of London. Charterhouse, one of the great English public schools, moved to Godalming in Surrey in 1872 and the buildings were taken over by Merchant Taylors' School. Merchant Taylors' in turn moved to Rickmansworth in 1933, and the buildings are now occupied by the medical school of *St Bartholomew's Hospital.* The Hospital itself is to the south of Smithfield Market. It was founded in 1123 in fulfilment of a vow by Rahere, Henry I's court jester, and belonged to the Priory. Over the gateway is a statue of Henry VIII, who was regarded as a second founder.

To the east of the Hospital is the street known as *Little Britain,* so called after a mansion belonging to the Dukes of Brittany which once stood here. Almost opposite the Hospital is a curious little Gothic gateway surmounted by an Elizabethan house. Through the gateway is a small courtyard from which a path runs past an old graveyard to the ancient west door of the church of **St Bartholomew the Great.** This is the oldest church in London, dated to soon after the Norman Conquest by its plain massive columns, its five round arches on each side and its narrow round-arched windows set deeply into the walls. It is in fact contemporary with the White Tower in the Tower of London. The church is spacious, though rather dark. The north clerestory is delicate late Gothic work, with a fine leaded oriel window known as *Prior Bolton's Window.* On the north side of the sanctuary is the *Tomb of Rahere,* also fine Gothic work. Round the outside of the church can be seen remains of the old monastic buildings (fragments of walls and doorways, etc.).

From the square in front of Smithfield Market, Giltspur St runs south to Newgate St. At the corner is the **Church of the Holy Sepulchre,** the largest City church. It dates from the time of the Crusades (hence its name), but all except part of the tower (15th century) and the south door was destroyed in the Great Fire. The interior was restored in 1677 by Wren, and again after 1945. The Lord Mayor and aldermen of the City of London attend services here. In the church is the tomb of Captain *John Smith* (1580-1631), "sometime Governor of Virginia and Admiral of New England", who landed at Jamestown, Virginia, in May 1607 and became governor of the new colony in the following year.

In Newgate St, which continues Holborn into the heart of
the City, stands the **Old Bailey,** the Central Criminal Court.
This building, opened in 1907 by King Edward VII, occupies the
site of the notorious Newgate Prison, built by George Dance
in the later part of the 18th century. Some of its rustic stone-
work and the somewhat macabre decorations are now incorporated in the Old Bailey. The *Central Hall* is the most imposing
part of the building, and there are four courts which sit in the
chambers adjacent to it. The north-west corner of the building
was demolished by bombs in 1940.

Also in Newgate St, to the east, is the huge building of the
General Post Office, near which is the tower of Wren's *Christ
Church* (1704).

B. The City

ST PAUL'S CATHEDRAL

To the south lies *Ludgate Hill*. At its foot there
once stood the old Lud Gate of the City, from which
in 1766 the statue of Queen Elizabeth was removed
to the church of Saint Dunstan in the West. Ludgate
Hill climbs up to and sweeps past St Paul's Cathedral,
which stands magnificently on the summit. On the
right is the small Wren *church of St Martin*, built
after the Great Fire.

St Paul's Cathedral, Wren's Baroque masterpiece,
was built between 1675 and 1710, in the shape of a
Latin cross. The cross surmounting the dome is
365 feet above the pavement; the golden ball immediately beneath the cross is capable of holding twelve
persons, and there is an unusual view from here of
the nave, 300 feet below, through a porthole in the
floor.

The Cathedral occupies the site of two earlier churches
dedicated to St Paul. The first was built some 1300 years ago,
and to judge from the number of stags' horns and objects
dedicated to Diana which were revealed during excavations in

the reign of Edward III (1327-77) there was probably a temple to Diana on the site in Roman times. The second cathedral, completed in the 13th century, was then the longest church in England, with a steeple over 450 feet high. It was burned down in the Great Fire (1666), blazing for five days. The new cathedral was designed to be one of the focal points of Wren's plan to build a new and well laid out city in the area between the Tower, St Paul's and Westminster Palace and Abbey, which before the Fire had been an intricate tangle of narrow streets and lanes. There was violent opposition to his plan, and it had to be dropped; but he did build the huge new cathedral he designed on the model of St Peter's in Rome. He spent 35 years (1675-1710) on the task, and completed it at the age of 80. St Paul's is a building of ample and noble proportions and is an imposing sight when seen from a suitable viewpoint, e.g. from the Thames. It is 515 feet long, 180 feet wide across the west front and 365 feet high (to the top of the cross above the dome).

The general effect, however, is rather cold — more like the solution of a mathematical problem than the creation of a building with a soul of its own: and some may feel that the two elaborate towers on the west front do not quite harmonise with the rest of the structure.

St Paul's was often in danger during the blitz of 1940-41, and was hit by a number of bombs. It survived, however, with relatively little damage; and the destruction of buildings in the surrounding area has made it possible to get a better general view of the Cathedral than before 1939.

The most impressive feature of the interior is the **dome** (painted by Sir James Thornhill in the reign of George I; scenes from

---

1 West doorway 2 North-west doorway 3 All Souls Chapel 4 St Dunstan's Chapel 5 North aisle 6 Nave 7 Monument to Wellington 8 Lord Mayor's Vestry 9 North transept 10 Dome 11 North transept chapel 12 North choir aisle 13 Chapel of the Modern Martyrs 14 Gates by Trijou 15 Choir 16 High altar 17 Jesus Chapel 18 South choir aisle 19 Lady Chapel 20 Effigy of Donne 21 Pulpit 22 Entrance to crypt and Chapel of Order of British Empire 23 South transept 24 Font 25 Stairs to Library, Whispering Gallery and Dome 26 "Light of the World" 27 South aisle 28 Chapel of St Michael and St George 29 Dean's Staircase 30 South-west doorway

ST. PAUL'S CATHEDRAL

N⟵

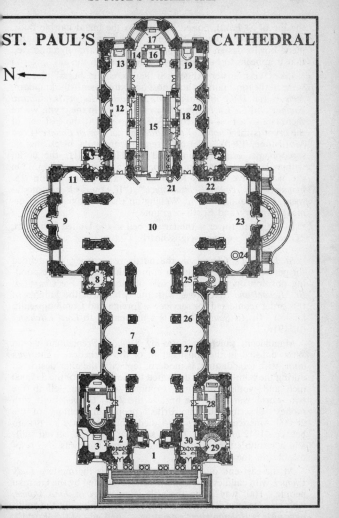

the life of St Paul), poised high above the inlaid marble floor. The dome, weighing 67,270 tons, rests upon four substantial piers, but its design and proportions are so carefully conceived that it appears to be suspended, weightless, in the air.

Like Westminster Abbey, St Paul's is the burial place of some of the most famous and most honoured men in the kingdom. *Nelson*, the *Duke of Wellington*, *Sir Joshua Reynolds*, *Admiral Rodney* and *Sir Christopher Wren* are buried in the crypt, where there is also a bust of George Washington. At the east end of the crypt is the *Chapel of the Order of the British Empire* (Lord Mottistone, 1960). Nelson's remains are in a black marble sarcophagus originally intended for Henry VIII: the coffin within it was made from the mast of a French warship. On the wall above Wren's tomb is the famous inscription "*Si monumentum requiris, circumspice*" ("If you seek his monument, look round you"). Wellington's sarcophagus is of Cornish porphyry and Scottish granite.

In the south tower is the largest bell in the United Kingdom, "Great Paul", which weighs nearly 17 tons.

St Dunstan's Chapel, in the north-west corner, is intended for personal devotions and for communion. In the corresponding position on the opposite side of the nave is the *Chapel of St Michael and St George*, with the banners of the knights of this order (conferred for services in foreign and Commonwealth affairs). In *All Souls Chapel* is a monument to *Lord Kitchener* (d. 1916).

Magnificent **sanctuary gates** by *Tijou*, a Frenchman whom Wren enlisted in the construction of the Cathedral. The *high altar*, with a baldaquin, is modern, replacing the altar destroyed during the bombing: it is dedicated to the memory of the 335,000 men and women from the Commonwealth who fell in the two world wars. In the apse is the *Jesus Chapel*, built with money subscribed by the British people in memory of the 28,000 American soldiers who died while stationed in Britain between 1942 and 1944. In the sanctuary are fine carved **stalls** and a bishop's throne by *Grinling Gibbons*, who was also responsible for the organ case.

At the east end of the south choir aisle is the modern *Lady Chapel*, with candlesticks and a crucifix presented by the German people. Half way along the aisle is an effigy of *John Donne*, who was Dean of St Paul's before the Great Fire. In the south nave aisle is *Holman Hunt's* painting, "The Light of the World", a replica by the artist of the original in Keble College, Oxford (1908).

A staircase leads up to the famous **Whispering Gallery,** notable for its unusual acoustic properties: a whisper at one side of the dome is heard clearly on the opposite side, though it is more than 100 feet across. Round the outside of the dome runs the *Stone Gallery*, from which there are very fine views of the City.

The *font* is by *Francis Bird.* The *pulpit* is modern, by *Lord Mottistone*, who was in charge of the post-war restoration of the Cathedral.

THE HEART OF THE CITY

Just south of St Paul's is Godliman St, a short street which runs down to meet **Queen Victoria Street** at right angles. To the right (west) are the *Faraday Building* (occupied by the telephone service), the little Wren church of *St Andrew by the Wardrobe* (1695, completely rebuilt after the last war) and the old "Times" building in Printing House Square (the "Times" offices moved in 1974 to New Printing House Square in Gray's Inn Road). Towards the river is *Blackfriars Station*, with Blackfriars Bridge beyond it. On the south side of Queen Victoria St is a modern building (1963) occupied by the Salvation Army. To the east, on the north side of the street, is the *College of Arms,* in a house dating from 1688. Beyond this is *St Nicholas Cole Abbey* (Wren, 1678; restored 1963). We now turn left into Bread St, which runs north across Cannon St into *Cheapside.* Turning right, we come to **Bow Church.**

St Mary-le-Bow, or **Bow Church,** was built by Wren in 1683. (Only the steeple is certainly his work; the attribution of the nave is uncertain). It was destroyed during the last war and rebuilt by Laurence King 1964-71: east windows by John Hayward. The crypt dates from 1090.

Farther east, King St runs north to the Guildhall, passing the Wren church of *St Lawrence Jewry* (1680; completely destroyed and rebuilt).

The **Guildhall** dates from the 14th and 15th century. The 15th century porch was badly damaged during the Great Fire of 1666 and again during the last war. The building is predominantly Gothic but was altered both inside and out, mainly in the 18th century. After the Great Fire Wren built a temporary roof, not at all in keeping with the general style of the architecture; this "temporary" roof lasted for about 200 years. The hall has been restored after war damage and is again the scene of the Lord Mayor's annual banquet, as well as many other official functions of the City of London.

The Guildhall is still the centre of the City's administration, and the official installation of a new Lord Mayor takes place here. For centuries its splendour has borne witness to the wealth of the City guilds or "companies". The companies, originally religious as well as trade associations, with their own patron saints and religious services, still play an active part in the life of the City. The Goldsmiths' Company is still responsible for controlling the quality of English gold and silver articles, to which its stamp must be applied; and it is still regarded as a distinction to be made an honorary member of, for example, the Fishmongers' Company.

At 55 Basinghall St, on the east side of the Guildhall, is the **Guildhall Museum** (open weekdays 10 to 5), with historical relics of the City and its companies.

Cheapside continues into *Poultry* (named after the market formerly held here) which leads to the Bank of England, the Mansion House and the Royal Exchange.

The **Bank of England** was enlarged by Sir John Soane, who for many years at the end of the 18th and beginning of the 19th century was the Bank's official architect. The façade which he built contains no windows, but is lit by skylights. The uniformity of the walls is relieved at intervals by massive but richly ornate doors flanked by Corinthian columns. Considerable alterations were made in 1931. The traditions of the past are preserved in the door-keeper's uniform of gold-braided robe, three-cornered hat and staff of office.

The square, well-proportioned building in late Renaissance style, faced with a Corinthian portico, at the corner of Lombard St and Cornhill, is the **Mansion House,** the official residence of the Lord Mayor of London and a police court. This mansion, the work of George Dance, was built about 1750 and is sumptuously appointed.

The Lord Mayor is elected for a year, and takes up office on 9 November. One of the great show occasions of the year is the Lord Mayor's Show, when he drives in procession through the City in a coach drawn by six horses to have his appointment confirmed by the Queen, accompanied by the sheriffs and aldermen of the City, also in coaches with liveried coachmen and footmen, and escorted by pikemen of the Honourable Artillery Company in their 17th century uniform. The route and timing of the Lord Mayor's Show are announced in the press. (Visitors are admitted to the Mansion House on written application).

The **Royal Exchange,** on the corner of Thread-needle St and Cornhill, opposite the Mansion House, dates from 1844 (William Tite). Founded in 1564 by Thomas Gresham (the first Royal Exchange was opened by Queen Elizabeth), it is the third Exchange on this site.

Old Broad Street leads to *Liverpool Street* and *Liverpool Street Station* (main lines to the Continent via Harwich, main

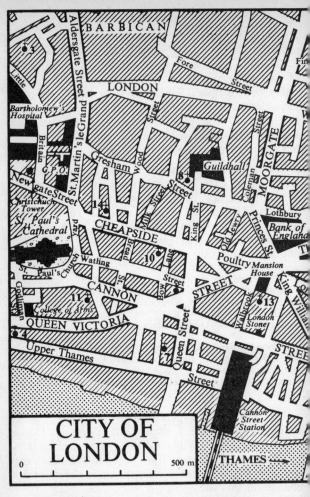

CITY OF LONDON

0   500 m

THAMES

1 Hallows Tower
2 St Andrew Undershaft
3 St Bartholomew the Great
4 St Benet

5 St Ethelbhurga
6 St Helen's
7 St James Garlickythe
8 St Lawrence

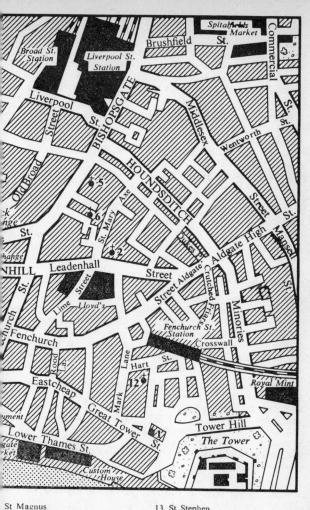

Broad St. Station

Liverpool St. Station

Brushfield St.

Spitalfields Market

Commercial St.

Liverpool Street

Old Broad St.

BISHOPSGATE

HOUNDSDITCH

Middlesex St.

Wentworth St.

Mansell St.

St. Mary Ave.

K
nge
St.
hange
hange

● 5

● 6

● 2

NHILL

Leadenhall Street

Lime Street

Lloyd's

Aldgate

Street Aldgate High

Crutched Friars

Aldgate High St.

Minories

Fenchurch St. Station

Crosswall

Royal Mint

Fenchurch

Rood La.

Mark Lane

Hart St.

12 ✝

Eastcheap

Great Tower

St.

Tower Hill

The Tower

Lower Thames St.

gate
ket

Custom House

St Magnus
Bow church
St Nicholas Cole
St Olave

13 St Stephen
14 St Vedast

lines to East Anglian seaside resorts, Cambridge, and suburban services to the east and north-east of London), which deals with 250,000 passengers daily. In this vicinity are the districts of **Whitechapel** (open air market, known as Petticoat Lane, in Middlesex St, offering an infinite variety of secondhand and new goods).

To the east is *Bethnal Green*, with a museum and art gallery (restored after being badly damaged during the last war) which are an annexe of the Victoria and Albert Museum in South Kensington, with British paintings, domestic pottery, porcelain, glass and silver. There is another museum, the *Geffrye Museum*, in Kinglands Road, with collections showing social and domestic history from Elizabethan times to the present day. The whole of this district, with its many small industrial establishments, power stations and gas-works, was devastated by wartime bombing.

From Liverpool Street Station *Bishopsgate Street* leads to the junction of Cornhill, Leadenhall St and Gracechurch St (all busy commercial thoroughfares lined with offices). Gracechurch St leads to the river and London Bridge, cutting en route the main thoroughfares of Fenchurch St and Cannon St.

Fenchurch St, the continuation of the great thoroughfare sweeping from one end of London to the other, leads to *Aldgate* (the site of one of the old City gates), Whitechapel Road and out of London to the east. On the right is *Fenchurch Street Station* (suburban services to East London and lines to Southend, Essex and Tilbury). Near the station are *Farthing Street* and *Ha' penny Street*, with some interesting old signboards.

Near the station, in Hart St, is the small Gothic church of *St Olave* (on this site a church has existed since 1100 or earlier), where the diarist Pepys and his wife are buried. Here too is a monument to John Watts (1789), "President of the Council of New York", a Loyalist who returned to Britain after the War of American Independence. The date when the church was built is not exactly known, but it survived the Great Fire: it was damaged by bombing in 1941.

From here we go south to *Tower Hill*, with a tablet commemorating the executions carried out here in the past.

TOWER OF LONDON

The **Tower of London** stands on Tower Hill. Of all the ancient buildings in the City of London it stands supreme. It is the very heart of the capital, a central feature in the country's history. Open: summer 9.30 to 5 on weekdays, 2 to 5 on Sundays; winter 9.30 to 4, closed on Sundays.

The Tower consists of a square central keep standing in a courtyard surrounded by a range of other buildings, the whole being enclosed within an outer wall and moat. The keep, known as the **White Tower**, stands 90 feet high and has walls up to 15 feet thick. The interior remains as it was in the Norman period. The tower was built by William the Conqueror astride the *Roman wall* which ran down to the Thames. Remains of this wall can be seen on the north side of Tower Hill, east of Trinity House.

Although built for defensive purposes, the Tower has featured largely in history as a **prison.** During the last war *Rudolf Hess,* Hitler's deputy, was confined here, and in earlier times many illustrious persons were imprisoned in the Tower, among them *John the Good,* king of France, *James I* of Scotland, the future *Elizabeth I* as a princess, *Sir Walter Raleigh* and the 18th century politician *John Wilkes.* A stone in the courtyard *(Tower Green)* marks the position of the scaffold on which many noted victims were beheaded, including two of Henry VIII's wives, *Anne Boleyn* and *Catherine Howard, Lady Jane Grey* and her husband, and the unfortunate *Earl of Essex.* Prisoners were brought to the Tower by boat, entering by the water gate known as the *Traitors' Gate.*

Each successive age has left an addition to the collection of buildings that now form the Tower of London. Henry III and Edward I built the outer defences (13th c.) and left the White Tower, with its corner turrets connected by a crenellated wall, much as we know it today. Richard I excavated the moat. It has in turn served as a citadel, a royal palace and a state prison, the mint, the treasury, and a repository of records.

Each tower has its name, derived usually from its history or former purpose, like the *Bloody Tower* in which the young Duke of York and his brother King Edward V were murdered by their uncle, Richard, Duke of Gloucester, known as Crookback. *Walter Raleigh* was confined here for more than 13 years of the 18 he spent in the Tower and wrote part of his "History of the World" here. Adjoining the Bloody Tower is a picturesque block of Tudor half-timbered buildings known as the *King's House*, inhabited by the resident Governor of the Tower.

The **White Tower,** the central feature of the Tower of London, was erected in 1078 by Gundulf, later Bishop of Rochester, for William the Conqueror, and this impregnable Norman keep is still very much as it was when first built. The walls between the rooms, one of which is 90 feet long, are 8 feet thick. The tower contains a fine collection of Renaissance arms and armour. Among the items on view is the impressive suit of armour weighing 93 1b which was presented to Henry VIII by the Emperor Maximilian of Austria in 1514, together with a massive coat of horse armour. **St John's Chapel,** on the second floor next the *Banqueting Hall*, is one of the finest examples of Norman architecture in England, with plain undecorated columns and vaulting which convey an impression of quiet beauty and serenity. In the Crypt are instruments of torture and the blade of an execution axe.

The military garrison (a Guards regiment) of the Tower of London is housed in the Waterloo Barracks (1845) to the north of the White Tower: at the south-east angle stand the ruins of the *Roman tower* known as the Wardrobe Tower. The surrounding stretch of lawn is a favourite haunt of the ravens which have for centuries been kept there. Immediately to the west of the barracks stands the church of *St Peter ad Vincula*, believed to have been built originally in the reign of Henry I (12th century), rebuilt at the beginning of the 14th century and restored after a fire in 1512. Many well-known persons are buried in or around the church, including Anne Boleyn, Lady Jane Grey, Catherine Howard, Sir Thomas More and the Earl of Essex.

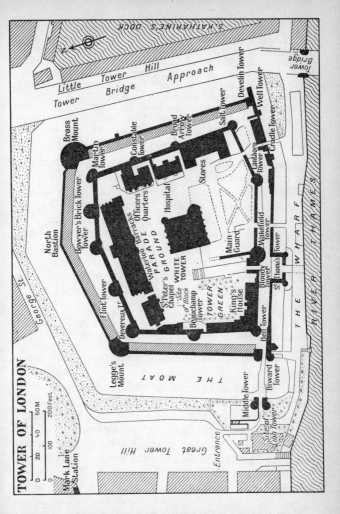

TOWER OF LONDON

N

ST. KATHARINE'S DOCK

Little Tower Hill Approach

Tower Bridge

Tower Bridge

Brass Mount

Martin Tower

Constable Tower

Bread Armoury Tower

Salt Tower

Devlin Tower

Well Tower

Cradle Tower

Landhorn Tower

Bowyer's Brick Tower

North Bastion

Stores

Hospital

Waterloo Barracks Officers Quarters

PARADE GROUND

Flint Tower

Devereux T.

St. Peter's Chapel

Site of Black

WHITE TOWER

TOWER GREEN

Main Guard

Wakefield Tower

Beauchamp Tower

King's House

St. Thomas's Tower

Bloody Tower

THE WHARF

RIVER THAMES

George St.

Legge's Mount

THE MOAT

Bell Tower

Biward Tower

Middle Tower

Site of Lion Tower

Mark Lane Station

0 20 40 60 M
0 100 200 Feet

Great Tower Hill

Entrance

7

To the south of the White Tower, connecting the outer wall with Tower Wharf, built by Henry III, is *St Thomas's Tower*, the old water gate to the tower, more commonly known as *Traitors' Gate*. Those condemned to death or imprisonment in the tower were conveyed there through this gate. Traitors' Gate leads directly to the *Bloody Tower*, whose entrance was sealed with a portcullis which is in working order to this day. In the *Wakefield Tower* is the room in which Henry VI was murdered by Richard III in 1461. Every year on 21 May boys from Eton College lay a wreath of lilies on the spot where he died, in pious memory of the king who founded Eton in 1440.

The **Crown Jewels** are kept in a strong room under the west corner of the *Waterloo Barracks*, north of the White Tower. Among the splendours on show behind a protective grille are the *Imperial State Crown*, set with 3000 diamonds and 300 pearls, and the famous *Black Prince's Ruby*, a gift from King Pedro the Cruel of Aragon, which Henry V wore at the battle of Agincourt. Among the other diamonds to be seen here are one of the "Stars of Africa", cut from the Cullinan diamond, and the famous *Koh-i-Noor*.

One of the few attempts to steal these immensely valuable treasures was made by Captain Blood in the reign of Charles II, and very nearly succeeded. The king was so impressed by Blood's daring that he released him and even granted him a pension for life.

Mention must be made of the *Yeomen Warders* of the tower, not to be confused with the separate "Queen's Bodyguard of Yeomen of the Guard", formed in 1485 to serve as the bodyguard of the sovereign; the Yeomen Warders were founded much earlier. Their uniform is still the original Tudor dress of scarlet and black and gold, with ruffs, long hose and halberds; this dress is only worn on state occasions. They are popularly known as *Beefeaters*, a name which has not been satisfactorily explained.

To the south-east of the Tower of London the **Tower Bridge** crosses the Thames. It is one of the landmarks of London, constructed in 1894. The lower span (200 ft) between the two Gothic towers is so built as to enable it to be raised in 1½ minutes to allow passage for vessels making for the open sea. The two towers are 120 feet in height over the piers, and the footway 142 feet. This is the last bridge over the Thames, here 250 yards wide.

The stretch of water between the Tower Bridge and London Bridge (upstream) is known as the *Pool of London*. A good view of the wharves can be had from either bridge. (The Governor of the Tower still holds ancient fishing rights in the Pool).

Just to the north-east of the Tower, off the square, stands the **Royal Mint,** built in 1811 on the site of a Cistercian abbey founded in the 14th century. Here until 1974 (when the Mint was transferred to Llantrisant, near Cardiff) the currency of the realm was minted and commemorative and war medals were struck.

Newly minted coins are still sent annually for assay (the "Trial of the Pyx") to the Goldsmiths' Company, under an authority originally granted by Edward I (1271-1307). The gold and silver standards, now preserved in the Mint, were formerly kept in the Chamber of the Pyx in Westminster Abbey (p. 147).

FROM THE TOWER TO LONDON BRIDGE

All Hallows Church stands to the west of the Tower, opposite Tower Hill Station. It was completely destroyed during the last war, only the walls and tower being left standing.

The tower, built in 1659, is a plain rectangular structure in red brick and was one of the few towers built during the Commonwealth (1649-60). It was from this tower that Samuel Pepys

watched the progress of the Great Fire in 1666 (see his diary,
5 September 1666). On the first floor of the tower a small
chapel has been arranged containing some interesting pieces of
woodwork salvaged from the wreckage of the church. It is
likely that All Hallows was first built at about the end of the
7th century. Under the church is a Norman crypt with a chapel
containing numerous relics of Roman London. The church
was rebuilt by Lord Mottistone in 1957.

On the north side of Trinity Square is **Trinity House** (1795).
The "Brethren" of Trinity House have had their headquarters
on this site for more than 400 years. The building was destroyed
during the last war but has been restored. To the west stands
the great white modern building (170 ft in height) of the *Port
of London Authority* (1912-1922), who are responsible for the
direction and management of the port of London and London's
bridges.

From the river end of Tower Hill, *Lower Thames
Street* runs west into Gracechurch St, where London
Bridge crosses to South London. We turn right to
reach the *Monument* in Fish St Hill. Nearby is *Billingsgate Market* (1877), named after an old water-gate
shutting off a wharf against piracy. It is the chief
fish market of London, where fish has been sold for
1000 years.

Note the porters' hats; similar hats were worn by English
archers at the battle of Agincourt. (The market is open from
5 a.m.). *Billingsgate Wharf* is one of the oldest of London's
wharves, mentioned as early as the 10th century. Adjoining
the fish market is the old *Customs House*, built in 1817 on the
site of five earlier customs houses, with a front 488 feet long.

The **Monument** is a tall column, 202 feet high, built
in 1675 to commemorate the Great Fire. Wren's
original plans envisaged a column able to be opened
and extended like a telescope by some ingenious
mechanical device: his modified column is fluted, and
bears a flaming urn. The base of the column bears
reliefs depicting the Great Fire and the rebuilding of

London. (Open daily May-September 9 to 6; winter on weekdays only, 9 to 4).

A flight of 345 steps leads to the top, from which there are magnificent views.

London Bridge is immediately south of the Monument. This is London's busiest bridge, and it is also the oldest, being the latest successor to the Roman bridge which crossed the Thames here. Many Roman objects have been recovered from the Thames near here.

The first stone bridge was begun by Henry II and completed in the reign of his son, John, at the beginning of the 13th century. It lay a little downstream from the present bridge. At each end was a fortified gate, on which the heads of traitors were displayed after their execution. This was for long the only bridge over the Thames; hence its name of London Bridge. The 13th century bridge remained until 1832, when it was replaced by a more modern structure, and this has in turn recently (1973) given place to a new bridge better adapted to the needs of present-day traffic.

At the north-east end of the bridge is the church of **St Magnus the Martyr** (Wren, 1687), with a very beautiful interior, unfortunately spoiled by stained glass windows inserted in the 1920s which are out of harmony with Wren's conception.

From the foot of Fish St Hill *Lower Thames Street* runs west under the viaduct which links Gracechurch St with London Bridge, and continues as Upper Thames St. Nearby is *Fishmongers' Hall* (rebuilt 1833), headquarters of the Fishmongers' Company. Upper Thames St continues west, passing under *Cannon Street Station* (services to Kent). Opposite the station there formerly stood *St Swithun's Church* (destroyed during the last war), in the wall of which was the *London Stone*, supposed to have been the starting point, in the Roman forum, of the Roman roads out of London. The stone is now built into the wall of the bank which occupies the site of the church.

Farther along Upper Thames St, at the foot of Garlick Hill, is the Wren church of *St James Garlick-hythe*, in which is preserved the mummified body of a mediaeval merchant. Nearby is another Wren church, *St Benet's*, a small church built in red brick with white stone façade, now occupied by a Welsh congregation. The interior has been completely spoiled by Victorian "improvements".

Before leaving this neighbourhood mention should be made of a number of other churches by Wren. **St Stephen's Walbrook** is in Walbrook, behind the Mansion House: the interior is notable for the beauty of its plan, and the exquisite dome has some of the finest plasterwork (damaged during the war) produced in the Restoration. It was Wren's parish church. At the other end of Cheapside, in Foster Lane, stands the small stone church of **St Vedast**: the tower, if not the most magnificent, is certainly one of the most charming that Wren ever designed. **St Margaret in Lothbury** (behind the Bank of England) is one of the few Wren churches left untouched by the air-raids. The interior, like all Wren's churches, contains some beautiful and interesting woodwork.

Also of considerable interest are three mediaeval churches in the City which escaped the Great Fire of London. *St Ethelburga* in Bishopsgate (said to be the oldest Christian foundation in London) is named after the daughter of the first Saxon king to become Christian. Nearby, in St Helen's Place, is the small and lovely church of *St Helen*. The third is *St Andrew Undershaft*, situated on the corner of Leadenhall St.

IV. THE SOUTH BANK

An itinerary to be followed by car. The southern districts of London are less visited by tourists than other parts of the city, but they should be seen by anyone who wants to get a complete impression of the sights and the life of the capital.

Starting from *Westminster Bridge*, we see on the left, beyond the bridge, *London County Hall*, and on the right *St Thomas's Hospital*.

London County Hall, an immense block 750 feet long, was opened in 1922. It houses the offices of the Greater London Council.

Beyond it, to the north, are a number of large modern buildings: the tower block, 320 feet high, of the **Shell Centre,** completed in 1962 (visitors can take lift to top, on payment, daily 10 to 5, Thursdays 8 to 5, closed Sundays); the **Royal Festival Hall,** just beyond Charing Cross railway bridge, a structure of concrete and glass (1965) with an auditorium seating 3000; and the **Queen Elizabeth Hall** (1951). Nearby is the *National Film Theatre*.

St Thomas's Hospital, founded in Southwark in 1213, moved to its present site in 1868. It suffered severe damage during the last war, but has now been largely rebuilt.

Turning right (south) into *Lambeth Palace Road*, we have a good view of the Houses of Parliament across the river. At the far end of Lambeth Palace Road, where it comes down to the Albert Embankment at Lambeth Bridge, is **Lambeth Palace,** which for more than 750 years has been the London residence of the Archbishop of Canterbury, Primate of All England. It was begun by Archbishop Baldwin, Primate from 1185 to 1190.

The name Lambeth means "muddy harbour", which no doubt reflects the condition of the Thames at that time. In the Palace grounds are some remnants of the original buildings, the oldest of their kind in London.

In 1829 the architect Edward Blore demolished the then existing Palace and erected in its place the present sham Gothic structure, second in size only to Buckingham Palace among London's buildings. Among the surviving parts of the older palace are the beautiful Norman *crypt*, built before Magna Carta, and the *chapel* above, dating from the reign of Henry III (1216-72). In this chapel in 1378 John Wyclif (1324-84), the English reformer, who with his assistants first translated the entire Bible into English, was arraigned before a council of bishops for his unorthodox ideas. His followers, however, compelled the council to disband. Three years later Wat Tyler marched against Archbishop Sudbury, who had taken refuge here. The unpopular archbishop escaped to the Tower of London, but Tyler later took the tower and beheaded Sudbury. *Lollard's Tower* was built in 1434. Here, in a chamber 12 feet by 9 feet, condemned heretics were lodged. The splendid early Tudor *gateway* at the Lambeth Bridge end of the palace grounds was erected in 1490, just after the Wars of the Roses, by Cardinal Morton, famous in history for the unpopular "Morton Fork", a scheme whereby Henry VII was able to extort money from his unwilling subjects. From the road can also be seen the upper section of the *Great Hall* with its curious cupola (1663). The first Great Hall was demolished by Cromwell, who also desecrated the chapel. At the Restoration, Juxton, the Bishop of London who had attended Charles I on the scaffold, became Primate and rebuilt the Great Hall. It now houses a library of some 40,000 books and many priceless manuscripts based on the 17th century collection of Archbishop Bancroft: some suffered damage during the 1941 blitz.

Immediately south of the Palace is the church of *St Mary Lambeth*, rebuilt in the 19th century, which retains a 16th century tower.

Going east along *Lambeth Road*, we come to the **Imperial War Museum,** in a park on the right. It occupies the former *Bethlem Hospital* for the insane ("Bedlam"), a neo-classical building erected in 1815. The Museum is concerned with the operations of British and Imperial Forces during the two world wars (open 10 to 6, Sundays 2 to 6).

A varied collection which includes uniforms, weapons, decorations, scale models of warships, aircraft, pocket submarines, relics of the Abyssinian campaign of 1941 and German flying bombs, together with pictures, posters and a bust of Sir Winston Churchill by Epstein. Library and cinema.

Continuing along Lambeth Road, we cross St George's Road, in which, to the left, is the Roman Catholic *St George's Cathedral*, a neo-Gothic building (1848) which has been restored after war damage. Lambeth Road continues to a roundabout, *St George's Circus*.

From here *Waterloo Road* runs north-west to Waterloo Bridge and the Strand. On the right-hand side is the **Old Vic Theatre**, notable for its performances of Shakespeare. On the left is *Waterloo Station* (lines to Southampton and the south-west).

London Road runs south-east from the roundabout to the busy traffic intersection of the *Elephant and Castle* (from the name of a tavern which flourished here in the 18th century).

Dickens enthusiasts will be interested in *Borough Road* (to the east) and *Blackfriars Road* (to the north), with their memories of Mr Micawber, Scrooge, Little Dorrit, Oliver Twist and many other characters in the novels.

Southwark Cathedral, one of London's finest churches and perhaps its most beautiful Gothic church after Westminster Abbey, stands near the south end of London Bridge.

There is said to have been a church on this site as early as 607, dedicated to *St Mary Overy* (supposed to be a corruption of "St Mary over the Ferry"). However this may be, the present Cathedral (St Saviour) has parts dating from 1207. The *Harvard Chapel* commemorates the founder of the famous American university, who was baptised here in 1607. The tomb of the poet John Gower, a friend of Chaucer's, is in the nave. The *Lady Chapel* is a graceful example of English Gothic. In the south transept is a monument to William Emerson (16th c.).

A little to the south is *Guy's Hospital*, one of the most famous of London hospitals, founded in 1721 by Thomas Guy, a bookseller.

Along the banks of the Thames, west of Southwark Bridge, is *Bankside*. In Elizabethan times this was noted for its pleasure gardens and theatres, and cock-fights and bear-fights were held here. Among the theatres was Shakespeare's famous "*Globe*", now replaced by a brewery.

On the east side of Borough High St, close to *London Bridge Station* (suburban services, South London and parts of Kent, Surrey and Sussex), stands the **George Inn,** which today is almost exactly as it was in the 17th century. It adjoins the site of the "Tabard", the inn from which Chaucer's pilgrims set out.

The present inn, built in 1677, is the last galleried inn left in London. The wooden galleries, with their heavy balustrades, form the only passage-ways from one room to another on the first and second storeys. Dickens must certainly have visited the George, for he mentions it in "Little Dorrit", and it is probable that Dr Johnson frequently found himself waiting for the stage coach here when visiting his friends the Thrales at Streatham. In coaching days the inn was the great terminus for the south east of England. Until the 1880s the building enclosed the three sides of a yard in which Shakespeare is reputed to have acted. The George Inn suffered bomb damage, but this has been repaired.

V. MUSEUMS AND GALLERIES

Although the various museums and galleries have been mentioned at the appropriate points in the preceding itineraries, it appears more convenient for the visitor to give a fuller account of their contents in this separate section. The British Museum and the National Gallery cannot be seen in a half-hour or so in the course of a sightseeing trip covering a whole district in London. Each requires at least half a day to get any general impression of their treasures; and even this could only be a preliminary exploration, to be followed by a fuller study of particular fields of interest.

Within the space available, however, it is not possible to give anything approaching a complete description of the contents of the various museums and galleries. This can be obtained in the guides produced by the institutions themselves, which are kept up to date and will enable visitors to make the most of their visit. In this section, therefore, only the items of particular importance are listed — the things which every visitor, whatever his particular interest, would be sorry to miss.

BRITISH MUSEUM

The building is described on p. 161. Main entrance: on south side, in Great Russell St, which runs parallel to Oxford St. Rear entrance in Montague Place. Underground stations: Holborn, Tottenham Court Road, Goodge St, Russell Square. Tel. 01-636 1555.

Open weekdays 10 to 5, Sundays 2.30 to 6.

The British Museum's ethnographical collections are in Burlington Gardens (p. 158). The Natural History Museum, originally part of the British Museum, is now separate (p. 171). In this section we describe only the departments housed in the main building.

To the rear of the entrance hall is the *Reading Room* (open to ticket-holders only).

In the following list the exhibits are grouped under the various departments of the Museum.

1. Department of Manuscripts: to the right of the entrance hall, beginning with the *Grenville Library* (bequeathed by Sir Thomas Grenville in 1846).

Manuscripts from various European countries. English, 10th to 15th centuries: Benedictional of St Ethelwold (10th c.), Evesham Psalter (mid 13th c.), Queen Mary Psalter (1320), Luttrell Psalter (1340), Bedford Hours (1422), etc. Spanish: Breviary of Queen Isabella (1490). French: La Somme le Roy, Maître Honoré (late 13th c.), etc.

Manuscript Saloon: papyruses, Codex Sinaiticus, Codex Alexandrinus, Lindisfarne Gospels (698), Magna Carta (1215), "Beowulf" (c. 1000), Chaucer manuscripts, autographs of Shakespeare, Nelson, various monarchs, etc.

Bible Room: Byzantine manuscripts, maps, etc.

2. Department of Oriental Printed Books and Manuscripts. Particularly rich in Hebrew, Arabic, Persian and Chinese manuscripts (6000 items, including the famous Diamond Sutra of 868). For most visitors it will be enough to see the items displayed at the entrance to the King's Library, immediately north of the Manuscript Saloon.

3. Department of Printed Books (King's Library). The Royal Library takes its name from George III, to whom it belonged. It was presented to the nation by George IV.

The room is used for temporary exhibitions. At other times it contains rare books (Shakespeare First Folios, a Gutenberg Bible, Caxton's edition of Aesop's Fables, printed in 1483, etc.) and collections of stamps.

From here we retrace our steps, keep straight across the entrance hall into the Publications Hall and turn right to reach the Egyptian gallery.

4. Department of Egyptian Antiquities. One of the richest Egyptian collections in the world. Unfortunately the exhibits are too numerous for the space available and the various items cannot be seen to advantage. The Department also occupies a number of rooms on the ground and upper floors.

The long gallery on the ground floor, the counterpart of the King's Library in the east wing, contains **Egyptian sculpture.** The original nucleus of the British Museum's holdings of Egyptian sculpture was the collection assembled by the team of scholars who accompanied Napoleon's Egyptian expedition, which was captured by Britain in 1801. The exhibits are, in general, arranged in chronological order, beginning at the far (north) end: statues of *Sesostris III* (c. 1850 B.C.); a colossal bust of *Amenophis IV* (c. 1440 B.C.); red granite lions (1360 B.C.); statues of *Ramesses II* (c. 1250 B.C.); at the south end of the gallery the famous **Rosetta Stone** (196 B.C.), which enabled Champollion to decipher the Egyptian hieroglyphic script.

In the *Egyptian Rooms* on the upper floor are human and animal mummies, wall paintings of the XVIIIth dynasty (c. 1400 B.C.), grave furnishings, *shabti*-boxes, papyruses (including in particular copies of the *Book of the Dead* ranging between 1400 B.C. to 200 A.D.), everyday domestic objects, etc. In the *Coptic Corridor* are Roman portraits and Coptic sculpture and textiles dating from the early centuries A.D.

5. Department of Western Asiatic Antiquities: several large rooms on the ground floor and a number of smaller rooms on the upper floor.

Upper floor. Persian Landing: bronzes from Luristan, sculptures from Persepolis, the Achaemenid gold Treasure of the Oxus. *Hittite Room. Syrian Room. Room of Writing* (examples of different alphabets). *Prehistoric Room* (finds from Western Asia). *Babylonian Room* (Sumerian art, including the famous "**Ram in a Thicket**" of 2600 B.C.).

Ground floor. Nineveh Gallery, with reliefs from the palaces of Sennacherib and Assurbanipal in Nineveh depicting military campaigns.

Nimrud Gallery: reliefs from the palace of Assurnasirpal at Nimrud, depicting hunting scenes and religious ceremonies.

Between the two galleries are reliefs from the palace of Tiglath-pileser III at Nimrud.

Assyrian Transept: winged human-headed lions from the palace of Assurnasirpal II (c. 860 B.C.) at Nimrud: bronze gates from a temple at Balawat; **black obelisk of Shalmaneser III** (858-824 B.C.); white obelisk of Assurnasirpal.

Assyrian Saloon: reliefs from the palaces of Sennacherib and Assurbanipal in Nineveh (in particular a representation of the **capture of Lachish** in Palestine).

Khorsabad Entrance: **winged human-headed bulls** and other reliefs from the palace of Sargon II at Khorsabad (722-705 B.C.).

Assyrian Basement (down staircase): reliefs from Assurbanipal's palace in Nineveh depicting warlike scenes.

6. Department of Greek and Roman Antiquities. On the ground floor mainly sculpture, on the upper floor vases and smaller objects.

Cycladic Room: Minoan and Mycenaean art.

Early Greek Room: lion and sphinx found near Miletus in Asia Minor.

Room of the Kouroi: archaic marble statues (6th c. B.C.) of *kouroi* (young men).

Room of the Harpy Tomb: classical **tomb** of the early 5th century B.C. from Xanthos in Asia Minor; *Chatsworth Head* (Apollo ?), c. 460; *Strangford Apollo.*

Mezzanine: frieze from the Temple of Apollo at Bassae (end of 5th c.).

Nereid Room: sculpture from the Temple of the Nereids at Xanthos (c. 400 B.C.), with a reconstruction of the façade.

Duveen Gallery: the famous **Elgin Marbles,** sculpture brought back from the Parthenon by Lord Elgin between 1802 and 1812, including the frieze representing the **Panathenaic procession** by *Phidias* (5th c.), and 15 of the 92 **metopes** of the Parthenon (battle between Lapiths and Centaurs). These are the greatest treasures of the British Museum.

Room of the Caryatid: the famous **Caryatid from the Erechtheion** on the Acropolis in Athens (end of 5th c. B.C.) and frieze from the Temple of Athena Nike.

Payava Room: reconstruction of Tomb of Payava from Xanthos in Asia Minor (c. 350 B.C.); vases from Magna Graecia.

Mezzanine: good view of the Caryatid.

Mausoleum Room: sculpture from the Mausoleum, the tomb of King Mausolus at Halicarnassus (4th c. B.C.), in particular a frieze depicting a **battle between Greeks and Amazons** by Scopas, Briaxis, Leochares and Timotheos; statue of Mausolus, attributed to Briaxis; reliefs from the *Temple of Artemis at Ephesus.* (The Mausoleum and the Temple of Artemis were two of the seven wonders of the world).

Hellenistic Room: **Demeter of Cnidus** (c. 330 B.C.).

First Roman Room: the famous **Portland Vase** (Early Empire), with cameo-like decoration.

Second Roman Room: Roman copies of Greek statues; mosaic in an impluvium.

On the *upper floor* (reached by a staircase near the entrance hall), in chronological order:

Terracotta Room: Etruscan, Greek and Roman bronzes and terracottas.

Greek and Roman Life Room: a variety of objects, including gold and silver articles and glass.

(Off this room opens a small room containing the **Department of Coins and Medals.** There are plans to move this department elsewhere).

Greek and Roman Corridor: objects relating to the gods and myths of classical antiquity.

Vase Rooms: three rooms containing vases of all periods from the 10th to the 3rd century B.C., together with some antiquities from Cyprus.

7. **Department of Prints and Drawings** (on first floor), reached from the Vase Rooms by way of the Persian and Egyptian Rooms, in a room situated between two rooms belonging to the Department of Oriental Antiquities (see below).

A magnificent collection, perhaps the most comprehensive in Europe. Woodcuts from the 15th century to the present day, including works by *Schongauer*, *Dürer*, *Lucas van Leyden* and *Rembrandt*. Collection of 20,000 watercolours by *Turner*. Engravings by *Michelangelo*, *Leonardo da Vinci*, *Raphael*, *Rubens*, *Claude Lorrain*, *Watteau*, etc.

8. Department of Oriental Antiquities: Islamic art, India, South-East Asia, Far East.

A small part of the Museum's collection is in the *Second Oriental Gallery* adjoining the Print Gallery (above); the main part is in the *King Edward VII Gallery* on the ground floor.

Islamic art: pottery, ceramics, glass, metalwork, ivories, etc. Note in particular an astrolabe from Cairo (1236 A.D.) and a Turkish lamp from the Mosque in Jerusalem (1549).

Asiatic art: *Tibet* and *Nepal* (bronzes); *India* (sculpture from Buddhist, Hindu and Jain temples in Orissa, Bihar, Bengal and South India, including a very delicately carved figure of a woman at her mirror, a 12th century work from the Deccan); *China* (Tang porcelain, funerary objects including a fine horse, bronzes, lacquerwork, etc.); *Korea* and *Japan* (a variety of objects including porcelain and bronzes); art of *Gandhara; Ceylon* (ivories and bronzes).

9. Department of Prehistoric and Romano-British Antiquities (on the first floor, south side, reached by the staircase on the left of the entrance hall).

Central Saloon: gold articles of the 2nd and 1st millennia B.C.; objects from tombs of the 1st century B.C.; early Christian mosaic from Hinton St Mary, Dorset.

Prehistory Rooms: Bronze Age weapons, Iron Age pottery and weapons, gold torcs.

Romano-British Room: frescoes from a villa at St Albans (Verulamium), **Mildenhall Treasure** (4th c. A.D.).

10. Department of Mediaeval and Later Antiquities: on first floor, immediately after the rooms just

described; some material displayed in King Edward VII Gallery. The department is being reorganised.

Fine gold cup from Paris (1380), ivory chess-men from the island of Lewis in Scotland, objects from the **Sutton Hoo burial**, watches of the 16th-19th centuries, etc.

NATIONAL GALLERY

In Trafalgar Square (see p. 151). Underground stations: Trafalgar Square, Piccadilly Circus, Charing Cross. Tel. 01-930 7618.

Open weekdays 10 to 6, Sundays 2 to 6; open until 9 on Tuesdays and Thursdays from June to September; closed on Christmas Eve, Christmas Day and Good Friday. Restaurant open 10 to 3 and 3.30 to 5 (Sundays 2.30 to 5).

The pictures are well displayed and not too crowded. It is perhaps a pity that so many of them are behind glass, which tends to produce undesirable reflections.

The National Gallery contains masterpieces by such prestigious names as **Michelangelo, Raphael, Botticelli, Piero della Francesca, Velazquez, Rembrandt, Goya** and **Holbein**. The Italian, Dutch and of course English schools are particularly well represented. The Italian primitives, mainly Florentine and Venetian, include *Filippo Lippi, Botticelli* and *Bellini*. Among Dutch masters are *Ruysdael, Hobbema, de Hooch* and *Rembrandt*. The English painters are mainly the famous landscapists and portrait painters of the 18th and 19th centuries *(Gainsborough, Reynolds, Constable, Turner)*. There are good examples of the satirical and genre work of *Hogarth*. French artists are rather thinly represented, apart from some fine works by *Poussin* and *Claude* and *Philippe de Champeigne*'s "Richelieu".

Convenient abridged catalogues are on sale at the entrance to the Gallery. A fuller catalogue, still of reasonable size and price, is Michael Levey's "Room-by-room Guide to the National Gallery", which is regularly re-issued and updated. Visitors who want to study the collection in detail — for which at least two days would be required — are referred to this guide. Here we can do no more than note the essential items, the works which no visitors would wish to miss.

The rooms are listed below in numerical order. In fact the visit begins with Room II (to the left of the entrance), with Room I opening off it on the left.

Room I; **Italian primitives.** *Margaritone of Arezzo*, Madonna and Child (564), the earliest work in the Gallery. Altarpiece with Madonna (4250), Venetian school. *Master of San Francesco*, Crucifix (6361), late 13th century. *Duccio*, **Madonna and Child** (566) and triptych (1330, 1140, 1139).

Room II; **Italian primitives** (continued). **Wilton Diptych** (4451), a work in the Italian style by an unknown English or French artist which belonged to Richard II and Charles I. Altarpiece by *Nardo*, Three Saints (581). *Giovanni di Paolo*, St John the Baptist (5421/2/3) and St John in the Desert (5454). *Matteo di Giovanni*, Assumption (1155). *Lorenzo Monaco*, Coronation of the Virgin (1897). *Sassetta*, Seven Scenes from the Life of St Francis (4757/63).

Room IIA: **Milanese and Veronese schools (15th c.).** Works by *Morone, Gerolamo dai Libri, Evangelista* and *Ambrogio de Predis, Boltraffio, Luini, Foppa, Bergognone* (Madonna and Child with Two Angels, 1077) and *Bramantino* (Adoration of the Magi, 3073).

Room III: **Florentine school (15th c.).** *Masaccio*, **Madonna and Child** (3064). *Masolino*, Pope and St Matthias (5963). *Filippo Lippi*, **Annunciation** (666), **Seven Saints** (667). *Pesellino*, The Trinity and Saints (727). *Paolo Uccello*, St George and the Dragon (6294), **Rout of San Romano** (533), painted for Lorenzo the Magnificent, illustrating a Florentine victory over Siena in 1432. *Piero della Francesca*, **St Michael** (769), **Baptism of Christ** (665), **Nativity** (908).

Room IV: **Central Italy (15th c.).** *Filippino Lippi*, **Virgin and Child with St Jerome and St Dominic** (altarpiece, 293), notable for the representation of landscape. *Piero de Cosimo*, Battle between Centaurs and Lapiths (4890), Mythological Subject (698). *Luca Signorelli*, **Coriolanus** (fresco, 3299). *Pinturicchio*,

Scenes from the Odyssey (911). *Perugino*, **Virgin and Child with St Michael and St Raphael** (altarpiece, 288).

Room V. Cartoon by *Leonardo da Vinci*, **Madonna and Child with St Anne and St John the Baptist** (6337).

Room VI: **Italian painters, excluding Venice (16th c.).** *Leonardo da Vinci*, **Madonna of the Rocks** (1093), one of his best-known pictures. *Michelangelo*, **Entombment** (790), Madonna and Child with St John and Angels (809). *Raphael*, the **Ansidei Madonna** (1171), St Catherine (168). *Andrea del Sarto*, Madonna and Child with St John and St Elizabeth (17), Portrait of a Young Man (670). *Pontormo*, Joseph in Egypt (1131). *Bronzino*, **Allegory with Venus and Cupid** (651). *Correggio*, Madonna of the Basket (23), The School of Love (10). *Parmigianino*, Madonna and Child with St John the Baptist and St Jerome (33).

Room VII: **Venetian school (16th c.).** *Veronese*, **Family of Darius before Alexander** (294), Consecration of St Nicholas (26), Allegories (1318, 1324, 1325, 1326), in the centre of the room. *Tintoretto*, **Origin of the Milky Way** (1313), St George and the Dragon (altarpiece, 16). *Jacopo Bassano*, The Good Samaritan (277). *Titian*, Holy Family with a Shepherd (4), **Bacchus and Ariadne** (35), commissioned by Alfonso of Este for his palace in Ferrara; **Portrait of a Gentleman** (1944), The Vendramin Family (4452), Madonna and Child (3948), Allegory of Prudence (6367), a work of his old age.

Room VIII: **Flemish school (16th c.).** *Joos van Wassenhove*, Allegories of Music and Rhetoric (756, 755). *Jan Gossaert*, Adoration of the Magi (2790), Portrait of a Girl (2211).

Room VIIIA: **German school (16th c.).** *Hans Holbein*, **The Ambassadors** (1314), Christina of Denmark,

Duchess of Milan (2475). *Dürer*, The Painter's Father (1938). *Stefan Lochner*, St Matthew, St Catherine and St John the Evangelist (705). *Hans Baldung*, Portrait of a Man (perhaps a self-portrait, 245), Pietà (1427). *Lucas Cranach*, Portrait of a Lady (281), **Cupid complaining to Venus** (6344). *Albrecht Altdorfer*, Landscape with Footbridge (6320). *Michael Pacher*, Virgin and Child (5786).

Room VIIIB: **Northern Italy (15th c.).** *Mantegna*, Introduction of the Cult of Cybele at Rome (902), Virgin and Child with St Mary Magdalene and St John the Baptist (274), **Agony in the Garden** (1417). *Antonello da Messina*, Crucifixion (1166), Portrait of a Man (1141). *Pisanello*, Vision of St Eustace (1436).

Room VIIIC: **Florentine school (15th c.).** *Botticelli*, **Venus and Mars** (915), one of his most celebrated works; Adoration of the Magi (1033), Portrait of a Young Man (626), Nativity (1034). *Filippino Lippi*, **Adoration of the Magi** (1124).

Room VIIID: **Flemish school (15th-16th c.).** *Jan van Eyck*, **Giovanni Arnolfini and his Wife** (186), painted in 1434; Man in Turban (222). *Master of Flémalle (Robert Campin)*, Virgin and Child (2609). *Roger van der Weyden*, Pietà (6265), The Magdalene Reading (654), St Ivo (6394). *Hans Memlinc*, the Donne Triptych (6275). *P. Brueghel the Elder*, Adoration of the Magi (3556).

Room IX: **Bellini, Giorgione and Titian.** *Giorgione*, Adoration of the Magi (1160), Sunset Landscape with St George and St Anthony (6307). *Titian*, Noli me tangere (270). *Bellini*, **Doge Leonardo Loredan** (189), one of his greatest works, painted in 1501; Madonna of the Meadow (599), **Christ in the Garden of Olives** (726).

Room X: **Dutch school (17th c.).** *Salomon van Ruysdael,* View of Rhenen (6348). *Jacob van Ruysdael,* Waterfall (627). *Aert van der Neer,* View of a River (732). *Frans Hals,* **Man wearing Gloves** (2528). *Gerhart ter Borch,* Peace of Munster (896). *Gabriel Metsu,* The Music Lesson (839). *Nicolaas Maes,* The Maid (207). *Jan Steen,* Young Woman playing the Harp (856). *Pieter Saenredam,* The Buurkerk in Utrecht (1896). *Karel Fabritius,* Portrait of a Young Man (4042, perhaps a self-portrait). *Thomas de Keyser,* Constantin Huyghens (212). *Karel Dujardin,* Woman and Child at Ford (827). *Hendrick Avercamp,* Winter Landscape (1346), Ice Scene near a Town (1479).

Room XI: **Dutch school** (continued). *Hobbema,* **Middelharnis** (830), Ruins of Brederode Castle (831). *Jacob van Ruysdael,* The Shore at Egmond-aan-Zee (1390). *Pieter de Hooch,* Courtyard of a House in Delft (835). *Vermeer,* **Young Lady at the Virginals** (1383), **Seated Figure of a Woman** (2568). *Gerard ter Borch,* Officer dictating a Letter (5847).

Room XII: **Rembrandt,** with many major works. Portrait of an Officer on Horseback (6300); The Woman Taken in Adultery (45); Christ before Pilate (1400); **Self-Portrait** (672), painted in 1640; **Self-Portrait in Old Age** (221), painted in 1669, the year of Rembrandt's death; **Saskia,** a portrait of the artist's wife (4930); and a number of other lesser known works. Also pictures by *Albert Cuyp* and *Jan van de Cappelle.*

Room XIII: **Northern Italy (16th c.),** entered through Room XIIIA (frescoes by *Domenichino* on themes from Ovid's "Metamorphoses"). *Lotto, Moretto, Moreni, Romanino, Dosso Dossi, Garofalo.*

Room XIIIB: **Italian painters of the 18th c.** *Guardi,* View with Ruins (2521), Malghera Tower (2524), Ruins on the Shore (2522). *Canaletto,* pictures of **Venice** (2515, 2516). *Ricci, Zais, Giaquinto. Tiepolo,* **Deposition from the Cross** (1333).

Room XIIIC: **Crivelli,** Annunciation (739); **Demidoff Altarpiece** (788), dated 1476.

Room XIV: **Flemish school (17th c.).** A number
of important works by *Rubens:* **Peace and War** (46),
presented to Charles I; **Judgment of Paris** (194, 6379);
Rape of the Sabines (38); **The Straw Hat** (852); Steen
Castle (66); Sunset (157). *Van Dyck:* **Charles I on
Horseback** (1172), perhaps his most famous work;
Abbé Scaglia adoring the Madonna and Child (4899);
Earl of Denbigh (5633). *Jordaens,* Double Portrait
(6293).

Room XV: **Flemish school (17th c.),** continued. *Teniers,*
The Conversation (950), Playing at Bowls (951), The Four
Seasons (857/60), View of Het Sterckshof (817). Works by
Coques, van Oost, van Huysum.

Room XVI: **English painters of the 18th and 19th c.**
Hogarth, **Marriage à la Mode** (113/8), **The Shrimp
Girl** (1162). *Sir Joshua Reynolds,* Captain Robert Orme
(681), General Tarleton (5985), **Lady Cockburn and
her Children** (2077), Lady Albemarle (1259), *Gainsborough,* The Morning Walk (6209), **Mr and Mrs Andrews** (6301), **Mrs Siddons** (683), The Watering Place
(109). *Constable,* **The Hay-Wain** (1207), The Cornfield
(130), **Salisbury Cathedral** (2651). *Turner,* Hero and
Leander (521), **Rain, Steam and Speed** (538), The
Evening Star (1991), The Fighting "Téméraire" (524),
Snowstorm at Sea (530).

Room XVII: **Canaletto.** Four pictures.

Room XVIIA: **Italian painters of the 17th c.** *Guercino, Cara-
vaggio* (Supper at Emmaus), *Preti, Le Valentin.*

Room XVIIB: **Italian and French painters of the 17th c.**
Domenichino, Landscape with Tobias and the Angel (48).
Salvator Rosa, Landscape (6298). *Claude le Lorrain,* Isaac and
Rebecca (12), Seaport (14), **Dido at Carthage** (498), **Sunrise** (479).

Room XVIIC: **Italian painters of the 17th c.** *Guido Reni*
(Adoration of the Shepherds, 6270), *Carraccio* (Pietà, 2923),
Giordano (Miracle of St Anthony, 1844), *Cavallino.*

Room XVIID: **Italian painters of the 18th c.** *Canaletto* (views of Venice), *Longhi, Pellegrini, Tiepolo, Batoni, Pittoni,* etc.
Room XIX: **French painters of the 18th c.** *Watteau* (La Gamme d'Amour), *Nicolas Lancret, Jean-Marc Nattier, Claude-Joseph Vernet, François Boucher, Chardin,* etc.

Room XVIII: **Spanish painters.** *Velazquez*, **Philip V** (745), Philip IV (129), Christ in the House of Martha and Mary (1375), St John on Patmos (6264), the **Rokeby Venus** (2057). *Zurbaran*, St Margaret (1930), St Francis (5655). *Murillo*, The Two Trinities (13), Christ at the Pool of Bethesda (5931), Self-Portrait (6153). *El Greco*, Garden of Olives (3476), Christ driving the Traders from the Temple (1457). *Goya*, **Dona Isabel Cobos de Porcel** (1473), one of the artist's finest works; Duke of Wellington (6322).

Room XX: **French painters of the 17th c.** *Claude*, **Cephalus and Procris** (2), Aeneas at Delos (1018). *Nicolas Poussin*, Worship of the Golden Calf (5587), Bacchanale (62), **Landscape with Snake** (5763), Adoration of the Shepherds (6331). *Philippe de Champeigne*, **Richelieu** (1449), **Triple Portrait of Richelieu** (798).

Room XXI: **French painters of the 19th c.** Ingres, **Mme Moitessier** (4821), on which Ingres worked for twelve years. *Delacroix*, Baron Schwiter (3286), Ovid among the Scythians (6262). *Boudin*, Beach Scenes at Trouville (6309/10). *Claude Monet*, Trouville (3951). *Courbet*, Demoiselles des Bords de la Seine (6355). *Edouard Manet*, **La Serveuse de Bocks** (3858), La Musique aux Tuileries (3260), Execution of Maximilian (3294).

Room XXII: **French painters of the 19th c.** (continued). *Cézanne*, **Les Grandes Baigneuses** (6359), La Vieille au Chapelet (6385). *Degas*, Après le Bain (6295), Lola at the Cirque Fernando (4121). *Seurat*,

Baignade (3908). *Van Gogh*, Cornfield with Cypresses (3861), **Sunflowers** (3863).

Room XXIII: **French painters of the 19th c.** (continued). *Monet*, Water Lilies (6343), **Nympheas** (4240). *Renoir*, Danseuses (3617/8), **La Première Sortie** (3859), Les Parapluies (3268).

NATIONAL PORTRAIT GALLERY

Entrance in St Martin's Place, behind the National Gallery. Open 10 to 5, Saturdays 10 to 8, Sundays 2 to 6.

The National Portrait Gallery, founded in 1856, displays some 4000 portraits in its 39 rooms, covering the whole range of British life (history, politics, literature and the arts).

Of particular interest are the self-portraits of *Hogarth, Reynold, Gainsborough* and *Angelica Kaufmann* and the portraits of sovereigns (George IV, by *Reynolds*) and other celebrities (Byron, by *Noel;* Sir John Moore, by *Lawrence,* etc.).

SOANE MUSEUM

This museum, situated at 13 Lincoln's Inn Fields, just off Holborn (p. 178), is in the house which *Sir John Soane* (1753-1837), architect of the Bank of England, built for himself in 1812-13. A great amateur of ancient art, with a particular interest in the excavations at Pompeii and Herculaneum, he assembled a considerable collection of works of art, which are displayed just as he himself arranged them. Open 10 to 5; closed on Sundays and Mondays and during the month of August.

From the vestibule we go right into the *Dining Room*, in Pompeian style, with ceiling paintings on mythological themes by *Howard* (1834). Above the fireplace is a portrait of Soane by *Lawrence* (1828). Near one of the windows is the **Cawdor Vase,** a mixing bowl (4th c. B.C.) found at Lecce in southern Italy in 1790, decorated with a representation of the sacrifices by Oenomaos and Pelops before the chariot race at Olympia for the hand of Hippodameia.

Passing through two small rooms (Italian Renaissance bronzes), we enter the *Picture Room*, with two series of **Hogarth's** finest works *(The Rake's Progress, The Election)*. We then come to the *Monk's Parlour*, with 15th century wood carving from Antwerp and 17th century German stained glass. In the *Crypt* are cinerary urns and copies of ancient works. The *Sepulchral Chamber* contains the famous Egyptian **sarcophagus of Seti I** (14th c. B.C.), of aragonite.

Returning to the ground floor, we come to the *New Picture Room*, with three views of Venice by **Canaletto** and **Turner's** "Admiral Tromp's Barge". In the Antechamber are **Watteau's** "Noces" and a fragment of sculpture from the Erechtheion in Athens. The *Breakfast Room* contains Chinese porcelain, Hindu statuettes and Napoleonic relics.

On the upper floor are Flemish and French illuminated manuscripts, Indian miniatures, medals, cameos, etc.

TATE GALLERY

The Tate Gallery stands on the banks of the Thames, south of Westminster (p. 147). It is easily reached from Westminster Abbey or the Houses of Parliament by following Millbank, a wide street lined with Victorian buildings (Thames House), with modern tower blocks farther along to the south (Millbank Tower, 380 ft high, erected 1965).

The Gallery contains the national collection of British art of the 17th to 19th centuries and modern British and foreign art (painting and sculpture). Open weekdays 10 to 6, Sundays 2 to 6. Restaurant. Tel.: 01-828 1212.

British art is displayed in the rooms to the left of the entrance, modern art to the right. Since the Gallery is in course of extension and rearrangement it is difficult to give a room-by-room description. We list below a selection of the most important works, with the warning that their placing in the various rooms is subject to alteration in the course of the next few years.

Sculpture: in a special room in the centre of the Gallery (works by Maillol, Epstein, Henry Moore and Barbara Hepworth, and temporary exhibitions).

BRITISH PAINTING TO 1900. Painters of the 16th and 17th century (Room 1), *Hogarth* (Room 2: Portrait of Dr Hoadly, The Calais Gate), *Reynolds, Gainsborough, Romney* and *Wilson* (Room 3), the neo-classical school (Room 4), *Fuseli* and *Loutherbourg* (Room 5).

Rooms 6 to 10 are devoted to **Turner,** the finest and most representative collection of his work (300 paintings and some 9000 watercolours). His development can be followed from his early imitations of Claude and Poussin to the later work, with its anticipation of Impressionist techniques. Among pictures of particular importance are Forum Romanum (504), Stormy Sea (4658), London from Greenwich (483), House by a Mountain Stream (2694), Evening of the Flood (530), Morning after the Flood (531), Chichester Canal (560) and Peace (528).

Room 11: **Constable** landscapes (Hadleigh Castle, 4810; Valley Farm, 327) and portraits (Mrs Andrew, 5966). Rooms 12, 13 and 14: painters of the Victorian period and the 1900s (*Steer, Whistler, Watts, Sargent, Mulready, Tissot, Egg,* etc.).

Beyond Room 11 we descend to the basement. Room 27 and the following rooms: works by the Pre-Raphaelites *(Millais, Rossetti, Holman Hunt), William Blake,* 19th century painters and watercolourists *(Cozens)* and British painters after 1920.

MODERN EUROPEAN ART. Room 24: **Impressionists,** *Pissarro, Sisley, Monet, van Gogh, Cézanne, Gauguin, Utrillo, Seurat, Bonnard, Vuillard, Renoir, Degas;* sculpture by *Rodin.* Room 23: **Matisse** and the **Fauves** *(Derain, Vlaminck).* Room 22: **Picasso** (Trois Danseurs, T 729, painted in 1925; Seated Nude, 6205, painted 1932; Femme en Chemise, 4720, painted 1905; Bust of Woman, 5915, painted 1903; etc.). Room 25: **Cubists and Futurists** *(Picasso, Léger; Braque,* The Mandoline, T 833; *Boccioni, Balla, Soffici,* etc.), **Vorticists** *(Wyndham Lewis, Bomberg;* sculpture by *Epstein* and *Gaudier-Breszka).*

Room 21: **Expressionists, Dadaists and Surrealists** (*Nolde, Munch, Kokoschka, Ernst, Delvaux, de Chirico, Dali, Klee, Miro, Chagall, Dufy, Rouault, Soutine, Modigliani, Magritte,* etc.). Room 18: **Giacometti.** Rooms 19 and 20: **Constructivists and Abstract Art** (*Kandinsky, Mondriaan, Pollock, Nicholson, Naum Gabo, Pasmore, Biedermann*).

European Art since 1945: *Poliakoff, de Stael, Hartung, Auerbach, Bacon, Sutherland, Gorky, Dubuffet,* the *Cobra group, Rothko, Davie, Soto, Stella,* the *Pop Art* school, *Vasarely,* etc.

WALLACE COLLECTION

This magnificent collection in Hertford House, Manchester Square (p. 164), is now one of the national collections. Open weekdays 10 to 5, Sundays 2 to 5. Tel.: 01-935 0687.

The main treasures of the collection are its paintings by French, Dutch, Spanish and Italian masters, but it also contains fine furniture and various objets d'art of first-rate importance.

The first eleven rooms are on the ground floor, the others on the first floor.

Entrance Hall: portrait of George IV by *Lawrence.*

Room I: portraits by *Lawrence, Hoppner* and others; candelabrum by *Caffieri* (18th c.); Louis XVI furniture.

Room II; pictures by *Nattier, Oudry, Largillière* and *van Loo;* furniture by *Boulle;* Sèvres porcelain; another candelabrum by *Caffieri.*

Room III (Renaissance): Italian bronzes, **Limoges enamels,** miniatures, **Italian pottery** (16th c. majolica from Siena, Urbino and Faenza: A 47, a dish dated 1525; B 98, a dish from Pesaro dated 1530; B 82, a dish from Urbino dated 1533); statuette of Hercules (S 273); pictures by *Crivelli, Memlinc* and *Corneille de Lyon.*

Room IV: **Limoges enamels;** mediaeval French ivories and silver; Adoration of the Shepherds by *Philippe de Champeigne;* bust of Le Brun by *Coysevox* and bust of Condé by Derbais.

Rooms V-VII: arms and armour of the 13th-17th centuries.

Room VIII: Oriental arms and armour.

Founder's Room; portraits by *Reynolds*, 18th century French furniture.

Room IX: 18th century French furniture, portrait of George III by *Ramsay*, pictures by *Canaletto* and *Guardi*.

Room X: French furniture; Italian paintings of the 15th and 16th centuries (*Foppa, Titian, Dolci, Luini, Andrea del Sarto, Cima da Conegliano,* etc.); Italian terracottas.

Room XI: pictures by *Murillo* and his pupils; miniatures.

Staircase: **forged iron balustrade** from the Bibliothèque Nationale in Paris (sold for scrap in 1862) dating from 1733-41; paintings by *Boucher* (**Sunrise** and **Sunset**); **bust of Louis XIV** by *Coysevox;* busts by *Houdon.*

Room XII: Sèvres porcelain; clock by the elder *Duplessis* (18th c.); bust of Louis XIV by *Coysevox* (S 165); library cabinet by *Levasseur* (F 390): pictures by *Guardi* and *Canaletto* (views of Venice); portrait by *Mme Vigée-Lebrun.*

Room XIII: works by *Rembrandt* (**Self-Portrait, The Good Samaritan,** Portrait of a Boy) and his pupils.

Room XIV: 17th century Flemish and Dutch painters (*Teniers, Gerard ter Borch, Jan Steen, van Ostade, van de Velde, Brouwer, Maes*).

Room XV: Dutch landscapists (*Hobbema,* The Mill; *van der Neer, van de Velde, van Ostade, Wijnants, Wouwerman, Cuyp, Ruysdael, van Huysum,* etc.).

Room XVI contains the **chief treasures of the Collection.** Among them are St John in the Desert, by *Reynolds* (P 48); a Self-Portrait by *van Dyck* (85); **Halt during the Chase,** by *Watteau* (416); **Perseus and Andromeda,** by *Titian* (11); Portrait of Nelly O'Brien, by *Reynolds* (38); Portrait of Miss Haverfield, by *Gainsborough* (44); Fête in a Park, *Watteau* (391); **Crucifixion,** by *Rubens* (71); Isabella Brandt, by *Rubens* (30); two portraits of Don Baltazar Carlos, son of Philip IV, by *Velazquez* (6, 12); Holy Family, by *Rubens* (81); **Christ and St Peter,** by **Rubens** (93); several paintings by *Rembrandt* (82, 90; 29, his son **Titus:** 86); several portraits by *Reynolds* (40, 35, 36, 45); pictures by *Salvator Rosa* (116), *Romney* (37), *Hobbema, Ruysdael, van Dyck* (79, 94), *Murillo, Philippe de Champeigne, Gainsborough;* **"The Laughing Cavalier"** by Frans Hals (84), dated 1624; **Lady with Fan,** by *Velazquez* (88); pictures by *Claude,*

Alonso Cano, etc.; **French furniture,** including a desk made by *Riesener* for Stanislas Leczinski of Poland.

Room XVII: **19th century French painters,** with works by *Delacroix* (Execution of Doge Marino Faliero, 282), *Delaroche*, *Prudhon, Meissonnier, Géricault, Corot, Vernet, Isabey* and *Couture.*

Room XVIII: **19th century French painters,** including *Lancret, Boucher, Watteau* (**Lady at her Toilet,** 439; Music Party, 410), *Nattier, Fragonard* (**The Swing,** 430; The Souvenir, 382; The Schoolmistress, 404), *Greuze, Mme Vigée-Lebrun,* etc.; 18th century French furniture, including two **secretaires** made by *Riesener* for Marie Antoinette (302/3).

Room XIX; *Boucher* (Madame Pompadour, 418) and 18th century French furniture.

Room XX: *Bonington;* portrait by *Reynolds;* French furniture made by *Dubois* for Catherine II of Russia.

Room XXI: cabinet by *Boulle;* pictures by *Lancret, Nattier, Oudry, Pater* and *Desportes.*

Room XXII: works by *Greuze, Pater,* and *de Troy;* furniture by *Leleu* and *Riesener;* marble vase by *Clodion;* porcelain; miniatures.

VICTORIA AND ALBERT MUSEUM

This very important museum of applied art is situated in South Kensington, with the entrance in Cromwell Road (p. 172).   Underground station: South Kensington. Open weekdays 10 to 6, Sundays 2.30 to 6. Restaurant. Tel.: 01-589 6371. Catalogues available at entrance.

The Museum is divided into two parts — the *Primary Galleries*, in which all the finest items in the collection are on display, arranged according to periods and styles, and the *Study Collections*, also open to visitors, where the rest of the material is grouped according to the type of object (pottery, silver, metalwork, sculpture, etc.).

The Victoria and Albert Museum is a museum of applied and decorative art of all countries, styles and periods. It is the successor to a museum of applied art founded in Marlborough House in 1852 on the initiative of the Prince Consort, and incorporates material from various other sources, including works acquired at the time of the Great Exhibition of 1851 and a collection assembled at Somerset House by the School of Design from 1837 onwards. Like the Marlborough House museum, it was established on the initiative of the Prince Consort.

From the beginning the Museum was specifically concerned with the applied arts, with the object of promoting interest in design in contemporary applied art. Soon, however, the fine arts also found a place in the Museum, following the gift of the Sheepshanks Collection of British painting and the acquisition by Sir John Charles Robinson of some fine examples of mediaeval art and Italian sculpture. The collection increased rapidly, and new buildings were added from time to time. By 1891, however, a major extension had become necessary. In a competition held for the erection of a new building the successful architect was Sir Aston Webb. The foundation stone was laid by Queen Victoria in 1899, and the new museum was opened by Edward VII in 1909. At the same time the scientific collections were transferred to the *Science Museum* (p. 171).

It is not possible in the space available to give anything approaching a complete account of the Museum's contents. Visitors who want a fuller description can obtain an excellent brief guide at the entrance to the Museum. Here we can do no more than give a general indication of the contents of the various rooms.

Immediately beyond the entrance hall is Room 49 (recent acquisitions, temporary exhibitions). Beyond this again is Room 43.

Room 43: early mediaeval art.

Rooms 23 and 24: English, German and French Gothic art.

Room 22: Italian Gothic art.

Room 25: Spanish and Hispano-Mauresque art.

Rooms 26-29: late mediaeval art.

Room 38: *mediaeval tapestries.*

Room 38A: temporary exhibitions. Beyond it is the restaurant.

Rooms 16 to 11: **Italian Renaissance** (works by *Donatello* in Room 16 and by *Luca della Robbia* in Rooms 14 and 12).

Rooms 17-20: Italian Renaissance.

Rooms 21A and 21: the **Renaissance in Europe** (16th c.). Note particularly *Bernini*'s Neptune and a Triton.

At the end of Room 21 steps lead down to Rooms 1-7.

Rooms 1-3: 17th century European art.

Rooms 4 and 5: **18th century European art.** Theseus and the Minotaur, by *Canova* (1782). Service of Meissen china which belonged to Frederick the Great. Bust of Voltaire by *Houdon.*

Rooms 6 and 7: **Jones Collection,** bequeathed by John Jones in 1882 (18th c. French furniture).

Returning to Room 21, go upstairs to the Exhibition Road entrance to the Museum, and turn left into Room 52, the beginning of the collection of **English art.**

Room 52: *Tudor art.*

Room 53: English embroidery from 1540 to 1640. The chair near the window is said to have been used by Charles I at his trial.

Room 54: 17th century English embroidery, pottery and furniture. Sculpture group by *Grinling Gibbons* (Stoning of St Stephen).

Room 55: miniatures *(Holbein, Hilliard, Oliver, Cooper).*

Room 56: English art in the second half of the 17th century and the early 18th century.

Rooms 57 and 57A: English art 1700-1750.

Room 58: English art 1700-1750, including fine *Chippendale furniture.*

The staircase at the end of Room 58 leads to the upper floor.

Rooms 126 to 122: *English art from 1750 to 1820* (Chelsea porcelain, rooms and decorative features from houses of the period).

Room 121: Regency art (1810-30).

Rooms 120 to 118: Victorian art.

Go down the stairs at the end of Room 118, return to the main entrance, keep across Room 49 and turn right into a corridor (Room 47D) and then left into Room 44.

Rooms 47A and 44: **arts of China, Korea and Japan.**

Room 45: temporary exhibitions.

Room 42: **Islamic art** (also in corridor, 47B). Beautiful *minbar* from a mosque in Cairo (late 15th c.). Persian pottery and silver. Persian carpets. Faience tiles.

Rooms 41, 47B and 47A: **Indian art,** with some outstanding examples. Torso from Sanchi; *Nataraja* (Shiva dancing): statue of the monkey god Hanuman; *jade cup* which belonged to Shah Jahan; illuminated manuscripts; tapestries and cotton paintings; "Tippoo's Tiger", a mechanical organ.

Room 40: **costume** from 1600 to 1947, an incomparable collection illustrating the history of European fashion. The staircase in the centre of the room leads up to the *Musical Instruments Gallery* (earlist known harpsichord, 1521).

Room 48: **cartoons by Raphael,** acquired by the future Charles I in 1623 and presented to the Museum by Queen Victoria in 1865. These are the only Raphael cartoons of this size outside Italy. They were used as patterns for tapestries made for the Sistine Chapel in the Vatican (scenes from the New Testament and the lives of the Apostles).

From here we return to the entrance hall, by way of the *Woodwork and Architectural Study Collection* and the stall selling guides and postcards. The last of the Primary Galleries are on the first floor (Rooms 102-106, at the north-east corner of the building).

Room 102: transparencies by *Gainsborough.*

Rooms 103 and 106B: **Constable Collection** (drawings, sketches, watercolours, oil paintings, including Cottage in a Cornfield, Salisbury Cathedral).

Rooms 104, 104A and 104B: pictures by *Gainsborough, Reynolds, Wilson, Turner, Landseer, Danby, Etty, Mulready, Leslie,* etc.

Room 105; the Ionides Collection, bequeathed by Mr C.A. Ionides in 1905 (*Rembrandt, Le Nain, Delacroix, Courbet, Ingres, Tintoretto,* the Barbizon group).

Rooms 106 and 106A: British and foreign watercolours.

The rooms containing the Study Collections of the Museum are not included in this list. For a description of these collections, which are likely to be of interest only to specialists or to visitors with a good deal of time at their disposal, see the "Brief Guide" produced by the Museum (pp. 55-65).

Other Museums and Galleries

There are of course a very considerable number of other museums and galleries, large and small, in London. The following is a list (in alphabetical order) of the most important of these museums, in addition to those mentioned in the various itineraries.

Baden-Powell House, Queen's Gate, South Kensington: mementoes of Lord Baden-Powell and the scout movement. Open daily 9 to 6.

Bromfield Museum, Broomfield Park, Palmers Green, N. 1 (Enfield): an old mansion in a park, with a collection of local antiquities, china, paintings and natural history. Open in summer 10 to 8, Saturdays and Sundays 10 to 6, closed Mondays; winter 10 to 5.

Chiswick House, Burlington Lane, Chiswick, W.4: a Palladian villa (1725) designed by the Earl of Burlington, with interior by *William Kent*. Open 9.30 to 7 in summer.

Cricket Memorial Gallery, Lord's Cricket Ground, N.W.8: objects and trophies relating to the history of cricket.

Cuming Museum, Walworth Road, Southwark: history of Southwark (Roman remains, mementoes of Dickens, material illustrating old superstitions). Open 10 to 5.30, except Sundays.

Darwin Museum, Downe, Kent: Charles Darwin's House. Open daily except Fridays 10 to 5.

Dulwich College Picture Gallery, College Road, S.E.21: pictures by *Rubens, Rembrandt, Claude, Poussin, Gainsborough, Watteau, Lancret*, etc. Open 10 to 6, except Mondays: Sundays 2 to 5 (summer only). See p. 234.

Federation of British Artists, The Mall Gallery: temporary exhibitions. Open weekdays 10 to 5, Saturdays 10 to 1.

Fenton House, The Grove, Hampstead, N.W.3: old musical instruments, china, furniture. Open 11 to 5, Sundays 2 to 5.

Forty Hall, Forty Hill, Enfield: a mansion of 1629 which belonged to Nicholas Raynton, Lord Mayor of London, with 17th and 18th century furniture and pictures. Open 10 to 8, Saturdays and Sundays 10 to 6.

Geffrye Museum, Kingsland Road, Shoreditch: daily life in England from 1600 onwards. Open 10 to 5, Sundays 2 to 5: closed Mondays. Underground: Liverpool Street.

Goldsmiths' Hall, Foster Lane, Cheapside, E.C.2: fine collection of plate. Seen by arrangement (tel. 01-606 8971). Underground: St Paul's.

Gordon Medical Museum, Guy's Hospital, St Thomas St, S.E.1. Open weekdays 9 to 5.

H.M.S. Belfast, Symons Wharf, Tooley St, S.E.1 (London Bridge): a cruiser which is now a museum. Open 11 to 5.

Hayward Gallery, Belvedere Road, South Bank, S.E.1: temporary exhibitions. Open 10 to 6, Sundays 12 to 6.

I.T.A. Television Gallery, 70 Brompton Road, S.W.3: exhibition of television techniques. Seen by arrangement (tel. 01-584 7011). No children under 16.

Jewish Museum, Woburn House, Upper Woburn Place, W.C.1. Open Monday-Thursday 2.30 to 5, Fridays and Sundays 10.30 to 1.

Dr Johnson's House, 17 Gough Square, E.C.4: the house in which Johnson lived from 1748 to 1759. Open weekdays 10.30 to 5.

Museum of London, London Wall, E.C.2. The history of London from prehistoric times to the present day (Roman remains, Great Fire exhibit, Lord Mayor's Coach). Open Tuesday to Saturday 10 to 6, Sunday 2 to 6.

National Army Museum, Royal Hospital Road, S.W.3: paintings, uniforms, weapons, etc., illustrating the history of the Army from 1485 to 1914. Open 10 to 5, Sundays 2 to 5.

National Film Archive, 81 Dean St, W.1: history of the cinema and of television. Seen on application (tel. 01-437 4355) 10 to 5.

National Postal Museum, King Edward St, E.C.1: collection of stamps. Open 10 to 4, closed Sundays.

Orleans House Gallery, Riverside, Twickenham: a Baroque mansion (James Gibbs, 1720) containing 18th and 19th century paintings, prints, and watercolours. Open 1 to 5.30, except Mondays.

Pharmaceutical Society Museum, 17 Bloomsbury Square, W.C.1: history of pharmacy. Seen by arrangement (tel. 01-405 8967).

Royal College of Music, Prince Consort Road, South Kensington, S.W.7. Mondays and Wednesdays 11 to 4, on application (tel. 01-589 3643).

Royal College of Surgeons Museum, Lincoln's Inn Fields, W.C.2; history of medicine. Seen by arrangement (tel. 01-405 3474).

Serpentine Gallery, South Carriageway, Kensington Gardens: exhibitions of contemporary art. Open 11 to 7.

South London Art Gallery, Peckham Road, Southwark: paintings, watercolours, drawings, engravings. Open 10 to 6.

Valence House Museum, Becontree Avenue, Dagenham, Essex (Barking): a 17th century manor-house containing local antiquities. Open Monday-Friday 9.30 to 12.

Wesley's House, 47 City Road, E.C.1: residence of the founder of Methodism. Open weekdays 10 to 1 and 2 to 4.

Whitechapel Art Gallery, High St, Whitechapel, E.1: modern art and design. Open weekdays 11 to 6, Sundays 2 to 6; closed Mondays.

VI. THE PORT OF LONDON

From the western districts of London we now pass to the Port of London and the East End, at the other extremity of the city. The atmosphere here is very different, but these areas are just as much part of London as Westminster and the West End, and the visitor who really wants to know what London is like must see them too.

From May to September the Port of London Authority runs sightseeing trips in motor launches, starting from Tower Pier, immediately west of the Tower of London (Tuesdays, Thursdays and Saturdays at 1.30, returning about 6.30). Other trips are run by private operators, starting from Westminster Pier (near the Westminster end of Westminster Bridge) and Charing Cross Pier.

History

When James I threatened to deprive London of its status as capital city of the kingdom the Lord Mayor replied that though the king could take his capital away from London he could not take away the Thames. And indeed throughout its history London has owed much of its importance to the river on which it stands. It has become, and remains, one of the great ports of the world; and although its relative importance in Britain's sea-borne trade has declined somewhat in recent years the Port of London still accounts for a third of the total traffic passing through British ports.

London was established and has developed at the point where the banks of the Thames are conveniently close to one another and offer stable ground for building (the City and Westminster areas). Below the Tower the river widens and the banks are low-lying and marshy, so that the city could not extend in this direction; but the softer alluvial soil downstream could readily be excavated to make docks and harbour basins. Hence the development of the Port of London, now extending for some 25 miles below Tower Bridge, from which point the Thames becomes London River.

In Roman times *Londinium* was already a busy trading centre, and Tacitus refers to the swarm of merchants to be found there in the first century of our era. In spite of the ravages of Saxon and Viking invaders the port remained an important centre of trade, whose greatness was proclaimed by the Venerable Bede in the 8th century; and it was protected and enriched by King Alfred. The Norman Conquest opened up new markets on the Continent, and London maintained regular trading relationships with Bordeaux, Caen and Flanders. The building of the Tower by William the Conqueror reflects his concern to defend the port as well as to watch over the town. At the same time London developed its trade with the countries round the North Sea, and a "counting-house" of the Hanseatic League was established in the city.

The discoveries of the late 15th and 16th centuries immensely enlarged London's commercial horizons. The Mediterranean countries now lost their maritime supremacy, and the hitherto powerful Venice stagnated. Henceforth the preponderance lay with the northern countries, more favourably situated in relation to America and the distant Indies. The Hanseatic counting-house in London was closed down in 1598, and new English trading companies were established — the Merchant Adventurers, the East India Company, the Hudson's Bay Company. Wharves were built along the Thames in the area now known as the City, and London Bridge, lined with houses, marked the farthest extent of the port.

The space available within these limits, however, was insufficient for the needs of the traffic. In the 18th century the overcrowded port could not accommodate all the ships seeking to enter it, some of which had to wait for weeks until there was room for them to berth. In the following century, therefore, new docks began to be built to cope with the steadily increasing traffic: the last of these docks, the George V Dock, was completed in 1921. In 1908 the *Port of London Authority* was established to administer the whole port area, although the wharves and warehouses remained in private hands. Subsequently the Authority deepened the main shipping channel in the Thames from 27 to 37 feet.

During the second world war, despite all enemy attacks, the Port of London maintained a high level of activity, handling a total of over 106 million tons of shipping during the war years. Three thousand convoys sailed from the Thames, and more than 200,000 tanks and military vehicles were despatched from this one port alone. In more recent times the busy activity to be seen in London River demonstrates that London has regained its place as one of the world's leading ports.

London has, however, lost a function which was formerly important — the role of an emporium or port of redistribution which stored tea, wool, rubber and other goods in its warehouses and shipped them to countries all over the world. It is now a regional port for south-eastern England, handling 60 million tons of goods annually, of which 40% is oil, 20% coal brought by coastal shipping and the rest bulk goods, timber, raw materials and semi-finished materials. The incoming traffic exceeds the outgoing in the proportion of 5 to 1.

The Port

Visitors will be struck by the large numbers of barges shuttling between the ships and the wharves and factories along the river. There are more than 7000 of these, hauled by smoke-blackened tugs. The huge warehouses in the port hold the country's main stocks of many products imported from distant lands — tobacco, rubber, cocoa, tea. The port's passenger traffic is much smaller than it was, but London is still the port of departure of the Peninsular and Oriental and Union Castle lines, sailing to India and the Far East and to South Africa and South America.

Passing under the Tower Bridge, below the busy Pool of London, the sightseeing launch enters the Port proper, through water polluted with flecks of oil and miscellaneous flotsam. Trains of barges make their slow and majestic way upstream against the current, while down river can be seen a confusion of cranes and ships and chimneys belching volumes of black smoke. The flags of every country in the world fly here, and all the different races of the world are found among the crews.

To the left are the *St Katharine Docks* and *London Docks* (1805), both now closed. The area of the St Katharine Docks has been redeveloped, and now houses the *World Trade Centre*. Captain Kidd and other pirates were hanged here, on the banks of the river. On the right bank are the **Surrey Commercial Docks,** mainly handling timber from Scandinavia and America. Beyond this, in a loop in the river, is the

Isle of Dogs, so called because it was once occupied by the royal kennels. On the Isle of Dogs are the **West India Docks** and *Millwall Docks*, handling colonial produce, wool, cane sugar, rum, coffee, bananas, tea and grain. The nearby **East India Docks** also handle goods of this type.

Farther downstream are the **Royal Victoria Docks** (no longer used) and **Royal Albert Docks** and the adjoining **King George V Dock,** with a total area of 1110 acres, handling mainly frozen meat from Holland, Denmark and Argentina. Finally, much farther downstream, are **Tilbury Docks,** much used by passenger traffic, with a direct rail link to the City (30 minutes).

Tilbury Fort marks the outermost limit of the Port of London. It is here that Queen Elizabeth I is said to have addressed her troops, then awaiting invasion by the Spanish Armada, with the stirring words: "I know I have the body of a weak and feeble woman, but I have the heart and stomach of a king, and of a king of England too."

The East End

The rather drab and dingy part of London known as the **East End** extends along both sides of the Thames from White-chapel to Poplar, but is mostly on the north bank. This area of narrow streets with rows of monotonously similar houses suffered severely from wartime bombing, and this has at any rate made it possible to improve the layout of the devastated areas. In **Whitechapel** is *Middlesex Street*, better known as *Petticoat Lane*, where a busy "flea-market" is held every Sunday. The whole of this district is a centre of the clothing industry. Most of the inhabitants are Jewish, and there is a special Jewish theatre giving performances in Yiddish. It was in Whitechapel that William Booth, seeking to bring the Gospel to the people of these slum areas, founded the Salvation Army in 1865.

Bethnal Green, Stepney and **Wapping** are also populous districts, with poor areas similar to those of Whitechapel and little of interest to offer the tourist. Stepney has a *church* dating in part from the 15th century, with an 11th century crucifix. *St Katharine's Hospital* has a chapel with 14th century stalls. At the north end of the *Rotherhithe Tunnel* under the Thames is the Danish Seamen's Church (1959), and at the south end are the Norwegian Church and the Finnish Seamen's Church.

In **Poplar** is one of the best known taverns in the world, known as "Charlie Brown's" after the name of a former land-lord who had amassed an extraordinary collection of curios from all over the world. Although Charlie Brown and his curios have gone, the pub is still frequented by seamen of all nationalities.

Beyond this is an industrial area into which the visitor will not wish to venture. *West Ham*, *East Ham* and *Barking* have factories producing rubber goods, concrete, chemicals, building materials, etc., and power stations. *Dagenham* is noted for the *Ford* car factory.

Thurrock, farther down river, has a variety of industry, including oil refineries, footwear factories, cement works, paper-mills and factories producing margarine and soap. In this district are *Tilbury Docks* (passenger traffic, repair yards).

Canvey Island (actually a peninsula on the north side of the estuary) is a popular holiday and weekend resort for Londoners, but is now acquiring some small-scale industry. Oil refinery. **Southend,** just beyond Canvey Island, is a popular seaside resort but is also a considerable industrial centre (radio-telephone equipment, silvering for mirrors, woollen and cotton goods, clothing).

Woolwich, on the south bank, is noted for its Royal Dock-yard and Arsenal. *Erith* and *Crayford* have heavy industry and oil refineries. *Dartford:* paper-making, engineering, chemi-cals. *Gravesend:* shipbuilding.

The main place of interest on the south side of the Thames is **Greenwich,** which is described in the next section.

VII. GREATER LONDON

The immediate surroundings of London are well served by buses and trains, and there are good roads for the motorist. There is ample scope, therefore, for a variety of day or half-day trips from the city.

1. Greenwich

Reached by bus (163 or 177 from Charing Cross or Cannon St), train (from Charing Cross or London Bridge: get off at Maze Hill) or boat (frequent departures in summer from Westminster, Charing Cross or Tower Pier). Travelling by car, leave by the Dover road (Great Dover St).

Greenwich lies a few miles downstream from London on the south bank of the Thames. It is principally known for its **Observatory,** founded in the 17th century: Greenwich Mean Time (G.M.T.) has been universally adopted, and most maps are based on the Greenwich meridian. The smoky atmosphere of modern London, however, interferes with astronomical observation and measurement, and the Observatory was transferred in 1948-49 to Herstmonceux in Sussex (p. 308).

The town itself is of no particular interest, and Greenwich's main attraction is **Greenwich Hospital,** now the *Royal Naval College.* Henry VIII and his daughters Mary and Elizabeth were born here, but most of the present buildings are no earlier than the beginning of the 18th century. In spite of the damage it suffered during the last war the Hospital still contains a number of fine rooms, including in particular the *Painted Hall.*

Another major feature is the **National Maritime Museum,** incorporating the *Queen's House,* an Italian-style palace built by Inigo Jones (1618-35). The Museum, opened in 1937, illustrates the whole of Britain's

maritime history. Open weekdays 11 to 6, Sundays
2 to 6.

The collection, displayed in chronological order, includes
pictures by *Hogarth*, *Reynolds*, *Kneller*, *Romney* (portrait of
Lady Hamilton) and *Gainsborough*, and mementoes of *Captain
Cook*'s voyages and of *Nelson*.

From Greenwich A 206 runs east to Woolwich, passing
Charlton House (1612). **Woolwich,** formerly important for its
Arsenal, is now an industrial suburb with a population of
170,000. It has an *Artillery Museum*, housed in the Rotunda
(Nash, 1814). To the south is *Eltham Palace* (18th c., with
some 15th c. parts).

2. Dulwich

Reached by bus (12 from Piccadilly Circus or Trafalgar
Square) or train (from Victoria Station: get off at West Dulwich).
Travelling by car, leave via the Elephant and Castle (p. 201),
Walworth Road and Camberwell Road.

The main feature of interest in this southern district
of London is the **Dulwich College Picture Gallery.**
The collection, bequeathed to the College in 1811, is
one of the most important private collections in
Britain. The Gallery was built by *Sir John Soane.*
Beside it are the Old College Buildings, erected by
Inigo Jones in 1619 for the actor Edward Alleyn, a
friend of Shakespeare's, now housing the offices of
the trust which runs the College.

The following list includes only the most important works
in the Gallery:

17th century Dutch painters: *Cuyp, Horst, Hobbema, Wouwer-
man, Ruysdael,* Gerard Dou, **Rembrandt** (Girl at Window, 163;
Portrait of the Artist's Son Titus, 221; Portrait of Jacob de
Gheyn, 99).

Italian painters: *Domenichino, Guercino, Reni, Veronese,
Piero di Cosimo* (Portrait of a Young Man, 258), **Raphael**
(St Francis and St Anthony, 241-3), *Tiepolo, Canaletto.*

Flemish painters: *Teniers*, **van Dyck** (Samson and Delilah, 127; Duke of Bedford, 170; Duke Emmanuel Philibert of Savoy, 173), **Rubens** (Hagar in the Wilderness, 131).

Spanish painters: *Velazquez* (Philip IV, 249), *Murillo* (Flower-Girl, 199).

English painters: portraits by *Reynolds*, *Gainsborough*, *Lawrence*, *Kneller*, *Romney*, etc.

South-east of Dulwich is *Crystal Palace Park* (sports facilities), to which the Crystal Palace, now destroyed, was moved from Hyde Park after the Great Exhibition of 1851 (see p. 128). Here now are the headquarters of the commercial television company ITV, in an ultra-modern building with an aerial mast 640 feet high. Farther south is **Croydon**, a suburban borough with a population of over 260,000 which suffered much damage during the last war. The site of London's first airport at Croydon is now a housing estate. The *Old Palace*, formerly an archiepiscopal palace, has parts dating from the 15th and 16th centuries. *Whitgift Hospital*, founded in 1596, also preserves part of the original building.

3. Kew and Richmond

The best approach is by underground (District line: Kew Gardens and Richmond stations).

In summer there are also motor launch services from Westminster Pier, passing attractive riverside scenery which contrasts with the busy activity of the Port farther downstream. The famous Oxford and Cambridge boat race is rowed annually between *Putney* and *Mortlake*. After the *Chiswick* bend the launch comes to the landing-stage for Kew Gardens, on the south side of the river. On the opposite bank is *Syon House* (Robert Adam, c. 1760), seat of the Duke of Northumberland, set in a beautiful riverside park and containing many artistic treasures. Legend has it that when Henry VIII's coffin was deposited here on the way from Westminster to Windsor it suddenly opened of its own accord, thus fulfilling a prophecy made to the king in 1535 by a Franciscan friar.

Kew Gardens, the *Royal Botanic Gardens*, established in 1840, cover an area of 250 acres and contain over 25,000 species of plants. Hot-houses (cactuses, orchids, etc.), Alpine garden, rock garden, water garden, arboretum, palm-house. In the park are a number of unusual buildings, including the famous Pagoda. Open 10 to 8 in summer, 10 to 4 in winter.

Above the Thames stands **Kew Palace,** a handsome mansion in the Dutch style (Samuel Fortrey, 1631), which was a favourite residence of George III, containing furniture, pictures and objets d'art. Open 11 to 6 in summer, Sunday 1 to 6.

Richmond Park (2350 acres, with a perimeter of 8 miles), stands on high ground above the Thames, with magnificent views. There are deer in the park. *White Lodge* was the birthplace of the future King Edward VIII, later Duke of Windsor. Queen Elizabeth I died in *Sheen Manor*, of which no trace now remains.

At *Petersham*, on the road from Richmond to Kingston (A 307), is **Ham House,** a fine 17th century mansion once occupied by the Duke of Lauderdale, one of Charles II's ministers, and still containing its original 17th century furniture, with pictures by English artists (in particular *Reynolds*). Open 2 to 6 in summer, 12 to 4 in winter; closed on Mondays.

From Ham House it is only a short distance to *Hampton Court* (see below), crossing the Thames at *Kingston* (so called because it was the place of coronation of Saxon kings in the 10th century).

Round Richmond are a number of places well known in the world of sport: **Wimbledon** for its tennis tournaments, **Twickenham** for its international rugby matches, **Kempton Park** and **Epsom** for their race-courses, and the Thames itself for its regattas. Here the river is very different from its lower reaches — a relatively narrow stream flowing gently past pleasant park-like landscape.

4. Hampton Court

Reached by bus (Green Line, 716 and 718 from Hyde Park Corner or Marble Arch), train (from Waterloo Station) or in summer by boat (from Westminster Pier).

Upstream from Richmond and Kingston (10 miles from London), **Hampton Court Palace** is one of the most popular tourist attractions in the outskirts of London, with many memories of the past, particularly the 16th and 17th centuries. Open 9.30 to 4, 5 or 6 according to season.

The Palace was built by Cardinal Wolsey, and in his day was a place of extraordinary splendour: it is said to have contained three hundred beds with silken sheets, together with gold and silver plate, tapestries and countless works of art. After Wolsey's fall Henry VIII took over the Palace and partly rebuilt it for his second wife, Anne Boleyn; but the unfortunate queen was beheaded before the work was completed. The Palace is said to be haunted by the ghosts of two of Henry's other wives, Jane Seymour and Cathe-'rine Howard. At the end of the 17th century it was enlarged and altered for William III by Wren, who died in the Palace in 1722. It has not been used as a royal residence since 1760, and most of it is now a museum.

The **gardens,** laid out in the French style in the reigns of Charles II and William III, are very beautiful, with carefully tended lawns and flower-beds and fine avenues of chestnuts and limes. There is also a celebrated maze. The Great Vine produces a magnificent crop of 500 bunches of grapes every year. The garden front of the Palace is imposing, in the style of a miniature Versailles. In the Lower Orangery is a painting by *Mantegna*, "**The Triumph of Julius Caesar**".

The Palace, built of mellow red brick, is laid out round a number of inner courtyards, the best known of which is the *Clock Court*, so called from the astronomical clock constructed for Henry VIII. The **State Apartments** are of great interest for their furniture and pictures, including particularly works by Italian masters, most of them bought by Charles I *(Titian, Tintoretto, Andrea del Sarto, Mantegna)*, and paintings by *Holbein* and *Jean Clouet*. The "Windsor Beauties" — portraits of the ladies of Charles II's court — are perhaps of more documentary than artistic interest. Two features which should not be missed, however, are the 17th century tapestries after cartoons by *Raphael* and the fine hammer-beam roof of Henry VIII's **Great Hall.**

Upstream from Hampton Court (14 miles by road on A 308) is **Windsor** (below). Rather more than half-way there, beyond Staines Bridge, is the meadow of **Runnymede,** the historic spot where the barons forced King John to sign *Magna Carta*, the Great Charter of English liberties (1215). Although the ceremony is traditionally believed to have taken place on *Magna Carta Island*, in the middle of the Thames, the actual scene of the signing is now thought to have been the Runnymede meadow, near the little town of Egham. If King John were now to return to earth and to Runnymede, he might well be surprised to find it surrounded by the industrial works of *Staines*, the airport at *Heathrow* and the Vickers arms factory at *Weybridge*. Less disturbing, perhaps, might be the quieter and more aristocratic atmosphere of *Ascot* race-course, some miles beyond Egham.

5. Windsor Castle

Reached by train (Paddington Station), bus (Green Line, 704 or 705) on in summer by boat from Kingston. Travelling by car, take the Great West Road (Cromwell Road, then motorway from Chiswick).

Opening hours: State Apartments 11 to 3 in winter, 11 to 4 or 5 in summer, Sundays from 1; St George's Chapel 11 to 4, Sundays from 2, closed on Fridays.

Windsor Castle presents a very different aspect according to the direction from which it is seen: from the river its high walls and massive keep give it the appearance of a mediaeval fortress, while from the park, on the Staines road, it is seen as a long and rather heavy façade of rectangular lines. This results from the fact that the castle was built at very different periods: the main structure dates from the time of Edward III and his successors, but considerable additions and alterations were carried out in the 19th century.

The original castle on this site was built by William the Conqueror, and each successive reign since then has left its mark on the structure. Here Edward founded the Order of the Garter; here his son the Black Prince was married in 1361; and here King John the Good of France was confined after the battle of Poitiers. Shakespeare was summoned to Windsor by Queen Elizabeth I and required to write a play in which Sir John Falstaff should reappear; and the result was "The Merry Wives of Windsor". The royal family still use the Castle as a residence, occupying the sumptuous private apartments in the Upper Ward, at the east end.

The Castle is entered by *Henry VIII's Gateway*, which gives access to the Lower Ward, a spacious courtyard surrounded by walls and massive towers. To the right is the Keep or *Round Tower*, straight ahead **St George's Chapel** and the *Albert Memorial Chapel*. St George's Chapel, dedicated to England's patron saint, was built by Richard Beauchamp, Bishop of Salisbury, in the 15th century, and is a fine example of Tudor architecture, related in style to Henry VII's Chapel in Westminster Abbey. In the choir hang the banners of the Knights of the Garter, and here too are buried a number of kings, including Henry VIII, Charles I, Edward VII and George V. The *Albert Memorial Chapel*, dedicated by Queen Victoria to the memory of the Prince Consort, was originally intended as a burial-place for Henry VII, who was in fact buried in Westminster Abbey. Thereafter the chapel was altered and embellished; the interior is richly decorated (mosaics).

Walking up towards the mound on which the Round Tower stands and keeping round it to the left, we pass through a gateway in the walls on to the *North Terrace*, a magnificent promenade over 500 yards long with wide views of the Thames and the green landscape of Buckinghamshire. From the terrace we enter the **State Apartments,** which are full of things of beauty and interest, including arms and armour, rare porcelain and a variety of historical relics (the splendid shield, set with gold and silver, presented to Henry VIII by Francis I of France on the Field of the Cloth of Gold; the cannon-ball which killed Nelson at Trafalgar). The greatest treasures to be seen here, however, are the tapestries and the pictures, many of them by the great European masters — *Rubens, van Dyck, Holbein, Titian, Rembrandt, Correggio, Brueghel, Mignard*, etc.

The view from the top of the Round Tower (actually elliptical in shape) is said to embrace nine counties. Just below the Castle, on the other side of the Thames, is the little town of **Eton**. *Eton College*, founded by Henry VI in 1440, is England's most famous public school. The main block, of mellow red brick, is built round two quadrangles: there is a very beautiful Perpendicular *chapel*. Among Eton's pupils — who still wear the traditional black jacket, grey trousers and top-hat — have been many of the country's greatest statesmen, including Wellington, Pitt, Fox, Canning and Gladstone.

For Windsor and Eton, see also p. 477.

6. The Northern Suburbs

The northern outskirts of London have less to offer the visitor than the area to the west, but there are a number of places which are well worth a visit if time permits.

A. Harrow

Harrow on the Hill is one of London's north-western suburbs, beyond *Wembley*, famous for its Stadium, the Mecca of football fans throughout the country. From the Hill there are fine views of London.

Harrow School (visiting by prior arrangement), stands on the top of the hill. It was founded by Elizabeth I in 1572, and has included among its pupils such famous names as Byron, Sheridan, Palmerston, Nehru and Winston Churchill. The *Fourth Form Room* dates from 1611.

St Mary's Church is said to have been founded by St Anselm in 1094. It contains some Norman work (tower). In the church is a *monument to John Nyon* (Flaxman, 1815).

West and north-west of Harrow are other suburbs on the edge of the green belt round Greater London — **Uxbridge, Rickmansworth, Watford.**

At **Uxbridge,** opposite the Underground station (terminus of the Piccadilly and Metropolitan lines) are the *Market House* (1789) and *St Margaret's Church.* Nearby, at 113 High St, is the *Treaty House,* in which there was a fruitless meeting between Charles I and representatives of Parliament in 1645 to discuss peace terms.

North of Uxbridge, on the road to Rickmansworth, is *Harefield.* In the church is the imposing tomb of the Countess of Derby (d. 1636).

In *Rickmansworth,* beyond the Grand Union Canal, are a number of old houses.

Watford (pop. 75,000) is an industrial town. *St Mary's Church* is a late mediaeval building with 17th century monuments. The Roman Catholic *church of the Holy Rood* is in late 19th century neo-Gothic style, with a large square tower.

From here we can return to Harrow and London by way of A 4140, via *Bentley Priory* (an Augustinian house rebuilt by Sir John Soane in 1758), *Stanmore* and **Edgware** (*St Lawrence's Church,* built 1715-20, with an organ played by Handel when choirmaster to the Duke of Chandos, whose mausoleum is in the church).

B. Hampstead and Kenwood

A visit to these places can be fitted into the return journey from the immediately preceding excursion.

Hampstead is a residential suburb which has grown up round an old village of winding tree-lined streets. *John Keats* lived in a house in Keats Grove from 1818 to 1820; small museum (open weekdays 10 to 6).

Some handsome 18th and 19th century houses still survive. **Hampstead Heath** is a large area of common land planted with trees and areas of woodland. On the highest point (443 ft) is *Whitstone Pond,* with a view extending over several counties. The Heath is particularly busy at the August bank holiday (fair, sideshows). There are two well-known inns, the Spaniards and Jack Straw's Castle, which in the 18th century were the haunt of highwaymen.

To the north-east is **Ken Wood,** a mansion built by Robert Adam in the second half of the 18th century which now houses a fine collection of pictures and furniture bequeathed to the nation by Lord Iveagh. During the last war the house was closed and the collection removed to a place of safety. The interior was damaged by bombs but has been restored. Open 10 to 5 or 7 according to season; Sundays from 2.

Beautiful **Library,** with a painted ceiling by A. Zucchi. Pictures by 18th century English painters *(Gainsborough, Reynolds, Raeburn, Romney, Lawrence),* 17th century Dutch masters *(Van Ostade. Cuyo. van Dyck, van de Velde,* etc.). French painters *(Pater, Rigaud, Boucher)* and Italians *(Guardi).* The chief treasures of the collections are works by **Rembrandt** (Self-Portrait), **Vermeer** (Guitar Player), **Van Dyck** (Portrait of James Stuart) and **Frans Hals** (Portrait of a Gentleman).

To the east of Ken Wood, in *Highgate,* is the cemetery in which Karl Marx is buried.

C. Epping Forest and Waltham

Take A 11 (the Norwich road), via *Bethnal Green* (p. 231), *Leyton* and *Walthamstow.* The road runs past *Chingford* (to left), with the *Epping Forest Museum,* and continues through **Epping Forest** itself, which covers an area of some 6000 acres and extends for a distance of some 11 miles, with a width of 1 to 2 miles.

At the Wake Arms Inn A 121 goes off on the left to **Waltham Abbey,** founded by King Harold in the 11th century. The Lady Chapel is 14th century, the west tower 16th century. Beautiful Norman interior, with the tomb of Edward Denny (early 17th c.). Small archaeological museum in the crypt. To the north is the abbey church, with a doorway of 1370.

Return to London by way of *Waltham Cross,* with one of the crosses erected by Edward I in 1291 to mark the stages in the funeral procession of his wife Eleanor of Castile, and then south on A 10 via *Enfield* and *Tottenham.*

II: SOUTH-EASTERN ENGLAND

The first part of the country encountered by travellers coming from the Continent is the county of Kent, through which they pass on their way to London. This "garden of England", as it is called, has every right to that title. During the flowering season the rolling countryside is perfumed with the scent of the Kent orchards, which are renowned for their fertility. The hop-fields, which for five centuries have produced the raw material for English beer, are invaded during the hop-picking season by thousands of Londoners, who are able to combine profitable employment with an open-air holiday; and throughout the year the rows of hop-poles and the oast-houses with their characteristic pointed roofs give the countryside its own particular stamp.

Kent and the neighbouring county of Sussex are lined with attractive beaches, and the nearness of London has led to the development of some of the best equipped seaside resorts in the country — places like Brighton, Eastbourne, Hastings, Folkestone, Ramsgate and Margate. But in between these large modern resorts there are still many picturesque old towns and busy little ports.

In this area too is one of England's great historical and architectural treasures — Canterbury Cathedral, towards which for centuries pilgrims wended their way along a route (the Pilgrims' Way) which can still be traced.

1. LONDON TO DOVER VIA CANTERBURY

This is the main road from London to the Continent, much of it now motorway (A 2, then M 2 to Canterbury). From Canterbury to Dover there is an alternative route which allows the visitor to see the extreme northern part of the county of Kent, the peninsula known as the Isle of Thanet.

The historic *Dover Road*, following the line of the Roman Watling Street, begins by running through the industrial districts on the south bank of the Thames. Starting from London Bridge, we follow Borough High St and turn left into Great Dover St, which runs into the Old Kent Road. At New Cross we turn left again into New Cross Road and continue east into Shooters Hill Road (A 207). At a roundabout Rochester Way (A 2) goes off on the right to bypass *Bexley* and **Dartford.**

16 miles: **Dartford** (pop. 46,000, E.C. Wednesday), situated on a navigable creek which is an outflow of the river Derwent. One of north Kent's oldest market towns, now an industrial centre. The first paper-mill in England was established here in the 16th century: there are now several paper-mills as well as engineering works and factories producing chemicals and pharmaceuticals. There is a tunnel under the Thames to Purfleet.

The *Dartford Borough Museum* in Market St contains material on local history, natural history and geology (open Mondays, Tuesdays, Thursdays and Fridays 1 to 5.30, Saturdays 9 to 5). Also of interest is *Holy Trinity Church* (13th-14th c., with an 11th c. Norman tower), in which is the tomb of *J. Spilman*, who brought the Carthusians to England (1607).

On the road to Northfleet (A 226) is *Stone*, with a 12th century church. Beyond Northfleet is *Gravesend*, on the south bank of the Thames, opposite Tilbury on the north bank.

A 2 skirts the south side of Gravesend.

28 miles: road on right to **Cobham**, a charming unspoiled village with quaint gabled roofs and the peaceful atmosphere of bygone days. It lies off the main road, at the end of a road

lined with trees. The town has associations with Dickens, and it was at the Leather Bottle inn here that Mr Tupman (in the "Pickwick Papers") contemplated suicide. On the other side of the road is the *church*, noted for its brasses. The almshouses behind the church were formerly the New College, built as living quarters for priests. *Cobham Hall*, set in a magnificent park of 700 acres, dates back to the reign of Queen Elizabeth. It is a typical red-brick Tudor building with imposing chimneys, all in beautiful proportion: in the interior there is an immense picture gallery, 125 feet long, with a marble Tudor mantelpiece. In the grounds is the Swiss chalet in which Dickens used to write, brought from the author's home at Gad's Hill, Higham.

Around Cobham. *Luddesdown.* With its peaceful church (interesting portrait of James Montacute, 1428, in the interior) and Luddesdown Court (Norman windows, minstrel gallery and a bear pit, etc.), it is worth a visit. *Sole Street:* Yeoman's House, 1 mile south-west, a typical high-halled Tudor house. Some Elizabethan additions were removed by Sir Herbert Baker, who restored the house and presented it to the National Trust in 1931. *Owletts*, at the junction of the road from Dartford and Sole St: a red-brick house of Charles II's reign, with five cottages and 25 acres of garden and orchard. There is a fine plaster ceiling over the main staircase, dated 1684. At *Cuxton* and *Halling*, to the east, the slopes of the North Downs have become the centre of the Kentish cement industry. Cuxton, mentioned in Domesday Book, was a Roman strongpoint. The Pilgrims' Way passes over the hill near the church. Halling, today a district of factories, was once renowned for its vineyards, which during Henry III's reign were known all over the country.

31½ miles: **Rochester** (pop. 56,000, E.C. Wednesday). The contiguous boroughs of Rochester, Chatham and Gillingham are so close to one another as to form a single town. They stand on the river Medway, a Kentish stream famous in England's maritime history. Strood, a residential suburb of Rochester on the left bank of the Medway, faces Rochester on the steep slope of Strood Hill.

Rochester

Rochester was a royal borough when the Normans built a castle on *Boley Hill*. The walls of this castle, 12 feet thick, are one of the finest existing examples of Norman military architecture. The Cathedral, also of Norman construction, has some of the oldest carved woodwork in England. In the reign of Edward III (1327-77) the building of a stone bridge of 11 arches was begun; it was completed in the reign of Richard II (1392). The present steel bridge, with three arches, dates from 1856.

The waterfront of Rochester is a few minutes' walk from the foot of Strood Hill along the narrow High St, and the best view of Rochester can be obtained from there. Flanking the esplanade are the ruins of the Norman castle, and behind, rising proudly from the trees surrounding it, stands the castle keep: beyond this again, to the left, can be seen the Cathedral, its squat spire dominating the buildings around it.

Rochester and the Medway are popular with sailing enthusiasts Lower down, however, the river is the scene of busy industrial activity, and the banks are lined with wharves, railway lines, repair yards and factories. Beyond this again are the Chatham dockyards, with higher ground behind them.

Over the bridge, the road enters Rochester High St.

The face of this street has changed little since the days of Dickens, who wrote of it: "The old High Street of Rochester is full of gables with old beams and timbers carved into strange faces. It is oddly furnished with a queer clock that projects over the pavement out of a grave, red-brick building, as if time carried on business and hung out his sign." This "queer clock" is still outside the *Corn Exchange*, which however is now a public hall. The *Bull Inn* is still there, well preserved and unaltered: it was an important coaching stage long before Dickens described it in "Pickwick Papers" and "Great Expectations" (the *Boar*). The *George* (formerly the George and Dragon) contains interesting cellars, although the exterior has been altered. At the *Crown* (entirely rebuilt in 1863) was the "inn yard at Rochester" of Shakespeare's "Henry IV", Part I. Opposite the ancient flint and stone archway of the *North Gate* is the *King's Head*, which still has some pleasant old panelled rooms. Opposite the Bull stands the *Guildhall* (1627), a handsome and well-proportioned building. The ceiling of the court room is by Grinling Gibbons. On the dome of the Guildhall

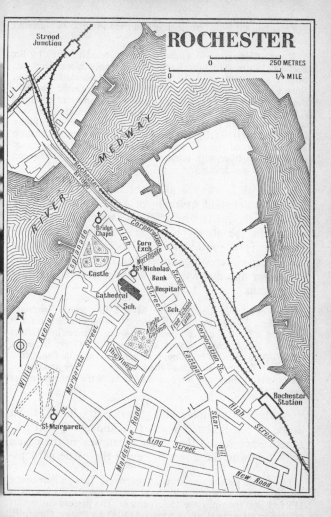

ROCHESTER

Strood
Junction

0   250 METRES

0   1/4 MILE

MEDWAY

Rochester Bridge

RIVER

Esplanade

Bridge
Chapel

high

Corporation

Corn
Exch.

Northgate

Castle

St Nicholas
Bank

Hospital

Cathedral

Sch.

Sch.

Street

Street

Avenue

Eagle
Alley Garden

Free School Lane

Corporation St.

N

The Vines

St Margaret's Street

Eastgate

Wills

Rochester
Station

St Margaret

King   Street

Maidstone Road

High

Star

Hill

Street

New Road

ι a magnificent gilded weathercock in the form of a two-masted sailing ship.

Watts' Charity, at 97 High St, was founded in 1579 by Sir Richard Watts, M.P. for Rochester. Farther along High St, on the same side, is the large red-brick *Mathematics School*, founded in 1701 by Joseph Williamson, M.P. David Garrick, the famous actor, was a pupil here in 1757. The present buildings (1840, 1882, 1893) stand on the site of the original school, which was built outside the town walls after the filling in of the moat. Nearby, in *Free School Lane*, is a corner bastion and a stretch of the old walls. There is another fragment of the walls, together with remains of a Roman wall, at the end of the narrow *Eagle Alley*.

A few yards away, still in the High St, is **Eastgate House,** a splendid example of late Tudor domestic architecture, erected in 1590 by Peter Buck, a paymaster in the Royal Navy at Chatham Dockyard. Eastgate House now serves as Rochester Museum; it houses an interesting collection of material about Rochester and district. One room is devoted entirely to Dickens.

The house was mentioned as Miss Twinkleton's Seminary for Young Ladies in "Edwin Drood", and the one on the opposite side of the road was Mr Sapsee's house in "Edwin Drood" and Uncle Pumblechook's home in "Great Expectations". The museum building, together with three half-timbered houses on the opposite side of the road, make a very fine group: the massive gables and three-tiered fronts of the houses project over High St.

At the top of Boley Hill stands *Satis House*, town house of Sir Richard Watts (see above): Queen Elizabeth once stayed there. By a gateway in the castle walls opposite the house we enter the castle gardens.

The **Castle Keep** stands directly before us. It is an immensely strong square structure with four corner towers; its height is 115 feet and the walls are 15 feet thick. The present castle was built soon after the Norman conquest (1080, by Bishop Gundulf), although it was not completed until 1126, when the Archbishop of Canterbury, William de Cortreuil, built the great tower. There is an excellent view from the tower.

In Maidstone Road is the Elizabethan *Restoration House*, in which Charles II spent the night in 1660 on his way back to London to reclaim the throne. On the other side of the street are the *Vines*, a pleasant garden and avenue of trees leading to *King's School*, founded by Bishop Justus in 604. The present buildings are modern.

The Cathedral. There are two main entrances to the precincts: *Prior's Gate*, which gives access to the south front of the cathedral, is very beautiful. The cathedral is an almost perfect example of early Norman architecture; it has for its ground plan a double cross, and closely resembles Canterbury Cathedral, having many similar features, including the double transepts, a choir higher than the nave, and an extensive crypt. It is really two churches one within the other, divided by the stone choir screen bearing the organ at the end of the nave. The nave served as the local parish church and the choir and presbytery were used by the Benedictine monks. The Norman w*est front*, with the magnificent **doorway,** is one of the finest in England. The whole building is notable for its sobriety of style.

According to the Venerable Bede, it was here that "King Ethelbert built the church of the holy Apostle Andrew." Little is known of the history of the church, except that it fell into ruin about 1075, when the last Saxon bishop, Siward, died. In 1076 Gundulf was ordained as bishop. It was he who built the White Tower in the Tower of London and Rochester Castle. He began to build the cathedral in 1080, probably with the tower whose ruins can still be seen. The walls and the massive piers at the west end of the nave and the two recesses at the west end of the crypt have survived all later restoration work. Part of the church was destroyed by fire, and in the late 12th and early 13th century Priors William de Hoo and Richard de Waldene carried out the first alterations. From this period date the crypt (except the recesses at the west end), the sanctuary,

the north and south transepts, the choir and part of the east
end of the nave. The reredoses in the north and south aisles
of the choir and the small doorway in the west front were added
in the mid 14th century.

In the **nave**, the style of the six arcades — that is, all except
the two most easterly bays — is Norman; the windows and
the clerestory are in Perpendicular style. An unusual feature
is the triforium which opens on to both the nave and aisles;
the arches are highly ornamented with diaper patterns. Directly
inside the small west door, marks on the floor indicate the
extent of the east end of the apse of the original Saxon church.

The style of the two **west transepts** is Early English; the north-
west transept was formerly the chapel and shrine of William
of Perth, a 12th century Scottish baker who as a pilgrim on
the **way** to Canterbury was murdered near Rochester. The
south-west transept contains the tomb of *Sir Richard Watts*,
and there is a brass plate to the memory of Charles Dickens;
in 1490 was added the Lady Chapel, in Perpendicular style.

The raised **choir** is Early English, On the modern stalls some
of the old misericord carvings have been retained. The pavement
also is modern but the tiles and designs are old, and the details
of the niches and capitals are curious. Very interesting is the
13th century wall painting of the *Wheel of Fortune* (opposite
the modern bishop's throne).

Beside the tomb of William of Perth is that of Bishop Walter
de Merton, founder of Merton College, Oxford. The *monument
of Bishop John de Sheppey* (14th c.) is also of great interest: it
was found during recent restoration work and has now been
placed on the east side of the transept between the choir and
the chapel. The stained glass windows in the south transept
of the choir commemorate Gen. Gordon. At the east end of
the choir is a stone coffin, believed to be that of *Bishop Gundulf*.

At the south-east corner of the ambulatory is a very beautiful
19th century doorway: the figures are copies from the original
doorway. Beyond this is the *Chapter House*, in which is housed
a very rich library.

The entrance to the **crypt**, one of the largest and finest in
England, is in the south aisle, beside St Edmund's Chapel.

Three of the original gateways into the cathedral precincts
still survive. The one nearest the west doorway leads into
High St. To the east, in the Deanery gardens, are the ruins

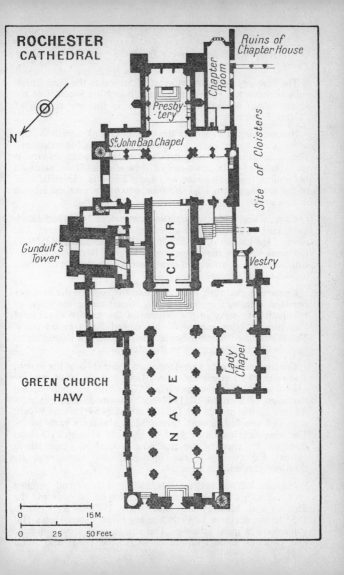

ROCHESTER
CATHEDRAL

N

Ruins of Chapter House

Chapter Room

Presbytery

St John Bap. Chapel

Site of Cloisters

CHOIR

Gundulf's Tower

Vestry

GREEN CHURCH HAW

NAVE

Lady Chapel

0   15 M.

0   25   50 Feet

of *St Andrew's Priory*, dating from the same period as the Cathedral.

The Hoo peninsula. North-east of Strood is the Hoo peninsula, between the Thames to the north and the Medway to the south, which is described by Dickens in the first chapter of "Great Expectations".

Beyond *Yantlet Creek* are the "Isle of Grain" and the village of the same name, swept by winds from the sea (oil refineries). Facing Southend, on the north side of the Thames estuary, is the village of Allhallows-on-Sea. Nearby is *Stoke*, with an old church (partly Norman and Early English). Splendid view of the marshes from *High Halstow*, one of the prettiest villages in this area.

Cliffe, a very old village, dates from before 742, when Ethelbald, king of Mercia, held an ecclesiastical council there. The nave of the church is 100 feet long, the chancel 50 feet. (Note the sand-glass in the pulpit). The village is now industrial, with limestone quarries and cement works which have destroyed its old-world atmosphere.

Upnor is a charming little village in the bend of the Medway opposite Chatham. *Upnor Castle*, built during the reign of Elizabeth I to serve in the defence of the royal dockyards of Chatham, is often mentioned by Samuel Pepys in his diary. The Whittington Stone indicates the boundary of fishing rights held by London fishermen in the Medway.

Cooling stands very near Upnor, in the middle of the marsh. The ruins of its *castle* are now a farm and the massive stone towers stand high over the village. The castle was built during the reign of Richard II (1377-99) by John de Cobham as a defence against pirates. In 1554 it was taken by Thomas Wyatt, who had rebelled against Queen Mary's alliance with Spain. The neighbouring churchyard is the one in which Dickens describes Pip meeting the escaped convict Abel Magwitch in "Great Expectations": the lozenge-shaped tombstones he mentions can still be seen.

Higham, halfway between Rochester and Gravesend, perched on a hill with a view over the surrounding countryside and the Thames and Medway marshes. Here Dickens lived (from 1857 to his death in 1870) in the big house called Gad's Hill Place (now a girls' school). The *church* is of great antiquity and contains some splendid carvings: the heads and floral designs on the church door, and the screen and pulpit in front of the 12th century Nun's Chapel are outstanding.

32½ miles: **Chatham** (pop. 41,000, E.C. Wednesday), a fortified town and naval dockyard and arsenal well placed on the Medway. The dockyards were once protected by the "Lines" (1758) but later separate forts were built both on the heights behind the town and on the Medway.

The royal dockyards were founded by Elizabeth I, although it is certain that King Alfred (871-901), founder of the British Navy, used the Medway when building his ships. The dockyards now extend more than 3 miles along the river and cover more than 500 acres. The installations include 3 huge basins joined by locks. There are 9 splendidly equipped dry docks, the larger of which can accommodate light cruiser class vessels, with building yards for all types of light naval craft and submarines. Many famous vessels, including the *Victory*, Nelson's flagship at Trafalgar, were built here.

36¾ miles: *Rainham*. Roman remains and pottery have been found in this area, particularly at Upchurch, 1½ miles north-east. In the hills to the south is *Hartlip*. St Michael's Church is 13th century, and contains 15th and 16th century brasses. On a path to the south of the village are the remains of a Roman villa.

38¼ miles: *Newington*, called Newstone or Newtown by the Saxons, on the site of a Roman station. Roman remains have been found in the surrounding area, and traces of fortifications can still be distinguished. St Mary's Church is Decorated, with some parts Early English; the tower is Perpendicular. In the interior are some interesting tombs.

The whole of this district is covered with hop-fields. When the hops are ripe some 40,000 Londoners emigrate to Kent for a hop-picking holiday. Each year they enjoy a festival, the

climax of which is the crowning of the Hop Queen. Characteristic features of the landscape are the "oast-houses", the kilns
for drying the hops. Their conical roofs and curious cowls
give a picturesque touch to the countryside.

2 miles north of Newington is *Lower Halstow*, on the river
Halstow, which has a charming church (St Mary's) with a
tiled roof and a squat Early English tower (Saxon and Norman
parts). Roman bricks in the external walls. A lead font was
discovered here in 1921.

40½ miles: road on left (A 249) to **Sheerness.**

3 miles: *Iwade*. The countryside here is embanked marshland
between the Swale narrows and Stangate Creek, but the
village stands on high ground. All Saints Church (13th c.) is
built in Kentish ragstone in the Perpendicular style. The road
crosses the Swale. 8 miles: short road on left to *Queenborough*
(pop. 3000, E.C. Wednesday). 10 miles: **Sheerness**, a fortified
town at the east end of the Isle of Sheppey, at the mouth of
the Thames, with large naval shipyards and docks. 3 miles
east is the small village of *Minster*, whose *church of SS. Mary
and Saxburga* is said to be the oldest abbey church in England
(founded in the 7th c. and later restored): some Saxon portions.

42¾ miles: **Sittingbourne** and *Milton Regis* (pop.
26,000, E.C. Wednesday), situated on Milton Creek,
which connects with the Swale. Brickfields. *St Michael's Church* was damaged by fire in 1750 but was
restored; it contains an octagonal font of 1400,
and an *Easter sepulchre* of 1500.

All this district has been inhabited since earliest times. Near
Grovehurst the site of a Neolithic village was found, and a
Neolithic boat, cut from an oak tree trunk, was excavated near
where the Creek joins the Swale. (See Rochester Museum; it
is now on view in the garden). After the departure of the Romans the towns in this area suffered from raids by Scandinavian
pirates. At the end of the 9th century a Danish chief named
Hoestan built a fortress (Castle Rough) on the Kemsley Downs,
which extend half a mile north of Murston church. King Alfred
also built a castle here; it was later used by the Normans, but
has now disappeared. The area south of the Swale is marshland,
a favourite haunt of wildfowl.

It is to the south of the Dover Road that Kent earns its title of the *Garden of England*. South of Sittingbourne lie the villages of Borden and Bredgar, surrounded by hopfields and orchards. *Borden* has a flint and brick church (SS. Peter and Paul), dating from Norman times; it has a massive Norman tower, square, with a dog-toothed arch. *Upchurch* is to the east. It was famous in Roman times for pottery works making a special bluish-black ware: many pieces have been excavated in the district. In the church, with a flint tower and shingled spire with an octagonal cap, are interesting carvings; the father of Sir Francis Drake is buried in the churchyard.

46 miles: *Teynham*, noted for its fruit and the beauty of its scenery. The cruciform church has several fine Early English lancet windows and contains four brasses, the most important of which, on the chancel floor, is that of William Palmer, Lord Teynham, and his wife.

To the south are the pleasant villages of Doddington, Eastling and Throwley. *Doddington* lies in a pretty valley. The church is mainly Norman; the Early English choir has a fine double lancet window (1290). Pleasant walks in the area. *Eastling*, on the road to Warren Street and Lenham, is also a good centre for walks in the surrounding woods and hills. St Mary's Church (Perpendicular); the yew in the churchyard is said to be over 1000 years old. The church of St Michael and All Saints at *Throwley* (Decorated) contains interesting tombs. The nearby mansion of *Belmont*, in a large wooded park, was built in 1770.

49½ miles: **Faversham** (pop. 15,000, E.C. Thursday). "The King's little town of Fafresham" received a charter from King Athelstan as early as 812. In 1147 King Stephen founded the abbey of St Saviour, and he, Queen Matilda and their son Eustace were buried there; their bones were afterwards transferred to the parish church of *St Mary of Charity*. This church, built on the site of a former church, is cruciform, and in Norman, Early English, Decorated and Perpendicular styles; in the crypt, Early English work;

in the interior ancient oak stalls, 14th century mural paintings and monuments. The fine half-timbered *Guildhall*, a rectangular building standing on 19 octagonal oak pillars, is Elizabethan.

1½ miles to the north lies *Faversham Without*, in the centre of the orchard district, chiefly cherries and hops. North and east of Faversham are interesting little villages, like *Graveney*, standing on high ground overlooking Seasalter Level and the Nagden Marshes, which stretch out to the Swale. In the village church of All Saints (Norman to Tudor styles) are brasses and mural monuments. A footpath leads through the orchards south to *Goodnestone*, lying amid the cornfields and orchards. The old church, in the Norman, Early English, Decorated and Perpendicular styles, has a wooden belfry. Farther east is *Hernhill*, with half-timbered cottages round a village green, amid wooded hills, orchards, hop-fields and cornfields. St Michael's Church (Perpendicular) has a carved oak pulpit and reredos, remains of an old rood-screen and a brass of 1667.

Boughton-under-Blean, 3½ miles south-east of Faversham, appears in Chaucer's "Canterbury Tales" as "Boghton under Blee". The Archbishops of Canterbury have been lords of the manor since the 10th century. The church of SS. Peter and Paul, with a Perpendicular tower, contains the alabaster tomb of Sir John Hawkins, the famous Elizabethan seaman and explorer, who played a major part in the defeat of the Armada. 4 miles south-east of Faversham is *Selling*, in a wooded area. St Mary's Church (Perpendicular) has a very fine 13th century stained glass window at the east end and a 16th century brass.

A 2 then runs through wooded country to **Canterbury,** 56 miles from London.

Canterbury

A town of 35,000 inhabitants (E.C. Thursday), during the Middle Ages a great pilgrimage centre and for many centuries the seat of the Primate of All England. Its Cathedral is one of the greatest architectural and historical treasures of England. The

peaceful town lies on the river Stour (which flows
through it) and is set within hills and gently undulating
farmland patterned with hop-fields, tree-lined lanes
and old-world hamlets.

The Roman town, *Durovernum*, which had been the British
village of Dwrwhern, became, owing to its position on the
military cross-roads from Lympne, Dover and Richborough,
an important station on the way to London. After the invasions
of the Jutes and Saxons it was named Cantwarabyrig ("stronghold of the men of Kent"), and in 560 Ethelbert, king of Kent,
made it his capital. In the year 587 Christianity sprang to life
again at Canterbury when Augustine with his forty monks from
Rome was welcomed by the king, whose wife, Bertha, was a
Frankish Christian princess. St Augustine dedicated a little
church on St Martin's Hill, upon the site of which Canterbury
Cathedral now stands; the king, who was baptised together
with a great number of his men, appointed Augustine Archbishop of all England. It was not until 1170, after the murder
of Thomas Becket, that the Archbishop of Canterbury was
recognised as the head of the English church. The subsequent
canonisation of Becket made the town the most frequented
centre of pilgrimage in England until the Reformation. Chaucer
in his "Canterbury Tales" immortalised these journeys.

The Dover Road continues through the town under
various names. Its first part is St Dunstan's St. On
the right stands *St Dunstan's Church;* it dates from
the 14th century and has two towers, one square and
the other semicircular. The head of St Thomas More
(who in 1535 was beheaded in the Tower of London)
is said to lie in the crypt, which contains the family
vaults of the Roper family; his daughter Margaret Roper placed it there. On the opposite side of the road
stands a brick archway, all that is left of the Roper
mansion.

The road continues, under the name of Westgate
Without, to the **West Gate,** the only gate still left of
the six that used to give access to the town, a fine

piece of 14th century building with massive twin towers.

In Broad St, east of the Cathedral, are remains of the old *town walls*. Just within the gate to the right is the *Church of the Holy Cross*, built by Archbishop Sudbury (1374-1381) at the same time as the gate; there are some interesting carved stalls and, in the chancel, an old panelled ceiling. The font is also very old. Farther along, on the left, is *St Peter's Church* (which now gives its name to the street), 13th century and of curious form, with some good stained glass.

Beyond the River Stour, by the old King's Bridge, we see on the left some quaint *Tudor half-timbered houses* with gables and lattice windows, once occupied by the Walloon and Huguenot refugee weavers who fled from the religious persecutions in France and the Netherlands at the time of the revocation of the Edict of Nantes (1685). Hand-weaving can be seen here much as it was practised in these actual buildings more than 400 years ago. Here is the beginning of the High St, and on the right is the ancient *Hospital of St Thomas*, built by Thomas Becket for poor pilgrims.

Canterbury *Museum* and *Public Library* (reading room) are housed in the Beaney Institute (1899), which stands on the left. The museum contains Roman, Saxon and other remains and geological specimens. The *Guildhall* (18th century) contains some interesting local portraits.

Mercery Lane, to the left (the way to the Cathedral), is named from the fact that here were once the shops and stalls and pedlars offering mementoes, crosses and images of the saint, etc., to pilgrims on their way to visit the shrine.

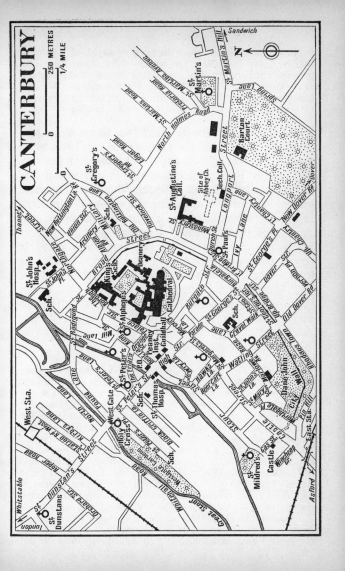

The *Chequers Inn*, in which the pilgrims stayed (cf. the "Canterbury Tales"), stood at the corner of this lane; traces can be seen in the courtyard of the present inn. In *Butter Market*, at the other end of Mercery Lane, is a statue of the Muse of lyric poetry, commemorating the Elizabethan poet and dramatist Christopher Marlowe, son of a Canterbury cobbler.

The Cathedral. The chief entrance to the monastery of Christ Church and the Cathedral is by *Christchurch Gateway;* it was built on the site of a Norman gateway in 1517 by Prior Goldstone and is a splendid late Perpendicular building. Within the gate a general impression of the whole cathedral, a splendid building in the Perpendicular style, can be best obtained; it is dominated by the beautiful **central tower,** but there are two towers on the west side and it has a double set of transepts. Its overall length is 515 feet, the length of the choir being 180 feet; the central tower is 235 feet high and the two west towers (that to the north-west is modern, having been built in 1834 to match the older south-west one) measure 150 feet; the height of the nave is 80 feet and that of the choir 70 feet; the nave and aisles are 70 feet wide.

Canterbury Cathedral reflects the whole architectural history of the 11th to the 15th century. It is the third church on the site. The original building is said to be that presented to St Augustine by King Ethelbert after his conversion to Christianity. St Augustine's church was burnt down by the Danes in the year 1011, and was later restored by Canute, the Danish king, whose church was also destroyed by fire. The oldest stones in the fabric of the cathedral as it is seen today belong to the church that was built by Lanfranc, first Norman Archbishop of Canterbury (1070-89), and they were brought from his native Caen. The choir was terminated in 1130 by Prior Conrad in exceedingly magnificent style, but this was destroyed during the fire of 1174; the present choir was completed by William the Englishman (1174-80) and the style shows the transition from Norman to Early English. It was not until 1421 that the present nave and transepts were added, replacing the old

Norman parts that had survived the fire; the central tower, the "Bell Harry Tower" (restored 1906), dates from 1495 (Prior Goldstone).

Canterbury Cathedral contained, for more than three centuries, the shrine of Archbishop Thomas Becket, who was murdered on 29 December 1170. His first resting place was in the crypt, and it was here that Henry II suffered his penitential scourging. Fifty years later Becket's body was placed in a golden shrine in the Trinity Chapel behind the high altar, where it remained until it was destroyed in 1538 during the Reformation.

The main entrance to the Cathedral is by the *south porch* (1400, Prior Chillenden). During the Reformation most of the statues were destroyed; those in the niches here, and also round the west front, are modern.

Nave. The graceful soaring lines of the columns carry the eye to the intricate vaulting of the roof and give a sense of light and majesty. This work was carried out by Prior Chillenden. The great west window is the only one which contains old stained glass.

Nave transepts. These too were built by Prior Chillenden, in the same style as the nave but with different details. Some of the masonry of the building erected by Lanfranc was retained (the walls and piers which support the central tower). The *Martyrdom Transept* was the one in which Thomas Becket was murdered: the four attackers followed the Archbishop, who had entered from the cloisters by the door on the west side (the same door is still to be seen) to attend Vespers which were then in progress. He refused to flee and was stabbed to death, falling to the ground in front of the wall between the chapel of St Benedict and the crypt entrance. (A mark in the stone indicates the probable spot, and the wall itself is part of the old building that has been left). The beautiful large window depicts Edward IV (1461-83) and his queen, who donated it; in another window are scenes from the life and the death of Becket. An open screen to the east leads to *Lady Chapel* (1499-68), or Deans' Chapel as it is called because of the number of tombs it contains; the fan-vaulting is very beautiful.

This chapel replaced the Norman chapel of St Benedict. To the south-west a similar chapel opens off the transept, St Michael's Chapel or the *Warriors' Chapel* (1370). In it is the tomb of *Archbishop Stephen Langton* (1207-29), who played a leading part in the struggle against King John. Between the nave and the choir is the magnificent 15th century rood-screen, with statues of six kings of England.

The **choir**, which is one of the longest in England, narrows towards the east end. The architect (William of Sens), not wishing to demolish the towers of St Andrew and St Anselm which had survived the 1174 fire, caused the walls to curve in slightly towards the end so that the new choir could incorporate the towers. The raised choir was a special feature of the work of this architect, repeated at Rochester and Chichester but rarely elsewhere. He is said to have used as his model for the choir that of the cathedral of Sens in France (1168), which also possesses this feature.

The simplicity and strength of the Norman arches, supported on piers which are alternately round and octagonal, are in striking contrast with the arches of the nave. The combination of rounded and pointed arches in the triforium, showing a transition between Norman and Gothic, is another link with Sens Cathedral. The altar, reredos and archbishop's throne are modern; the canons' stalls are attributed to *Grinling Gibbons*. The organ is concealed in the triforium, only the keyboard being visible. Prior Estria built in 1305 the magnificent screen wall which separates the choir from its lateral aisles; the tombs of the archbishops, covered by canopies, are in recesses in this wall. At the far end of the choir is the tomb of *Archbishop Chichele* (1414-43), founder, of All Souls College, Oxford, who blessed Henry V's army setting out for the Agincourt campaign and celebrated its victory in the Cathedral after their return. The stained glass, some of it 13th century, is very fine. The aisles and the north-east transept are largely the work of *Prior Conrad*, with later alterations by William of Sens.

In the *north-east transept*, the triforium windows are the work of Prior Ernulph; here is the tomb of Archbishop Tait (1811-22). At the east end of the north aisle is the door to *St Andrew's Tower*, a survival from the second church; the Decorated window was, however, added in 1335. In the chapel are the tombs of archbishops, restored in their brilliant mediaeval colours. At the east end of the south aisle is *St Anselm's Tower*, which corresponds to the Tower of St Andrew; here too in the chapel are the tombs of several of the archbishops: Anselm (died 1109), behind the altar, without a monument; Bradwardine (died 1319), and Meopham (died 1333), which form the chapel screen. The 12th century painting of *St Paul at Malta* was

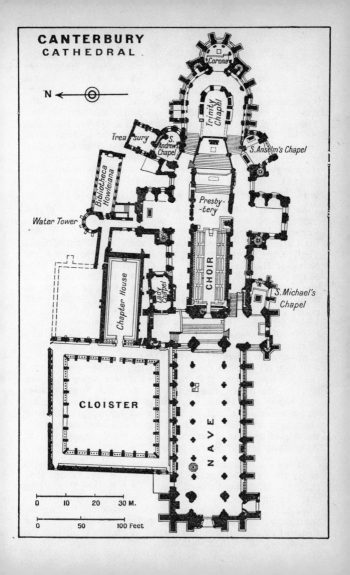

CANTERBURY
CATHEDRAL

N

Corona

Trinity Chapel

Treasury

S. Andrew's Chapel

S. Anselm's Chapel

Bibliotheca Howleiana

Water Tower

Presby-tery

Chapter House

Lady Chapel

CHOIR

S. Michael's Chapel

CLOISTER

N A V E

0   10   20   30 M.

0   50   100 Feet

discovered in 1890. Above this chapel is the *Watching Chamber*, or "excubitorium", from which the guardians of the treasure could, through the grating, obtain a view of the Trinity Chapel which once housed the shrine of Thomas Becket. Along the south aisle are the monuments of other archbishops — the unpopular Archbishop Sudbury (1375-81), beheaded by Wat Tyler in the Tower of London, Stratford (1333-69), Fitzwalter (1193-1207), Reynolds (1313-28) and many others. Near Archbishop Stratford's tomb are the remains of St Dunstan's shrine, formerly south of the high altar. Opposite the magnificent stained glass window in the south-east transept is the archbishop's throne, by *Grinling Gibbons* (1704).

The *Pilgrims' Steps* lead from the east ends of the choir aisles to the **Trinity Chapel** (which retains the name of the former chapel destroyed by fire) and to the **Corona** or Becket's Crown, both behind the high altar; they are the work of William the Englishman, who continued the work of William of Sens. The Trinity Chapel housed until the Reformation the magnificent Shrine of Thomas Becket. Henry VIII spared neither the body of the Archbishop, which was burned, nor the treasures, which were confiscated. The stained glass windows of this chapel depict Thomas Becket working miracles. Between the north pillars is the splendid *marble tomb of Henry IV*, the only King buried here (died 1413), and his second wife, Jeanne of Navarre. (Behind this monument in the north side aisle is the Chantry of Henry IV). Between the south piers of the chapel is the tomb of *Edward the Black Prince* (d. 1376), the redoubtable fighter who won his spurs at the battle of Crecy in 1346 and defeated the French again later at Poitiers. On the tomb reposes a brazen effigy of the prince, clad in heavy ornamented armour, chain mail hiding most of his face, and his gauntletted hands folded in prayer on his chest: above hang his helmet, shield, velvet surcoat, gauntlet and scabbard. Behind this monument, in the south side aisle, is the oldest tomb in the cathedral, that of Archbishop Hubert Walter (died 1205).

At the east extremity of the cathedral is the circular chapel called the "*Corona*" or *Becket's Crown* because at one time the head of Becket reposed in the altar there. Two tombs stand in the chapel: on the north side that of Cardinal Pole (died 1558), the last Roman Catholic archbishop, and on the south, the monument of Archbishop Temple (died 1902). The *Chair of St Augustine* stands here; it is on this chair that the archbishops sit at their installation.

Access to the **Crypt** is from the south-west transept. This is by far the oldest part of the Cathedral and if — as is believed — some of the pillars are not those of the original Roman building on this site, then certainly the east wall belonged to the church of St Augustine. It is chiefly, however, the work of Priors Ernulf and Conrad. The capitals are excellent examples of Norman stone sculpture: work on those that have not been completed was probably stopped owing to the fire of 1174. The 13th century column in the chapel of St Gabriel is interesting, as is also an old painting that has been brought to light. The splendid *Chantry of the Black Prince* occupies the south transept: this chapel, for the singing of mass for his soul, was endowed by the Black Prince on the occasion of his marriage in 1363 to his cousin; part of it was apportioned by Elizabeth I in 1575 to the French Huguenot and Flemish weaver refugees, and there is still a French Protestant chapel there.

From the central tower, the **Bell Harry Tower** (235 ft high, with 287 steps), there is a magnificent view over the surrounding countryside.

Cathedral precincts. There are remains of the Benedictine monastery founded by St Augustine and later re-established as a priory by Archbishop Lanfranc. The entrance to the **Cloister,** in late Perpendicular style, is from the north-west transept; between the arches are carved the arms of benefactors of the Cathedral. To the east of the Cloister is the *Chapter House*, begun in 1290 but only completed (particularly the upper part) in the early 15th century. Adjoining it is the *Library*, with a collection of Bibles, books and religious manuscripts. To the east is a round Norman baptistery, the *Water Tower* (12th c.). To the north-east is a lawn, round which the monastic buildings once stood: on its east side is the Deanery, on the north side the old guests' quarters. At the north-west corner is a Norman staircase leading up to *King's School*, founded in the 7th century and re-established by Henry VIII; at the north-east corner, near the Deanery, are the "Forrens"; at the south-west corner the Pentise. The ruins of the old monks' infirmary are at the east end of the Cathedral. Near here is the *Brick Walk*, on the right-hand side of which are early Norman arches. At the far end of Brick Walk is *Meister Omers*, an old house which formerly contained the great hall of the priory and lodgings for distinguished pilgrims.

In Palace St, to the north, is the *Archbishop's Palace* (1900); the present inconspicuous building is by no means so splendid as the magnificent palace after which the street is named and which was burnt out in the time of Laud. Following round the boundaries of the cathedral precincts into and along Burgate St, we reach Longport St, at the corner of which is the ancient **Monastery of St Augustine.**

In 1844 a missionary college was founded here in the beautifully restored buildings. When Thomas Becket was archbishop, this was the second largest Benedictine monastery in Europe, and excavations have revealed the foundations of a Saxon church, in the churchyard of which St Augustine, King Ethelbert and Queen Bertha were buried. The Norman *Abbey Church* ruins stand to the south of the court, and further to the east, in the park of the nearby hospital, are to be seen the bricks and tiles of the remains of the *Church of St Pancras*, the first church to be consecrated by St Augustine.

One of the most interesting sights in Canterbury is the old **Church of St Martin** (farther along Longport St), the first Christian church in England and one of the oldest in Europe, being erected during the Roman occupation in the 4th century, among the Roman villas which were numerous in this quarter.

It was much altered by a 13th century restoration, but there are still many Roman bricks to be seen in the walls. The choir is Early English and the nave Norman (at the south-east corner, note an interesting Norman piscina). The tower is 14th century. The sacristy and stained glass window are modern. Note the "squints" in the porch — narrow openings through which lepers could follow the service.

North of the cathedral are the *Royal Mint* and *St John's Hospital*, which Archbishop Lanfranc (1070-1089) founded. Near to the east station on the south-east of Canterbury are the *Dane John Gardens*, two sides of which are bounded by the moat (now dry) and the old town wall. The *Dane John* itself is an 80 foot high obelisk on a mound, from which there is a splendid view over the town. The obelisk was built to commemorate the opening of the gardens in 1790. In nearby *Castle Street* stands the massive Norman keep of the castle. *St Mildred's Church* stands in Stour St behind the castle: there are some Roman remains there. St Stephen's Church (Norman work) is adjacent. *St Margaret's Church* is in St Margaret's St near Mercery Lane and *St George's Church* further along down St George's St: both are worth a visit.

6 miles from Canterbury on the Sandwich road (A 257) is **Wingham,** one of the loveliest villages in Kent. The road approaches it by the Durlock Stream which follows it, passes under a bridge and flows into a millpond by the ancient mill. In the centre of the shady village is the church with its tall steeple and a series of chestnut pillars supporting the roof of the nave: traces of the first church (mentioned in Domesday Book) can be seen in the south wall of the chancel. The village street is very beautiful, with towering lime trees and chestnuts and 13th century buildings. — 10 miles: *Ash-next-Sandwich*, lying in the marshes, which is also mentioned in Domesday Book. The church of St Nicholas possesses a fine steeple which is a landmark for ships in the Downs: in the interior are the famous "procession of seven daughters" tombs. The windmill dates from the 18th century, and there are three old inns in the village. — 12 miles: *Sandwich* (p. 273).

Beyond Canterbury A 2 has no features of particular interest to offer. Rather more than half way towards Dover, to the left of the road, is the village of *Barfreston* (pronounced Barston), with a fine Norman church containing some of the best sculpture of the period. Outside the church is a yew tree, said to be over 1000 years old, in which the church bell is hung.

East of Barfreston is *Tilmanstone*, and between this and the main road is the village of *Eythorne*, with a church in which is one of the three lead fonts in Kent. Nearby is *Waldershare Park* (500 acres), with the seat of the Earl of Guilford: the park was laid out 250 years ago by Henry Furnese, first earl.

Shortly before Dover is **Ewell,** where King John had a meeting with the Papal legate before his abdication.

From Ewell A 256 runs north to Sandwich, 10 miles away.
5 miles: *Tilmanstone*, with one of Kent's coal-mines; there is
another at *Betteshanger*, 1 mile farther on. — 7 miles: *Fingles-
ham*. — 8 miles: **Eastry**. The fine 13th century *church* has a
Norman tower 63 feet high and an interesting interior. In front
of the altar is the tomb of *Thomas Nevyson*, with a recumbent
figure in armour (16th c.). Captain *John Harvey*, who served
under Nelson, is buried under an old oak in the churchyard.
Eastry Court stands close to Court Lodge, where Thomas Becket
often stayed and where he remained in hiding for a week in
1164 before crossing to France. In Woodnesborough Lane is
a magnificent labyrinth of caves with rock carvings, extending
for over 200 yards, of unknown origin. — Soon after this
A 256 runs into A 258 (Sandwich to Deal). — 10 miles: *Sandwich* (p. 273).

Canterbury to Dover by the Coast Road

Take A 290, which runs north-west from Canterbury.
9 miles: **Whitstable and Tankerton** (pop. 25,000, E.C.
Wednesday), a health resort with a bracing climate
and splendid views over the bay to the Isle of Sheppey
and the North Downs. There are sands flanked by a
shingle beach, good bathing facilities, a boating lake
and sailing.

St Augustine baptised more than 10,000 Saxons in the river
Swale on Christmas Day 597. The "Hundred of Witenstaple"
is mentioned in Domesday Book. The town used to be the
port for pilgrims to Canterbury. The original town, which by
1729 had become a fishing port for Canterbury, consisted of
the cottages and houses around the church of All Saints; the
harbour is still the picturesque centre of the town. Whitstable
oysters are renowned: the private oyster beds extend over
some 5000 acres.

All Saints' Church in Church St has some Saxon
work in the font and walls, but is mostly of the 15th
century. There is an old *Toll House*, and *Barn House*,
a 15th century manor, at the west end of the main
street where it becomes the Canterbury road. *Tankerton*

Tower is a 15th century castellated mansion where now the Council offices are housed, in beautifully kept grounds which were opened as a park on the Jubilee Day of King George V.

Tankerton is the newest part of the town, to the east, and is laid out on modern lines. Along the shore is the sea-front, with a grass promenade more than 1 mile long, bordered with grassy slopes leading down to the undercliff and the bathing cabins.

Around Whitstable. *Seasalter*, part of the old town of Whitstable; the shore by the meadows is a favourite camping site. — *Swalecliffe*, beyond Tankerton, is becoming a popular seaside resort owing to its bracing climate. The new railway station of Chesterfield serves this town. "Sivoleclippe" is mentioned in Domesday Book, when it was part of the possessions of the Bishop of Bayeux, Odo. Numerous interesting finds of bronze implements and fossilised remains of extinct animals have been made here. There is an old forge near the church of St John the Baptist (rebuilt 1875, founded very much earlier). — *Chestfield* (1 mile south-east) is an old-world village. The manor-house dates from the 12th century, and the *Tithe Barn* is at least 700 years old. The Golf Club occupies a house as old as the manor and can be said to be the oldest golf club house in the country. See also in this village the "*Shepherd's Cot*", "*Sparrer Court*", and the old oast-house. The pleasant Blean Woods lie near the town in beautiful hill country.

14 miles: **Herne Bay** (pop. 22,000, E.C. Thursday), a well-known seaside resort with a sunny, dry and bracing climate. The coast is flat with a background of wooded hills. Inland the country is hilly. The *pier* is the second longest in the British Isles; at the end of it there is fishing for bass, cod and a variety of flat fish. Rowing boats and motor boats can be hired for trips to Whitstable, Reculver and the mouth of the Thames. Good bathing facilities.

Around Herne Bay. *Reculver*, the site of a Roman fort *(Regulbium)*. The massive walls on the south and east sides are clearly to be seen, although much of the fort has been engulfed by the sea and the rest has still to be excavated. Excellent camping in the neighbourhood. — **Herne,** one of the most charming villages in this part of the country. In the parish church (St Martin's) the Te Deum was sung in English for the first time in Britain, when the living was held by Nicholas Ridley. The *Smuggler's Cottage* has an unusual window beside the fireplace giving a view of the coast of Herne Bay; a windmill adds a picturesque note. — *Fordwich* (5 miles): a peaceful village on the river Stour with a typical oast-house and a charming village church. The old ducking-stool on which scolds were immersed in the village pond can still be seen in the 15th century Town Hall. — *Wickhambreaux*, with a beautiful old mansion in which the "Fair Maid of Kent", who married the Black Prince, once lived. — *Grove Ferry* (5 miles), a well-known river angling centre. — A 299 runs through lavender fields, which are a magnificent sight during the flowering season.

21 miles: A 299 runs into A 28.

23 miles: *Birchington* (pop. 4000, E.C. Thursday), a seaside resort on the Thanet coast with broad sands, white cliffs, green swards and, nearby, a typically English countryside with cornfields, farms, lanes and cottages. The road follows the coast round two large bays, *St Mildred's Bay* and *West Bay*, flanked by low white cliffs. Pleasant walking along the seafront. Quex Park contains an astonishing collection of exotic curios and big game hunting trophies.

27 miles: **Margate** (pop. 48,000, E.C. Thursday). The borough of Margate is made up of five separate towns: Birchington, Westgate-on-Sea, Westbrook, Old Margate and Cliftonville. Nine miles of unbroken sands and every attraction for the thousands of visitors who flock there every summer.

The famous *Dreamland Amusement Park* is a permanent fun fair. There are three theatres and many cinemas, and during the season concert parties entertain in the pavilion and on the pier. **Cliftonville,** to the west, has a luxury swimming pool known as the Lido. The **Margate Grotto** consists of underground passages with symbols worked in shells on the 2000 square feet of walls: recent research on the passages and central chamber has advanced the theory that they form a Cretan tomb, probably 4000 years old. Excellent museum in the Public Library: rare prints depicting the history of many seaside places. *St John's Church* is a restored Norman building.

Broadstairs (pop. 20,000, E.C. Thursday), a quiet seaside resort with an extensive coastline of undulating chalk cliffs separated by seven sheltered bays. Along the whole foreshore are firm yellow sands.

The flint arch (*York Gate*, built as a defence against pirates and originally equipped with a heavy iron gate) in the Stairs — which are said to give the town its name — dates from 1540. Not far from the pier stands the famous chapel of *Our Lady of Bradstowe*, a shrine of St Mary, which according to some authorities dates from before 1070 since the first church of St Peter contained a model of it. The beautiful parish church *(St Peter's)* was built about 1070 and enlarged in 1184; the architectural style is Anglo-Norman and pointed. The tower is very old.

Broadstairs has many connections with Dickens, who completed many of his novels here, including the "Pickwick Papers", "Nicholas Nickleby", "Barnaby Rudge" and "The Old Curiosity Shop". The novel chiefly associated with the town is "David Copperfield". An annual Dickens Festival is organised by the Dickens Fellowship.

The picturesque village of **St Peter's** is a mile inland. It has a pretty 12th century *church* (16th c. tower). *Ranelagh Grove* is a park in which, 150 years ago, parties with dancing and music were held. The *Assembly Rooms* can also be seen, as well as other buildings with Gothic windows.

Ramsgate (5 miles on A 255, or a pleasant walk of 6 miles along the cliffs; pop. 40,000, E.C. Thursday), a popular seaside resort and seaport. The *Royal Harbour*, so named after George IV, who frequently came here, dominates the town's five mile coastline; it is a busy port whose picturesque quays and piers are crowded with yachts, motor cruisers, pleasure steamers and numerous small craft. The beach is of firm sand and bathing is excellent. The *Goodwin Sands* (10 mile long sandbanks which lie about 7 miles off the coast) can be visited by boat from the harbour. At low tide the Sands are firm, but when covered by water they constitute a menace to shipping, and despite being marked by lightships and the North Foreland Lighthouse several ships are lost every year. On the West Cliff is the Roman Catholic church of *St Augustine* (A. W. Pugin, 1848; it is regarded as one of his masterpieces).

5 miles west of Ramsgate, amid the meadows and gardens of the *Isle of Thanet*, is **Minster,** once a port, with ships sailing up to the very doors of the abbey. *Minster Abbey* was founded in 738 as a church for the nearby Benedictine monastery founded in 670 by King Egbert. It suffered so severely from a Danish plundering expedition in 840 that it was abandoned until 1028. The oldest part is the west wing, originally lit by rectangular openings which can still be seen. There is a 12th century vaulted passage. The ruined west tower dates from the first half of the 12th century; there was formerly a Norman chapel adjoining it. Mullioned windows (of which one still remains) were added in 1413, and the original roof was replaced by the present roof with king-posts. The upper storey was probably built in the 17th century, apart from the mullioned windows; the ornamentation dates from the 15th century restoration and the eastern part from the 19th century. There are remains of a *tithe barn* 325 feet long. The abbey is once again occupied by Benedictine monks. — *Minster church* is the mother church of Thanet. It has two towers, one Norman and the other Saxon. In the village is the oldest inhabited house in England. Nearby is a dyke built by the monks to provide protection from the sea. West of Minster is *Monkton*, where the old stocks can still be seen in front of the church.

From Ramsgate to Sandwich is 7 miles on A 256. 2½ miles: *Ebbsfleet*, the landing place of Hengist and Horsa, once a flourishing port. 4½ miles: *Rich-*

borough, a pleasant village, once — as *Rutupiae* on the River Wantsum — the gateway to Roman Britain, guarding the eastern extremity of the isle of Thanet, and used by the Romans for the landing of their legions. Here are to be seen *remains of Roman occupation* in Kent, among the finest in Britain: the ruins of the massive walls, a great defensive ditch 12 feet in width, 6 feet in depth and 100 feet long. In this district have been found relics of the everyday life of the Romans, many now housed in Richborough *Museum* — coins, thimbles, pins and needles, lamps, dice, hobnails, brooches, etc.

7 miles: **Sandwich** (pop. 46,000, E.C. Thursday). Now 2 miles from the sea but once an important port (dating from 665). It was the chief port for France and for pilgrims from the Continent visiting the shrine of Becket at Canterbury. Such was its importance and strength as a walled town that it was one of the oldest of the Cinque Ports; the Cinque Port emblems (a lion and a boat) are incorporated in the town seals and can be seen on many old buildings throughout the town.

The town is entered under the magnificent chequerboard-patterned walls of the *Tudor Tower*. This, with the *Barbican* (now the toll-gate to a bridge over the Stour) and *Fisher Gate*, is all that remains of the old town walls. From *Mill Wall* there is a fine view of the parish church *(St Clement's)*, with its Norman tower and interesting arcades. Among other notable buildings are the churches of *St Mary* in Strand St and *St Peter* in King St and Market St, both in the same style (restored). *St Thomas's Hospital* dates from 1392 and was restored in the 19th century. In Dover Road is *St Bartholomew's Hospital*, founded in the 12th century.

Strand St contains many houses of great interest. Manwood Court, the Weavers and the old Customs House in Upper Strand St are all worth a visit. From the Rope Walk a fine view can be had of the site of the monastery of the White Friars, which was founded in 1272; behind is the cattle market and the 16th century *Town Hall*, which has been recently restored. In the court room there can still be seen beautiful old oak panelling; note the sliding panels which used to conceal the jurymen from view when the court was in session. Also of interest are the *Guildhall* and the old *Dutch House* in King St and the Ferryway in Fisher St. From Mill Wall, near the remains of the old *Sandown Gate* and the site of the *King's Castle*, there is a good view of Roger Manwood's Grammar School.

From Sandwich to Dover is 14 miles on A 258.

1 mile: *Woodnesborough*, a picturesque village with many old half-timbered houses with Flemish gable ends in "the Street", which has borne this name since Roman times. On a hill stands *St Mary's Church*, with a wooden belfry on a square tower. The name of the village is said to be derived from a pagan temple to Woden which once stood on Fir Tree Hill.

3 miles: *Hacklinge* and the Lydden valley. 3½ miles: *Foulmead*. 4 miles: *Cottingtoncourt*.

5 miles: *Sholden*, where golfing visitors to the Royal Cinque Ports course can find accommodation. Part of the course lies within this parish, which has parish registers going back to 1591. There are a number of fine country houses in the area — Hill House, Sholden Lodge, Sholden Paddocks. Just north of Deal are the ruins of *Sandown Castle*, built by Henry VIII to defend the coast.

6 miles: **Deal** (pop. 27,000, E.C. Thursday) was one of the Cinque Ports. It is now a pleasant seaside resort noted for its golf courses. Deal Castle, now occupied by the Marquess of Reading, was built in the reign of Henry VIII for coastal defence, like Sandown and Walmer.

7 miles: *Walmer* (pop. 5500, E.3C. Thursday), which adjoins Deal on the south. Walmer Castle, the third of Henry VIII's coastal strongholds, has long been the residence of the Lord Warden of the Cinque Ports, a post held by the Duke of Wellington from 1830 until his death in the castle in 1852; his rooms, and others, are open to visitors. A more recent Warden was Sir Winston Churchill.

The old Roman road from Richborough to Dover runs inland from Deal and Walmer, going over higher ground with the famous Willow Woods. It passes near the village of *Sutton*, which has an old Norman church with a turret. *Northbourne* (2 miles west of Deal) stands on a hill in wooded surroundings. 14 miles: **Dover.**

Dover

Dover (pop. 38,500, E.C. Wednesday), the "gateway to the Continent", is situated in a small bay, on either side of which rise the famous "white cliffs of Dover". In addition to being an important port and naval base, it is a popular seaside resort, for its sheltered position gives it a mild and agreeable climate. The splendid pile of Dover Castle, which rises 400 feet above sea level, has been described as "the history of England in stone".

In Roman times *Dubrae* was of little importance except that it lay on the direct route to London. It became of greater consequence in the time of the Normans because it was directly opposite France. In 1216, during the reign of King John, Hubert de Burgh was able to resist a long siege laid by the French forces aiding the rebellious barons. In Tudor times Dover was the scene of the first successes against the Spanish Armada (1588). 60 years later it was taken by subterfuge by the Parliamentary forces. On his Restoration Charles II landed here. During the first world war Dover was the H.Q. of the Dover Patrol, organised to combat the German submarine menace. During the second world war it had a "front seat" in the battle of Britain and, eventually, in the invasion of occupied France by the Allies. It suffered heavy bombing by enemy aircraft and also lay for months under shellfire from German batteries behind Calais.

The Cinque Ports. Dover was the first of the Cinque Ports, which can claim to have been the birthplace of the British Navy. As early as Roman times the importance of guarding the narrow straits between England and the Continent was realised and a fleet was formed, based on ports commanding the coastline: *Rutupiae* (Richborough) and *Lemanis* (Studfall), *Regulbium* (Reculver), *Romelis* (Romney) and *Anderida* (Pevensey or Hastings). All these ports were connected by a system of fine highways; at Dover a lighthouse was built. Although the

Saxons were not a seafaring race, they maintained the Roman system, and Edward the Confessor, who established his capital at London and built Westminster Abbey, granted a royal charter to the Cinque Ports in recognition of their importance and the value of their services. William the Conqueror was not slow to recognise the strategic importance of the Cinque Ports in the defence of England and confirmed the royal charter of the Saxon King. The oldest document now extant is that granted by Edward I in 1278; by this date two other ports — called "ancient towns"-had been added by Richard I in 1190 to the original group. The Cinque Ports are to this day Dover, Hastings, Sandwich, Romney and Hythe and the additional "ancient towns" of Rye and Winchelsea. "Limbs" or "members" were certain other towns which were dependent upon these. The privileges accorded to the Cinque Ports were very valuable in those days: freedom from all customs, tolls and duties, and the right to administer justice independently of other courts in the kingdom. Matters of common interest were considered by a council which recognised no superior other than the king, his representative the Constable of Dover Castle and the Warden of the Cinque Ports. Except for Dover, where the port has been artificially maintained, the Cinque Ports have silted up and are of no naval significance, but they have preserved their traditions to the present day.

The *harbour* consists of the Commercial Harbour (80 acres, two docks: Granville and Wellington) and the Admiralty Harbour (nearly 700 acres), which is the best haven in the English Channel. Dover Marine Station and Ferry Berth is at the end of the Admiralty Pier (1550 yards long) on the west, and it is here that the cross-Channel steamers berth. The *Prince of Wales Pier* (1200 yards long), jutting out from below the castle, forms the east extremity. Nearly a mile from the shore to the south there is a breakwater about 1500 feet long, which forms the third side of the harbour: the entrances are approx. 700 feet wide. From the harbour the *Marine Parade* leads along the sea front. From here, along *Woolcomber St* (old church of St James) and up Castle Hill Road, the imposing

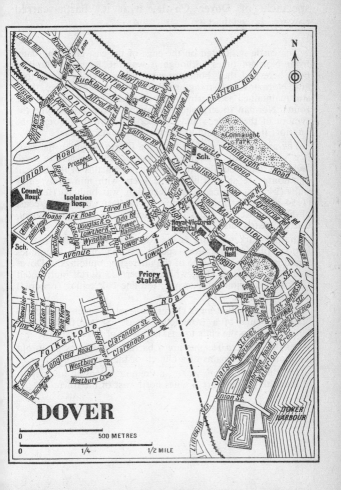

DOVER

spectacle of **Dover Castle,** with its battle-scarred towers, is reached.

The castle is situated on the edge of the east cliffs and dates from Norman times, although it was the Romans who first built here and their buildings were taken over by the Saxons and Normans and strengthened and restored by them. It is still maintained as a fortress and occupies some 35 acres. The round Norman tower, whose octagonal form has become the symbol of the castle, stands 50 feet high and is square in the interior: its origins date to the times of Julius Caesar.

The ancient church of **St Mary de Castro** stands to the east; it is an old Saxon building in which Roman bricks are used, and may date from the 7th century; the remains of the Roman lighthouse are still visible. The keep, with immensely thick walls (24 feet) and nearly 100 feet high, was built by Henry II (1154-89) and is now an armoury. In clear weather the coast of France, over 20 miles distant across the English Channel, can be clearly distinguished.

In the Market Square is the **Museum,** which contains collections of natural history specimens and of the antiquities found in the vicinity. One of the interesting buildings in Dover is the **Maison Dieu Hall,** which Hubert de Burgh built about 1215 as a hospital for pilgrims; the fine oak ceiling (restored) is very beautiful.

Beside Priory Station is Dover College, in which are incorporated remains of a Benedictine house, St Martin's Priory. Fine view from the cliffs to east and west of the town.

On the Western Heights are a barracks, the ruins of an old lighthouse and remains of a church of the Knights Templar.

The ruins of *Bradsole Abbey*, a Premonstratensian foundation of the 12th century, are 3 miles north-east of the town.

2. LONDON TO MAIDSTONE
AND FOLKESTONE

69 miles on A 20, with a section of motorway (A 20(M)) providing an alternative route past Maidstone (branching off the ordinary road just beyond Wrotham). Starting from London Bridge, we follow Borough High St and turn left into Great Dover St, which runs into the Old Kent Road. At New Cross we turn right into Lewisham Road, Lee High Road and the Eltham bypass (from which it is possible to reach the Rochester road, A 2, by way of Eltham High St and Bexley Road, to left) and continue along the Sidcup bypass, which takes us out of London.

11 miles: *Sidcup*. 12 miles: Foots Cray. 15 miles: *Swanley* (bypass). Very beautiful countryside: a landscape of soft hills patterned with rich orchards.

18 miles: **Farningham** (pop. 1600, E.C. Wednesday), an old village of pleasant houses on the banks of the river Darent at the point where it is crossed by the old London-Maidstone road.

Interesting archaeological investigations have been carried out in this area since the discovery of a **Roman villa** of the 1st century A.D. at *Eynsford* (1 mile south). 100 yards east of the river is the flint-and-stone **church of SS. Peter and Paul** (Perpendicular), with a 15th century tower. The east window has three lancets. Brasses and a 15th century font carved with representations of the seven sacraments. The church suffered damage during the second world war.

3 miles north of Farningham on the Dartford road (A 225) is the little town of **Sutton-at-Hone** (pop. 6500, E.C. Wednesday), in the middle of a rich fruit-growing district. The *church* is mainly Decorated, with a Jacobean pulpit and a Transitional piscina. The chief feature of interest is **St John's Jerusalem**, ¼ mile east of the village. The house, rebuilt in the late 17th century or early 18th century, was the home of Abraham Hill, one of the founders of the Royal Society, and later of Edward Hasted, historian of Kent. The building embodies the 13th century remains of a commandery of the Knights Hospitallers, the order established after the capture of Jerusalem in 1099

to protect pilgrims on their way to the Holy Land. The Priory Chapel dates from 1234. (The gardens and chapel are open to visitors on Wednesdays from 2.30 to 6.30).

From the south-east end of the village a road runs east to *Horton Kirby*, climbing steeply away from the river. The flint-and-stone village church, *St Mary's*, in Early English and later styles, contains 16th century brasses. There are a number of fine houses in the district, including *Franks Hall* (Elizabethan) and *Reynolds Place* (magnificent timber-work). At **Darenth** is the stone-built *St Margaret's Church*, one of the oldest churches in Kent (Saxon, Norman, Early English), with a wooden spire: tombs, stained glass and font, early 12th century. Near here was found a large Roman villa, with magnificent heating and bathing facilities, handsome pavements and fine decoration. Pottery, wall painting and coins from the Darenth villa are in Rochester Museum.

24 miles: **Wrotham** (pop. 1500, E.C. Wednesday), an agricultural village amid market gardens, hop-fields and orchards. *St George's Church* is mainly 13th to 15th century, with a tower under which is an unusual passage designed to allow the Sunday procession to pass without leaving consecrated ground. Fine 10th, 15th and 17th century brasses, 13th century font, 14th century choir screen.

Borough Green is contiguous with and forms part of the ecclesiastical parish of Wrotham. To the west is *Oldbury*, with one of the most impressive strongholds of prehistoric man in south-east England. To the south-east are *Platt*, amid hop-fields and orchards, *Mereworth Woods* (nearly 500 feet above sea-level) and the *Weald of Kent*, the centre of the region of hops and fruit. To the south is *Plaxtol*, whose church has a very fine hammerbeam roof and an exquisitely carved reredos. The village forge dates from the 15th century and the village is surrounded by mediaeval houses. *Old Soar Manor* (1½ miles east in the hilly wooded district between Ightham and Mere-worth) is a remarkably unspoilt example of part of a late 13th century knight's dwelling. It has an ancient chapel, is a National Trust property and is open to the public. (The adjoining farm, an early 18th century house in red brick, is not open to visitors).

Within 1¼ miles of Wrotham and Borough Green station is *Ightham Mote*, one of the best and most beautiful examples of a 14th century moated manor house in England. It is approached by a drawbridge through a lovely 15th century gateway; its chapel dates from the 16th century.

6 miles away on the Wrotham-Gravesend road (A 227) is **Meopham**, one of the show villages of the district, with a main street 4 miles long. The stone-built *church* has a very tall spire from which there are fine views of the surrounding countryside. The spacious interior contains some 15th century stained glass.

29 miles: *West Malling* (pop. 6000, E.C. Wednesday), a pleasant village in fruit-growing country. Ruins of a *Benedictine abbey* founded by Bishop Gundulf c. 1072. To the south is St Leonard's Tower, the keep of a castle built by Bishop Gundulf.

34 miles: **Maidstone** (pop. 65,000, E.C. Wednesday), the county town of Kent, situated on both banks of the Medway. Its industries are breweries, nursery gardens and paper-mills. In the 14th century Perpendicular *church of All Saints* are a number of carved stalls; adjoining is the *college of All Saints*, dissolved at the Reformation. A palace of the archbishops of Canterbury lies to the north; the outbuildings, with external staircase, are believed to be older even than the palace buildings. In Faith St is *Chillington Manor House*, a 16th century town house which now houses the Maidstone Museum and the Bentliff Art Gallery.

North of Maidstone, in the direction of Aylesford, is *Allington Castle*, surrounded by a moat and dating in its present form from the 13th century; it is now a religious house (open to visitors from 2 to 5). In *Aylesford* are a 15th century church (St Peter's) and a number of old houses. 1½ miles north-east is *Kit's Coty House*, a Neolithic burial chamber. To the east is the old Cistercian abbey of *Boxley*.

South of Maidstone is the village of *Loose*, in which is the *Woolhouse*, formerly used for the cleaning of wool (National

Trust property). Beyond this is *Boughton Place*, a 16th and 17th century mansion, with a magnificent park.

From Maidstone A 20 runs east, passing through the outlying district of *Bearsted*. To the south of the road is the village of *Otham*, in which is *Stoneacre*, a 15th century yeoman's house containing a varied collection of material, including Chinese porcelain (open on Wednesdays, Saturdays and Sundays in summer from 2.30 to 6).

A mile or two farther on, on the right of the road, is *Leeds Castle* (13th c.), in the middle of a lake. A 20 now runs along the foot of the North Downs, with the old *Pilgrims' Way* to Canterbury running parallel to it a short distance to the north. 47 miles: *Charing*, with a 15th century church and old houses.

In the hills to the north is *Otterden Place*, a 15th century manor-house, enlarged in the 18th century, in which experiments with electricity were carried out in 1729. To the north-east, on the Canterbury road (A 252), are *Chilham*, where there was a powerful Norman castle, and *Chartham*, with a very beautiful 14th century church.

53 miles: **Ashford** (pop. 32,000, E.C. Wednesday), an important railway junction and cattle market. *St Mary's Church* (15th c.) has a Perpendicular tower and contains some fine monuments.

To the north is *Godington Park*, a 17th century mansion with very beautiful gardens.

58 miles: *Smeeth*.   60 miles: *Sellinge*.   63 miles: A 20 turns left to bypass Hythe and Sandgate. 66 miles: *Newington*.

69 miles: **Folkestone** (pop. 45,000, E.C. Wednesday), a popular seaside resort situated on stately cliffs below the fine sweep of the North Downs. The port, recently

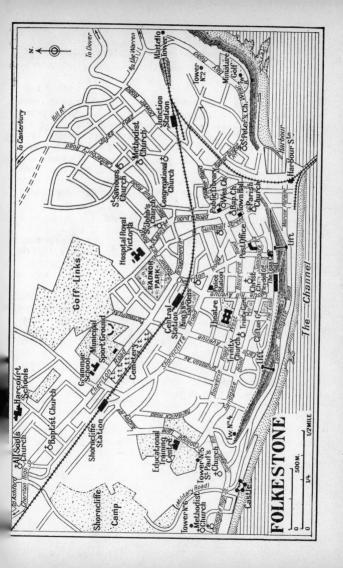

modernised, handles a busy passenger and cargo traffic. The movement of fishing boats gives a picturesque note to the old harbour.

Folkestone is a clean and attractive town whose charm was sensitively noted by Dickens. Among its chief attractions are the *Leas*, green lawns extending for more than a mile along the top of the cliffs and forming a pleasant promenade. Half way along is the *Leas Cliff Hall*, built into the cliffs: on a clear day the French coast can be seen from here. There are lifts down to the *Undercliff*, which offers more sheltered conditions for a walk when the wind is blowing off the sea. At the east end of the Leas is the *Road of Remembrance*, commemorating those who fell in the first world war.

The East Cliffs are on the east of the town. On this elevated tableland extending to the town boundary is the *East Cliff Pavilion*, conveniently situated for shelter and refreshments. Nearby is the first of the 74 *Martello Towers* built 1805-06 between Folkestone and Pevensey Bay as defences against an invasion by Napoleon. Some of the towers rendered service in the last war as anti-aircraft points. At the eastern end of East Cliff is the *Warren*, a wooded expanse between the cliffs and the sea formed of fallen rocks and earth. Along the foot of the cliff are sands with safe and pleasant bathing. There are also a bathing pool with purified sea-water, 165 feet by 75 feet, and — to the east — a motorboat pool and a games rotunda.

The *church of St Mary and St Eanswythe* dates from 1130, but has been altered and restored many times. It was built on the site of an even older church. William Harvey (1578-1637), who discovered the circulation of blood, was born in Folkestone, and there is a memorial to him on the Leas.

Folkestone is a "limb" of the Cinque Ports. An annual ceremony takes place in the narrow streets near the old harbour, when fishermen and boys and girls walk down in procession and the Bishop blesses the sea.

The *Museum*, on Grace Hill (open daily from 10 to 1 and 2.30 to 5.30), has material on the history and archaeology of the district, a scientific section and a few pictures.

3. FOLKESTONE TO HASTINGS

38 miles on A 259.

Adjoining Folkestone on the west is the little seaside resort of *Sandgate*, with remains of a castle built in the reign of Henry VIII.

5 miles: Hythe (pop. 11,000, E.C. Wednesday). Before its harbour silted up Hythe, now more than a mile from the sea, was one of the Cinque Ports. The town, mainly built along one main street parallel with the sea, is situated in a fine position at the foot of the cliffs at the east end of Rommey Marsh. The *church of St Leonard*, which is partly late Norman and partly Early English, stands on the hill above the town; the choir is raised like that of Canterbury Cathedral.

The surroundings of the town are very beautiful, with woods and lovely trees. The Royal Military Canal (23 miles from Sandgate to Rye and Cliffe End) was built in 1804-05 as the second line of defence to the Martello Towers to meet the threatened invasion by the troops Napoleon was collecting at Boulogne. Pleasant walks along its tree-lined banks, and opportunities for boating and fishing.

Saltwood (1 mile north): a small village with the ruins of a castle (13th-14th c.) which formerly belonged to the Archbishop of Canterbury. *West Hythe*, with the Roman camp of Stutfall Castle. *Lympne* (2 miles west): airport flying services to the Continent; the Roman station of *Portus Lemanis;* castle.

Hythe is the terminus of the smallest railway in the world, the Romney, Hythe and Dymchurch Light Railway (see below under New Romney).

8 miles: Dymchurch (pop. 1500, E.C. Wednesday), a seaside resort with a beautiful sandy beach. The town is a curious mixture of old half-timbered houses and modern bungalows. The *church of SS. Peter and Paul* is Norman (two doorways with zigzag moulding; high choir vaulting with some of the original herringbone tiles). Opposite the church is the historic *Court House*, named the New House in the 16th century when an earlier building was burned down; it now houses the town records.

Romney Marsh. The area in the south corner of Kent between the Royal Military Canal (immediately behind which is the range of hills once reached by the coastline) and the present seashore is called Romney Marsh, although it consists of three marshes proper — Romney, Wallend and Denge Marshes, making some 30,000 acres within borders 18 miles in length and 10 miles in breadth. All this was once a bay of the sea, and Julius Caesar sailed up the estuary of a river as far as Lympne. The estuary silted up and sandbanks appeared, and by Saxon times considerable extents of land were above the high water level; skilful irrigation and damming reclaimed further tracts of land. The Saxons began to settle here towards the end of the 6th century (the name Romney comes from the Saxon *ruimnea*, "marsh"). Later centuries have created the expanses of lush grass which provide pasturage for the renowned sheep of Romney Marsh.

St Mary's Bay, between Dymchurch and New Romney, is a seaside resort.

St Mary in the Marsh lies a mile or two inland. It consists of little more than a Norman church and an inn. The church was built on the site of an earlier Saxon building and was enlarged in 1250 in Early English style (the stalls and double piscina date from this period). Interesting brasses; Elizabethan pyx (1578). The graceful tower has interesting features in the lower part and a peal of three pre-Reformation bells.

14 miles: **New Romney** (pop. 2600, E.C. Wednesday), one of the Cinque Ports but now some distance from the sea. *Littlestone on Sea*, 1 mile away, is a seaside resort, with a beautiful church rebuilt in the 14th century.

New Romney is the headquarters of the *Romney, Hythe and Dymchurch Light Railway*, which runs between Hythe and Dungeness, calling at Dymchurch, St Mary's Bay, Greatstone and Maddieson's Camp. The miniature trains, drawn by small-scale locomotives on tracks about 1 foot in gauge, reach a speed of 30 m.p.h. The carriages seat two people side by side; in summer open carriages are used.

New Romney to Lydd and Dungeness: 7 miles on B 2075.

3 miles: **Lydd** (pop. 4500, E.C. Wednesday), the most southerly town in Kent. Its great 13th century *All Saints Church* is known, by reason of its size, as the *Cathedral of the Marsh*. The tower, 132 feet high, was built by Cardinal Wolsey, once rector here. In the north-west corner of the nave are some traces of the original Saxon walls. The 13th century arcade of seven arches supports some beautiful old roof beams with king-posts and carved spandrels. There are some old brasses. During the second world war a bomb landed on the choir, and further damage was caused by flying bombs. The *Town Hall* contains some interesting relics of the past — a 14th century charter, old sheep branding irons, an Elizabethan silver mace. Airport flying services to the Continent.

6 miles: **Dungeness,** the southern terminus of the Light Railway. Little to be seen here except miles of barren shingle along the seashore. For botanists and ornithologists, however, there are many attractions. The Royal Society for the Protection for Birds has created a bird sanctuary along the seashore, and it has become the nesting ground for countless gulls, terns and curlews, and is one of the few breeding grounds left of the Kentish plover.

The *Dungeness Lighthouse* (1904) dominates the landscape: its modern revolving incandescent paraffin lamp, the first of this kind in the world, emits a flash every 10 seconds and is visible for 21 miles out to sea. Large *nuclear power station*. During the second world war Dungeness was the scene of "Operation Pluto" (pipe line under the ocean) whereby 600 miles of pipeline laid across the Channel to the Calais area supplied more than a million gallons of petrol daily for the invasion forces.

14 miles: **Old Romney,** once a flourishing port but now, since the silting up of the old harbour, no more than a village.

Of the Saxon church which once stood here no trace remains, but the Norman *St Clement's Church* (with a tower and south porch of the 14th c.) has a font of Purbeck marble (1300) with beautiful carved capitals and a roof supported by curious beams.

16 miles: *Brenzett*. The parish church *(St Eanswyth's)* is largely Gothic, with a curious belfry.

17 miles: *Brookland*, an attractive and unspoilt village with many old tile-hung houses and old weathered roofs of Kentish weatherboarding. A very interesting *church*, with an octagonal wooden belfry.

20 miles: border between Kent and East Sussex.

26 miles: **Rye** (pop. 4,400, E.C.Tuesday), a quaint and quiet old town on the estuary of the river Rother, crowning the summit of a hill.

Before the Romans came to Britain there was a route running inland here for the transport of ore from the Sussex iron mines, and the Romans themselves used this road and built five large forts to defend it. In the 6th century this part of the country was surrounded by the Saxon conquerors of the forest of Anderida. In 1278 Rye and Winchelsea received their charters as "ancient towns" to be added to the Cinque Ports. In 1289 the town was created a royal borough.

In the 14th century, as a result of rivalry between Rye and Winchelsea on the one hand and the French on the other, Rye was sacked and burned down. In the 16th century it was ravaged by plague. Many French Huguenots settled here after the massacre of St Bartholomew, bringing their craft of weaving with them, and French names are still found among the old local families. During the second world war Rye suffered severely from air raids and flying bombs.

Remains of the old town wall can be seen in Cinque Ports St, with the town ditch on its outer side. The *Landgate* consists of two massive round towers over 40 feet high; it was part of the town wall, housing the machinery for the drawbridge over the moat. At the end of Cinque Ports St, to the right, is *Conduit Hill*, at the foot of which was a postern gate. Going along Conduit Hill and its continuation East St, we come to the **Old Flushing Inn**, which has been a hotel since the 18th century; the building itself dates from the 13th century. From here we go down **to the** cliffs, which formerly offered good landing places for smugglers. The **Ypres Tower,** damaged during the second world war, was built in the 12th century as one of the defences against the pillaging expeditions of the French: its walls are 4 feet thick and each tower is 40 feet high. It now houses a local museum.

Nearby, where once the alarm or watch bell stood, is *Watch-bell St*, cobbled, with houses of great antiquity. From the end of the street there is a magnificent view over the surrounding district. **St Mary's Church,** near the Ypres Tower, was built in 1120. The tower contains the oldest working clock with its original works in England (1561); the gilded oak *Quarter Boys*, 4 feet high, who strike the quarter hour, stand above the clock face. The belfry houses eight bells (1775).

In Lion St is the old *Grammar School* described by Thackeray in his uncompleted novel "Denis Duval". It was built in 1636 by Thomas Peacocke and is a splendid brick-fronted building of that time: the modern Grammar School has been transferred to Grove Lane and the building is now a club. Opposite is the 300 years old *George Hotel* with its beautiful banqueting hall and musicians' gallery: its Georgian front was added later.

The *Augustine Friary* was built in 1379. In the 16th century it provided shelter for the Huguenot refugees. Originally it was 70 feet long by 27 feet wide.

Mermaid St, famous among artists and lovers of the picturesque, remains unchanged with its cobbles, after a long history. The *Oak House* dates from the 15th century but contains many of the oak beams of the original 13th century house: there are fine frescoes and carvings. *Jeake's House*, opposite (1689), was built by the astronomer Samuel Jeake, who lived in the former building long before it was used as a hospital. The *Robin Inn* contains many oak beams and a fine timber and straw-plastered bedroom. The *Mermaid Inn* was damaged during the second world war but has been restored: it was built in the early 15th century and was a resort of smugglers and highwaymen.

The narrow lane known as the **Needles,** lined by closely huddled houses with overhanging upper storeys, is a characteristic feature of old Rye. It is paved with old gravestones, laid because the inhabitants complained of the poor quality of the footway.

A 259 now crosses *Tillingham Lock*. To the left
a mill (modern), on the site of an old gibbet. Then
on the right is a Martello tower, which formerly had
a moat and a drawbridge.

Beyond this, on the left, are the ruins of *Camber
Castle*. This was one of the five coastal fortresses
built by Henry VIII, erected in 1538 on the site of
an earlier blockhouse. Its five semicircular towers
and curtains can still be seen. From this point there
are magnificent views of Rye to the rear and Winchelsea ahead.

28 miles: **Winchelsea** (pop. 750, E.C. Wednesday).
The present town dates from 1292, when, after the
older Winchelsea had been engulfed by the sea,
Edward I laid out 800 plots on the hill of Iham—
an example of town planning without contemporary
parallel in England.

The majestic gateway to the town, the *Strand Gate*, wide
enough only for single line traffic, is a relic of mediaeval days.
Just inside the gate is the *Lookout*, affording splendid views
over the beach below, the sea walls, the unplanned array of
houses, bungalows and chalets in the new town, and right along
the coast and out over the Channel. The cottage near the gate
was once occupied by the famous actress Ellen Terry (d. 1928).
The Duke of Wellington also stayed here. The main structure
of the old *Court Hall* dates in part from the 13th century (restored). For many centuries courts were held here, and there
was a prison on the ground floor; the building is now a museum.

St Thomas's Church dates from 1290. The original plan was
cruciform, with a central tower, but today only the chancel
and two chapels can be seen. In the south aisle are two 14th century memorials, and the Alard Chantry contains a piscina and
sedilia. In the churchyard are some quaint epitaphs.

The **Greyfriars monastery** was built around 1300, and the
monks were dispersed at the Reformation. The present building
(1819) was used by Thackeray as the setting of "Denis Duval".
Of the old monastery there remains only St Mary's Chapel,

with picturesque ivy-clad arches and lancet windows. See also the *Pipewell Gate* (restored and much altered) and the New Gate, on the old town boundary ½ mile from the present town.

30 miles: **Icklesham.** *All Saints Church* is built on an unusual plan, with the tower on the north side. The nave, north chapel, south aisle and tower are early 12th century. St Nicholas's Chapel was rebuilt in the 14th century; in the south aisle are three Norman windows. To the south of Icklesham is *Pett*, and beyond this the Marsham valley and *Fairlight*, in a beautiful setting on cliffs standing 300 feet above the sea; from the church there are fine views of the surrounding countryside.

34 miles: *Guestling Green. St Lawrence's Church*, built in sandstone, is early 11th century; the north aisle and the crenellated tower date from around 1100 and *St John's Chapel* from the late 12th century. *St Mary's Chapel* (14th c.) and the "squint" between the chapel and the choir are interesting. In the choir are a 13th century piscina and two stalls of the same period.

36 miles: *Ore*, an old village, now part of Hastings, which forms a green and wooded approach to the town.

38 miles: **Hastings** (p. 301).

4. LONDON TO TUNBRIDGE WALLS AND HASTINGS

64 miles on A 21. Leave London by the Old Kent Road and Lewisham Way. Then turn right into Lewisham High St, which leads through Catford and out of London.

The Sussex Coast

Fine cliffs, backed by the noble line of the rolling downs and looking across wide stretches of golden sands to the coast of France — this is the aspect of the Sussex coast which makes a journey there a memorable experience. This exciting stretch of coastline has the added attraction of being dotted by ancient and historic towns of great charm and some of the finest holiday resorts of Britain.

Picturesque *Rye* has narrow winding streets which look like illustrations to a fairy tale. *Hastings* is the westernmost of the Cinque Ports and, with the contiguous St Leonards, one of the most popular of holiday centres on the south coast. Within the immediate neighbourhood are the castles of *Herstmonceux*, *Pevensey*, *Bodiam* and *Battle Abbey*. Bexhill and Eastbourne, farther to the west, are two well-known holiday centres. *Bexhill* has two good golf courses and an ancient church dating back to 1070, in which there is an interesting 13th century stained glass window. *Eastbourne* lies at the foot of the east end of the South Downs, those rolling sweeping turf-covered hills that give this part of Sussex a character and a charm all its own. Among features of interest in the neighbourhood are the *Long Man of Wilmington*, a figure of unknown origin cut out by removing the turf from the face of the chalk downs, and *Beachy Head*, a magnificent headland which falls a sheer 575 feet into the sea below. **Brighton,** the prince of seaside resorts, has a double appeal; it combines a joyous carefree holiday atmosphere with the elegant grace of the Regency style. *Littlehampton*, situated at the mouth of the River Arun, is a sea-bathing and golfing resort, from which may be visited *Arundel Castle*, the historic and imposing home of the Dukes of Norfolk. Other expeditions which may be made from Littlehampton include Goodwood, where the most picturesque race meeting of the year is held, and *Chichester*, a cathedral city which contains traces of Roman, Saxon and Norman origins.

Bognor owes its cognomen *Regis* to King George V, who convalesced there after a serious illness in 1929.

10 miles: **Bromley** (pop. 90,000, E.C. Wednesday), a pleasant well laid out garden city and dormitory town of London, situated on the Ravensbourne. Its name comes from *bromleag* (broom). On the main road, to the left, is a handsome 17th century house with wrought-iron railings bearing the date 1666: this is *Bromley College*, founded by the Bishop of Rochester to provide a home for forty widows of Church of England clergymen. The Gothic chapel was rebuilt in the 19th century. *Bromley Palace*, one of the official residences of the Bishops of Rochester, still stands in a superb park planted with elms and limes. The *church of SS. Peter and Paul* was destroyed during an air raid on London on 16 April 1941, leaving only the 14th century tower still standing. In the churchyard is the grave of Dr Johnson's wife; the Latin inscription composed by her husband, which was in one of the aisles in the church, escaped destruction. The original church was 13th century. The author H.G. Wells lived for some time in Bromley.

Around Bromley. *Hayes Place*, home of the Earl of Chatham and his son William Pitt, was demolished to make place for a later house, but the old oak-tree in the grounds of Holwood, near Keston, under which Wilberforce discussed his anti-slavery campaign with the younger Pitt is still to be seen. *Hayes parish church* is Early English (stained glass, brasses, monuments). At Warbank, Keston, are the remains of a Roman temple and an ancient cemetery. *"Caesar's Spring"*, also known as the "Roman bath", is the source of the Ravensbourne, which forms a chain of charming little lakes on Keston Common. At *Chislehurst*, north of Bromley via Sundridge, is Camden Place, a 16th century mansion in which the deposed French Emperor Napoleon III stayed after 1870. On Chislehurst Common is a large stone cross commemorating the Prince Imperial, Napoleon's son, who was killed in Zululand in 1879. The remains of the Emperor and the Prince Imperial were transferred in 1888 to a church at Farnborough built for the purpose by ex-Empress Eugénie. St Nicholas's Church is mainly Perpendicular, but the north side and the font are Early English; interesting epitaphs.

14 miles: **Farnborough.** 2 miles north on A 223 is *Orpington* (Perpendicular church with interesting brasses). 1 mile beyond this is *St Mary's Cray* (Early English church with a shingle spire).

22 miles: *Riverhead.* The road is more or less on the line of the old prehistoric track known as the Hard Way, which later became the *Pilgrims' Way* followed by pilgrims travelling from Southampton and Winchester to Canterbury.

26 miles: **Sevenoaks** (pop. 8500, E.C. Wednesday), picturesquely situated on a hill. The church (Perpendicular) contains several tombs of interest. The Grammar School was founded in 1432. At the Tonbridge end of the town is **Knole House,** former seat of the Sackville family and one of the largest private houses in England (open to visitors 10 to 12 and 2 to 5, except Sundays, Mondays and Tuesdays).

Begun by Thomas Bourchier, Archbishop of Canterbury, in 1456 and greatly extended in 1603 by Thomas Sackville, 1st Earl of Dorset. The *State Rooms* contain a large number of historic pictures, rare furniture (e.g. the Knole Settee) rugs and tapestries, dating from the early 17th century to the late 18th century. The Venetian Ambassador's Room, the King's Room (containing the Charles II silver furniture and state bed), the Reynolds Room, the Ball Room, the Cartoon, Brown and other galleries, are among the best-known state rooms of England. Knole House is built of Kentish ragstone, rough though silvery; its roofs are of reddish-brown tiles, giving the house a rather sombre aspect.

The **Garden** covers about 26 acres and is wholly enclosed within a high wall of Kentish ragstone. It is pierced at intervals by fine wrought-iron gates of the time of William III. The lawns and vistas can be seen from the house: the plan has not changed since the 17th century. The Park of 1000 acres is open freely to the public every day of the year. The main entrance is opposite St Nicholas's Church in Sevenoaks.

The road runs down a steep hill into a valley (rifle range) which is the dry bed of a former tributary of the Darenth. On the other side is *Icehouse Hill;* the mound containing the icehouse can be seen (on right) from the path which runs up the hill. As we emerge from the wood we have on the left, looking towards Knole, *Echo Hill.* Below, in the valley, is the *Duchess's Walk,* a long avenue of oak-trees. From the hill opposite (cricket field) there is an impressive general view of Knole House. The park also contains kitchen gardens, an aviary, decorative 18th century ruins and a wide avenue leading up to the lookout point known as the *Masthead,* with fine views over the Weald towards Tonbridge.

3 miles north of Sevenoaks on A 225 is **Ortford** (pop. 2200, E.C. Wednesday). 2000 years ago the whole of this area was settled by the Romans, and the ruins of many villas have been excavated; frescoes from one villa are in the British Museum. Roman cemeteries have been discovered on the Pilgrims' Way, which was originally a Roman road.

In the Middle Ages, standing as it did on the Pilgrims' Way, it was of considerable importance. Today it is a quiet and peaceful village of great charm with many houses and cottages displaying mediaeval features and containing massive oak timber-work. All that remains today of the *Palace of the Archbishops of Canterbury* is a ruined tower, gallery and gatehouse of the brick and stone-dressed Tudor palace of Archbishop Warham, but it once rivalled Hampton Court Palace in splendour and was occupied by Henry VIII before he moved to Knole. The *Bull Inn,* one of the oldest hostelries in Kent, owes its name to the Papal Bull authorising such houses to provide accommodation for travellers; it contains a well-panelled room and three beautiful Tudor fireplaces removed from the palace. In the charming 16th century *presbytery* are a beautiful reredos, old oak beams and two Tudor mantelpieces, one of which was discovered buried in the garden. The kitchens date from the time of Richard II (1377-99). **St Bartholomew's Church,** of Kentish ragstone, stands on the site of an earlier Saxon church. The massive tower is Norman; the main structure and most of the windows are 14th and 15th century; the wooden west porch dates from 1637; the south porch is modern. The church contains a 13th century font and interesting tombs and monuments. In the village are a number of charming old houses — Mill House, Bridge Cottage, Forge House, Pickmoss, etc.

33 miles: **Tonbridge** (pop. 28,000, E.C. Wednesday), a pleasant town (important railway junction and goods yards) on the Medway. Beautiful scenery on the banks of the river and along the Tonbridge-Maidstone road. The town was formerly a staging point on the old coach road. The *Angel* and the *Rose and Crown* are old coaching inns. Behind the Angel is a park, formerly Kent's county cricket ground, which was damaged during the second world war.

Tonbridge Castle was built by Richard de Tonebridge shortly after the Norman Conquest to guard the road from London to the coast and command the Medway, on the mound where it can be seen today. The entrance tower is one of the best examples of Norman castle architecture in existence. It was many times besieged. In 1793 the handsome stone residence adjoining the Castle was added (today the Council Offices). Of the castle only the magnificent gateway and part of the massive bulk of the outer wall and inner curtain remain. At the main entrance is a row of picturesque 15th and 16th century houses, now occupied by shops, some of them with curious overhanging gables and half-timbered fronts *(Chequers Inn)*. *Port Reeve House* in East St was formerly a tollhouse. Its squat shape and overhanging front are typical of the 15th century; it was badly damaged by a flying bomb during the last war but has been restored.

Tonbridge School, one of the great English educational institutions, was founded in 1553; the present buildings are modern. *Ferox Hall*, in the oldest part of the town, has a Georgian front but preserves parts of the original Tudor house; it is set in very attractive gardens. The *church of SS. Peter and Paul* is 12th century; the oldest parts are in the choir, the nave, the aisles and the porch.

Around Tonbridge. To the west is *Leigh*, with picturesque cottages, an old church and Hall Place, an old country house. To the south-west is *Penshurst*, a delightful old-world village which was the birthplace of William Penn, founder of Pennsylvania. The nearby **Penshurst Place** is a very beautiful old house, partly 14th century, belonging to Lord de Lisle and Dudley, a descendant of Sir Philip Sidney. Fine *picture gallery* with family portraits. Impressive state apartments and 14th century *Baron's Hall*.

West of Penshurst is the neo-Gothic mansion of *Chiddingstone* (early 19th c.), with Egyptian antiquities, 16th and 17th century pictures and old furniture.

Farther west is **Hever Castle** (13th-15th c.), once occupied by Anne Boleyn (open daily 2 to 7), with paintings by *Holbein*, *Jean* and *François Clouet*, *Antonio Moro*, *Titian*, *Cranach* and other artists. Magnificent Italian-style gardens.

TONBRIDGE TO LEWES.

27 miles on A 26.

5 miles: **Tunbridge Wells** (37 miles from London; pop. 42,500, E.C. Wednesday). Royal Tunbridge Wells was once a small village dependent upon Tonbridge (whose original name of Tunbridge was later changed to avoid confusion) but after the discovery in 1606 of chalybeate springs it developed into a spa which enjoyed great favour. Particularly during the 16th to 18th centuries it became a fashionable watering place and enjoyed a vogue with the aristocratic world; above all in the days of Queen Anne and the Georges, whence it takes the name "Royal" Tunbridge Wells. Situated on the borders of Kent and Sussex, in pleasant hilly country, it has a mild but invigorating climate; it has beautiful parks and recreation grounds. The famous *Pantiles* (note the curious pillars of the colonnade and the gabled roofs of the houses) are a handsome promenade lined with shops. At the far end are the *Assembly Rooms* or *Great Hall*. In the Town Hall is a memorandum written by Nelson before the battle of Trafalgar.

8 miles: *Eridge*, with Eridge Rocks, tower-like crags produced by erosion. 2 miles farther on are the Harrison Rocks. In Eridge Park (1000 acres) is *Eridge Castle*, seat of the Marquess of Abergavenny since the 15th century (not open to visitors). Lake (15 acres) and observation tower 60 feet high.

12 miles: **Crowborough** (pop. 8000, E.C. Wednesday), on the summit and slopes of Beacon Hill, between 750 and 800 feet above sea level. The golf course is justly renowned. From

the clubhouse terrace there is a magnificent view over some of the loveliest countryside in Sussex. To the south, some 20 miles away, extends a swathe of low-lying country between the wooded hills and the South Downs which runs west from the cliffs of Eastbourne to Birling Gap, the Devil's Dyke, Chanctonbury Ring and Ashdown Forest. The view extends to Lewes in the south-west, the Ouse gap in the Downs and Firle Beacon in the east, and Ditchling Beacon in the west. Little is known of the origins of the town; but it was on the route followed by smugglers from the east coast to East Grinstead, and no doubt the inhabitants helped in the trade by providing hiding places for smuggled goods in their cellars and farms. On one of the highest points was a beacon which could give warning of danger.

The woods of Sussex and Surrey are renowned for their bluebells, primroses and anemones, and honey with a very distinctive flavour is produced in the district.

Ashdown Forest. The Ashdown Forest covers a large, rolling stretch extending to the west from near Crowborough. It was once part of the ancient royal chase of the forest of Anderida, which extended over a large area of South-East England. In 1372 Edward III granted John of Gaunt, Duke of Lancaster, that part which lies between Tunbridge Wells and East Grinstead. This became part of the Duchy of Lancaster until the 17th century, and was known as the Free Chase of Ashdown. After the Restoration the forest was awarded to the Earl of Dorset; it was not until the 19th century that ancient common rights were confirmed by the establishment of a Conservators Board.

19 miles: *Uckfield* (pop. 5500, E.C. Wednesday), a quiet market town in the Weald, on the edge of the rocky part of Sussex with its red sandstone cliffs. The Uck, a tributary of the Sussex Ouse, divides it into the Old and New Town. From the 15th to the 18th century Uckfield, like most of the towns in the Sussex Weald, was a metal-working centre. Queen Elizabeth I stayed at the *Maiden's Head* inn. *Holy Cross Church*, built of stone in Perpendicular style, was rebuilt at the end of the 19th century. The tower is 15th century. Fine brasses in the choir.

20 miles: *Little Horsted*, a small village on the Uck. The stone church of St Michael and All Angels is in Norman and Perpendicular style. One of the six bells dates from the 15th century. It has Norman windows framed in quadruple arcading (11th c.). In the choir is a coffin dated 1270.

Isfield (just off A 26 1½ mile south of Uckfield) is very popular with trout fishermen and enthusiasts for coarse fishing. Two tributaries of the Ouse flow nearby. The church is 14th century: in the interior are monuments of the Shurley family, a Decorated Gothic window, and a finely carved piscina.

27 miles: **Lewes** (pop. 14,500, E.C. Wednesday), the old county town of Sussex, nestling in the heart of the Sussex Downs on the river Ouse. The town dates from Saxon times. Only the *keep* survives of the **castle** built in the 12th century by Count William de Warenne, who married Gundrada, William the Conqueror's stepdaughter. The castle is entered by the 14th century Barbican, which contains many carved stones from Lewes Priory, south of the town, which was founded by Gundrada. From the tower there are magnificent views. To the north can be seen Crowborough in its commanding position over the Weald; to the south are Newhaven and the sea. To the west the Downs extend into the distance. 2 miles north-west is Mount Harry, scene of the battle of Lewes (1264), in which Henry III was defeated by Simon de Montfort, Earl of Leicester.

Opposite the castle stands *Barbican House:* it now houses the museum of the Sussex Archaeological Society: there are some very fine 17th and 18th century tapestries, pictures of Sussex, and excellent collections of prehistoric implements, Roman and Saxon objects and Sussex ironwork. *St Michael's Church* (High St) has a Norman tower, and in the chapel (modern) of the Norman church of *St John's*, Southover, are the leaden coffins of William de Warenne and his wife. The 15th century house of Anne of Cleves (fourth wife of Henry VIII) contains beautiful fireplaces and Elizabethan panelling: it stands in Southover High St and has been converted into a museum: Sussex ironwork and numerous objects for domestic use. In the High Street is the interesting 16th century Bull House, once the Bull Inn. (Thomas Paine, author of "The Rights of Man", once lived here).

Around Lewes. 4 miles south on the Newhaven road is *Southease*. The tower of the 12th century *church* (dedication unknown) is round — one of the three such towers in Sussex. One of the bells bears the date 1310 and there is an old square Norman font. — 5 miles: *Piddinghoe*, on a height overlooking the River Ouse. St John's Church (Early English and Norman) has a round tower (see above). — 7 miles: Newhaven (p. 311).

Lewes to Pevensey: 19 miles on A274. 3 miles: Beddingham.
—Nearby is *Glynde*, one of the prettiest villages in the district.
In the vicinity is *Glyndebourne*, a beautiful country mansion
converted to an opera house under the great producer
Carl Ebert, whose exquisite productions of the operas of Mozart
are world-famed. Glyndebourne has become a centre of international importance in the music world. — 8 miles: *Alciston*,
a tiny village with an old stone-and-flint church. At Court
House farm are remains of a 14th century monastery.   —
12 miles: **Wilmington,** a small village on the slope of the downs.
The *church of St Mary and St Peter* is old: there is much 12th century work, including a small carving of the Virgin and Child
(outside north wall). *Wilmington Priory* was attached to the
Norman abbey of Grestain, until 1413, when Henry V gave
it to Chichester. After the Restoration it was a manor house
and then a farm house. The entrance doorway is 12th century.
The 14th century vaulting and the chapel window, found under
the plasterwork of the upper rooms, are very fine. The south-
west corner, now in ruins, is 14th century work; the doorway,
also ruined, is 15th century. Opposite is a large *tithe barn.*

One of the most interesting sights in the district is the *Long
Man of Wilmington:* the immense figure of a man, 226 feet
high, cut into the steep green slopes of Windover Hill (600 ft),
the largest such figure in the world. The arms are stretched
out and hold in each hand a staff or post 230 feet long.

14 miles: *Polegate.* — 16 miles: *Stonecross*, with one of the
last windmills in Sussex. — 19 miles: *Pevensey* (p. 304).

43 miles: *Lamberhurst* (pop. 1500), formerly an
ironworking centre. 53 miles: **Robertsbridge** (pop.
2500, E.C. Wednesday), a village on the Rother.

Robertsbridge Abbey (12th c.) was a Cistercian house. The
remains, now incorporated in farm buildings, are 1 mile down
the valley from the village: superb vaulting soaring up from
a central pier and supported on graceful columns, Early English
doorway. The *church of St Mary*, Salehurst, standing above
the river, is Early English, with a fine old tower.

58 miles: **Battle** (pop. 5000, E.C. Wednesday), an
important market town, shopping centre and holiday
resort, famous as the scene of the battle of Hastings

in 1066. The **ruins of Battle Abbey** are of great historical and architectural interest.

The abbey precincts are entered through the 14th century *gatehouse*, in late Decorated style, a great square battlemented tower with four battlemented octagonal towers at the corners. The old wall still extends to the east round the north and east sides of the precincts. The monks' *dorter*, now roofless, stands to the south of the position of the transepts. Each monk had a cell, and each cell had a lancet window: these can still be seen. Under the dorter is the *Common House*, with vaulting of great beauty and architectural interest.

The old market place was once in front of the Abbey gatehouse. The *Bull Ring* can still be seen. On the west side is the beautiful *Pilgrim's Rest*, a charming half-timbered inn dating from the 15th century, with parts going back to the 13th century. **St Mary's Church,** built by Abbot Ralph in the 12th century, stands opposite the massive walls of the Abbey. The chancel formed part of the original building, but the nave was added later in the 12th century and the aisles in the 14th. The piers supporting the arches between the nave and the aisles are alternately round and octagonal. In the interior is the tomb of Anthony Browne and his wife Alis, with alabaster effigies. There are some brasses in the chancel. Behind the church is the *Deanery*, a handsome Elizabethan house in red brick, with fine views of the valley towards Winchelsea and Fairlight.

64 miles: **Hastings** and *St Leonards* (pop. 68,000, E.C. Wednesday), a popular seaside resort, with a double-decked promenade, a pier with a restaurant, a theatre and a dance hall. *Old Hastings*, to the east, is still a picturesque old-world fishing port, with boats and net sheds, which attracts many artists.

Overlooking the town on West Hill are the scanty ruins of *Hastings Castle*. Little authentic is known of its history: William the Conqueror's name is connected with the castle as being either the builder or restorer. An excellent view can be had along the coast and cliffs as far as Beachy Head. North of the Castle are St Clement's Caves, originally hewn by sand-diggers but later used by smugglers for storing their wares;

they are lit by electricity and are open daily. A flight of steps beside the lighthouse runs down to the Perpendicular-style *St Clement's Church* (restored), near which is the Roman Catholic church of *St Mary Star-of-the-Sea*.

1 mile away along the cliffs, by way of Ecclesbourne Glen and Fairlight Glen, is *Lovers' Seat*, in a recess in the cliff path, with a splendid view of the sea. Beyond Lovers' Seat are the *Fire Hills*, so called because of a lighthouse which formerly stood there.

Surroundings of Hastings

1. Hastings to Maidstone: 33 miles on A229.

6 miles: **Sedlescombe Street,** a charming village in a very lovely part of the country. It lies on an old Roman road, of which remains have recently been excavated. Interesting walks through the woods from the village to Hurst Woods and the Reservoir. Old houses of the 16th and 17th centuries are grouped around the village green. The manor house, opposite Brichwall (which bears the date 1599 on the front of the chimney-stack) was built before 1611, the date of the west wing. The *Queen's Head* is an early 17th century posting inn. *St John's Church* has been rebuilt; the tower is, however, early 15th century.

12 miles: **Bodiam,** a pleasant little village on the Sussex-Kent border, chiefly famous for **Bodiam Castle.** The exterior is in an excellent state of preservation and is in plan nearly square, with circular towers at the corners and rectangular ones between: the parapets are machicolated. The rectangular moat is so large that it might be called a small lake; a stone causeway leads to an island in front of the castle, to which access was over two drawbridges. Inside, opposite the gateway, are the walls of the *Lord's Hall* and the *Lord's Kitchen*. (Visiting: interior and small museum, 10 to 7; Sundays 2 to 5).

St Giles' Church was built in the 13th century; most of the existing building dates from the 14th century. Considerable restorations have been carried out. The lancet windows on the south wall are of the 13th century.

15 miles: *Hawkhurst*. 19 miles: **Cranbrook,** in the midst of orchards. The 15th century *George Hotel* was used for centuries as a courthouse. The town is noted for its public school, founded in the 16th century. The church is Perpendicular. — 33 miles: **Maidstone** (p. 281).

2. Hastings to Ashford: 31 miles on A28.

6 miles: *Brede*, on the River Brede. *St George's Church* dates from the 12th century. The 12th century south arcade still remains. From the 13th century date parts of the north aisle and of the chancel and chancel arch. Most of the structure was rebuilt, however, during the 15th century when the crenellated tower, with its stair turret and tiled roof, were added. The three arches to the west end of the north aisle wall are transitional Norman or Early English in style. The church contains many interesting relics: a wooden cradle in which Dean Swift slept as a baby, and some old brasses. The 15th century font has a modern Spanish oak cover. The east window in the Oxenbridge Chapel is one of the finest examples in England of Perpendicular tracery. Over the pulpit is the old entrance to the rood loft. From the tower there is a magnificent view of the Brede valley. Charming old cottages in the village.

12 miles: **Northiam,** a beautiful village commanding a view over the Rother valley. The country here is hilly and wooded. *Great Dixter*, one of the most charming old houses in Sussex, dates from the mid 15th century; it has been restored, and has the original half-timbered front and Tudor porch. Nearby is another old house, brought from its original site at Benenden, together with a third, Brickwall, a black and white half-timbered house with wide bay windows and gables. *St Mary's Church* dates from 1190; the belfry and upper stories were added in the 15th century, the rest is 14th century; interesting brasses. The Rother marks the county boundary.

14 miles: *Newenden*, a peaceful hamlet with one church (Saxon font), one shop and one inn. — 17 miles: *Rolvenden*, a small village lying on high ground, once the home of Gibbon, author of the "Decline and Fall of the Roman Empire". Here is the edge of the Kent *Weald*, a country of magnificent views, of hop-gardens, orchards, fields of wheat and oats, and vegetable gardens. — 20 miles: *Tenterden* (pop. 5000, E.C. Wednesday), a small country town with wide streets and spacious green squares. St Mildred's Church (1491), with a tall square tower. Houses of many different periods and old cottages. — 23 miles: *High Halden*. — 26 miles: *Bethersden*. — 31 miles: **Ashford** (p. 282).

3. Hastings to Eastbourne: 17 miles on A259.

5 miles: *Bexhill-on-Sea* (population 33,000, E.C. Wednesday). 30 years ago Bexhill was a group of cottages; today it is a clean and spacious town with many attractions for holiday-makers. At *Cooden Beach* there is an excellent golf course, and the Highwood Club to the north-west also provides good golf. De la Warr Pavilion (1936).

13 miles: **Pevensey.** A seaside resort consisting mostly of bungalows now covers the coast where William the Conqueror landed in 1066, but in the old village are some interesting buildings. The 14th century *Mint House*, built on the site of a Norman mint, altered in the 16th century, is now a curiosity shop, and there are some beautiful frescoes, carvings and panellings to see. *St Nicholas's Church* (Early English) dates from the reign of King John (1199-1216). The ruins of **Pevensey Castle** are of very great interest. The walls date from 250, when this was a Roman fort *(Anderida)*. In 1372 John of Gaunt occupied the Norman castle which had been built on Roman foundations in the north-east of the original structure. At the beginning of the 15th century many royal prisoners were confined here.

17 miles: **Eastbourne** (p. 309).

5. LONDON TO EASTBOURNE

64 miles: A 23 to Purley, then branch left into A 22 for the rest of the way. Starting from Hyde Park Corner, turn right off Grosvenor Place into Halkin St, which runs into Belgrave Square. At the opposite corner of the square turn left into Belgrave Place and its continuation Eccleston St; then continue across Buckingham Palace Road into Belgrave Road. At the far end turn left into Lupus St and then bear right into Bessborough St, which leads to Vauxhall Bridge. Beyond the bridge turn right into South Lambeth Road (A 203). At a road junction with a clock tower (Stockwell Station) turn right into Clapham Road; then in ½ mile turn left into Bedford Road and straight ahead into King's Avenue. At the far end turn left into Thornton Road, which runs via Sternhold Avenue into Streatham Hill (A 23). Turn right, and at Streatham church fork left into Streatham High Road, continuing into London Road, still on A 23; then at Purley turn left into A 22.

Starting from London Bridge, take Borough High St (on the south side of the bridge), and at the Elephant and Castle roundabout keep straight ahead for Clapham Road, which joins the route just described at the Stockwell Station clock tower.

10 miles: **Croydon,** a suburb of London. The oldest building is the former *Palace* of the Archbishops of Canterbury, of which there survive the 14th century porch in Gothic style, the great hall (13th c.), which has a fine chestnut roof, the Guard Chamber (Arundel's Chamber) in which James I of Scotland was confined, and the long Gallery. The *church of St John the Baptist* stands on the site of a very early Saxon church. All over this area remains of prehistoric settlement and numerous fragments of Roman origin have been discovered. The present church (1867) incorporates the tower (120 ft high) of its 14th century predecessor, which was burned down in the 19th century. **Whitgift Hospital,** built in 1599, was endowed by Archbishop Whitgift (whose tomb is in St Nicho-

las's Chapel in St John's Church) as a home for the aged and infirm of Croydon and Lambeth. It is a rectangular red-brick building in Elizabethan style. The east end of the building is the most interesting part (warden's room, reception room with Elizabethan furniture, room with secret staircase on top floor).

Around Croydon. The old Croydon airport (330 acres) was on the Purley road. This was London's first airport, originally laid out in 1915 to contribute to the defence of the capital during the first world war and transferred to civil use in 1928. During the second world war it suffered severely from enemy attack.

At the Red Deer, south of Croydon, the road turns left and climbs steadily to *Sanderstead* (2 miles). Just after the station, on the right, are *Purley Beeches*, magnificent trees now designated as a bird sanctuary. Sanderstead is a quiet residential area with a 15th century church. Numerous remains of Stone Age man have been found in the district. A road goes off on the left to *Selsdon*, a modern garden suburb with a Saxon past. *Selsdon Park Hotel* is a fine Elizabethan house with mullioned windows, overgrown with creepers. Selsdon Court is a magnificent Queen Anne house. Parts of the house are late Tudor; the *Water Tower* and *Icehouse* are in the English Renaissance style. Selsdon Park (golf course) has an area of 230 acres and affords magnificent views of the Surrey and Kent hills.

Many remains dating from the Bronze Age (1900 B.C.) have been found at *Coulsdon*. Farthing Down, a beautiful chalk spur of the North Downs, was cultivated from 50 B.C. to the 2nd century A.D.; the small square fields and the trackway between them are still visible. The discovery of Roman villas and farms at Croham Hurst, Sanderstead and elsewhere has shown that the whole of this area was under cultivation in the late Iron Age and in the 1st century, after the Roman invasion. Saxon remains abound on Farthing Down: in 1871 fourteen burial mounds were discovered here, and excavations carried out in 1948 yielded further interesting material.

13 miles: *Purley*. On both sides of the road magnificent views over Riddlesdown and Kenley Heights, the North Downs of Surrey.

Turn left into A 22. 17¾ miles: *Caterham.* —
20¼ miles **Godstone,** a charming Surrey village
grouped round the village green on which cricket
matches are played. The *Clayton Hotel* dates from
1388. The *church* was 12th century, but was entirely
rebuilt in 1872 (Sir George Gilbert Scott). Near the
church are *St Mary's Almshouses* by the same architect,
successful copies of the Tudor style.

A 22 here follows the ancient Neolithic road, the
oldest highway in the country, which the Romans
used and which is called the *Pilgrims' Way* after the
12th century pilgrims who crossed this beautiful south
escarpment of the North Downs by what was then
a rough track leading to Canterbury.

To the east and south are lovely villages: *Tandridge* with its
Norman church (small Norman doorway, lancet window and a
very old tower); *Crowhurst,* to the south in the heart of the Surrey
Weald, with a beautiful old timbered house where Henry VIII
stayed; *Lingfield,* 2 miles to the south, famous for its beautiful
surroundings, with Chartham Park, Dormans Park, Ford Manor
and the ancient encampment on Dry Hill. There are some lovely
lakes and woodland amid the hills and valleys of the Eden and
Eden Brook. Bazing Farm is at the borders of Surrey, Sussex
and Kent, and nearby is the site of the ancient moated castle of
Starborough. The stone Perpendicular church of SS. Peter and
Paul, built in the 15th century (with the exception of the 14th century tower) occupies the site of a Norman and Saxon church.
In the interior are interesting tombs and brasses.

30½ miles: **East Grinstead** (pop. 18,000, E.C.
Wednesday). A market town in the midst of lovely
country through which flow the Medway and its
tributary the Eden.

On a hill is *Sackville College,* founded in 1609 by the 2nd Earl
of Dorset as an almshouse for 16 poor people; the pleasant old
gabled sandstone buildings comprise a chapel with screen and
stalls, the common room, the Dorset Lodgings, the warden's

quarters and hall. *St Swithin's Church*, rebuilt in the 18th century in local sandstone and Perpendicular style, is on the site of the first church (860); the tower dates from 1684.

33½ miles: *Forest Row*, in the Medway valley, amid wooded hills. A short distance above the river are the ruins of *Brambletye House*, a Jacobean mansion of which only the outer wall and moat and a few pieces of wall with mullioned windows are left.

36 miles: *Wych Cross*. The road is now running through Ashdown Forest. 39 miles: *Nutley*. 42 miles: *Maresfield*. St Bartholomew's Church, stone-built in Perpendicular style, has a small Saxon window belonging to the original church, built 1020. Timber porch (restored), holy water stoups.

44 miles: **Uckfield** (p. 298).

47¾ miles: *Halland*. 49¼ miles: *East Hoathly*. 54 miles: *Horsebridge*. In the vicinity is the village of *Dicker*, noted for its pottery. 4 miles east is **Herstmonceux Castle**, the oldest brick building south of the Thames.

The castle was built in 1440 by Roger de Fiennes. The interior walls and roof were demolished in 1778, but the outer wall is original. Access is by a long bridge over the moat. Since 1948 the castle has housed the Royal Observatory. (Open to visitors on Mondays, Wednesdays and Thursdays 2 to 5). On a nearby hill is *All Saints Church* (Early English and Perpendicular), which contains tombs with figures of knights in armour. On the floor of the choir is a brass of 1405 with a curious inscription (Sir William Fiennes). The old font was discovered at nearby Lime Park. Farther east, on a hill, is *Ninfield*, with a pre-Conquest church of St Mary, in Early English and Perpendicular style (rebuilt in the reign of Edward III, restored in 1885 and 1923).

Beyond Horsebridge is **Hailsham**. *St Mary's Church* (Early English) dates from the 15th century; of the older church, built in 1200, only the carved double capital in the small niche above the piscina in the south aisle chapel remains. There is a trefoil-headed piscina in the south wall of the chancel.

2 miles west of A 22 are the ruins of *Michelham Priory*, founded in 1229 by Gilbert de Aquila, Lord of Pevensey, on a small island (6 acres in extent); it is now privately owned. At *Arlington*, 3 miles south of Michelham, is a *church* dedicated to St Pancras, with architecture in many different styles; Celtic and Roman fragments in the chapel.

59¼ miles: *Polegate*, with a picturesque windmill.

64 miles: **Eastbourne** (pop. 65,000, E.C. Wednesday), one of the largest resorts on this coast, where the downs meet the sea. 4000 acres behind the town have been acquired to ensure the maintenance of a green belt round it.

Lewis Carroll (1832-98), author of "Alice in Wonderland", visited the town over a period of 17 years, staying at 7 Lushington Road. In 1905 the composer *Claude Debussy* stayed at Eastbourne while completing his three symphonic sketches, "The Sea".

Mentioned in Domesday Book as a fishing port, Eastbourne came into prominence during the 19th century, when it was laid out with broad tree-lined roads, three miles of promenades and fine shopping centres. *Helen Gardens* and *Holywell Retreat* stand at the end of the front. Principal points along the esplanade are the *Wish Tower* (one of the 74 Martello towers); the *Grand Parade Band Arena*, 1000 feet long, opened in 1865; the Redoubt, with a circular battery of guns, and the *Redoubt Music Gardens*. *Devonshire Park Winter Gardens* (1600 seats), built 50 years ago, are used for concerts, meetings, flower shows, dances, etc. The parks (four, extending to 180 acres) and gardens are always gay with flowers. The *Towner Art Gallery*, formerly the manor-house, is in the corner of the manor-house gardens; permanent collection of Sussex pictures. Opposite stands the 13th century Lambe Inn and nearby is the 700-year-old church of *St Mary* (Early English style with a vaulted crypt). The

Saffrons is a fine cricket ground not far from *Compton Place*, home of the Duke of Devonshire, within sight of the downs behind the town. To the east of the row are the Crumbles, an unbuilt expanse with wild bird life and a row of Martello Towers.

Beachy Head. To the south-west is the bold cliff headland where the downs reach down to the sea. It rises 575 feet sheer from the water; at the foot is the 141 foot high *Beachy Head Lighthouse* (1902) whose light is visible for 16 miles. To the west is Belle Tout, the old lighthouse, now a private residence. There is a pleasant walk of 3 miles from the town to Beachy Head, by way of Gow Cap and then along the cliffs. There are motorboat trips from the pier to the lighthouse at high tide. Off Beachy Head was fought a naval battle between British and Dutch ships and a French fleet on 30 June 1690.

Eastbourne to Brighton

22 miles on A 259. 4 miles: *Eastdean*, a village 1 mile inland from the cleft in the cliffs called Birling Gap, a favourite spot for picnics at the east end of the Seven Sisters. The **Seven Sisters** are great waves of chalk stretching along the seashore to the west, as far as Cuckmere Haven. The church of *SS. Simon and Jude* is a typical Sussex church, with a 14th century stoup, a carved oak Jacobean pulpit with the date 1623 on the panels above, and an aumbrey in the south wall.

7 miles: **Westdean,** in a secluded valley in the Downs. The church of *All Saints* (of flint and stone in the Decorated style) possesses a fine Norman tower arch. On the north wall of the chancel are two old canopied tombs; there is a square font and a shell-shaped piscina. The east wing of the rectory (restored 1894), dates from 1220; the walls are 2½ feet thick and have corbel-headed windows. In the interior are old ceiling beams and doors, and a newel stone staircase. Also of interest is *Charleston Manor* (13th-18th c.).

7½ miles: *East Blatchington*, a picturesque suburb of Seaford, with old cottages and modern houses. The flint-and-stone *church of St Peter* is Early English and Norman.

8 miles: **Seaford** (pop. 15,000, E.C. Wednesday). The discovery of numerous flint arrowheads has shown that there was a Neolithic settlement here, and Seaford Head was the site of a pre-Roman camp which the Romans took over. Seaford was

formerly a flourishing port, which in the 13th century was a dependency of Hastings. During the Napoleonic wars the most westerly of the Martello towers was built here; and in the second world war the town suffered from air attack. *St Leonard's Church* dates from the 11th century, but was later rebuilt. Of the Norman building there remains a carving of St Michael and the dragon on the wall of the nave; the tympanum of the south doorway and part of the north aisle with small Norman windows (12th c.) belong to the west end of the aisled nave which was built later. Also of Norman date are four arches in Transitional style. Note the figure carving on the capital of the central pier.

Around Seaford. B2108 runs north through the lovely *Cuckmere Valley* to **Alfriston** (4 miles). Dating from Saxon times (when its name was Aelfriceeshtun), Alfriston has some interesting old inns (including the 17th century *Star*) with secret passages used in smuggling days, when Cuckmere Haven offered excellent shelter for vessels and the inland villages provided hiding places for contraband. The 14th century cruciform village church of *St Andrew* is of such size that it is called the *Cathedral of the Downs;* the east window is very fine. Near the village green, known as the Tye, is the Clergy House, a pre-Reformation parish priest's house of about 1350, having one common living room and smaller apartments for individual use. The central hall, open to the roof, has large cambered tiebeams and moulded king-posts.

To the east of the Cuckmere river are the hamlets of *Litlington*, with attractive gardens, and *Lullington*, which has one of the smallest churches in the British Isles — the choir of what was once a much larger church. Between here and Alfriston is a high point on the road known as *High-and-Over* from which there are magnificent views over the windings of the Cuckmere and the fertile wooded region beyond.

13 miles: **Newhaven** (pop. 9000, E.C. Wednesday), one of the chief points of communication between England and the Continent. It had its origin in the village of Meeching, but when in 1579 after a great storm the river Ouse changed its course and found its outlet through the village, thereby creating a fine harbour, the town was re-named Newhaven. The 12th century church still retains its original chancel and has a Norman tower. There is a fort (modern) here.

17¼ miles; *Rottingdean.* — 21¼ miles: **Brighton** (p. 314).

6. LONDON TO BRIGHTON

53 miles on A 23; motorway for part of the way. Exit from London as in chapter 5.

15 miles: *Coulsdon* (pop. 60,000, E.C. Wednesday), a residential town. 18 miles: *Chaldon*. 19 miles: *Merstham*, with a picturesque old village street leading to the gates of Merstham House.

St Catherine's Church dates chiefly from 1200; the west tower has a fine wooden belfry, an interesting Gothic doorway with dog-tooth moulding and a cusped arch in the interior.

20 miles: *Gatton*, a village which has retained much of its charm, although now caught up in the expansion of the two neighbouring towns of Redhill and Reigate.

Gatton Park, an attractive old house magnificently situated in a fold of the North Downs, rebuilt after a fire in 1934. Entry to the park (on foot only) by the east and west gates and Tower Lodge. Near the house is *St Andrew's Church* (13th c., clumsily restored), with stalls and woodwork from Louvain (1834).

21 miles: **Nutfield.**

The *church of SS. Peter and Paul* (Gothic) dates from 1200; north aisle 1230; choir altered 1320; tower 1420; south transept 1450; 14th century reredos, Tudor pulpit, 17th century brasses.

To the east is the very picturesque village of *Bletchingley* (church, castle, old houses).

22 miles: **Redhill and Reigate** (pop. 60,000, E.C. Wednesday). The centres of these two towns in the lovely Holmesdale Valley at the base of the North Downs are only 2 miles apart.

Redhill, so called because of the colour of the sand on the Common, was transformed from a tiny rural village into the larger of the two towns as the result of the building in 1841 of the London-Brighton railway. *Reigate* was first mentioned in 1170, although there was a Saxon village of Cherchefelle

(Churchfield) — near the site of the present church — which had disappeared by the time the Domesday survey was made. The castle (of the motte-and-bailey type) was built by William de Warenne, and the old town grew up around it. Louis, the French Dauphin, took the castle in 1216. The *church of St Mary Magdalene*, in local stone, has a nave dating from 1180, with much later alteration in different styles. The choir (14th and 15th c.) contains a stone reredos and fine stalls. On the upper floor of the old sacristy is one of the oldest public libraries of religious books in the country, founded in 1701.

25 miles: *Horley*. B 2036 goes off on the left, providing an alternative route which rejoins the main road at Pyecombe.

Alternative route, Horley to Pyecombe: 27 miles. 5 miles: *Pound Hill.* 11 miles: *Balcombe*, a small village on the edge of the Ridge, Balcombe and East Ashdown Forests, with wide expanses of heath. Beyond Balcombe Forest is Tilgate Forest, with two lakes which were formerly used by ironworks. 15 miles: **Cuckfield,** with many old half-timbered buildings. The parish church is 13th century, on older foundations; enlarged in 14th century, with 15th century roof. Cuckfield Park is a lovely Elizabethan mansion with a 16th century gateway at the end of an avenue of lime-trees. 21 miles: *Burgess Hill*, at the foot of the Downs near Keymer and Clayton. 27 miles: *Pyecombe*.

28 miles: *Lowfield Heath*, near Gatwick Airport. 30 miles: **Crawley** (pop. 60,000, E.C. Wednesday), an attractively laid out "new town". B 2125 runs straight ahead through the town centre (level crossing), following the line of the old London-Brighton road, while A 23 bypasses the town, passes through Peas Pottage and climbs Handcross Hill to *Handcross*, a cluster of houses and shops.

40 miles: *Bolney*, lying within St Leonard's Forest in very lovely country. The Early English church of St Mary Magdalene has a quaint pinnacled tower and bells. 42 miles: *Twineham*, with St Peter's Church

(16th c., on older foundations) and Hickstead Place, a beautiful Tudor mansion.

47 miles: *Newtimber*, which has a small and interesting church with a 16th century carved pulpit. Newtimber Place (1600) is surrounded by a moat and stands in a 40 acre park. From the top of *Newtimber Hill*, overlooking the village, there are very fine views.

East of Newtimber, 5 miles beyond *Clayton*, is the village of **Ditchling.** To the south of the church is a 500 year old house in which Anne of Cleves is said to have lived. St Margaret's Church, in stone and flint, is Early English, with Decorated windows. 1½ miles south is *Ditchling Beacon* (813 ft), from which there are wide-ranging views; remains of a Roman camp and two reservoirs said to be 4000 years old. To the west is *Poynings*, a beautiful village below the Devil's Dyke, one of the widest of the valleys which cut through the Downs.

46 miles: *Pyecombe*. Nearby are Wolstonbury Beacon (670 ft) on which traces of a Saxon encampment are to be seen, and West Hill (680 ft). The small church (dedication unknown) is early Norman; its lead font (1180) is one of the only three remaining in England. — 51 miles: *Patcham*.

53 miles: **Brighton and Hove** (pop. 165,000, E.C. Wednesday, Thursday and Saturday). Brighton is one of the most popular and most frequented seaside resorts in the British Isles. Hove, to the west and contiguous with it, is a fashionable residential town.

The town is said to have been founded early in the 10th century by Brighthelm, an Anglo-Saxon bishop of Selsey. Domesday Book gives it as *Brightelmston*, and its feudal lord in the 11th century was Earl Godwin, father of King Harold. Until the 18th century it was a tiny fishing village, when a certain fashionable doctor, Dr Russell, recommended its sea bathing and invigorating air. It leaped into the highest fashion in 1783 when George IV, then Prince of Wales, chose it as his place of residence and built there his fantastic palace, the Pavilion.

From then on it became an aristocratic resort, patronised by
many members of the royal family, until the coming of the
railway made it a crowded popular "London-by-the-Sea".
Thackeray and Dickens and many other writers found a place
in their works for Brighton, and Harrison Ainsworth and other
novelists lived there.

Brighton, at the foot of the downs, has a frontage
of about 6 miles to the sea, most of it laid out in
spacious promenades which extend from Kemp Town
and Black Rock at the eastern extremity of the town
to as far west as Hove, where the Brunswick Lawns
continue the esplanade for another 2 miles. The
squares and crescents along the cliffs to the east and
in Hove are excellent examples of Regency domestic
architecture and town planning.

Royal Pavilion. Built for the Prince of Wales in
1787 by Nash in pseudo-Oriental style, with domes
and pinnacles and latticed balconies and arches. The
interior is decorated in Chinese style. The **Dome**
(once the royal stables) was so called from the immense
dome with which it is crowned. It is now used for
concerts and meetings, and also houses the *Museum*
and *Art Gallery* (open 10 to 7, Sundays 2 to 7).

The **Museum** is mainly devoted to archaeology, history and
local bygones. The **Art Gallery** contains a variety of works,
including a triptych by *Wohlgemut*, a *Botticelli* "Madonna and
Child", "The Centurion of Capernaum" by *Veronese*, and
paintings by Pater, Reynolds, Lawrence, Gainsborough, Canaletto, Vivarini, Mme Vigée-Lebrun, Kneller and others.

The *Booth Museum* in Dyke Road has a fine collection of
British birds. In Preston Manor is the *Thomas-Stanford Museum*.

The **Old Steine** gardens, with a fountain and a statue
of George IV (Chantrey), lead down to the sea front
and the *Aquarium* below ground level in the cliff,
with a fine collection of fish in natural settings. Nearby

is the *Motor Museum* (old cars). There are two piers, *Palace Pier* and *West Pier*.

At **Hove,** on the sea front, is the *King Alfred* (swimming pools, etc.), named after the naval training establishment for which it was used during the second world war. **Hove Museum** in Church Road contains works of art and material of local interest.

The *Sussex Room* reproduces the living room of a small Sussex landowner of the early 18th century. The *Georgian Room* is an 18th drawing room with some fine Chippendale furniture: note particularly a porcelain tray (1750) and two ladder-backed chairs. *Regency Room* (early 19th c.). *Victorian Room*, an early Victorian living room. Open daily 10 to 1 and 2 to 5.

Rottingdean, *Saltdean* and *Peacehaven* are suburbs of Brighton. **Rottingdean,** on the cliffs to the east, has developed from an old village: *St Margaret's Church* (Early English) and *Grange Museum* (mementoes of Kipling).

Brighton to Worthing

There are two alternative routes:

1. the *coast road*, 11 miles on A 259, through what has become in recent years a continuous built-up area. Leave Brighton by Hove and West Hove. 4 miles: *Southwick* (pop. 10,000, E.C. Wednesday), a seaside town on the site of a Roman camp, with many boatyards (yachts) round the harbour, beyond the road, which runs parallel to the river and the sea. 6½ miles: **Shoreham-by-Sea** (pop. 18,500, E.C. Wednesday), an old seaport close to the mouth of the river Adur. The *Marlipins*, one of a number of picturesque old buildings, is now a museum. Fine **Norman churches** in the villages of *Old Shoreham* and *New Shoreham*. The old timber bridge in Old Shoreham appeals to artists. 9 miles: *Lancing*. 11 miles: *Worthing* (p. 322).

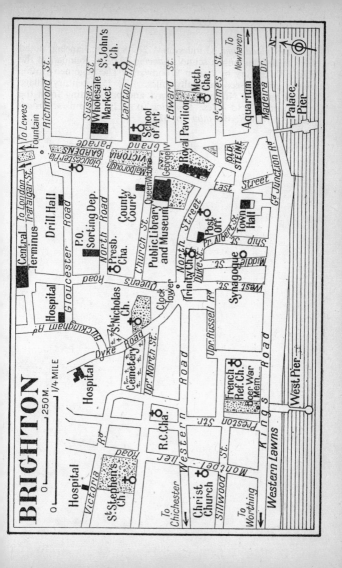

BRIGHTON

0   250 M.

0   1/4 MILE

2. the *inland road*, 13 miles on A 27. 8 miles: **Lancing**, noted for the famous public school, *Lancing College*, founded in the mid 19th century by Canon Woodward. The huge neo-Gothic chapel can be seen for many miles. The 15th century village *church* has two Norman doorways and parts dating from the 12th century. 10 miles: *Sompting* (p. 322). 12 miles: *Broadwater*. 13 miles: *Worthing* (p. 322).

7. LONDON TO WORTHING
AND SHOREHAM

58 miles. A 23 as far as Streatham High Road. At Streatham High Road turn right down Mitcham Lane and down Streatham Road through Mitcham.

8 miles: *Mitcham* (pop. 80,000, E.C. Wednesday), famous for factories making lavender-perfumed articles from locally grown lavender. — 12 miles: *Cheam*. — 15 miles: **Ewell** (pop. 75,000 with Epsom, E.C. Wednesday), favoured by Charles II (1680) as a spa, but now chiefly famous as a sporting centre.

Epsom Downs are famous the world over as the scene of the Derby, the classic of horse racing. Derby Week takes place during the last week of May or the first week of June: the Derby itself is usually run on a Wednesday; the second great event is the Oaks. The Derby Stakes were started in 1780. In the town itself there are many 17th and 18th century buildings.

17¾ miles: *Ashtead*, a small village, with a characteristic village green, occupying the site of a Roman settlement. In the woods on the Common to the north remains of a Roman villa were found, and the 13th century church was built on the site of a Roman camp: Roman brick and tiles are built into the north wall.

19¾ miles: *Leatherhead* (pop. 40,000, E.C. Wednesday), a pleasant town on the river Mole; the church dates from the 12th and 14th centuries. 23 miles: *West Humble*, with the ruins of a late 12th century chapel on the old road to Brockham, formerly part of the Pilgrims' Way. 24 miles: *Box Hill*. The village lies at the foot of the hill (690 ft). George Meredith lived in Flint Cottage during his last years.

25 miles: *Dorking* (pop. 23,000, E.C. Wednesday), an old country town amid some of the loveliest scenery in the North Downs. Bypass.

Near the town are *Ranmore Common* and *Leith Hill* (965 ft), from the top of which there are fine views of the well wooded countryside. 4 miles south-west, between Wotton Common and Coldharbour Common, is *Duke's Warren*, with one of the sources of the river Tillingbourne. *Leith Hill Place* (near the top of Leith Hill) is well worth visiting when the rhododendrons and azaleas are in flower. *Moss Wood*, between Coldharbour Common and the top of Leith Hill, is famous for its bluebells.

Polesden Lacey, 3 miles north-west of Dorking, stands in 910 acres of gardens and parkland. The house, built in 1824 in the form of a Regency villa, contains the Greville Collection of pictures, tapestries, furniture and works of art.

29 miles: *Holmwood.* — 31½ miles: *Capel.* — 34 miles: Kingsfold: A 24 branches right to Bognor Regis (see route 8). — 36 miles: *Warnham*.

38¼ miles: **Horsham** (pop. 25,000, E.C. Thursday), an important agricultural centre with four fairs a year, the "capital" of West Sussex. The most interesting part of the town lies to the south of Carfax, where the four main streets meet.

Note the roofs of Horsham stone (too heavy for modern houses). *St Mary's Church* with its tall shingled spire is chiefly Early English in style (two long central arcades and clerestory lancet windows); Norman door and window to the right of the north door, all that remain of the original building. In the interior are some interesting tombs (1396, Thomas Braose; 1453, Hoo), some brasses and two chantries.

3 miles north-west is *Field Place*, birthplace of Percy Bysshe Shelley (1792-1822). The public library bears his name.

39 miles: *Christ's Hospital.* The famous public school founded by Edward VI in 1553, formerly in London, came here in 1902. The pupils still wear the

original uniform (long blue tunic, knee-length breeches, yellow stockings and buckled shoes).

41 miles: *Southwater*. Just beyond this B 2224 goes off on the right, rejoining the main road at Dial Post Inn.

44 miles: A 272 cuts across both roads. 5 miles east is **Cowfold,** with the interesting *church of St Peter*, built in Sussex stone (Early English), in which is the famous *Nelond Brass*, 10 feet long, commemorating Thomas Nelond, prior of Lewes (d. 1433). The modern Carthusian *monastery of St Hugh* (1877) is south of the village: to visit, apply at porter's lodge.

51 miles: *Washington*, a pleasant village amid market gardens with fine views of Chanctonbury Ring (p. 222). An excellent centre for walls over the Downs.

Washington to Shoreham: 9½ miles on A283. A 283 crosses the village of Washington and, running along the foot of the Downs, follows the river Adur through a gap in the hills to Shoreham on the coast. On its way it passes charming villages built on the water springs flowing from the hills. — 2½ miles: *Wiston* (pronounced "Wisson"). The old church of St Mary, badly restored, has some interesting tombs. Beautiful Elizabethan manor house in a park. — 4 miles: **Steyning,** one of the most attractive old market towns in the south, full of peace and charm, said to have been founded in the 8th century. There are many old half-timbered houses and inns with roofs of Horsham stone and thatched cottages. See particularly Church St and the Grammar School, and Brotherhood Hall — a 16th century monastic institution. The *church* is one of the most splendid examples of Norman architecture to be found in England. It was restored in the last century, but the Norman south doorway and late Norman font are untouched.

Just beyond this are **Bramber** and *Botolphs*, two villages on the Adur, at one time reachable by quite large vessels. *Bramber Castle* was a fortress of some importance: situated on a hill commanding the village and the surrounding area, it was a Norman moated castle; it was destroyed in the time of Cromwell. The ruins of the main gateway and a stretch of walls stand more than 60 feet high. *St Mary's Guest House* is one of the finest and oldest examples of the local architectural style, with magnificent timbering and panelling. *St Nicholas's Church* was originally Norman (rebuilt).

On the other side of the river is Upper Beeding, which, like Bramber, was a port of some consequence in the days when the Adur was navigable. Boating and fishing in the river (mullet, pike, eels). The road continues down the banks of the Adur to Shoreham (9½ miles: see p. 316).

53¾ miles: *Findon* (pop. 900, E.C. Wednesday), a charming downland village lying beneath Cissbury Ring (see below), where a famous sheep fair is held every September. Many racing stables.

58 miles: **Worthing** (pop. 82,000, E.C. Wednesday), a popular seaside resort. The climate is bracing, and the average number of hours of sunshine in the year is among the highest in the country. The seafront is nearly 5 miles long. Small *museum* (open 10 to 7) in Chapel Road.

Around Worthing. *Sompting* (3 miles): Saxon church, notable for its unique early Norman tower with four high-pitched gables and a shingled roof. — *Broadwater*, with an old church, has now been swallowed up by the town. — *Tarring*, with fine 15th century half-timbered houses. — *Salvington*, birthplace of the lawyer and member of Parliament John Selden (1584-1654); the thatched cottage in which he was born can still be seen. Salvington Mill.

Cissbury Ring (alt. 603 ft, area 60 acres), on the north boundary of the town, derives its name from the Saxon chieftain Cissa. It is the finest of all the *prehistoric camps* of the South Downs, and famous for its flint implements. The fosse and vallum are in an excellent state of preservation. From the top are magnificent views of Beachy Head and the Isle of Wight. — *Highdown Hill* (270 ft) is an archaeological site rich in late Bronze Age, early Iron Age and Roman and Saxon remains. In the Saxon cemetery were found period jewellery and glass (now on exhibition in Worthing Museum.) — *Chanctonbury Ring* (760 ft), crowned with beech trees planted in 1760. In the grove can be seen clear traces of the fosse and vallum of the Roman camp, which was built on the site of a prehistoric encampment. From here there are beautiful and extensive views over the Weald as far as the North Downs at Reigate and the Hog's Back.

Worthing to Bognor Regis: 17 miles on A 259.

3 miles: *Goring-by-Sea*, with Goring Castle (19th c.), Greek on one side and Gothic on the other. 4 miles: *Ferring*. 6¼ miles: *Rustington*, now part of Littlehampton. Two convalescent homes, the Millfield Children's Home and a home belonging to the Worshipful Company of Carpenters. Notable features of the Early English church (restored 1861) are the oak arch and barge-board of the west porch, the low window at the south-west corner, the basin for washing liturgical utensils and the single-handed clock. 9 miles: *Littlehampton* (pop. 18,000, E.C. Wednesday), a seaside resort at the mouth of the Arun, under the Downs. Walks along the coast. The road then climbs to *Clymping*, with a 13th century church built on the site of an earlier Saxon church, the tower of which still remains. 16 miles: *Felpham*. 17 miles: *Bognor Regis* (p. 327).

8. LONDON TO BOGNOR REGIS

66 miles. On A 23 to Kingsfold (34 miles: see route 5), then turn right into A 29, which runs south-west on the line of the old Roman road (Stane Street) from London to Chichester.

34 miles: *Kingsfold*. Then A29 to (40 miles) *Slinfold*. Some picturesque cottages and a modern church (1861); there is an old altar-tomb, with a recumbent female effigy. In the neighbourhood is the lovely old mansion of *Strood Park*, standing in grounds and woods of 80 acres.

41½ miles: *Five Oaks*, where the A264 from Tunbridge Wells comes in.

43¼ miles: *Billingshurst*. The name is derived from a Saxon tribe, the Billings. The oldest parts of the Perpendicular church of St Mary are the lancet windows in the south chancel aisle and the tower; note the oak ceiling of the nave.

49 miles: **Pulborough** (pop. 3000, E.C. Wednesday). By reason of its position on a hill beside the ford at the confluence of the Rivers Arun and Western Rother, Pulborough has been of importance since early British times, and on *Nutbourne Common* many ancient British relics have been found. The name is derived from the Saxon "Pul" and "burh" — "stronghold by the pool". In Roman times it was the site of a fort on Stane Street, and excavations have revealed a large circular mausoleum. The town is beautifully situated in an area of lush green meadows.

The early 12th century **St Mary's Church** is one of the largest in Sussex: chancel Early English, nave Perpendicular; good brasses. The church, on top of a hill, is approached by a flight of steps and a 14th century lychgate. Around it are charming old buildings: *Chequers* (with the chapel of a 15th c. monastery in the garden); the *Old Cottage* (left exposed in 1825 when the road was lowered); *Old Place* (15th century manor house, once a priory; note the old doorways and windows); *New Place* (ingle-nook chimney in the old hall and 16th century gateway). — 1 mile to the west is Stopham. The *bridge* over the Arun is the finest in Sussex. It dates from the 14th century and has 8 arches.

50 miles: **Hardham.** *St Botolph's Church* (Early English), with Roman materials built into the walls and old wall paintings. Note the oak benches and pulpit and the Elizabethan chalice. Nearby are the ruins of an old priory and, built into a farmhouse, a 12th century refectory and chapter house.

51 miles: *Coldwaltham*, in one of the most beautiful parts of the Downs.

Beyond the village A 29 turns south, leaving the Roman *Stane Street* to continue south-west towards Chichester.

At **Bignor,** a mile or two away on the line of the Roman road, a *Roman villa* was discovered in 1901, with pavement mosaics (one of them representing a Medusa head), excellently preserved, very similar to those found at Brading in the Isle of Wight (p. 361). The villages of Sutton, Bignor and Fittleworth are all very attractive.

56 miles: *Bury.* 57 miles: **Houghton,** where A29 takes a sharp turn to the right.

From Houghton A 284 runs south through Arundel Park (1100 acres), with the beautiful Swanbourne Lake, to **Arundel** (pop. 2600, E.C. Wednesday), an ancient and picturesque town of red brick buildings set in tiers on the slopes of the South Downs.

Arundel Castle stands in a commanding position over the town. It is the seat of the Duke of Norfolk, who has the title of Earl of Arundel and the office of Chief Butler of England. Open 12 to 4.30 in summer. The oldest existing part of the castle is the *Keep* (of Saxon origin), which is now nothing but a shell. The entrance is by the *Lower Lodge*, which leads by the *Outer Tower* (with drawbridge and portcullis) and the *Clock Tower*, on the mound where the Norman keep formerly stood. There is a *well* 400 feet deep, dug in 1300. Of the residential portions the east towers and south-east front are the oldest (built by the first Norman owner, Earl Roger de Montgomery, to whom the castle was awarded after the battle of Hastings). The west wing was built in the middle of the 14th century with the ransoms of French prisoners taken at Crecy. The east wing was erected in the 16th century but was later incorporated in the large new north-west front built at the beginning of this century by the 10th duke, completing the restoration work begun in 1791. To the north-west of the keep, connected with it by a sentry-walk, is the barbican, *Bevis Tower*. The interior of the castle is beautifully furnished, with pictures by *Van Dyck*, *Teniers*, *Gainsborough* and other artists.

The Fitzalan Chapel, which dates from the time of Earl Roger de Montgomery, contains in the chapel and vaults the tombs of many of the Fitzalans and Howards. At the end of the long nave are the Lady Chapel and the main chapel, with very ancient altars. Part of the beautifully carved roof is original; note the east window.

St Nicholas's Church (Perpendicular) dates from the same period as the Fitzalan Chapel, from which it was at one time walled off following a 19th century lawsuit. The *church of St Philip Neri*, notable for its spires, was built by the Duke of Norfolk, in Gothic style, in 1863. In High St are the *Arundel Museum* (local history) and the *Totem Museum* (art of primitive peoples).

Houghton to Storrington: 6 miles on B 2139. 3 miles: **Amberley,** a charming old village with a long main street, in which most of the houses are thatched, leading to *St Michael's Church*. The west and north windows of the church, the chancel arch and the font are Norman; the nave (1100), the present chancel, the south aisle and the tower (1230) are Early English. The south doorway is one of the finest examples of the Decorated style in Sussex. Beyond the church are the ruins of *Amberley Castle*, a Norman structure which belonged to the Bishops of Chichester and was fortified in 1386 by Bishop William Rede. Still to be seen are the great gateway (the dungeons were under the houses on the right) and the curtain wall (restored 1908).

Parham Park (3 miles north-east) is a large Elizabethan mansion, standing in a magnificent park with groves of oak trees on grass slopes. The west wing was built before 1577, when the rest of the present E-shaped building was erected. *Great Hall:* portraits of Queen Elizabeth I, Edward VI, 16th and 17th century furniture, etc. *Great Parlour:* portraits including Louis XIII of France and Queen Anne of Austria, needlework and tapestry. *Salon* (1790, in cream and gold Adam style): portraits and occasional furniture, Royal Worcester dessert service. Upstairs: canopy and coverlet for a bed worked by Mary Queen of Scots during her imprisonment in England. Pictures by *Reynolds*, *Romney* and *Gainsborough*. (Visiting: Wednesdays, Thursdays and Sundays 2 to 5. 6 miles: **Storrington**, a little country town at the foot of the South Downs, with some fine Georgian houses. *Old Forge* (16th c.): oak beams, large chimney-piece, deep cellars used by smugglers. *St Mary's Church*, stone-built, dates from the Early English period but was restored in 1876. To the east is *Sullington Warren*, a large expanse of heathland and pinewoods, with magnificent views of the North and South Downs.

61 miles: *Slindon*, with St Mary's Church (11th c.) and a fine old Elizabethan mansion and park. 62 miles: *Walberton*. 66 miles: **Bognor Regis** (pop. 30,000, E.C. Wednesday). Of Saxon origin, Bognor was a fishing hamlet in mediaeval times and in the late 18th century became a bathing resort. It became popular after King George V went there in 1928 to convalesce after a severe illness. *Hotham Park* is a stately Georgian mansion built in 1792, standing in the centre of the town in its own grounds, which are now a public park. At *Felpham*, 1 mile east, is a thatched cottage in which *William Blake*, poet, painter and visionary, once lived.

9. LONDON TO CHICHESTER
AND PORTSMOUTH

To Portsmouth 75 miles on A 3. To Chichester 64 miles:
A 3 to Milford; then A 283 and A 285. Starting from London
Bridge, take Borough High St and at the Elephant and Castle
roundabout keep straight ahead into Newington Butts, Kenning-
ton Park Road and Clapham Road. At the end of Clapham
High St turn right along the north side of Clapham Common,
continue through Wandsworth and at the end of Wimbledon
Common turn left into the Kingston Bypass.

13 miles: **Kingston-upon-Thames,** an old Saxon town
in which the Anglo-Saxon kings had a riverside palace.
A great Council of State was held here in 838.

16 miles: *Esher.* Esher Place (ruins, 15th c.) was
Cardinal Wolsey's palace. 20 miles: *Church Cobham.*
22 miles: *Wisley.*

The gardens of the Royal Horticultural Society (250 acres,
with many rare plants) are on the road to *Ripley Green*, which
has a little Norman church with a small wooden belfry and
tower. A prehistoric site dating from 2500 B.C. has been excavated near here.

25 miles: **Ripley,** with a large and beautiful village
green surrounded by old houses.

Sutton Place, to the right of the main road between Ripley
and Guildford, is a fine Tudor mansion built in 1530 by Richard
Weston, one of Henry VIII's favourites, whose son was beheaded
as Anne Boleyn's lover. It contains a portrait of Henry VIII
by Holbein. The property belongs to the multi-millionaire
Paul Getty.

A 3 bypasses Guildford, joining up again with
A 3100 (which goes through the town) at Milford.

30 miles: **Guildford** (pop. 55,000, E.C. Wednesday),
on the river Wey, in the midst of peaceful country-

side, with a steep and attractive main street and many old buildings of architectural interest.

The most prominent remains of the past are the ruins of the *Norman castle*, with walls 10 feet thick, on an artificial mound on top of a hill; the grounds have been laid out as a park. *Abbot's Hospital* (1622), a home for old people. The *Guildhall* (1682), brick-built, contains some interesting pictures. **St Mary's Church** (late Norman) has grotesque carvings in the roof and some 13th century paintings in the Baptist's Chapel. The *Grammar School*, at the top of the hill, is a handsome 16th century building with an old library. See also the ruins of St Catherine's chapel. Among the most interesting buildings in the town are its inns. The *Angel*, the *Crown*, the *White Hart* and the *Lion* were all mentioned by John Taylor, the "water poet", in 1636, and Pepys recommends the *Red Lion*. **Guildford Cathedral**, dedicated to the Holy Spirit, stands on Stag Hill; it was begun in 1936 and completed in 1960.

Surroundings of Guildford

Loseley House (from Guildford on Aldershot and District bus 12, 22 or 24). A beautiful Elizabethan manor-house.

5 miles: **Godalming**, a small town which dates from at the latest the 6th century and is built in a district with many Roman settlements and Saxon villages. During the Middle Ages it was an important industrial centre for quarrying, tanning and the manufacture of gloves. Later knitting and weaving occupied the inhabitants. Pound Lane and Church St contain magnificent survivals of half-timbered buildings. The *church of SS. Peter and Paul* dates from the 11th century: much interesting Saxon and Norman work. *Charterhouse School*, one of England's leading public schools, was transferred to Godalming in 1872 from its original premises in London. The library contains interesting mementoes of Thackeray, Leech (the 19th century "Punch" writer) and Lord Baden-Powell. Museum open in the afternoon during term. Wyatt's Hospital, built in 1622, is a fine example of Jacobean architecture. — 2 miles beyond Godalming is *Milford*, where A 3100 runs into A 3 (the main Portsmouth road, which bypasses Guildford).

Compton, a very fine old village, whose church is unique. The tower with slit windows is Saxon, and red Roman tiles have been used in the construction. Above is a slender shingled spire (14th c.) and in the timbered roof, unchanged since it was built in Norman days, attractive gabled windows. The clock dates from 1688. There is an upper sanctuary over the low vaulting surrounding the main altar in the chancel: this is the only one in the country.

The sturdy arches are borne on round Norman piers of hard limestone. The *reredos*, carved from a single piece of oak, is Norman; it is believed to be the oldest wood carving in England. Nearby is beautiful *Eastbury Manor*, with ancient cedars. The painter G.F. Watts (1817-1904) lived in Compton; museum.

Guildford to Dorking: 12 miles on A25. The road follows A246 to *Merrow*, then turns right across the downs to *Newlands Corner*, from where there is a famous view. — 5½ miles: **Shere**, in the valley of the Tillingbourne, in a beautiful part of the downs. To the north is Netley Heath (616 ft), to the south Holmbury Hill (857 ft), with a prehistoric camp. Around Shere's Norman and Early English church of St James are narrow old-world streets of 16th and 17th century houses. At the foot of Albury Downs, just off the road, is the much visited and very beautiful *Silent Pool*. At *Abinger Hammer* are a clock with a figure which strikes the hours and an old mill. — 9 miles: *Wotton*. — 12 miles: *Dorking* (p. 320).

Guildford to Horsham: 20 miles on A281. 1 mile: *Shalford*, a large but attractive village in beautiful surroundings. The Pilgrims' Way runs nearby through Chantries Wood. To the south is *Tangley Manor*, one of the finest examples of timbered architecture in the country: it is said to have been a hunting lodge of King John (1199-1216). — 3 miles: *Bramley;* the hills between here and Godalming are thickly wooded. — 10 miles: *Dunsfold Green*. — 13 miles: *Alfold*. — 19 miles: *Broadbridge Heath*. — 20 miles: *Horsham* (p. 320).

38 miles: **Milford.** From here there are two roads to Chichester, A 283 via *Petworth* (28 miles) and A 286 via *Haslemere* (27 miles). The route via Petworth is described first, with the other route as an alternative. For **Portsmouth**, see below, p. 337.

15 miles from Milford on A 283 is the old town of **Petworth** (pop. 2600). It is a splendid example of a feudal town grouped round the lord's house, and

consists of winding and narrow streets with many 16th and 17th century houses. The *church of SS. Mary and Thomas* is on the site of a Saxon building, but is chiefly 14th, 15th and 16th century work.

Petworth House was rebuilt 1686-98 in the form of a rectangle, of freestone with Portland stone dressings. The south front was reconstructed between 1869 and 1872 by Anthony Salvin. The house includes the mid 13th century Percy Chapel and galleries, and state rooms magnificently carved by Grinling Gibbons, and contains one of the largest and finest private collections of paintings in England, including masterpieces by *Vandyck, Holbein, Hobbema, Correggio, Velazquez, Franz Hals, Murillo, Lely, Kneller, Reynolds, Gainsborough, Lawrence, Romney, Cuyp, Claude, Andrea del Sarto,* and some of the best landscapes that *Turner* ever painted. Park (735 acres) open to the public.

Alternative route from Milford to Chichester via Haslemere: 27 miles on A 286.

23 miles: *Upper Waltham.* 24 miles: the road runs into the old Roman *Stane Street* and follows it to **Chichester** (28 miles).

1 mile: *Witley,* a picturesque village in which George Eliot once lived. 7 miles: **Haslemere** (pop. 14,000, E.C. Wednesday), pleasantly situated on a hill, in wooded countryside which is known as the "Highlands of Surrey". A festival of 16th, 17th and 18th century music is held here every July. *Educational Museum* (science, local history).

15 miles: *Midhurst,* near which are the very interesting ruins of **Cowdray Castle.** Begun in 1530 by the Earl of Southampton, this was one of the finest country houses of the period, containing many treasures. The most interesting parts are the great hall with its minstrels' gallery and a large corbelled and mullioned window, the ruins of the chapel, the cellars and the gatehouse, now used as a museum. Very fine view from the south-east tower.

18 miles: *Cocking,* an excellent centre for exploring the Downs. Nearby is *Linch Down* or *Ball* (818 ft), one the high points of the Downs, with the pleasant villages of Bepton, Didling and Treyford nestling in the foothills. 21 miles: *Singleton.* 1 mile to the east is **Goodwood Park,** seat of the Duke of Richmond

(by Wyatt, 1780-1800). Picture gallery with fine collection (*Reynolds, Lawrence, Romney, van Dyck*: open on Wednesdays and Sundays in summer 2 to 6). On the estate is *Goodwood Racecourse*, where the race meeting — an informal version of Ascot — during the last week of July attracts fashionable crowds. *Charlton Racecourse* is also nearby. During the 17th century the Charlton Hunt was the most famous in England. 27 miles: **Chichester.**

Chichester (pop. 22,000, E.C. Thursday). The best vantage point from which the town and Cathedral of Chichester can be viewed is *St Roche's Hill* on Chichester Downs (4 miles north), which affords one of the best panoramas in South England, with the slender spire of the Cathedral rising in the near distance and, far away, the Isle of Wight behind Portsmouth and Spithead. At the top of the hill is the Trundle (circle), a hill stronghold of the Iron Age (1st century B.C.).

The Saxons landed in Wessex in 477, and the Roman town of Chichester *(Regnum)* was attacked and taken. Aella became king of the area, but the town takes its name from his third son, Cissa. Soon after the Norman Conquest the episcopal see of Selsey was transferred to Chichester, in line with William the Conqueror's policy of establishing the bishops in towns. Roger de Montgomery built a castle, the motte of which can be seen in Priory Park: it is not known whether the original timber ramparts were ever rebuilt in stone. During the 12th century Chichester suffered severely from fires. When there was a danger of French attack in the first half of the 14th century the town walls were repaired, and it is these walls that can still be seen today.

An interesting walk is the half-circuit from *East Gate* to *West Gate*. The *Market Cross*, at the intersection of the two main streets, called after the points of the compass, was erected by Bishop Storey shortly before 1500. (Restored 1724).

The **Cathedral** is one of the smaller cathedrals, but both the outside and the interior appear larger than

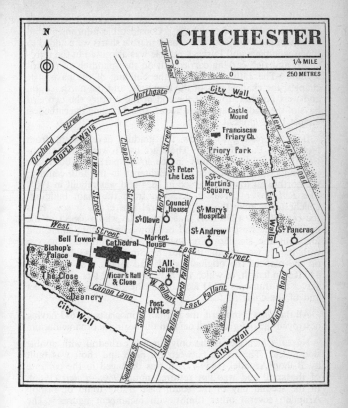

they really are because attention to proportion and balance has been paid in each successive addition.

In 1184, when the church was consecrated, it consisted of an aisled presbytery of three bays with an apse, aisleless transepts, and a nave of 8 bays with two west towers. The style was severely plain Norman. In 1187 fire again destroyed part of the church, which was restored. The clerestory was refashioned and the church vaulted to render it fire-proof, and at the same time the east end was rebuilt: the apse was replaced by a square-ended retro-choir of two bays. Considerable adornment and ornamentation was added: Purbeck marble shafts were added to the arcade piers and Purbeck marble was also used in the retro-choir, and rich carving carried out on the spandrels of the triforium. The 13th century saw the building of the nave aisle chapels, the chapels east of the transepts, and the north, south, and west porches: towards the end of the century the two east bays of the Lady Chapel were added, thus bringing the cathedral almost to its present form.

It is interesting to follow the gradual development from Norman to Early English. There are two towers. The south-west tower is 12th century in the lower part, but buttresses were added and the tower was heightened in the 13th century; the north-west tower collapsed in 1634 and was rebuilt in 1901. The *Bell Tower* (1440) is detached from the main building: Chichester is now the only cathedral where this is so. It is the *central spire* (292 feet) that unifies the whole aspect of the building: the west towers and bell tower are rather squat and low, but the slender spire soars skywards, drawing the eye with it. It was rebuilt in 1861 by Sir George Gilbert Scott on the plan of the original, which had fallen. The church is 410 feet in length, of which the nave is only 172 feet. The width across the transepts is 131 feet, and the height of the nave 62 feet and of the choir 65 feet.

All the glass is modern, the Puritan iconoclasts in 1643 having destroyed the old glass and defaced the beautiful ornamentation.

Nave. Chichester is the only English cathedral with double side aisles. The *screen* between the nave and choir was built by Bishop Arundel (1459-77); it was damaged in the collapse of the spire and was not restored until 1960. *Pulpit* (1966). In the second bay of the south aisle is the tomb of Bishop Arundel; several other tombs with recumbent figures. The *choir* is raised (four steps). The stalls are notable for their 14th century misericords, representing monsters and satirical subjects. Behind the high altar is an Aubusson tapestry to a design by John Piper (1966). At the east end are the tombs of several bishops. In the **south choir aisle** are magnificent *Saxon carvings* (Christ in the house of Martha and Mary, the raising of Lazarus) and the tomb of Bishop Sherburne (1508-36).

Transept. Bishop Langton (1305-37) was responsible for the large stained glass window. The large *paintings on the west* *wall* are 16th century, by Bernardi: portraits of English kings from William the Conqueror to Edward VI (the series was later continued to George I). Of the decorations in the vaulting there survive only some arabesques on one bay of the Lady Chapel: all the rest were whitewashed during restoration work in 1817. On *Plough Monday*, at the beginning of January each year, the traditional ceremony of blessing a plough is held.

To the west is the **Bishop's Palace,** a 12th century building with a kitchen dating from that period and a 15th century wing containing a dining room with a panelled ceiling painted by Bernardi. The south front has Georgian windows. The gatehouse is 14th century. The **cloisters** (15th c.) have a covered walk round three sides. The *Close* is very peaceful and beautiful. From the south end of the cloisters St Richard's Walk runs into Canon Lane, which leads to the gatehouse of the Bishop's Palace. The Residentiary and the Chantry are both of ancient date. Vicar's Close runs parallel to St Richard's Walk at the east end, near Canon's Gate; it was built in the 15th century for the Vicars Choral. In the court to the north is Canons' Hall, with a fine timber roof; below it is a vaulted crypt.

In North St is the tiny **St Olave's Church,** now a library; it is the oldest in Chichester, built on Roman foundations. It has a Norman nave 25 feet by 17 feet and a 13th century chancel only 13 feet square. There is an elaborate 14th century piscina. The church of *St Peter the Less* has a squat tower (14th c.) and a modern chancel. In East St is *St Andrew's*, dating from the 13th century.

In *St Martin's Square* and *Little London* are the most interesting houses. **St Mary's Hospital,** concealed behind its small gatehouse in a secluded square, is a mediaeval infirmary which has changed little in its planning and arrangements since it was built.

Founded during the reign of Henry II (1154-89), it was installed in 1229 on the site of the church of *St Peter in the Market* (corner of East and South St). In 1269 the hospital occupied the present building when its previous tenants, the

Grey Friars, moved to the site of the castle. The plan, like that of other old hospitals, is similar to a church, with the patients accommodated in the nave. The present building is an aisled hall, rather like a mediaeval barn, with a chapel at the east end. It is a magnificent timber structure with a light roof, borne on two rows of massive posts reinforced by diagonal ties and horizontal beams, overhanging the lateral aisles. The hall, originally 100 feet long, now measures only 79 feet. The chapel is built in stone. In mediaeval times pilgrims used to sleep here. The Hospital is now an almshouse.

Chichester Museum is in the old church of the Grey Friars in Priory Park (open in summer Tuesday-Saturday 10 to 5).

There is another *museum* at 29 Little London, with Roman remains, 17th century carving, etc. (open weekdays 10 to 5).

1¼ miles west on the Portsmouth road (A27) is the Roman site of **Fishbourne Palace** (open to visitors), a splendid mansion, the largest discovered in Britain, dating from the 1st-3rd centuries. There is a small museum.

8 miles south on B 2145 is **Selsey Bill,** with the seaside resorts of Wittering, Bracklesham, Selsey and Pagham. From West Itchenor Chichester Channel and Bosham Channel run inland, providing sheltered anchorages. This is a region of very attractive scenery.

4 miles east on the Arundel road (A 27) is **Boxgrove,** with an Early English priory (two bays of the earlier Norman nave still survive). From their similarity to the paintings in Chichester Cathedral the paintings in the vaulting can be attributed to Bernardi.

Milford to Portsmouth

41 miles (from London): *Thursley*. The name ("grove sacred to the thunder god, Thunor") reveals its Saxon origin. 44½ miles: *Hindhead* (pop. 2500, E.C. Wednesday). To the east of the village is the

Devil's Punch Bowl, and close by is the fine viewpoint of Gibbet Hill (895 ft).

All the magnificent heath and open woodland south of Gibbet Hill is now National Trust property, together with the adjoining open spaces and larch woods of Frydinghurst Common. Pleasant trips to Nutcombe Down, Tyndall Wood, Woodcock Bottom, Golden Valley and Whitmoor Valley. Highcombe Bottom, in the Devil's Punch Bowl, also belongs to the National Trust.

56¾ miles: *Petersfield* (pop. 7000, E.C. Wednesday), with an interesting Norman church (restored). 65 miles: *Horndean*.

74 miles: **Portsmouth** and (75 miles) **Southsea** (pop. 256,000, E.C. Wednesday and Saturday), Britain's chief naval base, affectionately known by inhabitants and by seamen the world over as "Pompey". Its magnificent harbour, nearly 5 miles long, is admirably situated between two projecting tongues of land, and its famous approach, the *Spithead* roadstead, is sheltered by the Isle of Wight. In addition to its large naval establishment Portsmouth has also an important military garrison and is the largest town on the south coast. The town consists of Landport (north-east), Southsea (south-east) and Portsea (north-west) and Old Portsmouth.

Royal Dockyard. First laid down about 1540 by Henry VIII and fortified within the general scheme of defences along the coast, the Royal Dockyard has developed into an immense establishment extending over more than 300 acres and comprising four large dry docks, 75 acres of fitting and repairing basins, an arsenal, building slips, and all the engineering, scientific and supply installations necessary for the building and maintenance of the Royal Navy.

"*Victory*" *Museum* (relics of Nelson, panorama of Trafalgar), Royal Naval College and Admiralty House. Visitors accompanied by official guides may view the dockyard daily from 10 to 6 (Sundays 1 to 6).

H.M.S. Victory. Nelson's flagship (launched 1765) at the Battle of Trafalgar, 1805, has been repaired and restored and now rests, flying Nelson's historic signal, in the Old Dock (King Charles's Dock: 1650). A simple plaque marks the spot where Nelson fell mortally wounded at the moment of victory.

City Museum and Art Gallery, Alexandra Road: furniture and china, pictures (open 10 to 6 or 7).

Portsmouth suffered severely from air raids during the second world war, losing many of its old buildings. One building which survived intact was *Buckingham House,* in which the first Duke of Buckingham was murdered (1628). Opposite it, at the end of High St, is the church of St Thomas Becket (1180, restored 1900; since 1927 the choir and sanctuary of **Portsmouth Cathedral**). In the right-hand aisle is the tomb of the Duke of Buckingham (1631). The Cathedral is in course of being enlarged.

At 393 Commercial Road is the **birthplace of Charles Dickens** (1812), now a museum (open in summer 10 to 6).

From the *Round Tower*, north of the harbour, there are fine views.

From the *Platform* (at the west end of High St, above *Grand Parade*) there is a splendid view of the port and Spithead. Boat trips round the harbour and to H.M. ships in port.

Southsea is now a popular seaside resort with two piers, the Clarence and West Parade. On D Day in June 1944 thousands of troops embarked here for France from specially built jetties.

Southsea Castle was built by Henry VIII (1540) and later altered. It now contains a *military and archaeological museum* (open 10 to 6 or 7).

Gosport, on the opposite side of Portsmouth Harbour, facing Portsmouth (pop. 60,000). The population consists almost entirely of employees of the Royal Clarence Victualling Yards.

PORTSMOUTH

Haslar Naval Hospital has an interesting museum.   At the
narrow entrance to the harbour is *Blockhouse Fort* (submarine
base).

Portsmouth to Southampton

22 miles on A 27. The road runs through the northern districts of Portsmouth (Cosham). From the old village of *Southwick* (on A 333 to Wickham) Gen. Eisenhower gave the order
to land in Normandy in June 1944.

7 miles: **Portchester,** the Roman station of *Portus Castra*
and the oldest port in this area, on the north side of Portsmouth
Harbour. The outer walls of Portchester Castle are Roman;
the keep and other parts are Norman. The church built within
the walls is 12th century. The monument to Nelson was erected
by the officers and crew of the "Victory".

9 miles: **Fareham** (pop. 70,000, E.C. Wednesday), a busy
town and harbour; railway junction for Gosport. 12 miles:
Titchfield. Henry VI was married to Margaret of Anjou in
the 13th century abbey. The nave of the old abbey is the part
with stone mullioned windows and Tudor chimneys. In the
village are a beautiful Early English church and the ruins of
Titchfield House (16th c.). — 15 miles: *Sarisbury*. 16 miles:
Swanwick. 22 miles: **Southampton** (p. 349).

10. LONDON TO WINCHESTER
AND SOUTHAMPTON

The quickest route to Winchester and Southampton is by motorway (M 3), which is entered from A 305 at Sunbury. The motorway runs roughly parallel to the old London-Salisbury road (A 30), described in Route 11.

The route described in this chapter is by A 31, which branches off A 3 at Guildford (p. 328). London to Winchester 68 miles, to Southampton 80 miles.

From Guildford A 31 follows the line of the *Pilgrims' Way*, the old Roman road used by pilgrims from 1174, when Henry II made his pilgrimage to the tomb of the murdered Archbishop Thomas Becket at Canterbury.

The road soon passes over the sharp ridge known as the *Hog's Back*, from which there are fine views of the heather-covered hills of Buckinghamshire to the north and Frensham Great Pond, the South Downs and Sussex to the south. To the west is wooded country in Hampshire and Berkshire.

34 miles: *Wanborough*, a small village on the north slope of the *Hog's Back*. St Bartholomew's Church is one of the smallest and oldest in England: it is of flint and stone, with Roman tile, in Early English style. To the south is *Puttenham*, with its red-roofed cottages: beyond Puttenham Common are a number of beautiful lakes. The caves are interesting. Barrows.

36 miles: *Seale*. Charming red-roofed cottages and a 13th century church (rebuilt 1860). 2 miles to the south stands the *Soldier's Ring*, an Iron Age camp at the place called the Sands. To the north are Aldershot and Farnborough (Route 11, p. 375).

39 miles: **Farnham,** in a hop-growing district.

The **castle** was the palace of the Bishops of Winchester, and the 12th century keep is incorporated in the present 17th century building. The park can be visited. William Cobbett (1762-1835), author of "Rural Rides", was born in the Jolly Farmer inn. *Walter House Museum* (local history). 1 mile away is *Moor Park*, where Swift worked as secretary for Sir William Temple (17th century) and met Stella.

On B 3001 to Milford (see p. 330) are (2 miles) the ruins of the 12th century *Waverley Abbey*, the first Cistercian foundation in this country; Scott is said to have taken the title of his first novel from it.

44 miles: *Bentley*, which has a Norman church with 13th century work.

49 miles: **Alton** (pop. 10,000, E.C. Wednesday), with *St Lawrence's Church* (interesting brasses) and *Curtis Museum* (Roman pottery). 50¾ miles: *Chawton*, in wooded country, with the house in which Jane Austen lived. *Chawton Park* manor-house (16th and 17th c.) has fine panelling. — 53 miles: *Four Marks*. The road climbs to nearly 700 feet. 60 miles: *New Alresford*.

To the south of *Ovington* is *Tichborne*, where bread is distributed to the people of the village on 25 March every year, under a bequest by Sir Roger de Tichborne's wife in the 12th century.

68 miles: **Winchester.**

Winchester

Winchester (pop. 31,000, E.C. Thursday), on the river Itchen, besides being one of the most ancient, is also one of the most graceful and unspoilt of English cities.

Its long history reaches back to the days of the Roman occupation, when it was called *Venta Belgarum*, and it was a capital city before London. The Cathedral is the longest Gothic

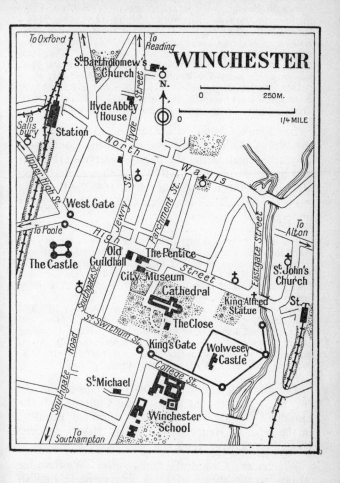

To Oxford
To Reading
St. Bartholomew's Church
WINCHESTER
N.
0   250 M.
0   1/4 MILE
Hyde Abbey House
To Salisbury
Station
Hyde Street
North Walls
To Poole
West Gate
Jewry St.
Parchment St.
Upper High St.
To Alton
The Castle
Old Guildhall
The Pentice
High Street
St. John's Church
City Museum
Cathedral
King Alfred Statue
St.
St. Swithun St.
The Close
Southgate St.
King's Gate
Wolwesey Castle
Eastgate Street
Southgate Road
St. Michael
College St.
To Southampton
Winchester School

church in Europe, with superb examples of Norman, Early English and Perpendicular work. Within the Cathedral are buried *William Rufus*, son of William the Conqueror, and *William of Wykeham*, who was responsible for rebuilding the nave and aisles. The only remaining portion of Winchester Castle, once the home of William the Conqueror, is the great hall in which hangs the Round Table of the legendary King Arthur and his knights. In this hall Sir Walter Raleigh, the great Elizabethan seaman, was sentenced to death in 1603. The town's prosperity for long depended on the woollen trade.

The **King's Castle,** on the hillside to the south of the West Gate, was built by William the Conqueror. It was besieged during the reign of Stephen (1135-54) and again during the Civil War, and was destroyed after it was taken by Cromwell in 1645. All that is left is the *Great Hall*, a postern gate and some curious underground passages.

It is in Early English style, with some traces of the original Norman work. The *Round Table of King Arthur*, first mentioned in the 14th century, is 18 feet in diameter and seats 25. The 14th century *West Gate* (museum) is one of the two surviving town gates, of which there were originally five. The drawbridge chains passed through openings under the grotesque heads on the outer side. Note carvings on the west wall by 16th and 17th century prisoners; the original Winchester Bushel and other standard measures of great historical interest, including Henry I's standard yard (based on the length of the king's arm); and a 10th century ship recovered from the river Hamble. (Visiting daily from 10 a.m. to dusk; admission free).

The graceful Gothic *City Cross* or *Butter Cross*, in the High St near St Lawrence's Church and the Guildhall (1713), was erected by Cardinal Beaufort in the reign of Henry VI (1422-61). It was restored by Gilbert Scott in 1865.

Winchester Cathedral ranks after Westminster Abbey as the shrine of kings and princes; English sovereigns were crowned here for many centuries — as

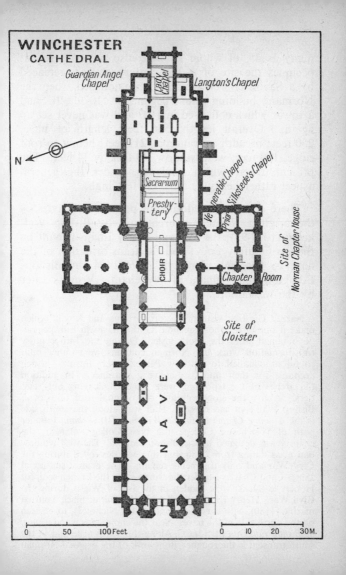

WINCHESTER
CATHEDRAL

Guardian Angel
Chapel

Lady
Chapel

Langton's Chapel

N

Sacrarium

Presby-
tery

Venerable Chapel

Prior Silkstede's Chapel

Site of
Norman Chapter House

CHOIR

Chapter Room

Site of
Cloister

NAVE

0   50   100 Feet

0   10   20   30 M.

many as 35, of whom 20 were also buried here. It occupies the site of a 2nd century church, replaced by a Saxon church which was demolished when the Norman building was begun in 1079. It had a tower which collapsed in 1107 and was never set up again. Overall length, 556 feet; length of nave, 250 feet; breadth at transepts, 217 feet; height to roof ridge, 109 feet; west window, 53 feet by 34 feet. The present tower, which tends to render the general aspect rather heavy, is only 138 feet high.

There are three predominant periods and styles — the original Norman church built by Bishop Walkelyn (1079-93); the east end (Early English) built by Bishop Godfrey Lucy; and the transformation of the nave to Perpendicular style (1360-1404) by Bishops Edington and William of Wykeham. Visitors enter by the west door.

Nave. The best vista of the proportions and length, which make it one of the most splendid Gothic naves in Europe, can be obtained from the south aisle. During the 14th century transformation work the Norman columns were either built round or chiselled to the new Perpendicular form — which accounts for their unduly massive appearance. In addition the arches of the triforium were removed, leaving only two tiers. Above the stone vaulting the original roof timbers of Bishop Walkelyn can be seen. Half way along the south side is the *Chantry Chapel of Bishop William of Wykeham*, founder both of Winchester College and New College, Oxford; the chantry was designed by the Bishop himself. The west window had glass dating from 1380, but this was destroyed during the Civil War and only fragments remain. The bronze statues of James I and Charles I under the window (by the French sculptor Hubert le Sueur) were hidden in the Isle of Wight during the Civil War. Henry III was baptised in the *font* of black Tournai marble (1180), with carved decoration (St Nicholas), to be seen on the north side of the nave. Near the choir steps is the *Chapel of Bishop Edington* (d. 1366). Along the south aisle and in the south transept is the rougher stonework of the original Norman church, in sharp contrast with the columns supporting the tower.

South transept. The 11th or 12th century *Pilgrim's Gate*, between the south transept and the choir, is said to be the oldest piece of iron grille work in the country. In the *Silkstede Chapel* is the tomb of Izaak Walton (d. 1683) whose name is associated with the Itchen.

Choir. The great thickness of the columns is due to the attempt of the builders to avoid a repetition of the collapse of the tower. The magnificent dark oak **choir stalls,** with beautifully carved and quaint misericord seats, date from the 14th century. The presbytery arches date from the 14th century and the wooden roof vaulting has interesting carving (1500) on the bosses. The pulpit was presented to Prior Silkstede in the early 16th century. The fine *Great Screen* is late 15th century work; the niches are ornamented with delicate fretted stonework; the images (1885) replace those destroyed at the Reformation. On the stone Renaissance side-screens round the presbytery (early 16th century) repose richly coloured mortuary chests containing the bones of Kings Ethelwulf, Egbert and Canute, and queens and bishops. In the centre of the choir is the black *tomb of William Rufus,* son of William the Conqueror.

Retro-choir. On the south side is the *chantry chapel of Cardinal Beaufort* (d. 1447), founder of Eton College. On the north side is the *chantry chapel of Bishop Waynflete,* founder of Magdalen College, Oxford. In the south aisle is the *chantry chapel of Bishop Fox,* secretary of Henry VII (1485-1509) and Lord Privy Seal, who founded Corpus Christi College, Oxford. In the north aisle is the *chantry chapel of Bishop Gardiner,* who married Mary Tudor and Philip II of Spain in the Cathedral in 1554. At the north-east corner is the *Chapel of the Guardian Angels,* with a statue (by Hubert le Sueur) of the Earl of Portland (d. 1634), Lord Treasurer of Charles I. In the centre is the *Lady Chapel,* with interesting Early English and early 16th century wall paintings. At the south-east corner is the *chantry chapel of Bishop Langton* (1501), who died of plague after being elected Archbishop of Canterbury.

North transept. Norman work which resembles the south transept. The entrance to the **crypt** is here: west part Norman, east section after Bishop Lucy's plans.

College St leads to **Winchester College,** founded by
Bishop William of Wykeham. The well-proportioned
and simple buildings of St Mary's College of Winchester are very much as they built in the 14th century:
the *chapel* is in great contrast and contains much
ornamentation. *Thurburn's Tower* was built in 1481.

The statue of the *Virgin and Child* over the great entrance
gate is ancient and was saved from the iconoclasts during the
Civil War. **Outer Court,** with the *Election Chamber* and, above
the central doorway, a statue of the founder with the Virgin
and the Archangel Gabriel. **Chamber Court,** with the *Hall* (panelling, tables and benches and ceiling beams, all of oak), the kitchen
and various domestic offices. At the entrance to the kitchen is a
curious painting, "The Trusty Servant", dating from 1560 but
repainted several times during the reign of George III. The
Perpendicular windows and the delicate wood carving in the
vaulting are original. In the centre is the *Fromond Chapel*,
commemorating a 15th century bursar. Visiting: 10 to 6 in
summer.

Wolvesey Castle, the castle of the Bishops of Winchester, was built by Prince Henry, Bishop of Blois,
King Stephen's half-brother. It was dismantled
during the Civil War, but part of the original Norman
walls can still be seen. The present Bishop's Palace
is the surviving wing of a palace built by Sir Christopher Wren on this site.

The oldest almshouse in England, the **St Cross
Hospital,** is on the west bank of the Itchen, a mile
outside the town walls. It was founded by Henry of
Blois in 1136. To the east are the old brewhouse and
domestic offices. To the west are the huge kitchens
and a quadrangle round which are the brothers'
lodgings, the refectory, the nave of the church and an
old courtyard of mellow brick. The chapel is a fine
transitional Norman building. Visiting: 9 to 5,
except Sundays.

The *City Museum* (open from 10 to 5 or 6) contains Iron Age, Roman and Saxon material from local excavations.

The **town walls** can be seen in an interesting walk, beginning in High St, down past the *statue of King Alfred* (erected in 1901 to commemorate the 1000th anniversary of his death), and turning right along the river bank.

Other features of interest are *Jane Austen's House*, 8 College St; *Kingsgate*, with *St Swithin's Church*; *Close Gate* and *Cheyney Court*; *Godbegot House*; *Abbey House* and gardens; the *City Mill*; and the old *Chesil Rectory*.

There are fine views from the two hills overlooking the city: St Giles' Hill to the east, where a large fair was formerly held, and St Catherine's Hill to the south, at the foot of which are earthworks dating from the early Iron Age (3rd c. B.C.).

Winchester to Southampton: 12 miles on A 33 (partly dual carriageway).

Southampton

Southampton (pop. 210,000, E.C. Wednesday) is a great transatlantic port, situated at the head of a deep and sheltered inlet.

The area was occupied in Stone Age times, and much material dating from this period has been found. In 43 A.D. the Romans established a port here to serve *Venta Belgarum* (Winchester), and built the fort of *Clausentum* (Bitterne), on the Itchen, to protect it. The first Saxon invaders landed here in 495. The township took the name of *Hamtun*, and a charter of 962, in the reign of Kind Edgar, refers to it as *Suthhamtune*. This was the embarkation point for the English forces who fought at Crecy and Agincourt, for the British expeditionary forces of 1914 and 1939, and for many of the Allied troops who landed in Normandy in 1944. During the last war Southampton was exposed to heavy air bombardment and suffered severe damage. It is well known as the home port of the famous transatlantic liners "Queen Elizabeth" and "Queen Mary".

Southampton Docks earn the town the title of the "Gateway to England". The harbour is 6 miles inland at the head of an estuary (600 feet wide at its narrowest) with an approach

channel 35 feet deep at low spring tide. No closed docks are
necessary since by reason of its position double tides ensure prolonged high water of long duration (two hours). In 1836,
216 acres of marshy land were reclaimed. *Ocean Dock* (North
Atlantic terminal) has a water surface of 15½ acres and a
minimum depth of 40 feet. Along the entire length of the berth
a new passenger terminal was opened in 1953. *New Dock*
provides a deep water quay 1½ miles long with accommodation
for 8 large liners. In all there are 28,922 feet of quays. The
King George V Graving Dock is 1200 feet long and 135 feet
wide and able to accommodate ships of up to 100,000 tons
gross. The dock railway system, connected with the main
lines, extends over 78 miles.

The docks have the most up-to-date equipment. *Town Quay*
is used by coastal shipping; the *Royal Pier* is the landing-stage
for local services and for trips in Southampton Water. The
car ferry terminal for services to the Continent (Le Havre,
Cherbourg) is to the east, on the Itchen. The port handles a
traffic of 30 million tons a year.

The old town lies to the south-west. Entering the
town by *London Road*, we pass on the right the Civic
Centre (see below) and continue along *Above Bar St*
to **Bar Gate**, the old north gate of the town.

Bar Gate, originally built in the late 12th century, was strengthened in the 13th and 15th centuries. On the first floor is the
old *Guildhall*, now a *museum of local history* (open 10 to 12
and 1 to 5).

To the right, a few steps away, are the old **town
walls,** dating from the Norman period, with a number
of well preserved **towers** and **gates:**

Arundel Tower, Catchcold Tower, Watergate (in striking
contrast with *Castle House*, built 1963), *Biddlesgate, King
John's House* (12th c.), *Westgate* (with a memorial to the Pilgrim
Fathers who left Southampton on the "Mayflower"). To the
south is **Wool House,** a late mediaeval house built by Italian
merchants, now the *Maritime Museum* (open 10 to 5); *Watergate Tower* and **God's House Tower,** now an *archaeological
museum* with Roman, Saxon and mediaeval material (open
10 to 5).

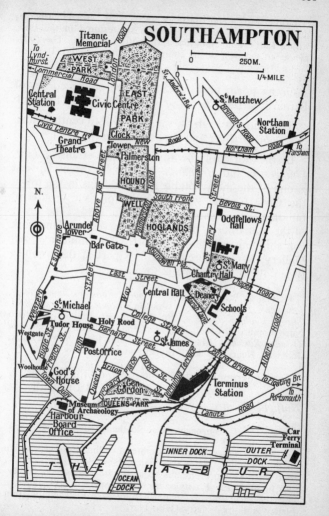

SOUTHAMPTON

0   250 M.
1/4 MILE

To Lynd-hurst

Commercial Road

Central Station

Titanic Memorial

WEST PARK

London Road

EAST PARK

Civic Centre

Clock Tower

Civic Centre Rd.

Grand Theatre

St. Andrew's Rd.

St. Matthew

Kingston Road

Northam Station

To Farsham

New Road

Palmerston

HOUND

WELLS

HOGLANDS

South Front

Bevois St.

Oddfellows Hall

St. Mary's Street

Kingsway

Northam Road

Above Bar Street

Arundel Tower

N.

Bar Gate

Hanover Pl.

St. Mary

Chantry Hall

Chapel Road

Esplanade

East Street

Way

Central Hall

Deanery

Schools

Marsh Lane

St. Michael

College Street

Western Esplanade

Tudor House

Holy Rood

Bernard Street

St. James

Westgate

Bugle St.

French St.

High St.

Post Office

Woolhouse

God's House

Queen's

Briton

Terrace

Oxford St.

Gen. Gordon

QUEENS PARK

Museum of Archaeology

Harbour Board Office

Central Bridge

Albert Road

Terminus Station

To Floating Br. to Portsmouth

Canute Road

Car Ferry Terminal

OCEAN DOCK

INNER DOCK

OUTER DOCK

T H E   H A R B O U R

To the west, a short distance away, is **St Michael's Church,** built in the 11th century and clumsily restored in the 19th, with a 12th century font and 15th century lecterns. The *Tudor House*, to the west of the church, dates from 1491-1518 (open 10 to 5).

Going north up High St, we see at the corner of Bernard St the *Church of the Holy Rood* (14th c.).

Returning to High St, we see two 18th century inns, the *Dolphin Hotel* and the *Star Hotel*.

In the north of the town are the extensive *East, Palmerston* and *Houndwell Parks*. To the north-west is one of the most notable new buildings in the town, the **Civic Centre,** which consists of four groups of buildings set in gardens, opened in 1934. The tower of the *Law Courts*, 182 feet high, serves as a landmark for shipping entering the port. The municipal **Art Gallery,** in Commercial Road, is part of the complex (open 10 to 7, Sundays 2 to 5).

Pictures by British painters *(Reynolds, Romney, Gainsborough, Lawrence, Turner)*, French (**Poussin,** *Millet, Delacroix, Corot, Sisley, Vuillard, Pissarro, Utrillo, Renoir*), Italian (**Allegretto Nuzi, Lorenzo di Credi,** *Vivarini, Cesare da Sesto*), Dutch *(van Ostade,* **Ruysdael, Maes,** *Hobbema)* and Flemish (**van Dyck, Jordaens, Roger van der Weyden**) and a bronze by *Degas*.

In the extreme north of the town, on the Winchester road, is the *University* (founded 1850), with the *Nuffield Theatre* (by Sir Basil Spence, 1964).

Surroundings of Southampton

1. **Netley Abbey,** 3 miles south-east. This *Cistercian abbey* on Southampton Water was founded by Henry III in 1237, after the transfer of monks from beautiful Beaulieu Abbey. It is in Early English style; the outer walls are still standing, with the exception of the north transept. Reached by train (Netley station) or ferry (Woolston).

2. Romsey, 8 miles north-west, with a very beautiful *abbey* (see p. 377).

3. Lymington, by way of *Beaulieu Abbey* and the **New Forest.** The New Forest, covering an area of over 92,000 acres between Southampton and Bournemouth, was once a hunting ground in which William the Conqueror hunted deer. It is a densely wooded region in which wild ponies roam. *Bolrewood, Whitleywood, Mark Ash* and *Denny Wood* have magnificent stands of beech, ash and oak. Some of the trees are of very large size, like the "Naked Man" and the "Knightwood Oak" (circumference 21 ft). The rhododendrons in Rhinefield Park are superb.

9 miles: **Lyndhurst** (pop. 2900, E.C. Wednesday), "capital" of the New Forest. In *St Michael's Church*, which has a beautiful spire, is a fresco (1864) by Lord Leighton, "The Wise and Foolish Virgins" (on the east wall). *Queen's House* is a handsome 17th century house in which the Verderers, who administer the New Forest, hold their meetings.

13 miles: *Brockenhurst* (pop. 2500, E.C. Wednesday), one of the many old villages in the heart of the New Forest which are the starting point of pleasant walks in the forest. *St Nicholas's Church*, in stone and brick, with some Norman work.

18 miles: **Lymington** (pop. 30,000, E.C. Wednesday), on a site which was occupied in prehistoric times. Nearby are **Buckland Rings,** an Iron Age earthwork. This sheltered resort on the Solent is a good centre for sailing. From Woodside Gardens there is a very fine view of the Isle of Wight. Fishing, water sports, bathing. Ferry service to Isle of Wight (p. 355).

6 miles north-east is **Beaulieu Abbey,** a Cistercian house founded in 1204 by King John which enjoyed the right of asylum. Picturesque ruins. The church is the former refectory of the abbey, and the north doorway opens into the ruined cloisters. The chapter house was to the east, approached through the cloisters, of which three beautiful arches remain. *Palace House,* the old gatehouse, is the residence of Lord Montagu of Beaulieu. In the grounds is an interesting **Motor Museum** (open 10 to 6).

2 miles away down Beaulieu Creek is **Bucklers Hard,** where some of the finest old timber ships of the Royal Navy were built, including the "Agamemnon" (commanded by Nelson in 1793), the "Bellerophon" which took Napoleon into exile in 1815, the "Illustrious" and the "Euryalus". Mariner's Chapel and *Maritime Museum.*

4 miles south is *Milford-on-Sea*, with a very beautiful Saxon and Norman church (11th c.). Leaning tower (Early English); picture attributed to Perugino. Beyond this, 6 miles from Lymington, is *Hurst Castle*, situated at the end of a promontory projecting into the sea. This was one of the castles built by Henry VIII for coastal defence; Charles I was confined here during his last journey from Carisbrooke to London. *Peterson's Tower* is a campanile-like structure built of concrete, one of a series of experiments in the use of concrete carried out at the end of the 19th century by A.T.T. Peterson. It is 24 feet square and has walls 2 feet thick.

7 miles south-west, in the middle of Christchurch Bay, is *Barton-on-Sea*, where there are four tides daily as a result of the accumulation of water in the bay. Beautiful sand and shingle bay at the foot of rugged cliffs 100 feet high. Interesting beds of clayey rock, in which many fossils have been found. Good walks along the cliffs to Chewton Bunny (to west) and Beckton Bunny and Milford-on-Sea (to east). *New Milton*, a pleasant holiday place joined on to Barton. To the north, at *Hinton Admiral*, is one of the oldest inns in England, the 12th century "Cat and Fiddle". This was a resort of smugglers, who landed their goods at Highcliffe and brought them up Chewton Glen to the inn. *Highcliffe Castle* was built with stone from an earlier Norman castle; William II, the German Kaiser, stayed here in 1907.

THE ISLE OF WIGHT

In the small compass of 147 square miles the beautiful Isle of Wight offers a tremendous variety of typical English scenery. Geological eccentricities have endowed it with striking cliffs and romantic gorges: its mild climate has made it bloom like a well-tended garden. The Romans conquered it and named it *Vectis* (or *Ictis*) in A.D. 43; in the 5th century it was settled by the Jutes. Queen Victoria's favourite residence was Osborne House, near *Cowes*, where she died in 1901.

There are three regular routes to the island: (1) Portsmouth Harbour to Ryde, half an hour; (2) Lymington to Yarmouth, 25 minutes; (3) Southampton to Cowes, 1 hour and then on to Ryde. In summer there are also many excursion steamers from various seaside resorts on the mainland. Buses run from the ports of entry to all parts of the island. In summer there is an air service from London. Car ferry from Portsmouth to Fishbourne.

The capital of the island is *Newport*, centrally situated at the head of the Medina estuary.

The three routes given below, A, B and C, will, if followed in that order, provide a complete 50 mile circuit of the island by the most interesting roads. We begin from Ryde, the customary "gateway" to the island, but the circuit can, of course, be joined at any other port of entry.

A: Ryde to Newport and Yarmouth: 22 miles.

Ryde (pop. 21,000, E.C. Thursday), the close rival of Cowes in the world of yachting, has been called the "gateway to the Garden Isle" because of its easy accessibility from Portsmouth Harbour by way of Ryde Pier. The town, sited on rising ground, commands a fine view of the busy waters of the Solent.

It is the island's chief resort, with the Esplanade Gardens, a pier ½ mile long, fine sandy beaches and a lake for boating (hire of motorboats and rowing boats).

2 miles: *Binstead*. In the neighbourhood are the ruins of the Cistercian *Quarr Abbey*, founded 1132, which derives its name from stone quarries nearby: 13th century cellarium, kitchen and refectory, and parts of the chapel. A French Benedictine monastery is now housed in Quarr Abbey House, and a church has been built.

3 miles: *Wootton Creek*. In the midst of magnificently wooded country is *Fishbourne*, terminal of the car ferry.

5 miles: A 3021 goes off on the right to Cowes (4 miles) via *Whippingham* (church designed by Albert, Queen Victoria's Prince Consort, with stained glass and other items presented by the queen). **East Cowes** and **Cowes** are built in terraces on both sides of the Medina estuary, and are connected by a ferry (passengers and cars) and a pontoon bridge.

Cowes (pop. 18,000, E.C. Wednesday). Along the broad parade, from which splendid views of the Solent and of the start and finish of the yacht races can be obtained, are the principal Cowes yacht clubs. The exclusive *Royal Yacht Squadron* has since 1856 occupied *Cowes Castle*, built by Henry VIII and formerly a State prison. The town is small and attractive, with old Georgian houses, and the harbour is the best in the island. *Northwood House* is the civic centre, and the park contains an admirable collection of trees and flowers. Along the esplanade to the west is the charming seaside village of *Gurnard*. Beyond this a path runs along the cliffs to beautiful Thorness Bay (magnificent views of the New Forest and of the Isle of Wight's Western Downs).

East Cowes, on the other side of the estuary, is the home of several aircraft and shipbuilding works. The *Shell House*, covered with shells of every kind and shape, is a curiosity. South-east is *Osborne House* (1846), one of the favourite residences of Queen Victoria and Prince Albert; the Queen died there in 1901. King Edward VII presented the mansion to the state in 1902 in memory of his mother, and it has since been converted into a convalescent home for officers. The state apartments contain magnificent pictures, furniture and objects of art. (Visiting: summer, Mondays, Wednesdays, Fridays, 11 to 5). In the grounds is the *Swiss cottage*, in which the Royal children had their playrooms; it is now a museum. Nearby are two fine mansions, *East Cowes Castle* and *Norris Castle* (1790, by Wyatt). In *St James's Church* is the tomb of the architect John Nash (1833).

13 miles: **Newport** (pop. 20,000, E.C. Thursday), the administrative centre of the island, in a hilly area on the banks of the Medina, which here is navigable by vessels of some size. In *St Thomas's Church* (1854) is a monument presented by Queen Victoria commemorating Princess Elizabeth, daughter of Charles I, who died in captivity in Carisbrooke Castle in 1650. In the *Grammar School* (1614) Charles I was confined in 1648 before being transferred to Hurst Castle in Hampshire (p. 354) and from there conveyed to London, where he was tried and executed. In Avondale Road are remains of a *Roman villa* (open to visitors in summer, Mondays, Wednesdays and Fridays, 2.30 to 5).

1 mile to the south-west is the village of **Carisbrooke,** with its old 12th century priory church and a lovely 15th century tower. On a wooded knoll is *Carisbrooke Castle*, formerly the residence of the lord of the island. The original building was Saxon, but the castle walls and stout keep, round which there is a sentry walk, are Norman. The rest of the buildings date chiefly from the 13th century. The ruins of the rooms in which Charles I was kept prisoner in 1647-48, and where three years later his 15-year-old daughter died, are indicated by wall tablets. St Nicholas in Castro (1070) was restored as a memorial chapel to King Charles in 1904. There is a museum in the gatehouse.

From Newport the road to Yarmouth runs north and then turns left to skirt the south side of Parkhurst Forest.   17 miles: *Shalfleet*.

To the north are the villages of **Newtown** (salt-pans), *Porchfield* and *Hamstead*, on Newtown Bay.   The old *Town Hall* in Newtown, of brick and stone, is a relic of its former status as a borough.   The doorway and square tower of the church are Norman.   The church in the village of *Calbourne* has fine brasses and stained glass.

22 miles: **Yarmouth** (pop. 900, E.C. Wednesday), a peaceful town and a favourite harbour for small yachts.   Ruins of one of Henry VIII's coastal castles. In the church is a monument to Admiral Robert Holmes (d. 1692) who in 1664 took New York from the Dutch.

Around Yarmouth.   2¼ miles: *Totland*, an attractive resort. Farther south is Alum Bay, interesting for the colours and strata of its cliffs.   The southern arm of the bay ends with the *Needles*, three famous and gigantic chalk rocks standing 100 feet out of the sea at the isle's most westerly point.   They are a well-known landmark for ships entering the Solent; there is a lighthouse on the endmost rock. — *High Down*, 1 hour's walk. A fine walk from Alum Bay across the cliffs (400-500 feet high with layers of flints) and downs.   On High Down is a memorial to Tennyson. — *Scratchell's Bay*, with a natural arch, 200 feet high, in the cliffs.

B: Yarmouth to Ventnor.   20 miles.

B3399 to Chale, then A3055.   An alternative route is A3055 (which runs round the island to Ryde), the "Military Road", following the coast to (10 miles) Chale, but this is less interesting.

2 miles: *Freshwater:* 1 mile south (across A 3055) is Freshwater Bay and, opposite, Freshwater Gate — interesting little seaside resorts.   1 mile west is *Farringford*, where Tennyson lived.   Lady Tennyson is buried in the churchyard.

7 miles: *Mottistone*. To the north is Mottistone
Down (750 ft), and beyond this Brightstone and Lime-
ston Downs, from which there are fine views of
moorland and heath. 8 miles: *Shorwell*. The village
church is 14th century, with a 12th century porch;
notable wall paintings. In the neighbourhood are
some fine country houses — *North Court* (1615), with
terraces and landscaped gardens in beautiful woods;
West Court (1590) and *Woolverton*. — 12 miles:
Chale Green.

Whale Chine and *Blackgang Chine* descend to the sea; pleasant
sandy coves. *St Catherine's Point* is the south extremity of
the island; the lighthouse is said to have the most powerful
beam in the world.

15¾ miles: *Niton* (pop. 1000), situated high above
the *Undercliff*, a series of terraces formed by landslides
as the chalk slips off the clay subsoil, stretching more
than 7 miles along the seashore to Bonchurch beyond
Ventnor.

One of the largest villages on the island. Nearby are two
pleasant bathing beaches, *Castle Haven* and *Puckaster Cove*.
Charles II landed here in 1675. Good walk along the Downs
above the sea to Chale and Blackgang.

18½ miles: *St Lawrence*, with what is said to be
the smallest church in England.

20 miles: **Ventnor** (pop. 7000, E.C. Wednesday),
built in terraces on the steep slopes of St Boniface
Down, the top of which (800 ft) is the highest point
on the island. Attractive esplanade, with pier. In
Steephill Castle, which dominates the upper town,
Elizabeth of Austria once lived.

Around Ventnor. *Bonchurch*, 1 mile east of Ventnor on A3055.
Old church, partly Norman. Modern church (1848) higher up
the hill. Swinburne (who lived at nearby East Dene as a boy)

is buried in the churchyard. Bonchurch is at the eastern end of the Undercliff, which extends from here to Blackgang Chine (see above).

Wroxhall, 2 miles away, a pre-Conquest village, now the centre of a farming district. *Appuldurcombe House* was at various times a country house, a school and a monastery.

C: Ventnor to Ryde. 12½ miles.

1 mile: *Bonchurch*. — 4 miles: **Shanklin** (pop. 11,000, E.C. Wednesday). Situated on top of the cliffs and facing the open sea, Shanklin is one of the chief scenic attractions of the isle. *Shanklin Chine* is a picturesque gorge. The *Old Village* is interesting both historically and architecturally. From the pier head the "Pluto" pipe-line fed fuel to the Allies on D-Day. The *Devil's Chimney* is a fine viewpoint.

From Shanklin A 3020 runs west to Newport (10 miles). **Godshill** is a picturesque village: in the churchyard are the graves of many members of the Worsley family, who lived here for centuries. The *church* contains a unique wall painting of the "Budding Cross", a representation of the Crucifixion in the form of a pale blue lily with three stems; the only other known example of this is in a window in St Michael's Church, Oxford. Beyond this is Blackwater, where A 3020 runs into A 3056 from Sandown. 4 miles from Blackwater, in a fold in the downs, is Arreton; the gabled flint manor-house with tall brick chimneys contains magnificent panelling behind which are secret rooms and cupboards. Charles I played bowls on its greens, and Queen Victoria also knew the house well.

5½ miles: *Lake*, where A 3056 goes off on the left to Newport via Arreton. 6½ miles: **Sandown** (pop. 14,000, E.C. Wednesday), a resort which holds the record for hours of sunshine on the south coast. The cliffs extend along Sandown Bay to Shanklin. The best view of the town is from the pier (1000 ft long). The *Geological Museum of the Isle of Wight* contains collections of local fossils. Keats wrote "Hyperion" at Sandown.

1 mile inland is *Alverstone*, a little village on the Yar in a beautiful setting, with a mill.

At the other end of Sandown Bay is *Culver Cliff*, where Bembridge Down reaches the sea. Nearby is the charming manor-house of *Yaverland*, with stone and brick gables and stone-paved floors: collection of Pre-Raphaelite paintings.

8½ miles: **Brading** (pop. 2000, E.C. Wednesday), a pretty village at the foot of Brading Down. The old bull ring can still be seen. *Nunwell Park* has been the home of the Oglander family since the Conquest; in the church is the family burial chapel. A *Roman villa* was discovered nearby, and its tesselated pavements can be seen. Roman glass, tiles and coins were found.

Beyond Brading a road leads east to **Bembridge** (pop. 2500, E.C. Thursday) situated near the Foreland, the isle's most easterly point. There is a wide harbour extremely popular with yachtsmen. Farther north is *St Helen's*, beyond the marsh. Between Bembridge Point and Rye is **Sea View,** to which toll road B3330 leads. A firm stretch of sand joins all the resorts along this coast: Seagrove and Priory Bays offer excellent bathing.

12½ miles. **Ryde** (see above, p. 355).

THE CHANNEL ISLANDS

How to get there. *By sea:* (1) Southampton-Guernsey;
(2) Southampton-Jersey (about 8 hrs); (3) Weymouth-Guernsey;
(4) Weymouth-Jersey (about 6 hrs); (5) St Malo (France) -
Jersey.

By air: frequent services from London, Southampton and
Bournemouth, and from Dinard and Rennes in France.

The *currency* is British. The *language* is English, but there
is a local Franco-Norman patois. Cars, motorcycles and pedal
bicycles are available for hire locally.

The local *licensing laws* allow drinking from 9 a.m. to 10
or 11 p.m. without any break. Duty on alcohol and tobacco
is much lower than in Britain, and prices are accordingly considerably less than on the mainland.

There are very strict regulations on the bringing in of *animals*
other than dogs, in the interests of protecting the world-renowned
Jersey cows.

The handful of islands, rocks, reefs thrown down
close to the shores of France, and known as the
Channel Islands, are not, in fact counties of Britain.
The last remnant of England's Norman possessions
lost by King John (1205), they are tied to the British
Isles by bonds of affection and historic partnership,
but they are independent members of the British
Commonwealth, and each of the two major groups,
Guernsey and Jersey, has its own parliament. The
four main islands are *Jersey*, *Guernsey*, *Alderney* and
Sark. There are many other smaller ones, Herm,
Brechou, Jethou and Burtou among them.

The total area of the islands is 75 sq. miles; the
population is 110,000.

The islands are notable for the quality of their light and their
beautiful sunsets. The secluded little villages and the tracks
linking them have retained something of the atmosphere of
their feudal past. There are interesting contrasts between

French culture and British traditions, and between the semi-tropical flora of the islands and the vegetation of almost northern European type found in the valleys near the coast. There are dangers for sailors round the islands, with shallow water and numerous reefs. The group of rocks known as the *Casquets*, seen when approaching the Channel Islands fromW eymouth, have claimed a heavy toll of shipwrecks.

No one knows when man first set foot here, but the islands are full of Stone Age remains. There are many megalithic monuments which seems to indicate that early inhabitants were of the Celtic (Breton) race; traces of the Roman occupation are numerous and many of the original Roman defences still remain. The islands became part of the duchy of Normandy in 932 and after the Norman conquest of England in 1066 were attached to the English crown; during the reigns of the first four Norman kings sovereignty was alternatively Norman and English until 1154 (Henry II), although the French continued to dispute possession. In 1360 English rights to the islands were recognised by the French; they have now been united with Britain for more than 800 years. The soil is very fertile: potatoes, fruit, flowers and garden produce of all kinds supply the markets of Britain with the first crop of the year. There is very rich pasture on which the splendid cattle thrive.

The only time the islands have been under foreign occupation was during the last war, when they were occupied by German forces from June 1940 to May 1945.

Guernsey

Guernsey is a triangular island 10 miles long and 6 miles across, lying some 20 miles north of Jersey. Its area is 24 sq. miles, and it has a population of 45,000. The south coast is particularly beautiful.

The old town of **St Peter Port** (pop. 16,000) rises tier upon tier on the hills behind the bay of Belle Grève and Havelet, whose blue waters on hot summer days reflect an almost Mediterranean scene.

Like St Helier on Jersey, St Peter Port has its guardian fortress, *Castle Cornet*, on an island over-

looking the port. It is an imposing example of mediaeval military architecture, but in the past it has not
always played its role of defending the town. During
the Civil War it was captured by Parliamentary forces,
and St Peter Port, which had declared for the king,
was subject to constant bombardment for several
years. In 1672 the powder magazine exploded, with
devastating consequences for the garrison.

The little town centres on the 13th century *St Peter's
Church*. Behind the church is the colourful market.

Two notable houses on the harbour are the ancient
Ville au Roi and *Hauteville House*, the home (1855-70)
of the exiled Victor Hugo.

While living in St Peter Port Hugo became familiar with
every aspect of the islands. which provided the setting for "Les
Travailleurs de la Mer". Here too he finished "Les Misérables".
The haunted house which features in the "Travailleurs" can
still be seen near *Pleinmont Point*, at the south-west corner of
the island. Hauteville House is open to visitors from 10 to 12
and 2 to 5, except Wednesdays and Sundays.

Guille-Alles Museum and Library contain extensive
collections relating to local history. The *Royal Court
House* (1800) in Manor St contains numerous portraits. The **Lukis Museum** has prehistoric material
excavated on the island (open 10 to 12 and 2 to 5,
except Sundays).

The **south coast** of the island has impressive scenery, with
cliffs rearing above the pretty inlets of *Moulin Huet* and *Icart
Bay*, their bases honeycombed with gloomy caves which were
much used by smugglers in earlier days. The **west coast** has
gentler but no less beautiful scenery, with the bays of *Rocquaine*
(and the offshore island of *Lithou*), *Perelle*, *Vazon* and *Cobo*.
Beyond these is *Grande Rocque*, and this stretch of coast cul-
minates in the jagged headlands which shelter *Grand Havre*,
Lancresse and *Fontenelle* Bays. All these bays have beautiful

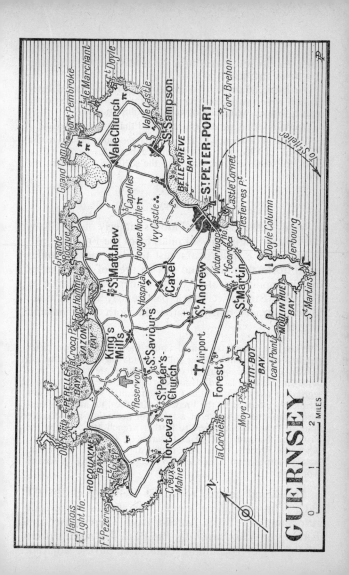

sandy beaches which cater both for bathers and for those who like peace and quiet.

One inland attraction of Guernsey is the *Water Lane*, a water channel with a path alongside it. The most popular part of it, with a wishing well, runs down to Moulin Huet Bay.

Guernsey cattle are no less renowned than those of Jersey.

The two little islands of *Herm* and *Jethou* also belong to the bailiwick of Guernsey. Herm has a beautiful beach half a mile long, with sand formed from the shells of various marine creatures.

Jersey

Jersey is the largest and most southerly of the Channel Islands, lying only 14 miles from the French coast. It measures 8 miles from east to west and 5½ miles from north to south, and has an area of 45 sq. miles and a population of 65,000. Under the influence of the Gulf Stream it has a particularly mild climate, which attracts many visitors in both summer and winter.

When the islands remained under the English crown after the loss of Normandy King John granted them a constitution (1205), confirmed by royal charters which are still in force. Jersey has its own lawcourts and Parliament, one of the smallest legislative assemblies in the Commonwealth. The island was frequently attacked by the French during the 14th and 15th centuries until the signature of a treaty of neutrality in 1483. In spite of this it was exposed to further French attack — by the Prince of Nassau in 1779 and Baron de Rullecourt in 1781, when the French forces were defeated. Thereafter the island was left in peace until the German occupation during the second woirld war.

The island centres round **St Helier** (pop. 28,000, E.C. Thursday), the capital, an attractive seaside resort and port on St Aubin's Bay. There is excellent bathing both at *Havre des Pas* Pool, the headquarters of the Jersey Swimming Club, and on the adjacent

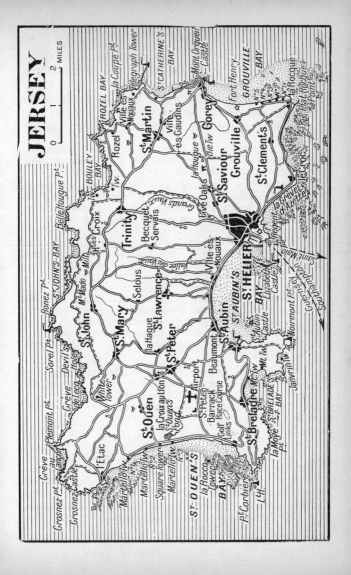

beaches. Public library in the impressive *Royal Court and States Building*. The *Castle* (1594), perched on a rock in the bay, broods over the lively little town, with the 6th century ruin of the *Hermitage of St Helerius* on a neighbouring rock. St Helerius was the missionary from whom the port derived its name.

A few miles north-east is **Mont Orgueil Castle** (13th-14th c.), with remains of Roman fortifications. The present structure is Norman, with much Tudor alteration and addition.

The coast from St Helier to *Gorey* is quiet and unassuming, but from this attractive little harbour northwards huge brooding cliffs begin to appear, and the scene changes to one of grandeur. St Catherine's Bay, Rozel, Bouley and Bonne Nuit Bays, Grève de Lecq, Plemont Point, Grève au Lançon, Grosnez Point, St Ouen's Bay and Corbière Lighthouse follow one another in a bewildering alternation of rocky headlands, caves, fine sweeping bays and sheer chasms. Travelling round this coast, it is easy to see how smuggling and piracy came to thrive on Jersey. A drive round the whole island is an unforgettable experience; and the fertile countryside of the interior is equally beautiful, much of it resembling the finest parts of Devon. The south coast of Jersey is less rugged, but has many fantastically shaped crags and beautiful bays, like St Brelade Bay, Portelet Bay and the wide curve of *St Aubin's Bay*, with its castle and its miniature tower.

La Hougue Bie, on the road from St Helier to Gorey, is an artificial mound dating from prehistoric times, topped by two chapels, of the 12th and 16th centuries respectively; large Neolithic burial chamber, and *underground museum* with mementoes of the German occupation.

St Martin has a 12th century church. To the north, near the coast, is the 13th century *Rozel Castle*, from which a road built by the Germans during the last war runs north, with magnificent views, via the villages of *Trinity*, *St John*, *St Mary* and *L'Etacq*. North of L'Etacq, at the north-western tip of the island, are the remains of **Grosnez Castle** (14th c.).

The return to St Helier is by way of *St Ouen* and *St Peter*. At *Tesson* an underground hospital constructed by the Germans during the last war can be seen.

Sark

Sark has an area of only 1035 acres and a population of 600. It is reached by motorboat from St Peter Port on Guernsey (daily service). The island is still owned by its feudal lord, and until recently no motor vehicles were allowed on it.

Sark has some dizzy and impressive cliffs, and it is a nerve-racking experience to cross the "coupee" or neck of land joining Great with Little Sark. There is room for a road here and nothing else, and on either hand the cliffs fall into the sea. There are no villages on the island, and *Creux Harbour* is the smallest harbour in the world. The south and west coasts present spectacles of rare magnificence, Dixcart and Derrible Bays in particular offering grim cliffs to ward off the ceaseless inroads of the tides. Les Autelets, or *Altar Rocks*, carved from the island mass by the waves, are a statuesque sight.

Alderney

Alderney is the most northerly of the Channel Islands, with an area of only 1962 acres and a population of 1500. It is separated from the French coast by the dangerous "race of Alderney", with fierce tides which have been the cause of many shipwrecks. It is only 8 miles from Alderney to the Pointe de la Hague on the French mainland.

Along the south coast are a succession of jagged cliffs. Inland is farming country on which cattle are bred, particularly dairy cows. The only little town on the island is St Anne. In earlier days the island was powerfully fortified in view of its strategic position off the French coast.

III: SOUTH-WEST ENGLAND

The romantic coast of Cornwall and the broad acres of lovely Devon are world-famous. Luxuriant flowers and palm-trees reveal the warm climate and fertile soil of their southern coasts fine; sands and coves and pleasure resorts line their cliffs; and this region is to the people of Britain what the Côte d'Azur is to the people of France.

But Cornwall and Devon have an added attraction for any visitor: the route to them from London takes him through some of the loveliest and most characteristic of English scenery. The routes in this section have been designed to reveal the beauties and the interest of the whole of the South-West of England, by inland roads and coastal roads.

From London the traveller journeys west through the beautiful Thames valley to the rolling Berkshire Downs. Southward lie Winchester, with its cathedral; Salisbury with its wonderful cathedral spire: Stonehenge, the most impressive relic of prehistoric Britain. West are the Cotswold Hills and the rich acres of Dorset sweeping south to a magnificent and varied coastline. Then Somerset with the Mendip Hills and the majestic Cheddar Gorge, and the granite uplands of Devon with its fine old cathedral town of Exeter.

Or travelling westward along the coast from Bournemouth the traveller sees the chalk cliffs give way to the warm red sandstone of Devon and the most colourful stretch of coast in England, with such fine resorts as Torquay. Farther west are the rugged granite rocks of Cornwall. The coastal scenery of the ancient duchy of Cornwall is often acclaimed as the finest in the country. In its creeks shelter old-world fishing villages beloved by artists, and on its southern coast is St Michael's Mount crowned by its fairytale castle. Land's End is the farthest point of this region of legends and age-old customs, and twenty miles west, lost in the Atlantic, lie the Scilly Isles, low islets basking in their warm sea breezes and famed for the flowers they send to the mainland.

Northward is the historic seaport of Bristol, and near it are two of the treasures of Britain — the spa of Bath, with its wonderfully preserved Roman baths and its superb classical architecture, and Wells with its beautiful cathedral.

11. LONDON TO SALISBURY
AND BOURNEMOUTH

83 miles to Salisbury (A 4 to Hounslow, then A 30). 112 miles to Bournemouth via Salisbury (A 338 beyond Salisbury).

A 4 (the Great West Road) to Staines is one of the busiest but one of the easiest routes out of London. From Hyde Park Corner keep west by way of Knightsbridge, Kensington Road, Kensington High St and Hammersmith Road, straight ahead into King St and along Chiswick High Road; at the end bear right into the Great West Road, bypassing Brentford and Hounslow to Staines. *Alternative route:* from Marble Arch due west along Bayswater Road, Holland Park Avenue, then Goldhawk Road (keeping right when Goldhawk Road forks left) straight on to Turnham Green, turning right along Chiswick High Road, and continuing as above.

Alternatively there is a rapid and easy route to Salisbury by way of M 3 from Staines, then via Winchester and Romsey (recommended).

17 miles: **Staines** (pop. 38,000 with Ashford, E.C. Thursday). The history of this busy town at the confluence of the Colne and Thames goes back to prehistoric times. Many Roman and Saxon remains have been found, and the name itself is of Saxon origin (from *stana,* a stone). The river is its main attraction.

On 1 August every year the "swan uppers" pass through Staines in their picturesque uniforms on their way up the Thames from Lambeth Bridge to mark the young swans. The *London Stone,* near the playing fields, marked the boundary between the up-river and down-river sectors of the Thames Conservancy and also between Greater London and the county of Buckinghamshire. It was erected in 1285 by the City of London; the base was added in 1781.

Around Staines. *Laleham,* 2 miles south-east, on an attractive stretch of the river with many house-boats. — *Chertsey,* 3 miles south (fishing, boating). — *Weybridge,* 6 miles north, beautifully situated at the confluence of the Thames and the Wey.

King Louis Philippe of France (d. 1850) is buried in the Roman Catholic chapel. From the top of St George's Hill (500 ft) there are fine views of the neighbouring valleys. — *Woking*, 9 miles south, a very busy town (pop. 60,000, E.C. Wednesday). 2 miles away, on the Wey, are the ruins of Newark Abbey. — *Knaphill*, 2 miles east, famous for its rhododendrons.

19 miles: **Egham,** near which is the *Field of Runny-mede*, where the barons compelled King John to accept Magna Carta (1215). The mansion of Milton Park is now occupied by the British Leather Manu-facturers Research Association, and its 43 rooms are now laboratories. On Cooper's Hill are the R.A.F. Memorial (fine view) and a monument to President Kennedy (1965).

21 miles: *Virginia Water,* with a large and beautiful park adjoining Windsor Great Park (p. 482). The 2 miles long lake was laid out in its present form in 1746 by the Duke of Cumberland.

Ascot (2½ miles away on A 329) is noted for its *racecourse*, the scene of England's most fashionable race meeting. This takes place on the Royal Heath during the third week in June, seven important races being run on each of four days. The Gold Cup, run over 2½ miles, sets the seal on the reputation of Derby and St Leger winners. The Queen and the Duke of Edinburgh are in residence for the week at Windsor Castle and drive in state up the course to the royal box, on the right of the Grand Stand, from which there is an uninterrupted view of the whole course.

27 miles: **Bagshot.** The Stuart kings hunted deer in *Bagshot Park*.

Splendid walks on the heath. The *Cricketers' Hotel* (1605) was the scene of the last highway robbery in the locality. At Bisley, 4 miles away on the Guildford road, the National Rifle Association's contests are held.

Bagshot to Farnham: 12 miles on A 325. 4 miles: **Frimley.** In St Peter's churchyard are the graves of *Admiral Sturdee*

(1850-1925), hero of the Battle of the Falklands (December 1914) and the American writer *Francis Bret Harte* (1839-1902), who died in Camberley (below). — 6½ miles: **Farnborough** (pop. 26,000, E.C. Wednesday). The *parish church of St Mary* (a 1537 will only recently established its dedication) has been rebuilt and restored; its rectors date back to 1290. The north door is original, the splendid wooden porch 13th century. Recently discovered frescoes inside are early 14th century; the pulpit and gallery are Jacobean. Of the six bells in the tower four are 17th century. "*Tumbledown Dick*" is an ancient hostelry on the site of the original inn of 1485. *St Michael's Abbey Church* (Perpendicular) was erected in 1887 by Empress Eugénie as a mausoleum for her husband Napoleon III (d. 1873) and the Prince Imperial of France (killed in action in Zululand 1879). The body of the Empress (d. Madrid 1920, aged 94) also rests here. The abbey itself was a monastery for monks of the Premonstratensian order, later for Benedictines and, from 1947, for monks from Prinknash Abbey near Gloucester. *Farnborough Hill* (now a convent college) was the Empress's residence after she left France in 1871. The *Royal Aircraft Establishment*, chief centre of aeronautical research and experimental development, dates from 1878. A large air show is held here every year. — 9 miles: **Aldershot** (pop. 40,000, E.C. Wednesday), famous for the largest permanent military camp (est. 1855) in the Commonwealth. Every arm of the service is here and every phase of instruction takes place. The R.A.S.C., R.A.O.C., R.E.M.E. and the Airborne Forces have headquarters here. The famous *Aldershot Command Searchlight Tattoo* is held in June. From the top of the hill (612 ft) called Caesar's Camp (equestrian statue of the Duke of Wellington) there is a fine view of the plains. — 11 miles: *Upper Hale*. 12 miles: **Farnham** (p. 341).

30 miles: **Camberley** (pop. 30,000, E.C. Wednesday). Very beautiful pinewoods. To the north is *Sandhurst Royal Military Academy* (founded 1800), where officer cadets are trained. *National Army Museum* (open 10 to 5). The historic mansion of *Elvetham Hall* occupies the site of an earlier house belonging to the Earl of Hertford in which Queen Elizabeth I stayed in 1591.

40 miles: *Hook*.

2 miles south is **Odiham** (pop. 3500, E.C. Wednesday). Charming old-fashioned High St; in the George Hotel is an interesting panelled room. Odiham Castle, of which only the ruins of the Norman keep remain, was besieged by the Dauphin of France in the reign of King John (1199-1216); Prince Edward, afterwards Edward I, was imprisoned here by Simon de Montfort 50 years later, and David II of Scotland after his defeat and capture in 1346. In the *church* are a 13th century font, a fine 17th century pulpit and old oak galleries. The stocks and whipping post and the old pest-house can still be seen.

41 miles: *Nately Scures*, with a very interesting little Norman church. A 30 bears left to bypass Basingstoke.

47 miles: **Basingstoke** (pop. 30,000, E.C. Thursday). The site of the town, at the entrance to a gap in the downs, has been occupied since Neolithic times, and in May St the remains of a Roman farm were discovered. It is a pleasant airy market town, and an excellent centre for sport, with three packs of foxhounds in the neighbourhood and good fishing.

Ruins of the **Holy Ghost Chapel** (1244), in an old churchyard beside the new one. There remain only the lower part of the west tower and parts of the adjoining walls (Early English window). Nearby are the more conspicuous ruins of the **Holy Trinity Chapel** (1542), to the south-east (hexagonal south-west tower, south wall with three lattice windows and end of apse). The chapels were abandoned after the Civil War, during which they were plundered by Parliamentary forces, but the school, founded in the reign of Mary Tudor, survived until 1855, when it was moved to Worthing Road. The large *St Michael's Church* (late Perpendicular, restored) preserves some 12th century work and a considerable amount of 16th century work. In New St is the *Willis Museum*, containing prehistoric material (open daily in the afternoon).

Around Basingstoke there are a number of splendid old houses: *Hackwood House* (1 mile south-east), designed by Inigo Jones; **The Vyne** (2 miles north), home of the first Lord

Sandys, built 1510, with 15th century Italian glass in the private chapel; *Bramshill House* (6 miles north-east), in a beautiful wooded park, a brick-built Jacobean mansion erected in 1612 for Lord Zouche; and *Kemshott House* (6 miles south-west). In the nearby village of *Dummer* is an interesting Early English church.

1½ miles east is **Basing,** a village of delightful brick and timber cottages and, nearby, the ruins of *Basing House*, on the site of a British settlement and a Norman castle. The remains (foundations, courtayrd, gatehouse, dovecote and barn) are of the stately Tudor mansion built by the first Marquess of Winchester in the 16th century, in which Queen Elizabeth I once stayed. During the Civil War Basing House was besieged for more than two years, but held out stubbornly in spite of the small number of defenders and the shortage of supplies. The *parish church*, with a massive tower, is Perpendicular but retains some Norman work. It was damaged during the siege, but still preserves an interesting "Virgin and Child" above the west door. Tombs of the Marquesses of Winchester; interesting font.

A 30 continues south-west. 6 miles beyond Basingstoke A 33 goes off on the left to Winchester and Southampton (route 10). A few miles farther on A 303 branches off on the right for Exeter via Andover.

60 miles: *Sutton Scotney*. To the north is the Roman camp of *Tidbury Ring*.

68 miles: **Stockbridge** (pop. 1000, E.C. Wednesday), once a centre of candle and parchment industries, but today an old-world village with one long wide street. 1000 years ago the Test was navigable a considerable way beyond the town; the Danes had a shipyard near Leckford, 3 miles upstream.

Stockbridge to Southampton: 17 miles on A 3057. The road follows the valley of the Test, and near Horsebridge crosses the old Roman road from Salisbury to Winchester. — 10 miles: **Romsey** (pop. 6500, E.C. Wednesdays), a little town grouped round **Romsey Abbey,** which contains some of the finest Norman work in the country. It was built on eth site of a Saxon

abbey founded in 907 which was sacked by the Danes and
formed part of the convent of St Mary and St Ethelfleda. The
present cruciform building dates mainly from the 12th century
(splendid view from the central tower). The west bays of the
nave, the vaulting and the east windows are Early English.
In the interior the arches and capitals of the choir, the clerestory,
the triforium and the nave are particularly notable. The crucifix on the south wall of the transept is 11th century. Nearby
is an interesting little 13th century house known as *King John's
House* or the *Hunting Box*. The ancient *White Horse Hotel*
preserves traces of an Elizabethan theatre, and has attractive
rooms with exposed beams. — 16 miles: **Southampton** (route 10).

79 miles: to the north-east of the road is Figsbury
Ring, an early Iron Age camp of 27 acres, with views
over Salisbury. The earthworks show signs of having
been enlarged several times (National Trust).

83 miles: **Salisbury** (pop. 36,000, E.C. Wednesday),
at the confluence of four rivers — the Avon and its
tributaries the Nadder, the Bourne and the Wylye —
and at the centre of a series of first-class roads. It
is a city rich in relics of the past. Its crowning glory
is the Cathedral, whose stately, slender spire can be
seen for miles around.

Salisbury

The present town was founded in 1220 when the see of *Old
Sarum* was transferred to it, and it is almost unique among
mediaeval towns in that it was laid out on a definite plan of
rectangular street blocks, with its large open market-place in
the centre.

Old Sarum, forerunner of the present city, stands on a spur
of the downs 2 miles north, and was a prehistoric fortified
settlement where the Romans established an important military
post *(Sorbiodonum);* from the summit the remains of at least
five converging Roman roads can be seen. The name dates
from the Saxon occupation *(Searobyrig,* "dry town", which
became *Saresberie).* The ramparts and ditches date from the
Norman period: it was a fortified stronghold as well as a reli-

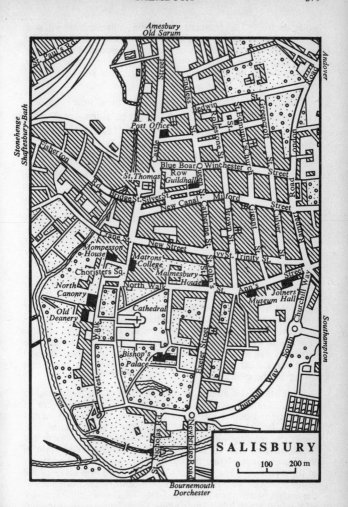

SALISBURY

0   100   200 m

gious centre.   The foundations of the cathedral, which was
burned down only five days after its consecration, can still be
seen.   Excavations in the inner bailey have revealed almost the
entire plan of the Norman town.   Access is by a new wooden
bridge on the old foundations.

Salisbury Cathedral dominates the "new" town.
The precincts are bounded on three sides by a wall
built with stone from Old Sarum (1328); the Avon
runs along the fourth side.   There are three gates to
the precincts: north, the High St Gate; south, Ann's
Gate and the Harnham Gate.   The fourth entrance
leads to the Bishop's Palace.

The **close,** with the beautiful turfed surround, old houses
and stately trees, makes a perfect setting for the majestic building.   On the north are the *College of Matrons* (1685), the *Judge's
Lodgings, Mompesson House* (1701) and the partly 14th century
Hemyingsby House.   To the west are the 15th century *Wardrobe*
(on 13th century foundations) with its double gables, the
17th century *Choristers' School,* and the *North Canonry.*   Nearby
are the *Jacobs House* (1720) the old deanery, the *King's House,*
partly 14th century and partly Elizabethan (now a teachers'
training college), and the 18th century *Walton Canonry.*   Along
the south side are the *South Canonry* and the partly 13th century
Leadenhall where Elias de Derham (from whose designs the
cathedral was built) is reputed to have lived.   The best vantage
point for a near view of the cathedral is from the north-east
corner of the close.

The Cathedral is an almost pure example of the Early English
phase of Gothic architecture (1220-58).   It is in the form of
a Greek (or double) cross and is 450 feet long; the principal
transept is 203 feet wide, the total area 55,000 square feet.
From the intersection of the great transept with the nave the
beautiful spire rises to a height of 404 feet (the tallest spire in
the country), completing the beautiful proportions and harmony
of the structure.   The steeple (1330) above the first stage of the
tower and the west front are in 14th century Decorated style;
the niches were never filled and the Te Deum sculptures are
all modern (1840-75).   The roofing vaults are not of stone but
of 13th century lime-concrete with imitation joints.   Repairs

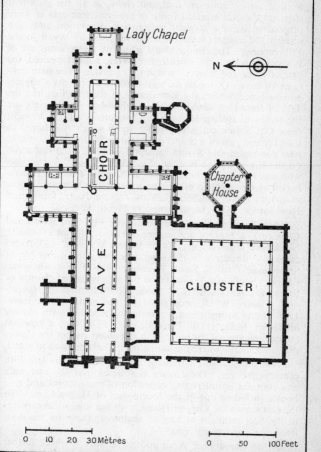

SALISBURY
CATHEDRAL

Lady Chapel

N ←⊚

CHOIR

Chapter House

NAVE

CLOISTER

0   10   20   30 Mètres

0   50   100 Feet

and restorations were carried out in the 18th century (Wyatt). Entry is by the west front.

The **interior** conveys an atmosphere of harmony and proportion: it seems, however, cold and chilly, as all the glass that survived the Reformation (only in the west transepts is there original glass), the original polychrome decoration and even screens and chapels were ruthlessly removed by Wyatt in the 18th century. The slender shafts adorning the columns are of Purbeck marble, and Christopher Wren himself praised the "air of grace and dignity" which they provide. The **nave** contains 10 bays. Owing to its height (80 ft) it presents a slightly narrow aspect. Note the adornments of the triforium and the Tree of Jesse (3rd window in the south aisle). On the right are the tombs of Bishop Herman and two other bishops, brought from Old Sarum cathedral, and a tomb which is believed to have formed part of a chapel dedicated to St Osmund (d. 1099), who completed Old Sarum cathedral in 1092. The last tomb on the left is said to be that of a "child bishop" (a chorister who was elected as "bishop" on St Nicholas's day, 6 December), but according to other authorities it is a miniature statue of a 13th century bishop, perhaps *Richard Poore*, founder of New Sarum. The pulpit is modern (Scott, 19th c.).

North Transept: three monuments (by Flaxman, Bacon and Chantrey), a bust of the author Richard Jefferies (1848-87). **North-east Transept:** a brass of Bishop Wyvil (d. 1375) who came into dispute with the King concerning the ownership of Sherbourne Castle. **South Transept:** 1914-18 War Memorial Chapel. **South-east Transept:** the beautifully carved chantry of Bishop Bridport (died 1262). **Choir.** To the north is the *Hungerford Chantry*, which once stood on the north of the nave: 15th century wrought iron; opposite, to the south, is the *chantry of Bishop Audley* (1520, Perpendicular). The *Lady Chapel*, at the extreme east of the building, is the oldest part of the Cathedral, and marks where the shrine of St Osmund used to stand.

From the south-west transept a door leads to the late 13th century *cloisters*. The *Library* is situated over the east walk and contains an interesting collection of manuscripts and rare books, including one of the four copies of Magna Carta. To the east stands the **Chapter House**, with fine allegorical carvings in the best tradition of English sculpture: those on the door itself are particularly good.

In 1668 Christopher Wren undertook work to check further settlement of west piers of the tower (from which there is a splendid view: access from the great transept); the apex of the steeple is today still 2 feet out of the perpendicular.

Leaving the Cathedral, we walk north between **Mompesson House** (1701) and *Matron's College* (1628) and through *North Gate* into the **High Street,** lined with old houses (note particularly the *Old George Hotel*). At the far end, to the right, is *Silver Street,* also lined with 15th and 16th century houses. At the intersection where Silver St runs into Butcher Row is the Gothic **Poultry Cross** (15th c.). A passage gives access to **St Thomas's Church.**

The church of St Thomas of Canterbury is 15th century, on earlier foundations. **Frescoes** of the *Last Judgment* (16th c.), the *Annunciation*, the *Visitation* and the *Nativity;* 15th and 17th century tombs.

From here it is a short distance east to the **Market Place,** with a number of old houses (in particular No. 17). To the north, at 35 Blue Boar Row, is another interesting old house.

The Duke of Buckingham was beheaded here in 1483, and many people were burned at the stake during the religious conflicts of the 16th century. To the south-east is the **Guildhall** (now the Town Hall), built in 1797 to replace the old Council House after its destruction by fire, on the site of the 14th century Guildhall and town prison. In the Banqueting Room are portraits of local notabilities.

The houses in **Butcher Row** and **Fisher Row** are almost all earlier than the 18th century. The gabled roof-line of many houses is an indication of 16th or 17th century date, although the fronts have often been altered in later periods.

The *House of John A'Port*, at 8 Queen St, is one of the finest examples of half-timbered work in the town, built in 1425 by the wealthy merchant whose name it bears. Fine stone fire-places with carved mantelpieces, panelling in the upstairs rooms, early Georgian staircase.

To the south of the Market Place is *New Canal*, so called after the open channels which ran down many streets until

1852. In this street is *"ye Halle of John Halle"*, a banqueting hall built by a rich wool merchant in 1470 (restored 1834).

Now return south along Catherine St and St John St, at the end of which, on the right, is Malmesbury House (1749). Turn left into St Ann St.

In St Ann St is *St Martin's Church* (Early English), on the site of a church dating back before the foundation of the town. The tower and font are 13th century, the nave and aisles 15th century. At No. 40 is the **Museum** (open 10 to 5), with objects discovered during excavations at Stonehenge and Old Sarum and local bygones (china and earthenware, costumes). At No. 56 is the 16th century **Joiners' Hall.**

Other features of interest. *St Nicholas's Hospital*, at Harnham Bridge, has a 13th century chapel (visiting only by special arrangement). *Trinity Hospital*, in Trinity St, dates from the 17th century. *St Edmund's Church* (15th c., on 13th c. foundations) was part of the collegiate church of St Edmund's College, dissolved at the Reformation. The Council Chamber is now incorporated in an 18th century building on the site of the College: collection of pictures of old buildings and old documents. In the park are fragments of the old town walls and the porch of the north transept of the Cathedral, deposited here at the time of the alterations carried out by Wyatt.

Salisbury plays a considerable part in English literature, featuring in the works of Fielding, Dickens, Trollope, Thomas Hardy and Hudson. Goldsmith's "Vicar of Wakefield" was first published in the town.

Surroundings of Salisbury

1. *Salisbury Plain*, to the north-west, is an area of open rolling downland some 20 miles long by 10 miles across. From *Beacon Hill* (625 ft), at *Bulford*, to the north-east, there is a good view of the whole plain. In 1900 the War Office acquired an area some 12 miles by 6 miles, and there are military camps at Bulford and at Tidworth, famous for its annual Tattoo.

2. Old Sarum and Stonehenge, to the north. Leave the town on A 345. 2 miles away is **Old Sarum** (see p. 378).

In the 18th century Old Sarum was a notorious "rotten borough", which continued to elect two M.P.s although nothing was left of the town. William Pitt was first elected to Parliament as member for Old Sarum in 1735.

8 miles: **Amesbury** (the Saxon *Ambresbury*), on a hilly site above the Avon, with a Norman and Early English *abbey church*. Gay wrote the "Beggars' Opera" while staying at Amesbury Abbey in 1727. The Abbey itself was built in 1661 (by J. Webb). To the west are the prehistoric and Norman earthworks known as Vespasian's Camp.

9 miles: **Stonehenge** (from the Saxon *Stanhengest*, hanging stones), the most imposing megalithic monument in Europe. The original form of Stonehenge was two concentric circles, within which were two ellipses or horseshoes of stones: the outer circle, just over 100 feet in diameter, was composed of mighty trilithons made up of 30 huge upright hewn stones (of which 16 still stand) in groups of pairs joined by a third horizontal slab over them (5 of which are still in position). The inner circle is about 10 feet smaller and comprised 30 (today 19) smaller upright stones, much more roughly hewn. In the first horseshoe were 5 trilithons of which two remain in perfect condition, and within this was the second ellipse consisting of 15 smaller stones. In the centre is the 15 feet long stone called the *Altar Stone*, across which now lies broken one of the immense transverse slabs, which were 3½ feet thick. The uprights of the trilithons were as much as 22 feet high and set 8 feet in the earth.

13

The larger circle and ellipse are of local sarsen sandstone, the inner circle and horseshoe (perhaps of earlier date) of a kind of blue granite or dolerite which was probably brought from the Prescelly Hills in Pembrokeshire, and the Altar Stone of micaceous sandstone from Milford Haven, both in Wales. Aerial photography and excavations clearly reveal traces of the earth rampart (300 feet in diameter) surrounding the circles and of the avenue leading to them. Directly to the north-east of the opening is a great isolated stone to which the name of *Friar's Heel* or Hele Stone has been given. Many people visit Stonehenge at dawn on the summer solstice to watch the sun rise on the longest day.

Neither historical nor scientific research has been able to decide exactly the origin or purpose of this monument. It is usually accepted that the stones have stood for nearly 4000 years and that they were erected in connection with some observation of the sun, probably for sun worship.

It is thought that the idea originated with migrating Mediterranean peoples who carried their cult of the sun and of stones and their burial practices all over Europe in the Bronze Age, and it is accepted also that the hundreds of barrows (tumuli) in the surrounding area have some connection with Stonehenge. The National Trust owns over 1400 acres of land round Stonehenge, including many barrows and other prehistoric remains, like the Cursus (a long earthwork to the north) and the avenue approaching Stonehenge.

Stonehenge is open to visitors daily from 9 a.m. to sunset. Excavations are still being carried out in the area, and recent finds are displayed in Salisbury Museum.

The return to Salisbury is through the beautiful Avon valley, passing through *Stratford*, where the elder Pitt lived. The road passes to the left of his first constituency, Old Sarum.

3. The Salisbury-Southampton road (A 36). 3 miles: *Alderbury*. On the left of the road are the ruins of *Clarendon Palace*, where the Constitutions of Clarendon were promulgated in 1164. — 5 miles: *Pepperbox Hill*, from which there is a very fine view of the spire of Salisbury Cathedral. The *Pepperbox* is a

17th century folly on top of the hill. To the right is *Trafalgar House*, which was presented to Nelson by the nation.

Salisbury to Bournemouth

29 miles on A 338.

2 miles: *Britford*, on the site of a Roman station. In the Saxon church is a monument to the Duke of Buckingham.

2 miles west is *Harnham*, with an old mill and mill-leet, in beautiful surroundings. This is believed to have been the scene of Constable's picture "The Rainbow". The mill is older than Harnham Bridge (built 1235), but has undergone alteration and restoration. Note the structure of the timber roof, with a queen-post, a type of construction abandoned after the 13th century.

3 miles: **Longford Castle,** on the Avon, the seat of the Earl of Radnor, built in 1591 by Thomas Gorges. Portrait of Erasmus by Holbein. There is also a famous steel chair of exquisite workmanship, presented to the Emperor Rudolf II in 1574 by the town of Augsburg. — 7 miles: *Downton.*

9 miles: *Breamore*, a small village with a 10th or early 11th century *church*, perfectly preserved, and the old village stocks.

Breamore House (open daily in summer, except Mondays and Fridays, from 2 to 6), a sumptuously furnished mansion of 1583 (tapestries, china, 17th century Dutch and Flemish pictures).

11 miles: *Fordingbridge*, with an Early English and Decorated church. — 17 miles: *Ringwood* (pop. 6000, E.C. Thursday), an old town which the modern world seems to have passed by.

26 miles: **Christchurch** (pop. 28,000, E.C. Wednesday), a former seaport and a prehistoric, British, Roman and Saxon site. Until the 12th century it was called *Twinham* ("between the rivers"), being situated between the Avon and the Stour.

Christchurch Priory (which became the parish church on the dissolution of the monasteries) dates from Saxon times. The nave, transept and apsed chapel at the south end of the transept are late 11th century. The aisles, the curious north porch and the clerestory (Early English) were added in the 13th century. The west tower and part of the choir are 14th century. The Perpendicular *screen* between the nave and choir was built in 1502. Magnificent carved **stalls**. Below the west tower is a monument to *Shelley* (d. 1822).

There are also ruins of a *Norman castle* (keep) and a Norman house. *Museum* in Red House (17th c.).

In Christchurch Bay is *Highcliffe Castle*, brought stone by stone from the Abbey of St Wandrille in Normandy and re-erected here. William II of Germany stayed in the house shortly before the first world war.

29 miles: **Bournemouth** (pop. 160,000, E.C. Wednesday and Saturday). Situated in the valley of the Bourne, on the sheltered *Poole Bay*, Bournemouth is an all-the-year-round seaside resort. The beach consists of 6 miles of sands, and a large proportion of the town has been preserved by the municipality for parks (1400 acres in all). The warm relaxing climate and the pine woods everywhere to be found have caused it to grow from a sandy desolate waste of heathland on which in 1810 there was not a single house, into one of the most fashionable resorts on the south coast.

The *Russell-Cotes Museum* contains pictures by *Turner*, *Corot* and their contemporaries. The *Rothesay Museum*, mainly devoted to china and pottery, the applied arts and ethnography, also has a number of pictures by Italian primitives.

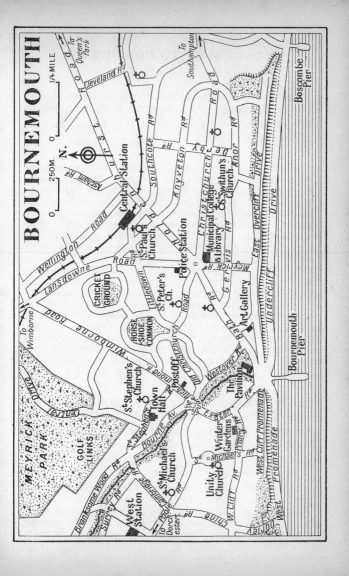

12. SALISBURY TO DORCHESTER
AND WEYMOUTH

From Salisbury (p. 333) the route follows A 338 to Britford, and then forks right on A 354. 3½ miles: Coombe Bissett. At 7½ miles is the boundary of the county of Dorset.

Dorset is a county of generous sweeping downland and fine coastline, of well-built old towns and ancient camps. It is in the "Wessex" of Thomas Hardy, whose towns and villages feature — thinly disguised under pseudonyms — in his stories. One of these is *Shaftesbury*, to which he gave the name of Shaston. It stands overlooking the fertile Blackmoor Vale and claims to be one of the oldest towns in England, dating from the time of King Alfred. *Maiden Castle*, one of the most famous of Britain's prehistoric camps, is south of *Dorchester*, which is itself noted for its Roman amphitheatre, the *Maumbury Rings*. The downs of Dorset reach a height of 900 feet, and along the lovely coastline are many pleasant seaside resorts. Due south is *Weymouth*, an attractive seaside town which was made fashionable by George III. Nearby, joined to the mainland by the remarkable shingle beach known as *Chesil Bank*, is the *Isle of Portland*, a naval stronghold where the famous Portland stone, used in so many of London's larger buildings, was quarried. *Lyme Regis*. a charming seaside town, lies to the west.

A 354 continues over the lonely downs to (11 miles) Woodyates and (12 miles) **Pentridge** (just off the main road and at the foot of Pentridge Hill, 500 feet). This is believed to be the Tantridge of "Tess of the d'Urbervilles".

There are many ancient monuments in the district: Bockerley Ditch, an ancient embankment along the Hampshire border; long barrows on Martin Down, and one on the wooded slopes between Oakley Down and Bottlebush Down; and a tumulus on the side of Penbury Knoll above the village. 1 mile north is Farnham, where there is an archaeological museum.

23½ miles: *Blandford* (pop. 3800, E.C. Wednesday), in the heart of Hardy's Wessex. — 28 miles: *Winterbourne Whitchurch.* — 31 miles: *Milbourne St Andrew.* 3 miles north is **Milton Abbas,** a village with a picturesque main street. *Milton Abbey* is a cathedral in miniature with a fine tower; the chapel of Athelstan is interesting. Weatherby Castle and an obelisk are to the south-east. — 35 miles: *Puddletown,* where A 35 comes in from Bournemouth. To the left is Higher Bockhampton, with the cottage in which Thomas Hardy was born. (Open Wednesdays, Thursdays and Sundays 2 to 6: National Trust property).

40 miles: **Dorchester** (pop. 13,500, E.C. Thursday), the county town of Dorset and a peaceful old market town. It features in many of Hardy's novels under the name of Casterbridge.

St Peter's Church (15th c.), at the intersection of the town's four main streets, has a magnificent Perpendicular tower. In front of the church is a statue of the Rev. William Barnes, author of poems in the Dorset dialect. The **Dorset Museum** is one of the best of England's provincial museums, with a varied collection, including fossils, Roman remains (mosaics), mementoes of Hardy. Opposite the Museum is *Judge Jeffreys' House,* and in the Town Hall is the chair in which he sat during the "Bloody Assize" of 1685 (when he condemned to death 60 of Monmouth's supporters in Dorchester alone). Also of interest are the *Nappers Mite Almshouses.*

There is a fine statue of Thomas Hardy (Eric Kennington, 1931) near the west entrance to the town. Nearby, in the West Walks, a section of the old Roman wall can be seen. **Maumbury Rings** (220 ft by 160 ft) near the railway station, is one of the best preserved Roman amphitheatres in the country. *Maiden Castle* (2 miles south-west) is one of the most perfect Iron Age camps in the country.

48 miles: **Weymouth and Melcombe Regis** (pop. Wednesday), a pleasant seaside resort at the mouth of the Wey in the middle of Weymouth Bay. In

Tudor times the castles of Portland (see below) and
Sandsfoot (in ruins) were built for defensive purposes
by Henry VIII.   Queen Elizabeth granted a charter
uniting Weymouth and Melcombe Regis.   It was not,
however, till the time of George III (1760-1820), who
had a summer residence here, that the town became
fashionable.   From the *Nothe Gardens* there is a
fine view of the town.

Around Weymouth.   To the south is the Isle of Portland
(pop. 11,600, E.C. Wednesday), a solid mass of limestone
4½ miles long rising out of the sea to a height of over 400 feet
and linked to the mainland by a pebble-covered ridge 12 miles
long. There are no rivers, and the villages have grown up round
wells — Fortuneswell, Castletown (the chief town), Chesilton,
Easton and, to the south, Weston and Southwell. In the garden
adjoining the offices of the Bath and Portland Stone Co. in
Easton Lane, Portland, is an interesting collection of fossils
(petrified trees, ammonites, cycads, stalactites, bones of prehistoric animals). After a rock fall in 1665 which made large
quantities of the local Portland stone accessible this stone was
selected by Christopher Wren for the rebuilding of London,
and it has continued to be used for public buildings in the
capital. The quarries can be visited. *Portland Harbour*, base
of the Home Fleet and a large submarine base, is enclosed by
the Great Breakwater (1869) and the New Breakwater (1903),
4 miles long, on the east side of the Isle. On the west is *Chesil
Beach*, 17 miles long, extending from West Bay to Abbotsbury.
There are fine views from Verne Citadel (490 ft); a magnificent
sight is a high sea over Chesil Beach. *Portland Castle* (1540),
which still retains its 14 ft thick walls, is now occupied by the
Army. Church Ope Cove is a pleasant bathing place. The
Undercliff at East Weare is ruggedly beautiful.

4½ miles offshore are the Shambles Sands, with the Shambles
lighthouse to the east. At the Race of Portland the tides meet,
producing a seething mass of water.

Portland Bill is at the southern tip of the Isle. At the point
is an obelisk; nearby is the Pulpit Rock, which makes an exacting but interesting climb. Rufus Castle, or Bow and Arrow
Castle as it is also called from its small loopholes, is a pentagonal
structure, presumably the keep of a castle erected by King

William Rufus, (1087-1100). Pennsylvania Castle is a modern residence built at the beginning of the 19th century (enlarged 1900) by John Penn, governor of Portland. Opposite the entrance to the castle is *Portland Museum*, housed in the old cottage described in Hardy's "The Well Beloved", which was presented to the Isle by Dr Marie Stopes.

Portland Prison is now a Borstal institution. During the second world war large numbers of American forces and the 2nd French armoured division embarked from Portland for the landing in France in 1944. Many old customs are still retained on the Isle.

To the east are *Osmington Mills* and Lulworth Cove. Osmington is noted for its lobsters. To the north-east are the prehistoric earthworks of Chalbury Camp, and 1 mile away the charming little village of Sutton Poyntz, with its thatched stone cottages reflected in the water. 1 mile to the north-east is the *White Horse*, the figure of a horseman, traditionally believed to be George III, cut out of the chalk of a hillside.

The *Hardy Monument* (to the west of Weymouth, 6 miles south-west of Dorchester on the Portesham-Martinstown road) is an octagonal tower 80 feet high, erected in 1846 to commemorate Vice-Admiral Hardy, in whose arms Nelson died. At Portesham on the Abbotsbury road is the house in which he lived. At *Abbotsbury* are the remains of a 12th century Benedictine abbey, with a 15th century church and a beautiful garden containing many exotic species (open April-September 10 to 5, Sundays 2 to 6).

Surroundings of Dorchester

A. Dorchester to Swanage: 27 miles (A 352 to Wareham, then A 351).

To the north of the road is *Clouds Hill*, to which T.E. Lawrence retired when he left the R.A.F., with many mementoes of Lawrence (d. 1935); open Wednesdays, Thursdays and Sundays 2 to 6. Nearby is *Bovington Camp*, with an interesting *Tank Museum*.

12 miles: *Wool* (pop. 3000), a quiet country town. Ruins of Bindon Abbey (12th c.).

16 miles: **Wareham** (pop. 2900). St Mary's Church, with a beautiful font. Monument to Lawrence of Arabia near St Martin's Church (founded 917).

21½ miles: **Corfe Castle** (pop. 1500, E.C. Thursday), a picturesque village of stone-built houses. The castle dates from soon after the Norman Conquest, with many 12th and 13th century additions. It was destroyed by Parliamentary forces during the Civil War after holding out for six weeks under the command of Lady Banks.

To the west are the Purbeck Hills. Half-way between Corfe Castle and Warbarrow Bay is *Creech Barrow;* magnificent views of the Channel and Portland Bill. Grange Arch, popularly known as Bond's Folly, stands out against the sky on top of the Purbeck Hills: it was built at the beginning of the 18th century by Dennis Bond (d. 1746) of Creech Grange. At Church Knowle, 2 miles west, are two old farms, Cocknowle and Church Farm, with 300 acres of cultivated land and gardens (National Trust property). *Creech Grange*, 5 miles west, is a Tudor-style mansion (open Tuesdays, Wednesdays and Sundays 2.30 to 5.30).

27 miles: **Swanage** (pop. 7000), at the south-east corner of Dorset in the *Isle of Purbeck* (actually a peninsula), set in a wide bay at the foot of verdant hills. Very beautiful sandy beach, pier 550 yards long. The area has much of interest to offer botanists and geologists. There is pleasant walking on the Downs, which here reach down to the sea, and superb views from the tops of the hills.

The carved façade of the *Town Hall* (1882) was originally designed by Sir Christopher Wren in 1670 for Mercers' Hall in Cheapside, London. Behind it is the old town gaol, with an interesting inscription. The *Mowlem Institute* (1863) contains a concert hall and the County Library. The quarries in the area date from the Norman Conquest and appear to have been worked in prehistoric times. The *Tilly Whim Caves,* quarries which have been out of use for a hundred years, are popular with visitors.

At *Durlston Head*, 1 mile south, is the Great Globe, a model of the world in Portland stone (made of 8 pieces weighing in total 40 tons), commissioned by the local landowner in 1887 from Greenwich Observatory. The steep cliffs here are eroded into bizarre shapes. This scenery is described by Hardy in "The Hand of Ethelberta".

Around Swanage. *St Alban's Head*, 5½ miles south, with steep cliffs rising to over 400 feet. The *Purbeck Hills* terminate to the west in Rings Hill (630 ft) above Worbarrow Bay. To the east is *Kimmeridge*, a small village of thatched cottages with a Norman church. To the west is beautiful *Lulworth Cove*. In the picturesque village of *East Lulworth* is Lulworth Castle, a splendid mansion begun in the 16th century and completed in Jacobean times, largely destroyed by fire in 1929.

B. Dorchester to Poole: 22 miles on A 35.

5 miles: *Puddletown*, a pleasant little village on the river Puddle, which also gives its name to (7 miles) *Tolpuddle:* Tola's Puddle — Tola was the wife of the steward of King Canute (1016-35).

From here were deported in 1834 to Australia the five "Tolpuddle Martyrs", agricultural labourers who suffered in the cause of trade unionism.

10½ miles: *Bere Regis*. Nearby Woodbury Hill is 360 feet high and affords a fine view over the rolling green countryside. The village is the Kingsbere of Hardy's "Tess of the D'Urbervilles".

22 miles: **Poole** (pop. 96,000, E.C. Wednesday), situated within a wide half-circle of hills whose arms extend into the sea and enclose the great tidal basin of *Poole Harbour*.

Affpuddle, *Bryants Puddle* and *Turners Puddle* are picturesque villages on the river, in the vicinity.

The *Old Town House* in Scaplen's Court, the Town Cellars or *Woolhouse*, the *Almshouses of St George* and remains of the seawall in *Thames St*, all date from the Middle Ages. A fine example of Tudor architecture is the *King Charles Inn*. Georgian buildings are the *Guildhall, Harbour Office* and *Customs House*, as well as many private houses, such as the *Mansion House* (Thames St) and *Peter Thompson's Mansion* (Market St), now the School of Art.

The harbour is separated from the English Channel by a 7 miles long sand barrier, through which the narrow entrance is pierced. The old town lies behind the port. Behind this again, on higher ground, are the pleasant modern districts of Branksome, Parkstone, Newtown, Canford, Broadstone, Creekmore and Upton. From Old Harry Rocks in the west to Christchurch in the east there is a beach 12 miles long. On the other side of the harbour (ferry) there is another beach, *Shell Bay*, behind which are dunes and heath.

There are two interesting museums in Poole, the *Old Town House Museum* (history, pottery, pictures) and *Poole Museum* (local interest).

There are several interesting islands: *Brownsea* (birthplace of the Boy Scout movement), *Furzey, Green, Long, Round, Pergin's*. Several yachting clubs with premises and private piers. *Poole Harbour Yachting Week* is now an annual fixture (the course extends from Poole to Bournemouth Pier) attended by many enthusiastic yachtsmen.

Around Poole. *Studland* (1 mile), an old village with a fine Norman church. Four *chines* (gorges hewn out of the cliff by streams) — Branksome Dene, Branksome Chine, Canford Cliffs and Flaghead Chine. At the end of Sandbanks peninsula is Chaddesley Wood, where there is a well equipped modern bathing beach.

D. Dorchester to Ringwood: 32 miles (A 35 to Bere Regis, then A 31).

10½ miles: *Bere Regis* (see p. 395). A 31 forks left through country rich in tumuli, primitive defence works, long barrows and Roman roads.

22½ miles: **Wimborne Minster** (pop. 4100, E.C. Wednesday), a quaint old town with narrow crooked streets. It stands at the junction of the Stour and the Allen on the edge of the New Forest.

The **Minster** dates from 1043, but has been much altered and added to since. The huge arches carrying the central tower and three bays of the nave are in transitional Norman style; the massive Norman central tower was built in 1600 when the spire collapsed. The west tower is in the Decorated style. The finest parts of the building are the Early English choir and presbytery. There are some remarkable tombs and brasses: one of the most interesting is that of John Beaufort (15th century) on the south side of the presbytery. There is a 14th century "orrery" clock (of the planetary system).

4 miles north-west are the remains of a pre-Roman camp, *Badbury Rings*, on the Dorchester-Old Sarum Roman road astride which the village of Shapwick today stands. Here, according to legend, King Arthur defeated the Saxons in battle. There is a fine view to the south as far as the Isle of Wight and the Needles. Beyond the woods, near Kingstone Lacy Park, is the meeting place of four Roman roads. On Summerlug Hill is a barrow; on Horton Common old earthworks.

14 miles: *Stupehill*. The road now begins to run almost imperceptibly downhill. — 26¾ miles: *Ferndown*. A 318 runs south-west via Kinson to Poole; A 347 runs south to Bournemouth. — 32 miles: *Ringwood*.

D. Dorchester to Sidmouth: 41 miles on A 35.

5 miles: *Winterbourne Abbas*. 15 miles: **Bridport** (pop. 6500, E.C. Thursday), a small port of historical interest, now a popular holiday resort. Fine bathing beach in West Bay. Local museum in South St.

18 miles: **Chideock** (pronounced "Chiddick"), a pretty village amid hills providing superb views.

In the *church of St Giles* is the tomb of John Arundel, with effigy, at east end of south aisle. Of the castle built in 1397 only part of the moat today remains. 1 mile south, on the coast, is *Seatown*, nestling in green cliffs, with a fine shingle beach.

20 miles: *Morecombelake*. From Hardown Hill (677 ft) there are fine views over the vale of Marshwood with its great oak trees. — 21¾ miles: *Charmouth* (pop. 900, E.C. Thursday), occupying a pleasant position at the mouth of the Char, with a broad sandy beach.

Lambert's Castle (842 ft), to the north on the Lyme Regis-Crewkerne road, is the site of an old Roman and British camp, with extensive earthworks. ½ mile to the north is *Racedown Farm*, where between 1795 and 1797 Wordsworth lived with his sister Dorothy, who described the lovely landscape.

24½ miles: **Lyme Regis** (pop. 3500, E.C. Thursday), seaside resort and harbour at the mouth of the Lyme. Good bathing on the shingle and sandy beach.

It was on the old stone harbour-pier, the Cobb, that the Duke of Monmouth landed in 1685. *St Michael's Church* (16th c.). *Philpot Museum*, with a large collection of fossils (open 10 to 1 and 2.30 to 5.30).

From Lyme Regis the road follows the course of an old Roman road and climbs immediately to 500 feet. To the south are *Rousdon* and the interesting cliff remains of Dowlands Landslip. The road turns inland and descends rapidly to the picturesque valley of the Axe, with its rich red mud. 2 miles south is *Seaton*, a seaside resort amid fine cliff scenery. 1 mile north is *Colyton*, with a church containing some unusual monuments.

31½ miles: *Colyford*, after which the road rises again to follow the ridge of the hill in the manner of Roman roads. 36 miles: B 3174 forks back on left to (2 miles) *Beer*, a quaint little fishing village; in the nearby chalk cliffs are Roman and Norman quarries with deep and interesting caves. — 39 ½ miles : *Sidford*.

41 ½ miles : **Sidmouth** (pop. 11,000, E.C. Thursday), a seaside resort in a sheltered position. Above the shingle beach (good bathing) is a pleasant esplanade, and the whole town lies within the sweep of the well-wooded red cliffs and hills which render the whole district so beautiful. Luxury hotels.

8 miles north is *Ottery St Mary* (pop. 3700, E.C. Wednesday). Samuel Taylor Coleridge (1772-1834) was born in the vicarage here. The very beautiful old church is built on the same general plan as Exeter Cathedral but on a smaller scale; it has two towers on the west front. This is the Clavering of Thackeray's "Pendennis".

13. SALISBURY TO EXETER

88 miles on A 30.

3 miles: **Wilton** (pop. 3500, E.C. Wednesday), former county town of Wiltshire and third oldest borough in the country. It is famous for the manufacture of Wilton carpets. (The Royal Carpet Factory can be visited; apply in writing.)

The Byzantine-style *church* (1844), built by the Earl of Pembroke, was designed by T.H. Wyatt, who was responsible for the deplorable restoration of Salisbury Cathedral. The 125 ft high campanile seems out of place in a small English town. The font is Italian. Fine French, English, German and Flemish *glass*.

Wilton House, seat of the Earl of Pembroke and Montgomery, is principally a 17th century building on the site of a Benedictine monastery. Scenes from Sir Philip Sidney's "Arcadia" are painted on the ceiling vaults of the great drawing room, and there is a famous collection of pictures by *Rubens, Holbein, Rembrandt, van Dyck, Lucas van Leyden, Mantegna* and others; old armour. In the Italian garden is a pavilion by Holbein. (Open April-September 11 to 6).

4½ miles: *Burcombe*. — 6 miles: *Barford St Martin*. — 8 miles: *Compton Chamberlayne*. — 10 miles: Favant: the road rises steadily. — 11 miles: *Sutton Mandeville*. — 12 miles: *Swallowcliffe*. To the right is Castle Ditches, an ancient British earthwork (670 ft). — 14 miles: Ansty. To the south-west is White Sheet Hill (766 ft). *Wardour Castle* (2 miles to the right), the residence of Lord Arundel, contains fine pictures and furniture.

20 miles: **Shaftesbury** (pop. 3500, E.C. Wednesday), a romantic little market town on a hill overlooking the beautiful Vale of Blackmore. It is the Shaston of Hardy's Wessex novels. Here are the foundations

of an abbey (founded by King Alfred) at which King Canute died (1035) and which later became a famous Benedictine nunnery. St Peter's Church (16th c.). Local museum.

Shaftesbury to Blandford: 13 miles on A 350. The road runs through peaceful old villages in a beautiful setting of hills and woodland, with thatched cottages and stone manor-houses which fit harmoniously into the landscape.

From Shaftesbury (700 ft) the road descends sharply. — 25 miles: *West Stour*, beyond which the road climbs to 250 feet and immediately runs down again to (27 miles) Five Bridges. — 29 miles: *Henstridge*. 33 miles: Milbourne Port.

35 miles **Sherborne** (pop. 7700, E.C. Wednesday), on the river Yeo in the Blackmore Vale. The houses, mostly built of stone, have stone-tiled roofs and mullioned windows.

The old **Abbey Church** still retains certain of its Norman characteristics, including the tower arches; the *Lady Chapel* is Early English. It was almost completely rebuilt in the 15th century in the Perpendicular style; the nave arches and fan-vaulting of the choir are particularly fine. The choir stalls with canopies and misericords are also 15th century. Tombs of two Kings of Wessex, Ethelbald and Ethelbert. — *Sherborne Grammar School* was founded in 1550 by Edward VI. The school buildings comprise the domestic buildings of the abbey. In the close there are some interesting old almshouses (1437).

East of the town is *Sherborne Castle*, standing in a magnificent deer park through which there is a public footpath. Nearby are the ruins of the 12th century castle built by Roger, Bishop of Salisbury. At Trent (to the north-west) King Charles II hid for several days after the battle of Worcester (1651) before going to Charmouth, from where he had arranged to sail for France.

From here A 352, 19 miles south to Dorchester. It climbs to (1 mile) West Hill Cottage (400 ft) and then follows

the gentle saucer-like slope to (10 miles) Minterne Magna
(600 ft), afterwards descending all the way to Dorchester. At
Cerne Abbas (12 miles) there stands the gatehouse of the old
abbey. On *Giant Hill* (north-east), cut in the chalk, is the figure
of a man dating probably from the Romano-British era.

The road here enters Somerset.

Somerset. A rich agricultural county, noted for its cheese
and its cider and also for the dialect of its inhabitants — that
slow rural intonation which makes of the county's name the
ever recognisable "Zummerzet". It is in Hardy's Wessex, and
many of its towns and villages are described in his novels. It
possesses many of the famous towns in English history and
also some of its finest buildings, and is particularly noted for
its Perpendicular church towers. Its most notable town is *Bath*,
the celebrated spa at which the Romans established a system
of baths about A.D. 44. One of the smallest yet most beautiful
cathedrals in Britain is at *Wells*, and 5 miles away at *Glastonbury* are the graves of King Arthur and his Queen Guinevere.
Nearby are the famous *Wookey Hole Caves* beneath the *Mendip
Hills*, and to the north is the impressive *Cheddar Gorge*. Its
county town is *Taunton*, in the lovely valley of Taunton Dene,
and it has popular seaside resorts in *Weston-super-Mare* and
Minehead.

42 miles: **Yeovil** (pop. 26,000, E.C. Thursday).
The town, on the river Yeo, is famous for glove-
making. The 15th century church is in Perpendicular
style; the old almshouses date from 1477. 2 miles
away are the ruins of *Naish Priory*.

Henford Manor is a Georgian house, now a museum
(open daily, except Thursdays and Sundays, 10 to 1
and 2 to 5).

4 miles west of Yeovil, on A 3088 to South Petherton, is
the village of **Montacute,** which derives its name from the
"sharp mount" (Mons Acutus) now called St Michael's Hill.
At its foot is the splendid two-storeyed gatehouse of early
Tudor days which marked the entrance to an important Cluniac
priory of which no trace now remains. Nearby is the village
church (15th century with Norman fragments). The houses in

the little square (locally known as the "Borough") are of architectural interest, especially the post office at the north-east corner, with its gable end and oriel window of Henry VII's time. In the Borough is the entrance to **Montacute House,** an exceptionally fine and complete specimen of a house dating from the end of the reign of Queen Elizabeth.

This magnificent mansion was begun in 1580 by Thomas Phelips and completed about 1600 by his son, Edward Phelips, Speaker of the House of Commons. It has an H-shaped ground plan with an east front (the original) and also a west front of three storeys, and is built of local warm yellow Ham Hill stone. The external features include beautiful oriel windows, curvilinear and finialled gables, open balustraded parapets, carved statues of the Nine Worthies standing in niches in the east front, and fluted angle columns. It contains some fine heraldic glass, plaster-work and panelling. The contemporary quadrangular garden contains two garden pavilions in the east forecourt, and has shaded alleys of trimmed yews bordering the smooth lawns. The rooms are panelled or decorated with fine plaster-work. Each room has its own particular character. The *State Bedroom* has 42 stained glass coats of arms in its four large windows. The *State Dining Room* has a richly carved mantelpiece and fine panelling. The *Grand Gallery* runs the full length of the house on the 3rd floor; it is 200 feet long, with walls 13 feet high. It has 14 large windows and contains period furniture, paintings and magnificent tapestries. Among the paintings are portraits of Edward Phelips in his Speaker's robes, James I, Sir Christopher Hatton, Sir Thomas Egerton, the Earl of Essex and many others. In one of the bedrooms is a carved four-poster bed known as the *Royal Bed.*

Open April-September daily, except Mondays and Tuesdays, 1 to 6.

1 mile beyond Montacute is the charming old village of **Stoke sub Hamdon,** with a Norman church and a museum in *Priory House* (15th c.), in the middle of the village. Beyond this the road runs into A 303, the main road from London to Cornwall. This passes on the right the Tudor manor-house of *Barrington Court;* and at Ilminster, 14 miles from Yeovil, is a beautiful 15th century church (Perpendicular).

5 miles north of Yeovil, on A 303, is **Ilchester,** with a church which is partly mediaeval; the nave dates from 1880. 1 mile east is the *Fleet Air Museum* (open April-September 11 to 5). 3 miles north-east is *Lytes Cary,* a stone manor-house with a

14th century chapel and a 15th century great hall; gardens laid out in Elizabethan style. (National Trust property: open Wednesdays and Saturdays in summer 2 to 6). 3 miles south-west is *Tintinhull*, with a 17th century manor-house set in beautiful gardens.

51 miles: **Crewkerne** (pop. 4500, E.C. Thursday), situated in a circle of hills. Richly decorated *church* (1430), built on the site of three earlier churches. The west front is particularly fine; the south side is unfinished. Note the sculptured figures of musicians and the north front. The *Grammar School* was founded in 1489. The town has a considerable textile industry, specialising in sailcloth, tarpaulins and conveyor belts.

7 miles south of Crewkerne is **Beaminster** (pop. 1600, E.C. Wednesday). Situated on the river Brit, it is an old town with a 15th century church. In Hardy's novels it is referred to as Emminster. Nearby *Parnham House* has been the seat of the Strode family since it was built in the 15th century.

From Crewkerne A 30 continues just within the Somerset county boundary. 52 miles: *Roundham*. At 55 miles the road rises sharply to the top of a wooded hill to Windwhistle Inn, afterwards descending to Chard.

58 miles: **Chard** (pop. 6000, E.C. Wednesday), a small country town on the south-east slopes of the Blackdown Hills. *St Mary's Church* (Perpendicular) is very beautiful. *Harvey's Almshouses* date from 1664. Among the other old buildings in the town is the Tudor manor house, where Judge Jeffreys sat in court after the battle of Sedgemoor. The courtroom with its fine ceiling still survives, although the rest of the building has been converted into shops.

4 miles away is **Forde Abbey,** one of the finest country houses in Dorset (private property). It incorporates the remains of a

12th century Cistercian abbey, with 15th century additions, altered in the 17th century by Inigo Jones. The salon, nearly 60 feet long by 25 feet high, has a magnificent ceiling and the famous Mortlake Tapestries, commissioned by Charles I from cartoons by Raphael. Open Tuesdays and Sundays in summer 2 to 6.

Chard to Axminster: 7 miles on A 358. The road, a continuation of the old Roman Fosse Way, goes along the top of the hills to (3 miles) Tyherleigh, and then descends to (7 miles) **Axminster** (pop. 2500, E.C. Wednesday), a pleasant little town which has given its name to a special kind of carpet formerly manufactured here. At *Ashe House*, 2 miles south-west, the 1st Duke of Marlborough was born. 2 miles away are the remains of *Newenham Abbey*.

64 miles: the road enters Devon.

Devon. A county of great contrasts, of rugged granite masses and high plateaus, and also of low wooded hills rising from lush valleys. It contains some of the best agricultural land in the country and some of the worst. The soil is red, and in full sunlight the ruddy cliffs of its south coast are a startling and unforgettable sight. It is the county of the cider apples and dairy produce; its clotted cream and junket are local delicacies. The county town is ancient *Exeter*, its great port and naval base is *Plymouth*. One can travel from Exeter to Plymouth across the high moorland of *Dartmoor* to the head waters of the lovely River Dart; or one can follow the road aloong the coast by way of such lovely resorts as *Teignmouth* and *Torquay*, past red cliffs, palm trees, and gardens of semi-tropical plants. Plymouth suffered terribly during the second world war. Devon's north coast is particularly fine. Great rocky hills slope steeply to the sea at the edge of which are pleasant resorts such as *Ilfracombe*, *Lynmouth* and *Lynton*, and, behind them, the heather-clad hills of *Exmoor*.

72 miles: **Honiton** (pop. 4400, E.C. Thursday), famous for the lace to which it has given its name, although it is mostly made in the neighbouring villages.

From Honiton A 30 follows the old Roman road, slowly descending to Fairmile, after which there is a

steep ascent to Straightway. The road again descends
sharply to Rockbeare and continues over low undulating country to Clyst Honiton. 88 miles: **Exeter.**

EXETER

Exeter (pop. 84,000) is the county town of Devon,
famed for its cathedral, its castle and its city walls.
The city, situated on a hillside sloping west to the
river Exe, contains many examples of ancient and
beautiful domestic architecture and is said to have
withstood more sieges than any other town in England.
It was severely damaged during the second world war.

Exeter, alone of all English towns, has been inhabited without
a break from pre-Roman times to the present day. Early in
the 3rd century a stone wall enclosing some 98 acres was built
round the town: almost three-quarters of the circuit can still
be seen. A castle was built on a mound by the first Norman
governor of the town, Baldwin. King John in 1200 granted
the town a charter. (Exeter was one of the first English cities
to be awarded rights of self-government.) The first stone bridge
was built over the Exe at the beginning of the 13th century.
When the water is very low, the piles of this bridge can still
be seen a little downstream from the present bridge. The first
ship canal in the country was cut by the city in 1563 to re-
establish its position as a port. During the Wars of the Roses
the city was presented by Edward IV with a sword as a mark
of approval. This sword, and another given by Henry VII
after the city had remained loyal and withstood Perkin War-
beck's rebellion, are the only swords of English kings still in
existence. *Moll's Coffee House*, in the Close, was the rendezvous of many of the famous seamen of the time, like Drake,
Hawkins, Frobisher and Raleigh. During the Civil War the
town was captured after a siege by royalist forces and Charles I
established his headquarters in Bedford House, Bedford Circus
(destroyed during the last war). His daughter Henrietta Maria
was born here. Exeter supported Monmouth during his rebellion, and Judge Jeffreys held his Bloody Assizes in the town.
In 1688 William of Orange spent 12 days here after landing
at Brixham and was proclaimed king. Thereafter Exeter was

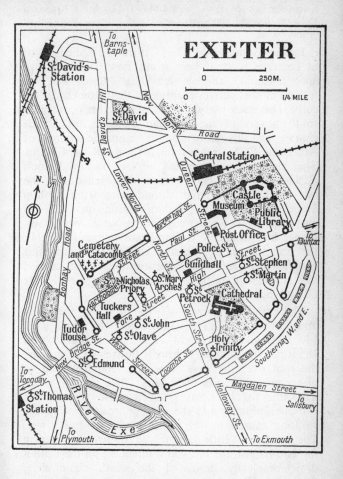

EXETER

0   250 M.

0   1/4 MILE

To
Barnstaple

St David's
Station

St David

New North Road

Central Station

St David's Hill

N.

Lower North St.

Queen Street

Castle
Museum
Public
Library

To
Taunton

Cemetery
and Catacombs

Northernhay St.

Paul St.

Post Office

Police Stn

St Stephen
St Martin

Street

St Nicholas
Priory

North St.

St Mary
Arches

Guildhall

High
Street

Bartholomew Street

St
Petrock

Cathedral

Tuckers
Hall

Fore

Street

St John

Southernhay W. and E.

Tudor
House

New Bridge St.

St Olave

West

Street

South Street

Holy
Trinity

To
Torquay

St Edmund

Coombe St.

Magdalen Street

To
Salisbury

St Thomas
Station

River   Exe

Holloway St.

To
Plymouth

To Exmouth

spared the ravages of war until 4 May 1942, when a large area including the old shopping district was entirely destroyed in an air raid.

Exeter Cathedral. The Cathedral, dedicated to St Peter, is built of Beer stone, now darkened with age. It is small and not immediately impressive, but it is an almost perfect example of the Geometrical (or early Decorated) style and retains the north and south towers of the Norman building. The first church on this site was the monastic church of Athelstan (932), rebuilt in 1017 by King Canute. The choir was completed under Bishop Bytoon (1292-1307). The choir screen (damaged during the last war), reredos and throne date from Bishop Stapeldon (1307-26). Bishop Grandison (1327-69) was responsible for the nave and splendid west front. Under his successor, Bishop Brantyngham (1370-94), the building was completed and the Perpendicular east window renewed. Restorations were carried out at the end of the 19th century by Sir George Gilbert Scott.

The cathedral is over 400 feet long, 75 feet wide and 65 feet high. The width across the transepts is 140 feet, and the height of the transeptal towers 165 feet. The building is heavily buttressed to support the roof over the nave: this roof, 300 feet long, is of stone and weighs 5000 tons. The interior is remarkable for its great symmetry and also for its extreme lightness and the long unbroken line in the vaulting caused by the absence of a central tower. The triforium is little more than a low arcade. During the bombing in the last war a direct hit on the Cathedral completely destroyed the south choir aisle, St James's Chapel, the crypt below and the *Muniment Room* above. Blast blew out every window, and the

EXETER CATHEDRAL

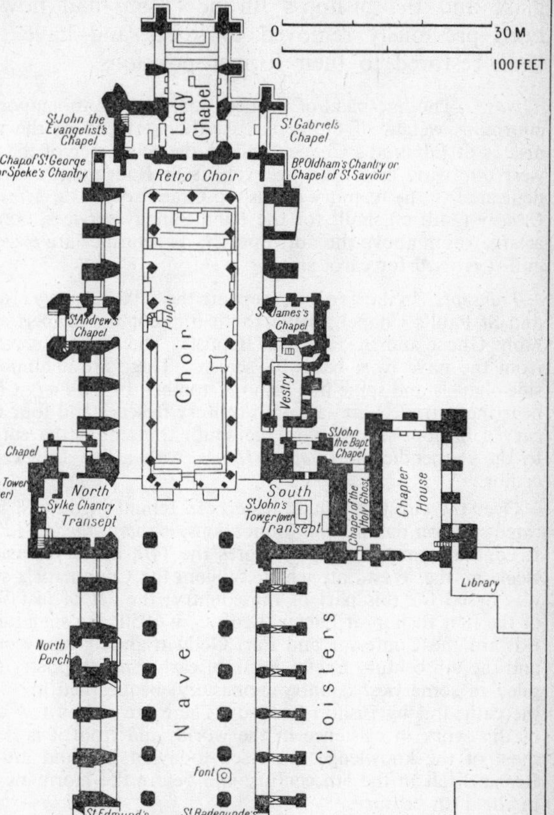

0 ——————————— 30 M

0 ——————————— 100 FEET

Lady Chapel

S.t John the Evangelist's Chapel

S.t Gabriel's Chapel

Chapel S.t George or Speke's Chantry

Retro Choir

B.p Oldham's Chantry or Chapel of S.t Saviour

S.t Andrew's Chapel

Pulpit

Choir

S.t James's Chapel

Vestry

S.t Paul's Chapel

S.t Paul's Tower (over)

North Sylke Chantry Transept

S.t John the Bapt. Chapel

S.t John's Tower (over)

South Transept

Chapel of the Holy Ghost

Chapter House

Library

North Porch

Nave

Cloisters

Font

S.t Edmund's Chapel

S.t Radegunde's Chapel

screens, organ and furniture were all badly damaged. The most important treasures, including the mediaeval glass and the bishop's throne (1465) had however been previously removed to safety and have since been restored to their former positions.

Nave. The fine piers of Purbeck marble help to support the enormous weight of the roof. At the west end of the north aisle is St Edmund's Chapel, and on the south side of the great west doorway, built into the wall, is St Radegunde's Chapel, dedicated to the memory of Bishop Grandison. The *Minstrels' Gallery* (14th c.), built for the Palm Sunday services, conceals a large room above the north porch; its acoustics are excellent, and it is used for carol singing.

Transepts. In the north transept are the Sylke Chantry (16th c.) and St Paul's Chapel, in the south transept the chapels of the Holy Ghost and St John the Baptist. The *choir* is separated from the nave by a beautiful screen. There are a number of side chapels and some fine bishops' tombs. In the *Lady Chapel*, near the entrance, are late 15th century frescoes and four richly carved bishops' tombs. In the south transept is the entrance to the Perpendicular *Chapter House*, with a fine 15th century ceiling.

Over the cloisters, which have been rebuilt in the old Decorated style on the original foundations, is the *Cathedral Library*. It contains among other treasures the 11th century **Domesday Book of the West,** on which William the Conqueror's survey was based for this part of the country; the act of installation of the first Bishop of Exeter, Leofric, in 1050; the signatures of Edward the Confessor and Earl Godwin among many others; and the 9th century Exeter Book of early English poetry (compiled in some west country monastery) bequeathed in 1072 to the cathedral by Bishop Leofric. There are only a few copies of this work in existence in the world, and from it is derived most of the knowledge possessed today of England after the Romans left in the 5th century and before the Normans came in the 11th century.

The works of the clock in the north tower are modern, but the square face dates from the 13th century and the minute dial from the 18th century: it depicts the earth at the centre and also records the phases of the moon. In the south tower is a ringing peal of 13 bells, the heaviest in the world.

Cathedral Close. The main building is the *Bishop's Palace*, which still retains much of the original work, including the 13th century chapel of St Mary and the entrance archway. In the *Law Library* there is a beautiful 14th century carved roof. In the *Annuellars' Refectory* (Murray's premises) there is a fine 15th century hall.

Mol's Coffee House, with its Elizabethan architecture, still retains a panelled room with coats of arms and a unique plaster ceiling.

Adjoining this old house is **St Martin's Church,** which was dedicated in 1065 (key next door). To the east is the archway to the quadrangle, with a splendidly carved early Jacobean oak door. In the centre of the close is a statue of the theologian *Richard Hooker* (1544-1600).

The best place to see the Roman *City Walls* is in Southernhay, where a considerable stretch was laid bare during the air raids. They were 10 feet wide, of squared local stone with rubble filling. Commemorative tablets mark the sites of the ancient city gates. There are many Roman remains: a tessellated pavement found in Waterbeer St has been relaid in the Magistrates' Court House entrance, and the museum contains many small objects dating from this period.

Behind the *Court House* is *St Pancras' Church,* the most ancient in the town: the pulpit and font are both Norman. The church of **St Mary Arches,** off Fore St, is mainly 12th century but the east wall contains Saxon work.

It is the only church in the county with a double Norman arcade. It contains many tombs of mayors of the town, of which the finest is that of Thomas Andrew, mayor in 1517. The church was badly damaged by bombing during the last war.

In Mint Lane is the Benedictine *St Nicholas Priory*, a pleasing example of mediaeval domestic architecture, with the original Guest Hall, prior's room, undercroft and red sandstone kitchen. There are also some good doorways. Half-way up Fore St is **Tucker's Hall,** the guild house of the Guild of Weavers, Fullers and Shearmen (founded 1490), whose coat of arms is above the door. In the 16th century the chapel, originally single-storied, was divided into two by the insertion of an intermediate floor. The upper floor has some of the finest panelling in England and a beautiful carved wooden ceiling, until recently concealed under a coat of plaster. Open on Tuesday, Thursday and Friday mornings.

The district near the site of the old west gate is one of the most interesting of the old town; the *Church of St Mary Steps* has a fine Norman font and a quaint old clock with figures striking the hours. Adjacent in Stepcote Hill, formerly a main thoroughfare to the High St, are old Tudor houses. — One of the most interesting houses in the town is the **Guild Hall,** in the High St, which is the oldest municipal building in use in the country. The present Guild Hall dates from 1330, when it was built on the site of a former town hall.

It has a fine façade, part of it projecting over the pavement, completed in 1595, with an interesting old carved door. The roof dates from 1468-69. Portraits of Queen Henrietta and Gen. Monk. The battle flag of the cruiser "Exeter", which fought the German pocket battleship "Graf Spee" in the battle of the River Plate in 1939, hangs in the great hall, which also contains the municipal insignia. In *Rougemont Gardens* are the ruins of a Norman castle (see p. 406).

Northernhay Gardens, laid out in the time of Charles II on the site of the old castle moat, were used as a militia training ground in the 19th century. The *Volunteer Memorial* (1895) commemorates the foundation in Devon of the Volunteer Force of Great Britain, which became the Territorial Army in 1908. The Wynard Almshouses in Magdalen St, founded in 1430, with old houses and a chapel, are set round a picturesque courtyard. Georgian houses in the town: *Barnfield Crescent*, some houses in *Southernhay West* and *Colleton Crescent* (Norworthy, 1784). *Pennsylvania Park* and *Pennsylvania Crescent* are Regency.

The *Royal Albert Memorial Museum and Art Gallery* (open 10 to 5, except Sundays), built in 1868, also houses the Art School and part of the University. The museum contains birds and mammals arranged by region, fauna of the British Isles, sections of ethnography and archaeology, classical antiquities and Stone and Bronze Age material (excavations of Hembury Fort). The art gallery contains pictures by Reynolds and Turner.

Exmouth

10 miles on A 377. 4 miles: *Topsham*, an ancient little town, where ships were built to fight the Armada. The Dutch houses on the Strand, the cobbled streets and the old inns still retain the atmosphere of the busy port of earlier days.

Exmouth (pop. 22,000, E.C. Wednesday), at the south end of the broad estuary of the Exe, in pleasantly undulating and well-wooded country, is a popular resort and favoured for sailing. To the west lie the *Halidon Hills*, famous for magnificent sunsets. *Littleham Church*, on the site of an older building dates from the 13th century.

In the churchyard is buried Lady Nelson, who lived on at the Beacon after having separated from her husband. In the churchyard of the 12th and 15th centuries church of St John's-in-the-Wilderness on the Withycombe Road are monuments of the families of Drake and Raleigh. In the churchyard of St Michael's Chapel is the grave of John Colleton (1754), governor of Virginia in America.

Around Exmouth. To the north and east is *Woodbury Common*, with fine views of the sea, the river, Dartmoor and the Tors. **Lympstone**, a village situated at the widest part of the Exe estuary, between red sandstone cliffs. From Cliff Field there is a very fine view, particularly at sunset. Interesting features of the village are its old houses and lanes, the quay and Darling's Rock. The *church* dates from 1409 (restored 1864): red sandstone tower, Saxon font, old beams in steeple, tombs of the Drake family. On the Exeter road is a house called *A la Ronde*, a replica of the church of San Vitale in Ravenna, with a rather inappropriate "seashell gallery" above the central hall. *Nutwell Court*, on the Exe, 3 miles away, was the home of the Drake family. *Ladram Bay* is a noted beauty spot.

East Budleigh and Otterton, 5 miles east of Exmouth: a quiet village on the Otter, which was formerly wide and navigable (Budleigh Haven was a considerable port). Nearby is *Hayes Barton*, a perfectly preserved Elizabethan mansion in which Sir Walter Raleigh was born; the actual room in which he was born can be seen (open 2 to 5 in summer). In a pleasant bay nearby is *Budleigh Salterton*, at the mouth of the Otter, surrounded by steep red cliffs. John G. Millais stayed here when painting his famous picture "The Boyhood of Raleigh".

Alternative Route from Salisbury to Exeter via Taunton

Follow route 12 13 from Salisbury to Barford St Martin, where B 3089 forks right to Mere.

8½ miles: *Dinton*, on the northern slopes of the Nadder valley, with 295 acres of parkland belonging to the National Trust. Phillips House, formerly the home of the Wyndham family, was completed in 1815 by Jeffrey Wyatt in the neo-Grecian style; it stands on rising ground with a screen of fine beech trees. Near the church is the Wren-style *Hyde's House*, probably dating from around 1725. In an older house on the site Edward Hyde, afterwards Lord Clarendon, is said to have been born. *Little Clarendon*, ¼ mile from Dinton church, is a stone building in Tudor style, probably late 15th century. Nearby is *Lawes Cottage*, also stone-built, a 17th century house once occupied by the composer William Lawes, a friend of Milton's.

10½ miles: *Teffont*. *Teffont Evias* and *Teffont Magna* are charming villages of thatched cottages. Interesting monuments in the church.

13 miles: *Chilmark*, a village of local stone from the nearby quarries built round the "Street". The road runs through pleasant country to (14 miles) *Fonthill Bishop:* road to the left to (1 mile) **Fonthill Gifford**, with *Beckford's Folly*, a great pseudo-Gothic "abbey" erected by William Beckford (1759-1844). It has a 300 feet tower and was shut off by a wall around the estate. Little remains of what was known as "Fonthill Abbey". 2 miles beyond on the north bank of the Nadder is *Tisbury*, on high ground in well-wooded and very beautiful countryside. There is a beautiful 12th century church with fine wood-carvings and monuments.

15¼ miles: *Hindon*, with a wide tree-lined High Street climbing up to the church on the hill.

17 miles: A 350 (Chippenham to Shaftesbury) cuts across B 3089. 2 miles along the road to Shaftesbury is *East Knoyle*, birthplace of Sir Christopher Wren (1632). Magnificent views over the Vale of Blackmore from the windmill on a nearby hill.

19 miles: B 3089 runs into A 303 (London to Exeter). 23 miles: **Mere** (pop. 3000), an ancient town. The *Old Ship Hotel* in the market-place is 17th century. *St Michael's Church* (Perpendicular) has a fine tower (94 ft, with pinnacles another 29 ft). Above the north porch is a museum.

3 miles north-west is the National Trust property of **Stourhead** (3000 acres), which includes the villages of Stourton and Kilmington. *Stourhead House* was built in 1722 by Colin Campbell for Henry Hoare, the banker, whose son Henry laid out the romantic gardens with their lakes and temples in 1741-50. They are among the finest examples in England of 18th century landscape design. Two wings of the house were added about 1800; it was partly burnt in 1892. Collection of works of art, notably furniture designed by Thomas Chippendale the younger. (Open 2 to 6, except Mondays and Tuesdays; gardens 11 to 7 daily). In front of the house is the 14th century Bristol Cross, removed from College Green, Bristol, in 1776 (p. 502). In the village there is a mediaeval church, and in the small valley are the six springs from which the River Stour rises.

25 miles: *Upper Zeals*. — 27 miles: half a mile north is *Penselwood*, with the strange "pen pits", curious excavations

of which the origin is unknown. — 30 miles: *Wincanton* (pop.
2100, E.C. Wednesday), at the beginning of the lovely Blackmore
Vale: medicinal springs. — 83 miles Holton. — 85 miles:
Blackford. — 35 miles: *Cadbury Castle*, an old British earthwork of 30 acres which tradition makes a second possible scene
of the Arthurian legends (see Camelford, p. 454). — 43 miles:
Ilchester. — 55 miles: Ilminster. — 123 miles: *Honiton.*
— 140 miles: **Exeter.**

14. EXETER TO PLYMOUTH
BY THE COAST ROAD

74 miles on A 379.

5 miles: *Exminster*. — 8 miles: *Kenton*. The church has a 15th century screen. — 10 miles: *Starcross* (ferry to Exmouth). Nearby is *Powderham Castle*, seat of the Earl of Devon (1420, restored), with pictures by Kneller and Reynolds and Brussels tapestries (open daily, except Saturdays, in summer, 2 to 6).

14 miles: **Dawlish** (pop. 7800, E.C. Thursday: ferry to Exmouth), an attractive seaside town, sheltered by Great Haldon Hill (820 ft). Good bathing from a sandy beach. *Newhays Falls* is one of the local beauty spots. In the parish church are tombs by Flaxman.

17 miles: **Teignmouth** (pop. 11,000, E.C. Thursday). The red cliffs crowned with fir-trees give this town on the mouth of the Teign a striking setting. The river forms a loop at the Salty, where there is an old harbour (ferry to Shaldon) with picturesque quays. Keats once lived at 35, The Strand. Commanding the entrance to the river and opposite the town is a magnificent landmark, the *Ness*, the grounds of which are open to the public. Access by ferry to Shaldon or over the Shaldon bridge.

Pleasant walks to the Labrador Cliffs (400 ft), Labrador Bay, Maidencombe, Bishopsteignton, Holcombe and Haldon Moors. 6 miles west is **Newton Abbot** (pop. 15,000, E.C. Thursday), with a 15th century tower. Just outside the village is *Ford House*, a fine Tudor mansion. In the neighbourhood are a number of other interesting villages — *Kingskerswell* and *Abbotskerwell*, noted for their cider, and *Coffinswell* with its thatched cottages. To the west of Newton Abbot is *Bradley*

Manor, a fine example of 15th century domestic architecture (open on Wednesdays in summer, 2 to 5).

26 miles: Torquay (pop. 53,000, E.C. Wednesday and Saturday). Set on seven hills around the red cliffs and blue waters of Torbay, Torquay is one of England's leading seaside resorts, noted for its regattas, its concerts and its golf. Its palm trees and semi-tropical vegetation have earned it the title of "Queen of the English Riviera".

Near the sea-front is the *Spanish Barn*, in which 400 prisoners from the Spanish Armada were imprisoned. There are numerous sea and river excursions (coastal and on the River Dart) and a ferry to Brixham. The ruins of *Torre Abbey* (12th-14th c.) are in Avenue Road; St Michael's Chapel has now been converted into an observatory. There is a well-preserved monastic out-house, known as the Monastic Barn. The Marine Drive conti-nues out to the east as Ilsham Lane; it soon passes *Kent's Cavern*, a limestone cave of great extent, with stalagmites. The road reaches Anstey's Cove, an unspoilt beauty spot, and Babbacombe Bay, which is lovely but inclined to be overcrowded. There is a fine view along the coast from the cliffs.

2 miles west is *Cockington*, a small fairy-tale village of that-ched roofs, clipped hedges and flowers. The forge is a great attraction. *Compton Castle*, a 15th century fortified mansion, is 3 miles beyond the village.

29 miles: Paignton (pop. 32,000, E.C. Wednesday), a popular seaside resort with extensive sands on Torbay. The church (Perpendicular) contains 15th century carving. Nearby is the 14th century *Bible Tower*, all that remains of the Bishop's Palace. The name of the tower is a reminder that the last bishop, Miles Coverdale, translated the Bible (1535). *Kirkham House* and *Oldway* are old houses, now museums.

6 miles west is **Totnes** (pop. 5000, E.C. Thursday), an old town built out on the side of a hill, with the castle ruins dominating the scene. Of the castle, built during the reign of William the Conqueror, only the oddly shaped keep, of two circular tiers

one upon the other, remains. The North Gate of the town is near by. In the 15th century *church* is one of the finest stone rood-screens in the country; the tower is very impressive. There is a 16th century *Guildhall*, and along the High St are numerous old houses. 2 miles: *Pomeroy Castle*. The ruins consist of the gateway, round tower and other portions of the 13th century. The rest is 16th century, an unfinished mansion; the whole was of immense size.

32 miles: *Churston Ferrers*. Road on left to *Brixham*.

Brixham (pop. 12,000, E.C. Wednesday), a venerable old town on Tor Bay with narrow and winding streets, famous for its fishing traditions and its modern fleet of trawlers. Here in 1688 William of Orange landed to claim the throne: a plaque marks the spot where he stepped ashore, and on the strand is a statue of him. On Berry Head are the ruins of two forts built to defend the town against Napoleon. Two minutes from Bolton Cross on Mount Pleasant is a cavern where many bones (cave lion, cave bear, etc.) and relics of prehistoric man were found.

36 miles: *Kingswear*. The road ends here on the estuary of the Dart. Hills thick with trees reach down to the water's edge, where charming villages nestle and bays shelter craft of all kind.

At Mount Ridley are the ruins of an old fort, and below Brookhill are the ruins of *Gommerock*, built by Edward IV (1461-83) to oppose Dartmouth Castle and fortify the Dart. *Kingswear Castle* farther along towards the estuary was also a work of defence.

Cross the river by ferry or by floating bridge.

37 miles: **Dartmouth** (pop. 6800, E.C. Wednesday and Saturday). Its many ancient buildings, its castles, its busy water-front and its soft climate make Dartmouth one of the outstanding west country beauty spots. The chancel of 14th century **St Saviour's Church** was built by John Hawley (d. 1408), a local hero, who is buried here with his two wives. The

south door, now inside the church, has fine ironwork.
Near the church, in Higher St, Collaford Lane and
Smith St, are some of the oldest houses in the town.
Tudor House, in Higher St, has been restored. *Butter
Walk* (17th c.), with its arcade of 11 stone columns
(carved signs of zodiac and dates), suffered severe
damage in the last war.   Among features which
survived were a genealogical tree on one of the ceilings
and the panelling in another room.   In the *Guildhall*
are relics of the Elizabethan and other periods, and
there is also an interesting collection of material in
the *Borough Museum*.

Dartmouth Castle, 1 mile from the centre of the
town, stands high above the Dart estuary, matched
by Kingswear Castle on the opposite bank.   It was
built in the reign of Edward IV (1461-83).   Just under
the Castle is *St Petrox Church*.

Returning to the town, we come to the end of Newcomen
Road.   On the right is the *Mansion House* (1750), with fine
carved ceilings.   The oldest part of the town is Bayard's Cove,
locally called *Monkeytown* and famous for the annual regatta
at which a mayor is elected for a day.   The streets are cobbled.
The *Customs House* (1729), is among the newest of its buildings.
Nearby Bearscove Castle (1502) was one of the fortifications
of the town.

The harbour of Dartmouth is very fine, and yachting is one
of the great attractions of the town.   There is an annual regatta
(last Thursday, Friday, and Saturday in August).   *The Royal
Naval College* (1905) is housed in an extensive range of buildings
on the hills above the town.   The cadets receive theoretical
and practical training for service in the Royal Navy.

The Dart. The lovely valley of the Dart leads to many pretty
villages.   3 miles upstream is *Dittisham*, particularly inviting
when the many plum orchards are in blossom.   *Sandridge*,
upstream, was the birthplace of Davis, the Arctic navigator.
Opposite is the attractive village of *Higher Dittisham*.   *Stoke-
mouth* and, a short distance inland, *Stoke Gabriel* are two
charming villages.   The Dart above here is at its most beautiful.

Sharpham, with its famous heronry and rookery. Then Totnes
Reach and *Totnes* (p. 418).

39 miles: *Stoke Fleming,* with Start Bay and Start
Point presenting a magnificent view. — 40 miles:
Blackpool Sands. In the bay is a submerged forest,
uncovered at certain tides. — 41 miles: *Strete.* —
42 miles: *Slapton.* The freshwater lake of *Slapton
Ley* is noted for its wildfowl. — 45 miles: *Torcross,*
where the road turns inland. Walkers should visit
Prawle Point and Start Point, where there is a rocky
and impressive coastline.

52 miles: **Kingsbridge,** at the head of the Salcombe
estuary.

7 miles south is *Salcombe*. Salcombe Harbour and, on the
opposite bank (ferry), East Portlemouth should be visited.
Some 1200 acres of cliff and farmland belong to the National
Trust: good walking and magnificent views. Youth hostel in
a modern building on the west side of Salcombe Harbour;
museum. On the east side, near Portlemouth, is another National Trust property — 290 acres of rocky country extending
from Mill Bay to Moor Sand and Decklers Cliff.

54 miles: road to *Thurlestone.* 59 miles: road to
Bigbury-on-Sea and *Burgh Island.* 60 miles: *Modbury.*
63 miles: road to *Newton Ferrers* down the beautiful
Yealm estuary. 65 miles: *Yealmpton,* at the head of
the Yealm estuary.

74 miles: **Plymouth** (p. 424).

15. EXETER TO PLYMOUTH
BY THE INLAND ROAD

43 miles on A 38.

1¾ miles: *Alphington*. 4 miles: *Kennford*. 10 miles: *Chudleigh*.

Nearby is the famous *Chudleigh Rock*, a bold limestone crag with a glen, waterfall and deep caverns. Near the Rock are the ruins of a chapel and palace built by Osbert, Bishop of Exeter, in 1080.

12 miles: *Chudleigh Knighton*.

Road on right to *Bovey Tracey*, a good centre for excursions on Dartmoor, near Bay Tor, Rippon Tor, Lustleigh Cleave and Becky Falls. Of the church built by Sir William Tracey, one of Thomas Becket's murderers, there survives only a small porch, to the south of the present chapel. The later church was built by the Countess of Beaufort, mother of Henry VII (1485-1509).

19 miles: *Ashburton* (pop. 2500, E.C. Wednesday), admirably situated as a centre for excursions on Dartmoor. The fine Early English church and the curious Card House should be visited.

Dartmoor. Some 23 miles by 11 miles, Dartmoor is a wild waste of more than 200 square miles and with an average height of about 1500 feet. Its bleak granite hills ("Tors") rise to some 2000 feet. Many streams famous for fishing rise in the hills and on the borders of the moors have cut their way into well-wooded ravines. There are prehistoric (Neolithic) menhirs, stone circles, "clapper" bridges and ancient monuments of every kind. The railway skirts the north and south edge of the moor and only two roads cross it: the Moretonhampstead — Yelverton and the Tavistock — Ashburton roads. Walkers should be careful to avoid the treacherous bogland.

North of Ashburton is the village of *Widecombe-in-the-Moor* (pop. 700). The century old Widecombe Fair is still held annually (early in September). There is a 16th century church built by the tin miners who once worked in the parish. To the north near the Hound Tor valley is *Manaton*, opposite a huge rock called *Bowerman's Nose*. Hound Tor crags are nearby, and Grimspound, a formation of stones 500 feet in diameter. *Becky Falls*, in the lovely woods, fall 70 feet over the rocky bed of the stream.

22 miles: *Buckfastleigh*. **Buckfast Abbey** (½ mile). which had been Celtic, Saxon and Norman, was suppressed at the Reformation and fell into ruin.

In 1883 Benedictine monks settled in the house and in 1907 began to build on the ancient foundations. The church, re-consecrated in 1932, was completed in 1938. It is in Transitional style, of the local grey limestone, and has a vaulting of red sandstone: length 224 feet, tower 158 feet high. Interior: fine modern art work, including a gilded metal altar, Stations of the Cross, candelabra and font.

2 miles north is the *Hembury* estate, comprising 374 acres, of which 200 acres are coppice and the remainder gorse and bracken. The land rises to a height of over 500 feet. Hembury Castle, site of an old camp, lies in the middle (National Trust).

25 miles: *Dean Prior*. Here Herrick (1591-1674) was rector and is buried. — 27¾ miles: *South Brent*. — 32½ miles: *Ivybridge*, another admirable centre for excursions in Dartmoor and also for the lovely Erme valley and the South Hams.

38 miles: **Plympton.** There are two Plymptons, St Mary and St Maurice, the former lying on the main road and St Maurice, an older township, clustered around the church and Grammar School (17th century Gothic style, with a fine cloister).

Dominating the countryside are the ruins of *Plympton Castle*, from the reign of Henry I (1100-35), scene of many sieges. The remains include the keep, built on a mound; the outline of the earthworks of a Roman camp can clearly be traced. The village is famous as being the birthplace (1723) of *Sir Joshua Reynolds*. In the *Guildhall* are the insignia of the old

corporation, dating from the time when the town sent its own
member to Parliament.

43 miles: **Plymouth.**

PLYMOUTH

Plymouth (pop. 215,000) is one of the leading naval
and commercial ports in the United Kingdom.

From here Francis Drake set out on his 3-year voyage round
the world. The Sound provides safe anchorage for the largest
ships, as does the Tamar where it widens into Devonport, in
which are the famous Royal Naval Dockyards, with the most
modern port installations.

Plymouth suffered severe bombing during the last war, and
much of the town was destroyed. The beauties of Plymouth
Hoe and the Sound, however, were not affected.

Certainly the first place to visit is *Plymouth Hoe*,
where, according to the old story, news was brought
to Francis Drake that the Spanish Armada had been
sighted, and where he finished his game of bowls
before he turned to the job of defeating Spain. From
the elevated esplanade there is a splendid view of the
Sound and Cawsand Bay.

In the centre is a statue of *Francis Drake* (1884), and nearby
is the *Armada Tercentenary Monument* (1890). A third monument on the Hoe is Smeaton's Lighthouse (95 ft), the third to
be erected on Eddystone island (12 miles to the south) which
was transferred here in 1884.

To the east, dominating the Hoe, is the **Royal
Citadel,** built 1666-74 by Charles II, one of the best
preserved and finest examples of a 17th century
fortress in the country. The statue on the central
green is that of George II (1727-60). There is a
splendid view from the ramparts (not open to visitors).
Beneath the walls of the Royal Citadel are the labo-

ratories of the Marine Biological Association of the United Kingdom: *aquarium* containing collections of living fishes and other marine animals found in the Channel. Below the Hoe is a promenade pier.

Sutton Pool, the first port and now the centre of the fishing trade, lies on the other side of the rock on which the citadel is built. This district is the **Barbican,** the Elizabethan part of the town, and many of the old characteristics have been retained, including the old narrow cobbled ways and the quaint old Cooksley and Camber Courts (off Castle St). *No. 32 New St* has been converted into a museum (period furniture): it is a Elizabethan style house, restored (open weekdays 10 to 1 and 2.15 to 6; Sundays, April-September, 3 to 5). Two other interesting houses are No. 16 (opposite) which dates from 1599, and the Island House (sometimes known incorrectly as the *Mayflower House*). Many of the houses have Tudor and Jacobean arches, windows and staircases.

The main church of Plymouth is **St Andrew's** (15th c.; restored by Sir George Gilbert Scott, 1875); it contains some interesting monuments but was damaged by bombing. Adjoining is *St Andrew's Prysten House* (1490), the residence of the chantry priests of the church: this is one of the best preserved examples of old domestic architecture in the town. In the neighbourhood are the municipal offices (interesting mayor's parlour) and the Guildhall, both modern Gothic.

On *Lambhay Point* are the ruins of a fortified tower, part of the system of defences erected by Henry VIII (1539). There are remains of other towers at Eastern Kings (Millbay Docks) and Devil's Point (foundations,

together with a vaulted chamber), and a better preserved example at Winter Villa, Stonehouse.

Other interesting old buildings: *Customs House* (1586), in
the Parade. 51 Southside St (James I, partly rebuilt) and 53
Southside St (1580, with a late 17th c. front). The *Blackfriars*,
now a gin distillery, was a Dominican monastery (15th c.);
wooden ceiling in the old main refectory. 31 Wolster St was
formerly the *Ring of Bells Inn*, adjoining the site of the old
Greyfriars monastery (Tudor interior with carved ceiling and
frieze, Tudor doorway). In this street also is the Mayoralty
Arch, formerly the entrance to the old Mayoralty House. At
3 Vauxhall St is a house with a Tudor carved ceiling and frieze.
At 12 Notte St is a Tudor house rebuilt in the 19th century,
and at No. 58 of the same street is a house once occupied by
William Cookworthy, manufacturer of Plymouth porcelain.
At 33 St Andrew St is a 16th century house which has pre-
served its granite doorways and handsome oak windows.

In Tavistock Road is the **Plymouth Museum and
Art Gallery,** with paintings by famous artists (*Watteau,
Rubens, Rembrandt, van Dyck, Tiepolo, Reynolds,* etc.),
the *Drake Cup* (1571), Oriental and English china,
industrial art, an Old Plymouth Room, natural
history, early printed books and engravings (open
weekdays 10 to 6, Sundays 3 to 5). In Duke St is
the *Devonport Museum* (ship models, industrial art):
open weekdays, except Wednesdays, 10 to 1 and 2
to 5.

At *Stonehouse* is the *Royal William Victualling Yard*, com-
menced in 1826 and designed by Rennie, with a stately entrance
gateway (statue of William IV). The yard covers some 20 acres.
To the south-west of St George's churchyard are the remains
of the wall of old Stonehouse Manor.

To the west, over the Stonehouse Pool, is **Devonport,** standing
on higher ground and including the industrial district of Plymouth and the *Royal Naval Dockyards* on the Hamoaze, which
is reserved for the Navy. The dockyards are not so large as
those of Portsmouth, but have all that is necessary for construct-
ing, maintaining and equipping naval vessels. At *Bunker's Hill*
(note the temple) are figureheads of historic ships.

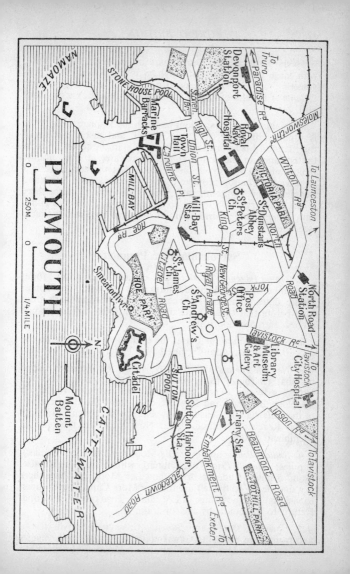

PLYMOUTH

0   250 M.

0   1/4 MILE

N.

NAMOAZE

STONE HOUSE POOL

Marine Barracks

MILL BAY

HOE RD

HOE PARK

Smeaton's Twr.

Citadel

Mount Batten

CATTEWATER

Devonport Station

Paradise Rd.

Royal Naval Hospital

STAFF

High St.

Union St.

Town Hall

Caroline Pl.

St. Peter's Ch.

St. Dunstan's

Abbey

Mill Bay Sta.

King St.

St. James Ch.

Citadel

St. Andrew's

Royal Parade

Post Office

St. George's

New St.

SUTTON POOL

SUTTON

Sutton Harbour Sta.

Friary Sta.

Embankment Rd.

PATTERDOWN Road

To Truro

To Launceston

MOLESWORTH

Wilton Rd.

VICTORIA PARK

North Rd.

York Rd.

North Road Station

City Hospital

To Tavistock

Tavistock Rd.

Library Museum & Art Gallery

Beaumont Road

Lipson Rd.

To Tavistock

FRIARY PARK

To Exeter

To the north are the Gun Wharf and Keyham Steam Yard, with large workshops. At Keyham is the Royal Naval Engineering College. Fine views from the top of the *Devonport Column* at the end of Ker St and from the Blockhouse on Stoke Hill.

Plymouth Sound is a spacious bay of some 3 square miles. West is Mount Edgcombe (ferry to Cremyll) and east the rocks of the island of Mewstone; *Drake's Island* is in the centre. Across the entrance to the sound is the Breakwater, a great granite mole built 1812-41: from the lighthouse at the end there is a good view. The top provides a fine promenade, and boats and steamers from Plymouth take visitors to view it. Here there is one of Henry VIII's forts. To the east is Mount Batten Point, with *Mount Batten Castle*, built at the same time as the citadel (see above).

Surroundings of Plymouth

1. *Mount Edgcumbe Park* (16th c.), seat of the Earl of Mount Edgcumbe, severely damaged during the last war. The Winter House dates from the 15th century and the deer park from long before that time. Note the splendid 16th century granite arched entrance doorway.

2. *Saltram House* (at Laira, the estuary of the Plym, on the way to Oreston). Another fine house Picture gallery.

3. *Newton Ferrers* and *Noss Nayo*, on the Yealm: reached by boat (Barbican to Wideslip), by bus (from St Andrew's Cross) or by car. There are two alternative routes: to the left via Noss, Bridgend and Newton, or to the right along the top of the cliffs via Old Cellars. Between Newton Green and Bridgend is Revelstoke church. Near Noss Mayo are the ruins of Membland Hall.

4. *Shaugh Bridge* and over Lee Moor to Cornwood (8 miles). 3 miles: *Shaugh Prior* (old church), with Shaugh lighthouse. 4 and 5 miles: Cadover Bridge and Lee Moor, of which there is a fine view. To the left are the Lee More China Works (open to visitors) and the village of Lee Moor. Then on to Cornwood. Return to Plymouth by bus or train.

5. *Cawsand, Penlee* and *Rame*. Cross to Cremyll (ferry), and from there by bus to Cawsand and Kingsand, twin villages with steep, winding, narrow streets. Alternatively direct to

Cawsand by motor-boat from the Barbican or Stonehouse Bridge. The road to Penlee passes through the Penlee woods (fine views over Drake's Island and the Breakwater) to the point, then along the precipitous cliffs to Rame Head. The church (1321) has a rood-loft staircase, and carved bench ends. A "squint" looks on to the altar, and there still exists the tympanum of the Norman building dating from 1259. On the summit of the headland is **St Michael's Chapel** (1425), formerly a hermitage.

6. **Weir Head** (19 miles). A pleasant half-day trip by boat up the Hamoaze to the mouth of the Tamar, which marks the boundary between Devon and Cornwall and is spanned by the *Royal Albert Bridge*, a large iron bridge built by Brunel in 1859 (the two main arches are each 500 ft long, and carry the railway over the river at a height of 100 ft). Just beyond the bridge (4 miles) is *Saltash*, an attractive little fishing village. Up river, to the left, is *Pentillie Castle*, at a point where the river widens out considerably beyond the first bend. To the north is *Great Mis Tor*. 12 miles away is *Cotehele*, on the Cornish side of the Tamar, 2 miles west of Calstock (see below). A narrow and winding road leads to **Cotehele House,** an intact example of a noble mansion of the late mediaeval period. The grey granite building is romantically situated in trees above the steep bank of the Tamar, just before it turns west. There are considerable remains of the old fortified manor-house (1353). The present house was built in the 15th century by Richard Edgcumbe and completed about 1520 by his son Piers, who added the great hall. (The main rooms are open to visitors on Wednesdays, Saturdays and Sundays from 2 to 4 or until dusk). 14 miles: *Calstock*, where the river takes a sharp bend: here you can get off the boat and continue by road to Morwellham Quay (17 miles). In the vicinity are the picturesque Morwell crags, 300 feet high. 19 miles: *Weir Head*, close to Tavisstock. This stretch of the river is very attractive, but is deep enough only for small boats.

7. *St Germans* and *Port Eliot*, with Trematon Castle (2 miles from Saltash). On the other side of the river is Anthony House. The mansion and estate of Port Eliot are very fine.

8. **Eddystone Lighthouse** (12 miles), on rocks commanding the entrance to the Sound. Steamers and launches arrange special trips round the lighthouse. There has been a lighthouse

here since 1697; the first was wrecked by storms within six years of its building, and the second was destroyed by fire in 1755. The next on the site was Smeaton's lighthouse (1757), but owing to its insecure foundations it was moved in 1882 to Plymouth Hoe, where it now stands. The present lighthouse is 135 feet high.

16. EXETER TO PENZANCE

Leave Exeter on A 30. 2 miles: *Pocombe Bridge*. 8 miles: *Tedburn St Mary*. 12 miles: *Crockerwell*. 16 miles: *Whiddon Down*. 19½ miles: *Sticklepath*.

23 miles: **Okehampton** (pop. 4000, E.C. Wednesday), a bright little town in the centre of the county of Devon, beneath a spur of Dartmoor. The main street runs between bridges crossing the East and West Ockments. *Okehampton Castle*, near the town, was one of the largest in the county. It was built after the battle of Hastings by Baldwin de Brionys; the ruins consist of the keep, the little chapel and the banqueting hall. Henry VIII demolished it, and there is not much to be seen. In the centre of the town is the mayoral *chapel of St James:* the curfew is still rung each night at 8 o'clock; in the morning the Angelus bell is sounded.

2 miles south-east is the old village of *Belstone*, near which are the *Nine Maidens*, a row of standing stones.

To the south are Yes Tor (2028 ft) and High Willhays (2039 ft), on Dartmoor.

Beyond Okehampton there are two alternative routes to the west, which meet again at Bodmin. The busier of the two is on A 30 via Launceston: in the first place, however, we describe the variant by way of *Tavistock* and *Liskeard*.

3½ miles: take left fork (A 386) to *Sourton*. — 8 miles: *Downtown*. On the right (2 miles) is *Lydford*, on the fringe of Dartmoor. Near the church are the ruins of a Norman castle of which the *keep* (fine door and windows) is all that can be distinguished. The grey stone church dates from Norman times, and was built on the site of a 7th century wooden structure: good mediaeval glass, wonderfully carved woodwork and oak reredos. *Lydford Gorge*, with a magnificent two-stage waterfall (120 ft).

12 miles: *Mary Tavy*, in the centre of rugged moorland. Mediaeval church; note again the stocks in the porch. Above the narrow ravine of the Tavy are *Nat Tor* and *Ger Tor*. North-west is **Brent Tor,** with a church perched on the summit on the edge of a 1100 foot precipice. In the village below there is a fine Early English *church* built like a fortress by the monks from Tavistock.

South-east of Mary Tavy is the charming village of *Peter Tavy*, in a gorge above the Tavy, with a peaceful little church surrounded by lime-trees.

16 miles: **Tavistock** (pop 6200, E.C. Wednesday), on the Tavy. Ruins of a 10th century *Benedictine abbey* near the Bedford Hotel: one of the richest foundations in the county, which produced the first printed books in Devon. Nearby is the *parish church* of St Eustachius (Perpendicular, restored 1846). The Tavy is crossed on Abbey Bridge, near the square. Note the doorway of the abbey.

Around Tavistock. 1 mile away is the site of *Crowndale Farm*, birthplace of Francis Drake; commemorative plaque. 3 miles away is the impressive *Morwell Rock*. To the south is *Meavy* village, once the home of Francis Drake. Yeo Farm, at the entrance to a charming dell, dates from 1610. From Sheepstor is a magnificent view of the Meavy Valley.

Buckland Monachorum village (6 miles south). The church has some interesting glass and a memorial to Baron Heathfield, conqueror of Gibraltar. **Buckland Abbey,** home of Sir Francis Drake, was a 13th century monastic establishment, with tithe barn, granted by Henry VIII in 1541 to Richard Grenville, whose famous grandson, Richard Grenville of the *Revenge*, altered the house in 1576 and added the fine plaster ceiling to the hall. In 1581 it was bought by Francis Drake on his return from circumnavigating the world; his arms are shown in plaster in a room of the top storey. Buckland Abbey is now a Drake Museum; much of the fine gardens, the great trees and yews, and the lawns have not been changed since the time of Drake. The 17th century two-storeyed Gift House in the village was built by a descendant of Drake.

From Tavistock A 384 (one of the two roads crossing Dart-moor), runs near the beautiful *Walkham Valley* to (4 miles) Merrivale and (8½ miles) Two Bridges, 1 mile from *Princetown Prison*, the renowned Dartmoor Prison. It was built in 1809 to house French prisoners, and was later used for Americans; a gateway commemorates the Americans who died there. It became a convict prison in 1850. Prisoners built the church in 1814.

20 miles: *Gunnislake*. Fine views of the Tamar valley. — 26 miles: *Callington*. The road descends abruptly to (27¼ miles) *Newbridge* and again climbs to 500 feet. — 34 miles: **Liskeard** (pop. 5000, E.C. Wednesday), an agreeable little town south of the wild Bodmin Moors. It is a fine centre for excursions. — 37 miles: Dobwalls. — 47 miles **Bodmin** (p. 434), where A 38 rejoins A 30.

A 30 runs west from Okehampton.

29 miles: *Bridestowe*. At 32 miles the road passes near the peaceful valley of the River Lew: to the south is *Lewtrenchard*. The church contains quaintly carved old stalls, benches and screens, and a dove candelabra with 18 lights. At *Lew House* are a 17th century Dower House and a 16 foot menhir. North is *Thrushellton*, on the river Thrushell: a lovely village on the steep bank of the river. — 34 miles: *Portgate*. — 37½ miles: *Lifton;* ancient camp in the vicinity. *Lifton Park* is a fine old mediaeval mansion.

40 miles: the road enters Cornwall.

Cornwall is a duchy. The eldest son of the monarch is Duke of Cornwall, and to this hereditary title certain privileges are attached. Cornwall is famous for its mild climate and its magnificent coasts. In its coves and creeks are some of the most picturesque fishing villages in Britain. The inhabitants were Celts, and the Cornish language was spoken until the 18th century; interesting survivals of it are found in place names and family names, and the old jingle "By Tre, Ros, Pol, Lan, Caer and Pen you may know most Cornish men", is still a reliable guide. On the south coast the boundary of Cornwall lies on the west of Plymouth Sound, and the people of Cornwall are fond of declaring that Cornwall is separated from England by the river Tamar, inferring that Cornwall is a land apart. Cornwall is indeed a land with its own unique customs and character. Cromlechs, monoliths and stone circles are to be found in many places, particularly at *Liskeard* in the Looe Valley, where the

Trevethy Stone is a well-known landmark. On the rocky promontory at *Tintagel* (p. 455) stand the ruins of what ancient
legend and romantic poetry claims to be King Arthur's castle.
The Cornish tin mines were world renowned: they were worked
by the Phoenicians centuries B.C.

41 miles: **Launceston** (pop. 4500, E.C. Thursday),
built on the side of a steep hill, at the summit of
which are the ruins (keep and 12 ft thick walls) of
a Norman castle. Small museum in south gatehouse
(admission charge). The outside of *St Mary Magdalene's Church* is covered with interesting carving.
Near the *King's Arms* is another gate, part of the
old town walls; and the Norman doorway of an
Augustinian priory is built into the White Hart Hotel.

A 30 now runs across *Bodmin Moor*.

64 miles: **Bodmin** (pop. 6000, E.C. Wednesday),
county town of Cornwall and one of the few Cornish
towns not in sight of the sea. The *parish church*
(St Petroc's) was built in 1470 on the site of an earlier
church, of which the tower and chancel still remain.
The views over the open spaces of Bodmin Moor are
superb.

Bodmin Moor is a great open region which has been inhabited
from earliest times. Cairns, barrows and earthworks, arrows,
implements, burial urns and countless relics of Palaeolithic man
have been found; there are many hut circles and stone monuments to be seen. In the vicinity of Bodmin are several ancient
hilltop camps: Castle-an-Dinas, St Columb, Berry Castle (with
a rampart of 260 yards), in the parish of Cardinham, and Kelly
Rounds (a fosse and vallum) in Egloshayle parish. 1 mile
south-east of Bodmin is *Castle Canyke* (500 ft); 1 mile north-
west is Dunmere Castle; 2 miles west is *Tregear*, of interest for
its Roman remains. Steep granite crags.

2 miles south of Bodmin is *Lanhydrock House* (17th c.;
gardens and art gallery; open 2 to 6 in summer, except Sundays).
5 miles away on the same road (B 3266, then B 3268) is the
little town of **Lostwithiel** (pop. 2200), on the Fowey. The 14th

century *church* has a lantern spire of curious openwork form. The Duchy House and bridge are also 14th century. 1 mile west are the ruins of *Restormel Castle*, dating from the reign of Henry III (1216-72).

67 miles: *Lanivet*. Soon afterwards A 391 branches off on the left and runs south to St Austell (8 miles).

St Austell (pop. 26,000, E.C. Thursday), in the heart of the china clay district, with deposits of disintegrated felspar which after treatment is similar to Chinese kaolin. Church of 12th and 15th centuries.

8 miles east of St Austell is **Fowey** (pop. 2400, E.C. Wednesday), formerly one of the West country's leading ports, now used for the shipment of china clay from the St Austell area to America. *St Nicholas's Church* (15th c.), with a beautiful tower. *Tudor Place House* (fine oriel windows). Ruins of St Saviour's Chapel and of a castle on St Catherine's Point, and of another of Henry VIII's fortresses on the other side of the river mouth (open from sunrise to sunset). In the Harbour Office are interesting old maps.

The **Roseland Peninsula**, south-west of St Austell Bay, is an unspoiled stretch of sea-bordered country. — 5 miles: *Mevagissey*. This small centre of pilchard fishing is now a popular resort. Just beyond is Port Mellon, with an excellent beach and woodland. — 8 miles: *Goran Haven*, with the church of St Goran, a Saxon saint. — 12¼ miles: *Veryan* (pop. 800), a quaint village whose history can be traced back to 1212, when it had the Cornish name of *Elerky* (Swan's House). Elerky farmhouse contains remains of the old manor-house. Three round houses with pointed thatched roofs; two other round houses and two holy wells at *Veryan Green*. Fifteen minutes' walk away is the fine sandy beach of *Pendower*, in sheltered coves; nearby is *Portholland Cove*, with rugged cliffs and peaceful beaches. The next cove is *Porthluney Cove;* to the left is *Caerhayes Castle* (1808), built on the site of the old castle on wild crags crowned with pine trees. There are interesting collections of minerals in the castle. 7 miles south-west of Veryan is the church of *St Just-in-Roseland*, founded in 550; the present building dates from the 13th century. Across Porthscuel River is *Gerrans*, with a church dating from 1262, and to the north-east is *Porthscatho*, a fishing village, where from the cliffs there is a splendid view of Gull Rock and Dodman

Point. South of St Just is *St Mawes*, another fishing village.
St Mawes Castle (1542), 117 feet above high water, is one of
the fortifications built by Henry VIII.

76 miles: *Indian Queen*. — 76½ miles: *Fraddon*.

Truro and Falmouth

12 miles: **Truro** (pop. 14,000, E.C. Friday and Saturday).
Situated on the Kenwyn, a tributary of the river Fal, Truro
is a busy market town. Its modern *Cathedral* (1880, Pearson)
was built when Truro was made the cathedral town of the
duchy, on the site of the 17th century church of St Mary. On
the south side of the choir the south aisle (Perpendicular) of
the original church can be recognised. The exceptionally wide
main street *(Boscawen St)* formerly contained the Market
House. One of the most interesting buildings is the *Red Lion
Hotel* (1671). In the *Town Museum* are good collections of
local antiquities and Cornish birds; pictures by Constable,
Gainsborough, Romney, Kneller and Rubens. Open 10 to 5,
except Sundays.

The journey from Truro to Falmouth can be made by steamer
down the beautifully wooded estuary of the Fal.

21 miles: **Penryn** (pop. 4250, E.C. Thursday), on the Penryn
Creek. From the quarries in the neighbourhood came the
granite for Waterloo Bridge in London. *Glasney Abbey* ruins
are nearby.

23 miles: **Falmouth** (pop. 18,000, E.C. Wednesday). Its
position on a peninsula jutting into the sea where the Gulf
Stream enters the Channel makes Falmouth the first town in
England to enjoy the benefits of the warm current, and in the
parks can be seen banana trees, orange and lemon bushes and
other Mediterranean and sub-tropical plants. Its harbour has
lost much of its former importance, but the bay still offers
a safe anchorage for large ships. The town itself dates only
from 1661; 17th century *church*. Ruins of *Arweneck Manor*.
At the tip of the peninsula is *Pendennis Castle* (1540), built
by Henry VIII to command the harbour entrance, along with
St Mawes Castle (above). Opposite Falmouth is the little
harbour of *Flushing* (ferry), originally founded by Dutch settlers. Oyster culture.

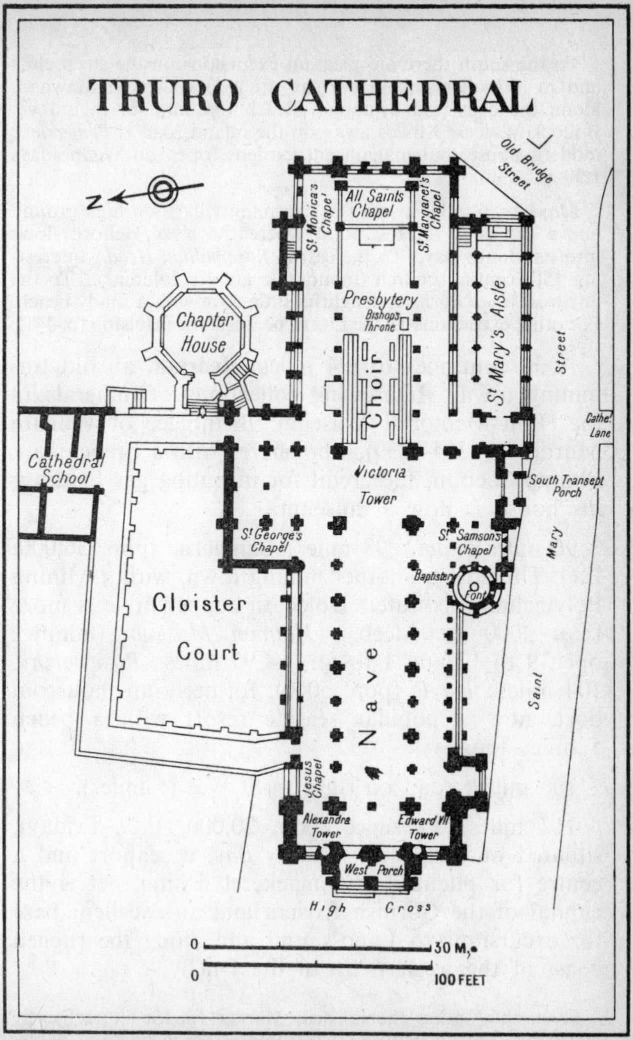

TRURO CATHEDRAL

Z

Old Bridge Street

St Monica's Chapel

All Saints Chapel

St Margaret's Chapel

St Mary's Aisle

Street

Presbytery

Bishop's Throne

Choir

Cathel Lane

Chapter House

Cathedral School

Victoria Tower

South Transept Porch

St George's Chapel

St Samsons Chapel

Baptistry

Font

Cloister Court

Nave

Mary

Saint

Jesus Chapel

Alexandra Tower

Edward VII Tower

West Porch

High Cross

| 0 | | 30 M. |
| 0 | | 100 FEET |

To the south there are pleasant excursions on the steep cliffs and in attractive valleys. There are two routes to Mawnan, along the coast via Swanpool Beach (bathing) or inland via Budock Water. 3 miles away on the inland road is *Penjerrick:* modern house, but magnificent gardens (open on Wednesdays 1.30 to 4.30).

Mawnan, 6 miles away, is a charming village on high ground above the coast at the point where the river Helford flows into Falmouth Bay. To the east is *Rosemullion Head*. Interesting 15th century church (monolithic granite columns). To the north is *Maen Porth*, a delightful little cove with a sandy beach. For other excursions on the Lizard peninsula see Helston (p. 441).

A 30 continues to (94 miles) **Redruth,** an old tin-mining town. Interesting collections of minerals in the Hunt Memorial Museum. Birthplace of William Murdock (1754-1839), who shares with a Frenchman, Philippe Lebon, the credit for inventing gas lighting; his house is now a museum.

96 miles: *Pool.* 98 miles: **Camborne** (pop. 36,000, E.C. Thursday), another mining town, with a Mining Polytechnic Institute. Dolcoath copper mine is more than 2000 feet deep. *Holman Museum* (mining: open 9 to 12 and 1 to 5). — 99 miles: *Roseworthy.* 104 miles: *Hayle* (pop. 5000), formerly an industrial port, now a popular seaside resort with a beach 5 miles long.

106 miles: road on right to St Ives (5 miles).

112 miles: **Penzance** (pop. 20,000, E.C. Friday), situated on beautiful *Mount's Bay*, a seaport and a centre for pilchard and mackerel fishing. It is the capital of the Cornish Riviera and an excellent base for excursions to Land's End and along the rugged coast of the western tip of the Duchy.

From the station the unusual Market Jew St slopes gently upward to Market House (1835); impressive façade and dome.

Here stands a statue of Humphrey Davy (1788-1829), philosopher and chemist, whose birthplace was Penzance. Beyond are the Market Place and Greenmarket. In Morrab Road is the Public Library: collection of prints and old books on Cornwall. Just below are the Penlee Memorial Gardens (15 acres), where in July and August the Cornish Shakespearean Festival takes place in the open-air theatre. Beyond are the *Morrab Gardens*, famous for many examples of rare plants and shrubs. Chapel St, formerly called Our Lady's St, the most important thoroughfare of the town, contains many graceful old buildings. St Mary's Church, on the seaward side, has a pinnacled tower. Down the hill is the harbour. *Lescudjack Castle* is an old British camp or hill-fort on the top of the hill. In Penlee Memorial Gardens is the *Antiquarian and Natural History Museum* (open 10 to 5).

North of Penzance, to the left of the St Ives road (B 3311), is the prehistoric village of *Chysauster*. From Castle Gate there are wide views. At *Halsetown* the famous 19th century actor Sir Henry Irving had a house.

To the south-east is **St Michael's Mount** (p. 441).

To the south-west there is a beautiful road along the coast (B 3315) via **Newlyn**, a fishing port which is a favourite with artists, *Mousehole*, another picturesque fishing village, *Penberth* and *Lamorna* to *Treen*, continuing to Land's End (see below).

To the north-west a road runs via Hea Moor and Madron to the sub-tropical gardens of *Trengwaiton* (National Trust) and the Neolithic burial chamber of *Lanyon Quoit*.

Scilly Isles. The Scilly archipelago consists of some 150 islands and islets, of which only five are inhabited. The climate is extremely mild in winter ($8°$ C) but relatively cool in summer ($15°$ C). Access is by boat from Penzance (daily in summer; about 2¾ hours) or by helicopter, also from Penzance (20 minutes). The main occupations are the growing of early fruit and vegetables and fishing. The largest island is St Mary's, with the port of *Hugh Town*. The most interesting is **Tresco**, with *Cromwell's Tower* (1651) and *King Charles's Castle* (actually built by Henry VIII), neither of which is open to visitors, and a modern *abbey* (open to visitors 10 to 4, except Sundays) surrounded by magnificent gardens.

10 miles from Penzance is **Land's End,** the most westerly point in Cornwall (longitude $5° 41'$ W.), an

impressive promontory standing 100 feet above the
sea.

On a rock 500 yards off the point is the *Longships lighthouse*
(120 ft high. In clear weather the Scilly Isles, 20 miles away,
can be seen from the cliffs. Isolated rocks emerge from the
sea, some of them of considerable size, like the Armed Knight
and the Irish Lady. To the south is the rocky point of Tol-
Pedn-Penwith. To the south-east, on a spur of Treryn Dinas,
is the *Logan Rock*, a 70 ton granite boulder so delicately ba-
lanced that it can be made to rock.

Land's End to St Ives (20 miles).

1¼ miles: *Sennen Cove*, a perfect Cornish village undisturbed
by the annual influx of holiday visitors. The fishermen still
use the centuries-old method of a communal net for catching
the fish. The coast is impressive, and the sea often rough.
The lifeboat — as in many of the villages on this coast — is
often called out to vessels in distress.

6 miles: St Just. 8¾ miles: *Pendeen*. 10 miles: *Morvah*,
near which are the *Nine Maidens* (remains of a stone circle),
the Hole Stone and the Written Stone. The Ding Dong tin
mine is said to date from prehistoric times. 15 miles: *Zennor*,
with the Zennor Quoit, one of the finest megalithic burial
chambers in the region; nearby is another, the Mulfra Quoit.

20 miles: **St Ives** (pop. 8700, E.C. Thursday), situated on
the north coast of Cornwall, on a promontory jutting out into
the Atlantic. It overlooks the graceful sweep of St Ives Bay
and commands some of the finest scenery in the Duchy. It
was a little fishing village until its attractions as a holiday
resort were discovered. As a result the importance of pilchard
fishing and tin-mining (Trenwith and St Ives Consols mines,
now disused, and others in the Stennack valley) has declined.
The church (Perpendicular) dates from the early 15th century.

There are many beautiful walks in the neighbourhood, but
the newcomer should first introduce himself to the *Island* — a
headland projecting into the bay and commanding fine views.
The headland is thus known locally because it is believed that
before the sand encroached and joined it to the mainland it
was an island. Rugged headlands jut out for miles in all directions, and when the sea is rough the crashing of the waves
is most impressive.

Penzance to Helston (13 miles) and the **Lizard peninsula** (A 30 for 1¾ miles, then A 394).

2 miles: *Long Rock*. A 394 forks right from A 30 for (3 miles) *Marazion*, a holiday centre in Mount's Bay. According to legend *Mount's Bay* was the lost land of Lyonesse and King Arthur. The chief attraction of the town is the romantic **St Michael's Mount,** an island in the bay, rising sharply 230 feet above the sea, and linked to the mainland each day at low tide by a sandy causeway. Crowning the summit of the hill is a castle almost fairy-tale-like in appearance, known as *Chevy Chase Hall* because of its stucco frieze portraying hunting scenes.

(Visiting: chapel, Chippendale Drawing Room and north and south terraces, Wednesdays and Fridays throughout the year 10 to 4; also on Mondays in summer).

St Michael's Chair, a turret on top of the tower, was formerly used as a lighthouse. At the foot of the Mount is a small fishing village.

4 miles away is *Perranuthnoe* and 4¼ miles away *Prussia Cove*, small villages on the coast. 8 miles away, also on the coast, is Prah Sands, near which, on Hoe Point, is *Pengersick Castle*, one of Henry VIII's coastal fortifications, now partly restored and occupied as a private residence.

13 miles: **Helston** (pop. 8000, E.C. Wednesday), a market town, which makes an admirable centre for the Lizard peninsula (see below), certainly one of the finest parts of the Duchy. *Borough Museum*, with local bygones (open 10 to 12 and 2 to 4).

St Michael's Church (18th c.) is built on the site of an earlier church burned down in 1763: fine 18th century stained glass in the old east window. *Loe Pool*, on the attractive Penrose estate, is a fresh-water lake, though it is separated from the sea only by a bar of sand and gravel. The Penrose grounds are open to visitors (pedestrians only) on weekdays until 8 in summer and 6 in winter. Ivy-covered ruins, old tin and copper mines.

The **Lizard Peninsula** is the area from Mount's Bay on the west to Falmouth Bay and the Helford estuary on the east. Along the coastline there is some of the most magnificent cliff scenery in Cornwall. The countryside to the north of Lizard Point is a high bare tableland (about 400 ft); nearer the Helford there is lovely wooded country.

The route to the Lizard crosses Goonhilly Downs. Along
the coast at *Gunwalloe Cove* there have been many wrecks on
the treacherous rocks. Gunwalloe *church* has a detached bell-
tower and a mediaeval screen. In the south aisle porch there
is a splendidly carved barrel-vaulted roof. Cory, 1 mile inland,
has an ancient church: fine east window in the Lady Chapel.
The next cove is *Poldhu*. A *Marconi Memorial* has been erected
on the spot where the first high-powered wireless transmitting
station stood when, on 12 December 1901, Marconi in Newfoundland received the morse signal sent from this cliff: the
first wireless message sent across the ocean. Here also, 22 years
later, the short-wave beam system, which revolutionised long-
distance communication, was successfully tested.

The next cove is *Polurrian Cove*, and then comes the famous
beauty spot of **Mullion Cove**: the cliffs are impressive and the
glowing colours of the serpentine rocks add to the beauty of
the scene. (Serpentine rock is a fine dark-green marble, streaked
like a snake skin with purples, scarlets, blacks, whites and
yellows.) Mullion Cove is the property of the National Trust,
as also are the three headlands at Predannack Wartha, known
as *Laden Ceyn*, *Mente-Heul* and *Pedn Crifton*. *Mullion Island*
and *Gull Rock*, only accessible at low tide, with two remarkable
caverns, and the harbour with its jetties and fish cellars should
be visited. 1 mile inland is the 15th century *church* with a
tower of local granite and serpentine stone, good mediaeval
stained glass and carved bench-ends.

Beyond Rill Head is the beautiful **Kynance Cove**, particularly
fine when the spray is blowing in from a rough sea. Picturesque
caves with curious names. (They can be reached only for
2 hours before and after low tide: before visiting them, therefore, it is important to check the times of the tides).

The inland road runs through Penhale to (26 miles) **Lizard
Point**, the southernmost promontory in England. The *lighthouse* is the most prominent feature (6,000,000 candle-power;
visible for 24 miles). There are also two foghorns; one long
blast and one short blast. (Visiting: weekdays, 1 p.m. to an
hour before sunset.) Below the headland is Polpeor Cove
The lifeboat station can also be visited (weekdays, 9.30 to 1).

At Housel Bay, a tiny cove just to the east, is the *Lion's Den*,
a huge vertical funnel within the cliffs open to the sea at the
bottom; at high tide this provides an impressive spectacle.
There is good bathing in the little bay. Ships rounding the
Lizard report to the Lloyd signal station on Penolver Point,

just to the east. At *Landewednack*, ¼ mile east, is England's most southerly church, an old building with Norman, Decorated and Perpendicular work in the rib-vaulted south porch (barrel-vaulted roof with carved bosses; 13th c. font).

East of Helston. *Gweek* is a small fishing village, once a busy port, lying at the head of the Helford River. From Gweek the road ascends to (3 miles) *Constantine*, a famous beauty spot. In the church is the fine monumental brass (1574) of Richard Gerveys. To the north is Piskey Hall, with an underground passage 30 feet long, 5 feet wide, made of granite slabs; its origin and purpose are unknown. To the north-east is *Mabe*, in the centre of the granite quarrying district. The 15th century church has interesting furniture and plate (including a Dutch 16th century cup with the head of Medusa. This piece is almost unique).

Mawgan in Meneage has one of the finest churches on the Lizard peninsula, mainly 14th century, with a 15th century turreted tower and west porch; 15th century barrel-vaulted roof, 13th century font. 1 mile south-east is Gulvingey Fiel, with a man-made cave of unknown origin and purpose. 1 mile north-west of St Martin in Meneage, the next village, is a ring-fort (14 acres), and there is a larger fort (100 acres), with a deep ditch, at Caervallack. At Newtown a road goes left to *Manaccan*, perched on an attractive hill round its old church, whose south porch is perhaps the finest example of Norman work (with Early English alterations) in the whole district. A huge fig-tree has established itself on the south wall.

St Anthony in Meneage has a pre-Reformation church with a 13th century font. The west tower is in Caen stone.

Helston to Crowan. To the north of Helston is *Sithney*, with an old church (mediaeval stained glass and early 15th c. brass). To the north-east is *Wendron*, on the edge of the heath, with a pre-Reformation church (cup-shaped 15th c. font, two 16th c. brasses; stocks in tower). Prehistoric remains in the neighbourhood: Beacon Hut stone circle; Celtic crosses at Polglasse, Trenethic, Manhay, Bodilly and Merthyr Uny; holy well at Treaill; stone-built mound on Crowan Beacon (721 ft). John Wesley preached at Black Rock, on the north side of Crowan Beacon, and at the foot of the hill is the village of *Crowan*, with a 15th century granite church (15th c. brasses in Lady Chapel). Some distance away, at *Tregear*, are old earthworks.

17. EXETER TO ILFRACOMBE
AND EXMOOR

Leave Exeter on A 377, going north.

2 miles: *Cowley Bridge*. Fork left to Newton St Cyres (4½ miles). 8 miles: *Crediton* (pop. 4000, E.C. Wednesday), a market town (15th c. church containing interesting relics). 12 miles: *Copplestone* (ancient cross).

A 377 runs through typical Devon scenery to *Lapford* (17 miles), at the end of the Taw valley. 25 miles: South Molton Road station, where a road goes off on the right to *South Molton* (9 miles). 38 miles: *Bishop's Tawton*.

40 miles: **Barnstaple** (pop. 16,200, E.C. Wednesday), one of the oldest boroughs in the country, situated on the north bank of the river Taw some 7 miles from its mouth. To the north-west, beyond the river Yeo (which flows into the Taw below the castle), is *Pilton*, the oldest part of the town. To the east is Dervy, to the south Newport and the modern housing suburb of *Sticklepath*.

Of the 14th century *parish church* (St Peter's) there remain the nave, steeple and chancel (Gothic); the tall spire has a noticeable tilt. Much restoration work has been carried out. *St Anne's Chapel*, in the churchyard, is early 14th century. Interesting crypt. It contains a museum of local antiquities. Near the river is *Queen Anne's Walk*, so called from the statue (1708) surmounting it: an interesting and beautiful old colonnade. The Taw is spanned by an old bridge of 16 arches. Some old alleys retain their mediaeval atmosphere: Theatre, Anchor and Green Lanes and Bengelwy's Court. Old houses with fine façades in High St (Nos. 97, 93 and 74). In Litchdon St are the Penrose almshouses (1624): 20 houses built round a courtyard entered through a granite colonnade. Other old almshouses are *Horwood's* almshouses in Church Lane (with adjacent school, founded 1659) and the *Paige* and *Salem* alms-houses (19th c.) in Trinity St. At the corner of High St and Joy St is the house in which John Gay (1685-1732), author of the "Beggar's Opera", was born; he attended the old Grammar School, originally in St Anne's Chapel. The walls of the hall of the old Norman castle built by Judhael of Totnes (who in 1107 also built the priory of St Mary Magdalene) are incorporated in the present *Castlehouse*, occupied by the municipal offices. In the grounds traces of the moat and the motte can still be seen.

A 361 leaves Barnstaple down the north bank of the Taw estuary to (46 miles) *Braunton* (pop. 4000, E.C. Wednesday), beautifully situated on low-lying hills. There is an interesting 14th century church (splendid wood carving). Nearby are Braunton Burrows. North of the burrows is *Saunton* (2 miles), with a good golf course. 47 miles: *Knowle*.

54 miles: **Ilfracombe** (pop. 8000, E.C. Thursday), a seaside resort south of the Bristol Channel, situated on a rocky coastline. In the High St is the Perpendicular church of the *Holy Trinity* (Norman and Early English parts still remain). From *Capstone Hill* (180 feet) there is a fine view of the town. Ruins of *St Nicholas's Chapel* (13th c.), converted into a lighthouse. Fine views from Hillsborough (447 ft). The main feature of the town is its promenade, *Torrs Walk*.

Around Ilfracombe. 3 miles west, beyond Torrs Walk, is the village of *Lee*, with the Old Maid's House. 3 miles farther west is *Mortehoe*, with an Early English church, one of the four churches founded by the murderers of St Thomas Becket in expiation of their crime. Very beautiful dunes. 1 mile west is the rocky headland of Morte Point. 8 miles from Ilfracombe is *Woolacombe:* superb dunes extending for 3 miles round a sheltered bay.

Ilfracombe to Minehead

The road runs along the coast between the Bristol Channel and Exmoor.

Exmoor. Chiefly in the county of Somerset, this fine plateau extends 35 miles from east to west and about 20 miles from north to south. It is most easily accessible from Dunster, Porlock, Lynton or Dulverton, but then only the fringe will be seen, and it is the walker who will see it at its best. The true heart of the Moor can be seen on a walk to Simonsbath and on to Moles Chamber, returning by Exe Head, where the River Barle rises, and *Pinkery Pond* (an artificial tarn) to Bedgworthy Water. Near here is *Oare Oak Hill*, from which the whole of Exmoor, with Dunkery Beacon in the distance, can be seen. It is a strikingly monotonous and wild expanse frequented by the blackcock and curlew, the sturdy Exmoor ponies and red deer.

3 miles: *Watermouth*, with a charming little harbour and a large castle (modern). Over a small stone bridge a little rocky valley leads down to the sea, where there are the Smallmouth Caves.

6 miles: *Combe Martin* (pop. 2000, E.C. Wednesday), a long straggling village of over 1 mile stretching down to the sea. Early English church with a fine Perpendicular tower 100 feet high. It is sheltered by two hills to the east, the *Little Hangman* (750 ft) and the *Great Hangman* (1080 ft). At Newbery is an interesting little church. In the village is a Perpendicular church.

10 miles: *Blackmoor Gate*. Turn left into A 39 (which to the right runs west to Arlington, 3 miles, and Barnstaple, 10 miles).

The *Arlington Court* estate (3750 acres) includes the hamlets of Arlington, Loxhore, Beccott and Loxhore Cott. Through it flows the Yeo, which supplies a large reservoir. In the centre is a nature reserve.

21 miles: **Lynton** and **Lynmouth** (pop. 2000, E.C. Thursday). The twin villages of Lynton and Lynmouth are really distinct, but they are now usually regarded as one. Lynmouth lies on the sea, at the mouth of the Lyn, and Lynton spreads over the beautiful cliff 400 feet above. In the height of the season crowds of tourists flock to the place.

Around Lynton. *Holiday Hill*, above the town, *Summer House Hill* (wide views), *Lyn Wood* and *Southcliff* are only a short distance from the centre of the town. Watersmeet Valley (National Trust, 360 acres) extends from Woodside to Wilsham Wood; mainly woodland. To the west are the Valley of the Rocks (associations with Lorna Doone: see below) and beyond it Woody Bay.

Brendon is a charming little village on the East Lyn, 600 feet above sea level in a beautiful open valley. The Gothic church of St Brendon was largely rebuilt in the 18th century. Trout-fishing in the East Lyn and hunting on Exmoor.

From Lynmouth the road climbs sharply to the top of the moors.

At 23 miles a minor road forks right (running along the fringe of Exmoor to rejoin A 39 at Porlock Hill) to *Oare*, famous for its associations with Blackmoor's "Lorna Doone". Of the eleven cottages in which the Doones once lived, there are now only low overgrown mounds to be seen. *Badgworthy Water* is one of the most beautiful valleys on the whole of Exmoor. Oare Church was where Lorna Doone was married and where at the altar she was shot by Carver Doone.

The road continues via the famous *Porlock Hill*, which has a gradient of 1 in 5 and drops in 3 miles from 1400 feet to sea level. The less difficult and almost disused private road (toll) is very picturesque and makes an attractive walk.

32 miles: *Porlock* (pop. 1350, E.C. Wednesday), a seaside resort in the midst of fields and woods and the centre for excursions to Exmoor.

In *Hawkcombe Valley* is an oval earthwork said to date from the Saxon period. There is an interesting Gothic church, with an unusual truncated spire. Porlock Weir at the end of the road to the coast is extremely picturesque, with a row of lovely old cottages. From here a delightful path runs along the top of the high cliffs through the woods to Culbone, in a deep and rather dismal combe, with the smallest church in England. On the other side of Porlock is the little village of *Bossington*, with its trim cottages and huge chestnut trees. Very fine views from Hurlstone Point. To the south is Dunkery Beacon (1707 ft), the highest point on Exmoor. To the west is another hill, Chapman Borrows.

34 miles: road on left to *Selworthy*, a noted beauty spot. The village stands near the Horner, a stream which flows between Selworthy and Luccombe.

Selworthy church is on the slopes of the hill. From *Selworthy Beacon* (809 ft) there is a fine view over the Bristol Channel to the Glamorgan coast, with the Welsh mountains in the background.

38 miles: **Minehead** (pop. 7500, E.C. Wednesday), a pleasant seaside resort in a wide bay, protected at one end by the North Hill with its woods. For more than 600 years three little towns have grown up side by side — round the old harbour, the market cross and the parish church respectively. Minehead began to overshadow Dunster as a port at the end of the 14th century, and Hugh Luttrell, whose family had owned the land for several centuries, enlarged the harbour in the 15th century. In 1616 George Luttrell extended the pier. Its trade was mainly with Ireland, importing cattle and wool for Dunster.

Around the quay are some *very old houses*, many of them with interior woodwork dating from the 15th century. (9 Quay St, circular stone staircase; No. 14, thatched roof and covered chimney top; No. 48, local Jacobean hinges; No. 33, the old Custom House). Quay St is continued along the water front by the Esplanade. The lower town is round the market cross, remains of which survive on its original position in Market House Lane; it was devastated by fire in 1791. The *Plume of Feathers Hotel* is another old building. In Wellington Square is a statue of Queen Anne (1719) by Francis Bird, a pupil of Grinling Gibbons, which was removed from the church in 1893. *St Michael's Church* has a late 15th century tower 90 feet high. On the east side are carved panels showing St Michael weighing souls. Late 15th century rood screen; unusual large oriel window at south end. Old houses at the Cross (Nos. 3, 7, 8).

1¼ miles west is *Bratton Court*, a fine example of mediaeval domestic architecture. Also to the west of the town is *North Hill*, which extends to Hurlstone Point, near Porlock. Many glens and deep gorges.

41 miles: **Dunster** (p. 450).

18. EXETER TO DUNSTER

Leave Exeter on A 377 as in route 17.

2 miles: *Cowley Bridge*. Fork right for A 396 to (11 miles) Bickleigh Bridge. 15 miles: **Tiverton** (pop. 14,000, E.C. Thursday), old town on the Exe, famous for its lace. There are the ruins of an old *castle* (the 14th century gateway can still be seen) and a fine 15th century *church*. The old premises of *Blundell's Grammar School*, founded 1604 (now transferred to the west of the town), can still be seen on the embankment of the river Loman, which here flows into the Exe.

22¾ miles: *Stuckeridge Bridge*. A 396 bears left; 2 miles north is *Bampton* (pop. 600, E.C. Thursday).

Bampton to Barnstaple: 29 miles on A 361.
2 miles: *Stuckeridge Bridge*. — 15 miles *Combesland*. — 17 miles: **South Molton** (pop. 3000, E.C. Wednesday). The town is built on top of a hill commanding a splendid view of Exmoor. There are traces of British and Roman earthworks in the vicinity. The chief industry is shirt-making. — 21 miles: *Filleigh*, with Castle Hill, seat of Earl Fortescue. — 24 miles: **Swimbridge.** The old church (restored 1880) has a 14th century spire and, in the interior, a beautiful screen (1500), 40 feet long, across the nave and aisles. From here a road runs west past Codden Hill (630 ft) to Bishop's Tawton (14th c. church). — 29 miles: **Barnstaple** (p. 444).

25 miles: *Exebridge*. A road branches left to *Dulverton* (pop. 4500, E.C. Thursday): Mount Sydenham and Pixton Park. Near Hawkridge is an ancient clapper bridge, *Tarr Steps*, over the Barle.

42 miles: **Dunster** (pop. 840, E.C. Wednesday). Dunster, off the main road, is a small town which still retains its mediaeval appearance. In the wide main street the chief feature is the *Yarn Market*

(1620), the last of several market buildings which previously formed a large island down the centre.

Near Sea Lane is a fresh-water lake, the *Hawn*. This was once the site of a seaport which in the 13th century rivalled Bridgwater in importance. When it silted up in the 14th century it was replaced by *Minehead*. **Dunster Castle** has changed ownership only once since the Norman Conquest: it was built by William de Mohun soon after the Conquest on the artificially scarped hill known as the Tor, and became the property of Hugh Luttrell in 1404, since when it has remained in the Luttrell family. The two gatehouses are all that remains of the original building. The inner one dates from the early 13th century, the outer one from the 14th century. The rest of the structure received its present form in 1617, apart from certain 18th and 19th century alterations. The magnificent moulded ceilings and the grand staircase were added in 1681. Open to visitors on Tuesdays, Wednesdays and Thursdays in summer 10 to 12.30 and 2 to 4.30. Thomas Hardy described it under the name of Standy Castle in "A Laodicean".

Many of the Luttrell family are buried in the **Priory Church,** which dates from the end of the 11th century, when a Benedictine priory from Bath Abbey was established here. The great rood-screen is the longest in England. In the south choir aisle is a chest, of a kind unique in England, made from a monk's desk cut off at the base. The church bells are rung every four hours, with a different tune for each day of the week.

8 miles south-east on the Bridgwater road (A 39) are the picturesque ruins of **Cleeve Abbey,** a 12th century Cistercian house. The surviving remains are mostly of monastic buildings (13th c. dorter, 16th c. refectory).

19. THE NORTH CORNISH COAST: BARNSTAPLE TO NEWQUAY

6 miles: *Instow* (pop. 650, E.C. Wednesday), a small port at the confluence of the Taw and Torridge, with a safe sandy beach. There is a ferry to Appledore and, on certain days, boats to *Lundy Island*.

Lundy. A lonely rock, 3¼ miles long and just over ¼ mile wide, 17 miles off Clovelly, from which there are excursion steamers. On its coasts are extraordinary rock formations, to which appropriate names have been given. The Shutter Rock at the south-west end of the island, for example, is so called because it appears to shut off the nearby formation known as the Devil's Limekiln. Near the quay are the ruins of Marisco Castle, once a pirates' and smugglers' lair.

Appledore (pop. 550, E.C. Wednesday), a colourful little port.

9 miles: **Bideford** (pop. 10,800, E.C. Wednesday), a historic town on the steep banks of the river Torridge, both a busy port and small fishing town. The main feature is the famous *bridge of 24 arches*, no two of them the same width, which replaced the wooden bridge in the 15th century.

On the promenade is a statue to Charles Kingsley, who wrote of North Devon in "Westward Ho!" and to whom we are indebted for the best description of the town and district. Rudyard Kipling and Hilaire Belloc also wrote on North Devon. The museum contains interesting collections of exhibits of local interest: an Armada treasure chest, ship's carpenters' tools, Bideford pottery, models of local boats, fossils and Palaeolithic material found in the area. From Chudleigh's Fort and the Memorial Park there are fine views of the river and the town.

Around Bideford. 2 miles north is *Northam*, with St Margaret's Church, the second highest in the county. Burrough in Northam was the home of Amyas Leigh, hero of Kingsley's novel "Westward Ho!". 3 miles north-west is the seaside resort of *Westward Ho*, named after the novel, founded in 1863. West of the village are the *Kipling Tors*, the scene of some episodes in Kipling's "Stalky and Co.", which Kipling left to the National Trust.   7 miles south-east is *Torrington* (pop. 2900, E.C. Thursday), an ancient borough perched on top of a hill, with some of Devon's most beautiful scenery in the surrounding area.   Very fine views from Castle Hill and towards Furzbeam.   1 mile away is *Frithelstock*, with the Perpendicular church of SS. Mary and Gregory.   In the vicinity are the ruins of a 13th century priory, with three fine ogival windows in the west gable.   The 13th century *Rothean Bridge*, now disused, spans the Torridge, in which there is good fishing.

14 miles: *Horns Cross*. — 18¾ miles: *Clovelly Cross*.   The road turns right to *Clovelly*, 1½ miles (pop. 550, E.C. Tuesday), a quaint fishing village of great charm, built into a cleft between cliffs and descending steeply to the sea in a series of steps, up which donkeys are still used to carry burdens to and from the shore.   In summer this beauty spot is crowded visitors.   From the end of the pier can be obtained the best view of the village.   The houses themselves, with their front doors looking out over the rooftops of neighbouring houses, are gay with colour.

Around Clovelly.   Clovelly has a most attractive promenade in *Hobby Drive* (toll for motor vehicles), which runs 3 miles east along the cliffs to join the Bideford road (A 39).   Another pleasant trip (2 miles) is through the grounds of *Clovelly Court* (entrance opposite New Road Gate: no cars beyond this point) to Gallantry Bower (387 ft), Mouth Mill and the quiet cove below Blackchurch Rock.   The prehistoric fort known as the *Dykes*, or Ditchen Hills, can be seen (taking care to check the time of high tide before setting out).   In calm weather it is a pleasant boat trip from Clovelly to *Mouth Mill Cove* (views of the cliffs and woodland of Gallantry Bower).

Hartland.   A district of great grandeur, unsurpassed anywhere along the coast, with cliffs rising 300 feet above the sea.   The 128 foot tower of **St Nectan's Church** is a landmark for shipping.   It contains a Norman font, a splendid Perpendicular rood-screen and fragments of 14th century figures from the old abbey. Note the roof (14th c.) of the *Lady Chapel*. The abbey, founded in 1168, was demolished at the Reformation and later reconstructed as a private residence. On St Catherine's Tor are remains of a chapel (14th c.) which belonged to the abbey. It is possible to continue to the tip of *Hartland Point* (lighthouse). At Speke's Mouth there is a beautiful waterfall. Good bathing in *Shipload Bay*, 2 miles north.

21 miles: *Boxworthy Cross*. 29 miles: *Kilhampton*, with a fine Norman church rebuilt in 1567, incorporating a porch from the original church.

Morwenstow (on the coast, 5 miles west) has a vicarage, with chimney stacks shaped like towers and rhymed inscriptions over the door, built by the Rev. Robert Steven Hawker (d. 1875) a writer of Cornish ballads. The church of St Morwenna, an ancient building with Norman remnants, is said to have been founded in the 5th century. To the south is *Tonacombe*, a grand 16th century mansion.

33 miles: *Stratton* (pop. 1000, E.C. Thursday). A 3072 forks right for Bude (2 miles).

Bude (pop. 5100, E.C. Thursday), a seaside resort in a sheltered bay, facing the Atlantic. For miles in both directions there are unhampered walks and drives over the magnificent cliffs.

41 miles: *Wainhouse Corner*.

52 miles: **Camelford** (pop. 1250, E.C. Wednesday). In the centre of magnificent Cornish moorland 600-700 feet above sea level, in that district of North Cornwall called *King Arthur's Country*, Camelford is said to be the Camelot of King Arthur. This peaceful old town lies on the banks of the river Camel, and this part of the west country was certainly one of the earliest inhabited regions. There is a menhir near the town, and many prehistoric remains lie scattered over the moors. The legendary grave of King Arthur is near the tiny *Slaughter Bridge:* it was

supposedly near here that the king was mortally wounded in the battle with the usurper Mordred. In the district there are many narrow, precipitous and winding roads. It is very beautiful and wild country. Rough Tor (1296 feet) and Brown Willy (1375 feet), the highest points in the Duchy, are 4-5 miles south-east; between the two is a dangerous bog.

2 miles west is *Delabole*, with slate quarries which have been worked since the time of Elizabeth I.

Port Isaac, on the coast 7 miles beyond Delabole, is an interesting little place (pop. 1000, E.C. Wednesday). The natural harbour, under lowering black cliffs, is surrounded by quaint old houses set along a narrow and winding main street. It is now a popular seaside resort.

Camelford to Tintagel: 11 miles (B 3266 to Boscastle, then B 3263).

7 miles: *Boscastle*, a small town at the mouth of the Valency with an unusual natural harbour; splendid views of the grim rocky coastline. Between Bude and Boscastle there is magnificent coastal scenery, with beautiful bays. To the south of Bude Haven are Compass Point and Efford Beacon, Widemouth Bay, Dizzard Point and Crackington Haven. At the end of the beach are the *Rock's End Pools* (excellent bathing).

Tintagel (pop. 1300, E.C. Wednesday), a small village in the centre of a district which legend connects with King Arthur. The surrounding countryside is very beautiful. The 12th century church of *St Materiana* (an Irish saint) has a 14th century tower; the north doorway is Saxon. The church, standing on top of the cliffs, is so exposed to the strong Atlantic winds that even the tombstones have had to be given additional support. The Old Post Office, in the centre of the village, has the windows with spy-holes, made from slabs of stone, which are common in the district (open to visitors 10 to 1 and 2 to 6). In *Trevena Village* is a 14th century stone house with an ancient tiled roof, built on the plan of a mediaeval manor-house.

In front of *Wharncliffe Arms Hotel* is a 9th century cross which was found serving as a gatepost in the village of Trevillett. King Arthur's Castle stands 1 mile away on the cliffs. Before going there, visitors should see *King Arthur's Hall*, a great granite building belonging to the fellowship of the Knights of King Arthur; there is an excellent collection of books, prints and manuscripts devoted to the subject, and the stained glass windows of the hall depict scenes from the stories of King Arthur and his knights.

King Arthur's Castle. Built on the headland, which is a natural fortress, and also on the "island", which is connected to the mainland by a narrow isthmus. In Norman days it is probable that the two parts of the castle were joined by a draw-bridge; today the only way into the great keep from the outer works is by winding steps cut into the cliff. The castle was built about 1150 by Reginald Earl of Cornwall, Henry I's adulterine son, used as a prison in the 14th century, and aband-oned soon afterwards. On top of the cliffs are the ruins of a 13th century chapel, and on the sheltered side of the headland are several groups of cells. (Visiting: the key to the nail-studded door of the keep can be obtained at a cottage in the valley on the way to the castle).

Around Tintagel. Interesting villages and several prehistoric forts to the south and south-east, on hills from which there are magnificent views. 2 miles south-west is *Lanteglos* (Norman church, with Perpendicular elements). In the vicinity are two forts — *Castlegoff*, near the church, with circular ramparts 200 feet in diameter, and *Newbury*, to the north. 4 miles south is *Michaelstox*. Other ancient forts in the surrounding area.

54½ miles: *Knightsmill*.

57 miles: to the left of the road (1 mile) is *St Tudy*, with a Perpendicular church (restored). In the neigh-bourhood are a number of fine country mansions: *Tremeer* (15th c.) and *Tinten* manor-house, where Captain Bligh of the "Bounty" is said to have lived.

59 miles: *St Kew Highway*. To the north-west is the old village of *St Kew*, formerly known as Landoho or Doceo, the earliest recorded place name in Corn-wall. Farther to the north is the circular earthwork known as *Tregeare Rounds*.

62 miles: *Wadebridge* (pop. 2800, E.C. Wednesday), a small town pleasantly situated on the river Camel.

The bridge was built in 1470 by the vicar of Egloshayle to replace a dangerous ford ("wade") where many travellers had lost their lives, and although very narrow still carries the weight of modern traffic. Only 13 of the original 17 arches are still to be seen. Beyond Wadebridge the railway runs along the left bank of the attractive Camel estuary.

64 miles: *St Breock* (13th c. church). On the neighbouring estate of Pawton Manor is an old tithe barn. Giant's Quoit (Neolithic burial chamber). To the south are St Breock's Downs, with several stone circles.

67 miles: *St Issey*, on a tributary of the Camel. 68 miles: *Little Petherick* (St Pethrock Minor), an ancient and very picturesque village, with St Pethrock's Church (Early English and Decorated, with a beautiful reredos).

70 miles: **Padstow** (pop. 2000, E.C. Wednesday), a small seaport whose entrance is obstructed by the notorious Doom Bar, a sandbank navigable only by small craft. The streets are narrow and picturesque. On the quay are the 15th century Abbey House, an old *Guild House* and *Raleigh's Court House* (16th c.). From the Style (the Promenade) there is a good view of the harbour mouth and of the two hills, Pentire (256 ft) on the right and Stepper (227 ft) on the left.

On the other side of the Camel estuary is *Rock* (frequent ferry service by motorboat from Padstow). The modern village occupies the site of a Roman establishment (3rd and 4th c.). *St Anodock* has an old church with a 13th century leaning spire; golf course. Beyond St Anodock are *Daymark Beach* and the beautiful Pentire Head.

On the top of Stepper Point is the *Daymark*, which can be seen for many miles out at sea. There are fine views from this point. At the foot of the point is St John's Well. Along the cliffs are *Pepper Hole*, *Butter Hole* and *Seal's Hole*. (Seals can sometimes be seen here). Farther to the west is **Gunver Head**. *Tregudda Gorge*, a deep chasm between massive rocks, is beyond Gunver Head: in bad weather, when there are high seas, it is an exhilarating sight. *Porth Missen Bridge* is a natural arch formed from the variegated rock of the cliffs. Another curious formation is the Round Hole, which gives access to the beach. *Trevone* is an attractive seaside resort with a beach of fine sand; surf-riding.

73 miles: Harlyn Bay (bathing and surf-riding).

In 1900 an Iron Age cemetery (350 B.C.) was discovered here under the sand on the beach. The skeletons were lying in the usual attitude on their sides with the knees beneath the chin, under slate slabs set north to south and end to end. To the left is Trevose Head (243 feet), on which stands Trevose lighthouse. (Visiting: daily till one hour before sunset.) Treyarnon Bay provides excellent opportunities for surf-riding. At Wine Cove to the west there is a cavern 100 yards deep.

76 miles *Porthcothan Bay* with many natural arches and rocks and beautiful cliffs. Among the cliffs are *Bedruthan Steps* and *Queen Bess Rock* (thought to resemble the profile of Queen Elizabeth I). Under the cliffs are caves, arches and tunnels. The "Samaritan" was wrecked in 1846 on the rock which bears its name, and it is said that fragments of the wreck are still occasionally cast up on the coast.

Inland is the village of *St Eval*. Its church tower (rebuilt in 1727) is a well-known landmark for shipping. The magnificent coastal scenery continues to St Columb Porth.

86 miles: **Newquay** (pop. 11,500, E.C. Wednesday). The town takes its name from the quay built as long ago as 1615. At the turn of the century Newquay was a tiny fishing village with a small harbour. Today it is one of the most popular seaside and holiday resorts on the north coast of Cornwall. The annual regatta is an attraction in summer. In the cliffs to the north and south are interesting caves.

Around Newquay. *Crantock*, on the other side of the Gannel estuary, in an area full of interest for botanists. *Columb Minor* (1 mile east) has an unusual church with a fine 15th century tower. Rialton farm, which formerly belonged to the priors of Bodmin, has magnificent oak ceilings in the mediaeval hall and the Tudor bedroom. In the courtyard is an old holy well. *Trerice Manor* (3 miles south-east), an Elizabethan house built in 1571 (open to visitors 12 to 6).

98 miles: *Perranporth* (pop. 2000, E.C. Wednesday), a seaside resort in beautiful Perran Bay, with 3 miles of sand below strangely shaped cliffs. There are numerous tiny coves, from which bathing is excellent. There are some remarkable rock-formations in the neighbourhood (Gap Rock, Chapel Rock). There is excellent bathing from Penhale Beach.

1½ miles from Perranporth, in a hollow in the dunes, is the *oratory of St Perran*, built in the 6th or 7th century. (Visiting: daily during July, August, September; at other times the key may be obtained from the vicar at Perranzabuloe Vicarage.) St Perran's Round, an amphitheatre 130 feet in diameter, is a good specimen of the ancient Cornish open-air theatre; in the Middle Ages miracle plays were performed here in Cornish and there was accommodation for 2000.

St Agnes Head. B 3285 from Perranporth to St Agnes (pronounced "St Anns"), 4 miles. But for the pedestrian there are two ways to the little town of *St Agnes* (which was also once a flourishing mining centre): at low tide, over the rocky shore; or, when the tide is in, by climbing the steep cliff by *Wheal Kitty Mine* and descending on the other side. From *St Agnes Beacon* (600 ft) there is a magnificent view, with curiously shaped rocks off the coast.

20. EXETER TO TAUNTON

32 miles on A 38 (the Bristol road).

3 miles: *Pinhoe*. — 13 miles: *Cullompton* (pop. 3000, E.C. Thursday), an old and interesting town. The 16th century parish church contains a unique Golgotha.

15 miles: *Willand*. B3391, forking right, offers an alternative route via *Uffculme* (pop. 2000, Thursday), whose church has a very long rood-screen, and Culmstock, at the foot of the Blackdown Hills.

25 miles: *Wellington* (pop. 12,000, E.C. Wednesday), with some attractive old houses. On the Blackdown Hills to the south is a monument to the Duke of Wellington, an obelisk in the form of one of the bayonets used at Waterloo.

32 miles: *Taunton* (pop. 37,000, E.C. Thursday), the county town of Somerset, situated in the fertile valley of Taunton Deane on the river Tone, from which it takes its name. It is a centre of cider manufacture and of considerable industries, including clothing and engineering. The site of the town dates from Roman times, but the first castle at Taunton was built c. 710 by the Saxon King Ina.

Remains of the **castle** built by the Bishop of Winchester in the 12th century can be seen in the Castle Hotel garden; the outer building and false portcullis date from the last century. The gate house of the inner ward (1495) is the best remaining feature. In the Great Hall where Judge Jeffreys had his courtroom there is now part of the collections of the Somersetshire Archaeological and Natural History Society Museum, installed here in 1873.

Items of particular interest include material from the lake dwellings on Lake Meare, relics of the battle of Sedgemoor, a pot-lid with one of Shakespeare's few known signatures and a Latin charter granted by King Ina in 705. There is also a library of some 35,000 volumes and manuscripts, mainly concerned with Somerset. (Open April-September 9.30 to 5.30, winter 9.30 to 1 and 2 to 5).

The 163 foot high tower of **St Mary Magdalen Church** (1508) is the most elaborate in the county. The church has five aisles and the decoration of the interior is chiefly with an angel motif on capital, bracket and corbel.

There are nearly 200 angels in stone and 28 in wood. There are fragments of old stained glass in the north windows and in the clerestory; the figures in the niches between are those of the 12 Apostles. The church contains numerous monuments, including a life-size figure of Robert Grey, who founded the almshouses in East St. The tower was restored in 1840 and rebuilt in 1862.

The church of *St James* dates from the 15th century; there is an old font and pulpit; the tower has been restored. An Augustinian priory (1127) stood near the church; it was destroyed at the Reformation and the only remains today are the large buildings known as the *Tythe Barn*. The south gable has windows of the late 13th century.

South of the town is *Vivery Park*, which takes its name from the fish-ponds (vivaria) of the monastery which once occupied the site.

Most of the older houses in the town have been swept away. Perhaps the most interesting that remain are Nos. 13 and 15 Fore St. No. 18 (a chemist's shop with a modern front) contains some fine mouldings; its 15th century porch now forms the entrance to Bath Place. The Grey Almshouses in East St have changed little since 1635; interesting chapel with good painted ceiling. Of the modern buildings in Taunton the *Somerset County Hall* (1935) and the public library are worthy of mention.

Taunton to Minehead.

A358 to Williton, then A39.

5 miles: *Bishop's Lydeard*. Interesting Perpendicular
church. — 10 miles: **Crowcombe.** In this pretty little
village at the foot of the Quantock Hills is the ancient
Perpendicular *church of the Holy Ghost*. The old
screen and the carved ends of the oak benches (1534)
are very fine. There is a 16th century cross in the
village and another in the churchyard. Nearby is
Crowcombe Court, a country house in a beautiful
park. Above the village is the *Triscombe Stone*,
where the local stag-hunt meets.

The *Quantock Hills*, stretching down almost to the sea,
contain some of the most lovely of English hill scenery, and
in the charming old villages in their folds there are many fine
churches and tiny cottages which have not changed for centuries, with fine old manor-houses in the vicinity.

The Quantocks are noted for their bluebells and rhododendrons. 3 miles east is *Stogursey*, with a beautiful church (restored)
In the *Halsway Aisle*, built by Cardinal Beaufort, are a double
"squint" (one of the only three in England) and 16th century
tombs.

13 miles: *Bicknoller*. One of the most charming villages in the Quantock foothills and an excellent
centre for exploring the Quantocks. In St George's
church good sculptured work includes a screen and
carved bench-ends. A yew tree grows on the top of
the tower.

15 miles: *Williton* (pop. 1200, E.C. Wednesday), a
very ancient village with a number of delightful old
cottages with thatched roofs. The church (restored
1588) was originally a chantry. *Nettlecombe Court*
is a Tudor mansion standing in a magnificent estate.

Williton to Bridgwater 18¼ miles. A 39.

1½ miles: *St Audries*. The church of St Etheldreda (early Decorated) is unusual with its marble monolithic piers and decorations. The ancient manor-house, now a girls' school, has a great hall 60 by 26 feet.

2½ miles: *West Quantoxhead*, and, near the sea, *East Quantoxhead*, two very charming villages. The church is very old. The Elizabethan manor-house *(Court House)* is worth a visit. (Visiting daily, except Sundays).

10 miles: *Nether Stowey*, another good centre for the Quantocks. To the west is a small cottage occupied by Coleridge from 1797 to 1800, in which he wrote "The Ancient Mariner" and the first part of "Christabel" (open daily).

17½ miles: *Washford*, chiefly interesting for the ruins of the Cistercian Cleeve Abbey, founded in 1188. The ruins comprise the 13th century gatehouse, the Chapter House, the sacristy and (best preserved) the refectory, which has a beautifully carved roof on angel corbels and on the north and south sides nine large Perpendicular windows, pieced together after being recovered from the earth. There is a fine mural of the Crucifixion.

2 miles north is the old port of *Watchet* (pop. 2200, E.C. Wednesday), now a seaside resort. *St Decuman's Church*, on the hill, is Perpendicular, with an Early English choir. 20 miles: *Carhampton*, an old village with a Perpendicular church (very fine painted screen, with eleven openings, between nave and choir).

Taunton to Chard

A 385, going south-east.

10 miles: *Horton*. In the church are brasses commemorating the founders of Wadham College, Oxford.

A 303 runs east to (2 miles) Ilminster (pop. 2500, E.C. Thursday). To the north-east of this little town, between the villages of Barrington, Knighton and Shepton Beauchamp, is *Barrington Court*, a house built of Ham Hill stone by Daubeny (1514-20). Along with its brick-built stables (1670) and 220 acres of arable land, it was acquired by the National Trust in 1907 and was restored by them. (House and gardens open on Wednesdays 10.15 to 12.15 and 2 to 6).

15½ miles: *Chard* (p. 404).

21. TAUNTON TO WELLS AND BRISTOL

43 miles by A 38 (the direct route); 48 miles via Glastonbury and Wells (the recommended alternative route).

A. On A 38

7 miles: *North Petherton*, one of the largest villages in Somerset. 15th century church with a beautiful tower. *Halswell House*, a fine country house (park with deer and a heronry).

10½ miles: **Bridgwater** (pop. 27,000, E.C. Thursday), a market town and port on the river Parrett, 6 miles from the sea, now also a holiday resort and industrial centre.

The town's outstanding landmark is the 175 foot spire of **St Mary's Church** (1367), a Gothic church which has remained in its original state apart from the modern glass, the roof of the nave and the clerestory windows. Above the altar is a "Descent from the Cross" attributed to *Murillo*. Wide views from the top of the tower, entered through a narrow 15th century doorway.

Mediaeval remains: castle gateway on West Quay, groups of old houses in Silver St, Rose and Crown inn. In Blake St is the *birthplace of Admiral Blake* (1599-1657), open 10 to 12 and 2 to 5. In the Town Hall are portraits of Blake and old tapestries. An interesting sight is the "bore", when the head of the tide rushes up the river in waves 3 to 6 feet high, splashing the banks.

Sedgemoor. The battlefield of Sedgemoor is one of the most interesting excursions from Bridgwater. The field can be seen east of the town from the Polden Hills, through which A 39 runs to Glastonbury. The battle was fought on 5 July 1685, when the Duke of Monmouth, after having been turned back on his way to Bristol, decided to stake all on a night attack on the King's forces, then camped at Westernzoyland. Monmouth's peasant troops crossed the Black Ditch, but at the Langmoor Rhine, the large irrigation ditch crossing the moor, their advance was detected, and Faversham's disciplined troops counter-attacked and routed the rebels. The slaughter and hanging continued long after the battle — the last to be fought on English soil — and in the autumn James II sent Judge Jeffreys to establish a commission of investigation. The "Bloody Assizes", as Jeffreys' court became known, sentenced leaders and men to transportation.

18 miles: *Highbridge*, a old cattle market. Good coarse fishing in the Brue.

1½ miles north-west is *Burnham-on-Sea* (pop. 6200, E.C. Wednesday), a seaside resort on the Bristol Channel, in the estuary of the Parrett. The land round the town, Burnham Level, is separated from the sea by dunes. 2½ miles north-east is *Brent Knoll* (fine views). St Andrew's Church (13th c.) has a leaning tower; the reredos of coloured marble came from Westminster Abbey.

21 miles: **East Brent.**

Alternative route from East Brent to Bristol via Weston-super-Mare (27 miles on A 370).

8 miles: **Weston-super-Mare** (pop. 44,000, E.C. Thursday), a popular holiday resort on a wide bay in the Bristol Channel. To the north is *Worlebury Hill*, to the south *Brean Down* (bird sanctuary). *Museum* above the Public Library: collections of historical, archaeological and local interest, including bones of early man from *Worlebury Camp* (open 9 to 6). In the south of the town is a *Railway Museum* (open Saturdays 2 to 6).

15 miles: **Congresbury.** 15th century church (Perpendicular) and large village cross. On nearby Cadbury Hill is an Iron Age hill-fort. B 3133 runs north-east to (7 miles) **Clevedon** (pop. 12,000, E.C. Wednesday), an attractive seaside resort in a bay on the Bristol Channel. In *St Andrew's Church* are buried the historian Henry Hallam (d. 1859) and his son Arthur (d. 1833), for whom Tennyson wrote "In Memoriam". Coleridge was born in the town. *Clevedon Court*, described by Thackeray in "Esmond" under the name of Castlewood, is a magnificent mediaeval manor-house (14th c. front with 16th c. additions). From Dial Hill there are fine views to the east. 1 mile away are the ruins of *Walton Castle*.

27 miles: **Bristol.**

25 miles: *Weare.* 26½ miles: road on right (1 mile) to **Axbridge** (pop. 1000, E.C. Wednesday), a pretty little town on the southern slopes of the Mendip Hills at the end of the beautiful Shute Valley. Fine square with Georgian houses; Perpendicular church with 17th century ceiling.

2½ miles: **Cheddar** (pop. 3000, E.C. Wednesdays), a picturesque old-world village, lying at the foot of the *Mendip Hills,* which here present some of the most striking rock scenery in Britain.

Cheddar village is remarkable in that it has on one side the precipitous limestone cliffs of the Mendip Hills and on the other the extensive plain known as Cheddar Moor. The scenery thus offers great variety. To the east are Long Wood (800 ft) and the Cheddar Cliffs with (near a disused quarry) the Lion and Monkey Rocks. The famous **Gorge** begins near the village and runs north-east between superb precipitous cliffs, sometimes as high as 400 feet. The gorge is more than 1 mile long, and from the end the road continues to climb to *Cheddar Head Farm* (896 feet). Near the village are the entrances to the **Cheddar Caves.** *Gough's Cavern* (discovered in 1877), at the foot of the gorge, is the finest of the caves and provides one of the most remarkable and beautiful sights in West England. The caves, like the Gorge, have been formed by the wearing action of water during centuries, which has carved out all manner of weird shapes and forms. There are stalactites and stalagmites of fairy-like beauty in all the colours of the rainbow. The wonders of this strange underground world are revealed by concealed floodlights. *Cox's Cavern,* discovered in 1837, is the smallest and perhaps the most beautiful. At the entrance to Gough's Cavern is a prehistoric museum, in which is the skeleton (discovered in 1903) of *Cheddar Man,* who lived in the caves perhaps 10,000 or 12,000 years ago. *Motor Museum* (old cars).

7½ miles: *Easton.* Minor road on left to **Wookey Hole.** Here the River Exe, which rises in the Mendip Hills to the north-west at 900 feet, near Priddy, and there plunges underground, emerges from the cave after an 18 hours' journey. In the great cave is a long passage in which have been found countless tools, ornaments, implements, querns and Roman coins dating from 250 B.C. to 450 A.D. Beyond "Hell's Ladder" is the first large chamber, containing a massive stalagmite known as the "Witch of Wookey". Excavations have suggested that ritual sacrifices took place here in prehistoric times. The colouring and carving on the walls are magnificent. The next chamber, Wookey Hall, is also a splendid sight. In the Witch's Hall, beyond the "Great Chimney", there is a curious sound effect produced by the movement of air caused by the river flowing underground. Large-scale exploration and excavation work has been carried out here since the last war, and one group of cavers reached the eleventh chamber. A museum at the entrance contains material found in the caves.

Wells (p. 471) is a short distance away to the south-east.

From the A371 road junction to Axbridge A38 begins to climb the west spurs of the Mendips.

28 miles: *Sidcot*. To the north-west is *Winscombe*, on the slopes of Wavering Down: the church has a fine embattled tower and 16th century glass.

30 miles: road on right to *Burrington*, with the entrance to Burrington Combe, a deep valley with on one side a nearly sheer cliff and on the other a steep grassy slope.

Opposite a fissure in the rock is *Aveline's Hole*, and after a sharp left-hand bend in the valley is *Lower Twin Brooke Combe*, in which is *Goatchurch Cavern*, the largest of the Burrington caves, in which prehistoric material has been found. To the south is the *Black Down* (2000 ft), the highest part of the Mendips, with ancient earthworks and barrows. The whole of this district abounds in prehistoric and Roman remains. 4 miles away, at *Charterhouse*, was an important Roman settlement. (Charterhouse can also be reached from Cheddar).

30½ miles: *Churchill*, in a beautiful valley where the road begins to run downhill. Nearby is *Dolbury Camp*, an Iron Age hill-fort (18 acres), oval in shape, on the top of a steep-sided hill: double ramparts, west entrance defended by three ditches.

34 miles: *Redhill*. 39 miles: road on right to *Dundry*, with a 15th century church: Dundry Hill (765 ft). 43 miles: **Bristol** (p. 495).

B. Via Glastonbury and Wells

Leave Taunton on A 38, as in the previous route, but in about 4 miles, at Walford, turn right into A 361, which runs past *Athelney* (on right), where King Alfred hid from the Danes in 878.

10 miles: *Burrow Bridge*, near which is a conical hill known as Burrow Mump. On top of the hill are an 18th century chapel (unfinished) and the ruins of an older chapel.

12 miles: *Othery*.

A 372 runs south-east to (5 miles) *Langport* (pop. 700, E.C. Wednesday).

Church (Perpendicular), with a very beautiful old window. *Hanging Chapel*. 2 miles south is *Muchelney*, an interesting little village where an abbey founded by King Athelstan in 937 is being excavated. *Priest's House*, a fine example of 13th century domestic architecture.

A 361 runs through the Polden Hills and across the battlefield of Sedgemoor (p. 465). At Street it runs into A 39 and continues to Glastonbury.

22 miles: **Glastonbury** (pop. 6200, E.C. Wednesday). In this ancient town, according to legend, Joseph of Arimathea founded the first Christian church in England, bringing to it the blood of the Crucifixion.

The town features in the tales of King Arthur and Queen Guinevere. **Glastonbury Abbey,** founded in 601, was destroyed by the Danes. About the middle of the 10th century St Dunstan, who had been a

novice in the monastery, became abbot, and erected
a stone building to the east of the older wooden
church built by King Ina.   A much larger abbey
church was built in the 12th century, but this was
destroyed by fire in 1184, together with the older
Lady Chapel.   Henry II (d. 1189) rebuilt the Lady

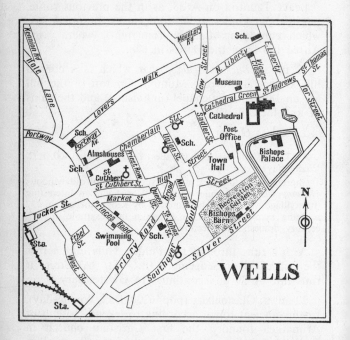

Chapel (sometimes called St Joseph's Chapel) and
also rebuilt the main church some 50 feet to the east.
This was completed in 1303.   At a later date the two
buildings were combined to form a single large church
550 feet long.   At the Reformation Abbot Richard

Whiting was tried in the Great Hall of the Bishop's Palace in Wells and hanged on Glastonbury Tor.

The remains are scanty. Some domestic buildings of the abbey remain intact: the 14th century *Abbot's Kitchen*, part of the Almonry, the *Pilgrims' Inn* (now the George Hotel) and the Great Barn. Open 9.30 to sunset.

St John's Church (**1485**, restored 1859), on the site of an earlier Norman church, has a tall Perpendicular tower, one of the finest in Somerset. The *Lake Village Museum*, on the ground floor of the Town Hall, contains material from the Meare and Godney lake villages.

Around Glastonbury. Magnificent views from *Glastonbury Tor* (500 ft). A 15th century tower is all that remains of a chapel dedicated to St Michael. It is said that Joseph of Arimathea buried the Holy Grail, the cup used at the Last Supper, at the foot of the hill, giving rise to the *Blood Spring*.

In the low-lying moors north-west of the town are the villages of *Meare* (B 3151) and, a little farther north, *Godney* (reached from A 39), where the almost complete remains of lake dwellings were discovered. At Meare is the *Abbot's Fish House* (14th c.).

28 miles: **Wells** (pop. 7500, E.C. Wednesday), a beautiful old town situated in a broad hollow, overlooking the plains to the south and sheltered to the north by the green Mendip Hills. In the centre of the town, at the east end of High St, is the spacious *Market Place*, and beyond it are two ancient gateways, the *Penniless Porch*, which leads to the Cathedral Green, and the Bishop's Eye, slightly larger, leading to the Bishop's Palace and moat. Both of these gates and the *Dean's Eye* (or *Brown's Gate*) in Sadler St were built by Bishop Bekynton (1442-64).

Wells Cathedral. The Cathedral of *St Andrew*, without doubt one of the finest in the country, is

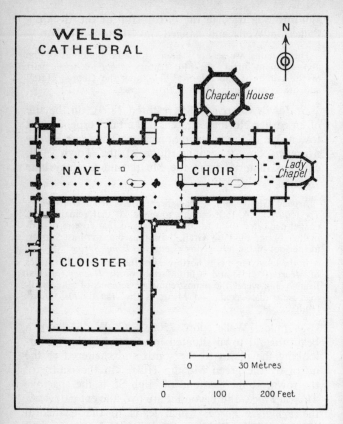

the third on this site. The first, built by the Saxon King
Ina in the 8th century, was probably a wooden building. The present Cathedral (dedicated 1239) is Early
English, dating from the 12th and 13th centuries,
although the central part of the building, the transepts,
the east bays of the nave and the west bays of the

choir are in late 12th century Transitional style. The east end dates from the early 14th century and is in Decorated style. The central tower (165 ft) dates from 1321; the west towers were added in the early 15th century in Perpendicular style. The west front, completed in 1239 by Elias of Dryham, is unique in this country both from the great beauty of the design and its splendid state of preservation. The towers were added later by William Winford. In the niches are 350 statues (completed about 1280), representing some of the finest work of this kind in England.

Interior. The outstanding note is one of simplicity. The vivid whiteness is unbroken except by the rood figures (1919) surmounting the **inverted arches** in the form of a St Andrew's Cross at the end of the nave; these three arches were added in 1330 to support the central tower. The main lines in the interior are horizontal rather than vertical. The triforium is supported to the rear, above the aisles.

Nave. At the east end are two interesting 15th century *chantries*. At the south-east corner, high up, is the Musicians' Gallery (Perpendicular). The glass of the lancet windows in the west end is early 16th century. The vault paintings are modern, following ancient models.

The *transepts* are similar in character to the nave, with aisles. South transept: Norman font and the fine alabaster tomb, with carved panels, of Bishop William of March (d. 1302). North transept: 14th century **astronomical clock.** The quarter-hours are struck by a seated figure who kicks two bells with his heels, while on the outside two figures strike two other bells with battle-axes. The west aisle is divided into two chapels by a Perpendicular screen wall.

The *choir*, separated from the nave by a Perpendicular screen, forms with the retrochoir and Lady Chapel one of the most beautiful examples of church architecture in the country. At the east end is a gilded window which dates, like its stained glass, from the mid 14th century. To the left are the tombs of Saxon bishops (with 13th c. effigies) and of Bishop William Bytton II (d. 1274). Side chapels dedicated to St Catherine (15th c., with stained glass and several tombs), St John the

Baptist (beautiful carved wood and a delicate 13th c. baldaquin over a tomb), St John the Evangelist (interesting tombs) and St Stephen. The *Lady Chapel*, forming the apse of the cathedral, is of the early Decorated period, with magnificent slender columns.

A door in the south transept gives access to the *tower* (admission charge), from which there are fine views. On the right-hand side of the north choir aisle is the entrance to the *crypt*, formerly the treasury. In the centre of this is a massive pier supporting the floor of the Chapter House, built at a later date. The **Chapter House** (Decorated, c. 1300) is an octagonal structure with magnificent fan vaulting radiating from the central pillar. It is reached from the north transept by an attractive staircase, which also leads to the gallery over the *Chain Gate*.

On the south side of the nave are the 15th century Perpendicular **cloisters,** entered through the doorway in the south transept. Over the east alley is the *Chapter Library*, with large numbers of original documents concerning the early history of the cathedral, many chained volumes, a 13th century crosier and a 13th century pyx canopy which is almost unique.

The subsidiary buildings of the Cathedral are part of its great charm. The most picturesque is the **Bishop's Palace** (south of the cathedral, beyond the cloisters), built by Bishop Jocelyn (d. 1242), who was also responsible for much of the cathedral. This is surrounded by a defensive wall and a moat fed by a number of wells (which gave the town its name), of which the largest is St Andrew's Well. The great hall, now in ruins, and the Decorated chapel, were added in 1292. North of the Cathedral, in the beautiful *Cathedral Green*, is the **Deanery,** a 15th century mansion with turrets and battlements built by Dean Gunthorpe and restored by Christopher Wren. Next door is the *museum:* objects from Wookey Hole and other caves in the neighbourhood and exhibits of varied interest. The several canon's houses are 15th century.

Beyond the old *Chain Gate* is the oldest complete street in Europe, the **Vicars' Close**. It was built in the 14th century by Bishop Ralph of Shrewsbury, and becomes gradually narrower as it climbs the hill, so that it appears longer than it really is. No. 22 has been restored in its original form; No. 5 still has its original door. Beside the Chain Gate is *Vicars' Hall*, built to house the vicars choral or "singing men", with old furniture. At the end of Cathedral Green is an old chapel, perfectly preserved.

St Cuthbert's Church is one of the most interesting buildings in Wells after the Cathedral. It is mainly Perpendicular, although some Early English work has survived in the nave and other parts. Major alterations were carried out at the beginning of the 15th century; in particular the piers and arches of the nave were removed and replaced by columns. The great west tower, which also dates from this period, is particularly fine. Opposite the tower are *Still's Almshouses*, with an ancient portico.

In Chamberlain St are *Bubwith's Almshouses* (early 15th c.) and, farther along, almshouses built by Archibald Harper. In the Georgian Town Hall (1779) are interesting portraits and other relics. The Cathedral School dates from the 12th century. From *Tor Hill* and *Dulcote Hill* (445 ft) there are good views of the town.

Around Wells. *Wookey Hole* (see p. 467) can be reached by way of Milton Hill. Beyond it is Ebbor Gorge, a quiet wooded area.

3½ miles east on A 371 is *Croscombe*. Church with a fine spire (rare in this area) and Jacobean woodwork.

5 miles east on A 371 is *Shepton Mallet* (pop. 5500, E.C. Wednesday), a quiet little town of the pre-industrial age. Beautiful market cross. Nearby are two mediaeval meat-shambles (slaughterhouses), the last of their kind in the country. The 15th century church has a fine ceiling. Some old houses.

From Wells the route to **Bristol**, continues on A 39, then left into A 37. Total distance from Taunton 48 miles. Features of interest on the way are the stone circle at *Stanton Drew*, near Pensford, and the Gothic church at *Whitchurch*.

22. LONDON TO BRISTOL

There is a motorway (M 4) from London to Bristol, continuing over the Severn on a large bridge and into Wales (Cardiff). It is the easiest way out of London, and can be left at Windsor if you have not already seen this major tourist attraction.

The motorway runs past **London Airport Heathrow** (to left) and the industrial town of **Slough** (pop. 85,000), to the right.

Surroundings of Slough: Eton and Windsor

3 miles north is **Stoke Poges,** with the churchyard immortalised in Gray's "Elegy". The poet is buried by the east wall. The church contains an interesting churchwardens' pew and old glass, particularly the "*Bicycle Window*" in the porch. Close to the churchyard is the *Garden of Remembrance* (12 acres), with a monument to Gray by James Wyatt (1799).

Eton, 1½ miles south on the Buckinghamshire side of the Thames, with Eton College, most famous of English public schools, founded in 1440 by Henry VI as a school for 70 pupils to be educated free. Today there are still 70 King's Scholars who live in the college itself and some 1100 "Oppidans" who live out in 25 boarding houses under the direction of masters.

The mellow red brick buildings of the College were originally built to the plans of William of Wykeham, who founded Winchester College. The two quadrangles, joined by the fine Tudor clock-tower (Lupton's Tower) and the cloisters (1523), are the oldest parts. In the larger quadrangle is a statue (1717) of the founder. On the south side stands the chapel (175 ft long by 82 ft high), built in 1476 on higher ground because of the Thames floods. The *Upper School*, built by Sir Christopher Wren, stretches over the arcades along the west side of the quadrangle. The *Lower School* is on the north side. On the south side of the inner courtyard are the *refectory* and *library*. The modern

Memorial Buildings contain the *School Hall* (seating for 1200) and the *Boys' Library*, in which there is also a well stocked museum (which can be seen on application). The Memorial Buildings were erected in honour of Etonians killed in the Boer War. From the courtyard a small gateway leads to the playing fields. Eton College suffered damage during the second world war. (Visiting: the main courtyard and cloisters are open to visitors from 10 to 5 during the school holidays).

Windsor (pop. 30,000, E.C. Wednesday), 2 miles from Slough and ½ mile beyond Eton, is one of Britain's most ancient boroughs, having received its charter from Edward I in 1276. Old Windsor (½ mile upstream) dates from Saxon times, when it was a royal residence. The Anglo-Saxon name was *Wyndesore*.

In High St are a number of fine buildings, including the *Corn Exchange* and the *Guild Hall* (Town Hall), designed by Wren. In Church St, opposite Henry VIII's gateway to the castle, with the original cobbled road, was the home of Nell Gwynn, and there are several Georgian buildings. Wren's dwelling house (the Old House Hotel) is near Windsor Bridge. A regiment of Household Cavalry and a battalion of the Guards are stationed in Combermere and Victoria Barracks. In the parish church are carvings by Grinling Gibbons.

Windsor Castle has been the chief residence of the sovereign since Norman times. When the royal family is in residence the royal standard can be seen flying from the Round Tower. The town is dominated by the massive Norman castle, which together with its precincts is almost 1 mile in circumference. The castle was founded by William the Conqueror, but the present building dates from the time of Edward III (1327-77), and additions and alterations have been made in practically every reign since. In the reigns of George IV, Queen Victoria and Edward VII extensive restoration work was undertaken.

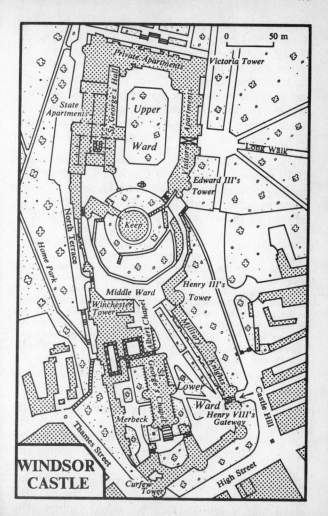

0   50 m

Private Apartments

Victoria Tower

State Apartments

St. George's Hall

Upper Ward

Visitors Apartments

Long Walk

Edward III's Tower

North Terrace

Keep

Home Park

Middle Ward

Henry III's Tower

Winchester Tower

Albert Chapel

Military Knights

St. George's Chapel

Lower Ward

Castle Hill

Henry VIII's Gateway

Thames Street

Merbeck

Curfew Tower

High Street

WINDSOR CASTLE

The castle comprises two main parts: *the Lower Ward*— St George's Chapel, the Albert Memorial Chapel, the Horseshoe Cloisters and the residences of the knights of Windsor; and the *Upper Ward*— the State Apartments, the Queen's private apartments and the south wing for royal guests and visitors. Between the two, in a charming garden, is the great *Round Tower;* from the top there is a magnificent view in which it is said twelve counties can be seen.

The main entrance to the castle is through **Henry VIII's Gateway** at the top of Castle Hill. On entering the Lower Ward, **St George's Chapel** is seen opposite: a fine example of late Perpendicular style begun by Edward IV in 1474 and completed by Henry VIII.

Very beautiful choir with fan vaulting; stalls of the Knights of the Garter, with their banners and coats of arms. At the west end, under the organ, is the royal pew. The wrought-iron grille below the royal pew is attributed to Quentin Metsys. The tombs of Edward VII and Queen Alexandra are to the south of the high altar, along with George V's tomb. A door in the choir leads down to the crypt, in which are the tombs of Henry VIII, Jane Seymour and Charles I. An underground passage leads to another crypt under the Albert Memorial Chapel, in which are the tombs, among others, of George III and IV and William IV.

Open to visitors 11 to 2.45; Fridays 1 to 3.45; Sundays 2.30 to 4.

The **Albert Memorial Chapel** was built by Henry VIII as his own mausoleum and afterwards presented to Cardinal Wolsey. Queen Victoria restored and decorated it in the style of the period (mosaic ceiling and marble walls) in memory of Prince Albert. It contains the cenotaphs of Prince Albert, the Duke of Albany and the Duke of Clarence (d. 1892, Edward VII's eldest son: tomb designed by Alfred Gilbert, who completed it in 1926 after leaving it unfinished for twenty years).

To the left of St George's Chapel are the brick and timber buildings round the Horseshoe Cloisters, dating from the time of Henry IV. In the *Curfew Tower*, which is the bell-tower of the chapel, are dungeons, which were used after the Wars of the Roses. The Chapter Library and canons' houses are to the north of St George's Chapel, from which a covered passage leads into the *Dean's Cloisters* and *Canons' Cloisters*, with the famous "Hundred Steps" leading directly down to the river, used only by the inhabitants of the Castle.

The **Round Tower** (or Keep) is 230 feet high and 300 feet in circumference. The entrance is by a doorway with a portcullis, still in working order, near the Norman Gate, which was one of the towers built by Henry II (1154-89).

On the left is a gate leading to the **North Terrace,** approximately a third of a mile long, from which there is a magnificent view of the River Thames, Eton and the Chiltern Hills. From the North Terrace is the entrance to the **State Apartments**. (Open daily 11 to 4; 11 to 5 in summer).

At the top of the Grand Staircase is *Charles II's Dining Room* (fine wood carvings by Grinling Gibbons). In the next room are paintings by Rubens. The *Bedchamber*, the *King's Closet* and the *Queen's Closet* contain paintings by Zuccarelli and Canaletto. To the left is the *Picture Gallery:* works by Holbein and other artists. Next is the *Van Dyck Room,* in which there are large portraits of Charles I, his family and the ladies of the Court. The *Queen's Presence Chamber* and the *Queen's Audience Room* have ceilings painted by Antonio Verrio; on the walls are Gobelins tapestries. Beyond these is the *Garter Chamber* with a magnificent roof and a rich collection of arms and armour. The next room is the 600-year-old *St George's Hall*, the assembly room of the Knights of the Garter. The ceiling, on which are emblazoned the coats of arms of the knights, is of later date. On the walls of the next chamber, the *Grand Reception Room*, decorated in Louis XV style, are Gobelins tapestries. The next room is the *Throne Room*. The upholstery and carpets are of Garter blue and around the walls are portraits of various sovereigns wearing Garter robes.

The *Waterloo Chamber*, built in the middle of a courtyard on the three sides of which are the three preceding rooms, is used for banquets and entertainments and has an immense carpet covering the entire floor. The portraits around the walls are those of personages of the Napoleonic wars.

Beneath the Throne Room is **Queen Mary's Doll's House** (entrance from the North Terrace).

From the East Terrace, relieved by four magnificent towers — the Prince of Wales, the Chester, the Clarence and the Victoria Towers — the exterior of the private apartments can be seen. The bay windows light the Crimson, White and Green Drawing Rooms and the Small Dining Room. The Sunken Garden was laid out by George IV.

On three sides of the castle is the *Home Park* (500 acres) of which only 70 acres to the north can be visited by the public. The *Royal Mausoleum* (where Queen Victoria and the Prince Consort are buried), *Frogmore House* and Royal Farm and Gardens are in the private park.

The Long Walk (3 miles, entrance in Park St) is a magnificent avenue leading from the castle to *Windsor Great Park*. At the end is an equestrian statue of George III, from which a splendid view of the castle can be obtained.

Windsor Great Park ($2\frac{1}{2}$ miles wide by $4\frac{1}{2}$ miles long, 1800 acres) consists of very beautiful park and woodland, where the only motor road is that of Windsor from Ascot. *Royal Lodge*, in the park, is a private residence of the Queen.

South of the park are the 12,000 acres of *Windsor Forest*, in which lies the famous *Ascot* race-course.

Maidenhead

Maidenhead can be reached from Windsor either direct on A 308, which passes under the motorway, or by returning to Slough and following A 4 to the west.

At Taplow is *Dropmore Park*, with superb trees planted by the landscape gardener Frost for Lord Grenville, George III's Prime Minister. Byron, Rogers, Hallam and other notabilities stayed in the house.

Maidenhead (pop. 40,000), 26 miles from London by the direct road, is a pleasant residential town on the Thames.

The *Reitlinger Museum*, in a riverside house built in 1895, is notable particularly for its Oriental porcelain (open Tuesdays and Wednesdays 10 to 12.30 and 2.15 to 4.30). At Cox Green, south-west of the town, a *Roman villa* (3rd-4th c.) was discovered in 1959.

Around Maidenhead. *Bray* (2 miles south-east, on the Thames) has a Perpendicular church dating from the reign of Edward I (1272-1307), with brasses and interesting 17th century monuments in the much restored interior. 2 miles west of Maidenhead is *Maidenhead Thicket* (375 acres), over which pass the old road to Bath and the road to Henley. In the centre is an Iron Age site known as *Robin Hood's Arbour*. To the north Maidenhead Thicket runs into Pinkney's Green (170 acres), with a further 75 acres in the Cookham Dean, Bigfrith and Togwood commons. 2 miles south of Maidenhead is *Ockwell's Manor* (1466), in grounds of 250 acres: one of England's best preserved manor-houses, with its original glass windows.

The Thames from Maidenhead to Henley

One of the loveliest reaches of the Thames lies above Maidenhead Bridge. Beyond Maidenhead the river enters the *Cliveden Reach*. Cliveden Reach is now National Trust property (263 acres), comprising **Cliveden House,** with pictures and tapestries, gardens, woods, and the reach along the Thames.   Cliveden House is the third house to be constructed on the great red-brick terrace, which dates from 1666 and is associated with George Villiers, Duke of Buckingham. It was built in 1851 by Charles Barry. The gardens contain temples by Giacomo Leoni, one of which has been converted into a mausoleum. (Open Wednesdays and Saturdays in summer 2.30 to 5.30). 1 mile east of Cliveden is *Dorney Wood*, south-west of Burnham Beeches. In 1942, the owner, Lord Courtauld-Thomson, bequeathed through the National Trust to the Prime Minister the house, contents and 250 acres of land as a future official residence for a Secretary of State or a Minister of Defence.

At the end of Cliveden Reach, on the other side of the river, is (4 miles) **Cookham,** in delightful Thames-side scenery. The Bell and Dragon and the King's Arms Inns are very ancient. The flint *church of the Trinity* is conspicuous from the river. It is an Early English and Perpendicular building built on the site of a Norman church. Square crenellated tower; 13th and 14th century pavement in the sanctuary. Gallery of works by *Stanley Spencer* (1891-1959).

8 miles: **Marlow** (pop. 6000, E.C. Wednesday), a quaint old town dating from the Saxon period, beautifully situated, with magnificent views of the Thames in both directions. The church (rebuilt 1835) contains some interesting monuments. Beside it are the old stocks and whipping post, and an old nail-studded prison door. Shelley stayed in a house on the north side of West St in 1817 (inscription). Great Marlow is still noted for its bobbin-lace. Fishing (barbel) near Marlow Lock. ¼ mile from the town, on the right bank of the river, is *Bisham* church: Norman tower of limestone and flint (restored 1849); interesting monuments with alabaster effigies. Warwick the King-Maker was buried here after the battle of Barnet. Bisham is a trim little village with charming old cottages. In the midst of the very beautiful countryside of woodland and hills is *Bisham Abbey*, which dates from the reign of Stephen (1135-54); it is now a pleasant Tudor house in an excellent state of preservation. The Great Hall was part of the original building, and there is still a large tithe barn.

9½ miles: *Temple Lock*, which derives its name from the associations of the Knights Templar with this district. — 10 miles: *Hurley*, a remote and unspoiled little village, originally established in Anglo-Saxon times (6th c.) at a ford. The *Olde*

Bell Inn was once the guest-house of a Benedictine monastery dissolved at the Reformation.

11 miles: *Medmenham*. The village is very charming and has a fine old church with some Norman work and two 15th century brasses. Its old-world atmosphere is enhanced by the old cottages and the inn. Medmenham Abbey, originally founded by Cistercian monks in the 13th century, is today a restored ruin. In the 18th century it became notorious as the headquarters of the "Hell Fire Club", with which the names of Sir Francis Dashwood and John Wilkes are associated. The manor-house (restored) is 15th century. Just off the main road is an ancient earthwork.

17 miles: **Henley-on-Thames** (pop. 9800, E.C. Wednesday), an attractive town, said to be one of the oldest in Oxfordshire, now the Mecca of rowing enthusiasts. This part of the river began to be fashionable in the late 18th century, with many fine country houses in the area. The Thames was then an important traffic route. *Henley Bridge* was built in 1786; the keystones of the central arch are carved with allegories by Mrs Damer, Walpole's cousin and Gen. Conway's daughter. The presence of this fashionable society in the neighbourhood led to the rise of **Henley Regatta**. The first boat race between Oxford and Cambridge was rowed in 1829 between Hambleden Lock and Henley Bridge. There were a number of other races during the next ten years, and the Henley Regatta was finally established in 1839. Prince Albert was patron of the 1851 regatta, and since then it has been known as the Henley Royal Regatta. It takes place on four days during the first week in July, and is one of the chief sporting and social events of the season. The course is run over 1 mile 550 yards upstream. There are many amateur rowing clubs in Henley.

The *Town Hall* contains an old portrait of George I. The *Red Lion* is an old inn. The *church* (square turreted tower, restored in the 19th c.) contains the tomb of the French General Dumouriez (1739-1823). In the north of the town is *Chantry House*, a 14th century timbered house. On rising ground to the west is *Friar Park*, another fine old house. (The gardens are sometimes open to the public: consult the local press).

From Henley A 321 runs south to join A 4 east of Reading, passing through *Wargrave*, one of the prettiest Thames-side villages, and east of *Shiplake*, another well known beauty spot. Upstream is *Sonning*, seat of a bishop and centre of a large diocese in Tudor times. The mellow red-brick bridge, the old houses in the village and the picturesque lock make a very attractive scene.

Reading

From Maidenhead A 4 runs west to Knowl Hill and past *Twyford*.

38 miles: **Reading** (pop. 125,000, E.C. Wednesday), at the junction of the Thames and the Kennet, county town of Berkshire, with a modern University and ancient grammar schools. It is an important centre for the Thames valley.

The site was occupied in Palaeolithic times. Reading became a royal borough in 871. In 1006 King Sweyn of Norway ravaged the area and the town was destroyed. Henry I founded a Benedictine abbey on high ground, and when he died in 1136 was buried in front of the high altar. At the Reformation the abbot was thrown into prison and the abbey demolished. The present *Greyfriars Church* stands on the site of a monastery founded in 1282. The University grew out of a College associated with Oxford (1860), and received its charter as an independent university in 1926. It has a *Museum of English Rural Life* (open 10 to 5.30, except Mondays).

Reading School, one of the most ancient in the country, was established even before the foundation of the abbey in 1121. In 1486 King Henry VII assisted the Abbot of Reading to convert the building of St John's Hospital into a school, and for centuries the school occupied the grounds of this building, before being transferred in 1871 to its present Redlands site.

The *Public Library* (Balgrave St) has a rich collection of books and material relating to Reading and Berkshire. The **Museum and Art Gallery's** collections comprise a fine series illustrating the prehistory of the district; the very important Romano-British remains from *Calleva Atrebatum* (Silchester), which flourished in the first four centuries A.D. Reading has the only full-size copy of the *Bayeux Tapestry*, made at Leek in Staffordshire. (Open 10 to 5.30).

The town has three churches: *St Mary the Virgin*, a tall building, with alternate courses of stone and flint, on the site of a Saxon church rebuilt in 1551 (16th c. roof); *St Lawrence*, in Market Place, built in the 12th century and rebuilt in the 15th (west end damaged during the second world war); and *St Giles*, in Southampton St, founded in the 12th century (but the present building dates only from 1873).

Reading is now increasingly coming within the London commuting area, but is also an industrial town in its own right. One of its oldest industries was milling, and at the *Abbey Mills* a large Norman arch can be seen over the mill leet. In the early 19th century the town already had engineering firms, sweet factories and printing works. There is a magnificent promenade along the Thames as far as Caversham Bridge.

Caversham Park, on the other side of the river, was in existence before Tudor times. The present house, built in 1723 by Gen. Cadogan, one of Marlborough's generals, was burned down in 1850 but was rebuilt by the owner. From 1922 to 1942 it was a school; it is now occupied by the B.B.C.

Reading to Wokingham: 7 miles on A 329.

1 mile: *Earley*, a residential suburb of Reading on the river Loddon, with Sutton's nurseries. — 7 miles: *Wokingham* (pop. 10,000, E.C. Wednesday), a market town with a history dating from pre-Saxon times. During the 14th-17th centuries the local industry was bell founding, and during the reign of Elizabeth I a prosperous silk industry was centred in Rose St, where old timbered houses may still be seen with mulberry trees in the gardens. *Ye Olde Rose Inne* opposite the Town Hall still has its 15th century interior. The *parish church*, much

restored, has 15th century galleries and a timber roof borne
on corbelled brackets.   There are a number of old people's
homes and, outside the town, Elizabethan almshouses founded
by Henry Lucas.   Near the town are old earthworks known as
"Caesar's Camp", with four small works which probably
date only from the 18th century.

Reading to Basingstoke: 16 miles.

6 miles: *Riseley*, on the line of the Roman London-Silchester
road called the "Devil's Highway". — *Silchester*, 3 miles
west, was the *Calleva Atrebatum* of the Romans, built on the
British site of Caer-Segeint.   The Saxon name was Silceastre.
The excavations are extremely interesting.   The almost complete
remains of a forum, a basilica, bath, gates and temples and
other buildings were excavated, only to be subsequently covered
up again.   The town was built on a hexagonal plan, not the
normal rectangular plan.   All that can now be seen is the stone
and flint town walls, 1½ miles long and 13 or 14 feet high in
places.   Outside the east gate is an earthen amphitheatre, within
which are an old farmhouse and parish church.   Excavations
have shown that there were a number of dyeing works.   Objects
discovered here are in Reading Museum.

2 miles east of Mortimer (the station for Silchester) is *Strath-
fieldsaye House*, presented to the Duke of Wellington by the
nation after Waterloo. 16 miles: *Basingstoke* (p. 376).

Newbury

43 miles: *Theale* (pop. 1000, E.C. Wednesday).
Old Lam Tea House, built of ships' timbers and red
brick, with a thatched roof.

To the north is *Bradfield*, in the Pang valley, in an area of
wooded hills where many prehistoric remains have been found.
Near *Bradfield College* (1850) a chalk pit has been made into
a Greek theatre modelled on the one at Epidaurus, in which
ancient classical plays have been performed every three years
since 1890.   To the north-west is *Englefield*, near which is the
very beautiful Tudor *Englefield House* (burned down and
modernised in the 19th c.).   Magnificent deer park, with Lake
Cranemoor.

48 miles: *Woolhampton*, with, nearby, the well-known public school of *Elstree* and beyond it *Douai Abbey* and *School*, built by English monks expelled from France in 1903 under the anti-clerical laws of the time. — 52 miles: *Thatcham* (pop. 2500, E.C. Wednesday).

55 miles: **Newbury** (pop. 22,000, E.C. Wednesday). In the 15th and 16th centuries Newbury was the centre of a thriving cloth trade founded by John Winchcombe ("Jack of Newbury"). When this trade began to decline at the beginning of the 19th century a canal was cut from Newbury to Reading along the Kennet, and in 1811 this was extended to Bath and Bristol.

There are several almshouses, including St Bartholomew's Hospital (1698). **St Nicholas's Church** (16th c.), with a brass commemorating Jack of Newbury (d. 1519). In the old Market Place are 17th and 18th century house fronts. Just off the Market Place is the **Cloth Hall** (1600), with an overhanging upper floor, which now houses a *museum* (Civil War and other local relics). The Granary dates from the 17th century; covered gallery on first floor.

From the old bridge (1769) over the Kennet there are fine views of the river. A path runs past the old mill to some 16th and 17th century houses. *Jack of Newbury's House*, with an overhanging first floor, also dates from the 16th century; it is half-timbered, with richly decorated brackets and cornices. There are a number of other old houses in the town.

Around Newbury. In the neighbourhood of *Donnington* village, 1 mile north, are old houses and interesting mansions. *Shaw House*, one of the finest Elizabethan houses in Berkshire, dates from 1581. The old brick two-storied house has a third gable storey under the tiled roof and contains fine old panelling and fireplaces. It is now used as a school. *Donnington Castle* (1386) stands on top of the hill; during the Civil War Col. John Boys withstood a siege by Roundhead forces and surrendered with the honours of war. All that is now left of the

castle, which was 150 feet long by 90 feet across, is the entrance
gateway.

To the south-east is *Speen*, believed to be the Roman *Spinae*,
an important staging post on the road to *Calleva Atrebatum*
(Silchester).

Newbury to Winchester: 25 miles on A 34.

3 miles: *Newtown*. — 8 miles: *Burghclere*, with an Early
English church and a fine old manor house. On neighbouring
Beacon Hill (860 ft) are remains of a British earthwork. Wonderful views.   At *Ashmansworth* (a charming village 2½ miles
west) is a Norman church with interesting 13th century murals.
— 8½ miles: to the left, the heights of *Seven Barrows* (ancient
burial mounds). — 10 miles: *Litchfield*. — 13 miles: **Whitchurch** (pop. 3500. E.C. Wednesday), a small market town on
the famous River Test in pleasant country.   The road runs
south over the chalk downs past Tidbury Ring (371 ft), an
old Roman camp, to (18 miles) *Sutton Scotney:* intersection
with A 30 London to Salisbury), and then over the Worthy
Downs to (25 miles) *Winchester* (p. 342).

Newbury to Salisbury: 35 miles.   A 343, joining A 30 at
Lobcombe Corner, 8 miles before Salisbury.

5 miles: *Highclere*. Near the village is *Highclere Castle*, seat
of the Earl of Carnarvon, a Jacobean mansion containing
some valuable pictures. — 11 miles: *Hurstbourne Tarrant*.
— 17 miles: *Andover* (pop. 13,000, E.C. Wednesday), an old
agricultural town.

18½ miles: *Bury Hill*, on top of which there is a large Romano-
British camp: fine view.   2 miles off the main road is the little
village of *Abbotts Ann*.

25 miles: the charming villages of *Over Wallop*, *Middle
Wallop* and *Nether Wallop*, in a secluded part of the Wallop
Brook, winding to join the Test. — 27 miles: A 343 joins A 30.
—35 miles: *Salisbury*.

Marlborough

63 miles: *Hungerford* (pop. 3,000, early closing
Thursday), a small town on the river Kent where
there is good angling; a well-known hunting centre.

Hungerford to Salisbury: 30 miles on A 388 and A 338.

4 miles: *Shalbourne*, on the Berkshire border, a charming village surrounded by trees and low hills. — 8 miles: *Easton* and the hamlet of *Easton Piercy*, birthplace of John Aubrey (1627-97). B 3087 runs west to *Pewsey* (3 miles) through the Vale of Pewsey. — 10½ miles: *Collingbourne Kingston.* — 12 miles: *Collingbourne Ducis.* The road intersects the A 342 to (14 miles) Tidworth below Sidbury Hill (735 ft), where there is an old encampment. — 16 miles: *Shipton Bellinger.* — 19 miles: *Cholderton.* The road follows the river Bourne south to *Salisbury.*

66 miles: *Froxfield*, a tranquil country village with a small flint church dating from the 12th century, and interesting 17th century red-brick almshouses. Many old half-timbered and thatched cottages.

The road continues over undulating country through *Savernake Forest*. The oldest tree is an oak with a trunk 24 feet in circumference.

73 miles: **Marlborough** (pop. 5000, E.C. Wednesday). Marlborough, situated on an ancient site in the centre of a district which has been occupied from very early times, is an important market and agricultural town. The High St is of great width; the old fair ground by St Peter's Church once continued the markets down the High St. The north side is higher than the south, and at one time the fine colonnade on the north side ran down the entire length. In the first week in October the Mop Fair booths present a picture similar to that of mediaeval days.

Old houses in the High St: the premises of *W. and H. Smith* (staircase, carving on first floor, sundial of coloured glass); *Cavendish House*, *Chantry ironworks* (15th c.); Nos. 13, 14 and 15 *Silverless St.*

St Mary's Church has a Norman porch. It was defended during the Royalists' attack on the town in 1642, and the north side of the tower still bears marks of the attack. In the west wall is a Roman altar dedicated to the goddess of Fortune. *St Peter's Church* is mainly 16th century (much restored), but the vaulting of the porch and choir go back to the original church.   Cardinal Wolsey was ordained as a priest here in 1498.   The curfew is still sounded every evening.   *St George's Church*, in Preshute, has a Norman arcade and a 12th century font, made from a large block of black stone, which was originally in St Nicholas's Chapel in the castle.

William the Conqueror built on the castle mound (which is believed to be of prehistoric date) a *castle*, of which no trace except the moat remains today.   The ruins were cleared away in 1700 and the present house, to which additions were made during the time of Queen Anne, was built.   In 1753 the great house became the *Castle Inn*.   In 1843 *Marlborough College*, one of England's great public schools, was opened in the house. (Visiting: apply at the main gate for permission to visit college and castle mound.)

Marlborough Downs.   To the north are the great green rolling Marlborough Downs, wild and beautiful, with admirable pasture for sheep and cattle.   Characteristic of the downs are the "grey wethers" or sarsen stones, blocks of siliceous sandstone, from the Eocene beds which in early times overlaid the chalk; these stones have been employed in building since the Stone Age.   *Piggle Dene*, to the east, is a source of the stones which is being preserved.   The highest point is *Milk Hill* (964 ft). An unusual sight is the number of white horses cut in the turf; there is one at Uffington, in the *Vale of the White Horse*, of unknown age (see below), others at Broad Hinton (1835), Chernhill (1780) and Alton Barnes (1812), and another at Marlborough itself cut by the boys at Gresley's School in 1804. The majority of these monuments are built along the old prehistoric track, the *Ridgeway*, which runs from south to north over the downs 5 miles east of the town and then turns northeast into the ancient Icknield Way.   The one nearest to Marlborough is at Piggle Dene, 1 mile west.   Here too is the famous *Devil's Den*, a Neolithic burial chamber.   At *West Overton* is a stone circle, starting point of the "Stone Avenue" between West Kennet and Avebury.

2 miles north-east is *Mildenhall*, the site (Folly Farm) of an ancient Roman station on the banks of the River Kennet. In the neighbourhood is one of the most interesting prehistoric monuments in the country.

76 miles: *Fyfield*.   Just off the main road is the *Devil's Den* (see above), a low arch of four great stones.   There are many sarsen stones scattered around.   Manton House, to the north, is a famous racing stable headquarters.

79 miles: *Silbury Hill*.   This originally covered 5 acres of ground, forming a mound 130 feet high. The diameter at the top was 300 feet, and the circumference of the base 1660 feet.   The origin and purpose of this, the largest artificial mound in Europe, is unknown.

80 miles: *Beckhampton*.

1 mile north-east on A 361 (the Swindon road) is the attractive village of **Avebury,** with an Elizabethan manor-house (open 2 to 6 in summer, except Tuesdays).

Avebury Circle, the largest stone circle in England, is believed to be even older than Stonehenge.   The circle was a place 0f worship and assembly and had a surrounding rampart round a ditch, and within that a circle of large stones.   Within this again was a smaller circle which is now incomplete.   Perry's Hotel covers a part of one of the inner stone circles.   Avebury itself stands unrivalled in size and importance among the megalithic monuments of the world.   The *museum*, to the north of the church and east of the manor-house, contains many objects found at Avebury and at Windmill Hill, 1½ miles north-west.   The monuments are under the guardianship of the Department of the Environment, and the ancient site, with over 900 acres of farm land, belongs to the National Trust.   To the north-east, at Barbury Castle (880 ft), where the Ridge Way bears off to the right, and at Liddington Castle (900 ft) are remains of Iron Age forts.   In the Vale of the White Horse, near Lambourn, is the megalithic structure known as *Wayland's Smithy*, and at Kinston Lisle is King Alfred's Blowing Stone.

Beckhampton to Devizes and Salisbury: 32 miles (A 361 to Devizes, then A 360).

7½ miles: *Devizes* (pop. 9000, E.C. Wednesday), a little town on the downs which was known to the Romans as *Castrum Divisarum* or *Ad Divisas*. An important corn market. Of the castle built in the reign of Henry I no trace is left. The churches of St Mary and St John have vaulted choirs from the original buildings. In the centre of the large market place is a *market cross* (1814). The museum, in Long St, contains prehistoric material found in the county (open 11 to 5, except Sundays and Mondays).

9 miles: *Pottern*, a picturesque village. 13 miles: *Lavington*, with a church in the style of Salisbury Cathedral. 18 miles: *Tilshead* (¾ mile south, the wedge-shaped *White Barrow*, 255 ft long). 22 miles: *Shrewton* (A 844 to Stonehenge and Amesbury). 32 miles: *Salisbury* (p. 378).

To Bristol

86 miles: *Calne* (pop. 7400, E.C. Wednesday), in the centre of a pig-rearing district. The *Lansdowne Arms* is a typical coaching inn of Georgian days, with the remains of the original old inn, the Catherine Wheel.

92 miles: **Chippenham** (pop. 19,000, E.C. Wednesday), a small industrial town famous for its cheese and corn. There is an interesting old Norman church.

3 miles south are **Lacock Abbey** and village, which along with *Manor Farm* and *Bewley Common* (315 acres) belong to the National Trust. Of the original abbey there remain the cloister, sacristy, chapter house and warming room (early 13th c.). After the Reformation, about 1540, William Sharington converted the monastic buildings into a *Tudor manor-house*. Magnificent octagonal tower overlooking the Avon; twisted chimneys, large courtyard with timber-framed buildings, clock. Alterations and additions in Gothic style (1753, 1828). Lacock is one of the prettiest villages in south-west England.

The direct road to Bristol (A 420) runs via Marshfield, Wick and Kingswood. 114 miles: **Bristol** (see below).

A 4 runs to Bristol by way of Bath.

96 miles: **Corsham** (pop. 9500, E.C. Wednesday). Good coarse fishing in the Avon.

The Methuen Arms is unique in possessing the original ancient lozenge or chequer design on the doorposts of the bar, indicating a tavern or house of refreshment. It is reputed to be the only inn in the country where the device has survived; it may be of Roman origin, since it is also found on inns in Pompeii. **Corsham Court,** the seat of Lord Methuen, in the vicinity, is a magnificent mansion built during the 16th to 18th centuries; it contains a great collection of pictures and period furniture. Paintings by *F. Lippi, van Dyck, Correggio, Reynolds* and *Gainsborough.* Open to visitors 11 to 12.30 and 2 to 6 in summer.

104 miles: **Bath** (p. 506).

Bath to Bristol: 13 miles on A 4.

BRISTOL

Bristol (pop. 437,000, E.C. Wednesday), an ancient inland seaport linked to the sea by 7 miles of the navigable River Avon, which enters the Bristol Channel at Avonmouth. From the old city docks of Bristol in 1497 John Cabot sailed on a voyage which led to the discovery of the northern half of the New World. In the neighbourhood of the old quays may still be found ancient taverns, once the haunt of pirates. The *Llandoger Trow* is supposed to be the inn which features in "Treasure Island", and it was at Bristol that Defoe met Alexander Selkirk, who gave him the idea of "Robinson Crusoe".

The town is an important industrial centre and carries on export trade with America, Ireland, the Mediterranean and the Middle East. It is chiefly famous for tobacco and chocolate factories and in addition are manufactured leather boots and shoes, glass, brass and copper wares, and modern machinery.

According to tradition the town was founded in the 6th century B.C. It is mentioned in Domesday Book, when it was the fourth largest town in England. In 1126 Robert Duke of Gloucester built the castle, in which Queen Matilda imprisoned Stephen in 1141. The castle was demolished by Cromwell during the Civil War, and no trace of it is left. The town was granted a charter by Edward III in 1373, and in the 15th and 16th centuries it was second only to London in importance. Its trade extended all over the world, centring mainly on the import of sugar and the slave trade to the West Indies. The town was besieged by the Royalists in 1643 and by Gen. Fairfax in 1645. The "Great Western", one of the first British steamships to cross the Atlantic, was built in Bristol and sailed from there in 1838. Bristol suffered heavy air attack during the second world war.

From Temple Meads Railway Station and the Bath road Victoria St leads to the centre of the town. To the right Temple St leads to *Temple Church;* it dates from the first half of the 12th century, when it was erected for the Knights Templar, but the present building is chiefly of the 14th to the 15th centuries. The tower stands 5 feet off the perpendicular. To the left, along Redcliffe Way, is the **Church of St Mary Redcliffe,** whose tapering *spire* can be seen from the station. It was founded in the 13th century, but with the exception of the Early English north porch (restored) it is today chiefly of the 14th and 15th century. Its bold flying buttresses, the delicate open parapets, the lofty spire (285 feet) and the richly decorated **north porch** (c. 1300) combine to make a harmonious and well-proportioned building.

The interior is worthy of the exterior. Outstanding features are the narrowness of the nave and transepts, the rich colouring lent by the reredos of Caen stone and the *Lady Chapel.* The window in the north-west corner (restored) is also very beautiful. Note the rib vaulting of the aisle. In the south transept

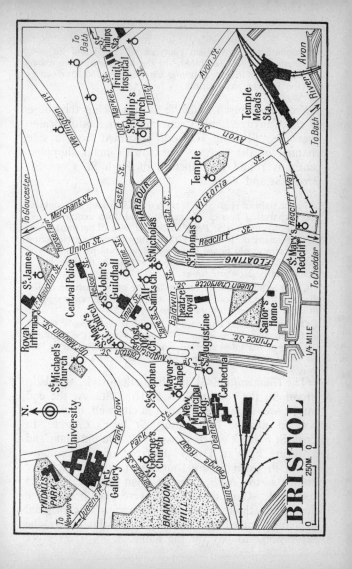

are monuments to William Canynge (d. 1396) and his son,
also named William (d. 1468). In the *Muniment Room* above
the north porch the poet Thomas Chatterton (1750-70) discovered the Rowley manuscript.

From the church Redcliffe St (in which is the house
of the Canynge family) runs north to Bristol Bridge
over the "Floating Harbour", formed from a side
channel of the Avon. The town's main shopping
centre is round the junction of High St, Corn St,
Broad St and Wine St.

To the right of High St is *Mary-le-Port St*, which still contains
many charming houses of the 14th and 15th centuries. At
the end of Peter St is *St Peter's Hospital*, one of the most splendid specimens of 16th and 17th century domestic architecture
in the county; old board room with fine wood panelling. The
mother church of Bristol, *St Peter's Church*, is close by; it
has an early Norman tower.

Castle St and Castle Green are the site of the Norman *castle:*
the only trace that can today be seen is the 13th century porch
situated at the end of the Green.

One of the oldest churches in Bristol is *St James's Church*
in Union St. There is much Norman work in the building;
the style of the small circular window is more often to be seen
on the Continent than in English architecture.

The *Guildhall* (1843), in Elizabethan style, stands in
Broad St, the continuation of High St. At the end
can be seen a gateway of the old city wall, now incorporated into the 15th century *St John's Church*. In
Corn St is the *Council House:* valuable old plate and
a picture by Van Dyck. In front of the *Exchange*
(1740) in Corn St are four metal tables which are
known as the *Nails*, three of them dated 1594, 1625
and 1631. Cash transactions were paid here at the
time when these tables formed part of the original
Exchange, called the *Tolsey*. From this comes the
expression "to pay on the nail".

There are a number of **old churches** in the business district of Bristol. *St Nicholas's*, near Bristol Bridge, rebuilt in neo-Perpendicular style in 1769, still has the original 14th century crypt. At the intersection of High St and Corn St are two churches: to the north *Christ Church* (1840, neo-classical), to the south *All Saints* (12th-15th c., Norman and Gothic, with later alterations).

In Clare St, which continues the line of Corn St, is *St Stephen's Church* (1740: on right). To the left is Marsh St, which leads to the old *Sailors' Home* (1696) in Great King St. Nearby is the **Theatre Royal,** opened in 1766, the smallest theatre in England but one of the most famous. Almost every great British actor and actress has appeared here. In the same street is the *City Free Library* (1740), with a magnificent mantelpiece by Grinling Gibbons and a fine collection of manuscripts and old books. Here too are the *Custom House* and the *Merchant Venturers' Hall* (1709), headquarters of the Society of Merchant Venturers of Bristol, founded in the reign of Henry II.

At the east end of King St is the Llandoger Trow restaurant (1664), the prototype of the inn in "Treasure Island". Here too Defoe may have met Alexander Selkirk.

On the south side of King St is **Queen Square,** named after Queen Anne, which at the time of its building at the beginning of the 18th century was the largest square in Europe. At No. 37 the first American consulate in Europe was opened in 1792. In the centre of the square is an equestrian statue of William III by *Rysbrack*.

Returning north-west along Redcliffe Way, we come to the **"Centre"**, occupying the position of an old harbour basin, now filled in. On the south side is a *statue of Neptune*, above the Floating Harbour. The central area is occupied by public gardens. There is very heavy traffic all day long. A number of large modern buildings have recently been built in this area, like the 17-storey offices of the Bristol and West Society.

Statues of Edmund Burke and Edward Colston (d. 1721, a great benefactor of Bristol: his tomb is in All Saints Church). War memorial. To the north is the church of *St Mary on the Quay* (classical-style doorway), whose name indicates that it formerly stood on the edge of the old dock. Beyond this are the *Christmas Steps* (1669), lined with bookshops and antique shops, leading to the tiny *Chapel of the Three Kings of Cologne*.

In Park Row, to the west beyond Colston St, is **Red Lodge**, a late 16th century house altered in the 18th century (period furniture: open 1 to 5, except Sundays).

Returning to the Centre, we take a street to the right (west) to reach the Cathedral.

Bristol Cathedral was built in the 14th century on the foundations of the 12th century church of an Augustinian abbey, and became a cathedral in 1542 when the bishopric of Bristol was founded by Henry VIII. The nave and west end, which had been demolished in the 16th century, were rebuilt by G. E. Street in 1868-88 to harmonise with the rest of the building. The Perpendicular central tower (125 ft high) dates from the 15th century (rebuilt 1893). The most beautiful part of the building is the *Chapter House*, which is Norman (1155-70). The *Elder Lady Chapel* adjoining the north transept (12th c., restored 1894) is good Early English. The Cathedral is 300 feet long, 65 feet wide and 55 feet high.

The church is unique on account of the absence of a clerestory and triforium; the nave and aisles are of the same height and the arches soar straight up to the springing of the vault and take the place of flying buttresses. The star-shaped tomb-recesses are copied in St Mary Redcliffe. To the east of the transept is the Elder Lady Chapel, with some original carvings.

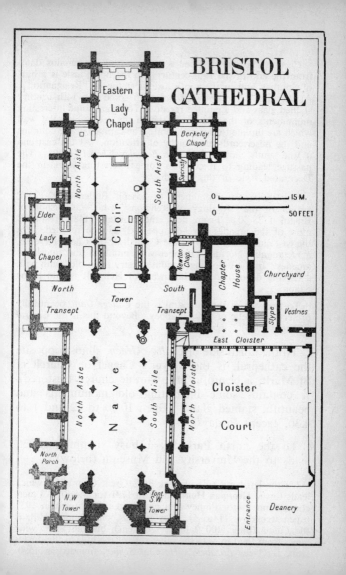

BRISTOL CATHEDRAL

Eastern Lady Chapel

Berkeley Chapel

Sacristy

North Aisle

South Aisle

Choir

0 _____ 15 M.
0 _____ 50 FEET

Elder Lady Chapel

Newton Chapel

Chapter House

Churchyard

North Transept

South Transept

Tower

Slype

Vestries

East Cloister

Nave

North Aisle

South Aisle

North Cloister

Cloister Court

North Porch

N.W Tower

Font S.W Tower

Entrance

Deanery

Choir. The marble floor is modern and the reredos dates from the end of the 19th century. In the north aisle is a bust of Southey and in the south aisle a statue of "Resignation". At the end is the *Lady Chapel*, with some fine 14th century stained glass and a painted reredos. There are some interesting monuments of the old abbots; note the recesses in the wall which are unique to this cathedral. The capitals of the columns and the misericords are worthy of attention. At the east end of the south choir aisle is the *Berkeley Chapel* (1340). The passage leading to it contains some interesting work in the Decorated style of this period.

South transept: monument to Joseph Butler (1692-1752), author of the "Analogy of Religion", who was Bishop of Bristol 1738-50. From here, the cloisters (1480, restored: most of the arcades have disappeared) can be reached. On the east side is the glory of the Cathedral, the **Chapter House,** a rectangular Norman chamber with moulded and interlaced arcades. In the adjoining Canons' Vestry is an old tomb with a carving depocting the Harrowing of Hell. It is said to be Saxon.

To the west of the cathedral is the *College Gate*, beautifully preserved, a relic of the old abbey. Beyond this is the *Central Library* (1900).

To the north side of *College Green*, almost opposite the cathedral, is the **Mayor's Chapel** or **Church of St Mark,** a beautiful little Gothic church (restored). It contains some interesting old monuments and beautiful stained glass. (Open 10.30 to 12 and 1 to 4.30, except Fridays).

To the north **Park St,** a busy shopping street, leads to the University and Museum (below).

On the left-hand side of Park St is Great George St, which leads to the **Georgian House,** built in 1791 for the Bristol merchant John Pretor Pinney and presented to the town in 1937 (open weekdays 11 to 5). Beyond this, on Brandon Hill, is the *Cabot Tower* (100 ft high, 170 steps), built in 1898: wide views from the top. On the other side of the hill, to the north-west, is *Queen Elizabeth's Hospital School*, founded in 1590.

At the north end of Park St is the **City Museum and Art Gallery** (open weekdays 10 to 5).

Material from excavations in the district; geological collections; seafaring and flying. Pictures by *Hogarth* and *Lawrence;* glass and china (particularly Chinese porcelain).

Beyond the Museum is the **University,** with a tower 220 feet high, designed by George Oatley, which was opened by King George V in 1925. To the east is *Royal Fort*, a mansion built in 1761 which now belongs to the University, as do the *Victoria Rooms* (1842) in Queens Road, to the north.

In **Clifton,** a high plateau overlooking the Avon, there are a number of large mansions. On the west it is bounded by the Avon, and of all the sights and scenes which Bristol can offer the visitor, none is more striking than the *Avon Gorge*, a rocky and wooded chasm descending over 200 feet to the River Avon, here navigable for vessels of large tonnage. The gorge is spanned by Brunel's graceful *Suspension Bridge* with its single span 700 feet long slung 250 feet above the water (1846-61).

In *Nightingale Valley*, a deep wooded hollow on the west bank of the Avon, are remains of British earthworks, with some evidence of Roman occupation. *Hotwells*, a spring of radioactive water at a temperature of 21° C, was once a fashionable watering place but fell out of use after the 18th century. It was later rediscovered, and now supplies the Grand Spa Hotel on top of the cliff. *Durdham Downs* (310 ft) run along above the river to Sea Walls: fine views. Tower, known as Cook's Folly, built into a house. On the other side of Durdham Downs is the *Zoo*.

Nearby *Clifton College* (1862) is one of England's leading schools.

In Clifton Park is a new *Roman Catholic Cathedral* (1972).

Surroundings of Bristol

3½ miles north-west of Clifton is *Kingsweston*, with a fine old castle commanding the Avon. Splendid view to the west from Penhole Point. On Kingsweston Down, to the east, is the site of a Roman camp. 1½ miles north is *Blaise Castle*, with an 18th century mansion and the "castle", a folly with four towers, set in an estate of 200 acres. The very attractive park offers fine sports facilities.

4 miles south-east is *Dundry*, with an interesting church. 7 miles north-west is *Avonmouth*, the port of Bristol, with extensive docks.

Severn Tunnel. 11 miles north, at Pilning. Built in 1886, the tunnel, 4½ miles long, is one of the greatest achievements of railway engineering. It is 26 feet wide and 20 feet high, has a double line of rails and passes under the river at a depth of from 40 to 100 feet. The estuary at this point is just over 2 miles wide.

Bristol to Clevedon: 15 miles.

9 miles: *Portishead* (pop. 4000, E.C. Thursday), an increasingly popular residential and holiday resort. There is good sailing and bathing. *Battery Point*, where ships approach very close to the land, is an interesting viewpoint. There is a phenomenal rise of the tide, which reaches 44 feet at "palm" tide (March) and 33 feet at the neap. Near the church of *St Peter* (Perpendicular, with a 15th century tower) is the fine old 15th and 16th century mansion Court House, now a farm house.

At *Wood Hill* is a prehistoric encampment which was possibly later a station on the Wansdyke, the Saxon fortified earthwork running from Portbury to Failand, Dundery and Bath and over the Wiltshire Downs.

Between Portishead and Clevedon the road passes through the beautiful "*Swiss Valley*".

2 miles south is *Weston-in-Gordano*, with a fine old church containing interesting monuments. There is a fine view of ths woodlands of Cadbury Camp (see below), which can be reached from Clapton-in-Gordano, whose church is notable for its early wooden domestic screen and bench-ends. The old manor house (modernised) has portions dating from 1310. The adjoin-

ing *Cadbury Camp* (391 ft) has a Neolithic heart-shaped fortress enclosure about 2000 years old.

13¾ miles: *Walton-in-Gordano*. On Walton Common is an Iron Age camp. Until the 19th century much of this area was marsh and was known by the name Gordano, of which the exact origin is unknown. - 15½ miles: *Clevedon* (p. 466).

23. BRISTOL TO BATH AND SALISBURY

A 431 follows the north bank of the Avon. 3 miles: *Hanham*. 5 miles: *Old Land*. 3 miles: *Kelston*. Alternative route by A 4.

13 miles: **Bath** (pop. 83,000, E.C. Thursday and Saturday). Beautifully situated in the valley of the Avon and on the surrounding hills, Bath is one of the most beautiful cities in the west country, and owes its fame throughout the world to the hot springs, around which from ancient times its life has centred.

History. Tradition puts the discovery of the springs at Bath well before the Roman era, but it was in the 1st century A.D. that the Romans founded a city round the baths, calling it *Aquae Sulis*. The Saxons occupied the town, where they built a monastery *(Akemanceaster)* in the 6th century. The Normans moved Bishop John de Villula from Wells to Bath in 1092, probably because of the increasing fame of the hot springs. Wells, which also had a sacred spring, strongly resisted the transfer, but did not get its bishop back until 1139; thereafter he was bishop of Bath and Wells. The historical link between the spring and the cathedral came to an end at the Reformation. It was not until the 17th century that Bath began to obtain a reputation as a spa and health resort. By the following century the town had become the most fashionable spa in the country. By the end of the 18th century almost the entire mediaeval city had been swept away and in its stead had arisen a magnificent town with well-planned buildings and carefully designed and laid out streets and terraces. All the eminent personages of this time came to Bath, and the town today is a museum of associations; plaques have already been placed on nearly 80 houses and more are being added. Literary references to Bath are numerous: "The Rivals" of Sheridan, the "Pickwick Papers" of Dickens, and very many others. During the second world war Bath suffered considerable damage from air raids and much of the beautiful Palladian architecture of John Wood and of his son and successor (also John Wood) was destroyed.

Springs and baths. In all there are three springs: the King's Spring (150 gallons a minute, 48° C), the Hot Spring (77 gallons per minute, 49° C), and the Cross Spring (25 gallons per minute, 45.5 °C). They are the only natural hot springs in the country, and gush what is known as lime-carbonated water, suitable for the treatment of rheumatic diseases, gout, certain conditions of high blood pressure and generally for disorders of the metabolism. The radioactive waters, which are cooled as required with the mineral waters from the Roman bath, are probably of volcanic origin.

The public buildings of Bath are grouped on the north bank of the River Avon. The great *Pump Room* near the Abbey was built in the classical style by John Wood the Younger in 1799. To the east of the Pump Room are the **Roman Baths,** said to have been built by the Emperor Claudius. They are 900 feet long and 350 feet wide, and the remains constitute one of the best examples of Roman architecture in Britain. The Baths are still lined with the original lead sheets (10 ft by 5 ft), each weighing a ton. The largest bath is rectangular and open to the sky. Note the hollow tiles with which the barrel vault is constructed. Open 9 to 6 (Sundays 11 to 6). Small museum.

From the Pump Room windows can be seen the disused *King's Bath*, which was the mediaeval bath, but of which the balustrade (1618) is now the oldest part. The dilapidated *Cross Bath* also dates from mediaeval times but has been completely transformed by subsequent alterations. The modern Bathing Establishment controls the *Queen's Baths*, the *Royal Baths* and the *Old Royal Baths*. To the north is the spacious *Royal Mineral Water Hospital* designed by the elder Wood; it provides free treatment with spa water for poor patients. Roman pavement in the basement. (Can be seen on application). Opposite the Hospital is a fragment of the mediaeval town walls.

One of Bath's most prominent buildings is the *Abbey Church* (in the decadent Gothic style of the 16th century), built on the site of the former church of the Benedictine priory of Bath. Traces of Bishop John de Villula's Norman building can be seen in

the round-arched window in the north choir aisle and
in the bases of the buttresses by the east wall. The
third building erected on the same site was begun in
1500 by Bishop King (1495-1503) after a dream in
which he saw angels descending from heaven on a
ladder (represented on the west front). When the
abbey was dissolved at the Reformation the church
was not finished. It was bought in 1560 and offered
to the town as a parish church, then restored and
completed from 1616 onwards by Bishop Montague.
In 1859 Sir George Gilbert Scott removed the 17th
century plaster ceiling and replaced it by stone vaulting in the style of its original period — one of the
great advances achieved by the Perpendicular style,
of which this modern work is a very fine imitation.
The tower is oblong; the transepts are narrower than
the nave and the choir.

Interior. The many large **stained glass windows** have earned
the Abbey the name of the "Lantern of England". The great
west window is particularly fine. Note also the beautiful fan
vaulting. In the southern arcade of the choir is the much restored *chantry* of Prior Birdie, who began the building of the
priory church in 1500, under the direction of Bishop King.
Monument to Beau Nash (d. 1761) at the east end of the south
aisle. In the south transept is a monument to Lady Waller,
wife of the famous Parliamentary general. Near the east doorway is a font (1710) with a carving of three lepers.

Just north of the Abbey is the **Guildhall,** a neo-
classical building by Baldwin (1775).

Banqueting Room (open 11.30 to 12.30 and 2 to 4, except
Saturdays and Sundays). In the north wing is the *Victoria Art
Gallery* (open 10 to 6), devoted to local art and exhibitions.

To the east *Pulteney Bridge* crosses the Avon.
Built 1769-74, it is the only work in Bath by the great
architect Robert Adam. Beyond it is Great Pulteney

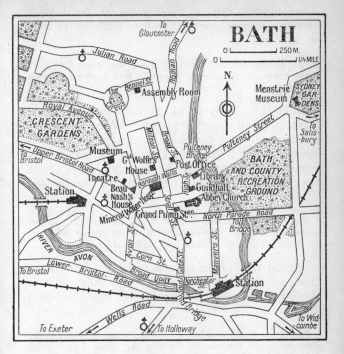

St, at the far end of which is the **Holburne of Menstrie Museum** (open 11 to 1 and 2 to 5), in an 18th century mansion: 19th century decorative and minor arts.

Now return to the right bank of the Avon.

Queen Square (1726-36) is John Wood's masterpiece; he himself lived at No. 24. The neighbouring streets are also in neo-classical style. To the south is the *Theatre Royal* (1720, façade rebuilt 1805). To the north is the **Circus,** with a central garden, laid out in 1758 to a plan by Wood.

Immediately east of the Circus are the famous
Assembly Rooms (open 10 to 6 in summer, 11 to 6
on Sundays).

This handsome neo-classical building was erected in 1771
to the designs of the younger Wood. It now houses a **Museum
of Costume.**

From the Circus Brock St runs west to **Royal
Crescent,** built by the younger Wood (1767-74).
Farther north are *Cavendish Crescent* (1730), *Lans-
down Crescent* (1792) and *Camden Crescent* (1788).
From the higher ground there are fine views of the
town. In *Victoria Park* (50 acres) are the Botanic
Gardens.

No. 1 Royal Crescent, built by Wood for his father-in-law,
is open to visitors. It was acquired by the city in 1968 and
has been completely restored and furnished in period style.

A good view of the town is to be had from *Sham
Castle* on Bathwick Hill, which Ralph Allen built to
"improve the prospect" from his own house in North
Parade.

Prior Park (2 miles south-east). The Palladian bridge in the
grounds of the mansion of Prior Park, which Ralph Allen
built for himself, is perhaps the most extraordinary example
of the application of the classical temple in English architecture.
Beside it is a round tower built to commemorate Allen.

Bath is surrounded by the *Downs*, which offer pleasant
walking and magnificent views.

2 miles south on the Salisbury road (A 36) is **Claverton Manor**
(1820), now an *American Museum* (open 2 to 5, except Mondays):
decorative arts of the United States in the colonial period and
the 19th century.

From Bath to Salisbury the route via Bradford-on-
Avon (described below) is recommended. Bradford

is 8 miles south-east of Bath on A 363, which branches off A 4 (the road to London) a short distance outside the town.

Bradford-on-Avon

Bradford-on-Avon (pop. 5500, E.C. Wednesday) is an ancient little town on the Avon. The river is spanned by two old **bridges,** one of which dates from the 13th century and consists of 9 arches, of which the two to the east are original. In the centre is a small chapel; the present building probably dates from the 18th century.

In the Abbey Yard stands the *Saxon church*, founded by St Aldhelm in the 8th century. In 1125 William of Malmesbury, who wrote a life of St Aldhelm, mentioned this little church of **St Lawrence**; during the Middle Ages, however, it fell into disuse. It was eventually used as a charnel-house, and later became a school, the chancel being occupied as a dwelling-house. In the 19th century the surrounding houses were demolished and the church restored. Today this old building exists in almost its original state. There are some interesting carvings. During the summer services are held. (Visiting: apply to the next-door cottage for keys).

Near the old Barton Bridge is a 14th century *Tithe Barn* (55 yards long by 10 yards wide) with its original stone-tiled roof. On the river bank is an old church, *Holy Trinity*, which dates from the 12th century (considerably altered and restored) with a 15th century tower. In the rebuilt porch is a Norman window, and inside are interesting brasses. Nearby is a 16th century chantry (17th and 18th century additions). Near the post office is the district known as the *Shambles*, with

a number of quaint old houses. At the end of Silver St
is the entrance to the *Hall*, formerly called *Kingston
House*, a magnificent Elizabethan mansion (1600) in
a perfect state of preservation.

On the outskirts of the town, in the Newtown
district, is *St Mary's Chapel*, built on the site of a
church founded in 652, which contains some Tudor
work. Very fine views from the top of the hill.

Around Bradford-on-Avon. 2 miles east on A 3053 is *Holt*.
The *Courts:* a house with a very ornate façade built about 1700,
in grounds of 7 acres, containing furniture, pictures and mementoes of William IV (open Wednesdays and Thursdays in
summer 2 to 6). 3 miles beyond Holt is *Melksham* (pop. 5500,
E.C. Wednesday), an old market town, now also a small industrial town, with a 14th century tithe barn now occupied
by a school. *Westwood Manor*, 2 miles away, is a late 15th
century stone-built house, altered in 1610, with late Gothic
and Jacobean windows and very elaborate mouldings. Beside
it is the tiny parish church.

11½ miles: **Trowbridge** (pop. 17,000, E.C. Wednesday). In the *church* (15th c., Perpendicular) is the
tomb of the poet George Crabbe. In County Hall
is the Savernake collection of 14th century documents.

Instead of continuing on A 363 to Warminster and
Salisbury, it is well worth while turning west into
A 366 to see the mansion of *Farleigh Hungerford*,
with a 14th century chapel containing the tombs of
many members of the Hungerford family (15th-17th c.).

At the next road junction turn left into A 36, which
runs south to *Beckington*.

From Beckington we can take A 359, which runs
south-west to **Frome** (pop. 12,000, E.C. Wednesday),
an old wool-manufacturing town with a beautiful
14th century church and many old houses. 3 miles

beyond it, on the road to Shepton Mallet, is the village of **Nunney,** with a very fine Perpendicular *church* and an imposing 14th century *castle* with enormous towers (destroyed during the Civil War).

From Frome take the Warminster road (A 362), to the right of which is the magnificent *Longleat House,* seat of the Marquess of Bath.

Longleat House, looking over Shear Water to fine parkland and girdled by woodland and rhododendron walks, is an Italian-style house with 365 windows and 70 main rooms. Its flat roof has carved domes and sculptured figures. Built in 1566-80 by John Thynne on the site of Longleat Priory, it is considered to be Britain's finest Elizabethan mansion, and possesses one of the finest private libraries in Europe containing, among other priceless books and manuscripts, Caxton's translation of "The Histories of Troye", the first book printed in English; the *Mainz Bible* of 1462; the 1st, 2nd, 3rd, and 4th *Shakespeare Folios*; Redouté's *Flower Books;* a letter from Queen Elizabeth congratulating the Earl of Shrewsbury upon the defeat of the Armada; and a signed Order in Council instructing the Earl of Shrewsbury to attend the execution of Mary, Queen of Scots. The Great Hall is a fine example of the work of the original builder, which remains practically unaltered. The ceilings of the **State rooms,** the work of Italian artists employed by the 3rd and 4th Marquesses, are beautifully moulded, painted and gilded. The doors are of inlaid walnut. The drawing-room walls are covered with Genoa velvet in red and gold. The dining-room walls are in embossed Spanish leather. In the Salon are 16th century *Flemish tapestries*. Interesting pieces of furniture include the table on which the Treaty of Vienna, 1815, was signed by Talleyrand, Wellington and Metternich; a set of William and Mary chairs with their original silk upholstery; German cabinets of fine craftsmanship; a pair of Louis XV tables, and many fine examples of Empire furniture.

The **collection of pictures** is famous: it includes a set of Hunting Scenes by *Wootton*, works by *Titian, Raphael, Longhi, Lorenzo Lotto* and *Bastiano Mainardi*, and portraits of Charles I when Prince of Wales, Charles II, Lady Arabella Stuart, Robert Devereux Earl of Essex, Henry of Navarre, the second Duke of Buckingham, the first Marquess of Bath by *Lawrence*, Lord

Thurlow by *Reynolds* and the fifth Marquess of Bath by *Sir William Orpen*. There are also pictures which came from the Alupka palace, near Yalta in the Crimea, then the property of a Prince Vorontsov, great-grandfather of the fourth Marquess of Bath.

The gardens in front of the house were laid out by Capability Brown about 1754. The small gardens to the north and east contain two interesting buildings, the Georgian *orangery* and the *boat-house* (by Wyattville, 1800). In the stables (also by Wyattville) is the *State Coach*, painted yellow with silver trimming, which took the fifth Marquess to the coronation of George V in 1911 and was also used on the occasion of a ceremony at Buckingham Palace in 1913. Visiting: 10 to 4 or 10 to 6 according to season. A more recent addition to the attractions of Longleat is the Lion Park through which visitors can drive in their cars.

In the neighbouring village of *Horningsham* is the oldest Presbyterian church in England, built by Scottish workmen brought here by John Thynne during the construction of Longleat.

Warminster (pop. 10,500), on the Bristol-Salisbury road, is an old wool-manufacturing town, with a Perpendicular church (restored) and Georgian houses.

The route continues on A 36 along the edge of the extensive *Salisbury Plain*. *Heytesbury* has a 13th-14th century church. Shortly afterwards A 390 goes off on the left to *Stonehenge* (p. 391). A 36 continues through *Deptford* and *Wilton* to **Salisbury**: (p. 378).

IV: EAST ANGLIA, CAMBRIDGESHIRE AND LINCOLNSHIRE

Between the estuary of the Thames and the Wash lies East Anglia, comprising the counties of Norfolk and Suffolk. These, with their neighbouring county of Essex, form a country of flat plains, of far stretching horizontal landscapes renowned for their gentle colouring and soft lights and studded with fine churches and tranquil villages. Across this territory Boadicea led the Britons against the Romans; amid its marshes Hereward the Wake made England's last stand against the Normans. At Colchester in Essex the Roman wall and the Norman castle bear witness to these two invasions separated by almost a thousand years.

Many Norman buildings have survived in this area, like the church at Clacton)on)Sea which now stands in the middle of a modern seaside resort. The suffix "on-Sea" appears in many Essex place-names, like Southend-on-Sea and Westcliff-on-Sea, on the estuary of the Thames. Southend, with a history going back to the time of William the Conqueror, is now a resort much favoured by Londoners.

Norfolk and its neighbouring county of Cambridgeshire contain some of the richest treasures of mediaeval England. Enshrined in the bend of the River Cam at Cambridge, one of the ancient university towns of England, are colleges and chapels which rank among the most glorious antiquities of Europe. At Ely is a sublimely beautiful cathedral. The cathedral town of

Norfolk, the quaint old port of King's Lynn, Sandringham, country home of the Queen and the Duke of Edinburgh, the placid inland waters of the Norfolk Broads and the lovely open coastline of Norfolk, all come within the geography of this richly historic and interesting corner of the country.

24. LONDON TO SOUTHEND

A. On A 127

44¾ miles to Southend (A 127); 49 miles to Shoeburyness
(B 1016 from Southend). From Hyde Park Corner follow
Route 25 on A 12 to Gallows Corner, then keep straight ahead
on A 127.

There are no features of particular interest on the
road. It cuts across the north side of *Basildon* new
town.

At the near end of Southend is **Prittlewell Priory** (open 11
to 5 or 6), the remains of a Cluniac house (12th c.). Refectory
with a fine doorway of 1170. Local museum.

Southend-on-Sea (pop. 170,000, E.C. Wednesday)
is a very popular seaside resort on the north side of
the Thames estuary.

As a resort it makes no pretensions to be anything other
than it is — a busy, crowded, jolly and companionable place.
Its attractions lie not in its historical interest or natural beauty
but in the facilities it offers for holiday entertainment. Its pier
is said to be the longest in the Commonwealth (1½ miles).
It has 5 miles of promenades, a Kursaal with 26 acres of sideshows, and a variety of other entertainments and amusements
for young and old. Included in its boundaries are *Leigh-on-
Sea*, which has an old church with a fine tower, *Westcliff-on-
Sea*, *Thorpe Bay* and *Shoeburyness*. Leigh and Westcliff-on-Sea
to the west and Thorpe Bay to the east are quieter outposts
of the popular resort; each have railway stations.

3 miles north is *Rochford*, with a mansion in which Anne
Boleyn, second wife of Henry VIII and mother of Queen Elizabeth I, once lived. The church has a 15th century brick
tower.

From Southend B 1016 runs round the coast to *Shoeburyness*.
To the north are the interesting villages of *Sutton*, *Shopland*
and *Barling*. Beyond a maze of creeks and waterways are the
islands of *Havengore* and *Foulness*, which a hundred years
ago were still the haunt of smugglers.

B. On A 13

This route runs through the *East End* of London,
great areas of which were completely devastated in
the months of bombardment during the last war.
South of the route, for more than half the way, lie
the great docks of the **Port of London.**

Road. 40 miles on A 13. From London Bridge leave by
King William St, Gracechurch St and Fenchurch St and along
to the end of Aldgate High St. A 11 forks north-east to Stratford. From the end of Aldgate High St A 13, continues straight
ahead along Commercial Road and East India Dock Road
to Poplar.

3 miles: **Poplar.** To the south are *Millwall* and the
Isle of Dogs, with the great *West India Dock* and,
across the water, the *Commercial Docks* at Rotherhithe.

The whole of this area is covered with acres of public and
private wharves equipped to handle every type of cargo. Within
the docks are bonded and free storage accommodation for one
million tons of merchandise, as well as accommodation in the
privately owned riverside warehouses for another million tons.
Despite the damage suffered during the war the Port of London is still one of the largest and best equipped ports in the
world.

3½ miles, on right: entrance to the *Blackwall
Tunnel*, which links by road the north bank and the
south bank of the Thames, emerging on the south
bank at Bugsby and Greenwich Marshes.

4 miles: *Limehouse.* The River Lee navigation
canal from Hertford and the Grand Union Canal
linking London by water with the Midlands enter the
Thames at Limehouse.

4½ miles: *Canning Town Station*. 4½ miles: A 13 forks right.

A 124, straight ahead, runs north-east to (3½ miles) *Barking*. Eastbury Manor House (¾ mile south of Upney station) is a fine example (c. 1550) of Tudor brickwork, standing in the centre of a modern housing estate. Inside are 17th century mural decorations.

A 13 continues along Beckton Road to East Ham. To the south are the *Royal Albert Dock*, the *Victoria Dock*, and the *King George V Dock;* across the river is **Woolwich** with its *Royal Dockyard* and *Royal Arsenal*. 10¾ miles: **Dagenham.** On the banks of the river, to the south, are the vast Ford motor works. — 13¾ miles: **Rainham** (pop. 6500, E.C. Wednesday). Near the church is *Rainham Hall*, a good example of late Renaissance architecture, built about 1729 in red brick with stone dressings.

16¾ miles: *Purfleet*, beyond which the access road to the Dartford Tunnel under the Thames goes off on the right. A 13 continues past **Grays** and **Tilbury** (on right), with a fort built by Henry VIII. *Tilbury* is an important Thames estuary port; regular ferry service across the river to Gravesend. 19¾ miles: *Stifford*. — 25 miles: *Stanford-le-Hope*. 35 miles: *Hadleigh*, with the ruins of a castle built by Hubert de Burgh, Earl of Kent, in the reign of Henry III (1216-72). The church of *St James the Less* dates from the 12th century.

3 miles north on A 29 is *Rayleigh:* old church and the ruins of *Rayleigh Mount*, an 11th century castle.

1½ miles south by B 1014 is **South Benfleet,** in the *Rochford Hundred*, a district of marshy pastures intersected by dykes and ditches. South Benfleet itself is an old-world fishing village at the head of the Hadleigh Ray. The oldest part of the church is 12th century; the roof of the south porch is very fine. B 1014

continues south to **Canvey Island,** an area of marshland reclaimed in the reign of James I (1603-25). Canvey Island has
an area of 4000 acres; it is 5 miles long and 2½ miles wide,
and surrounded by 18 miles of sea-walls. It is now a popular
holiday resort for Londoners from the East End. Oil refinrey.

40 miles: **Southend** (p. 517).

25. LONDON TO GREAT YARMOUTH

311 miles on A 12.

From Hyde Park Corner, take the East Carriageway in the Park (running parallel to Park Lane) and at Grosvenor Gate turn right across Park Lane into Upper Grosvenor St. Then turn left into Park St, cross Oxford St and Portman Square, and follow Gloucester Place to Regent's Park. Continue straight ahead into the Outer Circle, which runs round the west and north sides of the park, and at Gloucester Gate turn left into Parkway and under the railway bridge into Camden Road. In about a mile fork left into Parkhurst Road and cross Holloway Road into Seven Sisters Road. In about 2½ miles this runs into A 10: turn left, and almost immediately right into Broad Lane, Ferry Lane and Forest Road. At the end of Forest Road turn left into Woodford New Road and almost immediately, at a roundabout, right into Grove Road, Southend Road and Woodford Avenue. At Gants Hill station Woodford Avenue runs into A 12 (Eastern Avenue), which is followed to Romford.

19 miles: *Romford.* — 21 miles: *Gallows Corner.* — 26 miles: *Brentwood* (pop. 60,000, E.C. Thursday). The White Hart is an old coaching inn.

37 miles: **Chelmsford** (pop. 53,000, E.C. Wednesday). The Roman *Caesaromagus*, now the county town of Essex, was an important military station on the Roman highway to Colchester. It is now an industrial town (engineering). The rivers Chelmer and Can divide it into three parts. Over the Can is a bridge known as the Old Bridge (1788), but most of the ancient buildings in the town have been cleared to make way for modern expansion; what old building does remain is mostly no earlier than Georgian.

St Mary's Cathedral (raised to that status in 1913), a 15th century parish church, was rebuilt in the 19th century after falling down in 1800. Little is left of the original building apart from the fine south porch and the massive 15th century tower with a spire added in 1709. To the right of the Cathedral is the *Shire Hall* (1791).

At Oaklands in Mulsham St is the **Chelmsford and Essex Museum**: excellent collections of British birds, comprising 277 species and including an example of the needle-tailed swift (Acanthyllis caudacuta); birds' eggs of 234 species; British and foreign butterflies, moths and beetles, fossils and tropical molluscs and minerals; also exhibits of the ancient Egyptian and Romano-British periods and arms and weapons of colonial and native peoples. The library contains an old Bible and a book printed at Venice in 1475. Open weekdays 10 to 5 or 8, Sundays 2 to 5.

Surroundings of Chelmsford: Maldon

A 414 runs east to *Great Baddow*, a pleasant little village now almost swallowed up by Chelmsford; birthplace of Richard de Baddow, founder of Clare College, Cambridge. Interesting old church. — 2 miles: *Sandon*. Fine church with interesting brickwork and a tower said to have been built by Cardinal Wolsey; good wood carving. — 4¾ miles: **Danbury,** with *Danbury Palace*, residence of the Bishop of Rochester, a neo-Tudor house (1834) in grounds of 300 acres. The village of Danbury, situated on a hill (350 ft) and surrounded by an ancient earthwork, is one of the highest points in the area; it is mentioned in the preface to Scott's "Waverley". Old church with interesting wooden effigies of the 12th or 13th century. 1 mile south of Danbury Common on B 1418, at *Bicknacre*, are the ruins of an Augustinian priory (1175). 6½ miles: B 1010 goes off on the right to *Burnham-on-Crouch* (19½ miles): see below.

10 miles: **Maldon** (pop. 11,500, E.C. Wednesday), an old seaport and market town on a hill above the rivers Blackwater and Chelmer, occupying the site of a Roman settlement. The tower is all that remains of St Peter's Church, which collapsed in 1665. *All Saints Church* (14th c.) has a triangular tower surmounted by a hexagonal spire; sanctus bell, of a type characteristic of this part of England. Each of the windows on the south side has a different pattern of tracery. Stained glass window (1928) commemorating Lawrence Washington, an ancestor of George Washington. The oldest church in the town, and the oldest in Essex, is *St Mary's*, on the riverside, surrounded by interesting old houses. It was founded in Saxon

times, and the tower (rebuilt in brick in the early 17th century after it had collapsed) contains some Norman work.

There are a number of interesting old wrought-iron inn signs in the village (the White Horse, the Bell and the Blue Boar). The *Blue Boar Inn* is one of the most interesting inns in Essex, partly dating from the 16th century. Among other old buildings are the roofless ruins of *St Giles Hospital*, a 12th century leper-house, and the *Plume Library* (1704), on the site of St Peter's Church, with a rich collection of books, first editions and manuscripts, including Milton's "Paradise Lost" and "Paradise Regained". The Town Hall is 15th century.

There are many agreeable walks in the neighbourhood. **Beeleigh Abbey,** situated at the foot of a long slope on the banks of the Chelmer, was founded in 1180; the domestic buildings and chapter-house remain. Vaulted roofs carried on slender Purbeck marble columns.

Springfield is a charming village in which Oliver Goldsmith once stayed, with All Saints, an interesting old church. 2 miles north is *New Hall*, a fine old house, badly damaged during the last war, which is now occupied by a Roman Catholic monastery and school; the old chapel can be seen on application.

East of Maldon. **Burnham-on-Crouch** (pop. 4000) is a sailing centre 6 miles from the sea on the north side of the river Crouch: St Mary's Church (14th-18th c.). To the north of Burnham (B 1021) are *Southminster* (Perpendicular church) and **Bradwell-on-Sea,** near the south bank of the Blackwater estuary. *Bradwell Lodge* is a Tudor house with Georgian additions. 2 miles east, in the marshland by the sea, is the chapel of *St Peter-on-the-Wall* (7th c.), incorporating walls and foundations of a Roman fort; it was abandoned in the 11th century and was for long used as a barn. The walls are 2 feet thick.

40 miles: *Boreham*, an old-world village with a tiny church; interesting tombs. South-west is the beautiful mansion of *Boreham House*, standing in 100 acres of woodland.

43 miles: *Hatfield Peverel*. — 45½ miles: *Witham*. — 49 miles: *Kelvedon*.

B 1023 runs south-east to (4 miles) *Tiptree*, famous for its jam. North-east is the little village of *Layer Marney*. The manor house has a Tudor tower of interesting brick work, 70 feet high, the gateway of a mansion begun in the 16th century but never completed. In the church is a 16th century mural painting of St Christopher.

56 miles: *Marks Tey*. 1¾ miles south is *Copford*, with an interesting church (1100).

59 miles: **Colchester.**

Colchester

Colchester (pop. 68,000) is the oldest town in Essex, a centre of oyster culture and flower-growing (roses).

Before the Roman conquest this was the fortified capital of Cunobelinus (Shakespeare's Cymbeline), chief of the Trinobantes. It was captured in 44 A.D. by Claudius's forces, who established a camp here. In 50 this became a *colonia* and one of the most important Roman towns in Britain *(Camulodunum)*. In 62 it was pillaged by the Iceni, led by Boadicea, but the walls were rebuilt soon afterwards. Excavations have revealed the British fort and the Roman camp and town, which measured 1000 yards by 500 yards. Stretches of the wall survive, including the west gateway, the *Balkerne Gate*. In 1189 Richard I granted the town a charter, and during the Middle Ages Colchester enjoyed a thriving cloth trade, which was further increased by the arrival of Flemish refugees in 1570. The town withstood an eleven days' siege by Parliamentary forces under Gen. Fairfax during the Civil War. An earthquake in 1884 brought down the tower of a church and damaged more than 30 other buildings.

Colchester Castle dates from 1085. The keep, the largest Norman keep in the country (150 ft by 115 ft), resembles the White Tower in the Tower of London. It incorporates Roman tiles and was formerly surrounded by a ditch or moat. Excavations have shown that the castle was built on the site of the

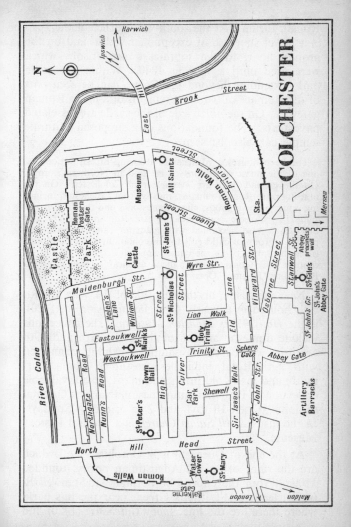

COLCHESTER

N

Harwich

Ipswich

East Hill

Brook Street

Priory Street

Roman Walls

Sta.

Mersea

River Colne

Castle

Roman Postern Gate

Museum

Park

The Castle

Maidenburgh Street

St. Helen's Lane

William Str.

St. Nicholas Street

Eastcukwells

St. Mark's

Westcukwell

Northgate Road

Nunn's Road

Town Hall

St. Peter's

High Street

Culver

Car Park

Shewell

Sir Isaac's Walk

Trinity St.

Holy Trinity

Lion Walk

Wyre Str.

Queen Street

St. James

All Saints

Eld Lane

Schere Gate

Vineyard Str.

Stanwell Str.

Osborne Street

Abbey precincts wall

St. Giles

St. John's Abbey Gate

St. John's Gr.

Abbey Gate

St. John Str.

Artillery Barracks

North Hill

Head Street

Water Tower

St. Mary

Roman Walls

Balkerne Gate

London

Maldon

Roman forum. At the south-west corner of the keep is a newel staircase of exceptional width, and on the ground floor, to the south-east, are prisons which were used until as late as 1840. Within the castle park, extending beyond the Colne, can be seen part of the Roman wall and the remains of a fallen Roman gateway. On the north side of the castle are tesselated pavements. The foundations of a supposed Mithraic temple can also be seen.

The keep houses a **Museum** of Romano-British antiquities, one of the finest collections of its kind in Northern Europe. On the ground floor are *mosaics* from Colchester. On the first floor are Roman remains, mostly from Colchester, including pottery, grave goods, glass, tombstones and the "*Colchester sphinx*". On the south balcony are Roman *jewellery* and bronzes, a vase decorated with gladiators and animals, and part of a group of children's tombs containing some 50 objects (near the sphinx). In the corner are Belgic objects of the 1st century B.C. (coins, pottery, metal articles). There is also a Prehistoric Room. Open 10 to 5.

Near the castle, on the east side of the War Memorial, housed in an early Georgian mansion (c. 1720), is the *Holly Trees Mansion Museum*. The collections include domestic articles of the 17th, 18th and 19th centuries, carved chests, samplers, exhibits connected with agricultural industries, costumes, china, furniture and many old prints and maps; also a valuable collection of Peruvian antiquities and various Oriental exhibits. Open 10 to 1 and 2 to 5, except Sundays. In the disused *All Saints Church* is a Natural History Museum.

At the end of Queen St is St Botolph St, off which are the ruins of an old Augustinian priory, founded 1109. From the end of St Botolph St, Stanwell St (right) leads to St John's Green, near the bus park, where there are the fine *Abbey Gatehouse* (1420) and the precinct wall, sole remains of the *Benedictine abbey of St John the Baptist*, founded in 1096 by William the Dapifer (steward) of William II, which was demolished at the Reformation.

The High St, reached via Abbeygate Road and the Scheregate Steps (Roman wall) is wide and pleasing. In nearby Trinity St is *Holy Trinity Church*, whose tower (c. 1050) is the oldest church tower in the town. There are remains of Saxon work at the west end of the nave.

The choir is 14th century, the south aisle a little later. In the north chapel is a monument to William Gilbert, physician to Queen Elizabeth I and a pioneer in the discovery of electricity.

Near the Town Hall is *St Martin's Church* (Decorated), with a nave and ruined tower dating from the 12th century and a 14th century choir and aisles. *St Peter's Church*, in North Hill, dates from the 16th century but was restored and altered in the 18th and 19th centuries; interesting brasses and monuments. In *St Giles' Church*, near the gatehouse of St John's Abbey (above), are monuments to Charles Lucas and George Lisle, Royalist leaders who were shot in 1648. The church dates from the 12th century. *St Leonard's Church* is 14th century.

There are many mediaeval houses in the town, several of them in East and West Stockwell St. In High St is the *Red Lion Hotel*, a fine Tudor building. The *Siege House* at the foot of East Hill still bears marks of the siege during the Civil War (1648); some good stained glass.

The *Town Hall* (1901) occupies the site of the Norman Moot Hall. From the tower (height to the top of the cross 160 ft) there is a fine view. The rooms on the second floor contain interesting pictures and other items. *Albert Hall Art Gallery:* paintings by

John Constable, van de Velde, Muirhead, etc.; also
water colours and graphic art collections.

Surroundings of Colchester

Mersea Island (5 miles long by 2 miles wide) lies 9½ miles
south on B 1025 at the junction of the Colne and the Blackwater,
separated from the mainland by the *Pyefleet Channel*, where
the famous Colchester oysters, the "Colchester natives", are
cultivated. The *Strood* is a causeway over the Channel. Numerous Roman remains have been discovered on the island —
in the church (which has a tower dating from 1100), at *West
Mersea Hall*, near Yew Tree House and elsewhere. 1 mile
from the church is a tumulus.

Colchester to Brightlingsea: 10 miles south-east by B 1027
and B 1029. 3½ miles: *Wivenhoe Cross* (13th c. church with
interesting brasses and monuments). — 7½ miles: crossroads,
at which B 1027 continues straight ahead, via the old village
of *Thorrington*, to **St Osyth** (4 miles), a small village with an
Early English and Perpendicular church. Near the village are
the remains of *St Osyth's Abbey*, a priory founded in 1118 by
Bishop Melmeis on the site of a convent in which a certain
Princess Osyth was killed by Danish raiders. In 1168 the priory
became an abbey, which was dissolved at the Reformation.
The remains include a handsome gatehouse, one of the finest
surviving examples of Norman architecture, and the Abbot's
Tower, together with a clock-tower and oriel window dating
from 1527. 4½ miles beyond St Osyth is *Clacton-on-Sea* (below).

From the crossroads B 1029 goes off on the right to *Brightlingsea* (pop. 4500, E.C. Thursday), a sailing and boatbuilding
centre which is becoming an increasingly popular seaside resort
on account of its bracing climate and sheltered situation. Many
Roman remains.

Colchester to Clacton-on-Sea: 16 miles on A 133.

4¾ miles: Elmstead Market. — 6½ miles: Frating, an old-
world village in the countryside of John Constable's paintings.
— 10 miles: Weeley. — 13 miles: A 136 forks left for *Harwich*
(10 miles): see p. 529.

16 miles: **Clacton-on-Sea** (pop. 25,000, E.C. Wednesday), a
popular holiday resort. At the end of the East Parade is *Holland-
on-Sea*, where the seaside and country blend; there are fine
sands and walks along the cliffs to Frinton-on-Sea.

24 miles: *Frinton-on-Sea* (pop. 3000, E.C. Wednesday), a resort developed since 1885.

26 miles: *Walton-on-the-Naze* (pop. 3000, E.C. Wednesday). There is a good golf course, and the neighbourhood is of interest to the geologist for the relics (shells) of the Pleocene period at Red Crag; flint axes, arrowheads, etc., can also be picked up here. Oyster culture.

Colchester to Harwich: 20 miles on A 604.

5 miles: *Ardleigh.* — 7½ miles: *Lawford.* — 8½ miles: *Manningtree* (pop. 800, E.C. Wednesday), an important railway junction and small port on the estuary of the Stour. An excellent centre for visits to the *Constable country* (see Stratford St Mary below). — 9½ miles: *Mistley*, a small port. — 20½ miles: **Harwich** (pop. 15,000, including Dovercourt, E.C. Wednesday), the "gateway to the Continent" (fast goods and passenger services to Hook of Holland, Antwerp, Esbjerg, Göteborg and Rotterdam).

The port, at the confluence of the Orwell and the Stour, has had a long history. Its prosperity and importance increased during the Norman period. Frobisher sailed from here on his quest for the North-West Passage. The town received its charter in 1603. Samuel Pepys was M.P. for the borough and mentions it frequently in his diary. The captain of the "Mayflower", Christopher Jones, was born at Harwich and lived in the town for many years. During the two world wars Harwich and Dovercourt were fortified, and during the last war many of the inhabitants were evacuated. 1750 bombs were dropped on the town, but many of them fell into the sea. Three hundred ships assembled here for the Normandy landings in 1944.

There are a number of ancient streets and buildings: King's Head St, King's Quay St, Eastgate St, Castlegate St and St Austin's Lane are all mediaeval in plan. In *Church St* there are some old houses, including Mead's Restaurant (14th c.). On the *Green* is the only specimen in the country of an old treadmill crane. There are also old lighthouses. The old *Guildhall* has an 18th century Council Chamber.

Dovercourt is the seaside and holiday resort of the town, with excellent sandy beaches.

66 miles: **Stratford St Mary,** in the heart of the countryside made famous by John Constable (1776-

1837), the most famous of English landscape painters, who was born at East Bergholt, 2 miles to the north over the border into Suffolk.

On the north bank of the Stour is *Flatford Mill*, which belonged to Constable's father and where he worked for a year. Here too he painted "The Hay-Wain". Nearby are *Mill House* and *Willy Lott's Cottage*, a 17th century house in characteristic local style, now a school and residence for artists (National Trust). — 1 mile east is *Dedham* (church tower) and 1 mile west is *Langham*, both painted by Constable.

77 miles: **Ipswich** (pop. 120,000, E.C. Wednesday), a port entered from the Orwell by a lock 300 feet long. Charles II is said to have hidden after the battle of Worcester in the *Ancient House* or *Sparrowe's House* (1567) in Butter Market. The *Great White Horse Hotel* in Tavern St, nearby, owes its fame to Mr Pickwick's adventure with the lady in yellow curl-papers, which took place here. Cardinal Wolsey, son of a butcher and innkeeper (1471-1530), was born in Ipswich. On the river is *Wolsey's Gate*, all that remains of a college of canons which he founded two years before his fall from power. In Christchurch Park (beyond St Margaret's St) is **Christchurch Mansion,** a Tudor house which is now a museum (open 10 to 5). The Municipal Museum is in High St (open 10 to 5).

12 miles away is **Felixstowe** (pop. 18,500, E.C. Wednesday), a popular holiday resort with a shingle beach, a swimming pool, and a long promenade along the cliffs on both sides of the town. To the north is the river Deben (ferry at the mouth). To the west and north-west is the Orwell estuary, too wide to be bridged at any point below Ipswich; motor ferries from Felixstowe to Harwich.

83 miles: *Martlesham*. On the heath is an aerodrome. B 1438 forks right for *Woodbridge*, 2 miles away, (pop. 6000), a market town on the north bank of the Deben estuary: fishing, wild fowling, sailing.

1 mile beyond is **Melton,** with one of the finest golf courses in the eastern counties. In the town are an interesting little 17th century Shire Hall and a Perpendicular church. Opposite the Shire Hall is the house where Edward Fitzgerald, translator of the "Rubaiyat of Omar Khayyam", lived for many years. At the *Crown Inn*, a former coaching house, recent restoration has uncovered much half-timber work and a great open fireplace in the dining-room.

From Woodbridge B 1084 runs through a desolate and little visited area of heath and woodland watered by tidal rivers. 9 miles away is **Orford,** a pretty village on the Ore estuary (sea and river angling, wildfowling). Ruins of a Norman *keep* built by Henry II in 1165; Norman chapel and underground dungeons. Fine views from the ramparts. The church has an interesting ruined tower, which collapsed in 1830.

A 12 bypasses Woodbridge and at Ufford is joined by B 1438. — 90 miles: B 1116 forks left for **Framlingham,** 5 miles away (pop. 2100, E.C. Wednesday).

An unspoiled and peaceful little town, dominated by the ruins of the **castle,** which dates mainly from the time of Edward I (gate tower, 15th c.). In the church are tombs of the Howards, Dukes of Norfolk. The *Crown*, a fine old posting inn, contains some splendid old woodwork.

96 miles: *Farnham*. A 1094 forks right for *Aldeburgh-on-Sea*, 5 miles away (pop. 3000, E.C. Wednesday), a quiet seaside resort. On the shore is the half-timbered 16th century *Moot Hall*.

Sea angling in the Alde estuary, river fishing above Snape Bridge, wildfowl shooting on the marshes and mudflats, sailing. In the church are interesting brasses and a memorial to George Crabbe (1754-1832), who was doctor and curate here and described the town in his poem "The Borough", made famous by Benjamin Britten in the opera "Peter Grimes".

98 miles: *Saxmundham* (pop. 1400, E.C. Thursday).

4 miles east on B 1115 is *Leiston*, with the ruins of a church (chapels and cloisters) belonging to a 14th century Premonstratensian abbey. 2 miles farther on (B 1353), on the coast, is

Thorpeness, a seaside resort laid out by a private company in 1913. The *Meare* (60 acres) is a shallow fresh-water lake.

104 miles: *Yoxford*. 3 miles south-east (by B 1122) is *Theberton*. At Theberton Hall was born the explorer Charles Doughty.

Dunwich, on the coast, was once a great town but is now almost completely engulfed by the sea. Many Roman remains have been found here, and in the museum are the seals and maces of the corporation of the town. The ruins of a Franciscan priory hospital and of two earlier churches may be seen in the churchyard of the modern church.

107 miles: Blythburgh.

2 miles west is *Wenhaston:* old church with a 13th century painting on oak of the Last Judgment.

On the coast, 4 miles west, is **Southwold** (pop. 2200, E.C. Wednesday), an attractive little seaside resort on a hill rising gently from the Blyth valley. Beautiful 15th century *church* (Perpendicular), with carved and painted pulpit of the period, three altarpieces painted on a plaster base, St George on a 14th century walnut chest and *Jack the Smiter*, in armour of the period of the Wars of the Roses. In High St is *Southerland House* (17th c.), with moulded ceilings and oak beams. *Museum* in Victoria St (archaeology, natural history, prints and photographs of the town). 1½ miles south is the charming fishing village of *Walberswick*, a great favourite with artists.

108 miles: *Henham*, with a magnificent rhododendron walk. — 110 miles: *Wangford*. — 113 miles: *Wrentham*. On the coast, 2 miles east, is *Covehithe*, a seaside village with the ruins of a fine old church. — 117 miles: *Kessingland*.

121 miles: **Lowestoft** (pop. 48,000, E.C. Thursday), an important fishing port and an agreeable resort. North of the harbour is the old town. From the High St the *Scores*, narrow lanes, run down to the beach. The fish markets are 63 acres in extent and have 5800

feet of quays. Near the Town Hall, in the *Sparrow's
Nest*, are a museum and summer theatre.

The *South Beach*, with an esplanade and two piers (1300 ft
and 760 ft) and with good sands, is the holiday resort proper.
One of the many parks is Normanston Park, in which is the
wildfowl sanctuary of Leathesham.

Ness Point, most easterly point of England, is at the end
of the Denes, an expanse of turf-covered sand. The lighthouse
is 123 feet high. (Visiting: weekdays, 9 a.m. to sunset.)

123 miles: 1 mile west is *Blundeston*, considered to
be the birthplace of David Copperfield. — 126 miles:
Hopton.

127½ miles: We enter **Norfolk,** a flat and fertile
region, famous for its windmills, its cornfields, its
fine old churches, its fishing ports and the 200 miles
of inland waterways known as the *Norfolk Broads*.

129 miles: *Gorleston-on-Sea*, part of Yarmouth.

4 miles west, at the junction of the Yare and Waveney rivers,
stand the ruins of Burgh Castle, a Romano-British fort on the
Saxon Shore, called *Garianonum*.

131 miles: **Great Yarmouth,** (pop. 52,000, E.C.
Thursday), one of the most important fishing ports
in the country, famous for its herrings, bloaters and
kippers, and also one of the most popular seaside resorts on the east coast. It is situated on the River Yare
at its confluence with the Bure.

Marine Parade nearly 5 miles long. At No. 25 is a *Maritime
Museum*. The old town still has many ancient buildings, including the picturesque *Rows* which lead from South Quay
to Middle Gate St, some of them only 3 feet wide. The 14th
century *Tollhouse*, once the gaol, is now a museum. Nearby
are the ruins of the 13th century Greyfriars cloisters. Parts
of the old town walls can be seen, including the interesting
south-east gate. In Church Plain, near the Market Place, are
the picturesque *Fishermen's Almhouses* (1702) and the church

of **St Nicholas,** the largest parish church in the country. It dates from 1119, but the oldest parts are the partly Norman tower (fine view) and the Transitional nave (1190). The *library* contains old books and manuscripts. On the South Denes is the *Nelson Monument*, a Doric column 114 feet high. On South Quay is an *Elizabethan Museum* (open 10 to 1 and 2 to 5). Boat trips up the Bure to the Broads and up the Yare to Norwich, starting from South Quay.

Near *Caister-on-Sea*, a small seaside resort 2 miles north, are the ruins of Caister Castle (15th c.), brick-built and surrounded by a moat.

26. THE NORFOLK COAST
FROM GREAT YARMOUTH TO KING'S LYNN

3 miles: *Caister-on-Sea.* — 4½ miles: *"First and Last" Inn*, where A 149 forks left for the inland route to Cromer. B 1159 keeps to the coast, east of the Norfolk Broads, to (8½ miles) *Winterton-on-Sea.* —12 miles: *Horsey.* Nearby *Horsey Mere* is a good centre for excursions on the Broads.

Horsey Estate (National Trust) comprises 1736 acres including Horsey Mere (120 acres), marshes and marram (a further 600 acres) and *Horsey Hall* with its farmland. Horsey Hall is not open to the public, but there is access to the mere by boat, and restricted access to the marshlands for naturalists. It is of great interest as a breeding ground for birds, plants and insects of marshland.

16 miles: *Palling.* — 22 miles: *Happisburgh* (pronounced Haizboro), at one end of the sea cliffs. Perpendicular church with a massive square tower. — 25 miles: *Bacton.* At this little seaside village are the ruins of the Cluniac Bromholme Priory (St Andrew's), which was founded in 1113 as a cell of Castle Acre Priory. — 27 miles: *Paston.* — 29 miles: *Mundesley-on-Sea*, a pleasant and quiet seaside resort with good bathing from the sands. From Mundesley A 148 continues along the coast to Cromer via *Trimingham*, where the cliffs rise to 300 feet. *Sidestrand* and *Overstrand*, villages which are now almost part of Cromer.

36 miles: **Cromer** (pop. 5000, E.C. Wednesday), a delightful holiday resort situated in a pretty valley bounded by some of the finest scenery in Norfolk. At the foot of the cliffs,which vary in height from 60 to 200 feet, are firm smooth sands. Behind the town are miles of woodland and heath.

The Perpendicular *church* (1387, restored) is a fine example
of the stone and flint masonry common in Norfolk. The tower
is 160 feet high.

2 miles inland, on A 148 to Holt, are the remains of an old
Roman camp, the highest point in Norfolk and a local beauty
spot. From the top (250 ft) of the hill there are fine views.

A 149 from Cromer is one of the most beautiful
roads in the country, particularly between Cromer
and Hunstanton.

40 miles: *Sheringham* (pop. 4500, E.C. Wednesday),
at the western extremity of the cliffs, an agreeable
and fashionable resort with a golf course. — 43 miles:
Weybourne. — 47 miles: *Cley-next-the-Sea* (pop. 2500),
a small town with an interesting church. — 48 miles:
Blakeney (pop. 700).

To the north is *Blakeney Point*, a shingled spit (1100 acres:
National Trust), of great interest, especially at nesting time,
for its birds, including the Sandwich tern, which are carefully
preserved in this sanctuary. Blakeney itself is a small but
extremely picturesque port. The church has a fine English
chancel, and there are the remains of a 13th century monastery.
Marshland and dunes.

53 miles: *Stiffkey*, one of the most charming villages
on this coast.

56½ miles: *Wells-next-the-Sea* (pop. 2250, E.C.
Thursday), a picturesque little port with a fairly large
harbour, quaint old streets and interesting houses.

58 miles: **Holkham** (pop. 340, E.C. Thursday), a
very beautiful model village on the sand dunes. Wildfowling, duck, widgeon and partridge shooting.

Holkham Hall (18th c.), seat of the Earl of Leicester, is beautifully decorated and furnished, with a picture gallery; magnificent
gardens. Open on Tuesdays in summer 2 to 5.

59 miles: B 1155 forks left for Burnham Overy (2 miles) and Burnham Market.

At *Burnham Overy* is the Mill, an attractive group of red brick buildings round the mill stream, consisting of the three-storied mill and maltings (c. 1795), the Mill House and 3 cottages standing in grounds. (No admission to interior). — *Burnham Market* (pop. 1100, E.C. Wednesday). There are in all six other Burnhams, including (2 miles south-east) Burnham Thorpe, birthplace of Nelson, which has a bust of the Admiral and a lectern made of timber from the "Victory".

61 miles: *Overy Staithe*, with a sandy beach. — 66 miles: *Brancaster* (pop. 980), a small village in the marshes, site of the Roman *Brandodunum*, a Saxon Shore fort. To the north is the island of *Scolt Head* (National Trust), 800 acres of dunes, salt-marshes and shingle: bird sanctuary (terns) and nature reserve, with interesting marine flora.

63 miles: **Hunstanton** (pop. 4000, E.C. Thursday), a resort on the shores of the Wash. There is excellent bathing from good sands, and a bathing pool. The cliffs to the north rise in layers of white, red, and brown to 80 feet and descend to the dunes and the little village of Old Hunstanton.

To the east is *St Mary's Church* (13th c.), with fine brasses of the Le Strange family (16th c.) and a Norman font.

66 miles: *Heacham*. In the church is a monument to Pocahontas, the Indian princess (the "Nonpareil of Virginia" of Thackeray's "Virginians") who became the wife of John Rolfe.

68 miles: *Snettisham*, with a fine Gothic church (tall steeple 190 ft high, interesting tombstones).

70 miles: *Dersingham* (13th c. church).

2 miles south on B 1440 is **Sandringham House,** country home of the royal family. The house, in neo-Tudor style, was built in 1862 by Edward VII, then Prince of Wales. The gardens and park are magnificent, with a row of coniferous trees bearing the names of the various distinguished people who planted them. Open Wednesdays and Thursdays in summer when the royal family is not in residence. Many royal memorials in Sandringham church.

74 miles: **Castle Rising,** formerly a flourishing port, now some distance inland. Norman *church* with fine west front. Ruins of a Norman *castle* with a 12th century keep. *Bede House* (1614), almshouses in Elizabethan style (brick-built), still containing their Jacobean furniture. The residents still wear red cloaks and beaver hats of the period when going to church.

82 miles: **King's Lynn** (pop. 28,000, E.C. Wednesday), an ancient borough and sea port belonging in Saxon times to the Bishop of Thetford. In the 12th century the town was extended by Bishop Turbe and granted a Tuesday market, as well as the Saturday market which was the privilege of the older town. *Saturday Market Place* and *Tuesday Market Place* still remain today. Henry VIII granted a new charter to the town, one of the kingdom's chief ports, which thereupon became known as King's Lynn.

One of the most interesting buildings is the *Custom House,* built in the 17th century as an Exchange by Henry Bell, who also built the fine *Duke's Head Hotel:* in the lounge are carvings by the sculptor who also did the carvings over the Custom House windows. In mediaeval days Lynn had important shipyards; in the 19th century two wet docks were added to the port. *St Margaret's Church* has some Norman work at the west end and outside the south tower. At the west end are two towers and the foundations of a central tower.

The nave was destroyed in 1741 but immediately rebuilt. The pillars rest on 13th century foundations, and there is good carving of the same period in the choir and on the walls. In the choir are two of the largest brasses in England (Flemish work, 14th c.); that of Robert Braunche depicts the "peacock feast" he gave in honour of Edward III. On the west side of the south tower is a clock showing the phases of the moon.

In the Walks is the *Red Mount Chapel* (late 15th century) an octagonal building. On the ground floor is the chapel, on the first floor the priest's living quarters, and on the top floor a rich cruciform chapel. The *Walks* are a public park built in 1753 on the site of the ancient ramparts.

Another of the handsome buildings of the town is the **Guildhall,** formerly the hall of the Holy Trinity Guild and now the Town Hall. It is a two-gabled building with chequer-work in flint and freestone. Items of interest to be seen here are *King John's Cup* (14th c., English enamel-work), a sword which belonged to King John and municipal charters. (For admission apply to the doorkeeper).

In King's St is **St George's Guildhall** (1406), used from Tudor times as a theatre. Shakespeare's company played here. (Apply within for admission). There are many old houses in the town — several half-timbered houses in Chapel St, and in Margaret's Lane half-timbered warehouses. *St Mary Magdalen's* in Gaywood Road is a 12th century group of almshouses destroyed during the 16th century and rebuilt in 1649.

In Market St is the *Borough Museum:* local antiquities, ethnographical, prehistoric and natural history exhibits. In Bridge St is the *Greenland Fishery Museum*, housed in an old merchant's house dated 1505: local antiquities.

Alternative Route from Cromer to King's Lynn by the Direct Road, A 148.

9 miles: *Holt*. — 22 miles: **Fakenham** (pop. 3000, E.C. Wednesday), which dates from the Anglo-Saxon period. The *parish church* (SS. Peter and Paul) has a tower 150 feet high, a well-known landmark. The north porch (Early English) is 200 years older than the church itself.

5 miles north on B 1105 is *Little Walsingham*, with the much visited shrine of Our Lady of Walsingham. Abbey and old priory (open to visitors on Wednesdays and public holidays). Some of the interesting old houses in the village were lodgings for pilgrims. In the church is a fine font (Font of the Seven Sacraments). — 2 miles beyond, still on B 1105, is *Wighton*, with an old earthwork known as *Crabbe's Castle*. B 1105 then continues to (3 miles) *Wells-next-the-Sea* (p. 536).

28 miles: *Harpley*. 35 miles: *Hillington*. 40 miles: *South Wootton*. 43 miles: **King's Lynn** (see above).

27. LONDON TO CAMBRIDGE, ELY AND KING'S LYNN

56 miles to Cambridge, 72 miles to Ely, 100 miles to King's Lynn. From Hyde Park Corner, take the East Carriageway in the Park (running parallel to Park Lane) and at Grosvenor Gate turn right across Park Lane into Upper Grosvenor St. Then turn left into Park St, cross Oxford St and Portman Square, and follow Gloucester Place to Park Road. Continue, bearing left, into Wellington Road and Finchley Road, and at Swiss Cottage station bear right into College Crescent and Fitzjohns Avenue for Hampstead. Then straight ahead into Heath St, and at Whitestone Pond bear right into Spaniards Road, then left into Bishop's Avenue for East Finchley. Bear left into North Finchley High Road, and in about a mile turn right into the North Circular Road. This continues north-east and east, with minor changes of direction and some changes of name, and crosses the main road to Cambridge (A 10). Soon afterwards, at the end of Silver St, turn left into A 1010 (Fore St), which runs north to join A 10 beyond Waltham Cross.

15 miles: *Waltham Cross*, with one of the "Eleanor crosses" erected by Edward I at the places where the funeral procession of his wife Queen Eleanor halted on its way from Harby in Nottinghamshire to Westminster (see p. 150). Across the river Lea and the canal to the east is Waltham Abbey. — 16 miles: *Cheshunt*. — 20 miles: *Broxbourne*. Nearby is the famous public school, Haileybury College. — 21 miles: *Hoddesdon* (pop. 15,000, E.C. Thursday). A 602 forks left to (4 miles) Hertford.

24¾ miles: *Ware* (pop. 12,000, E.C. Thursday). — 31 miles: *Puckeridge*. — 35 miles: *Buntingford*. — 42 miles: *Royston* (pop. 9000, E.C. Thursday). The *church of St John the Baptist* is an interesting old building. Near the post office is *King James's Cave*, with curious carvings and 13th century bas-reliefs.

The road enters Cambridgeshire.   56 miles: **Cambridge.**

Cambridge, seat of one of the two ancient universities of England, lies in a loop of the little river Cam.   Which is the more beautiful, Oxford or Cambridge, is a subject for eternal debate, but certainly some of the Cambridge colleges are of a loveliness second to none, and Cambridge has the advantage of its famous "Backs" — the wide lawns stretching in gracious tranquillity from behind the colleges to the willow-fringed banks of the little river.

CAMBRIDGE

The town on the Cam has a history reaching back many centuries as a border town on the edge of the Fens.   Lying an the direct route from London to the port of Lynn (now King's Lynn), it must have been a considerable trading centre in the Middle Ages.   It is not known with certainty how the University came into being, but it is believed that travelling scholars sponsored by the great Fenland monasteries and their daughter houses in Cambridge settled in the town and founded schools, which were formally recognised in the reign of Henry II (1217).   The first college was founded in 1284. In 1318 Pope John XXII recognised Cambridge as a *Studium generale*, the mediaeval equivalent of a university.   The first professorial chairs were established in the 16th century.   The colleges strongly resisted control by the University, but in recent years the role of the University authorities has increased, and the last sixty years have seen much new building by the University.

The relationship between the University and the colleges is not always easy to understand.   The University — which existed before the colleges — lays down degree programmes and grants degrees.   It is headed by a Chancellor and Vice-Chancellor, a Senate composed of all masters of arts, and an executive body called Regent House made up of holders of senior teaching posts.   The colleges were originally no more than students' lodgings, but took on teaching functions and came to supply most of the teaching staff, so that membership of a college became a requirement for admission to the University.   The development of scientific studies, involving expenditure beyond the means of the colleges, has enhanced the position of the

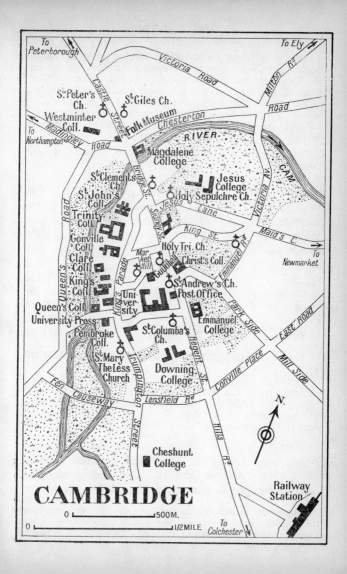

To Peterborough

To Ely

Victoria Road

Mitton Rd

Road

Castle Street

St. Peter's Ch.

St. Giles Ch.

Westminter Coll.

Folk Museum

Chesterton

To Northampton

Madingley Road

RIVER.

Magdalene College

CAM

St. Clements Ch.

Bridge St.

Jesus College

St. John's Coll.

Holy Sepulchre Ch.

Victoria Av.

Trinity Coll.

Jesus Lane

Sidney St.

Gonville Coll.

King St.

Maid's C.

Clare Coll.

Holy Tri. Ch.

Emmanuel Rd

To Newmarket

Road

Queen's Road

King's Coll.

Market Hill

Christ's Coll.

Guildhall

St. Andrew's Ch.

Queen's Coll.

King's Parade

University

Post Office

Park Side

University Press

St. Columba's Ch.

Emmanuel College

East Road

Pembroke Coll.

Regent St.

S. Mary The Less Church

Downing College

Conville Place

Mill Side

Fen Causeway

Trumpington Street

Lensfield Rd

Hills Rd

N.

Cheshunt College

Railway Station

CAMBRIDGE

0 ⸻ 500M.

0 ⸻ 1/2MILE

To Colchester

University in recent years, but the colleges are still powerful bodies, often well endowed financially. Relationships between the University and the colleges are, however, close: the Vice-Chancellor of the University is elected annually by the Masters of the colleges, and the proctors who are responsible for University discipline are supplied annually in rotation by the colleges. (See Ruth Mellanby's useful little guide, "Cambridge in One Day", published by Heffers).

The following are the 23 *colleges*, with the date of their foundation:

Peterhouse	1284	Magdalene	1542
Clare	1326	Trinity	1546
Pembroke	1347	Emmanuel	1584
Gonville and Caius	1348	Sidney Sussex	1596
Trinity Hall	1350	Downing	1800
Corpus Christi	1352	Girton	1869
King's	1441	Newnham	1871
Queens'	1448	Selwyn	1882
St Catharine's	1473	Fitzwilliam House	1869
Jesus	1496	New Hall	1954
Christ's	1505	Churchill	1960
St John's	1511		

The centre of the town is Market Place or **Market Hill.**

On the south side is the *Guildhall* (1939). On the west side is the church of *St Mary the Great* (Perpendicular, 1478-1608), 140 feet long by 65 feet wide. To the south of this church, in Peas Hill, is *St Edward's Church* (12th c. tower, pulpit of 1510).

West of Market Hill, on the far side of King's Parade and Trinity St, is the **Senate House** (Gibbs, 1730), with fine woodwork, used for ceremonial occasions (open in summer 3.30 to 4.30).

Behind the Senate House are the *Old Schools* (originally used for teaching purposes), which now accommodate University offices. The present buildings were erected between 1758 and 1840.

Taking the narrow lane which runs west along the north side of the Senate House, we pass on the right *Caius College*, founded in 1348 by Edward Gonville, Vicar General of the diocese of Ely, and re-founded in 1559 by Dr Caius, Edward VI's physician (see below). We then bear left past *Trinity Hall* (founded in 1350 by William Bateman, Bishop of Norwich) and *Clare College* (founded 1326) to enter the precincts of **King's College,** with the entrance to the magnificent *King's College Chapel* immediately to the left.

King's College is the oldest of Cambridge's royal foundations, having been founded by Henry VI in 1440, at almost the same time as Eton College (p. 477). Among its members have been Sir Robert Walpole, his son Horace Walpole and, in more recent times, John Maynard Keynes.

King's College Chapel has the finest fan vaulting in England. It was begun in 1446 and completed in 1515. It is 290 feet long, 40 feet wide and 80 feet high. There are 25 great windows with glass (except for the modern glass at the west end) dating from the 16th century. The organ screen dates from 1532-36 and the lower part of the stalls from the same period. From the top of the tower there are splendid views.

The rest of the college buildings date from the 18th century or later.

At the south end of King's Parade, in Benet St, is *St Benet's Church*, with one of the finest Saxon towers in the country. The nave was rebuilt in its present form in the 13th century. The rest of the building is 19th century. **Corpus Christi College** was founded in 1352 by the guilds of Corpus Christi and St Mary. The front court and west front date from the 19th century, but the splendid *Old Court* (restored 1919) to the north still remains much as it was first built.

In the chapel (1579) are some 16th century French glass and stalls from the earlier chapel. The library (to the right of the entrance) contains one of the richest collections of **manu-scripts** in England, including the bequests of Matthew Parker, Archbishop of Canterbury (1559-75). There are manuscripts of the 10th, 11th and later centuries, two books by Caxton and another by the first Cambridge printer, Siberch. Among distinguished members of the college were Marlowe and Fletcher, the Elizabethan dramatists.

On the opposite side of Trumpington St is *St Catharine's College*, founded in 1473 but re-built in the 17th century. The fine chapel dates from 1704. Silver St leads west to *Queens' College* (behind St Catharine's College), founded in 1448 under the patronage of Mary of Anjou, wife of Henry VI and refounded by Elizabeth Woodville, wife of Edward IV.

Through the handsome vaulted gateway with its four turrets is a First Court of red brick, built soon after the foundation, in which are the *Hall* (restored), *Library* and *Old Chapel*, which is now used as a lecture room and library. To the left is the picturesque *Cloister Court* (c. 1460) north of which is the half-timbered **President's Lodge** (16th c.). Beyond the south cloister is the small Pump Court. In 1510-13 Erasmus was professor of Greek here, and tradition has it that he occupied the rooms adjoining the south-west corner. *Walnut Tree Court*, dating from 1618, is to the north-east of the principal court.

The *New Chapel* on the north side was built in the 19th century.

There is an attractive view of the river from the pretty little bridge to the west of the college, the "Mathematicians' Bridge". On the way back, note the sundial on the north wall of the first court.

Now return to Silver St, on the south side of which is the Cambridge University Press. On the river is a landing-stage for boats. To the south is the Garden House Hotel.

Going back (east) along Silver St, we come into Trumpington St. A little way south, at its junction with Pembroke St, is **Pembroke College,** founded by the Countess of Pembroke in 1347 but almost completely rebuilt since then.

The *Old Chapel* (14th c.) is all that remains of the original building. The *New Chapel* (1663) was one of Wren's first works and one of the first classical-style buildings in England. *Hitcham's Building* and the adjoining cloister are 17th century; all the rest of the buildings of Pembroke are modern. Distinguished former members of Pembroke have included William Pitt, Edmund Spenser and Thomas Gray.

On the other side of Trumpington St, to the west, are **Peterhouse College** and the *church of St Mary the Less*.

The church (clumsily restored) dates from 1352, and for 350 years served as the college chapel. To the west of the churchyard is the Museum of Classical Archaeology, with casts of classical sculpture and a fine library of standard works on art and archaeology.

Farther south is **Peterhouse College,** founded in 1280 by Hugh of Belsham, Bishop of Ely, and moved to this site in 1284. It is the oldest college in Cambridge and despite additions the buildings still retain sufficient of the original style to display the stages through which the college passed to arrive at the present quadrangular arrangement.

Christopher Wren's uncle was Master of Peterhouse in 1632, when the present chapel was built. In the Hall and Combination Room is stained glass by William Morris. Lord Kelvin was a member of the college.

Beyond Peterhouse is the **Fitzwilliam Museum,** built with a legacy of £100,000 from the seventh Viscount Fitzwilliam to house the splendid art collection he had assembled. The classical façade is the masterpiece of George Basevi, who was selected as architect after a competition (1835).

The Museum contains pictures, sculpture, tapestries, Egyptian antiquities, coins, pottery, china, etc. The *Library* has original scores by Bach, Blow, Handel, Purcell and other composers.

Among the chief treasures on display are a jade buffalo of the Han dynasty (206 B.C. to 220 A.D.), a copy of a statue by Franz Anton Bustelli (1760), pictures by *Constable*, a portrait of G.B. Shaw by Augustus John, a number of valuable manuscripts including Keats's "Ode to a Nightingale", and pictures by Italian (Titian, Veronese), Dutch (Rembrandt) and French (Corot, Renoir, Degas) masters.

Pembroke St, opening off Trumpington St next Pembroke College, runs into Downing St, in which is a group of laboratories and museums, including the famous *Cavendish Physical Laboratory*, the Archaeological and Ethnological Museum, the Museum of Geology and the Museum of the History of Science (mostly open 2 to 4).

Opposite the end of Downing St is *Emmanuel College*, founded in 1584 by Walter Mildmay, Chancellor of the Exchequer, who adapted the buildings of a 13th century Dominican priory on the site. In the front court stands the chapel, designed in 1666 by Christopher Wren. There is a window in commemoration of John Harvard, who founded Harvard University in America.

Turning left along St Andrew's St, passing the Post Office on the left, we come to **Christ's College** (on right).

Originally founded in 1436 as Godshouse, on the site now occupied by King's College Chapel, it was moved to its present position in 1446. Sixty years later, now called Christ's College, it was enlarged by Margaret Beaufort, Countess of Richmond and Derby and mother of Henry VII. The buildings round the First Court were erected before the foundress's death and incorporate parts of the old Godshouse College. The chapel is pre-Reformation. The rest of the buildings date from the 18th century. Among distinguished members of the College have been Milton, Philip Sidney, Darwin and Gen. Smuts.

Along Sidney St (the continuation of St Andrew's St), on the left, is Holy Trinity Church (14th and 15th c.).

At the end of Sidney St, on the right, is *Sidney Sussex College,* founded in 1589 by a bequest of Lady Frances Sidney, Countess of Sussex. This was the second college to be founded after the Reformation. The buildings date from 1598 (altered in 1832 by Jeffry Wyatt). In 1602 the former refectory was converted into a chapel, which was altered in 1912. Oliver Cromwell was a student here, and there is an interesting portrait of him in the hall. The gardens are very fine.

To the north-east of Jesus Lane is **Jesus College,** founded by John Alcock, Bishop of Ealing, in the Benedictine nunnery of St Radegund which was suppressed in 1496. It is entered by a fine tower gateway, which originally led into the nunnery garden. The *chapel* (Early English) was the nunnery church, but most of the nave has been demolished. There is some Norman work in the crypt, and the *Chapter House* doorway is particularly fine. Among members of the college have been Coleridge and Sterne.

Bridge St continues to the **church of the Holy Sepulchre,** one of the four round churches in England. It was built in about 1130 (restored 1841). At the end of Bridge St is a bridge over the Cam.

On the other side of the bridge is **Magdalene College** (pronounced Maudlen) the only college on the west bank of the river. It was founded in 1542 by Lord Audley of Walden to replace Buckingham College, a hostel for Benedictine monks dating from 1428. In the Second Court is the beautiful 17th century **Pepysian Library,** which contains the library bequeathed by Samuel Pepys in 1724 and the shorthand manuscript of his diary. One of the new buildings, Benson Court, was designed by Sir Edward Lutyens.

Beyond Magdalene College stand the churches of *St Giles* (with Norman chancel arch) and *St Peter's-by-the-Castle,* rebuilt in 1718. *Castle Hill* (right) is an artificial mound on which there stood the keep of a castle built by William the Conqueror in 1068; to the north can be seen the line of the ramparts and moat. At 2 Castle St is a *Folk Museum*.

From the round church St John's St leads south to **St John's College,** one of the most beautiful in Cambridge, founded under the will of Lady Margaret Beaufort in 1511. The two-storeyed college gateway, with four turrets, is the finest gateway tower in Cambridge.

The *chapel* dates from 1869 (Sir George Gilbert Scott), but the interior is older. The mellow brickwork of the **Second Court** (late 16th c.) makes it one of the most beautiful in Cambridge. On the south wall is a monument to Wordsworth. The *Hall*, enlarged by Scott (1865), on the west side of the court, has the original panelling and hammerbeam roof. The Combination Room is one of the finest panelled galleries in England. Good portraits. In the Third Court is the Jacobean *Old Library* (1628), with its original layout and bookcases. From this court we reach the picturesque *"Bridge of Sighs"*, with a beautiful view of the Cam. To the left, through the gardens, is the *Old Bridge* (1696-1712). The river front of the college is very fine.

Famous "Johnians" have included Wordsworth (who describes his rooms in the "Prelude"), William Wilberforce and Samuel Butler. The college boat club (the Lady Margaret Boat Club) is said to have given the word "blazer" (from the brilliant scarlet colour of their jackets) to the English language.

Farther down St John's St, on the right, is **Trinity College,** founded in 1546 by Henry VIII, who amalgamated King's Hall (founded in 1336 by Edward III), Michael House (founded in 1323) and several hostels.

Trinity College, with 800 students, is the largest of the colleges. The *entrance gateway* is magnificent, with rich ornamentation; in the central niche is a statue of the founder. The *Great Court* within is 334 feet by 228 feet and contains on the right the **chapel** (1564), whose fittings date from the early 18th century; there are many interesting monuments. King Edward's

Gate to the west (rebuilt here 1600) is opposite Queen's Gate (1597). The *Hall* (1604-1608) is a copy of the hall of the Middle Temple, London. Tradition has it that Field Marshal Lord Montgomery's father was the first man to jump up all the steps in a single bound (1866). Famous members of the college have included Newton, Byron, Fitzgerald, Macaulay and Thackeray.

The next college is **Caius** (pronounced Keys), founded in 1348 by Edmund Gonville. It was moved to its present site in 1351 and re-founded in 1557 by Dr John Caius, court physician. Its full name is *Gonville and Caius College.*

The *Gate of Humility*, now removed to the Master's Garden, was once the entrance to the college through which students passed. A second vaulted gateway, the *Gate of Virtue*, gives access to the undergraduates' rooms in Caius Court. The *Gate of Honour* leads to the old examination rooms. Among members of the college have been Judge Jeffreys and Jeremy Taylor.

Behind, at the end of Senate House Passage to the west, is **Trinity Hall,** founded by William Bateman, Bishop of Norwich, in 1350. It is the only college in Cambridge which still retains the name of Hall (Aula) and is popularly known as "The Hall". The library is a delightful Elizabethan building of mellow red brick with step-gables; the original locks and bars which once chained the books to the bookcases can still be seen.

To the south is **Clare College,** second oldest college in Cambridge, founded by the University and re-founded in 1338 by Lady Elizabeth de Clare as Clare Hall. In the 16th and 17th centuries the present magnificent buildings were erected; note the very fine ironwork of the college gates (1714).

In the chapel, above the altar (1769), is a painting of the *Annunciation* by Cipriani. The hall has a fine ceiling and chimney-piece. The very attractive *Clare Bridge* (1640) across the Cam has a curious decoration of spheres on either side. The New Court, beyond Queens Road, was designed by Sir Giles Gilbert Scott (1924-35).

Farther west, in Burrell's Walk, is the imposing *University Library* (Sir Giles Gilbert Scott, 1931-34), with a main front 420 feet long and a tower 160 feet high.

Other Features of Interest

Downing College (1800) is housed in modern buildings in a park. There are also *Selwyn College* (1882) and *Girton College*, established for women students at Hitchin in 1869 and moved to Cambridge in 1873, and *Newnham College*, also for women students (established 1871, transferred to its present site in 1875).

In Huntingdon Road are two of Cambridge's younger colleges — **Fitzwilliam College**, founded in 1869, which moved in 1968 to its present modern buildings, and **New Hall,** a women's college founded in 1954 (refectory with a huge concrete dome and barrel-vaulted library built in 1967).

Also in this north-western part of Cambridge (Madingley Road, with entrance from Storey's Way) is **Churchill College,** which specialises in scientific and technological research. In front of the college is a piece of sculpture by Henry Moore. To the west is an observatory (open 8 to 12 on the first Saturday of the month).

The *Backs*. Queen's Road, which runs behind the colleges on the west bank of the Cam, offers attractive views of the college lawns. An even pleasanter way to see them is from a boat on the river.

In Lensfield Road, which goes off on the left at the end of Trumpington St, is the *Scott Polar Research Institute*, with an interesting museum (open 2 to 4, except Saturdays and Sundays).

South from Trumpington St on the London road are the **Botanic Gardens** (40 acres), laid out in 1847. The glasshouses, second only in importance to those of Kew (p. 235), are open to the public in the afternoon.

Farther south are *Trumpington* (13th c. church with a very early brass) and *Grantchester*, a pretty little village remembered for its association with Rupert Brooke.

To the east of Cambridge, at *Cherry Hinton*, is a fine 13th century church (sculpture).

To the north-east, just beyond the railway bridge on the outskirts of the town, is *Stourbridge Chapel*, built in 1120 as the chapel of a leperhouse. A little farther along the same road is the church of *St Andrew the Less*, also known as the *Abbey Church* (13th c.). To the north of the road, approaching Newmarket, is *Swaffham Prior* (church and windmills).

Cambridge to Colchester: 48 miles on A 604.

8 miles: *Great Abington*. — 11 miles: *Linton*. — 18 miles: *Haverhill*. — 27 miles: *Great Yeldham*. The road follows the valley of the Colne. — 30½ miles: *Sible Hedingham* (pop. 3000, E.C. Saturday). There are charming houses in Swan St, the entrance to the village. North-east (1 mile on B 1058), at *Hedingham* are the ruins of a Norman castle with a fine keep. — 34 miles: *Halsted*. Little Maplestead (to the north) has one of the only four round churches in the country. — 37½ miles: *Earls Colne*, in the wide Colne valley. — 48 miles: **Colchester** (p. 524).

From Cambridge A 10 continues over flat country and soon swings left to join the route of the old Roman road, *Akeman Street*.

68 miles: *Stretham*.

72 miles: **Ely** (pop. 20,000, E.C. Tuesday). The "Island City of the Fens" stands on the margin of the Fenlands on a slight hill formerly surrounded by water, so that as one approaches the town across the flat countryside the graceful and harmonious lines of Ely Cathedral are seen against the sky.

The written history of the Fenlands begins in the 8th century, when St Etheldreda, Queen of Northumbria, withdrew from the world and founded an abbey on an island in the fens. Her church was destroyed by the Danes in 870, but a hundred years later St Dunstan founded a new church and a Benedictine monastery. A small settlement grew up round the monastery, and it was in the "Isle of Ely" that Hereward the Wake offered the last Saxon resistance to the Norman invaders. In 1083 William the Conqueror appointed Simeon, brother of Bishop

Walkelin of Winchester, as abbot, and thereafter the building of the great Cathedral was begun. The monastery became the seat of a bishop in 1109.

Ely Cathedral. The "Monarch of the Fens", as this great building is called, is remarkable for its size and magnificence. The central tower, a fine octagon in Decorated style (1328), replaced the original tower, which collapsed in 1322. The Lady Chapel was added between 1321 and 1349, and the Perpendicular chantries adjoining the retro-choir between 1486 and 1550. Towards the end of the 14th century the massive west tower (270 ft) was built to harmonise with the magnificent central octagon. In the 19th century the Cathedral was restored by Sir George Gilbert Scott. The Cathedral, harmonious despite its mingling of styles, is the third longest church in England (537 ft), and its situation in the midst of dead flat country is such that from wherever it may be approached it stands out like "a great solitary ship at sea". Its great length can best be appreciated when approached from the south but from all sides can be appreciated the beauty of the Octagon and lantern ("the crown of Ely") which in 1322, as today, represented a great feat of architectural and engineering skill.

The entrance is by the *Galilee Porch* at the west end (Early English, c. 1200). Above is the west tower, to the right the south-west transept, and opening off the east aisle, *St Catherine's Chapel* (very beautiful Norman work). To the left a white wall marks the spot where until its collapse in the 14th century stood the north-west transept (although some authorities state that this was never completed). The great length of the *nave* (208 ft) and its 12 Norman bays can best be appreciated from the south aisle; the height of the triforium and clerestory from the nave itself. The original roof was flat, but when the central Octagon was built it was given its present domed form. In the middle of the *south transept* is a *Saxon cross.*

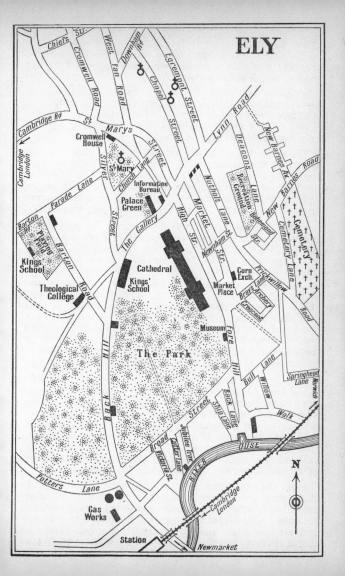

At the end of the transept is the monks' doorway into the cloisters. The glass is modern, with the exception of the last window in the north triforium.

Seen from outside, the **Octagon,** built by Alan de Walsingham, sacrist of the monastery, has the appearance of a dome, and is unique of its kind in England. The lantern which crowns it (140 ft) is a magnificent piece of timber construction, the only example of its type in wood.

There are remains of the original Norman church in the north and south transepts. In the east aisle of the south transept is the *Chapter Library*, and in the corresponding position in the north transept **St Edmund's Chapel** (restored in the 19th c.), which contains a 14th century reredos, a 12th century fresco and *St George's Chapel*, the county war memorial.

Choir. The oak screen between the chapel and the Octagon is modern. The east end (Early English) dates from 1252, the three bays at the west end (Decorated) from the 14th century. The upper row of choir stalls is also 14th century. All the rest of the woodwork is modern. Interesting *monuments:* on right, to Bishops de Luda (1290-98), Barnet (1366-73) and Northwold (1229-54). Interesting old chapels. At the east end of the north aisle is **Bishop Alcock's Chantry,** recently restored with the help of Jesus College, Cambridge (which was founded by Bishop Alcock). At the east end of the south aisle is *Bishop West's Chantry* (1515-34). In the floor of the south aisle is what is believed to be the base of the shrine of St Etheldreda (St Audrey), a place of pilgrimage in the Middle Ages.

The **Lady Chapel** is entered through the north door in the north-east corner of the north transept. For 400 years the Chapel was used as the parish church of Holy Trinity, but reverted to the cathedral in 1938; cleaning and restoration work was undertaken in 1939. This beautiful building dates from 1320-49 and was designed by Alan of Walsingham. Restoration has brought to light much of the beauty of the carving of the roof bosses and the roses which adorn the vaulting.

From the west tower there are magnificent views. South of the nave are the scanty remains of the *cloisters*, but there are still to be seen some interesting remains of the old monastic buildings. These comprise the very beautiful *Ely Porta* or *Walpole Gate* which was the principal gateway to the Benedictine priory and dates from 1396-97; the Guesten Hall, now

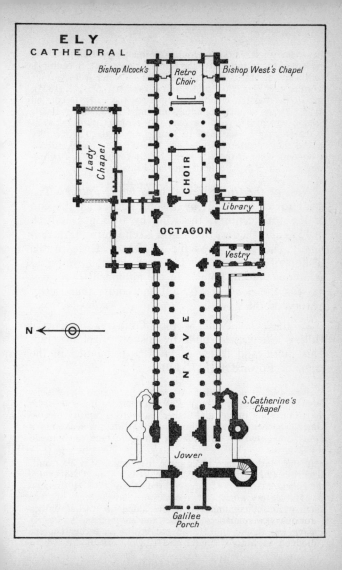

ELY
CATHEDRAL

Bishop Alcock's   Retro Choir   Bishop West's Chapel

Lady Chapel

CHOIR

Library

OCTAGON

Vestry

N A V E

N

S. Catherine's Chapel

Tower

Galilee Porch

the Deanery; the Prior's House (Norman crypt) and part of
the late Norman Infirmary; the Monks' Granary (15th century),
in which was stored the grain brought by water from various
centres; the *Fair Hall* and Prior Crauden's Chapel (1325),
one of the most wonderful examples of the early Decorated
style.   Many of these buildings are now occupied by *King's
School*, which claims to be one of the oldest public schools
in the country by virtue of its foundation in the 11th century
in the monastic seminary where Edward the Confessor was
a student.   One of the best views of Ely Cathedral can be obtained from King's School playing fields.

West of the Cathedral is the *Bishop's Palace*.   The
front tower was built by Bishop Alcock at the end
of the 15th century, the wing by Bishop Goodrich
in 1550 and the rest by Bishop Keene in the 18th century.   The Palace was the official residence of the
Bishop of Ely until the last war, when it was used
as a convalescent home.   In the muniment room can
be seen the *Book of Ely*, a 12th century manuscript
history of the city.

To the east of the Monks' Granary, on Cherry
Hill, is *Ely Castle*, built by Bishop Nigel in 1135.
This motte and bailey castle was dismantled in the
reign of Edward I (1271-1307).

Of the old town itself there are some very interesting remains.
High St, once called *Steeple Row*, still has on the south side
the picturesque plaster-and-timber, early 16th century Steeple
Gate.   Farther along on the south side are the *Goldsmith's
Tower* and *Sacrist's Gate*, dating from the time of Alan de
Walsingham.

In the **Market Place** takes place the annual May Fair and,
since the 12th century, on St Etheldreda's Day, October 17,
the Etheldreda Fair.   The quay at the foot of Fore Hill retains
its 15th century aspect.   In mediaeval times the river was the
chief means of communication and along the various hithes
(or quays) were numerous granaries and warehouses. *St Mary's
Church* was rebuilt in 1215 on the site of an earlier church.
Adjoining St Mary's Churchyard is *Cromwell House*, where

Oliver Cromwell lived 1638-47. To the west are 15th century almshouses. At the west end of *St John's Farm* are two buildings which formed part of the 13th century St John's Hospital.

Around Ely. Ely is a magnificent centre from which to explore the **Fens,** with their 300 miles of navigable waterways. There is pleasant boating on the Cam, the Ouse, the Lark, the Wissey and other rivers. The Fens are noted for the good fishing they offer, and there are four fishing clubs in Ely itself. The very characteristic fenland landscape extends widely to the north of the city, but almost all that is left of the once extensive fens of the Great Level, the Wicken and Burwell Fens (National Trust), to the south-east, is the 730 acres of Wicken, Adventurer's and St Edmund's Fens and Lapwing Hall Farm. During the last war part of Adventurer's Fen became arable land, but the district is now maintained as a bird sanctuary and nature reserve. Rich insect, plant and bird life, with some insects not known elsewhere in England, are to be found here. 3 miles south of Isleham is the *Chippenham Fen* (also National Trust), 125 acres of fenland maintained as a nature reserve. (Visiting: accessible to naturalists by ticket on application to the Zoological Department, Downing St, Cambridge.)

Ely to Newmarket: 13 miles on A 142.

2 miles: *Stuntney*, with the house of Oliver Cromwell. — 6 miles *Soham* (pop. 4750, E.C. Wednesday). — 7 miles: B 1085 (right) leads to *Wicken*, a village to which Richard, son and successor of Oliver Cromwell, retired and where he was buried. Here is also the nature reserve of *Wicken Fen* (see above). 4 miles south is *Swaffham Prior* (p. 576), connected by water with Reach Lode and the Cam. B 1087 continues beyond Wicken to (7 miles) Stretham and (13 miles) *Newmarket*.

77 miles: Littleport, from which A 1101 runs south-east to (14 miles) *Mildenhall* (p. 564). — 81 miles *Brandon Creek*, beyond which the road enters Norfolk. — 83 miles: *Southery*. — 89 miles: *Downham Market* (pop. 2650, E.C. Wednesday). — 100 miles: **King's Lynn** (p. 538).

28. LONDON TO NORWICH

114 miles on A 11. Leave London as in Route 25 to Forest Road and into Woodford New Road, but from there continue straight ahead beyond Woodford Green via Woodford to Epping.

15 miles: *Buckhurst Hill*, the highest point in *Epping Forest*, which extends north from here. A favourite hunting area; good riding in the forest. 20 miles: *Epping* (p. 242).

Epping to Chelmsford: 18 miles on A 122.

A 122 forks right off A 11 half a mile beyond Epping. — 5 miles: *Greensted-juxta-Ongar*, a very interesting little village with the only timber-built Saxon church, *St Andrew's*. The nave is made of planks from two large oak trees. The wooden tower with its shingled belfry dates from the 17th century; the tiled roof and skylight windows replace the original thatched roof. — 7 miles: **Chipping Ongar**, a pleasant little town on the site of an ancient fort above the river Roding. *St Martin's Church* (12th c.) has fine Norman windows and a 15th century tower. Nearby are the remains of an Elizabethan moated building on the site of an earlier castle. Small museum. — 7½ miles: *High Ongar. St Mary's Church*, with a fine Norman porch and an interesting 16th century brass. Six 16th century almshouses. Other old churches in the neighbourhood. — 18 miles: *Chelmsford* (p. 521).

27 miles: *Harlow*, a rapidly developing "new town" (pop. 70,000).

29 miles: *Sawbridgeworth* (pop. 3500, E.C. Thursday). — 33 miles: **Bishop's Stortford** (pop. 20,000, E.C. Wednesday), a small market town. Birthplace of Cecil Rhodes (museum). Church, with fine stalls. Famous Grammar School.

3 miles east is beautiful **Hatfield Forest** (National Trust), formerly part of the Essex royal forests: over 1000 acres of hilly woodland, with some magnificent trees. Old fort on

Portingbury Hills. Lake (boating and fishing). Access from Bush End and Woodside Green. Ruins of Waytemore Castle.

Bishop's Stortford to Colchester: 32 miles (A 120 to Marks Tey, then A 12).

A 120 follows the course of the old Roman Stane Street along the north of Hatfield Forest (see above). 9 miles: *Great Dunmow* and *Little Dunmow* (pop. 3300, E.C. Wednesday), famous for its "flitch of bacon" trial on Easter Monday. The trial is of married couples who claim to be perfectly happy together. To the east, near *Felsted*, are the ruins of Dunmow Abbey. Trout fishing in the Chelmer and the Roding. — 17 miles: *Barintree* (pop. 15,600, E.C. Wednesday). — 23 miles: **Coggeshall** (pop. 2700, E.C. Wednesday). There is an interesting old church, and at Little Coggeshall (south on B 1024) are the ruins of Coggeshall Abbey. There is also the lovely gabled *Paycocke's House*, a merchant's house, richly ornamented, dating from about 1500; exceptionally fine panelling and wood-carving. 32 miles: *Colchester* (p. 524).

11 miles north-east on B 1051 is the charming village of **Thaxted,** with old houses, a 15th century Guildhall and the 16th century church of St John the Baptist.

36 miles: *Stansted Mountfitchet*. — 42 miles: *Newport*. — 44 miles: B 1052 goes off on the right for Saffron Walden. — 45½ miles: **Audley End,** where another road goes off to Saffron Walden (1 mile).

Audley End takes its name from Sir Thomas Audley, Speaker of the House of Commons from 1529 to 1535, when the legislation for the dissolution of the monasteries was passed. As a mark of gratitude Henry VIII granted him Walden Abbey. Of the house he built after demolishing the monastery nothing now remains. — The present mansion was built in two stages — in the early 17th century (Great Hall, with magnificent woodwork) and from 1721 onwards, by Vanbrugh and Robert Adam (state apartments). The neo-Gothic chapel was added in 1786. Splendid *furniture* (including a fine clock by Boulle) and pictures by van Goyen, Canaletto, Lely, etc. The *gardens* were laid out by Capability Brown in 1763.

Saffron Walden (pop. 8500, E.C. Wednesday). The town's history can be traced in its many interesting old buildings. Its name is derived from the saffron or autumn crocus, introduced into England about 1340, which was once extensively cultivated here.

St Mary's Church (1300, with parts dating from the 15th and 16th c.) is notable for the height and breadth of the nave. There are a number of other old buildings. *Sun Inn* (now a private house), at the intersection of Church St and Market Hill, a gabled building with a 15th century hall (fine woodwork and 17th century plaster decoration). Almshouses (1400, rebuilt 1550). *Rose and Crown Hotel* (16th c.). Two houses in Gold St have old doorways, and there are other old houses in Cross St and King St. The *Museum*, on Castle Hill, contains zoological (foreign birds), geological, ethnological and archaeological collections, manuscripts and prints. Near the Museum are the remains of *Walden Castle* (early 13th c.).

West of the town are the remains of an earthwork fortification, *Battle Ditches*. In the north-west corner of the earthworks a Saxon cemetery was discovered in 1830.

At *Great Chesterford* the road enters Cambridgeshire. Soon afterwards A 130 goes off on the left to *Cambridge* (p. 542).

On this road, to the right, is *Sawston Hall*, built in 1553 (furniture, tapestries: open 2 to 5.30 on Sundays from May to September, and on Saturdays as well in July and August).

Just beyond Great Chesterford A 11 cuts across the Cambridge-Colchester road (A 604) and continues, following the line of an old Roman road, to join the the Cambridge-Newmarket road just at the *Devil's Ditch*, a mediaeval fortification. 65 miles: **Newmarket,** in a narrow strip of Suffolk which projects into Cambridgeshire.

Newmarket is the recognised headquarters of flat racing. There are between 30 and 40 racing stables in the town, and more than 1000 horses are trained every day on Newmarket

Heath. The first meeting of the season is held in the second week of April, and in all there are eight weeks of racing — the second and fourth weeks in April, the second week in May, the first and third weeks in July, the last week in September and the second and fourth weeks in October. At the second spring meeting the main events are the 2000 Guineas and 1000 Guineas (confined to fillies), run over a straight course of 1 mile, the first of the classic races of the season for three-year-olds. At the autumn meetings the chief races are the Jockey Club Stakes (for three- and four-year-olds), the Cambridgeshire Stakes and the Cesarewitch Stakes. At these autumn fixtures there are also the Middle Park Stakes and the Dewhurst Stakes for two-year-olds, which usually serve to indicate likely winners of the classic events of the following year.

Newmarket to Ipswich: 40 miles (A 11 for 1½ miles, then A 45).

14 miles: **Bury Saint Edmunds** (pop. 23,000, E.C. Thursday). This pleasant little town became a centre of pilgrimage after the 8th century, when the body of St Edmund, last king of East Anglia, was transferred there. An **abbey** was erected over his shrine in the 11th century; on Angel Hill is the *Abbey Gateway* (14th c.: Decorated style), and at the entrance to the *Botanical Gardens* are the abbey ruins. These are rather scanty and include the remains of the church and the Abbot's Palace. In the north-east corner, across the river Lark, is the picturesque 13th century Abbot's Bridge. **St James's Church,** near the Abbey Gateway, is a 15th century Perpendicular edifice which is the cathedral of the diocese of St Edmundsbury and Ipswich: fine old glass in the interior. Nearby stands the **Norman tower,** built in the 11th century as a belfry tower and a main approach to the abbey church.

The 15th century **St Mary's Church** has a splendid timber roof; note the rare Flemish glass and the memorial to Mary Tudor.

In the market place is a late Norman house called *Moyses Hall,* said to have been a Jewish synagogue and now a museum. The *Angel Hotel,* in which Mr Pickwick and Sam Weller stayed, is still one of the town's leading hotels. The "Westgate House Establishment for Young Ladies", where Mr Pickwick got himself into a situation of some difficulty, was at 42-43 Southgate St.

There are a number of large country houses in the neighbourhood — *Barton House* (2 miles away), *Culford Hall*, *Ickworth House*, *Hengrave Hall*.

22 miles: *Woolpit*. — 28 miles: *Stowmarket* (pop. 7000, E.C. Tuesday). The town is noted for the manufacture of gun-cotton and is an important grain market. The church has an unusual wooden spire. — 32 miles: *Needham Market* (pop. 31,000, E.C. Tuesday). — 36 miles: *Claydon*, on the River Gipping. — 40 miles: **Ipswich** (p. 530).

Newmarket to Lowestoft: 66 miles (as above to Bury Saint Edmunds, then A 143 to Bungay, then A 1116 to Beccles, then A 145 to Lowestoft).

20 miles: *Ixworth* (remains of a 12th c. abbey, built into a 17th c. house). — 29 miles: *Botesdale*. — 34 miles: A 1066 forks back left to (1 mile) *Diss*, a quiet old market town on the Little Ouse. *Diss Mere*. — 36 miles: *Scole*. A 143 runs along the valley of the river Waveney (here the boundary between Norfolk and Suffolk). — 40 miles: *Brockdish*. 3 miles south is *Wingfield*, with the remains of an old moated castle. — 44 miles: *Harleston* (pop. 1700, E.C. Thursday), a small and sleepy little market town with the *Old Swan* (1551, rebuilt in the early Georgian period).

51 miles: **Bungay** (pop. 3100, E.C. Wednesday), an attractive little town in the Broadland district, with the attractive little river Waveney. There are a number of old houses and, in the market-place, the old market cross, known as the *Butter Cross*. *St Mary's* and *Holy Trinity* churches; ruins of a Norman castle.

56 miles: **Beccles** (pop. 6500, E.C. Wednesday), a pleasant town which dates from before Saxon times, built on a hill overlooking the river. The Perpendicular church of *St Michael* dates from the middle of the 14th century; the south porch is very fine, and there is a detached tower. St Benet's R.C. church, called the Minster (1908), is a fine example of early 20th century religious architecture.

64 miles: *Oulton Broad*, a popular centre for sailing on the Norfolk Broads (p. 573). 66 miles: **Lowestoft** (p. 532).

73 miles: *Barton Mills*. 1 mile west is *Mildenhall*, where a splendid hoard of Roman silver (now in the British Museum) was discovered during the last war.

84 miles: *Thetford*, a peaceful little town on both banks of the Little Ouse, which here forms the boundary between Suffolk and Norfolk.

Castle Hill is a large earthwork 100 feet in diameter, probably either a British or a Roman fort. Gatehouse and ruins of a Cluniac priory founded in 1104. The *Bell Hotel* is very old: in 1938 remains of wall paintings were found in the building, and in 1948 part of a 15th century wattle and daub wall. 1 Brick Lane was the birthplace of Thomas Paine (1734-1809).

Thetford is in the centre of the *Breckland*, an area of heathland, meres and pinewoods. A large part has been requisitioned by the Ministry of Defence as a training area, and the roads are closed. — 6 miles north-west on B 1107 is *Brandon*, also on the Little Ouse, where flint knapping, one of the oldest crafts in the world, is still practised: flints for guns are made in the same way as flint instruments in the Stone Age. 3½ miles north-east are *Grime's Graves* (prehistoric flint mines).

Thetford to Colchester: 44 miles on A 134. 8 miles: *Ingham.* — 10 miles: *Fornham St Martin.* — 12 miles: **Bury St Edmunds.** — 15 miles: *Sicklesmere.* — 18 miles: *Bradfield Combust.* — 19 miles: B 1141 goes off on the left to (4 miles) **Lavenham** (pop. 1450, E.C. Wednesday), one of the most notable villages in Suffolk, a 15th century weaving town, with many houses of that period. The 16th century *Guildhall* is the finest timber-framed building in England, and there is a beautiful Perpendicular *church*. The *Swan Inn* dates from the 15th century, the cottages in Shilling St (National Trust) from the 17th. — From Lavenham B 1141 continues to (2 miles) *Brent Eleigh* and (4 miles) *Monks Eleigh*, two charming little villages. In another 3 miles a road runs south to *Kersey*, reputed to be the prettiest village in the county. Near this is *Lindsey*, an old weaving village, which has given its name to linsey-woolsey. At *Hadleigh* B 1141 runs into A 1071 from Sudbury (see below) to Ipswich.

23 miles: *Bridge Street.* — 26 miles: **Long Melford** (pop. 2400, E.C. Wednesday), with a Perpendicular *church* which is one of the glories of Suffolk. Formerly a settlement of Flemish weavers, the town has some fine old houses. The *Bull Inn* (early 15th c.) has carved and moulded beams. Two fine Tudor houses, *Melford Hall* (near the Bull Inn) and *Kentwell Hall* (beyond the church).

29 miles: **Sudbury** (pop. 7000, E.C. Wednesday), a little town on the Stour (here the boundary between Suffolk and Essex) which was the centre of the Suffolk cloth trade in the 15th and 16th centuries. Many half-timbered houses. The *Moot Hall* and *Salters' Hall* are fine old buildings. In the vestry of St Gregory's Church is preserved the skull of Simon Sudbury, Archbishop of Canterbury, who was beheaded in the Tower of London. Two other interesting churches are *All Saints* and *St Peter's*, both Perpendicular. In Gainsborough St is the birthplace of the painter Thomas Gainsborough.

32 miles: *Neston*. — 35 miles: B 1068 goes off on the left to the little village of *Stoke-by-Nayland*. In Back St are two half-timbered cottages, the Old Maltings and the Guildhall (c. 1620). 2 miles beyond the village is *Thorington Hall* (built 1600, enlarged c. 1700, repaired 1937: National Trust), an intact example of local architecture (oak-framed with plaster filling, gable with interior bearing wall). B 1087 then continues to join A 143 at (38 miles) Nayland. — 44 miles: **Colchester.**

98 miles: *Attleborough* (pop. 2500, E.C. Wednesday). The parish church is an interesting Norman and Perpendicular building.

104 miles: *Wymondham* (pronounced "Windham": pop. 6250, E.C. Wednesday), a quaint old market town. Its church, one of the finest in the county, dates from the 12th century and retains its Norman nave. Its double towers are very impressive. In the market place is the old Market Cross (1616). Chapel of St Thomas Becket. The *Green Dragon* is a very old inn.

114 miles: **Norwich.**

NORWICH

Norwich (pop. 120,000, E.C. Wednesday), chief town of Norfolk and of East Anglia, is situated in flat country on the river Wensum. It is an industrial city and a considerable agricultural centre, with corn and cattle markets.

In Saxon times Norwich was a populous settlement which the Danes destroyed in 1004. It was rebuilt, the Norman castle was constructed, and the bishopric of East Anglia transferred here from Thetford. A Benedictine priory using the cathedral as a convent church was also founded. The prosperity of the town dates from the 14th century, when the establishment of the wool market here, with the influx of Flemish weavers, caused it to become the staple town (official wool market of East Anglia). The walls date from this time.

Norwich is exceedingly rich in beautiful old buildings and parish churches, many of then constructed of chipped flints and dating from the 15th century. The streets are narrow and built to no regular plan.

In the centre of the town on a great artificial mound rises the *Castle*, a large 12th century Norman keep (refaced 1834). The building, almost a cube, is 70 feet high. It was built by William Fitz Osborn, and in the Middle Ages was converted into a prison.

In 1894 King George V, then Duke of York, opened it as the *Castle Museum*. It contains collections of art, archaeology and natural history and mementoes of Nelson. In the *Art Gallery* there is a good collection of Norfolk artists including Crome, the Cotmans, and other landscape painters of the Norwich school, and some works by Sir Alfred Munnings. From the battlements there is a very fine view over the city. The *city archives* are housed in the Muniment Room of the Museum: extensive collections of documents relating to the administration of the city from the 13th century. Museum open 10 to 5, Sundays 2 to 5.

To the west of the Castle is the **Market Place,** one of the largest open-air markets in the country.

On the west side of the square is the new **City Hall** (1938), with a campanile 185 feet high. The municipal regalia, brought here from the old Guildhall, are second in magnificence only to the regalia of the City of London ("cap of maintenance" dating from the reign of Henry VII, crystal mace, sword of St George's Guild and many other interesting articles). Open Mondays and Tuesdays 10 to 1 and 2 to 5, Saturdays 10 to 12.

To the north is the **Guildhall** (1407-13, now mainly 16th c.), which replaced the thatched Norman Tolbooth as the centre of municipal administration.   Good glass, period furniture. Council Chamber of 1535. Open 2 to 4.30; closed on Sundays.

At the south-west corner of the Market Place is the magnificent **church of St Peter Mancroft,** the largest and most important of Norwich's 35 surviving pre-Reformation churches, still very much as it was in the 15th century (hammerbeam roof; font-canopy; some good glass; interesting brasses). In the vestry, formerly the Lady Chapel, are some beautiful liturgical utensils. Sir Thomas Browne (1605-82), author of "Religio Medici", who lived in Norwich from 1637 until his death, is buried in the church. The bells (a tenor and 12 other bells) are the city's finest.

In *Theatre Street*, which runs from east to west to the south of the Market Place, are *St Stephen's Church* (16th-17th c.), the *Assembly Rooms* (1754, in neo-classical style) and the Central Library (1963). To the west is the Roman Catholic *church of St John the Baptist* (19th c., Sir George Gilbert Scott). Returning along St Giles St, we pass on the left St Giles Church (Gothic).

To the north of the Market Place is the Gothic *church of St John Maddermarket* (stained glass). In the narrow St John's Alley is the *Maddermarket Theatre*, an 18th century replica of an Elizabethan theatre.

A lane opposite St Gregory's Church leads to **Strangers' Hall,** a Tudor house which is now a museum, with furniture and other objects of various periods (open 10 to 5, Sundays 2 to 5).

To the west, in St Benedict St, are a number of other Perpendicular churches — *St Lawrence's*, *St Margaret's*, *St Swithin's*, *St Benedict's* (with an 11th c. tower).

In Coslany St, just north of the river, is *St Michael's Church* (Gothic), and in St Mary's Plain, off this street on the right, is the church of *St Mary Coslany*, with a Saxon tower and a 15th century wooden roof. In Colegate St, which also runs east off Coslany St, is the 15th century church of *St George Colegate*. From here we can return to the city centre by way of St George St, which runs south across the river.

Just south of the river is **St Andrew's Hall,** once a Dominican church (Perpendicular, 1460), now a

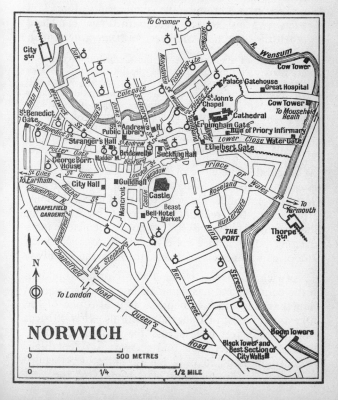

public hall.   Just beyond it is *St Andrew's Church* (1506), near which is the 16th century *Suckling House*. Beyond the church to the south is the **Bridewell,** now houses a museum of local industries (open 10 to 5, except Sundays).

In Princes St, to the east in the direction of the Cathedral, is the church of *St Peter Hungate*, now a **Museum of Church Art** (open 10 to 5, except Sundays). We then pass through the picturesque **Elm Hill** district, with old houses, and south down **Tombland** to reach the church of *St Peter Parmentergate* (1486).

To the left of the entrance to the Cathedral precincts is **Palace Street,** with old town houses, the 14th century *Norwich School* (open to visitors), founded by Edward VI, which still uses as its chapel the old monks' charnel-house, and the *Bishop's Palace* (enlarged 1963), which preserves some 14th and 15th century work. To the east, in Bishopgate, is the *Great Hospital*, with the 15th century *St Helen's Church*. Bishopgate continues east to *Bishop Bridge* (partly 13th c.), with the *Cow Tower*, where tolls used to be collected from boats using the river.

Cathedral. The close of Norwich Cathedral, which dates from 1094, is entered through the **Erpingham Gate** in Tombland. The gate was built by Sir Thomas Erpingham, the redoubtable knight mentioned in Shakespeare's "Henry V" (who is depicted in a kneeling position in a relief on the gate). Norwich School can be seen to the left, through the archway.

Norwich Cathedral is the finest Norman building in the country, and has departed less from its original plan than any other cathedral. It is also one of the largest and oldest of English cathedrals. It is 407 feet long and 178 feet wide across the transepts, with a choir over 80 feet high and a *spire* 315 feet high, exceeded in England only by the spire of Salisbury Cathedral.   The building was begun by the first

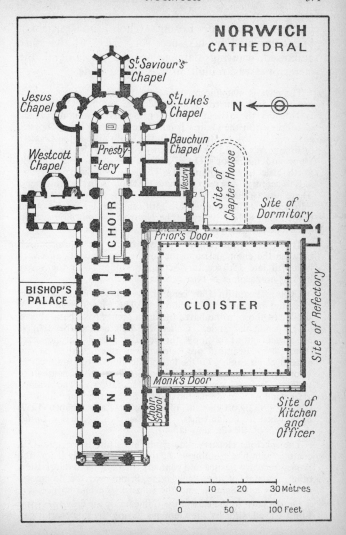

NORWICH
CATHEDRAL

St. Saviour's Chapel

Jesus Chapel

St. Luke's Chapel

N

Westcott Chapel

Presby-tery

Bauchun Chapel

Vestry

Site of Chapter House

Site of Dormitory

CHOIR

Prior's Door

BISHOP'S PALACE

CLOISTER

Site of Refectory

NAVE

Monk's Door

Choir School

Site of Kitchen and Officer

0   10   20   30 Mètres

0   50   100 Feet

bishop, Herbert de Losinga (choir and transepts), and completed by his successor. In 1361 the spire collapsed, causing damage to the choir, and the clerestory was rebuilt in Decorated style.

The **nave** is magnificent. Note the triforium arches, which are equal in height to those of the nave and choir. The nave is Norman throughout except for the lierne vaulting, which is continued in the choir. In all there are 1500 carved bosses, each one worthy of attention. In the south aisle is the *Chantry of Bishop Nix* (d. 1535). The Cloister is entered by the Monks' Door and the Prior's Door, also in the south aisle. In the north aisle is a monument to Thomas Wyndham; the glass is 19th century. A screen separates the choir from the presbytery. There are a number of 15th century stalls, with 60 interesting misericords. The canopies are 15th century. Under the pulpit is the Dean's chair (ivory). The Norman *central tower* has an open lantern and rests on four large round arches.

Transepts. 16th century vaulted roof. The Norman arch between the choir aisle and the south transept contains a very beautiful late 15th century screened window. In the vestry by this transept is a 14th century altar.

Choir. Beautiful 15th century *clerestory*. Rounded apse, a feature rare in English churches. The triforium arches are similar to those in the nave; the main arches have been altered in Perpendicular style. Under the arch behind the altar is an ancient stone bishop's throne; the present throne dates from 1895. Beautiful pre-Reformation lectern with a pelican instead of an eagle. To the left of the altar is the tomb of Sir Thomas Erpingham. In the south aisle is a monument to William Boleyn, Anne Boleyn's grandfather. The stained glass window is modern. Beyond the apse is the War Memorial Chapel (1932), on the site of an earlier Lady Chapel (1257) demolished in Tudor times. In St Luke's Chapel is a *Gothic polyptych* of the Passion (1380).

The spacious **cloisters** date from late 13th to the mid 15th century, with fine groining in the roof and with many sculptured bosses (recently cleaned and painted). In addition to the cloisters other remains of the Benedictine Priory are the Locutory, now the Choir School, and the ruins of the infirmary.

On the lawn to the east of the Cathedral is the grave of Nurse Edith Cavell, shot by the Germans during the first world war.

In the walls enclosing the old 11th century monastery precincts are four well preserved gates — the *Erpingham Gate* (above); *St Ethelbert's Gate*, dating from the reign of Edward I (1272-1307); the gateway to the Bishop's Palace (15th c.); and the 15th century *Water Gate*, at Pulls Ferry, on the river. There are a number of interesting houses in the Close (the Deanery and Nos. 32 and 50).

Surroundings of Norwich

1. **Immediate surroundings.** *Mousehold Heath* (190 acres), an area of rolling heathland from which there are fine views of the city. *Earlham Park* (75 acres), with woodland and gardens running down to the river; in the centre is *Earlham Hall*, now a maternity hospital. In the city and its immediate surroundings are more than 25 parks and gardens, with a total area of some 570 acres.

3 miles south is *Caister St Edmunds*, with earthworks marking the site of the important Roman town of *Venta Icenorum*.

2. **The Norfolk Broads.** Norwich is a good starting point for a tour of the Norfolk Broads, an area of shallow lagoons connected by placid streams, lying roughly in the triangle Norwich-Great Yarmouth-Palling. There are more than 200 miles of navigable waterway in the dozen large broads and nearly two score smaller ones linked by the rivers Bure, Yare, Waveney, Ant and Thurne. Here and there can be seen windmills erected to drive the draining machinery.

The Broads cannot be appreciated to the full from the road even by walkers, and the best way of gaining an impression if time is limited is to take a steamer from Norwich down the Yare to Yarmouth and from Yarmouth up the Bure as far as Wroxham. An enjoyable way of spending a holiday is to hire a sailing barge of shallow draught, called a wherry; crafts of various sizes for 2 to 10 or more persons can be hired and excursions for any length of time from days to weeks can be planned. Good centres are *Wroxham*, 8 miles by A 1151; *Stalham*, 7 miles beyond on A 1151; *Potter Higham*, 16 miles

by A 1151 to Wroxham, then B 1354; — *Hickling*, 5 miles
beyond; — *Acle*, 11 miles on A 47; and *Oulton*.

Of the main broads on which the public are allowed to sail
the most suitable are Wroxham. Salhouse, Ranworth, Hoveton
and South Walsham Broads; Barton Broad, which the river
Ant joins to the Bure; the largest, Hickling Broad; Horsey
Mere, Somerton and Martham Broad, which the Thurne joins
to the Bure; and, on the river Yare, Rockland, Surlingham,
Hassingham and Upton.

3. Norwich to Ipswich: 43 miles (A 140 to Claydon, then A 45).

3 miles: B 1113 forks right for *Swardeston*, where
Nurse Edith Cavell was born. A 140 follows the
line of an old Roman road. — 17 miles: *Dickle-
burgh*. — 20 miles: *Scole*. The famous mid 17th century Great Inn of Scole can still be seen near the
Norwich road.

B 1077 goes off on the left to **Eye** (pop. 1730, E.C. Tuesday),
an unspoiled little country town with many old houses. In
the 16th century *White Lion* is a charming Adam style ballroom
(mid 18th c.) in white and gold, with a musicians' gallery reached
by a ladder. In the church is a beautiful painted rood-screen.
The countryside to the east is delightfully quiet and unspoiled,
with narrow little roads, scarcely more than footpaths, winding
about between sleepy villages and remote hamlets.

39 miles: *Claydon*, where A 140 joins A 45 to
(43 miles) *Ipswich*.

4. Norwich to Cromer: 23 miles (A 140 for 20 miles, then A 149).

12 miles: *Aylsham* (pop. 3600, E.C. Wednesday).
B 1354 leads north-west to (1 mile) *Blickling*, with
the National Trust property (acquired in 1940) of
Blickling Hall and 4500 acres including a deer park,

woodlands, 17 farms, an inn and 138 smaller houses and cottages.

Blickling Hall, one of the most splendid of England's ancestral halls, stands on the site of the reputed birthplace of Anne Boleyn. The present hall was built of red brick in 1619-24 by Robert Liming for Henry Hobart, and was altered in 1765-70 by a Norwich family of architects named Ivory, who built the Orangery and the Temple in the grounds. The state apartments contain furniture, family portraits and tapestries. The gallery has an elaborately carved Jacobean plaster ceiling. The Ivorys altered the double staircase. The Mausoleum in the park was designed by Joseph Bonomi about 1793. The extensive grounds contain magnificent trees and an artificial lake half a mile long. Open April to October 2 to 6 except Fridays.

From Aylsham B 1145 runs north-east to **North Walsham** (pop. 4400, E.C. Wednesday), a market town in the centre of a prosperous farming district, wooded and well watered by rivers and lakes.

In the market-place is an octagonal *cross* (1602). The Perpendicular **parish church** dates from 1330, but the building of the church was held up by the lack of masons following outbreaks of plague in the town in 1338, 1361 and 1369. The tower (which was 140 ft high) is now a ruin, having twice collapsed (in 1724 and 1735).

5. Norwich to King's Lynn: 44 miles on A 47.

8 miles: *Honingham*. — 16 miles: **East Dereham** (pop. 5800, E.C. Wednesday), which has preserved its old-world charm in spite of modern industrial development.

The town is believed to have been founded in 642. Fine Early English and Perpendicular *church* (font with Seven Sacraments). There are a number of old buildings. *Bonner's Cottages* (1502), near the church, have unusual coloured pargeting. William Cowper spent the last years of his life in Dereham and is buried in the parish church. The archaeologist John Fenn, first editor of the 15th century "Paston Letters", lived in Hill House, in the Market Place. George Borrow was born (1803) in a farm opposite the Jolly Farmers Inn in Dumpling Green (1½ miles south-east on the Yaxham road), and refers to Dereham in "Lavengro". — 3 miles north-east on B 1147 (the Bawdeswell road) is *Swanton Morley*, with a Perpendicular church (14th c.). In the 17th century the landlord of the Angel Inn was Richard Lincoln, whose son Samuel emigrated to America in 1637 and had as one of his descendants Abraham Lincoln.

28 miles: **Swaffham** (pop. 3000, E.C. Thursdays). There is an interesting 15th century church of which the roof is noteworthy. The ancient market Cross is a relic of Swaffham's past prosperity.

4 miles north on A 1065 is Castle Acre, near the village of Newton, built by William de Warenne (see Lewes Castle). The north gateway and earthworks are all that remain. There are more remains, however, of the **Cluniac priory** — one of the greatest in the county — which he founded: the west front of the church (late Norman), the rear wall of the cloisters and the Tudor gatehouse. In the old village can be seen many remains taken from the castle and priory.

34 miles: *Narborough*. — 44 miles: **King's Lynn**.

5. Norwich to Fakenham: 25 miles on A 1067.

8 miles: *Attlebridge*. — 10 miles: *Lenwade*. — 14 miles: *Bawdeswell*, home of the Reeve in Chaucer's "Canterbury Tales".

Chaucer House, in the High Street, is an old half-timbered house which Chaucer is reputed to have known. *All Saints Church* was demolished when a British plane crashed into it in 1944.

29. LONDON TO LINCOLN

137 miles. A 1 (the Great North Road) to Grantham, then A 607.

A. Via Grantham

Lincolnshire is a vast expanse of fens and agricultural land, in the centre of which rise the tall and graceful towers of Lincoln's beautiful Cathedral. The ancient city of *Lincoln* — which possesses one of the four existing contemporary copies of Magna Carta — is packed with delightful examples of early domestic architecture, including one of the few bridges on which houses still stand, and is also famed for its horse-racing: the Lincolnshire Handicap is the first big event of the flat-racing season. Another great landmark in this flat country is *Boston Stump*, the tower of the parish church of Boston. Higher up the coast are Skegness, Mablethorpe and Grimsby. *Woodhall Spa* lies a short distance inland on the edge of the Lincolnshire Wolds. To the north of Lincoln industry (iron and steel, brick-making, engineering, dyestuffs) has grown up round *Retford*, *Gainsborough* and *Scunthorpe*. The southern gateway of Lincolnshire is the ancient and picturesque town of *Stamford*, the first Lincolnshire town reached by the Great North Road.

78 miles: **Norman Cross.** (For the road from London to Norman Cross, see Route 31). At Norman Cross A 15 goes off on the right for Peterborough, offering an alternative route to Lincoln (56 miles): see below.

92 miles: **Stamford** (pop. 12,600, E.C. Wednesday) retains much of its old atmosphere in spite of the modern development of industry.

The Normans built a castle here on the site of an earlier Saxon settlement which was a royal borough by 972. In the 12th century the town was famous for its cloth, and in the Middle Ages the town walls had eleven towers and seven gates. The town then contained six monasteries, six religious colleges and 17 churches. After the battle of Wakefield (1460) the Lancastrian army under Queen Margaret plundered and almost

destroyed Stamford. In the Elizabethan period its most notable
magnate was the great Lord Burghley. During the Civil War
Cromwell captured the town and seized Burghley House,
2 miles away. All Stamford's churches and most of its houses
are built in stone from the quarries at Barnack, 3 miles east.

Of the Norman castle some portions of the curtain
wall with a postern gate can be seen in King's Mill
Lane; and there is a Norman arch on St Mary's
Hill. Of the six remaining old churches the finest is
St Mary's on the slopes beyond the river. The tower
(Early English) has a 14th century Decorated spire.
The main body of the church dates from the 13th
century. There are interesting monuments, including
the tomb of D. Phillips (1506).

St Martin's Church (Perpendicular) also contains
some fine monuments (tomb of the sixth Earl of
Exeter, by Monnot, 1703), as well as good glass.
All Saints has preserved much of the original 14th
century building (the beautifully arcaded external
walls and the arches of the nave and chancel); there
are some brasses and a double piscina (13th c.) in
the east chapel. The nearby *church of St John the
Baptist* (174) (1478) shows some similarity with St
Martin's; the roof is particularly fine.

Brasenose Gate marks the site of Greyfriars School.
St Leonard's Priory, the earliest of the monastic
buildings, was founded in 658; portions of the rebuilt priory dating from 1082 are to be seen. The
west front is very fine. *Brown's Hospital* was founded
in the 15th century but altered in 1870 (open 8 a.m.
to 9 p.m., except Sundays). *Stamford School* dates
from the 14th century; here Burghley was educated.

2 miles east is **Burghley House,** seat of the Marquess of
Exeter. The splendid Tudor mansion, built by Lord Burghley
in the second half of the 16th century, is set in a park with a

picturesque lake. The house contains fine period furniture, pictures (Rembrandt, Holbein, Brueghel, etc.), tapestries and china. Open April to October 11 to 5, except Mondays and Fridays; Sundays 2 to 5.

93 miles: the road enters the former county of Rutland, once the smallest in England (150 sq. miles). Gentle pastoral landscape; villages roofed with Colly Weston slates.

94 miles: *Great Casterton*. — 99 miles: *Stretton*. We pass again into Lincolnshire.

104 miles: *Colsterworth*. To the east is Woolsthorpe Manor, the birthplace in 1641 of Isaac Newton.

The apple orchard in front of the house still remains and contains a descendant of the tree from which the famous apple is reputed to have fallen. The small stone-built early 17th century house is let as a residence (National Trust) but is open for visiting (Mondays, Wednesdays and Saturdays 11 to 1 and 2 to 6).

112 miles: **Grantham** (pop. 26,000, E.C. Thursday), an old country town with one of the finest parish churches in England: the 13th century church of **St Wulfram** (Early English). The carvings and ornamentation, including the gargoyles, are very fine; the slender spire is 280 feet high. In the library are many chained books. Immediately east of St Wulfram's Church is **Grantham House,** with gardens and 20 acres of park, which provide an open space in the very centre of the town. The house dates from the late 14th and early 15th century; it was extensively altered in the 18th century, when the pleasant south front with sash windows and stone architraves was built. Open Wednesdays and Thursdays 2 to 5.

The *Angel and Royal Hotel* is one of only three mediaeval hostelries in the kingdom. The fine stone front dates from the late 15th century. King John and his court lodged here in 1213. In what is now the Coffee Room Richard II signed the Duke of Buckingham's death warrant.

7 miles west is *Belvoir Castle*, residence of the Duke of Rutland, situated in beautiful countryside, with pictures by Rubens, Rembrandt and other masters. Open Wednesdays, Thursdays and Saturdays 12 to 6, Sundays 2 to 7.

Grantham to Boston: 30 miles (A 152 to Donington, then A 154).

12 miles: *Threekingham*. — 20 miles: *Donington*. — 21 miles: *Bicker*. — 23 miles: *Drayton*. — 25 miles: *Swineshead*. This small fen village has an impressive church (fine tower, interesting monuments). Shakespeare (wrongly) makes this the scene of King John's death. To the west are the *Manwarings* (Danish earthworks). — 30 miles: **Boston.**

Grantham to Grimsby: 67 miles (A 607 for 5 miles, then A 16).

2½ miles: *Belton*, with *Belton House*, seat of Earl Brownlow. In the village church are some superb tombs of the Brownlow family (including one by Canova). — 5 miles: turn left into A 153. — 8 miles: *Ancaster*, once a Roman station on the military road, Ermine Street. — 14 miles: *Sleaford*, with St Denis's Church (14th c.: old tombs).

28 miles: **Tattershall** (pop. 400, E.C. Wednesday), a village situated above the plains traversed by the river Witham, with *Tattershall Castle*, one of the finest brick-built structures in England, erected about 1440 by Ralph Cromwell (d. 1456), Henry VI's Lord Treasurer. It is a harmoniously proportioned building with a tower 110 feet high. The mantelpieces with their heraldic carvings were sold in 1911, but Lord Curzon bought them back and restored the building, bequeathing it in 1926 to the National Trust. (Open weekdays and public holidays 9.30 to 7, Sundays 1 to 7, or until dusk if earlier). There is a magnificent view from the top; south-east can be seen "Boston Stump" and in the opposite direction the towers of Lincoln Cathedral. In the village is a fine *church* built by Ralph Cromwell: there are some fine old brasses and a beautiful stone screen. In the churchyard is an almshouse. The 15th century *Market Cross* is still standing.

— B 1192 runs 5 miles north to *Woodhall Spa* (pop. 460, E.C. Wednesday), on the edge of the Lincolnshire wolds amid lovely woodland and moorland scenery. The medicinal waters can be taken internally or as baths; there are also mud baths. All forms of rheumatism are treated. At nearby *Kirkstead* are the ruins of a 12th century Cistercian abbey.

30 miles: *Tumby*.

35 miles: B 1183 goes off on the right to *Scrivelsby*, with *Scrivelsby Court*, ancestral home of the Dymoke family, hereditary King's or Queen's Champions, descended from Scott's Marmion. The present house is modern. The village church contains monuments to members of the Dymoke and Marmion families.

37 miles: *Horncastle* (pop. 3500, E.C. Wednesday), the Roman station of *Banovallum*, with traces of walls. Interesting old church. — 5 miles north-east is the little village of *Somersby*, where Tennyson was born in 1809 in the old rectory; monument in church. — 39 miles: *West Ashby*. — 44 miles: *Scamblesby*. Nearby is *Cadwell Park*, in wooded country, one of the most beautiful parts of the Lincolnshire Wolds. — 51 miles: *Louth* (pop. 10,000, E.C. Thursday). The fine old *St James's Church* has a spire 294 feet high. Outside the town are the ruins of an old abbey.

115 miles: Bleton. 120 miles: Normanton. 124 miles *Boothby Graffoe*. 1 mile west are the ruins of 13th century *Somerton Castle*, in which the Black Prince held King John of France prisoner in 1359-60.

137 miles: **Lincoln**

LINCOLN

Lincoln (pop. 70,000, E.C. Wednesday), on the river Witham, the county town of Lincolnshire, is one of the oldest towns in the country, rich in historic monuments and remains of the past.

There was a settlement on the site before the arrival of the Romans, who built a fort on the summit of the steep hill near the river three years after their invasion of Britain. Its name, *Lindum*, came from the Celtic *Lindon* (*llwn* = "pool"). In 75, after the repression of Boadicea's rising, the town became a *colonia* (of which there were only nine in Britain). When

the Danes invaded Britain and occupied all this part of the
country (as the ending -*by* found in so many place names in
this area indicates) Lincoln became an important Danish town.
After the Norman Conquest William the Conqueror built a
castle here, and it became the fourth largest town in the kingdom.
Its prosperity increased in the 13th century through the cloth
trade, but this began to decline at the end of the 14th century.
Thereafter Lincoln sank into obscurity for four centuries,
until the industrial revolution, the development of nearby
Yorkshire and the draining of the fens gave it a fresh lease of
life, which continued in the 19th century with the establishment
of industry on a considerable scale (agricultural machinery,
engineering).

A 15 enters the town from the south by the High
St.

Soon, on the right, can be seen the church of *St Peter-at-
Gowts*, with some Early English work, a Saxon tower and a
nave with long and short quoins. Nearby is *St Mary's Guildhall*,
a rare example of Norman domestic architecture (1180-90), the
headquarters of the most important mediaeval Lincoln guild;
today only very few remains can be seen, including a Norman
gateway (12th c.). There is an interesting old half-timbered
house in Akrill's Passage, behind 333 High St. Beyond the
railway line right is *the church of St Mary Wigford*, with a fine
Saxon tower and an Early English nave and chancel; note in
the west wall a stone with a Roman and a Saxon inscription.

To the left is *St Benedict's Church* (restored), with an Early
English choir and a Saxon tower rebuilt after the Civil War.
Farther west is *Brayford Pool*, fed by the Witham, alongside
which are some fine half-timbered houses (1540). The "*Glory
Hole*" is delightfully picturesque: a black-and-white half-
timbered gabled house over an arch with water flowing beneath.

Over the Witham runs *High Bridge*, portions of
which date from the 12th century. Farther up High
St, at the junction with Silver St, stands the **Stonebow,**
on the site of the south gate of the Roman fortification, which was later extended from the original fortress on the hill down to the river. Over the present
gate, which dates from the 15th and 16th centuries,

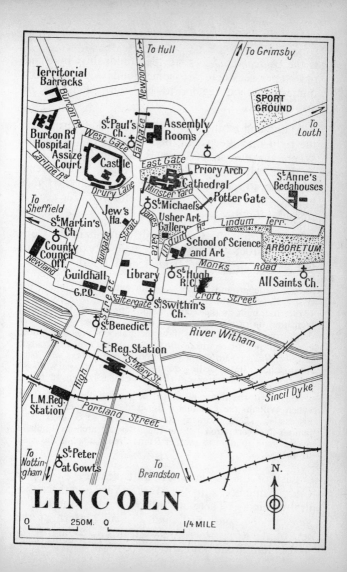

LINCOLN

Territorial Barracks

Burton Rd

Burton Rd Hospital

Assize Court

Carline Rd

St Paul's Ch.

West Gate

Castle

Drury Lane

Assembly Rooms

To Hull

Newport St

Bailgate

East Gate

Priory Arch

Cathedral

Minster Yard

Potter Gate

To Grimsby

SPORT GROUND

To Louth

St Anne's Bedahouses

ARBORETUM

Jew's Ha.

To Sheffield

St Martin's Ch.

County Council Off.

Newland

Guildhall

G.P.O.

Strait

Danes Gate

St Michaels

Usher Art Gallery

Lindum Rd

Lindum Terr.

School of Science and Art

Monks Road

Library

St Hugh R.C.

All Saints Ch.

Croft Street

Saltergate

St Swithin's Ch.

St Benedict

E. Reg. Station

River Witham

High

St Mary St.

Portland Street

Sincil Dyke

L.M. Reg. Station

To Nottingham

St Peter at Gowts

To Brandston

N.

0   250M. 0   1/4 MILE

is the *Guildhall.* Access to the Guildhall is by a fine oak staircase; there are some good woodwork and interesting civic regalia to be seen. (Visiting by arrangement).

At the end of the High St the *Strait* climbs up on the right into Steep Hill, once the site of the ghetto. Where the two streets meet is the old Bullring, and in the Strait itself is the *Jew's House*, which seems to have been a synagogue in the 13th century. Higher up, at the corner of Christ's Hospital Terrace, is *Aaron's House.*

At the top is the **Castle,** built by William the Conqueror in 1068. The west gate (still in existence, but not used) can be seen from Union Road.

The castle grounds are 6 acres in extent and contain the *Assize Court* (1826), the old county prison (1787, disused in 1878); and, built on the second mound, the Observatory Tower, from the top of which there is a fine view. The *Round Tower* dates from the 19th century; note the graves of prisoners whose execution took place within the castle. At the north-east angle is *Cobb Hall*, a 13th century bastion of two storeys with cells for prisoners. In the castle gatehouse is a beautiful oriel window. (Visiting: April-September 10 to 6, October-March 10 to 4).

Bailgate is the name given to the part of the upper town which William the Conqueror annexed as an outer bailey to his castle. There are many Roman remains to be seen. The famous **Newport Arch** — the only Roman arch in England over a main road — is another Roman relic: it spans the road to Brigg.

East of the castle is the 14th century *Exchequer Gate*, giving access to the **Minster Yard** and theca the-dral precincts. There are two other gates: the *Potter-gate*, to the south-east, and a small postern at the top of the *Greenstone Stairs* (13th c.) leading down to Lindum Road and the lower town.

In the precincts are the *Chapter House*, which suffered severe damage during the Civil War; the Subdeanery, which has a fine 15th century oriel window, and the Cantilupe Chantry House. Adjoining is the old Palace Gateway, with the ruins of the Great Hall (13th c.) in the garden. East is *Bishop Alnwick's Tower* (15th c.). From the Vicars' Court, the earliest part of which dates from the 13th century, there is a fine view of the Cathedral tower. The Chancery (early 14th c.) and the Choristers' House (17th c.) are nearby.

Lincoln Cathedral, some 200 feet above the lower city, is one of the most beautiful ecclesiastical buildings in the country. In 1074 Bishop Remigius, appointed by William the Conqueror on the death of the Saxon bishop, moved the see from Dorchester to Lincoln and chose the highest part of the city for his cathedral. Of the massive building, more castle than church, the base of the west front and the lower portions of the Norman towers remain. In 1141 the third Norman bishop, Alexander, restored the church after a fire. Of this period are the three ornamented Norman doorways, the arcading over the lateral recesses, the upper stages of the Norman towers and the gables on the north and south faces of the towers. Later in the 12th century an earthquake damaged the building, and under Bishop Hugh of Avalon (later canonised) restoration work was begun. It is to this period that the outstandingly beautiful examples of the Early English style belong: the choir, the east transept and the two bays in the east wall of the Great Transept all date from before 1200. By the middle of the 13th century the nave, the chapter house and the lower stages of the central tower were completed. The Angel Choir for the shrine of St Hugh (see above) was added in 1220. Here can be seen splendid examples of the transition from Early English to the Decorated style. In 1320 the central

tower was finished; the cloisters date from the end
of the 13th century. From 1922 to 1932 and from 1935
onwards extensive restoration work was carried out.
The Cathedral is 480 feet long by 80 feet wide (230 feet
across the west transept) and 80 feet high; the tower
271 feet high.

The **west front** is impressive despite the various styles, and
perhaps the severe Norman work of Bishop Remigius makes
the most suitable background for the richer ornamentation of
Bishop Alexander. From the south side there is a splendid
view of the nave and the **central tower,** still the highest cathedral
tower in England even without the wooden steeple, rising to
a height of over 520 feet, which was blown down by a storm
in 1548. In the lantern is the bell known as Great Tom. In
the south-west transept is the *Galilee Porch,* with a superb
Decorated rose window. On the south side of the Angel Choir
is the magnificent **Judgment Porch.**

Interior. The doorway by which the church is entered is
Norman and survives from the original church. The *nave*
consists of seven Early English bays (1253) and despite the
rather low vaulting, which has richly carved bosses, the effect
is one of great lightness. At the west end are two lateral chapels
with fine Early English vaulting. The piers are of Purbeck
marble and freestone, with rich ornamentation on the capitals.
The Norman font dates from 1150. In contrast with the slender
pillars in the nave are the massive stone columns supporting
the four lofty arches beneath the central tower.

Great Transept. The double arcading in the north and south
chapels by the choir date from the time of Bishop Hugh; the
remainder of the work is later. At the north and south end
are the two great *Rose Windows* known from their supposed
power to ward off evil as the "Dean's Eye" (to the north)
and the "Bishop's Eye" to the south. The glass in both is
old: that in the "Dean's Eye" dates from the 13th century,
and the window itself is a fine example of "plate tracery".
There are several chapels in the transepts, that in the south
transept near the choir aisle being the *Works Chantry.*

Choir. Between the choir and the nave is a magnificent
14th century screen which still bears traces of its original colouring. The fine doorways to the choir aisles date from after 1239,

LINCOLN CATHEDRAL

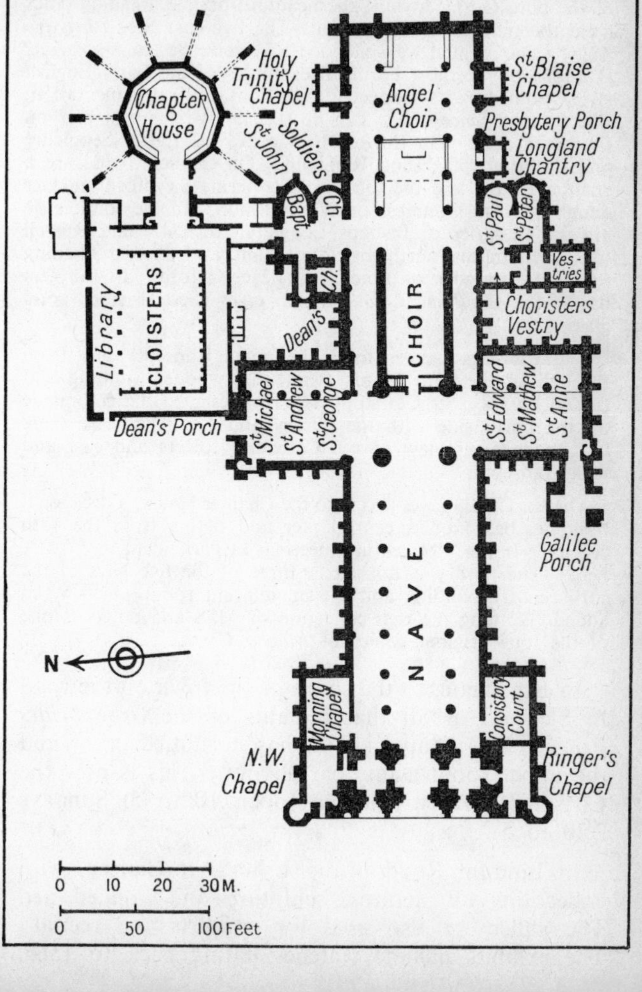

Chapter House

Holy Trinity Chapel

St. John Bapt.

Soldiers' Ch.

Angel Choir

St. Blaise Chapel

Presbytery Porch

Longland Chantry

St. Paul

St. Peter

Vestries

Choristers Vestry

Library

CLOISTERS

Dean's Ch.

CHOIR

Dean's Porch

St. Michael

St. Andrew

St. George

St. Edward

St. Matthew

St. Anne

Galilee Porch

N

NAVE

Morning Chapel

N.W. Chapel

Consistory Court

Ringer's Chapel

0   10   20   30 M.

0   50   100 Feet

when the tower collapsed. The choir itself is the oldest example of the pure Gothic style. The beautiful double arcading dates from the time of Bishop Hugh. The five east bays form the **Angel Choir,** which was intended to receive St Hugh's shrine. It is one of the most beautiful examples of the Early English style, both for its perfect proportions and ornamentation. The famous *Lincoln Imp* can be seen above the east pier on the north side. On the north side are the Easter Sepulchre and the tomb of Bishop Remigius. On the south side are a chantry chapel and the tombs of Catherine Swynford and her daughter Joan, Countess of Westmorland. In the south aisle are the chantries of Bishops Longland (d. 1547) and Russell (d. 1494), in the north aisle the chantry of Bishop Fleming (d. 1431), founder of Lincoln College, Oxford. In the east bay is the *Cantilupe Chantry* (14th c.). There is some good glass.

The **Cloisters** (access from the north transept) date from the end of the 13th century: note the wooden vaulting and carved bosses. Sir Christopher Wren designed the colonnade on the north side with the library above. From here there is a magnificent view of the Cathedral towers and east and west transept.

The East Walk gives access to the **Chapter House,** a decagonal building, based on a central pier and dating from the 13th century. In the 14th century meetings of Parliament took place here. The library is housed in three of the five bays of the 15th century building and the magnificent room which Wren added. Among the rich collection of MSS and books is one of the four original copies of *Magna Carta.*

In Broadgate, to the south of the town on the road to Sleaford, is all that remains of the *Grey Friars Priory.* The chapel (1230) has a vaulted crypt and the upper room a fine barrel roof. This is now the **City and County Museum** (open 10 to 5, Sundays 2.30 to 5).

In Lindum Road is the **Usher Art Gallery,** with collections of pictures, sculpture and applied art. The gallery is also used for concerts and recitals. The exhibits include watches dating back to 1566, miniatures, Nanking blue and white porcelain, English and continental china, ancient jewellery, etc. Open weekdays 10 to 5.30, Sundays 2.30 to 5.

B. Via Peterborough

Norman Cross to Lincoln: 56 miles on A 15.

78 miles: Norman Cross. Turn off on the right into A 15. — 5 miles: **Peterborough** (pop. 65,000, E.C. Thursday), an old town, now semi-industrial, and an important railway junction, situated on the river Nene. It has been the see of a bishop since 1541, and its chief attraction is its **Cathedral,** one of the most important Norman buildings in the country.

Peterborough Cathedral. The present building dates from 1140; the foundations of the Saxon church are beneath the south transept. The *Great Transept* dates from 1115-57. The late Norman nave was added by 1193 and the west transept (Transitional style) was completed by 1200. There is a notable 13th century front; the flanking turrets have Decorated and Perpendicular spires and pinnacles. The Decorated windows are 14th century. The *retro-choir* or "New Building", a Perpendicular construction with fan vaulting, dates from 1438-1528. The *north-west tower* dates from 1265-70 and the Perpendicular west porch from about 1370. The *central tower* replaced the Norman lantern in the 14th century (rebuilt 1884). The length of the Cathedral is 470 feet; it is 80 feet wide and 80 feet high. The north-west tower is nearly 190 feet in height, and the Great Transept measures 200 feet.

Interior. The first impression gained on entering the Cathedral is one of the lightness of the architecture. Much of the beautiful decoration and ornamentation work was destroyed in 1643 by the iconoclasts. The 12th century **painted wooden ceiling** is considered to be one of the best in Europe. In the north choir aisle is the *grave of Queen Catherine of Aragon* (d. 1536). In the south aisle is a slab marking the grave of Mary Queen of Scots (d. 1587); her remains were removed to Westminster Abbey by her son, James I.

Laurel Court is the name given to the *cloisters* (on the south side of the nave). In the Minster Close are the remains of the old abbey building, but these are not very interesting.

Entrance to the Cathedral precincts is by three old gateways of which the west gateway dates from 1193. The *Bishop's Palace*, *Deanery* and *Prior's House* are outside the Court, facing the west front of the Cathedral.

St John's Church (restored) is interesting; 15th century tower. Nearby is the *Guildhall* (1671). The **Museum** (open 10 to 1 and 2 to 5, except Sundays and Monday mornings) contains Roman and Saxon relics, collections of natural history and ceramics, and bone and other articles made by French prisoners during the Napoleonic wars.

Around Peterborough. 7 miles east on A 605 is *Whittlesey* (pop. 9000, E.C. Wednesday), an old market town. From here B 1040 runs south through the fens to (9 miles) *Ramsey* (pop. 5100, E.C. Thursday). A Norman chapel and the ruins of a porch are all that remains of the great Benedictine abbey which formerly stood here.

3 miles west is *Longthorpe Tower*, a mediaeval fortified house (frescoes).

11 miles: *Glinton*. — 14 miles: *Market Deeping*. — 15 miles: Langtoft. — 19 miles: *Thurlby*. — 21 miles: **Bourne** (pop. 4900, E.C. Wednesday), an old town at the western end of the fens, which had associations with Hereward the Wake and was the birthplace of Lord Burghley, Elizabeth I's Lord Treasurer. The *parish church* contains remains of an Augustinian abbey. To the north-west on B 676 is *Grimsthorpe Castle*. — 30 miles: *Folkingham*. — 33 miles: *Osbournby*. — 39 miles: *Sleaford* (pop. 7500, E.C. Thursday). There are some old houses, but little remains of the castle which once stood here. In St Denis's Church (Gothic) are some interesting monuments and a fine screen. A 17 runs east to King's Lynn. — 56 miles: **Lincoln** (p. 581).

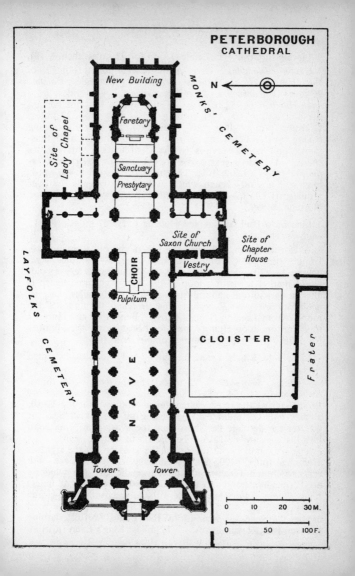

PETERBOROUGH
CATHEDRAL

N

New Building

MONKS' CEMETERY

Site of Lady Chapel

Feretory

Sanctuary

Presbytary

Site of Saxon Church

Site of Chapter House

Vestry

CHOIR

Pulpitum

LAYFOLKS CEMETERY

CLOISTER

Frater

N A V E

Tower

Tower

0   10   20   30 M.

0   50   100 F.

Lincoln to Grimsby: 37 miles (A 46 for 32 miles, then A 18).

6 miles: *Dunholme.* — 16 miles: *Market Rasen* (pop. 2100, E.C. Thursday). — 23 miles: *Nettleton.* — 24 miles: *Caistor.* 26 miles: *Cabourne.* — 28 miles: *Swallow.* — 30 miles: *Irby-upon-Humber.* — 32 miles: A 46 runs into A 18. Just beyond the junction, where A 18 turns left, is Laceby. — 37 miles: **Grimsby** (pop. 95,000, E.C. Thursday), the world's leading fishing port, situated on the right bank of the Humber (passenger and goods services to the Continent). 13th century *church.* 1½ miles east is the popular seaside resort of *Cleethorpes* (pop. 29,500, E.C. Thursday), with a pier 400 yards long and a sandy beach which at low tide extends for over a mile. At *Old Clee* is an interesting church with a Saxon and Norman tower.

Lincoln to Hull via the New Holland ferry: 37 miles on A 15 to New Holland.

A 15 runs north, following the line of the old Roman road, Ermine Street, to (11 miles) *Caenby Corner.* — 18 miles: *Redbourne.* — 20 miles: *Hibaldstow.* — 23 miles: *Brigg,* an old-world market town in a loop in the river Ancholme which is also an agricultural and industrial centre. — 34 miles: *Barrow-upon-Humber.* — 37 miles: *New Holland,* terminus of the railway from London (King's Cross). Ferry over the Humber to Kingston upon Hull. (A new road bridge over the Humber from Barton to Hull is nearing completion).

Lincoln to King's Lynn: 62 miles (A 15 to Sleaford, then A 17).

17 miles: *Sleaford.* — 22 miles: *Heckington.* — 29 miles: *Swineshead.* — 34 miles: *Sutterton.* — 38 miles: *Fosdyke Bridge,* across the river Welland at its outflow into the **Wash,** a wide gulf (22 miles by 15) opening off the North Sea. It was on the desolate flats bordering the Wash that King John lost his treasure in 1216. To the north can be seen *Boston Stump* (p. 594). — 42 miles: B 1168 goes off on the right to *Holbeach* (pop. 6100, E.C. Wednesday), with a large 16th century church (Decorated and Perpendicular; the windows are Perpendicular). — 29 miles: *Gedney* (church). — 48 miles: *Long Sutton.* Norman church with an interesting two-storey vestry (14th c.). — 52 miles: *Sutton Bridge,* where the road crosses the Nene. — 54 miles: the road enters Norfolk, running between two Roman dykes. — 62 miles: **King's Lynn** (p. 538).

30. THE LINCOLNSHIRE COAST
(VIA BOSTON AND SKEGNESS)

Leave Peterborough (p. 589) on A 15, which runs north via *Glinton* to (6 miles) *Northborough*. A mile beyond this turn right into B 1162, which in another mile cuts across B 1166 at *Deeping Gate* and just beyond the village runs into A 16.

To the right along B 1166 is **Crowland,** with the ruins of the *Benedictine abbey of St Guthlack*, founded by Ethelbald, king of Mercia (d. 757). The splendid 12th century west front with its old statues can still be seen. The west tower (1428) and the north aisle of the nave (now the parish church) are well preserved. The town itself lies on the confluence of the Welland, which here forms the boundary of Lincolnshire, and the Nene. There is an unusual 14th century *triangular bridge*. On the south side is an effigy of King Ethelbald, older than the bridge. From Crowland B 1040 runs south-east to (5 miles) Thorney.

14 miles: *Deeping St Nicholas*. — 19 miles: **Spalding** (pop. 14,000, E.C. Thursday). This busy market town in the centre of the fen district owes much, if not its very existence, to the draining of the fens. The surrounding fenland, a flat landscape criss-crossed by streams and dykes, and with here and there a windmill, closely resembles the countryside of Holland. Its resemblance is even more striking from March to May, when hundreds of acres are filled with tulips, daffodils, narcissi, and hyacinths, and other bulb flowers in bloom. Every year millions of parcels of bulbs are despatched from Spalding. Sugar beet is also grown in the area.

Excavations to the east of the town have revealed evidence of Roman occupation. Spalding Priory, founded in 1051, was dissolved at the Reformation; the only remains are a turret cell in Hole-in-the-Wall Passage and a stone building in the Sheep Market which was used as a prison. One of the oldest buildings in the town is the *White Horse Inn*, which has records going back to 1377. Near **Ayscoughfee Hall** (a 15th c. house in Dutch style, now an *ornithological museum*) is the **church of St Mary and St Nicholas** (1240: Early English, with Decorated and Perpendicular alterations), with a good rood-screen and the large chantry chapel of St Mary and St Thomas.

In Broad St are the library and hall of the Spalding Gentlemen's Society, a learned society founded in 1710.

21 miles: *Pinchbeck.* — 23 miles: *Surfleet.* — 29 miles: *Sutterton.* — 31 miles: *Kirton.*

35 miles: **Boston** (pop. 25,000, E.C. Thursday), an ancient market town and seaport near the mouth of the river Witham. The name is derived from that of the town's saint, St Botolph. During the 13th century Boston was one of the leading seaports in the country.

St Botolph's Church is a beautiful building in the Decorated style with a tall Perpendicular tower known as **Boston Stump.** It is 272 feet high and is a well-known landmark for miles around. From the top there is a magnificent view. There are interesting monuments and fine wood-carving and misericords on the choir stalls.

Hussey Tower dates from the 15th century. Also of interest is *Fydell House* (1726). The *Guildhall* (15th c.) contains the splendid civic regalia. Many old half-timbered buildings, including the *Shodfriars' Hall.*

2½ miles south-east is *Fishtoft*, with an interesting old church and village stocks. 3 miles east is *Freiston*, with a church which incorporates parts (the nave) of a 12th century abbey church.

8 miles: *Old Leake.* — 11 miles: *Wrangle.* — 13 miles: off the road to the right, the village of *Friskney*, with an old church containing some fine woodwork. — 17 miles: **Wainfleet,** the Roman *Bainona*, birthplace of William of Wayneflete, founder of Magdalen College, Oxford (1548), who also built Magdalen School

here to provide students for his college. 9 miles
north-east is *Spilsby* (pop. 1380, E.C. Tuesday), with
St James's Church (interesting monuments).

22 miles: **Skegness** (pop. 14,000, E.C. Thursday),
a seaside resort on the flat coast, with a pier, a broad
sandy beach and amusement parks. 1 mile south is
another resort, *Seacroft*.

Interesting villages with beautiful churches. Near *Burgh-le-
Marsh* (5 miles inland on A 158) is *Gunby Hall* (1700), a brick
house with stone dressings, Tennyson's "haunt of ancient
peace". Very fine oak staircase; almost all the rooms are
panelled.

38 miles: *Sutton-on-Sea* (pop. 1200, E.C. Thursday).
— 39 miles: *Trusthorpe*. — 40 miles: **Mablethorpe**
(pop. 5400, E.C. Thursday).

The three places are combined into one developing seaside
resort enjoying a splendid situation on the bracing coast of
the North Sea, with miles of sand hills and a dry climate. *Trusthorpe* is a typical Lincolnshire village with a 13th century
church.

Markby (2 miles inland on B 1197) has a thatched church
(1672).

45 miles: *Theddlethorpe St Helen*. In the beautiful
All Saints Church, known as the *Cathedral of the
Marshes*, there are traces of Norman work; note also
the fine oak screens and the font.

49 miles: *Saltfleet*, a small village on the sea with a
fine old manor-house built in 1347. — 51 miles:
North Somercotes. — 57 miles: *March Chapel*. —
64 miles: *Humberston*. — 68 miles: *Cleethorpes*.
— 70 miles: **Grimsby** (p. 592).

Peterborough to Wisbech and King's Lynn.

34 miles on A 47.

5 miles: *Eye* — 7 miles: *Thorney*. — 15 miles: *Guyhirne Bridge*. 20 miles: **Wisbech** (pop. 18,000, E.C. Wednesday). On the river Nene, in a district favoured by market gardeners and seed cultivators. On the brink of the Nene stands *Peckover House*, built in 1722. The interior is a fine example of Rococo, possibly executed by French artists from Houghton Hall about 1730-40. (Open May-October, Wednesdays, Thursdays, Saturdays and Sundays 2 to 5 or 6). To the east of Peckover House, at 14 North Brink, is an early 18th century house with a fine carved balustrade on the steps in the entrance courtyard. To the west, at No. 19, is a coach-house of the same period, with recent alterations. Opposite the *church* (Norman and Gothic) is the *Museum* (open 10 to 4 or 5).

27 miles: *St John's Highway*. This part of the fens is known as *Marshland*. Many of the local villages have names referring to the dyke on which they are built (*Walpole, Walton, Walsoken*, etc.). The "seven churches of Marshland" are at *Clenchwarton* (Perpendicular), *Tilney All Saints* (Norman and Perpendicular), *Terrington St Clement* and *Walpole St Peter* (Perpendicular), *West Walton* (Early English), *Walsoken* (Norman) and *Emneth* (Early English and Perpendicular). Most of these churches are built in hard grey Ancaster stone. — 34 miles: **King's Lynn** (p. 538).

V: THE MIDLANDS

The Midlands are, as their name denotes, the midland counties of England — the heart of the country. They comprise all the territory between the rivers Thames and Trent and between Wales and East Anglia. Although within this region are such important and busy industrial towns as Birmingham, Coventry and Wolverhampton, there are vast expanses of unspoiled countryside and some of England's loveliest villages and towns. For instance, only a few miles south of Coventry lies the old-world town of Stratford-on-Avon, birthplace of Shakespeare and home of the Shakespeare Memorial Theatre, surrounded by beautiful wooded country. East of Birmingham are the shires — Leicestershire, Northamptonshire and the old pocket county of Rutland — famous as the region of foxhunting. This area is of great historic interest, with many castles and fine houses.

Along the western frontier of the Midlands is the enchanting country of the Welsh border, and to the north stretch Sherwood Forest and the grandly mountainous landscape of Derbyshire.

Visitors to England always remark upon the rich green of its fertile landscape; nowhere in England is this characteristic colouring more striking than in the West Midlands, a region of grassy hills, noble valleys and luxuriant woodland, noted for its picturesque villages and cathedral towns. One of the best routes from London to the west Midlands takes the traveller through Oxford, city of exquisite ancient architecture, with its famous colleges and chapels. Farther west are Gloucester and Worcester, with beautiful cathedrals. Chief town and port of the west is Bristol.

31. LONDON TO NORTHAMPTON

70 miles by motorway (M 1); 69 miles by A 5 from St Albans.

London to St Albans: see p. 604.

22 miles: *St Albans.* — 26 miles: *Redbourn.* — 30 miles: the road enters Bedfordshire, one of London's "market garden" areas; a pleasant county, mostly flat, but with the bare chalk of the Chiltern Hills rising to 700 feet.

34 miles: **Dunstable** (pop. 30,000, E.C. Wednesday), an industrial town on the site of the Roman station of *Durocobrivae*, at the intersection of Watling Street and the old British track, Icknield Way.

An Augustinian priory was founded here by Henry I in 1110, and was completed in 1220. Its remains are incorporated in the **church of SS. Peter and Paul**, which has an interesting west front (Norman with later alterations). When the two towers collapsed in a storm in 1222 the façade was damaged and later rebuilt in Early English style. The tower and crenellations are Perpendicular. *Interior:* ten pillars erected by Mary Tudor, interesting brasses, an ambroidered shroud (the Fayrey Pall).

Priory House, formerly part of the priory, still has its original gatehouse and a vaulted room added in the 13th century. *Civic Hall* (1964).

2 miles west is the *Maiden Bower*, an early Iron Age camp (10 acres). 2½ miles south is *Whipsnade Zoo*, on the Dunstable Downs, where the animals roam freely in large enclosures.

B 489 (the Icknield Way) runs south-west to *Ivinghoe*, a small market town at the foot of the Chilterns, with some old houses and a fine Town Hall. To the west is Ivinghoe Mill, one of the oldest post-mills in the country; it is a notable landmark from neighbouring Ivinghoe Beacon (811 ft). Excavations

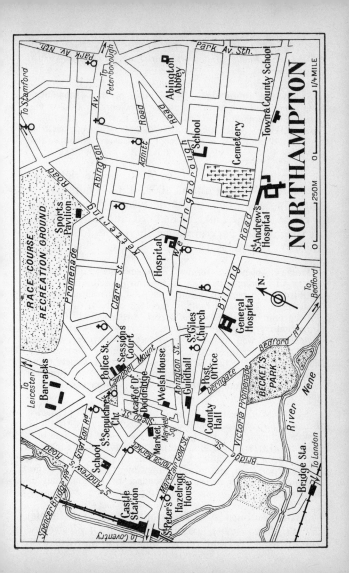

of the *Five Knolls* (prehistoric burial mounds) have yielded interesting results.

5 miles north is *Toddington*, a market town which has retained its old-world atmosphere. — 12 miles north is **Ampthill**, a small market town with a number of Georgian houses and inns. Near *Ampthill Park* was the castle in which Catherine of Aragon, Henry VIII's first wife, was confined during her trial. In the old church is a monument to Richard Nicholls, first governor of New York. — 20 miles: *Bedford* (p. 612).

38 miles: *Hockliffe*. Take A 50, to the right. — 43 miles: **Woburn** (pop. 1000, E.C. Thursday), a charming and interesting little town. **Woburn Abbey** is the seat of the Duke of Bedford, and the house and its magnificent park are open to visitors (daily 11.30 to 5.30, Thursdays 12 to 9).

Woburn Abbey is a former Cistercian abbey, presented by Henry VIII along with its lands to John Russell, first Duke of Bedford. The present splendid mansion, surrounded by magnificent gardens, was built in the 18th century. It contains French and English *furniture*, *porcelain* (particularly Chinese), 18th century *silver* and a **picture gallery** with 24 pictures by *Canaletto* as well as works by Poussin, Velazquez, Teniers, van Dyck, Murillo, Moroni, Reynolds, Kneller, Gainsborough and Tiepolo. The fine **park** (300 acres) offers a variety of attractions — amusements, hothouses, a Safari Park with deer and other wild animals through which visitors can drive in their own cars.

5 miles south-west of Woburn, on the other side of A 5, is *Leighton Buzzard* (pop. 12,000, E.C. Wednesday), with a 13th century church. A short distance away, on the Aylesbury road (A 418), is **Ascott House** (open to visitors on Wednesdays and Saturdays in summer 2 to 6), with Chippendale furniture, Chinese porcelain and pictures by Cuyp, Hobbema, Gainsborough and other artists. The village of *Wing* has an interesting church.

From Woburn A 50 runs north-west over *Aspley Heath* (fine views), passing close to *Aspley Guise* (mansion). It then runs under the motorway at

Broughton (church with wall paintings). 52 miles: *Newport Pagnell*, a little town noted for its lace.

67 miles: **Northampton** (pop. 122,000, E.C. Thursday), county town of Northamptonshire, on the north bank of the river Nene, noted for the manufacture of boots and shoes.

St Sepulchre's Church, built by Simon de Senlis in 1084 on the model of the Church of the Holy Sepulchre in Jerusalem, is one of the four round churches in England (the others being in Cambridge, at Little Maplestead in Essex and in the Temple in London). The interior is particularly impressive, with its eight massive Norman piers carrying pointed arches.

St Peter's Church, one of the finest examples of Norman religious architecture, has remained almost unchanged since the 12th century. Note the finely carved arch above the window on the west side of the tower. The exterior is very characteristic Norman work.

All Saints Church, at the south end of Mercer's Row, was built in 1675 after a great fire had destroyed the previous church, leaving only the 14th century tower. The central dome shows some resemblance to the dome of St Paul's in London. In Marefair is the *Hazelrigge Mansion*, dating from before the 1675 fire, now a ladies' club. In Bridge St is the old *St John's Hospital* (1138).

In Guildhall Road is the **Museum and Art Gallery** (open free of charge on weekdays 10 to 6, Thursdays and Saturdays 10 to 8): footwear since Roman times, British, Saxon and Norman antiquities found in the area, 15,000 fossils, 17th and 18th century pottery, fine porcelain, old coins, pictures of the Flemish and Italian schools, a *Titian*, a *Turner* and a *Bonnard*, a piece of 12th century Hindu sculpture, a VIth dynasty Egyptian statue, etc.

Outside the town, near Abington Park, is **Abington Museum**, in a 17th century mansion with a large Gothic *Oak Hall*. A room to the front contains a collection of china, an adjoining room displays Chinese porcelain, and other ground floor rooms contain Egyptian antiquities, animals, old woodwork and ironwork, and a collection of old bicycles. An Elizabethan staircase (portraits of local notabilities) leads to the first floor, with rooms devoted to the actor David Garrick, local prints, natural history, minerals, ethnology, the local sculptor Eli Johnson, cottages and old pipes. Open weekdays 10 to 6, Sundays 2 to 5.

Behind the Museum is St Matthew's Church, in the left transept of which is a "Madonna and Child" by Henry Moore (1944).

Surroundings of Northampton

1 mile south is an *Eleanor cross*, the best preserved of the three surviving crosses (out of the original 14) erected by Edward I at the places where the funeral cortege of his wife Queen Eleanor (d. 1290) halted on the journey from Harby in Nottinghamshire to Westminster. Nearby are the ruins of *Delapre Abbey*, on the site of a former Cluniac house (open to visitors on Thursday and Saturday afternoons).

4 miles north-west on A 428 is *Harlestone*, just beyond which is **Althorp**, seat of Earl Spencer, in beautiful grounds: very fine furniture and many paintings by leading masters (*van Dyck*, *Lely*, *Reynolds*, *Murillo*, *Gainsborough*, *Rubens*, etc.). Open May-September on Tuesdays, Thursdays and Sundays 2.30 to 6. — 11 miles: *Thornby*, from which a minor road runs north-east to (3 miles) *Naseby*, where Parliamentary forces won a decisive victory over the Royalists in 1645.

6 miles north on A 508 is *Brixworth*, with a large and interesting church which may have been built with Roman materials in the 7th century, or may even have been a Roman building adapted for the purpose.

Northampton to Wellingborough: 10 miles on A 45.

5 miles: *Ecton*. In the churchyard are the graves of Thomas and Eleanor Franklin, uncle and aunt of the great American statesman. The church register contains the names of the Franklin family as far back as 1558. Benjamin Franklin when on a visit to England stayed at the *manor-house*, which is still standing. In the church is a modern monument to his memory. — 7 miles: off the main road to the right is *Earls Barton*, where there is a church with one of the finest late Saxon towers in England. — 10 miles: **Wellingborough** (pop. 30,000, E.C. Thursday), an industrial town manufacturing boots and shoes, situated on the north bank of the Nene. The most interesting of the few buildings which escaped a fire in 1738 is the *Hind Inn*, which contains, among some very fine rooms, the Cromwell Room. In Gold St and Cheap St are some old houses.

There is a Perpendicular church with Norman portions and grotesque misericords in the choir. To the south of the town is the very beautiful *Irchester Park*.

Northampton to Bedford: 21 miles on A 428.

3 miles: *Little Houghton*, to the north of which is Billing *Aquadrome*, with a museum in Billing Mill. — 7 miles: *Yardley Hastings*, 1 mile north of which is **Castle Ashby House,** seat of the Marquess of Northampton. The house, built of grey local stone, consists of three wings set round a courtyard, the oldest part dating from 1574. The south wing was designed by Inigo Jones (1635). There are 30 principal reception rooms and bedrooms, with fine moulded ceilings and oak panelling; several of the staircases and mantelpieces date from 1600-35. Many of the tapestries and much of the furniture date from 1660-1700. There are paintings of the English school (Reynolds, Romney, Lawrence, Hoppner, etc.), some fine pictures of the Italian Renaissance (Mantegna, Bellini, Sebastiano del Piombo, Botticelli) and works of the Dutch school (Rubens, van Dyck, Jan Steen, etc.). Open May-September 2 to 6 on Thursdays, Saturdays and Sundays.

From Yardley Hastings B 5388 runs south-east to *Olney* (pop. 2500, E.C. Wednesday). The church of SS. Peter and Paul is 14th century (Decorated). At the corner of the Market Place is the Cowper Museum, with mementoes of the poet William Cowper (1731-1800).

32. LONDON TO LEICESTER
AND NOTTINGHAM

99 miles to Leicester, 125 miles to Nottingham. A 6 to Leicester, then A 46 and A 606 to Nottingham. Leave London as in Route 31 as far as Barnet, then fork left on A 1081 to join A 6 to St Albans.

Motorway: M 1 (direct and fast).

18 miles: *Salisbury Hall*, a mediaeval manor-house altered in 1668.

22 miles: **St Albans** (pop. 52,000, E.C. Thursday), situated on a hill in the middle of a large area of low-lying land at the intersection of two main roads to the north, A 5 and A 6.

The history of the town goes back almost 2000 years. In the 1st century A.D. *Verulamium* was a Roman *municipium* whose inhabitants were automatically Roman citizens. A Roman soldier named Albanus was executed here for embracing the Christian faith and giving shelter to a Christian priest, and became the first Christian martyr in England. On the hill above the river Ver a Saxon monastery was founded to contain his shrine, and this was followed by a Norman abbey founded in the 11th century by Bishop Paul of Caen, the first Norman bishop. The mediaeval town of St Albans grew up round this religious house.

The Roman town occupied an area of some 150 acres at the crossing of the Camlet Way (Colchester to Silchester) and Watling Street (Dover to Chester).

The remains of the **Roman town** lie to the west of the present town. They include a *theatre* (the only one discovered in Britain) built about the middle of the 2nd century A.D., with seating for 2000 spectators, the forum and some remains of houses. The site is open to the public from 10 a.m. to sunset. There is a **Museum** at the entrance to the excavations (frescoes, mosaics, a bronze statue of Venus, etc.): open 10 to

4 or 5.30, Sundays from 2; May to August, Saturdays and Sundays to 8.30. Behind the Museum is a small zoo.

Opposite the Museum, on higher ground, is **St Michael's Church,** one of the three parish churches erected in the 10th century by Abbot Ulsinus.

The fabric contains many bricks taken from the Roman city. Saxon work can be seen in the blocked doorway in the north of the chancel, and over the nave arcade are round-headed windows. In the 12th century a Norman church was built, and the aisles date from this period; the clerestory is 13th century. To the south-east is the 13th century *chapel of St Mary the Virgin* (the *Leper Chapel*) with a 15th century clerestory and belfry. There is a unique double piscina in the south wall, an ancient font (1350) and an old brass lectern. Of outstandingly fine workmanship is the beautiful Jacobean carved pulpit with tester. In a recess in the choir is a life-size statue of Francis Bacon, first Lord Verulam and Viscount St Albans (d. 1626). In the vestry are remains of 15th century paintings on wood (Last Judgment). The north-west tower was built in the 19th century.

From here St Michael's St and Fishpool St (fine Georgian houses) lead to the Cathedral.

Cathedral. In the north transept are traces of a Saxon church built c. 795, when the abbey was founded by Offa II, King of Mercia, on the hill above the site of the Roman city.

The *nave* (285 ft) is one of the longest in the world, and the total length (555 ft) is more than that of any church in England except Winchester Cathedral. The transepts are 175 feet wide and the massive Norman tower, faced with tiles from the ruins of Verulamium, is 145 feet high. The Norman church extended for the same length as the church of today without the Lady Chapel. Many Roman bricks were used in the construction.

The *interior* was decorated with *painted plaster work*, of which traces can be seen on some of the pillars on the north side of the nave. In the 13th century the five west bays on the south and four on the north of the nave were rebuilt in the Early English style. The five bays at the east end of the south side (containing some of the finest arcading work in

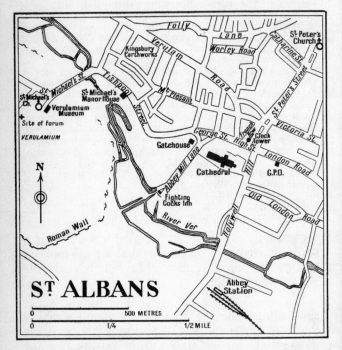

the church) date from the 14th century. The Lady Chapel was also added in the 14th century and the west front in the 19th century.

Perhaps on first seeing the nave the visitor feels a sense of disappointment, but the beauty of the building is appreciated on closer acquaintance with its detail. Great care has been taken with the restorations, and the result is impressive despite the mixture of Norman, Early English and Decorated styles.

In the north aisle of the nave are some 15th century stained-glass windows. Between the nave and the choir is a 14th century *rood-screen*. The **choir** has a *painted ceiling* dating from the 14th century; that of the chancel dates from the 15th century. Before the Reformation when there were paintings on most of the surfaces, the abbey must have presented a magnificent sight. Murals now remain only in the choir, south transept and north transept. Behind the high altar is one of the treasures of the cathedral — the delicately carved high **screen** built by Abbot John of Wheathampstead. There are also some 15th century brasses. In the south choir aisle is a fine 14th century **Abbot's Door.** An outstanding feature of the cathedral is the chapels. The *chantry of Abbot Ramryge* (Perpendicular, 1520) has fine fan-tracery and carvings. In the chantry of Abbot John of Wheathampstead is the famous *brass of Abbot de la Mare* (1385, Flemish work) which survived the Puritan period only because during the Civil War it had been turned face down. The **shrine of St Alban** was destroyed at the Reformation, but in the 19th century the base was reconstructed from fragments and restored to its original chapel. The windows are Decorated. In the north-east corner is a superb portrait (14th c.) of William FitzHerbert, Archbishop of York (1143-54). To the south is the tomb of Humphrey Duke of Gloucester, Henry V's brother.

Of the monastic buildings all that remains today is the massive *Abbey Gatehouse* (1365), which was besieged during the Peasants' Revolt of 1381 and until 1868 was used as a prison. It is now part of *St Albans School*, which was founded in the 10th century.

The town contains a number of interesting old buildings. The **Clock Tower** (1403-12, restored in 1866 by Sir George Gilbert Scott), built of flint and rubble, was originally a curfew tower. From the top there are fine views of the town.

The Eleanor Cross (see p. 150) which formerly stood in front of the Clock Tower was removed in the 17th century.

To the left is *French Row*, a narrow street of mediaeval aspect, so called because French prisoners were quartered here in 1216 when the future Louis VIII of France intervened in the civil war which followed the signing of Magna Carta. It leads to *St Peter's Street*, where in 1455 the Yorkists attacked the Lancastrians and Henry VI was taken prisoner in a baker's shop. At the end of the street is **St Peter's Church,** the second of the churches built by Abbot Ulsinus (Perpendicular, restored in the 19th c.), with a monument to Edward Strong (d. 1723), a master mason who worked with Wren on the construction of St Paul's in London.

To the left of the church are *Pemberton's Almshouses* (1629). In Hatfield Road (to the right) is another group of almshouses (1736) built by Sarah, Duchess of Marlborough. Opposite is the **County Museum** (open 10 to 4, except Sundays and Mondays): books and prints relating to Hertfordshire, Roman and British coins, Saxon objects, Bronze Age axes, mediaeval material.

Abbey Mill Lane runs from the Abbey Gatehouse to the river Ver, a tributary of the Colne. On the river is the *Fighting Cocks Inn*, the oldest inn in England (13th c.), for long a famous cock-fighting centre.

Another of St Albans' old inns is on Holywell Hill, the *White Hart Hotel*, a typical timber-and-plaster building of the 15th-16th century, containing some fine original panelling; of the Saracen's Head Inn, however, only the yard remains. Almost opposite the clock tower is the *Fleur de Lys Inn*, on the site of the house in which King John of France was imprisoned after the battle of Poitiers in 1356. The *George Inn* is an old coaching inn built in the 15th century; it was originally a monastic hostel, but today has been converted into shops.

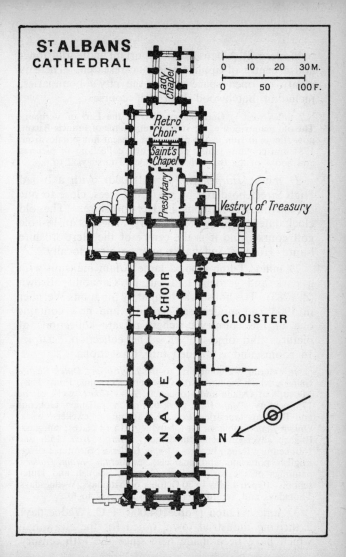

ST. ALBANS
CATHEDRAL

0   10   20   30 M.

0   50   100 F.

Lady Chapel

Retro Choir

Saint's Chapel

Presbytery

Vestry of Treasury

CHOIR

CLOISTER

NAVE

N

Modern St Albans is an important industrial town
and a centre of applied scientific research. There is
plenty of open space within the city's boundaries,
including Batchwood Hall golf course.

2 miles west is **Gorhambury,** seat of the Earl of Verulam.
The old manor-house, the 16th century home of Francis Bacon,
now stands in ruin in the park. The present house dates from
1784 and contains family portraits and collections of pictures
and books of the Bacon family. Open Thursdays 2 to 6.

27 miles: *Harpenden* (pop. 18,000), with a broad
High Street bordered by grass and trees, close to one
of the finest commons in Hertfordshire. The old
clock dates from the 18th century. There is an 18-hole
golf course, and it is the centre of the Hertfordshire
hunt. Hunters and hacks may be hired locally.

29 miles: **Luton Hoo,** a large Adam mansion with
a park and gardens laid out by Capability Brown
(d. 1783). The house was bought by Sir Julius Wernher
in 1903 and modernised by him, and now contains
one of the country's richest private collections of
pictures and objets d'art. The collection occupies
14 rooms and is divided into 12 sections.

On entering we come first to the *English and Dutch Picture
Gallery*, which includes works by Lely, Reynolds, Frans Hals,
Metsu, van Ostade and Hobbema. *Ivory Court:* work of the
17th century. *Main Hall:* work of French craftsmen, Gobelins
and Beauvais tapestries, Louis XV furniture, jewellers' work.
Dining Room: table set for a banquet with 18 places; cut glass;
English silver-gilt plate; tapestries. *Marble Hall:* 15th and
16th century Italian bronzes. *Upper Galleries:* furniture; silver;
English porcelain and enamels; jewellery. *Main Gallery:*
paintings of the early Italian, German, Spanish and Dutch
schools. (Open 4 May to 30 October on Mondays, Wednesdays,
Thursdays and Saturdays 11 to 6, Sundays 2 to 6).

32 miles: **Luton** (pop. 104,000, E.C. Wednesday),
a thriving industrial town, noted for the straw hats
which have been made here since the 17th century.

St Mary's Church, one of the largest parish churches in the country, is predominantly 15th century Perpendicular, though it contains work in every style from Norman onwards.

In the church is a canopied baptistery (14th c.), of which there are only two other examples in England. The choir has fourfold sedilia (15th c.). The *Wenlock Chapel* commemorates John Wenlock, who was killed in the battle of Tewkesbury (1461). The screen between the chapel and the choir is particularly fine.

In Wardown Park is a **Museum** (open 10 to 5 or 6): history of the straw hat industry, prehistoric material and historical relics, local crafts (including the making of pillow lace), a hoard of coins discovered locally in 1961, etc.

Luton to Baldock: 13 miles on A 505.

5 miles: *Great Offley.* — 8 miles: **Hitchin** (pop. 25,000, E.C. Wednesday), an ancient town on the river Lea at the edge of the Chiltern Hills. There is a large *parish church.* In Sun St, close to the Market Place, is the old *Sun Hotel;* the present house is an early 18th century rebuilding of an Elizabethan inn. There are many ancient houses in the town, including a *priory* and 17th century *almshouses.* 2 miles south on A 600 to Welwyn is *St Ippollitts,* where there is a very beautiful old church on the top of a hill amid charming countryside. At nearby *Chapel Foot* are the ruins of Minsden Chapel. To the west is *St Paul's Walden,* with some of the most delightful scenery in Hertfordshire.

11 miles: **Letchworth** (pop. 26,500, E.C. Wednesday). Founded in 1904 by Ebenezer Howard, Letchworth was the first "garden city" to be built in England. Good planning has enabled it to develop industrially without losing its attraction as a residential town. — 13 miles: *Baldock* (15th c. church).

38 miles *Barton-in-the-Clay.* At Sharpenhoe nearby is the National Trust property of the Clappers and

Robert's Farm; 136 acres of downland farm, including a fine spur (524 ft) of the Chilterns, crowned by Clappers Wood, a notable viewpoint. — 49 miles: *Elstow*, birthplace of John Bunyan. On the site of the cottage in which he lived after his marriage is Bunyan Cottage. The Norman and Early English church was attached to a Benedictine abbey founded in 1078 (few remains). The detached tower is in Perpendicular style. In the church are two windows commemorating Bunyan. The *Moot Hall* (15th c.) is on the old village green, which is described by Bunyan.

52 miles: **Bedford** (pop. 68,000, E.C. Thursday), a quiet agricultural town on the Ouse, the county town of Bedfordshire. There is some industry in the surrounding area.

A 6 enters the town by St John's St, in which is *St John's Church*. Adjoining are the 13th century buildings of *St John's Hospital*, founded in the 10th century, and the Rectory. In St Mary's St, the continuation of St John's St, is the Norman *St Mary's Church*, with some fine round-arched double windows and, inside, semicircular arches; in the chancel are three interesting 17th century brasses. St Mary's St leads over the Ouse, with fine riverside promenades and excellent boating. South of the bridge is an artificial mound, 15 feet high and 150 feet in diameter, on which there once stood a Norman castle. In Castle Close is the *Cecil Higgins Art Gallery* (open 11 to 6, Sundays 2 to 5): decorative arts, watercolours. Close to the bridge in High St is the *Swan Hotel*, with a staircase from Houghton House, Bunyan's "House Beautiful". In St Paul's Square is **St Paul's Church** (central tower built in 1868, with the old steeple). The choir still has its original timber roof. The east window commemorates William Harpur and his wife Alice, who founded the Harpur Schools. The *Shire Hall* dates from 1753, and has been rebuilt and enlarged since; here the county's archives are kept. At the corner of Silver St is the site of the County Gaol, where for 12 years (1660-72) Bunyan was imprisoned. It was, however, in the Town Gaol (demolished in 1765) on Bedford Bridge that during six months' imprisonment in 1675-76 he wrote "Pilgrim's Progress". On the right, opposite Silver St, is Mill St, with the *Bunyan Meeting House*, rebuilt in 1849 on the site of a barn in which Bunyan preached from 1762 to 1788: Bunyan relics, and ten panels with scenes from "Pilgrim's Progress". Adjoining is a Bunyan museum (open Tuesdays and Fridays 10 to 12 and 2 to 4). The *Howard Congregational Church* (1772) was built by John Howard, the prison reformer, whose house can be seen in Mill St.

Farther along, on the right, is St Peter's St, in which is a statue of John Bunyan (Boehm, 1874). **St Peter's Church** contains a mixture of many styles, including a Saxon tower. At No. 38 is the *Doll Museum:* dolls, period dolls, houses, miniature china services, toys, hats, shoes, etc., from 1800 onwards. (Visiting: apply to the Moravian Manse, No. 24; charge.)

In Harpur St is the **Bedford Modern School and Museum** (open 11 to 5, Sundays 2 to 5): local antiquities from the Stone Age to the present day; lace and straw mats; birds' eggs, insects and mammals; objects from Cyprus, Greece, Rome and the Far East. *Bedford School*, in Burnaby Road, was founded in 1150 and re-founded by William Harpur in 1552; the present building is 19th century.

9 miles south on A 600 (the Hitchin road) is *Shefford*, an old-world little country town. A 428 runs north-east for Cambridge (29 miles), passing through the market gardening town of *Eaton Socon* (10 miles), the Eton Slocombe of "Nicholas Nickleby".

56 miles: *Milton Ernest*. — 58 miles: *Bletsoe*. This picturesque village was the birthplace of Countess Margaret Beaufort, mother of Henry VII, foundress of Christ's and St John's Colleges, Cambridge. Edward Fitzgerald, translator of the "Rubaiyat,, of Omar Khayyam, used often to visit the Falcon Inn.

62 miles: the road enters *Northamptonshire*, a pleasant agricultural county famous for its fine churches and country houses. It is also famous for its boot and shoe manufacture, and Northampton is considered as the capital of the footwear industry.

62 miles: *Rushden*. — 63 miles: **Higham Ferrers.**
There is a fine Early English and Decorated church
with a splendid west porch. Inside are several brasses;
the stalls and rood-screen date from the time of
Archbishop Chichele (1362-1443), who was born
here and founded a college for secular canons, of
which the gateway survives, together with the school-
house and bede-house in the churchyard which can
still be seen.

10 miles west on A 45 (to St Neots and Cambridge) is *Kimbolton*, with an old castle in which Catherine of Aragon, Henry VIII's first wife, died in 1536.

67 miles: *Finedon*. — 73 miles: **Kettering** (pop.
40,000, E.C. Thursday). The late Perpendicular
church has a graceful spire.

Wicksteed Park (150 acres) was laid out after the first world
war by Charles Wicksteed, a 19th century pioneer of modern
agriculture; it was intended particularly for the enjoyment of
children.

At *Isham*, a small village just south of Kettering, is a falconry
centre, where visitors can watch the birds being trained (open
on Thursdays, Saturdays and Sundays in summer from 2 p.m.
to dusk).

Kettering to Peterborough: 29 miles on A 6, A 604 and A 605.

9 miles: *Thrapston*, 4 miles south of which is *Raunds*, with
a very beautiful church. — 14 miles: *Barnwell*, just before
which (on left) is *Lilford Park* (interesting fauna, particularly
birds). — 16 miles: **Oundle** (pop. 3000, E.C. Wednesday),
a small town on the Nene. The church is a mixture of Early
English, Decorated and Perpendicular work. The *Talbot Inn*
has a fine staircase and some mullioned windows from Fotheringhay Castle (see below). Several old inns and almshouses.
Oundle School (1544) was founded by William Laxton, Lord
Mayor of London. South-west of Oundle is *Lyveden New
Building* (National Trust: to visit, apply to caretaker), a curious
four-winged house begun about 1600 by Sir Thomas Tresham
but never finished. — 19 miles: *Warmington*, with a beautiful

Early English church which has a groined timber roof over the nave. 2 miles north-west is *Fotheringhay*, the site of the castle in which Mary Queen of Scots was tried and executed; the castle was demolished by her son James I and VI. In the fine Perpendicular church are several interesting monuments, including those of Edward Duke of York, killed at Agincourt, and Richard Duke of York, killed at Wakefield, which were erected by Queen Elizabeth I. To the south (3 miles east of Oundle) is *Ashton Wold* (National Trust), 520 acres of woodland and farmland preserved as a nature reserve. — 21 miles: *Elton*. — 24 miles: *Alwalton*. — 29 miles: *Peterborough*.

Kettering to Stamford: 22 miles on A 43.

3 miles: *Geddington*, with an Eleanor Cross (see p. 150). — 8 miles: *Great Weldon*. — 11 miles: to the left, *Deene Park*, with a very beautiful interior (open to the public at irregular times), and **Kirby Hall,** a 16th and 17th century mansion, partly ruined. — 16 miles: *Duddington*, on the Welland, an attractive village with a picturesque water-mill. — 18 miles: *Colly Weston*, another very picturesque little village, with the remains of a splendid mansion which belonged to Margaret, Countess of Richmond, Henry VII's mother. 19 miles: *Easton on the Hill*, one of the highest points in the district (300 ft) with old cottages. From the church tower Ely Cathedral and Boston Stump can be seen. — 20 miles: *Wothorpe*, a hamlet with the ruins of a turreted Elizabethan house, built in 1600 and demolished in the 18th century. Fine views from the hilltop. — 22 miles: *Stamford*.

Kettering to Oakham: 21 miles north on A 6003.

The road runs past (on left) the village of Rushton, with an Elizabethan house, **Rushton Hall,** now a school for the blind, which has a curious triangular lodge built in 1595 (open to visitors on the first Thursday in the month from 10 to 6). Beyond this, to the right, is the steel-working town of *Corby* (pop. 45,000). — 8 miles: **Rockingham Castle,** a Norman building altered in the 16th century, for centuries a royal residence (open Thursdays and Sundays 2 to 6). Charles Dickens stayed in the village. — 14 miles: *Uppingham* (p. 619). — 21 miles: *Oakham* (p. 620).

77 miles: *Rothwell*. — 79 miles: *Desborough*. — 82 miles: the road enters *Leicestershire*, chief of the "Shires", the famous foxhunting country, hunted by

the most noted packs of foxhounds, including the Quorn, the Cottesmore, the Pytchley and the Belvoir. Leicestershire is the home of the famous Stilton cheese (although *Stilton* itself is in Cambridgeshire) and of the equally famous Melton Mowbray pie. It has its industrial fame too: *Leicester* is noted for its hosiery, and *Loughborough*, noted for electrical work and for its bell-founding, produced the great bell of St Paul's Cathedral.

84 miles: **Market Harborough** (pop. 12,000, E.C. Thursday), a small town, famous as a hunting centre, built on the site of a Roman settlement. In the neighbourhood are the remains of a Roman camp. The *Grammar School* is 17th century. The Perpendicular *church* (14th and 15th c.) has a broach spire. The town is on a branch of the Grand Union Canal, and a Boat Festival and Rally is held here annually in August.

99 miles: **Leicester** (pop. 300,000, E.C. Thursday), on the river Soar, county town of Leicestershire and an important industrial centre.

LEICESTER

The earliest remains found here are those of the Roman town of *Ratae Coritanorum*, on the Fosse Way. Beside St Nicholas's Church are remains of Roman baths, with a sizeable stretch of wall, and 14 Roman pavements have been found in the city. Leicester was one of the five boroughs of the Danelaw, granted to the Danes under the treaty of Wedmore (878) and recovered by King Edmund in 941. In 1485 Richard III stayed in the town before the battle of Bosworth, and after his death in the battle was buried in the Greyfriars church. During the Civil War the town was taken by Prince Rupert.

A 6 enters the city from the south-east as London Road and runs straight into the centre, a Victorian

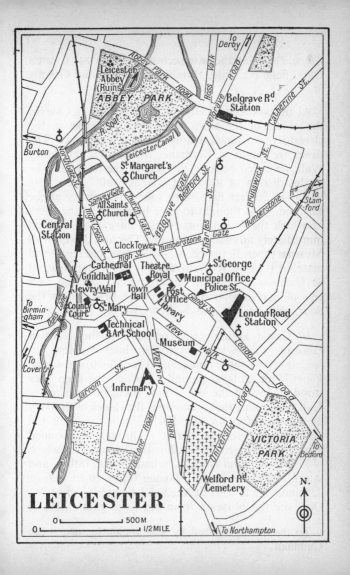

To Derby

To Burton

Leicester Abbey (Ruins)

ABBEY PARK

Abbey Park Road

Ross Walk

Belgrave Road

Belgrave Rd Station

Catherine St.

R. Soar

North Gate St.

Leicester Canal

St. Margaret's Church

Belgrave Gate

Bedford St.

Brunswick St.

Humberstone Rd

To Stamford

Sanvey Gate

Church Gate

All Saints Church

High St.

Central Station

High Cross St.

Clock Tower

Humberstone Gate

Charles St.

Humberstone Gate

To Birmingham

Cathedral

Guildhall

Theatre Royal

St. George

Municipal Office

Police St.

Jewry Wall

Town Hall

Post Office

Canby St.

London Road Station

To Coventry

Dun's Lane

County Court

St. Mary

Library

Technical & Art School

Museum

New Walk

London Road

Welford Road

Jarrom St.

Infirmary

Aylestone Road

University Road

VICTORIA PARK

To Bedford

Welford Rd Cemetery

LEICESTER

0 ———— 500M

0 ———— 1/2 MILE

To Northampton

N.

Clock Tower at the intersection of High St, Church Gate, Belgrave Gate, Humberstone Gate and Granby St.

At the west end of High St is **St Nicholas's Church,** the oldest in the town, with Roman bricks in the clerestory and much Saxon and Norman work. The tower (restored) is Norman. Beside it is the **Jewry Wall,** so called because the Jewish ghetto used to be in this district: a stretch of Roman wall 70 feet long and over 20 feet high, with four large arches at the east end. It is thought to have been part of the baths of which the foundation courses have been exposed immediately adjoining the wall. The new **Jewry Wall Museum** (open 10 to 6) contains Roman and mediaeval material. More Roman remains can be seen at 50 St Nicholas St and in Blackfriars St. At the west end of St Nicholas St is the West Bridge over the Soar, and beyond this is Bow Bridge.

In Castle St are some remains of the Norman *Leicester Castle* incorporated in later building (to see, apply to the caretaker). The *Mount* (or *Castle View*) is an artificial mound on which the keep once stood. Most of the site is now occupied by County Hall. Adjoining the gatehouse is the **church of St Mary de Castro** (Norman and Early English, with a tall and slender modern spire). Through the ruined Turret Gateway to the south is the Newarke, in which is *Trinity Hospital* (14th c., rebuilt in the 18th c. and later). *Newarke House Museum* (open 10 to 5, 6 or 7, Sundays 2 to 5) is devoted to Leicester's industries. Opposite the Museum is an old town gate (1410).

To the north, reached by way of Southgates, is the **Guildhall.**

This was originally the **Chantry House** (14th c.) of the Corpus Christi Guild. Mayor's Parlour, with fine woodwork; Library (1632). Open 10 to 5, 6 or 7, except Sundays.

St Martin's Church (mainly Early English, with a Perpendicular choir) was raised to cathedral status in 1926.

In Horsefair St, south of the Market, is the *Town Hall* (1876), with a tower 150 feet high.

To the south, near London Road Station, is the **Museum and Art Gallery,** built in 1836 (open 10 to 5, 6 or 7, Sundays 2 to 5).

Sculpture by *Moore* and *Epstein;* pictures by *Maes, S. van Ruysdael* and *Luti;* silver, Chinese, Arab and English porcelain; Japanese objets d'art; works by *Constable, Turner, Opie, Fernley, E. Nolde, Sisley, Pissarro, Degas, Renoir, Vlaminck,* etc.

To the north, in *Abbey Park,* are the remains of **Leicester Abbey,** founded in the 12th century by Augustinian monks but altered in later centuries (particularly the 16th).

To the north-east, in Belgrave Road (the Loughborough road), is *Belgrave Hall,* an early 18th century mansion which is now a museum (open 10 to 5, 6 or 7).

5 miles north-west (reached either via the village of *Cropston* or via *Anstey,* on B 5327, and *Newtown Linford,* with charming 16th and 17th century cottages) is **Bradgate Park** (800 acres), on the edge of Charnwood Forest. *Bradgate House,* now in ruins, was the birthplace of Lady Jane Grey (1537). The house, built in 1501 by the Marquess of Dorset and his son, was allowed to fall into ruin in the 18th century. Interesting chapel; magnificent park.

Surroundings of Leicester

Leicester to Peterborough: 41 miles on A 47.

8 miles: *Billesdon.* — 13 miles: *East Norton.* — 19 miles: **Uppingham** (pop. 3000, E.C. Thursday), with a famous public school founded in the 16th century by Robert Johnson, Archdeacon of Leicester.

6 miles north of Uppingham on A 6003 is **Oakham** (pop. 4000, E.C. Thursday). Of the Norman *castle* only the great banqueting hall, with fine carving on the capitals, remains. In the Market Place is the octagonal *Butter Cross*, beneath which are the old stocks. In the nave of the fine old church are some notable carved capitals. Jacobean library. Near the church is the original building of *Oakham School*, also founded by Archdeacon Johnson.

23 miles: A 6121 goes off on the left to *South Luffenham*, with *North Luffenham* (interesting Gothic church) to the north. — 27 miles: *Duddington*. — 33 miles: *Wansford*. — 41 miles: **Peterborough** (p. 589).

Leicester to Grantham: 30 miles on A 46 and A 607.

5 miles: *Syston*. — 15 miles: **Melton Mowbray** (pop. 17,500, E.C. Thursday), centre of the fox-hunting country of the Midlands, an attractive little town which is also noted for its pork pies. The church is a small Early English structure with a tower and steeple, richly ornamented west porch and 48 fine windows. There are a number of mediaeval houses. *Bede House* (almshouse, 1540). *Egerton Lodge* (neo-Tudor, 1829), a hunting lodge of the Earl of Wilton, now houses local government offices. 4 miles east is **Stapleford Park** (miniature railway, lion reserve), with a 16th and 17th century mansion (open Thursday and Sunday afternoons during the season). The *church of St Mary Magdalen* (Richardson, 1783) contains interesting monuments.

20 miles: *Waltham on the Wolds*, with a Norman church standing on high ground above the village. — 23 miles: *Croxton Kerrial*, from which there are some of the finest views in the district. Over the park walls can be seen remains of a Premonstratensian abbey, where King John's body lay before his burial in Worcester. 3 miles north is *Belvoir Castle*, built by Robert de Todeni, William the Conqueror's standard-bearer at the battle of Hastings. It was badly damaged during the Civil War, but restoration work was begun in the 18th century and completed in 1807. Very fine views. — 26 miles: the road enters Lincolnshire. — 30 miles: *Grantham*.

Leicester to Derby: 28 miles on A 6, which follows the valley of the Soar, through very beautiful country.

7 miles: *Mountsorrel*. — 11 miles: **Loughborough** (pop. 40,000, E.C. Wednesday), the second largest town in Leicestershire, a pleasant market town noted for its bell foundries, which have

produced, among other famous bells, Great Paul (17 tons, 1881), now in the south-west tower of St Paul's in London. The War Memorial Tower (1923), 150 feet high, has a carillon of 47 bells. — To the south-west is *Charnwood Forest*, 60 sq. miles of craggy hills. The highest point is Bardon Hill (921 ft). Ruins of two Augustinian priories, in beautiful parks: *Ulverscroft* and *Grace Dieu*. *Rothley Temple* is an early Tudor mansion (now a hotel) in which Lord Macaulay was born in 1800. — 25 miles: *Elvaston*. — 28 miles: *Derby*.

Leaving Leicester on A 46, the old Fosse Way, we pass through *Thurmaston* (102 miles) and enter Nottinghamshire (105 miles).

Nottinghamshire. Perhaps the feature for which it is most renowned is *Sherwood Forest*, haunt of Robin Hood and his merry men. Much of what was forest in ancient days is now arable land, but north of the county town of Nottingham — particularly round Ollerton — are surviving stretches of woodland famous for their grand and ancient oaks. To the west are the spreading coalfields of the county, but the northern stretches of the forest were preserved from despoliation by their development into vast parks which, by reason of their noble owners, gained for the area the title of the *Dukeries*. Of these great parks *Welbeck*, home of the Duke of Portland, is most widely known, mainly for the great underground reception rooms and passages and galleries constructed there by the eccentric and now almost legendary Duke of Portland in the 19th century. His neighbour dukes were the Dukes of Norfolk, Newcastle and Kingston.

110 miles: *Six Hills*. — 113 miles: to the left is *Willoughby-on-the-Wolds*, near which is the site of the Roman town of *Vernometum*. — 115 miles: *Widmerpool* cross-roads. The Fosse Way continues north-east to Newark-on-Trent (6 miles) and Lincoln (22 miles). At the crossroads we take the left fork for West Bridgford.

125 miles: **Nottingham.**

NOTTINGHAM

Nottingham (pop. 320,000 E.C. Thursday), a university town, has played a leading part in English
history. Here in 1642 Charles I raised his standard
on Standard Hill, the first act in the Civil War. The
town also has associations with Byron. It has been
famous for generations for its lace and hosiery, and
more recently has acquired other industries — cigarettes (Players), pharmaceuticals (boots), hosiery
(Morleys), bicycles (Raleigh).

The town, probably built on the site of a Roman station,
was known in Saxon times as *Snodengahane*, and was one of
the five boroughs of the Danelaw (see Leicester, p. 616). During
the industrial revolution of the early 19th century Nottingham
was the centre of the Luddite movement, in which the hosiery
workers banded themselves together against their employers
and destroyed the newly installed machinery.

The *Market Place* is the largest in the country,
although no market is now held there.

The famous *Goose Fair* formerly held in the square (first
Thursday in October and the two following days) is now held
in the Forest Recreation Ground, once part of Sherwood
Forest. There are some picturesque old houses round the
square. At one end is the fine new City Hall (1928).

From the south-west corner of the square Prior
Lane and Park St climb up to the **Castle,** on a steep
crag above the town. 150 feet below flows the river
Leen, which joins the Trent just to the south of the
town.

The original castle was built by William the Conqueror. It
was rebuilt by the Duke of Newcastle in 1674 on the site of
the older keep, and was burned down in 1831 during a riot
against the Duke of the day, an opponent of the Reform Bill.
It was acquired by the town in 1878 and made into a **Museum
and Art Gallery** (open 10 a.m. to dusk): pictures by the Not-

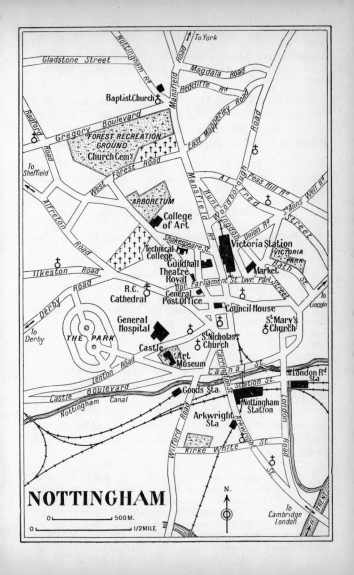

NOTTINGHAM

To York

Gladstone Street

Magdala Road

Redcliffe Rd

Baptist Church

Gregory Boulevard

East Mapperley Road

FOREST RECREATION
GROUND

Church Cemy

West Forest Road

To
Sheffield

ARBORETUM

Peas Hill Rd

S.Anns Well Rd

College
of Art

Union Rd

Victoria Station

VICTORIA
PARK

Technical
College

Shakespeare St

Bath St

Market

Ilkeston Road

Guildhall
Theatre
Royal

Upr. Parliament St. Lwr. Parl. Street

R.C.
Cathedral

General
Post Office

To
Lincoln

Council House

Derby Road

General
Hospital

St Nicholas
Church

St Mary's
Church

THE PARK

Castle

Art
Museum

Trinity St

Carrington St

Station St

London Rd
Sta

Lenton Road

Castle Boulevard

Goods Sta.

Nottingham Canal

London Road

Nottingham
Station

Arkwright
Sta

Wilford Road

Arkwright St

Kirke White St

N.

0 — 500 M.

0 — 1/2 MILE

To
Cambridge
London

R. TRENT

To
Derby

Alfreton Road

Radford Road

Nottingham Rd

Mansfield Rd

Mansfield Rd

Woodborough Rd

tingham artists *Richard Bonington* and *Paul Sandby;* Greek and Roman antiquities; mediaeval alabaster sculpture, Wedgwood ware, textiles, Nottingham lace.

St Mary's Church (15th c., with a later tower and choir) is the finest of the city's churches. University College, in Highfields Park (at the end of University Boulevard), is the most notable of its modern buildings.

2 miles west is *Wollaton Hall*, an Elizabethan mansion which now houses an industrial museum.

Surroundings of Nottingham

1. Nottingham to Worksop via Mansfield: 27 miles on A 60.

9 miles: entrance to the park of **Newstead Abbey,** home of Byron (now owned by Nottingham). The abbey incorporates part of an old priory, including the Early English west front, the rectory, the chapel (originally the chapter house) and the cloisters. Byron succeeded to the title and property in 1798. There are many Byron relics, and his bedroom and sitting room.

14 miles: **Mansfield** (pop. 56,000, E.C. Wednesday), a flourishing town on the river Maun and a good centre for excursions to Sherwood Forest. It occupies the site of an old Roman town. *St Peter's Church* was rebuilt in the 14th century on the site of a Norman building, but has undergone constant alteration and restoration.

3 miles north-west on A 617 is *Pleasley*, the best way of approach to **Hardwick Hall,** property of the Duke of Devonshire and one of the finest of England's Elizabethan mansions, built in 1590-97 by the Countess of Shrewsbury. The house contains magnificent portraits, tapestry and furniture, and stands in 620 acres of park. (Open Wednesdays, Thursdays, Saturdays and Sundays 2 to 6).

From Mansfield A 60 follows the Roman *Leeming Lane* through the woodlands of Sherwood Forest and the parks of the Dukeries.

19 miles: *Market Warsop*. — 21 miles: *Cuckney*. To the right is *Welbeck Park*, with **Welbeck Abbey,** former seat of the Duke of Portland.

The house dates chiefly from the 17th century but includes parts of the old 12th century abbey. The main interest of the mansion lies in the 1½ miles of underground rooms and tunnels constructed by the 5th Duke (d. 1879). Among them are the Picture Gallery and the Ballroom (160 ft long by 65 ft wide) which, when it was built, was the largest room in England without columns.

27 miles: **Worksop** (pop. 35,000, E.C. Wednesday), a small mining town at the north end of the Dukeries, a good centre from which to explore this area.

The old **Norman church** was formerly the nave of a larger priory church built in 1103. Magnificent *Norman door* between the towers, and two other doorways on the north side. The Lady Chapel (Early English) is now a war memorial chapel. Remains of cloisters; 14th century gatehouse (Decorated). Interesting *museum* (prehistoric cup, sculpture from Pergamum).

Worksop Manor (to the west) stands in beautiful grounds; it was originally built by the Countess of Shrewsbury (see Hardwick Hall, above), but was destroyed by fire in 1761. The present house is much less magnificent.

2. Worksop to Nottingham via Ollerton: 28 miles A 6009 from Worksop to Budby, then A 616 to Ollerton, then A 614 to Nottingham).

A 6009 runs through the Dukeries, east of Welbeck (see above) and west of **Clumber Park,** seat of the Dukes of Newcastle until 1928.

The beautiful 18th century **Clumber House** was demolished in 1928 on the death of the 7th Duke. The extensive park is maintained by the National Trust and contains a superb avenue of limes, 3 miles long. The park and lake are open to the public.

7 miles: *Budby*. To the east is **Thoresby House,** seat of Earl Manvers, a 19th century mansion in Elizabethan style.

The park is ten miles in circumference and contains some of the oldest oak-trees in England. Here in 1689 was born Lady Mary Wortley Montagu, noted for her amusing "Letters from Turkey". (Park open to pedestrians and cars on Wednesdays, Thursdays and Saturdays 2.30 to 6, Sundays 12.30 to 6).

9 miles: *Ollerton*, a splendid centre for excursions in Sherwood Forest and the Dukeries and a charming village. 2 miles west on B 6033 is *Edwinstowe*, also a good centre.

10 miles: A 611 forks right to Mansfield, via (3 miles) *Clipstone*, with the ruins of "King John's Palace". A 614 now runs to the west of *Rufford Park*.

Rufford Abbey, seat of Lord Savile until 1931, is one of England's most beautiful country houses. A Cistercian abbey was founded here in 1148; the present house is 16th century.

16 miles: *Farnsfield*. Intersection with A 617 from Mansfield to Newark. 5 miles east on A 617 is **Southwell** (pop. 4500, E.C. Thursday), a peaceful little town whose fine **Minster** in 1884 became a Cathedral.

It is a beautiful example of a Norman church; the nave, transepts and three towers all date from 1150. The interior is very impressive; the choir (Early English) is 13th century and has a combined triforium and clerestory with round windows. The Decorated stone screen between the nave and the choir is 14th century. There is some fine carving on the capitals and mouldings on the exterior of the tower arches. The most beautiful part is the Decorated chapter house, with magnificent carvings (1300). To the south are the remains of the 15th century palace of the Archbishops of York.

3. Nottingham to Grantham: 24 miles on A 52.

5 miles: *Radcliffe-on-Trent*. — 9 miles: *Bingham* (pop. 1680, E.C. Wednesday). — 16 miles: *Bottesford*, a charming little village on the banks of the Devon, amid picturesque and peaceful rural countryside. The Perpendicular church has a 222 foot high tower; inside are monuments to the Earls of Rutland, whose seat is *Belvoir Castle*, 4 miles south (p. 620). — 16 miles: the road enters Lincolnshire. — 24 miles: *Grantham*.

4. Nottingham to Stamford: 40 miles on A 606.

12 miles: *Upper Broughton*. — 13 miles: *Nether Broughton*, with a fine church which has survived almost without alteration since it was built in 1500. It contains interesting monuments to members of the families living in nearby *Broughton Hall*. — 15 miles: *Ab Kettleby*, a charming village on top of the Wolds. The church (restored) has a lofty spire. In the main street is a curious gabled cottage of ironstone and brick with a thatched roof. — 19 miles: **Melton Mowbray** (p. 620). — 21 miles: *Burton Lazars*, named after a leper-house founded in the 12th century. 13th century church with fine arcades and an old font. The Wolds lie all round this rich and fertile farming district. — 29 miles: **Oakham** (p. 620). — 35 miles: *Empingham*, a delightful little village of thatched cottages on the river Gwash. Early English church. — 40 miles: *Stamford* (p. 577).

33. DERBYSHIRE AND THE PEAK

Derbyshire is famous for its Peak District, a region of bold moorland hills, often precipitous and intersected by steep valleys through which wander streams of great beauty. It lies in the north-west corner of the county, is some 22 miles broad and 30 miles long, and extends from Chesterfield on the east to Buxton on the west, and from Glossop on the north to Ashbourne on the south. The highest points are *Kinder Scout* (2088 ft) in the High Peak; *Axe Edge* (1810 ft), south-east of Buxton, and *Mam Tor* (1710 ft), near Castleton. Among the many excellent centres from which to explore the Peak, one of the best-known is **Buxton:** it is also one of the noted spas of England. Situated 1000 feet above sea level, it is surrounded by places of great interest and beauty, of which Chatsworth, Haddon Hall, Dovedale, Monsal Dale, Peveril Castle and Castleton are but a few. *Chatsworth*, the stately home of the Duke of Devonshire, is of interest not only for its fine collection of pictures but as the place of detention of Mary Queen of Scots. *Haddon Hall* is a fortified mediaeval house of great beauty, the property of the Duke of Rutland, associated with the romantic Dorothy Vernon, who eloped with John Manners in the 16th century. The picturesque town of *Bakewell* is another centre from which the beauties of the Peak District may be explored, and other good centres are Macclesfield, Chesterfield and Matlock. *Chesterfield* is known for its beautiful parish church with a twisted spire. Nearby is the rich coalfield of *Staveley*. To the north of the Peak District is *Macclesfield*, centre of the British silk industry, only a short distance from Manchester.

DERBY

Derby (pop. 220,000, E.C. Wednesday), county town of Derbyshire, situated on the river Derwent in the first foothills of the Pennines, is a well planned industrial town noted for such important industrial establishments as the Rolls Royce factory and the Crown Derby china manufactory.

Derby's history dates back to the Roman station and *colonia* of *Derventio*, which grew up on the east bank of the Derwent

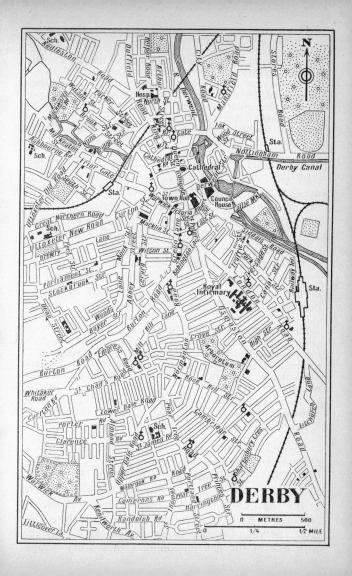

DERBY

METRES 500

1/4 1/2 MILE

and later became one of the five boroughs of the Danelaw (see Leicester, p. 616). After the Norman Conquest William the Conqueror's natural son built a castle which has long since disappeared, and Derby features in Domesday Book as a town of some consequence. During the Civil War it was taken by Parliamentary forces after their victory at Tissington. It was the most southerly point reached by Bonnie Prince Charlie in 1745.

In Market Place are the *Guildhall* (1841) and *Assembly Rooms* (1764). To the west, in the Ward-wick, is the *Museum* (open 10 to 5, Sundays 2 to 5): archaeology, a magnificent collection of Derby and other china, an exhibition illustrating the industrial development of the town, and a variety of pictures.

All Saints Church, which was raised to cathedral status in 1927, is a fine Perpendicular building with a crenellated tower 174 feet high. There are four corner pinnacles, one of which was cut off by a stray barrage balloon during the last war.

The main structure was built by James Gibbs in the 18th century. There are a number of interesting monuments, including the ornately carved alabaster tomb of "Bess of Hardwick", Countess of Shrewsbury (see Hardwick, p. 624), and others by Roubiliac, Nollekens and Chantrey. Note also the beautiful wrought-iron screen and the Devonshire Chapel.

Nearby is *St Alkmund's Church*, with a spire 30 feet higher than the Cathedral. The church (10th c., rebuilt in 1841) contains a Saxon sarcophagus and a 13th century font.

Beyond the Shire Hall (17th c.) is *St Werburgh's Church*, with the very fine chantry of Sarah Whingates (d. 1828). The Wardwick and Victoria St lead to St Peter's St, in which is *St Peter's Church*, the oldest in the town (14th c.). A modern Council House, a rectangular building in russet brick, stands above the river. Between Derwent Bridge and St Mary's Bridge, with one of the few remaining 13th century bridge chapels, *St Mary's of the Bridge*, is the first silk mill in Britain (1717). In St Michael's Lane are a number of picturesque old houses, including *Ye Olde Dolphin*, an ancient inn, and the *Mayor's Parlour*, a quaint half-timbered building.

There are a number of **parks** in the town: the *Arboretum*, established in 1840, with rare trees and shrubs; *Darley Abbey Park*, with a Georgian mansion (1737), famous for its gardens; *Markeaton Park* (200 acres); the *Racecourse Park*, *Riverside Gardens*, etc. Boating on the Derwent; motorboats can be hired.

4 miles north-east on the Heanor road (A 608) is the village of **Morley**, with a fine *church* (15th-16th c.) containing notable tombs (15th to 18th c.).

5 miles north-west is **Kedleston Hall** (open Sundays 2 to 6), an 18th century mansion in neo-classical style. South front and *Great Hall* by Robert Adam; *Dining Room*, with paintings by Angelica Kaufmann. Beautiful *park*, with a bridge by Adam. In the village is a 13th century *church*, with Curzon family tombs, including a fine 15th century tomb of the Lord Curzon of the day.

Derby to Buxton via Matlock

A 6 runs north from Derby through the beautiful Derwent valley.

4 miles: *Duffield*. Situated at the junction of the Derwent and the little river Ecclesbourne, where there was once a Roman fort, Duffield is a growing modern town set in wooded hills. The church has parts dating from the 12th and 15th centuries and contains a number of alabaster monuments.

7 miles: **Belper** (pop. 15,000, E.C. Wednesday), on the Derwent. One of the first five cotton mills in England was opened here in 1776 by Richard Arkwright. The town now produces not only cotton goods but hosiery, gloves, textiles and hardware.

10 miles: *Ambergate*, an important road junction.

Ambergate to Nottingham: 18 miles on A 610.   4 miles:
Ripley (pop. 17,500, E.C. Wednesday), an industrial town,
with collieries, foundries, iron and steel works and local manufactures. — 19 miles: *Eastwood* (pop. 9000, E.C. Wednesday).
The town, situated in Nottinghamshire, depends chiefly on
the collieries in the neighbouring west corner of Derbyshire.
— 14 miles: *Kimberley*. — 18 miles: *Nottingham* (p. 622).

12 miles: **Whatstandwell** (E.C. Wednesday), in a
very picturesque part of the Derwent valley, with
good trout fishing and walking in the neighbourhood.
To the west are Shining Cliff Woods, 200 acres of
woodland on the west bank of the river.   2 miles
west of the woods is *Alport Height*, from the top of
which (1034 ft) there are wide views: in clear weather
the Derbyshire coalfields can be seen.

B 5035 runs east to *Crich* (2 miles), a small town on a hill,
with splendid views in all directions.   On the top of Crich
Stand (950 ft), a hill to the north, is the *Sherwood Foresters
War Memorial* (1923); limestone quarry. — 4 miles: *South
Wingfield*, with the ruins of the historic Wingfield Manor
House, built by Ralph Cromwell in the 15th century, the fortifications of which were destroyed by the Parliamentarian forces
during the Civil War.   The house (particularly the banqueting
hall and cellars) is a fine example of Gothic architecture. —
7 miles: *Alfreton*.

13 miles: B 5036 goes off on the left to **Wirksworth**
(4 miles), a lead-mining town surrounded by hills.

The town has associations with George Eliot, and there is
a tablet commemorating Elizabeth Evans, the Dinah Morris
of "Adam Bede".   Cruciform church with Norman and Early
English work.

Pleasant walking in the neighbourhood.   In the hillsides
are ancient mine shafts, some of them Roman and Saxon,
some dating back even earlier to the time of the Phoenicians.

15 miles: *Cromford.* The hills begin to crowd in over the road, which is dominated by massive tors. This wild scenery of crags thrusting through the dense woods continues until the Matlocks (see below) are passed. On A 5012 (running west) is the *Via Gellia*, a ravine 2 miles long between towering cliffs covered with vegetation.

16 miles: **Matlock** (pop. 18,760, E.C. Thursdays). "The Matlocks" is the name given to Matlock Bath and Matlock, now regarded as one town. They lie beneath the massive limestone High Tor (673 ft) which descends abruptly to the River Derwent. On the other side of the gorge is Masson (1110 ft), part of which is known as the Heights of Abraham in commemoration of Gen. Wolfe's death at Quebec.

In the surrounding woodlands are the Rutland, Cumberland and Masson caverns, ancient Roman lead mines (open to the public). From Victoria Prospect Tower there is a magnificent view.

Matlock Bath is a spa, with thermal springs (20° C) for the treatment of rheumatic and allied conditions. The first spa establishment was Smedley's, opened in 1850. From Matlock can be seen *Riber Castle*, built by Smedley, on the hill (800 ft) opposite Masson.

Beyond Matlock the valley opens out, and the road continues through green meadowland, with hills on either side.

19 miles: 3 miles south-west is *Winster.* The old market-house dates from the late 17th or early 18th century. 2 miles north of Winster is the bold gritstone escarpment of Stanton Moor Edge, over 900 feet high, commanding fine views over the Derwent Valley.

22 miles: **Rowsley** (pop. 200, E.C. Tuesday), at the junction of the Derwent with its tributary Wye,

one of the most beautiful spots in the Peak District and famous for angling. The main road turns left from the Derwent valley and ascends the valley of the Wye, which is remarkably beautiful in every part.

Rowsley to Chapel-en-le-Frith: 20 miles on A 623.

1 miles: *Beeley.* The road passes west of Chatsworth Park (below) to (3 miles) Edensor and (5 miles) Baslow. — 7 miles: *Calver,* where an 18th century bridge spans the Derwent. — 7¾ miles: *Stoney Middleton,* a charmingly picturesque village of colour-washed cottages, nestling in a steep valley. There is a unique 15th century octagonal church. 1 mile north on A 6010 is *Eyam* (pronounced "Eem"), a picturesque village situated on a steep hillside.

12 miles: *Tideswell,* a village with steep hills and limestone peaks on every hand. There is a 14th century church with monuments and brasses.

16 miles: *Peak Forest.* — 18 miles: *Sparrowpit.* — 20 miles: *Chapel-en-le-Frith* (p. 639).

24 miles: **Haddon Hall,** a magnificent mediaeval mansion unspoiled by additions or reconstruction, with splendid state apartments and a banqueting hall. It is associated with the story of Dorothy Vernon's elopement; after her marriage to John Manners it passed to the Dukes of Rutland. Open April-September 11 to 6, except Sundays and Mondays.

Chapel of 1427 (stained glass, frescoes). Magnificent **Great Hall** (14th c.). *Parlour* (1550) and *Solar* (early 16th c.). **Long Gallery** (early 17th c.), 120 feet long. Splendid **gardens** of the same period.

26 miles **Bakewell** (pop. 3900, E.C. Thursday), a delightful town on the river Wye, situated amid green meadows, high wooded hills and spreading moorlands. The **church** (dating from Saxon times) was rebuilt in the 11th century and contains much Norman work. In the churchyard is an 8th century

Saxon cross. The 14th century *Vernon Chapel* (rebuilt in the 19th c.), contains the monuments of Dorothy Vernon and John Manners and their children (see above). There are other interesting monuments. The **bridge** over the Wye, with five pointed arches and triangular quoins over the buttresses, is one of the oldest in the country. Bakewell's Agricultural Show (on the Thursday in August bank holiday week) is one of the most important in the Midlands. Bakewell is a centre for some of the finest scenery in the Peak District.

Bakewell to Chesterfield: 13 miles (A 622 for 1 mile, then A 619).

1 mile: turn right into A 619 for (2 miles) *Baslow* (pop. 845, E.C. Thursday), one of the prettiest villages in the district, set in a beautiful valley. 2 miles south is **Chatsworth House,** a large Palladian mansion begun by the first Duke of Devonshire in 1687. There are some remains of the house built by the Countess of Shrewsbury, "Bess of Hardwick" (see p. 624), when the property was bought by her second husband, Sir William Cavendish. The north wing dates from 1820-27. The house contains **magnificent collections of furniture paintings and porcelain.** The **gardens** cover some 8 acres. Near the bridge over the Derwent, which flows through the deer park (with a perimeter some 12 miles long), is *Queen Mary's Bower*, where Mary Queen of Scots is supposed to have sat during her captivity. Open April-September 11.30 to 4, Sundays 2 to 5; closed Mondays and Tuesdays.

13 miles: **Chesterfield** (pop. 70,000, E.C. Wednesday), the "town of the twisted spire", is an industrial centre (coal-mining, foundries), but is well planned, with wide streets and open spaces.

The town was made a borough by King John. In the 16th century it was ravaged by plague, and during the Civil War was the scene of a battle in which the Royalists defeated the Parliamentary forces. In the 18th century it developed into an industrial town. Stephenson, who invented a miner's safety lamp and the railway engine, lived in Tapton House (now a school), and was buried in Trinity Church.

The 14th century Decorated *church of St Mary and All Saints* is a cruciform building, 170 feet by 110 feet across the transepts, containing traces of the Norman church. Its chief curiosity is its twisted spire, 230 feet high, octagonal in plan, with lead tiles in herringbone pattern. The shape of the spire is due to the warping of the timber or to some constructional fault: it first leans 12 feet to the south, then 12 feet to the south-west, and finally 3 feet to the west.

6 miles east on A 632 is *Bolsover*, an industrial town with many collieries. Bolsover Castle, which dominates the land-scape, was built on a peak (600 ft) by William Peveril, son of William the Conqueror, and rebuilt in 1613 by the son of the Countess of Shrewsbury. The keep incorporates work of both periods.

28 miles: *Ashford-in-the-Water*. A charming village where the curfew still rings each night. There are several old mansions in the district: *Churchdale Hall*, *Ashford Hall* and the Tudor *Thornbridge Hall*. On the nearby hills are several ancient tumuli.

The road climbs through increasingly beautiful scenery. At 31 miles it reaches *Monsal Dale*, where the Wye winds round the foot of Fir Cop at a particularly lovely spot.

33 miles: road on right to *Miller's Dale*, where the Wye is no more than a foaming mountain stream.

38 miles: **Buxton** (pop. 19,000, E.C. Wednesday), a spa situated 1000 feet above sea level, with a bracing climate. There are nine springs, giving at least 250,000 gallons a day at a constant temperature of 28 °C; chalybeate water. To the east of the *Crescent* (in the style of Wood's crescents in Bath) are the *Thermal Baths*, to the west the *Natural Baths*, where all kinds of modern treatment are administered. The thermal and chalybeate water of *St Ann's Well*, supplied to the Pump Room in front of the Crescent, is efficacious in the treatment of rheumatism.

The *Devonshire Royal Hospital* occupies what was originally the ducal riding school. *St Anne's Church* (1625), in Bath Road, has massive oak beams. The **Museum,** in Peak Buildings, Terrace Road, contains prehistoric material found in caverns in the area or recovered by excavation (open weekdays 10 to 1 and 2.30 to 6). In *Poole's Cavern* (in Green Lane, off Temple Road) are stalactites and stalagmites.

Around Buxton. There are many noted beauty spots. 1 mile south are *Grin Low* and Solomon's Temple, with magnificent views. 2 miles south is *Axe Edge* (1800 ft), the second highest point in the Peak District, 1 mile from which are *Ashwood Dale*, *Sherwood Dell* and *Lover's Leap*.

Derby to Buxton via Ashbourne

A 52 to Ashbourne, then A 515.

13 miles: **Ashbourne** (pop. 5700, E.C. Wednesday). This old market town situated in a narrow valley, with Thorpe Cloud and the Dovedale mountains behind, is an excellent centre for Dovedale and the Izaak Walton country. *St Oswald's Church* (spire 212 ft high) is principally in the Early English style: 13th century brasses and finely ornamented tombs. The adjoining Ashbourne Grammar School dates from 1585, although the school itself has been transferred to new premises. The fine park of *Ashbourne Hall*, a Jacobean mansion, is now a public park. There are numerous associations with Dr Johnson and Boswell, George Eliot and other literary figures.

4 miles south-west on B 5082, in the Dove valley, is *Ellastone*, the Hayslope of George Eliot's "Adam Bede". To the north of Ellastone is *Wootton Hall*, where Jean-Jacques Rousseau stayed in 1766 and wrote the greater part of his "Confessions".

15 miles: *Fenny Bentley*. In the old church is a monument to Thomas Beresford, who fought at Agincourt (1415), with eight of his sons.

B 5056 goes off on the right to *Haddon Hall* and *Bakewell* (p. 634). To the east of this road is the little village of *Brassington*. Interesting discoveries have been made in the caverns and quarries of this area (see Buxton Museum, p. 637). Curious geological formations at the *Rainster Rocks* and *Harboro Rocks*.

17 miles: *Tissington*, an old "model village" near the beautiful valley of Dovedale. To the west is *Thorpe*, north of which extends the *Dovedale Gorge*, which along with the neighbouring Manifold valley makes up the Peak District National Park. The valley of the Dove is of outstanding beauty, with tree-clad limestone escarpments sloping down to the banks of the crystalline river.

Dovedale is the setting of the "Compleat Angler", the angler's classic. Charles Cotton, its co-author with Izaak Walton, was born and lived in *Beresford Hall* (now in ruins), and the "Fishing Temple" used by the two friends still exists. The Dove has maintained its reputation, particularly as a trout stream. Dovedale is mentioned in the works of Dr Johnson, Byron, Tennyson, Ruskin and other writers. At Ilam, 2 miles west, are 85 acres of park and woodland (National Trust), extending over both banks of the Manifold at the point where it emerges from its subterranean course to join the Dove. Ilam Hall (19th c.) has been converted into a youth hostel. Nearby is *Paradise Walk*, with the remains of a Saxon cross.

19 miles: *Alsop-en-le-Dale* (E.C. Wednesday). Entrance to the magnificent National Trust property extending on both banks of the Dove from *Biggin Dale* in the north to Ilam in the south, 825 acres of woodland and open country.

A 515 then runs along the line of a Roman road to *Buxton* (34 miles): see above.

Surroundings of Buxton

1. Buxton to Glossop: 15 miles on A 624.

3 miles: Doveholes. — 6 miles: **Chapel-en-le-Frith** (pop. 6500, E.C. Wednesday), an ancient market town built of grey millstone grit, on a spur of Eccles Pike (1½ miles west). To the south, at the end of the beautiful valley below the town, is Combs Moss.

Chapel has retained its old-world appearance: the market cross dates from 1634, and the old stocks stand in front of the Roebuck Inn. Among a number of fine houses in the district are Ford Hall; Bowden Hall, containing parts of a very ancient mansion; and Bradshaw Hall, with a Jacobean gateway, dating from 1620.

8 miles: *Chinley Head*, an important railway junction and an excellent centre for the north Derbyshire hills. — 10 miles: *Hayfield* (pop. 2300, E.C. Wednesday), an excellent approach to Kinder Scout and an industrial centre. From South Ridge Farm (1000 feet, National Trust) to the west there are excellent views of Kinder Scout and the Peak. From the moor and hilltop of *Lantern Pike* (1 mile northwest) there are wide views to the north, south-west and east. — 15 miles: **Glossop** (pop. 20,000, E.C. Tuesday).

Situated among the gritstone hills, Glossop is an industrial town on the Manchester-Sheffield railway line, and the gateway to the Peak (reached by way of the Snake Pass road). Walkers can follow the old Roman road known as *Doctor's Gate;* nearby is the Roman fort of *Melandra Castle* (370 ft by 330 ft).

2. Buxton to Sheffield, via Chapel-en-le-Frith: 29 miles (A 624 to Chapel, then A 625).

13 miles: *Castleton* (pop. 600), the best centre for the Hope Valley (see below) in the heart of the High Peak district, dominated by the *castle* founded in 1176 by William Peveril, son of William the Conqueror, which features in Scott's "Peveril of the Peak".

The *church of St Edmund* dates from 1269 and contains an early Norman arch and a valuable library.

In the neighbourhood are lead ore mines, and under the ruins of *Peveril Castle* at the end of a gorge is Peak Cavern, penetrating 2000 feet underground. Another interesting cave, which can be visited by boat, is *Speedwell Cavern*, under the Winnats. The *Treak Cliff Cavern*, an old mine shaft, with electric lighting to show up the rock formations, is at the foot of Treak Cliffs.

Edale, 5 miles north, is a little hill village in the centre of the High Peak country, on the river Noe. It is the southern approach to the magnificent *Kinder Scout*. One possible route is by way of Upper Booth and Jacob's Ladder to the wild *Edale Moor* and from there to Kinder Scout. The National Trust has considerable holdings in this area — Edale End Farm, near the bend in the Edale road, at the foot of Jagger's Clough on the western slopes of Kinder Scout, and the farms of Harrop and Fullwood Holmes in the valley to the north of Hope (below). *Harrop Farm*, with its fields extending down to the Noe, is a typical Derbyshire valley farm. There are two other farms, Lee and Orchard Farms, to the west of Barber Booth, at the end of Edale. Other interesting excursions are to Lord's Sea, Ashton Bank and Lose Hill Pike, between the Hope and Edale valleys, 55 acres of bleak plateau. To the south are Mam Tor (1700 ft) and the Winnats. *Mam Tor*, or the *Shivering Mountain*, crowned by a hill-fort, commands magnificent views over Kinder Scout and the uplands above Castleton and Edale. It is called the "shivering mountain" because of its frequent landslides, due to the alternate layers of shale and grit in its make-up. Nearby are the *Blue John Caverns*, in Treak Cliff (above), which yield the colour-banded fluorspar known as "Blue John". The magnificent rocky gorge, the famous *Winnats Pass*, is also National Trust property. Winnats Head Farm is one of the highest farms in England. From Edale the highest point that can be seen is Crowden Head (2070 ft). Around the valley are *Win Hill*, with a Roman road, and a stone pillar dating from 1737 called Hope Cross.

14 miles: Hope (pop. 600 E.C. Tuesday), in the centre of the Hope valley. St Peter's Church has

Early English work and some remarkable gargoyles. South is *Bradwell* (pop. 1450, E.C. Tuesday), amid wild scenery with overhanging crags and rocks. The *Bagshaw* Cavern (discovered in 1800) contains interesting rock formations.

18 miles: **Hathersage** (pop. 1500, E.C. Tuesday), a village in a moorland setting. In the 14th century church on the hill above the village are interesting brasses. Old mansions around the village are: Highlow, North Lees, Hazleford, Offerton and others. Hathersage features in Charlotte Bronte's "Jane Eyre" as Morton.

3 miles south is *Froggatt Wood*, 75 acres of woodland and grass under Froggatt Edge, and a short distance east the *Longshore* estate (National Trust), 1000 acres of moor and woodland extending from Fox House to below the *Surprise View*, a stretch of barren heathland above a fertile valley, and including Padley Woods and Owler Tor. Nearby are an old hill-fort, *Carl Wark*, and *Higgar Tor*. Near the church is a circular earthwork known as the *Green Camp* or the *Danes' Camp*.

A 625 continues down to **Sheffield** (29 miles): see p. 802.

3. Buxton to Stockport: 18 miles on A 6.

7 miles: *Whaley Bridge*, a grey stone village in a beautiful setting in the Goyt valley. — 10 miles: *New Mills* (pop. 8250, E.C. Wednesday), an industrial town, with iron and brass foundries and cotton and textile spinning mills. The surrounding area is agricultural, and there are pleasant excursions to the Rowarth hills. — 11 miles: **Disley** (pop. 2900, E.C. Wednesday). To the west of the village is the entrance to *Lyme Park*, a large mansion standing in 1300 acres of park and moorland. The house, of Elizabethan origin, was enlarged and altered by Giacomo Leoni in 1726, and added to by Lewis Wyatt in 1817. It contains some finely decorated rooms and collections of furniture, pictures and tapestries. — 18 miles: *Stockport*.

4. Buxton to Macclesfield and Congleton: 20 miles.

5 miles: *Cat and Fiddle Inn* (1690 ft). From here a road runs down the beautiful Goyt valley. — 6 miles: minor road on right to *Macclesfield Forest*, an old village with views of the Langley reservoirs to the south-east. — 12 miles: *Macclesfield* (pop. 34,800, E.C. Wednesday), situated at 500 feet above sea level, the centre of the British silk industry for over two centuries. — 15 miles: *Gawsworth*, a charming old village with the black-and-white ("magpie") half-timbered houses characteristic of Cheshire. Magnificent Perpendicular *church;* fine rectory and *Old Hall.* — 20 miles: *Congleton.*

5. Buxton to Leek: 12 miles on A 53.

The road climbs up the magnificent *Axe Edge* (1700 ft), affording some of the finest views in the Peak District. Five rivers rise here — the Dane, Dove, Goyt, Manifold and Wye. — 7 miles: *Upper Hulme.* The sharp contours of the *Roaches* can be seen to the north-west. — 12 miles: *Leek* (see below).

Derby to Stockport and Manchester

This route is not so attractive as the route via Buxton, but it avoids the high ground. *Derby to Ashbourne:* see p. 637.

Leave *Ashbourne* (13 miles) on A 52, which soon crosses the Dove, here the boundary between Derbyshire and Cheshire. — 18 miles: turn right into A 523, which runs over the moors to (20 miles) *Waterhouses*, on the river Hamps. — 28 miles: *Leek* (pop. 19,500, E.C. Thursday), a silk-making town. The *church* (Decorated) contains interesting monuments and Saxon crosses. 1 mile north are the remains of *Dieulacresse Abbey* (1214). 30 miles: *Rudyard* (1 mile west), from which Kipling got his Christian name. — 32 miles: the road runs past Rudyard Lake, a 2½ mile long reservoir constructed in 1793. — 35 miles: *Rushton Marsh.* The church has an Early English wooden arcade in the nave. — 41 miles: *Macclesfield* (above). — 44 miles: to the west, on A 538, is *Prest-*

bury, a village with many half-timbered houses, among them the old Priest's House. The 13th century church has the ruins of a Norman chapel in the churchyard. — 47 miles: **Adlington.** Half a mile from the station is *Adlington Hall*, a magnificent Cheshire manor-house.

The oldest part is the Great Hall, built between 1450 and 1505. The "black and white" half-timbered wing was added in 1581, the Georgian south and west wings in 1757. Open to visitors in summer, Saturdays and Sundays 2.30 to 6.

48 miles: *Poynton*. 3 miles west is *Bramall Hall*, one of the most splendid examples of Cheshire 16th century "black and white" architecture (open to visitors 11 to 1 and 2 to 5, except Thursdays). — 52 miles: **Stockport** (pop. 142,000, E.C. Thursday), an industrial town in the Mersey valley, now part of Greater Manchester.

Underbank Hall, a 15th century half-timbered building. *St Mary's Church* (rebuilt 1813) has a 12th century choir and a 14th century window with modern glass. In Vernon Park is the **Municipal Museum** (open weekdays 10 to 6, Sundays 2 to 5): local flora, fauna and geology, British birds, zoology, local records, ceramics, botany, local industries.

59 miles: **Manchester** (p. 793).

34. LONDON TO SHREWSBURY

22 miles: *St Albans*. — 38 miles: *Hockcliffe* (p. 600). See Route 31.

46 miles: *Fenny Stratford* (pop. 6400, E.C. Wednesday). Nearby was the Roman station of *Magiovinium*. — 53 miles: *Stony Stratford* (pop. 4000, E.C. Thursday).

61 miles: **Towcester** (pop. 2500, E.C. Thursday), a peaceful old town with an Early English church (St Lawrence's). The Pomfret Arms features in the "Pickwick Papers".

A 43 runs north-west to *Northampton* (p. 601) via *Blisworth*, an attractive village with old cottages and an old church.

4 miles south of Blisworth, at **Stoke Bruerne,** is the *Waterways Museum* (opened 1963), devoted to the story of the English canals (daily 10 to 12,30, 2 to 5 and 6 to 8).

69 miles: *Weedon*. 3 miles north-east is **Little Brington,** in the main street of which is *Washington House*, occupied by the Washington family after moving from Sulgrave Manor (p. 658). The family tombs are in the church at *Great Brington*, 1 mile north.

75 miles: minor road to (1½ miles) *Ashby St Legers*, where there is a Saxon church with interesting frescoes.

85 miles: A 5 crosses A 426, on which, 2 miles away on the right, is *Lutterworth* (pop. 3000, E.C. Wednesday). John Wyclif was rector here from 1374 until his death in 1384. There are a number of Wyclif relics in the church, which also has 14th century frescoes.

92 miles: A 447 runs north to *Hinckley* and *Bosworth Field*, where Henry Tudor defeated Richard III in 1485.

97 miles: A 47 runs west to (2 miles) *Nuneaton* (p. 669). — 102 miles: *Atherstone* (pop. 6500, E.C. Thursday). Henry Tudor stayed here before the battle of Bosworth. To the south-west are the ruins of *Merevale Abbey*.

109 miles: *Fazeley*. 1 mile north is **Tamworth** (pop. 32,000, E.C. Wednesday), an old town on the river Tame. The *Castle*, built by Robert Marmion, the Norman baron who features in Scott's poem, is now the *Municipal Museum*. *St Edith's Church* has interesting windows.

2 miles south of Fazeley is *Drayton Bassett*. John Peel is buried in the church, and the Peel family home, *Drayton Manor*, is close to the village.

Tamworth to Nottingham: 35 miles on A 453.

8 miles: *Appleby Magna*, a small village in an attractive situation. Mediaeval manor-house with moat and guard-room. At *Appleby Parva*, 1 mile south, is a *Grammar School* (1697) by Wren, the only school he designed. — 10 miles: *Measham*, a small industrial town with a 14th century church and the *Midland Motor Museum* (open 10 to 6). — 13 miles: **Ashby-de-la-Zouch** (pop. 7500, E.C. Wednesday), a pleasant market town which still retains its charm in spite of its situation in a mining district. Its name comes from its first Norman owner, Alain de Zouch. The ruined *castle* (15th c.) was built by Lord Hastings, who features in Shakespeare's "Richard III". The tournament in Scott's "Ivanhoe" took place near the town. Fine *church* (Perpendicular, restored and enlarged in 1880), with some interesting monuments, particularly in the Huntingdon Chapel.

A 50 runs south-east to Leicester (13 miles) through the beautiful *Charnwood Forest*. In *Ravenstone* (3 miles) is *Alton Grange*, home of George Stephenson. 18th century almshouses. 2 miles farther on is *Coalville* (pop. 25,000, E.C. Wednesday).

2 miles north-east of Coalville, in Charnwood Forest, is the modern Cistercian *monastery of Mount St Bernard*.

15 miles: A 512 goes off on the right to *Cole Orton*, on the edge of the oldest coalfield in the district. Scott, Byron, Southey, Wordsworth and many other noted writers stayed at *Coleorton Hall*, home of the Beaumont family. — 18 miles: *Breedon-on-the-Hill*, with a fine Early English church, formerly belonging to a priory. — 28 miles: *Long Eaton*. — 31 miles: *Beeston*. — 35 miles: **Nottingham** (p. 622).

114 miles: A 446 forks right to (3 miles) **Lichfield** (pop. 18,000, E.C. Wednesday), a delightful country town with one of the smallest cathedrals in England, known for its associations with Dr Samuel Johnson, whose birthplace it was in 1709.

Standing in its pleasant close, with 18th century courtyards and historic buildings, is the **Cathedral of St Mary and St Chad.** A beautiful red sandstone building, mainly Early English and Decorated, it has three spires, the two at the west end being 198 feet high. The first church on the site was built in 699 by Bishop Hedda, the second was built by Bishop Robert de Clinton. It suffered greatly during the Reformation and even more so during the Civil War, when the central tower was demolished and much of the fine carving and splendid monuments were broken up. The outstanding part of the building is the **west front** (1280), beautifully proportioned, with very fine doors. The Cathedral measures 370 feet in length (interior); width across the transepts 150 feet, height 58 feet. Entrance is by the west door.

The **interior** is notable for its lightness. The nave (early Decorated) has a fine triforium and unique clerestory windows; the aisles are very narrow. Monuments to Lady Mary Wortley Montagu, the great actor David Garrick (with an epitaph by Dr Johnson) and Anna Seward, the "Swan of Lichfield". The **transept** is Early English with Perpendicular additions; in the

LICHFIELD CATHEDRAL

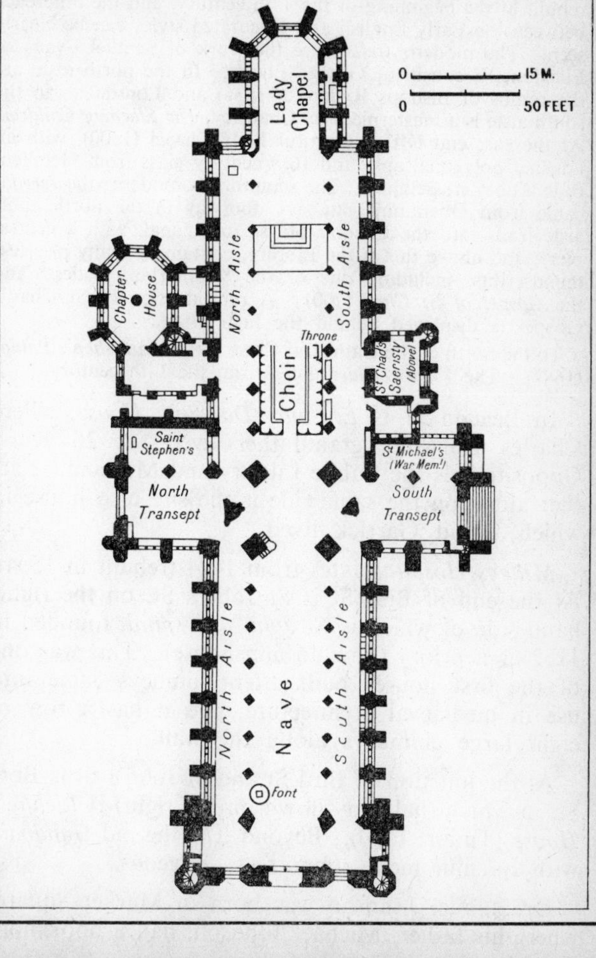

0 — 15 M.

0 — 50 FEET

Lady Chapel

North Aisle

South Aisle

Chapter House

Throne

Choir

St Chad's Sacristy (Above)

Saint Stephen's

St Michael's (War Mem!)

North Transept

South Transept

North Aisle

South Aisle

Nave

font

north transept is a striking effigy of Dean Heywood. The **choir** (1200) is the oldest part of the Cathedral. The east end was rebuilt at the beginning of the 14th century, and the difference between the Early English and Decorated styles can be clearly seen. The modern *stalls* were the work of Samuel Evans of Ellastone, a cousin of George Eliot's. In the north aisle are the tombs of Bishops Ryder (d. 1836) and Lonsdale. In the south aisle is a masterpiece by Chantrey, *The Sleeping Children*. At the east end is the beautiful **Lady Chapel** (1300), with an unusual polygonal apse and 16th century glass from Herckenrode Abbey in Belgium. The sculpture is modern; the *reredos* came from Oberammergau. A doorway in the north choir aisle leads into the **Chapter House** (octagonal, with a central pier); and above this is the Library, containing many priceless manuscripts, including one of the "Canterbury Tales" and the *Gospel of St Chad* (700). A reproduction of St Chad's Gospel is displayed behind the high altar.

To the north of the Cathedral Close is the old *Bishop's Palace* (1687). The *Vicars' Close* dates from the 14th century.

In Beacon St is *Erasmus Darwin's House*, where Charles Darwin's grandfather lived for 26 years. Opposite it is the Public Library and Museum. Farther along on the same side is the site of a house in which David Garrick lived.

Milleys Hospital dates from 1424 (rebuilt in 1504). At the end of Bird St is St John's St, on the right-hand side of which is *St John's Hospital*, founded in 1252 as a priory (now an almshouse). This was one of the first houses built after chimneys came into use in mediaeval architecture, and it has a row of eight large chimneys along the wall.

At the junction of Bird St and St John's St is Bore St, in which (half-way down on the right) is *Lichfield House* (Tudor, 1510). Beyond it is the old *Guildhall*, with its muniment room and dungeons.

Dr Samuel Johnson was born in Market Square, where his father, Michael Johnson, had a bookshop.

The house is now the **Johnson Birthplace Museum**, with mementoes of the great lexicographer. In a nearby house was born Elias Ashmole (1617), founder of the Ashmolean Museum in Oxford.

In Market Square is *St Mary's Church* (rebuilt 1868). In front of the church is a large *statue of Johnson* (1838). Behind it is a *statue of James Boswell* (1906).

To the north-east of the town is **Stowe Pool,** with *St Chad's Church* (14th c.). Beside it are two fine old houses, *Stowe House* and *Stowe Hill.* Johnson's father and mother were baptised and are buried in St Michael's Church in Church St. To the south is *Borrowcop Hill*, with an old Saxon camp. 3 miles south, at **Wall,** are the remains of the Roman town of *Etocetum*, including baths; museum.

124 miles: *Bridgetown.* 5 miles south, off A 460 to Wolverhampton, is *Moseley Old Hall*, an old house, formerly half-timbered, retaining many internal features of great interest. Here Charles II took refuge in 1651 after the battle of Worcester.

Bridgetown to Stafford: 12 miles on A 34.

A 34 runs north to (½ mile) **Cannock** (pop. 50,000, E.C. Thursday), a pleasant little town which is rapidly becoming industrialised. To the north are the ruins of *Beaudesert Hall*, once the residence of the Bishop of Lichfield and later seat of the Marquess of Anglesey. Cannock stands on the borders of *Cannock Chase*, an area of 25 square miles of moorland, scarred in the south by collieries. A 34 runs west of the Chase to (12 miles) **Stafford** (pop. 50,000, E.C. Wednesday), county town of Staffordshire (see below), an ancient borough on the river Sow and a busy industrial centre. In *St Mary's Church* — with a Norman nave (1190) and an octagonal tower — is a memorial to *Izaak Walton* (1593-1683), who was born in the town and baptised in the church. Nearby, at the corner of Greengate and St Mary's Gate, stands High House (1555), and opposite is the Norman *St Chad's Church* (restored). In Greengate are the noted *Stafford Royal Brine Baths:* for rheumatism, sciatica and muscular complaints. In Eastgate stands the Borough Hall, in which are the public library and the *Wragge Museum*. In Bank Passage is the *William Salt Library*, which contains a rich collection.

½ miles west stands *Stafford Castle*, on the site of a Saxon fortification. The Norman castle was altered and strengthened in 1348. It is a square building, with walls 8 feet thick and turrets at the corners. The large banqueting hall has fine oak panelling.

Staffordshire. Although an industrialised county, with the *Black Country* of coalmines and foundries within its borders, it also has some pleasant untouched country. *Wolverhampton* for instance, known as "capital of the Black Country", lies close to some of the loveliest country in England. The neighbouring town of *Walsall*, centre of the leather goods trade, has nearby *Cannock Chase*, a stretch of delightful moorland between Stafford and Lichfield (see above).

Around Stafford. 6 miles east on A 513 is *Colwich*, an attractive little village in Cannock Chase, on the Trent. Beyond it (9 miles) is *Rugeley* (pop. 16,000, E.C. Wednesday), with the interesting ruins of St Augustine's Church. 4 miles north is *Blithfield Hall*, an Elizabethan house in beautiful gardens, with a museum (costume, toys, etc.): open Wednesdays, Thursdays, Saturdays and Sundays 2.30 to 6. Shakespeare Festival in July.

129 miles: *Gailey*. Intersection with A 449 (north to Stafford, 8 miles; south to Wolverhampton, 8 miles).

145 miles: **Wellington** (pop. 16,000, E.C. Wednesday), an industrial town and an important railway junction, with some interesting old houses. To the south-west is the *Wrekin* (1335 ft), an isolated hill from which there are wide views.

15 miles north on A 442 is **Bridgnorth** (pop. 7800, E.C. Thursday), a historic old town in an area of beautiful scenery. It is divided by the Severn into two parts — the High Town, standing 200 feet above the river on a red sandstone crag, and the Low Town — linked by steps cut in the rock and by a rack railway. Of the *Castle* (1101) there remain only the ramparts and the Leaning Tower (the remains of the keep).

The *church of St Mary Magdalene* (1794), near the Castle, was designed by the engineer Thomas Telford. From Castle Walk, 100 feet above the river, there are magnificent views (lift from Low Town). To the north of Castle Walk is the Cartway, with *Bishop Percy's House* (1580), standing in the middle of the road (to see, apply to caretaker). In High St are some "black and white" houses. To the north, in Church St, is *St Leonard's Church* (rebuilt in the 19th c.), with cast-iron tombstones (14th c.). Beyond the bridge, in the Low Town, is *Cann Hall*, an old gabled house in which Prince Rupert stayed in 1642.

Around Bridgnorth. Very fine views from *High Rock*. The Hermitage is a cave occupied by hermits in the reign of Edward II (1307-27); beside it is a chapel. Fine views also from Queen's Parlour, higher up. 6 miles east on A 454 (the Wolverhampton road) is the attractive village of *Claverley*, with half-timbered cottages and a church with some Saxon and Norman work.

A 453 runs north-east to Shrewsbury via (8 miles) *Much Wenlock*. Nearby are the ruins of a Cluniac priory (1080), containing Norman and Gothic work; interesting old *Guildhall* and mediaeval whipping post.

151 miles: B 4380 goes off on left to *Wroxeter* (1 mile). Nearby is the site of the Roman *Uriconium*, a military station and town. Although the site has not been completely excavated it is of considerable interest. There is a small local museum.

152 miles: **Attingham Park,** an estate of 4300 acres (National Trust), with a house (1785), built by George Stewart for the first Lord Berwick, which is notable for its interior decoration. The park was laid out by Humphrey Repton in 1797 for the second Lord Berwick. Most of the house is now occupied by a college of adult education. Open to visitors Wednesdays and Thursdays 2 to 6.

156 miles: Shrewsbury (pop. 52,000, E.C. Thursday), county town of Salop (Shropshire), situated on a hill (250 ft) on the Welsh border. The Severn is here crossed by four bridges: the English Bridge (1770), the Welsh Bridge, Kingland Bridge and Greyfriars Bridge.

The name of the town is derived from the Old English *Scrobisbrig*, a citadel surrounded by shrubs. The town has many old houses of the native red sandstone and mellow old brick, principally with red tiled roofs, and many narrow steep streets on the hillside. A great attraction of the town are its gardens, and its important Horticultural Society organises a popular annual event, the Shrewsbury Flower Show.

Near the station is the **Castle,** rebuilt in the 13th century by Edward I; only the shell of the great hall with three towers adjacent remains.

The finely carved wooden roof dates from the Stuart period. At the end of the 18th century it was converted into a mansion, when Laura's Tower was also built. From the top of the *Watch Tower* there are superb views. In 1924 the house was presented to the town. Open 9 to 12 and 2 to 5, Sundays 2 to 5.

Opposite the Castle is the *Old Grammar School* (1600), now the *public library, natural history museum* and *gallery of local art*. Opposite a statue of Charles Darwin is a beautiful Jacobean timber building, Castle Gates House, and in Water Lands stands the *Council House* (1620), with fine woodcarving and decoration. Down a steep lane is *St Mary's Water Gate* on the river, the only remaining gateway to the town.

On the right is **St Mary's Church** (various styles from Norman to late Perpendicular). Old stained glass windows from Trier, Germany; the *Jesse window* at the east end is English (1345). The roof of the church collapsed during a storm in 1894. Opposite is the *Royal Salop Infirmary* (1745).

Butcher Row and *Fish Street* contain many picturesque mediaeval buildings: note the beautiful half-timbered *Abbot's House*. *Grope Lane*, nearby, is very

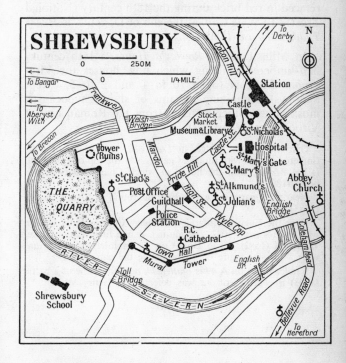

narrow (St Alkmund's Church, with a Gothic tower and glass of 1795). The *Cross Keys*, at the corner, dates from 1600.

In High St is *Ireland's Mansion* (1575), and opposite *Owen's Mansion* (1592). There are many old timber-framed houses in this street «*Shire Hall*». In Dogpole (No. 20) is the **Old House,** a typical mid 16th century house, of which the street front preserves its original character. The garden front above the river was refaced in red brick during the 18th century (National Trust). In Wyle Cop, at the end of Dogpole, is *Henry Tudor's House* (15th c.).

In Mills Lane is *Rowley's House,* a 16th century half-timbered building which now houses the **Viroconium Museum** (open 10 to 1 and 2 to 5, except Sundays), containing remains of shops, hypocausts, mosaics and other material from the Roman city of Viroconium (Wroxeter).

Over the Welsh Bridge, in *Frankwell*, is a group of half-timbered houses with timbered gables. At the top of Frankwell is the *Mount*, with the house in which Charles Darwin was born (1809).

Near the Quarry (now a park) is the round *St Chad's Church* (1785).

Over the English Bridge is the **Abbey Church** (Holy Cross), which dates from 1083. Beside it is a fine Elizabethan house, *Whitehall* (1582). The Dun Cow is an interesting old inn, with a life-size figure of a cow above the entrance.

5 miles north on A 49 is *Battlefield*, near the scene of a battle (1403) in which Hotspur was defeated by Henry V.

35. LONDON TO BIRMINGHAM

110 miles on A 41. From Hyde Park Corner follow Route 32 to Mill Hill; then keep left into Edgware Way (A 555) and the Watford Bypass (A 500) to join A 41 at Hunton Bridge.

By motorway: M 1 and M 6.

20 miles: *Hunton Bridge*.

3 miles south-east on A 41 is **Watford** (pop. 73,000, E.C. Wednesday), on the Coln, an important railway junction. *St Mary's Church* (12th c., Early English) contains interesting monuments. Near the church are *Russell's Almshouses* (1580, restored). To the north is *Aldenham*, with a 14th century church and one of England's leading public schools (1597). See also p. 241.

21 miles: *King's Langley*, a pleasant village. Nearby are *Abbot's Langley* and the old-world hamlet of Bedmond, with many 17th century cottages. Birthplace of Nicholas Breakspear, who became Pope Adrian IV in 1154 — the only Englishman to become Pope.

23 miles: **Hemel Hempstead** (pop. 62,000, E.C. Wednesday). Norman church. *Piccotts End* (open to visitors 10 to 5.30), with 14th century frescoes.

28 miles: **Berkhamsted** (pop. 15,000), birthplace of the poet Cowper (1731). *St Peter's Church* (Decorated, with a Saxon porch). Ruined castle. 17th century almshouses.

Ashridge Park, 3 miles north-east, a fine mansion built by Wyatt in 1808 (now used as a management training centre), in splendid grounds noted for their fine beech-woods. (Open to visitors April to October at weekends and on public holidays). 5 miles south-west on A 416 is *Chesham*. 15th century church with interesting monuments. The town lies on the south side of the Chiltern Hills.

33 miles: **Tring** (pop. 7500, E.C. Wednesday), a small town prettily situated in a gap in the Chilterns. The fine church (Perpendicular) has parish registers recording the baptisms of members of the Washington family.

Nearby is the fine Wren mansion of **Tring Park,** now housing a *Zoological Museum* (open 2 to 5). B 488 runs north on the line of the prehistoric *Icknield Way* to Ivinghoe and Dunstable (10 miles).

36 miles: 3 miles south-east is *Wendover* (pop. 50000, E.C. Thursday), an old market town. Local crafts are straw-plaiting and pillow-lace. 1½ miles south-east is *Chequers*, a Tudor mansion presented to the nation in 1917 by Viscount Lee of Fareham as the country residence of the Prime Minister.

40 miles: **Aylesbury** (pop. 35,000, E.C. Thursday), county town of Buckinghamshire, situated on a low hill. *St Mary's Church* (Early English) has a Lady Chapel over the Norman crypt; Norman font and 15th century choir stalls. To the north-west of the old Market Square is the *King's Head*, an inn (National Trust) partly dating from the 15th century. The hall is a fine example of mediaeval architecture; fine stained glass window. In Church St, in the town centre, is the *County Museum* (open 9.30 to 5, except Sundays).

1 mile south-west on A 418 is **Hartwell House,** an 18th century mansion which is now a training college. This was the home from 1804 to 1818 of the exiled Comte de Provence, brother of Louis XVI of France, who became king as Louis XVIII.

10 miles north on A 413 (the Buckingham road) is **Winslow,** a picturesque old town. See in particular the *Market Square* and the old *Bullring*. The *White Hart Hotel* is a coaching inn dating from the mid 18th century. *St John's Royal Latin School* dates from the 16th century.

3 miles away is *Stowe School*, established in 1923 in a former seat of the Dukes of Buckingham, a handsome 18th century mansion in classical style, with a façade 900 feet long, approached by a double avenue of elms. 6 miles north is *Silverstone* motor-racing track.

Buckinghamshire is one of the smallest English counties, but rich in historic and literary interest and, although now invaded by the suburbs of London, still with much rural charm. One of the finest stretches of the Thames lies within its borders, and south-west of the *Vale of Aylesbury* are the beautiful *Chiltern Hills*.

46 miles: *Waddesdon* (pop 1300, E.C. Thursday), a picturesque little village in a beautiful setting.

Waddesdon Manor (National Trust: open Wednesdays and Sundays 2 to 6) is a Renaissance-style mansion built for the Rothschild family in 1889 by the French architect G.-H. Destailleur and offered to the National Trust in 1957. 18th century furniture, Sèvres porcelain; pictures by *Rubens, Guardi, Watteau, Lancret, Boucher, Greuze, Mme Vigée-Lebrun, Fragonard, Gainsborough, Reynolds* and minor Dutch masters; sculpture by *Falconet* and *Lemoyne*.

57 miles: *Bicester* (pop. 50,000, E.C. Thursdays), a small country town with a Norman church (some Saxon work) formerly attached to the priory whose ruins can be seen.

65 miles: *Aynhoe Park* (17th c.).

72 miles: **Banbury** (pop. 22,000, E.C. Tuesdays), an old town on the Cherwell. *Whately Hall*, now a hotel, has a Georgian front, with stone gables to the rear dating from 1652. In the stagecoach era the central part was known as the Three Tuns Inn, and the old gardens give the place the atmosphere of an agreeable private house. Visitors can see the bakery which became famed for its Banbury cakes (1638).

3 miles south-west is the Elizabethan *Broughton Castle* (open Wednesdays 2 to 6).

3 miles north-east is *Chacombe*, with an 11th century priory, rebuilt in the 17th century (picture gallery).

7 miles north-east on B 4525 (the Northampton road) is **Sulgrave Manor,** home of George Washington's ancestors. The property was purchased in 1539 by Lawrence Washington, mayor of Northampton in 1532 and 1545. The family lived here until 1610 and then moved to the village of Little Brington (p. 644), 15 miles away. The house was bought in 1914 to commemorate a century of peace between Britain and the United States and is now a *Washington Museum*, run by the Sulgrave Manor Board. Above the entrance are the arms of the Washington family.

7 miles north-west on A 422 (the Stratford-on-Avon road) is **Upton House,** a late 17th century house standing on a hill 700 feet high, splendidly furnished (tapestries; *Hieronymus Bosch*, Nativity). 3 miles south-west of Upton House is **Compton Wynyates,** a Tudor mansion (end of 15th and beginning of 16th c.) in which Henry VIII resided (open Thursdays, Saturdays and Sundays in summer, 2 to 6).

10 miles east on A 422 (the Buckingham road) is **Brackley** (pop. 3000, E.C. Tuesday), a small industrial town (boots and shoes). *St Peter's Church* has an Early English tower. *St John's Hospital* (12th c., restored) is now a school.

83 miles: *Gaydon.*

92 miles: **Warwick** (pop. 18,000, E.C. Thursday), county town of Warwickshire, with many interesting old houses in its narrow streets. The town dates back to the Saxon period, and was fortified by Ethelfleda, King Alfred's eldest daughter.

In the centre of the town is **St Mary's Church,** a Norman foundation rebuilt after a fire in 1694; only the east end and the crypt escaped destruction.

The choir and chapter house date from the mid 14th century. In the crypt is an old ducking-stool, of which only two others remain in existence. The **Beauchamp Chapel** to the south of the choir is the finest part of the church and one of the finest pieces of architecture in the town. It dates from the mid 15th century and contains the tomb of Richard Beauchamp, Earl of Warwick, and those of the Earl of Leicester, Queen Elizabeth I's favourite, and his brother Ambrose Dudley; 15th century glass and a 17th century Last Judgment. Under the choir is a Norman **crypt** (1120).

To the west, reached by way of Old Square, is the *Market Place*, with the *Market Hall*, which now houses the *County Museum* (open 10 to 5.30, except Fridays and Sunday mornings): birds, fossils, local antiquities. In the square are some fine old houses.

To the south, along Market St, is the *West Gate* (of four different periods, including early Norman), surmounted by St James's Chapel (14th c.). Nearby are the fine 15th century half-timbered buildings of *Leycester's Hospital*, converted into a hospital by the Earl of Leicester in 1571, which now contains a regimental museum. Open 10 to 6, except Sundays.

Among other very attractive old houses in the town are **Thomas Oken's House** (16th c.) in Castle St; a fine 15th or early 16th century house in High St, at the intersection with Swan St and New St; the *Court House*, farther east at the end of Jury St; and 41 Mill St. Outside the *East Gate*, on the north-west slopes of the hill, are two fine stone-built Jacobean houses, St John's Hospital and Marble House.

The imposing **Castle,** to the south-east, was enlarged in the 12th and 13th centuries; the present building dates from about 1330. Magnificent gardens laid out by Capability Brown in the 18th century. Open 10 to 5.30, except Sunday mornings.

Caesar's Tower, the *gateway*, *Guy's Tower* and the walls were all finished at the end of the 14th century; the Clarence and Bear Towers were added in the 15th century. In the early 17th century the Castle was restored by Fulke Greville after suffering severe damage by fire in 1594. It was enlarged after a further fire in 1871. The **State Apartments** contain a collection of art treasures and items of historical interest.

2 miles east of Warwick on A 425 is **Leamington** (pop. 45,000, E.C. Thursday), a pleasant and well laid out town on the Leam, a tributary of the Avon. The thermal springs were discovered in the 16th century and became fashionable in the 18th. Their chalybeate, saline and sulphureous waters are efficacious in the treatment of cardiac, circulatory and rheumatic conditions.

In Avenue Road is the *Art Gallery and Library* (open 10 to 5, Sundays 2 to 5): Delft and Wedgwood ware.

To the north of Warwick on A 46 are **Kenilworth** (5 miles) and **Coventry** (10 miles).

Kenilworth (pop. 19,000, E.C. Thursday). *St Nicholas's Church* has Norman and Gothic work. Beside the church are the ruins of *Kenilworth Priory*, which features in Scott's novel. In *Castle Green* are some pretty half-timbered cottages and charming Georgian houses.

Kenilworth Castle was built in 1120 by Geoffrey de Clinton, Treasurer to Henry I. In 1254 it was acquired by Simon de Montfort, and in 1266, under his son, it withstood a six months' siege by Henry III. In 1362 it came into the hands of John of Gaunt. From 1399 it was Crown property until 1562, when Elizabeth I presented it to her favourite Robert Dudley, Earl of Leicester, who spent large sums on enlarging the castle, in which the Queen was his guest. Cromwell granted the castle to Col. Hawkesworth and other officers, who dispersed the magnificent furniture and demolished much of the structure for the sake of its materials. After the Restoration it passed to Lord

Hyde and his descendants, the Earls of Clarendon, in whose family it has since remained.

The entrance is near *Leicester's Gatehouse* (1570), now a private residence (open to visitors). At the end of the wall, to the right, is the Norman keep, *Caesar's Tower*, originally of three or four storeys, with walls 16 feet thick. Beyond this to the west is *Mervyn's Tower* (1392), in which was Amy Robsart's room. Close by is the *Pleasance*, with the grotto in which Scott makes the Queen discover Amy Robsart.

At right angles to Mervyn's Tower are the *Banqueting Hall* (with two beautiful oriel windows), the *White Hall*, the *Presence Chamber* and the *Privy Chamber*. The buildings at the south-east corner, with the roof supported on piers, were added by Leicester. The line of the outer walls can still be followed, with the Swan Tower, Lunn's Tower, the Water Tower and Mortimer's Tower; in front of Mortimer's Tower is the tilt-yard.

Coventry (pop. 330,000, E.C. Thursday), an industrial town which expanded rapidly from 1875 onwards as a centre of bicycle and later motor-car manufacture. The first British bicycle was made at Coventry in 1869, and the first motor-car in 1896 (by Daimler). The first flight by a monoplane in 1906 was the result of experiments carried out at Coventry by A. Weaver.

Excavations have suggested that there was a settlement here in the 9th century. The town grew up round a Benedictine monastery founded by Leofric, Earl of Mercia, and his wife Lady Godiva. It was granted three charters, the earliest in 1153, and originally had twelve gates (of which only two remain). During the second world was Coventry suffered very extensive damage, 67,670 houses being destroyed or damaged. The heaviest attack was on 14 November 1940, the first "blitz" by the Luftwaffe on a British town. The town has since been rebuilt and is still in course of redevelopment. Many of its old mediaeval streets have in consequence disappeared.

The old **Cathedral** was destroyed in 1940. The **New Cathedral,** designed by Sir Basil Spence, stands the ruins of its predecessor.

The old Cathedral (Perpendicular) dated from the 13th-15th centuries, and had a **spire** 295 feet high, which survived the bombing. The new Cathedral was consecrated in 1962. It is linked with the old one, and measures 270 feet long by 80 feet wide. Huge glass screen by *John Hutton* at west end. Carved group, "St Michael and Lucifer", by *Epstein* on outside of nave wall. The nave has two lateral aisles. To the left of the entrance is the octagonal **Chapel of Unity,** open to all Christian denominations (mosaics by *Einar Forseth,* glass by *M. Traherne*). To the right of the entrance is the **Baptistery** (large stained glass window, font made of stone from Bethlehem). On the altar, which stands in the choir, is a *crucifix* by *G. Clarke,* and behind the altar is an immense tapestry by *Graham Sutherland,* representing **Christ in Majesty.** To the right of the choir are the circular **Chapel of Industry** and the little *Chapel of Gethsemane (mosaic* in Byzantine style by *Steven Sykes).*

To the west of the Cathedral is **Holy Trinity Church,** built between 1360 and 1540, in Perpendicular style, with a spire 260 feet high. 15th century stalls; modern glass (1955). On the north side of the church is *Priory Row,* lined with houses in 18th century style.

Still farther west is **Broadgate,** the hub of city life, with a *statue of Lady Godiva* (Reid Dick, 1949) in the centre. To the south-west is a modern building (1953) designed by Donald Gibbons, who was responsible for the post-war planning of Coventry.

High St leads from the south-east corner of the square to **St Mary's Hall.**

Above the vaulted passage is very fine carving. From the courtyard we enter a crypt under the *Great Hall* (old stocks and a 13th c. sarcophagus). The Great Hall has an oak roof and contains a 16th century tapestry. The most interesting of the other rooms are the kitchen, the mayoress's parlour and the muniment room.

COVENTRY

0   100   200 m

Just to the east of St Mary's Hall is the *Herbert Art Gallery and Museum* (open 10 to 6, Sundays 2 to 5): industrial history, local antiquities.

In Greyfriars Lane, towards the south of the town, is **Ford's Hospital,** built in 1509, damaged during the last war and since restored, with a very beautiful courtyard (open 10 to 5 or 7 according to season). Farther south is the *octagonal tower* (260 ft high) of a 14th century Franciscan church.

Around Coventry. 1½ miles south-east is *Whitley Abbey,* on high ground above the river Sherbourne, where Charles I stayed in 1642 while besieging Coventry; the house was burned down in 1874. To the south is **Stoneleigh Abbey,** seat of Lord Leigh, in a large and very beautiful park. Of the Cistercian abbey, founded in the 12th century, there remains a very fine 14th century doorway. The house, in Renaissance style, dates from 1720 and contains valuable furniture, pictures and reliefs by Cipriani.

103 miles: **Knowle,** with an old *church* and *Guildhall.* To the north is the very fine mansion of *Grimshaw Hall.* — 106 miles: *Solihull.*

113 miles: **Birmingham** (pop. 1,130,000, E.C. Wednesday and Saturday), one of the world's great industrial cities, situated in the heart of England on a series of low hills, surrounded by beautiful countryside. The city covers a total area of 80 sq. miles. Plan in colour at end of volume.

BIRMINGHAM

Birmingham is an ancient town, originating as a small hamlet clustering round the manor of Bermingeham, which was valued in Domesday Book at no more than 20 shillings. It is now Britain's second city. In the Tudor period it was observed that the town was largely inhabited by blacksmiths, using Staffordshire iron and coal, and a century later Birmingham was described as a populous place resounding to the clang of hammer on anvil. During the Civil War the town supplied 15,000 sabre blades to the Earl of Essex, in command of the

Parliamentary forces. It was, however, later captured by the Royalists, led by Prince Rupert.

During the 18th century Birmingham increased rapidly in size and importance, launching itself into new activities which drew men of an inventive cast of mind and forward-looking views from all over the country. Men like *James Watt, Matthew Boulton* and *William Murdock* made the name of Birmingham known throughout the world. Working in partnership with Watt, who perfected the steam engine, and Murdock, a pioneer in the use of gas for lighting, Boulton decided to bring together in his factory not only the production of different kinds of hardware but the commercial organisation required to sell the goods produced, and was thus able to demonstrate the advantages of mass production. It was to the efforts of men like these that Birmingham owed its reputation for the high quality of its products, a reputation maintained by successive generations of craftsmen. Present-day Birmingham is a city of contrasts, with a plant which employs 17,000 workers and turns out more than 3000 cars every week but also with small workshops employing mo more than two or three highly skilled craftsmen and producing exquisite hand-made jewellery. Small family firms established more than a century ago are found side by side with large establishments using the most modern methods. In many workshops in Birmingham's back streets the machine tool has still not supplanted the skilled hand of the craftsman.

The roads from Warwick and Coventry both lead to the wide street called *Digbeth*, which ends in the **Bull Ring.**

In the Bull Ring is *St Martin's Church* (Decorated, 13th c., rebuilt 1873), with some Norman work. In the church are the tombs, with monuments, of the old lords of the manor; some good glass. Beside the church is a large modern block, *St Martin's House* (1961).

Along the north side of the Bull Ring, beyond a monument to Nelson (Westmacott, 1809), are a number of ultra-modern buildings, including in particular the *Bull Ring Centre*, a vast shopping centre built in 1964, and the cylindrical tower of the *Rotunda*, a glass and aluminium structure of 22 floors, 300 feet high (1965).

New Street, Birmingham's main shopping street, leads to **Victoria Square,** in which is the *Town Hall* (1834, built by Joseph Hansom, who gave his name to the hansom cab), a classical-style building modelled on the temple of Jupiter Stator in Rome, with 40 Corinthian columns. The first performance of Mendelssohn's "Elijah" was given here in 1840. To the north is the Renaissance-style *Council House* (Thomason, 1874), dominated by the 160 foot high clock tower known as "Big Brum".

To the rear is the **Corporation Art Gallery and Museum,** with a rich collection of works of art and objects of interest.

The **Art Gallery** contains works belonging to the various European and British schools, and is particularly notable for its Pre-Raphaelite works and for the finest collection of *David Cox*'s pictures and watercolours. In the Round Room is *Epstein*'s "Lucifer". The **Museum** has fine displays of Italian Renaissance art, European silver and ceramics, arms and armour, and "treen" (articles made from wood). The natural history section contains a fine collection of British birds and their eggs and a gallery of mineralogy. Open daily 10.30 to 6, Sundays 2 to 5.30.

To the north-west of Victoria Square, by way of Great Charles St and then left into Newhall St, is the **Museum of Science and Industry.**

The industrial history of Birmingham. Early machines, including those of Watt, Boulton and Murdock; bicycles, motor-cycles and cars; scale models; special collections (mechanical organs, watches and clocks). Open 10 to 5, Sundays 2 to 5.30.

To the north of the Museum, in a shady square, is the neo-classical *St Paul's Church* (1780).

From the north-east corner of Victoria Square Colmore Row runs up to Colmore Circus, passing on the right *St Philip's Cathedral*, with some good stained glass by Sir Edward Burne-Jones (1833-98), who was born in Birmingham.

From Colmore Circus Snow Hill Ringway runs north-west into St Chad's Circus. To the right, in Bath St, is the Roman Catholic **St Chad's Cathedral**, a neo-Gothic church by Pugin (1839-41): old carving, including an oak pulpit from Louvain, Belgium, dated to 1520, and 15th century carving from Cologne; modern glass.

Outer Districts

To the south extends the residential district of *Edgbaston*, with a large park. Beyond this is the **University,** dominated by the *Chamberlain Tower*, 360 feet high, named after Joseph Chamberlain.

Nearby, to the east, is the **Barber Institute of Fine Arts,** erected in 1939. In front of the building is a statue of George I (1722), formerly in Dublin. Picture gallery (open on the first Saturday in the month 10 to 4, and on the following Wednesday 2 to 5).

Farther south is the district of *Bournville*, with two restored 14th century houses (*Selly Manor House*, at the corner of Pale Road and Sycamore Road: open Tuesdays, Wednesdays and Fridays 2 to 5).

To the west of Bournville are the excavated remains of the 13th century *Weoley Castle* (open 2 to 5).

To the north of the city centre is the district of **Aston.** The fine Jacobean mansion of **Aston Hall,** set in a large park, is now a museum of decorative art (open 10 to 5, Sundays 2 to 5). To the north of the park is the *church of SS. Peter and Paul*, with a 15th century tower and monuments of different periods. Aston has given its name to the famous football club, Aston Villa. It now also contains Birmingham's second university, *Aston University*.

To the north-west is the industrial suburb of Hansworth, where Watt and Boulton's famous Soho Foundry (see above) stood until 1850, and where coins were minted during the reign of George III. The front of the foundry was illuminated by gas to celebrate the Peace of Amiens in 1802 — a demonstration of the use of coal gas for lighting, in which William Murdock, manager of the foundry, was a pioneer. **Hansworth church** contains monuments to Watt, Boulton and Murdock.

To the south-west of the city are the *Lickey Hills* (500 acres) — Bilberry Hill, Lickey Warren, Cofton Hill and Rose Hill, with an obelisk commemorating one of the Earls of Plymouth. Very fine views from Beacon Hill (1000 ft).

7 miles north-east on A 38 is **Sutton Coldfield** (pop. 45,000, E.C. Thursday). *Church* (much restored), with a Norman font and interesting monuments. *Sutton Park* covers more than 2000 acres (lakes). 1 mile south-east is *New Hall*, a moated house with parts dating from the 12th century.

Surroundings of Birmingham

1. Birmingham to Northampton: 49 miles on A 45.

10 miles: *Stonebridge* (intersection with A 446. — 12 miles: *Meriden* (pop. 4500, E.C. Thursday), with an old market cross. — 16 miles: *Allesley*, on the outskirts of Coventry (bypass), with an Early English church. — 18 miles: *Coventry* (p. 661). — 21 miles: *Willenhall*, where the bypass rejoins the road through the town. — 22 miles: *Ryton on Dunsmore*. The road continues over Dunsmore Heath. — 29 miles: *Dunchurch*, an old-world village with several ancient inns and a smithy. The village stocks can still be seen.

3 miles north on A 426 is **Rugby** (pop. 55,000, E.C. Wednesday) a pleasant town situated on a plateau, famous as a hunting centre and for **Rugby School,** founded by Laurence Sheriffe in 1567. In the chapel (1809-94) are monuments to the poet Rupert Brooke and C.L. Dodgson (Lewis Carroll) and statues of Rugby School's famous headmaster Dr Thomas Arnold (1828-42) and Dean Arnold. The school has an observatory and a valuable library. Rugby was the scene of "Tom Brown's Schooldays", and there is a monument in the school to the book's author, Thomas Hughes. The school has given its

name to rugby football, the originator of which was William Webb Ellis (1823). *St Mary's Church* is a fine Gothic building. *St Andrew's Church* (rebuilt 1879) has a 14th century tower. Opposite the church are almshouses founded by Laurence Sheriffe. The Derby College of Technology (electrical engineering) is one of the finest in the country.

7 miles north-east of Rugby is **Stanford Hall,** a fine classical mansion (1700), with later additions; museum (aircraft, cars), open Tuesdays, Saturdays and Sundays 2 to 6.

2. Birmingham to Leicester: 39 miles (A 47 to 2 miles beyond Nuneaton, A 5 for ½ mile, then A 47).

6 miles: *Castle Bromwich* (pop. 1050).

Near the village is *Castle Bromwich Hall* (National Trust), formerly the seat of Viscount Newport. Built in the early 17th century and little altered since, it was bought in 1657 by John Bridgeman, ancestor of the Newport family. A characteristic early Jacobean building, brick-built, with pointed gables and a Restoration porch added by Bridgeman.

9 miles: *Coleshill.* — 21 miles: **Nuneaton** (pop. 62,000, E.C. Thursday), an industrial town (textiles, pharmaceuticals). It is the centre of the George Eliot country and the Milby of her novels; the suburb of Chilvers Coton, to the south, is the Shepperton of her "Scenes of Clerical Life". 1 mile south-west of Chilvers Coton is Arbury Farm, where George Eliot (Mary Ann Evans) was born in 1819; she lived at nearby Griff House until 1840. Arbury is the Cheverel of her novels. Nuneaton has a church with fine 16th and 18th century tombs.

26 miles: *Hinckley.* — 39 miles: **Leicester.**

3. Birmingham to Shrewsbury: 45 miles (A 41 for 20 miles, then A 464).

5 miles: *West Bromwich*, on the edge of the Staffordshire "Black Country", with many industries

(mainly heavy engineering).　　Home of the famous West Bromwich Albion football club.　— 8 miles: *Wednesbury*, another industrial town (engineering). — 10 miles: *Bilston* (iron and steel).

13 miles: **Wolverhampton** (pop. 150,000, E.C. Wednesday), capital of the "Black Country", the Staffordshire coal and iron country.

In Queen's Square is **St Peter's Church** (13th and 15th c.), on the site of an earlier 10th century church. Pre-Reformation stone pulpit, old font; monument to Col. Lane, who helped Charles II to escape after the battle of Worcester.　From the tower there are wide views over the Black Country.

In Lichfield St is the **Art Gallery and Museum** (open 10 to 6).　Pictures, in particular works by Dame Laura Knight, Sir Frank Brangwyn and Spencer Watson.　Ground floor: decorative and industrial art (Wedgwood ware, Roman material from Wall Heath).　A section of the Museum is in *Bantock House* (old furniture, ivory and porcelain, Bilston enamel-work, objects from Wall).

3 miles south is **Wightwick Manor,** in 15 acres of gardens: built in 1887, it shows the influence of the Pre-Raphaelite school and contains works of art of the period. Residence of Sir Geoffrey Mander, who presented it to the National Trust in 1937. Open Saturdays 10.30 to 12.30 and 2.30 to 5.30, and on Thursday afternoons.

4 miles north-east is *Moseley Old Hall*, an 18th century house with some Elizabethan work.

8 miles north-west is **Chillington Hall** (Sir John Soane, 1785), with gardens by Capability Brown. Nearby is **Boscobel House,** a 17th century mansion with mementoes of the future Charles II's flight during the Civil War. Here, according to tradition, he hid in an oak-tree after the battle of Worcester.

18 miles: road junction, where A 41 continues (right) to Chester via Newport, passing through **Tong,** a charming village with the ruins of a Norman castle and a Perpendicular church containing fine *tombs* of the Vernon family (14th-17th c.).

From Tong a side trip can be made to **Weston Park** (on Watling Street, A 5), seat of the Earl of Bradford. The house, built in 1671, with 18th century gardens by Capability Brown, has some *magnificent rooms* and contains splendid works of art (pictures by *van Dyck, Gainsborough, Reynolds, Brueghel, Claude, Vernet, Constable, Bassano, Salvator Rosa, Teniers,* etc.). Open 2 to 6, except Mondays and Fridays.

28 miles: *Shifnal,* a market town dating back to Saxon times, in wooded country. Mediaeval church (14th c. *Moreton Chapel*). Old houses.

34 miles: *Wellington* (p. 650) and **Shrewsbury.**

4. Birmingham to Stoke-on-Trent: 50 miles (A 456 for 4 miles, then A 4123 to Wolverhampton, A 449 to Stafford and A 34 to Newcastle-under-Lyme).

4 miles: turn right into A 4123. 4 miles west is **Dudley** (pop. 60,000, E.C. Wednesday), noted since mediaeval times for its coal and iron.

On a hill north of the town are the ruins of *Dudley Castle,* burned down in 1750. The keep is 13th century, the rest of the castle 16th century. From the top of the keep (66 ft high, 580 ft above sea level) there are wide views of the Black Country. In the grounds of the castle is Dudley Zoo. In Priory Park are the ruins of a priory. At nearby *Holbeach House* the Gunpowder Plot conspirators were run to ground in 1605.

15 miles: **Wolverhampton** (p. 670). — 23 miles: *Gailey.* — 26 miles: *Penkridge.* — 28 miles: *Dunston.* — 32 miles: *Stafford.*

48 miles: *Newcastle-under-Lyme* (pop. 77,000, E.C. Thursday), an industrial town in the centre of the "Potteries" (see below). Museum in Queen St.

2 miles east is **Stoke-on-Trent** (pop. 265,000, E.C. Thursday), in the North Staffordshire coalfields. Stoke-on-Trent, together with the adjacent Tunstall, Burslem, Hanley, Fenton and Longton, make up the *Potteries*. The six towns were amalgamated in 1910 into a single borough under the name of Stoke-on-Trent, the twelfth largest town in England.

In addition to the potteries themselves there are other important industrial plants (foundries, steelworks, tyre manufacture, etc.). The development of the potteries dates from the time of *Josiah Wedgwood*, although there were potteries in the area before his time. Wedgwood (born 1730) evolved the famous "Wedgwood blue" and "cream ware", which were so successful that he bought an estate outside the town in 1766 and established his works there, under the name of *Etruria*. Other famous makers like Minton and Copeland also established themselves here. The Etruria works closed down in 1940, but since the war the production of Wedgwood has been resumed at *Barlaston*, with ultra-modern electric kilns, in a garden city. Visitors should see the show rooms of the main potteries. Hanley was the birthplace of the novelist Arnold Bennett (1867-1931).

In Church St is the *Spode-Copeland Museum* (open 10 to 5): ancient pottery.

The *City Museum and Art Gallery* in Hanley (open 10 to 6) displays pottery and pictures by local artists.

At Burslem, north of Hanley, is *Ford Hall Green*, a 16th century house (open 10 to 5 or 7).

Stoke to Derby: 34 miles (A 5007 to Fenton, A 50 to Sudbury, then A 516).

15 miles: **Uttoxeter** (pop. 8000, E.C. Thursday), a charming little town. In the *Market Place* is a bas-relief commemorating Dr Johnson's self-imposed penance, when he stood bareheaded in the rain to atone for his refusal as a boy to serve at his father's book-stall. — 26 miles: A 50 goes off on the right to Burton-upon-Trent, via *Tutbury*, on the river Dove (castle built by John of Gaunt in which Mary Queen of Scots was confined).

Burton-upon-Trent (pop. 50,000, E.C. Wednesday), long famous for its breweries. By the 16th century there were already many malt-houses here, and the trade was facilitated in the early 18th century when the Trent was made navigable as far as Gainsborough. The Bass breweries were established in 1777, the Worthington breweries in 1744. The parish church occupies the site of an earlier abbey church; in the churchyard are remains of the abbey. *Museum and Art Gallery* (prehistoric remains, ornithology).

34 miles: **Derby** (p. 628).

36. LONDON TO OXFORD

56 miles. From Hyde Park Corner, follow the East Carriage Road (just inside the Park) or Park Lane to Marble Arch and turn left along the north side of the Park into Bayswater Road, Notting Hill Gate and Holland Park Avenue. At the end of Holland Park Avenue fork right into Uxbridge Road, and almost immediately turn right again into Wood Lane. At White City Stadium turn left into Westway, continuing along Western Avenue (A 40, the Oxford road).

Motorway: M 40.

24 miles: **Beaconsfield** (pop. 11,000, E.C. Wednesday). The original name was *Bekenesfeld*, the "clearing in the beech-wood", and there are still many beeches in the area. Edmund Burke (1730-97), the statesman and writer, lived in Butler's Court, formerly called Gregories, and is buried in the parish church. In the churchyard is the grave of the poet Edmund Waller (d. 1687), who lived in Hall Barn. The rectory is a charming old half-timbered building. This was the birthplace of Benjamin Disraeli (1804-81). In the park are a model village and miniature railway (open 10 to 6).

Around Beaconsfield. North-east is the charming little village of *Jordans*, with the old Quaker meeting-house, which has changed little since its erection in the 17th century. In the burial ground lie William Penn (founder of Pennsylvania and Philadelphia,) his two wives and five of his children. Nearby is the old Jordans Hostel, used by the Quakers before their meeting-house was built. — 4 miles north-east is *Chalfont Saint Giles*. In the little building called *Milton's Cottage* John Milton lived while the plague was raging in London in 1665, and wrote *Paradise Lost*. The cottage is now a museum containing Milton relics. — 4 miles north (off B 473) is *Coleshill*, a charming village 560 feet above sea level, with splendid views over the surrounding countryside. Edmund Waller was born in the *Manor*, now a farm. — 5 miles north on B 473 is *Amersham*, an old market town now swallowed up in the London commuting area. In St Mary's Church are brasses and monuments of the Drake family, who lived in *Shardeloes Manor*, 1½ miles west. The present building dates from the 18th century (Adam). The park is always open to the public.

30 miles: **High Wycombe** (pop. 55,000, E.C. Wednesday), with factories producing beechwood chairs. *All Saints Church* dates from the 13th and 15th centuries. There are some quaint old houses. In the *Guildhall* is a picture by van Dyck. Desborough Castle occupies the site of a Saxon settlement; remains of a Roman villa.

1 mile north is **Hughenden Manor,** bought in 1847 by Benjamin Disraeli, who rebuilt the house and lived there until his death in 1881. The house (National Trust) contains much of his furniture, pictures, books and other relics. (Open 2 to 6; closed Tuesdays, Saturdays and Sunday mornings).

32 miles: **West Wycombe,** an ancient village with a classical-style church on top of a hill. 240 acres of the hill and most of the village's many 17th and 18th century buildings are National Trust property.

At the west end of the village, south of the road, is *West Wycombe Park* (300 acres), with a house built about 1765 for Sir Francis Dashwood in Adam style. The interior has been preserved in its original form, with ceiling paintings by an Italian artist, Borgnis. Open 2 to 6 daily in summer, except Saturdays.

A 4010 forks north-west through lovely country to (6 miles) **Princes Risborough,** in the Chiltern Hills, a pleasant town with many old houses. Close to the church is the *Manor House*, a brick house of the 17th and early 18th century, with a fine oak staircase of the earlier period and wainscoting of the later. To the north-east are *Whiteleaf Fields* (opposite the Nag's Head Inn at Monks Risborough). These and 200 acres on either side of the *Icknield Way*, south of Whiteleaf Cross, have been made National Trust property to safeguard the splendid view from the Cross over the vale of Aylesbury. 3 miles north-east is *Coombe Hill*, 106 acres of downs (rising to 852 ft), with views towards Aylesbury and the woods surrounding Chequers

(p. 656). *Great Hampden* (3 miles south-east) has an old church
in which John Hampden (1594-1643) is buried; the monument
dates from 1755.

37 miles: *Stokenchurch*. — 41 miles: B 4009 goes
off on the right to *Aston Rowant* (½ mile). Nearby
is Aston Wood (National Trust), 100 acres of beech-
woods on the escarpment of the Chilterns. To the
south is *Watlington Hill* (National Trust), one of the
bastions of the Chilterns, with 150 acres of woodland;
fine views.

41 miles: *Postcombe*.

Road on right to **Thame** (5 miles), with an interesting Early
English church. John Hampden died here in 1643. *Prebendal
House*, to the north-west, is an interesting country house. 2 miles
north, at *Long Crendon*, is a 14th century Court House, partly
half-timbered, probably first used as a wool store. The upper
room, with a fine timber roof, is now occupied by the local
authority child welfare service. To the north-west is *Boarstall
Tower*, the gatehouse of a 14th century fortified manor-house,
altered in the 16th and 17th centuries, with loopholes for archers.

50 miles: *Wheatley*. To the south is *Cuddesdon
Palace*, residence of the Bishop of Oxford.

53 miles: *Headington*. A 40 goes off on the right,
bypassing Oxford to the north and continuing to
Witney, Cheltenham and Gloucester. See Route 38.

56 miles: **Oxford** (pop. 108,000, E.C. Thursday),
known to all visitors as one of England's two ancient
university towns, the "city of dreaming spires". Its
chief glory is the High St ("the High"), running
between beautiful old colleges on either side. In all
there are 31 colleges, and it is a difficult task to decide
which is the finest and which has the most beautiful
gardens. Perhaps for most visitors, however, pride

of place would go to Magdalen College, with its harmoniously proportioned tower, its graceful bridge over the Cherwell and its ancient gardens.

OXFORD

Oxford began as a small settlement round a church built by St Frideswide in the early 8th century. Before the Norman Conquest the place suffered greatly from attacks by the Danes. William the Conqueror built the castle and the town walls, remains of which can be seen in the gardens of New College. The foundation of the University is traditionally ascribed to King Alfred, but in fact it was in the 12th century that students began to come to Oxford to study at the monastic establishments. Merton College was founded in 1264, the first formally constituted college — although University and Balliol Colleges also claim to be the oldest foundations.

Charles I held a Parliament in Oxford, and during the Civil War the town supported the Royalist cause.

Oxford has now 31 colleges, including five women's colleges, and there are many other educational establishments not attached to the University. In the 20th century Oxford has also become an industrial town, with the Morris car works, established in 1912, as well as firms producing electrical equipment, furniture and foodstuffs.

A convenient focal point from which to explore the town is the traffic intersection known as **Carfax,** at which are *Carfax Tower*, built in the reign of Edward III (1327-77), all that remains of *St Martin's Church* (demolished 1886), and the modern *Town Hall.*

Itinerary 1

From Carfax St Aldate's St runs past the Town Hall (on left) and the Post Office (on right) and comes (left) to the noble front of **Christ Church College,** founded by Cardinal Wolsey in 1525. The fine gateway *(Tom Gate)* was begun by Wolsey in 1525, and the upper part of the tower was added by Sir Christopher Wren in 1682. In the tower hangs "*Great Tom*", a bell weighing 7½ tons dedicated to St Thomas Becket. The great quadrangle, *Tom Quad*, is the largest in Oxford (90 yds square). In the south-east corner is the entrance (with fine fan vaulting) to the **Hall,** built in 1529, which is also the largest in Oxford, 115 feet long by 40 feet wide and 50 feet high. It contains a number of fine paintings — portraits of Wolsey and Henry VIII by Holbein, a portrait of Elizabeth I by *Zucchero* and works by *Lely*, *Gainsborough*, *Reynolds*, *Millais* and others. The oldest part of the college is the *kitchen*, adjoining the Hall. (The Hall is open to visitors daily 10 to 12 and 2 to 4).

On the east side of the quadrangle, near the entrance to the Hall, is the way to **Christ Church Cathedral,** which is also the college chapel. The Dean of Christ Church is also Dean of the Cathedral, whch was made an episcopal see by Henry VIII in 1546. The present church is chiefly late Norman or Transitional of the 11th century, containing some 12th century work, and is built on the site of an 8th century nunnery, portions of which can be seen in the east wall. The *Lady Chapel* dates from the 13th century and the *Latin Chapel* from the 14th century. The lower stage of the tower (145 ft high) is Norman; the Early English belfry and octagonal spire are the oldest in the country. The cathedral is the smallest in England. Wolsey demolished half the nave to provide space for Tom Quad. Open to visitors 7 to 6.

Inside, the double arches, with the lower ones rising from the corbels on the massive columns, alternately octagonal and round, are the most interesting feature of the nave. The timber roof dates from Wolsey's day: the pulpit and organ screen are Jacobean. In the *nave* are the tombs of Bishop Berkeley (d. 1753),

the philosopher, and Dr Pusey (d. 1882), the theologian. Burne-
Jones designed the glass in the west window of the south aisle.
From the dais in the south transept the proportions of the
interior can be best appreciated. The choir has a magnificent
roof of 1490. In the *east aisle* wall is a window representing
St Thomas of Canterbury. By the north choir aisle is the 13th
century *Lady Chapel;* tombs of Sir George Nowers (d. 1425)
and of Elizabeth Montacute (d. 1353), with interesting statues,
and the tomb of a Prior (1300). Adjoining is *St Frideswide's
Chapel* (15th c.), probably a "watching chamber". On the
north side is another 14th century chapel, known as the *Latin
Chapel* because the college prayers are read here every day in
Latin. Finely carved windows; the east window, by Burne-
Jones, represents St Frideswide. On the east side of the Perpendicular *cloisters* (to the south of the nave) is the Early
English *Chapter House.*

From the north-east corner of Tom Quad the
passage known as "Kill-Canon" (statue of Dr Fell,
with the well known inscription, "I do not love thee,
Dr Fell") leads into **Peckwater Quad** (1705). On
the south side is the *Library* (1761), with many valuable
books and pictures (a *Raphael*, a "Nativity" by
Titian, works by *Giotto*, etc.).

Opposite Christ Church is *St Aldate's Church.* To
the south are *almshouses* founded by Cardinal Wolsey
and endowed by Henry VIII; the buildings were not,
however, completed until 1834. Behind the church
is **Pembroke College,** founded in 1624 on the site of
Broadgates Hall. The chapel dates from 1732, but
was redecorated in the 19th century. The Library
contains many valuable books and a splendid collection of the works of Aristotle. Dr Johnson and
Thomas Browne were members of Pembroke.

Itinerary 2

Going east from Carfax along High St, we pass
on the left *All Saints Church*, and beyond this, on
the right, come to Oriel College, founded in 1326
by Adam de Brome.

The present attractive buildings date from 1630-42, the
Library from 1788. *St Mary's Hall*, a little farther along, was
founded by Oriel in 1335. Members of Oriel have included
Sir Walter Raleigh and Thomas Arnold.

Passing the Canterbury Gate of Christ Church, we come to
Merton St, in which is **Corpus Christi College,** founded in 1616
by Bishop Fox of Winchester.

A vaulted gateway leads into the *Quadrangle*, in which is a
curious sundial with a perpetual calendar. In the south-east
corner is the *Chapel*, which has an altarpiece by Rubens. A
passage outside the Chapel leads into the newer part of the
college (1706). The Library contains valuable manuscripts and
incunabula.

Also in Merton St is **Merton College,** the oldest
in the University, founded in 1264 by Walter de
Merton at Malden in Surrey and transferred to
Oxford in 1274.

The beautiful **Chapel** dates from 1276, the ante-chapel from
the 15th century; the tower is one of Oxford's landmarks. The
twelve windows in the choir (early Perpendicular) still have
their original glass. Fine 14th and 15th century brasses. From
the quadrangle a passage below the Treasury (13th c.) leads
to the **Library** (14th c.), containing rare manuscripts and chained
books. The inner quadrangle is Jacobean. From the gardens
there are splendid views of Magdalen bell-tower to the east
and Christ Church Cathedral to the west, with Christ Church
Meadow in the foreground. *St Alban Hall* (1230) is part of
Merton; the façade dates from 1600.

Continuing along Merton St, we come back to
the High St above Magdalen Bridge. On the left
can be seen the beautiful bell-tower of Magdalen

College. On the right is the *Botanic Garden*, one of the oldest in the country, established in 1621.

Magdalen College was founded in 1458 by Bishop William of Waynflete. The buildings date from 1475-81 and are among the most beautiful in the University; the entrance gateway is modern (1885).

To the left is St Swithin's Quadrangle (1881), with part of the old Magdalen Hall. Straight ahead is the President's Lodging. The *Founder's Tower* contains the fine banqueting room and two state apartments (restored 1856), with beautiful tapestries. The **Chapel** (restored 1853) is interesting, with an altarpiece by Ribalta and a west window designed by Christopher Schwartz. On one side of St Swithin's Quadrangle are the *Cloisters*, in the south-east corner of which is a staircase leading up to the magnificent *Hall*, with fine oak panelling (1541). From the Cloisters a narrow passage leads into the *Chaplain's Quadrangle*, from which there is a very fine view of the *bell-tower*, built 1493-1505. The Library contains valuable manuscripts. Cardinal Wolsey, Joseph Addison and Charles Reed were members of Magdalen.

Returning along High St, we pass on the left the *Examination Schools* (Thomas Jackson, 1882) and on the right the corner of Queen's Lane, from which the architectural beauty of the *"High"* can best be appreciated.

Immediately on the right is **Queen's College,** founded in 1340 by Robert de Eglesfield, confessor of Philippa, wife of Edward III. The buildings date from the end of the 17th century and the chapel from 1714. There is a splendid *Hall* designed by Christopher Wren and a fine library.

Queen's Lane leads between Queen's College and *St Edmund Hall* (built 1660; chapel built 1682), passes the *church of St Peter in the East* (fine 12th c. crypt), and comes to **New College.**

New College was founded in 1379 by William of Wykeham, Bishop of Winchester. It is, despite its name, one of the most ancient buildings in the town, and most of the buildings retain their original form. The upper storey of the main quadrangle was added in 1678 and the garden wing in 1684.

The beautiful **garden** is surrounded on the north and east by a well preserved stretch of the old town walls, beyond which are 19th century buildings (Sir George Gilbert Scott) and the Robinson Memorial Tower (Champneys). The **Chapel** is one of the earliest buildings in the country entirely in Perpendicular style and contains 14th century glass. The large west window was designed by Sir Joshua Reynolds. To the north of the altar is the founder's silver-gilt crosier. The *Treasury*, in the Muniment Tower, contains the college's mediaeval plate.

West of New College is **Hertford College,** founded in 1740 on the site of the 13th century Hertford Hall and re-founded in 1875. Among its members have been Thomas Hobbes and Dean Swift.

Passing under a bridge over the street on the north side of Hertford College, we see on the right the *Clarendon Building* (1713), used by the Clarendon Press until 1830, which now contains University offices.

Farther on, in Broad St, is the *Sheldonian Theatre* (Wren, 1667), built by Archbishop Sheldon. The interior is well proportioned, with a ceiling (restored 1900), by Robert Streater, court painter to Charles II. From the cupola (1838) there is a fine view of the town.

To the right of the Sheldonian is the Old Ashmolean Museum (1683), now housing the *Museum of the History of Science* (open 10 to 1 and 2 to 4.30).

Behind the Sheldonian is the **Divinity School** (1480), a notable building with a beautiful groined roof.

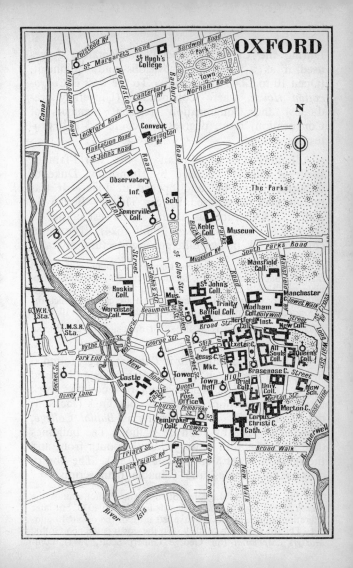

OXFORD

During the Civil War the Parliamentarian forces used it as a store for provisions and equipment. (Open 10 to 12.45 and 2 to 5). To the west is *Convocation House*, where Convocation (University graduates) and Congregation (resident members of Convocation) meet, degrees are conferred and professors elected.

Adjoining the Sheldonian is the world-famous **Bodleian Library,** founded by Humphrey, Duke of Gloucester, in 1450 and opened in 1488. It was rebuilt and reorganised by Sir Thomas Bodley in 1602. The entrance is at the south-west corner of the *Old Schools Quadrangle* (built 1624). The tower contains work in five different architectural styles.

The Bodleian contains more than 2½ million volumes and many valuable manuscripts, including the Anglo-Saxon Chronicle and the "Chanson de Roland". There is also a large collection of coins. In the reading room are cases in which the autographs of famous people are displayed. Open 10 to 5.

The New Bodleian is in Broad St opposite the Sheldonian Theatre.

To the north of Broad St is *Trinity College*, founded in 1554 on the site of a Benedictine college dissolved at the Reformation. The chapel (1694) contains work by Grinling Gibbons. The new buildings (Jackson) date from 1887. Beside Trinity is *Balliol College*, founded in 1268 by John de Balliol. The buildings date from the 15th century, but the south front and the massive tower were rebuilt in 1870. The library contains old Bibles and valuable manuscripts.

In the middle of Magdalen St, opposite Balliol, stands the *church of St Mary Magdalen;* it was founded in 1320, but later alterations and restorations have left little of the original building. The tower is 16th century. To the north is the neo-Gothic *Martyrs' Memorial* (Sir George Gilbert Scott, 1841), commemorating Cranmer, Latimer and Ridley, burned at the stake outside Balliol in 1555 and 1556.

Opposite Balliol in Broad St is Turl St, in which, on the right, is **Jesus College,** founded by Queen Elizabeth I in 1571. It was rebuilt in 1667 and restored in 1856. In the Chapel (1621) is some period oak panelling, and in the Hall is a fine Jacobean screen, with portraits, including one of Charles I by *van Dyck*.

Facing Jesus College is **Exeter College,** founded in 1314 by Walter of Stapleton, Bishop of Exeter. The buildings have been subjected to frequent restoration, and many date from the 19th century. The *Chapel* is 13th century Gothic (restored); the *Hall* (1618) was restored in 1818. From the Fellows' Garden there are good views of the Bodleian Library and the Divinity School.

Farther along Turl St is **Lincoln College,** founded by the Bishop of Lincoln in 1427. The Chapel dates from 1631; interesting Italian glass. The Hall has a fine chestnut roof. John Wesley was a fellow of the College.

Turl St brings us back to the High St. Turning left, we come to *Brasenose College* (1509), renowned for its sporting achievements, particularly in rowing and athletics. The entrance tower and Hall date from the original foundation.

Farther along the High St is **University College** (1249). The present buildings date from 1637-74 and 1980. The impressive Gothic front with two tower gateways is one of the ornaments of the High St. On the west gateway are statues of Queen Anne (outside) and James II (inside); the east gateway has figures of Queen Mary and Dr Radcliffe. Shelley was a member of the college but was sent down; a passage on the right-hand side of the main quadrangle leads to the Shelley Memorial (Onslow Ford, 1803).

On the other side of the High St is **All Souls College** (1437). The gateway and the first quadrangle remain as they were when first built.

The **Chapel** has exquisite fan vaulting and a magnificent carved screen. The second quadrangle was built by Nicholas Hawksmoor in 1720; from here there is a very fine view of the Radcliffe Camera (see below). The *Library* contains Wren's original designs for St Paul's Cathedral.

Beside All Souls is *St Mary's Church*, and immediately behind this is the **Radcliffe Camera,** built to house the Radcliffe Library, a fine rotunda (James Gibbs, 1737-39) with columns and a superb dome.

Itinerary 3

From Carfax **Cornmarket Street** runs north. On 23 April (the accepted date of Shakespeare's birthday) town and universitary dignitaries walk in procession to the *Painted Room* in this street, formerly part of the Crown Tavern, which Shakespeare must have visited when it was kept by his friend John Davenant.

In Cornmarket St is **St Michael's Church.** The oldest part of the church is a Saxon tower, formerly built into the town walls. On the other side of the street, in St Michael's St, are the Union Society Rooms, home of the famous debating society (founded 1823).

Continuing north along Cornmarket St, we reach (beyond Balliol and the Martyrs' Memorial) the wide St Giles St, in which is **St John's College** (1555).

The Hall and quadrangle date from the original foundation, the *Chapel* from 1530 (restored in the 19th c.). The second quadrangle was built by Archbishop Laud (1631). Between the two is a passage with magnificent **fan vaulting.** On the south and east sides of the second quadrangle is the *Library,* with two fine oriel windows; it contains valuable manuscripts and early printed books, together with relics of Archbishop Laud.

Opposite St John's is *Pusey House,* founded in 1884 to contain Dr Pusey's library. At the corner of Beaumont St are the *Taylor Institution* (founded 1845: modern languages) and, in the same building, the **Ashmolean Museum,** the oldest museum in the country. The basis of the collection was the material assembled by the 17th century travellers John Tradescant and his son.

The Tradescant collections were bequeathed to Dr Elias Ashmole (1617-92), who added further material and presented the museum to the University in 1683. The Ashmolean moved into its present accommodation in 1874. Its holdings have been considerably increased since then, and it is now one of the most important museums of art and archaeology in the country. Among its many treasures are the *Alfred Jewel* (gold cloisonné work), discovered at Newton Park, near the Isle of Athelney, and the *Minster Lovell Jewel,* which dates from the same period. Magnificent **Greek vases.** The collection of material from **excavations in Crete** is larger and finer than that of the British Museum. The Ashmolean also contains a collection of classical sculpture assembled by the Earl of Arundel (d. in the reign of Charles I).

Works of art in the Ashmolean include portraits of Charles II and busts of Oliver Cromwell and Sir Christoper Wren by Edward Pierce; drawings, including 200 attributed to *Raphael* and many to *Michelangelo* and *Rembrandt;* miniatures; watercolours, including works by Blake and Turner; etchings; engravings; and pictures by *Fra Angelico, Filippo Lippi, Crivelli, Bronzini, Andrea del Sarto, Rubens, Teniers, Maes, Hogarth, Reynolds, Gainsborough, Richard Wilson, Zoffany, Constable, Turner* and the leading Pre-Raphaelites. There is a fine collection of silver.

The Ashmolean Museum is open daily from 10 to 4.

At the end of Beaumont St is **Worcester College,**
founded in 1714, which incorporated six earlier
monastic houses. The present buildings date from
1714. The interior of the *Chapel* is in pure Renaissance style. The *Library* contains a number of valuable
manuscripts.

In South Parks Road is the **University Museum** (open 10 to
4), with geological, chemical, anatomical, zoological, anthropological and other collections. Nearby are the *Clarendon
Laboratories* (chemistry, physiology and experimental physics)
and, immediately to the south, the *Radcliffe Science Library*,
established by a bequest from Dr Radcliffe (d. 1714).

To the west of the Museum is *Keble College*, founded in 1870.
The Chapel (1876) contains some beautiful mosaics; in the
Library and Hall are relics of the Rev. John Keble (d. 1866).

To the south, in Parks Road, is *Wadham College*, founded
in 1613, with a fine entrance tower; early 17th century glass
in the Chapel.

Surroundings of Oxford

Oxford to Winchester: 52 miles on A 34.

6 miles: *Abingdon-on-Thames*, a pleasant little Berkshire
town, with remains of the gateway of a once important Benedictine abbey. *St Helen's Church* has a fine spire. *Christ's
Hospital* almshouses date from 1553. The market house was
built in 1678. The County Hall and Guildhall and the 15th
century bridge are interesting, and there is a 16th century
grammar school. — 3 miles north-west is *Cothill*, with the
Ruskin Reserve. (National Trust). — 10 miles: *Steventon*,
with some old cottages, belonging to a former monastic house,
grouped round three sides of a court. The cottages have been
converted into two houses (National Trust). — 17 miles:
East Ilsley. — 27 miles: *Newbury*. See Route 22. — 52 miles:
Winchester.

Oxford to Hungerford: 28 miles (A 420 for 6 miles, then
A 338).

6 miles: turn left into A 338. — 8 miles: *Frilford*. — 11 miles:
East Hanney. — 15 miles: *Wantage*, where Alfred the Great
(849-901) was born. There is a statue of Alfred in the market

place. The church is 14th century. — 23 miles: *Shefford.* — 28 miles: *Hungerford.*

Oxford to Reading by the Thames valley: 29 miles (A 423 to Shillingford, then A 329).

2 miles: *Iffley.* Fine Norman *church.* Iffley Lock is the starting point of the college eights races. — 3 miles: *Littlemore.* — 4 miles: *Sandford-on-Thames,* with a Norman church. — 5 miles: *Nuneham Courtenay,* a model village. Beautiful woods; boating. — 10 miles: **Dorchester.** This little village on the Thames was the see of a bishop from the 7th century until after the Norman Conquest, and an Augustinian abbey was founded here in 1140. The *abbey church* (13th c.) contains some Norman work; interesting Jesse windows in choir. — 11 miles: *Shillingford.* The Thames here forms the boundary between Oxfordshire and Berkshire. Turn right into A 329, which runs south down the Thames valley. — 13 miles: *Wallingford* (pop. 3500, E.C. Wednesday), a historic old town with an old stone bridge of 17 arches extending over the fields and the river. *St Leonard's Church* dates from the Norman period. Ruined castle; prehistoric earthworks. Part of the Lamb Hotel dates from the 16th century. — 17 miles: *Moulsford.* Old cottages and a 14th century church (restored) with a timber steeple. — 19 miles: *Streatley,* opposite which, on the other bank of the Thames, is *Goring-on-Thames,* a charming village with a Norman church. — 23 miles: *Pangbourne,* on the opposite bank, one of the prettiest Thames-side villages. 1 mile north is *Coombe End Farm,* with a house dating in part from the 17th century and 230 acres of arable land at the south end of the Chilterns. (National Trust: access by footpaths; house not open to public). — 29 miles: *Reading.*

Oxford to Reading via Henley-on-Thames: 32 miles (A 423 to Henley, then A 4155).

Follow the previous route to *Shillingford,* and continue straight ahead to *Nettlebed* (19 miles), situated on the southern slopes of the Chilterns at 700 feet above sea level, with magnificent views over the Thames valley. — 24 miles: *Henley-on-Thames.* Continue on A 4155 to *Shiplake* (with the church in which Tennyson was married). — 31 miles: *Caversham.* — miles: *Reading.*

Oxford to Bath: 61 miles (A 420 to Chippenham, then A 4).

17 miles: *Faringdon,* with an interesting old market place and church. Faringdon Hall is an 18th century mansion built

by the poet Henry Pye. From Faringdon there is an alternative
route to Swindon on B 4019, passing *Coleshill House* (Inigo
Jones, 1650) and *Highworth*, with a Perpendicular church which
played a part in the Civil War. Beyond Faringdon A 420
continues to *Shrivenham*, enters Wiltshire and comes to **Swindon**
(pop. 66,000, E.C. Wednesday). 1 mile north is the important
Swindon railway junction, with a new town which developed
round the railway workshops. Birthplace of Richard Jefferies.
1 mile west on A 419 (the Hungerford road) is the very beautiful
Coate Water reservoir. — 49 miles: *Chippenham*. Chippenham
to Bath: see Route 22. — 61 miles: **Bath.**

37. OXFORD TO BIRMINGHAM
VIA STRATFORD-UPON-AVON

Leave Oxford on A 34, running north-west.

8 miles: **Woodstock** (pop. 1900, E.C. Wednesday), an ancient town, birthplace of the Black Prince (1330). Its name was made famous by Sir Walter Scott.

Town Hall designed by Sir William Chambers (1766). *Chaucer's Cottage*, which belonged to a son of the poet. *Oxford City and County Museum* (open May-September 10 to 6, Sundays 2 to 6; winter 10 to 5, closed on Sundays): local history and way of life.

To the south is **Blenheim Palace,** the magnificent mansion, set in a beautiful park, presented to the Duke of Marlborough after his victory at Blenheim (Bavaria) in 1704. The house, in massive classical style, was designed by Vanbrugh. Sumptuous rooms decorated with period furniture and furnishings. Open to the public 1 to 6. The park was laid out by Capability Brown. Sir Winston Churchill, a descendant of the great Duke, was born in Blenheim in 1874.

23 miles: *Long Compton*, in Warwickshire. — 29 miles: *Shipston-on-Stour* (pop. 7600, E.C. Thursday).

5 miles east on B 4035 is **Compton Wynyates,** seat of the Marquess of Northampton, a splendid mansion of pink brick, with battlemented walls and twisted chimneys. The interior has changed little since 1520. The four main wings date from 1480; the towers and turrets were added in 1520.

31 miles: *Tredington*. — 40 miles: **Stratford-upon-Avon** (pop. 18,000, E.C. Thursday), a pleasant town beautifully situated on the banks of the Avon, known the world over as the birthplace of William Shakespeare and the place to which he retired to end his days. The *New Place Museum* contains many relics

of the old town, which seems to have moved from
the left bank to the right bank during the Middle
Ages.

STRATFORD-UPON-AVON

William Shakespeare. Of the life of the poet himself very
little has really been substantiated, and much legend surrounds
him. It is known that William Shakespeare was baptised on
26 April 1564, the third of the seven children of John Shakespeare and Mary Arden, of Wilmcote. John Shakespeare was
a glover and agricultural trader, who in 1565 became alderman,
and in 1568 high bailiff. Tradition says that Shakespeare
attended the "King's New School of Stratford-upon-Avon",
the grammar school (in Church St) and that he left school at
the age of 14 to be apprenticed either to a butcher or a glover.
It is not known where Shakespeare married, but on 27 November 1582 the Bishop of Worcester granted a special licence
for a William Shakespeare to marry Anne Whateley, of Temple
Grafton; there also exists a bond of security dated the following
day for a marriage between William Shakespeare and Anne
Hathaway. Shakespeare was aged 18, and Anne Hathaway
seven or eight years older. A daughter, Susanna, was born
the next spring, and in February 1585 twins, Hamnet and
Judith. Hamnet died when he was 11. About 1584 Shakespeare
left Stratford. Tradition ascribes this to the necessity for avoiding punishment for deer poaching at Charlecote, the estate of
Sir Thomas Lucy. In 1590 Shakespeare appeared in London.
In 1597 he purchased New Place, and in 1607 Susanna, his
eldest daughter, married Dr John Hall, a local doctor. Shakespeare lived at New Place from about 1610, spending part of
the year in London, which he visited during 1613 and 1614.
On 23 April 1616 he died, and was buried in the church of
the Holy Trinity.

Rother Street contains the oldest half-timbered
buildings in the town (Masons Court). In the Market
Place is the *American Fountain* (19th c.), a tribute to
Shakespeare. At the corner is the *White Swan Hotel*,
which contains a remarkable mural painting of the
apocryphal story of Tobit, dating from about 1550
and discovered in the course of alterations in 1927.

Wood St leads to a traffic roundabout beyond which, to the left, is *Henley Street*, in which is **Shakespeare's birthplace.**

The house is now the property of a trust, and the half-timbered exterior has been restored to represent the original appearance. It is known that John Shakespeare lived in the west house in 1552, and that he bought the east house in October 1556. The house, arranged as a museum, contains documents relating to the family, including a letter to the poet (the only one extant addressed to him) from Richard Quiney, and several portraits. The walls and ceiling of the room where he is reputed to have been born are covered with signatures, including those of Scott (on the windows), Carlyle, Thackeray and Browning.

To the left of the house is the *Shakespeare Centre*, a building erected in 1964 for Shakespeare study and research (library). To the right is the *Public Library*, in a restored 16th century building.

To the south is the **High Street.**   Shakespeare's daughter Judith lived in a house at the corner of Bridge St. At the far end of the High St, on the left, is **Harvard House,** birthplace of Katherine Rodgers, who became the wife of Robert Harvard and mother of the founder of Harvard University. (Open 9 to 1 and 2 to 6).

Nearby, at the corner of Chapel St and Sheep St, is the *Town Hall*, in which the old municipal charters can be seen.

In Chapel St is the **Shakespeare Hotel,** said to have been the original "Great House", built by Hugh Clopton (d. 1496). The rooms are named after Shakespeare plays. In this street too are the town's information office and (at the far end, on the right) the ancient *Falcon Hotel* in which the Shakespeare Club used to meet. Opposite is *Nash's House*, now the **New Place Museum,** near the site of the house which Shakespeare bought in 1610 and in which he died. (Open May-October 9 to 6, Sundays 2 to 6).

The museum contains archaeological finds from the district (Iron Age, Roman and Saxon). One room is devoted to the Stratford guilds, another to the actor David Garrick and his celebration of the Shakespeare jubilee in 1759. Adjoining are the foundations of Shakespeare's house. The entrance to the Great Garden of New Place — Shakespeare's garden — is in Chapel Lane.

At the corner of Church St and Chapel Lane stands the **Guild Chapel of the Holy Cross** (wrongly called the chapel of the Holy Trinity), founded in 1269 and rebuilt after 1496. In the nave, between the windows, are quaint carvings, and the walls have mediaeval frescoes: note the *Last Judgment* on the chancel arch. (Open 9.30 to sunset in summer, except Saturday afternoons, Sundays and public holidays). Nearby is the **Grammar School,** incorporating the *Guildhall* where Shakespeare probably saw plays performed by strolling players. The school dates from before the Reformation, and when Edward VI (1547-53) assigned the guild property to the Corporation, the school met in the upper room. Shakespeare was almost certainly a pupil here. (Open Sundays 9 to 12 and 2 to 4.30). Nearby are some old half-timbered houses (guild almshouses).

In *Old Town* (to the left at the end of Church St) are *Hall's Croft*, the house of Shakespeare's son-in-law Dr John Hall, and Avoncroft, the town house of the Clopton family. At the far end of Old Town, on the banks of the Avon, is **Holy Trinity Church,** with the tombs of Shakespeare and members of his family in the chancel.

The church is largely 15th century; the tower and wall of the north aisle are 14th century, the transept 13th century.

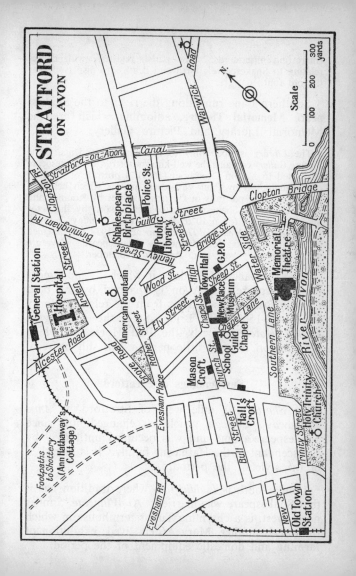

Interesting misericords. The parish registers, with entries
relating to Shakespeare's birth and death, are displayed near
the old font.

Southern Lane runs along the river to the **Shakespeare Memorial Theatre,** adjoining which are the Memorial Library and Picture Gallery.

The *Library* is open only to Shakespeare students. The *Picture Gallery* contains the well-known portrait of Shakespeare attributed to Martin Droeshout (1609), a portrait of the Earl of Southampton by Paul Vansomer, articles which belonged to Shakespeare, portraits of Garrick, pictures by Romney and an exhibition of Shakespearean costumes worn by the actor Sir Henry Irving (open 10 to 1 and 2 to 5, Sundays 2 to 5). The *Shakespeare Memorial Theatre,* opened in 1932, was designed by Elizabeth Scott; performances of Shakespeare's plays are given here every year from April to September.

Near the Bancroft Gardens, in which is a monument to Shakespeare, the Avon is spanned by the bold *Clopton Bridge,* which dates from the reign of Henry VII (1485-1509).   In Bridge St is the *Washington Irrving Hotel,* formerly the Red Horse, in which Washington Irving's little parlour can still be seen.

Surroundings of Stratford

At *Shottery,* 1 mile west of Stratford, is *Anne Hathaway's Cottage,* which has changed little since Shakespeare's time and was occupied until 1899 by a descendant of the Hathaway family. It is furnished in the style of the period.

1 mile south is *Luddington,* where tradition has it that Shakespeare was married. At *Wilmcote,* 5 miles north-west, is a charming Tudor farmhouse in which the poet's mother, Mary Arden, lived: exhibition of farming and domestic equipment of the period.

SURROUNDINGS OF STRATFORD   697

1 mile north by way of Clopton Road is **Clopton House,** meeting-place of the Gunpowder Plot conspirators, who trained their cavalrymen in the park and dined together for the last time in the great hall. The house contains fine furniture (mediaeval, Adam, Chippendale, Louis XV and Louis XVI) and a number of pictures, including some panels by *Fragonard* and a full-length portrait of Sir Walter Raleigh by Zucchero. (Open 10 to 5).

4 miles north-east by A 46 or B 4086 is **Charlecote Park,** the beautiful mansion of the Lucy family (1558). Shakespeare is supposed to have been brought up before Sir Thomas Lucy in the Great Hall for poaching deer in the park, and to have taken his revenge by burlesquing Lucy as Mr Justice Shallow in "The Merry Wives of Windsor". The red brick gatehouse remains exactly as Shakespeare knew it. The house contains magnificent furniture and pictures; in the dining room are the Lucy silver-gilt cups, in the morning room an autograph letter of Oliver Cromwell and a 1632 Shakespeare folio. (Open 11 to 6).

5 miles east is *Wellesbourne Mountford,* and just beyond this is *Wellesbourne Hastings* (pop. 1300, E.C. Thursday). 2 miles farther on is *Edgehill*, scene of the first battle between Parliamentarians and Royalists in 1642. A pseudo-Gothic castle was built in 1750 on the top of Edge Hill to commemorate the event.

Stratford to Birmingham

8 miles: *Henley-in-Arden* (pop. 1400, E.C. Wednesday), a quaint old town with an ancient Guildhall and market cross. — 13 miles: *Hockley Heath.* 1½ miles east is *Packwood House*, a timber-framed Tudor house with 17th century additions in brick, standing in 115 acres of park and woodland, with very fine formal *gardens*. The house (open in summer

2 to 7, except Mondays and Fridays) contains an important collection of tapestry, needlework and furniture.

25 miles: **Birmingham** (p. 664).

38. OXFORD TO WORCESTER

56 miles. Leave Oxford by Woodstock Road (A 34) and continue on A 34 for 18 miles before turning left into A 44. From London to Gloucester, follow Route 36 (London to Oxford) as far as Headington, where the Oxford bypass begins, joining the route described in this chapter before Woodstock.

14 miles: *Enstone*. — 18 miles: fork left on A 44 for (19 miles) *Chipping Norton* (pop. 4000, E.C. Thursday), an ancient market-town standing 700 feet above sea level, with a fine Perpendicular church: interesting monuments and brasses.

On the right of Church St are old almshouses (1640). At 20 High St is a former monastic chapel, with 14th century stone vaulting. (Visiting: by arrangement with occupier.) There are many old houses in the town. Behind the picturesque Georgian stone front of the *White Hart Hotel* are carefully restored rooms of a much earlier period. — 3 miles north-west are the *Rollright Stones*, a very ancient monument. There are 73 stones, ranged in a circle 100 feet in diameter. To the north is a single monolith, 8 feet high, called the "King's Stone", and ¾ mile southeast are the "Whispering Knights", five great stones in a group.

23 miles: B 4450 goes off on the left for Stow-on-the-Wold, passing **Chastleton House**, built by Walter Jones in 1603 on land bought from Robert Catesby, one of the Gunpowder Plot conspirators. The interior contains fine mouldings and some of the finest oak panelling in the country, period furniture, tapestries, china, etc., and the Bible which Charles I had with him on the scaffold. The *Box Garden* (c. 1700) is famous. Open 10.30 to 1 and 2 to 5.30, except Wednesdays.

Stow-on-the-Wold (pop. 1800, E.C. Wednesday), an ancient village perched at a height of 750 feet in the Cotswold Hills, for which it is an excellent centre. There is a 14th century Gothic *church* (restored).

The Cotswolds. Some of the loveliest villages in England are to be found among the Cotswold Hills, where every building and every roof is made of the local honey-coloured stone, and where the graceful domestic architecture of the Tudor period can be seen at its best. There is not a single ugly village in this

district, and all are worth seeing. Among the finest are Chipping
Campden, Broadway, Burford, Bourton-on-the-Water and
Moreton-in-Marsh. Painswick and its ancient yews, Bibury
and its lovely Arlington Row, and the view from the top of
Birdlip Hill should not be missed. Nor must we omit Chipping
Norton, sitting picturesquely on the side of a hill and overlooking a valley in which tweeds were formerly made. Witney,
at the foot of the Cotswolds, has succeeded in retaining all its
charm although engaged in the manufacture of blankets which
have made the name of Witney famous all over the world.
Cheltenham and Stroud are other good centres for the Cotswolds.

25 miles: the "*Four Shire Stone*", marking the
meeting place of Gloucestershire, Warwickshire,
Oxfordshire and Worcestershire.

27 miles: *Moreton-in-Marsh* (pop. 2000, E.C.
Wednesday), a picturesque and typical Cotswold
village with a 13th century church rebuilt and restored
1859-91. King Charles I slept at the White Hart
Hotel on 2 July 1644.

36 miles: **Broadway** (pop. 3000, E.C. Thursday),
a picturesque little village with many Tudor houses.
From the tower on the hilltop there is a fine view.
The *St Eadburgh's Church* dates from the 12th century.

3 miles east is **Chipping Campden** (pop. 2000, E.C. Thursday),
a delightful unspoiled market town with houses built of the
local tawny coloured stone. There are a number of old houses,
which date mainly from the 14th century to the beginning of
the 17th century. The *market hall* is a Jacobean building dating
from 1627, resting upon arcades over a cobbled floor. The
High St sweeps round in a curve to reach the market square.
Here are the *grammar school* (1487), and, nearby, one of the
most beautiful 14th century houses in England, the *Grevel
House*. Its numerous windows include a two-storey bay window
with a gable. Opposite is the *Woolstaplers' Hall*. The almshouses
were endowed by Baptist Hicks in 1612. Beautiful Perpendicular
church (restored 1884), with a fine carved altar.

6 miles north-east on A 46 (the Stratford-upon-Avon road)
is *Mickleton*, near which is *Hidcote Manor Garden* (289 acres),

the first garden acquired under the Gardens Scheme of the National Trust and the Royal Horticultural Society.

41 miles: **Evesham** (pop. 13,000, E.C. Wednesday), an ancient little town with the remains of a Benedictine abbey.

Within the abbey precincts are *All Saints* and *St Lawrence's Church*, both built by the monks, with fine fan vaulting. Evesham lies in the *Vale of Evesham*, a fertile valley famous for its fruit orchards and market gardens. 2 miles away is *Wickhamford:* in the church is the tomb of Penelope Washington (d. 1697), who lived in the nearby manor-house.

Evesham to Birmingham: 30 miles (A 435 to Arrow, then A 422 to Alcester, then again A 435).

10 miles: *Alcester* (pop. 2500, E.C. Thursday), situated at the junction of the Alne and the Arrow. Pre-British settlement; Roman camp. Town Hall of 1618, church of 1730. 2 miles south-west is **Ragley Hall,** seat of Earl Seymour, built in 1690, with a Great Hall and a picture gallery (*Rubens*, *Reynolds*, etc.): open 2 to 6, except Mondays and Fridays.

12 miles: *Coughton.* **Coughton Court** was bequeathed to the Throckmorton family in 1409; the gatehouse dates from 1509. To the east are two Elizabethan wings. The house contains many Jacobite relics.

14 miles: *Studley*, with the ruins of an Augustinian priory. Half way up Gorgott Hill is a fine half-timbered house, *Gorgott Hall* (15th c.). The church is 12th century.

21 miles: to the east, *Earlswood Lakes* station, with *Earlswood Moat House* and the Roundabouts beyond it. A small half-timbered house (end of 15th c.) in 65 acres of meadows and woodland, now a nature reserve (National Trust). — 30 miles: *Birmingham.*

48 miles: *Pershore* (pop. 4000, E.C. Thursday). *Holy Cross Church* contains remains of an old Benedictine abbey church: Early English choir, Norman south transept, 14th century square tower. — 52 miles: *Stoulton.*

57 miles: **Worcester** (pop. 67,000, E.C. Thursday), an ancient and handsome town and cathedral city situated in one of the richest parts of the Severn valley, with magnificent views of the Bredon, Crook Barrow and Abberley Hills. It is an industrial centre noted for its gloves, its porcelain and its sauce.

WORCESTER

There was a settlement here in pre-Roman times, and under the Romans the place was an important military station. Its Saxon name was *Wigorna Ceaster*. The town became an independent episcopal see in 680. The castle was built in the 11th century, and was the residence of several of the early post-Conquest kings. The town suffered many vicissitudes during the Middle Ages, being besieged and destroyed on several occasions. The last siege was during the battle of Worcester in 1651, when Cromwell routed Charles II's forces and almost captured the king himself,

In the south of the town is the **Cathedral,** built on high ground above the east bank of the Severn. To the north of the Cathedral is the *Bishop's Palace*, now the offices of the Worcestershire Agricultural Committee. On the south side, entered by the Edgar Tower, is **College Green,** in which are the ruins of the guest-house, the Chapter House, the cloisters and the Refectory (now part of King's School).

The Cathedral is built in the form of a double cross, with short transepts. It is 415 feet long; the width of the nave is 80 feet and across the west transept 130 feet. The height over the nave is 68 feet. The central tower is 196 feet high.

The style is mainly Early English and Decorated, but there is also other work to be seen. The earliest parts of the present building are the crypt and some sections of the walls, which date from 1084, when

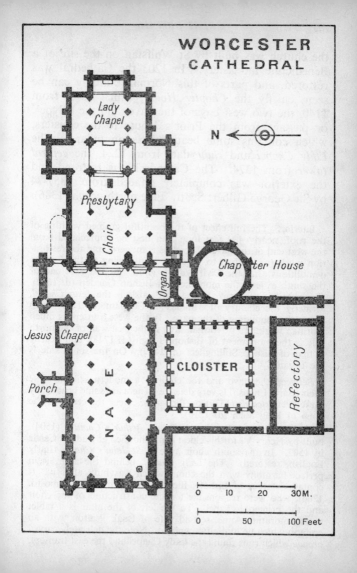

WORCESTER
CATHEDRAL

Lady Chapel

N

Presbytary

Choir

Chapter House

Organ

Jesus Chapel

Porch

NAVE

CLOISTER

Refectory

0   10   20   30 M.

0   50   100 Feet

the church was built by St Wulfstan on the site of a Benedictine monastery. In 1203 the Cathedral was restored, and parts of this Norman building can be seen, chiefly the *Chapter House*, which dates from 1140, the two west bays of the nave, and the "slype" or passage from the Prior's House to the cloisters, which contains some beautiful Saxon pillars. The *Lady Chapel* and *choir* date from 1224, the *central tower* from 1374. The Cathedral was restored and the exterior was completely refaced from 1857-74 by Sir George Gilbert Scott. Fine north porch (1386).

Interior. The full effect of the beautiful groined vaulting of the roof, nearly 400 feet long, can best be appreciated from the west end of the nave. The glass is modern, and the restoration work (which had to be carried out owing to the Puritan demolitions after the Civil War) is good. At the west end of the south aisle is the monument of Bishop Gauden (d. 1662). The pulpit is modern. In the north aisle is the *Jesus Chapel*, formerly the chantry of Thomas de Cobham (d. 1327), who began the rebuilding of the nave. In the west transept is much Norman work. In a Norman arch in the east wall of the north side is the monument of Bishop Hough (d. 1743), and nearby is that of Bishop Stillingfleet (d. 1699). On the south side is the organ.

Between the nave and the choir is a modern screen. The **choir** (Early English) is very delicate. There are some beautifully carved *misericords* (1379) on the stalls. Near the centre is the **tomb of King John** (d. 1216).

To the right of the altar is *Prince Arthur's Chantry* (1504), built by Henry VI for his eldest son, who died at Ludlow Castle in 1502. In the south choir aisle is *St John's Chapel* (Early English, restored). The *Lady Chapel*, behind the altar, is in perfect harmony with the choir, which was built after it. It contains statues of Bishops Blois (d. 1236) and Cantilupe (d. 1266), who were responsible for the construction of the choir and the principal chapel. To the left of the altar is a tablet commemorating Anne, second wife of Isaak Walton, with an epitaph which he himself composed. Note the delicately carved *arcade* which runs round the Lady Chapel and the east transept.

The **crypt** (reached from the south-west transept), which was originally intended to contain relics, is notably light, with beautiful groined vaulting borne on tall Norman columns.

A magnificent Norman doorway in the south aisle of the nave gives access to the red sandstone **cloisters,** with the tombstone which inspired one of Wordsworth's sonnets. The cloisters have very fine carved ornament, including a rare Tree of Jesse on the south side. On the east side of the cloisters is the entrance to the **Chapter House,** one of the earliest examples of a vaulted chamber with the roof supported on a single central pier.

From the top of the tower there are wide views. The *Library* contains many valuable manuscripts.

To the south of the Cathedral, in Severn St, are the *Royal Porcelain Works,* founded in 1751 (open to visitors Monday-Friday 10 to 1 and 2 to 5), with a porcelain museum (open 10 to 6).

In **Sidbury,** to the south-east, is the **Commandery,** a hospice for travellers founded by St Wulfstan, entered through an iron gate. This is one of the most interesting old houses in the town, dating from the 11th century, when the hospice was founded. The present building dates from the time of Henry VII: the great hall is the former refectory, with a magnificent *musicians' gallery.* The hospice was abolished in 1524; the building is now a private house. (The great hall, Elizabethan staircase and some other rooms can be seen at certain times, or by arrangement).

Returning along Sidbury, turn right into **Friar Street,** in which are some old half-timbered houses.

On the left-hand (west) side of the street is **Tudor House,** now a museum of local life (open 10.30 to 5, except Thursdays and Sundays). On the right-hand side is **Greyfriars House** (1480), a former Franciscan friary now occupied by the Worcestershire Archaeological Society (open on the first Tuesday in the month 2 to 5).

Farther north, in *New Street,* are other old houses (16th c.), in one of which Charles I once stayed.

Turning left into Pump St, we come to the **High Street,** in which, almost immediately in front, is the **Guildhall.**

This is a fine Queen Anne building (1723) designed by one of Wren's pupils, Thomas White. The **Assembly Hall** is very handsome and contains a number of paintings, including a portrait of George III by Reynolds (1788). The *Lower Hall,* 120 feet long, contains two bronze cannon and armour from the battlefield of Worcester. Open 9 to 5, except Saturdays and Sundays.

On the other side of the street is the *Market Hall.*

Farther north in a short street on the right, Church St, is *St Swithin's Church,* with a Perpendicular tower; the rest was rebuilt in the 18th century. Behind the church, in Trinity St, is a house from which Queen Elizabeth I spoke to the townspeople during her visit to Worcester in 1574.

Beyond this point the High St runs into the street called The Cross. On the right-hand side is St Nicholas's Church (1732); on the left-hand side is All Saints Church, of the same period.

At the corner of High St and Fish St is St Helen's Church (founded 680, rebuilt 1450; restored). In Fish St is *St Alban's Church,* founded in the 8th century; the present building dates from the 12th century. In Deansgate is St Andrew's Church, with a slender spire 245 feet high (end of 15th c.). One of Gloucester's pleasantest churches is St John in Bedwardine (12th c.).

Around Worcester. Boating in the Severn; steamer trips. To the north-west is the village of *Broadheath,* where Sir Edward Elgar was born; the house contains mementoes of the composer (open on Thursdays, Saturdays and Sundays, or can be seen by appointment: tel. Cotheridge 224).

Worcester to Monmouth: 39 miles (A 449 to Ross-on-Wye, then A 40).

8 miles: **Great Malvern** (pop. 28,000, E.C. Thursday), one of the most beautiful holiday towns in England, situated at between 350 and 850 feet above sea level on the gentle slopes of the Malvern Hills (see below). It has long been noted as a spa.

The principal thermal springs are *St Anne's Well* (756 ft: free) at Great Malvern, the *Royal Well* (1150 ft) near West Malvern, and the *Holy Well* (675 ft) above Malvern Wells. The beautiful **Priory Church** contains fine examples of the Early English, Perpendicular and Renaissance styles, with a nave dating from 1085; good glass and 15th century misericords. Nearby is the gatehouse of a Benedictine priory.

A celebrated dramatic festival is held annually in August. The plays of George Bernard Shaw (who used to attend the festival) always figure prominently in the programme.

1 mile south of Little Malvern is an old church built into a Norman castle and tower.

Malvern Hills. One of the most arresting landscapes in England is the long range of the Malvern Hills, rising steeply and unexpectedly, like a series of volcanic heights, out of the low-lying pastoral Vale of Evesham. The ascent from Malvern is not unduly exacting, for the paths have a gentle and easy gradient. From the summit is a magnificent vista over 15 counties. The highest point is the *Worcester Beacon* (1395 ft), which rises immediately above Great Malvern. North of the Worcester Beacon is the *North Hill* (1326 ft) which is reached by the Ivy Scar Rock. Much of this area belongs to the National Trust; one of their properties extends from Little Malvern to Chase End Hill, including almost the whole of the ridge and part of the *Herefordshire Beacon* (1370 ft), on which is one of the finest hill-forts in the country. The National Trust also owns Shady Bank, Castlemorton and Hollybed Commons, to the east. 1½ miles south-west of Little Malvern is *Broad Down*. 1½ miles north of Midsummer Hill are remains of another hill-fort.

15 miles: A 438 runs south-east to *Eastnor*, where there is a castle in mediaeval style with an excellent collection of paintings and armour.

The *church*, which has a detached bell-tower, contains many architectural styles, including Norman. In the north aisle is a monument to the parents of Elizabeth Barrett Browning, who lived at Hope End. The old *Market House* (1633) rests on wooden pillars. There is an institute (1895) dedicated to Elizabeth Barrett Browning. The Knapp, a house near the market place, was John Masefield's birthplace.

17 miles: **Ledbury** (pop. 3600, E.C. Thursday), with many old half-timbered buildings.

29 miles: *Ross-on-Wye*. For the rest of the route see Route 40 from Ross-on-Wye to *Monmouth*.

Worcester to Shrewsbury: 48 miles (A 449 for 12 miles, then A 442 to Kidderminster and Bridgnorth, then A 458).

6 miles: *Ombersley*. — 9 miles: *Crossway Green*. — 10 miles: *Hartlebury*. Hartlebury Castle, seat of the Bishops of Worcester (built in the 18th century on a 13th century site), contains a valuable library. Now a County Museum (open Wednesdays and Sundays).

12 miles: fork left on A 449 for **Kidderminster** (pop. 41,000, E.C. Wednesday). The nonconformist preacher Richard Baxter was minister here 1641-66, and his pulpit can be seen in the Unitarian Chapel. In the *Bull Ring* is a statue of Baxter, and (near the Town Hall) of Sir Rowland Hill (1795-1879), who introduced the penny post. The town, situated on the Stour, is famous for its carpet manufacture.

3 miles south-east on A 449 is **Harvington Hall,** a moated house belonging to the Roman Catholic diocese of Birmingham. It was built in 1570-78 for John Pakington, and contains some remarkable 17th century wall paintings on Biblical themes and a collection of oak furniture.

27 miles: *Bridgnorth* (p. 650). — 35 miles: *Much Wenlock*. — 48 miles: *Shrewsbury* (p. 652).

Worcester to Birmingham: 26 miles on A 38.

7 miles: **Droitwich** (pop. 8500, E.C. Thursday), a country town and brine spa, situated on the Salwarpe, a tributary of the Severn, surrounded by picturesque hills.

The brine is pumped from 200 feet below the surface, where it is assumed there is an underground lake created by water filtering through a rock salt bed. The brine contains 30% natural salts, about ten times as dense as sea water. It is radio-active, and the natural temperature is 7° C. It is efficacious in cases of rheumatism, after the treatment of certain diseases and injuries, and for certain disorders of the circulatory system. As a spa the town has earned a reputation out of all proportion to its size. The centre for treatment is *St Andrew's Brine Baths*.

There are a number of fine half-timbered and stone houses in *High St* and *Prior St*. Owing to the pumping of the brine the foundations of many of the houses have subsided: the interesting old *Crooked House* is an example. The *Old Cock Inn* is attractive. *St Andrew's Church* was rebuilt after the former church was destroyed in 1290: *St Richard's Chapel*, with a Tudor altar, dates from 1200. Note the carved stone supports of the arch in a chapel in the south aisle (Henry III and a female head).

At *Dodderhill* is the Norman church of St Augustine (restored). ½ mile south is *St Peter de Witton*, a Norman church on an old Saxon site; fine stained glass and an early 16th century timbered roof over the nave. The Roman Catholic *church of the Sacred Heart and St Catherine* (1921) is built on the plan of a Roman basilica: interesting mosaics. — 13 miles: *Bromsgrove* (pop. 30,000, E.C. Thursday), an old town which still has some gabled houses.

The road climbs between the Clent Hills and the Lickey Hills to (17 miles) *Chadwick Manor Estate* (National Trust, 431 acres), including Chadwick Manor House (c. 1700), the neighbouring spring pools and the spinney field. Public access only by footpaths, except at *Highfield* (873 ft) where there is a fine view to the Malvern Hills. — 18 miles: *Rubery*. The road passes into Warwickshire. — 26 miles *Birmingham* (p. 664).

51 miles. Leave Oxford by Woodstock Road: A 34 for 3 miles to end of bypass, then A 40 to Gloucester. London to Gloucester direct: Route 36 to Headington (beginning of bypass), then join A 40 at end of bypass.

3 miles: end of bypass. Turn left for Witney.

An alternative way out of Oxford is by Queen St, New Road and Parkend St, then fork right into A 4141, joining A 40 beyond *Eynsham*, where the old tradition of mummers' plays at Christmas is still preserved.

12 miles: **Witney** (pop. 9500, E.C. Tuesday), an ancient town famous for its blankets and its woollen industry.

In Corn St and Church Green are interesting old stone houses. *Butter Cross* (1683). Very fine *Town Hall*, by a pupil of Wren's. **St Mary's Church** (13th c.) has an Early English tower and a Norman porch. The very beautiful river Windrush flows near the town, which lies between the Cotswolds and the quiet scenery of the Thames valley.

2 miles south is **Ducklington**, a pleasant stone-built village. The church has a south arcade in Transitional style, an Early English choir and a Decorated north aisle. Interesting brackets and roof lights. 1½ miles beyond this village is *Cokethorpe*, which has a 15th century church with a Norman font (key at cottage opposite Park Gate). To the south-east of Cokethorpe is *Stanton Harcourt*, an old-world village with charming old houses. The church has one of the oldest rood-screens in England; other features are the Harcourt Chapel, the Early English piscina and the Decorated altar. The old manor-house (15th c.) has an interesting kitchen. Alexander Pope lived in *Pope's Tower* in 1716-18 and here completed the translation of the 5th book of the "Iliad". Beautiful gardens. Nearby are three prehistoric standing stones known as the Devil's Quoits.

20 miles: **Burford** (pop. 1300, E.C. Wednesday), on the Windrush. Old stone-built gabled houses with

mullioned windows and charming old doorways. The *church* has a Norman west doorway and central tower; the rest is Early English and Perpendicular. Beside the church are 15th century *almshouses*. *Tolsey Museum* (open 2.30 to 5.30 during the season): local history.

22 miles: the road enters Gloucestershire.

29 miles: **Northleach** (pop. 1250). Church (15th c.), with interesting tombstones in the south porch.

At *Chedworth*, 4 miles south-west on A 429 (the Cirencester road), are the remains of an exceptionally fine **Roman villa** dating from 180-350, with a museum (open 10 to 1 and 2 to 5).

42 miles: **Cheltenham Spa** (pop. 75,000, E.C. Wednesday and Saturday), on the river Chelt, still has the elegant and leisured air of a fashionable spa. The springs were discovered in 1716, and after 1788, when George III visited the town, it became a fashionable resort. Cheltenham is a well-known educational centre.

The *High Street* (2 miles) runs east to west. Pittville St leads north to Pittville Gardens, with the Pump Room.

St Mary's Church dates from the 12th-15th centuries (restored): there is a very fine rose window. In Clarence St are the public library, museum and picture gallery.

Throughout the year fine concerts of music are held. These reach their peak in July with the annual Festival of British Contemporary Music, Opera, Drama and Art.

Important events at the Racecourse (at the foot of the Cotswolds) include the National Hunt Festival Meeting in March. Chief events are the Champion Hurdle Cup, the Cheltenham Gold Cup, and the National Hunt Steeplechase for amateurs, run over 4 miles, during which no fence is jumped twice.

Cheltenham to Broadway: 15 miles.

4 miles: *Cleeve Hill* (1031 ft), with wide views. — 7 miles: **Winchcombe** (pop. 3100, E.C. Thursday), once capital of the

kingdom of Mercia and now a little town with quaint old houses and a beautiful church (grotesque gargoyles). Nearby is *Sudeley Castle*, home of Henry VIII's last wife, Catherine Parr, who is buried in the church near the castle. 2 miles north-east are the ruins of *Hailes Abbey*, a Cistercian house: museum with statuettes, pottery and other relics of the abbey.

10 miles: east of the road is *Stanway*, with magnificent views of the nearby hills. — 15 miles: *Broadway* (p. 700).

51 miles: **Gloucester** (pop. 91,000, E.C. Thursday), pleasantly situated on the banks of the Severn, the county town of Gloucestershire and the see of a bishop.

GLOUCESTER

There was a British settlement here, and since then Gloucester has continued to play an important part in the history of Britain. Like Colchester, Lincoln and York, it was a Roman *colonia (Glevum)*, and a Roman road (Ermine Street) ran east from the town up the Birdlip Hills in the Cotswolds (from which there are some of the finest views in western England). The town's four main streets, meeting at right angles, still reflect the Roman layout, and there are many remains of the Roman town walls.

Gloucester is also a seaport linked with the Atlantic by the Ship Canal. Among its industries are engineering and the manufacture of railway rolling stock, aircraft, transport vehicles, foodstuffs and cameras.

The beautiful **Cathedral** which dominates the city was built on the site of a Benedictine house founded in 760; in 822 was established a college for priests, which in 1020 became a monastery. Fire destroyed the building, and in 1100 a new church (by Abbot Serlo) was consecrated; it became a cathedral in 1541. The timber roof structure was destroyed by fire on several occasions; the stone vaulting of the nave dates from 1242. In the 14th century alterations to the Norman building gave a Perpendicular style to

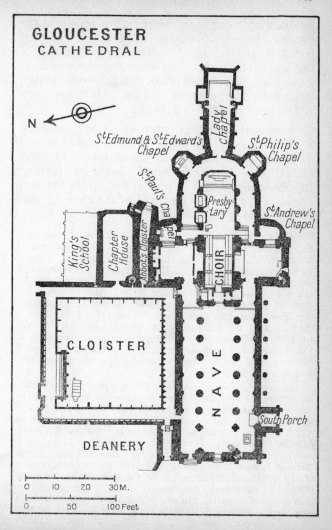

GLOUCESTER
CATHEDRAL

N

St Edmund & St Edward's Chapel

Lady Chapel

St Philip's Chapel

St Paul's Chapel

Presbytary

St Andrew's Chapel

King's School

Chapter House

Abbot's Cloister

CHOIR

CLOISTER

NAVE

South Porch

DEANERY

0   10   20   30 M.

0   50   100 Feet

the building. The main structure, the *crypt* and the *Chapter House* are Norman. The *cloisters*, with their beautiful fan vaulting, date from the second half of the 14th century; the south porch and the west front from 1425. The *tower* (220 ft high), with delicate stone-work and pinnacles, and the *Lady Chapel* were added between 1460 and 1483.

During the Civil War, when Gloucester withstood a Royalist siege for a month, the Cathedral was damaged by the Parliamentarian troops. Sir George Gilbert Scott restored the building in the 19th century. Its measurements are: length 420 feet; width 145 feet; height of the nave 69 feet; and of the choir 85 feet. It is entered by the very beautiful south porch.

Interior. The solid Norman pillars of the *nave*, which are exceptionally high (30 ft), and the delicacy of the east end of the choir, which contains more glass than stone-work, make a strikingly beautiful contrast. The Early English **clerestory** and vaulting are very fine; the *triforium* is almost miniature. In the north aisle there are two old stained glass windows; the rest are modern. There are some interesting monuments: *Dr Jenner*, the discoverer of vaccination (1749-1823, statue); memorials to the *Machen* family (17th c.) and *Mrs Morely* (d. 1784) by Flaxman. In the transept is the first example of the Perpendicular style in the country, applied over the solid Norman base. In the south transept is the *Prentice Bracket*, a projection for a lamp.

The **choir,** a splendid example of the purest Perpendicular, is perhaps the most magnificent in the country, and the tracery, vaulting, walls and great east window produce an outstanding effect of beauty and delicacy. The *glass* in the east window (72 ft by 39 ft) is 14th century. Behind is a *Whispering Gallery* reached from the west turrets of the transept. The 14th century *stalls* have grotesque misericords. In the presbytery is the **tomb of Edward II** (murdered at Berkeley Castle in 1327), with a richly ornamented canopy. In the 14th century pilgrims flocked to the tomb of the "martyr king". There are also an oak statue of Robert Curthose, William the Conqueror's eldest son, and a monument to King Osric, who founded the first abbey in 681. The *Bracket Tomb* is said to be that of Abbot Serlo.

The *Lady Chapel* (1483), at the east end, suffered severely during the Civil War. 15th century glass; old reredos; lierne vaulting. In the lateral aisles and the choristers' gallery above are the tombs of abbots.

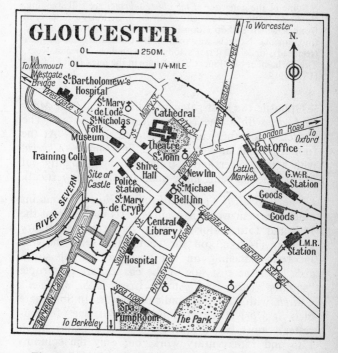

The **Cloisters** are reached from the east end of the north nave aisle. The fan vaulting is the earliest in the country, and is outstandingly beautiful. The monks' scriptorium is in the south walk. The Norman *Chapter House* (Perpendicular east window) is reached from the east walk. It was here that, traditionally, William the Conqueror gave instructions for the compilation of Domesday Book. The cathedral library is above: many valuable manuscripts and old books.

In the south transept is the entrance to the **crypt,** which is almost entirely Norman. The walls were strngthened in the 11th century. There are very fine views from the top of the tower.

Some of the *gateways of the abbey precinct* are still standing, the finest being the west gate (13th c.) in St Mary's Square, in front of which Bishop Hooper was burned at the stake in 1555 (monument). Near the west front of the Cathedral is the *Deanery* (restored), once the Prior's lodging, with fine Norman work. The Parliament of Gloucester met here in the reign of Richard II (1377-99).

Opposite the west gateway is the *church of St Mary de Lode*, with a fine Norman tower and choir. The church was rather clumsily restored in 1825. At the foot of the hill, in Westgate St, is *St Nicholas's Church*, with a fine tower and a truncated spire (slightly out of true, the top being more than a yard off the vertical).

The *Chapel of St Bartholomew's Hospital* contains much Norman work, as well as parts dating from the 14th and 15th centuries. Note the bronze sanctuary knocker (14th c.) on the south door and the fine Jacobean panelling on the west wall of the south aisle. On the east side of the chancel are quadruple "squints" (12th c.). At the Cross is *St Michael's Church*, with a fine Perpendicular tower. In Southgate St is *St Mary de Crypt* (founded 1080), one of Gloucester's most beautiful churches. It contains much 13th and 15th century work, but only the columns supporting the vaulting date from the original Norman building. George Whitfield, one of the founders of Methodism (born at the Bell Inn in 1714), was baptised in this church and preached his first sermon here.

There are a number of ancient inns in the town. From the gallery of the *New Inn* in 1553 Lady Jane Grey was proclaimed Queen. The *Bell* is another mediaeval building; in the *Fleece Hotel* is an underground room called the Monks' Retreat, and an old wisteria in the galleried courtyard.

Every street in the ancient centre of this historic city contains something of interest. Just beyond the Fleece Inn, on the other side of the street, is a small alley, at the end of which is *Maverdine House*, with one of the best Elizabethan fronts in the town. Beyond the Shire Hall in Westgate are the *Old Booth Hall* and **Bishop Hooper's Lodging**, a half-timbered house where Bishop Hooper is said to have lodged before his execution. It is now a *museum*, with collections illustrating the past life of the city and county.

The docks can be reached from the Cross by way of Southgate St. From the bridge the Severn bore can be observed. In Northgate St, beyond the New Inn, is *St John's Church* (1732), on the site of an earlier Saxon foundation. From here Hare Lane continues past the Old Raven Inn. At the end of this street, where St Catherine's St goes off on the left, is the site of an old Roman cemetery and a royal palace. In Priory Road are the ruins of *St Oswald's Priory*, a Norman building (12th c.) which was damaged during the Civil War.

Gloucester to Bristol

35 miles on A 38. Motorway: M 5.

4 miles: *Hardwick*. — 11 miles: *Cambridge*. — 15 miles: road on right to **Berkeley** (pop. 1000, E.C. Wednesday), birthplace of Dr Jenner (1749-1823), the originator of vaccination. The cottage in which he was born can still be seen.

Berkeley Castle, with a keep, is surrounded by a moat. It contains interesting furniture and portraits. Edward II was murdered here in 1327. (Open 2 to 5, except Mondays). The *church*, which has a separate tower, contains some interesting monuments, some of them with epitaphs by Swift.

Beyond Berkeley is *Sharpness*, Gloucester's outer port, connected with the city by a canal.

18 miles: *Stone*. — 19 miles: *Falfield*. B 4061 runs
west and then south to *Thornbury*, which has an old
church and a Tudor castle (unfinished) dating from
1511. — 24 miles: *Alveston* (pop. 1200, E.C. Thursday), with an old church (St Helen's). Nearby are
remains of an ancient hill-fort and tumuli. 5 miles
west is *Aust* (ferry to Chepstow and South Wales).

28 miles: *Almondsbury*. A road goes off on the
right to *Westbury-on-Trym* (4 miles), with a 15th century gateway, all that remains of the 13th century
Westbury College where John Wyclif was a prebendary.
Beside it is an 18th century house.

To the west, beyond the village of Henbury, is the hamlet
of Blaise, a picturesque group of ten small cottages, each one
different from the others, set irregularly round a green. The
hamlet was built by John Wash in 1809 to house old servants
of the Blaise estate (National Trust).

30 miles: *Filton*, a settlement dating from Roman
times, now with large aircraft factories. To the east
is *Frenchay Moor* (National Trust), an area of meadowland and scattered copses. — 35 miles: **Bristol** (p. 495).

Gloucester to Worcester

26 miles on A 38. Motorway: M 5.

7 miles: *Coombe Hill*. — 11 miles: **Tewkesbury**
(pop. 5300, E.C. Thursday), one of England's most
attractive old towns, situated at the junction of the
Severn and the Avon. It is a mingling of many architectural styles, in which half-timbered Tudor and
finely proportioned Georgian buildings predominate.

Tewkesbury Abbey, whose great pinnacled Norman
tower (132 ft) is a notable landmark, is one of the

oldest and most remarkable foundations in the country (715), and the late 12th century church is one of England's finest Norman buildings.

The **west front,** with its recessed arch and its fine window, is unique. Of particular interest is the Early English chapel on the east side of the north transept. The nave contains thirty pillars over 6 feet in diameter, contrasting in their massive simplicity with the slenderer Gothic arches. The **choir** (14th c.) is Decorated; many misericords and seven large windows with 14th century glass. Very fine vaulting in both nave and choir. In the north choir aisle are the *Beauchamp Chantry* (1425) and the tomb of High le Despenser. At the east end is the *Founder's Chapel*, with the tomb of Robert Fitz-Hamon (d. 1107), who built the Norman church. Below the central tower is a brass marking the grave of Prince Edward, son of Henry VI and Margaret of Anjou, who was killed at the battle of Tewkesbury. In the north choir aisle are the *Warwick Chapel* (1425) and monuments to a number of abbots. In the south transept is a tablet commemorating Mrs Craik, author of "John Halifax, Gentleman", which is set in Tewkesbury.

Tewkesbury is noted for the number and excellence of its ancient inns, some of which are mentioned in the "Pickwick Papers" and in "John Halifax, Gentleman". The Swan Inn (rebuilt in the 18th century) was already old when it was the focal point of an attack of plague in the town in 1579.

1 mile south is the *Bloody Meadow*, scene of the battle of Tewkesbury (1461), when the Yorkists defeated the Lancastrians in one of the most bitterly fought engagements in the Wars of the Roses. — 4 miles south is *Deerhurst*, which has a fine pre-Norman church with a Saxon tower. An inscribed stone dated to 1056, now in the Ashmolean Museum in Oxford, indicates that part of this building was the oldest in the country.

26 miles: **Worcester** (p. 702).

40. THE WELSH BORDER, THE WYE VALLEY AND THE FOREST OF DEAN

Shrewsbury to Chepstow via Ross-on-Wye

13 miles: *Church Stretton* (pop. 2900, E.C. Wednesday), a pleasant little town. The church still has part of the original Norman structure. Picturesque old market hall. To the west are the Stretton Hills and the Long Mynd (1696 ft). 2 miles north-east is the old British camp of *Caer Caradoc.*

6 miles east is *Longville in the Dale.* On the wooded slopes of Wenlock Edge is *Wilberhope Manor,* a limestone building erected in 1586 which has remained unaltered except for the addition of 17th century plaster ceilings.

15 miles: *Marshbrook.* — 23 miles: to the west, *Stokesay Castle* (13th c.), which has preserved its moat. — 25 miles: *Bromfield,* with a ruined abbey (12th-15th c.).

28 miles: **Ludlow** (pop. 7000, E.C. Thursday), a historic and interesting old town situated in one of the richest and most beautiful parts of the county of Salop, on the banks of the Teme and the Corve. In the 12th century Ludlow was surrounded by a wall with seven gates (of which only one survives); it was the residence of the Lord President of the Marches (see below).

Ruins of **Ludlow Castle** (11th c.). Milton's masque, "Comus", was performed in the Great Hall (late 13th c.) in 1634. Samuel Butler wrote much of "Hudibras" while he was keeper of the castle. Open 10 to 1 and 2 to 4.30.

On top of the hill is **St Lawrence's Church** (1199). Magnificent views from the tower (100 ft). *St John's Chapel* (15th c.) has a Saxon font, fine *glass* and carving. In the *choir* is more beautiful *glass* (1445), together with some very fine misericords.

The *Lady Chapel* (14th c.) also has old glass. There are a number of interesting monuments and old tombs. A.E. Housman, author of "The Shropshire Lad", is buried in the church.

There are many old half-timbered houses in the town; the *Feathers Inn* is a splendid example. On the east side of the churchyard is the Reader's House, a 10th century stone church hall, with Tudor timber additions and a beautiful Jacobean court. In the Teme and its tributaries there is good fishing; it is also a hunting district.

The **Marches** are the district on the Welsh border from the mouth of the Dee to the Severn estuary, in ancient times the scene of constant struggle and battle. Many castles and fortified mansions were built to dominate the Marches, among them Clun, Bishop's Castle, Hopton, Siddon, Stokesay, Downton, Wigmore, Richard's Castle and Croft. The castles at Chester, Shrewsbury, Ludlow and Hereford were fortified military stations from which expeditions could be launched against the surrounding countryside.

Ludlow to Kidderminster: 22 miles (A 4117 for 16 miles, then A 456).

6 miles: *Cleehill*. North is Clee Hill (1749 feet). — 12 miles: *Cleobury Mortimer*, with an interesting 12th-13th century church. — 19 miles: *Bewdley*, a pleasant market town, south of the beautiful Wyre Forest. — 22 miles: *Kidderminster*.

32 miles: *Woofferton*, at the head of the Teme valley.

5 miles west is *Croft Castle* (14th c.).

5 miles south is *Tenbury Wells* (pop. 2000, E.C. Thursday). There are some interesting monuments in the old church.

36 miles: *Ashton*. To the right is *Berrington Castle* (18th c.), with beautiful gardens laid out by Capability Brown.

39 miles: **Leominster** (pop. 6800, E.C. Thursday). The town takes its name (pronounced Lemster) from the 7th century priory on the site. The *church* of *SS. Peter and Paul* (restored 19th century), is one of the most splendid parish churches in England, and con-

tains a mixture of all styles from Norman to Perpendicular. The ball-flower ornamentation on the south aisle windows is very fine. In the north aisle is an old ducking stool. There are many interesting old buildings, including *Clarke's Almshouses* (1736, rebuilt 19th c.) and the former *Market House* (1634) in the Grange pleasure grounds, to which it was moved in the 19th century from the centre of the town. Woollen industry.

Leominster to Worcester: 26 miles on A 44.

11 miles: **Bromyard.** There are a number of old houses in this little town: the Tower House (1630), a 16th century building now occupied by the News and Record office, the Phineas Jackson almshouses (1656) and a number of 16th and 17th century inns. The Downs (800 ft) dominate the scene. — 14 miles: **Brockhampton,** with Brockhampton Park, a modern house in Georgian style. At *Lower Brockhampton* (1 mile off the road) is a comparatively unspoiled moated manor-house (late 14th c.), half-timbered, with an unusual detached gatehouse built a century later. — 18 miles: *Knightswood*, where the road crosses the Teme. — 26 miles: *Worcester* (p. 702).

52 miles: **Hereford** (pop. 45,000, E.C. Thursday), on the left bank of the Wye. Originally a Saxon town, and a royal demesne from the time of Edward the Confessor until 1189, Hereford is one of the most picturesque towns in the west of England.

Of the *Castle*, once one of the chief points in the domination of the Marches, little is left apart from some remains of walls. In the wide street known as High Town is the *Old House*, a fine half-timbered dwelling (1620, restored in the 19th c.), containing relics of Mrs Siddons and David Garrick. In High St is *All Saints Church*, with fine 15th century choir stalls and a library of 315 chained books in the vestry. From here Broad St runs south, with the Public

Library and Museum on the right-hand side. The Museum contains an interesting collection of Roman antiquities, including an altar from the town of *Magna* (*Kenchester*, 5 miles west, on the old Roman road).

The **Cathedral** (St Mary and St Ethelbert), the fourth church on the site, dates from 1079, the previous building having been destroyed in 1055. Built of the warm-coloured local sandstone, it shows the successive stages in the development of Gothic, not being completed until 1530.

The Norman work, done in the time of Bishop Robert de Losinga, comprises the nave, the south transept, the arches in the choir and the triforium. The *Lady Chapel* (Early English) dates from 1226-47. The north-west part of the transept, with its floral ornament in Decorated style, was built between 1250 and 1290, and the inner part of the north doorway (Perpendicular) in 1290. The *central tower* (165 ft) was built in the 14th century. The outer part of the north doorway was added in 1530. James Wyatt restored the west front and the upper part of the nave, which had been damaged in 1786, and Sir George Gilbert Scott carried out further work during the 19th century.

The Cathedral is 340 feet long, the nave and aisle 75 feet across, and the length of the transepts 146 feet; the nave is 65 feet high. Entrance is by the north porch.

Interior. The heavy, plain columns and arches make a striking contrast to the Decorated features of the exterior, and there is a similar extreme between the north (Norman) and south transepts. There are several monuments: in the north aisle, Bishop Booth (1516-35); the south aisle, *Richard Pembridge* (d. 1375). Nearby is a Norman font. Hanging in the north

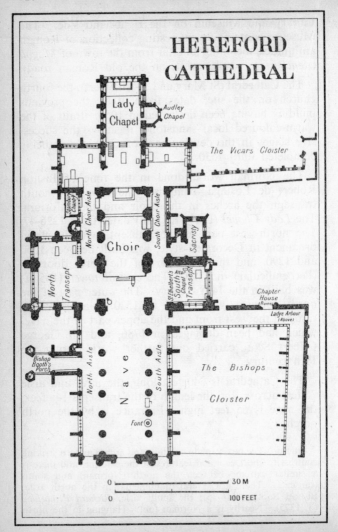

HEREFORD
CATHEDRAL

Lady
Chapel

*Audley
Chapel*

The Vicars Cloister

North Choir Aisle

Stanbury
Chapel

South Choir Aisle

Choir

Sacristy

North
Transept

St. Ethelbert's
Chapel

Altar

South
Transept

*Chapter
House
(Ruins)*

*Ladye Arbour
(Above)*

*Bishop
Booth's
Porch*

North Aisle

N a v e

South Aisle

*The Bishops
Cloister*

Font

0   30 M

0   100 FEET

aisle is the **Mappa Mundi,** a mediaeval map belonging to the
late 13th or early 14th century, one of the earliest in existence.
The north-west transept is Early English. The glass is modern.

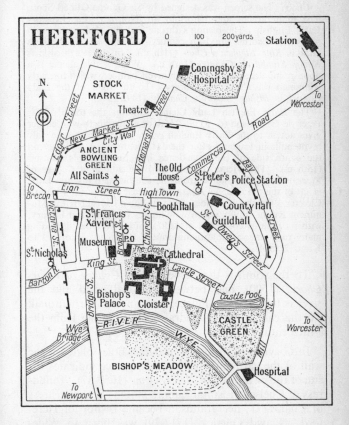

Monuments to *Bishop Peter d'Acquablanca* (1240-68) and
Bishop Thomas de Cantilupe (1275-82), the last Englishman to
be canonised before the Reformation. The south-west transept

is Norman, perhaps one of the oldest parts of the structure. Note the fireplaces in the west wall and the glass cabinet in the east aisle. The great **central tower** rises above the crossing, with some marvellous stonework in the lantern.

Choir. The screen was designed by Sir George Gilbert Scott. The main arches and triforium are Norman, the clerestory Early English. The bishop's throne and the **choir-stalls,** with many misericords, are 14th century. To the left of the high altar is *King Stephen's Chair* (11th c.). In the north aisle is *Bishop Stanbury's Chantry* (15th c.). West of this chapel is a door giving access to the old Archive Chamber, which formerly contained the Cathedral Library. To the right of the Lady Chapel is *Bishop Audley's Chantry* (1492-1502).

The Early English **Lady Chapel** contains the tomb of Sir Peter de Grandison (d. 1358). A door at the north-west corner gives access to the Early English *crypt*, believed to be the only crypt built in England after the 11th century. A doorway on the south side of the nave leads into the Bishop's Cloister (15th c.). The **Vicars' Cloister** and the adjoining *College of Vicars Choral* are entered from the south-east transept. Little is left of the old *Chapter House*, in the east walk of the Bishop's Cloister. On the west side of the Bishop's Cloister is the Muniment Room (1898), which now houses the **Cathedral Library,** with its famous collection of 1450 chained volumes, including many rare and valuable manuscripts. (Open to visitors 11 to 1 and 2 to 4).

To the south is the Perpendicular *College of Vicars Choral* (1500), and between the Cathedral and the river is the Bishop's Palace, with an old Norman hall. To the east is the Cathedral School, dating from the 14th century.

In Gwynne St, near the bridge, a brass plate on the wall of the garden of the bishop's palace indicates the site of the birthplace of *Nell Gwynne* (1650-87), "foundress of Chelsea Hospital", more famous as the mistress of Charles II; her grandson became Bishop of Hereford. David Garrick (1717-79) was born in Widemarsh St, in what is now the Raven Inn. Here too is *Coningsby Hospital*, a 17th century almshouse, also known as the Black Cross Hospital because in the garden are the ruins of a Blackfriars priory.

After the battle of Naseby (1645) Charles I regrouped his forces at Hereford. Over the bridge (at the end of White Cross Road) is the 14th century *White Cross*, erected in 1349 after an early visitation of the plague.

60 miles of the beautiful *Wye Valley* lie between Hereford and Chepstow, at the mouth of the Wye and the Severn estuary, and to the west of Hereford are as many, or more, miles of beautiful valley through which the river winds on its way from the hills of Wales. Until south of Monmouth the main road does not follow the extravagant loops of the Wye, and as there are many points on the river which are of outstanding beauty it is advisable to see the scenery from the water itself. Boats may be hired at all the towns and villages en route.

60 miles: *Llandinabo*. The churchyard is famous for its enormous yew, and the church has a screen believed to be 13th century. — 61 miles: *Harewood End*. — 63 miles: *Pengethly Park* (National Trust), 109 acres of farm and woodland, chiefly north of the main road; access by footpath.

66 miles: **Ross-on-Wye** (pop. 6000, E.C. Wednesday). Ross stands above a large horseshoe bend on the Wye, built on a red cliff overlooking the river.

The town owes much to John Kyrle (1637-1724), who appears in Pope's writings as the Man of Ross. Opposite the Town Hall, in the *Market Place*, is Kyrle's house. The *Town Hall* or Market House dates from the 17th century; built of red sandstone, it is supported on pillars. There is a fine 13th century **church** with a tall spire; monuments of John Kyrle and the Rudhall family. In the building are two tree trunks overgrown with creepers. From Prospect Walk, near the churchyard, there is a beautiful view of the Wye. In the *Royal Hotel* Dickens first met his biographer, John Forster. Ross-on-Wye is one of the best centres for excursions to the Wye Valley, the Forest of Dean, the Breconshire mountains and the borderland of Wales with its historic towns and ancient abbeys.

71 miles: B 4228 turns back on the left to *Goodrich*, on the west bank of the Wye. On a wooded hill above the village are the ruins of a famous 12th century moated *castle*, including the Norman keep, the chapel and the banqueting hall (13th c.).

73 miles: *Whitchurch.* 1 mile south-east is **Symond's Yat,** one of the most remarkable beauty spots in England, at the narrow neck, no more than a few hundred yards wide, of a 5 mile loop in the Wye. From the top of *Symond's Yat Rock* (475 ft) there are magnificent views of the valley and the *Forest of Dean* on the left bank.

77 miles: **Monmouth** (pop. 5800, E.C. Thursday), at the junction of the Monnow and the Wye. In the Middle Ages it was a walled town with four gates, of which one survives at the end of the old bridge over the Monnow — the only *Norman gate* of its kind in England. There are some remains of the castle, with the room in which Henry V (1382-1422) was born. There are an interesting *church*, a number of picturesque old houses and the ruins of a priory. *Museum* with relics of Nelson. The chronicler Geoffrey of Monmouth (d. 1154) was born in the town, and there is a 17th century building known as "Geoffrey's Window".

1 mile east is *Kymin Hill* (850 ft), from which there are wide views of the Wye and Monnow valleys. On top of the hill are a tower known as the Round House, built by a dining club in 1794, and a "Naval Temple", erected by the club in 1802 in honour of the Royal Navy. 1 mile south-east is a rocking stone known as the Buckstone. There is trout and salmon fishing in the Wye and the Monnow.

Below Monmouth the Wye valley narrows again, and extensive woods cover the steep hills. Both the road and the railway follow closely the course of the river, through some of the most beautiful scenery in England.

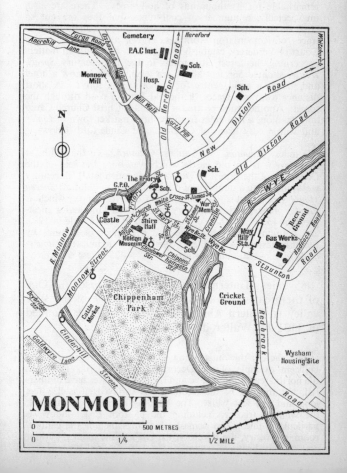

MONMOUTH

Monmouth to Gloucester: 25 miles. The road runs through the **Forest of Dean,** one of William the Conqueror's hunting preserves — a wild and beautiful tract of woodland extending over some 20,000 acres between the Wye and the Severn and remarkable for its thousands of holly-trees. There are also, unexpectedly, a number of coal-mines, but they are not so large or so numerous as to spoil the scenery. There are also traces of Roman iron workings, known as "scowles". The Court of Verderers, established in 1016 to deal with all matters concerning the forest, still meets in the 17th century *Speech House,* situated 566 feet above sea level, which is now a hotel and makes a good centre for exploring the forest. A short distance away are traces of the old Roman road through the forest. Another good centre for visitors is Christ Church Camp and Pavilion, a few miles from the little market town of *Lidley* and within easy reach of Coleford and Cinderford (below).

3 miles: *Staunton.* — 6 miles: **Coleford.** To the south, at *St Briavels,* is an old castle which was once the seat of the Constable of the Forest of Dean. It has much late 13th century work, including a dungeon of oubliette type. — 9 miles: *Speech House* (see above). — 11 miles: **Cinderford,** near which is *Flaxley Abbey,* with a refectory dating from 1148 and a guest-room of 1356. The house was enlarged in Adam style in 1780, and contains period furniture and a number of pictures by Flemish masters. — 13 miles: *Little Dean.* — 16 miles: *Westbury-on-Severn.* — 20 miles: *Minsterworth.* — 25 miles: *Gloucester.*

88 miles: **Tintern** (pop. 750, E.C. Thursday). One of the greatest beauty spots in the whole of the Wye valley is **Tintern Abbey,** a Cistercian house founded in 1131 by Walter de Clare of Chepstow.

The **church,** the outstanding feature of the ruins, is a magnificent example of the Decorated style (1288). The roof, the north arcade of the nave and the central tower have disappeared, but the rest of the building has survived: it is 228 feet long and 150 feet wide. The building is richly ornamented; the window tracery, including the 65 foot east window, is particularly fine. The domestic buildings include the canons' room, the vestry, the refectory, the kitchen, the monks' parlour and the lay brothers' rooms.

90 miles: a road on the right runs past Moss Cottage, from which there is a path to the top of *Wyndcliff* (650 ft), with one of the most beautiful views of river scenery in Europe.

93 miles: **Chepstow** (pop. 7500, E.C. Wednesday), at the junction of the Wye and the Severn. Perched high on a cliff above the river are the ruins of *Chepstow Castle*, first built by William Fitz-Osborn, who fought at Hastings. The present building dates from the 12th, 14th and 19th centuries. In one of its massive towers Henry Marten, one of Charles I's judges, was imprisoned for 20 years; he is buried in the churchyard (d. 1680). Nearby is a small *local museum*. Many steep and crooked streets give character to the town, which still preserves something of its mediaeval atmosphere. *St Mary's Church* has a fine Norman nave and west doorway and a 14th century font. In the garden of the George Hotel is a good example of the half-round towers which were set at intervals on the town walls. The railway bridge was built by Brunel in 1852.

4 miles south is *Beachley*, dominated by the large new **Severn Road Bridge,** opened by the Queen in 1966. Built in 3½ years, this magnificent suspension bridge is the seventh longest in the world (5340 ft). Toll charge. The average daily number of vehicles using the bridge in the years 1967-73 was 25,000, with peaks of 52,000. The bridge carries the London-Cardiff motorway (M 4).

5 miles south-west is **Caerwent,** on an old Roman road. This was the Roman town of *Venta Silurum:* remains of walls, an amphitheatre, hypocausts.

A short distance south of Caerwent is **Caldicot Castle,** a Norman stronghold completed in 1396. Historical museum. Banquets in mediaeval style (advance booking necessary).

41. GLOUCESTER TO READING
(CIRENCESTER)

72 miles (A 417 to Streatley, then A 329). Leave Gloucester by Northgate St and London Road, then turn right into Barnwood Road.

9 miles: *Birdlip* (pop. 300, E.C. Tuesday), with fine views of the Severn valley and the Welsh hills.

19 miles: **Cirencester** (pop. 12,700, E.C. Thursday), which occupies the site of the Roman *Corinium*, the second largest town in Roman Britain, situated at the intersection of Ermine Street and the Fosse Way.

The Saxons conquered the town in 577, and by the reign of Ethelred (978-1016) it already had a church, markets and a castle. Henry I often stayed in the castle, and founded an Augustinian abbey and St John's Hospital (1116). The castle was destroyed in the reign of Stephen (1135-54). In the Middle Ages Cirencester was a centre of the cloth trade. During the Civil War the town was captured from the Parliamentarians, but later retaken by the Earl of Essex.

The **parish church** was built on the site of a Saxon church and contains many styles of architecture. Of the Norman church only a small doorway between the north end of the nave and the north chancel aisle and a similar one on the south side of the nave are to be seen. The north and south chancel aisles date from the Transitional period, the north aisle arcades from 1150. The magnificent Perpendicular style nave was rebuilt in 1515. The *Lady Chapel* (rebuilt 1450) is early 13th century, and the *Trinity Chapel* dates from 1430. The south porch was rebuilt in 1500. Rebuilding and repairs were carried out in the 19th century. The roof of St Catherine's Chapel incorporates stone groining from the great abbey suppressed at the Reformation. The fine *tower* (162 ft) dates from 1400.

In the *Corinium Museum* are the finds excavated from the site of the old Roman town. (Open 10 to 4.30). Remains of Roman building include the earthwork ampitheatre. *Cirencester Park*, 3000 acres of park and woodland with the seat of Earl Bathurst, is open to the public.

7 miles north-east is *Bibury*, one of the prettiest villages in the country, in a picturesque setting on the river Colne. *Arlington Row* is a row of early 17th century cottages in Cotswold stone with pointed gables and steeply pitched tiled roofs.

Cirencester to Stroud: 12 miles (A 429, then A 419).

1 mile: turn right into A 419. Royal Agricultural College, the first agricultural training centre in England. — 7 miles: *Frampton*. Road on left to (3 miles) **Minchinhampton** (pop. 3700), an old cloth-making town, with a 17th century *Market House*. — 12 miles: *Stroud* (pop. 18,000, E.C. Thursday), a centre of the cloth industry. At *Lansdown* is a Technical College, with a *museum* containing a collection of fossils from oolitic limestone (including some magnificent fossil reptiles), coins and mediaeval pottery and glass.

Between Stroud and Nailsworth is *Woodchester*, where in a National Trust property of 26 acres is one of the largest Roman villas in the country (not now visible), dating from about 117 A.D. and discovered in 1796. 3 miles north-east of Chipping Sodbury (see below) is *Horton Court*, a Cotswold manor-house with a 12th century Norman hall.

2-3 miles north-west of Stroud are *Haresfield Beacon* and *Standish Wood* (National Trust), on the north edge of the Cotswolds. The property includes Ring Hill, Randwick Wood (long barrow), Stockend Wood, Broad Barrow Green and Halliday's Wood. On the Beacon itself is a hill-fort, with fine views over the Severn.

North of Stroud is **Painswick** (pop. 3100, E.C. Thursday), a charming little town amid some of the most beautiful scenery in the Cotswolds, with a number of interesting old buildings.

Fine Perpendicular church with a ribbed stone spire; the church-yard is notable for its 99 clipped yews. In the centre of the town is *Little Fleece*, a small town hall in traditional Cotswold style, built and roofed with stone, probably dating from the 17th century (National Trust). To the north of the town is *Painswick Beacon* (920 ft), crowned by *Kimsbury Camp*, a typical hill-fort with a triple line of ramparts.

Cirencester to Bristol: 37 miles (A 429 for 4 miles, then A 433 to Dunkirk, A 46 for 3 miles and finally A 432).

3 miles: nearby is the source of the Thames. — 4 miles: turn right into A 43. — 11 miles: *Tetbury* (pop. 6500, E.C. Thursday). At *Beverstone*, 2 miles west, is a ruined castle. — 19 miles : *Dunkirk*. — 25 miles: **Chipping Sodbury** (pop. 2000, E.C. Thursday), a picturesque town of pleasant houses with many gables. In the background are the beech-clad hills known as the Wagon and Horses. The old *church* contains some interesting monuments. Some of the oldest houses are in *Hatters Lane* (15th c.). Picturesque old Cotswold farmhouses at *Old Sodbury* and *Little Sodbury*, to the north-east. Near *Portway* is an ancient earthwork. The manor-house of *Little Sodbury* dates from 1485; the north wing was added in the 18th century. William Tyndale, translator of the Bible, was tutor here in 1522. — 37 miles: *Bristol*.

Cirencester to Swindon: 15 miles on A 419.

7 miles: **Cricklade,** a market town of grey stone, situated on the old Roman road, Ermine Street, and on the Thames, here still a small stream. 17th century grammar school. *St Sampson's Church* has an Early English nave, a Decorated choir and a Perpendicular tower. *St Mary's Church*, near the bridge, preserves some Norman work. Cricklade is a hunting town in the Vale of the White Horse. 3 miles south-east on B 4040, the road to Malmesbury (see below), is *Leigh*, to the north of which is *Ashton Keynes*, on the Thames. The Bruderhof, a German community, moved here in 1936: to visit, apply at entrance. — 15 miles: *Swindon*.

Cirencester to Chippenham: 23 miles on A 429.

11 miles: **Malmesbury** (pop. 9000, E.C. Thursday), a quiet little town, the birthplace of Thomas Hobbes (1588-1679). Ruins of a Norman *abbey church* belonging to a Benedictine abbey; six of the nine bays of the nave still survive, together with the very fine south porch. The church contains what is traditionally believed to be the tomb of King Athelstan. In

the triforium is a small watching chamber. There is a notable choir screen. The chronicler William of Malmesbury (d. 1143) was a monk in the abbey. In the market place is a fine *Market Cross* (15th c.), 40 feet high. 3 miles east, to the right of B 4040 (the Cricklade road), is *Garsdon* church, with a monument (restored 1905) to Lawrence Washington (d. 1613). — 23 miles: *Chippenham.*

28 miles: *Fairford* (pop. 1500, E.C. Thursday), an old-world stone-built village on the fringe of the Cotswolds, with a *church* built in 1493, notable for its 28 windows filled with magnificent 16th century glass.

32 miles: *Lechlade-on-Thames* (pop. 2500, E.C. Thursday). — 38 miles: *Faringdon,* with picturesque old inns and a market hall (18th c.). Nearby, in a large park, is *Faringdon House,* rebuilt in the 18th century by the poet laureate Henry Pye.

47 miles: *Wantage.* — 62 miles: *Streatley.* From Streatley to Reading, see Route 36. — 72 miles: **Reading** (p. 486).

VI: THE NORTH OF ENGLAND

The North of England is a region of grand and varied country, of high hills and widespread moorland, of magnificent coastal scenery and noble river valleys.

England at her most representative is to be seen in her largest county, **Yorkshire,** and its north-eastern neighbours, the counties of **Durham** and **Northumberland.** Here are rock-strewn hills, moors stretching their purple folds as far as the eye can see, and fine cliffs fronting the North Sea. Here too are coal-mines, shipyards, blast furnaces and textile mills. Industrial Yorkshire, one of the most highly industrialised areas in England, includes *Sheffield*, centre of the steel trade; *Bradford*, capital of the woollen industry; and *Doncaster*, a railway engineering town. Northward are the coalfields of the county of *Durham* and the furnaces and shipyards of Tyneside and Teeside.

Yet neighbouring these industrial tracts are great areas of open country and unsullied coast, with villages in high remote dales, lovely market towns amid rich farmland, and magnificent cathedrals, abbeys and minsters. Perhaps the most beautiful of all the buildings of the north is *York Minster*, an architectural jewel in the beautiful setting of a walled mediaeval city; but this rich gallery of architectural treasures also includes *Durham Cathedral*, *Ripon Cathedral*, *Beverley Minster* and *Rievaulx Abbey*. Also here are many famous inland and coastal resorts, and such renowned spas as gracious inland *Harrogate* and seaside *Scarborough*.

West of Yorkshire stretches the "cotton county" of **Lancashire,** with its great "cottonopolis" of *Manchester*, and *Liverpool*, second seaport in England. Around Manchester is a congested territory of satellite cotton-towns, but Lancashire also has much lovely country. On its coasts are many seaside resorts; the most renowned of them is, of course, *Blackpool* with its promenade and its famous tower. Lancashire's northern boundary takes us into the geography of the **Lake District,** which stretches north into the wildly beautiful county of *Cumbria*. The Lake District, a region of statuesque mountains and romantic lakes and gorges, is claimed by many to be the most beautiful part of all England.

42. THE GREAT NORTH ROAD TO SCOTLAND

London to Berwick-upon-Tweed

332 miles: A 1 (the Great North Road) all the way. Much of the road is of motorway standard (A 1 (M)).

From London Bridge follow King William St into Poultry and Cheapside; then turn right into St Martin's le Grand and Aldersgate St, continue straight ahead into Goswell Road, and at the Angel bear right into Islington High St and Upper St. At Highbury and Islington station bear left into Holloway Road, and at Archway bear slightly right into Archway Road for East Finchley; then continue across the North Circular Road for North Finchley and Barnet.

A quicker way out of London is by way of the Barnet bypass (see Route 32); then follow A 55 to join A 1 just beyond Hatfield.

12 miles: *Barnet.* At East Barnet is a Norman church, St Mary the Virgin. At nearby *Hadley* is a church with a beacon.

21 miles: **Hatfield** (pop. 25,000, E.C. Thursday), a small market town with an interesting old *church.*

To the east is **Hatfield House,** seat of the Marquess of Salisbury, built by Robert, first Earl of Salisbury, in 1607-11. Henry VIII kept his daughter Mary prisoner here, and when she became queen she in turn confined her sister Elizabeth in the house.

The *State Apartments* contain pictures, furniture, tapestries, armour and various historical relics. Open 12 to 5, Sundays 2 to 5; closed on Mondays.

7 miles east on A 414 is **Hertford** (pop. 17,500, E.C. Thursday), an old town on the river Lea, with the ruins of a 10th century castle and a 17th century building which is now a school.

23 miles: road on right to **Welwyn Garden City** (pop. 40,000, E.C. Wednesday), founded in 1920 by

Ebenezer Howard, the pioneer of town planning and founder of Letchworth, the first garden city. It is being developed as a "new town" and is now a rapidly growing industrial centre.

26 miles: *Old Welwyn*, where traces of Roman occupation have been found.

2 miles north-west on A 600 (the Hitchin road) is *Codicote* (pop. 1600, E.C. Wednesday), with the George and Dragon, an Elizabethan inn originally founded in the 14th century. From here a minor road runs west to **Ayot St Lawrence,** at the south-west end of which is *Shaw's Corner*, a red brick house built at the beginning of this century, where George Bernard Shaw lived from 1906 until his death in 1950. Shaw made over the property to the National Trust in 1944 and it is now a museum (open 11 to 1 and 2 to 6; closed on Mondays).

28 miles: *Woolmer Green*. — 29 miles: *Knebworth* (pop. 2500, E.C. Wednesday). Adjacent is Knebworth House, with towers and turrets, once the home of the Lyttons. At Water End is a beautiful Jacobean house once occupied by Sarah Jennings, the famous Duchess of Marlborough. — 30 miles: *Broadwater*, where A 602, coming from Hertford, joins A 1.

32 miles: **Stevenage** (pop. 60,000, E.C. Wednesday), an ancient town with many old buildings which is now a "new town" taking overspill from London. The High St (300 ft above sea level) is the highest point on the Great North Road between London and Darlington.

There are many picturesque little villages in the surrounding area. *St Nicholas's Church* (early 12th c.). *Old inns:* White Lion, Old Castle Inn, Swan (now the Grange), all mentioned by Pepys in his diary. South of the town are the "Six Hills" (British or Roman tumuli).

38 miles: *Baldock* (pop. 8000, E.C. Thursday), an 18th century town, mainly built in red brick. There is an attractive modern factory designed by T. Burdett.

46 miles: *Biggleswade* (pop. 6000, E.C. Thursday). 2 miles north-east on B 1040 is a 13th century pack-horse bridge over the Ouse at Sutton. — 50 miles: *Girtford.* — 53 miles: B 1043 goes off on the right to *Little Barford* (earthworks of a 12th century castle, the Hillings).

56 miles: *Eaton Socon.*

1 mile east is **St Neots** (pop. 5000, E.C. Thursday), on the Ouse. The town grew up round the 10th century monastery of Eynesbury, to which the bones of St Neot, formerly at the place of that name in Cornwall, were transferred.

The town is well planned and has many pleasant old buildings. The Ouse is spanned by a 16th century bridge. *St Mary's Church* has a pinnacled tower resembling that of Gloucester Cathedral. On the other side of the Henbrook is *Eynesbury* with its old church. The annual fair held on Ascension Day and the third Thursday in September goes back to the 13th century. Local industries are brewing, flour-milling, paper-making and woodworking. The countryside in the *Ouse valley* is very beautiful.

62 miles: *Buckden*, with the ruins of the palace of the Bishops of Lincoln. Bypass on west side of the town.

63 miles: A 141 goes off on the right to **Huntingdon** (pop. 13,000), 3 miles north-east, on the Ouse. Oliver Cromwell (1599-1658), who was M.P. for the town for 12 years, was born here; *Cromwell House* in the High Street occupies the site of his birthplace. He was educated at the *Grammar School* (restored: some Norman work), which still stands on the east side of the market place. Another pupil at the school was Samuel Pepys. Opposite the Grammar School is

the *Old George Hotel*, parts of which date back to Stuart times; interesting galleried courtyard. The poet Cowper lived in the town for two years; a tablet marks the house.

Around Huntingdon. A 14 runs south from the market place, crosses the Ouse on a mediaeval bridge and comes in 2 miles to **Godmanchester**, the Roman *Durolipons*. *Farm Hall* is a small-scale version of an elegant early 18th century mansion; the house, built in 1746, consists of a three-storey main block with a south wing and a service wing added on the north side in 1860 (National Trust). ½ mile south-west is *Hinchingbrooke*, just off the Great North Road, a mansion built by Henry Cromwell, grandfather of Oliver Cromwell; magnificent gardens, particularly the Dutch rose garden.

Huntingdon to Stretham: 19 miles (A 141 for 1½ miles to Hartford, then A 1123).

1½ miles: *Hartford*. A 1123 goes off on the right to Wyton, and turns right for **St Ives** (pop. 3000, E.C. Tuesday), an old town dating from Saxon times which still has many mediaeval buildings. *All Saints Church* has a fine spire. The Ouse is spanned by a mediaeval bridge with a *chantry chapel*. In Market Hill are a statue of Oliver Cromwell and a late 14th century building, *Cromwell's Barn*. A house in which Cromwell lived is now demolished. Nearby, on the river, is *Houghton*, with an old water-mill once occupied by Potto Brown and Joseph Goodman, two millers noted for their philanthropy.

11 miles: *Earith*. At the bridge the road enters the *Isle of Ely*, formerly a separate administrative unit within the county of Cambridgeshire. From here the Old and New Bedford Rivers run north-east in a straight line to join the Ouse at Denver Sluice. These two large drainage canals were cut by Dutch engineers during the draining of the Fens in the 17th century. — 16 miles: *Haddenham*. — 19 miles: *Stretham* (p. 553), on A 10 (Cambridge-Ely).

70 miles: *Alconbury Hill*. A 1 now follows the line of the old Norman road, *Ermine Street*, which passed through Huntingdon. — 77 miles: *Stilton*, which has given its name to the famous Stilton cheese.

78 miles: *Norman Cross*, where French prisoners were confined during the Napoleonic wars. A 16 goes off on the right to Peterborough and Lincoln (see Route 29).

85 miles: *Wamsford Station.* — 92 miles: *Stamford* (p. 577). — 94 miles: *Great Casterton.* — 112 miles: *Grantham* (p. 579). — 114 miles: *Great Gonerby.* 120 miles: *Long Bennington.* — 123 miles: the road enters Nottinghamshire. Newark bypass goes off on the left.

127 miles: **Newark-on-Trent** (pop. 25,000, E.C. Thursday), an old town on the Roman *Fosse Way*. In the public gardens are the ruins of a 12th century *castle* in which King John died in 1216; it was demolished by Cromwell. ½ mile south-east is the *Queen's Sconce*, the remains of Civil War siege works. Fine 15th century Perpendicular church, *St Mary Magdalene*, with an Early English spire: interesting wood carvings, rood-screen (1506), misericords and a large brass (Alan Flemyng, d. 1363). At the intersection of the Great North Road with the Fosse Way is the *Beaumont Market Cross* (15th c.).

129 miles: A 1 crosses the Trent, the principal river of Nottinghamshire; its tributary the Devon flows through Newark. — 135 miles: *Sutton-on-Trent.* — 140 miles: *Tuxford* (pop. 1300, E.C. Wednesday).

9 miles west is *Ollerton*, a good centre for Sherwood Forest and the Dukeries (p. 621). To the east is **Darlton,** with magnificent views of the surrounding countryside. *Kingshaugh*, now a farmhouse, contains part of the walls and outbuildings of a hunting lodge which belonged to King John. The church tower has a fine Norman porch and a 12th century lancet window; interesting brasses (1510). 3 miles farther on is *Dunham* (church with 15th c. tower).

142 miles: A 638 goes off on the right to *East Retford* and *Bawtry* (below). 148 miles: A 614 comes in on the left, at a point where A 1 bears right to run almost due north.

154 miles: to the left, *Blyth*. — 155 miles: A 1 (M) bears left for Doncaster and the north, while A 614 goes off on the right to *Bawtry*, passing on the right *Serlby Hall*, an 18th century mansion with beautiful gardens, and the village of *Scrooby*.

William Brewster, leader of the Pilgrim Fathers, was born in the *Old Manor House*. His pew can be seen in the church, with a memorial tablet put there by the Pilgrims Society of Plymouth, Massachusetts.

We now enter South Yorkshire, one of the three new counties formed out of **Yorkshire**, formerly England's largest county, which was divided into three "ridings". The new counties of South, West and North Yorkshire are related to the circumstances of the present day and bear no relationship to these historic divisions. South and West Yorkshire, almost entirely industrial, have been carved out of the old West Riding, the largest of the three. North Yorkshire, mainly rural, takes in some of the upland parts of the West Riding, the dales of the old North Riding and its beautiful coastal regions on the North Sea. Most of the old East Riding is now incorporated in the new county of Humberside.

The *Yorkshire dales* are notable for their beautiful scenery and their stone-built villages, and the county also contains some of the finest remains of Cistercian abbeys in Europe. The people of Yorkshire are a well defined and individual type: they claim to be hardheaded and thrifty, but their ready hospitality is proverbial. The housewives of the Dales have maintained their reputation as good cooks, and the sturdy Yorkshire dialect has held out against the standardising effect on the language of compulsory education, radio and television.

11 miles east of Bawtry on A 631 is **Gainsborough** (pop. 18,000, E.C. Wednesday), an old port on the Trent and now an industrial town; the St Ogg's of George Eliot's "Mill on the Floss". The "eagre" (bore) on the Trent (which is linked by canals with the Humber, the Midlands and East Anglia) is a tidal wave resulting from the surge of water into the narrow

river. *All Saints Church* has a tower dating from 1300. The *Old Hall* (15th and 16th c., restored in the 19th c.) is a fine example of Tudor architecture.

1½ miles north-east on A 614 is **Austerfield**. The manor-house was the birthplace of William Bradford, who sailed on the "Mayflower" and became the second governor of Plymouth, Massachusetts. In the Norman church is a tablet recording that the present south aisle was built by the descendants of the Pilgrim Fathers.

165 miles (to the right of the motorway or by A 638 from Bawtry): **Doncaster** (pop. 86,000, E.C. Thursday), a busy industrial town on the Don, with iron-working (locomotives) as its main industry and many coal-mines in the area. It is also an important agricultural market centre. There has been racing on its famous Town Moor course since 1615.

In the centre of the town is the 18th century *Mansion House*. In Chackell Road is the *Museum* (open 10 to 6), mainly devoted to Roman archaeology. To the north-west of the town is *Cusworth Hall*, a mid 18th century house with a beautiful chapel.

Doncaster to Scunthorpe and Grimsby: A 18.

7 miles: *Hatfield*. — 12 miles: the road enters Lincolnshire. — 15 miles: intersection with A 161. To the north is *Crowle*, a small and ancient market town on the moors near the Yorkshire boundary. To the south is *Epworth*, where John and Charles Wesley were born (1703, 1708); Wesley Memorial Chapel. *Haxey*, where the old ceremony of "throwing the hood" has been performed since the 14th century (6 January). — 23 miles: **Scunthorpe** (pop. 70,000, E.C. Thursday), with blast furnaces, foundries, steel-works and many factories. *St Lawrence's Church* was built in 1236 and enlarged in 1913. In High St are the Municipal Library and *Museum* (geology, prehistoric and Roman material, natural history, local fossils).

4 miles north on B 1430 is *Burton-upon-Stuther*, with a splendid view northward over the Humber towards York. The village lies on a ridge of high ground above the east bank of the Trent estuary. The old church contains interesting features. Near

the village is the old mansion of *Normanby Hall*, in a park of over 300 acres.

Beyond this, near the outflow of the Trent into the Humber, is *Alkborough*, with a church dating from Norman times (tower, font). To the west is a cliff on top of which is a 12th century maze, known as *Julian's Bower*.

A 1077 runs north from Scunthorpe to *Winterton* (5 miles) and *Barton-upon-Humber* (12 miles), which has a church with a fine Saxon tower.

A 18 continues east from Scunthorpe through attractive scenery. 27 miles: B 1207 runs south to *Scawby* (1 mile). The Blackhead Ponds of Scawby and Manton are a bird sanctuary, one of the two breeding places in England of the lesser black-backed gull.

52 miles: **Grimsby** (p. 592).

Doncaster to Sheffield: 19 miles (A 60 for 1 mile, then A 630).

1 mile: *Balby*. Turn right into A 630. — 5 miles: *Conisbrough*, with a 12th century Norman castle standing above the Don valley, the home of Athelstane in Scott's "Ivanhoe". The church contains interesting old monuments. — 12 miles: **Rotherham** (pop. 80,000, E.C. Thursday), an industrial town with many blast furnaces (heavy industry, manufacture of railway rolling stock). *All Saints Church* (14th and 15th c., restored) retains some traces of the earlier Saxon church; Norman font, 15th century stalls and pews, brasses, modern glass. On the old Rotherham Bridge is the *Lady Chapel* (1483), one of the four surviving bridge chapels in England. Modern Town Hall. In *Clifton Park* (60 acres) is a museum containing Roman material from local excavations. *Grange Park* (275 acres), with attractive woodland.

Around Rotherham. 7 miles east on A 631 is *Maltby*, with **Roche Abbey** (1½ miles south), the ruins of a Cistercian abbey in a setting of woodland and crags. Nearby is *Sandbeck Park*, seat of the Earl of Scarborough. — 4 miles north is *Wentworth Woodhouse*, the magnificent seat of Earl Fitzwilliam. In the park are Hoober Stand (viewpoint and landmark), a Mausoleum and Kettle's Column in Scholes Coppice (fine views of the surrounding countryside and woodland).

170 miles: *Robin Hood's Well*, legendary scene of the fight between Robin Hood and Friar Tuck. —

180 miles: *Ferrybridge* (pop. 2000, E.C. Thursday). — 189 miles: *Aberford*. From here the Great North Road follows the line of the old Roman ridge road.

196 miles: *Wetherby*. — 209 miles: *Boroughbridge*. From here A 167, following the line of a Roman road, runs south-east to *Aldborough* (1 mile), with the remains of the Roman station of *Isurium* (museum, with material from excavations).

Boroughbridge to Darlington via Thirsk: 36 miles.

4 miles: turn right into A 167. — 7 miles: *Topcliffe*. — 12 miles: **Thirsk** (pop. 4000, E.C. Wednesday), an interesting old town with a cobbled market place. There is a fine Perpendicular *church* (14th-15th c.). The Golden Fleece Hotel (early 18th c.) is an old coaching inn. — 21 miles: **Northallerton** (pop. 5000, E.C. Thursday), an agricultural town with a main street more than 100 feet wide in which a horse fair and weekly market used to be held. The *parish church* contains some fragments of Saxon crosses; Norman north arcade with three fine Early English lancet windows in the transept. Earthworks of an old castle on Castle Hill Farm. There are a number of old houses in the town. Opposite the church is *Porch House* (1584), and near it *Vine House*, now a hospital. — 23 miles: *Stone Cross*, scene of the Battle of the Standard (1138), in which King Stephen defeated Matilda and King David I of Scotland. — 36 miles: **Darlington** (p. 748).

Boroughbridge to Sunderland: 69 miles.

Follow the preceding route to *Thirsk* (12 miles). 20 miles: *Jeater Houses*. Nearby is *Mount Grace Priory*, the only remaining Carthusian house in England.

24 miles: A 172 runs north-east to **Middlesbrough** (pop. 160,000, E.C. Wednesday), an ancient town, centre of the Cleveland iron-mining area. Situated on the Tees, it has been one of England's leading ports since 1854. Iron and steel works, chemical plants, oil refineries. Very modern dry docks for ship repairing. It is now a district within the new county of Cleveland, part of a conurbation which also takes in Stockton, Thornaby and various outlying areas. A notable feature of the town is the huge *transporter bridge* (1911), 990 feet long, standing 260 feet above the river. There is a municipal museum,

the *Dorman Museum* in Linthorpe Road (open 10 to 6, except Sundays): geology, science, local history. 3 miles south-east on A 174 is an 18th century mansion, *Ormesby Hall.*

32 miles: *Yarm*, in the county of Durham. The *county of Durham* has the richest coalfields in Britain, but much of the county remains unspoiled, and the western part has scenery as fine as any to be seen in the north.

36 miles: **Stockton-on-Tees** (pop. 85,000, E.C. Thursday), an old market town on the north bank of the river Tees, navigable for large vessels up to the *Victoria Bridge* (1887), which links the town with Thornaby-on-Tees. The docks are of prime importance; heavy industry includes the I.C.I. works at Billingham, iron foundries and steel-works.

Thomas Sheraton, the famous furniture-maker, was born here in 1751. John Walker (1827), a Stockton chemist, invented the friction match. The first railway line was laid here on 23 May 1822, and the first passenger service, between Stockton and Darlington, was opened in 1825.

40 miles: *Wolviston*. A 689 runs north-east to *West Hartlepool* (6 miles), a modern seaport on Tees Bay with many docks, mainly handling coal. The old town, *Hartlepool*, to the east, has a Norman church. Remains of town walls.

53 miles: *Easington*. — 69 miles: **Sunderland** (pop. 190,000, E.C. Wednesday), an important shipbuilding centre; its other industries include the manufacture of furniture, glass, lime and jam. *Seaburn and Roker* are seaside resorts within the area of the town; in Roker is a stone cross commemorating the Venerable Bede. At *Monkwearmouth*, above the Wearmouth Bridge, is *St Peter's Church*, in which the west wall of the nave dates from the 7th century; the church belonged to the monastery which Bede entered as a boy. The *Museum* contains collections of local historical and geological interest, models of ships built in Sunderland and material recovered from the tumuli on nearby Hastings Hill. Art gallery, with periodic exhibitions. To the west of the town centre is *Hylton Castle* (15th c.).

228 miles: **Scotch Corner.** 4 miles south-west is the ancient and attractive little town of **Richmond** (p. 831).

Scotch Corner to Carter Bar and Scotland

Leave Scotch Corner on A 1 and turn off into B 6275, which runs due north in a straight line, via the Roman site of *Piercebridge*, to join A 68: turn left for West Auckland. (Alternatively continue on A 1 for another 6 miles and take the exit into A 68).

3 miles north-east of West Auckland is **Bishop Auckland** (pop. 35,000, E.C. Wednesday), an old town on the river Wear, with *Auckland Castle*, palace of the Bishop of Durham (interesting glass in the Bishop's Chapel). 1 mile south is *Southchurch*, with a 13th century church, and to the west is *Escomb*, with another old church which preserves parts of the original 7th century building.

19 miles: *Witton-le-Wear*. — 45 miles: **Corbridge** (pop. 2100, E.C. Thursday), with the excavated site of the Roman station of *Corstopitum* (museum). The church has a Saxon nave and entrance tower. 7 miles east is *Wylam-on-Tyme*, with the cottage in which George Stephenson was born in 1781; he carried out his first experiments with wooden rails laid in front of the house.

48 miles: A 68, following the line of a Roman road, crosses Hadrian's Wall (p. 759). — 50 miles: to the east, at Great Whittington, is a B.B.C. transmitter. — 61 miles: *West Woodburn*.

65 miles: A 696 comes in on the right from Newcastle. 2 miles south-east on A 696 is **Otterburn**, with Otterburn Castle and the 14th century Percy's Cross. From Otterburn B 6341 runs down the Coquet valley to *Rothbury*, a little town in the beautiful Rothbury Forest. 5 miles south-east is *Brinkburn*, with Brinkburn Priory (fine 12th c. church in Transitional style).

A 68 continues north-west up the Rede valley and through the Cheviots to **Carter Bar** (81 miles), on the Scottish border: see p. 940.

Beyond Scotch Corner A 1 continues north (motorway) towards Newcastle. To the right of the road is **Darlington** (pop. 85,000), an important industrial town on the site of a Saxon settlement.

The opening of the Stockton-Darlington railway line (which Stephenson brought to Darlington on the urgent insistence of his Quaker friend Edward Pease)

led to the development of the extensive railway
workshops of the present day.

Darlington's situation on the Tees enabled it to develop
into a shipbuilding town, and it is also world-famous as a
bridge-building centre. Other industries include textiles, agricultural engineering and heavy and electrical engineering. At
Aycliffe a former ordnance factory site has become the nucleus
of a modern industrial area and the "new town" of *Newton
Aycliffe* has been developed. The *Museum* in Tubwell Row
contains interesting collections of material on natural history,
geology and local history. Art Gallery in Crown St. *St Cuthbert's Church* is 13th century, with 16th century stalls.

254 miles: *Neville's Cross*. The cross commemorates the victory of 1346 in which Neville's army
took King David II of Scotland prisoner.

⌐ 1 bypasses Durham (1 mile to the east).

DURHAM

Durham (pop. 25,000, E.C. Wednesday), county
town of Durham, is a fine old town with many 16th,
17th and 18th century buildings. It is not itself an
industrial town but is the centre of the Durham
coalfield, one of the largest in the country. At the
north end of the old town is *Duamrh Castle*, built
by William the Conqueror, and to the south of this
is the **Cathedral,** which was begun in 1093. The
site, originally surrounded by walls, is a commanding one, towering over the modern town.⌐

The **Cathedral** stands on the site of a Saxon church
built in 995 as a shrine for the relics of St Cuthbert.
In 1072 William the Conqueror made it a bishop's
palatine see, making it almost autonomous, and it
retained its temporal power until 1836. In 1092
Bishop William de St Calais planned the cathedral,

and the choir was completed and the transepts and
nave begun. By 1140 these and the chapter house
were completed and by 1175 the Lady Chapel, or
Galilee Chapel. The east transept formed by the
Chapel of the Nine Altars (Early English) dates from
1280; it is a copy of that at Fountains Abbey. The
Perpendicular cloister and other parts of the central
tower were built from 1400 to 1490. Between 1660
and 1685 the refectory (south side of the cloisters)
and the library were rebuilt. In the 18th century
Wyatt carried out extensive restoration.

The measurements of the Cathedral are: length
510 feet, width 80 feet, across the transepts 170 feet,
and height 70 feet. The central tower (325 steps) is
215 feet high, and the west towers 140 feet.

Entry is by the north porch.

Interior. The *north porch* comprises five recessed Norman
arches with unsuitable modern pinnacles. *The nave.* The first
impression received on entering the building and surveying
its uninterrupted length is one of massive strength. The columns
are alternately circular, ornamented with deep incisions of
zigzag and lattice patterns, and square, with subsidiary piers.
The stone vaulting is late Norman. The porches are all very
fine. The most interesting monument in the nave is that of
the *Nevilles* (now dilapidated). At the west end is the west
doorway, which was formerly the principal entrance; it now
leads to the **Galilee** or **Lady Chapel,** which contains excellent
transitional Norman work, and has an almost oriental effect
with its Moorish arches. In this chapel is the tomb of the
Venerable Bede (d. 735). In the recess with fresco ornamentation, walled up in the 15th century, stood an altar to Our Lady
of Pity.

The great transept and the choir resemble the nave, and are
of slightly earlier date; the large windows were added later.
The fine *reredos* dates from 1385; the choir stalls and font are
18th century. The *bishop's throne* is also the monument of
Bishop Hatfield (14th century). Behind the high altar is the
feretory of St Cuthbert, where once stood his shrine; his relics

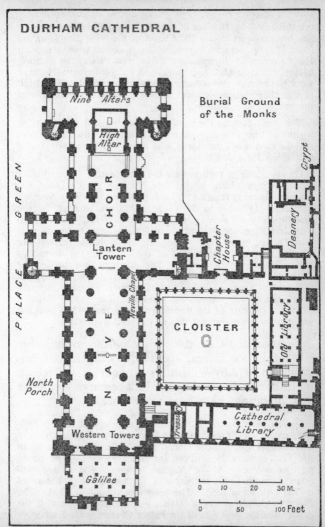

DURHAM CATHEDRAL

Nine Altars

Burial Ground of the Monks

High Altar

CHOIR

PALACE GREEN

Lantern Tower

Chapter House

Deanery

Crypt

Neville Chapel

CLOISTER

Old Library

NAVE

North Porch

Treasury

Cathedral Library

Western Towers

Galilee

0   10   20   30 M.

0   50   100 Feet

are still below it. In place of the original apse, the east transept has been converted into the **Chapel of the Nine Altars,** dating from 1230-80, and an interesting study of the transition from Early English to the geometrical Decorated style; the addition of this intricate Gothic construction to the massive Norman work has been carried out ingeniously and artistically. The detail in the chapel repays careful attention, with the exception of the modern rose window.

The stone cow on the exterior of this transept relates to the legend of the founding of the cathedral by Bishop Aldhun and the monks of Lindisfarne, who are said to have been guided to the site by a dun cow.

On the south of the nave are the 15th century Perpendicular cloisters from which, by the late Norman Prior's Door, the **Chapter House** is reached. This was one of the finest Norman chambers (1135-40) in the country, but was marred by the demolition of the semi-circular east end in Wyatt's restoration. This has been rebuilt and the original design restored; it is now 78 feet by 35 feet. Other original monastic remains are on the west and south sides of the cloisters, the dormitory and refectory of the monks. The refectory now houses the Cathedral Library, with valuable manuscripts and relics from St Cuthbert's coffin. Below this chamber is the early Norman crypt, the oldest part of the building. The monks' kitchen (to the south-east of the dormitory) dates from 1380, and the great gateway on the east side of the yard from 1500.

Opposite the Cathedral to the north, on the other side of Palace Green, stands the *Castle*, built originally in 1072 by William the Conqueror and rebuilt by Bishop Pudsey during the 12th century. Additions and alterations have been made since.

In *Tunstall's Gallery* is the original doorway of Bishop Pudsey's castle, which resembles the Prior's Door of the Cathedral. The **Chapel** (carved oak *stalls*) and Gallery were altered in the 16th century by Bishop Tunstall (1530-38). The upper portion is known as the *Norman Gallery*. The *Dining Hall* dates from the 14th century and the fine *Black Staircase* of carved oak from 1665. The keep was rebuilt in 1840. The Norman chapel or crypt (11th c.) is the earliest part of the castle. On the west side of the Palace Green are the Exchequer

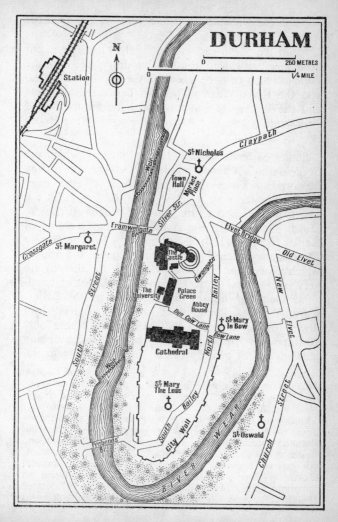

DURHAM

0 250 METRES

0 ¼ MILE

N

Station

Claypath

St Nicholas

Town Hall

Market Place

Silver Str.

Framwellgate Bri.

Elvet Bridge

Old Elvet

Crossgate

St Margaret

Owengate

The Castle

Saddler Street

Milburngate

Wear

The University

Palace Green

Abbey House

Dun Cow Lane

St Mary le Bow

Bailey

New

Elvet

Bow Lane

North

Cathedral

Wear

St Mary The Less

Bailey

RIVER WEAR

South Wall

City Wall

South

Street

Prebends Bri.

Church Street

St Oswald

and Bishop Cosin's Library. (Open weekdays 9 to 12.30 and 2 to 5.30 or dusk).

From the south-east corner of the Green a quaint little lane with 18th century buildings leads to the Bailey, which runs between the Castle, the Cathedral and the River Wear. The part between Bow Lane and the Watergate is a fine and harmonious unit of 18th century houses. At the other end of the Bailey is *Hatfield Hall*.

Sadler St leads to the Market Place, in which are *St Nicholas's Church* (modern) and the *Town Hall* (restored). From the Market Place up the steep Giles Gate the way is to *St Giles' Church* (12th c.), and over the road to the ruins of *Magdalen Chapel*. Down the hill are the *Sands*, and the remains of Kepier Hospital (12th c., Bishop Pudsey). The *Market Place* is also reached along the river bank: the bridges which cross near Framwellgate (11th c., altered) are very interesting. and *Old Elvert* is a street of handsome Georgian houses only equalled by the Bailey. Curious little alleyways known as "vennels" run down to the riverside. *Silver St* is in places only 10 feet wide. In Silver St is Luke's Cafe, comprising part of a 17th century house; magnificent staircase.

Around Durham. 4 miles north are the ruins of *Finchale Priory* (13th c.), in a beautiful setting on the banks of the Wear. — 4 miles south-west is *Brandon*, with an interesting church. Nearby is *Brancepeth Castle*, home of the Neville family. — 3 miles south is *Butterby Grange*, which has preserved its ancient moat. — 5 miles south-east is *Cowhoe*, birthplace of Elizabeth Barrett Browning (1806). Fine view of Durham Cathedral and Castle. 5 miles behond Cowhoe on A 177 (the road to Stockton-on-Tees) is *Sedgefield*, an old market town with a beautiful church. — 7 miles east of Durham is *Houghton-le-Spring*, an important mining town with an Early English and Decorated church. Houghton Colliery (1829) has a shaft going down to over 700 feet.

260 miles: **Chester-le-Street** (pop. 20,000, E.C. Wednesday), an ancient town on the site of the Roman *Condercum*, now an important mining centre. The very interesting *parish church* (fine monuments with remarkable effigies) has an unusual spire. — 261 miles: 1 mile east is *Lambton Castle*, seat of the Earl of Durham. A little farther on, by the main road, is the *Penshaw Monument* (1884), a Doric temple commemorating the first Earl of Durham, Governor-General of Canada. — 265 miles: to the west, *Lamesley*, with the fine mansion of *Ravensworth*.

269 miles: **Gateshead** (pop. 101,000, E.C. Wednesday), a busy port and industrial town (shipbuilding, engineering, foodstuffs, etc.). There are five bridges, linking Gateshead with Newcastle, including the *King Edward Bridge* (1906) and the *Tyne Bridge* (1928), 1800 feet long with a great parabolic arch carrying the road at a height of 200 feet above the river.

The county of **Northumberland** has some of the most famous shipyards in the world on the Tyne, and *Newcastle*, 9 miles from the mouth of the river, is an industrial centre and a cathedral city which has figured prominently in England's history. The Tyne is navigable for a distance of 15 miles, and its banks are lined with docks, quays and shipbuilding yards. Other thriving industries are the manufacture of electrical equipment, flour-milling, furniture and the production of china, glass and clothing. The development of a concentrated and productive industrial area here has been promoted by the availability of coal and ease of access by sea. Farther north is the rugged *Border country*, over which English and Scots fought for centuries.

The most remarkable of all ancient monuments in Northumberland is undoubtedly the **Roman wall** (Hadrian's Wall), which cuts across the country from coast to coast, running up hill and down dale according to the lie of the land. See p. 759.

270 miles: **Newcastle-upon-Tyne.**

NEWCASTLE-UPON-TYNE

Newcastle-upon-Tyne (pop. 260,000), situated on the left bank of the Tyne 9 miles from its mouth, is one of Britain's leading coal-shipping ports and the centre of a rich mining district. It is noted for the manufacture of railway rolling stock and has large and important shipyards. It is linked by regular shipping services with London, Antwerp, Rotterdam, Hamburg, Amsterdam, Ghent and many other continental ports.

The town occupies the site of the Roman *Pons Aelii*, named after a bridge at the end of Hadrian's Wall. In Saxon times it had many monasteries and was known as Monkchester, but thereafter its importance declined until Robert Curthose, William the Conqueror's son, made it a stronghold in the defensive system of the Border. During the Civil War the Royalists were besieged here for ten weeks, and at a later stage Charles I was held prisoner in the castle for ten months. In 1847 the Armstrong works were established at Elswick, and in 1849 Robert Stephenson built the High Level Bridge over the Tyne gorge. Newcastle became an episcopal see in 1882. The University was founded in 1963.

In the Central Station can be seen Stephenson's first locomotive, "*Locomotion No. 1*". Near the station, to the left, is St Mary's Cathedral (Roman Catholic). Collingwood St, to the north-east, leads to the **Town Hall,** which incorporates the municipal buildings and the Corn Exchange, on the site of a former open market; cf. the streets named *Cloth Market* and *Groat Market* on either side of the Town Hall. Opposite, on the far side of Moseley St, is **St Nicholas's Cathedral** (14th c.), with a fine 15th century lantern tower and a spire 195 feet high. In the interior are a number of interesting monuments and an ancient font cover (1500). St Nicholas St

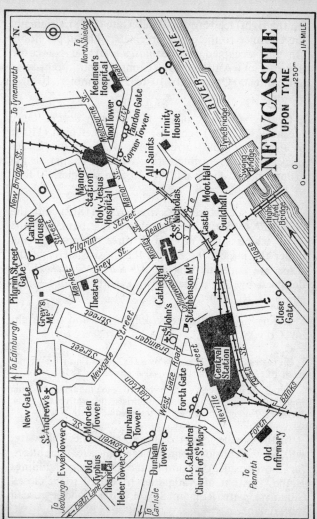

NEWCASTLE UPON TYNE

1/4 MILE
0 250m

(to the right) leads to the **Black Gate** (1248), originally the entrance to the castle precincts. The upper floors are now occupied by the *museum* of the Newcastle Society of Antiquaries (Roman and prehistoric antiquities). Open daily 10 to 5 in summer, 10 to 4 in winter.

Nearby is the site of the 11th century *castle*. Only the **keep** (1172-77) remains; it is 85 feet high (110 ft to the top of the turret), with walls 15 to 18 feet thick. There is an interesting Norman chapel on the ground floor. Open daily 10 to 5 in summer, 10 to 4 in winter.

To the south are the *Moot Hall* (1812) and the *Guildhall* (1658), standing above the banks of the Tyne, which is here crossed by three bridges. Passing under the large *Tyne Bridge*, the most easterly of the three, we continue east to *All Saints Church* (1796, designed by David Stephenson), with the fine tombstone of R. Thornton.

Returning west, we cross Pilgrim St and turn right up **Grey Street.**

On the right is the *Theatre Royal* (1838), and near it a monument to the second Earl Grey, also erected in 1838.

At the end of Grey St we turn right to reach the **Laing Museum** (open 10 to 6): English watercolourists, decorative art. The *Plummer Tower* formed part of the mediaeval town walls.

In the northern part of the town is the **University,** which was considerably enlarged in 1961 (architect, Sir Basil Spence). Among the University buildings is the **Museum of Antiquities** (open 10 to 5, closed Sundays), with Roman, Saxon, Greek and Etruscan material.

Just beyond the University is the *Hancock Museum* (open 10 to 12): natural history and geology. Still farther north, in Exhibition Park, is the *Museum of Science and Engineering* (open 11 to 8).

Newcastle has a number of very fine parks. *Town Moor* (900 acres) is a favourite place of resort; the Town Moor Festival takes place every year in the third week of June, the week after Ascot, when the chief race meeting of the north-east is held in Newcastle. *Jesmond Dene* (60 acres), in the residential district between A 1 and Kesmond Road, is one of the pleasantest parks in the country. To the west of Jesmond Dene Road are the ruins of the *chapel of St Mary of Jesmond* (12th c.). Nearby (in private grounds) is a holy well which still attracts pilgrims.

Newcastle to South Shields. 12 miles (A 184 for 3 miles, then A 185). The excursion can be done by boat on the Tyne.

3 miles: turn left into A 185. — 5 miles: *Jarrow*, where the Venerable Bede died in 735. *St Paul's Church*, which incorporates parts of a 7th century monastery, contains relics of Bede. — 12 miles: **South Shields** (pop. 110,000, E.C. Wednesday), an important coal-exporting and shipbuilding town. The *Museum* in Ocean Road contains Roman material, and there are remains of a Roman fort. 2 miles south is *Marsden Bay*, a popular seaside resort (fishing, golf). A model of the first lifeboat (1797) hangs from the roof of *St Hilda's Church*.

Newcastle to Tynemouth and Whitley Bay: 9 miles on A 695.

4 miles: *Wallsend*, the terminal point of **Hadrian's Wall,** a Roman defensive work which extended for a distance of 75 miles to Bowness on the Solway.

The Wall was intended to mark out the frontier of Roman rule, to cut off the barbarian tribes to the north from the related tribes south of the frontier, and to provide a base for offensive operations against the northern tribes. The construction of the Wall was begun about 120 A.D., and it suffered many vicissitudes, being several times destroyed and later reoccupied, before finally being abandoned during the 4th century. For most of its length the Wall was built of stone, 20 feet high and either 10 or 8 feet thick; west of the river Irthing, where stone was not availiable, it was of turf, 15 feet high and 20 feet thick. In front of the wall itself was a ditch 27 feet wide and 9 feet deep. A short distance to the rear was a further defensive work, the *Vallum*, consisting of a ditch 20 feet wide at the top and 10 feet deep flanked by turf banks 20 feet wide and 6 feet high. Along the Wall were 16 forts, supported by a number of other forts to the rear on the old Roman road from east to west, the Stanegate, and at intervals of a Roman mile (1620 yds) were mile-castles, with two smaller turrets between the mile-castles.

The very striking remains of this massive defensive system are easily seen from the road which runs along the line of the Wall for most of the way (B 6318, the continuation of A 69 from Newcastle). The most notable features are to be seen at *Corbridge*, a Stanegate fort (p. 748); *Chesters*, the Roman Cilurnum (fort, impressive remains of bridge abutment); *Carrawburgh* (Brocolitium: mithraeum); *Housesteads* (Vercovicium: fort, with a fine stretch of the Wall); *Chesterholm* (Vindolanda), a large site with a Roman fort on the Stanegate and a settlement where large-scale excavations are in progress, to the south of Housesteads; *Walltown Crags*, 7 miles west of Housesteads, with a fine stretch of wall; *Willowford*, near Gillsland, with another fine stretch; and *Birdoswald* (Camboglanna), a fort with particularly well preserved defences. For those with sufficient time at their disposal there is pleasant walking to be had along some of the exposed stretches of the wall, striding impressively over the windy moorland.

8 miles: *North Shields*, an important seaport and industrial town, connected by ferry with South Shields. — 9 miles: *Tynemouth* (pop. 72,000, E.C. Wednesday), a popular seaside resort. On the cliffs at the end of Front St are a Norman *keep* and the ruins of a priory built in the 11th century by monks from St Albans. The Percy Chapel (15th c.) is well preserved. To the north is *Cullercoats*, an old fishing village. In the north-west corner of the bay, below Bank Top, is the *Dove Marine Laboratory*, which is concerned with the scientific study of the local fishing industry. 2 miles north of Tynemouth is the seaside resort of *Whitley Bay*, and 6 miles north is *Seaton Delaval Hall* (1729), a large mansion designed by Vanbrugh.

272 miles: *Gosforth*. 3 miles north-east is *Killingworth*, where Stephenson built his first locomotive. —282 miles: *Morpeth* (pop. 14,000, E.C. Thursday), a small town with the ruins of a Norman castle. The church has an unusual bell-tower. Nearby is Newminster Abbey. To the south-east, on the coast,

is *Blyth* (pop. 33,000, E.C. Wednesday), a modern port exporting coal, steel and iron; shipyards.

303 miles: **Alnwick** (pop. 7000, E.C. Wednesday), an old town on the Alne. Old town gates — *Hotspur Tower Gate* and *Town Gate*. Old town cross. Church (15th c.) and ruins of abbey. Remains of *St Leonard's Hospital* and *Farmer's Folly*.

Dominating the town is the **Castle,** seat of the Duke of Northumberland, one of the most magnificent feudal castles in the country; it has been restored, not always very judiciously. The main features of interest are the keep, the armoury, the gatehouse, the state apartments, the dungeon, a fine state coach and a collection of Roman and Celtic antiquities. The beautiful Hulne Park can also be seen. (Open May-September Sunday to Thursday from 1 to 4.30). Nearby are the ruins of *Hulne Priory*, a Carmelite house.

3 miles south-east on A 1068 is *Alnmouth*, a seaside resort. 4 miles south of this is **Warkworth,** a charming little red and grey town near the mouth of the Coquet, entered by a mediaval bridge and gateway. There is an interesting old Norman church. The town is dominated by the ruins of the *castle* (12th-14th c.), with an unusual 14th century keep. Also of interest are the entrance, the Lion Tower, the great hall and the chapel. From the foot of the castle we can walk up the river to *Warkworth Hermitage* (three caves in the cliff).

From Alnmouth a path runs north along the basalt cliffs, and walkers can enjoy splendid scenery. 6 miles north is *Embleton*, with an interesting 14th century vicarage. 2 miles east, perched high on the cliffs, are the ruins of *Dunstanburgh Castle* (1313). 13 miles: Seahoughton, where boats can be hired for the **Farne Islands**, about 20 islands, some 80 acres in extent, 2-5 miles off the coast, opposite Bamburgh. The islands are preserved by the National Trust as a breeding place for sea-birds and seals. The *Longstone Lighthouse* was made famous by Grace Darling who, with her father, rescued the survivors of the "Forfarshire" in 1838. The Brownsman is closed to visitors in the nesting season.

318 miles: *Belford*, a convenient centre for exploring the coast. 5 miles east is *Bamburgh*, an ancient town

with a great *Castle* on the site of a Saxon settlement.
The castle has been restored, but the keep is Norman.
St Aidan's Church (Early English) has a very fine
choir and an interesting crypt. In the churchyard is
the grave of Grace Darling, who was born in a nearby
house (tablet). In the *Grace Darling Museum* is the
original lifeboat. Boats can be hired here for the
Farne Islands.

324 miles: *West Mains*, from which a road runs
east to *Holy Island*, or **Lindisfarne**. Access is difficult,
and there is no ferry service. The sands can be crossed
at low tide; the distance is 2½ miles. The route is
marked by posts, and taxis cross even when the
sands are covered by the sea.

Lindisfarne Abbey was founded by St Aidan in the 7th century, and St Cuthbert later became Bishop of Lindisfarne.
The ruins are those of the 11th century Benedictine priory
church, which resembles Durham Cathedral. The *Castle*,
picturesquely situated on a high crag, with stout bastions and
thick walls, was built about 1550. It was restored by Sir Edwin
Lutyens after 1900, and given to the National Trust in 1934
along with his collection of furniture.

333 miles: **Berwick-upon-Tweed** (pop. 11,800, E.C.
Thursday), an ancient town at the mouth of the
Tweed, for centuries a bone of contention between
England and Scotland.

Of the *Tudor walls* (1558) there remain the Cumberland, Brass Mount and Windmill bastions and
the Meg's Mount and King's Mount half-bastions.
Three bridges cross the Tweed at Berwick: the Jacobean bridge (1634) between the old town and Tweed-
mouth, the Royal Tweed Bridge (1928), a reinforced
concrete structure with four arches, and the Royal
Border Railway Bridge (1847), designed by Robert
Stephenson.

There are a number of old houses in the town. The most interesting are in Coxon's Lane, West St, Palace Green and Bishop's Entry; and there are also some handsome Georgian houses in Palace St, Ravendowne and Quay Walls. In Marygate is the Museum and Art Gallery. The *Barracks* (1717-21) near Wallace Green now contain a regimental museum.

To the north-west of the town is *Halidon Hill*, where Edward III defeated the Scots in 1333. From the hill there are fine views of the town and the sea, extending to the Farne Islands (above) and the Cheviots to the south-west. 3 miles north on A 1 is *Lamberton*, where runaway couples could in earlier days be married very speedily by the toll-keeper. To the south-east is the seaside resort of *Spittal*.

Beyond Berwick A 1 continues to **Edinburgh** (57 miles): see Route 58.

Berwick to Carlisle: 88 miles (A 698 to Hawick, then A 7). The first stretch of the road, as far as Coldstream, runs parallel to the Scottish border.

7 miles: *Norham*, a picturesque village on the south bank of the Tweed. The road runs across the large artificial ditch which was part of the castle defences. Norham Castle, to the east, was a stronghold of the Bishops of Durham, and is mentioned in Scott's "Marmion"; the keep is Norman. — 11 miles: the Till flows into the Tweed in a densely wooded gorge. — 14 miles: *Coldstream*, a small town on the Scottish side of the Tweed.

23 miles: *Kelso* (p. 938). — 43 miles: *Hawick* (p. 933). For the road from Hawick to Carlisle, see Route 59.

Coldstream to Newcastle: 60 miles.

6 miles: *Branxton*. Near the church is a monument commemorating the battle of Flodden (1513), an English victory in which King James IV of Scotland was killed.

14 miles: *Wooler*, a small town which is mentioned in Scott's "Marmion". 1 mile west, on *Humbleton Hill*, is the Battle Stone, marking the spot where the Earl of Northumberland and his son Hotspur routed the Scots in 1402. Wooler is the best starting point for climbing the curiously shaped Cheviot (2676 ft), 7 miles south-west (taking the road up Harthope Glen to Langleeford). This is the highest point of the Cheviot Hills, which extend along the border with Scotland. Magni-

ficent views. — 6 miles south-east is *Chillingham Castle*, seat
of the Earl of Tankerville (14th c., with later buildings dating
from 1600). In the park of over 700 acres, which dates from
the 13th century, are the last wild cattle in England. — 46 miles:
Morpeth (p. 760). — 60 miles: **Newcastle-upon-Tyne** (p. 756).

43. YORK AND THE YORKSHIRE COAST

Doncaster to Scarborough by York

Leave Doncaster by High St, French Gate and Marsh Gate; then fork right into Bentley Road (A 19).

7 miles: *Askern*. — 20 miles: **Selby** (pop. 10,700, E.C. Thursday). Toll bridge. A small market town on the Ouse, birthplace of Henry I, with one of the finest abbey churches in the country.

The **Abbey,** a Benedictine house, was founded in 1069 by William the Conqueror, the first established by the Normans in the north of England. It was badly damaged by fire in 1906. The transepts and part of the nave are in 12th century Norman style; part of the fine west front is Early English; the choir and Lady Chapel are Decorated. The exquisite *east window* has delicate Perpendicular tracery and 14th century glass (restored).

34 miles: **York.**

YORK

York (pop. 106,000, E.C. Wednesday) is one of the great historic centres of western civilisation and one of the finest mediaeval cities in existence, still girdled by its fortifications, with a curfew bell which, with but few interruptions, has nightly tolled from the tower of St Michael's church in Spurriersgate since the first curfew was ordained in 1066.

The outstanding features of York are its *Minster* and its city *walls*. The long history of the Minster, an incomparable masterpiece of architecture, goes back to 627 when Paulinus, first Bishop of York, baptised Edwin king of Northumbria in a wooden chapel which stood on the site. The building as it

appears today was completed towards the end of
the 15th century and took 250 years to build.

The city walls, along the top of which runs a walk-
way, make an almost complete circuit of the city
and afford many fine views of the Minster. The
walls, with their grim "bars" or gates, date from the
time of Edward III. Among the many interesting
buildings to be seen in York are the 14th century
hall of the Merchant Adventurers' Company, the
13th century Clifford's Tower, the Treasurer's House
with its 17th century furniture and King's Manor,
seat of the Council of the North. Visitors should
not miss the many quaint side streets which in many
cases still possess their mediaeval names and mediaeval character.

The first traces of the town are of the British settlement
of Caer Evrauc. In 71 A.D. it achieved importance under the
Romans as *Eboracum*, a military outpost; the Romans remained
for 330 years. It subsequently fell to the Saxons, who in 627
built the first church, founding at the same time a university.
It was then called Eoforwic. The Danish invaders seized the
town in 876. In 1069 the Normans completely destroyed the
town, which was burnt out, and re-established a magnificent
city on the site. In the 18th century York enjoyed a period of
prosperity, and its finest buildings date from this period. It
is an important industrial town, with its railway workshops,
its factories producing optical instruments and a variety of
light industries. The University was founded in 1963.

The walls. The present walls date mainly from
the time of Edward III (1327-77), and there is no
better introduction to the treasures enclosed within
their circuit than to walk round the battlements and
see the old buildings clustered round the largest of
England's historic cathedrals. In Tower Place is a

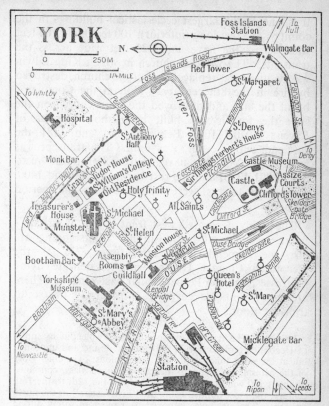

stretch of the walls where we can see the rampart walk with the openings through which the defenders launched their projectiles against the enemy.

Itinerary 1

York Minster. The Minster contains so much that it would in itself justify a prolonged stay in the city.

It is one of the largest ecclesiastical buildings in the country, 485 feet long (interior), 100 feet high, 104 feet wide across the nave, and 225 feet wide across the transepts. The wooden church in which King Edwin was baptised was replaced by a stone church, destroyed by fire in the 8th century. William the Conqueror burnt the city and destroyed the third church on the site; the fourth was built by Bishop Thomas of Bayeux (1070-1110). Between 1154 and 1181 the east end, with a crypt, was built. The transept was built in 1220-60; the nave, chapter house and vestibule, 1291-1350; and the rest between 1360 and 1400. The three towers were added during the period 1405-72.

The richly decorated **west front** is one of Britain's finest architectural compositions. Outstanding are also the Perpendicular **central tower** (215 ft), the Decorated **Chapter House,** with its delicate flying buttresses, and the Perpendicular **east window.** There are many fantastic gargoyles. Enter by the south transept door.

Interior. The nave is one of the most splendid examples of Decorated architecture in the country: grand and imposing, but at the same time simple and harmonious. The chief glory of the Minster is its superb mediaeval stained glass, contained in about 120 windows of all periods from the 12th to the 16th century, the most famous being the "Five Sisters" in the north transept. The glass was removed to a place of safety during the last war. The oldest part of the building is the **transept,** in pure Early English style. Monument to *Archbishop Greenfield* (1306-15), and in the east aisle the finely decorated monument of *Archbishop de Gray* (1215-55). Nearby is the tomb of *Dean Duncan* (d. 1880; by Boehm). Between the nave and choir (Perpendicular) is a superb and richly decorated *roodscreen* (15th c.) with effigies of English kings. The presbytery, the Lady Chapel and the east end date from the earliest building period; the altar screens and timber vaulting are reproductions.

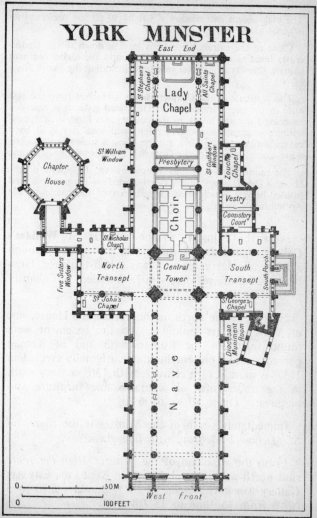

YORK MINSTER

East End

St Stephen's Chapel

Lady Chapel

All Saints Chapel

St William Window

Chapter House

Presbytery

St Cuthbert Window

Zouche Chapel

Choir

Vestry

Consistory Court

St Nicholas Chapel

Five Sisters Window

North Transept

Central Tower

South Transept

South Porch

St John's Chapel

St George's Chapel

Nave

Diocesan Monument Room

0 ___ 30M
0 ___ 100 FEET

West Front

25

The magnificent **east window** (78 ft by 30 ft) has preserved its original glass.

Close to the entrance are steps leading down to the **Undercroft:** remains of Roman praetorium and the earlier Norman church. Display of Minster treasures, including the Saxon *Horn* of *Ulf*.

The vestibule of the **Chapter House** is reached from the east aisle of the north transept. In Decorated style, it is regarded as being the most lovely in the country: its form is octagonal without a central supporting pillar, and each bay is lit by a magnificent window. Here are the Minster treasures, including a pre-Conquest copy of the Gospels. There is very fine carving.

The muniment room and vestry are to the south of the choir. The *Deanery* and *Library* (priceless manuscripts and printed books), which once formed part of the chapel of the Archbishop's Palace, are to the north.

Near the Minster, to the east, is **St William's College** (open 9 a.m. to dusk), which is entered through a Perpendicular gateway. It is a half-timbered Jacobean building (restored 1903) founded for chantry priests by Warwick the Kingmaker.

Nearby, to the north, is the **Treasurer's House,** one of York's oldest buildings. In the basement were found traces of the Roman road and of Roman barracks. The present building, originally erected in 1137, is mainly 17th century, with 13th century work in the undercroft. It contains fine furniture and pictures. Open 10.30 to 6.30.

Immediately south of the Minster is the *church of St Michael le Belfrey*, with fine glass.

From the west end of the Minster *High Petergate* runs north-west through Bootham Bar to the **City Art Gallery** (on left). Open 10 to 5, Sundays 2.30 to 5 (to 8 from 16 June to 15 July).

Pictures of various schools from the 14th century to the present day, many of them bequeathed by F.D. Lycett Green in 1955. "Dead Christ" by the *Master of the San Lucchese Altarspiece* (Florentine, 1350); portrait of Cardinal Aggucchi, by *Domenichino* (1620); seascape by *Berchem*; many works by the York painter **William Etty** (1787-1849); "Storm", by *Isabey;* pictures by *Rousseau, Daubigny, Courbet, Pissarro, Guillaumin,* etc.

Adjoining the Art Gallery to the south-west is **King's Manor,** formerly the palace of the Abbots of St Mary's (below), built about 1280 but altered and enlarged in the 15th and 16th centuries. It is now occupied by the University.

By way of *St Leonard's Place*, turning right into *Museum Street*, we come to Lendal Bridge over the Ouse. Before reaching the bridge, just after the Library and City Information Bureau, we turn right into the **Museum Gardens.**

On the north side of the Gardens is the *Multangular Tower*, on Roman foundations, one of the defensive towers on the mediaeval city walls. In the centre of the Gardens is the **Yorkshire Museum** (open 10 to 5, Sundays 1 to 5), with local antiquities, natural history collections and a fine display of china.

Behind the Museum are the picturesque ruins of **St Mary's Abbey** (same opening hours), dating from the 13th century. To the west is *St Olave's Church* (old glass).

On the south side of the Gardens is the *Hospitium*, the mediaeval guest-house of the abbey, with a collection of Roman material (same opening hours).

Returning to the entrance to the Gardens, we go along Lendal St, immediately opposite, passing on the right, in Museum St, the remains of *St Leonard's Hospital* (13th c.). In Lendal St are the Post Office (on right) and beyond this the neo-classical *Mansion House* (1726), behind which, on the river, is the 15th century **Guildhall** (open 9 to 5). Beyond the

Mansion House, in Coney St, is *St Martin's Church* (16th c.).

North-east of the Mansion House, on the far side of St Helen's Square, is *St Helen's Church* (Perpendicular, 15th c.). Turning left along Blake St, we pass the *Assembly Rooms* (mid 18th c.: fine interior). From here we turn right along Duncombe Place to return to the Minster.

Itinerary 2

Starting from the Castle (parking), this takes us through the southern part of the old town.

Of the *Castle* there remains only the keep, known as **Clifford's Tower.** The southern part of the site is occupied by the neo-classical *Assize Courts* (late 18th c.).

Clifford's Tower, built in 1245 on an artificial mound, occupies the position of an earlier wooden keep which was burned down in 1190. The site was chosen by William the Conqueror for his second stronghold in England, which became known as "the eye of Yorkshire".

Opposite the Assize Courts is the old *Female Prison* (1780: designed, like the Assize Courts, by John Carr), at the south end of which is the former *Debtors' Prison* (Vanbrugh, 1705). The prisons now house the **Castle Museum** (open 9.30 to 7.30).

The special feature of this museum is its reconstruction of old streets, with shops and craftsmen's workshops, furnished and equipped in the style of the period.

From here Tower St and Castlegate lead north to *St Mary's Church*, with a Perpendicular tower and old glass. Beyond this, at the intersection with Low and High Ousegate, is *St Michael's Church* (12th-15th c.). Turning right into High Ousegate, we come (far end, on right) to *All Saints Church* (15th c.), flanked by an octagonal tower. Beyond this we turn right into Piccadilly. On the right-hand side of this busy street, in a small garden, is **Merchant Adventurers' Hall** (open 10 to 12.30 and 2 to 5.30, except Sundays).

This very interesting building dates from 1368. The **Great Hall** is a magnificent example of a mediaeval guildhall. It is mainly built in wood — because, it is said, the Great Plague of 1349 carried off all the stonemasons in York but spared the carpenters, who led a healthier life. The *chapel* was altered in the 17th century.

From here we can find our way north towards the Minster through the picturesque old streets of the mediaeval town, the most interesting of which is the *Shambles*.

Itinerary 3

This takes us along the *right bank of the Ouse*, over which looms the large new *Viking Hotel*. The entrance is in North St, between two churches, *St John's* to the south, now an institute of archaeological studies, and *All Saints* (12th-13th c.), which has a 15th century steeple 130 feet high and superb glass.

In Micklegate, on the other side of the Ouse, are a number of other churches: *St Martin-cum-Gregory* (13th c.), now a Church of England youth centre; *Holy Trinity*, an abbey church founded in the 12th century by monks from Marmoutier in Touraine, where mystery plays were performed in mediaeval times; and *St Mary Younger*, with an 11th century steeple.

At the far end of Micklegate we pass out of the old town through Micklegate Bar and turn right into

Queen St, on the left-hand side of which, before the station, is the **Railway Museum** (open 10 to 5).

This interesting museum contains early steam locomotives (one from Hetton colliery, 1822; the Agenoria; Stirling No. 1, etc.), models of rolling stock, signals, prints and pictures, etc.

Other Features of Interest

For visitors who have sufficient time at their disposal York has a wealth of interest to offer. They will find it well worth while to obtain the very full illustrated guide produced by the City Information Bureau. Here we mention only a selection of the more interesting sights additional to those already described.

Holy Trinity Church, Goodramgate (not to be confused with Holy Trinity in Micklegate, mentioned above). The present church was built between 1260 and 1500 on the site of an earlier church. 18th century box-pews; fine *window* in apse, with 15th century **glass.** The church is rarely used for worship. Beside it is *Lady Row*, believed to be the oldest row of cottages in York (mid 14th c.).

St Margaret's Church, Walmgate, in the east of the town. Restored 1852. Fine doorway.

St Denys, Walmgate. Fine Norman doorway; 12th century glass.

St Cuthbert's, Peasholme Green. Founded 687. Re-used Roman materials are visible in the structure. The family of Gen. Wolfe, hero of the capture of Quebec in 1760, lived nearby in the Black Swan inn.

St Anthony's Hall, at the corner of Peasholme Green and Aldwark. A 15th century guildhall, now occupied by a University institute of historical research. Fine chapel and great hall.

Merchant Taylors' Hall, immediately north of St Anthony's Hall. Built in the 14th century by the brotherhood of St John the Baptist, it was occupied by the Merchant Taylors' Guild from the 15th century onwards. Fine 17th century window.

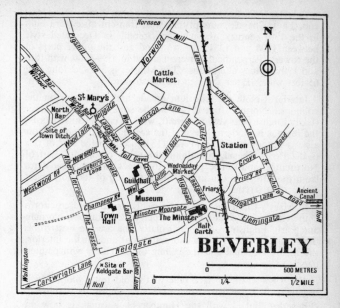

Roman Bath. In Sampson Square, in the heart of the old town, is the Roman Bath Inn (formerly the Mail Coach Inn), on the site of a Roman bath (one of the few built within a fortified Roman station).

York to Hull

58 miles east on A 1079, via Beverley.

11 miles: *Barmby-on-the-Moor.* At *Pocklington*, 2 miles east, are an ancient grammar school and an Early English church with a Perpendicular tower. — 19 miles: *Market Weighton.* — 28 miles: *Bishop Burton*, a charming little village. — 30 miles: **Beverley** (pop. 17,000, E.C. Thursday), an interesting old market town dominated by its splendid **Minster.**

Beverley Minster was founded in Saxon times. The east end, Lady Chapel, transept and west transept aisle were built in the 13th century; the nave was rebuilt in Decorated style between 1308 and 1331; the west end and the upper parts of the towers (Perpendicular) were restored in 1399-1400, with 18th and 19th century alterations. The Minster is 335 feet long and 65 feet wide. Enter through the north porch.

Interior. Note the triforium arcade and the angels on the columns. Norman font (1140) in the south aisle. The choir (Early English) has very fine *stalls*, with 68 curious misericords; the reredos is modern. Beyond the east end of the north choir aisle is the tomb of Lady Percy (1340), and to the east of this is the **Percy Chapel,** containing the tomb of the 4th Earl of Northumberland. The glass in the great east window dates from the 13th-15th centuries. From the top of the north-west tower (200 ft) there are wide views.

St Mary's Church is a splendid richly ornamented cruciform church in Decorated and Perpendicular style, with some Norman and Early English work. Particularly fine are the west front, the south doorway (with a Norman arch) and, in the interior, the Flemish Chapel and the ceiling of the choir, with painted panels.

North Bar (14th c.) is a relic of the old town walls, which originally had five gates and were surrounded by a ditch.

Beverley, linked with the Humber by a canal, is now an industrial town (shipbuilding, tanning, car accessories, etc.). The town has a number of interesting old streets with names that are reminders of the past — Wednesday Market, Saturday Market, Butchers' Row, Toll Gavel, Hengate, etc.

37 miles: **Hull** (pop. 300,000, E.C. Thursday), the country's third largest port, situated at the junction of the river Hull and the Humber. The docks extend for 7 miles along the Humber, with 12 miles of quays and 3 miles of railway lines.

The first settlement here grew up about 1160 on land belonging to Meaux Abbey and was known as *Wyke*. It received its first charter from Edward I in 1293, under the name of *Kingston-upon-Hull* (still its official name). The town was fortified in 1322. The Pilgrim Fathers sailed from the Humber for Holland, and went on from there to join the "Mayflower" at Plymouth.

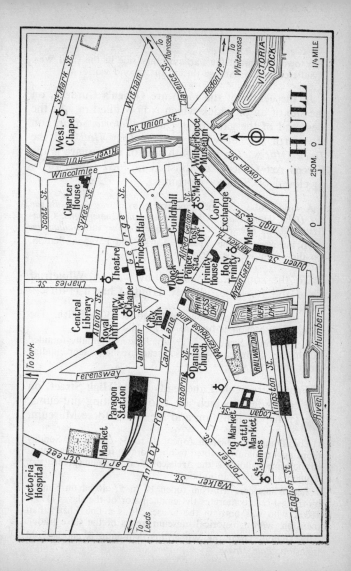

The town supported the Parliamentary side in the Civil War.
It suffered severe damage during the second world war.

In the centre of the town are **Queen's Gardens,** on
the site of an old dock which is now filled in. At the
west end of the gardens is *Queen Victoria Square*, on
the north side of which are the *City Hall* and the
Dock Offices. On the south side of the square is the
Ferens Art Gallery, established in 1937 (open 10 to
5; closed on Sunday mornings).

A varied collection, including works by *J. van Cleve, B. van
der Helst, Frans Hals, Ribera, Philippe de Champeigne, Canaletto, Guardi, Hogarth, Pissaro, Fantin-Latour* and *Guillaumin*.

To the west are the business district and Paragon Station.
To the south are the docks.

To the south-east, reached by way of Whitefriar
Gate and Lowgate, is **Holy Trinity Church** (14th c.).

The church is 272 feet long, with a tower 150 feet high. The
Early English choir is built in brick. Old font.

In front of the church is *Trinity House*, originally founded
in 1369 for the relief of distressed seamen; the present building
dates from 1753.

From here Scale Lane leads to the **High Street,** on
the east side of which are two interesting museums,
the Transport Museum and the Wilberforce Museum.

The **Transport Museum** (open 10 to 5; closed on Sunday
mornings) is mainly devoted to horse-drawn forms of transport.
In the same building is the **Archaeological Museum** (prehistoric,
Roman and Saxon antiquities).

The **Wilberforce Museum** (open 10 to 5; closed on Sunday
mornings) commemorates the emancipator of the slaves (1759-
1833), who was born in the house. It is a fine Elizabethan
mansion, with a historical museum (relics of the slave trade).

In High St, near the Wilberforce Museum, is another old
mansion, *Pole House.*

From here we return to Queen's Gardens by way of Salt House Lane and Lowgate, in which is *St Mary's Church*, founded in the 14th century by the Knights Hospitallers of North Ferriby; the passage under the tower was opened up in the 19th century.

Surroundings of Hull

To the east. *Hedon* (pop. 1800, E.C. Thursday), with a fine cathedral-like church. Old cross at Holyrood House. — *Patrington*, with a fine church (St Patrick's) which is known as the "Queen of Holderness". B 1445 runs south-east to *Basington*, a village on the coast. Beyond this are *Kilmsea* and, to the south, *Spurnhead*, a hook-shaped promontory at the mouth of the Humber (lighthouse and lifeboat station). — *Withernsea* (pop. 5000, E.C. Tuesday), a seaside resort popular with the people of Hull, with a firm, flat sandy beach.

To the south. The new *Humber Bridge* (toll), opened in 1981, crosses the Humber to *Barton-upon-Humber* (pop. 7000), formerly a flourishing port, with two interesting churches, particularly St Peter's (11th c. Saxon tower).

A short distance south-east is *Thornton Abbey*, a 12th century Augustinian foundation, later rebuilt, with a very fine gatehouse (1382).

From here continue via Wootton and then A 1211 to Ulceby and *Keelby* (1 mile from which is the 18th c. mansion of *Brocklesby Park*, with a mausoleum in the shape of a rotunda designed by Wyatt, 1792).

Beyond this is **Grimsby** (pop. 96,000), the largest fishing port in the world. St James's Church (13th c.). Large industrial installations; also at *Immingham*, to the north, and *Cleethorpes*, to the south.

South of Grimsby is *Louth* (pop. 12,000). St James's Church (Perpendicular), with a tower over 300 feet high.

To the north. A 165 runs from Hull to **Bridlington** (30 miles), a seaside resort on the North Sea, passing on the way the resort of *Hornsea*.

The older part of Bridlington has preserved much of the charm of the past. The *church* incorporates the nave of a chapel belonging to a 12th century Augustinian priory, and has parts representing the various phases of Gothic. The west front with its great window is particularly fine. Picturesque old *Bayle Gate*. 5 miles north-east is **Flamborough Head,** with sheer cliffs rising more than 400 feet above the sea. 6 miles south-west on A 166 (the York road) is *Burton Agnes Hall*, a splendidly furnished Elizabethan mansion (open 2 to 5).

York to Scarborough

Leave York on A 64. 12 miles: to right, **Kirkham Priory,** founded by Walter L'Espec in 1122. Church built in 1180 (tombs of Helmsley family). Fine gatehouse.

13 miles: road on left to **Castle Howard** (open during the season 2 to 5; closed Mondays and Fridays).

A splendid classical mansion built by Vanbrugh (his first major work) in 1726 for Charles Howard, 3rd Earl of Carlisle, and still occupied by the Howard family. *Hall*, *Long Gallery* (190 ft), Chapel (restored 1878). **Magnificent pictures,** including works by *Holbein* (Henry VIII), *Rubens* (Herodias and Salome), *Tintoretto* (Sacrifice of Isaac), *Reynolds*, *Gainsborough*, *Veronese*, *Parmigiano*, *Poussin*, *Salvator Rosa*, *van Dyck*, etc. Fine furniture. **Costume Museum** in the Stables, with a unique collection of costume from 1640 to the present day.

17 miles: **Malton** (pop. 4200, E.C. Thursday), an ancient town where many Roman remains have been found, now an important market town, situated on the west bank of the river Derwent.

At Old Malton is a priory, now the **parish church,** with a beautiful west front (fine Norman arch) and much old work in the interior; 12th century crypt. *Malton Lodge* is a Jacobean country house with magnificent oak carving. The *Museum*, in Milton Rooms (Market Place), contains Roman and pre-Roman antiquities and other material of local interest.

On the other side of the Derwent is *Morton*, a centre of racehorse training.

29 miles: *Sherburn* (pop. 650, E.C. Thursday). — 33 miles: *Staxton*.

41 miles: **Scarborough** (pop. 44,000, E.C. Wednesday), a popular seaside resort splendidly situated on two bays separated by a headland on which the old town stands, and linked by the superb *Marine Drive*. To north and south are cliffs, and inland are the Yorkshire moors.

The **Castle** (12th c.) is in the old town, standing on the headland 300 feet above the harbour. Nearby is *St Mary's Church*, with Anne Brontë's grave in the churchyard. The harbour is crowded with fishing boats. The lighthouse contains a museum. Fast motor launches start from Lighthouse Pier on trips round the bay, and there are steamers to Whitby and Bridlington. Near the harbour is *Richard III's House* (1350), with interesting relics. In Vernon Road is a *Museum*, with collections of birds' eggs, fish, shells, fossils, minerals, antiquities, etc.

The Art Gallery, in the Crescent, contains pictures of local interest. Nearby is Woodend, home of the Sitwell family, which is mentioned in Sir Osbert Sitwell's autobiography, "Left Hand, Right Hand". Remains of a Roman signal station. Magnificent gardens. From *Oliver's Mount*, behind Southcliff, there are fine views.

Surroundings of Scarborough

7 miles south is **Filey** (pop. 5000, E.C. Wednesday), a seaside resort with a large expanse of fine sand in a wide bay facing east. To the west rise the Yorkshire Wolds. The *Brigg*, a rocky spit ½ mile long extending into the sea, is a splendid sight, particularly in stormy weather. *St Oswald's Church* (Early English).

A road runs north to Whitby via Scalby and Burniston.

Scalby. 2 miles west is the village of *Hackness*, with an old church (St Peter's). *Hackness Hall* is the seat of Lord Derwent.

Burniston. 3 miles north by a minor road is *Ravenscar*, a holiday resort on cliffs standing 600 feet above the sea.

Shortly before Whitby a road runs east to **Robin Hood's Bay,** a quaint fishing village spoiled by modern building. The charming steep main street (no through road for cars) is lined with narrow lanes which wind about among the fishermen's houses.

21 miles from Scarborough is **Whitby** (pop. 12,600, E.C. Wednesday), a seaside resort of great charm, with historical associations. The town is situated on the Esk, the valley of which is bounded by steep cliffs, from which there are very fine views of the town. Alum was discovered here in the 17th century. The port has been a fishing and boatbuilding centre for many centuries. Captain Cook sailed from here on his first voyage, as cabin boy on the "Free Love". *St Mary's Church*, on the cliffs above the harbour and reached by a flight of 199 steps known as Jacob's Ladder, contains some Norman work. Beside it are the ruins of **Whitby Abbey,** which dates in its present form from the 12th to 14th centuries; it was damaged by fire from German cruisers in 1914.

Beyond Whitby is the delightful little village of Sandsend. — *Hinderwell*, near which, nestling in a wide bay at the foot of high cliffs, is *Runswick*, sometimes called the "Clovelly of the north". — *Staithes*, with small red-roofed houses huddled on both sides of the steep and narrow main street. The pict-uresque cliffs north of Staithes are the highest in the country. — *Saltburn-by-the-Sea* (pop. 7000, E.C. Tuesday) is a very popular seaside resort.

5 miles inland on A 1268 is **Guisborough Priory,** which dates from the 12th century (fine Norman entrance near the road; beautiful east end of choir, in 14th c. Gothic style).

From Guisborough it is 8 miles to **Middlesbrough** (p. 746).

44. SCARBOROUGH TO THIRSK

From Scarborough B 1262 runs up the beautiful Forge Valley to join A 170 at *Ayton*, an old village at the south end of the valley, on the quiet river Derwent. Ruins of *Ayton Castle*.

7 miles: *Brompton*, with an old church in which Wordsworth married Mary Hutchinson in 1820. — 10 miles: *Ebberston*, with a Palladian villa built in 1718 (open to the public Tuesdays 2 to 6). — 14 miles: *Thornton-le-Dale*, regarded by many as the prettiest village in Yorkshire, with the old market cross and stocks. — 17 miles: **Pickering** (pop. 4600, E.C. Wednesday), an old market town, the gateway to the Yorkshire moors.

Excavation has shown that there was a British settlement here, and many finds have been made in the barrows of the surrounding area. The **Castle** (13th c.) was an impregnable fortress; the outer walls and towers date from the 14th century. The *church of SS. Peter and Paul* (12th c.) has a massive Norman nave, with *frescoes* (discovered 1851, restored 1859) above the arcade.

Pickering to Whitby (A 169).

The north Yorkshire dales spread out fan-like from Pickering to the North Sea on the east and to the Hambleton and Cleveland Hills in the west and north-west. Towards the east end are Staindale, Givendale and Troutdale (old dykes and earthworks). In the direction of Scarborough are Crosscliffe, Langdale and Hackness. To the west are Rosedale and Farndale. **Saltergate,** in the midst of a wide expanse of moorland (Bridestones Moor, Grime Moor), is National Trust property. The *Bridestones* are rocks carved into curious shapes by erosion.

A road runs north-west from the Pickering-Whitby road to **Goathland** (pop. 600, E.C. Thursday), a beautiful and typical moorland village. In the vicinity are many waterfalls, in beautiful scenery. Nearby are the Bridestones (above) and the remains of a Roman road on *Wheeldale Moor*.

Just before Whitby is *Sleights* (pop. 1000, E.C. Wednesday), on the edge of the moors, with splendid views.

19 miles: *Wrelton*. — 21 miles: *Sinnington*, with a charming bridge over the river Seven. Very beautiful scenery (woods).

22 miles: road on left to *Lastingham*, a beautiful moorland village. Fine church with a well preserved Saxon crypt. Grouse and wild duck shooting. To the north is *Rosedale Abbey*, a little village nestling in a valley in the middle of moors and heather-clad hills. Ruins of a 12th century Cistercian priory, damaged in 1322.

24 miles: *Kirby Moorside*, a charming little old town. Nearby is *Kirkdale church*, which dates from Norman times, with a Saxon sundial.

30 miles: **Helmsley** (pop. 1600, E.C. Wednesday), with the ruins of a 12th century *castle*.

The castle was built by Walter L'Espec, founder of Kirkham Priory and Rievaulx Abbey. The earliest parts of the present building date from the 12th century, but most of it, including the fine quadrangular *keep*, is 14th century work. The castle withstood a three months' siege by Fairfax's Parliamentary forces during the Civil War (1644).

3 miles north-west on B 1257 is **Rievaulx Abbey,** the first Cistercian abbey in Yorkshire, founded by Walter L'Espec in 1132.

The building of the Abbey, on the banks of the Rye, may have been carried out under the direction of St Bernard himself. No doubt because of the local topography, the church is oriented nearer south to north than to the usual east to west. The very picturesque ruins have recently been cleared and tidied up. In its heyday the abbey had as many as 500 monks and lay brothers. Of the original 12th century buildings there remain the nave and transept of the *abbey church* and the cloisters; the **choir** and *monks' refectory* date from the 13th century. From Rievaulx Terrace, above the ruins, there are very fine views of the site. On the Terrace are two Greek temples, 18th century follies (restored).

B 1257 continues over the moors and the Cleveland Hills, through magnificent scenery, to Stokesley and Middlesbrough.

6 miles south of Helmsley on B 1363 is **Gilling Castle,** now a school, with a superb Elizabethan dining room. Open to visitors 10 to 12 and 2 to 4, except Sundays.

At *Sproxton*, beyond Helmsley, the Thirsk road turns west through hilly country. Soon afterwards a minor road goes off on the left to **Byland Abbey.**

Byland Abbey, lying just under the southern slopes of the Hambleton Hills, was founded in 1177. It was one of the three great Cistercian abbeys in Yorkshire (the others being Rievaulx and Fountains). Fine ruins of the *abbey church* (end of 12th c.), particularly the west front.

39 miles: **Coxwold,** where Laurence Sterne was curate (1760-68). He wrote "Tristram Shandy" and the "Sentimental Journey" at Shandy Hall here. The *church* (Perpendicular) has an old pulpit, interesting monuments and curious gargoyles. Nearby is *Newburgh Priory*, a fine old country house.

27 miles: **Thirsk** (p. 746).

Doncaster to Harrogate and Ripon

Leave Doncaster on A 1, the Great North Road.
To *Bramham* (28 miles), see Route 42.

Bramham to Skipton

31 miles (A 1 for 2 miles, then left into A 659, then A 65).

8 miles: *Harewood*. Nearby is **Harewood House,** in a wooded
park overlooking Wharfedale. The estate dates from Norman
times. The Aldburgh family built a castle here in the 14th
century; remains can still be seen, with walls over 6 feet thick
and towers 90 feet high. The present house was built by John
Carr for Edwin Lascelles, later Lord Harewood, in the 18th century, and was decorated by the Adam brothers and furnished
by Chippendale. The rooms contain magnificent *furniture*,
with interior decoration by *Angelika Kauffmann*, *Zucchi* and
Rebecchi. The collection of pictures includes works by *Reynolds*,
van Dyck, *Turner* and *Titian*. Sèvres porcelain and celadon
china. This is one of the most valuable private collections in
the world. (Open during the season 11 to 6).

16 miles: **Otley** (pop. 12,000, E.C. Wednesday), an ancient
and busy market town in lower Wharfedale (paper-mills,
manufacture of printing machinery). Early English church
with some Norman work. Otley was the birthplace of Thomas
Chippendale (1711). Above the town rises the Chevin (841 ft),
from the top of which there are fine views of Wharfedale and
the hills to the north. 1 mile north-east is *Farnley Hall*, with
a large collection of pictures by *Turner*, relics of Cromwell
and mementoes of the Civil War.

22 miles: **Ilkley** (pop. 19,000, E.C. Wednesday), an attractive
town in the midst of heather-clad moorland. In the churchyard
of *All Saints Church* (Early English, restored) are three fine
Saxon crosses. The *Museum*, in Manor House, contains local
antiquities from the Stone Age to the present day, Roman
material, mediaeval glass and carving, implements used in
the early days of the woollen industry, etc. (Open 10 to 12
and 2 to 5, except Mondays).

The moors round the town provide ample opportunity for
walking. Among the local beauty spots are *Almescliffe Crag*

and the *Cow and Calf Rocks*, from which there are splendid views; *Heber's Ghyll*, one of the most delightful ravines in the moors; and the *Panorama Rocks*, east of the head of Heber's Ghyll. 1 mile south are the *White Wells*, and nearby is the Tarn, a pleasant lake. In Rocky Valley are a number of caves. — 3 miles farther off are the *Doubler Stones*, traditionally associated with Druidical rites. Over the Wharfe is an old packhorse bridge, and at *Ben Rhydding* there are stepping stones. *Middleton Lodge* is an Elizabethan mansion which is now a Passionist monastery (open to visitors). — 4 miles: *Beamsley Beacon* (1314 ft), with wide views.

32 miles: **Skipton** (pop. 13,000, E.C. Tuesday), chief town of the district of Craven, in Airedale. The town dates from Saxon times and has a Norman *parish church* with a fine open roof, an old screen (1533) and tombs of the Clifford family. The *Castle* (late 11th c.) was built by Robert de Romelli, and rebuilt in the 13th century. The east part and the octagonal tower date from 1536; the west entrance was added in the 17th century. The castle is entered by the great gateway in High St (open 10 a.m. to dusk). In High St is the *Craven Museum* (open 2 to 5, except Tuesdays and Sundays): prehistoric material, local history.

Around Skipton. 10 miles north-west is *Malham*, near which is *Gordale Scar*, an impressive deep ravine. North of Malham is *Malham Cove*, a rocky amphitheatre 300 feet high, and beyond this is *Malham Tarn*, where the National Trust has a property of 875 acres, including the tarn, Malham Tarn House and Waterhouses Farm. The first chapter of Charles Kingsley's "Water Babies" is set in this area.

9 miles south-east is *Keighley* (pop. 56,000, E.C. Tuesday), a town built on hills, with important textile mills, engineering works, foundries and factories producing electrical equipment. 1 mile north-east, on the north bank of the Aire, is *East Riddlesden Hall*, a typical local manor-house (17th c.) with a fishpond and two fine old barns in its 12½ acres of grounds; small collection of oak furniture. 2 miles south-west is **Haworth,** home of the Brontë family. The school attended by the sisters at Cowan's Bridge appears as Lowood in "Jane Eyre". The wild beauty of the surrounding countryside is well depicted in "Wuthering Heights". In the village, opposite the museum, is the parsonage in which the family lived (open 11 to 6, Sundays 2 to 6). The school in which Charlotte Brontë and her husband taught can also be seen. The church contains the tombs of

the whole family, except Anne. In the Black Bull inn is the room occupied by Branwell Brontë. 2 miles from the parsonage is the Brontë Waterfall, and 1 mile beyond this is Withens Farm (Wuthering Heights).

32 miles: *Wetherby.*

41 miles: **Harrogate** (pop. 60,000, E.C. Wednesday), one of the country's leading spas, situated on the Yorkshire moors 450 feet above sea level. The *Stray* (200 acres) is a common extending beyond High Harrogate. The springs are in the lower town.

There are more than 80 springs of all kinds — chalybeate, sulphur, saline. There are fine spa establishments with the most modern facilities for treatment. The waters are recommended for rheumatism, gout, arthritis, lumbago, sciatica, fibrositis, neuritis, circulatory disorders including high blood pressure, arteriosclerosis, cardiac disease, liver disorders including cirrhosis, gallstones, intestinal disorders, chronic skin conditions of all kinds, anaemia, general debility and the after-effects of tropical diseases.

Harrogate to Skipton: 21 miles on A 59.

The road crosses the wild *Forest of Knaresborough* to (10 miles) Blubberhouses, a moorland village. — 16 miles: *Bolton Bridge,* in the heart of Wharfedale. Nearby are the ruins of the lovely old priory known as **Bolton Abbey,** founded in 1120 at Embsay and transferred to the present site in 1151. The present buildings were built by Alice, daughter of Robert de Romelli, but today only the church remains. The ruins of the choir, north transept and old central tower stand roofless and ruined on a green bank by the river. At the west end is the 15th century Perpendicular tower, left uncompleted when the priory was dissolved at the Reformation. — Nearby are *Barden Bridge* and *Barden Tower,* with pleasant walks along the river. 1 mile away, on the edge of Bolton Woods, is the *Strid,* a narrow gorge carved out of the rock by the river, 50 yards long. In the beautiful Valley of Desolation — which does not deserve its name — are two waterfalls.

Harrogate to York: 21 miles.

3 miles: **Knaresborough** (pop. 9500, E.C. Thursday), on the river Nidd, one of the pleasantest old towns in Yorkshire. Of the *Castle* (14th c.) only the ruins of the *keep* and four towers remain. The *church* contains interesting monuments. *St Robert's Chapel* is a cave hewn out of the limestone, with the crudely carved figure of an armed man. Near Mother Shipton's Inn is the *Dropping Well*, with petrifying properties, unique in England. — 11 miles: *Green Hammerton.* To the south-east is *Marston Moor*, scene of a battle in 1644 in which Cromwell defeated the Royalist forces. — 21 miles: **York.**

45 miles: **Ripley** (pop. 200, E.C. Thursday). The *church* (Decorated and Perpendicular) has interesting brasses and tombs. Cromwell stayed in Ripley Castle (16th c.) before the battle of Marston Moor.

10 miles west on B 6165 is *Pateley Bridge*, a quaint little town of steep winding streets with picturesque old houses and inns. 3 miles away are *Brimham Rocks* (100 ft), covering an area of 60 acres and affording magnificent views. Within easy reach are the glens of Ravensgill, Burn Ghyll, Rhyddings Ghyll and Ramsgill. Near the How Stean gorge are *Eglin's Hole* and *Stump Cross Cavern.* At *Goyden Pot* the Nidd surges turbulently through a canyon and then flows for more than 2 miles underground; it can be followed for a distance of more than 500 yards.

52 miles: **Ripon** (pop. 11,000, E.C. Wednesday), an attractive town and spa on the banks of the Ure. The curfew is still sounded at 9 o'clock every night by the blowing of a horn in front of the mayor's house.

From the Market Place Kirkgate leads to the **Cathedral.** The transept and parts of the choir are Transitional (1150-80). The beautiful west front is Early English (1215-50). The east end of the choir is Decorated (1290-1300), and the nave, some of the south part of the choir and the central tower are Perpendicular (15th c.). Under the crossing is the crypt of the church built by St Wilfrid in 699. Sir George Gilbert Scott restored the building in the 19th century. The Cathedral is not very large: its length is 270 feet, but it is nearly 90 feet wide across nave and aisles.

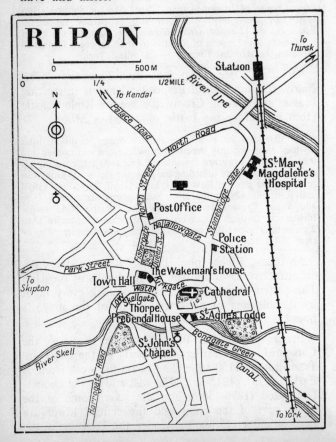

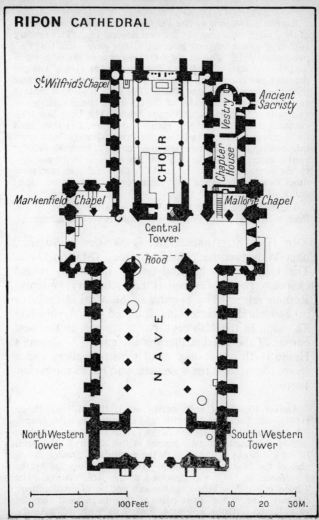

RIPON CATHEDRAL

St Wilfrid's Chapel

Ancient Sacristy

Vestry

CHOIR

Chapter House

Markenfield Chapel

Mallorie Chapel

Central Tower

Rood

NAVE

North Western Tower

South Western Tower

0   50   100 Feet

0   10   20   30 M.

Interior. The *nave* is late Perpendicular, with the exception of the Early English bays by the west towers. In the 15th century two of the four original Norman arches were rebuilt in Perpendicular style. The transept (1185) contains much work in Transitional style. There is a fine *rood-screen* (1480) between the nave and choir. The nave has no triforium, but in the choir the triforium openings are glazed. The *stalls* have 15th century carving. On the south side of the choir are the chapter house and vestry (Norman), with a crypt below. The *Lady Loft* (Decorated), above the chapter house and vestry, has been used for a century or more to house the chapter library, with some rare books, and has interesting misericords. From the churchyard is entered one of the only two Saxon crypts in the country. In the north-east corner is *St Wilfred's Needle;* in mediaeval times women who could not pass through this were presumed guilty of adultery.

The best view of the Cathedral is from the Market Place, from which the Early English west front is seen to advantage.

In High St, Agnes Gate, is *St Anne's Hospital,* once known as the "Maiden's Due" (Maison Dieu). The 15th century hospital has an interesting ruined chapel. *Thorpe Prebend* is now the city museum: Roman relics. The *hospital of St Mary Magdalene* in Stonebridge Gate was founded by Archbishop Thurston in the 12th century for lepers. In the west corner of the Market Place is the gabled **Wakeman's House** (13th c.), with a small minstrel gallery and a secret room. It is the wakeman who blows the curfew horn.

Around Ripon. 1 mile north-west is the *Bishop's Palace* (1841), in Tudor style, with a Perpendicular-style chapel. 1½ miles south-west are the famous ruins of **Fountains Abbey,** one of the finest monastic houses in the country. The ruins lie on the banks of the Skell in the grounds of *Studley Royal,* seat of the Marquess of Ripon. The Abbey, founded by the Cistercians in 1132, was dissolved at the Reformation. The *Chapel of the Nine Altars,* at the east end, is of extraordinary delicacy; one of the finest parts of this magnificent complex of buildings. (Open 9.30 to 4, 5.30, 7 or 9 according to the time of year). There is a magnificent view of the Abbey when approaching it from Studley Royal through the 12th century gatehouse, by the 13th century *Mill Bridge*. The west front, with its fine window and tower, dates from Tudor times, the rest from the 12th and 13th centuries; the *Chapel of the Nine Altars*, now roofless, is 13th century. The extra transept at the east end containing the Chapel is similar to the Chapel of the Nine Altars in Durham Cathedral. The monastic buildings lie to the south: the double-aisled *Cellarium*, the Chapter House (with Norman arches), the Parlour, the Refectory, the Buttery, the Warming House, the Kitchen. To the east are the ruins of the Infirmary and the remains of the *Abbot's Chambers*. The *Vyner Chapel* is modern.

9 miles north is *Masham* (pop. 2000, E.C. Thursday), a pleasant market town on the Ure. Late Gothic church with an octagonal tower and spire. — 14 miles: **Jervaulx Abbey,** on the south bank of the Ure, a large 12th century Cistercian house founded in 1156. The remains of the cruciform church, chapter house and monastic buildings date from the Transitional and Early English periods. The *Chapter House* is a fine example of Early English architecture, with the tombstones of the early abbots and an old altar in the north transept. — 16 miles: *Middleham*, with the ruins of a large castle which belonged to Warwick the Kingmaker.

4 miles south-east on B 6265 is **Newby Hall,** built by Robert Adam in 1770 round an earlier house attributed to Wren. Curious collection of chamber pots. Magnificent interior decorated with Roman statues, etc., and fine *tapestries*, with medallions by Boucher. Beautiful park, with miniature railway.

London to Manchester

Motorways M 1 and M 6. Leave M 6 at New-castle-under-Lyme (p. 671) and continue north on A 34.

157 miles: **Little Moreton Hall.** This moated building, which took its present shape between 1559 and 1589, is one of the most perfect specimens of the "black and white" style in the country; it is remarkable for its carved gables and Elizabethan wood and plaster work. There is a long wainscoted gallery, a chapel, and a great hall; it contains some oak furniture, a service of pewter, and four 17th century Flemish tapestries. (Open 2 to 6, except Tuesdays).

159 miles: *Astbury*. Old church, with interesting monuments (effigies) in churchyard.

161 miles: **Congleton** (pop. 16,000, E.C. Wednesday), an old town with a number of ancient houses and inns.

5 miles south is *Mow Cop Castle* (National Trust), an artificial ruin built in 1750, in 5 acres of hilly ground over 1000 feet above sea level. To the north is the *Old Man of Mow*, a prominent crag on the borders of Staffordshire.

7 miles west is *Sandbach* (pop. 9000, E.C. Tuesday), with a Perpendicular church and two dilapidated Saxon crosses in the market place. — 13 miles: *Crewe* (pop. 60,000, E.C. Wednesday), an important railway junction with large railway workshops. Nearby is *Crewe Hall*, seat of the Marquess of Crewe, a rebuilding (1870) of a Jacobean mansion designed by Inigo Jones, destroyed by fire in 1866.

169 miles: *Monks Heath*.

8 miles north-west on A 537 is **Knutsford**, the model for Cranford in the novel by Mrs Gaskell (1810-75), who lived as a child in Heath House, in Gaskell Avenue. She is buried

in the churchyard of the Unitarian Chapel. Also of interest is the *Italian House*.

173 miles: *Wilmslow* (pop. 15,000, E.C. Wednesday). 1 mile north-west is the *Styal* estate (National Trust), 252 acres of natural beauty and historical interest. *Quarry Bank*, the *Cotton Mill* and the village of *Styal*, built soon after the mill, form a fine example of an early industrial community.

185 miles: **Manchester.**

MANCHESTER

Manchester (pop. 650,000, E.C. Wednesday and Saturday) is one of England's leading industrial centres, situated at the junction of the Irk and the Irwell. Its name is synonymous with cotton and textiles, but since the last war other industries (electrical equipment, aircraft, chemicals, heavy engineering) have also developed. Plan at end of volume.

The town was originally a Roman settlement, *Mancunium.* The Saxon town, known as *Manigceaster*, was fortified in the 10th century. It developed into a thriving industrial town in the Middle Ages, particularly through the manufacture of woollen goods and cloth, which was brought in by Flemish weavers towards the end of the 14th century. By Tudor times it had become the county town, although its population was still relatively small. The industrial revolution brought amazing prosperity to Manchester, and the population rose from 20,000 in 1750 to nearly 100,000 in 1800. The abundant water power provided by the streams flowing down from the Pennines promoted this industrial development, and at the end of the 18th century the rich local coalfields made possible the change-over to steam power. The damp climate was very suitable for cotton spinning. In 1894 the construction of the Ship Canal, linking Manchester with the sea 35 miles away, made it a great inland port.

The tour of the town begins in **Piccadilly Gardens,** in and around which are the air terminal, the bus station and the principal hotels (the Piccadilly, the Grand Hotel, Queen's Hotel).

From here Moseley St runs south-west to the **City Art Gallery** (open 10 to 6, Sundays 2 to 5), a 19th century building on the left-hand side of the street.

Silver, mediaeval pottery. Paintings by artists of various schools: 17th century Dutch (*Steen, van Ostade, Wouwerman, Potter, Hobbema, Rembrandt, Teniers, P. de Hooch, G. Terborch,* etc.), Italian (*Guardi, Bordone, Maestro di 1518,* etc.), French *(Fantin-Latour)*, English (*Blake, Turner, Lely, Reynolds, Hogarth, Lawrence, Rossetti,* etc.).

Moseley St runs into **St Peter's Square.** Straight ahead is the Midland Hotel, to the right the *Central Library* (1934) and *Town Hall.* In the centre of the square is a *War Memorial.*

From here John Dalton St runs west into one of the city's main thoroughfares, **Deansgate,** running north and south. Almost opposite is the **John Rylands Library.**

Magnificent collections of *manuscripts* (including a 2nd century St John's Gospel) and *early printed books.* The library contains a total of 700,000 volumes.

Going north up Deansgate, we pass on the right, in neighbouring streets, *St Ann's Church* and the *Royal Exchange* (1870, with a Corinthian façade and a campanile 190 ft high), and after some public gardens come to the **Cathedral.**

In 15th century Perpendicular style (restored), this is the smallest of English cathedrals, 220 feet long but, with its side chapels, relatively wide (112 ft), with a square tower 140 feet high (rebuilt 1868) and much curious carved ornament. The north porch, muniment room and baptistery are modern.

The choir and nave have flat timber roofs; the *nave* is interesting on account of its width. The *choir stalls* (1505) have fine carved misericords. *Lady Chapel* (1518). The Cathedral suffered severe damage during the last war.

The *Corn Exchange* stands to the east of the Cathedral, and beyond is Smithfield Market in Shudehill, which is particularly lively on Saturday evenings. Nearby is Withy Grove, with Kemsley House, northern headquarters of the Kemsley newspapers. The home of the world-famous "Guardian", formerly the "Manchester Guardian", is in Cross St, near the Royal Exchange. North of the Cathedral is **Chetham College** or **Hospital** (founded 1651) with the oldest *free library* in Europe. The building, arranged round a quadrangle, is one of the oldest in the town, and dates from the 15th century. Adjoining is the *Grammar School*, and to the north the *Exchange* and *Victoria Station*. New Bridge St intersects with Great Ducie St, which leads to the Assize Courts (1864).

South of the city centre, in Oxford Road, is **Manchester University** (oldest building 1873; much recent building). There is a *Museum* of natural history and ethnography in the old University buildings.

Farther out on Oxford Road is the **Whitworth Art Gallery** (open 10 to 5, except Sundays).

Pictures by *Rembrandt, Vernet, Blake, Lawrence, Cézanne, Picasso, Rodin.* Watercolours by many English and foreign artists — *Sutherland, Moore, Turner, Rossetti, Gauguin, van Gogh,* etc. Works by contemporary artists — *Vasarely, Epstein, Miró,* etc. Magnificent collection of **Chinese porcelain.**

Still farther south, in the district of **Rusholme**, is *Platt Hall*, a Georgian mansion (1760) containing a Gallery of English Costume from the 17th century to the present day.

In **Salford**, north-west of the city centre, is an Art Gallery devoted to modern art (works by Epstein). Opposite it is Joule

House, with relics of the physicist J.P. Joule (1818-89). To the west is the *Science Museum*, with a reproduction of a coal-mine.

To the north, in the district of *Collyhurst*, is the *Queen's Park Gallery* (decorative arts, toys, military uniforms).

Manchester has forty parks with an area of over 2200 acres. To the north is *Heaton Park*, formerly the property of the Earl of Wilton; the house, Heaton Hall, is now a museum containing a collection of Oriental armour. The *Fletcher Moss Gardens* in Didsbury have an interesting collection of English flowers, trees and shrubs. In *Wythenshawe Park* is an Eliza-bethan mansion, Wythenshawe Hall, now a museum (bronzes, pictures, furniture, Chinese porcelain, dolls' houses). In *Belle Vue Gardens* (80 acres), opened in 1820, are a zoo, an amusement park, a lake, a circus and a motor racing track. Very popular race meetings are held here.

Lancashire, the Cotton County

Lancashire, together with certain parts of Cheshire and Derbyshire, has within its borders four-fifths of the workers employed in cotton-spinning and weaving.

The various parts of the industry are distributed in different geographical areas. Ordinary spinning is done in the towns to the north and east of Manchester — Oldham, Bolton, Roch-dale, Royton, Ashton-under-Lyme and Stockport; more deli-cate work at Bolton and Leigh. Most of the weaving is done farther north, in Blackburn, Darwen, Burnley and Accrington and in an area extending by way of Nelson and Colne into Yorkshire. Most of the finishing work is done in south-east Lancashire, including Manchester itself and extending into Cheshire and Derbyshire. This distribution, however, is by no means rigid. There are spinning, weaving and finishing shops in Manchester; there are many weaving looms in Bolton and spinning mills in Blackburn; and both spinning and weaving are done at Bury, Ramsbottom, Heywood and Radcliffe, in the towns in the Rossendale valley and at Preston. The main warehousing and sales centre is Manchester; yarns and cotton fabrics are bought and sold on the Royal Exchange, and the shipping firms which handle cotton have their offices in the city. Liverpool is the principal port of the cotton trade, import-ing raw cotton from overseas and exporting the finished products.

Manchester to Chester via Altrincham: 38 miles.

5 miles: *Sale.* — 8 miles: *Altrincham* (pop. 40,000, E.C. Wednesday), a favourite Manchester residential area. Dunham Park is very fine. St Margaret's Church, Dunham Massey, should be seen. — 12 miles: A 56 runs east to *Warrington* via *Lymm* (pop. 6000, E.C. Wednesday): old market cross and stocks. — 21 miles: **Northwich** (pop. 19,600, E.C. Wednesday). Near the beautiful Delamere Forest (4000 acres), the town is the centre of Cheshire's great salt industry. It is a quaint topsy-turvy town, where the houses and roofs and walls crack and sag in strange disorder as the result of the subsidence of the soil through the gradual dissolving of the salt foundations. There is a large salt museum. — 38 miles: **Chester.**

Manchester to Leeds

Motorway (M 62) or A 62. The route on A 62 is described.

7 miles: **Oldham** (pop. 120,000, E.C. Tuesday), one of the world's leading cotton centres, with 50 spinning mills, over 3½ million mule and ring spindles, 150,000 doubling spindles and 1500 looms in use. Other industries include aircraft engines, textiles and brewing. *Art Gallery* (19th c. watercolours).

4 miles south is *Ashton-under-Lyme,* another important cotton town. *Stalybridge* in Cheshire, 2 miles east, also belongs to the cotton-spinning region. Beyond Oldham the road begins to climb over hills and moors.

25 miles: **Huddersfield** (pop. 130,000, E.C. Wednesday), one of the centres of the textile industry, noted for the quality of its worsted fabrics.

Other industries include dyeworks, chemical plants, clothing factories and breweries; in the hills are coal-mines. To the west and south are bleak moors rising to 2000 feet above sea level. Parts of the town are above 1000 feet. *Tolson Museum* (local and industrial history).

40 miles: **Leeds.**

LEEDS

Leeds (pop. 510,000, E.C. Wednesday) is a great
industrial and commercial centre, mainly noted for
its woollen industry but with a variety of other industries as well (iron and steel, locomotives, electrical
engineering). It is also a university city. Lying almost
in the centre of northern England, half way between
the North Sea and the Irish Sea, it is an important
cultural and commercial centre for the region.

Roman remains have been found in the area, and there is
known to have been a Roman station at *Adel*, now a suburb
of the city. A palace was built near the site of the town in the
7th century. In the 9th century the whole region fell into the
hands of the Danes, who have left many traces of their presence in local place names. From the 13th to the 16th century
the woollen trade brought prosperity to the town, but this
later gave place to engineering, which was favoured by the
availability of iron and coal. Since then the clothing trade
has again moved into first place.

Leeds has few old buildings.

In front of City Station is **City Square,** with the
General Post Office on the north side and *Holy
Trinity Church* (1727) on the east side. In the centre
of the square is a *statue of the Black Prince*.

From the square Park Row runs north to the
Roman Catholic *Cathedral* (1904). From here we
turn left along Great George St to reach the **Town
Hall,** with the **City Museum** and **City Art Gallery**
opposite it.

The **Town Hall,** a neo-classical building erected in the 1850s,
has a tower 225 feet high. Every three years the Leeds Musical
Festival is held here; the next occasions are in 1982 and 1985.

Behind the Town Hall, to the west, is *St John's Church*
(1634).

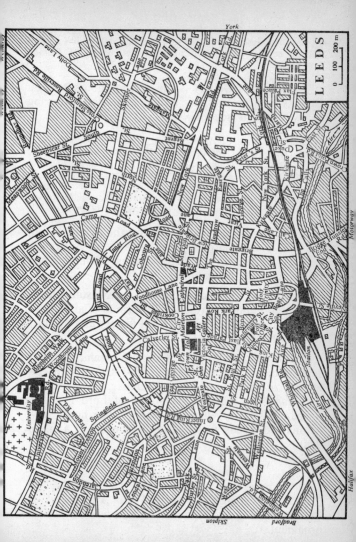

LEEDS

0 100 200 m

York

Woodhouse Moor

Spencer Pl.

Roundhay Rd.

Sheepscar St.

Meanwood

Leylands

South

Camp. Road

Inner Ring

Cobourg

Woodhouse Lane

Calverley St.

Cookridge

Portland

Civic Museum

City Art Gallery

City Museum

East Parade

Park Row

Park Square

St. George

Victoria Queen

City

Church

Eastgate

Briggate

Regent St.

New York St.

Marsh Lane

New Market

The Calls

Holy

Town Hall

Park Street

King St.

Wellington St.

Inner Ring Rd.

Infirmary St.

Aire

Station

City

Call

Dark Arches

Neville St.

Aire

Motorway

University

Woodhouse Lane

Blenheim Terr.

Clarendon

Springfield Pl.

Town Factory

Great George St.

Merrion

Skipton   Bradford   Halifax

26

The City Museum (open 10 to 6, except Sundays) has natural history collections and an important collection of Roman antiquities.

The City Art Gallery (same opening hours, and on Sunday afternoons) has a fine collection, covering many different schools:

Italian (*Cima, Carracci, Bissolo, Francia, Guardi, Guido Reni*, etc.); Dutch (*van der Neer, Ruisdael, Berchem, Stomer*, etc.); French (*Marquet, Sisley, Renoir, Vuillard, Bonnard, Pissarro, Signac, Géricault, Courbet, Corot, Fantin-Latour, Rousseau*, etc.); English (Pre-Raphaelites, watercolourists, *Turner*, etc.). Contemporary sculptors (*Moore, Mestrovic, Hepworth, Ralph Brown*) and older masters (*Canova*).

In the north-west of the city (on the Skipton road, A 660) is the University of Leeds, with a circular Library containing 500,000 volumes (including manuscripts and incunabula).

To the west of the city, on A 65, is Kirkstall Abbey, with the imposing ruins of Norman and Gothic buildings. Small *museum* of local history and bygones (open 10 to 5).

To the east, on A 63, is Temple Newsam, a former seat of the Earls of Halifax (17th-18th c.): rich collection of furniture, Chinese archaeology, pictures by *Guardi*. It was the birthplace of Lord Darnley, husband of Mary Queen of Scots. The house now belongs to Leeds Corporation (open 10.30 a.m. to dusk).

Surroundings of Leeds

5 miles north on A 660 is Adel. The *church of St John the Baptist* (Norman, 12th c.) has fine carved ornament.

Leeds to Sheffield: 32 miles on A 61.

9 miles: **Wakefield** (pop. 58,000, E.C. Wednesday), an industrial town (woollens, chemicals, engineering) connected with the Mersey and Humber by canals.

The *Cathedral* (All Saints) dates from the 14th-15th centuries. It has a fine crocketed spire (249 ft) and is Perpendicular in style. The retro-choir dates from 1900. Over the Calder is a bridge with *St Mary's Chantry Chapel*, begun about 1342. The original façade is in the grounds of Kettlethorpe Hall, just outside the city. There are only three other mediaeval bridge chapels in the country (see Rotherham). To the south are the ruins of *Sandal Castle*, near the site of the battle of Wakefield (1460). In Manygates Lane is a monument (1897) to Richard Plantagenet.

The **Municipal Museum** in Holmfield Park, Denbydale Road (open weekdays 11 to 5 or 7.30 according to the time of year, Sundays 2.30 to 5.30 in summer) contains collections of pottery and ceramics, furniture, pewter, and prehistoric and mediaeval antiquities. The *Municipal Art Gallery* (open weekdays 11 to 7, Wednesdays and Saturdays until 8, Sundays 2.30 to 5.30) is in Wentworth Terrace.

Around Wakefield. 6 miles west is the industrial town of *Dewsbury*, where on Christmas Eve the "Devil's Knell" is still tolled (one stroke for every year that has passed since the birth of Christ). Nearby is *Batley*.

5 miles south-east on A 638 (the Doncaster road) is *Wragby*, near which is **Nostell Priory,** a large mansion begun by James Paine in 1733 and completed by Robert Adam after 1765: fine interior with Chippendale furniture (open Wednesdays, Saturdays and Sundays during the season from 2 to 6); there is also a small motorcycle museum.

19 miles: *Barnsley* (pop. 75,000, E.C. Thursday). In the neighbourhood are the ruins of Monk Bretton Priory and Wentworth Castle. — 24 miles: to the west, *Wortley*, in the wooded area of Wharncliffe Chase. Lady Mary Wortley Montagu lived in Wharncliffe Lodge.

32 miles: **Sheffield** (below).

Manchester to Sheffield

The direct route is on A 628 via Stocksbridge. We describe
the alternative route by A 57 (38 miles), which has less traffic
and more attractive scenery. It follows the line of an old Roman
road.

7 miles: *Hyde*. — 14 miles: *Glossop* (pop. 20,000,
E.C. Tuesday), an industrial and residential town on
the edge of the Derbyshire moors and within easy
reach of the Peak (p. 639). — 20 miles: *Snake Inn*.
— 27 miles: *Ashopton*, most of which has been submerged by the construction of a reservoir. The whole
valley between the Derwent moors and Win Hill is
now under water, a large new artificial lake (area
500 acres, depth 100 ft) having been created by the
building of a series of dams; fine views.

38 miles: **Sheffield.**

SHEFFIELD

In the 11th century this area belonged to Earl Waltheof, the
last of the Saxon barons, who organised a rebellion against
the Normans and was executed. Sheffield Castle, in which
Mary Queen of Scots was held prisoner for 14 years under the
care of the Earl of Shrewsbury, was demolished after the
Civil War. Sheffield steel, and particularly Sheffield cutlery,
is known throughout the world, and enjoyed considerable
reputation from the earliest times. In the early 18th century
the population was under 15,000, and a century later was still
less than 50,000. The city's innumerable foundries and factories
produce every conceivable article made of steel, using extremely
complicated and intricate machinery. The population is now
500,000. Sheffield is now also a university city.

The centre of Sheffield is round *City Hall* (1932).
To the east is the Grand Hotel, and at the end of
the busy street known as Barker's Pool is the **Town
Hall** (1897), with a tower 210 feet high crowned by

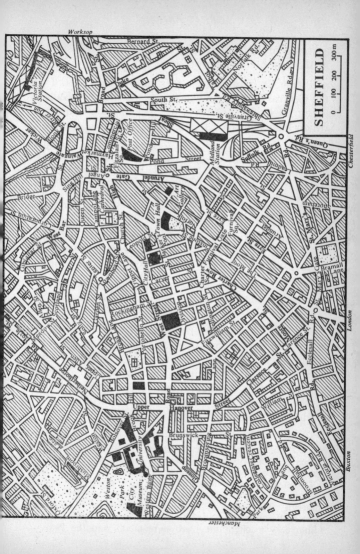

a statue of Vulcan (who, as the god of blacksmiths, is the symbol of the city).

Surrey St continues east from the Town Hall to the Central Library, in which is the **Graves Art Gallery** (open 10 to 8, Sundays 2 to 5), a private collection which has been open to the public since the last war.

Works by painters of various schools: French *(Boudin, Rousseau, Gauguin, Cézanne, Matisse, Daubigny, Corot);* Spanish *(Ribera, Murillo, A. Moro);* Italian *(Verrocchio,* the Ruskin Madonna; *Bonfigli, Giambellino, Pinturicchio, Canaletto, Maestro di 1518);* and English *(Gainsborough, Turner, Constable, Cotman, Richard Wilson).* Sculpture by *Despiau* and *Epstein.* Greek, Indian, Chinese and Moslem art.

To the north is the **Cathedral of SS. Peter and Paul** (14th-15th c., restored). The beautiful *Shrewsbury Chapel* contains tombs of the Earls of Shrewsbury.

South of the Cathedral, in Church St, is **Cutlers' Hall,** a neo-classical building (1832) belonging to the Company of Cutlers (founded 1624).

Sheffield University (founded 1905) occupies a large complex of buildings to the west of the city centre, near *Weston Park;* among the buildings is a tower block 290 feet high. On the west side of the park is the **City Museum** (open 10 to 5 or 8 according to the time of year, Sundays 1 to 4), with material related to the industries of the area.

Around Sheffield. 1½ miles south is the very pleasant *Meersbrook Park.* 1 mile south-east is *Manor Castle,* in which Mary Queen of Scots was held prisoner for many years. Nearby, in Clarke House Road, is the *Botanical Garden.* — 6 miles south is **Dronfield,** a small industrial town with stone-built houses both old and new (steel instruments, mining equipment, machinery). The *church* (14th c.) has old glass; fine Jacobean choir stalls and 14th and 15th century tombs. The town is within easy reach of the Derbyshire moors and the Peak.

47. LIVERPOOL AND CHESTER

Liverpool (pop. 740,000, E.C. Wednesday), situated on the right bank of the Mersey some 3 miles from the sea, is England's second seaport and one of the world's leading maritime and commercial cities, with fine docks and a magnificent river frontage. Plan at end of Guide.

The town received its first charter in 1207 from King John, who established a settlement round the castle he built here (destroyed in the 18th c.). At the end of the 16th century Francis Bacon was Member of Parliament for the borough. During the Civil War the town withstood a siege by Prince Rupert. At the beginning of the 18th century the port became prosperous through the trade with the New World, and by 1730 Liverpool had a population of 12,000, a figure which increased to 80,000 by the end of the century. In the 1840s steamship services to New York were established, and the traffic on this route increased very rapidly. During the second world war Liverpool was the scene of busy shipping activity, with an Allied command headquarters, and was subjected to severe air bombardment.

Liverpool is not only a busy seaport, handling some 30 million tons a year, but an industrial city with a wide range of activities — shipbuilding, engineering, foodstuffs, chemicals and pharmaceuticals, electrical equipment, etc. It imports cotton, timber, foodstuffs and tobacco, and exports textiles and machinery.

A central point in the city is **St John's Gardens** (just to the east of the entrance to the Mersey Tunnel), round which stand a number of important buildings.

On the south-east side is **St George's Hall,** a large building in the form of a Greek temple (1854), designed by H.L. Elmes.

It contains court-rooms and offices. The *Great Hall*, with statues of local celebrities, is used as a concert hall; it was damaged during the last war but has been restored. In front of the Hall are a number of statues, including one of Queen Victoria.

To the north of St George's Hall is the *Wellington Monument*,
120 feet high. On the south side of the square is the *St John's*
shopping centre, with a *tower* 450 feet high (1967: revolving
restaurant at top).

Also to the north of St George's Hall, beyond
William Brown St, are the **City Museum** (to left,
lower down) and the **Walker Art Gallery** (to right,
higher up).

The **City Museum,** which was damaged during the
last war but has since been rebuilt and enlarged,
contains varied collections (open 10 to 5, Sundays
2 to 5).

Basement: aquarium, vivarium, transport museum (locomotive of 1838, the "Lion").

Ground floor: history of the town and port (ship models).
Mayer Collection (archaeology, mediaeval French ivories, Saxon
jewellery, manuscripts, Byzantine, Etruscan and Roman art,
English porcelain, etc.).

First floor: history of navigation.

Third floor: planetarium; collection of clocks and watches.

The **Walker Art Gallery,** named after the Lord
Mayor of Liverpool who gave the money for its
construction in 1873, has the finest collection of
pictures in England outside London. Open 10 to 5,
Sundays 2 to 5.

All schools are represented, from the 14th to the end of
the a 19th century. Italian masters and Flemish primitives;
Bellini ("Portrait of a Young Man"), *Giordano* ("Adoration
of the Magi"); 17th century Dutch masters, including a self-
portrait by *Rembrandt*; Flemish artists *(Rubens)* and Spanish
(Murillo). English painting is represented by a "Henry VIII"
belonging to the school of Holbein, a portrait of Elizabeth I
by *Nicholas Hilliard* and works by *Hogarth, Reynolds, Wilson,
Stubbs* (born in Liverpool), *Turner, Millais* and other Pre-
Raphaelites (the Liverpool School). A few French Impressionists
(Degas). Sculpture by *Renoir, Rodin, Epstein*.

Between the Museum and the Art Gallery is the **Picton Reading Room** (1879), and adjoining this the **Brown Library** (established by William Brown, an American merchant in Liverpool).

Beyond the Walker Art Gallery is *County Sessions House* (1884).

To the east of St John's Gardens is the very busy *Lime Street Station*.

The other main sights of Liverpool lie east, south and west of the centre. To the east are the University and the Roman Catholic Cathedral; to the south is the gigantic Protestant Cathedral; to the west are the Town Hall and the docks.

1. East of the centre. On the north side of Brownlow Hill, a wide street running east and west, is the **University**; on the south side is the Roman Catholic **Cathedral of Christ the King.**

The **University,** founded in 1881, has five faculties and some 9000 students. The original building dates from the end of the 19th century, but many new buildings have been erected since the end of the last war.

The **Cathedral of Christ the King** was begun in 1933 and completed in 1957, after an interruption during the war. The architect responsible for its completion was Frederick Gibberd. It is a strikingly original building, circular in plan, with a huge *dome* 320 feet high borne on reinforced concrete buttresses. It can accommodate a congregation of 2250. Fine *crypt*, with tombs of archbishops.

2. South of the centre. The Anglican **Liverpool Cathedral,** reached by way of Rodney St and St James Road, is in a very different architectural style.

Designed by Sir Giles Gilbert Scott, the Cathedral is in a 20th century interpretation of Gothic. The foundation stone was laid in 1904, and in 1924 the choir and east transept were consecrated in presence of King George V. The building was damaged during the last war, but work was resumed in 1948 and carried on under Sir Giles Gilbert Scott's direction until his death in 1960, still using the same red sandstone from quarries at Woolton, near the city. The dimensions of the Cathedral are impressive: length 610 feet, width 280 feet, tower 330 feet high, vaulting 175 feet high. Fine glass ("Te Deum" in east window). Organ with 9704 pipes.

3. West of the centre. Dale St runs down from the city centre towards the docks. To the left are the *Municipal Buildings* (1866) and behind them the General Post Office. Farther down, on the right, is the **Town Hall.**

This is a handsome neo-classical building (1754), designed by John Wood of Bath, on the site of an earlier building dating from 1515. It was damaged by fire in 1795 and restored by J. Wyatt in the early 19th century. Fine reception rooms.

To the south of the Town Hall, at the end of Castle St, is *Derby Square*, with a large monument to Queen Victoria in the centre.

Water St continues the line of Dale St down to the *banks of the Mersey* (**Pierhead**).

To the north (on right) is *St Nicholas's Church* (14th c., restored).

Straight ahead, from right to left, are the *Royal Liver Building* (1910), with two towers 295 feet high; the former Cunard Building (1916: a copy of the Farnese Palace in Rome), now the *Custom House;* and the *Dock Board Offices* (1907).

To north and south extend the **Docks.**

The Docks stretch for 7 miles along the Mersey. The first dock was constructed in 1715 near the present Canning Place, to the south of Pierhead. The present docks, from north to south, are the *Gladstone Docks*, the largest, with a lock over 1000 feet long (trade with America, Asia and Oceania); the *Container Terminal;* the *Alexandra Docks* (with cold stores); the *Langton* and *Canada Docks*, recently modernised; the

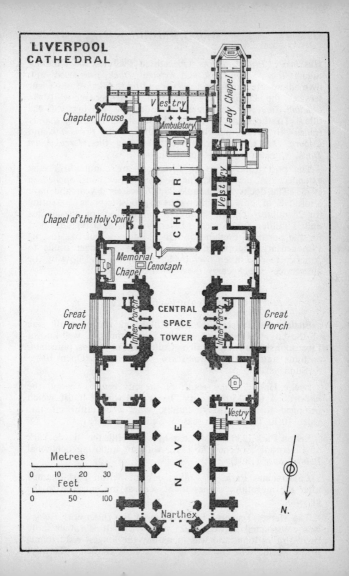

LIVERPOOL CATHEDRAL

Chapter House

Vestry

Ambulatory

Lady Chapel

CHOIR

Vestry

Chapel of the Holy Spirit

Memorial Chapel

Cenotaph

Great Porch

Inner Porch

CENTRAL SPACE TOWER

Inner Porch

Great Porch

Vestry

NAVE

Metres

0   10   20   30

Feet

0   50   100

Narthex

N.

Huskinsson Branch Docks (specialised facilities for handling sugar); the *Nelson Dock* and *Princess Dock*, now used only by medium-sized and small vessels and by the Belfast passenger service; the *Victoria Dock* (Dublin passenger service); the *Landing Stage* for passengers, 1/2 mile long, moving with the tide. To the south of Pierhead are docks handling mainly trade with Africa and the West Indies — the *Brunswick* and *Coburg Docks*, with grain elevators, and the *Herculaneum Dock*, with facilities for handling oil.

The port installations of Liverpool are continually being extended. A new dock, the *Seaforth Dock*, was opened in 1973. The docks now handle 27,000 vessels a year and have a turnover of some 30 million tons of goods, imports accounting for 25 million tons (including 18 million tons of oil) against only 5 million for exports. Liverpool acts as a regional port for the north of England and the Midlands, but has lost its 19th century importance as a centre of passenger traffic to America (a role taken over by Southampton, and now by the air services which carry most of the traffic).

Other Features of Interest

Sudley Art Gallery, Mossley Hill Road, on the south side of the city. Bequeathed by the Holt family, a well-known Liverpool ship-owning family. Collections of ivories, porcelain, costume and pictures *(Gainsborough, Turner)*. Open 10 to 5, Sundays 2 to 5.

Speke Hall, 7 miles south of the city centre, beyond the airport. A fine 15th century "black and white" house which belonged to the Norreys family, with a beautiful interior. Open 10 to 7 during the season, Sundays 2 to 7.

Sefton Park (230 acres), near Mossley Hill, the "Hyde Park of Liverpool", opened in 1872, with an imposing octagonal *Palm House* (1894).

Calderstones Park, 1 1/2 miles east of Sefton Park, named after the megalithic stones to be seen at the entrance to the glasshouses.

The Mersey Tunnels. The first tunnel, the *Queensway Tunnel*, was constructed between 1925 and 1934. It is rather more than 2 miles long, and was in its day the longest road tunnel in the world. The entrance is in St John's Gardens. To meet the needs of the increasing traffic a second tunnel, the *Kingsway Tunnel*, was built between 1966 and 1971; it connects Liverpool (entrance at north end of Cazneau St) with Wallasey, and was doubled in size in 1974.

Surroundings of Liverpool

Liverpool to Southport: 20 miles.

3 miles: *Bootle* (pop. 71,000, E.C. Wednesday), a modern industrial town, densely populated, adjoining Liverpool on the north; docks. Connected with Liverpool by elevated electric railway. — 13 miles: *Formby* (pop. 10,000, E.C. Wednesday). The old parish church (St Luke's) has a 12th century font. — 20 miles: **Southport** (pop. 80,000, E.C. Tuesday), an attractive holiday resort with parks and gardens; one of England's best known golfing centres. *Lord Street*, the fine main street, runs parallel to the promenade for a mile.

Liverpool to Preston: 31 miles on A 59.

5 miles: *Aintree*. — 12 miles: **Ormskirk** (pop. 22,000, E.C. Wednesday), a prosperous market town. The *church*, with a massive tower and spire, contains interesting 12th century monuments (Earls of Derby). In the neighbourhood is the fine mansion of Scarisbrick Hall. — 14 miles: *Burscough*, with the ruins of a priory. — 17 miles: **Rufford.** At the north end of the village is *Rufford Old Hall*, a Tudor building of timber and plaster, with wings added in 1662 and 1821. The great hall has fine beams. In one of the wings is a local museum (open weekdays and public holidays 10 a.m. to dusk, Sundays 1 p.m. to dusk). — 31 miles: **Preston** (p. 825).

Liverpool to Warrington: 18 miles on A 562.

8 miles: 1 mile off the road, **Speke Hall** (p. 812). — 12 miles: *Widnes*, with important chemical plants. — 18 miles: **Warrington** (pop. 75,000, E.C. Thursday), an important industrial town on the Mersey. The Manchester Ship Canal passes through the town. *Church* (14th-15th c., restored) in Decorated style. Old houses in Church St. Museum and art gallery.

Liverpool to Bolton: 30 miles on A 58.

8 miles: *Prescot*. — 11 miles: *St Helens* (pop. 108,000, E.C. Thursday), in a coal-mining area, noted mainly as a leading centre of the glass industry. Glass Museum. Also factories producing chemicals and pharmaceuticals. Just west of the

town is the charming old village of *Eccleston*. 4 miles north
is *Billinge*, with a parish church of 1718. — 16 miles: *Ashton
in Makerfield*. —21 miles: *Hindley*. — 30 miles: **Bolton**.

Liverpool to Manchester: 35 miles on A 580. New motorway
(M 62).

Liverpool to Chester

Leave Liverpool by the Mersey Tunnel.

2 miles: **Birkenhead** (pop. 145,000, E.C. Thursday),
a modern seaport on the Mersey, connected with
Liverpool by the Mersey Tunnel, the railway tunnel
and a ferry service. Many shipyards and flour-mills.

In the handsome and spacious Hamilton Square is the *Town
Hall* (1877), with the Public Library and the **Williamson Art
Gallery and Museum** (porcelain, pictures by English artists of
the 18th, 19th and 20th c.). In Church St are the ruins of *Birkenhead Priory*, founded in 1152, dissolved at the Reformation
and destroyed during the Civil War; the crypt survives.

North of Birkenhead is **Wallasey** (pop. 105,000), part of the
same conurbation, also an important shipbuilding town, connected with Liverpool by the new *Kingsway Tunnel* (p. 813).

At the north end of the peninsula is **New Brighton,** a seaside
resort popular with the people of Liverpool. To the west are
other resorts — *Hoylake*, *West Kirby*, etc.

From Birkenhead A 41 runs south through a
heavily industrialised and urbanised area. It passes
through *Bebington* and *Port Sunlight* (chemicals,
soaps and detergents) and to the west of *Ellesmere*
(oil refinery), and comes to **Chester,** 18 miles from
Liverpool.

CHESTER

Chester (pop. 60,000, E.C. Wednesday), county
town of *Cheshire*, on the river Dee, is one of the most
picturesque old towns in England.

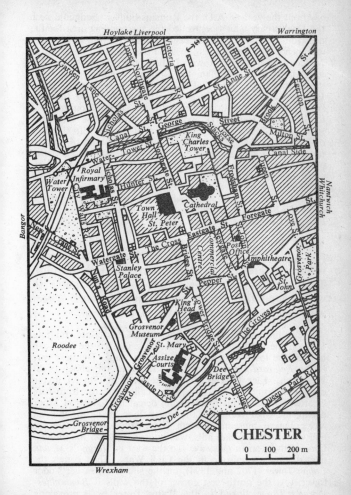

Hoylake Liverpool — Warrington

Victoria

St. Anne St.

St. George Street

King Charles Tower

Canal Side

Royal Infirmary

Water Tower

Bangor

Cathedral

Town Hall
St. Peter

Foregate

The Cross

Eastgate

Post Office

Amphitheatre

Watergate

Stanley Palace

Pepper

St. John

King Head

The Groves

Grosvenor Museum

Roodee

St. Mary
Assize Courts

Dee Bridge

Grosvenor Rd.

Castle Dr.

Dee

Grosvenor Bridge

Queen's Park Rd.

Wrexham

Nantwich Whitchurch

CHESTER

0   100   200 m

About the year 68 A.D. the Romans built a stronghold near the Dee estuary which controlled the surrounding area for the next four centuries. At the beginning of the 10th century the imminence of Danish invasion led Ethelred and Ethelfreda of Mercia to re-fortify the town. It did not surrender to the Normans until 1072. William the Conqueror attached so much importance to the town that he granted it to his nephew Hugh Lupus as a county palatine, with royal powers and the task subduing the neighbouring Welsh. In 1237 the earldom reverted to the crown (Henry III), and since then the eldest son of the sovereign is Prince of Wales and Earl of Chester. In the time of Richard II (1377-99) the town enjoyed its period of greatest prosperity, in spite of the ravages of plague and fire and frequent Welsh raids. In the 15th century, however, the river silted up. During the Civil War the town was besieged by Parliamentary forces for two years (1644-46) and was finally reduced by starvation, after which the townspeople suffered great hardship and destitution. In 1541, during the reign of Henry VIII, Chester became the see of a bishop.

The **town walls** have a circuit of 2 miles. The present walls, which follow the line of the Roman walls on three sides, date from the 14th century. They are built of red sandstone. It is possible to walk round them on a paved footway some 6 feet wide which affords fine views of the town.

The main entrance to the town is the **East Gate,** built in 1769 on the position of the mediaeval gate. To the right can be seen the lower courses of the Roman wall. The next gate is the *Kaleyard Gate*, once the entrance to the abbey of St Werburgh. **King Charles's Tower** (restored in 17th c.), at the north-east corner of the walls, is so called because from here Charles I watched his forces being defeated at Rowton Moor during the Civil War. On the upper floor of the tower is an archæological museum. **North Gate,** from which there are fine views of the Welsh hills, was built in 1808 on the foundations of the Roman gateway. To the west is *Morgan's Mount,* named after an episode in the Civil War. Then comes the *Goblin Tower* (1702 and 1894), on the site of an earlier Tudor tower. At the north-west corner of the walls is *Bonewaldes-thorne's Tower*, linked to the **Water Tower** by a projecting wall.

To the south is the **Water Gate** (rebuilt in 1788 50 yards south of its previous position), formerly the main entrance to the harbour. Outside the walls is the *Roodee* racecourse. Next comes the *Bridge Gate* (1782), near the old bridge over the Dee. In the stretch of walls running north from here (fine views) are the *Recorder's Steps* (1700) and the *Wishing Steps* (1785). In Park St are nine old half-timbered almshouses. The next gate, the **New Gate,** is modern, built to replace the old *Wolf Gate*, which was too narrow for modern traffic. Near here can be seen remains of the Roman wall (1st c.). To the north is the *Wolf Gate* or *Thimbleby's Tower*. To the east of the New Gate are the excavated remains of the largest **Roman amphitheatre** in Britain (314 ft by 286 ft). A short distance farther east is **St John's Church,** on the site of an earlier church built by Peter, the first Norman bishop in Mercia, who incorporated in his church the remains of an even earlier foundation of 689. When the episcopal see was transferred to Lichfield St John's became a collegiate church. All that remains standing is the nave and transept crossing (12th c.): note the triforium and the Gothic clerestory. To the east are the ruins of the *choir* (12th c., rebuilt in 14th c.). Near the church is a *Hermitage* (16th-17th c., incorporating some mediæval work).

The street layout of the old town still shows the regular Roman pattern, with the *cardo* and *decumanus* intersecting at right angles (with a slight offset). The **Rows** — Chester's most distinctive feature — are picturesque old streets, dating from the Middle Ages and the 16th century, with wooden galleries running along at first floor level.

The central intersection in the heart of the old town is known as the **Cross.** The stone cross which formerly stood here is now in the Grosvenor Museum. On the north side of the intersection is *St Peter's Church*.

Eastgate Street, with the Grosvenor Hotel on the south side, runs through the East Gate and is continued by *Foregate Street* (A 51), in which there are a number of old houses; No. 70 dates from 1645.

Watergate Street runs west from the Cross, with many old houses.

No. 11 has a fine crypt dating from 1180. Beyond this is **God's Providence House** (1652, restored 1862). At No. 17 is the 16th century *Leche House* (enlarged in 17th c.). At No. 36 is the base of a Roman column. At No. 47 is **Bishop Lloyd's House** (early 17th c.), with a richly carved exterior and the original panelling and mouldings in the interior.

On the right, at the corner of Weaver St, is *Trinity Church* (rebuilt in 19th c.).

Beyond this, on the left, is **Stanley Palace**, built in 1591, with later additions (open Monday-Friday 10 to 5).

The whole of the west side of *Nicholas Street*, which runs south from Watergate St, dates from the late 18th century.

Northgate Street runs north from the Cross into a square, on the left-hand side of which is the *Town Hall* (1869).

On the opposite side of the square are *Folliott House* (1778) and the *Pied Bull Hotel*, on a site which has been occupied by an inn since 1471; the present front is 18th century, but there are fine examples of 16th and 17th century work in the interior.

In St Werburgh's St is the old *Theatre Royal* (1773), now a cinema, in which Dickens gave readings from his works in 1867.

The *Abbey Gateway* (1377) gives access to the Cathedral close.

The **Cathedral,** built of red sandstone, is in various styles from Norman to Perpendicular. A Benedictine monastery was founded here in 1093 on the site of an earlier Saxon church. At the Reformation the abbey church became a cathedral. Although much altered by later building, its plan is still that of a monastery built round its cloisters. It is 350 feet long, 75 feet wide, 200 feet across the transept and

CHESTER CATHEDRAL

78 feet high, with a tower 125 feet high. The Benedictine abbey was not completed until the 14th century, and the church itself was rebuilt in Gothic
style in the early 13th century. The Early English
Lady Chapel and Chapter House date from the
13th century, but the choir is in early Decorated
style, with geometrical tracery. The uncompleted
central tower, the west front, the upper parts of
the nave and the south transept date from the 15th
century and are in the late Perpendicular style. Entrance is by the south doorway.

Interior. The late Perpendicular west end of the nave is
raised, and from here can be obtained a splendid view of the
warm-coloured interior. The east bays of the nave, the south
aisle and the south transept are Decorated. Norman work
can be found in the north aisle wall and at the west end. At
the other end of the north aisle is a Norman doorway leading
to the cloisters. Notice in the second bay from the east in the
north clerestory the quaint carving of the "Chester imp."
The oak fan vaulting is modern (Sir George Gilbert Scott).
Within the tower at the west end of the south aisle is the *Consistory Court*, with Jacobean stone and wood carving.

In the *Children's Corner* are some 12th century arches and
a 6th century marble font. There is fine Norman work in the
north transept. The windows and roof are Perpendicular.
The *south transept* is four times the size of the north, and equal
in size to the choir. The reason for this was that the monks
who wished to enlarge the church could, on account of the
monastic buildings to the north, build only to the south. The
south transept was built in the 14th and 15th centuries. Fine
stalls in the choir.

The Early English *Chapter House* (entered from the north
transept or from the cloisters) contains very fine carving and
gracefully moulded pillars with varied capitals. In it is housed
the *Library*, with early manuscripts and printed books and an
ancient ironwork cupboard.

At the east end of the church is the Early English *Lady Chapel*
(restored).

Cloisters and **Refectory.** As noted above, lack of space influenced the plan of the cathedral; and for the same reason the monastic buildings were sited on the north side of the church rather than the more normal south side. The Perpendicular cloisters have double arcades (Norman work) on the south side, and also some on the west side.

The entrance to the *Monks' Dorter* is at the north-east corner of the cloisters. On the south side of the cloisters are monuments to the early abbots. To the west is the 12th century *Norman undercroft*, with groined vaulting and squat pillars. On the north side is the Early English *Refectory*, with a fine lector's pulpit in the wall.

Bridge Street, running south from the Cross, is lined with very picturesque old houses, now fronted by shops. On the east side of the street, extending to Eastgate St, is a modern shopping area, constructed without interfering with the old house fronts.

No. 12 has a 13th century crypt. At No. 39 are remains of Roman baths. Farther along are the *Falcon Café* (1626, on 15th c. foundations) and *Ye Olde King's Head* (1621). Near the bridge is the 17th century *Bear and Billet Inn*, with fine windows.

Grosvenor St goes off on the right to the **Grosvenor Museum** (open 10 to 5), with Roman remains, local bygones and coins.

At the far end of Grosvenor St is the **Castle.**

Chester Castle was originally built in timber in 1069, but in the time of Henry III (1216-72) was rebuilt with stone walls and towers. The present buildings, including the entrance and the assize courts, date from 1789. The *Agricola Tower* is 13th century; on the first floor is a chapel, and on the ground and second floors the *museum* of the Cheshire Regiment.

To the east of the Castle is the little church of *St Mary on the Hill* (14th-16th c.).

Surroundings of Chester

Cheshire, although extending into the industrial suburbs of Manchester and Liverpool, also contains much attractive rural scenery, with quiet villages and fine timber and plaster houses with checkerboard fronts. The Dee, rising in the distant Welsh mountains, winds its way down through the flat plains to Chester.

At **Upton,** 2 miles north, is a *Zoo* (open daily 10 a.m. to dusk), noted for its lions. — 4 miles south is **Eaton Hall,** a seat of the Duke of Westminster; it can be reached by boat on the Dee or by road. — 6 miles west is **Hawarden Castle,** the home of Mr Gladstone (d. 1898), with the ruins of an old castle in the park. In Hawarden church are monuments and relics of Gladstone. Beside it is *St Deiniol's Library* (1902), devoted to Gladstone. 2 miles north-west of Hawarden are the ruins of *Ewloe Castle*.

Chester to Nantwich: 20 miles on A 51.

A 51 leaves Chester by Foregate St and the Bars and follows the line of the Roman *Watling Street*. At *Tarvin* (5 miles) A 54 goes off on the left, continuing along Watling Street: A 51 bears right. — 10 miles: *Tarporley*. 1 mile south is *Beeston Castle*, on a precipitous crag commanding wide views (13th c.), dismantled after the Civil War). — 20 miles: **Nantwich** (pop. 11,000, E.C. Wednesday), a centre of the Cheshire salt industry, with medicinal brine baths. Perpendicular church of red sandstone with an octagonal tower; carved choir-stalls. "Black and white" half-timbered houses.

Chester to Shrewsbury: 41 miles (A 41, then A 49).

20 miles: *Whitchurch* (pop. 7200), an important railway junction. St Alkmund's Church (1713), with the tomb of John Talbot (16th c.).

4 miles north-east is *Combermere Abbey*, a fine country house in a beautiful park.

48. MANCHESTER TO BLACKPOOL

48 miles: A 6, or by motorway (M 6) as far as Preston.

A 6 leaves Manchester by Chapel St.

3 miles: *Irlams o' th' Height*. A 666 goes off on the right to (8 miles) **Bolton** (pop. 160,000, E.C. Wednesday): spinning, manufacture of clothing, cotton goods. The *Old Man and Scythe* is an old inn. The *Grammar School* (founded 1641) still has its library of chained books. In Nelson Square is a statue of Samuel Crompton (1763-1827), inventor of the spinning mule. (The invention was made at *Hall i' th' Wood*, 2 miles away). In Victoria Square, in the town centre, is a *Museum and Art Gallery* (local history).

In the north-east of the town, in Tonge Moor Road (A 676), is a *Textile Machinery Museum*. At *Hall i' th' Wood* (see above), on the same road, is a museum of local bygones, in a house dating from the 16th and 17th centuries. 2 miles north-west is **Smithills Hall** (mainly 14th c.). 5 miles north on B 6391 is **Turton Tower,** a 16th century mansion with a mediaeval tower (small museum). 6 miles east on A 58 is **Bury** (see below).

Bolton to Bradford

6 miles: **Bury** (pop. 63,000, E.C. Tuesday). The humid atmosphere and heavy rainfall have promoted the development of cotton spinning in this area. The town is surrounded by high moorland, rising to 1500 feet in the Holcombe, Scout and Knowl Hills (5 miles away). The invention of the flying shuttle by John Kay of Bury and of the drop box loom by his son Robert did much to enable the cotton industry to supplant the older woollen industry. The **Art Gallery** at the corner of Manchester Road and Moss St has paintings and water-colours by English artists of the 19th century, including *Turner, David Cox, Constable* and *Landseer*. The associated *Museum* contains material illustrating the history of the town and its

industrial activities. There is easy access from the town to
the surrounding moorland. *Holcombe Hill* is a noted beauty
spot, with a tower commemorating Sir Robert Peel (1788-
1850). The *Grant Tower* was built by the Grant brothers, the
models for the Cheeryble brothers in Dickens's "Nicholas
Nickleby"; they lived in *Ramsbottom*, another spinning town
5 miles north of Bury.

12 miles: **Rochdale** (pop. 95,000, E.C. Tuesday), an important
spinning town on the river Roch. Public Library and *Art
Gallery*, with works by Augustus John, Sir Gerald Kelly and
J. Wilson Steer. On the ground floor is the *Museum* (mementoes of John Bright, flints from Rochdale Moor, natural history).
Rochdale is famous as the place of origin of the cooperative
movement: the original shop in *Toad Lane* (opened 1844) has
been restored to its original form. John Bright is buried in
the Friends' Meeting House graveyard.

A 58 bypasses Rochdale and continues to *Littleborough*.
— 17 miles: *Blackstone Edge*, with a fine stretch of **Roman
road**. The modern road, like the Roman one, climbs up and
over great open moors. — 23 miles: *Ripponden*. — 26 miles:
Sowerby Bridge. — 29 miles: **Halifax** (pop. 95,000, E.C. Thursday), a woollen town situated at an average height of 800 feet
above sea level, above the valleys of the Hebble and the Calder.
The town's importance in the woollen trade dates back to
Norman times. In the part of the main street known as *Wool
Shops* are the old warehouses of the woollen merchants. Fine
Town Hall (1863), with a tower 180 feet high. The Perpendicular
parish church, the third on the site, dates from about 1450:
Rokeby Chapel.

Daniel Defoe wrote part of "Robinson Crusoe" in the Rose
and Crown Inn, and there are descriptions of Halifax in his
works. Near the People's Park is the Public Library and *Museum* (natural history). In Ackroyd Park is the *Bankfield Museum
and Art Gallery:* art, ethnography, textiles, old weaving looms,
works on textiles, Balkan needlework; Halifax Room; exhibitions of contemporary art. *Shibden Hall*, a fine 15th century
house in Shibden Park, contains a Folk Museum (old agricultural implements); period furniture. *Wainhouse Tower*
(1871), a stone chimney 270 feet high (fine views), originally
built for a dyeworks. — 4 miles south-east is *Brighouse* (pop.
30,000, E.C. Tuesday), in the Calder valley, in the centre of
one of the most highly industrialised parts of the country.

37 miles: **Bradford** (pop. 300,000, E.C. Wednesday), the centre of the Yorkshire woollen trade, specialising in worsteds; also cotton goods, carpets and engineering. **St Peter's Cathedral** (Perpendicular) has a fine oak roof. To the north-west, in Lister Park, is the Cartwright Memorial Hall, with an *Art Gallery and Museum* (natural history and archaeology, painting and sculpture). 1 mile south is *Bolling Hall*, a fine old manor-house (14th and 17th c.), now a museum of the textile industry. 4 miles north is *Thornton*, birthplace of the Brontë sisters.

A 6, bypassing *Bolton* (p. 823), continues north-west to (22 miles) *Chorley* (pop. 33,000, E.C. Wednesday), another cotton-spinning town. To the north-east is the fine Elizabethan mansion (restored 1666) of *Astley Hall* (open 2 to 8). — 31 miles: **Preston** (pop. 110,000, E.C. Thursday), a Lancashire cotton which also has engineering and other industries. *Town Hall* designed by Sir George Gilbert Scott. *Harris Museum.*

Preston has seen much fighting between the English and the Scots. During the Civil War the Parliamentary army defeated the Royalists near the town, and Cromwell defeated a Scottish army led by the Duke of Hamilton. The cotton manufacturer and inventor Richard Arkwright was born in Preston in 1732.

5 miles south-east is **Hoghton Tower,** home of the Hoghton family since it was built in 1565, a magnificent example of a 16th century fortified manor-house. State apartments with fine panelling; famous *banqueting hall*; period furniture and portraits. From *Hoghton Hill* (600 ft) there are fine views of the river Darwen. — 7 miles north-east is **Ribchester,** site of the Roman station of *Bremetennacum*, built about 80 A.D. (museum).

Preston to Skipton: 36 miles on A 59.

6 miles: A 677 goes off on the right to (4 miles) **Blackburn** (pop. 103,000, E.C. Thursday), one of the most important textile centres in the world. *Lewis Textile Museum* (open 10 to 5). The *Cathedral* occupies the site of a church founded in

569 (rebuilt in the 19th c.); old glass. 11 miles east is **Burnley** (pop. 79,000, E.C. Tuesday), a grimly industrial town, though situated in beautiful countryside. The fine mediaeval mansion of *Towneley Hall* contains an art gallery. The town has associations with Sir Walter Scott, and there are a Scott Memorial and a Scott Park. Remains of stocks and old crosses.

13 miles: *Whalley* (pop. 1000, E.C. Wednesday), a picturesque village with the ruins of a *Cistercian abbey* of 1296. The *parish church* (13th c., Early English) has stalls (1430) from the abbey church, with misericords bearing inscriptions in Latin, French and English. In the churchyard are three Saxon crosses (10th c.). 5 miles north-west is *Stonyhurst*, a fine country house which has been a Jesuit college since 1794.

17 miles: *Clitheroe* (pop. 11,000, E.C. Wednesday), a very ancient town with the keep of an old *castle* (1150), the smallest in England. To the north is the hilly region of the Forest of Bowland. — 36 miles: **Skipton** (p. 787).

39 miles: *Kirkham*. — 48 miles: **Blackpool** (pop. 150,000, E.C. Wednesday), Britain's largest holiday resort, situated on the Irish Sea, east of the Fylde, the farming district between the Ribble and the Lune. The world-famous *Blackpool Tower*, on the model of the Eiffel Tower, is 500 feet high; the *Tower Circus* contains a dance hall, a menagerie and an aquarium. Other attractions are the *Winter Gardens*, the *Empress Ballroom*, the *Baronial Hall* and the *Spanish Hall*.

The coast road (A 584) runs south to **Lytham St Annes** (pop. 36,000, E.C. Wednesday), a seaside resort on the Ribble estuary, incorporating Lytham, Ansdell, Fairhaven and St Annes. Beach 7 miles long; golf courses.

8 miles north is **Fleetwood** (pop. 29,000, E.C. Wednesday), a fishing port on a peninsula in Morecambe Bay, with the Irish Sea on one side and the river Wyre on the other. Magnificent view of the Lake District hills on the far side of the bay. Fleetwood is the most important fishing port on the west coast.

On the east bank of the Wyre (ferry service) is *Knott-on-Sea*, another seaside resort.

49. THE WEST COAST ROUTE TO SCOTLAND

There is a fast route by motorway (M 6), through beautiful scenery. In this section we describe the route on A 6 (119 miles).

31 miles: **Preston** (p. 825). — 41 miles: *Garstang*. — 52 miles: **Lancaster** (pop. 48,000, E.C. Wednesday), county town of Lancashire, at the head of the Lune estuary. On the other side of Morecambe Bay are the hills of the Furness peninsula, to the north are the Cumbrian hills, to the east the moors rising to Burn Moor and the Forest of Bowland. Lancaster is an industrial town (linoleum).

Reached by cobbled streets and paths, the **Castle** on its hilltop dominates the town. The base of *Hadrian's Tower* is partly Roman, but the present castle was begun in 1094 by Roger de Toictou.

The *Lungess Tower* contains some Norman work, but the present castle dates almost entirely from the Tudor period. John of Gaunt, father of Henry V, built the magnificent *Gateway Tower* (9 ft thick); the *gatehouse* served for many years as a prison. The **Shire Hall** houses the assize courts; here can be seen a "holdfast" (used to secure prisoners while they were branded).

St Mary's Church, on the north side of Castle Hill, is another prominent landmark. The present building is mainly Perpendicular (15th c.); the tower is 18th century. The canopied *choir-stalls* (1340) are among the finest examples of carved woodwork of their kind in the country.

In Meeting House Lane is a Quaker meeting house established in 1690. In King St is *Penny's Hospital* (1720). In the *Old Town Hall* (1783) in Market Square is the **Municipal Museum** (open 10 to 5): local history since the Stone Age. Williamson Park is on top of

a hill; magnificent views from the Palm House, the
Observatory and the *Ashton Memorial*, a large domed
building which contains natural history collections.

4 miles west is **Morecambe** (pop. 40,000, E.C. Wednesday),
a very popular seaside resort with magnificent views of Morecambe Bay. Adjoining Morecambe is **Heysham,** from which
there are steamer services to the Isle of Man and Ireland. On
a rocky headland are the ruins of *St Patrick's Chapel* (5th c.),
with some remarkable stone coffins.

Lancaster to Sedbergh: 27 miles on A 683.

From Lancaster A 683 follows the beautiful Lune valley
to (3 miles) *Halton* (ancient cross), through some of the most
attractive scenery in the country. — 4 miles: *Caton*, at the
Crook of the Lune, a wide bend in wooded country. — 7 miles:
Claughton, where the Wenning flows into the Lune. The church
has an old bell (1296). — 9 miles: *Hornby*, with the ruins of
a 16th century keep and *Castlestede*. — 13 miles: *Tunstall*,
where Charlotte Brontë attended the church (described in
"Jane Eyre"). Nearby is *Thurland Castle*, which was captured
and gutted by Parliamentary forces during the Civil War.
— 17 miles: the road bypasses **Kirkby Lonsdale** (pop. 1400,
E.C. Wednesday), an ancient market town with picturesque
old streets. *St Mary's Church* is very fine; it has some Norman
pillars (1100) with lozenge ornament like that found in Durham
Cathedral, and the tower contains some 12th century work.
To the south of the town is the *Devil's Bridge* (16th c.), with
fine ribbed arches. — 18 miles: *Casterton*, on the Roman
road to Carlisle. On the nearby fells is an ancient stone circle.
— 27 miles: **Sedbergh** (p. 829). To the south-east is Langth-
waite Bridge; to the east are Littledale, Cator Moor and the
beautiful Roeburn valley (no access for cars). Many of the
hill farms were originally manor-houses; they are mostly stone-
built.

59 miles: *Carnforth* (pop. 3500, E.C. Thursday), a
railway junction. — 61 miles: to the west, the little
village of *Warton*, where the Washington family lived
for 300 years. — 66 miles: *Milnethorpe* (pop. 1200,
E.C. Thursday). — 70 miles: *Levens Hall* (1590),

with beautiful gardens. — 72 miles: *Sizergh Castle* (beautiful interior; picture gallery).

74 miles: **Kendal** (pop. 19,000, E.C. Thursday), a picturesque market town, the gateway to the Lake District, known as the "auld grey town" from the colour of the local limestone of which it is built. In the 14th century Flemish weavers introduced the making of woollen cloth, the famous "Kendal green".

In Kirkland is *Holy Trinity Church* (13th c.), one of the largest parish churches in the country, with five aisles; interesting monuments and brasses. Little is left of the Norman castle in which Catherine Parr was born in 1512; fine view from the ruins.

In Wildman St is *Castle Dalry* (rebuilt 1564); oak beams with fine carvings and bosses. Near the parish church is the old *Grammar School* (founded 1525). George Romney, the artist, lived in Kendal for many years; he died in *Romney House* in 1802.

Abbot Hall (J. Carr, 1759) now houses a *local museum* (open 10.30 to 5.30, except Saturday and Sunday mornings), with china, furniture and paintings by Romney, Lawrence, Reynolds, Turner and others. Beside it is the *Lakes Museum* (local bygones).

Kendal to Leyburn: 42 miles on A 684.

11 miles: *Sedbergh* (pop. 2200, E.C. Thursday). Nearby is the beautiful waterfall of *Cautley Spout*. The road runs over the moors. — 26 miles: *Hawes*, a good centre for excursions. — 30 miles: **Bainbridge,** a centre for exploring *Wensleydale*, the largest of the Yorkshire dales. Remains of a Roman fort on *Brough Hill*; prehistoric tumulus on Addlebrough (1564 ft). To the south is *Semer Water*, a lake with an area of 100 acres. To the north is *Askrigg*, a good excursion centre. — 34 miles: **Aysgarth.** The church (rebuilt in the 19th c.) contains a screen from Jervaulx Abbey. ½ mile away is one of the most noted beauty spots in Wensleydale, *Aysgarth Force*, a waterfall on the river Ure. — 37 miles: *Swinithwaite*. To the north is *Redmire*, with Castle Bolton (14th c.), in which Mary Queen of Scots was imprisoned in 1568. — 42 miles: **Leyburn,** another good centre from which to explore Wensleydale.

There is a very attractive route from Kendal to Carlisle via Keswick. It is a little longer, but runs through the heart of the Lake District: see Route 50.

A 6 climbs from Kendal over Shap Fell to (90 miles) **Shap,** an old village in a valley almost 1000 feet above sea level, which grew up round the 12th century *abbey of St Mary Magdalene* (interesting ruins). *St Michael's Church* is partly Norman. At Shap Wells Hotel are sulphur springs. Splendid views.

101 miles: **Penrith** (pop. 10,000, E.C. Thursday), an old market town on the river Eamont, the northern gateway to the Lakes. Opposite the station are the ruins, in red stone, of *Penrith Castle*, built by Bishop Strickland and the future Richard III. In the square known as *Great Dockray* are old inns. *St Andrew's Church* (rebuilt in the 18th c.) occupies the site of an earlier 12th century church. Samuel Plimsoll, who devised the "Plimsoll line", lived in Page Hall, in Foster St.

West of the town is *Penrith Beacon*, with the Pike (1720 ft): magnificent views. 1 mile south-east are the ruins of *Brougham Castle* (1214), near which is the site of the Roman station of *Brovacum*. 5 miles south is *Lowther Castle* (1802). 3 miles south-west is *Dacre Castle*.

Penrith to Barnard Castle.

7 miles: *Temple Sowerby*. — 13 miles: **Appleby,** on the river Eden, attractively built of red stone and surrounded by beautiful scenery. *Castle* (1685). Historic *Moot Hall*. *St Michael's Church*, founded in Saxon times. — 21 miles: *Brough*, with a ruined castle. 5 miles south is *Kirkby Stephen*, with the ruins of *Hartley Castle* 1 mile away. — 34 miles: **Bowes,** site of the Roman fort of *Lavatrae*.

6 miles east on A 66 (which follows the line of a Roman road) is *Greta Bridge*, a favourite spot with artists. Local beauty spots are the "Meeting of the Waters" and Mortham Tower on the Tees.

To the south-west is **Richmond** (pop. 5600, E.C. Wednesday), a charming little town on the Swale, which flows down from the fells near the town, and a good centre for Swaledale. High over the river stands *Richmond Castle*, with its massive keep. In Market Place is *Holy Trinity Church*, with an unusual interior. *Tower* of the former monastery of the Grey Friars. 1 mile north is the fine mansion of *Aske Hall*. 1 mile south-east, down the Swale valley, is **Easby Abbey,** a Premonstratensian house (1152), notable particularly for the gatehouse, the chapter house and the refectory. Little is left of the abbey church. Easby parish church (Early English) has 12th century frescoes, a Norman font and a cross of 1300. 8 miles south-east on B 6271 is *Kiplin Hall*, built in 1616 by Lord Baltimore, founder of Maryland.

39 miles: **Barnard Castle** (pop. 5600, E.C. Thursday), an excellent centre for excursions in *Teesdale.*

The **Castle** from which the town takes its name dates from the 12th century and was built by Bernard Baliol, who also built the church (1129). The castle has a massive circular keep. In the round tower to the south is a window with Richard III's emblem, a boar. The great hall contains much 13th and 14th century work. The castle was the setting of Scott's poem "Rokeby". In Newgate are **Bowes Park** and **Bowes Museum,** in a‍ French Renaissance-style mansion (1892), with a magnificent collection of pictures and works of art from the earliest times to the 19th century (*El Greco*, "St Peter"; *Goya*, "Prison Scene"). Open 10 to 4 or 5.

Around Barnard Castle. To the west, on the banks of the Tees, is *Flatt's Wood*. 1 mile south-east is the *Abbey Bridge* (1773), near which are the ruins of **Egglestone Abbey,** a Premonstratensian house founded in 1190. 7 miles north-east is *Raby Castle* (1380), in a beautiful park.

Penrith to Alston

5 miles: *Langwathby*. The road crosses the Eden. 2 miles north are *"Long Meg and her Daughters"*, a group of 67 standing stones. The road runs over wild and lonely fells to (12 miles) *Hartside Height* (1900 ft). — 20 miles: *Alston* (pop. 2600, E.C. Tuesday), the highest market town in England, 960 feet above sea level on the slopes of the Pennines.

119 miles: **Carlisle** (pop. 72,000, E.C. Thursday), an ancient border town lying only 8 miles from

Scotland at the confluence of the Eden, the Caldew and the Petteril; county town of Cumbria. It is an important railway centre, the see of a bishop, with thriving industries (engineering, biscuit-making, manufacture of carpets).

Carlisle was the British *Caer Luel* and became the fortified Roman station of *Luguvallium*, near the west end of Hadrian's Wall. In Norman times a castle was built and the town became a strong point in the defence of the border. The bishopric was founded in 1133. The town was taken by the Young Pretender in 1745 but was later recaptured by Hanoverian forces.

From the *Market Place*, in which are the *Town Hall* (1709) and the 17th century *Market Cross*, Castle St leads to the **Cathedral,** one of the smallest in the country. It was originally the church of an Augustinian priory founded by William Rufus in the 12th century.

In the 13th century most of the Norman church was destroyed by fire. The Early English choir was burned down in 1292 and replaced in Decorated style in 1404. The central tower dates from 1408. In 1645 Scottish troops destroyed most of the nave. The whole building was restored in 1852. The most interesting features are the choir and the Decorated **east window**, with 14th century glass. The *stalls* (15th c.) have crude paintings on them. From the top of the tower there are fine views. Walter Scott was married in the nave in 1797. To the south is the refectory of the original priory. The Deanery has a square tower.

In Castle St is **Tullie House** (17th c.), with the Public Library and Museum (natural history, Roman material). At the end of Castle St is *Carlisle Castle*, now a barracks, which incorporates the Norman keep built by William Rufus. Fine views from the battle-

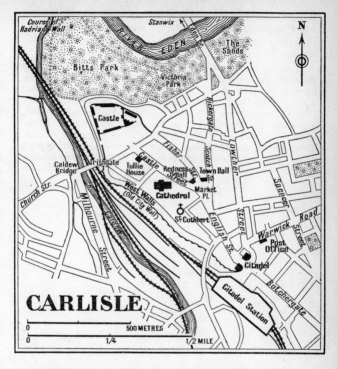

CARLISLE

ments. Mary Queen of Scots was imprisoned here in 1568. The dungeons can be visited.

Carlisle to Newcastle-upon-Tyne: 58 miles on A 69. The road runs parallel to Hadrian's Wall, a short distance to the south. See p. 759.

9 miles: **Brampton,** a picturesque old town with a Moot Hall, stocks and an old bull ring. In the modern church (1875) are windows by Burne-Jones. The parish church contains some Norman work. 3 miles north-east is *Naworth Castle,* seat of the Earl of Carlisle. To the north is the Augustinian priory of *Lanercost* (1169); the nave (restored), now the parish

church, has windows by Burne-Jones and interesting monuments. The Roman wall is ½ mile to the north.

18 miles: *Greenhead*. — 22 miles: *Haltwhistle*. — 31 miles: *Haydon Bridge*.

38 miles: **Hexham** (pop. 10,000, E.C. Thursday), an ancient town on the Tyne, see of a Roman Catholic bishop. A **monastery,** built by St Wilfred in the 7th century, was burned down by the Danes in the 9th century. The present building (1112) contains very little of the original Early English work, and dates almost entirely from the early 13th century. In the choir is the *"Frid Stool"*, brought back from Italy by St Wilfred. There are an old *Moot Hall* and a *Manor Office* dating from 1330. The Roman wall passes a short distance away (*Housesteads:* — 41 miles: *Corbridge* (p. 748). — 51 miles: *Heddon-on-the-Wall.* — 58 miles: **Newcastle-upon-Tyne** (p. 756).

50. THE LAKE DISTRICT

The Lake District is an area some 35 miles square in which hills and valleys, lakes and woods, rocks and rich green grass combine to produce scenery of incomparable beauty. Hills rising to 3000 feet, lakes miles in length, soft wooded valleys, wind-tossed clouds casting their shadows on the hills, white-washed cottages, grazing sheep, the ever changing light on the surface of the water, and above all the rich soft colouring: these are the delights of this loveliest part of England.

The area is rich in literary associations. Its chief figure is *William Wordsworth*, who, apart from visits by his friends Southey and Coleridge, lived almost a hermit's life among the hills. Among more recent literary figures who have lived in the Lake District are Hugh Walpole and Beatrix Potter, author of the world-famous children's books, who spent her whole life here.

The Lake District is easy to explore: the roads are good and there is no lack of excellent hotels. From most of the main centres — Grange-over-Sands, Kendal, Penrith, Keswick, Windermere, Ambleside, Appleby, Ulverston — there are organised coach trips. A variety of holiday pursuits are available. For those whose tastes incline towards strenuous climbing Pillar Rock, Great Gable, and parts of Scafell and the Langdale Pikes offer a test of skill for the most experienced. The highest peaks are *Scafell Pike* (3210 ft, highest peak in England); *Scafell* (3162 ft); *Helvellyn* (3118 ft) and *Skiddaw* (3054 ft). All the summits can be reached, however, by means of fine paths for mountain walkers. Other peaks are Saddleback, Saint Sunday Crag, Red Screes, Fairfield and Wansfell Pike. The lakes themselves (the largest are Windermere, Ullswater, Coniston and Derwentwater) provide boating, sailing, trips in steamers and motor launches, bathing.

Kendal (see Route 49), the "gateway to the Lake District", is a good departure point. 8 miles north-west of Kendal is **Windermere,** largest and most accessible of the lakes. The circuit of the lake can be made by steamer or motor boat. Its scenery is sylvan and less rugged than that of the others.

From *Windermere* the road south leads via Newby Bridge to the Furness district, a quiet countryside with small market towns, and thence north along the coast road to Carlisle. North of Windermere one road leads over Kirkstone Pass to *Ulls-*

water, perhaps the most beautiful of all the lakes, and so to **Penrith**, a quaint and busy old market town. Another road from Windermere leads north to *Ambleside*, a good centre for rock climbing, and then south to Coniston, Hawkshead, Coniston Water and the Furness district. Another road goes by Rydal Water to *Grasmere*, on which is the village where William Wordsworth and Thomas de Quincey, the "opium eater", lived. This road runs north past Thirlmere to *Keswick*, capital of the Lake District, close to *Derwentwater*, known as "Queen of the Lakes". Keswick also has its literary associations: for many years it was the home of Coleridge and of Southey; and for a short while Shelley, after his marriage to Harriet Westbrook, lived in Keswick. From here expeditions can be made to Crummock Water, thence through Buttermere Fells and over the Honister Pass to Rosthwaite, starting point for the ascent of Great Gable, and so through *Borrowdale*, judged by many as the most beautiful valley in the Lake District. The scenery in this area is as rugged and wild as any to be found in England.

8 miles from Kendal is **Windermere** (pop. 7000, E.C. Thursday), magnificently situated at the foot of Orrest Head, 400 feet above sea level and 300 feet above Lake Windermere. Magnificent views of the lake, the largest in England (10½ miles long, ranging in width between ¼ mile and 1¼ miles). On its wooded banks are many attractive houses. To the north rise the hills, at the south end of the lake is *Lakeside*, and just south of the town is *Bowness* (ferry across the lake).

At Bowness is *St Martin's Church* (1483), with good glass.

On *Belle Isle*, in the middle of the lake, is a neoclassical villa (1775).

Windermere to Penrith
via Kirkstone Pass and Ullswater

Leave Windermere on A 591 (signposted to Ambleside) and in 1 mile turn right into A 592 for (3 miles) *Troutbeck* (*Townend*, a yeoman's house of 1626). The road then climbs sharply on to a terrace above the Troutbeck valley, runs through beautiful wooded country and continues to climb to the **Kirkstone Pass** (7 miles), with magnificent wide views to the west over Windermere, Esthwaite Water, Coniston Water and many small circular tarns.

From the pass (1489 ft) we look down on a scene of unrivalled beauty. In the foreground is the small lake of *Brothers Water* (so called, according to the local tradition, because two brothers were drowned in the lake), and beyond are the upper reaches of *Ullswater* and the massive bulk of *Place Fell*.

12 miles: **Patterdale,** a village at the foot of Kirkstone Pass and at the head of Ullswater where Wordsworth lived for some time.

Ullswater is generally held to be the most beautiful of the lakes; it is 7½ miles long, ½ mile wide and over 200 feet deep in parts, in the shape of a giant S, with jutting headlands and rocky foothills. Much of the area is National Trust property.

The road now runs along the very brink of Ullswater for its whole length, passing on the left the foothills of Helvellyn and the romantic *Grisedale* valley, where, climbing between *Fairfield* and the *Dollywagon Pike* of the Helvellyn massif, is one of the finest footpaths in the Lake District, leading west to Grasmere.

13 miles: *Glenridding*, at the foot of Helvellyn. — 15 miles: *Aira Force*, a magnificent waterfall, 65 feet high, in a deep gorge, the scene of Wordsworth's "Somnambulist". Lyulph's Tower, a castellated shooting lodge on the side of the road, figures in the poem. Here also is the best approach to *Gowbarrow Park*

(750 acres, National Trust) of Wordsworth's "Daffodils". The road (left) skirts the park and crosses the
fells to Troutbeck and Keswick. — 20 miles: *Pooley
Bridge*, at the foot of Ullswater; magnificent views up
the lake to the hills round its upper reaches. —
28 miles: *Eamont Bridge*. — 30 miles: **Penrith** (p. 830).

Windermere to Grange-over-Sands

2 miles: *Bowness*. — 9 miles: *Newby Bridge* (pop.
200), with a graceful bridge opposite an old inn.
— 15 miles: *Lindale*. — 17 miles: **Grange-over-Sands**
(pop. 2700, E.C. Thursday), a seaside resort on the
north side of Morecambe Bay, in a beautiful setting
at the foot of the Lake District hills.

Castlehead, now a missionary college, was the home of
Wilkinson, who built the first iron boat, launched on the Winster. At Humphrey Head the last wolf in England was killed.
— 4 miles away is *Cark Hall* (1597), where George Fox, founder
of the Quakers, spent a night in 1663 on his way to Lancaster
prison. — 3 miles north-west is **Cartmel,** with a fine 12th century church. The church and the picturesque gatehouse (c. 1300)
are all that remains of an Augustinian priory. *St Anthony's
Church*, Cartmel Fell, is pre-Reformation. From *Hampsfell
Hospice* there are wide views of the hills and the coast.

Windermere to Barrow-in-Furness

9 miles: *Newby Bridge* (see above). — 17 miles:
Ulverston (pop. 10,300, E.C. Friday), a quaint old
market town with winding streets and an old church
(Norman doorway, Perpendicular tower). — 22 miles:
Dalton, an iron-mining village, birthplace of the artist
George Romney, who is buried here. — 24 miles:
Furness Abbey, ruins of a Cistercian house (12th c.)
built of red sandstone, one of the most beautiful in
the country. Of particular interest are the choir and

transept of the *abbey church*, the chapter house (Early English), the infirmary, the west tower and the Abbot's Chapel (with two 12th century effigies of Norman knights with flat helmets, the oldest of the kind in England). — 26 miles: **Barrow-in-Furness** (pop. 65,000, E.C. Thursday), a modern seaside resort, with the Vickers-Armstrong armament factory and shipyards, and other related industries. The docks can take the largest warships. A bridge leads to Vickerstown, on *Walney Island*.

Barrow-in-Furness to Carlisle

4 miles: *Dalton* (see above). — 15 miles: **Broughton-in-Furness,** a market town with a 14th century peel tower, near the beautiful *Duddon* valley (or *Dunnerdale*). In the valley are (12 miles away) the *Wrynose Pass* and *Hardknott Pass*, the *Three Shires Stone*, the *Grey Friar* (2530 ft), the *Carrs* (2550 ft), Cockley Beck and Dale Head. Near Birks Bridge and Thrang are Broadside and the Thrang farms (National Trust).

19 miles: A 5093 runs south to (3 miles) *Millom* (pop. 7000, E.C. Wednesday), an industrial town with the ruins of a 14th century castle destroyed during the Civil War. — 24 miles: *Whitbeck*, at the foot of Black Combe (1990 ft). — 27 miles: *Bootle*, an ancient little town. — 34 miles: **Ravenglass,** an old town looking out towards the Isle of Man, with *Walls Castle*, a well preserved Roman bath-house.

A miniature railway runs to Boot in *Eskdale* (iron and copper mines). Inland is Wastwater.

Wastwater, 3 miles long by ½ mile wide, is one of the deepest lakes, reaching in parts 250 feet in depth. It is situated amid wild and impressive scenery; at its head are the magnifi-

cent mountains of Scafell, Lingmell, Great Gable, Kirk Fell
and Yewbarrow. On one side the *Screes* rise precipitously
from the water's edge; great cliffs reaching 1980 feet at *Illgill
Head*, the highest point. There are fine woods on the south
side of the lake.

40 miles: *Gosforth*. In the churchyard is a cross
dating from the 7th century. 2 miles west is *Seascale*,
a small seaside resort. — 42 miles: **Calder Bridge,**
On the river Calder stand the ruins of a 12th century
Cistercian abbey. From here is a fine walk over the
moors to Ennerdale Bridge and *Ennerdale Water*.

Ennerdale. The lake is 2½ miles long. At the head of it
are some of the rockiest peaks in the district: *Great Gable*
(3000 feet) and *Pillar* hills. The river Liza flows through the
Upper Dale (youth hostel).

46 miles: *Egremont* (ruined castle). A good road
runs up the valley to Ennerdale Bridge and Ennerdale
Water. A 5086 goes off on the right through the
mining district (haematite) of Cleator to Cockermouth.

51 miles: road on left to (1 mile) **Whitehaven** (pop.
27,500, E.C. Wednesday), a small seaport (steamers
to the Isle of Man) situated in an unattractive iron-
mining district. To the south-west are the rocky hills
of *St Bees Head*.

8 miles beyond Whitehaven is *Workington* (pop.
29,700, E.C. Thursday), a small seaport at the mouth
of the Derwent, with important steel works.

63 miles: **Cockermouth** (pop. 6000, E.C. Thursday),
situated at the junction of the Derwent and the Cocker
in the centre of a farming district. In the main street
is *Wordsworth House*, where the poet was born (1770)
and lived until his mother's death. Ruined *castle*.

Around Cockermouth. 2 miles north is *Bridekirk*; the church
of St Bridget has a 9th century font. — 8 miles south is *Lowes-*

water, at the foot of Loweswater Lake (1½ by ½ mile). Loweswater is the most northerly lake of a magnificent string of three, the next being *Crummock Water*, and the farthest lovely **Buttermere**. On the west shore of Crummock Water (2½ miles long by 1000 yards wide) are the sheer *Screes of Mellbreak* (1678 ft). 2½ miles west is *Scale Force*, the Lake District's highest waterfall (120 ft). On the west wall of the Dale is *Sour Milk Ghyll*. From the town Red Pike (2480 ft) and High Stile are easy of access. From Buttermere the road climbs Honister Pass and drops to *Rosthwaite* (good centre for climbing Great Gable) and *Seatoller* for Keswick by way of lovely *Borrowdale* and the shores of Derwentwater.

82 miles: *Thursby*, from which A 596 runs south-west to Wigton. B 5302 continues to *Silloth* (pop. 2500, E.C. Tuesday), a small seaside resort. 2 miles away are the ruins of *Worsty Castle*. — 88 miles: **Carlisle** (p. 831).

Windermere to Keswick

13 miles: **Ambleside** (pop. 2600, E.C. Thursday), beautifully situated in the Rothay valley, near the head of Lake Windermere. To the north-west is *Wansfell Pike* (1597 ft), with Roman remains (mosaics). In *Borrans Field*, ½ mile south on the left bank of the Brathay, is the site of the Roman fort of *Galava*. This is one of the best centres from which to explore the southern part of the Lake District.

Around Ambleside. *Wansfell Pike*; *Fairfield* (2865 ft); *Mab Scar*, from which there are fine views; Troutbeck, and the Troutbeck Valley; Clappersgate (south-west), a hamlet with picturesque houses and cottages; Elterwater, Force How and Skelwith Force. 1½ miles south-east, *Kelsickscar* and *High Skelgill Farm*, with fine view over Windermere, *Coniston Old Man*, and Langdale Fells. 2 miles south (on the west side of Windermere) is *Wray Castle*, a modern castle let to the Fresh Water Biological Association. Grounds open to the public, but not the castle.

B 5286 runs south-west to tranquil **Esthwaite Water,** at the head of which is *Hawkshead*, a quaint village much loved by artists, with charming old cottages and quiet empty lanes. Wordsworth went to the Grammar School (16th c.). B 5286 runs alongside Esthwaite Water to the west side of Windermere (ferry to Bowness and Windermere).

2 miles: *Skelwith Bridge*, romantically situated on the Brathay at the foot of wooded hills and at the mouth of a ravine. B 5343 runs west to Dungeon Ghyll through the wildly beautiful Langdale valley, past the village of Langdale, in the magnificent setting of the Langdale Pikes. Beyond Dungeon Ghyll a path runs between the Pikes and Bowfell to *Styhead Pass*, north of Scafell, and on to Wasdale Head.

8 miles: **Coniston** (pop. 1100, E.C. Wednesday). John Ruskin, who chose this romantically situated village for the last years of his life, is buried in the churchyard. Ruskin Museum. From 1870 he lived at Brantwood, 2 miles down the east side of the lake; now a Ruskin Society hostel. A 595 runs along the west side of **Coniston Water** (5½ miles long, ½ mile wide, 260 ft deep). The north end of the lake, with its background of hills, is the most beautiful part; the lower part is attractively wooded. The National Trust owns a continuous tract of country extending north from Coniston to *Little Langdale* (see above), in one of the most beautiful parts of the district: a magnificent estate of over 4000 acres, including Waterhead House, Thwaite Farm, the famous Tarn Hows (magnificent views), Tilberthwaite and, to the west, Wetherlam (2500 ft) and Broad Slack. The Nibthwaite woods, Peel Island (near the south end of the lake) and Fir Island also belong to the National Trust. From the *Coniston Old Man* (2635 ft) there are wide views.

On Coniston Water in 1959 Donald Campbell set up a new world water speed record.

15 miles: *Rydal*, with the little lake of Rydal Water and *Rashfield*, a very beautiful property acquired by Wordsworth in 1826.

The road now runs alongside *Grasmere*. The village of Grasmere is at the north end of the lake, just to the east of the road.

Grasmere is a charming village in a very beautiful situation, and the lake (1 mile long, ½ mile wide) is one of the most famous and most beautiful in the Lake District.

St Oswald's Church, in Grasmere Vale, dates from the 14th century. ½ mile east of the village is *Town End*, with *Dove Cottage*, where Wordsworth lived with his sister Dorothy in 1799 and where he brought his wife in 1802. In 1813 they moved to *Rydal Mount*, where the poet died in 1850.

Thomas de Quincey lived for 20 years in Dove Cottage after Wordsworth's departure. The house is now a memorial to the two writers. Opposite is a Wordsworth Museum.

From Grasmere the road climbs over *Dunmail Rise* and descends to skirt the shores of *Thirlmere* (3½ miles long, ½ mile wide). — 24 miles: *Thirlspot*.

30 miles: **Keswick** (pop. 4500, E.C. Wednesday), the "capital of the Lake District", beautifully situated in a river valley near Derwentwater; a good centre for the northern lakes and hills. The *Moot Hall* is built with stone from Lord's Island. In the *Museum* is a relief model of the Lake District. In *St Kentigern's Church*, Crosthwaite, is a monument (with an inscription by Wordsworth) to Robert Southey, who is buried in the churchyard.

Around Keswick. On *Castlerigg*, 2 miles east, near the old road to Penrith, is a stone circle of 48 stones covering an area of 10 acres. — 1 mile south is *Castle Head* (wide views). — 1 mile south-west is *Crow Park*, near Cockshott Wood. Nearby is *Friar's Crag*, a noted viewpoint, with a memorial to John Ruskin.

Derwentwater (3 miles long, 1½ miles wide) lies in a beautiful setting of hills. The river Derwent flows into the lake, passing Borrowdale (pop. 400), and links it with *Bassenthwaite Lake* (4 miles long, 3¼ miles wide). For the route from Keswick via Borrowdale to Buttermere, Crummock Water and Loweswater, see under Cockermouth (above, p. 840).

Three peaks lie within easy reach of Keswick — *Skiddaw* (3053 ft), *Saddleback* or Blencathra (2847 ft) and, farther to the south, *Helvellyn* (3118 ft), on the west side of Ullswater. In a walk of some 7 hours from Keswick it is possible to take in a number of other less known peaks — *Grasmoor* (2791 ft), *Grisedale Pike* (2593 ft) and *Causey Pike* (2000 ft).

THE ISLE OF MAN

Access

By sea. Steamer services (carrying cars) between Liverpool and Douglas (daily in summer: time 3¾ hours) and between Heysham and Douglas (summer only, on certain days: time 3 hours). In summer there are also irregular services between Belfast and Douglas, Ramsey and Douglas, and Dublin and Douglas.

By air. Services by Caledonian Airways between Ronaldsway airport (7 miles south of Douglas) and London, Liverpool, Manchester and other towns.

The Island and its History

Lying in the centre of the Irish Sea, at almost the same distance from the coasts of England, Scotland, Ireland and Wales, the **Isle of Man** is one of the most interesting of the many islands of the British Isles. The nearest point on the mainland is Burrow Head in Galloway, 16 miles away. The island is 32 miles long by 12 miles across and has an area of 227 sq. miles.

The Isle of Man, the home of the smallest nation in the Western world, has the Parliament with the longest continuous existence. Its attractions are many. It has a great variety of scenery, with lonely moorland, glens with luxuriant semi-tropical foliage, wide sandy beaches and bold rocky headlands. The centre of the island is hilly, and from the top of Snaefell (2034 ft) there are wide views of the island itself and the mainland of Britain.

The streams which rise in the hills form beautiful waterfalls in the rocky glens through which they find their way to the sea. Sulby Glen marks the northern end of the hilly region, with plains and moorland beyond. Along the south coast are steeply scarped hills.

In summer the chief town, *Douglas*, and the surrounding area are crowded with visitors, but the rest of the island preserves its tranquil and peaceful beauty.

Nothing is known with certainty of the early history of the island, though there are abundant legends. It is, however, known that invaders arrived on the island from Europe with the first wave of Celtic incomers, and that after a period under the rule of Welsh chieftains the island fell under Norwegian control from the 10th to the 13th century. It was invaded by Alexander III of Scotland and sought the protection of Edward III of England. Thereafter it was ruled by viceroys appointed by the English king, who were crowned in Peel Cathedral; notable among them were William Montacute, Earl of Salisbury, and Earl Percy (1399). From 1405 to 1825 the island was held by the Earls of Derby, but in the 18th century the Duke of Atholl, a descendant of the seventh Earl of Derby, sold his sovereign rights to the Crown.

The period of Norwegian occupation has left its mark on the island. The most picturesque of the ancient customs of Man is the annual meeting of the Tynwald (the Manx Parliament) on 5 July, held for the last thousand years, when the laws passed by the Tynwald during the year are read out to the people on Tynwald Hill (an artificial mound said to have been built up of earth from the 17 parishes on the island). The government consists of a Lieutenant Governor appointed by the Crown, the Council and the *House of Keys* (a chamber of 24 elected members), which together form the Court of Tynwald.

The Manx language, a branch of the Celtic language family related to Gaelic, has almost died out.

The Isle of Man's motor and motorcycle races, the Tourist Trophy and the Manx Grand Prix, which take place in summer over the island's famous road circuits, attract competitors of all nationalities.

The Isle of Man is the setting of Hall Caine's novel "The Manxman".

Douglas (pop. 18,000, E.C. Thursday), the capital of the island, attracts increasing numbers of holiday-makers every year: more than a million and a quarter people annually arrive in the town. The town, situated in a wide bay, has a 2 mile long esplanade and three piers (the Victoria Pier, 1625 ft long, and the Red Pier, 550 ft long, being the most popular). Across the harbour is *Douglas Head* (ferry), where there is good bathing. In Finch Road is the *Manx National*

Museum, with interesting prehistoric exhibits. *Nunnery Mansion* is a picturesque house (modern) on ancient foundations. 3 miles south is *Port Soderick:* good bathing. 1½ miles north-west is *Braddan,* with an old church containing some of the runic inscriptions for which the island is famous.

Douglas to Port Erin via Castletown: 19 miles.

9 miles: *Ballasalla,* with the island's airport, *Ronaldsway.* Nearby are the ruins of 11th century *Rushen Abbey.* — 12 miles: **Castletown,** formerly the capital and seat of the island government. *Castle Rushen,* once the palace of the kings of Man, is a fine specimen of a mediaeval fortification. From the castle tower there is a magnificent view. The *Nautical Museum* has an interesting collection. 1 mile east is *Derbyhaven,* a pleasant seaside resort in a small bay. Ruined chapel on St Michael's Isle.

18 miles: **Port Erin,** an attractive seaside resort in a deep bay sheltered on the north by Bradda Head. Marine biological station. 1 mile south-east is *Port St Mary* (pop. 1200, E.C. Thursday), a fishing village which is developing into a holiday resort. Folk Museum. Some of the finest cliffs on the island extend for some 3 miles beyond Port Erin, with Chicken Rock (lighthouse) and Spanish Head. The north coast is rugged and much indented. Beyond Fleshwick Bay is a desolate area where the hills come down almost to the sea. To the south-west is the *Calf of Man,* an island of 616 acres with two lighthouses (one ruined). From the highest point (300 ft) the Mourne Mountains in Ireland and the Scottish and Welsh hills can be seen. Nature reserve.

Douglas to Peel

2 miles: *Union Mills.* — 5 miles: *Crosby.* — 9 miles: *St John's.* To the north is *Tynwald Hill.* 2 miles north is *Glen Helen,* one of the most attractive glens on the island, with the Rhenass Falls. 4 miles south is *Glen Maye* (waterfalls), which runs down to the sea. — 11 miles: **Peel** (pop. 2500, E.C. Wednesday), a seaside resort in a small bay at the mouth of the Neb. Offshore, linked with the mainland by a causeway, is *St Patrick's Isle,* with the picturesque ruins of *Peel Castle* (15th c.), surrounded by 16th century walls. In the centre of the enclosure is a round tower similar to those found in Ireland,

the only one on the island. Also within the enclosure are the
ruins of *St Germanus's Cathedral*, with a 13th century Norman
choir. Fenella's Tower (the one nearest the sea) is the scene
of Fenella's escape in Scott's "Peveril of the Peak". *Murray
Museum* (arms, motor cars).

Douglas to Ramsey

2 miles: *Onchan*, a very popular seaside resort. — 8 miles:
Laxey, a charming fishing village and holiday resort, with a
large wheel (1854), a relic of the lead mines which used to be
worked here. Starting point for the trip to the top of Snaefell.
Museum of old cars. — 9 miles: *Bulgham Bay*. The road runs
through a very attractive area, with fine views of the glens
inland. — 13 miles: on the left, North Barrule (1860 ft); on
the right, Maughold Head (lighthouse), at the south end of
spacious Ramsey Bay.

18 miles: **Ramsey** (pop. 3800, E.C. Thursday), the island's
second largest holiday resort, less popular with visitors than
Douglas, though it is more attractively situated and has a fine
sandy beach. *Queen's Pier* (2230 ft long); promenade; *Mooragh
Park* (with lake).

The surrounding countryside is very beautiful and offers
plenty of good walks and other excursions. 1 mile away is
the *Albert Tower*, a fine viewpoint; then over North Barrule
and along the ridge to Snaefell (4 miles). Another pleasant
walk is along the coast to Maughold Head, passing a number
of charming little bays like Port Lewaigue. At *Kirk Maughold*,
on the hill, is an interesting church with runic inscriptions and
45 ancient crosses. The novelist Hall Caine is buried in the
churchyard. To the north are Sulby Glen and Glen Auldyn.
Magnificent waterfalls at Ballaglass and Ballure Glen.

Ramsey to Peel

The road runs along the foot of the hills. To the north the
country is flat apart from a few sand dunes. 3 miles north-
west is *Andreas*, with a church containing more ancient crosses.
1 mile south, at *Ballachurry*, is a prehistoric fort. At the northern
tip of the island is the *Point of Ayre*. Down the west coast are
dunes. — 5 miles: *Sulby*. — 6 miles: *Ballaugh*. To the north,
at the *Curragh*, interesting fossils have been found. — 9 miles:
Kirkmichael, with ancient crosses in the churchyard. From
here a secondary road runs south-east to the Neb valley and
St John's. — 16 miles: **Peel** (see above).

VII: WALES

Because of its rich coalfields South Wales is much industrialised, and along its coast are the important ports of **Cardiff,
Swansea** and **Newport.** Northward however, behind this busy
coastline, lies some of the loveliest country in the British Isles.
The valley of the River Usk, which flows into the sea at Newport, vies with that of the Wye in its scenic beauty. Close to
its source the river flows past *Brecon* with its ruined castle
and ancient priory church. To the east are the **Black Mountains,**
a tract of wild, open country where neither man nor progress
has laid a hand, and to the south are the *Brecon Beacons*, a
country dear to the hearts of walkers. Thence the valley runs
past Crickhowell and Abergavenny, Usk and Caerleon, and so
through green and pleasant places to Newport and the sea.

Between Newport and Swansea are many places of interest
and beauty. Caerphilly Castle, north of Cardiff, is one of the
largest and finest castles in Wales.

Swansea, on the edge of one of the richest coalfields in Britain,
is situated on the Gower peninsula, a good centre for exploring
the coast. On the peninsula are a number of ruined castles,
among them Oystermouth and Penrice.

Farther west are Kidwelly and Carmarthen with their ruined
castles and *Tenby*, a very modern resort which still retains its
old town walls. From Tenby a wide variety of excursions in
the extreme western part of Wales offer themselves — to Pembroke Castle, the historic old port of Milford Haven, Haverfordwest with its ruined castle and old buildings, *St David's*
with its cathedral, the smallest in Britain.

Northward, both along the coast and inland, Wales becomes
a country of steep hills, impressive mountains and fine fertile
valleys, with a landscape in which wild and rocky grandeur
mingles with green luxuriance. Along the coasts are fine seaside
resorts; inland are villages beautifully situated amid the hills.

The resorts on the northern coast are widely known. One
of the most popular is *Llandudno* in Orme's Bay. *Colwyn Bay*
is noted for its mild and equable climate. Rhyl, Prestatyn and
Abergele are other seaside places on the north coast.

On the west coast is *Barmouth*, fringed with a wide expanse
of bathing beaches and backed by some of the finest scenery
in Wales. South of it is the fine range of Cader Idris; inland,

to the west, is Dolgellau, an ancient town where the curfew is still rung nightly. Beyond the Menai Straits is the fertile **Isle of Anglesey,** one of the largest of the islands on the coast of Britain.

An outstanding feature of North Wales is the great massif of **Snowdonia,** which presents scenery on the grand scale. The ascent to the top of Snowdon, the highest mountain in Wales, can be made by a number of routes of varying difficulty or by a mountain railway from Llanberis.

51. THE SOUTH WALES COAST
(CHEPSTOW TO CARMARTHEN)

2 miles north-east on the Usk road (A 449) is **Caerleon,** on

Chepstow (p. 731). — 5 miles: *Caerwent*, the Roman station of *Venta Silurum*. To the south is the Severn.

16 miles: **Newport** (pop. 110,000, E.C. Thursday), at the mouth of the Usk, a market town and one of the largest ports on the Bristol Channel; also a railway centre for the nearby mining area. The port has a deep water area of 125 acres, with an entrance lock 1000 feet by 100 feet. The Usk is spanned by a transporter bridge with two steel lattice towers 240 feet high.

There are the remains of a 14th century *castle* destroyed by Cromwell during the Civil War, on the site of an earlier Norman castle.

The **Cathedral,** on Stow Hill, is a Norman foundation, altered and enlarged in the 13th and 15th centuries, which became a cathedral in 1942. An interesting feature is that it incorporates the 13th century St Mary's Church (Norman porch; Norman pillars and arches with dog-tooth moulding) between the 13th century nave and the 15th century west tower.

The *Civic Centre* in Clytha Park is an attractive group of modern buildings with a campanile. It contains the **Museum and Art Gallery,** with Roman remains from *Venta Silurum* and *Isca* and collections of historical material. The Art Gallery has pictures of the English and Dutch schools.

2 miles north-east on the Usk road (A 449) is **Caerleon,** on the site of the Roman town of *Isca*. Its present name is a corruption of *Castra legionis* (it was the camp of the Roman Second Legion). Remains of an amphitheatre of the late 1st

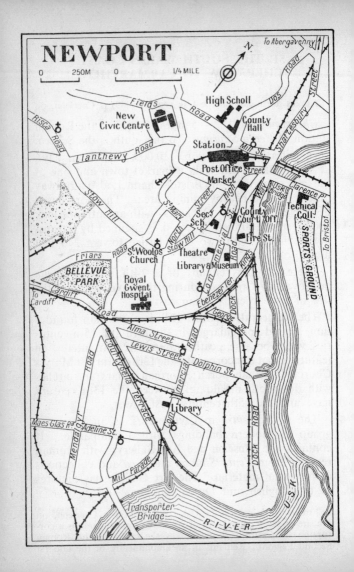

century A.D. Near the church (15th c.) is a small *Roman museum.*

28 miles: **Cardiff.**

CARDIFF

Cardiff (pop. 292,000, E.C. Wednesday), situated on the Taff, 2 miles above its mouth, was until 1939 the largest coal-exporting port in the world. It also handles considerable quantities of iron, steel and tinplate from the industrial valleys of Glamorgan. Half the population of Wales lives within 30 miles of Cardiff, mostly in the Glamorgan and Monmouthshire valleys.

The extensive and modern **Bute Docks** consist of five main basins, cover 180 acres and have 7 miles of quays. There are also docks at Penarth, on the other side of the Taff estuary (ferry service). Cardiff Docks were originally built on the initiative of the Marquess of Bute (d. 1848). The port has an annual traffic of 3,600,000 tons.

Cardiff Castle, reached by way of High St, was formerly the seat of the Marquess of Bute; it was acquired by the city in 1947. The original castle was built in 1090. William the Conqueror's eldest son, Robert Curthose, died in captivity here. The *keep* is 14th century; the rest of the present castle was built in 1861. Interesting mural paintings in the large banqueting hall.

South-east of the castle is *St John's Church* (15th c.).

Cardiff's main features of interest lie to the north of the castle, round a large open space (**Cathays Park**) bounded on the east by Park Place and on the west by North Road.

In the centre is the Renaissance-style **City Hall,** built at the beginning of this century, with a tower 240 feet high. To the left of the City Hall are the *Law Courts* (1904), and beyond this *Glamorgan County Hall* and the *College of Technology*, dating from the same period. Farther to the north-west is the *Welsh Board of Health* (1938).

To the right of the City Hall is the **National Museum of Wales,** opened in 1927, and beyond this is the *University* (1883-1933).

The **National Museum** (open 10 to 5, Sundays 2 to 5) has large collections, mainly related to Wales.

Prehistoric, Roman, Welsh and early Christian material. Mediaeval art, exotic art. Botany and zoology. Section on the mining industry.

The **Thomson Gallery** and the **Art Gallery** are well stocked with works by old and modern masters — Italian, Flemish (*Rubens, van Dyck*), Dutch (*Rembrandt*), British (*Reynolds, Gainsborough, Romney, Raeburn, Turner, Constable, Lawrence, the Pre-Raphaelites*) and French (*Corot, Daumier, Boudin, Courbet, Daubigny, Cézanne, Derain, Bonnard, Van Gogh, Marquet, Sisley, Berthe Morisot*, etc.). Of particular importance are **Monet's** "Rouen Cathedral" and "Charing Cross Bridge" and works by *Renoir*. Sculpture by *Carpeaux, Rodin, Epstein, Degas, Bourdelle* and others.

In the suburb of **Llandaff,** to the west of the city centre, is the magnificent **Llandaff Cathedral,** situated on the banks of the Taff on the site of an earlier 6th century church. The present building was begun by Bishop Urban (1107-33); from this period there remains a *Norman arch* between the Lady Chapel and the presbytery, which has also Norman work in the south wall and the doorways in the aisle walls. The *Chapter House* is Early English (end of 13th c.). The *Lady Chapel* is in early Decorated style; the presbytery, walls of the nave and choir aisles are late Decorated.

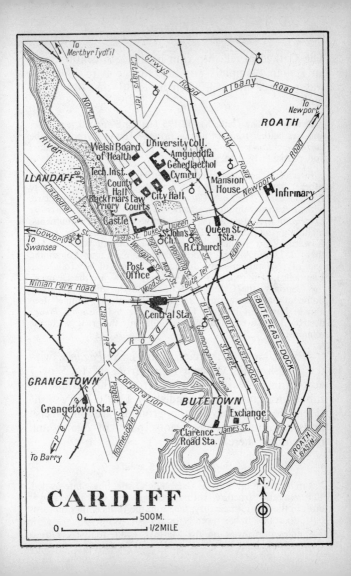

The Cathedral fell into ruin in the 18th century, and an Italian "temple" was built inside it in 1740. It was restored in 1843, when the south-east tower was built.

Exterior. The Cathedral is 175 feet long and 70 feet wide, and has neither transept nor triforium. The *west front* and the *north-west tower* (built by Henry VII's uncle Jasper Tudor) are particularly fine.

Interior. There is an unobstructed view from one end to the other. Between the presbytery and the Lady Chapel is a fine *Norman arch*. The *Lady Chapel* and the *Chapter House* (square, with a central column) are also very fine. *Figure of Christ by Epstein* on a bold parabolic arch. Some interesting monuments, including the tomb of David Matthew, standard-bearer to Edward IV, in the north choir aisle, and that of William Matthew (d. 1528). Also in the north choir aisle is a tomb containing one of the miraculously duplicated bodies of St Teilo (see Llandeilo). The roof and glass are modern, as are the Deanery, the Canonry, the Cathedral School and the Bishop's Palace. Some of the decoration from the 18th century "temple" (see above) has been brought here. Of the old *Bishop's Palace* destroyed by Owen Glendower in 1402 only the great gatehouse remains.

4 miles west of the city centre is *St Fagan's*, with the **Welsh Folk Museum** (open from 11 to 5 or 7 according to season; Sundays from 2.30), in an Elizabethan mansion surrounded by 13th century walls (Flemish tapestries; in the grounds are old Welsh houses, brought from various parts of Wales and reassembled here).

Surroundings of Cardiff

7 miles north on A 469 is **Caerphilly Castle,** now State-owned. This majestic structure, with imposing walls and towers, was built in the late 13th century, but from the 16th century onwards fell into ruin. It has recently been partly restored.

5 miles north-west on the Merthyr Tydfil road (A 470) is *Castle Coch*, built on a triangular plan (restored).

South of Cardiff, on the other side of the harbour, is **Penarth** (docks, beach). In Plymouth Road is a small *Turner Museum* attached to the National Museum of Wales.

A 4055 runs south-west to **Barry** (pop. 40,000, E.C. Wednesday), a very popular seaside resort on the wide arch of Whitmore Bay, with a full range of holiday entertainments on *Barry Island* (which is an island only in name). From Knap Point there are fine views of the beach and Porthkerry Bay. In Watchtower Bay is the old harbour of *Watch House*. In *Porthkerry Park* are a large viaduct and a ruined castle.

Along the coast to the west are the picturesque villages of *Rhoose* and *Fontygary Bay*. *Gileston* lies a little inland in the pretty valley of the Thawe. At *Llancarfan*, to the north-west, is a monastery founded in 550. *Llantwit Major* has a very interesting church and a mediaeval town hall. Nearby is *St Donat's Castle*, a fine 14th century fortress altered in Elizabethan times.

40 miles: *Cowbridge* (pop. 1100, E.C. Wednesday). Ruins of *Beaupre Castle* (16th c.).

47 miles: **Bridgend** (pop. 15,000, E.C. Wednesday), a market town divided by the river Ogmore into *Newcastle* (to the west) and *Oldcastle* (to the east).

Near the church in Newcastle are the ruins of *Bridgend Castle:* 12th century doorway. The *Hospice of St John* dates from the 15th century (restored).

Around Bridgend. 1½ miles south-east is **Ewenny Priory,** a fortified ecclesiastical building founded 1146. 3 miles south-west, ruins of *Ogmore Castle*, dating from Norman times. 3½ miles south-west, ruins of a 15th century fortified mansion, *Candleston Castle*. 2 miles north-east, **Coity,** where there is a 14th century *church* with an unusual 15th century central tower: interesting monuments. *Coity Castle* dates from the 13th-14th centuries. 2 miles east, *Coy Church*, a fine 13th century church with interesting monuments.

B 4524 runs south to 6 miles *Southerndown*, a small seaside resort. East is the modern *Dunraven Castle*, a great house in a splendid situation on the cliffs. Rugged cliffs continue down the coast south-east to *Nash Point* (lighthouse).

52 miles: *Pyle* and, 3 miles south, **Porthcawl** (pop. 12,000, E.C. Wednesday), a popular seaside resort with five sandy beaches. *St Nicholas Field:* interesting stone circle.

Margam: 12th century *Cistercian monastery*, recently restored and modernised.

60 miles: *Aberavon*, with **Port Talbot** (pop. 51,000, E.C. Thursday), the port for the mineral, coal, copper and iron-working district of the vale of Afon and the beginning of the Welsh "black country".

64 miles: to the right, **Neath** (pop. 30,000, E.C. Thursday), a manufacturing town at the mouth of the Neath and Dulais valleys, in a district of coal, iron, tin, copper and brickworks. Near the old Market St are the ruins of a *castle* built by a Norman baron, Fitzhamon.

1 miles north is **Neath Abbey** (1129), originally founded by the Grey Friars, later occupied by Cistercians, dissolved at the Reformation. Remains of west front, transepts, walls of the nave and a beautiful undercroft. In the beautiful *Vale of Neath* are numerous waterfalls — Aberdulais Cascade; Melincourt, near Resolven; Lesser Clwydd, above Rheola; Scwd-y-Rhyd, on the Pergwm; the magnificent Upper Cilhepste Falls and Lower Cilhepste Falls; the cataract and cave at Pwll-yr-Ogof on the Mellte; Upper Clymgwyn, Middle Clymgwyn and Lower Clymgwyn; Scwd-y-Oannwr; Scwd Einion Gam and Scwd Gwladys (the Lady Fall) on the Pyrddin; and Scwd Dwli. Beautiful old country houses — Glyn Castell, Rheola, etc.

72 miles: **Swansea** (pop. 170,000, E.C. Thursday), at the mouth of the Tawe, on the north-west side of Swansea Bay, a great commercial and industrial centre and seaside resort. It lies in the centre of a steel-producing, smelting and copper-manufacturing region and is also a leading oil port.

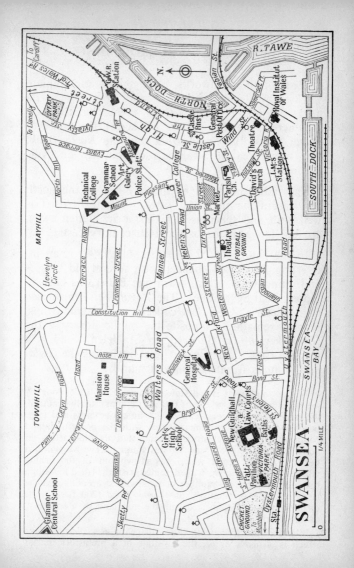

SWANSEA

¼ MILE

SWANSEA AND SURROUNDINGS

Most of the steelworks, rolling mills and tinplate works of Wales are within 15 miles of Swansea. Its docks can take the largest ships — the *Queen's Dock* (150 acres), the *King's Dock* (72 acres), the *Prince of Wales Dock*, the *South Dock* and the *North Dock*. The total area of Swansea's deep water docks is 270 acres.

The industrial parts of the city are to the north and east along the river Tawe. The town itself is well built and spacious. In *Castle St*, hidden away, are the few remains of the 14th century castle.

In the church of *St Mary* (rebuilt 1897) is an interesting Decorated chancel, with several old brasses and monuments. Beau Nash (see Bath) was born in Upper Goat St (plaque). The *Royal Welsh Institution* is in Victoria Road: art collections and engravings, Roman remains. Opposite the public library is the *Glynn Vivian Art Gallery*. In St Helen Road is a modern *Civic Centre* (campanile), including the *Guildhall*, famous for its Brangwyn murals.

To the south-west is the **Gower peninsula,** 15 miles long by 4-8 miles wide. The whole of this area is remarkably beautiful, the much indented coast edged with limestone cliffs and large beaches forming a striking contrast with the peaceful inland country, with its prehistoric remains and its old castles set amid woods. A 4067 runs 5 miles south to **The Mumbles,** a popular seaside resort which has grown out of the fishing village of *Oystermouth*, with a ruined castle (11th c.). Along the south coast are a number of bays with steep cliffs and the large outlying promontory of *Worms Head* (200 ft), 1 mile offshore, which is connected with the mainland by a causeway usable at low tide.

Inland is the interesting little village of *Reynoldston*, near which is *Arthur's Stone*, the capstone of a prehistoric burial chamber, 15 feet long and weighing 25 tons. To the north are the ruins of *Weabley Castle* (14th c.).

From Swansea to Carmarthen there are two possible routes:

(a) The *coast road*, A 4070, runs west to *Loughor* (6 miles), crosses the river Loughor and enters Carmarthenshire. 11 miles: **Llanelly** (pop. 30,000, E.C. Tuesday), an industrial town, with the *Howard Park Museum* (local interest). — 20 miles: *Kidwelly*, on Carmarthen Bay: ruined castle (14th c.), interesting Decorated church. — 30 miles: *Carmarthen*.

(b) The *inland road*, A 48, runs north to *Pontardulais* (86 miles), in the Loughor valley. 87 miles: *Hendy*, in Carmarthenshire. — 95 miles: *Cross Hands*, at the intersection with A 476 (Llanelly to Llandeilo). — 99 miles: *Llanddarog*. 106 miles: **Carmarthen** (pop. 13,000, E.C. Thursday), in a splendid situation on the right bank of the Towey, 16 miles from its mouth. Of its 11th century *Norman castle* there remain two massive round towers and fragments of walls and other towers, from one of which there is a very fine view.

Behind Christ Church can be seen remains of the earthworks built to protect the town during the Civil War. Between the main streets is a network of narrow winding lanes. In *St Peter's Church* (14th c., Decorated) in Spillman St is the altar-tomb, removed from the priory of the Grey Friars, of Rhws ap Thomas (d. 1527), who crowned Henry Tudor on Bosworth Field. Nearby are monuments to Anne Vaughan (interesting inscription) and Bishop Ferrars, burned at the stake in the market place in 1555.

At 4-5 Quay St is the **County Museum,** one of the richest in Wales. The collection includes Neolithic material from western Wales, stones with Romano-British and ogham inscriptions, including the important 6th century stone of Voteporix, Roman jewellery and local bygones. The library contains valuable manuscripts and important printed works. Carmarthen has interesting memories of the old guilds, including the fishermen's guild; fishing is still practised in the Towy with coracles and nets.

6 miles south is *Llanstephan*, with a ruined castle and *St Andrew's Wishing Well*.

Beyond Carmarthen: see the next route.

52. MONMOUTH TO FISHGUARD

129 miles on A 40.

Monmouth: see p. 728.

8 miles: **Raglan** (pop. 1300, E.C. Thursday), at the junction of roads from Monmouth, Abergavenny, Usk and Chepstow. Ruins of *castle* (14th-15th c.), destroyed during the Civil War.

1 mile south-east is *Coed Arthur*, a wooded hilltop (c. 25 acres) with an Iron Age fort (National Trust property). 5 miles south is **Usk**, with a Norman and Gothic church, the remains of an old abbey and a ruined 13th century castle.

17 miles: **Abergavenny** (pop. 10,000, E.C. Thursday), at the confluence of the Usk and the Gavenny, surrounded by beautifully wooded hills. Remains of a Norman *castle* built by the first Norman adventurers who advanced into Wales soon after the battle of Hastings: 13th century curtain-wall and tower ruins. **St Mary's Church** was the church of the 14th century Benedictine priory: magnificent monuments, original choir stalls. Interesting old houses in the town include the former *Cow Inn* in Neville St, and buildings in St John's Lane, Flannel St and Tudor St. *District Museum* (local history).

Abergavenny makes a splendid centre for visiting the *Brecon Mountains*, the valleys of the Wye and Usk, and the castles of the Welsh border. Between the Black Mountains and Brecknock and Glamorgan, where are all the important coal valleys of South Wales, is the *Vale of Usk*.

Around Abergavenny. The landscape is dominated by three hills — Blorenge (1833 ft), 1 mile south-west; the Sugar Loaf (1955 ft), 4 miles north-west; and Skirrid Fawr (1601 ft), 3 miles north-east. — 6 miles north-east on A 485 (the road to Hereford) is *Pandy*, 5 miles north-west of which, in the heart of the Black Mountains, are the ruins of the Cistercian *Llanthony*

Abbey, founded in 1108. The remains include the church and chapter house, in transitional Norman style (12th c.), with some 14th century work. — 6 miles beyond Pandy is *Pontrilas*, and 6 miles south-east of this is the Norman *Skenfrith Castle*, with a keep, 13th century walls and a number of towers. 3 miles north of Pontrilas on B 4347 are the remains of **Abbey Dore**, a Cistercian foundation of 1147, with a beautiful late 12th century church. 5 miles north-east of Pontrilas on a narrow country road is the village of **Kilpeck,** with a beautiful 12th century church, originally belonging to a Benedictine abbey (very fine south doorway, richly carved).

To Merthyr Tydfil (A 465). The road runs through the industrial towns of *Brynmawr, Ebbw Vale* and *Tredegar*, from which mining valleys run down to the sea. 19 miles: **Merthyr Tydfil** (pop. 60,600, E.C. Thursday), an iron and steel town. 1 mile north-west, on a hill, is *Cyfarthfa Castle*, formerly the home of the owners of the great Cyfarthfa works, now a museum and art gallery. 2 miles north is *Pontsarn*, with the ruins of Morlais Castle (13th c.). A 470 runs south to *Pontypridd* (pop. 40,000, E.C. Thursday), on the river Taff, which is crossed by a graceful single-spanned bridge (1755). Off this road to the right is *Aberfan*, the scene of the Aberfan disaster of 1966, when the subsidence of a spoil heap caused the death of 144 people, including 116 children.

North-west of Pontypridd is the heavily industrialised *Rhondda Valley*.

23 miles : **Crickhowell** (pop. 1400, E.C. Wednesday), a village on the Usk, which is spanned by an old bridge (1308) of 13 arches.

There are the ruins of a Norman castle. The village makes a splendid centre for the Vale of Usk and the Black Mountains. 14th century *church*. 2 miles north-west is Table Mountain, with a British fortification (1200 ft in circumference) called in Welsh "Crug Hywel" (fort of Howell-ap-Rhys).

27 miles: junction with A 479, on which is *Tretower*, with the ruins of an old castle with two chimneys in the tower. — 29 miles: *Bwlch*, in the beautiful Usk Valley (wide views).

37 miles: **Brecon** (pop. 5000, E.C. Wednesday), situated 450 feet above sea-level in the hollow of the hills at the confluence of the Usk and Honddu. It was strongly fortified by the Romans, and derives its name from the 5th century Welsh chieftain Brychan.

The Norman Bernard de Newnarch built the *castle* with many stones of the Roman castrum; three towers and part of the wall can still be seen. In the *Ely Tower* Bishop Morton of Ely signed the agreement with the Duke of Buckingham to support Henry Tudor against Richard III.

On the hill stands the old 11th century priory, since 1925 **Brecon Cathedral.** Early English *choir*, massive crenellated *tower*. Norman font and very rare triple piscina. The priory was attached to Battle Abbey, near Hastings, and the north transept is called *Battle Chapel*. The south transept is called *Capel-y-Cochiaid* ("chapel of the red-haired men").

In High St are a number of old houses. Very beautiful view from the seven-arched bridge over the Usk. At Llanfaes is *Christ's College*, founded by Henry VIII. **Museum** (prehistoric, Celtic and Roman material, furniture, natural history) and *library* in Glamorgan St. Part of the old town walls can be seen in *Captain's Walk*.

A 438 runs north-east to *Glasbury* (11 miles), a charming village in the Wye valley, with a magnificent view of the river. *Maesllwh Castle* (1829) is a combination of Norman and Gothic. To the south are the *Black Mountains*.

4 miles north-east of Glasbury is **Hay-on-Wye** (pop. 1300, E.C. Tuesday), a pleasantly situated little town on the boundary between Wales and England, with the station in Wales and the main part of the town in England. The remains of the old *castle* are incorporated in a Jacobean house. 1 mile south of Hay is *Mouse Castle*, a British camp. 2 miles north is *Clifford*, at the north end of the Golden Valley, with a ruined castle. Near the church are the ruins of an 11th century Cluniac priory. 4 miles south-east is the ruined 13th century *Craswall Abbey*. 1 mile north-west is *Clyro*, with remains of a Roman camp.

49 miles: *Trecastle*, near which is the beautiful pass of Cwm Dwr. 58 miles: **Llandovery** (pop. 1980, E.C. Thursday), a picturesque market town on the

Towy. The town has associations with George Borrow, author of "Wild Wales" and "Lavengro". Ruins of a *Norman castle*.

Above the town is the beautiful Vale of Towy. An excursion to *Ystradffin* (10 miles) is a good way of seeing most of the magnificent scenery. Nearby is the cave of Twn Shon Catti a 17th century Welsh Robin Hood; and through the Cwrt-y-Cadno Pass, near Pumsaint, north-west on A 482, is *Ogofau*, where there are disused gold mines worked by the Romans. At *Dolaucothi* is an ancient gold-mine worked intermittentl since Roman times.

70 miles: **Llandeilo** (pop. 2000, E.C. Thursday), in a beautiful setting on the river Towy (attractive stone bridge), a good centre for excursions. The name means "church of St Teilo", and this is one of several burial places attributed to the saint (others being Llandaff, Penally and Bridgend).

1 mile west is *Dynevor Castle* (ruins of a Norman castle in the grounds of a 19th century country house). — 3 miles east is *Carreg-Cennen Castle* (13th c.), magnificently perched on a crag 300 feet high. — *Dryslwyn Castle* (13th c.), with the chapel and part of the great hall. On a nearby hill are remains of pre-Roman fortifications. — 8 miles north are the ruins of *Talley Abbey* (1197). — 7 miles south is *Ammanford* (pop. 8000, E.C. Thursday), a mining town at the junction of the Amman and the Loughor. Near Llandybie is *Glynhir*, a 17th century mansion, with a beautiful park and a waterfall.

85 miles: **Carmarthen** (p. 861). 94 miles: **St Clears** (church with some Norman work), the scene of the Rebecca riots in 1843 against toll gates.

St Clears to Pembroke. 12 miles: *Kilgetty*, from which A 478 runs 5 miles south to **Tenby** (pop. 4700, E.C. Wednesday), one of the most attractive seaside resorts in Wales, situated on a narrow promontory jutting out into Carmarthen Bay. On both sides are sandy bays with high cliffs. Sails to Bristol and other places in summer.

There are some fragments of the town walls (13th and 15th c.),
a 12th century watch-tower and the ruins of *Tenby Castle*.
Local *museum* in the gatehouse of the Castle. The church is
13th century (Early English and Perpendicular). On Quay Hill,
facing Bridge St, is the *Tudor Merchant's House*, one of the
few surviving mediaeval merchants' houses in Wales (15th-
16th c.: National Trust property). The adjoining *Plantagenet
House*, also National Trust property, dates from the same
period.

Around Tenby. At the south end of the beach is *St Catherine's Rock* (cut off from the mainland at high tide), with a
disused fort (1860). — 1 mile south is *Penally*, one of the supposed burial places of St Teilo (see Llandeilo). — 3 miles,
Lydstep, which can be reached by a path along the cliffs. Many
caves, which can be seen at neap-tide. Skrinkle Haven, in a
military area, is of geological interest for the juxtaposition of
red sandstone and Carboniferous limestone. — 5 miles, *Manorbier*, in a very beautiful bay, with the remains of a Norman
castle, part of which is occupied as a house. Interesting church;
dolmen. 1 mile west is *Gumfreston*, with three springs in the
churchyard of the curious old church. — Offshore is **Caldey
Island** (regular motor-boat services from Tenby harbour).
Remains of a 13th century priory, now a Trappist monastery.
The church has a leaning spire. — 3 miles north is *Saundersfoot*,
a little village with a very beautiful beach.

20 miles: **Carew,** with a ruined castle (13th, 14th, and 15th c.)
Carew Cross (9th-10th c.). The *church* has a 15th century
tower and interesting monuments.

24 miles: **Pembroke** (pop. 14,000, E.C. Wednesday), centred
on its long main street. The **castle,** in which Henry VII was
born in 1456, is notable for its Norman keep, 80 feet high.
Handsome gatehouse, with towers; fine *domed roof* in great
hall. On a hill opposite the castle is the ruined *Monkton Priory*
(Norman); the Decorated choir was the original church.

Around Pembroke. 5 miles south, *St Gowan's Head*, where
cliffs (165 ft) jut out into the sea. There is a 13th century chapel,
a hermitage high on the downs. 3 miles west are the *Stack
Rocks*, great limestone crags where, in season, myriads of
sea birds nest. The *Devil's Punch Bowl* is a natural cauldron.
Other rocks and passes on the rocky coast are the Huntsman's
Leap, the Green Bridge, Pen-y-holt, Stack, and (west beyond
the Wash) Linney Head. — 3 miles south is *Stackpole Court*,

seat of the Earl of Cawdor.   Nearby is Bosherton, where in
summer magnificent water lilies cover the picturesque lakes.
— *Pembroke Dock*, a modern town with important docks.

99 miles: *Whitland*.   115 miles: **Haverfordwest,** on
the River Cleddau, a picturesque old county town,
with crooked steep streets and many riverside quays.
The *Shire Hall* is in the High St, at the top of which is
the 13th century *St Mary's Church*, still retaining
parts of the Norman edifice: Early English arcading,
curious carvings on the capitals.   Another old church
is the Norman *St Martin's* (rebuilt in the 14th century).

7 miles south-west is **Milford Haven** (pop. 11,000, E.C.
Thursday), a fishing and oil port within the wonderful natural
harbour of the Milford Haven, in which the whole of the Royal
Navy could anchor.   Associations with Lord Nelson's Emma
Hamilton, who lived at *Castle Hall*, 1 mile east.   Off the very
beautiful coast to the west (with the jagged *St Ann's Head*)
are the islands of Skomer and Skokholm, which are bird sanctuaries and breeding grounds.   West is *St Bride's Bay*, magnificent
cliffs, rugged headlands and secluded beaches, forming part
of the Pembrokeshire Coast National Park.

Haverfordwest to St David's.   16 miles on A 487.   8 miles:
Roch, with a 13th century castle rising from the gorse-covered
plain. 13 miles: *Solva*, a charming little seaport with a picturesque
harbour behind the hills which run down to the sea.   Nearby is
the lovely glen of Porth-y-rhaw, with cliffs towering on both
sides.   16 miles: **St David's** (pop. 1600, E.C. Wednesday), at
the most westerly point of the Welsh peninsula on the wind-
swept height over the river Alan.   It is the smallest cathedral
city in Britain.   *The Popples* lead from the Cross to the main
gate of the cathedral close, where is obtained the first glimpse
of **St David's Cathedral,** nestling in a deep hollow in rough
moorland country.   39 steps lead down to it.

St David (born at St Non's, 1 mile away, died *c.* 600), patron
saint of Wales, founded the cathedral.   The present building
dates from 1176.   Of this building some parts remain, including
the arcading and narrow arches.   In 1220 the tower collapsed
and destroyed the transepts and choir, which were rebuilt by

1250. The Early English *Lady Chapel* was finished by 1327. During the 14th century the aisle walls were inserted, and the Decorated windows were added; the uppermost stage of the *tower* is also Perpendicular (c. 1515). Sir George Gilbert Scott (19th century) restored the building and improved the 18th century *west front*. The exterior of the building is severe, with little decoration. The length is 289 feet, and the breadth 130 feet. Access is by the south porch.

The interior, with its rich ornamentation and warm red colour, makes a striking contrast with the exterior. The 12th century nave is very varied, a feature unusual in Norman architecture. The clerestory and triforium are richly ornamented. In the interior of the tower there is a roof lantern of beautiful Decorated work. Between the transepts and nave are fine Norman doorways, and a 14th century *rood-screen* separates the choir from the nave. A doorway on the east side of the north transept leads into the chapter house and sacristy (1220), formerly St Thomas's Chapel. Beautiful Early English piscina. The choir, below the tower, has 15th century *stalls*. To the east is the presbytery (13th c.), showing the transition to Early English. At the east end are two tiers of lancet windows. Mosaics by Salviati (19th c.). On the north side is the base on which St David's shrine formerly stood, and opposite this is a monument commemorating Bishop Anselm (d. 1247). In the centre is the tomb of Edmund Tudor (d. 1456), father of Henry VII. To the east is *Bishop Vaughan's Chapel* (16th c., Perpendicular). The Lady Chapel has an ante-chapel with fan vaulting. On the south side is the tomb of Bishop Martyn, the founder.

To the north are the ruins of *St Mary's College* (14th c.). The chapel has a beautiful slender spire. The cloisters, between the College and the Cathedral, are not open to visitors. On the other bank of the Alan are the magnificent ruins (restored) of the fine **Bishop's Palace** built by Bishop Gower in 1348: great hall 90 feet long with a very fine rose window and a balustrade of delicate arches.

Around St David's. The coast is impressive, though not particularly high. *St David's Head* (100 ft), together with Carn Llidi and Llaethdy farms, belongs to the National Trust, which owns the coastal strip extending from Tywyn Fach, south-east of Carn Llidi, along the coast from Porthwuch to Pen Lledwen and from Upper Solva to Cwm Bach, Newgale. Other notable features are the cliffs between Whitesands Bay and Porth Clais;

Penrhyn Dalar Head, with St Justinian's chapel and well;
Treginnis Isaf; Rhosson farm, Rhosson Isaf and Trefeiddan.
Also on this magnificent stretch of coast are Treginnis Uchaf,
Upper and Lower Porthlysky, Pen Porth-clais and Porth-clais,
extending eastward to Porth-y-Fynnon.

120 miles: *Trefgarn.* — 122 miles: *Wolf's Castle*,
with an inscribed gilded cross of late Saxon or Norman
date. — 124 miles: *Letterston.*

129 miles: **Fishguard** (pop. 5000, E.C. Wednesday),
one of the most picturesque towns on the Pembrokeshire coast. In 1908 the Great Western Railway
established a harbour and port providing direct communication between the mainland and Ireland (frequent services to Rosslare).

The surroundings are very beautiful, with wild jagged cliffs,
sandy beaches, vegetation reaching down almost to the sea,
rocky estuaries and hill streams. Inland are wind-swept hills
and rugged crags, alternating with peaceful pastureland, woods
and moorland. At *Carreg-gwastad*, 2 miles north-west, a
French force of 1400 men landed in 1797 but was defeated
by the local militia. 5 miles away is lonely *Strumple Head*,
with high rocky cliffs. At *Ynis Michael* is a modern lighthouse.

53. WORCESTER TO ABERYSTWYTH AND CARDIGAN

Worcester to Leominster: see p. 722.   26 miles: **Leominster** (p. 721).

40 miles: **Kington** (pop. 1800, E.C. Wednesday), on the Arrow, with an Early English and Decorated church. Associations with Mrs Siddons, the actress.

Kington to Shrewsbury: 48 miles. B 4355 to Knighton, then A 488.

7 miles: **Presteigne** (pop. 1130, E.C. Thursday). The border country in which it stands is little known to visitors, but has many beauties — the hilly Radnor Forest area, the tributaries of the Wye, the glens and streams of the Welsh spas. The parish church has Saxon, Norman and later work; 16th century Flemish tapestry on the north wall. *Radnorshire Arms* (1616). Part of Offa's Dyke (see below) can be seen near here, and there are remains of a Roman camp at *Watley.*

13 miles: **Knighton** (pop. 2200, E.C. Thursday), a little agricultural town on the Teme, in a magnificent setting. 2 miles away is the *Garth* (1000 ft), from which there are very fine views. 4 miles away, near the road to Frydd, remains of Offa's Dyke can be seen.

Offa's Dyke was built by King Offa of Mercia in the 8th century, reaching from the Dee in North Wales to the banks of the Severn near Chepstow, as a boundary between his kingdom and Welsh territory. In places the dyke was 15 feet high.

20 miles: *Clun,* on the river of the same name, with the ruins of a 12th century castle destroyed during the Civil War. — 25 miles: *Bishop's Castle,* an interesting old town with the remains of a 12th century castle. At *Lea,* 1 mile east, are the ruins of another castle (14th c.). — 38 miles: *Minsterley.* — 48 miles: *Shrewsbury* (p. 652).

46 miles: *New Radnor.* To the north-west is Radnor Forest. Norman earthworks near the church. The village has a rectangular street pattern, like Winchelsea in Sussex. — 49 miles: *Llanfihangel Nant Melan.*

— 55 miles: *Penybont*. 5 miles away is the Cistercian *Cwmhir Abbey* (12th c.). — 57 miles: **Cross Gates**.

3 miles south is **Llandrindod Wells** (pop. 3300, E.C. Wednesday), a spa and holiday resort (alt. 700 ft) in beautiful surroundings. Its water is saline and contains sulphur, magnesium and iron. There are three spa establishments — Pump House, Rock Park Spa and the Recreation Ground Spring (New Spring). *Museum* (Roman objects, local bygones). — 2 miles north-east is *Cefnllys Castle*, where the Court of the Marches met in the 15th and 16th centuries. — 2 miles north is *Castell Collen*, a Roman station. There is a museum containing a prehistoric dugout boat found in the river Ithon.

11 miles south is **Builth Wells** (pop. 1600, E.C. Wednesday), 400 feet above sea level on the Wye, in a saucer surrounded by high hills. There are three springs — saline, chalybeate and sulphur — which are recommended for conditions of the kidneys and heart and for gout. Earthworks of an old *castle*. At *Cilmeri*, 1½ miles west, is a monument to Llewelyn, a 13th century Welsh prince defeated by Edward I.

65 miles: **Rhayader** (pop. 1000, E.C. Wednesday), on the Wye some 20 miles from its source, 700 feet above sea level. From St Clement's Church there are magnificent views.

3 miles away is the Welsh lake district, the **Elan Valley**, with the artificial lakes created to provide a water supply for Birmingham. The first dam is at Caban Coch, the second at Garreg Ddu. A bridge over the dam links the Dol-y-Mynach reservoir with the river Claerwen, where a new dam 1000 feet long with a fall of 180 feet has been built.

In 1811, after being sent down from Oxford, Shelley spent the summer at *Cwm Flan* in the Elan valley and at the old manor-house of *Nant Gwyllt*, both submerged by the Caban Coch reservoir. Francis Brett Young describes this area in his novel, "The House under the Water".

75 miles: *Llangurig* (pop. 1100, E.C. Thursday), on the Wye 900 feet above sea level, surrounded by beautiful moorland, a good centre for walking. The church has a massive 12th century tower.

A starting point for the climb of *Plynlimon* (2468 ft), on which are the sources of the Wye, the Severn, the Rheidol, the Ystwyth and the Clywedog. The route goes by way of the Eistedfa Curig pass (1350 ft). There was a Roman station at *Cae Gaer*.

85 miles: *Dyffryn Castell*.

100 miles: **Aberystwyth** (pop. 10,000, E.C. Wednesday), a seaside resort in a great bay into which the rivers Ystwyth and Rheidol flow united and form a small harbour. To the south-west are the ruins of the *castle*, built in 1277 by Edmund of Lancaster, brother of Edward I. Aberystwyth is also a spa, with a chalybeate spring. Near the castle is the **University College,** established in 1872. The present building dates mostly from 1898. Museum of arts and crafts: unique collection of Welsh slip ware. Attached to the Agriculture department of the college is the *Welsh Plant Breeding Station*, at which new strains of plants are bred. On a hill at the back of the town is the *National Library of Wales* (1937): collections of Welsh printed books and manuscripts, exhibitions. (Visiting: weekdays 10 to 5, except Sundays).

Around Aberystwyth. 12 miles south-east are the *Devil's Bridge* and the beautiful Rheidol Falls (350 ft). The Devil's Bridge is in fact three bridges, one on top of the other. From the mountain railway which winds round the hills there are fine views of the Rheidol valley.

The road runs round Cardigan Bay. 103 miles: *Llanfarian*.

A 485 runs south-east to *Tregaron* (15 miles). 5 miles north-east of Tregaron on B 4343 is **Pontrhydfendigaid,** 2 miles from which is **Strata Florida Abbey** (12th c.), with a late Norman arch and little else. 3 miles away are the *Teifi Pools*, the source of the river Teifi.

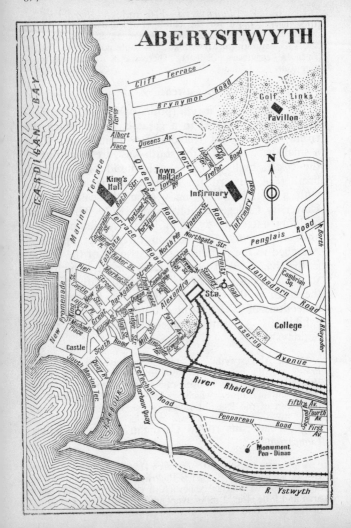

ABERYSTWYTH

109 miles: *Llanrhystyd*. 116 miles: *Aberaeron*, a quiet little port.

A 482 runs south-east to **Lampeter** (13 miles), a holiday resort 400 feet above sea level. *St David's College*, a theological college founded in 1827 by Thomas Burgess (1756-1837), bishop of St David's and later of Salisbury. The main library consists of 50,000 volumes and a number of illuminated manuscripts, including the only copy in Britain of the *Lübeck Missal*. *Olwen Camp*, an ancient British earthwork. *Alltgoch Camp*, a Roman station. 8 miles north-east is *Llanddewi Brefi*, a small village of grey and white houses with a 13th century church (carved Celtic crosses) at the entrance to a picturesque glen.

123 miles: *Synod*. 4 miles north-west is *New Quay*, a small harbour and seaside resort on the slopes of the Neuadd and Penywig hills.

138 miles: **Cardigan** (pop. 4000, E.C. Wednesday), a holiday resort with easy access to the country inland. Ruined *castle*. The church (rebuilt) dates from the Norman period.

Around Cardigan. 3 miles north-west is *Gwbert-on-Sea*, a seaside resort at the mouth of the river Teifi. 3 miles south-east is **Cilgerran**, a charming village on the Teifi. On a crag above the river are the ruins of a *Norman castle*, rebuilt in the 13th century, which have been painted by many artists, including Turner. 1 mile south-west is *St Dogmaels* (ruins of 12th century Benedictine monastery).

7 miles south-east is *Cenarth* (beautiful waterfalls). — 10 miles: *Newcastle Emlyn*, on the Teifi. Of the castle, built about 1240, only the gateway remains. Pleasant walks in the hills.

22 miles south-east is *Narberth*, a market town with a ruined castle. 4 miles north-west of this is *Llawhaden*, with an interesting church and a ruined castle, formerly residence of the Bishops of St David's.

10 miles south-west is **Newport**, a fishing port and seaside resort at the mouth of the Nevern. Ruins of 13th century castle, incorporated in a modern house. 2 miles south-west is the *Pentre Evan* dolmen. 1 mile north north-east is *Nevern* (church with a beautiful Celtic cross).

54. SHREWSBURY TO BARMOUTH

Leave Shrewsbury on A 458 over Welsh Bridge.

13 miles: *Middletown*, at the foot of Breidden Hill.
19 miles: **Welshpool** (pop. 6500, E.C. Thursday), an
old town in the Severn valley (foundries, timber
yards, cattle market). *St Mary's Church* is 13th
century, with a 14th century chancel and porch and
a 16th century nave. *Powysland Museum* (prehistoric
and later material relating to the ancient kingdom
of Powys; fossils). 1 mile south is **Powis Castle,** seat
of the Earl of Powis. Practically nothing remains of
the original 12th century castle; the present building
is almost entirely 19th century.

3 miles north is *Guilsfield*, with the very interesting church
of St Aelhaearn; remains of an ancient camp at Gaerfawr.
— 5 miles south is *Berriew*, an old village at the end of the
beautiful Rhiew valley (falls). — 4 miles north-east are the
Breidden hills. On top of *Craig Breidden* (1202 ft) is a monument
commemorating Admiral Rodney's victory in 1782. The highest
point is *Moel y Golfa* (1323 ft).

Welshpool to Aberystwyth: 57 miles (A 483 to Newtown,
A 492 to Llangurig, then A 44).

10 miles: *Abermule*. 4 miles north-east is **Montgomery,** an
old town with the ruins of an 11th century castle in a commanding position on a hill. From the British camp on a neighbouring
hill there are magnificent views. 1 mile east is Offa's Dyke
(see p. 871). 1 mile south-east is the beautiful old mansion
of *Lymore House*. — 14 miles: *Newtown* (pop. 5500, E.C.
Thursday), which owes its prosperity to the development of
the woollen industry in the Wye and Severn valleys. The church,
which is modern, has a rood-screen from the older church.
Robert Owen (1771-1858), pioneer of the cooperative movement,
was born in Newtown, left at the age of 17 to work in Manchester, but died and was buried in the town. There is a small
Owen Museum in his birthplace.

Beyond Newtown A 492 runs down the Severn valley. —
20 miles: *Caersws*, a Roman station. 5 miles north-west is

Carno, in a beautiful wooded valley south-west of three charming lakes. — 28 miles: *Llanidloes*, on the Severn, 10 miles from its source. The Market Hall of this pleasant old town dates from Tudor times. — 32 miles: *Llangurig* (p. 872). *Llangurig to Aberystwyth:* see route 53.

27 miles: Llanfair Caereinion. — 45 miles: *Mallwyd*, a charming village on the river Dyfi. — 46 miles: *Dinas Mawddwy*, a picturesque village at the junction of the Cerist and the Dyfi, with impressive waterfalls (particularly at Craig Wen and Abercowarch).

56 miles: **Dolgellau** (pop. 2500, E.C. Wednesday), in the centre of some of the loveliest glen country in Britain, at the foot of *Cader Idris*.

Immediately above the town is the *Precipice Walk*, which winds up the steep slopes of Moel Cynwch (1000 ft), with magnificent views of Cader Idris, the Mawddach estuary, Barmouth and Cardigan Bay. — At Tyn-y-Groes is the beautiful Black Cataract. — 6 miles north, reached by way of the Precipice Walk, is Nannay, 2 miles from which are the ruins of *Cymer Abbey* (1200). — **Cader Idris** (2927 ft), from the top of which there are splendid views of Wales, with Snowdonia to the north and Plynlimon to the south. Among the lakes which surround the hills is the famous *Tal-y-llyn*. The river Dysynny rises here amid the steep crags. The village at the end of the lake is one of the best starting points for the climb of Cader Idris, via Llyn-y-Cau to the highest point of the range, Pen-y-Gader.

Dolgellau to Aberystwyth by the coast road: 56 miles. A very pleasant round trip from Dolgellau is to follow this route to Machynlleth and return through the inland hills.

6 miles: *Arthog*. 8 miles: *Fairbourne*, a small seaside resort. Ferry service to Barmouth (below). — 11 miles: *Llwyngwril*. — 20 miles: **Towyn** (pop. 4500, E.C. Wednesday), a pleasant seaside resort. *St Cadfan's Church*, which has a Norman nave, occupies the site of an earlier 7th century church. When the Norman tower collapsed in the late 17th century a new tower was built, but this was demolished in the 19th century. Small *Railway Museum*. — 24 miles: *Aberdovey* (pop. 1200, E.C. Wednesday), a seaside resort at the mouth of the Dovey, with

beautiful beaches. — The road now follows the coast round
a series of wooded coves. 35 miles: **Machynlleth** (pop. 2000,
E.C. Thursday), a market town at the junction of the Dovey
and the Dulas. *Plas Machynlleth*, formerly a residence of the
Marquess of Londonderry, was presented to the town in the
1930s, and the grounds are now a public park. — The road
follows the Dovey valley, and then bears left along the coast
to *Glan Dovey*. — 50 miles: *Rhyd-y-pennau*, 2 miles from which
is the little seaside resort of Borth. — 56 miles: **Aberystwyth**
(p. 873).

A 496 runs along the north bank of the beautiful
Mawddach estuary via *Bontdud* (61 miles) to (66 miles)
Barmouth (pop. 2500, E.C. Wednesday), a seaside
resort magnificently situated between the hills and
the sea.

Around Barmouth. 2 miles from the town centre is *Llanaber*,
with a beautiful church (nave, choir and clerestory in very
pure Early English style). — 5 miles away is *Corsy-y-Gedol*,
an old manor-house with a gateway designed by Inigo Jones.
— 5 miles north-east is the *Dolmelynllyn* estate (1365 acres:
National Trust), with Tyn-y-Droes Hotel and several cottages
in the village of Ganllwyd. Beautiful meadows on the slopes
of Y Garn and, 3 miles north-west, two areas of sheep grazing
land rising to 2400 feet. The *Rhaiadr Du* waterfall (the Black
Falls), on Gamlam, one of the most impressive falls in Wales,
is easily reached on a path.

Up the coast to the north is **Harlech Castle** (p. 890).

55. SHREWSBURY TO HOLYHEAD

Leave Shrewsbury on A 458 over Welsh Bridge and at Shelton (2 miles) fork right into A 5.

14 miles: Queen's Head.

A 4083 goes off on the left and runs north-west 4 miles to **Oswestry** (pop. 11,500, E.C. Thursday), in the centre of an agricultural region between the valleys of the Dee and the Ceiriog, the Vyrnwy and the Severn, with wonderful views of the Shropshire plain and the Welsh hills. The *parish church* (rebuilt 1873) has some 13th and 14th century work. Remains of a *Norman castle*. Old houses in Church St, Albion Hill and Willow St. *Grammar School* in Bailey St.

At *Old Oswestry* is a prehistoric fort.

17 miles: *Whittington* (ruins of mediaeval castle). — **19 miles:** *Gogowen.* — **22 miles: Chirk** (pop. 3600, E.C. Thursday), on the river Ceiriog, with a castle dating from the reign of Edward I (1272-1307). Ebony cabinet presented to Thomas Myddleton by Charles II. Fine view from the ramparts.

24 miles: road on right to Wrexham and Chester.

4 miles along this road is **Ruabon,** a railway junction near a coal and iron district. In the parish church are tombs of the Williams-Wynn family. 1 mile south is *Wynnstay*, home of the Williams-Wynn family, with family portraits and a magnificent park. — **9 miles: Wrexham** (pop. 36,000, E.C. Wednesday), with a Perpendicular *church* (15th c.); west tower (1506), 140 feet high, with statues of saints. In the churchyard is buried Elihu Yale (1648-1721), who gave his name to Yale University; curious epitaph (1874). 1 mile north is *Acton Park*, birthplace of Judge Jeffreys (1648-89). 1 mile south-west is *Erddig Park*, home of Elihu Yale's parents.

29 miles: Llangollen (pop. 3260, E.C. Thursday), a small spa town on the Dee in a setting of verdant hills. Four-arched *bridge* built by John Trevor,

Bishop of St Asaph, in 1345. The church is 13th
century, with a 15th century tower.

Around Llangollen. *Dinas Bran Castle* (13th c.), on top of
a hill 910 feet high. The ruins include part of the gatehouse,
the windows of the great hall, the state bedroom and an apsed
tower. Fine views from Moel-y-geraint (1000 ft), — ½ mile
south is *Plas Newydd*, the residence (1780-1831) of the eccentric
"ladies of Llangollen", Eleanor Butler and Sarah Ponsonby.
— 2 miles north is the ruined **Valle Crucis Abbey,** a 12th century Cistercian foundation in a superb setting. Very fine carving in a whole range of styles from Transitional Norman (choir)
to late 13th century (west front). Nearby is the *Pillar of Eliseg*,
the shaft of a 9th century cross. The *Eglwyseg Rocks* vie with
the Pennines and the Mendips in the magnificence of their
scenery. Prehistoric remains. Some of the little valleys are
particularly beautiful, like the one leading to *World's End*.
— 3 miles away is the *Pontcysyllte Aqueduct*, 500 yards long
and 120 feet high, built by Thomas Telford in 1805 to carry
the Shropshire Union Canal over the valley.

39 miles: *Corwen*, a small town which is a good
centre for anglers. The church contains some interesting monuments; outside it is the shaft of an
8th century cross. 3 miles north-east is *Bryneglwys*,
with a Yale Chapel in the parish church. — 41 miles:
Druid.

Druid to Bala. The road runs through magnificent scenery.
4 miles: *Llandderfel*, an attractive little village within easy
reach of some of the finest inland scenery in North Wales.
In the ancient church are two curious wooden relics. — 9 miles:
Bala, in a magnificent setting near Lake Bala (530 ft above
sea level), the largest natural lake in Wales (4½ miles by 1 mile),
from which springs the river Dee. The sheepdog trials during
the summer months are a great attraction. — 2 miles away,
near Rhosygwaliau, is the attractive manor-house of *Rhiwaedog*.
In this area are many lakes, and good hills for climbers, like
Aran with its two peaks, Aran Benllyn (2901 ft) and Aran
Fawddwy (2970 ft), and Arenig (2800 ft).

49 miles: *Cerrig-y-Druidion*. The scenery becomes increasingly fine. — 55 miles: *Pentre Foelas*. The road follows the Conwy valley.

62 miles: **Betws-y-Coed,** beautifully situated at the junction of the Conwy and the Llugwy. A charming 15th century bridge, the *Pont-y-Pair*, crosses the Llugwy, with the stream tumbling over the boulders below.

67 miles: *Capel Curig*, a popular tourist centre, with a very fine view of Snowdon. — 77 miles: **Bethesda** (pop. 4800, E.C. Wednesday), 5 miles from the sea and 550 feet above sea level. Nearby is the largest slate quarry in the world, the Penrhyn Slate Quarry.

The peaks of Carnedd Dafydd (3426 ft) and Carnedd Llywelyn (3484 ft) can be climbed from Bethesda. There is a stiff climb between the two Black Ladders (Ysgolion Duon) by way of Ogwen to Nant Ffrancon, with a succession of peaks. At the head of the Nant Ffrancon pass are the two beautiful lakes of *Llyn Ogwen* and *Llyn Idwal*.

80 miles: *Llandegai*. Old church with the tomb of Archbishop Williams (see under Conwy).

82 miles: **Bangor** (pop. 14,000, E.C. Wednesday), a tourist centre consisting of *Lower Bangor* (to the south-east, in the narrow valley in which is the station) and *Upper Bangor* (a residential district in the valley above the Menai Strait, extending north to Garth Point).

The present **Cathedral** dates from the 16th century, apart from the 15th century choir; it was, however, thoroughly restored by Sir George Gilbert Scott in the 19th century. The interior is well proportioned. The nave and aisles have flat timber roofs, but the choir is vaulted. The windows are Perpendicular, those in the transept and south aisle Decorated.

Tombs of Welsh princes, including Owen Gwynedd (d. 1169), in the south transept. The Lady Chapel contains some tomb-stones. Beside the Cathedral are the Deanery and Canonry. To the north is Friar's School, a 16th century grammar school. In College Road, Upper Bangor, is the *University College of North Wales*, near which is the *Museum* (archaeology, local bygones). From the Menai woods there are wide views of the Menai Strait and bridges.

1 mile east is *Port Penrhyn*, a small harbour for shipping slates from the Bethesda quarries. Nearby is *Penrhyn Castle*, a modern building in Norman style. Large park. Picture gallery; Railway Museum.

The road skirts the picturesque and fast-flowing **Menai Strait** (14 miles long by 200 yards to ½ mile wide) which divides the Isle of Anglesey from the mainland. The road crosses the Strait by the *Menai Suspension Bridge*, the longest suspension bridge in the country (1826, Telford). The other bridge is the *Britannia Tubular Bridge*, which carries the railway (1850, Robert Stephenson).

The **Isle of Anglesey,** or *Mona*, has an area of 300 square miles, with a landscape of heather-covered common land and wide fields divided by low stone walls.

5 miles north-east of *Menai Bridge*, along the coast of the island, is **Beaumaris** (pop. 1960, E.C. Wednesday), a small market town and seaside resort at the north end of the Menai Strait, overlooking Conwy Bay to the Snowdon range. The *church* (14th century) has a 16th century chancel, with old stalls and quaint misericords, interesting monuments and brasses. Ruins of the 13th century **Beaumaris Castle**, built by Edward I in 1298. This was an almost perfect example of a circular castle, with two completely independent defence systems. The Great Hall, 70 feet by 25, was never completed. The round towers are particularly fine.

The County Hall (1614) has fine municipal insignia. At 32 Castle St is one of the oldest houses in the county (1400, altered in the 17th century), now a museum.

1 mile north is *Llanfaes Friary*, a 13th century Franciscan foundation. — 4 miles north is **Penmon,** with the church (restored) of a 7th century priory. The buildings are almost all Norman; 15th century glass. — 1 mile offshore is *Puffin Island,* a sanctuary for puffins and other seabirds. Ruins of a Norman tower. — 3 miles north is *Llangoed*, with the ruins of Lleiniog Castell (11th c.).

86 miles: **Llanfairpwllgwyngyllgogerychwyrndrob-wllllantysiliogogogoch** (pop. 1000), famous only for its name, which, for postal purposes and conversational convenience, is shortened to Llanfair P.G. The 58 letters and nineteen syllables describe the village as "the church of St Mary in a white-hazel hollow by a rapid whirlpool and St Tysilio's church near a red cave".

A 4080 goes off on the left (in a short distance, path to the right) to *Bryn Celli Ddu*, a perfectly preserved prehistoric hypogaeum (2nd millennium B.C.).

102 miles: *Valley.*   Aerodrome.

106 miles: **Holyhead** (pop. 10,000, E.C. Tuesday), a commercial centre, with a harbour which was rebuilt at the end of the 19th century for the railway passenger services to Ireland, and a small seaside resort. A breakwater nearby a mile and a half long protects the *New Harbour* (1873). Magnificent cliff scenery on both sides of the town, particularly near the South Stack to the east (lighthouse).

On the south-west coast of Anglesey there are many bays — Trearddur Bay, Cymyran Bay, Malltraeth Bay, off which is the bird sanctuary of Llanddwyn Island. St Cybi's church, semi-fortified (13th and 15th c.).

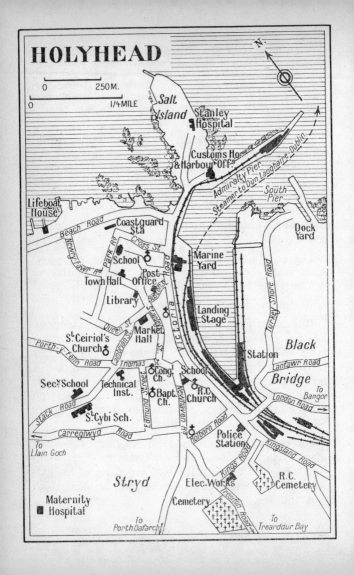

56. BANGOR TO BARMOUTH
VIA CAERNARVON

The road runs down the shore of the Menai Strait to *Port Dinorwic* (4½ miles). From here the slate from Llanberis quarries is shipped.

8½ miles: **Caernarvon** (pop. 10,000, E.C. Thursday), an ancient and picturesque town with narrow streets; its castle is one of the most splendid in the country. From the Twt Hill (194 ft), there is a good view of the town and castle.

The Castle stands west of the town at the confluence of the Seiont and Menai Strait. From the Toll Swing Bridge crossing the Seiont a splendid view of it can be obtained. This massive fortress built solely of hewn stone, one of the key points on the chain of fortifications erected by Edward I in 1283, was begun by the great architect Henry de Elreton, who also built Beaumaris Castle. It was not completed until the reign of Edward II (1307-27). The damaged figure over the great north King's Gateway is that of Edward I. The ground plan of the castle is of two courts in irregular oval shape divided by a wall. At intervals polygonal towers with slender turrets strengthen the walls, which in places are nearly 15 feet thick.

The King's Gate leads into the *Outer Bailey*, near the dividing wall. At the west end of the castle, in the Inner Bailey, is the *Eagle Tower*, one of the most interesting features, dating from the original building. From the sentry walk which runs round at first floor level there are fine views of the Menai Strait. The top of the Eagle Tower also offers magnificent views.

The *Queen's Tower* (restored) and the smaller *Chamberlain Tower* also belong to the original structure. There are four other large towers.

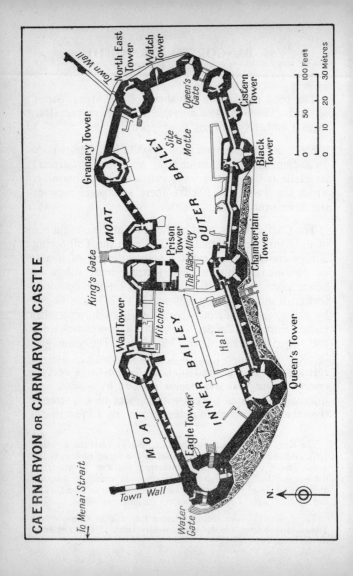

CAERNARVON or CARNARVON CASTLE

Town Wall
North East Tower
Watch Tower
Queen's Gate
Granary Tower
MOAT
BAILEY
Site of Motte
Cistern Tower
King's Gate
OUTER
Black Tower
Prison Tower
The Black Alley
Chamberlain Tower
Wall Tower
Kitchen
BAILEY
Hall
Eagle Tower
INNER BAILEY
Queen's Tower
MOAT
To Menai Strait
Town Wall
Water Gate
N.

100 Feet
50
0
0 10 20 30 Métres

The **town walls,** which originally linked up with the castle walls at the east and west ends, still survive, and it makes a pleasant walk to follow them round from the castle, turning right to begin at the side facing the river. There is an attractive promenade running along the river bank from the Eagle Tower.

1 mile east is *Segontium*, a Roman station covering an area of 3 acres. The museum contains many objects found on the site. — 2 miles away is *Llanbeblig*, the mother church of Caernarvon, with an interesting Tudor tower and fine monuments.

The Lleyn Peninsula

3 miles: *Llanwnda*. — 9 miles: **Clynnog Fawr.** In the magnificent Perpendicular *St Beuno's Church* note the old strongbox in which offerings were kept and a pair of "dog-tongs" (used to control fighting dogs). A short distance away is St Beuno's Well, and near this is a large dolmen. The village lies at the foot of Bwlch Mawr (1670 ft). — 14 miles: **Llanaelhaearn,** at the foot of the *Rivals* (Yr Eifl, 1849 ft), three peaks in the form of two forks: hence the Welsh name. On *Tre'r Ceiri* ("Giants' Town") is one of the largest and best preserved prehistoric forts in the country. There are parts of the walls 15 feet high and 10 feet long, enclosing an area of 5 acres. — 20 miles: **Pwllheli** (pop. 4000, E.C. Thursday), a seaside resort on Cardigan Bay near the mouth of the river Erch. The town faces south and is sheltered by the Rivals, the Bedfean Mountains (920 ft) and the two peaks of the Mabryn Mountains (1220 ft). The beach is one of the best in the country. West of the harbour is Gimlet Rock (Carreg-y-Rimbill).

Around Pwllheli. 5 miles south is *Llandebrog*, a pleasant seaside village. *Bardsey Island* (Ynis Enlli) is 2¼ miles from Braich-y-Pwll, at the tip of the peninsula, with very beautiful coastal scenery; it can be reached by boat from *Aberdaron* (pop. 1000, E.C. Wednesday), a popular little resort. Little is left of St Mary's Abbey (13th c.). — 5 miles north-east of Aberdaron, on the hill of Mynydd Rhiw, is *Plas-yn-Rhiw*, a 17th century mansion.

Snowdonia

A 4086 from Caernarvon to Capel Curig. *Bryn Bras*, a country house (1830) with beautiful gardens, lies to the right of the road.

The road runs alongside the lakes of *Llyh Padarn* and *Llyn Peris*. 7 miles: **Llanberis** (pop. 2200, E.C. Wednesday), at the end of Llyn Padarn, dominated by the bulk of Snowdon to the south-east. The beauty of the scenery tends to be marred by slate quarries. From the single tower of *Dolbadarn Castle* (13th c.) there is a fine view up Llanberis Pass, one of the wildest in the country. Near the Victoria Hotel is the *Ceumant Mawr* waterfall (60 ft). Down the valley is *Ceumant Bach*, which is even more beautiful.

Snowdon, in Welsh *Eryri* (3560 ft), is the highest mountain in England and Wales but still falls short of Ben Nevis in Scotland by 850 feet. It is a hill of majestic outline, with five peaks linked by ridges. On the central peak, Yr Wyddfa (3560 ft), a cairn marks the traditional burial place of the giant Rhitta Gawr. The other peaks are Grib Goch (the Red Peak, 3023 ft), Grib-y-Ddysgyl (3500 ft), the first to be encountered when climbing from Llanberis, Lliwedd (2947 ft) and, to the south towards Beddgelert, Yr Aran (2451 ft). *Snowdonia National Park*.

Snowdon, created by the Cambrian and Silurian folding movements, consists mainly of porphyry and schist. A mountain railway climbs to the summit from Llanberis (about 1 hour). The ascent can be made on foot by five routes — from Llanberis, Capel Curig, Beddgelert, the Snowdon Ranger and Nant Gwynant. The second route is the most rewarding; the first is the fastest and easiest.

10 miles: *Nant Peris*. To the north-east is Glyder Fawr (3279 ft). The road goes over the Llanberis pass. — 14 miles: *Pen-y-Gwryd*, one of the starting points for the climb of Snowdon and the beginning of the shortest ascent of Glyder Fawr. — 18 miles: *Capel Curig*.

13 miles: *Betws Garmon*.   Nearby is beautiful *Hafodty Park*.   To the north-east is Moel Eilioand; to the south-east Mynydd Mawr (2290 ft). — 18 miles: *Rhyd-ddu*, after passing Llyn Cwellyn.

To the north of this lake a path goes off for the ascent of Snowdon by the *Snowdon Ranger* route. From Rhyd-ddu it is 3 miles to the summit (terminus of the mountain railway). A road climbs west from here, passing Llyn-y-Dywarchen, to Bwylch-y-Felin (750 ft), and then runs past Mynydd Mawr to Nantle.

21 miles: **Beddgelert** (pop. 400, E.C. Wednesday), a charming village situated at the confluence of the Colwyn and Glaslyn on the south foot of Snowdon. It is one of the best tourist centres in North Wales, within easy reach of the most famous beauty spots, and itself very beautiful.

23 miles: **Pont Aberglaslyn** over the little River Glaslyn where it runs through the superb *Aberglaslyn Pass* between sheer rock cliffs 800 feet high. This pass is one of the most famous beauty spots in Wales. — 29 miles *Penrhyndeudraeth*.

7 miles east, on the road to Bala, is **Ffestiniog** (pop. 9100, E.C. Thursday), in a charming situation on a hill between the valleys of the Dwyrd and the Cynfal. In the neighbourhood are the lovely Cynfal Falls. Rhaeadr-y-Cwm is another beautiful district. Remains of a Roman amphitheatre near Tomen-y-Mur. 3 miles north of Ffestiniog is *Blaenau Ffestiniog* (pop. 9160, E.C. Thursday), a small town in a beautiful situation at the head of the Dwyryd valley, in a district of slate quarries cut into the surrounding mountain sides. The largest, the Palmerston Quarry, has been worked since 1775.

3 miles west are **Porthmadog** and *Borth-y-Gest* (pop. 4100, E.C. Wednesdays). A fine centre for excursions, particularly for the Snowdon district; it was founded just over 100 years ago in connection with the Ffestiniog slate quarries by W.A. Madocks, who reclaimed 10,000 acres of land from the sea by building the stone dyke, the "Cob", over the Glaslyn estuary. Formerly a busy port, it is now a quiet little market town and seaside resort. 1 mile away is *Woodlands*, birthplace of Lawrence of Arabia. 5 miles west is **Criccieth** (pop. 1600, E.C. Wednesday), a seaside resort on Tremadoc Bay. There are the ruins of a castle built by Edward I. 1½ miles north-east, *Llanystumdwy*, with the grave of Llloyd George. He lived at *Brynawelon* nearby; in the village is the Lloyd George Museum. — *Ystumcedig Cromlech*, the largest prehistoric remains in the district. From *Ednyfed Hill* there are magnificent views. *Cwmystradllyn*, a beautiful lake.

32 miles: *Talsarnau*. Fine views over Snowdonia.
— 36 miles: **Harlech** (pop. 1020, E.C. Wednesday),
a small town famous for its *Castle*, one of the defensive
fortifications of Edward I, erected high on the rock
in the shape of a square with impregnable walls and
round towers. The remains are very complete. From
the castle are fine views over sea and mountains.
1½ miles east is *Moel-y-Senicl* (1018 ft), with magnificent views.

45 miles: *Llanaber*. — 46 miles: **Barmouth** (p. 878).

57. THE NORTH WALES COAST
(CHESTER TO BANGOR)

7 miles: *Hawarden*. 8 miles: **Ewloe Green,** with the ruins of a fine 13th century castle.

Ewloe Green to Druid: 28 miles on A 494.

4 miles: **Mold** (pop. 5680, E.C. Thursday), a busy coal-mining centre on the river Alyn. The church (15th c.) has good glass and interesting ornamentation. The landscape painter Richard Wilson (1714-82) is buried in the churchyard.

1 mile south is a manor-house with a 15th century battlemented tower and a Jacobean wing. — 8 miles: the *Loggerheads Inn*. — 10 miles: *Llanferres*. — 2 miles away is Bwlch Pen Barras, from which Moel Fammau (1817 ft), the highest hill in the Clwydian range, can be climbed: magnificent views. — 15 miles: **Ruthin** (pop. 3500, E.C. Thursday). Favourably situated above the Vale of Clwyd in one of the loveliest districts of North Wales, Ruthin is a picturesque little town. The 14th century *St Peter's Church* (modern spire) contains a black oak roof of 500 panels, and interesting brasses. The ruins of the *Castle* of the time of Edward I (1272-1307) are in the grounds of a house. Old houses.

The *Castle Hotel* in the centre of the town has many features of historical interest, including the old Dutch building, with seven dormers, formerly known as the Myddleton Arms. There are a 16th century *Grammar School* and *Almshouses*, both founded by Dean Goodman of Westminster. — 28 miles: **Druid** (p. 880).

11 miles: *Northop*. 3 miles north is *Flint* (pop. 14,000), a centre of the chemical industry, with a 13th century castle.

17½ miles: **Holywell** (pop. 8500, E.C. Wednesday), a small town on the Dee estuary nearly 1000 feet above sea level, commanding magnificent views. The town is so called because of St Winefride's Well, one of the "seven wonders of Wales". Until 1917, when the course of its flow was altered by mining operations, the spring produced nearly 3000 gallons of crystal-clear water per minute at approximately 50 F. The water still flows — at a reduced rate — into the basin in the chapel of St Winefride.

28 miles: **St Asaph** (pop. 2000, E.C. Saturday), a quiet little cathedral town on the Clwyd. The *Cathedral* — the smallest in the country but also the oldest, dating from the 6th century — stands on top of a hill.

It is 180 feet long, mainly in 15th century Decorated style. Parts of the nave and aisles date from the 13th century. The whole building was restored by Sir George Gilbert Scott in the 19th century. Large square tower (100 ft): wide views. The 18th century *choir* preserves some older work, with carved oak stalls; modern glass. The *Chapter Museum* contains a collection of Bibles and prayer books.

6 miles south is **Denbigh** (pop. 8500, E.C. Thursday), an old town on the site of a Roman station, situated on a hill, with fine views over the Vale of Clwyd. The **castle** (1282) was one of the chain of fortresses built by Edward I to maintain order in Wales. In 1563 Queen Elizabeth I presented it to Robert Dudley, Earl of Leicester. During the Civil War it was held by the Royalists. The *museum* contains many interesting relics from the castle and the surrounding area. **St Hilary's Church** (170 ft by 71 ft) was begun by the Earl of Leicester, but work stopped on his death in 1588; only the tower is left. Nearby is the entrance to the *town walls*, contemporary with the oldest part of the castle (Burgess and Goblin Towers). H.M. Stanley, the African explorer, was born in Denbigh and brought up in St Asaph workhouse; his real name was John Rowlands, but he took the name of the New Orleans broker who adopted him. *Howell's School* was founded in 1540 by Thomas Howell, who left 12,000 gold ducats for its upkeep, and is now one of the country's leading public schools for girls; the present building dates from 1850. — 2 miles north-west is *Henllan*. St Sadwrn's Church (1807) has a separate tower, built on a rock at the north-east corner of the churchyard. — 8 miles: *Llanrhaiadr*, with an interesting church (fine east window with a *tree of Jesse*).

A 525 runs north from St Asaph to *Rhuddlan Castle* (built by Edward I about 1280) and **Rhyl** (pop. 22,000), a seaside resort popular with families. East of Rhyl is *Prestatyn*, another resort. It is possible to return to St Asaph via the village of *Dyserth*, near which is *Bodrhyddan Hall*, a 17th century manor-house with a beautiful interior (open Tuesdays and Thursdays 2 to 5.30).

30 miles: **Bodelwyddan,** famous for the "*Marble Church*" (1860) of white magnesium limestone. The spire is 202 feet high, and there are interesting carvings and ornamentation in the interior.

35 miles: **Abergele** and *Pensarn* (pop. 9000, E.C. Thursday), a seaside resort, with fine sands in a great sheltered bay. *St Michael's Church* was rebuilt in the 13th century; subsequent additions. The tower dates from 1879. On Tower Hill is *Gwrych Castle*. The frontage is 480 yards, and there are seventeen turrets, with the tallest tower 95 feet high. The *Castle* (formerly seat of the Earl of Dundonald) is now a centre of attractions for visitors; massed choirs and silver prize bands, etc. Higher up Tower Hill (600 ft) are the natural caverns of *Cefn-Yr-Ogo*. Magnificent views from the summit. Nearby is the British camp of *Castell-y-Cawr*.

The tiny hamlet of *St George*, 2 miles away, is traditionally the site of the battle between St George and the Dragon. The annual agricultural show and sheepdog trials are an important event in the district. Other seaside resorts are *Kinmel Bay*, *Llanddulas* and *Rhydyfoel*.

42 miles: **Colwyn Bay** (pop. 22,000, E.C. Wednesday), a very popular seaside resort on a bay 3 miles long, flanked by two large promontories and backed by a ridge of hills (400 ft). At one end of the bay is *Llysfaen*, and to the west are the hill of Euryn and

Rhos-on-Sea, formerly the fishing village of Llan-drillon-y-Rhos; very beautiful parks.

47 miles: **Llandudno** (pop. 18,500, E.C. Wednesday), one of the best known of the Welsh seaside resorts, an excellent centre for excursions in North Wales. It is uniquely situated on a peninsula, has a sandy shore on either side of the town, and is overlooked by *Great Orme's Head* (670 feet). Llandudno Bay extends between the two headlands of Great Orme and Little Orme; the west side looks on to the hills beyond Conwy Bay.

St Tudno's Church was built in the 15th century (restored 19th century). In the 7th century it was the anchorite cell of St Tudno.

The *rocking stone* was, according to legend, used by the druids; the cromlech also dates from prehistoric times. Shafts of disused copper-mines are to be seen — remains of mines once worked by the Romans and by even earlier dwellers. Little Orme's Head resembles closely the larger crag, but measures only 465 feet. From the summit there is a magnificent view over the town and Snowdonia.

2 miles south are the ruins of *Deganwy Castle*.

52 miles: **Conwy** (pop. 10,000, E.C. Wednesday), a picturesque town at the mouth of the river Conwy, which retained until 1934 the complete circuit of town walls built in 1284. The Welsh form of the name, Conwy, has recently replaced the English form, Conway.

There were originally four gates in the walls: *Porth yr Felin* (Mill Gate), *Porth Uchaf* (Upper Gate), the main exit towards Bangor, with a drawbridge and barbican, *Porth Isaf* (Lower Gate) and *Porth Bach*, a postern gate on the quay. There is also a gate in the spur of wall at the end of the quay, *Porth yr Aden* (Wing Gate). It is possible to follow the line of the walls for most of their circuit; particularly fine views along the river. (Enter by Upper Gate and the quay).

The **Castle** is splendidly situated on a rock over
the river. It was the third castle that Edward I built
in North Wales. The plan is oblong. It is protected

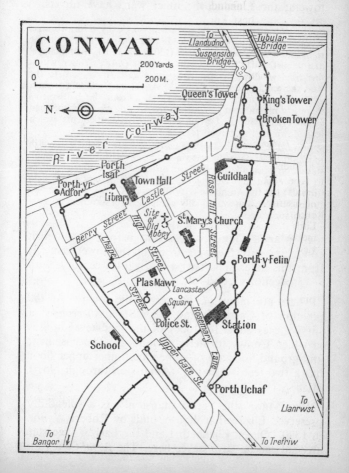

on three sides by the Conwy, while the fourth is incorporated into the town defences. The walls, 12-15 feet in thickness, were strengthened by eight towers; those round the inner ward have turrets.

The entrance is at the north-west angle by a drawbridge. A gateway with a portcullis leads to the *Great Hall*. On the right stood the *Banqueting Hall* (130 ft by 32 ft), with a chapel at the east end. To the north-east is the *Queen's Tower*, with a fine oriel window. Opposite is the *King's Tower*, and to the west the rebuilt "*Broken Tower*". At the east end is a terrace, where was formerly the River Gate. From the battlements there is a magnificent *view* of the town. The *garden* (mentioned as early as 1316) is beyond the massive battlements which lead down to the garden terrace.

Edward was besieged in the castle in 1294 during the Welsh rebellion. The garrison was on the point of surrender through starvation when a fall in the level of the Conwy enabled supplies to be brought in. During the Civil War the castle was held for the king by Archbishop Williams of Conwy and later by Prince Rupert, but was finally compelled to surrender to Parliamentary forces.

St Mary's Church dates from before the English conquest; only the west front of the tower remains from this date. The nave is early 14th century, with a 15th century rood-loft.

There are many *old houses* in the town. At the junction of Castle St and High St is *Aberconwy*, a surviving example (c. 1500) of the mediaeval houses in which Conwy formerly abounded. The basement and ground floor are of stone; the timber upper floor has a two feet overhang. (Admission through No. 1 High St).

Plas Mawr (the "great mansion") is a splendidly preserved Elizabethan house, built by Robert Wynne in 1580. Queen Elizabeth I and the Earl of Leicester are said once to have stayed here. The *Royal Cambrian*

Academy of Art now have their headquarters here: annual summer exhibitions. (Visiting: daily, except Sundays, 10 to 4 or 6).

There are several old inns in the town. The *Boot Inn* and *Cae Coch* were one house in the 15th century. The *Black Lion Inn* in Castle St was built by a vicar of Conwy, and is sometimes known as the *Old Vicarage*.

The *Quay* (restored in the 19th century) retains its mediaeval charm and tranquillity. It is now used only by the Conwy fishermen. On the Quay is the *smallest house in Britain*, which is also interesting for the mid-Victorian Welsh cottage interior it depicts.

For centuries Conwy has been an important centre of mussel fishery. There are three golf courses. Yachting.

Around Conwy. 5 miles away, on *Penmaenmawr*, is a circle of standing stones. At Conwy begins the great mountain mass known as **Snowdonia.** Between the Conwy and Ogwen valleys are Carnedd Llywelyn (3485 ft), Carnedd Ddafydd (3424 ft), Yr Elen (3150 ft) and Foel Fras (3091 ft), this last being the most easily accessible by way of Aber and the Anafon valley. The four peaks can be climbed in turn without descending below 3000 feet.

12 miles away is **Llanrwst** (pop. 2600, E.C. Wednesday), a picturesque town on the Conwy, here spanned by the *Pont Fawr*, built in 1636 by Inigo Jones, who was also responsible for the *Gwydir Chapel* adjoining the parish church (19th c. tower and north aisle). The church has a carved rood-screen (15th c.) and a beautifully carved oak ceiling. 1 mile away is *Gwydir Castle*, on the west bank of the river, amid the dense woodland and high crags of the surrounding countryside. The chief attractions are the gardens — very beautiful lawns, the Royal Garden, the Statesman's Garden, the Dutch Garden, the Chinese Walk and the Rhododendron Walk. 1 mile north is *Trefriw*, at the foot of pine-clad hills, with two thermal springs (water containing iron, sulphur, alum and silicon): spa establishments.

51 miles: **Penmaenmawr** (pop. 3700, E.C. Wednesday), seaside resort protected by a semicircle of high hills, situated on the north Gwynedd coast between

the two headlands of Penmaenmawr and Penmaen-
bach, the northernmost spurs of the Snowdon range.
— 1½ miles: *Fairy Glen*, a charming little valley. —
1¼ miles: *Druid Circle* (Y Meini Hirion), which
consists of ten upright stones in a circle 80 feet in
diameter.

54 miles: *Llanfairfechan* (pop. 3166, E.C. Wednesday). 56 miles: *Aber*, some distance from the coast
at the mouth of a picturesque glen. On the other
side of the Menai Strait is *Beaumaris*. Before the
building of the bridge access to Anglesey was over
Lavan Sands at low tide — a hazardous crossing in
which many travellers were drowned.

In the centre of the village is the mound known as the *Mwd*,
said to be the site of a castle built by Llywelyn the Great, where
Edward I finally brought the Welsh forces to bay and compelled
Llywelyn to surrender.

Inland from Aber is the beautiful *Aber Glen*. The road goes
over the Pont Newydd. To reach the very fine *Aber Falls*
(Rhaeadr Fawr, 210 ft), 1½ miles away, it is necessary to cross
the small bridge higher up. The Afon Bach is another beautiful
waterfall.

62 miles: **Bangor** (p. 881).

VIII: THE LOWLANDS OF SCOTLAND AND THE BORDERS

The term **Lowlands** may mislead the visitor, for within this geographical division of Scotland is country which is anything but low, and although its high country nowhere achieves the craggy grandeur of the Highlands some of its hills are steep and impressive. The Lowlands are the most productive and consequently the most thickly populated region of Scotland, and it is claimed that all the heavy industries and most of the light industries known to the British Isles are represented here. The world-famous Clyde shipyards are within the Lowlands, and the woollen mills of the Border country are no less widely known. But agriculturally the area is equally famous and its advanced farming, particularly in the rich Lothians, is justly renowned.

Edinburgh claims to be considered as among the loveliest cities in Europe. History, romance and natural beauties have made it a city indeed worthy of being the capital of a country rich in all those attributes. South of Edinburgh to the Borders is a countryside of hills and wooded slopes studded with compact border towns lying in sheltered valleys on the banks of fine rivers. This is the country beloved by Walter Scott, and around Abbotsford, his home on the banks of the River Tweed, is the gracious countryside known now as the Scott Country. Within this romantic territory are the abbeys of Melrose and Dryburgh and Jedburgh. Eastward lies Berwick, a town which has changed hands so often that one may be excused for not knowing whether it belongs to Scotland or to England. Geographically it could be in Scotland, but politically it is in England, for the border is not crossed until one has reached Lamberton tollhouse three miles north of the town. Northward stretches up to the mouth of the Firth of Forth a magnificent coastline.

In the south-west corner of the Lowlands are lovely Galloway and Dumfriesshire, and here we are in the country of another great Scots writer. This is the Burns Country. At Dumfries is the tomb of the poet, and at Alloway on the outskirts of Ayr is the cottage where he was born. This gentle and lovely countryside is rich in scenic and historic interest, and through it all runs the bright thread of the Burns tradition, enlivening with his verse each bridge and river bank and loch.

The Lowlands stretch up to the two great Firths of Forth and Clyde; the Forth, on which stands Edinburgh, spanned by the mighty railway bridge which is still more than eighty years after its building one of the engineering marvels of the world, as well as by a fine new road bridge, and the Clyde, the great highway to the vast industrial city of Glasgow and the site of some of the finest shipyards in the world. Along the shores of both these Firths are fine seaside resorts, and beyond the mouth of the Clyde and the Ayrshire coast are such beauties as the Isle of Arran and the Kyles of Bute.

58. EDINBURGH

Berwick-on-Tweed to Edinburgh

58 miles on A 1. London to Berwick, by the Great North Road: see Route 42.

4 miles: the *Border*. — 8 miles: *Ayton*.

3 miles north-west is the little fishing port of *Eyemouth*. 3 miles beyond this on A 1107, at *Coldingham*, are the ruins of a Benedictine priory (1099) in Transitional style. Nearby is *St Abb's Head*, a fine headland (310 ft) with a lighthouse and the ruins of a 14th century church. Along the coast to the west are the picturesque ruins of *Fast Castle*, on a precipitous crag jutting out from the cliffs.

22 miles: *Cockburnspath*, where the road comes back to the coast. Here we enter the Lothians. The road and railway follow the low land east of the Lammermuir Hills. — 29 miles: stone (on left) marking the site of the *battle of Dunbar* (3 September 1650), in which Cromwell defeated the Scots. The road bypasses **Dunbar.**

30 miles: **Dunbar** (pop. 5000, E.C. Wednesday), a popular seaside resort. On the rocks above the new harbour are the ruins of *Dunbar Castle*, which was burned down five times during the wars between Scotland and England. At the entrance to the old harbour is a barometer.

35 miles: A 198 goes off on the right to *Tynninghame*, near which is *Tynninghame House*, seat of the Earl of Haddington, a turreted red sandstone building in well wooded country.

12 miles north is **North Berwick** (pop. 4200, E.C. Thursday), a seaside resort on a bay with numerous islands. Picturesque old harbour. Wide views to the south-east from Berwick Law (613 ft). Ruins of a Cistercian nunnery (1216) at the end of the town.

Around North Berwick. *Bass Rock* (350 ft), a rocky mass rising out of the sea, the haunt of many seabirds (gannets). Lighthouse; ruins of castle and chapel. — 3 miles east are the ruins of *Tantallon Castle* (1350), magnificently poised on the top of high cliffs.

A 198 continues along the coast via *Gullane* and *Aberlady*, pleasant seaside resorts (golf-courses). At *Prestonpans* is a monument to Col. Gardiner, killed in the battle of Prestonpans (1745). — 28 miles: A 198 runs into A 1.

33 miles: *East Linton*.

41 miles: A 1 bypasses **Haddington** (pop. 5700, E.C. Thursday), an attractive old market town. Fine *church* (12th c.). Jane Welsh, wife of Thomas Carlyle, is buried in the churchyard.

43 miles: *Tranent* (pop. 5600), a mining town.

2 miles south is *Elphinstone Tower* (15th c.), with many rooms and secret passages. To the east is *Fawside Castle*, another feudal stronghold, near which the battle of Pinkie was fought in 1547. To the north is *Preston Tower* (15th c.).

47 miles: **Musselburgh** (pop. 17,100, E.C. Thursday), an industrial and mining town and fishing port. Old Tolbooth. *Pinkie House* (1613) is a handsome old mansion (now occupied by a school). Nearby is *Carberry Tower*, formerly seat of Lord Elphinstone; to the south, *Carberry Hill*, where Mary Queen of Scots surrendered. Famous golf-course.

51 miles: **Portobello,** now part of Edinburgh. Beach; fine modern open-air swimming pool. 2 miles south is *Craigmillar Castle* (14th c.), on a rocky hill commanding the surrounding area.

A 90 continues (to right) along the Firth of Forth to **Leith** (pop. 77,400), Scotland's second largest seaport, and *Granton*, with a spacious harbour built in the early 19th century, used by North Sea trawlers.

58 miles: **Edinburgh.**

EDINBURGH

Edinburgh (pop. 470,000), capital of Scotland and one of the most prestigious cities in the United Kingdom, and indeed in Europe. This "Athens of the North" is an intellectual centre noted for its Universities and its printing and publishing firms, and also an industrial town (brewing, engineering, electrical equipment, chemicals, clothing, etc.).

From the battlements of the castle — within a few steps of St Margaret's Chapel, one of the oldest sacred buildings in Scotland — one looks down on the city, on the spires and crescents of the New Town of Stevenson and Scott, of Raeburn and Alexander Nasmyth. Beyond, the blue waters of the Forth wash the shores of the ancient kingdom of Fife, and, in the far distance, the shadowy ranges of the Highlands form the horizon.

Edinburgh is magnificently built on a series of hills and ravines: to the east is *Arthur's Seat* (823 ft), to the west *Corstorphine Hill* and to the south *Blackford Hill* and the *Braid Hills*, with the long Pentland range beyond. The Firth of Forth is the northern boundary. Plan in colour at end of Guide.

There are two main aspects of the town — the **Old Town,** which covers the long ridge from Castle Rock to the palace of Holyroodhouse, and — on the other side of the valley — the **New Town.**

History

The history of Edinburgh is bound up with the castle, which was first built in the 7th century. Holyrood Abbey was founded in the 12th century, the Blackfriars Monastery in the 13th, but it was not until 1437, when Edinburgh became the recognised capital (see Perth), that it reached any size and importance.

The town walls date from soon after this time (1455). In 1544 and again five years later, after the battle of Pinkie, Henry VIII sacked Edinburgh. From 1555 onwards the capital was the scene of the bitter struggles between Queen Mary and the Reformers. James VI founded its University.

1603 saw the departure to London of James VI of Scotland to become James I of England, and the importance of the city as a capital decreased. In 1650 Cromwell seized the castle. After the Restoration, Edinburgh witnessed the persecution of the Covenanters. On the signing of the Act of Union the Scottish Parliament was moved to London in 1707. In 1745 Prince Charles Edward occupied the city and held court at Holyrood, but was unable to take the castle.

The end of the 18th and beginning of the 19th century saw Edinburgh's renaissance. It was a period of literary brilliance, when many famous figures lived here. Some of the great names were David Hume (d. 1776); Adam Smith (d. 1790); the historian, Robertson (d. 1793); Smollett (d. 1771); Henry Mackenzie (d. 1831); Scott (d. 1832); John Wilson (d. 1854); Lockhart and Jeffrey (d. 1850); and many others. Walter Scott and James Boswell (biographer of Dr Johnson) were born in Edinburgh; and Thomas Babington Macaulay, perhaps the greatest English historian, and Charles Dickens, who received the freedom of the city, were also closely associated with the capital.

Also born in Edinburgh were several distinguished Americans, including James Lorraine Geddes (1829), who became a brigadier-general in the Civil War; James Blair, chief founder and first president of William and Mary College; and Alexander Graham Bell (1847), inventor of the telephone.

The New Town began to be built in the 18th century, and since then Edinburgh has continued to increase in size. Since 1947 the city has been noted for its *International Festival of Music and Drama*, held annually in August-September; associated with this is the spectacular *Military Tattoo*.

Edinburgh Castle

Edinburgh Castle is the most immediately striking feature in the city, perched on a volcanic crag 443 feet high (260 ft above the city) with sheer rock faces on three sides. The easiest way of reaching it from Princes St (Edinburgh's most famous street, running from east to west across the centre of the city) is to go up the *Mound*, a wide street which sweeps up to the old town, and turn right into the narrow street leading steeply uphill to the Castle Esplanade. The Castle is open from 9.30 to 6 in summer (Sundays 11 to 6), the outer parts until 9.

In the course of its long and stormy history the Castle changed hands many times. It was captured in 1296 by Edward I and thereafter was held by the English until 1313. The apartments occupied by Mary Queen of Scots are of particular interest. In a small room on the ground floor she gave birth in 1566 to a son, who was to become James VI of Scotland and I of England. Charles I stayed in the Castle in 1633. It was besieged in 1689, when it supported James II against William and Mary, and unsuccessfully blockaded by Prince Charles Edward in 1745.

The *Esplanade* was laid out in the early 19th century as a military parade ground. Every summer it is the scene of the Military Tattoo during the Edinburgh Festival.

A drawbridge leads over the moat to the *Gatehouse* (modern). Built into the walls of the arched entry are two 17th century carved panels depicting cannon. In front is the ticket office, and from here the roadway climbs steeply up to the **Portcullis Gate,** at the foot of the curtain wall under the Half Moon Bastion.

The Portcullis Gate (1574), with *Argyll's Tower* above it, had two outer double doors and an inner double door, with the portcullis between them. The tower is named after the Marquis of Argyll, who was imprisoned here in 1661.

Beyond the Portcullis Gate, on the right, is a battery of cannon, and beyond this barracks and other buildings. The roadway then turns up to the

left, passing the *Governor's House* on the right, with
hospital buildings and barracks behind it.   Then,
turning left again through an old gateway, *Foog's
Gate*, we come to the highest point in the Castle, the
Citadel.

The highest point, the *Bomb Battery* (443 ft above sea level),
commands a magnificent view over the city. In the foreground
are Princes St and the New Town, the straggling Old Town
and Royal Mile stretching downhill to Holyrood Palace, and
the ancient Grassmarket, and beyond this the Firth of Forth
and the North Sea, Arthur's Seat and the Pentland Hills. On
the farther horizons can be seen the peaks of the Grampians.

On the ramparts is a famous cannon familiarly known as
Mons Meg, believed to have been cast at Mons in Flanders.
According to the popular legend, however, it was made in
Kirkcudbrightshire for James III, then laying siege to Threave
Castle.   It became a kind of national symbol: having been
carried off to London in 1754, it was returned to Scotland in
1829, after a campaign for its recovery led by Sir Walter Scott.
It was probably cast in the 15th century. It is 13 ft 4 in. long,
with a bore of 1 ft 8 in., and could project an iron cannonball
¾ mile or a stone one 1½ mile Below the platform on which
Mons Meg stands is a small bastion, now used as a burial
place for soldiers' dogs.

St Margaret's Chapel was built in 1076 by Malcolm III's
Saxon queen, Margaret. It is a charming little Norman building
with a fine ornamented *arch*, still used for the marriages of
members of the garrison. The flowers on the altar are supplied
by Edinburgh women named Margaret. The chapel is the
oldest religious building in Edinburgh still in use.

From here we walk south-east past the *Forewall
Battery* and the *Fore Well*, which formerly supplied
the Castle with water; it is 110 feet deep, the lower
90 feet being hewn from the rock.   Beyond is the
curved **Half Moon Battery** (16th c.), with the **"one
o'clock gun"** which is fired regularly every day at
1 o'clock,

Turning right, we enter the **Palace Yard** or "Close", on the north side of which (on right) is the **Scottish National War Memorial.**

The Memorial was built to commemorate those of Scottish birth who fell in the first world war, and consists of a shrine and a gallery of honour. Entirely the work of Scottish artists, it is perhaps the finest and most moving war memorial ever built. The *Hall of Honour* has a barrel-vaulted roof borne on octagonal columns which form twelve bays, one for each of the twelve Scottish regiments. In the Shrine is the *Stone of Remembrance*, standing on the native rock, with a steel casket containing the names of the fallen. Every branch of the armed forces is remembered in the friezes and panels and windows in the gallery of honour.

On the south side of the Palace Yard is the **Great Hall,** which is believed to have been the meeting place of the early Scottish Parliaments.

The Great Hall, built by James IV, is notable for its fine hammerbeam roof, with carved human and animal masks at the ends of the beams. It was used as a banqueting hall, and Charles I and Cromwell were among those entertained here. It now contains a collection of arms and armour (two-handed Scottish swords, models of old guns, pistols, cannon; the gun carriage used in the funeral of Queen Victoria and King Edward VII).

On the west side of the Palace Yard is the *Scottish United Services Museum* (uniforms, ship models, mementoes of the Napoleonic wars, an R.A.F. section, etc.).

On the east side of the square are the **Royal Apartments,** including the small room in which Mary Queen of Scots gave birth to James VI on 19 June 1566.

Mary stayed in the Castle for the last time after the murder of Darnley and before her marriage to Bothwell. In other rooms are relics of the Stuarts. In the **Crown Room** are the "Honours of Scotland", the Scottish regalia (crown, sceptre and sword of state). The origin of the crown is unknown; it was remade for James V in 1540. It is made of Scottish gold and is set with 94 pearls, 10 diamonds and 33 other precious stones. The velvet cushion on which it rests is over 300 years old. At the Union in 1707 the Honours were hidden away in the oak chest to be seen in the Crown Room, since it was feared that they might be carried off to England, and remained hidden for more than a century until they were rediscovered in 1817 by a Commission which included Walter Scott among its members.

The Royal Mile

The **Royal Mile** runs down the ridge from the Castle to Holyrood Palace, a distance of a mile, under the successive names of Castle Hill, the Lawnmarket, High Street and Canongate. For many centuries, until the building of the New Town in the 18th century, this was the centre of Edinburgh life. Plan: pp. 914-15.

On the left-hand side of Castle Hill is the **Outlook Tower** (18th c.), containing a small museum and a camera obscura (open weekdays 10 to 6, Sundays 12.30 to 6). Opposite, on the right-hand side of the street, is *Tolbooth St John's Church* (19th c.), with a spire 240 feet high modelled on the spire of Salisbury Cathedral: services in Gaelic as well as English.

Below, to the right, is the *Grassmarket*, scene of the Porteous riots in 1736: see p. 910.

Lawnmarket. On the left is *Lady Stair's House* (17th c., restored), in which is one of the city museums, with mementoes of Scott, Burns and Stevenson and local antiquities (open weekdays 10 to 4, Saturdays 10 to 1). Beyond this, also on the left, is **Gladstone's Land** (1620), restored by the National Trust in 1930 and now the headquarters of the Saltire Society (open Monday-Friday 2 to 5).

Beyond this is the **High Street,** the core of the old town. On either side are "closes" and "wynds", little courts and narrow passages, each bearing some great Scottish name and each with its own history.

On the left, at the junction with the Mound, is the Sheriff Court. A little farther down, on the right, is **St Giles Cathedral** (not now strictly a cathedral, but

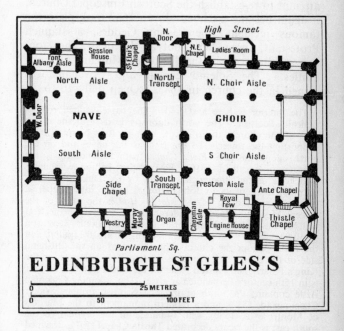

EDINBURGH ST GILES'S

styled the High Kirk of St Giles). The exterior was clumsily restored in the 19th century; the interior is severe but impressive. It has a 14th century lantern tower modelled on that of the Cathedral of St Nicholas in Newcastle.

The church dates mainly from the 14th and 15th centuries, after a fire in the 14th century had destroyed most of the earlier Norman church. At the Reformation fanatics defaced the building and later divided it into four separate churches. John Knox often preached in St Giles. In 1634, during Charles I's attempt to re-establish the Scottish Episcopal Church, it again became a cathedral. In 1637 took place the famous incident when Jenny Geddes, a staunch Protestant, threw her stool at the dean; the stool can still be seen in the National Museum of Antiquities. The Solemn League and Covenant was signed in the church in 1643. (Open daily 10 to 5).

The interior is bare and cold. The barrel-vaulted roof is typically Scottish. The north doorway leads into the oldest part of the church, the transept, with its four Norman piers supporting the tower. To the right is the nave, and on the north side of this is *St Eloi's Chapel*, with a monument to the Marquis of Argyll (d. 1616). Beyond this, behind a wrought-iron grille, is the *Albany Aisle*, built by the Duke of Albany in 1402 (monuments to John Knox). In the little chapel at the south-west corner of the *Moray Aisle* is the tomb of the Regent Moray (d. 1570). Underneath the window in the west wall of the aisle is a memorial to Robert Louis Stevenson (1850-94). The west porch is modern, as are the pulpit and the royal pew in the choir. The last pillar on the left-hand side of the choir, with the arms of James II, is known as the King's Pillar. The Preston Aisle on the south side of the choir is in 15th century Perpendicular style. The adjoining Chepman Aisle contains the tomb of the first Scottish printer, Walter Chepman (d. 1532), and a modern monument to the Marquis of Montrose (d. 1650), who is buried in the crypt. To the south-east is the richly decorated **Thistle Chapel** (1911, designed by Sir Robert Lorimer), the chapel of the Order of the Thistle.

In the roadway outside the west end of St Giles is a heart-shaped pattern of paving-stones.

This marks the position of the entrance to the *Tolbooth*, the old prison (built 1466) which stood here and was besieged by the mob during the Porteous riots in 1736. The Tolbooth features in the opening chapters of Scott's novel "The Heart of Midlothian".

Outside the east end of St Giles is the **Mercat Cross,** in a little square in which markets were held, condemned prisoners were executed, royal proclamations were made and popular celebrations and rejoicings took place.

The cross is first referred to in the 14th century. The present cross (with the original shaft) was set up by Mr W.E. Gladstone in 1885, with a Latin inscription which he himself composed. Royal proclamations are still read out here by Lord Lyon King of Arms, standing on the high octagonal platform round the cross.

Behind St Giles is **Parliament Square,** on the position of the old churchyard. In the square is an equestrian statue of *Charles II* (erected 1685), and nearby is a stone with the inscription "I.K. 1572", the supposed site of *John Knox's grave.*

On the south side of the square is **Parliament House,** formerly the meeting place of the Scottish Parliament and now occupied by the Law Courts. (Open 10 to 4.30, except Saturday afternoons and Sundays). *Parliament Hall* has a fine oak roof, and contains many statues and portraits of leading Scottish statesmen and lawyers. Stained glass window depicting the foundation of the College of Justice by James V in 1537. At the end of the hall is a corridor 300 feet long giving access to the courts.

Opposite St Giles, on the north side of the High Street, are the **City Chambers.**

The building was erected in 1753 as the Royal Exchange (architect John Fergus, using plans by John Adam). In the courtyard is a statue of "Alexander and Bucephalus", by Sir John Steell. At the entrance is the city's *Stone of Remembrance* (war memorial). The rear part of the City Chambers is eleven storeys high, one of the tallest buildings in the Old Town. (Open 10 to 3, except Saturdays and Sundays).

At the junction with South Bridge St is the *Tron Church* (17th c.), outside which there once stood the weighing-beam or "tron". The present steeple dates from 1848, the earlier one having been destroyed by fire.

Here the Royal Mile crosses an important north-south thoroughfare. To the left the *North Bridge* runs down to Waverley Station and the New Town; to the right the *South Bridge* runs past the University and into the road to the south (A 7).

On the left-hand side of the High Street, beyond the junction, a narrow passage called Carrubber's Close runs down to the Episcopalian church of *St Paul's* (1883), built on the site of an old wool store.

A little farther down on the same side, projecting into the street, is **John Knox's House.**

It is not absolutely certain that this was really the house in which John Knox lived between 1561 and 1572. Whether the name is justified or not, however, it is a picturesque old house dating from the end of the 15th century, with wooden galleries. The *Oak Room* (1600, has a decorated ceiling. Museum devoted to Knox (open 10 to 5, except Sundays).

Opposite John Knox's House, on the south side of the street, is the **Museum of Childhood** (open 10 to 5, except Sundays), with toys, dolls, clothes, etc., mostly of the 19th and 20th centuries.

From here the **Canongate** runs down the hill to Holyrood Palace. This was once a fashionable residential quarter, with some fine old houses, many of which have recently been restored or rebuilt.

On the right-hand side is **Moray House** (1629), now housing a College of Education. Charles I lived in this house, and Cromwell made it his head-quarters. In a summerhouse in the garden the Act of Union between Scotland and England was signed in 1707.

Opposite, on the north side of the street, is the **Canongate Tolbooth** (1591), with a projecting clock, originally a court-room and prison (open 10 to 5, except Sundays). Beyond it is the **Canongate Church** (1688, restored since the last war), the local parish church. In the churchyard are the graves of Adam Smith, Robert Ferguson and Burns's Clarinda.

Opposite the church, on the south side of the Canongate, is the main **City Museum,** in *Huntly House* (1517, restored).

Many relics of Scottish life in bygone days; glass, pottery; a copy of the National Covenant (1638); mementoes of Field-Marshal Douglas Haig, commander-in-chief of the British armies in France in 1918. Open 10 to 5, except Sundays; also Wednesdays 6 to 8 in summer and Sundays 2 to 5 during the Edinburgh Festival.

Next door is *Acheson House* (1633), which now houses the Scottish Craft Centre.

Farther down the Canongate, on the left, is the *White Horse Close*, an old coaching inn preserved in its 17th century aspect (restored 1965).

At the foot of the Canongate is the entrance to **Holyrood Palace,** officially the *Palace of Holyrood-house* (open 9.30 to 6, Sundays 11 to 6, in summer; it may be closed without notice on the occasion of state visits or when members of the royal family are in residence).

The palace, once the residence of Scottish kings and queens, is now unoccupied, except when the Queen is in residence or when the Queen's representa-tive at the annual General Assembly of the Church of Scotland, the Lord High Commissioner, resides there with his suite. From the time of the Stuarts

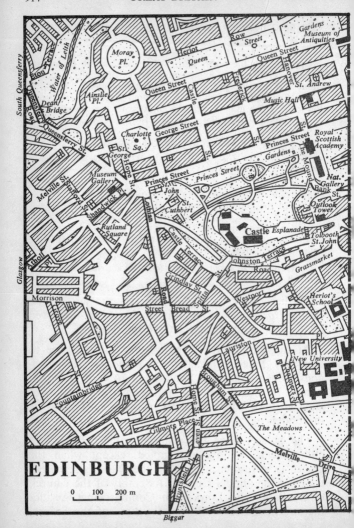

EDINBURGH

0   100   200 m

Biggar

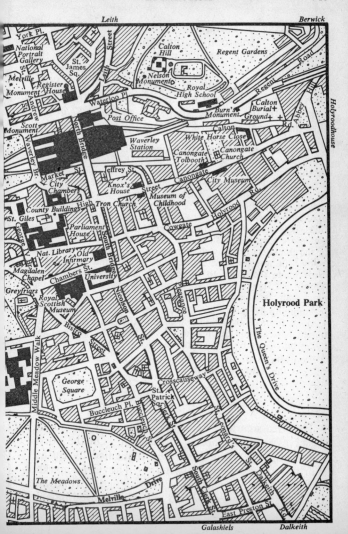

to the reign of Victoria no British monarch lived in the palace. Holyrood is a miniature palace in French and Italian style, rebuilt in its present form in the 17th century, and set in spacious surroundings which contrast with the confined spaces of the Royal Mile. Beyond the palace and to the right extends the *King's Park*, with the leonine shape of *Arthur's Seat* and the sheer rock faces of *Salisbury Crags*.

The palace contains much of historical interest, though it must be confessed that the portraits of 110 kings of Scotland in the Picture Gallery (mass produced by a visiting Dutch artist in the 17th century) are of little artistic interest. It was in this gallery that Prince Charles Edward gave his famous ball in 1745, although only a mile away the Castle was still holding out against him. The palace's main historical associations, however, are with Mary Queen of Scots. Her apartments, which are surprisingly small, are connected by a staircase built in the thickness of the wall with those of Darnley on the floor below. It was up these stairs that Darnley and the Scottish lords made their way to the Queen's apartments to murder Rizzio, her Italian secretary. A brass plate at the head of the main staircase marks the spot where he fell.

Adjoining the palace are the ruins of **Holyrood Abbey** (12th-15th c.), founded by David I in 1128. Rizzio and Darnley are buried here. Note the fine detail on the west front and the flying buttresses on the south side.

From the 12th to the 19th century the Abbey precincts enjoyed the right of sanctuary.

South of the Royal Mile

The **Grassmarket,** below the Castle to the south, preserves many memories of the past. On the north side is the old *White Hart Inn*, frequented by Burns, Wordsworth and other writers. The Grassmarket was the scene of many executions; in the roadway at the east end is a cross laid in pink-coloured paving stones, marking the spot where over 100 Covenanters preferred to die rather than renounce their convictions. In the *Cowgate*, formerly a fashionable street, which leaves the east end of the Grassmarket, is the **Magdalen Chapel,** containing records of charitable bequests, mostly dating from the 17th century.

The chapel at one time served as a mortuary, and the Earl of Argyll's body was taken there after his execution in 1685. The stained glass is the only mediaeval glass in Scotland surviving in its original form. Tower built 1618. (Open 10 to 12 and 2 to 4, except Sundays).

Farther along the Cowgate is *St Cecilia's Hall* (1762), still used as a concert hall.

The Cowgate then runs under George IV Bridge. It is preferable to return to the point where the Cowgate leaves the Grassmarket and take a little street to the left, Candlemaker Row, which runs uphill to the south end of George IV Bridge. At the top, on the right, is **Greyfriars Church** (1614), where the National Covenant was signed in 1638.

The churchyard contains handsome monuments and tombstones commemorating many noted citizens of Edinburgh. In the north-east corner is the *Martyrs' Monument*, erected in honour of the Covenanters who died for their faith. Outside the entrance to the churchyard, at the top of Candlemaker Row, is the figure of *"Greyfriars Bobby"*, the faithful dog which stayed on the grave of its master John Gray in Greyfriars churchyard from 1858 until its own death 14 years later.

To the west of the church (entered from Lauriston Place) is *George Heriot's School*, a 17th century Gothic and Renaissance building, founded by George Heriot in 1624 for the education and maintenance of the sons of poor citizens of Edinburgh.

In and around George Square, to the south, are the new *University buildings*, erected to meet the steadily expanding needs of the University, most of them since the last war. *Hume Tower* (1963). Fine new *Library*.

Half way along George IV Bridge, on the east side, is the **National Library of Scotland,** founded in 1682, which now possesses 3 million volumes, with fine manuscripts and incunabula (open 9.30 to 5, except Saturdays after 1 and Sundays; during the Edinburgh Festival open weekdays 9.30 to 8, Sundays 2 to 5).

Almost opposite Greyfriars Church is the end of *Chambers Street*, which runs down to the South Bridge. On the right-hand side is the imposing building occupied by the **Royal Scottish Museum.** Founded in 1854, this has four sections — art and archaeology, natural history, technology and geology. Open 10 to 5, Sundays 2 to 5.

The Museum has very extensive collections, and a thorough visit would take several hours. Among the outstanding exhibits are the zoological and geological collections, the scale models of machinery, aircraft, etc., the scientific apparatus, the Benin bronzes, the Italian ceramics (Gubbio, Deruta) and the old silver (the Lennoxlove toilet service, the Watson mazer).

Opposite the Museum is Edinburgh's second university, the *Heriot-Watt University*, formerly a technical college. The Campus is on a new site at Riccarton, on the western outskirts of the city. Farther down Chambers St on the left-hand side is *Adam House*, with Edinburgh University's examination rooms, also used for exhibitions and dramatic performances.

At the bottom of Chambers St, on the right-hand side, is the original building of Edinburgh University, the **Old College,** with its main front on the South Bridge.

The University of Edinburgh was founded in 1582. The present Old College was built between 1789 and 1834, the original design by Robert Adam being altered by William Henry Playfair. The *portico* on South Bridge is one of Adam's finest works. The *dome*, designed by Rowand Anderson, was added in 1884.

In Infirmary St, which runs down from the opposite side of the South Bridge, is the *Old Infirmary* (1777-1830), now occupied by the University.

Turning left along South Bridge, we come to the junction with the Royal Mile and then cross the railway lines on the North Bridge to reach the New Town (below).

The New Town

To the north of the Royal Mile, separated from it by the low-lying *Princes Street Gardens* (formerly a loch, which was drained in the 18th century), is the **New Town**, laid out on a plan drawn up in 1767 by James Craig, then only 23 years old. The layout and buildings are basically Georgian, with wide streets meeting at right angles and spacious squares and crescents.

The main street of the New Town, running east and west, is *George Street*, named after George III. To the north is *Queen Street* and to the south *Princes Street* (completed in 1805), Edinburgh's best known street, whose attraction lies rather in the view of the Castle, the old town and the gardens to the south than in its mostly undistinguished modern buildings.

At the east end of Princes St, a busy junction with the North Bridge on one side and Leith St on the other, are the *General Post Office* (south-east corner) and the *North British Hotel* (south-west corner). On the north side of Princes St, opposite the end of the North Bridge, is the **Register House,** containing the Scottish Record Office, built 1774-89 to the design of Robert Adam and completed in 1827 by Robert Reid.

The Register House (open 9 to 5 and on Saturday mornings) contains Scottish historical, administrative and legal records from the 13th century onwards. In the adjoining *New Register*

House are the registers of births, marriages and deaths and the offices of the Lord Lyon King of Arms, the Scottish heraldic authority. The building, erected 1859-63 to the design of Robert Matheson, is in the Italian style and contains an impressive steel stack housing the current registers together with the old parish registers and Scottish census records.

Behind the Register House is a vast modern block housing government offices (New St Andrew's House), shops and a hotel.

To the east can be seen the **Calton Hill** (350 ft), with the *Nelson Monument* (1816), in the form of a telescope, and the unfinished *National Monument*, in the form of a Greek temple, which was intended to commemorate the defeat of Napoleon. On the hill, from which there are fine views, there are also some Russian cannon captured during the Crimean War.

Under the Calton Hill, in Regent Road, is the old **Royal High School,** now the City of Edinburgh Art Centre (pictures and statues: open 10 to 4.30, except Sunday mornings). The building is a copy of the Theseion in Athens (1825), designed by Thomas Hamilton. Opposite it is the *Burns Monument*, also by Hamilton (1830). On the opposite side of Regent Road is *St Andrew's House* (1939), the headquarters of Scottish administration, recently supplemented by New St Andrew's House (above).

Going west along **Princes Street,** with the gardens on the left and an uninterrupted line of shops on the right, the eye is caught at once by the **Scott Monument,** one of Edinburgh's most notable landmarks.

The Monument, a Gothic spire 200 feet high, was designed by G.M. Kemp (1844) and houses a statue of Scott by Sir John Steell (1846). In the niches are figures of characters from Scott's novels. 287 steps lead up to the top (fine views). Open weekdays 10 to 7, Sundays 1 to 7; in winter 10 to 3, except Sundays.

Opposite the Monument South St Andrew St runs up to spacious **St Andrew Square,** surrounded by banks and insurance companies (*Royal Bank of Scotland*, in a classical mansion built by Sir William Chambers in 1772 for Sir Laurence Dundas). In the centre of the square is a *column* 150 feet high bearing a statue of Henry Dundas, first Lord Melville (1828).

To the north North St Andrew St runs down to **Queen Street.** Immediately on the right is a large neo-Gothic building housing the **National Museum of Antiquities** and the **National Portrait Gallery.**

The **National Museum of Antiquities of Scotland** is devoted to the history and archaeology of Scotland from prehistoric times to the present day: mediaeval jewellery, the *Monymusk Reliquary* (8th c.), gold objects dating from the Bronze Age, Roman material, the *St Ninian's Treasure* (Saxon, 9th c.), the *Traprain Treasure* (Roman, 5th c.). Open 10 to 5, Sundays 2 to 5.

The **Scottish National Portrait Gallery** has a large collection of portraits of historical personages Scottish and foreign: Mary Queen of Scots by *Oudry*, George IV by *Lawrence*, Sir Walter Scott by *Raeburn*, the fourth Duke of Argyll by *Gainsborough* and many other portraits by noted artists (*Reynolds, Lely, Kneller, Mignard, Romney, Turner*, etc.). Sculpture by *Rodin, Epstein, Mestrović*, etc.

Now return to St Andrew Square and turn west along **George Street.** On the right is *St Andrew's Church* (1785), to the left the *Music Hall* (1787). Beyond this turn left down Hanover St to return to Princes St. Immediately opposite is the *Royal Scottish Academy*, and behind it the **National Gallery of Scotland** (see below).

At the corner of West Princes Street Gardens, beyond the Royal Scottish Academy, is a *floral clock*, the oldest of its kind in the world (1903).

A cuckoo appears at the quarter hours. The flowers are frequently changed, the layout sometimes being related to a particular event taking place in the city. The hands measure respectively 8 feet and 5 feet, and the circumference of the dial is 36 feet. When filled with flowers the hour hand weighs 50 lb and the minute hand 80 lb.

In the *Ross Bandstand* in the centre of the gardens open-air performances are given throughout the summer (variety shows, concerts, bagpipe recitals, Scottish country dancing, etc.).

At the west end of Princes St a path leads down on the left to *St Cuthbert's Church* (1894), with the graves of many noted Scotsmen. At the corner of Princes St and Lothian Road (to left) is the neo-Gothic *St John's Church*, with the tomb of the painter Henry Raeburn.

The line of Princes St is continued by Shandwick Place.

To the west can be seen *St Mary's Cathedral* (Episcopalian, 1879), designed by Sir George Gilbert Scott, with a spire 280 feet high.

From the west end of Princes St either Hope St or South Charlotte St leads north to **Charlotte Square,** at the west end of George St.

This magnificent square (Robert Adam, 1791) was one of the first parts of the New Town to be completed. The north side is the finest section of the square, and is one of the accepted masterpieces of European town architecture. In the centre of the square is the *Albert Memorial* (1876). On the west side is **St George's Church,** a classical building designed by Robert Reid (1814), now used to house some of the national records. At No. 6 is the official residence of the Secretary of State for Scotland.

The National Gallery of Scotland

This stands on the *Mound*, which was artificially built up to provide convenient access from Princes St to the old town and the Castle.

In front of the Gallery is the *Royal Scottish Academy* (1836), which puts on temporary exhibitions.

The **National Gallery** occupies a neo-classical building erected in 1845-48 (with a recent extension), and contains a very fine collection covering all European schools, with a good representation of Scottish artists. Since 1946 it has been enriched by the loan of part of the Duke of Sutherland's collection, acquired by one of the Duke's ancestors at the sale of the Duke of Orleans' property during the French Revolution. Another valuable acquisition was a collection of pictures (including particularly French Impressionists) presented by Sir Alexander Maitland in 1960. Open 10 to 5, Sundays 2 to 5.

Room 1: Daddi (Altarpiece); *Duccio* (Crucifixion); *Vitale da Bologna* (Adoration of the Kings); *Lucas Cranach* (Venus and Cupid); *Gerard David* (Three Legends of St Nicholas); *Ferrarese school* (Madonna and Child with Angels); *Filippino Lippi* (Holy Family); *Lorenzo Monaco* (Madonna and Child); *Perugino* (Four Male Figures); **Raphael** (Holy Family with a Palm Tree, Madonna del Passeggio, Bridgewater Madonna); **Hugo van der Goes** (Trinity Altarpiece); *A. Benson* (Madonna and Child with St Anne); *Quentin Metsys* (Portrait of a Notary).

Room 2: Bacchiacca (Moses Striking the Rock); *Andrea del Sarto* (Portrait of a Man); *Lotto* (Madonna and Child with Four Saints); **Tintoretto** (Descent from the Cross, Portrait of a Venetian); **Titian** (Three Ages of Man, Venus Anadyomene, Diana and Actaeon); *Veronese* (Mars and Venus).

Room 3: Temporary exhibitions.

Room 4: Bassano (Adoration of the Kings, Portrait of a Gentleman); *Domenichino* (Adoration of the Shepherds); **van**

Dyck (The Lomellini Family, St Sebastian Bound for Martyr-dom); **El Greco** (Saviour of the World, St Jerome Penitent); *Guercino* (St Peter Penitent); *Procaccini* (Raising of the Cross); **Rubens** (Fest of Herod, Head of St Ambrose); *Teniers* (Peasants Playing Bowls); **Velazquez** (Old Woman Cooking Eggs); *Zur-baran* (Immaculate Conception).

Rooms 5 and 6: Avercamp (Winter Landscape); *P. Bril* (Land-scape with Figures); *Claude* (Landscape with Apollo, the Muses and a Sea God); *Cuyp* (Landscape with a View of the Valkhof, Nijmegen); *Gerard Dou* (Interior with Young Violinist); **van Dyck** (Portrait of a Young Man); *Elsheimer* (Stoning of St Stephen); *Frans Hals* (Portrait of Verdonck, Portraits of a Gentleman and his Wife); *Hobbema* (View of Deventer); *P. de Hoogh* (Courtyard with an Arbour); *Lievens* (Portrait of a Young Man); **Rembrandt** (Woman in Bed, Self-Portrait, Young Woman with Flowers in her Hair, Hannah and Samuel (?), Study of Man's Head); **Rubens** (Adoration of the Shepherds); *Ruysdael* (Banks of a River); J. Steen (The Schoolroom); *Terborch* (Singing Practice); *Terbrugghen* (Decollation of St John the Baptist); *van Goyen* (River Scene); **Vermeer** (Christ in the Home of Martha and Mary).

Rooms 7 and 8: Temporary exhibitions.

Rooms 9-13 (upstairs): **Poussin** (seven pictures representing the Seven Sacraments, Moses Striking the Rock); **Gainsborough** (Landscape with Distant View of Cornard Village, The Hon. Mrs Graham, Mrs Hamilton Nisbet, Rocky Landscape); *Hogarth* (Sarah Malcom); *Allan Ramsay* (Sir Peter Halkett Wedderburn, The Painter's Wife, Mrs Bruce of Arnot, Jean-Jacques Rousseau); *Pater* (Ladies Bathing); **Watteau** (Fêtes Vénitiennes); *Richard Wilson* (Italian Landscape); *Sisley* (Molesey Weir, Hampton Court); *Pissarro* (The Marne at Chennevières); **Monet** (Haystacks, Snow Effect; Poplars on the Epte); **Renoir** (Mother and Child); *Greuze* (Girl with Dead Canary); **van Gogh** (The Olive Trees, Orchard in Blossom, Head of a Peasant Woman); **Gauguin** (Martinique Landscape, Vision after the Sermon, Three Tahitians); **Degas** (Diego Martelli, Before the Performance, Woman Drying Herself); *Delacroix* (Chess-Players); *Daubigny* (La Frette, Sunset); *Daumier* (The Painter); **Courbet** (River in a Mountain Gorge, The Wave); **Corot** (Landscape with Castle, The Artist's Mother,

Entrance to a Wood); *Chardin* (Vase of Flowers); **Cézanne** (Mont Sainte-Victoire); *Boucher* (Madame de Pompadour); *Bonnard* (Lane at Vernonnet); *Vuillard* (La Causette).

Room 14: Canaletto (Entrance to Grand Canal); *Guardi* (San Giorgio Maggiore, Santa Maria della Salute); **Tiepolo** (Finding of Moses, Meeting of Anthony and Cleopatra); *Pittoni* (Altarpiece with Apotheosis of St Jerome); *Goya* (El Médico); **Reynolds** (The Ladies Waldegrave).

Rooms 15-17: Bonington (Grand Canal, Venice; Landscape with White House); **Constable** (Vale of Dedham); *Crome* (The Beaters); **Turner** (Somer Hill, near Tunbridge); *Andrew Geddes* (The Artist's Mother); *W.Y. Macgregor* (Rocky Solitude); *W. McTaggart* (Spring, The Young Fishers, The Storm); **Raeburn** (Sir John Sinclair of Ulbster, Rev. Robert Walker Skating on Duddingston Loch, Sir P. Inglis, J. Wauchope, Miss Lamont, Mrs Scott-Moncrieff, Self-Portrait); *D. Scott* (The Traitor's Gate); *D. Wilkie* (Self-Portrait, The Irish Whiskey Still, Pitlessie Fair and other genre paintings).

The arrangement of the pictures is subject to alteration.

Other Features of Interest

South of the city centre

Royal Observatory, Blackford Hill (replacing an earlier observatory on Calton Hill, at the east end of Princes St). Conducted tours on Wednesdays at 3 p.m.

The Observatory is attached to the department of astronomy of Edinburgh University. Observations are made with four telescopes at Blackford and another in Italy, where the Observatory has an outstation. The Observatory specialises in the application to astronomy of automatic methods of observation, measurement and data processing, and in the design and construction of advanced instruments. It also follows the trajectory of artificial satellites from an outstation in the Borders and carries out extra-atmospheric observation of rockets and satellites with the help of astronomical instruments.

South-west of the city centre

In Colinton Road is *Napier College* (1964), named after
John Napier (1550-1617), the inventor of logarithms. The
15th century tower in which he lived is incorporated in the
new buildings.

East of the city centre

In the King's Park is **Arthur's Seat** (823 ft), a
volcanic hill from the top of which there are wide
views. The name is popularly associated with the
legendary King Arthur who is dated to the 6th century;
alternative derivations are the Gaelic *Ard na Said*,
"Hill of Arrows", and *Ard Thor*, "Hill of Thor".

North of the city centre

The *Water of Leith* flows through the northern and
north-western districts of the city. It rises in the
Pentland Hills and reaches the sea at Leith, with a
total course of 20 miles.

There were formerly many water-mills on the Water of
Leith, and the official Scots pint was defined in 1621 as "three
Scots pounds of water from the Water of Leith". The stream
flows through the old village of **Dean**, now part of the city,
with many old buildings reconstructed by the municipal authorities. The Dean Bridge, 120 feet above the Water of Leith,
was built in 1832.

The Water of Leith flows close to the **Botanic Gardens** in
Inverleith Row (parking at the rear entrance in Arboretum
Road), open 9 a.m. (Sundays 11) to dusk. Beautifully laid
out, with many exotic plants. The Gardens were originally
founded (on another site) in 1670. In the centre is *Inverleith
House* (1774), in which is the **Museum of Modern Art** (open
10 to 6), with displays of 20th century art. Immediately west
of the Botanic Gardens is spacious *Inverleith Park* (tennis,
bowling; pond, with swans).

A short distance farther north are the shores of
the Firth of Forth, with **Leith**, Edinburgh's seaport,

which was formerly a separate burgh but is now incorporated in the city. It handles both passengers and freight.

Among old buildings in Leith are *St Mary's Church* (15th c.), in Kirkgate, and nearby *Trinity House*, founded in the 14th century but dating in its present form from 1816. Round the docks are a number of old inns. On the Shore is a stone commemorating the landing of King George IV in 1822. In 1561 Mary Queen of Scots landed at Leith and was entertained by a merchant named Andrew Lamb, whose house still exists. *Lamb's House*, in Burgess St, is a typical merchant's house of the period, both dwelling and warehouse, with a crowstep gable and an outside staircase; it is now an old people's welfare centre.

East of Leith is **Portobello,** now also part of Edinburgh, with a sandy beach and an esplanade 2 miles long. It was formerly a fashionable seaside resort, and was also noted for its potteries, founded in 1786. Walter Scott stayed in Portobello as an officer of the Volunteers. The famous Scottish singer Harry Lauder was born in Portobello in 1870. One modern attraction is the largest open-air swimming pool in Europe (artificial waves).

Newhaven, west of Leith, is a fishing port, founded in 1500. Among the first ships built here was the "Great Michael", launched in 1507. The Newhaven fishwives in their traditional costume were formerly a colourful feature of Edinburgh life, but they have now almost disappeared. The harbour still presents a lively scene at the early morning fish auction. Nearby is *Starbank Park*, overlooking the Firth of Forth.

West of the city centre

The magnificent *Saughton Rose Garden*, at the corner of Gorgie Road and Balgreen Road, is reached by going west from Princes St to Haymarket, bearing left into Dalry Road and then right into Gorgie Road (A 71). Roses and dahlias, Italian garden, scented garden for the blind.

The road to the airport and to Glasgow (A 8) runs
past **Edinburgh Zoo,** on the right-hand side of Corstorphine Road, which has an area of 75 acres. Open
9 to 5 in winter, 9 to 7 in summer.

Magnificent and unique colony of *Antarctic penguins*. A
wide range of mammals, Highland cattle, bisons, deer (including
the almost extinct Père David's deer), exotic birds. Children's
farm. Carnegie Aquarium.

Farther out on the same road, before the entrance to the
Glasgow motorway (M 8), is **Ingliston,** with the *Royal Highland
Show* grounds. The Royal Highland Show itself is held in
the third week in June, but the grounds are used for sports
and other purposes during the rest of the year. A motor racing
track was opened in 1961.

North-west of the city centre

Lauriston Castle is reached by way of Queensferry
Road (A 90), which passes through Blackhall and
Davidson's Mains. Opposite Corstorphine Hill turn
right into Quality St. This runs into Cramond Road
South, with the entrance to the castle grounds on the
right. Open 11 to 1 and 2 to 5, except Fridays.

Lauriston Castle was built about 1590 by Archibald Napier
and remained almost intact until its acquisition in 1823 by
Thomas Allan, a lawyer and banker. Allan bought it from a
descendant of John Law, the financier and speculator who
founded the Royal Bank in France, whose family had owned
it for 140 years. It is now an attractive mansion-house in fine
grounds overlooking the Forth (period furniture, Flemish
tapestries, porcelain, etc.).

Beyond Lauriston Castle, at the mouth of the little
river Almond, is the village of **Cramond,** on the Firth
of Forth.

Cramond was originally a Roman station, founded in 142.
Recent excavations have yielded pottery, coins, glass and other
objects now displayed in the City Museum in Huntly House

(p. 913). There are some remains of the fort in a garden in the village, which also shows a plan of the site.

The 18th century houses formerly occupied by workers in the ironworks on the river Almond have recently been restored by the municipal authorities. There is a 15th century *tower*, believed to have belonged to the Bishop of Dunkeld. Cramond is now a popular sailing centre.

59. THE BORDERS

The area south of Edinburgh is known as the Southern Uplands or as the Borders — the frontier region long disputed between Scotland and England and the scene of much fighting in earlier centuries. In the centre of the area is the Scott Country, with the Border abbeys.

A. EDINBURGH TO CARLISLE VIA BIGGAR

96 miles (A 702 to Abington, then A 74). Leave central Edinburgh by Lothian Road, at the west end of Princes St, and at Tollcross bear right into the Biggar road (A 702).

13 miles: *Ninemileburn*, so called because it was nine Scottish miles from the capital. The road runs along the west side of the Pentland Hills; magnificent walking country. The highest points are Scald Law (1898 ft) and Carnethy (1890 ft). The hills stretch from 3 miles south of Edinburgh for a distance of 16 miles. — 15 miles: *Carlops*. — 17 miles: *West Linton*. — 21 miles: *Dolphinton*.

28 miles: **Biggar** (pop. 1340, E.C. Wednesday). 1 mile south are the ruins of *Boghall Castle* (tower).

34 miles: *Lamington*, with the ruins of a 16th century tower. — 39 miles: *Abington*. — 42 miles: *Crawford*. — 44 miles: *Elvanfoot*. Here the Elvan Water flows into the Clyde. Soon afterwards the road turns south-east and climbs to 1000 feet. Scanty remains of Lindsay Tower.

46 miles: *Little Clyde* (remains of a Roman camp). — 51 miles: the border of Dumfries and Galloway, continued along the crest of the *Lowther Hills*, which sweep away in a semicircle to the south-west.

52 miles: A 719 goes off on the left, offering an alternative route to Beattock (below) via **Moffat** (pop. 2000, E.C. Wednes-

day), a small spa town on the Annan, 5 miles from its source, amid sheltering hills. The springs, well known for the last 250 years, are 1 mile east (640 ft). 4 miles north, on Hartfell, are other springs (sulphureous and chalybeate). The town has a wide main street with a double row of lime-trees. Near the Colvin Fountain is *Moffat House* (Adam), now a hotel. In the old churchyard is the grave of John McAdam (1756-1836), inventor of the macadamised road, who lived in nearby Dumcrieff House.

Around Moffat. Good walks. — 8 miles north is the *Devil's Beef Tub*, a large circular hollow in the hills, beyond which is *Tweed's Well*, source of the river Tweed. — 4 miles north is *Hartfell* (2651 ft), to the east of which is White Coomb (2695 ft), and below this a picturesque waterfall, the Grey Mare's Tail. *Garpol Glen* (chalybeate spring): fine views.

57 miles: *Beattock*. — 71 miles: **Lockerbie** (pop. 2800, E.C. Tuesday), in Annandale, centre of a rich agricultural district.

On nearby *Burnswark* (920 ft) are the remains of two Roman camps. — 4 miles north-west is *Lochmaben*, a small town surrounded by seven lochs, with a ruined castle. — 6 miles south on B 723 is *Hoddam Castle* (16th c.).

76 miles: **Ecclefechan** (pop. 600, E.C. Thursday), famous as the birthplace of *Thomas Carlyle* (1795-1881).

His house, on the right in the main street, contains furniture from his Chelsea house and other relics (open 10 to 6). He is buried in the local churchyard, along with his parents and brother.

To the north-east are the remains of the Roman station of *Blatobulgium*. Nearby is *Kirkconnel*, where "fair Helen of Kirkconnel Lea" is buried with her lover Adam Fleming.

80 miles: to the right, Robgill Tower and, beyond it, Bonshaw Tower.

83 miles: *Kirkpatrick*. — 86 miles: **Gretna Green,** where the village blacksmith used to perform a quick marriage ceremony for eloping couples from England. — 88 miles: the *Border*. — 96 miles: **Carlisle** (p. 831).

B. EDINBURGH TO CARLISLE VIA SELKIRK

97 miles.   Leave central Edinburgh by the South Bridge and Nicholson St (A 7), then via Eskbank and Newtongrange.

13 miles: *Fushiebridge*. 1 mile north is *Gorebridge*, to the north-west of which is *Dalhousie Castle* (12th c.). — 14 miles: to the east, *Borthwick Castle* (15th c.), splendidly preserved and still inhabited.

The road climbs up the valley of the Gala Water to 1000 feet.

18 miles: *Heriot*. — 28 miles: *Stow*, beautifully situated in the Wedale valley, on the left bank of the Gala Water.

35 miles: **Galashiels** (pop. 12,000, E.C. Wednesday), situated in a valley between Meigle Hill (1387 ft) and Buckholm Hill (1064 ft), at the junction of the Gala Water and the Tweed.   A tweed-making town.

Among ancient remains in the neighbourhood are the *Catrail*, a hill-fort on *Torwoodlee* (the Brock) and the site of a Roman camp at *Newstead*.

2 miles away is *Abbotsford* (p. 938).

41 miles: **Selkirk** (pop. 5700, E.C. Thursday), magnificently situated on a hill (600 ft) overlooking the Ettrick. Tweed-making. Statues of Sir Walter Scott (who was Sheriff here for 32 years) and, at the end of High St, Mungo Park, the great African explorer. In the Town Hall are Scott manuscripts and mementoes.

To the west are the beautiful valleys of the Yarrow and the Ettrick Water. Magnificent views from Black Andrew (1364 ft) and Newark Hill (1450 ft). At Howden is the *Mote of Howden*, an ancient British fortification.

Selkirk to Moffat: 34 miles on A 708.

A 708 runs along the Yarrow valley past (4 miles, on left) the ruins of *Newark Castle*. 9 miles: the village of *Yarrow*. 14 miles: a private road on the right runs up the Douglas Burn to the ruins of *Blackhouse Castle*. 1½ miles beyond this, on right, is the ruined *Dryhope Tower*. The road now comes to *St Mary's Loch*, the largest loch in southern Scotland (3 miles long, 1 mile wide). Beyond this is the Loch of the Lowes (1 mile long, ¼ mile wide). A 708 runs alongside the loch and then down beautiful Moffatdale to *Moffat* (p. 930).

Selkirk to Langholm via Ettrick Forest: 44 miles (B 7009 to Tushielaw, then B 709).

B 7009 runs south-west past *Bowhill*, seat of the Duke of Buccleuch, to (6 miles) *Ettrick Bridge*. 7 miles: *Kirkhope* (old tower). — 14 miles: *Tushielaw Inn*, in a fishing area. To the west, on Tushie Law (1431 ft), is a ruined tower. There is another at *Thirlestane*, in wildly beautiful scenery. Good walks from Tushielaw to Penistone Knowe (1807 ft), Muckra Hill (1738 ft) and Ramsey Knowe (1951 ft). — 44 miles: *Langholm*.

53 miles: *Hawick* (pop. 17,000, E.C. Tuesday), a thriving Border town manufacturing tweed and hosiery. The town is mostly modern but has a long history. At the end of the main street is the *Motte Hill*, a prehistoric mound. *Museum* in Wilton Lodge Park (local antiquities). There are a number of fine old houses in the neighbourhood.

3 miles south-west is *Branxholm Park*, with a ruined castle which features in Scott's "Lay of the Last Minstrel". — 5 miles north-east is *Minto House*, seat of the Earl of Minto. The gardens are open to the public during the season. Nearby, on the Minto Hills (905 ft), are the ruins of *Fatlips Castle*. — 1 mile south-east is the village of *Denholm*, near Melgund, with a superb *New Garden*.

57 miles: *Stobs Camp*, a military training camp. Nearby is an old castle. — 62 miles: *Teviothead*. To the south-east are Millstone Edge (1961 ft), Cauldcleuch Head (1996 ft), Greatmore Hill (1960 ft) and the Maiden Paps (1677 ft).

66 miles: the road enters Dumfries and Galloway. *Mosspaul*, near Whisp Hill (1950 ft). The road continues through the hills, following the valley of the Ewes Water, to (76 miles) *Langholm* (pop. 2400, E.C. Thursday).

The road now runs down beautiful Eskdale to *Canonbie* (82 miles).

B 6357 runs north-east up Liddesdale, through magnificent scenery, to *Hermitage Castle*, one of the oldest baronial castles in Scotland still standing to its full height.

88 miles: *Longtown*. The road enters England. A 6071 runs west to (4 miles) *Gretna Green* (p. 932). 97 miles: **Carlisle** (p. 831).

C. THE SCOTT COUNTRY

Edinburgh to Carter Bar: 57 miles on A 68.

The road out of Edinburgh passes on the left **Craigmillar Castle.**

The castle, badly ruined, dates from the 15th century (the oldest parts from 1374). It was a favourite resort of the Stuart kings, and Mary Queen of Scots stayed here after the murder of Rizzio in 1566. Open 9.30 to 7.

7 miles: **Dalkeith** (pop. 9000, E.C. Tuesday), a small industrial town. *Dalkeith Palace*, a seat of the Duke of Buccleuch, dates from the 14th century (portraits, pictures, furniture).

1 mile north-east is *Newbattle*. In the church are the pulpit of Archbishop Leighton, interesting memorials and fine modern glass. Nearby is *Newbattle Abbey*, a former seat of the Marquess of Lothian, now an adult education college; a mansion built on the foundations of a 12th century Cistercian abbey, of which there remain the crypt and a chapel (restored).

Dalkeith to Haddington. 10 miles: *Pencaitland*. A short distance away is *Ormiston*, a mining village with a wide tree-lined main street which has preserved much of the charm of the past. — 6 miles south-east is *Gifford*, a secluded and attractive village. In the vicinity are the ruins of *Yester Castle* (13th c.), with an underground chamber (40 ft by 20) called *Goblin Ha'*. — 14 miles: *Haddington*.

11 miles: *Pathhead*. The road climbs over Soutra Hill, affording fine views. To the east are the heather-covered Lammermuir Hills. On the far side of the hill the road runs down into Lauderdale.

27 miles: *Lauder*.

Lauder to Berwick-upon-Tweed: 34 miles on A 6105.

12 miles: *Greenlaw*. — 19 miles: **Duns** (pop. 2000, E.C. Wednesday), an old Border town, the centre of a farming region. Manufacture of blankets; iron foundries. The *Castle* was originally built in the 14th century, but the present building is modern with the exception of the east tower (1320). 1 mile north, on *Duns Law*, are the remains of fortifications erected by the Covenanters' army. 7 miles west is *Longformacus*, under the Lammermuir Hills; on the way there Harden's Hill (1153 ft) and Dirrington Great Law (1309 ft), with three Bronze Age cairns on the summit, can be climbed. 2 miles south is of Duns is *Nisbet House*, a modern country house incorporating an old border castle. — 26 miles: *Chirnside*. — 34 miles: **Berwick-upon-Tweed** (p. 762).

34 miles: *Earlston*. — 39 miles: **St Boswells,** an agricultural market town in good fox-hunting country. A good centre from which to visit the Border abbeys.

1½ miles north, in an area of meadowland enclosed within a great loop of the Tweed, are the picturesque

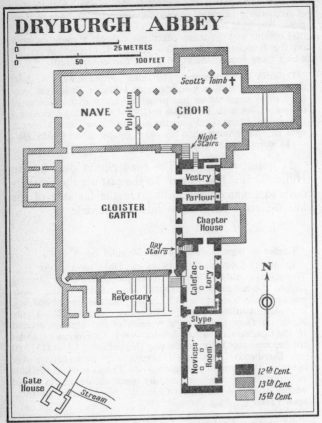

ruins of **Dryburgh Abbey.** There are remains of the
church, the chapter house, the cloisters, the refectory
and some of the domestic buildings. Here are buried
Sir Walter Scott (1771-1832), his son in-law and
biographer John Gibson Lockhart (d. 1854) and

Field-Marshal Earl Haig (d. 1928).   Open weekdays
8 a.m. to 8 p.m., Sundays 1 to 5. — To the north,
on Bemerside Hill (wide views), is a statue of William
Wallace.   Nearby is *Bemerside House*, seat of the
Haig family, now a museum (open daily July-Septem-
ber 10 to 12 and 1 to 6).

St Boswells to Melrose and Abbotsford (A 6091).

4 miles: **Melrose** (pop. 2000, E.C. Thursday), a
small town and holiday centre in an attractive setting.

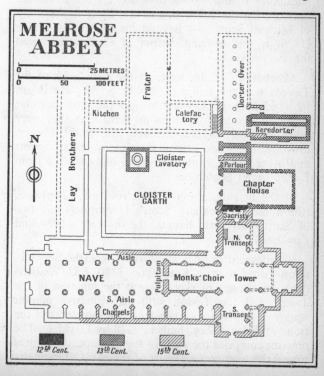

At the end of the High Street is a 14th century *Mercat Cross*. Nearby is St Dunstan's Well. The ruins of **Melrose Abbey** are architecturally the most beautiful in Scotland. They consist of the late Gothic *choir* (c. 1450), with large and delicately carved windows (note in particular the east window). Near the east end is the transept crossing. Practically nothing remains of the nave apart from two Norman arches on the north side. At the east end, by the altar, Alexander II and the heart of Robert the Bruce are buried. On the south side of the choir is the tomb of Michael Scott. — Beyond the suspension bridge (1826) is the outlying district of *Gattonside*, noted for its orchards.

Abbotsford (2 miles west, on the right bank of the Tweed) was the home of Walter Scott. He began to build it in 1812, when he was the most popular writer of his time. The rooms remain as they were when he died; in the entrance hall, study, library, drawing rooms and armoury are many relics of Scott and other items of interest. Open daily 10 to 5 from Easter to 30 September.

In the neighbourhood of Melrose are *Chiefswood* (the home of Lockhart, Scott's biographer) and two of Scott's favourite haunts, the *Rhymer's Glen* and *Cauldshiels Loch*.

10 miles east of St Boswells on A 699 (the Berwick-upon-Tweed road) is **Kelso** (pop. 3880, E.C. Wednesday), an ancient market town at the junction of the Tweed and the Teviot, with an attractive market square. A short distance from the square are the ruins of **Kelso Abbey,** built in 1128 by David I. The remains comprise the walls of the transept, the central tower, the west end and part of the choir. Originally

the abbey was more than 300 feet long and 80 feet wide. In the cloisters are the tombs of the Dukes of Roxburghe.

Around Kelso. *Pinnacle Hill*, from which there are fine views of the Tweed. — *Floors Castle*, seat of the Duke of Roxburghe, one of the most splendid specimens of Tudor architecture in Scotland, altered by Sir John Vanbrugh (1718). — William Hooper, one of the four Scottish signatories of the Declaration of American Independence, was born near Kelso, the son of a minister of religion. — 3 miles north is *Newton Don*, a fine country house in extensive grounds, in which is the Stichill Linn, a waterfall (45 ft high) on the river Eden. — 5 miles north is Hume (old castle). — 6 miles west is *Smailholm Tower*, an old peel tower, with fine views of the surrounding country. — 2 miles south-west is *Roxburgh* (ruins of 12th c. castle, destroyed 1460). — 2 miles north-east is *Ednam*, birthplace (1700) of James Thomson, who wrote "Rule Britannia" (obelisk).

46 miles: **Jedburgh** (pop. 3800, E.C. Thursday), an industrial town (tweed and rayon) on the Jed Water. **Jedburgh Abbey,** on the banks of the river, is a picturesque ruin which bears witness to the ferocity of Border warfare. It was founded by David I in 1118 and became an abbey in 1147. Early English and Norman in style, the remains are among the largest in Scotland. From the 86 foot high tower (restored) there are wide views. The great west doorway and the cloister doorway are very fine; large rose window.

The old county prison (1823) stands on the site of the castle, demolished in 1409. In Queen St is *Queen Mary's House,* in which Mary stayed when ill after a long ride to visit Bothwell at Hermitage Castle. The house has been restored and is now a museum (open 10 to 12 and 2 to 5). Between Canongate and Richmond Row is an old *mediaeval bridge* (10th c.) with three ribbed arches, one of the few surviving in the country. Many associations with Sir Walter Scott.

A 68 continues toward the Cheviot Hills. — 49 miles: *Ferniehirst Castle* (1598), now a youth

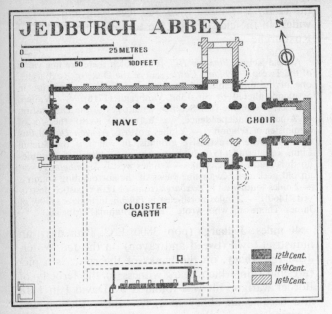

hostel. — 57 miles: *Carter Bar*, where the road runs over lonely Carter Fell into England.

For the route from Carter Bar to Newcastle and on to London, see Route 42.

D. EDINBURGH TO PEEBLES

23 miles on A 702 and A 703. Leave Edinburgh by way of Lothian Road, from the west end of Princes St, and at Tollcross bear right into the Biggar road. At Hillend, on the outskirts of the city, fork left for Penicuik. From the east end of Princes St, North Bridge runs into the direct road for Penicuik.

7 miles: 1 mile east is *Roslin*, with a ruined *castle* and **Roslin Chapel** on the hill above the village.

The *castle*, which features in Scott's "Rosabelle", was burned down in 1542, demolished by the English in 1544 and twice subsequently reduced to ruins. The **chapel** is the choir of an unfinished church and is noted for its rich ornament (the beautifully carved *Prentice Pillar*, the three-bayed roof, the elaborate pillars and lintels). Open 10 to 1 and 2 to 5 during the season.

10 miles: *Penicuik* (pop. 5000, E.C. Wednesday), a paper-making town on the Esk.

13 miles: *Leadburn*. The road climbs to 1000 feet and then enters the valley of the Eddleston Water. To the east are the beautiful Moorfoot Hills, with Gladhouse reservoir.

18 miles: *Eddleston* (pop. 640). To the east is Blackhope Scar (2137 ft). On a lower hill just above the road (1 mile south-east) are the *Milkieston Rings*, a hill-fort with an impressive ring of ramparts.

23 miles: **Peebles** (pop. 5500, E.C. Wednesday), an old town on the Tweed. On the north side of the town are the ruins of the *Cross Kirk* (1261), which was allowed to fall into ruin and was abandoned in 1784. To the west is the tower of *St Andrew's Church*, founded in 1195 and closed at the Reformation. The tower was restored in 1882; interesting old tombstones. In Northgate is the *Cross Keys Hotel* (1653). In High St is the *Chambers Institute* (1857), with a reading room, library, museum and picture gallery. The Tweed is spanned by a 15th century bridge (altered in 1900).

1 mile west are the ruins of *Neidpath Castle* (14th c.), magnificently situated above the Tweed. — 4 miles: near Woodhouse Farm, south of the Tweed in the Manor valley, is the *Black Dwarf's Cottage*, where Scott stayed in 1797 and which

features in "The Black Dwarf". — 5 miles: *Lyne*, with the remains of a Roman camp.

Peebles to Galashiels: 18 miles on A 72.

6 miles: **Innerleithen** (pop. 2300, E.C. Tuesday), a former spa town making cloth and hosiery. ½ mile north-west is Lee Pen (1647 ft), from which there is a fine view of the town and surrounding countryside. In the neighbourhood are a number of prehistoric fortifications, including *Caerlee Fort* (double ring of ramparts). The highest point in the surrounding area is Windlestraw Law (2161 ft). — 1 mile south is *Traquair House* (17th c.), originally built in the 11th century. At the end of the avenue are fine iron gates which were Scott's model for the Tullyveolan gates in "Waverley". Beyond this, to the right of the road, is *The Glen*, seat of Lord Glenconner, in beautiful grounds.

9 miles: *Walkerburn*. — 13 miles: *Ashiesteel*, where Scott wrote much of "Marmion" and "The Lay of the Last Minstrel". — 15 miles: *Clovenfords*, noted for its hothouse grapes. — 18 miles: **Galashiels** (p. 932).

60. EDINBURGH TO STIRLING

Instead of taking the recently opened motorway, it is preferable to leave Edinburgh by way of Barnton and Cramond Bridge (A 90), branching off into A 904 near *Queensferry*, with a view of the two **bridges over the Forth** (p. 949).

13 miles: to the right of the road, on the Firth of Forth, is **Hopetoun House,** the imposing seat of the Marquess of Linlithgow, built by the Adam brothers in the first half of the 18th century and decorated by James Cullen between 1753 and 1768. Magnificent interior, with pictures by *Rubens, Rembrandt, van Dyck, Gainsborough* and other artists. Beautiful park (deer). Open in summer 1.30 to 5.30, except Thursdays and Fridays.

A 904 continues to **Bo'ness** (pop. 10,000, E.C. Wednesday), an industrial town on the Firth of Forth. The name is an abbreviation of *Borrowstounness*.

West of the town is **Kinneil House** (16th and 17th c.), a seat of the Duke of Hamilton (frescoes: open 10 to 7). On the coast to the east is **Blackness Castle** (15th c.), boldly perched on a rocky crag.

From Bo'ness A 706 runs south to (3 miles) **Linlithgow** (pop. 4500, E.C. Wednesday).

An ancient town on the edge of a loch, with the noble ruins of a palace that was for centuries a royal residence. The present **Linlithgow Palace** was built between the 14th and the 17th centuries. Here were born James IV (1542) and his daughter Mary, the future Queen of Scots. The Regent Moray was murdered in the streets of Linlithgow in 1570. Near the palace is *St Michael's Church* (12th c.), founded by David I: a splendid building in various styles, but mainly Decorated.

A 9 runs parallel to the motorway (on right), passes on the right the industrial town and port of *Grangemouth* (oil refineries) and comes to **Falkirk**,

Falkirk (pop. 38,000) is an industrial town, with foundries, breweries, refineries and soap-works. At a battle fought here in 1298 Edward I's English army defeated a Scottish army led by William Wallace. Mary Queen of Scots and Prince Charles Edward stayed in *Callendar House*. Remains of the *Roman wall* (the Antonine Wall) from the Forth to the Clyde.

At the far end of Falkirk A 9 forks right for *Larbert* (pop. 10,000, E.C. Wednesday). 5 miles north-east is Kincardine Bridge, which crosses the Forth to *Kincardine* (pop. 3000, E.C. Thursday).

A 9 continues to **Bannockburn,** a small mining village near which in 1314 a Scottish army led by Robert Bruce defeated Edward II's English army (see below). 3 miles south-west is *Sauchie*, where James III was defeated in 1488 by his rebellious nobles. Nearby is Beaton's Mill, where the wounded king was murdered after the battle.

37 miles from Edinburgh is **Stirling** (pop. 27,000, E.C. Wednesday), an ancient and attractive town which, like Edinburgh, is dominated by a great castle built on a rock. Stirling Castle was a favourite residence of Scottish kings.

There was a Roman station on the castle rock in 81 A.D. After the departure of the Romans in the 5th century the Picts established themselves here, remaining until they were defeated in 843. In the 10th century the castle served as a base against the Danes. Alexander I died here in 1124. The royal mint was established in the castle, which in the 13th century was considered one of the most formidable strongholds in the country. In 1296, after the battle of Dunbar, Edward I of England seized the castle; in the following year it was recaptured by Wallace; after the battle of Falkirk Edward I reoccupied it, lost it again and again recovered it in 1304 after a siege; Robert Bruce took it in 1314; in 1337 Edward III had it repaired; in 1339 it again fell into Scottish hands. Many kings of Scotland were born in the castle, and Mary Queen of Scots spent her early years there, as did her son James VI. The castle underwent sieges in 1651 and 1746.

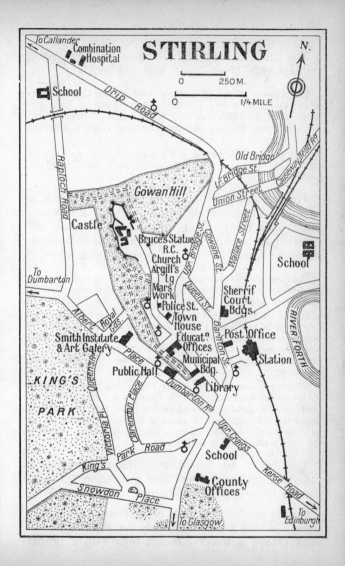

The castle is reached by way of the steep street called **Castle Wynd,** lined with old buildings.

The **Church of the Holy Rude** retains some 15th century work; the choir is 16th century. Mary Queen of Scots was crowned in the church in 1543 at the age of 9 months, and her son James VI was also crowned here in 1567, when he was a year old.

To the left of the church is the *Guildhall* (17th c.). On the right is *Mar's Wark* (1570), and beyond this is **Argyll's Lodging** (1630).

The Esplanade leads up to the **Castle,** which is entered by a drawbridge (open 10 to 7 in summer, Sundays 11 to 6). Long occupied by the army, the Castle has recently been evacuated and restored. From the top of its crag it commands wide views.

The outer ditches were cut in the early 18th century. Beyond the *Gatehouse* (15th c., built by James III) is an inner courtyard, the Lower Square or *Parade.*

To the right are a well and batteries. Straight ahead is the south end of the Great Hall. To the left is James V's **Palace,** built round a central court called the *Lion's Den.* The building was designed by English, French and Portuguese architects (note the affinities with the Manueline style). The interior can be visited.

A narrow passage between the Palace and the Great Hall leads into the Upper Square. On the right is James III's **Great Hall**; straight ahead is the **Chapel Royal** (1594, built by James V), under the left-hand end of which is a passage leading to the gardens (view). On the left-hand side of the Upper Square is the *King's Old Building* (museum).

The *Smith Art Gallery and Museum* contains a collection of watercolours and a museum (geology, natural history, local antiquities): open 10 to 5.

On the northern outskirts of the town is the Abbey Craig (362 ft), on which stands the **Wallace Monument** (1869), a tower 220 feet high with a bronze

statue (13 ft high) of Wallace. In the *Hall of Heroes*
are busts of noted Scotsmen. Fine views from the
top of the tower.

On the left bank of the Forth, over the graceful *Old Bridge*
(1400), is **Cambuskenneth Abbey,** an Augustinian house founded
by David I in 1147. This is a magnificent example of early
Gothic, with remains of the tower, the east doorway, the north
aisle and transept, the base of the high altar and parts of the
chapter house and cloisters. Monuments (new tombs, erected
1865) to King James III, murdered after the battle of Sauchie,
and his queen.

1 mile south of Stirling, in the district of St Ninians, is a
memorial commemorating the battle of **Bannockburn,** with an
equestrian statue of Robert Bruce (C. d'O. Pilkington Jackson,
1964) and an information centre with an audio-visual presentation, "The Forging of a Nation".

Stirling to Perth

34 miles on A 9.

Just beyond the Wallace Monument, in the grounds
of Airthrey Castle, is the new **University of Stirling,**
with beautifully laid out modern buildings in an
attractive setting.

3 miles: **Bridge of Allan** (pop. 3300, E.C. Wednesday), a residential town on the left bank of the Allan
Water, which flows into the Forth 1 mile to the south.
The town is built round the foot and on the lower
slopes of the Ochil Hills.

Before the accidental discovery of mineral springs, the Wells
of Airthrey, Bridge of Allan was no more than a few houses
built round the bridge, but during the 19th century it developed
into a fashionable spa: a role it has now lost.

The Allan Water is a very beautiful stream which rises on
one of the northern Ochils and flows down in a course of some
20 miles to join the Forth. Below Dunblane (below) the gorge

is wild and densely wooded. Burns wrote a poem about it
("By Allan's Stream", 1793).

6 miles: **Dunblane** (pop. 3400, E.C. Wednesday),
agreeably situated on the Allan Water. At the top
of the High Street is the early Gothic **Cathedral,** one
of the few such buildings spared by the fanaticism
of the Reformers in Scotland. It was founded by
David I in the 12th century and enlarged by Bishop
Clemens in the 13th. It was completely restored in
1892; Ruskin thought highly of it. Interesting monuments, including those of Margaret Drummond and
her two sisters.

At Sheriffmuir, 3 miles east, an indecisive battle was fought
in 1715 between the Jacobites and the royal forces.

11 miles: *Greenloaning.* At Ardoch are the remains
of the Roman fort of *Lindum,* one of the best preserved in the country. To the north-west are the
ruins of Braco Castle. — 17 miles: *Blackford,* with
the remains of *Ogilvie Castle.* To the south are the
Ochil Hills, extending from north of Stirling to the
Firth of Tay. — 20 miles: *Auchterarder* (pop. 2600,
E.C. Wednesday), a pleasant little town 430 feet
above sea level. To the south is *Gleneagles House*
(17th c.), home of the Haldane family. — 34 miles:
Perth (p. 999).

61. FIFE

A. Edinburgh to St Andrews by the Fife Coast

63 miles. Leave Edinburgh by Queensferry Road (A 90).

9 miles: **South Queensferry,** under the south end
of the Forth road bridge. (Bypassed by A 90).

This ancient royal burgh owes its name to Queen Margaret,
wife of King Malcolm Canmore, who frequently used the ferry
on her way between Dunfermline and Edinburgh. *Church*
(14th c.). *Plewlands House* (17th c., restored by National Trust).
Nearby is the little village of *Dalmeny*, with a Norman church
(12th c.).

The Firth of Forth is crossed on the magnificent
new **Forth Road Bridge,** opened in 1964, when it
was the longest suspension bridge in the world.

Including the approaches, the total length of the bridge
is 1 mile 588 yards. The distance between the two main pylons
is 3300 feet. 40,000 tons of steel and 150,000 cu. yards of concrete
were used in its construction, and the total cost was £20,000,000.

To the east can be seen the railway bridge, the original *Forth
Bridge*, built 1883-90. It is over 1½ miles long including the
approaches, with towers rising to 360 feet above the water.
It has two main spans of 1700 feet and two smaller spans of
690 feet. It cost £3,000,000.

11 miles: **North Queensferry,** in Fife. The motorway
(M 90) continues north (p. 956).

4 miles north-west is **Dunfermline** (pop. 50,000, E.C. Wednesday), a linen-making town and the home of the Carnegie Trust,
a philanthropic foundation established by Andrew Carnegie,
who was born in Dunfermline and became a millionaire in
America.

Dunfermline Abbey was founded by Queen Margaret and
King Malcolm III on the site of an earlier church. In the 12th
century their son David I built what is now known as the Old
Nave and founded a Benedictine monastery. The church was
enlarged in the 13th century. In 1303 Edward I of England

destroyed the monastery, but it was later rebuilt. In the 19th century a modern church was built incorporating the fine Norman remains. For centuries the church was the burial place of Scottish kings and queens. It contains the tombs of Queen Margaret and (below the pulpit) Robert Bruce.

Near the abbey are the ruins of a *royal palace* (1500), a favourite residence of the Scottish kings and the birthplace of Charles I.

To the north-east of the abbey, in Maygate, is the *Abbot's House*, a fine example of 16th century Scottish domestic architecture. Part of the building contains the collections of the Dunfermline Naturalists' Society. To the east is the *Carnegie Public Library*, notable in particular for a collection of 3800 volumes relating to Dunfermline and Fife, 152 illuminated manuscripts dating back to 1300 and a collection of Burns's works.

In beautiful Pittencrieff Glen to the west of the Abbey, presented to the town by Carnegie, is *Pittencrieff House* (17th c.), containing a museum.

The modest cottage in which Andrew Carnegie was born is at the corner of Priory Lane and Moodie St. Adjoining it is the *Carnegie Memorial Hall*.

7 miles west of Dunfermline, off A 985, is **Culross,** a remarkably complete survival of a little Scottish town of the 16th and 17th centuries, largely National Trust property. *Culross Palace* (1597-1611), with painted rooms and walled garden; the *Study* (16th c.), with 17th century panelling and period furniture; picturesque streets of old houses.

12 miles: *Inverkeithing*, an old royal burgh. *Town Hall* (1775). In the church is one of the few old *fonts* still surviving in Scotland. — 17 miles: *Aberdour* (pop. 1800, E.C. Wednesday), a seaside resort with an excellently restored Norman church. Ruined castle. Boats to the island of *Inchcolm* (old monastery). — 20 miles: **Burntisland** (pop. 6000), a seaside resort and shipbuilding town on the site of a Roman naval station. Very fine square *church* (1590), with an octagonal central tower and good carving. Old houses. Fine views of the Firth of Forth from

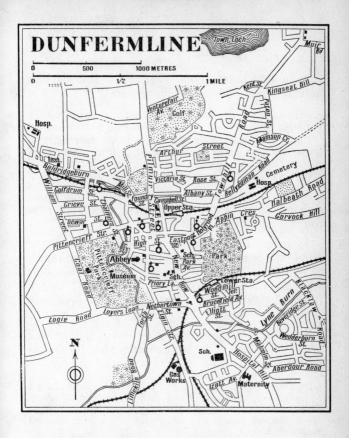

Dunearn Hill. — 22 miles: *Kinghorn*, with a monument to Alexander III (1249-89), who was killed near here. — 25 miles: **Kirkcaldy** (pop. 53,000, E.C. Wednesday), an old town with a main street 4 miles long, an industrial centre and holiday resort.

Raith Tower contains a fine mineralogical collection. Opposite the station is a *Museum of Local History*. The town was the birthplace of the economist Adam Smith (1723) and the architect Robert Adam (1728).

35 miles: Leven (pop. 9000, E.C. Thursday), a holiday resort and coal-shipping port.

Beaches, dunes covered with marram grass, a fine golf course. Industries: iron and steel, paper, jute, weaving, timber products.

3 miles south-west are *Buckhaven* and *Methil*, twin industrial towns which were little fishing villages until the discovery of coal. At Denbeath is the Wellesley pit, the largest in Britain. Methil was formerly an important coal-exporting port.

37 miles: *Lundin Links*, with three impressive standing stones and an old tower. The road runs round beautiful Largo Bay.

38 miles: *Upper Largo*. ½ mile south is *Lower Largo*, the birthplace of Alexander Selkirk, the prototype of Defoe's Robinson Crusoe. Attractive harbour. A 915 runs north-east to St Andrews (12 miles). Instead of taking this direct route, turn right into A 917.

43 miles: *Elie and Earlsferry* (pop. 1100, E.C. Wednesday), one of the most attractive holiday resorts on the Fife coast.

On *Chapel Ness* are the ruins of a 12th century chapel. *Lady's Tower* (18th c.), near the swimming pool. Ruined castle (16th c.). Near Earlsferry is *Macduff's Cave* (accessible at low tide), in which Macduff is said to have sought refuge when pursued by Macbeth.

45 miles: St Monance, with a fine *church* (14th c.) on the edge of the cliffs. Ruins of *Newark Castle* and, beyond Croupie Bay, *Ardross Castle*. The road runs along the coast, with a fine view of the *Isle of May* (below).

47 miles: **Pittenweem** (pop. 1500, E.C. Wednesday), with a picturesque harbour and old 17th century houses. Ruins of a *priory* associated with St Fillan, with a cave shrine.

49 miles: *Anstruther*, a typical East Neuk fishing town of great charm. The pier was built by R.L. Stevenson's father. *Scottish Fisheries Museum.*

53 miles: **Crail** (pop. 1080, E.C. Wednesday), the most easterly of the fishing villages in the East Neuk of Fife, and an increasingly popular holiday resort.

The *Town Hall* (1602, rebuilt in 19th c.) has a charming Dutch tower. Ruins of Crail Castle, which commanded the harbour.

6 miles offshore is the *Isle of May* (reached by boat from Crail harbour), with a ruined 13th century chapel and a modern lighthouse. Large numbers of seabirds nest on the cliffs.

To the east is *Fife Ness*, a headland with tall cliffs and fine views (lightship). *Balcomie Castle*, with a fine golf course overlooking the sea. Nearby are the interesting *Caiplie Caves*.

63 miles: **St Andrews** (pop. 10,000, E.C. Thursday), an ancient town, with the oldest of the eight Scottish universities; the traditional "home of golf" (with five famous courses) and a pleasant holiday resort. The episcopal see of St Andrews was founded in the 8th century. The first and last of the martyrs of the Reformation in Scotland, Patrick Hamilton (1527) and Walter Myln (1558), died in St Andrews; and after the death of George Wishart at the stake in 1545 Cardinal Beaton was murdered by Reformers in St Andrews Castle.

At the east end of the town are the romantic ruins of the Cathedral, founded in 1160 but completed only in the early 14th century (Norman and Gothic). At the Reformation it fell into ruin and was used as a quarry of building materials.

In the old cloisters is a small *museum*. Near the apse is the little *St Rule's Church* (12th c.), with a tall tower.

Opposite the entrance to the Cathedral, to the south, is *Queen Mary's House*, in which Mary Queen of Scots once lived.

From here **South Street** runs west. On the right is *Dean's Court* (16th and 17th c.); to the left are the **Pends,** with a 14th century gateway giving access to *St Leonard's Chapel* (16th c.). Along South St, on the left, are *St Leonard's College* (1512), **St Mary's College** (1537) and the *Town Hall*, opposite which is *Holy Trinity Church* (restored).

At the far end of the street, on the left, are the remains of *Blackfriars Chapel* (1525) and, across the street, the *West Port* (1560).

On the north side of the town, above the sea, are the ruins of the **Castle,** originally an episcopal residence. James III was born in the Castle.

The **golf courses** are to the west of the town; the most notable is the famous Old Course.

On the road from St Andrews to Dundee is *Leuchars*, which has a fine church with a Norman east end (12th c.). Beyond Newport is the new *road bridge* over the Tay to Dundee, opened in 1966 (2850 yds long).

B. St Andrews to Stirling

53 miles on A 91.

10 miles: *Cupar* (pop. 5500, E.C. Thursday), with the ruins of a Dominican monastery. In County Hall are interesting old portraits. — 19 miles: *Auchtermuchty* (fine views of the Lomond Hills, 1713 ft). 3 miles south is **Falkland Palace** (16th c.), in Italian Renaissance style, a former royal residence (Flemish tapestries). — 21 miles: *Strathmiglo*. — 26 miles: A 91 runs into A 90, the Edinburgh-Perth road (see below). — 29 miles: *Milnathort* (below). — 35 miles: *Yetts of Muckhart*. — 38 miles: *Dollar* (pop. 2000), near which are the ruins of *Castle Campbell* (15th-17th c.). To the north are the Ochil Hills (2363 ft). — 46 miles: *Alva*. 3 miles south is *Alloa*, with a tower (13th c.) 90 feet high. — 53 miles: *Stirling* (p. 944).

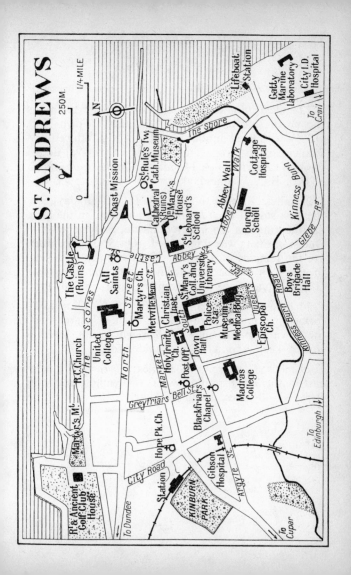

C. Edinburgh to Perth

Motorway (M 90). The places mentioned below are bypassed.

12 miles: *Inverkeithing*, an old harbour town on the north side of the Firth of Forth. Town Hall (1755), with local antiquities. Ruins of a 14th century Franciscan hospice. 2 miles west is the naval dockyard of *Rosyth*. — 14 miles: *Cowdenbeath* (pop. 13,000, E.C. Wednesday), an old mining town.

22 miles: **Kinross** (pop. 2300, E.C. Thursday), on the west side of *Loch Leven*. On an island in the loch are the ruins of **Loch Leven Castle,** in which Mary Queen of Scots was imprisoned. On *St Serf's Island* are the remains of a priory. On the north-west side of the loch is the Renaissance-style *Kinross House* (17th c.), one of the finest country houses in Scotland.

24 miles: **Milnathort** (pop. 1000, E.C. Thursday), formerly a noted wool-making town. Just east of the town are the ruins of *Burleigh Castle*, with a square keep and a vaulted undercroft.

29 miles: *Glenfarg*. — 33 miles: *Aberargie*. 1 mile east is *Abernethy* (round tower). — 36 miles: *Bridge of Earn*. — 40 miles: **Perth** (p. 999).

62. GLASGOW

Carlisle to Glasgow

Carlisle to Abington (57 miles): see p. 930.

A 73 runs to the east of the Tinto Hills and turns north-west to (74 miles) **Lanark** (pop. 8400, E.C. Thursday), an industrial town on the Clyde. Above the porch of the church is a statue of William Wallace; the site of his house (tablet) is opposite the church. Ruins of *St Kentigern's Church* (12th c.).

Around Lanark. **Falls of Clyde.** Upstream, immediately above the town, are *Corra Linn* (three falls, 83 ft) and *Bonnington Linn*. Downstream are *Stonebyres Falls* (100 ft), near Braxfield, home of Robert Owen, the pioneer of the cooperative movement and founder of the New Lanark works. Opposite Corra Linn are the ruins of *Corra Castle*. Cartland Crags and Cleghorn Woods, and, beyond this, *Craignethan Castle*.

83 miles: **Hamilton** (pop. 40,000, E.C. Wednesday), a busy industrial town in the centre of a mining area near the junction of the Avon and the Clyde. To the north is *Hamilton Park*, in which formerly stood Hamilton Palace, seat of the Duke of Hamilton. The palace was demolished because of subsidence caused by underground mine workings. The extensive park now belongs to the town. To the west is the ducal Mausoleum.

2 miles south-east, on the Avon, are the ruins of *Cadzow Castle* (13th c.), in a magnificently wooded park. On the other side of the river is the small country house of *Chatelherault*, now used as stables and farm buildings, an 18th century imitation of the French château from which the Dukes of Hamilton took one of their subsidiary titles. — At *Bothwell Bridge*, 2 miles north of Hamilton, the royal forces defeated the Covenanters in 1679 *(Bothwell Castle)*. — *Blantyre*, north-west of Hamilton, was the birthplace of the famous explorer David Livingstone (1813-73): museum.

Glasgow (pop. 1,000,000, E.C. Wednesday or Saturday) is Scotland's largest city, with one-fifth of the total population, and the third largest city in Britain after London and Birmingham. Although it has fewer old and historic buildings than Edinburgh,

Glasgow deserves more than a passing visit, for its Cathedral and its fine museums and galleries have much of interest to offer. Plan at end of Guide.

Situation and History

Glasgow is situated on the Clyde and owes its rise to prosperity and importance to the river and its estuary. Glasgow University is the second oldest in Scotland, and there is now a second university, *Strathclyde*, in the city. Although the city itself is a hive of commercial activity and is surrounded by extensive industrial areas, it is within surprisingly easy reach of great expanses of wild and beautiful country — the silent wind-swept moors and hills of Argyll, the quiet waters of Loch Lomond, the sea lochs of the Clyde estuary.

From the earliest times Glasgow played a leading part in the history and development of Scotland. It saw the coming of Christianity, was involved in the struggle for independence, became an important centre of the tobacco trade (early 18th c.) and later of the sugar trade, and then developed into one of the chief centres of the industrial revolution. The coming of steam increased its trade in the various goods it produced, and the coal and iron mines in the surrounding area further enhanced its prosperity. In 1811 Henry Bell's steam-driven "Comet" marked the beginning of the rise of the great Clyde shipyards.

The *Port of Glasgow*, on the Clyde, lined with shipyards, extends from Port Glasgow to the Albert Bridge, the highest point on the river navigable by seagoing vessels. It handles an annual tonnage of more than 18 million tons. There are 15 miles of quays and six main docks — Kingston Dock, Queen's Dock, Prince's Dock, Yorkhill Basin, King George V Dock and Rothesay Dock. During the second world war more than 2000 ships were launched on the Clyde, some 650 were converted to naval use and more than 23,000 were repaired. Altogether there are 80 shipyards on the Clyde, most notable among the ships built here being the two famous liners, "Queen Mary" and "Queen Elizabeth".

Glasgow, Scotland's largest city, is also its commercial capital. It is well provided with excellent shops which attract customers from a wide area. It has also much to offer in the field of sport and entertainment. It was the birthplace of the

Scottish Opera Company and of the Scottish National Orchestra,
and has one of the best known repertory theatres in Britain,
the Citizens' Theatre. It is also notable for having more parks
and public open spaces per head (61 at the latest count) than
any other town in Britain.

1. The city centre. Glasgow's central point is
George Square, in which is the city's tourist information office.

On the east side of the square are the **City Chambers,** a
massive and imposing building erected in 1888 (some rooms
open to the public 10 to 12.30 and 2 to 4, except Thursdays
and Saturdays).

On the south side is the *General Post Office.*

On the north side, behind the North British Hotel, is *Queen
Street Station.*

In the centre of the square is a column 80 feet high with a
statue of Sir Walter Scott (John Greenshields, 1837), the first
statue erected in Scott's honour. Also in the square are the
Cenotaph and statues of Queen Victoria and Prince Albert,
Gen. Moore, James Watt and other notabilities.

A short distance south is *Royal Exchange Square*, with the
neo-classical Royal Exchange (1830) and a statue of the Duke
of Wellington.

2. The Cathedral. The Cathedral is reached by
following George St east from George Square and
turning left into *High Street.* **Glasgow Cathedral,**
dedicated to St Mungo, was founded in the 12th
century. The first cathedral (1137) was destroyed by
fire; the present building was begun in 1197. It is
285 feet long, 65 feet wide and 60 feet high, with a
spire 220 feet high.

Interior. The 14th century nave has a timber roof. The
screen between the nave and the choir is 13th century (Early
English). At the end of the choir are the Lady Chapel and
Sacristy. The **crypt** has fine vaulting and decoration. In the
crypt is the tomb of St Mungo, Glasgow's patron saint.

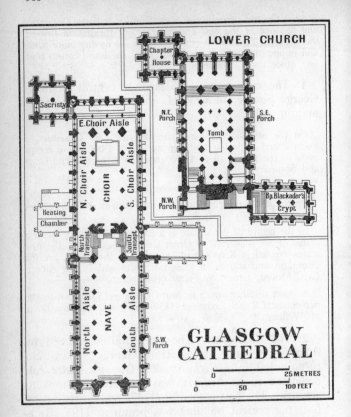

LOWER CHURCH

Chapter House

Sacristy

E. Choir Aisle

N.E. Porch

S.E. Porch

Tomb

N. Choir Aisle

CHOIR

S. Choir Aisle

N.W. Porch

Bp. Blackader's Crypt

Heating Chamber

North Transept

South Transept

North Aisle

NAVE

South Aisle

S.W. Porch

GLASGOW CATHEDRAL

0   25 METRES

0   50   100 FEET

North of the Cathedral is the **Royal Infirmary** (1792), built on the site of an ancient fort. To the east is the *Necropolis*, with numerous impressive monuments, including a column commemorating John Knox.

On the other side of Castle St, to the west of the square in front of the Cathedral, is a little house called **Provand's Lordship**, the oldest house in Glasgow (1471), now housing a small museum (open 10 to 12.30 and 2 to 5).

3. The Art Gallery and University. The Art Gallery
and Museum and the University, 2 miles west of
George Square, are reached by following St Vincent St,
which runs out of the south-west corner of the square,
and its continuation Argyle St. Both buildings are
in the extensive Kelvingrove Park. On the south side
of Argyle St is the large *Kelvin Hall* (1926), with the
Art Gallery and Museum (open 10 to 5, Sundays 2
to 5) opposite it on the north side.

The **Museum** was founded in 1807 and moved into the present
building in 1902. It contains a number of interesting specialised
collections — arms and armour (including a very fine suit of
15th c. armour from Milan and a suit of 16th c. horseman's
armour); models of steamships and sailing ships; engineering
(James Watt's steam engines and other machinery and engines);
historical items; crafts; archaeology (an Egyptian sarcophagus;
Scottish prehistoric material); ethnography; natural history
(geology, zoology, botany).

The **Art Gallery,** on the first floor, has British and foreign
sections. Pictures by *Giorgione* ("The Woman taken in Adul-
tery"), *Botticelli, Filippino Lippi, Bellini, Domenichino, Bordone,
Guardi, Salvator Rosa*; *Rubens* ("Nature embellished by the
Graces"), *Jordaens* ("The Fruit-Seller"), *Bernard van Orley*
("Virgin at the Fountain"), *Memlinc, Teniers* and other Flemish
masters; *Velazquez* ("Philip IV"), *Ribera* ("St Peter"); *Rem-
brandt* ("Man in Armour"), *Ruysdael* ("View of Egmond-aan-
Zee"), *Cuyp* ("Christ's Entry into Jerusalem"), *Frans Hals,
Honthorst, Saenredam, Wouwerman, J. Maris: Master of Mou-
lins* ("St Victor and Donor"). Very fine collection of French
art: *Delacroix, Corot, Rousseau, Millet, Harpignies, Daubigny,
Daumier, Courbet, Boudin, Jongkind, Fantin-Latour, Degas,
Manet, Monet, Pissarro, Sisley, van Gogh, Renoir, Cézanne,
Signac, Guillaumin, Gauguin, Seurat, Bonnard, Vuillard, Derain,
Marquet, Utrillo, Matisse, Braque, Picasso*, etc. *Salvador Dali*'s
controversial "Christ of St John of the Cross".

British artists represented include *Raeburn* (Mrs Urquhart",
"Mr and Mrs Robert Campbell of Kailzie"), *Allan Ramsay,
Geddes, Reynolds, Hogarth, Romney, Hoppner, Zoffany* ("The
Minuet"), *Gainsborough* ("Wooded Landscape near Bath"),
Whistler ("Thomas Carlyle"), *Turner* ("The Pifferari"), *Constable*
("Hampstead Heath"), *Millais, Rossetti*, members of the *Glas-*

gow school and contemporary artists (*Moore, Nicholson, Sutherland, Spencer,* etc.).

To the north is **Glasgow University,** reached by
going north along Kelvin Avenue (to the left on
leaving the Art Gallery) and then turning west along
University Avenue. The University, founded in 1451,
moved into the present buildings in 1870 (neo-Gothic,
designed by Sir George Gilbert Scott; spire 300 ft
high).

In the west courtyard is a mobile by George Rickey (1972).
The *University Library* is entered from this courtyard.

In the east courtyard is the entrance to the **Hunterian Museum**
(open 9 to 5; closed Saturday afternoons and Sundays), named
after the noted 18th century doctor William Hunter (1718-83).
Roman archaeology (material from the Antonine Wall), Egyptian and Oriental archaeology, Scottish antiquities (prehistoric
material); ethnography; Newcomen's steam engine; pictures
by *Reynolds, Whistler, Raeburn, Corot, Pissarro, Rembrandt*
("Entombment"), *Rubens* ("Head of an Old Woman"), *Chardin*
and *Le Nain.*

4. Other Features of Interest.   South-west of the
city centre, on the south side of the Clyde, are two
interesting museums, the **Transport Museum** and
Pollok House.

The **Transport Museum** (open 10 to 5, Sundays 2 to 5) is
at the junction of the important thoroughfare Pollokshaws
Road with Albert Drive. This museum, opened in 1964 to
house vehicles from the Kelvingrove Museum which could not
be adequately accommodated there, has a fine collection of
old cars, trams, horse-drawn carriages, bicycles, etc.

Pollok House (open 10 to 5, Sundays 2 to 5) is a splendid
mansion built by William Adam in 1752, with a *magnificent
collection of pictures,* mainly Spanish *(El Greco, Murillo, Goya),*
Italian *(Guardi, Signorelli, Sebastiano del Piombo)* and British
(portraits by *Hogarth, Romney* and *Kneller* and six works by
Blake).

South-east of the city centre, in the spacious *Glasgow Green* (140 acres) on the north bank of the Clyde, is the **People's Palace,** with the *"Old Glasgow" Museum.*

To the east, in Tollcross Road, is the *Children's Museum.* Farther out is *Calderpark Zoo.*

8 miles west of Glasgow is the industrial town (thread manufacture) of **Paisley** (pop. 96,000, E.C. Tuesday), with *Paisley Abbey* (13th-15th c.) and an interesting *Museum* (Paisley shawls). Between Glasgow and Paisley, to the south of the road, is *Crookston Castle* (15th c.).

7 miles south-east of Glasgow, in the north-eastern part of the "new town" of East Kilbride, is *Hunter House* (late 17th c.), which belonged to the father of the two famous 18th century doctors John and William Hunter and since 1961 has been a museum.

63. DUMFRIES AND GALLOWAY
AND THE BURNS COUNTRY

Dumfries and Galloway. The Dumfries and Galloway region, formerly the counties of Dumfries, Kirkcudbright and Wigtown, offers almost every aspect of Scottish scenery. In the east is an area of rich farmland, extending from the rolling hills in the north by way of the green meadows round the old county town of Dumfries to the sandy shores of the Solway estuary in the south. Farther west are rough hills along the northern border of the region, with lonely moors and solitary lochs, but these grey hills of Galloway merge into the lush country-side along the coast to the south. The most westerly part of the region also runs down from the hills to the sea, but the ruggedness of the hills is softened to great rolling moorlands stretching down to a rock-bound coast in the west and a sea-board of sandy bays in the south, where the former country of Wigtown meets the Atlantic.

The area offers a wide variety of beauty spots and places of interest. To the east are *Langholm*, nestling in a shady valley at the junction of the Esk and the Ewes; *Annan*, a small town astride the main road running along the coastal plain; *Ecclefechan*, birthplace of Thomas Carlyle; *Lockerbie*, watching over the lower part of Annandale; and **Moffat,** a charming town amid moors and hills. *Sanquhar*, with its castle, guards the upper valley of the Nith, which then flows southward past Drumlanrig Castle, seat of the Duke of Buccleuch, and through the great area of pasture land round *Thornhill*. East of the Nith lies the pretty little village of *Moniaive*, in a rich farming district.

New Galloway is a quiet little town in the Stewartry of Kirkcudbright, at a meeting place of roads. Many artists have made their home in this beautiful part of the country. To the west are *Creetown* and *Newton Stewart* on the river Cree, within easy reach of the lofty Merrick and lonely Loch Enoch, the luxuriant coastal area round *Gatehouse of Fleet*, the old county town of *Wigtown* and the historic burgh of *Whithorn*. The Isle of Whithorn, Port William, Glenluce and Drummore are seaside resorts on Luce Bay. *Portpatrick*, on the Atlantic, is only some 20 miles from the coast of Ireland. *Stranraer*, at the head of Loch Ryan, is an attractive little town and port (services to Ireland). *Ballantrae* and *Girvan*, at the outermost

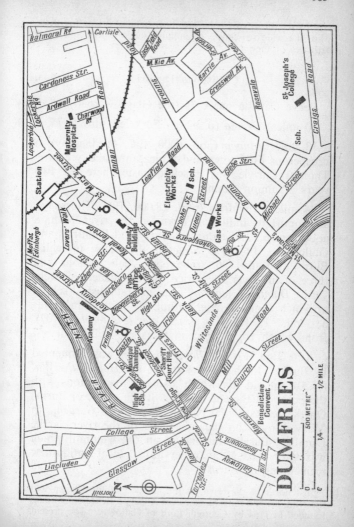

end of the Firth of Clyde, are ideal holiday places for those who like wide seascapes, green hills, quiet valleys and great expanses of moorland.

Carlisle to Dumfries

Leave Carlisle on A 74 (the Glasgow road).

10 miles: *Gretna* (p. 932). Fork left into A 75.

18 miles: *Annan* (pop. 6000, E.C. Wednesday), a prosperous little town and a pleasant holiday centre. Thomas Carlyle was a schoolmaster here for two years. Salmon fishing.

34 miles: **Dumfries** (pop. 28,000, E.C. Thursday), an important industrial town on the river Nith, a good centre for the Burns country and Dumfries and Galloway. In *Burns Street* is the house in which Burns died in 1796. The poet, Jean Armour and three of his sons are buried in St Michael's church-yard. *Dumfries Academy* is an old-established school at which James Barrie, author of "Peter Pan", was a pupil. In High St is the old *Midsteeple* (1707), from which royal proclamations are still made.

At 6 High St is the *Globe Inn*, which was frequented by Burns. In the same street is the *Hole i' the Wa'* (1620), an old inn which also has associations with the poet. At the end of High St is a statue of Burns. On the banks of the Nith is *Peter Pan's Garden*. In Maxwelltown, on the other side of the river, is the Dumfries **Burgh Museum,** in an old windmill which was later used as an observatory: local antiquities, mementoes of Burns.

Just north of the town, at the junction of the Cluden and the Nith, are the ruins of **Lincluden Abbey,** a Benedictine house founded in 1164 by Uchtred, Lord of Galloway. The present remains date mostly from the 14th century; beautiful choir. Princess Margaret, daughter of King Robert III (1390-1406), is buried here.

Around Dumfries. Delightful excursions in Nithsdale, Annandale, Eskdale, Galloway and the Solway area. — 6 miles northwest is the farm of *Ellisland,* where Burns lived for three years and wrote "Tam o'Shanter". — 7 miles south, on the Solway, is **Caerlaverock Castle,** a stronghold of the Earls of Nithsdale. It was the first triangular castle to be built in the British Isles. The interior is 17th century, but the rest dates from the 15th century. — 14 miles south-west on A 711 is **Dalbeattie** (pop. 3100, E.C. Thursday), a pleasant town built of grey granite from the local Craignair quarries, in the beautiful valley of the Urr. 1 mile north is the *Mote of Urr*, a magnificent ancient fortress commanding the Urr valley.

An alternative route from Dumfries to Dalbeattie is along the coast on A 710. 7 miles: *New Abbey*, near which are the picturesque ruins of **Sweetheart Abbey,** founded in 1275 by the Lady Devorguilla, wife of John Balliol (founder of Balliol College, Oxford). From here the nearby hill of Criffell (1868 ft) can be climbed. 3 miles east, on the east side of the Nith estuary, is the charming village of *Glencaple*. From New Abbey A 710 runs south, passing between Criffell to the west and the rocky shore of the Solway to the east. To the east, on the coast, is *Arbigland*, birthplace of the American privateer John Paul Jones; there is a museum in the house in which he was born. Dr Craik, Washington's personal physician, was also born in Arbigland.

Dumfries to Stranraer

18 miles: **Castle Douglas** (pop. 3000, E.C. Thursday), founded in the 18th century by a merchant named William Douglas near the old village of Carlingwark. 2 miles west are the ruins of **Threave Castle** (14th c.), on an island in the Dee, built by Archibald the Grim, Lord of Galloway; it can be reached by boat or by stepping stones.

Castle Douglas to Ayr via New Galloway: 50 miles on A 713.

The road follows the impressive valley of the Dee and soon reaches the banks of *Loch Ken*. The scenery is among the wildest and finest in southern Scotland. — 13 miles: *New Galloway* (pop. 400, E.C. Thursday), a little burgh with a single street on a hill above the Ken valley; a good centre from which to explore the surrounding countryside. *Kenmure Castle* (15th c.) overlooks the north end of Loch Ken. — The road runs up the valley of the Water of Ken. To the west are the *Rhinns of Kells*, the highest point in which is Corserine (2669 ft). — 25 miles: *Carsphairn*. — 31 miles: the road enters Strathclyde region. To the west is Loch Doon (5½ miles long). Glen Ness can be seen in the distance. — 35 miles: *Dalmellington*, a mining town. — 50 miles: **Ayr** (p. 977).

23 miles: A 711 forks left for (5 miles) **Kirkcud-bright,** pronounced Kircoobry (pop. 2520, E.C. Thursday), one of the oldest towns in Scotland, a seaport and agricultural centre, situated at the head of the Dee estuary.

The name of the town means "St Cuthbert's church", referring to the monks of Lindisfarne who fled from the Danes, bringing the body of St Cuthbert with them, and later settled at Durham (see p. 749). Of the first *castle* built here there remains only the mound on which it stood *(Mote Brae)*. *McLellan's Castle*, near the remains of a *Franciscan friary* (15th c.), dates from 1582. At the end of the High St is the Tolbooth (17th c.). In *Broughton House* is a museum devoted to the painter E.O. Hornel (d. 1933).

½ mile south is *St Mary's Isle*, on which was the seat of the Earl of Selkirk (burned down 1939). — 6 miles south-east on A 711 is *Dundrennan Abbey* (1142), which contains interesting monuments.

33 miles: *Gatehouse of Fleet* (pop. 800, E.C. Thursday), a holiday resort sheltered by the Anwoth hills and the Cairnsmore range.

From Gatehouse of Fleet the road runs round the edge of Wigtown Bay, passing *Cardoness Castle* (15th c.) and *Barholm Tower*.

43 miles: *Creetown* (pop. 900, E.C. Wednesday).

53 miles: **Newton Stewart** (pop. 2000, E.C. Wednesday), a little market town, delightfully situated on the
west bank of the river Cree.

A 714 runs south to (7 miles) **Wigtown** (pop. 1470, E.C.
Wednesday). The old county town of Wigtownshire, situated
on a hill from which there are fine views. Outside the town,
on Windy Hill, is the *Martyrs' Monument* (1685), commemorat-
two Covenanters, Margaret Maclachlan and Margaret Wilson,
who were tied to stakes in the Solway and drowned by the
rising tide; their graves are in the churchyard. To the south-
west is the village of *Bladnoch*, on the river Bladnoch, where
"barley bree" (whisky) is distilled. Nearby Baldoon Castle
provided Scott with the model for Bucklaw in "The Bride of
Lammermoor". — 8 miles south-west is *Garlieston*, once a
thriving port. Galloway House, formerly seat of the Earl of
Galloway, can be visited. — 11 miles south is **Whithorn**, one
of the oldest Christian centres in Britain ("Candida Casa").
Ruins of a 12th century priory founded by St Ninian, entered
through a 16th century archway; museum with inscribed stones
and fragments of carved crosses. A 5th century oratory was
excavated here in 1949. 3½ miles south-west, on the coast,
is St Ninian's Cave. — A 714 runs up the beautiful Cree valley,
with many streams flowing down attractive side valleys, to
(9 miles) *House o' Hill*, near the magnificent Glen Trool,
under Lamachan Hill (2350 ft), and (30 miles) *Girvan*.

A 712 runs north-east up the valley of the Palmure Burn,
with a *rocking stone*. To the right is Cairnsmore of Fleet (2331 ft),
and farther on, on the left, the *Grey Mare's Tail* waterfall.
The road reaches 700 feet in places. After passing the very
beautiful *Clatteringshaws Loch* (on left) it comes to *New Galloway* (18 miles).

56 miles: B 735 runs south-west to the lonely weaving
village of *Kirkcowan*.

66 miles: **Glenluce** (pop. 700, E.C. Wednesday), a
village which is developing into a popular seaside
resort, near beautiful Luce Bay; a good centre from
which to explore the surrounding countryside. *Abbey*
founded in 1192, with a fine chapter house (15th c.).

A 747 runs south-east along **Luce Bay,** past the smaller
Auchenmalg Bay (5 miles), to (14 miles) *Port William* (pop. 600,
E.C. Thursday), a quiet little harbour town on a rocky coast.
The road from Port William to Whithorn is one of the most
beautiful in this part of Scotland.

73 miles: on right, *Castle Kennedy*, near the magnificent White Loch. Beyond it is *Lochinch Castle* (19th
c.), seat of the Earl of Stair, with crowstep gables
and gargoyles in the Scottish baronial tradition.

76 miles: **Stranraer** (p. 980).

Dumfries to Ayr

From Dumfries A 76 runs up beautiful Nithsdale
to (49 miles) *Thornhill* (pop. 1200, E.C. Thursday).

A 702 runs west to *Moniaive* (8 miles), a very pretty hill
village. 9 miles south-east of Moniaive is *Dunscore*, with the
grave (modern) of Robert Grierson of Lag, the prototype of
Scott's Robert Redgauntlet. 5 miles west of Moniaive, in a
lonely moorland area, is the farm of *Craigenputtock*, where
Thomas Carlyle lived from 1828 to 1834 and wrote "Sartor
Resartus". *Maxwelton House*, near Moniaive, was the birthplace of Annie Laurie; she died at Craigdarroch, 2 miles west
of Moniaive.

There are a number of castles near Thornhill: 2 miles north,
the ruins of *Tibbers Castle*, destroyed by Robert Bruce in 1311;
3 miles north, *Drumlanrig Castle* (17th c.), seat of the Duke of
Buccleuch; 3 miles north-east, *Morton Castle* (11th c.).

The road continues up the wooded valley, passing
the end of the *Devil's Dyke*, an ancient defensive
earthwork. To the north-east are the Lowther Hills,
with Ballencleuch Law (2268 ft) and the Green Lowther (2403 ft). 8 miles north-east are *Wanlockhead*
and *Leadhills*, the highest villages in Scotland.

61 miles: *Sanquhar* (pop. 2000, E.C. Thursday),
with a ruined castle. Here Richard Cameron in 1680

and James Renwick in 1685 affixed the Declarations of Sanquhar to the old mercat cross (the position of which is marked by a granite obelisk). — 64 miles: *Kirkconnel*, beyond which the road crosses to the south bank of the Nith. — 72 miles: *New Cumnock*, on Burns's "sweet Afton".

78 miles: **Cumnock** (pop. 4000, E.C. Wednesday), an old mining town on the Lugar Water, with a monument to the Covenanters and Covenanting relics in *Baird's Institute*. Nearby are *Dumfries House*, a seat of the Marquess of Bute, and the ruins of *Terringzean Castle*.

6 miles north is **Mauchline,** where Burns married Jean Armour in 1788. At *Mossgiel Farm*, 1 mile north, he wrote some of his best poems. Nearby is the *National Burns Memorial*. Graves of Gavin Hamilton and others associated with Burns.

3 miles south-east of Mauchline on B 713 is *Catrine*, with *Ballochmyle Bridge*. Catrine's cotton-spinning mills are worked by twin water wheels (1829) 50 feet in diameter and 12 feet wide. — 3 miles east of Catrine on B 713 is *Sorn*, with an old bridge and a 17th century church. Sorn Castle dates in part from the 15th century.

94 miles: **Ayr** (p. 977).

64. THE AYRSHIRE COAST AND THE ISLE OF ARRAN

Glasgow to Stranraer

The sandy beaches of the Ayrshire coast are a joy to holiday-makers. Gailes, Troon and Prestwick have fine golf courses bordering their sandy shores. *Ayr* is a town with a long history behind it, the town of Burns, and for many a favourite holiday resort.

Visitors can enjoy magnificent cruises down the Clyde estuary and along the coast. As soon as the ship rounds Cloch Point, near Gourock, passes the village of Inverkip and turns down the coast towards Skelmorlie and Largs the distant horizon is dominated by the hilly outline of the *Isle of Arran*. At Fairlie the view widens out, and when the ship approaches the coast at Portencross, near West Kilbride, the blue waters of the Clyde provide a foreground for the magnificent spectacle of the island to the west. On the east side of Arran are two fine bays, Brodick Bay and Lamlash Bay, the latter sheltered by Holy Island. Landing on Arran, the visitor enters a new world in which he can enjoy the silence of Glen Sannox, the peace of Lochranza, the gentle pace of life in Pirnmill or the tranquillity of Machrie Bay. It is possible to drive right round the island by way of Blackwaterfoot, with magnificent views of the Kintyre peninsula to the west: and there is also a road which cuts through the hills in the centre of the island from Lamlash to Black-waterfoot.

Farther up the Firth of Clyde are the island of *Bute*, with the popular holiday resort of Rothesay, and two smaller islands, the *Great Cumbrae* and *Little Cumbrae*, with their little town of Millport set in a beautiful bay.

Glasgow to Ayr via Kilmarnock

33 miles on A 77.

21 miles: **Kilmarnock** (pop. 50,000, E.C. Wednesday), the industrial capital of Ayrshire: mining, loco-motive construction, hydraulic and general engineer-

ing, carpet-making, brass and iron founding, sanitary ware, whisky.

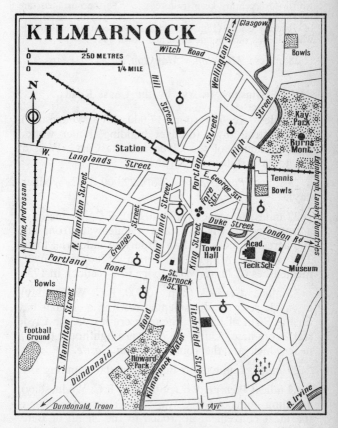

In Waterloo St a tablet marks the site of *John Wilson's printing office*, where the first edition of Burns's poems was printed. *Burns Monument* and *Burns Museum*. In a house in

London Road (tablet) lived the poet's friend Tam Samson, celebrated in "Tam Samson's Elegy".

To the north is **Dean Castle,** seat of Lord Howard de Walden, with a 12th century keep (restored). — To the north-east are the ruins of *Crawfurdland Castle.* — 5 miles east are the remains of *Loudoun Castle* (15th c.) and the 19th century building in which it was incorporated (burned down 1941).

28 miles: *Monkton.* *Monkton to Ayr:* see p. 977.

Glasgow to Ayr by the Coast Road

6 miles: *Renfrew* (pop. 17,000, E.C. Wednesday), an industrial town (dredger building, boiler works) at the junction of the Clyde and the Cart. West of the town is Glasgow Airport.

19 miles: *Port Glasgow* (pop. 22,000, E.C. Wednesday).

22 miles: **Greenock** (pop. 70,000, E.C. Wednesday), a port on the Clyde with a 4 mile waterfront and 100 acres of docks, and an important industrial town. The *McLean Museum* in Union St contains many mementoes of James Watt, born in Greenock in 1736.

25 miles: **Gourock** (pop. 10,000, E.C. Wednesday), a seaside resort and residential town in a circular bay on the Firth of Clyde. Steamer cruises on the Clyde start from here. On *Cloch Point* is a lighthouse (1791), near which are the ruins of *Levan Castle.*

29 miles: Lunderston Bay, a popular camping site.

33 miles: *Wemyss Bay* (pop. 1400, E.C. Wednesday), a calling point of the Clyde steamer services. This is the most convenient approach to the island of **Bute.**

Bute (which can also be reached by the ferry service from *Colintraive* in the Cowal peninsula, on A 886 running south from Strachur on Loch Fyne) is 15 miles long, hilly at the northern end (Windy Hill, 930 ft) and flat at the south end. The chief town is *Rothesay* (pop. 8000, E.C. Wednesday), one of the most popular holiday resorts on the Clyde. Ruins of a 14th century castle. Fine views from Baron Hill (530 ft). — 5 miles south-east is *Mount Stuart*, seat of the Marquess of Bute. — 2 miles north is *Port Bannatyne*, a holiday resort on Kames Bay. To the north is the tower of *Kames Castle* (14th c.), with the old tower-house of Wester Kames in its grounds. — In the centre of the island are Lochs Dhu, Fad and Quien. — Near *Ettrick Bay*, on the west side of the island, is a stone circle.

39 miles: **Largs** (pop. 9000, E.C. Wednesday), a seaside resort on the Clyde, sheltered by its background of hills. Pleasant walks and excursions in the surrounding moorlands and hills.

Interesting *Stevenson Institute*. Ruins of *Kelburn* and *Knock* castles. In the old churchyard is the Skelmorlie Aisle, with 18th century painted ceilings and carving. On *Bowen Craig*, to the south, is a round tower commemorating the battle of Largs (1263).

42 miles: *Fairlie* (pop. 1000, E.C. Wednesday), a picturesque little town. In a charming glen are the ruins of Fairlie Castle (16th c.). Steamer service to Campbeltown.

46 miles: *West Kilbride* (pop. 4640, E.C. Wednesday), a small town with the ruins of *Law Castle* (15th c.). 2 miles west are the ruins of *Portincross Castle*.

51 miles: **Ardrossan** (pop. 9000, E.C. Wednesday), an important port and seaside resort. Near the station

are the ruins of *Ardrossan Castle*. Daily steamer services in summer to Arran, the Isle of Man and Ireland. *North Ayrshire Museum* (local history). 5 miles inland are the remains of *Kilwinning Abbey*, founded in the 12th century.

The Isle of Arran

The island (20 miles long by 12 to 13 miles wide) is one of the most beautiful and most easily accessible in Scotland. To the north are Goat Fell (2866 ft) and Ben Bharrain (2345 ft).

Brodick, the largest place on the island, is on the east side, in beautiful Brodick Bay. This is the point of arrival of the steamers from Ardrossan. *Brodick Castle*, seat of the Duke of Montrose, is a 19th century building, with parts dating from the 16th century. 6 miles west is the magnificent Glen Rosa. To the south is Glen Cloy, with a prehistoric fort.

A 841 runs round the island. 6 miles north of Brodick is *Corrie*, a charming fishing village. The road runs round Sannox Bay and then inland through beautiful Glen Sannox to *Lochranza* (14 miles), with Lochranza Castle (16th c.). — The road then turns down the west side of the island and continues round the south coast. Off Dippin Head is the island of Pladda (lighthouse). — 47 miles: *Whiting Bay* (Eais a Chraneig waterfall, 200 ft). — 51 miles: *Lamlash*, a pleasant holiday resort. In the bay is *Holy Island* (associated with St Molaise), with a small village.

56 miles: *Kilwinning* (pop. 6400, E.C. Wednesday). Nearby are the ruins of a 12th century priory, and **Eglinton Castle** (18th c.), now a hospital. — A 737 runs north to *Dalry*, a woollen town (blankets, rugs) in a magnificent situation.

59 miles: **Irvine** (pop. 17,000, E.C. Wednesday), a seaside resort on the river Irvine, now being developed as a "new town". The *Burns Club* possesses Burns manuscripts and relics. Edgar Allan Poe went to school here as a small boy.

65 miles: A 759 runs west to *Troon* (pop. 10,000, E.C. Wednesday), a holiday resort noted for its golf courses. — 66 miles: *Monkton*.

68 miles: **Prestwick** (pop. 12,000, E.C. Wednesday), a holiday resort and golfing centre (5 courses). International airport. Ruins of an old church; ancient **Mercat Cross** (rebuilt 1777). On the way to Ayr is the ancient *Kingcase Well*.

71 miles: **Ayr** (pop. 46,000, E.C. Wednesday), the county town and a popular bathing resort. Birthplace of Burns, who is commemorated by a statue (1891). Beautiful Esplanade, with fine views of the Arran hills. The 130 foot high *Wallace Tower* (1832) is built on the site of an earlier tower in which Wallace was imprisoned. To the west, in Forth St, is *Ayr Academy*, founded in the 13th century. In Cromwell Place is *Fort Castle*, the tower (restored) of the 12th century St John's Church. *Belleisle House* and its grounds now belong to the town. The *Tam o' Shanter Inn* (museum) at the end of High St was the starting point of Tam's ride, as described in Burns's poem. The *parish church* dates from 1665.

To the south is the *Brig o' Doon*, with a statue of Burns. 2 miles south is *Alloway*, with the **Burns Cottage** (now a museum), in which Burns was born in 1759. Beyond this the Doon is spanned by two bridges, the older of which is the single-arched **Auld Brig o' Doon,** where Tam o' Shanter escaped from his pursuers.

Continuing south from Ayr, there are two alternative routes. — A 719, the coast road, and A 77 via Maybole. The two routes join at Turnberry (21 miles). The coast road is described below.

76 miles: *Dunure*, with a ruined *castle*, formerly a Kennedy stronghold. To the east is *Brown Carrick Hill* (910 ft), with wide views.

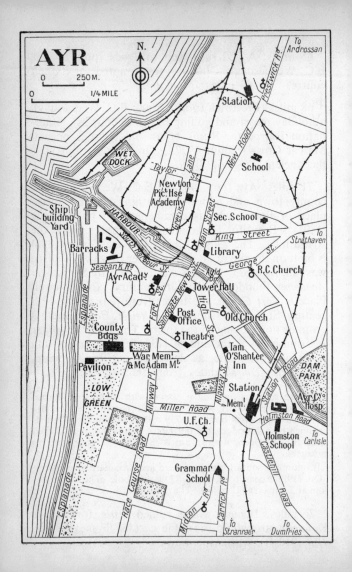

86 miles: *Glenside*. Nearby, on the coast, is *Culzean Castle* (Robert Adam, 1777-92), with a Gothic tower. A flat in the castle was put at the disposal of Gen. Eisenhower for his lifetime in 1946. — 89 miles: *Maidens*, an attractive old village and seaside resort. —96 miles: *Turnberry*, with the ruins of a castle where Robert Bruce landed in 1307.

Here the coast road joins A 77, coming from Ayr via **Maybole,** 6 miles north-east. Maybole (pop. 4700, E.C. Wednesday) is an industrial town (boots and shoes) situated in delightful countryside at a height of 300 feet above sea level. Old *Tolbooth*, formerly a house belonging to the Kennedy family; *castle*; ruins of an old collegiate church. 2 miles south-west are the ruins of *Crossraguel Abbey*, the most complete remains of a 13th century monastic house in Scotland.

3 miles from Turnberry on the Maybole road is **Kirkoswald,** which has Burns associations: *Souter Johnnie's House* (National Trust: museum); graves of Tam o' Shanter and Souter Johnnie in churchyard.

93 miles: **Girvan** (pop. 6200, E.C. Wednesday), a seaside resort surrounded by hills. Boats can be hired in the harbour for trips to Lendal Bay and Turnberry Point, or up the Water of Girvan on which the town stands.

10 miles offshore is **Ailsa Craig,** a volcanic rock rising to a height of over 1000 feet, with a circumference of 2 miles, reached by boat from Girvan. Ruins of *Ailsa Castle* (16th c.). It is the haunt of many seabirds, and is particularly interesting in the nesting season (June and July).

3 miles north-east of Girvan are the ruins of *Killochan Castle*. To the south is *Ardmillan House*, which was visited by Mary Queen of Scots.

99 miles: *Lendalfoot*, a holiday resort. Ruins of *Carlton Castle*.

106 miles: **Ballantrae** (pop. 800), a popular holiday resort on the river Stinchar, dominated by the mas-

sive ruins of *Ardstinchar Castle*, a stronghold of the
Kennedys. Stone circles in the area. The Stinchar
valley is very beautiful, with attractive scenery and
little hamlets.

2 miles south is *Glenapp Castle*, seat of Lord Inch-
cape.

The road runs through fine scenery along the
rugged coast, passes Carlock Hill (1046 ft) and runs
down Glenapp to *Cairnryan* (116 miles). It then
continues south along the shores of Loch Ryan,
with steep cliffs.

116 miles: **Stranraer** (pop. 9200, E.C. Wednesday),
a busy port and holiday resort at the south end of
Loch Ryan. In the centre of the town is *Stranraer
Castle*, an old peel tower which features in Scott's
"Guy Mannering".

Pleasant excursions in the *Rhinns of Galloway*, a peninsula
which extends some 6 miles north-west and 20 miles south to
the *Mull of Galloway*.

8 miles south-west on A 77 is *Portpatrick* (pop. 500, E.C.
Thursday), a coastal village which is becoming one of the
favourite holiday resorts in south-western Scotland. From
the cliffs of *Dashers Den* there are magnificent views extending
as far as the Irish coast 21 miles away.

IX: THE HIGHLANDS

There is no scenery more beautiful or more impressive in the British Isles than that of the Highlands of Scotland, and indeed there are many who claim that its qualities of colour and light make it more beautiful than anything to be seen anywhere in the world. It is a land of magic, an ancient land of great and moving beauty which has almost escaped the hand of man. Before history began to be written the silhouette of the Highlands was as we see it todays, and for countless centuries the hills have echoed the challenge of the deer and heard the dry complaint of the grouse, while in the torrents of the rivers the salmon have leapt upward to the spawning grounds in the upper waters.

The Highlands are divided by the *Great Glen*, that majestic valley with its chain of lochs. Centrally situated in the mountainous area south of this divide are the ancient towns of *Stirling* and *Perth*, and to the north-east the granite-built seaport of *Aberdeen*. Within this vast area are such notable beauty spots as the *Trossachs*, with lovely Loch Katrine, Loch Achray and Loch Vennachar in the shadow of Ben Ledi, Loch Earn and Loch Tay.

From the lovely Trossachs, west of Stirling, the traveller can pass through the foothills of the Grampians to Loch Earn and Loch Tay. From Loch Tay the river Tay runs past the little burgh of Aberfeldy to join the river Tummel. The valley of the Tummel, with Pitlochry, Blair Atholl and Struan, is well worth a visit, and to those who love the wilder stretches of the hills the route northward to the Spey valley will beckon. Eastward lie the shires of Angus and Aberdeen and the rich farming country of Strathmore.

On the east coast are famous towns — *Dundee*, Arbroath, Montrose — and fine cliff scenery. Northward lies Deeside with Balmoral Castle, country home of the Queen, set amid a vast territory of beautiful mountains. West of Stirling is Scotland's greatest loch, *Loch Lomond*, and farther west are the sea lochs of Loch Fyne and Loch Long.

The west coast is wondrously indented with sea lochs of unparalleled beauty, a bewildering succession of peninsulas and firths along the whole of the coast and beyond it the beautiful shapes of the Western Isles. At the southern tip of the Great Glen is *Ben Nevis*, Britain's highest mountain. At the

northern tip is *Inverness*, justly entitled "capital of the Highlands".   North of the Great Glen is a country of untouched
wild beauty, of vast moors, far-spread deer forests, craggy
glinting mountains and deep tree-clothed gorges, immense and
lonely lochs and a western seaboard of incredible grandeur
along which can be found, on the sheltered white-sanded shores,
quiet villages, filled with the soft scent of the peat-smoke and
the soft sound of Gaelic voices, little villages of indescribable
tranquillity and charm.   Beyond this magical coast lie the
Hebrides, a galaxy of lovely islands, each with its particular
appeal and its own romantic legends.

65. GLASGOW TO OBAN

The route runs through the old county of **Argyll,** now the Argyll district of the Strathclyde region. With an area of over 3000 sq. miles, no part of the county is more than 11 miles from the sea or from the shores of a sea loch. The coast is slashed by innumerable sea lochs and fringed with innumerable islands, the largest of which are Mull, Coll, Tiree, Colonsay, Jura and Islay. The inland regions offer a wide variety of scenery and are well provided with accommodation for the visitor. The busy holiday resort of *Dunoon*, on the west side of the Firth of Clyde, is popular with Glasgow people. Near the head of Loch Fyne is *Inveraray*, a picturesque little burgh with an imposing castle, seat of the Duke of Argyll. Beyond Inveraray the road runs through Glen Aray to the longest fresh-water loch in the country, Loch Awe.

Oban, in a bay sheltered by the island of Kerrera, is a leading holiday resort and the shopping centre for a large surrounding area. It is an important communications centre, the terminus of the railway from the south and the port of embarkation for the Hebrides.

An attractive road runs south from Oban to the quiet little burgh of *Lochgilphead*, on Loch Fyne, and *Ardrishaig*, at the east end of the Crinan Canal, which cuts across the head of the Kintyre peninsula to the pretty village of Crinan on the Sound of Jura. Beyond Ardrishaig the road continues south down the shores of Loch Fyne to the little town of *Tarbert*, much frequented by sailing boats. In then runs down the west side of Kintyre and cuts across to *Campbeltown*, the chief town of the peninsula.

The best way out of Glasgow is by Great Western Road (to the north of the University), which runs into a fast road, A 82. This is preferable to the road which runs along the north bank of the Clyde through the crowded industrial areas on the outskirts of Glasgow (particularly *Clydebank*, an industrial town with a population of 50,000).

16 miles: to left, **Dumbarton** (pop. 27,000, E.C. Wednesday), in a fine situation at the junction of

the Leven and the Clyde. The main activities are shipbuilding, the manufacture of machinery and aircraft construction.

The town is dominated by the **Castle** on its rock (300 ft). It was a royal residence, first established in the 13th century, and changed hands several times during the wars with England (1571). From the top (orientation table) there are wide views. In the High St is the *Greit House* (1623), once the residence of the Earl of Glencairn. Very beautiful parks: *Levengrove Park* (30 acres), on the Clyde, and the grounds of *Overtoun House* (80 acres), with Spardie Linn and the beautiful Overtoun Glen.

From Dumbarton there is an alternative route to *Arrochar* (below) on A 814 up the east side of Loch Long. It runs via *Cardross* (with a castle in which Robert Bruce died in 1329) to **Helensburgh**, a popular Clyde holiday resort, magnificently situated at the mouth of the Gareloch. The town is well and spaciously laid out. On the Esplanade is an obelisk commemorating Henry Bell (1767-1830), who in 1812 launched the first steamship to sail on the Clyde, the "Comet". The road then runs up the east side of the Gareloch, via Rhu and Shandon, to *Garelochhead* (pop. 1600, E.C. Wednesday), finely situated at the head of the loch, and continues up the east side of Loch Long, with splendid views, to *Arrochar*.

A 82 bypasses Dumbarton and comes to *Bonhill* (18 miles). 1 mile south-west is *Renton*, with a monument to Tobias Smollett (1721-71).

20 miles: *Balloch* (pop. 4000, E.C. Wednesday), with earthworks marking the position of an old castle. The road now runs along the west side of **Loch Lomond**, the largest lake in Britain (24 miles long, up to 5 miles wide at the south end). *Ben Lomond* (3192 ft) rises majestically on the east side of the loch.

27 miles: *Luss* (pop. 450, E.C. Wednesday), magnificently situated on the shores of the loch, which becomes gradually narrower towards its northern end. — 36 miles: **Tarbet,** with fine views of the loch and Ben Lomond. An important road junction.

(a) Tarbet to Oban via Inveraray

2 miles: *Arrochar*, at the head of Loch Long (fine view). The road climbs up Glencroe, to the south-west of Ben Arthur, also known as the Cobbler (2891 ft). — 7 miles: the pass of *Rest and Be Thankful*. To the east is Ben Ime (3318 ft), to the west Beinn an Lochain (3021 ft). The road now runs down to Loch Fyne.

To Dunoon. A 815 goes off on the left and runs down the south-east side of Loch Fyne to *Strachur*, where it turns inland and runs through the hills, skirting Loch Eck, to reach the Clyde coast in the Holy Loch shortly before *Sandbank*. Beyond this, on the coast, is *Hunter's Quay*, a sailing centre, and adjoining it **Dunoon** (pop. 9500), a holiday resort. Beyond this there is a pleasant run down the coast to Toward Point, opposite the island of Bute (p. 974).

From Strachur A 886 runs south to *Colintraive*, from which there is a ferry service to Bute (p. 974).

A 83 runs round the north end of Loch Fyne and comes to **Inveraray** (pop. 500), a fine example of an 18th century planned village.

Inveraray was laid out by the Duke of Argyll, with regular streets of attractive whitewashed houses, when he moved the older village from its previous site near Inveraray Castle. Church of 1795.

Inveraray Castle (entrance just before the beginning of the town) is a magnificent Gothic mansion (Adam, 1780) with a richly decorated and furnished interior (pictures, mainly family portraits, by *Raeburn*, *Gainsborough*, *Hoppner*, *Landseer* and others; display of swords and muskets).

It is possible to continue south-west along Loch Fyne on A 83 to *Lochgilphead*, and from there turn north on A 816 to **Oban** (below, p. 987).

From Inveraray A 819 runs north up Glen Aray to **Loch Awe** and then skirts the loch to join A 85,

the road to Oban, just west of *Dalmally*. Dalmally
to Oban: see below.

(b) Tarbet to Oban via Crianlarich

A 82 to Tyndrum, then A 85.

44 miles: *Ardlui*, at the northern tip of Loch Lomond. — 53 miles: *Crianlarich* (pop. 430, E.C.
Wednesday), at the junction of Strath Fillan, Glen
Falloch and Glen Dochart, an excellent centre for
walks and climbs in the surrounding hills. To the
east is Ben More (3843 ft), to the west Ben Dubh-
chraig (3204 ft).

56 miles: on the banks of the Fillan are the ruins
of a 14th century priory. *St Fillan's Pool*, a holy
well formerly believed to cure madness.

58 miles: *Tyndrum*, situated 870 feet above sea
level in Strath Fillan, a railway junction. From here
A 82 continues north to *Glencoe* (p. 1032).

A 85 runs down Glen Lochy to (70 miles) *Dalmally*
(pop. 1000, E.C. Thursday), at the foot of beautiful
Glen Orchy, and continues along the north end of
Loch Awe, through magnificent scenery, passing the
imposing ruins of *Kilchurn Castle* (15th c. keep, the
rest 17th c.), on a headland jutting out into the loch.

75 miles: the village of *Loch Awe*, after which the
road enters the **Pass of Brander** and follows the Awe
down to *Taynuilt* (pop. 600, E.C. Wednesday), on
Loch Etive.

Goods walks and excursions round Loch Etive. To the east
is Ben Cruachan (3689 ft), with its double peak, from which
there are wide-ranging views. There are footpaths up both
sides of Loch Etive to Kinlochetive, from which there is a
magnificent hill road to Glencoe. Boat trips on the loch.

90 miles: *Connel Ferry*. Road on right to bridge for Fort William.

92 miles: *Dunstaffnage Castle*, with massive battlemented walls. From here the "Stone of Destiny" was taken in the 9th century to Scone Castle near Perth, where it was seized by Edward I and removed to Westminster Abbey. It is now under the Coronation Chair.

95 miles: **Oban** (pop. 6700, E.C. Thursday), a very attractive town, sheltered by hills, in a beautiful bay on the Firth of Lorne, which is almost completely closed by the island of Kerrera.

The harbour is the departure point for steamers to the islands and along the coast, and these services by water combine with the roads and the railway to earn Oban the name of "the Charing Cross of the Highlands". On the hill behind the town is *McCaig's Tower*, a "folly" built by a local banker who died in 1902, an imitation of the Coliseum in Rome; it remained unfinished.

Around Oban. Island of *Kerrera* (ferry from Gallanach road). At the south end are the ruins of Gylen Castle. — 4 miles south-west is *Loch Nell* ("Loch of the Swans"). Near the south side of the loch is the *Serpent Mound*, a prehistoric tumulus. — 2 miles north is *Ganavan*, with beaches of fine sand. — 3 miles north is *Dunollie Castle*, commanding the northern entrance to the bay. The ruins can be reached from the Ganavan road (on right).

Oban to Campbeltown: 89 miles on A 816.

8 miles: *Kilninver*, on Loch Feochan. — 8 miles: south-west is *Ardmaddy House*, on Seil Sound. A 816 continues south through Glen Euchar and the *Pass of Melfort*, with fine views. — 15 miles: *Kilmelfort*, on Loch Melfort. — 23 miles: *Kintraw*. To the south is Craignish Point, to the north the ruins of *Craignish Castle*. — 27 miles: B 840 runs north-east to *Ford*, at the south end of beautiful Loch Awe. — 29 miles: *Kilmartin*.

— 37 miles: **Lochgilphead** (pop. 1200, E.C. Thursday), at the head of Loch Gilp, from which the Crinan Canal (1800) runs 9 miles north-west to Crinan, on Loch Crinan. — 39 miles: *Ardrishaig* (pop. 1020), from which the famous Loch Fyne herring are fished. — 41 miles: **Tarbert.** 1 mile west is *West Loch Tarbert*, a sea loch opening off the Atlantic. At the end of the loch are the remains of a 14th century castle. A 83 runs down the south-east side of the loch and then continues down the west coast of the Kintyre peninsula. — 62 miles: *Clachan*. — 70 miles: *Tayinloan*, near which is Largie Castle. — 81 miles: *Bellochantuy*. — 89 miles: **Campbeltown** (pop. 6400, E.C. Wednesday), a fishing port and holiday resort with many interesting excursions in the surrounding area. Local museum (history and antiquities). The Public Library contains a catalogue of 25 standing stones in the Kintyre peninsula. — To the east is the island of *Arran* (p. 976). — 5 miles west is *Machrihanish* (pop. 190, E.C. Thursday), with a well-known golf course. Airfield. — 10 miles south through the Conie Glen is *Southend*, an attractive village near the mouth of the Conieglen Water.

Oban to Fort William: see p. 1031.

66. THE HEBRIDES

The visitor who travels along the much indented western seaboard of Scotland will constantly catch glimpses of romantically shaped islands lying out to sea. Some of them are near the coast and easily accessible, others lie far out into the Atlantic. All are of remarkable beauty, but each has its own characteristics and its own way of life. A trip to one of these islands, either by sea or by air, will be an experience to remember. The most visited islands are the two most easily accessible, Skye and Mull — the former notable for the magnificent Cuillin Hills, the latter for the sacred island of Iona off its western coast.

Access

There are regular air services between Glasgow and all the larger islands, but the best way to see the Hebrides is to use one of the regular steamer services and take your car with you. Information from Caledonian MacBrayne, Gourock PA 19 1QP (tel. Gourock 31261). The main services are the following:

Mallaig to Lochboisdale (South Uist)

Mallaig to Castlebay (Barra)

Oban to Coll and Tiree

Oban to Castlebay and Lochboisdale

West Loch Tarbert to Port Ellen (Islay)

Oban to Craignure (Mull)

Mallaig to Armadale (Skye)

Ullapool to Stornoway (Lewis)

Kyle of Lochalsh to Kyleakin (Skye)

Uig (Skye) to Lochmaddy (North Uist)

Uig to Tarbert (Harris)

Oban to Colonsay

Tour of Mull.

MULL

The island of Mull lies on the north-west side of the Firth of Lorne and is reached by regular boat services from Oban, on the other side of the firth (enquire locally about timetables). Roughly triangular in shape, it is 30 miles long, with many inlets and lochs. The highest point is *Ben More* (3169 ft), in the south-west, and most of the island is hilly moorland, with spacious bays round the coast. Its main features of historical interest are *Duart Castle* in the south and *Bloody Bay* in the north, scene of the last sea battle between the island clans.

From Craignure A 849 runs north-west past *Salen* and the ruins of *Aros Castle* to (20 miles) **Tobermory** (pop. 700), a holiday resort.

The Spanish galleon "Florida", a treasure ship laden with gold, sank in Tobermory Bay in 1588. Attempts to recover the vessel have been unsuccessful.

From Craignure A 849 runs south-west, passing *Duart Castle* (open to visitors), a Maclean stronghold. From Fionnphort, at the end of the road, there is a ferry service to Iona (no cars allowed).

Iona saw the first coming of Christianity to Scotland, the first Norse invasion of the Hebrides and, in a later century, the establishment of the Lordship of the Isles. This small green island set in a sapphire sea, with its little cathedral, is an epitome of the eventful history of this part of Scotland. Here St Columba landed in 563, coming from Ireland to bring the Christian faith to Scotland.

The oldest building on Iona is **St Oran's Chapel** (11th c.), dedicated to the saint who gave his name to the island of Oronsay (see below). It contains the *tombs of 49 Scottish kings*. The *abbey church* (Transitional style, 13th-16th c.) has been restored. Of the many **Celtic crosses** formerly on the island there remain only St Martin's and St John's. The **Cathedral** (13th-16th c.) has beautiful *cloisters* (carved group, "Pentecost", by Lipchitz, 1960).

Staffa is one of the smallest but perhaps the most remarkable of all the islands, enclosed in the great sweep of Mull's west coast. It can be reached by hired boat from Iona. It is a basaltic mass, formed by volcanic action into fantastic shapes. Its most striking feature is its column-like structure — huge octagonal pillars of lava rising vertically out of the sea and pierced by giant caves. The most imposing of these is the famous **Fingal's Cave** which inspired Mendelssohn's overture, 200 feet long, with a vaulted roof borne on columns of dark-coloured basalt. Among the many other caves is the *Clam Shell Cave*. Staffa is at the Scottish end of the wave of volcanic activity which created the Giant's Causeway in Northern Ireland. The island is uninhabited.

COLL AND TIREE

These two islands, lying west of Mull, are holiday resorts (small hotels, accommodation in croft houses). Coll has a permanent population of 150. Tiree is a flat elongated island with a population of 1000. still speaking Gaelic. Crofting (small-scale farming) is more important than fishing in the island's economy.

The two islands were converted to Christianity in the 6th century. Originally Macdonald country, they passed to the Macleans of Duart and then to the Campbells of Lochawe. Out in the Atlantic off Tiree is the *Skerryvore* lighthouse (1843).

ISLAY

Islay, west of the Kintyre peninsula beyond the Sound of Jura, is noted for its rolling moorland and its magnificent beaches. The largest places on the island are **Port Ellen** and **Port Askaig,** and there are many small villages and hamlets round the coasts and in the interior. Islay is reached by the Clyde

steamers from West Loch Tarbert or by air. The
population is 4000. Important whisky distilleries.

Port Ellen has a well-known golf course. *Bridgend* and
Bowmore are good centres from which to explore the island.
Fine scenery along the Rhinns in the west and the Oa peninsula
in the south-west. Near *Port Charlotte* are the graves of American soldiers drowned when the "Tuscania" was torpedoed
in 1918.

JURA

North-east of Islay, beyond the Sound of Islay, is the island
of Jura (pop. 250). Access by Clyde steamers from West Loch
Tarbert to Craighouse, or by air to Islay and ferry from Port
Askaig to Feolin Ferry.

The island's most conspicuous feature is the *Paps of Jura*
(Ben an Oir, 2571 ft, and neighbouring peaks), a landmark
over a wide area of the Hebrides. The island, almost cut in
two by *Loch Tarbert*, is separated from the coast of Kintyre
by the Sound of Jura and from the island of Scarba, off its
northern tip, by the famous Corrievreckan whirlpool. The
largest villages, both on the east coast, are Lagg and Craighouse.

COLONSAY AND ORONSAY

West of Jura and north of Islay are the two small islands
of Colonsay and Oronsay, separated by a shallow strait, the
Strand, which is dry for three hours at low tide. They are
named after St Columba and St Oran. *Colonsay* attracts visitors
with its solitude and its fine beaches. Colonsay House has a
beautiful garden of semi-tropical plants. On *Oronsay* are the
remains of a 14th century priory founded by the Lord of the
Isles, with a fine cross.

SKYE

Skye has a much indented coast, with a total
coastline of over 1000 miles. It is 50 miles long, but
no point on the island is more than 5 miles from the
sea. The population is 8000, living by farming,
fishing and tourism.

Kyleakin, a little village of quaint charm on the east coast, is the gateway to the island. *Armadale* and *Broadford* in the south, *Sligachan* in the centre and *Dunvegan* in the north-west are good centres. **Portree,** beautifully situated in Portree Bay, is the only town on the island.

Access. Ferry services (cars carried) from Mallaig on A 830 to Armadale; Kyle of Lochalsh on A 87 to Kyleakin; and Glenelg to Kylerhea. Mallaig is the terminus of the railway (sleeping cars from London, King's Cross, and trains from Glasgow, Queen Street).

Kyleakin to Portree and Dunvegan: 50 miles on A 850.
A 850 runs west along the coast to Lusa. 6 miles: A 851 goes off on the left and runs south to reach the coast on the Sound of Sleat, which it follows to (17 miles) *Armadale,* terminus of the ferry from Mallaig (neo-Gothic castle). — 8 miles: *Broadford* (pop. 980, E.C. Wednesday), a holiday resort in Broadford Bay.

From Broadford A 881 runs south-west round Beinn na Caillich (2403 ft) to the head of Loch Slapin and then down the Strathaird peninsula on the west coast, passing Blaven (3042 ft) and Garbh Bheinn (2648 ft), to *Elgol* on Loch Scavaig, a wild and picturesque inlet. To the north-west are the **Cuillin Hills** (Sgurr Alasdair, 3309 ft), at the foot of which is *Loch Coruisk,* one of the grandest and most impressive spots in the whole of Scotland.

A 850 continues north-west along the coast, with magnificent scenery. To the north is the island of Scalpay. — 15 miles: *Luib,* on Loch Ainort. To the south is Glas Bheinn Mhor (1852 ft). The road runs round the loch and continues north through more beautiful scenery to Loch Sligachan, at the head of which (26 miles) is *Sligachan,* a good centre for walks and climbs in the Cuillins.

From Sligachan A 850 continues north to (36 miles) **Portree** (pop. 1000, E.C. Wednesday), capital of the island and a good centre for excursions, situated in a small loch opening off the *Sound of Raasay*, on the opposite side of which cna be seen the cliffs of the bare island of Raasay.

The Trotternish peninsula: a round trip of 50 miles (A 855) from Portree.

4 miles: in the cliffs to the east is *Prince Charles's Cave*, where the Prince is said to have hidden in 1746. — 7 miles: the road passes to the east of the *Storr* (2341 ft), with strange rock formations; on the east side of the hill is a curious natural pillar, the *Old Man of Storr*. — 18 miles: **Staffin,** with the offshore Staffin Island. To the north-west is the *Quiraing* (1779 ft), with high rock faces and crags, one of the most impressive hills in the area. — A 855 now runs round the north end of the island to (23 miles) *Kilmaluag* and (25 miles) *Duntulm* (old castle). — 27 miles: to the east, on the road to Peingown, is a monument to Flora Macdonald. — 30 miles: a path runs west to Monkstadt, beyond which is *Prince Charles's Point*, where the Prince landed with Flora Macdonald in June 1746. — 35 miles: *Uig*, from which the road runs south to Portree.

From Portree A 850 runs north-west to *Loch Snizort* and turns west to reach *Fairy Bridge* (54 miles), from which B 886 runs north to *Stein*, on Loch Bay. A 850 turns south to (58 miles) **Dunvegan,** with the splendid ancient castle of the Macleods.

South-west of Skye are the islands of *Muck, Eigg, Rhum, Canna* and *Soay*, beloved of artists.

THE OUTER HEBRIDES

The Outer Hebrides are a chain of islands extending for 130 miles from the *Butt of Lewis* in the north to Barra Head in the south — **Lewis and Harris** (a single island), **North Uist, Benbecula, South Uist** and **Barra.** The scenery is magnificent, though bare and empty, for the full force of the Atlantic beats against the western seaboard, broken by innumerable sea lochs. *Stornoway* is the chief town of Lewis and Harris, *Lochmaddy* of North Uist, *Lochboisdale* of South Uist and *Castlebay* of Barra. These are pleasant little towns with long traditions and associations with the Scottish clans. 15 miles west of Stornoway are the 47 standing stones of *Callanish*, dating from 2000 B.C.

The islands can be reached either by the steamer services from the mainland or by air from Glasgow and Inverness.

Lewis and Harris. This is the largest island of the group, 60 miles long by 20 miles wide, with a population of 25,000. The centre is flat, and to the west becomes a maze of lochs and waterways which offer good sport to the fishermen. To the south the island's main ranges of hills rise steeply round Clisham and form the backbone of Harris. Lewis and Harris are so nearly separated by two deeply indented sea lochs, West Loch Tarbert and East Loch Tarbert, that they are often thought of as separate islands. The chief town, and the administrative centre of the whole of the Outer Isles (which were formed into an independent local authority in 1975), is **Stornoway** (pop. 5200). *Tarbert* has a harbour used by fishing boats. To the south-west are the hills of Tirga More (2227 ft), Ullaval (2153 ft), Oreval (2185 ft), Uisgnaval More (2392 ft) and Clisham (2622 ft). The island is famous for its hand-woven Harris tweed.

North Uist, Benbecula and South Uist. South of Harris, separated from it by the Sound of Harris, is **North Uist**, the chief place in which is *Lochmaddy*. A 865 and A 867 run round the island. North Uist is connected with Benbecula, and Benbecula with South Uist, by causeways. **South Uist** (chief town *Lochboisdale*) has a much indented coastline and a number of offshore islands. There are many hills, including Ben More (2035 ft) and Hecla (1988 ft). **Barra** is the most southerly of the main islands and the most barren. Near *Castlebay*, which has the island's harbour, are the ruins of Kisimul Castle (12th c., restored). The beach at Traigh Mhor Bay in the north-east of Barra serves as the landing strip for the air services.

67. THE TROSSACHS

Glasgow to Perth

Leave Glasgow by Maryhill Road (A 81, sign-posted to Aberfoyle).

4 miles: bear left into the Bearsden road (A 809), leaving A 81 to continue north to *Milngavie*, a dormitory suburb of Glasgow. Beyond Milngavie are the Campsie Fells (Earl's Seat, 1897 ft) and the Kilsyth Hills.

5 miles: *Bearsden* (remains of the Antonine Wall). — 12 miles: to the east, *Duntreath Castle* (15th c.: old dungeons).

18 miles: *Drymen* (pop. 380, E.C. Wednesday).

27 miles: A 81 runs east to Stirling, passing the Lake of Menteith, in which is *Inchmahome Priory* (associations with Mary Queen of Scots).

29 miles: **Aberfoyle** (pop. 1500, E.C. Wednesday), a pleasant village and a good centre for the Trossachs.

B 829 runs west along beautiful *Loch Ard* and the north side of Loch Chon, climbing to 500 feet, and then runs down to *Inversnaid* on Loch Lomond.

From Aberfoyle we climb the magnificent Duke's Road (A 821) and then run down to the end of beautiful **Loch Katrine** (9 miles long). This is the heart of the Trossachs, the lovely green and wooded valley linking Loch Achray and Loch Katrine, one of the best-known beauty spots in the Highlands. In Loch Katrine is *Ellen's Isle* (steamer services). To the south-west is the jagged peak of Ben Venue (2393 ft) with the Silver Strand and the Goblin's Cave on the shores of the loch at its foot.

The road now runs east along the north side of *Loch Achray* (magnificent views) and *Loch Venachar*, at the far end of which (4 miles) is **Callander** (pop. 7130, E.C. Wednesday), a pleasant little town and a good centre for excursions. 16 miles south-east of Callander, via *Doune* (ruined castle), is **Stirling** (p. 944).

A 84 runs north from Callander via *Kilmahog* and the *Pass of Leny*, a picturesque gorge with fine waterfalls, to Loch Lubnaig. To the west is Ben Ledi (2873 ft). At the far end of the loch (52 miles) is *Strathyre* (pop. 150, E.C. Wednesday), a pretty little village (fishing). — 53 miles: *Kingshouse*. To the west are the Braes of Balquhidder. In the churchyard at Balquhidder is the grave of Rob Roy, and to the west of the village is Loch Voil.

58 miles: *Lochearnhead* (pop. 390, E.C. Wednesday), on Loch Earn. Magnificent views.

Lochearnhead to Killin and Pitlochry. From Lochearnhead A 85 climbs up the impressive *Glen Ogle* and descends again, with fine hill views in every direction. *Killin* (pop. 600, E.C. Wednesday) is a pretty little village on the Dochart just above its entry into Loch Tay. The houses cluster round a handsome bridge over the falls. Beyond Killin A 827 crosses the Lochay, with the fine Falls of Lochay and the impressive ruins of *Finlarig Castle*. It then runs along the north side of **Loch Tay** (14½ miles long, 3 miles wide). — 16 miles: *Kenmore* (Taymouth Castle, now a school). Beautiful scenery. — 22 miles: *Aberfeldy* (pop. 1680, E.C. Wednesday), a pleasant town at the junction of the Moness and the Tay. Monument commemorating the mutiny of the Black Watch regiment in 1740. Large bridge over the Tay (1733). In the Urlar Glen, to the south-west, are

the *Falls of Moness* (50 ft). — 32 miles: *Ballinluig*.
— 37 miles: *Pitlochry* (p. 1009).

From Lochearnhead A 85 runs along the north
side of Loch Earn to *St Fillans* (pop. 190, E.C. Wednesday), a quiet lochside village. (There is another road,
narrow but very attractive, on the south side of the
loch).

61 miles: **Comrie** (pop. 1000, E.C. Wednesday), at
the meeting of the wild Glen Artney and Glen Lednock.

At midnight on New Year's Eve a torchlight procession is
held here, with "guisers" wearing strange costumes and horned
headdresses. — In Glen Lednock is the Devil's Cauldron, an
impressive waterfall in the hills. From the top of Dunmore
Hill, on which is the Melville Monument, there are wide views.

68 miles: **Crieff** (pop. 6000, E.C. Wednesday), a
holiday resort in a beautiful setting. The *County
Court* (1853) stands on the site of the old town hall.
Near the entrance is a cross (1688) placed there in
1868; in front of it are the remains of the old stocks.

Immediately behind the Knock of Crieff (911 ft) there is
an orientation table: splendid views. — 3 miles south is the
magnificently situated *Drummond Castle*. — 2 miles north is
Monzie Castle, a fine country house dating from the 17th century. — 4 miles south-east is *Innerpeffray*, with a ruined castle
and chapel, and a valuable old *public library* (1691). — 2 miles
north-west is the fine old house of *Ochtertyre*, where Burns
wrote "Blyth, blyth and merry was she" (1787). — 4 miles
east is **Abercairney**, a very ancient settlement with the ruins
of a 13th century abbey. Just beyond this is the old village of
Fowlis Wester, with an old stone cross 10 feet high. Pleasant
walking in the Glen o' the Muckle Burns. — 5 miles north
is the *Sma' Glen*, with the remains of a Roman fort and signal
station and an Iron Age hill-fort.

85 miles: **Perth** (p. 999).

68. PERTH TO ABERDEEN

Perth

Perth (pop. 42,000, E.C. Wednesday), on the river Tay, is one of Scotland's most historic cities and was for centuries its capital. It is an important livestock market, and has whisky distilleries.

There was a Roman station here. It was occupied by the Picts in the 6th century. Perth was a royal residence long before Edinburgh, and during the 13th, 14th and 15th centuries was the scene of bitter fighting between the clans and between England and Scotland. In 1482 James III moved the court and the seat of government to Edinburgh.

St John's Church (restored) is in Decorated style, with an older tower; it was founded in 1126. In Tay St is the site, now occupied by local authority offices, of *Gowrie House*, the scene of the Gowrie Conspiracy (1600) to kidnap James VI. Immediately south is the old Greyfriars Burial Ground, on the site of one of the four monasteries in the town.

At the corner of High St and Tay St are the Tudor-style municipal buildings, with stained glass windows depicting scenes from Scott's "Fair Maid of Perth". At the junction of George St and Charlotte St is the **Art Gallery and Museum,** with an excellent collection of pictures, including works by contemporary artists. In Curfew Row is the *Fair Maid's House*, one of the oldest houses in the town (16th c.), the supposed home of Catherine Glover, the "fair maid" of Scott's novel.

King James VI's Hospital, founded in 1569, stands at the junction of King St and Leonard St, on the site of a former Carthusian monastery. The original building was demolished by Cromwell in 1651 in order to build a citadel; the present building dates from 1750.

Perth Bridge (1771: fine view) leads to the Bridgend district.   John Ruskin lived in *Bridgend House* (tablet). Some of the houses along the riverside are very attractive.

Near the river are the *North Inch* and *South Inch*, areas of parkland in the heart of the city, which feature in Scott's novel.   There is a monument to Scott on the South Inch.   The novelist John Buchan was born in Perth.

Around Perth.   To the south-west is *Kinnoull Hill*, a fine viewpoint (orientation table).   On top of the hill is a ruined tower. — To the north-west is *Huntingtower Castle*, formerly Ruthven Castle, seat of the Earls of Gowrie. — 2 miles north is **Scone Palace,** seat of the Earl of Mansfield.   Nearby is the site of the abbey where Scottish kings were crowned, from which Edward I in 1297 transferred the *Stone of Scone* to Westminster Abbey.   (In 1950 it was stolen from the Abbey by a group of young Scots, but was later recovered). — 4 miles south are the ruins of *Elcho Castle* (13th c.), associated with Wallace's attempt to recover Perth from the English. — 5 miles south-west is *Dupplin Castle*, seat of Lord Forteviot, commanding the wide valley of the Earn (Strathearn).   The present building dates from 1927, when the earlier Tudor building was destroyed by fire.   Dupplin is a model village. — 3 miles east is *Kinfauns Castle*, a former seat of the Earl of Moray, now a hotel.

(a) Perth to Aberdeen vie Balmoral

109 miles on A 93.

15 miles: **Blairgowrie** (pop. 5000, E.C. Thursday), a holiday resort and the centre of a raspberry-growing area.   West of the town is the beautiful *Loch of Clunie*, with Clunie Castle; to the north are the Forest of Clunie and the mansion of *Craighall*.

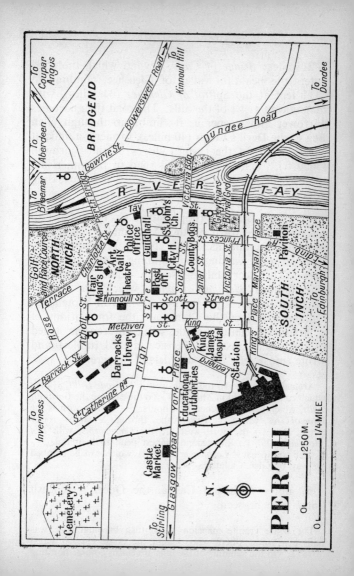

PERTH

21 miles: *Bridge of Cally*, beyond which the road enters the beautiful valley of **Glenshee,** climbing to 1111 feet at the *Spittal of Glenshee* (34 miles), with magnificent views of the hills. The road then becomes narrower and steeper as it climbs up through Glen Beg to the **Devil's Elbow** (40 miles), formerly a difficult zigzag bend on the eastern slopes of the Cairnwell (3059 ft). This is the highest road in Britain, rising to 2199 feet at the Cairnwell pass. A popular skiing area.

49 miles: **Braemar** (pop. 640, E.C. Thursday), an attractive little town on the Dee, amid wooded hills and high mountains. The climate is bracing, and there is good walking and climbing in the surroundings. The deer stalking season begins in August. The famous *Highland Games*, which are usually attended by the royal family, are held in September. On the banks of the Clunie are the foundations of a large 11th century castle. R.L. Stevenson stayed in a house in Castleton Terrace in 1881 (tablet), and wrote most of "Treasure Island" there.

Around Braemar. To the south-west is *Morrone Hill* (2819 ft), which can be climbed in 2 hours. — To the east are the *Garawalt Falls*, which can be reached in 3 hours. — 7 miles west is the *Linn of Dee*, where the river rushes through a narrow rocky gorge. — To the north-west are the *Cairngorms*, with *Ben Macdhui* (4296 ft), the second highest peak in Scotland. — To the south-east is *Lochnagar* (3768 ft), which can be climbed by way of Glen Callater.

57 miles: **Balmoral Castle,** the Queen's Scottish home, can be seen.

The white granite mansion in Scottish baronial style was built by Prince Albert, who bought the estate (11,000 acres) in 1852. On the summits of the hills are cairns commemorating various members of the royal family. The beautiful grounds can be seen when the royal family is not in residence.

58 miles: *Crathie*, with the church attended by the royal family when at Balmoral. Monument erected by Queen Victoria to her faithful attendant John Brown (d. 1883). — 59 miles: *Abergeldie Castle* (16th c., enlarged in the 19th), a royal residence occupied by the Duke of Windsor when Prince of Wales.

66 miles: *Ballater* (pop. 1000, E.C. Thursday), a delightful holiday resort amid fine Highland scenery. To the south is Mount Keen (3077 ft), which can be climbed from Ballater.

72 miles: *Dinnet* (pop. 600). To the west is the lonely Muir of Dinnet, extending north-west to Culblean Hill and Morven (2862 ft). To the south-east are the Forest of Glentanar and beautiful Glen Tanar.

78 miles: *Aboyne* (pop. 1000, E.C. Thursday), a charming little place among birch and pine woods. *Highland Games* in the first week of September. To the north-west is *Aboyne Castle* (17th c.), in the grounds of which are a stone circle and an ogham stone.

83 miles: *Kincardine O'Neil*, where Edward I of England spent a night in 1296.

90 miles: **Banchory** (pop. 1900, E.C. Thursday), a pleasant town on the southern slopes of a hill overlooking the Dee and a good centre for excursions.

To the south-west is *Scolty* (983 ft), with a round tower on the summit. — 2 miles south-east is *Tilquhillie Castle* (1575), now a farmhouse. — 3 miles north is *Hill of Fare* (1545 ft); fishing.

From Banchory two roads lead to Aberdeen —
A 943 south of the Dee, A 93 north of the Dee. Just
beyond the town A 943 crosses the Water of Feugh
at *Bridge of Feugh* (18th c. bridge), with waterfalls
where the salmon can be seen leaping upstream in
late summer.　A 93 passes close to *Crathes Castle*
(late 16th c.) and (98 miles) *Drum Castle*, a fine 17th
century mansion, the home of the Irvine family, with
a mediaeval tower.

109 miles: **Aberdeen** (p. 1009).

(b) Perth to Aberdeen by the Coast Road

90 miles (A 85 to Dundee, A 972 to bypass Dundee
if not visiting the city, then A 92).

A 85 runs east over the fertile *Carse of Gowrie*,
with the Sidlaw Hills to the north and the Tay to
the south.

13 miles: *Inchture*.
3 miles west is *Kinnaird*, with a 12th-15th century castle
(restored). — ½ mile north-east is *Huntly Castle* (15th c.).
— 1 mile north is *Rossie Priory*, seat of Lord Kinnaird.

21 miles: **Dundee** (pop. 185,000, E.C. Wednesday
and Saturday), Scotland's fourth largest city and an
important industrial and commercial centre, well
situated on the Tay estuary.　It is linked with Fife by
the large new *road bridge* and the *railway bridge* over
the Tay (over 2 miles long).　Industries: jute (the
traditional Dundee industry), plastics, electrical equipment, clothing manufacture, oil refineries.　There is
a modern industrial estate on Kingsway.　Large
docks and shipyards.

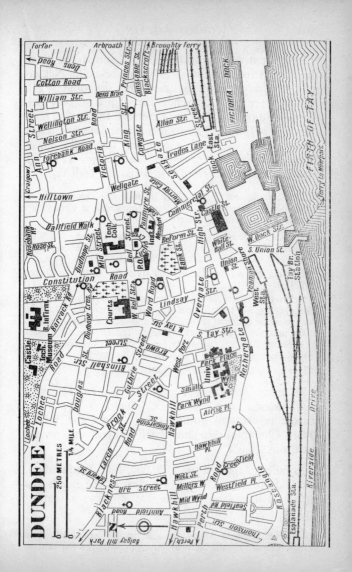

In the centre of the town is *City Square*, from which the High Street runs west. Off this branches **Nethergate,** the city's main business and shopping street, in which are three churches linked in a single cruciform building — *St Mary's* (rebuilt 1844), *St Paul's* (rebuilt 1847) and *St Clement's* or the Steeple Church (built 1788). St Mary's contains interesting glass. Magnificent views from the *Old Steeple* (190 ft). Nearby is the old *Town Cross* (partly 16th c.).

In Albert Square is the **Albert Institute** (Sir George Gilbert Scott, 1867), a group of buildings containing a library, art gallery and museum (archaeology).

St Paul's Cathedral (1853), with a graceful spire, stands on Castlehill Rock. To the east, reached by way of Murraygate, is Cowgate, with the *Wishart Arch* (restored 1877).

In King St is the Renaissance-style *St Andrew's Church* (1722).

In **Broughty Ferry,** 4 miles east, is *Broughty Castle*, a 19th century copy of the original 15th century castle. *Dudhope Park Museum* contains the technical and archaeological sections of the museum in the Albert Institute. The *Orchar Art Gallery* at 31 Beach Crescent, Broughty Ferry, shows work by contemporary Scottish artists. *Claypotts Castle* (1598).

7 miles north-east is **Affleck Castle** (15th c.).

31 miles: *Muirdrum*. 2 miles south, on the coast, is *Carnoustie* (pop. 5600, E.C. Tuesday), a popular seaside resort and golfing town, where the British Open Championship has been played on several occasions.

38 miles: **Arbroath** (pop. 20,000, E.C. Wednesday), a seaside resort on the North Sea, at the north-east corner of a bay outside the Tay estuary; a seaport and industrial town.

Ruins of **Arbroath Abbey,** founded by William the Lion in 1178, where in 1320 the Scottish barons drew up the *Declaration* *of Independence*. Here in 1951 was deposited the Stone of Scone, which had been stolen from Westminster Abbey by a group of young Scots. There is a local museum in the 16th century *Abbot's House*. Scott describes the town and surrounding area in "The Antiquary".

A fine stretch of cliff-fringed coast begins near Carnoustie and extends for some 12 miles to beyond Arbroath. On *Whiting Ness* are a number of caves and the curious rock formations known as the Needle's E'e and the Mermaid's Kirk.

43 miles: *Inverkeilor*. To the south-east are the impressive cliffs of Red Head, *Ethie Castle* (restored) and *Prail Castle*. To the north-east, in the wide sweep of Lunan Bay, is *Lunan*, with the ruins of the Red Castle.

52 miles: **Montrose** (pop. 10,000, E.C. Wednesday), a seaside resort on a flat promontory between the North Sea and the Montrose tidal basin. Recent industrial developments connected with North Sea oil.

The old Town Hall (1768) contains the museum of the Montrose Natural History and Antiquarian Society. In *Montrose Academy* (1534) Greek was taught for the first time in Scotland. Church of 1791.

58 miles: *St Cyrus*. — 65 miles: *Inverbervie* (pop. 1100, E.C. Wednesday). 1 mile west is the little *Allardice Castle*, on the Bervie Water.

73 miles: to the right, above the sea, can be seen the ruins of *Dunnottar Castle* (13th c.).

75 miles: **Stonehaven** (pop. 4400). *Tolbooth* (17th c.). Fishing.

90 miles: **Aberdeen** (p. 1009).

(c) Perth to Aberdeen vie Forfar

83 miles on A 94.

5 miles: *Balbeggie*. To the right are the Sidlaw Hills, with Dunsinane Hill, on which are the ruins of an old stronghold known as Macbeth's Castle.

13 miles: *Coupar Angus* (pop. 2300, E.C. Wednesday), with the ruins of a large 12th century Cistercian abbey. 4 miles west, at *Meikleour*, are the remains of a Roman camp and signal station.

18 miles: *Meigle* (pop. 760), in the heart of Strathmore. Museum with a famous collection of 20 carved stones dating from the 7th-11th centuries.

To the south is *Belmont Castle*, now an old people's home. On Barry Hill is an ancient hill-fort. 5 miles north-west is *Alyth*, at the foot of beautiful Glenisla. Very attractive run up Glenisla, by way of the picturesque Reekie Linn (waterfall, 70 ft) on the Isla, to the head of the glen and into Glenshee. Other beautiful glens in the area are Glen Prosen and Glen Doll.

24 miles: **Glamis.** 1 mile south is *Glamis Castle*, seat of the Earl of Strathmore and birthplace of Princess Margaret. Here, according to tradition, King Malcolm II was murdered in 1039. Open Tuesdays, Thursdays and Saturdays in summer, 2 to 5.30.

5 miles north on A 928 is *Kirriemuir* (pop. 3000, E.C. Thursday), birthplace of Sir James Barrie, author of "Peter Pan". The house in which he was born is now a museum, with the wash-house in which he had his first theatre.

The surrounding country is very attractive. To the north, by B 955, is *Glen Clova*, with *Cortachy Castle* and (15 miles) *Clova*, surrounded by fine hills.

30 miles: *Forfar* (pop. 10,300, E.C. Thursday), at one time a royal residence.

43 miles: **Brechin** (pop. 7100, E.C. Wednesday), a pleasant town, with a *Cathedral* founded in 1150,

The present building dates from 1220 (clumsily restored in the 19th c.); it is now the parish church. At the south-west corner, separate from the Cathedral, is a large **round tower,** of which there are only two other examples in Scotland (at Abernethy on the Tay and at Egilsay).

Brechin Castle stands on the site of a castle destroyed by the Danes in 1012. The building has been modernised.

Around Brechin. Beautiful Glenesk: road up to Lochlee, path through the hills via Glenmark to Deeside. — Off the road which runs along the South Esk are Glen Ogle, Glen Clova and Glen Prosen. — 3 miles south is *Kinnaird Castle.* — To the south-west is *Aldbar Castle*, in a picturesque setting. 5 miles south-west is the well preserved old house of *Careston.* — To the north is *Farnell Palace*, formerly the residence of the Bishop of Brechin, now an old people's home. Beyond this are twin hills, the White Caterthun and the Brown Caterthun. On the higher of the two, the *White Caterthun* (978 ft) is one of the best preserved hill-forts in the country; it is oval in shape, 500 feet long by 220 feet wide.

54 miles: *Laurencekirk* (pop. 1300, E.C. Wednesday), centre of the district known as the *Howe of the Mearns.*

4 miles west is *Fettercairn*, a picturesque village, with *Balbegno Castle* (16th c.). — 4 miles north-west are the ruins of *Kincardine Castle.*

68 miles: **Stonehaven** (p. 1001). — 83 miles: **Aberdeen.**

Aberdeen

Aberdeen (pop. 187,000, E.C. Wednesday and Saturday) is known as the "granite city", being built almost entirely of the local grey granite, which gives it a clean but rather severe aspect.

William the Lion granted Aberdeen a municipal charter in 1179, and the town's privileges were confirmed and extended by Robert Bruce in the 14th century. It developed in two distinct parts — the episcopal and later the university city at the mouth of the river Don, to the north, and the commercial town which developed later on the Dee estuary to the south. The two parts of the town were joined in 1891.

Until the discovery of oil in the North Sea, which brought a major new industry to Aberdeen, the town's main activities were related to livestock farming, which is highly developed in the surrounding area, horticulture (roses), textiles (man-made fibres), paper-making, etc. It is also the third largest fishing port in Britain, coming after Hull and Grimsby. The great days of the Aberdeen herring fisheries are over, and the main catches are now white fish from the North Sea and cod from the Atlantic fishing grounds.

The sights of Aberdeen fall into two distinct groups, the old town to the north and the newer districts to the south.

1. The old town. This is reached from the city centre (with the railway station and the main hotels) by going north along *King Street* (the Fraserburgh road, A 92), a wide street which leaves the east end of *Union Street*, Aberdeen's principal street. In rather more than a mile turn left into University Road and then right into College Bounds. On the right of this street is **King's College.**

King's College was founded in 1494 by Bishop Elphinstone. In 1641 Charles I joined it to Marischal College, but the two colleges were separated again by Charles II, and it was not until 1860 that they came together again to form the University of Aberdeen. King's College houses the faculties of arts and divinity (theology). The present buildings were erected between 1825 and 1965, but they incorporate a *tower* dating from 1525 and another dating from 1658, together with a 16th century **chapel** (stalls. tombstones). To visit the chapel and the library, apply to the porter (Monday-Friday 9 to 5).

Continue north along the ancient and picturesque **High Street,** past the **Town House** (1787), to **St Machar's Cathedral,** the only cathedral in Britain built entirely of granite. It has a rather squat appearance

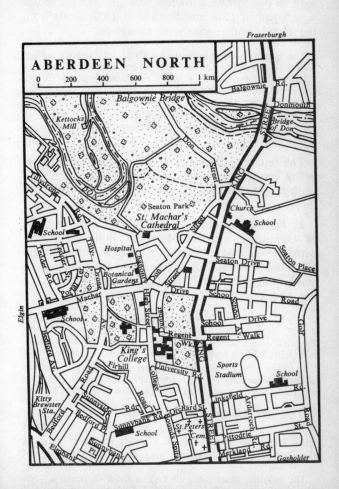

ABERDEEN NORTH

0 200 400 600 800 1 km

Fraserburgh

Balgownie Bridge

Balgownie Rd.

Donmouth

Bridge of Don

Kettocks Mill

KING STREET

Tillydrone

DON

Seaton Park

St. Machar's Cathedral

Church

School

School

Hospital

Seaton Drive

Seaton Place

Botanical Gardens

Elgin

Bedford Rd.

School

Machar

Drive

School Avenue

Road

High Street

St. Machar

Drive

School

Drive

Golf Road

Regent Wk.

Regent Walk

King's College

Firhill

University Rd.

Sports Stadium

School Rd.

Kitty Brewster Sta.

Bedford Rd.

Sunnyside Rd.

College Rd.

Orchard St.

Linksfield

Ardarroch Rd.

Bedford Pl.

Sunnybank Rd.

Mounds Nora

St. Peters Cem.

Pittodrie

Road

Elmbank

Sunnybank Pl.

School

Merkland Rd.

Gasholder

with its two low west towers (16th c.). The Cathedral
was begun in 1378 and finished in 1552, apart from
the choir, which was never completed.

The interior has an interesting 16th century **painted ceiling,**
with the coats of arms of various great personages (the Emperor
Charles V, Pope Leo X, kings of Scotland, England, France
and Spain, Scottish bishops and other notabilities). Interesting
glass, 15th century tombs.

Beyond St Machar's is the **Brig o' Balgownie,** a bridge over
the Don originally built in the 14th century and rebuilt in
the 17th.

The return to the city centre is by the same route,
or by continuing down College Bounds past King's
College to reach Union St at the Municipal Buildings
(below).

2. The new town. In *Broad Street*, off the east end
of Union St, are the **Municipal Buildings** (1968),
with the tourist information office. Immediately
north is **Marischal College** (founded 1593); the present
neo-Gothic building (1906) houses the faculties of
law and agriculture.

In Marischal College is the **Anthropological Museum** (open
9 to 5, except Sunday mornings, and Wednesdays 6 to 9.30):
Egyptian, Greek and Roman antiquities; ethnography; Chinese
porcelain; Scottish prehistory; various antiquities (old weapons).

In a narrow street behind the Municipal Buildings is **Provost
Skene's House** (open 10 to 5, except Sundays), a charming
old 16th century town house, now a museum of local history.

The **Art Gallery and Museum** is in Schoolhill,
which is reached by taking St Nicholas St, which
runs north from Union St a short distance west of
the Municipal Buildings, and then turning left.

The building dates from the end of the 19th century. The
Museum covers natural history and Scottish antiquities and

Elgin · Fraserburgh

Terrace · Powis Pl · Canal Rd · Causewayend St · Advocates Rd · KING · Trinity Cemetery · Rd

GEORGE · Fraser Rd · Holland St · Canal St · School · Seaforth · Sch

Hutcheon · Nelson · STREET · Urquhart · Roslin Ter · City Hospital

Ch. · Maberley St · Ch. · Ch. · North · Jasmine Ter. · Park · Constitution St

Kintore Pl · Charlotte St · John St · Galloway · STREET · Marischal College · St Andrew · Commerce St

Baker St · Museum · Schoolhill · Town Hall · Queen · Barracks · Virginia St

Crimon Pl · Union · Diamond · Netherkirk · Plough · St. Nicolas · Castle St · Ship Row · Trinity Quay · Regent Quay · Regent Bridge

Chapel · Summer St · Cath. · Back Aconsti St · Crown · Guild St · Upper Dock · Regent Rd

Ch. · Post Office · Bus Station · Fish Market · Pontoon Dock

UNION · Station

Dundee · Portland Street · Millburn St · Esplanade West · DEE · Victoria Bridge

ABERDEEN SOUTH

industries, with a special section in the basement (separate entrance) devoted to the fishing industry.

The **Art Gallery** has a very interesting collection, including sculpture by *Zadkine* and *Henry Moore*, Indian art, portraits by 90 English painters of the 19th and 20th centuries, works by *Reynolds* and *Hogarth*, pictures by *Raeburn* and other Scottish artists, and a very fine collection of works by French artists (*Pissarro, Monet, Sisley, Guillaumin, Boudin, Daubigny, Théodore Rousseau, Courbet, Marie Laurencin, Vlaminck, Fantin-Latour, Toulouse-Lautrec, Fernand Léger,* etc.).

On the west side of St Nicholas St, near Union St, is **St Nicholas's Church** (13th-15th c., altered in the 17th and 18th c.), with a fine peal of bells and tapestries on Biblical themes by Mary Jamesone.

Union Street, Aberdeen's main shopping street, is so called in honour of the union with Ireland in 1800. Towards its east end is the important junction with St Nicholas St to the north and Market St to the south. At the far end is the beginning of King St, the route to the old town (above). At the near end of this street, on the right-hand side, is the Episcopalian *St Andrew's Cathedral* (1817).

Beyond Union St is *Castle Street*, in which are the **Mercat Cross** (1686), topped by a unicorn, one of the supporters of the Scottish arms, and the *Old Town House* (1874), with a fine collection of portraits. To the south-west is *Shiprow*, in which is **Provost Ross's House** (1593), the oldest house in Aberdeen.

In the south-west of the town is the old *Brig o' Dee* (1527).

An interesting feature of Aberdeen life is the fish auction in the *Fish Market* (Monday to Friday at 7.30 a.m.).

69. PERTH TO INVERNESS

115 miles on A 9.

15 miles: **Dunkeld** (pop. 1060, E.C. Thursday), a small town pleasantly situated on the left bank of the Tay, opposite *Birnam*. Large bridge (Telford, 1809).

Dunkeld Cathedral. (12th-14th c.) stands in grounds belonging to the Duke of Atholl. The nave and aisles are roofless but the choir has been restored and serves as the parish church. Many interesting monuments and statues. Near the main doorway are the tombs of the Wolf of Badenoch (see Elgin Cathedral, p. 1021) and Bishop Gavin Douglas (d. 1522), who translated Virgil into Scots.

On the other side of the river (ferry) are the falls on the Braan and the very picturesque Hermitage (National Trust). — To the south is Birnam Hill (1320 ft), with wide views.

28 miles: **Pitlochry** (pop, 2500, E.C. Thursday), a pleasant holiday resort in a setting of woods and hills. To the north-east is Ben Vrackie (2760 ft). Hydro-electric station (salmon ladder), with a very beautiful reservoir.

Pitlochry to Rannoch Station: 36 miles (A 9 for 3 miles, then B 8019 and B 896).

3 miles: turn left into B 8019, near the junction of the rivers Garry and Tummel (hydroelectric installations). The road runs along the Tummel valley and the north side of Loch Tummel. — 13 miles: *Tummel Bridge.* — 20 miles: *Kinloch Rannoch* (pop. 240, E.C. Wednesday), a lonely village amid wild scenery. In all this area there is good fishing. To the south-east is Schiehallion (3547 ft). The road runs along the north side of Loch Rannoch (10 miles long, 1 mile wide: fishing) and continues to Rannoch Station (36 miles) through wild country in the valley of the Gaur.

From Pitlochry A 9 follows the valley of the Garry to (31 miles) the **Pass of Killiecrankie,** where William

III's troops were defeated by Jacobite forces in 1689. A stone marks the spot where Viscount Dundee was killed.

The road and railway run through the pass to **Blair Atholl** (35 miles), a small village in a beautiful setting at the junction of the rivers Tilt and Garry.

To the north is **Blair Castle**, seat of the Duke of Atholl, which dates in part from the 13th century: interesting family portraits and other relics (open 10 to 6 in summer). — 1 mile south is *Tulach Hill* (1541 ft), with fine views. Pleasant walk up Glen Tilt. 2 miles: Fender Bridge (waterfall). To the north are Carn Liath (3193 ft), Ben Vuroch (2961 ft) and the magnificent Beinn a' Ghlo (3671 ft).

40 miles: *Struan.* To the north are the Falls of Bruar. A 9 continues up Glen Garry to *Dalnaspidal.* To the south-east is *Loch Garry*, with Meall na Leitreach, on which the Garry rises.

The road and railway now leave the course of the Garry and turn north-west, passing on the left two rounded hills, the Atholl Sow and the Boar of Badenoch, and climb to the *Pass of Drumochter* (1484 ft), the highest point reached by any railway line in Britain. To the east is the Forest of Atholl.

59 miles: *Dalwhinnie*, in a bleak situation at the head of Glen Truim. To the south-west is *Loch Ericht* (15 miles long), with Ben Alder (3757 ft) on its west side.

69 miles: immediately after crossing the river Spey, *Newtonmore* (pop. 840, E.C. Wednesday).

72 miles: **Kingussie,** a pleasant holiday resort and winter sports centre on the river Spey.

In the village is the **Highland Folk Museum** (Am Fasgadh): furniture, various implements and utensils, clothing and ornaments, old crafts (dyeing, spinning, weaving). In the grounds are various cottages showing the different types of Highland dwelling. Open 10 to 1 and 2 to 5 in summer, except Sundays.

A 9 runs along the north-west side of beautiful Strathspey. A secondary road (B 970) runs along the south side. — 79 miles: *Kincraig*. In the *Highland Wildlife Park* visitors can watch from their cars a wide range of mountain creatures (deer, bears, wolves, lynxes, foxes, wild cats, eagles, etc.). Open 10 to 6.

84 miles: **Aviemore** (pop. 900, E.C. Wednesday), a well equipped modern holiday resort and winter sports centre (skiing); a good centre for walking and climbing in the Cairngorms.

3 miles away is Loch an Eilean, one of the most picturesque of Highland lochs. On an island in the loch are the ruins of a castle which belonged to the Wolf of Badenoch, son of Robert II (see Elgin Cathedral, p. 1021), who held sway in the Rothiemurchus area to the south. — 9 miles east is **Cairngorm**, at the foot of the Cairngorm range (highest point 4296 ft).

88 miles: 3 miles east, *Boat of Garten;* 10 miles north-east, on A 95, *Grantown-on-Spey* (p. 1024).

91 miles: *Carrbridge* (pop. 320, E.C. Thursday), a summer and winter resort on the Dulnain. To the north are Duthil and the charming Duthil Glen.

The road and railway now climb over the wild Slochd Mor pass (1327 ft), with magnificent views, to (102 miles) *Freeburn*, on the Findhorn. — 106 miles: *Moy*, near Loch Moy. On an island in the Loch are the remains of an old Mackintosh stronghold. Nearby is the modern mansion of *Moy Hall*, seat of the clan chief.

115 miles: **Inverness.**

Inverness

Inverness (pop. 30,000, E.C. Wednesday), a market town on the river Ness, at the west end of the Moray Firth and the east end of the Great Glen. Justly called the "capital of the Highlands", it is the centre of Highland cultural, commercial and sporting life and the venue of Gaelic Mods, Highland games and gatherings and Highland shows which perpetuate the ancient traditions of the Highlands.

The town was granted a charter by William the Lion in 1174, and in 1312 Robert Bruce held a Parliament here. Under the Commonwealth a strong garrison was installed in the town. The Duke of Cumberland made Inverness his headquarters after the battle of Drummossie Moor.

The site of the old *castle* is now occupied by local authority offices. Nothing is left of the original 12th century building but the old well. Below the castle site is the **Town House,** in front of which is the ancient *Town Cross.* At its base is the *Clach na Cudainn*, an ancient stone which Scott called the "charter stone" of Inverness. Behind the Town House are the Public Library and Museum, with an interesting collection including Jacobite relics. Opposite, at the corner of Bridge St, is the spire of the old *Tolbooth.*

In Church St, opposite the High Church, is an old house called *Dunbar's Hospital* (1668). The *High Church* (1772) is built on the site of an earlier church. In the adjoining Gaelic Church is an old pulpit formerly used as an auctioneer's rostrum. *St Andrew's Cathedral* (Episcopalian), on the left bank of the river, was built in 1869 in Decorated style.

The *Citadel*, on the northern outskirts of the town, is all that remains of the fortress built by Cromwell

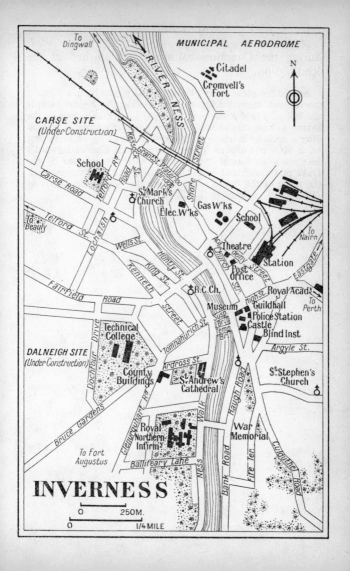

INVERNESS

during the Commonwealth and demolished at the Restoration.

Around Inverness. Very pleasant walks up the Nith, a winding stream with many thickly wooded islands. — 2 miles west is the hill of *Craig Phadrig* (fine views). — 1 mile west is the fishing village of *Clachnaharry* ("watchman's stone"), named after a rock from which there are wide views. — 6 miles east on B 9006 is **Culloden Moor,** where Prince Charles Edward's Jacobite army fought its last battle and was defeated by the Duke of Cumberland in 1745. A cairn and tombstones mark the scene of the battle. Nearby are the prehistoric *Stones of Clava* (2nd millennium B.C.).

70. INVERNESS TO ABERDEEN

105 miles on A 96.

16 miles: **Nairn** (pop. 5000, E.C. Wednesday), a pleasant holiday resort on the Moray Firth. The town is said to have been founded in the 12th century; its municipal charter was confirmed by James VI in 1589. Nothing is left of the old royal castle. Pottery works, open to visitors, in Viewfield St (9 to 5).

6 miles south-west is *Cawdor Castle*, one of Scotland's most romantic castles, where according to legend King Duncan was murdered by Macbeth. The present buildings are no older than the 15th century. Very beautiful gardens.

19 miles: *Auldearn*, scene of a battle during the Civil War.

27 miles: **Forres** (pop. 4700, E.C. Wednesday), a pleasant holiday resort where Macbeth is supposed to have had a castle in the 11th century. The *Falconer Museum* (open 10 to 5) in Tolbooth St has an interesting collection of fossils.

3 miles north are the Culbin Sands, which in 1695 engulfed the house of the local laird. — 1 mile north-east is **Sweno's Stone**, 23 feet high, covered with interesting carving, which is thought to date from 1010 and to commemorate a victory over the Danes. Nearby, to the east, is the granite *Witches' Stone*, marking the spot where three witches were burned. It was near here, according to the popular legend, that Macbeth and Banquo met the witches. — Farther along the coast is the small harbour town and holiday resort of *Findhorn*.

38 miles: **Elgin** (pop. 16,500, E.C. Wednesday), a pleasant town on the south bank of the river Lossie, 5 miles from the sea: woollen weaving, net-making, foundries. The **Cathedral,** founded in 1270 and then rebuilt after a fire in 1270, was burned down again

in 1390 by the famous Wolf of Badenoch, brother of
Robert III. The present building fell into ruin after
the lead was removed from the roof in 1569 to provide
money for paying troops. Of the original five towers
there remain only the two at the west end. Beautiful
entrance doorway to the nave and fine *clerestory*
in the choir, with double and triple lancet windows.
The best preserved part of the structure is the 15th
century *chapter house*, with its central pier and vaulting. The remains also include (to the north-west) a
wing (15th c.) of the bishop's palace and the ruins of
a Franciscan friary (15th c. chapel).

Among other features of interest in the town are *Lady Hill*,
on which the castle formerly stood, and the *Museum*, in High St,
with fossils and Bronze Age material (open 10 to 12 and 2 to 5,
except Tuesday afternoons and Sundays).

Around Elgin. 6 miles south-west are the remains (restored)
of **Pluscarden Priory**, a 13th century Cistercian house. — 2 miles
north is beautiful Loch Spynie, with the ruins of the *Palace of
Spynie* and *David's Tower*, formerly the principal residence of
the Bishops of Moray. — 3 miles north-west are the ruins of
Duffus Castle (a few fragments of the keep and outer walls).
— 6 miles north on A 941 is **Lossiemouth** (pop. 6000, E.C.
Thursday), on the Moray Firth. In the past the history of
the town was affected by changes in the course of the river
and in the position of the sand-banks along the sea. It is now
a quiet holiday resort (golf) and fishing port. Birthplace of
Ramsay Macdonald (1866-1937), a poor Lossiemouth boy who
became Prime Minister.

47 miles: **Fochabers** (pop. 1200, E.C. Wednesday), a
well planned little town laid out in 1770, magnificently situated among fine woods on the banks of
the Spey. Parish church of 1798.

From Fochabers there are two possible routes to
Aberdeen: the coast road via Fraserburgh and Peter-

head, the more attractive route; and the inland route
via Keith and Huntly, which is shorter and quicker.

(a) Fochabers to Aberdeen via Fraserburgh

A 98 to Fraserburgh, then A 92 and A 952.

6 miles: A 942 goes off on the left and runs along the coast,
through fine scenery and the fishing villages of *Portgordon*,
Buckie, *Findochty* and *Portknockie*, to rejoin the main road
(10 miles).

12 miles: **Cullen** (pop. 1350, E.C. Wednesday), a
fishing village and holiday resort. *Cullen House*
(16th c., with a fine interior) can be visited. In the
church are 16th century *tombs*. 2 miles east, on the
cliffs, are the ruins of *Findlater Castle*.

18 miles: *Portsoy*, a small fishing port. To the east
are the ruins of Boyne Castle.

29 miles: **Banff** (pop. 3490, E.C. Wednesday), a
port at the mouth of the Deveron.

Little is left of the old castle. *Duff House*, formerly seat of
the Duke of Fife, was presented to the town along with its
140 acres of grounds, now a public park. — A 947 runs direct
to Aberdeen via Turriff and Old Meldrum.

30 miles: **Macduff** (pop. 3600, E.C. Wednesday), a
busy fishing port.

54 miles: **Fraserburgh** (pop. 10,800, E.C. Wednesday), a herring fishing port.

72 miles: **Peterhead** (pop. 14,500, E.C. Wednesday),
a herring fishing port, with new industrial developments connected with North Sea oil; chief town of
the old district of Buchan. In front of the *Town*

House (18th c.) in Broad St is a statue of Field-Marshal Keith (d. 1758).

78 miles: A 975 goes off on the left along the rocky coast, offering a pleasant, and slightly shorter, alternative route to Aberdeen. 1 mile along this road are the *Bullers of Buchan*, rock cauldrons at the foot of a 200 foot cliff in which the waves thunder impressively in a high sea. Beyond this point are Port Errol and the adjoining resort of *Cruden Bay* (golf). Still farther down the coast, near the village of Collieston, is *Old Slains Castle*, which was destroyed by James VI in 1594. Beyond Newburgh A 975 joins the main road (95 miles).

84 miles: A 952 joins A 92, coming direct from Fraserburgh. — 89 miles: *Ellon* (pop. 3000, E.C. Wednesday), a market town. 6 miles west are Pitmedden Gardens (National Trust) and Tolquhon Castle.

106 miles: **Aberdeen** (p. 1009).

(b) Fochabers to Aberdeen via Keith and Huntly

8 miles (55 miles from Inverness): **Keith** (pop. 4200, E.C. Wednesday). Whisky distillery (Chivas Regal), the oldest in Scotland (1786).

Keith to Carrbridge via Grantown-on-Spey: 46 miles on A 95.

12 miles: *Craigellachie* (pop. 460, E.C. Thursday), where the Fiddich flows into the Spey. — 4 miles south-east on A 941 is *Dufftown*, a pleasant little town 640 feet above sea level, with the Grant whisky distillery. Surrounded by hills; to the north Ben Aigan (1544 ft). Just north of Dufftown are the ruins of Balvenie Castle. A 941 continues south-east past the ruins of *Auchindoun Castle*, passes to the west of the Scalp (1599 ft) and climbs to 1370 feet beyond Cabrach (15 miles).

From Craigellachie A 95 runs up beautiful Strathspey to (36 miles) **Grantown-on-Spey** (pop. 1600, E.C. Thursday), a fine Highland town in the centre of the Grant country. Whisky distillery (Long John). 6 miles north-west is Lochindorb, with a ruined castle on an island in the loch.

39 miles: *Dulnain Bridge.* From here A 95 runs south-west to join A 9 (Perth-Inverness), passing (7 miles: 2 miles east) *Boat of Garten,* a very attractive little place in Strathspey. To the east, beyond the river, is the Abernethy Forest. From Dulnain Bridge A 938 runs west to (46 miles) *Carrbridge* (p. 1017).

Grantown-on-Spey to Balmoral: 38 miles on A 939, through some of the finest scenery in the central Highlands. Splendid views of the Cairngorms to the south. The road climbs to 1400 feet and comes (14 miles) to *Tomintoul* (pop. 600, E.C. Wednesday), the highest village in Scotland (1160 ft), a holiday place in the middle of the moors and within easy reach of the hills. The road (the Lecht road) runs up the valley of the Conglass Water through wild country, reaching a height of 2090 feet above sea level. — 23 miles: *Cock Bridge* (1285 ft). To the south is Corgarff Castle. — 38 miles: *Balmoral* (p. 1002).

66 miles: **Huntly** (pop. 3900, E.C. Thursday), a pleasant little country town whose history is bound up with the Earls of Huntly and with Huntly Castle (rebuilt 1602), a picturesque ruin north of the town. Fishing in the Deveron and the Bogie.

Huntly to Balmoral: 44 miles (A 97 for 24 miles, then B 973 and A 939).

9 miles: *Rhynie.* — 12 miles: *Lumsden.* To the east are the Correen Hills (1588 ft). — 14 miles: *Mossat.* 7 miles east on A 944 is **Alford,** in the beautiful Howe of Alford. 4 miles north-west are the ruins of *Terpersie Castle* (16th c.). The Don flows through the gorge called My Lord's Throat, the entrance to the Howe of Alford, under the ridge of Bennachie (2070 ft), with six peaks. To the south-west of this hill is *Castle Forbes* (19th c.), seat of Lord Forbes, premier baron of Scotland.

16 miles: *Kildrummy,* with the ruins of *Kildrummy Castle,* once a royal residence. — 27 miles: *Strathdon.* To the north are the ruins of *Glenbuchat Castle* (16th c.). — 32 miles: B 973 joins A 939 (from Grantown-on-Spey) and comes (44 miles) to *Balmoral* (p. 1002).

89 miles: **Inverurie** (pop. 5500, E.C. Wednesday). In the churchyard on the east side of the town is the Bass, a mound on which the castle formerly stood.

2 miles north-west is *Harlaw*, where a savage battle was
fought between Highlanders and Lowlanders in 1411. — 2 miles
west are the ruins of *Balquhain Castle*, where Mary Queen of
Scots stayed in 1562; it was burned down by the Duke of Cumberland in 1746. — 3 miles north-east is *Barra Castle*, just
south of Oldmeldrum. Nearby, on Barra Hill (634 ft), is a
prehistoric ring-fort.

93 miles: *Kintore* (pop. 1000, E.C. Wednesday).
— 105 miles: **Aberdeen** (p. 1009).

Banff to Aberdeen: 46 miles on A 947.

11 miles: *Turriff*, in a beautiful situation on the hills above
the Idock Water. 3 miles east is *Delgatie Castle*. — 13 miles:
1 mile east is *Hatton Castle*, with an old tower. — 19 miles:
Fyvie, with **Fyvie Castle,** one of the finest of Scotland's old
castles, in an excellent state of preservation (four towers dating
between the 15th and 18th centuries). — 28 miles: *Oldmeldrum.*
— 35 miles: *Newmachar.* The road crosses the Don and comes
(46 miles) to *Aberdeen* (p. 1009).

71. THE GREAT GLEN,
THE NORTH-WESTERN HIGHLANDS
AND GLENCOE

Inverness to Fort William

The **Great Glen** is a geological fault extending south-west across Scotland from Inverness to Loch Linnhe on the west coast and containing a chain of long narrow lochs — Loch Dochfour, Loch Ness, Loch Oich and Loch Lochy — linked by the Caledonian Canal (62 miles long). The scenery throughout is of true Highland magnificence. The Caledonian Canal was built in 1847.

Alternative route. From Inverness A 862, a very narrow road, runs along the south side of Loch Ness, joining the main road at Fort Augustus. This road provides an excellent return route for a round trip from Inverness (77 miles).

8 miles: *Lochend*, at the north-east end of Loch Ness. A 82 now follows the shore of **Loch Ness** (famous for its monster, much discussed but still a mystery) to (15 miles) *Drumnadrochit* (pier used by steamers on the Caledonian Canal).

The road runs round a little bay and past the ruins of **Castle Urquhart**, on the edge of the loch. The castle, built in the 14th century, was destroyed after the Jacobite rising in 1689. Fine view of Loch Ness.

28 miles: *Invermoriston* (pier), on the river Moriston, which here flows into Loch Ness.

A 887 goes off on the right and climbs up wild Glen Moriston and past Loch Cluanie to rejoin the main road at Cluanie Bridge (A 87, from Invergarry to Kyle of Lochalsh: see below).

34 miles: **Fort Augustus** (pop. 900, E.C. Wednesday), at the south-west end of Loch Ness, a good centre from which to explore the beautiful glens in the area. The remains of the fort, built after the 1715 rising to command Glen Tarff and the Corrieyairack pass, are incorporated in a Benedictine monastery built at the turn of the 19th century.

From Fort Augustus A 82 continues south-west to (38 miles) *Loch Oich* and then follows the north side of the loch to **Invergarry.**

Invergarry to Kyle of Lochalsh: 52 miles on A 87.

This very typical Highland road can rank among the most beautiful in Europe.

A 87 runs west up the valley of the Garry and along the north side of *Loch Garry*. A minor road (difficult) continues along the shores of the loch to Quoich Bridge (11 miles), on the north side of Loch Quoich, and continues to *Kinlochhourn*, at the head of Loch Hourn. A 87 turns up from Loch Garry and climbs north through wild scenery before running down to the river Moriston, with fine views of Glen Moriston to the right. To the left is Aonachair Chrith (3342 ft). A 87 turns left along the north side of Loch Cluanie and comes to Cluanie Bridge, at the west end of the loch, where it begins to climb into **Glen Shiel**. From the pass at the top of this road, between the *"Five Sisters"* on the right and the jagged ridge of the Saddle on the left, there are magnificent views to the west of hills and lochs, and the road down to Loch Duich is of unequalled beauty. — 36 miles: *Shiel Bridge*. From here it is possible to walk to the *Glomach Falls*, the highest (750 ft) and most beautiful in Scotland. The road then runs along the steep shores of Loch Duich, with fine views of the Five Sisters to the rear. — 42 miles: *Dornie*, at the meeting of three lochs — Loch Duich, Loch Long and Loch Alsh. On an islet in Loch Duich is the castle of **Eilean Donan** (13th c., destroyed 1719, restored 1913). — 45 miles: A 890 runs north to (8 miles) *Strome* (ferry over Loch Carron to Strome Castle). A 87 continues along the north side of Loch Alsh to (48 miles) *Balmacara*. — 52 miles: **Kyle of Lochalsh** (pop. 410, E.C. Thursday), a beautifully situated village from which there are ferry services to *Skye* (p. 992).

From Invergarry A 82 continues south-west to
(45 miles) *Loch Lochy*. It runs along the south-east
side of the loch and turns south to reach (56 miles)
Spean Bridge (pop. 200). Memorial to the commandos
of the second world war, who had a base near here.

From here A 86 runs east along Glen Spean to *Roy Bridge*,
at the south end of Glen Roy, continues along the *Braes of
Lochaber* (to the right, Loch Treig), climbs to 900 feet along
the north side of *Loch Moy* and continues along Loch Laggan
to reach (29 miles) *Laggan*, on the Spey, and (33 miles) *Newtonmore* (p. 1016), on the Perth-Inverness road.

From Spean Bridge A 82 continues south-west,
with fine views of **Ben Nevis** (4406 ft), the highest
point in the British Isles. After passing the ruins of
Inverlochy Castle (13th c.) it comes (65 miles) to **Fort
William** (pop. 2800, E.C. Wednesday), a good centre
for the western Highlands and an industrial town
(pulp-mill). In High St is the *West Highland Museum*
(open 10 to 6, except Thursday afternoons): local
history and bygones.

Fort William is the starting point for the climb of
Ben Nevis. In clear weather there are fine views
from the top. Even on the hottest days extra clothing
should be taken to wear on the top, where it can be
cold (there is always snow on the north-east preci-
pices). There are several good routes to the top, but
the bridle path is advised for those without climbing
experience.

Pleasant walking to the south up *Glen Nevis*.

Fort William to Mallaig: 45 miles on A 830. This splendid
Highland road, the famous "*Road to the Isles*", runs past a
succession of remote and beautiful lochs and through wildly
beautiful glens to the green seas and silver sands along the
beautiful indented coast, with enchanting views of the islands

south of Skye. The road has many bends and often climbs steeply, but the surface is good.

2 miles: *Banavie*, at the south end of the Caledonian Canal. 1 mile south of Corpach is the beginning of the series of locks known as *Neptune's Staircase*. The road then runs along the north side of Loch Eil. — 13 miles: *Kinlocheil*. From here to Morven and Ardnamurchan: see below.

17 miles: the road comes to the end of the long narrow **Loch Shiel.** *Monument* marking the spot where Bonnie Prince Charlie landed in 1745 and sought to rally the clans in his support. — 18 miles: *Glenfinnan*, at the foot of picturesque Glen Finnan. A 830 descends steeply and runs along the north side of Loch Eilt to (28 miles) *Lochailort*, at the head of the sea loch of the same name. To the south-east are Druim Fiaclach (2851 ft) and Fros Bheinn (2876 ft). — 37 miles: *Arisaig* (pier). — 44 miles: *Morar*, at the west end of Loch Morar, Scotland's deepest loch (1080 ft), with a bay of white sand sheltered by hills. — 47 miles: **Mallaig** (pop. 1000, E.C. Monday), a busy little fishing port at the terminus of the railway. From here Skye can be reached either by the ferry to Armadale in the south of the island or by steamer to Portree via Kyle of Lochalsh. There are also regular services to the Outer Hebrides.

Morven and Ardnamurchan.   Kinlocheil to Ardnamurchan Point, 71 miles on A 861.

From Kinlocheil A 861 runs east along the south side of Loch Eil to the promontory where this loch meets *Loch Linnhe*, a sea loch. It then runs down the beautiful west side of Loch Linnhe to (22 miles) *Ardgour* (ferry to the Fort William-Ballachulish road) and continues south-west to (29 miles) *Inversanda*, from which it runs west to (35 miles) *Strontian*, at the head of Loch Sunart. To the south is the magnificent **Morven peninsula,** a region of rugged hills and jagged rocks. From Strontian A 884 runs south-west for 19 miles across the peninsula to Lochaline on the Sound of Mull, opposite the island of Mull (p. 990).

From Strontian A 861 continues west along the north side of Loch Sunart to (47 miles) *Salen*, from which B 8007 winds along the beautiful coast of the Ardnamurchan peninsula to (66 miles) *Kilchoan* and (71 miles) **Ardnamurchan,** the most westerly point on the Scottish mainland.

SOUTH OF FORT WILLIAM

A. Fort William to Oban

49 miles (A 82 to Glencoe, then A 828). The old
road round Loch Leven is now short-circuited by
the new Ballachulish bridge.

From Fort William A 82 runs down the east side
of Loch Linnhe. 9 miles: ferry to Ardgour (above).
— 11 miles: *Onich* (pier). — 13 miles: *North Ballachulish* (ferry).

A 82 runs east along the north side of picturesque **Loch
Leven,** with Mam na Gualainn (2603 ft) to the north. — 23 miles:
Kinlochleven (pop. 1100, E.C. Friday), a little industrial town
at the head of the loch. A 82 now runs west along the south
side of the loch, with Garbh Bheinn (2835 ft) and the Pap of
Glencoe (2430 ft) to the south. — 29 miles: the village of
Glencoe (Carnach), from which A 82 runs south-east up the
famous Pass of Glencoe (below, p. 1032).

32 miles: **Ballachulish** (pop. 800, E.C. Wednesday),
a good holiday centre at the foot of Loch Leven.
Large slate quarries. To the south-west is Beinn a
Bheithir (3362 ft). A 828 runs west and then south-
west along the shores of *Loch Linnhe.*

38 miles: *Duror,* with an old cairn marking the
scene of the "Appin murder" which is referred to in
Stevenson's "Kidnapped". — 44 miles: *Portnacroish.*
— 46 miles: *Appin.*

To the south-west is *Port Appin,* from which there is a ferry
to Port Ramsay on the island of **Lismore,** at the mouth of
Loch Linnhe (remains of an old *cathedral*; at *Auchindown*
ruins of an episcopal castle).

48 miles: *Creagan,* on Loch Creran. The road runs
round the east end and along the south side of the
loch to reach (58 miles) *Benderloch.* To the north-
west is *Barcaldine Castle* (15th c.).

63 miles: *Connel Ferry*, where there is a large bridge (toll) over Loch Etive. *Falls of Lora*, where the sea surges over the rocks at the foot of Loch Etive. — 68 miles: **Oban** (p. 987).

B. Fort William to Tyndrum and Glasgow, Stirling or Edinburgh via Glencoe.   47 miles to Tyndrum on A 82.

Follow Route A above to the village of *Glencoe*, from which A 82 runs up to the **Pass of Glencoe.**

This wild and picturesque glen, perhaps the grandest of all the Scottish glens, is flanked along its whole length by majestic mountains with sheer rock faces and great frowning buttresses. To the north is the *Chancellor* and at the top of the pass, to the south, *Buchaille Etive Mor*. *Ossian's Cave*, to the south, is a great gash on Aonach Dubh, one of the *Three Sisters*, behind which is a mountain well known to rock climbers, *Bidean nam Bian* (3766 ft).

The whole area abounds in rock climbs. Only experienced climbers should attempt any of the peaks, and even the hill tracks require care.

Glencoe was the scene of a massacre in 1692, when forty members of the Macdonald clan whose chief had failed to take the oath of allegiance to the king were killed by troops.

38 miles: an easy path on the left, following the line of an old military road, leads over the Devil's Staircase to Kinlochleven, at the head of Loch Leven.

40 miles: to the right is **Glen Etive.** A difficult road runs up (11 miles) to the end of Loch Etive. — 41 miles: *Kingshouse Hotel*. The road runs over desolate Rannoch Moor, passing a number of lochans (small lochs), to Loch Tulla (50 miles). — 53 miles: *Bridge of Orchy*. To the north-east is Beinn an Dothaidh (3267 ft), to the south-east Ben Dorain (3524 ft). — 60 miles: *Tyndrum* (p. 986).

72. THE FAR NORTH

A. Inverness to Dingwall

From Inverness A 9 runs west along the *Beauly Firth*.

12 miles: A 831 runs south-west via Kilmorack and Struy and then along Strath Glass, through magnificent scenery, to **Cannich** (17 miles). To the west is Glen Cannich and to the south-west, beyond Tomich, *Glen Affric*, dominated by the massive bulk of Mam Soul (3862 ft) and Cairn Eige (3877 ft). From Cannich A 831 runs east for 12 miles along Glen Urquhart to Drumnadrochit on Loch Ness.

13 miles: **Beauly** (pop. 900, E.C. Thursday), a little town dating back to the 10th century, in a beautiful situation on the river Beauly. It is a popular holiday place.

Remains of a 13th century *priory* (in the north transept, tombs of the Mackenzies, 14th-16th c.).

To the south-west are the *Killmorack Falls*.

16 miles: *Muir of Ord*.

The **Black Isle,** actually a peninsula surrounded by the Beauly, Moray and Cromarty Firths, lies to the east (A 832). — 10 miles: *Munlochy*, from which B 9161 runs south to the Beauly Firth (ferry from North Kessock to South Kessock and Inverness). — 14 miles: *Fortrose*, a small harbour town, with the ruins of the cathedral (14th c.) of the old see of Ross. — 15 miles: *Rosemarkie* (pop. 860, E.C. Thursday), a seaside resort. The cliffs to the north-east are described in the works of Hugh Miller (see below). — 24 miles: **Cromarty** (pop. 860, E.C. Wednesday), in a wide bay. Hugh Miller, the 19th century geologist, was born in a thatched cottage in the main street (National Trust). From Cromarty B 9163 runs along the north coast of the Black Isle, on the Cromarty Firth, which can take the largest warships. 23 miles: *Conon Bridge*.

20 miles: *Conon Bridge* (pop. 460, E.C. Thursday),
a pleasant village (fishing) near the head of the Cromarty Firth. — 23 miles: **Dingwall** (pop. 3800, E.C.
Thursday), on the Cromarty Firth. The Tolbooth,
in the main street, dates from 1730.

B. Dingwall to Wester Ross

4 miles: **Strathpeffer** (pop. 700, E.C. Thursday), a
holiday resort, formerly noted as a spa. Two thermal
springs, one sulphureous, the other chalybeate, recommended for the treatment of rheumatism, arthritis
and gout, digestive disorders, liver conditions and
anaemia.

The little town lies in a picturesque and fertile area and is
a good centre for excursions. — To the north is Ben Wyvis
(3429 ft). Just north of the village is *Castle Leod* (1600). —
2 miles south-west are *Loch Achilty* and the Falls of Rogie
on the Blackwater.

7 miles: *Contin*, from which A 832 runs south-east
to Muir of Ord (p. 1033). The main road runs north-
west, through beautiful scenery, to *Garve* (13 miles).

14 miles: *Gorstan*, where A 832 goes off on the left
to *Achnasheen* (below). A 835 bears right for Ullapool.

19 miles: *Inchbae*, at the end of picturesque Strath
Rannoch. To the east are Little Wyvis (2497 ft) and
Ben Wyvis (3429 ft). — 21 miles: foot of Strath
Vaich. — 23 miles: *Altguish*. The road runs along-
side Loch Glascarnoch, climbs to the desolate **Dirrie
More** pass (915 ft) and runs down to *Braemore* (33
miles), on the river Broom, passing the *Falls of*

Measach, in the deep *Corrieshalloch Gorge*. — 39 miles:
Inverlael, at the head of **Loch Broom,** one of the finest
sea lochs on the north-west coast. The road runs
down the east side of the loch to (45 miles) **Ullapool**
(pop. 700, E.C. Tuesday), a pleasant fishing village
and holiday place. Boat services to Stornoway on
the island of Lewis. Beautiful scenery in the surrounding area.

Tour of Wester Ross. A magnificent circuit through
some of the finest scenery in this wild and remote
part of northern Scotland.

At *Gorstan* (above) turn left into A 832 for *Achnasheen*, and from there turn left again into A 890,
which runs south-west to *Loch Carron*.

The road climbs to 564 feet, passing Loch Gowan and the
larger Loch Sgabhain, and runs down Glen Carron to the
village of **Lochcarron.**

From Lochcarron a magnificent new scenic road runs north
through the hills to *Shieldaig*, a fishing village in a beautiful
situation on Loch Torridon. At the head of Loch Kishorn
a difficult minor road goes off on the left, climbs steeply to the
Bealach nam Ba (Pass of the Cattle), at 2053 feet, and then
runs down, equally steeply, to the remote little fishing village
of *Applecross*.

From Lochcarron A 890 runs along the north-west side of
the loch to **Strome Ferry,** with the ruins of Strome Castle.
(Ferry to A 87, the road from Invergarry to Kyle of Lochalsh:
p. 1028). 5 miles south-west, on the far side of the ferry, is
Plockton, which is claimed to be the most beautiful village in
Scotland.

Beyond Achnasheen A 832 runs along the north
side of Loch a' Chroisg. To the north is Meall a'
Chaoruinn (2313 ft), and beyond it Fionn Bheinn
(3059 ft). The road climbs to 815 feet and then runs
down to *Kinlochewe*.

To the north are Beinn a' Mhuinidh (2231 ft) and Slioch (3217 ft), which can be climbed. From Kinlochewe B 858 runs south-west to *Torridon*, at the head of Loch Torridon, and *Shieldaig* (above).

The road continues north-west to **Loch Maree,** a wildly beautiful loch 12 miles long surrounded by high hills. After the Loch Maree Hotel the road leaves the loch, climbs to 600 feet and then runs down through the beautiful Kerrysdale gorge to **Gairloch** (pop. 750), a straggling village at the head of the loch of the same name.

From Gairloch the road turns right and climbs over the hills to **Loch Ewe,** in which convoys to Russia were assembled during the second world war. At the head of the loch is *Poolewe*. Inland, to the east, is the large Fionn Loch. — The road runs north along the loch to *Aultbea*, off which is the Isle of Ewe, and then cuts across a promontory to *Laide*, in Gruinard Bay. In the bay is Gruinard Island. After running round the shores of the bay the road climbs through the hills to Little Loch Broom, which it follows to *Dundonnell*, at the head of the loch. It then continues south-east up the valley of the river Dundonnell, passing An Teallach (3484 ft), and runs down to Braemore (above, p. 1034).

C. Dingwall to Wick

From Dingwall A 9 follows the west side of the Cromarty Firth to *Evanton* (28 miles from Inverness), at the foot of Glen Glass. At the head of the glen, to the north-west, is Loch Glass. — 32 miles: *Alness*. Just before the town A 836 runs due north to rejoin A 9 after its loop to the east (cutting 10 miles off the distance).

36 miles: *Invergordon* (pop. 1650, E.C. Wednesday), an important naval base.

43 miles: B 9165 runs east to *Hill of Fearn*, to the south of the little Loch Eye. An abbey was founded here in 1230; the church has been restored. 10 miles north-east is the fishing village of *Portmahomack*, 3 miles from Tarbat Ness (lighthouse).

47 miles: **Tain** (pop. 1700, E.C. Thursday), a town of Viking origin on the Dornoch Firth.

The 17th century *Tolbooth* with its conical spire has been incorporated in the modern local authority offices. Adjoining is the church of *St Duthus* (14th c., restored in the 19th), in Decorated style.

52 miles: *Edderton*. To the east is an old cairn.

56 miles: **Bonar Bridge** (pop. 500, E.C. Wednesday), at the Kyle of Sutherland.

Bonar Bridge to Lochinver: 50 miles (A 836 and A 837).

The road runs up the Kyle of Sutherland, the valley of the rivers Shin and Oykell. — 3 miles: *Invershin* (pop. 100, E.C. Wednesday), at the junction of the Shin and the Oykell. Nearby is Invershin Castle. — 4 miles: *Inveran*. A 837 runs up Strath Oykell to (12 miles) *Rosehall*, near which are the beautiful *Cassley Falls*. — 18 miles: *Oykell Bridge*, a good fishing centre, surrounded by many peaks. The road leaves the Oykell valley, climbs to 570 feet and runs down to *Altnacealgach* (28 miles), on Loch Borralan (good fishing). — 31 miles: *Ledmore*. 3 miles west on A 835 (to Ullapool) is *Elphin*. Between Ledmore and Elphin, to the south, is *Loch Urigill*. From Ledmore A 837 continues north, climbs to 542 feet and then runs down the valley of the Loanan to *Inchnadamph* (37 miles), at the east eud of the long Loch Assynt. From here Ben More Assynt (3273 ft), Canisp (2779 ft), Breabag (2338 ft) and Quinag (2653 ft) can be climbed. — 39 miles: *Skiag Bridge*, with the ruins of Ardvreck Castle (15th c.). From here A 894 runs north to Kylesku, Scourie, Laxford Bridge and Durness (see below). A 837 continues west along the north side of majestic Loch Assynt to (50 miles) **Lochinver** (pop. 200), an attractive little holiday place on Loch Inver (bathing, fishing). From here Suilven (2399 ft) and Canisp can be climbed. Boats to the Outer He-

brides. From Lochinver B 869 runs round the beautiful coast
to the north, fringed with islands, past scattered crofts and
hamlets, to (25 miles) *Kylesku* (below).

Inchnadamph to Durness: 47 miles (A 894 and A 838).

From Inchnadamph A 894 climbs to 849 feet, passing to
the east of Quinag, and runs down through a beautiful landscape of craggy hills and sea lochs to (10 miles) *Kylesku* and
the ferry to Kylestrome. — 21 miles: *Scourie* (pop. 350, E.C.
Wednesday), a small fishing village between Scourie Bay and
Loch a' Bhadaidh Daraich. 2 miles north-west, beyond the
Sound of Handa, is the island of Handa (bird sanctuary).
— 28 miles: *Laxford Bridge*. — 47 miles: *Durness*.

74 miles: *Clashmore*. Nearby is *Skibo Castle*,
which belonged to Andrew Carnegie.

76 miles: 3 miles east on A 949 is **Dornoch** (pop.
1000, E.C. Thursday).

The **Cathedral** was consecrated in 1223, and was almost
completely rebuilt in the 18th and 19th centuries. Bishop's
palace, called Dornoch Castle.

79 miles: *Mound Rock*. A 839 goes off on the left
to **Lairg,** 15 miles west, an important road junction.

Lairg to Durness via Laxford Bridge: 56 miles.

A 838 runs along the north-east side of Loch Shin (17 miles
long) to *Overscaig* (16 miles). — 20 miles: *Loch a' Ghriama*.
— 22 miles: *Loch Merkland*. — 27 miles: *Achfary*, on Loch
More. The road runs along Loch More and continues along
the south side of Loch Stack, passing under Ben Stack (2364 ft).
— 37 miles: *Laxford Bridge*, at the head of the sea loch of the
same name (excellent fishing). A 894 comes in on the left from
Kylestrome (above). — 42 miles: *Rhiconich*, at the head of
Loch Inchard, another sea loch. B 801 runs along the north
side of the loch to the villages of Badcall, Kinlochbervie and
Oldshore More. — 54 miles: *Keoldale Hotel*. From here to
Cape Wrath: see p. 1042. — 56 miles: *Durness*.

Lairg to Tongue: 38 miles on A 836.

From Lairg the road runs north past the end of Loch Shin.
In 2 miles A 838 (to Laxford Bridge) goes off on the left: A 836

continues straight ahead. — 13 miles: *Crask*. The road climbs
to 869 feet and runs down Strath Vagastie, with Ben Klibreck
(3154 ft) to the right. — 21 miles: *Altnaharra*, at the west end
of Loch Naver. The road climbs again and then runs down
to *Loch Loyal*. It then continues north along the west side of
the loch, with Ben Loyal (2506 ft) above the road on the left.
— 38 miles: *Tongue* (p. 1042).

83 miles: *Golspie* (pop. 900, E.C. Wednesday), a
fishing village which is an increasingly popular holiday place.

85 miles: to the right of the road, **Dunrobin Castle,**
a seat of the Duke of Sutherland, now a school.
Remains of the 11th century castle are incorporated
in the present 19th century building. 1 mile west,
on Beinn a' Bhragaidh (1293 ft), is a large monument
(by Chantrey) to the first Duke of Sutherland.

88 miles: **Brora** (pop. 1100, E.C. Wednesday), a
seaside resort at the mouth of the river Brora, with
fine beaches, sea angling and river angling (salmon),
and golf. The town has the most northerly coal-mine
in Britain, which has been worked since the 16th
century. Weaving; distilleries.

There are a number of Pictish remains in the neighbourhood,
including brochs (stone towers) at Kintradwell on the Blackwater, Caisteal na Coille and Carrol. The other brochs in the
area are not much more than piles of stones. At *Clyne* is a
small square tower dating from the 17th century.

100 miles: *Helmsdale* (pop. 600, E.C. Wednesday),
a herring fishing port at the mouth of the river Helmsdale, with the ruins of a 16th century castle.

103 miles: *Ord of Caithness* (fine view).

108 miles: *Berriedale*, with a ruined castle. To the
west are Scaraben (2055 ft) and, farther away, Morven
(2313 ft).

115 miles: *Dunbeath* (pop. 600, E.C. Thursday). Dunbeath Castle has a 15th century keep (restored in the 19th c.). The Duke of Kent was killed in an air crash on nearby *Eagle's Rock* in 1942.

A 9 runs along the coast through flat and treeless country.

119 miles: *Latheron*. — 123 miles: *Lybster*, a fishing village.

137 miles: **Wick** (pop. 7400, E.C. Wednesday), a fishing town with a fine harbour, which presents a lively scene when the herring boats come back with their catch.

1 mile south is *Old Wick Castle*, a square tower dating from the 12th century. — 2 miles south, on the coast, is a strange rock formation called the *Gote o' Tram*. — 3 miles north is *Noss Head* (lighthouse), with the ruins of Castle Girnigoe and Castle Sinclair a short distance away. — 2 miles north-west, in Sinclair's Bay, is *Ackergill Tower* (65 ft high), formerly a residence of the Earl Marischal.

D. The north coast

From Wick A 9 runs north-west to *Reiss* and then round Sinclair's Bay. Many brochs. Ruined castle on *Tang Head*. Broch at *Freswick*.

The road continues to **John o' Groats,** popularly regarded as the most northerly point in Britain ("from Land's End to John o' Groats" being equivalent to "from end to end of the country"). In fact *Dunnet Head* (12 miles west) is farther north than John o' Groats.

2 miles east are the cliffs of *Duncansby Head* (210 ft), from which there are fine views of the Orkneys and of the coast. South of the headland are the *Stacks of Duncansby*, three pillars of rock emerging from the sea.

From John o' Groats A 836 runs west along the coast, with much of interest for the naturalist and the archaeologist.

1 mile: *Huna*, a quiet little fishing village. Boat services and hires to the island of *Stroma*. — 6 miles: *Mey*, another small fishing village. *Castle of Mey*, formerly known as Barrogill Castle, was a seat of the Earls of Caithness, and is now owned by Queen Elizabeth the Queen Mother. — 12 miles: *Dunnet*.

3 miles north is *Dunnet Head*, the most northerly point in Scotland (bird sanctuary). In the cliffs 30 feet above high tide level is a large cave, the *Aukies' Hole*, in which puffins nest.

15 miles: *Castletown* (pop. 630, E.C. Thursday). To the east is the mansion of *Hill House*. Many disused quarries in the area.

20 miles: **Thurso** (pop. 800, E.C. Monday), a holiday resort situated in a pleasant bay. In Wilson's Lane, near the old *St Peter's Church* (which contains some 12th c. work), lived Robert Dick (d. 1866), a local baker who made a name as a botanist and geologist. In the Public Library and Museum are collections of Dick's work, including his herbarium, and the Skinnet and Ulbster Stones (ancient Christian monuments). Thurso Castle, built in the 19th century on the site of an earlier 17th century structure, is a curious turreted and battlemented building.

To the east is *Harold's Tower*, marking the spot where Harold, the Norwegian Earl of Caithness, was killed. In Murkle Bay is a ruined castle. *Scrabster*, to the west, is a harbour town (services to the Orkneys and Shetlands).

25 miles: *Forss* (fishing). — 29 miles: **Dounreay,** the site of an important atomic reactor. *Atomic Energy Exhibition* (open in summer 9 to 4, except

Sundays). — 31 miles: *Achvarasdale*, where Robert
Dick (see under Thurso) planted his ferns. — 32 miles:
Reay, with a church built in 1739. — 38 miles:
Melvich, on magnificent cliffs. — 40 miles: *Strathy*.
— 51 miles: *Bettyhill*. The road turns inland up the
valley of the river Naver. — 64 miles: *Tongue* (pop.
700, E.C. Monday), on the Kyle of Tongue, which
is spanned by a bridge. Extensive beaches.

75 miles: *Loch Hope*, with Ben Hope (3042 ft) to
the south. Magnificent scenery, with rugged cliffs
and high mountains in the background. — 77 miles:
the road reaches *Loch Eriboll*, a large sea loch, turns
south along its east side and then runs up the other
side to the north coast. — 92 miles: the *Smoo Cave*,
a group of cave chambers in the limestone cliffs at
the head of a narrow inlet (access by boat).

94 miles: **Durness** (pop. 600, E.C. Wednesday).

2 miles south-west, at Keoldale Hotel on the east side of
the Kyle of Durness, is a ferry across the Kyle to the promontory
in the extreme north-west of Scotland, at the tip of which is
Cape Wrath (12 miles). The scenery is wildly magnificent, the
cliffs being 600 feet high in places and never less than 250 feet.
There are wonderful views across the Minch to the Hebrides.
Lighthouse.

73. ORKNEY AND SHETLAND

Access. *Boats* leave daily from Scrabster (Thurso) for Stromness. It is advisable to book in advance if you are taking your car. There are regular boat services from Leith (Edinburgh) and Aberdeen to Kirkwall in Orkney and Lerwick in Shetland.

There are *air services* to Kirkwall and Lerwick from Aberdeen, Edinburgh, Glasgow and London.

ORKNEY

The Orkney Islands are a group of 68 islands, only 29 of which are inhabited, separated from the Scottish mainland by the Pentland Firth. Their total area is about 244 sq. miles, their population 18,000.

The islands have fine rocky coasts, with many inlets and bays, usually edged with golden sand. Everywhere there are innumerable seabirds. The largest island, known as *Mainland* (traditionally, Pomona), is 24 miles long by 16½ miles across, and on it are the two principal towns, *Kirkwall* and *Stromness*. The best way of seeing the most northerly islands is on one of the excursion services run by the Orkney Steam Navigation Co., leaving Kirkwall four times a week; but it is now also possible to use the inter-island air service. The climate is mild and equable. During the summer the days are very long, particularly at the end of June and the beginning of July, when there is practically no darkness; the glow from the north at this time of year is strikingly beautiful. The main industry is the weaving of tweed; there are also distilleries.

There are many stone circles, megalithic monuments and other prehistoric remains in the islands (e.g. at Stenness, Maeshowe, Skara Brae, Aikerness and Rousay). The islands were known to the Romans. Orkney was annexed to Norway in the 9th century by Harold Fairhair, but was ceded to Scotland in 1468 as a pledge for the dowry of Margaret of Norway, who married King David III of Scotland. Orkney is the setting of Scott's "Pirate".

Stromness is a beautifully situated port at the south-west corner of Mainland. Sheltering the entrance to its natural harbour are the islands of Hoy and Graemsay. There is an interesting *museum* containing specimens of the large numbers of fossils found in the area.

Boats leave the New Pier daily, except Fridays and Sundays, for Graemsay, Hoy, Cava, Fara, Lyness, Rinnigall, Longhope and Flotta.

North of Stromness on A 57 is the prehistoric village of **Skara Brae** (2nd millennium B C.), discovered in 1850 when a storm cleared the sand which had covered it. Farther north is **Birsay**, with the remains of an *Earl's Palace* (12th c., further building in 16th c.) and *St Peter's Cathedral* (11th c.), which is on an islet accessible at low tide.

On the island of Hoy, south of Stromness, is a striking crag 450 feet high, the *Old Man of Hoy*, which can be visited by boat.

Kirkwall (pop. 4300), capital of Orkney, is situated in an attractive bay which forms a natural harbour. The town is unusual in form, the houses being built along very narrow winding streets. In Broad St a tablet on a modern building marks the site of the old castle (14th c.).

St Magnus's Cathedral (Norman and Early English) was founded in 1137 but was not completed until the 16th century. It is perfectly preserved. The *choir*, with a 16th century rose window, serves as the parish church. In the nave (very beautiful arches in the aisles) are interesting tombs and monuments, including the tomb of John Rae (1813-93), the Arctic explorer. Very fine views from the top of the tower (130 ft).

Beside the Cathedral is the *Earl's Palace*, built by Patrick Stewart, Earl of Orkney, about 1600, which features in Scott's "Pirate". To the west are the

Bishop's Palace and *Bishop Reid's Tower* (13th c.). King Haakon of Norway died in the palace in 1263 after his defeat at the battle of Largs.

There are a number of interesting old houses in the town, including *Tankerness House* (16th c.), in Broad St, opposite the Cathedral.

1 mile south of Kirkwall is the north side of the great anchorage of **Scapa Flow,** a British naval base in both world wars, in which the German High Seas Fleet was scuttled in 1919 and the British battleship "Royal Oak" was torpedoed by a German submarine in 1939.

In 1942-44 the *Churchill Barrier* was built along the east side of Scapa Flow (between Mainland and the islands of Burray and South Ronaldsay) in order to prevent German submarines from entering the anchorage. A road runs from Kirkwall to Burwick, crossing from island to island on the causeway on top of the Churchill Barrier, and passing through the village of *St Margaret's Hope*, where Queen Margaret of Norway died in 1290.

West of Kirkwall, reached from the Stromness road (A 965), are the prehistoric tumulus of *Maeshowe* and beyond this (to the right on B 9055) the *Standing Stones of Stenness*, both dated to the 2nd millennium B.C.

Hoy (reached by steamer or motorboat from Stromness) is the most striking of the Orkney islands, offering every variety of scenery, with hills and glens and magnificent rocks round its coasts. The highest points are Ward Hill (1565 ft) and the Cuilags (1420 ft), above St John's Head.

Below Ward Hill is the Dwarfie Stone, a prehistoric passage grave. On the west coast are picturesque cliffs extending from the Kame of Hoy to Rora Head. 1 mile north of Rora Head is the *Old Man of Hoy*, an isolated crag of rock 450 feet high. There are a number of tumuli and Pictish structures on the island, and two fine lochs, Heldale Water and Hoglinns Water. At *Lyness*, to the south-east, is a naval base. Long Hope (4 miles long) is a sea loch defended by a round tower on each side of the entrance.

Westray is the most interesting of the northern islands. Above the straggling houses of the village of *Pierowall* (beach) are the ruins of *Noltland Castle*. There are fine rock formations. The islands of *Rousay* and *Eday* (no hotels) are picturesque. *Sanday* and *Stronsay* are flat and cultivated. On the little islet of *Eynhallow* are the ruins of a Cistercian monastery and church (12th c.).

SHETLAND

The hundred islands of this group, of which 15 are inhabited, are separated from Orkney by a turbulent arm of the sea called the *Roost*, in which the Atlantic and the North Sea meet. The total area of the islands is about 560 sq. miles, the population 17,000.

The principal island, *Mainland*, is over 50 miles long, from the Point of Fethaland in the north to Sumburgh Head in the south, but it is almost cut in two by deep voes (fjords) at several points, particularly at a point where the road passes over a narrow strip of land between Sullom Voe to the north and Busta Voe to the south. To the north and east of Mainland are the islands of *Yell*, *Fetlar* and *Whalsay*. *Fair Isle*, the most southerly island in the group, lies 20 miles south-east. *Foula* is 20 miles south-west. The main islands are connected by boat services and by the inter-island air service.

One of Shetland's main industries is the knitting of garments from the famous Shetland wool; the Fair Isle patterns are world-renowned.

Lerwick (pop. 6000), the most northerly town in the British Isles, is surprisingly large and busy. It is situated on a ridge overlooking a fine natural harbour. It is a busy herring fishing port, and in recent years has enjoyed something of an industrial boom as a result of the discovery of North Sea oil.

Above the fish market is *Fort Charlotte*, dating from the time of the Commonwealth, which is now used as offices. In *Commercial Street*, the main shopping street, which winds about through the oldest and quaintest part of the town, are many old houses. The "lodberries", enclosed courtyards with steps leading down to the sea, are relics of the time when the houses were approached mainly by water. There is a well arranged new museum, the *Shetland Museum* (archaeology, local bygones). Old *Tolbooth*.

The passenger steamers moor at the *Victoria Pier*, from which there is a view of the harbour. From the Knab, south of the town, there are fine views of the island of Bressay, which encloses and shelters the harbour to the east. On the little island of Noss, beyond Bressay, is the *Noup of Noss*, a sheer cliff 600 feet high.

6 miles west is **Scalloway,** once capital of Shetland but now a quiet village with the ruins of a 16th century castle.

At the south end of Mainland, near Sumburgh Airport, is the prehistoric site of **Jarlshof** (Bronze and Iron Ages), which was later occupied by Vikings; remains of a 16th century palace.

The cliffs round the coasts of Shetland are the haunt of innumerable seabirds, and seals are often seen round the islands.

Practical
Information

GREAT BRITAIN

CONTENTS

	Pages
Where to get information about Great Britain	1051
I. Where to go	1054
II. When to go	1058
III. Recommended itineraries	1059
IV. Passports and customs	1060
V. Currency	1062
VI. Sea connections	1063
VII. Rail services	1072
VIII. Air services	1074
IX. Motoring	1079
X. Sport	1084
XI. Entertainments	1087
XII. Food and drink	1090
XIII. Shopping in London	1094
XIV. Foreign consulates in Britain	1099
XV. Miscellaneous	1107
Welsh and Gaelic glossaries	1114
Hotels	1119

WHERE TO GET INFORMATION ABOUT GREAT BRITAIN

Tourist information about Britain is supplied and coordinated by the British Tourist Authority, whose headquarters are at 64 St James's St, London. Information about particular parts of the country can be obtained from the various regional tourist boards. Addresses from which information can be obtained are listed below.

OUTSIDE BRITAIN

Argentina: Piso 2, Avenida Cordoba 645, Buenos Aires (tel. 392 99 55).

Australia: ASL House, Clarence and King Sts, Sydney, N.S.W. 2000 (tel. 29 8637).

Belgium: 23 Place Rogier, Bruxelles 1000 (tel. 18 67 70).

Brazil: Avenida Ipiranga 318A, 12° Andar, Conjunto 1201, 01046 São Paulo-Sp. (tel. 257 1834).

Canada: 151 Bloor St West, Toronto M5S IT3, Ontario (tel. 416-925 6326); 602 West Hastings St, Vancouver 2, B.C. (tel. 604-682 2604).

Denmark: P.O. Box 46, 1002 København K.

France: 6 Place Vendôme, 75001 Paris (tel. 260 34 50).

Germany (Federal Republic): 6 Frankfurt-am-Main 1, Neue Mainzer Strasse (tel. 28 81 47).

Italy: via Torino 40, 00184 Roma (tel. 46 19 56).

Japan: Room 246, Tokyo Club Building, 2-6 3-chome Kasumigaseki, Chiyoda-ku, Tokyo 100 (tel. 581 3603).

Mexico: Piso 6, Tiber 103, México 5 D.F. (tel. 5 11 39 27).

Netherlands: Leidseplein 5, Amsterdam (tel. 23 40 04).

Norway: Postboks 1781 Vika, Oslo 1.

New Zealand: P.O. Box 3655, 19 Tory St, Wellington (tel. 553 223).

Spain: Torre de Madrid 6/4, Plaza de Espana, Madrid 13 (tel. 241 13 96).

Sweden: Malmskillnadsgatan 40, P.O. Box 40097, 10342 Stockholm 40 (tel. 21 24 44).

Switzerland: 8001 Zurich, 78/v Limmatquai (tel. 47 42 97).

Union of South Africa: P.O. Box 6256, 51/55 St George's St, Capetown (tel. 3 4946).

U.S.A.: 680 Fifth Avenue, New York NY 10019 (tel. 212-581 4700). Suite 2450, John Hancock Center, 875 North Michigan Avenue, Chicago, Illinois 60611 (tel. 312-787 0490). 612 South Flower St, Los Angeles, California 900017 (tel. 213-623 8196).

IN ENGLAND

Tourist Information Centre (B.T.A.), 64 St James's St, London SW1A 1NF (tel. 01-629 9191).

London Tourist Board, 26 Grosvenor Gardens, London SW1W ODU (tel. 01-730 0791). Kiosks at British Airways Terminal (open 9 to 2 during the season) and at Victoria Station (open all year round).

East Anglia Tourist Board, 14 Museum St, Ipswich IP1 1HU, Suffolk (tel. 0473-214 211).

North-West Tourist Board, 119 The Piazza, Piccadilly Plaza, Manchester M1 4AN (tel. 061-236 0393).

Northumbria Tourist Board, Prudential Building, 140-150 Pilgrim St, Newcastle-upon-Tyne NE1 6TH (tel. 0632-28795).

East Midlands Tourist Board, Bailgate, Lincoln LN1 3AR (tel. 0522-31521).

Cumbria Tourist Board, Ellerthwaite, Windermere, Westmorland (tel. 4444).

West Midlands Tourist Board, P.O. Box 15, Worcester WR1 3QQ (tel. 0905-29511).

Yorkshire Tourist Board, 312 Tadcaster Road, York YO2 2HF (tel. 0904-67961).

Thames and Chilterns Tourist Board, P.O. Box 10, 25 Bridge St, Abingdon, Berks (tel. 4344).

South-East England Tourist Board, Cheviot House, 4-6 Monson Road, Tunbridge Wells, Kent (tel. 0892-33066).

Dover Tourist Information Centre, Townwall St, Dover (tel. 202915).

West Country Tourist Board, Trinity Court, Southernhay East, Exeter EX1 1QS, Devon (tel. 0392-76351).

Isle of Man Tourist Board, 13 Victoria St, Douglas, Isle of Man (tel. 0624-4323).

Isle of Wight Tourist Board, 21 High St, Newport, I.O.W. (tel. 098381-4343).

Jersey Tourism Committee, Weighbridge, St Helier, Jersey, Channel Islands (tel. 0534-21281).

IN SCOTLAND

Scottish Tourist Board, 23 Ravelston Terrace, Edinburgh EH4 3EU (tel. 031-332 2433). Londonffice: 137 Knightsbridge, of London SW1X 7PN (tel. 01-589 2218).

Borders Tourist Association, 66 Woodmarket, Kelso, Roxburghshire (tel. Kelso 2125).

Clyde Tourist Association, c/o Information Centre, George Square, Glasgow G2 1ES (tel. 041-221 9600).

East Central Scotland Tourist Association, Marshall Place, Perth (tel. 0738-22900).

Edinburgh and Lothians Tourist Association, c/o Publicity Department, Edinburgh District Council, Cockburn St, Edinburgh EH1 1BP (tel. 031-225 2424).

Grampian Tourist Association, 17 High St, Elgin, Moray (tel. 0343-2666).

Highlands and Islands Development Board, Bridge House, Bank St, Inverness (tel. 0463-34171).

South-West of Scotland Tourist Association, Douglas House, Newton Stewart, Wigtownshire (tel. 549).

IN WALES

Wales Tourist Board, Welcome House, High St, Llandaff, Cardiff CF5 2YZ (tel. 0222-567701); Information Centre, 3 Castle St, Cardiff CF1 2RE (tel. 0222-27281).

Mid Wales Tourism Council, 3 China St, Llanidloes, Mont. (tel. Llanidloes 644).

North Wales Tourism Council, Civic Centre, Colwyn Bay, Denbighshire (tel. 0492-55222).

South Wales Tourism Council, Dark Gate, Carmarthen (tel. 0267-7557).

I. WHERE TO GO

There are of course many different ways of visiting Britain. Some visitors prefer a package tour, which saves trouble and may well save money as well; others prefer the greater reedom of travelling in their own car or in a hired car and making their own arrangements for accommodation. In the latter case they should bear in mind the need to make hotel reservations in advance, particularly ih summer.

There is so much to see in Britain that any kind of complete tour is out of the question within the normal compass of a few weeks' stay in the country. The best plan is to select one or more regions, stay in a suitable centre and make trips from there. For this purpose it may be helpful to give a brief summary of the main tourist areas.

The larger cities of the north and the smaller towns all over the country are good centres from which to explore the surrounding area, though some visitors may prefer to establish themselves in some quiet little village in the heart of the country. The roads are excellent, and there are good public transport services, so that getting from place to place presents no problems.

For those with specialised interests there are many possibilities—a tour of the cathedral cities, of old abbeys or famous castles, or a visit to some part of the country associated with a great writer or artist. With the help of the information given in this section and in other parts of this Guide each visitor will be able to decide for himself how best to spend his time.

London.   Most visitors choose to spend at least some of their time in London, although they will be well advised not to confine themselves to the capital but to vary their stay with a visit to some other part of the country as well. It is also possible to visit a variety of places of historic or scenic interest from a base in London, like *Windsor Castle*, the oldest and largest royal palace in the world.

The other royal residence, *Buckingham Palace*, is one of London's great tourist attractions, particularly for the changing of the guard in their full-dress scarlet uniform and tall bearskins. Even more impressive is the sight of the Horse Guards parading along the Mall, with waving plumes and gleaming breastplates, on their way to change the guard in Whitehall. Other world-famous London sights are the *Tower of London*, *St Paul's Cathedral*, the *National Gallery*, *Westminster Abbey*, *Parliament* and *Hampton Court Palace*, to say nothing of a whole series of green and attractive parks, the brightly coloured London buses and the London policemen. The museums and art galleries of London are among the richest in the world, and these, no less than the many historic old buildings, draw large numbers of people to visit the capital.

Edinburgh. Edinburgh is second only to London in its historical associations. Centred on the castle towering above the houses on its rock, it is one of the world's most beautiful and most appealing cities, notable for the festival of music and the arts held there every summer.

The Cotswolds and the Shakespeare Country. This is the most rural, most tranquil and most typical part of England. Stratford, Warwick, Kenilworth, Leamington Spa and Rugby are served by fast trains from Paddington and Euston.

The South-East Coast: Kent with its idyllic orchards, the delightful county of Sussex with the wide expanses of the South Downs, and the many seaside resorts along the coast.

The West Country. This is the country of King Arthur, a region of many ancient buildings and a beautiful coastline. Among its relics of the past are Tintern Abbey and Chepstow Castle, in the beautiful Malvern Hills and Wye valley. Beyond the Severn estuary is *Gloucester*, with one of England's finest cathedrals. To the south, at *Bristol*, the Avon gorge is spanned by the Clifton suspension bridge, carrying the road into Somerset and North Devon. Among the many beauties of the West Country are Clovelly perched on its cliffs, the jagged coast of North Cornwall, St Ives, a favourite with artists, *Land's End*, the most westerly point in England, Newlyn, St Michael's Mount, the wild scenery of Dartmoor, the historic old towns of *Plymouth* and Taunton, the attractive resort of Torquay, Wells Cathedral and *Bath* with its Roman remains.

East Anglia and the Norfolk Broads. This flat low-lying region contains some of the country's finest architectural treasures. The *Broads* offer 200 miles of navigable waterways to explore, interesting bird sanctuaries and enchanting scenery in which land, sea and sky merge into a delightful whole.

Oxford and Cambridge. It is difficult to decide which of these two university towns is the more attractive. Oxford can claim the most beautiful street in the world, Cambridge the most beautiful river; Oxford has the loveliest tower that ever pointed skyward, Cambridge the most marvellous chapel (King's College).

The Peak District: an area of majestic grandeur only half an hour by car from the busy and populous cities of Manchester, Sheffield and Derby.

Yorkshire and the Brontë Country: splendid churches and abbeys, great stretches of wild moorland, well stocked trout streams flowing down through rocky valleys.

The Lake District. This area with its eleven lakes set amid magnificently wild scenery, with its moors, hills and woods reflected in the calm waters of the lakes, attracts all those to whom the beauties of nature appeal. The heart of the Lake District is *Keswick*, and other good centres are Windermere, Grasmere, Ambleside and Kendal. In a trip of less than 100 miles visitors can seen at least eight lakes and some of the finest hill scenery in Europe. Other attractions are sailing and fishing; and for some the sheepdog trials will be a new experience.

Wales and the Welsh Border. A land of mountains and hills with green valleys sloping gently down towards the sea, of huge castles, occupied by a music-loving people. The approaches to Wales pass through some of the most attractive towns in England. Cardiff, Penarth, Carmarthen, Llandrindod Wells, the seaside resorts of Aberystwyth, Llandudno, Colwyn Bay and Rhyl, and Snowdonia are served by trains from Paddington and Euston.

Scotland. A marvellous country which is worth coming to see even if you see nothing else in Britain. To the south of Edinburgh is the Scott country, to the north are the wildly beautiful Highlands, which can be explored from Inverness, Aberdeen, Fort William or Oban. In the Grampians there are winter sports (Aviemore).

Spas. There are numerous spa towns all over the country, though few of them are still in business as spas. The leading spa towns are Bath, Harrogate, Leamington Spa and Tunbridge. Other pleasant resorts are Cheltenham, Malvern, Matlock, Woodhall Spa, Moffat, Strathpeffer and Llandrindod Wells.

Seaside resorts. Britain has some of the best equipped seaside resorts in the world. Their number and variety may appear almost disconcerting until it is remembered that the country has a total coastline of something like 6000 miles. From the rugged solitude of Shetland and the Hebrides to the almost tropical luxuriance of the Channel Islands and the Cornish coast every kind of coastal scenery is to be found. Bare hills sloping steeply down to the sea, rocks swarming with seabirds, marshes and fenland, sand dunes, jagged rocks and sheer limestone cliffs, empty stretches of sea and crowded beaches: all this and much more is to be seen round the coasts of Britain. This variety of scenery is matched by the variety of interests catered for—sea angling and shrimping, sailing and boating of all kinds, swimming for children and for the expert—and by the range of different types of resort, from the quiet little fishing villages and the secluded bays to the larger places offering a full programme of entertainments and attractions for large numbers of people.

The following is merely a selection of some of the leading resorts:

South coast: Margate, Ramsgate, Folkestone, Hastings, Eastbourne, Brighton and Hove, Worthing, Bognor Regis, Isle of Wight, Bournemouth, Weymouth, Torquay, Falmouth, Penzance, St Ives, Newquay, Tintagel, Bude, Ilfracombe, Minehead.

Wales: Penarth, Mumbles, Tenby, Cardigan, Newquay, Aberystwyth, Criccieth, Pwllheli, Nevin, Caernarvon, Beaumaris (Anglesey), Conwy, Llandudno, Colwyn Bay, Prestatyn.

East coast: Clacton, Aldeburgh, Southwold, Lowestoft, Great Yarmouth, Cromer, Skegness, Bridlington, Scarborough, Whitby, Saltburn, Redcar, Whitley Bay.

West coast. New Brighton, Southport, Lytham St Annes, Blackpool, Morecambe, Ravenglass.

Cathedral cities. If one had to select a typically English town—one with no counterpart in any other country—it would undoubtedly be one of the cathedral cities. A cathedral city is not necessarily the largest town in the area—Ely, for example, has a huge cathedral but is itself little more than a large village—but it is almost certainly the oldest and often the most picturesque. It is also—at any rate the part of it round the cathedral itself—the most peaceful. The "closes" of cathedrals like Canterbury, Salisbury and Wells must be the most tranquil places to be found anywhere in the world. Surrounded by green lawns and protected from the tumult of the everyday world by a screen of mellow old houses occupied by the dean and other church dignitaries, the cathedral seems to live a life quite apart from that of the town, though in fact it exerts a dominant influence on the life of the community.

Visitors interested in architecture will notice certain differences between the cathedrals of Britain and those of the Continent—the prominence of the towers and spires, all the more striking because of the relatively low roof and the great length of the nave (Winchester and St Albans are the two longest Gothic cathedrals in the world); the large size of the windows (the east ends of Gloucester Cathedral and York Minster, for example, seem to contain more glass than stone); and the fine auxiliary structures like cloisters and chapter houses, a result of the monastic origin of most of the cathedrals.

Cathedrals in England: St Paul's, Southwark and Westminster Abbey in London, Canterbury, Rochester, Guildford, St Albans, Chichester, Portsmouth, Ely, Chelmsford, Derby, Gloucester, Bristol, Winchester, Leicester, Norwich, Oxford, Coventry, Birmingham, Bury St Edmunds, Wells, Lichfield, Salisbury, Worcester, Newport, Chester, Exeter, Truro, Hereford, Lincoln, Peterborough, Southwell, Blackburn, Bradford, Ripon, Sheffield, Wakefield, York, Durham, Newcastle, Liverpool, Manchester, Carlisle. *Scotland:* Edinburgh, Glasgow, Dunblane, St Andrews, Aberdeen, Elgin, Kirkwall (Orkney). *Wales:* Brecon, Llandaff, St Asaph, Bangor, St Davids.

II. WHEN TO GO

The British Isles enjoy the pleasantest climate to be found in their latitude. The mean annual rainfall is around 600 mm, being slightly higher in Edinburgh than in London. The average range of temperature between the coldest and the warmest month is no more than 12 °C in England and 10° in Scotland, and falls to 8° on the Atlantic coast. The maximum day temperature in summer (June to August) is around 22 °C over almost the whole of south-east England, including London, and around 16° in northern and north-western Scotland. There are an average of 6 or 7 hours of sunshine a day in London in summer, and 4 to 5 hours in spring. In almost all the country's seaside resorts there are more than 7 hours of sunshine a day in summer.

Extreme cold and extreme heat are accordingly rare in Britain. Each season has its own particular charm, but for visitors with only limited time at their disposal, who naturally want to have good weather, the best chances lie between April and October.

July and August are the favourite holiday months, and accordingly accommodation in the seaside resorts during this period must be booked well in advance. Often, however, the weather is better before or after these two peak months. Moreover the countryside is at its loveliest in spring and autumn, and there is frequently a "St Martin's summer" of fine weather lasting into November.

London can be visited at any time of year. Even in the heat of summer its parks and gardens and the river Thames offer pleasant coolness, and the city is surrounded by a "green belt" within which building is not permitted. The possibility of excursions into the surrounding countryside makes London an ideal holiday centre, and it has of course innumerable attractions of its own in the form of theatres, concerts, sporting events and other entertainments in addition to its museums and other tourist sights.

It is worth remembering also that rates for hotel accommodation, car hire, etc., tend to be lower outside the main holiday season; and during the off-season there are often special trips (e.g. winter weekends) organised by the travel agencies.

III. RECOMMENDED ITINERARIES

The choice of an itinerary will of course depend on the time available. Those who can spare only one or two weeks will want to see London and the surrounding area: other possibilities—particularly for those travelling by car—are suggested below.

1. *A week in London.* The historic buildings, museums and art galleries of the capital, plus a trip to Windsor.

2. *A week in the south-east* (perhaps preceding or following a week in London). Canterbury, the coast from Margate to Portsmouth, Winchester and Southampton, with side trips to Salisbury and Stonehenge.

3. *A week in the south-west* (perhaps combined with either of the previous suggestions). Devon and Cornwall (along the south coast to Penzance, returning along the north coast to Wells and Bristol).

4. *A week north of London.* A tour of traditional England,
with its cathedrals and museum towns. Oxford, Stratford and
the Shakespeare country, Warwick, Coventry (a town rebuilt
after war damage), Leicester, Lincoln; then through the Fens
to Norfolk (possible side trip to Ely), Norwich and Yarmouth;
return via Cambridge.

5. *A week in Wales.* Via Oxford, Stratford and Birmingham
to Shrewsbury and Chester, then along the Welsh coast (Conwy,
Bangor, Caernarvon, Harlech, Aberystwyth, St Davids), returning by way of Swansea, Cardiff and Newport to Gloucester
and London. Could be combined with one of the two preceding
routes to make a fortnight's tour.

6. *Two weeks in central and northern England.* From London
or Southampton (a possible point of disembarkation) to Bristol;
then Gloucester-Worcester-Shrewsbury-Chester-Liverpool; then
via Manchester to the Lake District, Carlisle, Hadrian's Wall
and Newcastle; Durham, Barnard Castle (museum), Ripon,
York and Lincoln; then either Leicester-Stratford-Oxford or
Norwich and Cambridge.

7. *Two weeks in England and southern Scotland.* London
to Manchester by motorway, then the Lake District, Carlisle,
Glasgow (Loch Lomond), the Trossachs, Perth and Edinburgh;
return by way of the Scott country to Durham, York and
Lincoln; then via Ely and Cambridge to London.

8. *Two weeks in Scotland.* Pass quickly through England
on the motorway (one day each way) or by car sleeper. Glasgow,
Oban, Fort William and Skye; then Wester Ross (Ullapool),
Sutherland and the far north; return by Inverness, the Grampians, the Dee valley, Aberdeen, Perth and Edinburgh.

9. *Three weeks or a month in Britain.* Combine two or more
of the preceding routes according to taste.

IV. PASSPORTS AND CUSTOMS

Passports

For a stay of up to 3 months a valid passport without visa
is sufficient for nationals of most states; for certain countries
a visa may be necessary (enquire of the British Tourist Authority). Nationals of the E.E.C. countries need only a national
identity card not more than ten years old. All foreign nationals
must fill in a landing card and present it to the immigration
officer.

Health

Except in case of epidemic an international vaccination certificate is not required.

Foreign currency

There are no restrictions on the bringing or taking out in of British or foreign currency, letters of credit or traveller's cheques.

Motor vehicles

The following documents must be produced on entry:

(a) the car's registration book or similar document;

(b) a national or international driving licence;

(c) an international insurance certificate ("green card"), failing which temporary insurance must be taken out on landing. This requirement does not apply to nationals of E.E.C. countries.

The vehicle must also bear a national identity plaque.

Customs

If you have nothing to declare, take the "green lane" when passing through the customs; if you have dutiable goods to declare, take the "red lane".

Nationals of E.E.C. countries can bring in the following items duty-free provided that they were obtained in ordinary shops within the E.E.C.: 300 cigarettes or 150 cigarillos or 75 cigars or 400 gr. of tobacco; 1½ litres of spirits over 38.8° proof (22° Gay-Lussac) or 3 litres of spirits under 38.8° proof or 3 litres of fortified or sparkling wine: 3 litres of still table wine; 75 gr. of perfume; .375 litre of toilet water; and £120 worth of other goods. The allowances of tobacco and alcoholic drinks do not apply to persons under 17. Where the goods are bought in duty-free shops at airports or on ships or aircraft the allowances are reduced to those applicable to nationals of non-E.E.C. countries (next paragraph).

For nationals of non-E.E.C. countries the duty-free allowances are: 200 cigarettes or 100 cigarillos or 50 cigars or 250 gr. tobacco (double these amounts for visitors who live outside Europe); 1 litre of spirits over 38.8° proof (22° Gay-Lussac) or 2 litres of spirits under 38.8° proof or 2 litres of fortified or sparkling wine; 50 gr. of perfume; ¼ litre of toilet water; and £28 worth of other goods.

Visitors staying in Britain for less than 6 months pay no duty on their personal effects (clothing, jewellery, a camera or ciné-camera, a watch, etc.).

Full information can be obtained from H.M. Customs and Excise, King's Beam House, Mark Lane, London EC3R 7HE).

Animals

See p. 1107.

V. CURRENCY

Decimal currency was introduced in Britain in 1971. The unit is still the pound sterling (£), now divided into 100 pence. There are banknotes for £20, £10, £5 and £1 and coins in the following denominations: 50 pence (silver, seven-sided), 10 pence and 5 pence (silver), and 2 pence, 1 penny and ½ penny (bronze). (Note that the new penny is abbreviated *p* and not *d* like the old non-decimal penny).

The Scottish banks issue their own banknotes, which are not always readily accepted in other parts of Britain. The Channel Islands also have their own notes. It should be remembered that British money is current in the Republic of Ireland but Irish money is not accepted in Britain.

Foreign currency can be changed in banks and exchange offices (the latter being found at airports and seaports and in the larger towns) and in some of the larger hotels and shops.

Banking hours are as follows:

England: Monday to Friday, 9.30 to 3.30.

Scotland: Monday to Wednesday, 9.30 to 12.30 and 1.30 to 3.30; Thursday, same times and also 4.30 to 6; Friday, 9.30 to 3.30.

Wales: Monday to Friday, 9.30 to 3.

In addition banks in England and Wales remain open on one evening a week (varying according to local arrangements) from 4.30 to 6. All banks are closed on Saturday.

There are *exchange offices* at the main ports and airports, open for the arrival and departure of all boats and aircraft. There are also the following exchange offices in central London:

Victoria Station, S.W.1: winter 8.15 a.m. to 10 p.m., summer
7.30 a.m. to 10.30 p.m.

Air Terminal, Victoria, S.W.1: daily (except between Christmas
and Easter) 7 a.m. to 11 p.m.; between Christmas and Easter
7 a.m. to 10 p.m.

West London Air Terminal, Cromwell Road, S.W.7: April-
October 7.30 a.m. to 10 p.m., November-March 7.30 a.m.
to 7.30 p.m.

Dorfman and Co., Oxford Street Arcade, 527 Oxford St,
Marble Arch, W.1: Monday to Friday, 10 to 7; Saturday,
10 to 6.

VI. SEA CONNECTIONS

With France

Sealink (British Rail and French National Railways): services
for passengers arriving by train and for cars:—

Calais-Dover, 1 hr 40 min. (2 departures daily in winter, 8 in
April, May, June and September, 12 in July and August).

Boulogne-Dover, 1 hr 40 min. (one departure daily in winter,
4 or 5 in spring and autumn, up to 12 in July and August).

Dunkirk-Dover, 3 hrs 45 min. (one departure in winter, 4 in
summer).

Calais-Folkestone, 1 hr 40 min. (2 to 5 departures daily according to season).

Boulogne-Folkestone, 1 hr 40 min. (one to 4 departures daily
according to season).

Dieppe-Newhaven, 3 hrs 45 min. (2 to 6 departures daily according to season).

Passengers should arrive at the embarkation point not less
than 45 minutes before departure (1 hour on the Dover-Dunkirk
service, 90 minutes on night services). Places should be booked
in advance, either at the addresses given below or through a
travel agency.

London: British Rail Car Ferry Centre, P.O. Box 303, 52 Grosvenor Gardens, London SW1W OAG.

Paris: Chemins de Fer Britanniques, 12 Boulevard de la Made-
leine, 75009 Paris (tel. 073 56 70).
Air Transport, 4 rue de Surène, 75008 Paris (tel. 265 05 41).
Bureau de Tourisme S.N.C.F., Gare du Nord (tel. 878 15 66).
Bureau de Tourisme S.N.C.F., Gare St Lazare (tel. 387 61 89).

Boulogne: Gare Maritime, B.P. 327/1 (tel. 31 45 45).

Calais: Gare de Transit S.A.G.A. (tel. 34 48 40).

Dunkirk: Société A.L.A., Gare Maritime (tel. 66 80 01).

Dieppe: Gare Maritime, B.P. 85 (tel. 84 24 87).

In summer the Sealink services connect with car-sleeper trains arriving at Dieppe, Calais and Boulogne and leaving Dover for Scotland.

Normandy Ferries: Le Havre to Southampton. Two departures daily in each direction (one by night and one by day). The crossing takes from 7 to 8½ hours.

Townsend-Thoresen Car Ferries: Calais-Dover, Le Havre-Southampton, Cherbourg-Southampton.

Brittany Ferries: Roscoff-Plymouth.

Seaspeed (British Rail and French National Railways): Boulogne-Dover by hovercraft (35 min.). Cars carried. Also Calais-Dover. During the season six services daily in each direction between Dover and the two French ports.

Apply to the addresses given above, or to the hoverports at Boulogne, B.P. 359/2 (tel. 31 71 22); Calais, B.P. 428 (tel. 34 65 70); and Dover, 7 Cambridge Terrace.

Hoverlloyd: Calais-Ramsgate by hovercraft (40 min.). Cars carried. Apply to International Hoverport, Calais (tel. 34 67 10); Ramsgate (tel. Thanet 54761); London (tel. 01-499 9481).

With Belgium

Sealink: Ostend-Dover (3 hrs 30 min.), Ostend-Folkestone (4 hrs), Ostend-Harwich (4 hrs 45 min.).

Townsend-Thoresen: Zeebrugge-Dover (4 hrs).

With Holland

Tor Line: Amsterdam-Immingham (12½ hrs), once weekly.

Sealink: Hook of Holland-Harwich (6 to 8 hrs), one day and one night departure daily.

Transport Ferry Service: Rotterdam (Europort) - Felixstowe (about 7 hrs), 16 departures weekly.

North Sea Ferries: Rotterdam (Europort) - Hull (about 14 hrs), one departure daily.

Norfolk Line: Scheveningen-Yarmouth (8 hrs), 2 departures daily.

With Germany

Prins Ferries: Bremerhaven-Harwich (16 hrs), 3 or 4 departures
weekly; Hamburg-Harwich (20 hrs), 3 or 4 departures weekly.

With Denmark

DFDS: Esbjerg-Harwich (18 hrs), 3 to 7 departures weekly
according to season; Esbjerg-Newcastle (10½ hrs), one
departure weekly.

Iceland Steamship Co.: Copenhagen-Leith (Edinburgh) (about
36 hrs), 3 departures monthly.

With Finland

Finnlines: Helsinki-Felixstowe (3½ days).

Baltic Shipping Co.: Helsinki-Tilbury (London 3½ days).

With Sweden

Tor Line: Göteborg-Immingham (25 hrs), 3 departures weekly.

Swedish Lloyd: Göteborg-Tilbury (London) (c. 38 hrs), 7 to
8 departures monthly.

With Norway

Bergen Line: Bergen-Newcastle or Stavanger-Newcastle (18 or
23 hrs), 2 to 5 departures monthly.

Fred Olsen Lines: Kristiansand-Harwich (22 hrs), 7 departures
monthly; Kristiansand-Newcastle (24 hrs), one departure
weekly; Oslo-Newcastle (36 hrs).

With the Soviet Union

Baltic Shipping Co.: Leningrad-Tilbury (London) (5 days),
irregular frequency, summer only.

With Spain

Swedish Lloyd: Bilbao-Southampton (37 hrs), 6 to 8 departures
monthly.

With Portugal

Southern Ferries: Lisbon-Southampton (43 hrs), 4 to 7 departures
monthly.

With Iceland

Iceland Steamship Co.: Reykjavik-Leith (Edinburgh) (60 hrs), 3 departures monthly.

Channel Islands

Services in summer only between Granville (France) and Jersey (75 min.) by *Navifrance-Vedettes Armoricaines;* Carteret (France) and Jersey by *Service Maritime;* St Malo (France) and Guernsey-Alderney by *Condor.* Services, summer and winter, between St Malo and Jersey by boat and hydrofoil. (Services between Weymouth and Jersey or Guernsey (4 to 6 hrs) by *Sealink.*

Isle of Wight

Very frequent services between Lymington and Yarmouth, Portsmouth and Fishbourne, Southampton and Cowes; hovercraft services between Southsea and Ryde.

Scilly Isles

Penzance to St Mary's (about 3 hrs) by *Scilly Steamship Co.*

Isle of Man

Douglas-Liverpool (4 hrs), one to 6 departures daily; also from Douglas to Fleetwood, Heysham, Dublin, Belfast, Ardrossan and Llandudno.

Northern Ireland

Liverpool-Belfast, Heysham-Belfast, Preston-Belfast, Rotterdam-Belfast (with return via Dublin and Le Havre). Other services between Stranraer and Larne (about 2 hrs), the most frequent service, with one to 6 departures daily; and between Campbeltown and Red Bay.

Republic of Ireland

Dublin-Liverpool (7 hrs), 2 or 3 departures daily; Dublin-Holyhead (3½ hrs), same frequency; Rosslare-Fishguard (Wales) (3¼ hrs); Cork-Swansea (9 hrs). *Sealink* or *B + I.*

Hebrides

For details of services, consult the timetables issued by *Caledonian MacBrayne* (address below).

Orkney and Shetland

Services from Aberdeen and Thurso. Consult the timetables of the *North of Scotland, Orkney and Shetland Shipping Co.*

Addresses of Shipping Companies

Baltic Shipping Co.

Sea Travel Centres (UK) Ltd., 10 Haymarket, London SW1Y 4DD (tel. 01-839 8844).

Danish State Railways Bureau, Frederiksborggarde 42, København K.

John Nurimen Oy, Snellmaninkatu 13, Helsinki.

Baltic Shipping Co., 35 Herzen Street, Leningrad.

Belfast Steamship Co.

94 High Street, Belfast BT1 2DH (tel. 23636).

P & O Short Sea Shipping Ltd, Reliance House, Water Street, Liverpool L2 8TS (tel. 051-236 5464).

Bergen Line

Bergen Steamship Co. Ltd, 21-24 Cockspur Street, London SW1Y 5BY (tel. 01-839 4631).

Det Bergenske Dampskibsselskab, 505 Fifth Avenue, New York NY 10017, USA (tel. 210020).

B + I Line

British & Irish Steam Packet Co. Ltd., 155 Regent Street, London W1R 7FD (tel. 01-734 4681).

16 Westmoreland Street, Dublin 2 (tel. 778271).

8 Bridge Street, Cork (tel. 54100).

Reliance House, Water Street, Liverpool L2 8TS (tel. 051-227 5151).

Exchange Buildings, Swansea (tel. 52016).

Brittany Ferries

Millbay Docks, Plymouth (tel. 21840).

Port de Roscoff (France) (tel. 69 76 10).

Caledonian MacBrayne

The Pier, Gourock PA19 IQP (tel. 31261).

Channel Islands Ferries

Falcon House, 17a York Street, St Helier, Jersey (tel. 37422).

Condor Ltd.

28 Conway Street, St Helier, Jersey (tel. 36331).

Morvan Fils, 4 rue des Cordiers, Saint-Malo (tel. 34 98 35).

DFDS Seaways

8 Berkeley Square, London W1X 6HJ (tel. 01-629 3512).

Tyne Commission Quays, North Shields NE29 6EE (tel. 78115).

Parkeston Quay, Harwich CO12 4SY (tel. 4411).

Axelborg, Vesterbrogade 4A, København (tel. 01-15 6341).

Finnlines

Gloverbros Ltd, 8-9 Bond Street, London W1 (tel. 623-1311).

Hoverlloyd

Hoverport, Pegwell Bay, Ramsgate (tel. Thanet 54761).

Iceland Steamship Co

Icelandair, 73 Grosvenor Street, London W1X 9DD (tel. 01-499 9971).

Currie Line, 16 Bernard Street, Leith (tel. 031-554 5581).

Posthusstrætti 2, Reykjavik (tel. 21460).

Isle of Man Steam Packet Co.

P.O. Box 5, Imperial Buildings, Douglas (Isle of Man) (tel. 3824).

McBride's Shipping Agencies, 93 Hope Street, Glasgow C2 (tel. 041-248 5162).

W.E. Williams & Co. 82/86 High Street, Belfast (tel. 29281).

British & Irish Steam Packet Co., 16 Westmoreland Street, Dublin (tel. 777345).

Shipping and Port Manager, Heysham (tel. 52373).

Branch Office: India Buildings, 40 Brunswick Street, Liverpool 2 (tel. 051-236 3214).

Isles of Scilly Steamship Co.

16 Quay Street, Penzance (tel. 2009/4013).

Navifrance-Vedettes Armoricaines

1er Bassin, Port de Commerce, B.P. 88, Brest Cedex (tel. 44 44 04).

12 rue G. Clemenceau, B.P. 24, 50400 Graville (tel. 50 09 87).

Norfolk Line

Atlas House, Southgates Road. Great Yarmouth (tel. 56133).

Keizerstraat 2, Scheveningen, Holland (tel. 514601).

Normandy Ferries

Arundel Towers, Portland Terrace, Southampton SO9 4AE (tel. 32131/34141).

Route du Môle Central, 76 Port du Havre, France (tel. 48 19 81).

North of Scotland, Orkney & Shetland Shipping Co.

P.O. Box 5, Matthews' Quay, Aberdeen AB9 8DL (tel. 29111).

Scrabster Pier, Caithness (tel. Thurso 2052).

Harbour Street, Kirkwall (tel. 3330).

The Esplanade, Lerwick (tel. 491/2).

New Pier, Stromness (tel. 216).

North Sea Ferries Ltd.

King George Dock, Hedon Road, Hull HU9 5QA (tel. 74106).

Haringvliet 100, P.O. Box 1476, Rotterdam 1 (tel. (010) 14266).

Fred. Olsen Lines

229 Regent Street, London W1R 9AP (tel. 01-437 9888).

Fred. Olsen, Fred. Olsens Gate 2, Oslo (tel. 41 72 70).

P.H. Matthiesen & Co., Passenger Department, 54 Pilgrim Street, Newcastle-upon-Tyne, Northumberland (tel. 26171).

Vestre Strandgate 42, Kristiansand (tel. 26500).

Interolsen Agencies Inc., 160 Sansome Street, San Francisco, California 94104, (tel. 415-433 4990).

Vereenigd Cargadoorskantour, 16 Koningsplein, Amsterdam, Holland (tel. 248303).

Prins Ferries

Prins Ferries (Lion Ferry AB), Halmstad, Sweden (tel. 01-629 7961).

67 Grosvenor Street, London W1X OEA (tel. 01-491 7641).

Karl Geuther & Co., Martinistrasse 58, 2800 Bremen (tel. 31 49 70/81).

Hadag Seetouristik und Fahrdienst AG, Johanisbollwerk 6-8, Hamburg 11 (tel. 31 24 21).

Sealink

Sealink Car Ferry Centre, P.O. Box 303, 52 Grosvenor Gardens, London SW1W OAG (tel. 01-730 3440).

French Railways House, 179 Piccadilly, London W1V OBA.

Sealink, 50 Liverpool Street, London EC2M 7QM (tel. 01-623 1831).

Chemins de Fer Britanniques, 12 Boulevard de la Madeleine, 75009 Paris (tel. 073 56 70).

Gare Maritime, Boulogne, B.P. 327/1 (tel. 31 45 45).

Gare Maritime, Calais (tel. 34 48 40).

Gare Maritime, Dieppe (tel. 84 24 89).

A.L.A., Gare Maritime, Dunkerque (tel. 66 80 01).

Harwich Ferry Agency, Hoek van Holland (tel. 01747-2681).

British Rail, Rosslare Harbour; North Wall, Dublin 1.

British Rail, 24 Donegall Place, Belfast (tel. 27525).

Shipping & Port Manager, British Rail, Heysham Harbour (tel. 52373).

Sealink (Scotland) Ltd, Stranraer Harbour, Wigtownshire, Scotland (tel. 2262).

Central Reservations Office: Isle of Wight Car Ferry Services, Portsmouth Harbour Station, Portsmouth, Hampshire PO1 3EU (tel. 22571).

Sealink Car Ferry Booking Office: Lymington Pier, Hampshire (tel. 3301).

Seaspeed British Rail Hovercraft

Royal London House, Finsbury Square, London EC2P 2BQ (tel. 01-628 3050).

Reservations Office: 7 Cambridge Terrace, Dover (tel. Dover 2501/3).

See also under Sealink.

Southern Ferries

Arundel Towers, Portland Terrace, Southampton SO9 4AE (tel. 32131).

20 Praça Duque da Terceira, Lisboa, 2 Portugal (tel. 36 15 81).

Service Maritime

Service Maritime, Carteret (Manche), France (tel. 121 Barneville).

Swedish Lloyd

Swedish Lloyd, Lloyd House, 94 Baker Street, London W1M 1LA (tel. 01-289 2151/6).

Svenska Lloyd, Skandia Harbour, Göteborg 2 (tel. 031/530080).

Alberto Jentoft, Calle José Luis Aznar y Zabala 4, Bilbao

Tor Line Ltd

West Gate, Immingham Dock, nr. Grimsby, Lincolnshire DN4O 2PH (tel. 3131).

34 Panton Street, London SW1Y 4DY (tel. 01-930 3828).

Tor Line Travel Service, Södra Vägen 41, Göteborg (tel. 20 09 50.

Tor Line Travel Service, Birger Jarlsgatan 6, 114 34 Stockholm (tel. (08) 24 18 80).

Tor Line, Coenhaven Weg, Amsterdam W., Holland (tel. 62666).

Townsend Thoresen Car Ferries Ltd

Car Ferry Centre: P.O. Box 12, 1 Camden Crescent, Dover (tel. 204040).

Eastern Docks, Dover (tel. 206079).

Car Ferry House, Canute Road, Southampton SO9 5GP (tel. 29241).

127 Regent Street, London W1R 8LB (tel. 01-437 7800).

Car Ferry Terminal, Zeebrugge, Belgium (tel. 54874).

Gare de Transit, Calais (tel. 34 38 36).

41 Place d'Armes, Calais (tel. 34 41 90).

41 Boulevard des Capucines, 75002 Paris (tel. 073 81 37).

Gare Maritime, Cherbourg (tel. 53 29 98).

Quai de Southampton, Le Havre (tel. 42 72 81).

Transport Ferry Service

25 Whitehall, London SW1A 2BT (tel. 01-930 2363).

Herdman Channel Road, Belfast BT3 9AL (tel. 745407).

A.M.A. Agence Maritime Anversoise S.A., Bordeauxstraat 8, Antwerp (tel. 31 16 36).

Transport Ferry Service (Nederland) N.V., Beneluxhaven, Europoort, Rotterdam (tel. 01-1888 2366).

VII. RAIL SERVICES

Services to Britain

Various combinations are possible—train and boat, train and hovercraft, train and aircraft.

Train and boat: services operated jointly by British Rail and the French National Railways (or the Belgian National Railways for the Ostend line) under the general name of *Sealink*. It is necessary to change at the port of embarkation, except on the Paris-London night service with through sleepers.

Paris (St Lazare) - Dieppe - Newhaven - London (Victoria): total time about 8 hrs, including 3 hrs 45 min. in the boat.

Paris (Gare du Nord) - Calais - Folkestone - London (Victoria): total time 7 hrs 30 min. on the morning service, 7 hrs on the afternoon service (boat 90 min.).

Paris (Gare du Nord) - Dunkirk - Dover - London (Victoria): night service (11 hrs), 1st class sleepers only.

Via Dieppe the fare is slightly less than via Calais or Dunkirk. There are through carriages from the Côte d'Azur, Marseilles and Lyons to Calais and from Basle, Strasbourg and Metz to Calais via Lille.

Customs formalities are often carried out on the train.

Train and hovercraft: special rail-car from Paris (Nord) to Boulogne, then Seaspeed hovercraft to Dover (35 min.) and connecting train to London (Victoria or Charing Cross). Total time 6 hrs.

Train and aircraft: special train from Paris (Nord) to Le Touquet, then by air to Gatwick (20 min.) and electric train to London (Victoria); total time under 4 hrs (the Silver Arrow service). There is also a service via Le Touquet and Southend, arriving at London (Liverpool St). Return tickets from France to Britain are valid for 2 months (on the Silver Arrow service 3 months). Through tickets can be obtained between the principal towns in France and Britain.

On the French rail system certain reductions are available—family tickets giving a reduction of 75% from the third person onwards and annual holiday tickets giving a reduction of 30%. On international services there are reductions for groups of 10 or more.

Refunds for unused tickets can be obtained only in one of the countries on the route. Partly used tickets must be noted accordingly at the station where the journey is interrupted.

Seats can be booked at railway stations, French Railways tourist offices and travel agencies. Booking begins 1 month in advance. Applications for bookings can be made by letter or by telegram (or by telephone 1 week in advance).

For further information apply to:

Air Transport, 4 rue de Surène, 75008 Paris (tel. 265 05 41).

Chemins de Fer Britanniques, 12 Boulevard de la Madeleine, 75009 Paris (tel. 073 56 70).

French Railways, 179 Piccadilly, London W1V OBA.

Sealink (addresses on p. 1070).

British Rail

An extensive network with frequent services. A return ticket, normally valid 3 months (except in Greater London), costs twice the single fare. First class costs roughly 50% more than 2nd class. Fares are related to distance travelled, scaled down as the distance increases. There are, of course, restaurant cars, sleeping cars (the charges for which are very reasonable) and Pullman cars. Seats can be booked at a small charge.

The *Inter-City* trains provide fast and very comfortable services between the main cities, at speeds of up to 100 m.p.h. Almost all of them provide meals and drinks and are timed at regular intervals (every half hour, every 2 hours, etc.), varying according to the route.

Rail Drive is a car hire service run jointly by British Rail and Godfrey Davis at 73 stations with Inter-City services. Cars can be hired through any Godfrey Davis office or at their blue and white Rail Drive kiosks in stations. If you have not booked in advance, use the free telephone at a Godfrey Davis kiosk.

Brit Rail Passes provide unlimited travel on all rail rervices in England, Scotland and Wales, including Continental ferries, excursion trains, steamers on Lake Windermere and services to the Isle of Wight. They are available from May to October for periods of one, two or three weeks. They must be bought before arrival in Britain. Information from British Rail offices in Europe.

The following special tickets can also be brought in Britain:

Circular Tour tickets, valid for 3 months over routes covering at least three separate journeys.

Rail Rover tickets, providing two weeks' unlimited travel in specified areas or in the whole of England, Scotland and Wales.

VIII. AIR SERVICES

Services to Britain

Britain is connected by air with every country in the world, and it is not possible within the compass of this Guide to list all the services flown by British and foreign airlines. Full information can be obtained from the various offices of the British Travel Authority or from travel agencies.

Many services are flown by *British Airways* jointly with foreign airlines. There are also a number of independent airlines, e.g. *British Caledonian* (connections with France), *North-East Airlines* (Austria), *TAT* (*Touraine Air Transport:* Tours-London).

Although most international services go through London (Heathrow or Gatwick) there are also connections with other British towns:

Birmingham (Amsterdam, Dublin, Düsseldorf, Paris)

Bournemouth (Paris)

Bradford (Amsterdam, Dublin)

Bristol (Paris, Dublin)

Cardiff (Paris, Dublin)

Edinburgh (Amsterdam)

Glasgow (Berlin, Düsseldorf, Frankfurt, Paris, Reykjavik, Copenhagen)

Jersey (Amsterdam, Paris, Rennes, Dinard)

Leeds (Amsterdam, Dublin)

Liverpool (Dublin)

Manchester (Amsterdam, Berlin, Brussels, Copenhagen, Dublin, Düsseldorf, Frankfurt, Geneva, Innsbruck, Milan, Munich, Nicosia, Paris, Zurich)

Newcastle (Dublin)

Southampton (Paris)

British Airways Offices in Europe

Amsterdam: Leidseplein 23 (tel. 22 93 33).

Ankara: 127 Atatürk Bulvari (tel. 12 84 02).

Athens: 10 Othonos Street (tel. 323 04 76).

Barcelona: Paseo de Gracia (tel. 215 21 12).

Basle: Centralbahnplatz 3/4 (tel. 22 40 11).

Belgrade: General Ždanova 33 (tel. 33 94 82).

Berlin: Kurfürstendamm 16 (tel. 69 10 21).

Bonn: Münsterplatz 5 (tel. 65 70 25).

Brussels: 142 Bd Adolphe-Max (tel. 18 35 00).

Bucharest: Bd Balcescu 22 (tel. 16 30 22).

Budapest: Apaczai Scere Janos utca (tel. 18 94 93).

Cologne: Burgmauer 12 (tel. 23 52 52).

Copenhagen: Vesterbrogade 2 B (tel. 14 60 00).

Dublin: 39 Westmoreland Street (tel. 77 28 21).

Düsseldorf: Berliner Allee 26 (tel. 800 31).

Florence: Piazza Antinori 2/7 (tel. 28 37 49).

Frankfurt: Friedenstrasse 1 (tel. 208 21).

Geneva: Chantepoulet 13 (tel. 31 40 50).

Hamburg: Ballindamm 17 (tel. 32 27 01).

Helsinki: Keskuskatu 5 (tel. 76 06 77).

Istanbul: Cumhuriyet Caddesi 10 (tel. 47 67 75).

Lisbon: Liberdade 23/27 (tel. 331 61).

Madrid: José Antonio 68 (tel. 247 53 00).

Marseilles: 75 Canebière (tel. 39 77 10).

Milan: Piazza Diaz 7 (tel. 87 81 51).

Moscow: National Hotel, Gorky Street, Room 375 (tel. 203 55 87).

Munich: Promenadenplatz 10 (tel. 29 21 21).

Naples: via Partenope 38 (Royal Hotel) (tel. 40 01 44).

Nice: 25 Promenade des Anglais (tel. 88 37 36).

Nicosia: c/o Cyprus Airways, 11 Stassinos Avenue (tel. 43 054).

Oslo: Kronprinsesse Marthas Plass 1 (tel. 41 77 50).

Paris: 129 Champs Elysées (tel. 742 46 30).

Prague: Stepanska 63 (tel. 24 08 47).

Reykjavik: Bankastraeti 11 (tel. 23112).

Rome: via Nazionale 6A (Hotel Quirinale) (tel. 48 99 56).

Shannon: Airport (tel. 61477).

Stockholm: Norrmalmstorg 1 (tel. 23 39 00).

Stuttgart: Bolzstrasse 6 (tel. 22 30 01).

Tel Aviv: 59 Ben Yehuda Street (tel. 22 92 51).

Turin: via Arsenale 25 (tel. 51 32 32).

Valletta: 12 Kingsgate (tel. Central 29324).

Vienna: Kärntner Ring 10 (tel. 65 76 91).

Warsaw: 49 Krucza (tel. 28 94 31).

Zurich: Bahnhofstrasse 100 (tel. 25 54 54).

In London, for information and bookings (by letter only) apply to West London Air Terminal, Cromwell Road, S.W.7.

Booking by telephone (24 hour service): Dorland Hall, Lower Regent Street, S.W. 1 (tel. 370 5411).

Information about departures and arrivals: Heathrow Airport (tel. 759 3131); West London Air Terminal (tel. 370 4224).

Air France

The French national airline, Air France, operates numerous services between France and Britain. Among the main routes are Paris-London (very frequent daily services), Paris-Manchester Nice-London, Marseilles-London, Lyons-London and Lille-London. Services from Dinard to Jersey and London and from Nantes to London are also operated by other companies: apply for information to Air France.

Addresses of Air France

Paris: 119 Champs Elysées (tel. 225 70 50).

   30 rue Faubourg-Poissonnière (tel. 824 46 00).

   Esplanade des Invalides (tel. 468 96 20).

   2 rue Scribe (tel. 073 41 00).

   4 bis Place Pereire (tel. 425 75 93).

   Bookings by telephone: 535 66 00.

   Bookings by letter: B.P. 33-813, Paris (CCP Paris 21 272 08) 535 66 00).

   Flight information: tel. 535 68 00.

Ajaccio: 3 Bd Roi-Jérôme (tel. 1076-263 061).

Algiers: Immeuble Mauretania, Carrefour de l'Agha (tel. 64 90 10); Dar el Beïda Airport (tel. 76 10 18, 77 07 95, 77 14 33).

Beirut: Immeuble Esseyli, Place Riad-Sohl (tel. 25 10 20).

Bordeaux: 29 rue Esprit des Lois (tel. 52 47 00).

Brussels: 48 Bd Adolphe-Max (tel. 18 67 00).

Deauville (summer only): 66 Avenue Gén. Leclerc (tel. 88 27 21).

Geneva: 12 Quai Gén. Guisan (tel. 25 83 50).

Istanbul: Cumhuriyet Caddesi 7 (tel. 47 11 30).

London: 158 New Bond Street, W. 1 (tel. 499 9511).

Lyons: 10 Quai Jules Courmont (tel. 42 57 01).

Marseilles: 14 Canebière (tel. 21 08 60).

Montreal: 1265 Peel Street (tel. 861 5813).

Nantes: Palais de la Bourse (tel. 73 45 52).

New York: 683 Fifth Avenue (tel. 765 3000).

Nice: 7 Avenue Gustave V (tel. 80 38 80).

Rome: via Vittorio Veneto (tel. 47 88 41).

Strasbourg: 11 rue Vieux Marché aux Vins (tel. 32 00 67).

Teheran: 307 Avenue Shah Reza (tel. 66252).

Toulouse: 2 Boul. de Strasbourg (tel. 62 84 04).

Other Airlines

British Caledonian Airways: 65-67 Regent Street, London W.1 (tel. 828 9711).

Skyways International: Victoria Coach Station, 33 Elizabeth Street, London S.W.1 (tel. 730 9681); 8 bis Place de la République, Paris (tel. 357 85 59). Services from Paris to London (via Beauvais Airport), Montpellier and Clermont to London, Ostend to London, and Paris to Derby (East Midlands Airport).

Domestic services

There are regular services from London to the larger towns in Btitain, and between these other towns, operated by *British Airways* and a number of independent airlines (*North-East Airlines, British Midland Airways, British Island Airways, Cambrian Airways, Caledonian/BUA, Channel Airways, Danair Services*, etc.). There are bus services throughout the day and night between Heathrow Airport and West London Air Terminal, Cromwell Road, S.W.7; the journey takes 50 minutes. Gatwick Airport is connected with Victoria Station by rail-car (20 minutes).

By way of example, the flight from London to Edinburgh takes 1 hr 20 min., London-Jersey 50 min., Glasgow-Southampton 75 min., Aberdeen-Lerwick 55 min., Penzance-Scilly 15 min. There are 6 flights daily between London-Liverpool and London-Manchester, 2 flights daily between London and Inverness.

Addresses:

Aberdeen: British Airways, 335-7 Union Street, AB9 1WH (tel. 53311).

Barra: British Airways, Northbay (tel. Northbay 201).

Belfast: British Airways, Commonwealth House, Castle Street, BT1 GW (tel. 40522).

Birmingham: British Airways, 100 New Street (tel. 643 9955).

Bristol: British Airways, 35 College Green (tel. 298181).

Campbeltown: British Airways, Machrihanish Airport (tel. and 2571 and 2686).

Cardiff: Air Booking Centre, Wood Street (tel. 397071).

Edinburgh: British Airways, 135 Princes Street (tel. 225 2525).

Glasgow: British Airways, 122 St Vincent Street (tel. 332 9666).

Guernsey: British Airways, 4 South Esplanade, St Peter Port (tel. 24433).

Inverness: British Airways, Station Square, Academy Street (tel. 33821).

Islay: British Airways, Glenegedale Airport (tel. Port Ellen 22).

Isle of Man: Cambrian Airways, Coach/Air Terminal, Lord Street, Douglas (tel. Douglas 3606).

Isles of Scilly: British Airways Helicopters Ltd, Airport, St Mary's (tel. Scillonia 646).

Jersey: British Airways, 59 Esplanade, St Helier (tel. Central 22201).

Leeds: British Airways, 32 The Headrow (tel. 36801).

Liverpool: British Airways, 66 Lord Street (tel. 709 0123).

London: **West London Air Terminal,** Cromwell Road, S.W.7.
British Airways, Dorland Hall, Lower Regent Street, S.W.1 (tel. 370 5411).

British Airways, 101-2 Cheapside, EC1V 6DT.

British Airways, 107 New Bond Street, W.1.

British Airways, Hilton Hotel, Park Lane, W.1.

British Airways, Terminal House, Grosvenor Gardens, S.W.1.

British Airways, 457 Strand, W.C.2.

Manchester: British Airways, Speakers House, 39 Deansgate (tel. 832 7234).

Newcastle: British Airways, 21 Blackett Street (tel. Durham 64949).

Nottingham: British Airways, 6 Beastmarket Hill (tel. Loughborough 68641).

Orkney: British Airways, 69 Albert Street, Kirkwall (tel. Kirkwall 3359).

Penzance: British Airways Helicopters Ltd, Penzance Heliport (tel. 3871).

Shetland: British Airways, Sumburgh Airport (tel. Sumburgh 203); Ganson Bros, Lerwick (tel. Lerwick 11).

Southampton: British Airways, 161 High Street (tel. Fareham 82721).

Stornoway: British Airways, 81 Cromwell Street (tel. 3105).

Wick: British Airways, 82 High Street (tel. 2294).

IX. MOTORING

Travelling by car is certainly the best way to see Britain. It enables you to work out your own route, select the particular sights you want to see, stay as long as you like in each place; and above all it allows you to visit the remotest little villages. The roads throughout the country are excellent.

Bringing in your car; see p. 1061.

Motoring organisations

Automobile Association (AA), Fanum House, Leicester Square, London W.C.2 (tel. 01-839 8811).

Royal Automobile Club (RAC), 83-85 Pall Mall, London S.W.1 (tel. 01-930 4343); Paris office 8 Place Vendôme (tel. 742 40 01).

Royal Scottish Automobile Club (RSAC), 242 West George Street, Glasgow C.2 (tel. 041-248 4444).

The motoring organisations have offices throughtou Britain, and at the main ports and airports, which provide an excellent information service and sell road maps and a variety of useful publications, including the AA Touring Guides to England, Scotland and Wales and the RAC Guide and Handbook.

Information about road conditions, weather and traffic conditions round London can be obtained by telephoning 01-246 8021. Similar information for other areas is available from telephone numbers shown in the local telephone directory or from the AA.

Motorways. Although Britain was behind some other countries in starting the construction of motorways, there is now a considerable network, which is still being developed. The motorways are designated by the letter M followed by a number. Among the motorways of most interest to visitors are the following:

M 1: London-Leicester-Leeds, with continuation via M 18 to Newcastle.

M 2: London-Dover.

M 3: London-Winchester-Southampton.

M 4: London-Bristol-Wales.

M 5: Birmingham-Bristol, for Cornwall.

M 6: branches off M 1, providing a connection from London to Birmingham, Manchester and Carlisle.

There are shorter stretches of motorway in other areas with heavy traffic, e.g. M 62 between Leeds and Manchester, M 8 between Edinburgh and Glasgow, M 40 between London and Oxford. Much of A 1 (the Great North Road) is of motorway standard.

No tolls are payable on British motorways.

Roads. Both main and secondary roads in Britain and well made and well maintained. The secondary roads tend sometimes to be winding, but they are less crowded than the main roads, which carry a heavy traffic, particularly at weekends.

Main trunk roads are designated by the letter A, secondary roads by the letter B. The whole country is divided into nine zones related to the nine principal roads A 1 to A 9, the numbering of intermediate roads being related to that of the principal road. The following are the nine principal roads, with their traditional names:

A 1, London to Edinburgh by the east coast route, the Great North Road.

A 2, London to Dover via Canterbury, the Dover Road.

A 3, London to Portsmouth, the Portsmouth Road.

A 4, London to Bristol, the Bath Road.

A 5, London-Shrewsbury-Holyhead, the Holyhead Road (Watling Street).

A 6, London-Manchester-Carlisle, the Carlisle Road.

A 7, Edinburgh-Carlisle.

A 8, Edinburgh-Glasgow.

A 9, Edinburgh-John o' Groats.

Bridges. A number of large new road bridges have been built in recent years, considerably shortening the distance between some of the principal towns on the main tourist routes: over the Firth of Forth (Edinburgh-Perth), the Firth of Tay (Dundee-St Andrews), the Clyde (the Erskine Bridge, downstream from Glasgow) and the Severn (Bristol-Cardiff). Tolls are payable on these bridges.

The Highway Code. Visitors from abroad will find it useful to study the Highway Code, which can be bought at a very modest price; leaflets summarising the main provisions of the code are available (with editions in French and German) at ports.

The main thing for a foreign visitor to remember is that traffic goes on the left, with overtaking on the right. Road signs and markings (illustrated in the Highway Code) mostly follow the international pattern.

At the junction of a minor road with a major road a continuous white line with the word "Stop" means that a car emerging from the minor road must stop on the line, whether there is any traffic on the main road or not. A double line of white dashes, sometimes with the words "Give way", means that the car on the minor road must slow down, ready to stop if there is traffic on the main road.

A pattern of crisscross yellow lines at a road junction means that you cannot enter the junction until your exit is clear.

Zones within which parking is controlled are usually marked by yellow lines along the edge of the pavement (double, single or broken). The timing and extent of the restrictions are indicated either on plaques on the pavement or at the beginning of the controlled zone.

Speed limits should be strictly observed. The present limits are 30 m.p.h. in built-up areas, 40 or 50 m.p.h. on roads so marked, 60 m.p.h. on ordinary roads outside built-up areas, and 70 m.p.h. on roads with dual carriageways and motorways.

Car sleepers. Trains carrying cars and their passengers, with reserved seats, couchettes or sleepers, operate all over Britain between April/May and the end of September. At other times of year there are limited services in which the passengers travel in a different train from the car. For further information and booking forms, apply to the *Motorail Reservation Office*, British Rail, Kensington (Olympia) Station, London W 14, or in Paris to the British Rail office, 12 Boulevard de la Madeleine.

Road maps. The British Tourist Authority produces a map of Britain for tourists and regional folders with maps. Road maps are also published by some of the big petrol companies. For more detail there are the excellent Ordnance Survey maps on the 1:50,000 scale.

Car hire. There are numerous car hire firms with offices all over Britain, hiring cars of all types, with or without driver; addresses can be obtained from British Tourist Authority offices. Formalities are reduced to the minimum. As a rule the hirer must have held a driving licence for not less than a year, and for insurance reasons cars are not usually hired to drivers under 21 or over 65-70.

Arrangements can be made to have a hired car waiting for you on arrival in Britain. It can then be left at your point of departure (which need not be the same as your point of arrival). Cars without drivers (self-drive hire) are usually hired by the day, week or month: there is often a reduction for hires of three weeks or more. The rates are much lower in spring and autumn than in the main season.

Ferries in Scotland. It is worth remembering that some ferries in Scotland, particularly in the north and west, do not operate on Sundays.

Travel by bus. There are bus services, with comfortable modern buses, covering every corner of the country, and bus travel is one of the cheapest ways of getting about Britain. Apart from the scheduled services there are a variety of excursions, ranging from day or half-day trips to longer circuits of 3 days or 3 weeks. Seats on these excursions, particularly for weekend trips, are best booked some time in advance.

Information about bus services in Britain can be obtained from the Victoria Bus Station, Buckingham Palace Road, London S.W.1.

Coachmaster tickets, bought through a travel agency before departure, provide unlimited travel on the main through bus routes and on day and half-day trips throughout England, Scotland and Wales. These tickets can also be bought by foreign visitors, on presentation of their passport, from Coastal Coaches Ltd, at Victoria Bus Station, or from other bus companies.

In London the *Red Rover* tickets issued by London Transport allow unlimited travel in central London (red buses). *Green Rover* tickets cover travel on the Green Line buses. *Golden Rover* tickets cover travel on Green Line buses and provincial bus services. For visitors spending a week or a fortnight in London the "Go as you please" tickets issued by London Transport are a good bargain; see p. 1113.

Measurements. Visitors from abroad may find it helpful to have some tables of equivalence between British and metric measurements;

Distances

1 metre	39.37 inches
1 kilometre	5/8 mile
1.6 km	1 mile
50 km	31 miles
100 km	62 miles
160 km	100 miles

Volumes

0.56 litre	1 pint
1 litre	1.76 pints
4.54 litres	1 gallon
5 litres	1.1 gallon
20 litres	4.5 gallons
50 litres	11 gallons

Temperature

Centigrade	Fahrenheit
0°	32°
10	50
15.6	60
21	70
26.7	80
32	90
37.8	100
49	120
100	212

Tyre pressure

lb per sq. in.	kg per sq. cm
18	1.26
20	1.40
22	1.54
24	1.68
26	1.82
28	1.96
30	2.10
32	2.25
34	2.39
36	2.53

In Britain *petrol consumption* is expressed as so many miles per gallon—the converse of the Continental practice of expressing it as so many litres per 100 kilometres. A consumption of 10 litres per 100 km is roughly equivalent to 28 miles per gallon on the British calculation.

X. SPORT

Britain has long been known as a country addicted to sport, and some varieties of sport are peculiar to the British.

Cricket. The two best known cricket grounds in the world are Lord's and the Oval in London, but every town in England and many villages have their own cricket ground, where visitors

may spend a pleasant and restful afternoon, even if they find
the proceedings a little puzzling. It is well to have a friend
with you who can explain the intricacies of the game, but this
is not essential for enjoyment of the occasion. The cricketing
season begins in May. The game is much less popular in Scotland than in England.

Association football. This is a game which needs no further
explanation; born in England, it has become international.
The season begins on the last Saturday in August and ends
on the first Saturday in May. Wembley Stadium in London
is the Mecca of football fans. Most of the big games are played
by professional teams, of which there are over a hundred: in
addition there are some 30,000 amateur clubs, and the smallest
village has its own team. Football is particularly popular in
Scotland, and big matches in Edinburgh and Glasgow excite
an almost religious enthusiasm.

Rugby football. Although there are professional teams in
the North of England (Rugby League), rugby is mainly an
amateur game, played under Rugby Union rules. The big
events of the year are the international matches between England,
Wales, Scotland, Ireland and France, played at Twickenham
(London), Cardiff, Edinburgh, Dublin and Paris.

Tennis. There are innumerable tennis courts all over the
country on which visitors can play on payment of a modest
fee. The main event is the international championship played
at Wimbledon (London) in June and early July.

Golf. Golf has become a very popular sport all over the
country, as it has long been in Scotland. There are more golf
courses in Britain than in any other country in the world,
and they are of course particularly numerous (and relatively
cheap) in Scotland. St Andrews, on the Fife coast is the "home
of golf", and the Old Course there is its most sacred shrine.
There are other noted courses at Gleneagles and Troon in
Scotland and at Sunningdale and Sandwich in England.

The rules for the admission of visitors vary in the different
clubs, but visitors may be assured of finding a good course
and a warm welcome wherever they go. Charges are much
lower than on the Continent.

Horse racing. There are over 100 racecourses in Britain,
and race meetings are held almost every day of the week except
Sundays. The flat racing season begins with the Lincolnshire

Handicap in March and ends with the November Handicap at Manchester.   There is steeplechasing throughout the year except in July and August.   There are a number of important racecourses in the London area—Ascot, Epsom (scene of the Derby, late May or early June), Kempton Park, Lingfield Park, Newbury, Windsor, Newmarket.

Greyhound racing.   This is also a popular sport in Britain, and there are greyhound tracks in all the larger towns.

Riding.   All over the country there are stables where horses can be hired by the hour, by the day or for longer periods. Pony trekking is a popular way of seeing the country, and many hotels in country areas offer facilities and have horses for hire.   Hotels with accommodation for horses bear the plaque of the Horse and Pony Club.   Before undertaking an independent tour on horseback it is well to check the route with the stable from which you hire your horse.

Hunting.   Fox hunting takes place during the winter.   There are hunts in many parts of the country, but the great fox-hunting country is in central England (Northamptonshire and Leicestershire).   Vivitors will be welcome to join the hunt, but they will be expected to contribute towards expenses (the "cap").

Stag hunting is practised on Exmoor: the season begins in August.

Visitors from continental Europe may care to be reminded that in Britain "hunting" does not involve the use of guns. The pursuit of game with guns is "shooting", not "hunting".

Shooting and fishing.   Shooting is a popular sport in may parts of the country.   In some places it is free: elsewhere a modest fee is payable.   Some hotels offer shooting to residents. Deer-stalking is a great Highland sport but tends to be exclusive and expensive: the same can be said of grouse-shooting.

There is good trout and salmon fishing in Scotland.   Hampshire is fly-fishing country: wet-fly fishing is to be had in many areas, particularly in Wales.

A permit for fishing salmon and sea trout costs a few pounds for the whole season.   A special permit valid for two weeks in a particular area can be obtained at modest cost, and can be extended to other areas at additional charge.   No permit is necessary for fishing brown trout, but fishing is prohibited by law before 15 February.

Sailing and boating. There are many sailing clubs along the coasts of England, Scotland and Wales. Cowes on the Isle of Wight and the Clyde in Scotland are notable sailing centres. Most clubs hold regattas in summer. There is also plenty of scope for sailing without belonging to a club.

There is pleasant rowing on many rivers and lakes and along the coasts. Well known competitive events are the Henley regatta on the Thames in July and the famous Oxford and Cambridge boat race from Putney to Mortlake, also on the Thames, in spring.

Swimming. There are many swimming pools, indoor and open-air, throughout the country, and there is also sea bathing at the many coastal resorts (though the temperature of the water is low by Mediterranean standards).

Climbing. There is ample scope for climbing and hill walking in Scotland, North Wales and the Lake District. Scotland offers the widest range of opportunities, with Ben Nevis, the highest peak in Britain (4406 ft), and the mighty Cairngorm range, with six peaks over 4000 feet. There is also skiing in this area in winter.

Full information about sport in Britain can be obtained from the British Travel Authority.

XI. ENTERTAINMENTS

Admission to museums and art galleries is often free. The hours of opening vary from place to place; museums and galleries are usually closed on Sunday mornings and sometimes on one day during the week, but they may have a late opening on one evening in the week. Frequently the opening hours are shorter from October to April, and some places (including particularly the historic old country houses which are still lived in) may be closed during this period.

Many ancient and historical monuments (castles, abbeys, Roman remains, etc.) are in the care of the State. There are small charges for admission, but a season ticket can be obtained at reasonable cost. Other old buildings and beauty spots are the property of voluntary bodies concerned with their preservation, the National Trusts for England and Wales and for Scotland.

Churches in England and Wales are usually open daily, from 8 or 9 in the morning to 6, but visitors are not admitted during services. In Scotland the hours of opening may be more limited.

Excellent illustrated booklets giving full details about museums and galleries and about historic buildings are published by ABC Travel Guides Ltd and are brought regularly up to date. They can be easily obtained through tourist offices.

Cinemas. These usually open about 12.30 or 1 (3 p.m. on Sundays), with the last showing beginning about 8.30. In the larger towns some cinemas open at 10.30 and have a late showing on Sunday evenings (at 10.30 or 11). Foreign films are usually shown in the original version with sub-titles. No tips are expected by staff. Smoking is permitted.

Theatres. The London theatres offer a wide range of excellent productions. Companies from the capital often tour in the provinces, but a number of towns have companies of their own—e.g. Birmingham, Liverpool, Manchester, Bath, Norwich (Maddermarket Theatre), Glasgow (Citizens' Theatre), Bristol (Old Vic) and of course Stratford. Shakespeare's plays are performed daily during the summer at Stratford, and frequently throughout the year in London. Performances usually begin between 7.30 and 8.30.

There are also theatre clubs which give performances on Sundays. Admission is restricted to members and their guests.

The prices of seats are always shown at theatre booking offices, which are usually open from 10 a.m. to 10 p.m. Seats in boxes, the stalls, dress and upper circles can be booked through ticket agencies, either directly or by telephone, at a small additional charge. In some theatres the cheaper seats (pit and gallery) can also be booked.

Music. The music season in London and other towns in Britain offers abundant opportunities for the music-lover. There are a number of well-known orchestras—the London Symphony Orchestra, the Royal Philharmonic Orchestra, the London Philharmonic Orchestra, the B.B.C. Symphony Orchestra, the Liverpool Philharmonic Orchestra, the Halle Orchestra, the Scottish National Orchestra—and among conductors there have been such well-known personalities as Sir Thomas Beecham, Sir Adrian Boult, Sir Malcolm Sargent, Sir John Barbirolli, George Weldon and Ian Whyte.

In London ballet and opera are produced at the Royal Opera House, Covent Garden, and the Sadlers Wells Theatre. The

Promenade Concerts organised by the B.B.C. in the Royal Albert Hall are a popular annual feature.

Festivals. A visit to one of Britain's famous festival towns can make a memorable holiday. Apart from the beauty of the towns themselves there is a particular charm in enjoying in the pleasant setting of a holiday town a series of concerts, operas, plays and exhibitions of a quality normally associated with a great capital city. The festival season begins early in the year: the main events are the Shakespeare Festival in Stratford-upon-Avon (March to September); festivals at Bath (May), Cheltenham (July), Glyndebourne (July) and Haslemere (July): the Malvern Festival of Dramatic Art (August); the Royal National Eisteddfod at Caerphilly (August); the International Eisteddfod, Llangollen (July); the Edinburgh International Festival of Music and Drama (August-September); the Three Choirs Festival in Gloucester Cathedral (September); and the Pitlochry Festival of Music and Drama (May-September). The festivals usually last for two or three weeks in the months indicated.

The *Edinburgh* Festival has become an annual event of international importance at which musicians, actors and artists of world reputation perform. It is accompanied by the famous Military Tattoo on the Castle Esplanade.

The Shakespeare Festival at *Stratford* takes place in one of the most up-to-date theatres in Britain. Visitors attending the festival also have the opportunity of seeing an attractive little country town and its beautiful and typically English surroundings.

The *Malvern* Festival can claim credit for the first performances of a number of plays by G.B. Shaw and other noted playwrights.

The *Bath* Assembly has become a popular spring event. It has a programme of opera, drama and music, and describes itself as a festival for the young of all ages.

The famous Three Choirs Festival held at *Gloucester* is devoted to sacred music. The choir of some three hundred singers is drawn from the Worcester, Gloucester and Hereford choirs.

Cheltenham's annual Festival of British Contemporary Arts is one of the most important musical events of the season. It includes concerts, opera, drama and an exhibition of contemporary painting.

The *Canterbury* Festival includes special services in the Cathedral, a festival play and concerts in the cloisters.

Folk dancing, singing, etc. Some visitors may have the opportunity of watching traditional folk dancing on a village green, in front of a cathedral or elsewhere (Lincoln, Hereford, etc.), but no spectacle of the kind holds so much popular appeal as the famous Highland gatherings and Highland games of Scotland, held between June and September. Every little town in the Highlands seems to have its own, usually associated with the local clan. The most popular events of this kind are the Braemar and Inverness gatherings.

The Welsh have their Eisteddfods, with folk singing and dancing and poetry recitals. The Lake District has its rush-bearing ceremonies in July and August—harvest thanksgiving celebrations in which the churches are decorated with flowers: and throughout the country the churches have harvest thanksgiving services in the early autumn, in which the fruits of the harvest are displayed.

Radio and television. The B.B.C. (British Broadcasting Corporation), an independent public corporation drawing its revenue from licence fees, transmits two television programmes, BBC 1 and BBC 2 (PAL system), and four radio programmes, including one (Radio 3) largely devoted to music. There are also a number of independent television companies financed by revenue from advertisements in the different parts of the country, under the general supervision of the Independent Television Authority, and a small number of local radio stations also financed by advertisements. Programmes are published in the newspapers.

XII. FOOD AND DRINK

British cooking has a worse name than it deserves. It has the advantage of using ingredients of high quality; the meat in particular is excellent.

Roast meat of any description (besides beef, there are mutton, pork, poultry and all types of game) forms the staple item in restaurant menus all over the ountry. The accompaniments to the "roast" are all-important, and admirable in their ingenuity. Roast beef demands roast potatoes, a generous slice of Yorkshire pudding, and, of course, horseradish sauce, as essential to roast beef as mint sauce is to roast lamb. Mutton demands red currant jelly or a sauce made from onions or capers: red currant jelly is also the accepted companion of venison. Apple sauce, together with a herb stuffing, is considered necessary for the full enjoyment of pork, duck or goose. Chicken and turkey, on the other hand, are served with bread sauce and a sausage or slice of bacon.

Fish is another food with which British cooks can generally be relied upon to excel, even in the cheapest restaurants. No visitor should return home without having sampled a Dover sole fried or grilled, and a Torbay or lemon sole. Halibut and turbot are also usually well cooked, but far more exclusively British is the kipper, a herring matured in wood-smoke, which is a popular breakfast dish in all districts. The Scots excel in the cooking of fresh herring. Generally speaking, the sauces which accompany fish follow continental recipes.

Continental visitors accustomed to a simple meal of rolls and coffee to start the day will find a British breakfast a highly interesting, if lengthy, experience. It commences with a substantial dish either of cereals served with milk, or, more traditionally, of porridge—an oatmeal gruel which is flavoured with salt in Scotland, where it originated, and with sugar or syrup in the south. An alternative to this is grapefruit. Then follows the main course, which may consist of a fried egg with bacon, or some other egg dish, or else a kipper. The meal concludes with buttered toast spread with orange marmalade. (Note that in Britain "marmalade" is always made with orange or lemon. All other preserves are called jams). Either tea or coffee is drunk at breakfast.

Afternoon tea is another occasion which the British may properly claim to have invented. This is also a fairly lengthy affair, which may comprise, besides buttered bread or toast with jam, sandwiches and a wide variety of rich cakes, such interesting delicacies as crumpets, scones, splits (in Devonshire and Cornwall), parkin (a form of gingerbread common in Yorkshire, Cumberland and Westmorland) and baps and bannocks (in Scotland).

In Scotland the visitor may encounter the old-fashioned Scottish "high tea", usually served at any time between 5 and 7, consisting of meat or fish as well as tea and its accompaniments of bread or scones. In many families this takes the place of dinner—supplemented perhaps by a late evening cup of tea while watching television.

The main course, both at lunch and dinner, is invariably followed by a sweet. This can consist of ice cream, fruit or cake (such as is customary on the Continent) but the visitor who is determined to sample the traditional native fare is recommended to order instead a "pie" or a "pudding". The pie, in which the fruit (normally apple) is entirely enclosed in delicious pastry, is another notable triumph of the British kitchen. Pies may sometimes form the main course of a meal, in which case it is meat that is enclosed by the pastry: steak and kidney, and veal and ham, are among the most popular constituents.

Britain produces many fine cheeses, of which Cheddar and Stilton are the most celebrated. Though they still retain the names of the districts in which they originated they can usually be obtained in all parts of the country. Among the more localised cheeses are Caerphilly (South Wales), Dunlop (Scotland) and Wensleydale (Yorkshire).

It must be admitted that many of the restaurants of London are nowadays so cosmopolitan in character that newcomers to the capital may sometimes experience difficulty in choosing the right place in which to sample the traditional food of the country. It is often the older houses that have best preserved the secrets of fine English cooking. Hence it is that the inns of London, some of them dating back for centuries, are reliable strongholds of the native cuisine. Of these, the Cheshire Cheese, situated in an obscure alley off Fleet Street, is particularly well known to overseas visitors.

Almost every part of the country has its own specialised local dishes, which will be proudly set before the visitor from abroad. Devon and Cornwall are famous for their clotted cream and their junket (made from curdled milk). In Cornwall there is the added attraction of Cornish pasties—delicious small pies to which clotted cream is added to the main ingredients. The other well-known pies are the superb pork pies of Melton Mowbray in Leicestershire and the partan (crab) pie of the Isle of Skye. Whitstable (Kent) and Colchester (Essex) are noted for oysters: Aylesbury (Buckinghamshire) for its ducks, and Norfolk for its turkeys. And it should be mentioned that the delicately-flavoured red grouse is found nowhere else in the world but in Britain, and may be ordered for dinner any time after the "Glorious Twelfth" of August when the shooting season begins.

Among the infinite variety of local cakes one should mention Scottish shortbread, which melts in the mouth like the butter of which it is made: the delicious and prettily-named Maids of

Honour obtainable in Richmond, Surrey: the sugary buns of Bath and Chelsea: and the miscellaneous oat-cakes, of which the Staffordshire version is particularly good. Lancashire hot-pot is a celebrated stew: stargazy pie is a rich west country dish comprising fish, eggs and cream: and the haggis of Scotland is a highly spiced dish made up of the heart, lung and liver of a sheep or calf, chopped up with oatmeal, onions and other seasoning and enclosed in a sheep's stomach.

There is no doubt that when properly cooked the best British dishes—Lancashire hotpot, fresh grilled salmon, Dover sole or roast pork with sage and onion stuffing and bread sauce—can stand comparison with the traditional masterpieces of French cuisine. Visitors will do well, therefore, to seek out the typical British restaurants which can be found all over the country, from Land's End to John o' Groats.

Drinks. Wine is not drunk in Britain to anything like the same extent as in some continental countries, though good vintages are obtainable everywhere and there is a good range of reasonably priced wines. The usual everyday drink is beer or in some parts of the country cider, either bottled or draught. The hop-fields of Kent and Herefordshire and the apple orchards of the West country bear witness to the scale on which these two national drinks are consumed. The hop-picking season is one of the events of the year in Kent, and the traditional old ceremony of "wassailing" still takes place in the West country orchards as a means of ensuring a good crop.

Beer is the real national drink, accompanied in Scotland by the national specialty of Scotch whisky. Particularly in England the pub is an important centre of social life, noted for its friendly atmosphere: in Scotland the pub has been by tradition a more exclusively male preserve, but the tendency now is for Scottish pubs to approximate more closely to the English pattern.

Beer is divided into four main types: ale, mild ale, stout and Burton. *Pale ale*, more generally known as "*bitter*" when on draught, is made from highest quality malt. The light colour is no guide as to its strength, and it is not necessarily weaker than darker beers. Varieties of pale ale include "light ales" and "family ales". *Mild ale* is a dark, full-flavoured beer which, again, is brewed from malt but by a slightly different process. Brown ale in bottle is usually a mild ale, but may also be beer of the Burton type. *Stout* is sold in bottle and on draught. It is a beer brewed from highly dried full-flavoured malts, with the addition of a proportion of roasted malt or barley which gives it its colour and characteristic flavour. *Burton* is a strong ale (of the same type as pale ale but darker) which has had prolonged cellar treatment. Although not necessarily made in Burton it is based on the types of strong beer made famous there.

Lager is the name given in Britain to light beers of continental type, which have become increasingly popular in recent years. Lagers are served chilled, unlike ordinary British beer, which is drunk at room warmth.

Whisky, or *Scotch*, is the indigenous product of Scotland par excellence. Most of the whisky drunk in Scotland is blended from anything up to twenty kinds of grain and malt whisky, all fully matured and carefully selected by the blender (the particular blend for each brand being of course a carefully guarded trade secret). For connoisseurs there are the unblended malt whiskies, each associated with the name of a famous distillery.

A pleasant drink on a warm summer day is *cider cup*, a long drink consisting of chilled cider with the addition of fruit and a little white wine. Among refreshing non-alcoholic drinks are *ginger ale* and *ginger beer*.

In the south of England there are a few vineyards producing excellent wine, but the traditional British wines are made from a variety of ingredients other than grapes, some of them rather unexpected—elderberries, blackberries, damsons, dandelions and nettles. They can be pleasant drinks, and surprisingly strong. In the cherry-growing region of Kent *cherry brandy* is made. In Cornwall the old drink, *mead*, is still made from honey.

It should be remembered that public houses have strictly controlled opening hours.

XIII. SHOPPING IN LONDON

London can claim to be one of the oldest shopping centres in the world, and down the centuries its shops have acquired characteristics and traditions which almost make them national institutions. Thanks to the maintenance of a family tradition, many London shops have preserved into our own day something of the grace of an earlier age, and shops with 18th century fronts can be found side by side with modern establishments glittering with glass and chrome-plating. In Holborn the visitor will find a row of shops sheltering under the wooden galleries of London's only surviving Tudor domestic building.

In this section we give a brief account of the main West End shopping streets. For fuller information see the British Tourist Authority publication "Shopping in London".

Piccadilly runs west from Piccadilly Circus. The largest shop in the Circus is *Swan and Edgar's* department store, founded a century and a half ago as a small draper's shop. On the opposite side is *Boot's*, the large chemist's with so many branches that there are two in Piccadilly Circus itself.

On the south side of Piccadilly are many shops which have become almost synonymous with the goods they sell. To the west of Prince's Arcade, in which there are a variety of small shops, is *Hatchards*, a bookshop which has been in business since 1797, with a graceful bow-windowed front giving it something of the distinction of a private library. In a handsome building farther along the street are *Fortnum and Mason*, provision merchants who have been here for 200 years and are still flourishing. Beyond the Piccadilly Arcade is *Robert Jackson*, grocer and wine-merchant since 1720.

No passer-by should miss the shop window of *Rowland Ward*, the beauty specialist. At the corner of St James's St is *Lincoln Bennett*, the famous hatter.

The **Burlington Arcade,** on the north side of Piccadilly, has survived for 130 years without apparent change. It is lined with small specialist shops.

Sackville Street, a short distance beyond the Piccadilly Hotel, still preserves the charm of the 18th century, with shops offering wares of the highest quality.

Off the south side of Piccadilly is a network of little streets, each with its own character—**Jermyn Street,** with three French restaurants, the Ecu de France, the Apéritif and Monseigneur: **Bury Street,** with a famous restaurant, Quaglino's, and many shops selling objets d'art: **King Street** and **Ryder Street,** also with many art shops: and **Duke Street,** which runs from Jermyn St to King St.

On the left-hand side of **St James's Street,** going down from Piccadilly, are two old and famous shops, *James Lock*, hatters since 1725, and *Berry Bros*, wine merchants whose records go back to 1765 and whose shop-front is even older. On the other side of the street, under two massive gilded hooks, is *Ogden Smith* (fishing tackle). Other noted shops in this street are *Hoopers* (coachbuilders) and *Sifton Praed* (books and maps).

In **Knightsbridge** there is a concentration of fashion shops—*Paul Elliot and Shwartz, Margaret Marks, Eve Valere, Wooland Brothers* and *Harvey Nichols*. From Knightsbridge **Sloane Street** runs south to **Sloane Square,** in which is the astonishing glass-fronted building occupied by *Peter Jones*. At the west end of Knightsbridge is the *Scotch House* (clothing made in Scotland).

Brompton Road is dominated by the great domed building of *Harrods*, the famous department store.

Kensington High Street, though not one of the great shopping streets, has much of interest to offer. On both sides of the street is *John Barker's*, who claim to supply all the needs of everyday life.

Between the Green Park and St James's Park and **Victoria Street** to the south is a labyrinth of little streets—Buckingham Gate, York St, Caxton St, etc.—with many antique shops.

Bond Street is to London what the Rue de la Paix is to Paris. On the west corner are *Scotts*, the famous hatters. Between Piccadilly and Burlington Gardens, where Old Bond St becomes New Bond St, are two theatre ticket agencies, *Ashton and Mitchell* (where Ascot racegoers receive their tickets) at No. 2 and *Alfred Hays* at No. 26. Here too are travel agencies covering every country in the world and four famous art dealers—*Agnew, Ackermann* (specialising in hunting pictures), *Leger and Son* and *Knoedler*. At the north end of Bond St are *Benson's*, one of Britain's leading watchmakers and jewellers.

In New Bond St French jewellers are well represented. The famous house of *Cartier* has its London headquarters at No. 175: at No. 26 is *Tessiers*, at No. 180 *Boucheron*. At the corner of Grafton St is *Asprey*, established here for over 120 years. Hatters are represented by *Henry Heath* (No. 172), *Herbert Johnson* (No. 38) and *Hillhouse*, at No. 11, in the narrowest part of the street. Charles Dickens was a customer of Hillhouse's shop, and one of his bills can still be seen there. Two centres of female fashion in New Bond St are *Fenwicks* (No. 63) and *Yves Saint-Laurent* (No. 113). At No. 143 is London's oldest chemist's shop, *Savory and Moore*, with an old-world shop front which is one of the finest things to be seen in the whole of Bond St.

The streets opening off both sides of Bond St have many of London's most elegant shops. In **Bruton Street,** at the far end of which is the green oasis of **Berkeley Square,** is the establishment of the Queen's dressmaker, *Norman Hartnell.* In **Conduit Street,** on the other side of Bond St, are the *Rolls-Royce* showrooms. **Brook Street,** where Handel lived during his stay in London, is dominated by *Claridge's Hotel* and is the centre of London's fashion trade. To the east are **Savile Row** and **Sackville Street,** with the world's best tailors.

South-west of Berkeley Square is **Curzon Street,** an old and fashionable street which runs into **Park Lane,** past the long white Regency-style front of Crewe House. Parallel to Bond St on the west are **Berkeley Street, Dover Street** and **Albemarle Street,** with more shops of the highest quality.

Regent Street, originally a fine conception by Nash, now rebuilt, is lined with shops on both sides. *Aquascutum* (No. 100), *Austin Reed* (No. 103) and *Jaeger* (No. 204) specialise in clothing for men. At No. 153 are *Hedges and Butler,* wine merchants since 1677 and still in the same family. Farther north are the gleaming *Galeries Lafayette.* **Carnaby Street,** parallel to Regent St on the east, is noted as the home of lively fashions for the young. The north end of Regent St runs into **Oxford Street,** a busy shopping street with many large department stores.

In **Haymarket** is the bay-windowed shop of *Fribourg and Treyer,* one of the oldest tobacconist's in the world. On the opposite side of Haymarket, behind His Majesty's Theatre, is the old-world *Royal Opera Arcade,* with a row of shops which might well pass unnoticed but which will satisfy the most discerning buyer, selling a wide variety of objets d'art, silver and hosiery.

Charing Cross Road is the book-hunter's paradise, with more new and secondhand bookshops than any other street in London, including the famous *Foyle's,* which claims to be the largest bookshop in the world. Many of the shops, particularly in the little side streets opening off Charing Cross Road, have open-air stalls which offer a tantalising range of choice for the browser.

Bargain-hunters and other addicts of open-air markets will find a happy hunting ground in *Portobello Road* (Saturdays), the *New Caledonian Market*, Bermondsey Square, S.E.1 (Fridays) and *Petticoat Lane*, the famous "flea-market" in Middlesex St (Sunday mornings).

Clothing sizes

Clothing and underwear

British	10	12	14	16	18	20
USA	8	10	12	14	16	18
Continental	42	44	46	48	50	52
Inches	32/34	34/36	36/38	38/40	40/42	42/44
Centimetres	81/88	86/91	91/96	96/102	102/107	107/112

Hats

British and USA	8	8½	9	9½	10	10½	11
Continental	0	1	2	3	4	5	6

Shirts

British	14	14½	15	15½	16	16½	17	17½
USA	14	14½	15	15½	15¾	16	16½	17
Continental	36	37	38	39	40	41	42	43

Shoes

British	3	3½ 4	4½ 5	5½ 6	6½ 7	7½ 8	8½ 9
USA	4½ 5	5½ 6	6½ 7	7½ 8	8½ 9	9½ 10	10
Continental	36	37	38	39	40	41	42

XIV. FOREIGN CONSULATES IN BRITAIN

In London

Afghanistan: 31 Princes Gate, SW7 1QQ, tel. 01-589 8891/2.
Algeria: 6 Hyde Park Gate, SW7, tel. 01-584 9501.
Andorra: French Consulate General.
Argentina: 53 Hans Place, SW1X OLB, tel. 01-584 1701/3.
Austria: 18 Belgrave Mews West, SW1X 8HU, tel. 01-235 3731.
Bahrein: 98 Gloucester Road, SW7 4AU, tel. 01-370 5213/3.
Belgium: 103 Eaton Square, SW1W 9AB, tel. 01-235 5422.

Bolivia: 106 Eccleston Mews, SW1, tel. 01-235 4255.

Brazil: 6 Deanery Street, W1Y 5HL, tel. 01-499 7441/4.

Bulgaria: 12 Queen's Gate Gardens, SW7 5NA, tel. 01-584 9400.

Burma: 19a Charles Street, W1X 8ER, tel. 01-499 8841.

Cambodia: see Khmer Republic.

Cameroun, United Republic of: 84 Holland Park, W 11, tel. 01-727 0771/3.

Central African Republic: French Consulate General.

Chad: French Consulate General.

Chile: 12 Devonshire Street, W1N 2DS, tel. 01-580 1023.

China, People's Republic: 31 Portland Place, W1N 3AG, tel. 01-636 5746.

Colombia: 140 Park Lane, W1Y 3DF, tel. 01-493 4565.

Congo (Brazzaville): French Consulate General.

Costa Rica: 8 Braemar Mansions, Cornwall Gardens, SW7 4AF, tel. 01-937 7749.

Cuba: 57 Kensington Court, W8 5OY, tel. 01-937 8226.

Czechoslovakia: 25 Kensington Palace Gardens, W8 4QY, tel. 01-229 1255.

Dahomey: Standbrook House, 2/5 Old Bond Street, W1X 3TB, tel. 01-493 7681.

Denmark: 67 Pont Street, SW1X OBQ, tel. 01-584 0102.

Dominican Republic: 4 Braemar Mansions, Cornwall Gardens, SW7 4AG, tel. 01-937 7116.

Ecuador: 3 Hans Crescent, SW1X OLN, tel. 01-584 2648.

Egypt: 19 Kensington Palace Gardens, W8 4QL, tel. 01-229 8818/9.

El Salvador: Flat 16, Edinburgh House, 9b Portland Place, W1N 3AA, tel. 01-636 9563.

Estonia: 167 Queensgate, SW7 5HE, tel. 01-589 5473.

Ethiopia: 17 Princes Gate, SW7 1PZ, tel. 01-589 7212.

Finland: 66 Chester Square, SW1W 9DX, tel. 01-730 0771/5.

France: 24 Rutland Gate, SW7, tel. 01-584 9628.

Gabon: 66 Drayton Gardens, SW10, tel. 01-370 6441/2.

Germany, Democratic Republic: 34 Belgrave Square, SW1, tel. 01-235 9941.

Germany, Federal Republic: 23 Belgrave Square, SW1X 8PZ, tel. 01-235 5033.

Greece: 49 Upper Brook Street, W1Y 2LB, tel. 01-499 2323/4.

Haiti: 17 Queen's Gate, SW7, tel. 01-581 0577.

Honduras: 48 George Street, W1, tel. 01-486 4880.

Hungary: 35b Eaton Place, SW1X 8BY, tel. 01-235 4462.

Iceland: 1 Eaton Terrace, SW1W 8EY, tel. 01-730 5131.

Indonesia: 38 Grosvenor Square, W1X 9AD, tel. 01-499 7661.

Iran: 50 Kensington Court, Kensington High Street, W8, tel. 01-937 5255.

Iraq: 21 Queen's Gate, SW7, tel. 01-584 7141.

Ireland: 17 Grosvenor Place, SW1X 7HR, tel. 01-235 2171

Israel: 2 Palace Green, W8 4QB, tel. 01-937 8091.

Italy: 38 Eaton Place, SW1X 8AN, tel. 01-235 4831/3.

Ivory Coast: 2 Upper Belgrave Street, SW1X 8BJ, tel. 01-235 6991.

Japan: 43/46 Grosvenor Street, W1X 0BA, tel. 01-493 6030.

Jordania: 6 Upper Phillimore Gardens, W8 7HB, tel. 01-937 3685/6.

Khmer Republic: 26 Townshend Road, NW8 6LH, tel. 01-722 8802.

Korea: 36 Cadogan Square, SW1X OJN, tel. 01-581 0247 and 0240.

Kuwait: 40 Devonshire Street, W1N 2AX, tel. 01-580 8471/6.

Laos: 5 Palace Green, W8, tel. 01-937 7001.

Latvia: 6 Holland Park Road, W14 8LZ, tel. 01-602.

Lebanon: 15 Palace Gardens Mews, W8, tel. 01-229 8485.

Liberia: 21 Prince's Gate, SW7, tel. 01-589 9405/7.

Libya: 58 Prince's Gate, SW7 2PW, tel. 01-589 5236.

Liechtenstein: see Switzerland.

Lithuania: 17 Essex Villas, W8 7BP, tel. 01-937 1588.

Luxembourg: 27 Wilton Crescent, SW1X 8SD, tel. 01-235 6961.

Malagasy (Madagascar): 33 Thurloe Square, SW7, tel. 01-584 3714.

Mexico: 8 Halkin Street, SW1X 7DW, tel. 01-235 6393/6.

Monaco: 4 Audley Square, W1Y 5DR, tel. 01-629 0734.

Mongolia: 7 Kensington Court, W8, tel. 01-937 0150.

Morocco: 49 Queens Gate Gardens, SW7, tel. 01-584 8827.

Nepal: 12a Kensington Palace Gardens, W8 4QU, tel. 01-229 1594 and 6231.

Netherlands: 38 Hyde Park Gate, SW7 5DP, tel. 01-584 5040.

Nicaragua: 8 Gloucester Road, SW7, tel. 01-584 3231.

Niger: French Consulate General.

Norway: 42 Lancaster Gate, W2 3NE, tel. 01-235 7151.

Oman: 33 Hyde Park Gate, SW7, tel. 01-584 6782.

Pakistan: 35 Lowndes Square, SW1X 9JN, tel. 01-235 2044.

Panama: Wheatsheaf House, 4 Carmelite Street, EC4Y 0BN, tel. 01-353 4792/3.

Paraguay: Braemar Lodge, Cornwall Gardens, SW7 4AQ, tel. 01-937 6629.

Peru: 52 Sloane Street, SW1X 9SP, tel. 01-235 6867.

Philippines: 9a Palace Green, Kensington, W8 4QE, tel. 01-937 3646.

Poland: 19 Weymouth Street, W1N 4EA, tel. 01-580 4324.

Portugal: 47 Wilton Crescent, SW1 8RU, tel. 01-235 6216.

Qatar: 10 Reeves Mews, South Audley Street, W1Y 3PB, tel. 01-499 8831 Ext. 7.

Romania: 4 Palace Green, W8, tel. 01-937 9667.

San Marino: see Italy.

Saudi Arabia: 27 Eaton Place, SW1X 8BW, tel. 01-235 8431.

Senegal: 11 Phillimore Gardens, W8 7QG, tel. 01-937 0925.

Somalia: 60 Portland Place, W1N 3DG, tel. 01-580 7148.

South Africa: Trafalgar Square, WC2 N5DP, tel. 01-930 4488.

Southern Yemen: 57 Cromwell Road, SW7, tel. 01-584 6607.

Soviet Union: 5 Kensington Palace Gardens, W8 4QS, tel. 01-229 3215/6.

Spain: 3 Hans Crescent, SW1, tel. 01-589 3234.

Sudan: 3 Cleveland Row, St. James's, SW1, tel. 01-839 8080.

Sweden: 23 North Row, W1R 2DN, tel. 01-499 9500.

Switzerland: 16-18 Montagu Place, London W1H 2BQ, tel. 01-723 0701.

Syria: 5 Eaton Terrace, SW1, tel. 01-730 0384.

Thailand: 39 Queen's Gate, SW7 5JB, tel. 01-589 2857.

Tunisia: 29 Princes Gate, SW7 1QG, tel. 01-584 8117.

Turkey: 46 Rutland Gate, SW7 1PE, tel. 01-589 0360.

United Arab Emirates: 30 Princes Gate, SW7, tel. 01-581 1281.

United States: American Embassy, Visa Unit, 5 Upper Grosvenor Street, W1A 2JB, tel. 01-499 5521.

Uruguay: 48 Lennox Gardens, SW1X 0DL, tel. 01-589 8735.

Venezuela: 71a Park Mansions, Knightsbridge, SW1 (Visa section), tel. 01-589 9916.

Vietnam: 12 Victoria Road, Kensington, W8 5RE, tel. 01-937 3765/6.

Yemen Arab Republic: 41 South Street W1, tel. 01-499 5246.

Yugoslavia: 19 Upper Phililmore Gardens, W8, tel. 01-937 3671.

Zaire: 26 Chesham Place, SW1, tel. 01-235 6137.

Outside London

Austria

Birmingham: 24 Harborne Road, Edgbaston, BI5 3AD, tel. 012-454 5131.

Edinburgh: 16 Heriot Row, EH3 6HR, tel. 031-556 2896.

Manchester: Dennis House, Marsden Street, M2 FD, tel. 061-832 5994.

Belgium

Aberdeen: 23 Market Street, tel. Aberdeen (0224) 29015/6.

Birmingham: 77 Colmore Row, tel. 021-236 5417.

Bristol: Gloucester Road, Avonmouth, B511 9BH, tel. 0272 3671.

Cardiff: Dascoe House, 54 Bute Street, tel. 0222-21491.

Edinburgh: 16 Bernard Street, EH6, tel. 031-554 5581.

Glasgow: Scottish Legal Building, 80 Blythswood Street C2, tel. 041-221 8550.

Hull: St. Andrew's Buildings, St. Andrew's Dock, tel. Hull (0482) 27464.

Liverpool: Wingate & Johnson Ltd., Cunard Building, L3 1EU, tel. 051-236 9931.

Manchester: Television House, Mount Street, M2 5WS, tel. 061-834 0482, 061-832 5331.

Newcastle-on-Tyne: Milburn House, tel. Newcastle (0632) 20523.

Southampton: Oxford House, College Street, tel. Southampton (0703) 22766/7.

Finland

Birmingham: Royal Mail House, Five Ways, 15, tel. 021-454 4381.

Bristol: 11/12 Queen Square, BS99 7JU, tel. (0722) 20461.

Cardiff: Pascoe House, 54 Bute Street, tel. Cardiff (0222) 21491.

Dover: 134/5 Snargate Street, Dover, tel. Dover 1201.

Glasgow: 259-261 Broomloan Road, SW1, tel. 041-427 74961.

Hull: 71 High Street, tel. Hull (0482) 25781.

Immingham: Immingham Dock, tel. Immingham (04692) 2387.

Leith: 50 East Fettes Avenue, EH4 1EQ, tel. 031-552 7101.

Liverpool: Percival Lane, Runcorn Ches, tel. Runcorn (09285) 75951.

Manchester: Northern Assurance Buildings, Princess Street, M2 4DN, tel. 061-834 1361.

Newcastle-upon-Tyne: Trapp and Co. Ltd., C Floor, Milburn House, NE 99 1CL, tel. Newcastle (0632) 28767.

Sheffield: Capital Steel Works, 3, tel. Sheffield (0742) 22071.

Southampton: Unity Chambers, Latimer Street, tel. Southampton (0703) 22248, 22157.

France

Cardiff: 129 Queen Street, tel. Cardiff (0222) 22742.

Edinburgh: 28 Regent Terrace, tel. 031-556 6266.

Jersey: 2 Westaway Chambers, Don Street, St Helier, tel. Central 21741.

Liverpool: Cunard Building, Pier Head, tel. 051-236 8685.

Germany (Federal Republic)

Edinburgh: 16 Eglinton Crescent, EH12 5DG, tel. 031-337 2323.

Liverpool: Pearl Assurance House, 55 Castle Street, tel. 051-236 0294.

Greece

Birmingham: 70/90 Coventry Road, 81D OSE, tel. 021-772 5757.

Bradford: 17 Manor Row, tel. Bradford (0274) 24211.

Bristol: Gloucester Road, Avonmouth, BS11 9BH, tel. Bristol (02752) 3671.

Cardiff: 45/47 George Street, CF1 6BU, tel. Cardiff (0222) 22026.

Edinburgh: 9 Regent Terrace, tel. 031-556 1701.

Glasgow: 91 West George Street, tel. 041-248 7111.

Grimsby: Lock Pit, Immingham Dock, tel. Grimsby (04692) 2166.

Hull: Ocean Chambers, 54 Cowgate, tel. Hull (0482) 224151.

Leeds: Vauvelle Ltd, Clayton Wood Close, tel. Leeds (0532) 784261.

Liverpool: Royal Liver Building, tel. 051-236 1942.

Manchester: 60 Whitworth Street, 16LV, tel. 061-236 7111.

Newcastle-upon-Tyne: Milburn House, Dean Street, tel. Newcastle (0632) 25141.

Plymouth: 7 The Parade, Barbican, tel. Plymouth (0752) 60604.

Portsmouth: 16 Landport Terrace, tel. Portsmouth (0705) 27231.

Southampton: 1 Paget Street, tel. Southampton (0703) 27971.

Iceland

Aberdeen: 62 Marischal Street, AB9 8AZ, tel. Aberdeen (0224) 54112.

Bristol: 9 Whiteladies Road, Clifton, tel. Bristol (0272) 38205/6.

Dover: Limekiln Street, tel. Dover 1201.

Edinburgh-Leith: 13 South Charlotte Street, EH2 4AS, tel. 031-226 4259, 031-332 5856.

Felixstowe: c/o McGregor, Gow and Holland Ltd, Trelawny House, The Dock, tel. Felixstowe (03942) 5651.

Glasgow: 166 Buchanan Street, G1 2LP, tel. 041-332 7101.

Grimsby: c/o Fylkir Ltd, Fish Dock Road, tel. Grimsby (0472) 50721.

Hull: Ferensway Chambers, tel. Hull (0482) 224715.

Lerwick: Mr Lindsay Robertson, Vice-Consul, Alexander Wharf.

Liverpool: 24 Fenwick Street, L2 7NE, tel. 051-236 9554.

Manchester: Warwick House, Warwick Road, M16 0RR, tel. 061-872 3177.

Newcastle: 26-30 Jesmond Road, tel. Newcastle (0632) 811212.

Italy

Cardiff: 15 West Bute Street, tel. Cardiff (0222) 29887.

Edinburgh: 21 Albany Street, tel. 031-556 1603.

Glasgow: 9 Park Street South, C3, tel. 041-332 3563.

Manchester: St James's Building, 77 Oxford Street, tel. 061-236 9024.

Netherlands

Birmingham: 77 Colmore Row, tel. 021-236 5417.

Cardiff: Pascoe House, Bute Street, tel. Cardiff (0222) 21491.

Edinburgh: 10 Atholl Crescent, tel. 031-229 2251.

Glasgow: Standard Buildings, 102 Hope Street, C2, tel. 041-221 0605.

Hull: Jenning Street, tel. Hull (0482) 29841.

Liverpool: 32 City Buildings, 21 Old Hall Street, L39 BS, tel. 051-236 7499.

Manchester: c/o English Calico, 56 Oxford Street, M60 1HJ, tel. 061-228 1144.

Newcastle-upon-Tyne: B Floor, Milburn House, NE1 1LE, tel. Newcastle (0632) 27314.

Plymouth: c/o W.D. Tamlyn and Co. Ltd, 16 Parade, PL1 2JT, tel. Plymouth (0752) 63444/5/6.

Southampton: c/o Phs. Van Ommeren Ltd, 150 High Street, SO9 5DN, tel. Southampton (0703) 29051.

Norway

Birmingham: Reynolds and Co., Rutland House, 148 Edmund Street, tel. 021-236 8065.

Bradford: Mount Street Mills, Mount Street, BD3 9RL, tel. Bradford (0274) 22 226.

Bristol: Portview Road, Avonmouth, BS11 9YX, tel. Avonmouth (02752) 5081.

Cardiff: Empire House, Mount Stuart Square, CF1 6QT, tel. 0222-32911.

Glasgow: 141 West Nile Street, G1 2RN, tel. 041-332 9353.

Hull: Ocean Chambers, 54 Lowgate, HU1 1XJ, tel. Hull (0482) 36921.

Leith/Edinburgh: 50 East Fettes Avenue, EH4 1EQ, tel. 031-552 7101.

Liverpool: 509 Tower Building, Water Street, L3 1BA, tel. 051-236 2787.

Manchester: Ship Canal House, King Street, M2 4PA, tel. 061-602 3322.

Newcastle-upon-Tyne: 54 Pilgrim Street, NE1 6TJ, tel. New-castle (0632) 26171.

Southampton: 28 Queen's Terrace, SO9 2UJ, tel. Southampton (0703) 23555.

Sunderland: 11 Toward Road, tel. Sunderland (0783) 70101/2.

Swansea: 61 Wind Street, SA1 1EX, tel. Swansea (0792) 50564/5.

Portugal

Aberdeen: 52 Marischal Street, tel. Aberdeen (0224) 28347.

Birmingham: 41 Church Street, tel. 021-236 8574/5/6.

Bristol: 39/40 Queen Square, tel. Bristol (0272) 22421.

Cardiff: 178 Cathedral Road, tel. Cardiff (0222) 26991.

Dover: Limekiln Street, tel. Dover (0304) 1201/2/3.

Edinburgh: 43 Hanover Street, tel. 031-354 36664.

Glasgow: 200 St Vincent Street, C1, tel. 041-221 9591.

Hull: Moran House, 79 Beverley Road, tel. Hull (0482) 35342.

Leeds: Mount House, Boston Spa, nr. Wetherby, tel. Leeds (0523) 32506.

Liverpool: 1 Falkner Square, L8 7NU, tel. 051-709 5712.

Manchester: 2 Mount Street, tel. 061-834 0595.

Middlesborough: County Chambers, Marton Road, tel. Middles-brough (0642) 44402.

Newcastle-upon-Tyne: 8a Saville Row, tel. Newcastle-upon-Tyne (0632) 25256.

Southampton: 12 Carlton Road, SO1 2HL, tel. Southampton (0703) 23609.

Swansea: 8 Alexandra Terrace, Brynmill, tel. Swansea (0792) 50021.

South Africa

Glasgow: South African Consulate General, Stock Exchange House, 69 St George's Place, G2 1BX, tel. 041-221 3114.

Sweden

Birmingham: Crown Works, Rubery, B45 9AG, tel. 021-453 3701.

Bristol: Portview Road, Avonmouth, BS11 9YX, Avonmouth, tel. (02752) 5081.

Cardiff: Cory's Buildings, 57 Bute Street, CF1 1SE, tel. Cardiff (0222) 31141.

Glasgow: 209 West George Street, G2 2NJ, tel. 041-221 9414.

Liverpool: 470 India Buildings, Water Street, L2 0QT, tel. 051-236 3516.

Manchester: Ship Canal House, King Street, M2 YNX, tel. 061-832 7290.

Newcastle: Clayton House, Regent Centre, Gosforth, NE3 3HW, tel. Newcastle (0632) 850621.

Switzerland

Manchester: Sunley Building, 18th Floor, Piccadilly Plaza, M1 4BH, tel. 061-236 2933.

United States

Edinburgh: 3 Regent Terrace, EH7 5BW, tel. 031-556 8315/8.

Liverpool: Cunard Building, Pier Head, L3 1ED, tel. 051-236 8501/2.

XV. MISCELLANEOUS

Animals

It is not possible for foreign visitors to take dogs or cats with them on a holiday in Britain, since the requirement for 6 months' quarantine is strictly maintained.

Bed and breakfast

A room in a private house offering "bed and breakfast" (indicated by a sign in the window or on the garden gate) is a popular and economical form of overnight accommodation. It is advisable, particularly in summer, to start looking for accommodation fairly early in the evening (before 5.30). Convenient lists of houses providing bed and breakfast are published, with new editions from time to time: e.g. "Bed, Breakfast and Evening Meal" (Starfish Books), 94 West Grove, Walton on Thames, Surrey), "Bed and Breakfast in N. Wales, N. England and Scotland" (Herald Advisory Services, 23a Brighton Road, South Croydon, Surrey), "Bed and Breakfast in South and S.W. England" (Herald Advisory Services).

Accommodation can also be had in farmhouses, but usually for longer periods than one night (most commonly by the week), A free booklet on this subject is issued by the British Tourist Authority. Accommodation is also available in some country houses, for stays of from 3 days to a week: information from the British Tourist Authority.

Camping and Caravanning

The British Tourist Authority publishes a useful list, "Camping and Caravan Sites".

The Camping Club of Great Britain and Ireland admits visitors from abroad as temporary members on payment of a very modest fee. Temporary members receive the Club's List of Sites and Year Book and can use the Club's sites. Visitors who belong to a club affiliated to the International Federation of Camping Clubs are admitted to temporary membership free of charge provided that they apply to their own club for this facility before departure. For all information about camping in Britain apply to the Camping Club of Great Britain and Ireland, 38 Grosvenor Gardens, London SW1.

For Scotland (which is covered by the BTA and Camping Club lists) see also the Scottish Tourist Board publication, "Scotland for Touring Caravans".

Dress

As noted in the introductory section of this Guide, the British climate is mild, but sometimes quite cool in summer and sometimes wet. Light clothing is adequate in summer, but it is advisable to take a raincoat and a pullover or light coat for wear on cool evenings. In winter, of course, warm clothing should be taken.

Electricity

The commonest voltage is 240 volts A.C. (50 c/s), though there are still some areas using 220 volts. In the few places with direct current this is indicated by notices.

Emergencies

For fire, police or ambulance dial 999.

Emergency medical service in London: Middlesex Hospital, Mortimer St, W1 (tel. 636 8333).

Emergency dental service in London: St George's Hospital, Tooting Grove, SW17 (tel. 672 1255).

Emergency ophthalmological service in London: Moorfields Eye Hospital, City Road, EC1 (tel. 253 3411).

Chemists' shops in London open day and night: Boots, Piccadilly Circus (tel. 930 4761); Bliss, 50-56 Willesden Lane, NW6 (tel. 624 8000).

Farm camps

These offer students and young people generally the opportunity of working in the country and meeting other young people of all nationalities. There are farm camps (harvesting, forestry work or general farm work) in all parts of the country. A deduction is made from the wages paid to cover board and lodging. For further information apply to the Farm Camps Organiser, National Union of Students, 3 Endsleigh St, London WC1, or to Concordia (Youth Service Volunteers), 11a Albemarle St, London W1.

Language-learning on holiday

A stay in Britain is undoubtedly the best way of learning English. There are a number of organisations which make arrangements for young people to spend some time in Britain—preferably in a family, with or without formal language lessons, often with facilities for sport, perhaps on an au pair or exchange basis. These organisations have local agents whose responsibility is to find suitable families and to maintain contact with the young visitors during their stay so as to ensure that all goes well.

The British Tourist Authority can provide a list of organisations making arrangements of this kind, so that those interested can select the one which seems most likely to meet their needs.

Liquor licensing

The sale of alcoholic liquor in Britain is controlled by a statutory licensing system which limits the number of establishments where alcohol may be sold and the hours during which it may be sold. Public houses in England are normally open from 11 to 3 and 6 to 11, with shorter opening hours on Sunday. In Scotland the hours are slightly different. Pubs in some parts of Wales are closed on Sundays. Children under 14 are not admitted, and young people between 14 and 18 may be served only with non-alcoholic drinks. Young people between 16 and 18, however, may be served with certain alcoholic drinks along with a meal. Clubs, restaurants and hotels can sometimes obtain special licences enabling them to serve alcoholic drinks until later hours than normal; and clubs and hotels can be licensed to serve drinks to residents and their guests at any time of day. An establishment without a licence cannot serve alcohol of any kind.

Lost property

For property lost in the streets of London, apply to any police station. For property lost in taxis, apply to the Lost Property Office, 15 Penton St, N1 (open 10 to 4.30 except at weekends). For property lost in London Transport vehicles or on London Transport premises, apply to 200-202 Baker St, NW1 (open 10 to 6 except at weekends).

Anywhere outside London, apply to the nearest police station.

Postal, telegraph and telephone services

London. The principal post offices are usually open on week-days (except public holidays) from 8.30 to 6.30. The District Office in King Edward St, EC1, and the Leicester Square branch office, 39 Charing Cross Road, WC2, are open until 8 for postal and telegraph services, and are open permanently for telephone calls, including telegrams by phone, and the sale of stamps. The post office in Trafalgar Square stays open all night.

Outside London. Main post offices are usually open from 8.30 to 5, smaller ones from 9 to 6. Some close in the afternoon on the local early closing day.

Sundays and public holidays. In London the office in King Edward St and the Leicester Square office (see above) remain open all the time, and some others are open from 9 to 1 for telephone and telegraph services and the sale of stamps. Outside London head post offices and some others are open from 9 to 10.30 or 11 (10 in Scotland) for telephone and telegraph services and the sale of stamps.

Stamps. These can be bought in any post office; they are not sold, as on the Continent, in cafés and tobacconists' shops. There are stamp machines outside some post offices and in other places, so that stamps can be obtained at any time of day. Pillar-boxes for posting letters (so called even though they are not all in the form of the traditional pillar) are painted bright red and are usually easy to find.

Telephoning: see below, p. 1111.

Poste restante. For the convenience of travellers letters may be addressed poste restante, for a period of 3 months, at any post office (other than a sub post office). If not collected within two weeks (a month in the case of letters from abroad) letters are returned to the sender. There is no extra charge for poste restante letters. They should be clearly marked "Poste restante" or "To be called for".

Public holidays

The main public holidays are *in England* Good Friday, Easter Monday, the last Monday in May and the last Monday in August (bank holidays), Christmas Day and Boxing Day (26 December), and *in Scotland* New Year's Day and 2 January, Good Friday, the first Monday in May, the first Monday in August and Christmas Day.

Shop hours

Shops are usually open from 9 or 10 to 5.30 on weekdays; on Saturdays they close at 1. They are often closed on Monday mornings, at least in the larger towns. On one afternoon in the week, varying from place to place, the shops close at 1 o'clock: this is the "early closing day", indicated in the descriptive part of this Guide by the letters E.C. after the name of a place. Some shops, particularly department stores, remain open later than usual on one evening in the week.

Telephoning

There are public telephone kiosks (call-boxes) in post offices and in the streets, painted red and white and readily recognisable. There are operated by coins (2p and 10p pieces), not by tokens as in some continental countries.

Over most of the country calls can be dialled direct, without the intervention of an operator. Each area has a dialling code (e.g. 01 for London), used only when telephoning from outside the area concerned. The dialling tone, which must be heard before a number is dialled, is a continuous purring sound. The ringing tone is a repeated burr-burr. The "engaged" tone is a repeated single note; a steady note means "number unobtainable". When dialling from a "pay on answer" call-box (the normal type) the "pay tone" (a series of rapid pips) will be heard: you must then insert money, or you cannot be heard by the person you are calling.

In case of difficulty, dial the operator (100).

Full information about how to use the telephone, and about special services, will be found in the introductory pages of any telephone directory.

Special services:

Teletourist (information for tourists about the main events of the day): in London dial 246 8041 (in English), 246 8043 (in French), 246 8045 (in German), 246 8047 (in Spanish) or 246 8049 (in Italian); in Edinburgh (1 May to 30 September only) dial (031) 246 8041.

Weather forecasts: dial 246 8091 in London; for other parts of the country see the front pages of the local telephone directory.

Motoring information: dial 246 8021 in London for information about road conditions within a radius of 50 miles; for other parts of the country see the front pages of the telephone directory.

Time (the "speaking clock"): dial 123 in London. In other parts of the country: see telephone directory.

Other services include skiing information (Edinburgh), "dial a disc" and a summary of business news (London).

Tipping

There are no fixed rules on this subject, but it is the custom to tip taxi-drivers, hotel and restaurant staff, railway porters, hairdressers and cloakroom attendants. No tips are expected in theatres and cinemas. The following general indications may be helpful.

Hotels. Many hotels add a service charge of 10 or 12½ (sometimes 15) per cent to their bills. When service is not included it is customary—though there is no absolute obligation—to distribute 10 to 15 per cent of the bill to those members of the staff who have been of service.

Restaurants. It is customary to leave a tip of 10 per cent of the bill (unless it specifically includes a service charge).

Porters. The amount of the tip depends on the luggage carried and the distance it has to be carried. For carrying a medium-sized suitcase from the train to a taxi the tip might be 5p; for heavier luggage or a longer distance proportionately more.

Taxis. For a short distance a tip of 25% would be regarded as normal; for longer distances 15-20% would be adequate. When a driver has performed some additional service like carrying luggage a higher tip will be expected.

Urban transport services

A number of towns, including London, Liverpool and Glasgow, have underground railway systems. All towns have buses, usually double-deckers.

On the London *underground* (the "tube") the fare varies according to the distance. Tickets are issued by ticket-machines, but there are also ticket-offices. Trains with different destinations and on different routes may arrive at the same platform: you should therefore check where a train is going before boarding it by looking at the illuminated signs on the platform (or the destination board on the front of the train).

The London *buses* are run by the same authority as the underground, London Transport. On routes within London the buses are red; the country services are green. Fares vary according to distance. Smoking is allowed only on the upper deck.

Taxis are numerous, and are a very convenient way of getting about London and other large cities. The driver is paid after getting out of the taxi (the front of the taxi being separated from the passenger compartment by a glass screen). There is an extra charge for heavy luggage.

There are *motor launch* services on the Thames (scheduled services, plus excursions in summer), leaving from Charing Cross Pier or Westminster Pier. There are hydrofoil services from Tower Pier to Greenwich.

There are two kinds of *special tickets*, for foreign visitors only, issued by London Transport, enabling visitors to save both time and money:

Master Tickets, covering unlimited travel for a week on all normal London Transport services, the London Country Bus services, the Green Line buses and London Transport's "Round London Sightseeing Tour"; and *Tourist ("Go as you please")* *Tickets*, issued for either 4 or 7 consecutive days, covering travel on the London buses and underground and the sightseeing tour.

Foreign visitors can obtain these special tickets from the Tourist Ticket Office, London Transport, 55 Broadway, SW1 (above St James's Park underground station) on production of their passport or identity card. The office is open Monday to Friday from 9 to 5 (5.30 in July and August) and on Saturday from 9 to 12.

Weights and measures

Although the metric system is gradually being introduced in Britain, the old measures are still in use. It may be useful for foreign visitors, therefore, to give some equivalences.

Weight:

1 gramme	= 15.43 grains	28.35 gr	= 1 ounce (oz)
100 gr	= 2½ oz	453.6 gr	= 1 pound (1b)

Area:

1 cm2	= 0.155 sq. in.	1 m2	= 10.76 sq. ft
1 ha	= 2.417 acres	259 ha	= 1 sq. mile

Volume

1 cm3	= 0.061 cu. in.	16.387 cm3 = 1 cu. in.

Length

1 m	= 39.37 in.	1 km	= 5/8 mile
1 yard	= .914 m	1 mile	= 1.609 km

Youth hostels

There are more than 500 youth hostels throughout Britain. For further information apply to the Youth Hostels Association, 29 John Adam St, London WC2 (tel. 839 1722) or the Scottish Youth Hostels Association, 7 Glebe Crescent, Stirling FK8 2JA.

WELSH AND GAELIC GLOSSARIES

The following brief glossaries of elements occurring in place names may help visitors to interpret some of the unfamiliar names they will come across in Wales and the Highlands of Scotland. The spelling is frequently variable, since many names have undergone varying degrees of anglicisation.

WELSH

Aber	river-mouth
Ban	hill, peak

Bryn	hill.
Cae	field, enclosure
Caer	fort
Coed	wood, forest
Crymlin	round pool or lake
Cwm	valley
Derw	oak-tree
Derwydd	druid
Dolau	meadows
Dwfn	deep
Dywffryn	valley
Eglwys	church
Fan	hill, peak
Ffridd	mountain pasturage
Glas, gwyrdd	blue, green
Llan	church
Llwydd	grey
Llyn	lake
Mor	sea
Mynachdy	monastery
Mynydd	mountain
Pen	hill, hilltop
Penmaen	headland
Pentre	village
Rhyd	fort
Tad	father
Traeth	beach
Tre	town
Tywod	sands

GAELIC

Aber	river-mouth
Ach	field
Allt	stream
Ard	high point

Avie	water
Avon	river
Bal	town, place
Ban	white
Beallach	pass
Beg	little
Beinn, ben	hill, mountain
Blair	field
Brae	hill, mountain
Can, caen	head
Carn	heap, pile
Clachan	group of houses
Clunie	meadow
Coir, corrie	hollow
Dal	field
Dearg	red
Drum	back, ridge
Dubh	black
Dun	fort
Eilean	island
Garve	rough
Glas	grey
Glen	valley
Gorm	blue
Inch, innis	island
Inver	river-mouth
Kil	monk's cell, enclosure, parish
Kin	head
Knock	knoll
Kyle	strait
Linn	pool, narrow channel
Mam	rounded hill
Meall	do.
Mor	big

Ross	point
Tarbet	narrow strip of land between two arms of the sea
Tigh	house
Uam	cave

HOTELS

Britain is well equipped with hotels. The best guide to British hotel resources is the British Tourist Authority's published list of "Hotels and Restaurants in Great Britain", which is available through bookshops. This very useful publication lists some 5000 hotels in all categories, including guest-houses (pensions), giving the number of rooms, the number of rooms with private bathrooms, the rate for bed and breakfast and where appropriate the weekly rate for full board. It also shows hotels catering for special diets and includes a list of restaurants in London and other large towns. Finally it gives information about the various towns and regions which may be helpful in planning your trip.

Booking

Rooms in hotels in London should be booked well in advance whatever the time of year. This can be done either through a travel agency or direct. In the main tourist centres the hotels are under heavy pressure during the months of July and August, and if you are travelling on your own in any part of Britain during the summer it is desirable to book in advance wherever possible. If you have no firm itinerary mapped out you should at least telephone in the morning to reserve accommodation for that night. From September to April there is usually no difficulty in finding a room, except in London.

During the summer months the rates charged by hotels in London are considerably higher than in other towns. It should be noted that the charge for a room generally includes breakfast.

Other accommodation

Accommodation in guest-houses (pensions) is usually cheaper than in hotels, and an even more economical possibility is "bed and breakfast" accommodation in private houses, widely available in country areas (see p. 1107). There are also large numbers of caravan and camping sites (see p. 1108). Young people can take advantage of the many youth hostels throughout the country (see p. 1114). Still another possibility is one of the holiday camps on the seaside or in the country, providing family holidays with a wide range of entertainments and facilities at very reasonable prices; for further information apply to the National Association of Holiday Centres, 10 Bolton St, London W1Y 8AU.

Abbreviations

In front of the name of each hotel is a letter (A, B, C, or D) indicating the price bracket into which the hotel falls. Since prices are subject to variation it is not possible to give precise tariff rates. The classification is broadly as follows;

A luxury hotels and hotels offering a very high standard of comfort and amenity

B first-class hotels offering excellent comfort and amenity

C hotels offering comfortable accommodation at reasonable prices

D more modest but good and comfortable hotels

After each hotel the list shows the telephone number and the number of rooms, followed by various symbols, which have the following significance;

G   garage or parking space

CW closed in winter

CH central heating in all rooms

NP night porter

UL unlicensed (i.e. not authorised to sell alcoholic drinks)

H   building of historic or architectural interest.

Arrangement

For convenience the hotels have been arranged under geographical regions (and within these regions under the old counties), following roughly the order in which the regions are described in the Guide.

In the first section (London and surroundings) hotels in London proper are listed first, followed by hotels at Heathrow Airport and hotels in outer London.

I. HOTELS IN LONDON AND SURROUNDINGS

LONDON

Hotel	Tel.	Rooms		Notes	
A **Athenaeum**, 116 Piccadilly W1V 0BJ	01-499 3464	200		CH NP	H
A **Belgravia Royal**, 20 Chesham Place SW1	01-235 6040	111		CH NP	
A **Berkeley** Wilton Place SW1X 7RL ...	01-235 6000	152	G	CH NP	
A **Bristol** 1-3 Berkeley Street W1	01-493 8282	183	G	CH NP	
A **Britannia** Grosvenor Square W1	01-629 9400	448	G	CH NP	H
A **Brown's** Dover Street W1A 4SW ...	01-493 6020	123		CH NP	
A **Cadogan** 75 Sloane Street SW1	01-235 7141	84	G	CH NP	H
A **Capital** 22-24 Basil Street SW3 1AT	01-589 5171	60	G	CH NP	
A **Carlton Tower** Cadogan Place Sloane Street SW1	01-235 5411	272	G	CH NP	
A **Cavendish** Jermyn Street SW1Y 6JF	01-930 2111	255	G	CH NP	
A **Charles Dickens** 66 Lancaster Gate W2	01-262 5090	193		CH NP	H

A **Churchill**
Portman Square
   W1H 0AJ ....   01-486 5800   489   G   CH NP

A **Claridge's**
Brook Street
   W1Y 2AS ....   01-629 8860   250   G   CH NP

A **Connaught**
Carlos Place W1 .   01-499 7070   84   G   CH NP

A **Cumberland**
Marble Arch
   W1A 4RF ....   01-262 1234   900   CH NP

A **Curzon**
Stanhope Row,
   Park Lane W1 .   01-493 7222   75   G   CH NP   H

A **Dorchester**
Park Lane
   W1A 2HJ ....   01-629 8888   285   G   CH NP

A **Dukes**
35 St. James's Place
   SW1 ....   01-493 2366   44   CH NP   H

A **Europa**
Grosvenor Square
   W1A 4AW ...   01-493 1232   272   CH NP

A **Gloucester**
4-18 Harrington
   Gardens SW7
   4LH ....   01-373 6030   575   G   CH NP

A **Grosvenor House**
Park Lane W1A
   3AA ....   01-499 6363   467   G   CH NP

A **Hilton**
22 Park Lane
   W1A 2HH ....   01-493 8000   509   G   CH NP   H

A **Holiday Inn**
George Street,
   Marble Arch
   W1 ....   01-723 1277   243   G   CH NP

A **Holiday Inn**
King Henry's Road,
   Swiss Cottage
   NW3 ....   01-722 7711   300   G   CH NP

A **Hyde Park** Knightsbridge SW1 7LA	01-235 2000	182	G	CH NP	
A **Inn on the Park** Hamilton Place, Park Lane W1A 1AZ	01-499 0888	228	G	CH NP	
A **Kensington Hilton** Holland Park Ave. W11 4UL	01-603 3355	611	G	CH NP	H
A **Kensington Palace** De Vere Gardens W8 5AF	01-937 8121	314	G	CH NP	
A **Londonderry** 19 Old Park Lane W1	01-493 7292	159	G	CH NP	
A **London International** Cromwell Road SW5	01-370 4200	424	G	CH NP	
A **London Metropole** Edgware Road W2	01-402 4141	555	G	CH NP	H
A **Lowndes** 19-21 Lowndes Street SW1	01-235 6020	90	G	CH NP	
A **May Fair** Berkeley Street W1A 2AN	01-629 7777	392		CH NP	
A **Meurice & Quaglino's** Bury Street, St James's SW1Y 6AJ	01-930 6767	41	G	CH NP	
A **Montcalm** Great Cumberland Place W1	01-402 4288	111	G	CH NP	H

A **Park Plaza**
Bayswater Road
  W2 .... 01-262 5022   282   G   CH NP   H

A **Piccadilly**
Piccadilly W1A
  2AU .... 01-734 8000   219   CH NP

A **Portman**
22 Portman Square
  W1 .... 01-486 5844   293   G   CH NP

A **Ritz**
Piccadilly W1A
  2JS .... 01-493 8181   120   CH NP   H

A **Royal Garden**
Kensington High
  Street W8 4PT . 01-938 70000   50   G   CH NP

A **Royal
Kensington**
380 Kensington
  High Street W14 01-603 3333   414   G   CH NP

A **Royal
Lancaster**
Lancaster Terrace
  W2 2TY ...... 01-262 6737   433   G   CH NP   H

A **Royal
Westminster**
Buckingham Palace
  Road SW1 .... 01-834 1302   142   NP

A **St. George's**
Langham Place
  W1A 2JW .... 01-580 0111   500   G   CH NP

A **Savoy**
Strand WC2R 0BP 01-836 4343   500   G   CH NP

A **Selfridge**
Orchard Street
  W1   307   CH NP

A **Sherlock Holmes**
108 Baker Street
  W1 .... 01-486 6161   149   G   CH NP   H

A **Skyline Park
Tower**
Knightsbridge SW1   300   G   CH NP

A **Stafford** 16 St James's Place SW1A 1NJ	01-493 0111	51	G	CH	NP	
A **Tower** St Katharine's Way E1 9LD	01-481 2575	826	G	CH	NP	
A **Waldorf** Aldwych, WC2 4DD	01-836 2400	310		CH	NP	
A **Westbury** Bond Street W1Y 0PD	01-629 6755	255	G	CH	NP	
A **West Centre** Lillie Road SW6	01-381 0331	508	G	CH	NP	
A **White's** Lancaster Gate W2 3NR	01-262 2711	61	G	CH	NP	
B **Astor Lodge** 45 Marlborough Place NW8 ...	01-624 0181	73	G	CH	NP	
B **Barkston** Earls Court SW5 .	01-373 7851	74			NP	
B **Basil, The** Knightsbridge SW3 1AH	01-730 3411	127	G	CH	NP	H
B **Bedford** 83 Southampton Row WC1	01-636 7822	182	G	CH	NP	
B **Berners** Berners Street W1A 3BE	01-636 1629	163		CH	NP	
B **Bonnington** Southampton Row WC1B 4BH ..	01-242 2828	268		CH	NP	
B **Buckingham** 94-102 Cromwell Road SW7	01-373 7131	63			NP	
B **Central Park** Queensborough Terrace W2 ...	01-229 2424	360	G	CH	NP	

B Charing Cross Strand WC2N 5HX	01-839 7282	205	G	CH NP	H
B Charles Bernard 5 Frognal NW3 6AL	01-794 0101	57	G	CH NP	
B Clifton Ford Welbeck Street W1M 8DN ...	01-486 6600	219	G	NP	
B Clive Primrose Hill Road NW3	01-586 2233	84	G	CH NP	
B Coburg 129 Bayswater Road W2 4RJ .	01-229 3654	120	G	CH NP	
B Cora Upper Woburn Place WC1H 0HT	01-387 5111	145		CH NP	H
B Cranley Gardens Cranley Gardens SW7	01-373 3232	87		CH NP	
B Cunard International Hammersmith W6	01-373 8425	640	G	CH NP	
B De Vere 60 Hyde Park Gate W8	01-584 0051	76		CH NP	
B Drury Lane Shorts Gardens, Drury Lane WC1		123	G	CH NP	
B Elizabetta 162 Cromwell Road SW5	01-370 4282	84	G	CH NP	
B Flemings Half Moon Street W1	01-499 2964	76	G	CH NP	
B Georgian House 87 Gloucester Place W1Y	01-935 2211	19		CH NP	

B **Goring** Grosvenor Gardens Beeston Place SW1W 0JW ...	01-834 8221	100		CH NP	
B **Green Park** Half Moon Street W1Y 8BP	01-629 7522	83		CH NP	
B **Grosvenor Victoria** Buckingham Palace Road SW1W 0SJ	01-834 9494	58		CH NP	
B **Hallam** 12 Hallam Strret W1	01-580 1166	28		CH NP	H
B **Harewood** Harewood Row NW1	01-262 2707	82		CH NP	
B **Henry VIII** Leinster Gardens W2	01-262 0117	110		CH NP	
B **Hertford** Bayswater Road W2 3HL	01-262 4461	175	G	CH NP	
B **Hyde Park Towers** 41-49 Inverness Terrace W2 ...	01-229 9461	120		CH NP	
B **Imperial** Russell Square WC1B 4HD ...	01-837 3655	457	G	CH NP	
B **Julius Caesar** Queens Gardens, Hyde Park W2	01-262 0022	118		CH NP	
B **Kennedy** Cardington Street NW1 2LP	01-387 4400	323	G	NP	
B **Kensington Close** Wrights Lane W8 5SP	01-937 8170	539	G	CH NP	

B **Kingsley**
Bloomsbury Way
  WC1A 2SD ..   01-242 5881   174   NP

B **Leinster Towers**
25-31 Leinster
  Gardens W2 ..   01-262 4591   163   CH NP

B **London
  Embassy**
150-152 Bayswater
  Road W2 4RT .   01-229 1212   194   G   CH NP

B **Londoner**
Welbeck Strret
  W1M 8HS ...   01-935 4442   125   CH NP

B **London Penta**
97-109 Cromwell
  Road SW7 4ON   01-370 4511   914   G   CH NP

B **London Tara**
Wrights Lane W8   01-937 7211   850   G   CH NP

B **Majestic**
158-160 Cromwell
  Road SW5 ....   01-373 3083   93   CH NP   H

B **Mandeville**
Mandeville Place
  W1M 6BE ....   01-935 5599   161   NP   H

B **Mostyn**
Portman Strret
  W1H 0DE ....   01-935 2361   100   CH NP

B **Mount Royal**
Marble Arch
  W1A 4OR ....   01-629 8040   665   G   CH NP

B **Old St James's
  House**
7 Park Place Sw1 .   01-493 2412   34   G   CH NP

B **Park Court**
Lancaster Gate
  W2 ....   01-402 4272   443   G   CH NP

B **Park Lane**
Piccadilly
  W1A 4UA ...   01-499 6321   320   G   CH NP

B **Pastoria** St Martin's Street WC2	01-930 8641	52		CH NP	
B **Post House** Haverstock Hill, Hampstead NW3 4RB	01-794 8121	140	G	CH NP	
B **President** Russell Square WC1N 1DB ...	01-837 8844	447	G	CH NP	
B **Rathbone** **Piccadilly** Charlotte Street W1	01-636 2001	60	G	NP	
B **Regent Centre** Carburton Street W1	01-388 2300	350	G	CH NP	
B **Regent Palace** Piccadilly Circus W1R 6EP	01-734 7000	1130		NP	
B **Rembrandt** Thurloe Place SW7 2RS	01-589 8100	153		CH NP	
B **Royal Angus** Coventry Street W1	01-930 4033	94		CH NP	
B **Royal Court** Sloane Square SW1	01-730 9191	104		CH NP	H
B **Royal** **Horseguards** Whitehall Court SW1	01-839 3400	277		CH NP	
B **Royal Scot** 100 Kings Cross Road WC1 ...	01-278 2434	349	G	CH NP	H
B **Royal Trafalgar** Whitcomb Street WC2	01-930 4477	108		CH NP	
B **Rubens** Buckingham Palace Road SW1 0PS	01-834 6600	87		CH NP	

B **Russell**					
Russell Square					
WC1 5BE	01-837 6470	330		CH NP	H
B **St Ermins**					
Caxton Street					
SW1H 0QW ..	01-222 7888	250	G	CH NP	H
B **Somerset House**					
6 Dorset Square					
NW1 6QA ...	01-723 0741	23	G	CH NP	H
B **Strand Palace**					
Strand WC2 0JJ .	01-836 8080	786		CH NP	
B **Stratford Court**					
Oxford Street					
W1N 0BY	01-629 7474	114		CH NP	
B **Tavistock**					
Tavistock Square					
WC1H 9EU ...	01-366 8383	301	G	CH NP	
B **Viceroy**					
9 Lancaster Gate					
W2	01-723 1144	51		CH NP	
B **Victoria Garden**					
100 Westbourne					
Terrace W2 ...	01-262 1161	70	G	CH NP	
B **Washington**					
Curzon Street					
W1Y 8DT	01-499 7030	162	G	CH NP	
B **Wilbraham**					
Wilbraham Place,					
Sloane Street					
SW1 AE9	01-730 8296	32	G	CH NP	
B **Windsor**					
56-60 Lancaster					
Gate W2 3NG .	01-262 4501	51	G	CH NP	
C **Adelphi**					
127 Cromwell Road					
SW7	01-373 7177	63		CH NP	
C **Adria**					
88 Queen's Gate					
SW7 AA5 ...	01-373 3391	43		CH NP	

C **Airways**
16 Collingham Road
  SW5 . . . . 01-373 1075 100   G   CH NP

C **Alexandra**
  National
330 Seven Sisters
  Road N4 2PF . 01-800 8090 193   G   CH NP

C **Alwin Court**
61 Gloucester Road
  SW7 4PE . . . . . 01-584 8314 61   CH NP UL

C **Ambassador**
12 Lancaster Gate
  W2 . . . . 01-262 7361 66   CH NP

C **Andora**
44-48 West
  Cromwell Road
  SW5 9QL . . . . . 01-373 4546 43   CH NP

C **Ascot**
11 Craven Road
  W2 . . . . 01-402 5448 52   CH NP   H

C **Ashburn**
111 Cromwell Road
  SW7 4DR 01-370 3321 26   CH NP

C **Atlantic**
1 Queens Gardens
  W2 . . . . 01-262 4471 200   CH NP

C **Aviva**
1 Platts Lane NW3 01-794 6756 18   G   CH

C **Bailey's**
140 Gloucester Road
  SW7 . . . . 01-373 8131 150   CH NP

C **Bedford Corner**
Bayley Street
  WC1B 3HD . . . 01-580 7766 85   CH NP

C **Bloomsbury**
  Centre
Coram Street
  WC1N 1HT . . . 01-837 1200 250   G   CH NP

C **Bryanston Court**
Great Cumberland
  Place W1 . . . . . 01-262 3141 55   CH NP   H

C **Burns**					
18-26 Barkston					
Gardens SW5 .	01-373 3151	100		CH NP	H
C **Carlyle**					
27 Devonshire					
Terrace W2 ...	01-262 2204	80		CH NP	
C **Casserly Court**					
125 Gloucester					
Terrace W2 ...	01-262 3161	71		CH NP	
C **Central City**					
Central Street EC1		508	G	CH NP	
C **Clarendon Court**					
Edgware Road,					
Maida Valle					
W9 1AG	01-286 8080	189		CH NP	
C **Commodore**					
52 Lancaster Gate					
W2	01-402 5291	67		CH NP	
C **County**					
Upper Woburn					
Place WC1	01-387 5544	174		CH NP	
C **Croft Court**					
44-46 Ravenscroft					
Avenue WN11					
8AY	01-455 9175	10	G	CH NP UL	
C **Currant's**					
George Street					
W1H 6BJ	01-935 8131	71		CH NP	H
C **Ebury Court**					
26 Ebury Street					
SW1	01-730 8147	37		CH NP	
C **Eccleston**					
Gillingham Street					
SW1V 1PS	01-834 8042	115		NP	
C **Eden**					
27 Harrington					
Gardens SW7					
4JT	01-370 6161	130		CH	
C **Eden Park**					
35-39 Inverness					
Terrace W2 3JR	01-229 1453	140	G	CH NP	

C **Eden Plaza**
68-69 Queen's Gate
  SW7 . . . . 01-370 6111   61   CH NP   H

C **Edward**
Spring Street W2 . 01-262 2671   57   G   CH NP

C **Edwardian**
40-44 Harrington
  Gardens SW7 . 01-370 6262   85   CH NP

C **Embassy House**
31 Queen's Gate
  SW7 5J1 . . . . . . 01-584 7222   94   CH NP

C **Fielding**
4 Broad Court,
  Bow Street WC2 01-836 8305   25   CH NP   H

C **Freemantle**
West Cromwell
  Road SW5 9QJ. 01-373 4494   65   CH NP

C **Gore**
189 Queen's Gate
  SW7 5EX . . . . . 01-584 6601   53   CH NP   H

C **Grand**
Southampton Road
  WC1B 5AD . . . 01-405 2006   88   CH NP

C **Great Eastern**
Liverpool Street
  EC2 P2AN . . . 01-283 4363   163   G   CH NP   H

C **Great Northern**
King's Cross
  Railway Station
  N1 . . . . 01-837 5454   68   G   CH NP

C **Great Western
Royal**
Praed Street W2 . 01-723 8064   169   G   CH NP

C **Harrington Hall**
Harrington Gardens
  SW7 4JW . . . . . 01-373 4477   90   G   CH NP

C **Hotel Europe**
131-137 Cromwell
  Road SW7 . . . . 01-370 2336   95   CH NP

C **Hotel George**
11 Templeton Place
  SW5 . . . .   01-370 1092   100   CH NP

C **Hyde Park View**
52-56 Inverness
  Terrace W2 3LB   01-229 8841   45   G   CH NP   H

C **Ivanhoe**
Bloomsbury Street
  WC1B 3QD . . .   01-636 5601   250   CH NP

C **Kenilworth**
Great Russell Street
  WC1B 3LB . . .   01-636 3283   200   CH NP

C **Kingshill**
55 Westbourne
  Terrace W2 . . .   01-723 3434   147   G   CH NP

C **Lancaster Gate**
106 Lancaster Gate
  W2 3NU . . . . .   01-402 5111   60   G   CH NP

C **Leicester Court**
41 Queen's Gate
  Gardens SW7
  5NB . . . .   01-548 0512   68   CH NP UL H

C **Lexham**
32-38 Lexham
  Gardens W8 5JU   01-373 6471   66   CH NP UL

C **London
Elizabeth**
4 Lancaster Terrace
  W2 3PF . . . . . .   01-402 6641   50   G   CH NP

C **London Ryan**
Gwynne Place
  WC1Y 9QN . .   01-278 2480   213   G   CH NP

C **Milestone**
8 Kensington Court
  W8 5PA . . . . .   01-937 0991   88   CH NP   H

C **Milton Court**
68-74 Cromwell
  Road SW7 5BU   01-584 7851   105   CH NP UL

C **Montague**
Montague Street
  WC1B 5BJ . . . .   01-637 1001   130   NP

C **Montana**
67 Gloucester Road
  SW7 4PG ..... 01-584 7654   53   CH NP

C **New**
  Ambassadors
Upper Woburn
  Place WC1 .... 01-387 1456   98   CH NP   H

C **Ninety nine**
99 Eaton Place
  SW1 .... 01-245 9791   30   CH   H

C **Norfolk Towers**
Norfolk Place W2 01-723 6632   60   CH NP

C **Oliver**
198 Cromwell
  Road SW5 .... 01-370 6881   48   CH NP

C **Onslow Court**
109-113 Queen's
  Gate SW7 5LR 01-589 6300   162   CH NP UL

C **Park Royal**
147 Cromwell Road
  SW7 5DZ ..... 01-370 4341   44   CH NP

C **Parkway**
Inverness Terrace
  W2 3HZ ...... 01-229 9222   86   NP

C **Prince of Wales**
De Vere Gardens
  W8 5AG ..... 01-937 8080   310   NP

C **Queensway**
Prince's Square
  W2 4NT ...... 01-727 8621   125   NP

C **Regency**
100-105 Queen's
  Gate SW7 .... 01-370 4595   200   CH NP

C **Richwood**
25 Cranley Gardens
  SW7   01-589 5281   58   CH NP

C **Royal Norfolk**
25 London Street
  W2 .... 01-402 5521   58   CH NP

C **St James**
Buckingham Gate
  SW1   01-834 2360 520   G   CH NP

C **Senator**
78-82 Westbourne
  Terrace W2   01-262 4521 100   G   CH NP   H

C **Shaftesbury**
Monmouth Street
  WC2H 9HD ..   01-836 4422 192   NP

C **Southway**
Gillingham Street
  SW1V 1HL ..   01-834 0642   41   NP

C **Stanhope**
46-52 Stanhope
  Gardens SW7
  5RT ....   01-370 2161 102   CH NP UL

C **Suncourt**
57-67 Lexham
  Gardens W8 6JJ 01-373 7242 111   CH NP UL

C **Swiss Cottage**
4 Adamson Road
  NW3 ....   01-722 2281   67   G   CH NP

C **Tudor Court**
58-66 Cromwell
  Road SW7 5BY 01-584 8273 100   CH NP UL

C **Vanderbilt**
76 Cromwell Road
  SW7 5TB ....   01-584 0491   86   NP

C **Viscount**
Victoria Road W8 01-937 0752   49   CH NP

C **Waverley**
Southampton Row
  WC1B 5AH ...   01-837 6292   10   CH NP

C **White Hall**
9-11 Bloomsbury
  Square WC1A
  2NA ....   01-242 5401   70   CH NP   H

C **White Hall**
2-5 Montague
  Street WC1B
  5BU ....   01-580 5871   60   CH NP   H

				G	CH	NP	UL	H
C	**White House** Albany Street NW1 3UP	01-387 1200	600		CH	NP		
C	**York** Queensborough Terrace W2	01-229 9511	80					
D	**Durand** 109 Warwick Road SW5	01-370 4474	17		CH	NP		
D	**Eden House** 111 Old Church Street SW3	01-352 3403	21		CH		UL	H
D	**King's Arms** 254 Edgware Road W2	01-723 2461	16		CH	NP		
D	**Lexham Lodge** 134-136 Lexham Gardens W8	01-373 5892	25		CH	NP	UL	
D	**Lindsay Motel** 4 Lindsey Street EC1	01-600 2502	48	G	CH	NP		
D	**London Park** Longville Road SE11 4QU	01-735 9191	375	G	CH	NP		
D	**Mardis Court** 15-23 Hogarth Road SW5	01-373 3063	143			NP		
D	**Morton Court** 25 Courtfield Gardens SW5 0PG	01-370 2277	64	G			UL	
D	**Mount Pleasant** Calthorpe Street WC1X 0HL	01-837 9781	450			NP		
D	**Pembridge Court** 34 Pembridge Gardens W2 4OX	01-229 9977	35	G	CH	NP		

D **Phoenix**
1-7 Kensington
   Gardens Square
   W2 4BH ...... 01-229 2494 105   NP

D **Plaza**
42 Princes Square
   W2 .... 01-229 1292 400   CH NP

D **Queensborough**
44-52 Queensborough
   Terrace W2 ... 01-229 9611 87   CH NP

D **Rosemount**
  Guest House
17-18 Parsifal Road
   NW6 .... 01-435 5856 23   CH   UL

D **Royal Court**
  House
51 Gloucester
   Terrace W2 ... 01-262 1177 65   G   CH NP UL

D **Sandringham**
25-26 Lancaster
   Gate W2 ..... 01-262 4401 52   G   NP   H

D **Shellbourne**
1 Lexham Gardens
   W8 6JN ...... 01-373 5161 41   CH NP

D **White House**
17 Earl's Court
   Square SW5 ... 01-373 1031 36   NP   H

D **Whiteness**
45-48 Queen's
   Gardens W2 .. 01-723 2051 54   CH NP

LONDON AIRPORT (HEATHROW)

A **Berkeley Arms**
Bath Road
   Cranford ..... 01-897 2121 42   G   CH NP

A **Excelsior**
Bath Road, West
   Drayton ...... 01-759 6611 662   G   CH NP

A **Skyline**
Bath Road,
   Harlington Hayes 01-759 2535 360   G   CH NP

A **Skyway**					
Bath Road Hayes .	01-759 6311	440	G	CH NP	H
B **Ariel**					
Bath Road Hayes .	01-759 2552	182	G	CH NP	
B **Arlington**					
Shepiston Lane,					
Hayes	01-573 6162	80	G	NP	
B **Centre Airport**					
Bath Road,					
Longford	01-759 2400	360	G	CH NP	
B **Heathrow**					
Hounslow	01-897 1055	725	G	CH NP	H
B **Holiday Inn**					
Stockley Road,					
West Drayton .	01	301	G	CH NP	H
B **Post House**					
Sipson Road, West					
Drayton	01-579 2323	596	G	CH NP	
B **Sheraton-**					
Heathrow					
Colnbrook Bypass,					
West Drayton .	01-759 2424	440	G	CH NP	H

OUTER LONDON

BLACKHEATH

C **Westcombe Park**					
Westcombe Park					
Road SE3 0SB .	01-858 3697	130	G	CH	H

BROMLEY

C **Bromley Court**					
Bromley Hill, BR1					
4JD	01-460 0055	140	G	CH	H
C **Crest**					
16 Blyth Road . . .	01-460 3070	15	G	NP	

CROYDON

B **Selsdon Park**					
Addington Road .	01-657 8811	150	G	CH NP	H

C Aerodrome
Purley Way CR9
  4LT .... 01-681 1572   69   G   CH NP

C Alpine
Moreton Road .. 01-688 6116   11   G   CH

C Quendale Lodge
70-74 St. Augus-
  tine's Avenue
  CR2 6JH ..... 01-688 2839   9   G   UL H

CRYSTAL PALACE

C Queen's
Church Road SE19 01-653 6622   213   G   CH NP   H

EALING

B Carnarvon
Hanger Lane,
  Ealing Common
  W5 .... 01-992 5399   150   G   CH NP

B Kenton House
5 Hillcrest Road
  W5 .... 01-887 8436   50   G   CH NP

ELTHAM

D Eltham
31 Westmount Road
  SE9 1JF ..... 01-850 8222   13   G   CH NP UL

ENFIELD

C Enfield
52 Rowantree Road
  EN2 8PW .... 01-366 3511   39   G   CH

HAMPTON COURT

C Greyhound
Hampton Court
  Road .... 01-977 1878   10   G   CH

HAREFIELD

C Old Orchard
Park Lane ...... *Harefield*
                 3211   7   G   CH

HARLINGTON

B Garth
Brickfields Lane,
Hayes .... 01-759 9400   18   G

HARROW-ON-THE-HILL

C King's Head
High Street ..... 01-422 5541   16   G   NP   H

HENDON

B Excelsior Motor
 Lodge
Scratchwood NW7
3HB .... 01-906 0611   100   G   CH
C Brent Bridge
Brent Street NW4   01-203 0066   53   G   CH NP   H
C Hendon Hall
Ashley Lane NW1
1HF .... 01-203 3341   53   G   CH NP   H

HILLINGDON

B Master Brewer
 Motel
Western Avenue,   *Uxbridge*
 Hillington Circus   51199   64   G   CH NP

HOUNSLOW

B Master Robert
 Motel
366 Great West
 Road .... 01-570 6261   63   G   CH NP

ILFORD

C Cranford
22-26 Argyle Road   01-478 8403   35   G   CH

ISLEWORTH

B Europa Lodge
Great West Road   01-568 9981   32   G   CH NP

KINGSTON-UPON-THAMES

D **Antoinette**
26 Beaufort Road   01-546 1185   78   G   CH NP UL

D **Griffin**
Market Place ....   01-546 0924   6   G

RICHMOND

B **Star and Garter**
Nightingale Lane   01-940 5451   59   G   CH NP   H

C **Richmond Gate**
Richmond Hill
   TW10 6RP ....   01-940 0061   59   G   CH NP   H

C **Richmond Hill**
Richmond Hill ..   01-940 2247   131   G   CH NP

D **Quinn's**
Sheen Road
   TW9 1AW ....   01-940 5444   33   G   CH

STRATFORD

C **Harleen Motel**
162 Romford Road
   E15 ....   01-534 7861   27   G   CH NP

STREATHAM

C **Thrale Hall**
38 Mitcham Lane
   SW16 6NP ....   01-769 0094   46   G   NP   H

TOTTENHAM (South)

D **Granham House**
97 Philip Lane ...
   N15 4JR ......   01-801 2244   8   G

WEMBLEY

A **Esso Motor**
   Empire Way ..   01-902 8839   335   G   CH NP

RESTAURANTS IN LONDON

There are thousands of restaurants in London: clearly, therefore, there can be no question of presenting a comprehensive list, particularly since the numbers of restaurants and the standards they offer are constantly changing. In this section we give a select list of restaurants drawn up by the British Tourist Authority. The letters A, B and C give some indication of the price level — A for luxury establishments, B for restaurants of first-class quality, C for more modest places. The letters VM (visitor's menu) indicate a restaurant offering a special menu for visitors at an all-in price. It should be noted that in most London restaurants dinner is normally à la carte.

A **April and Desmond** 8 Egerton Garden Mews, Knightsbridge, SW3. Tel. 584 9576. Dinner only (Saturdays lunch only).

A **Athenaeum (Athenaeum Hotel)** 116 Piccadilly, W1. Tel. 499 3464.

A **Belvedere** Holland House, Holland Park, W8. Tel. 602 1238. Closed Sunday evenings.

A **Café Royal (Grill Room)** 68 Regent Street, W1. Tel. 930 6611.

A **Caprice** Arlington House, Arlington Street, SW1. Tel. 493 5154. Lunch only.

A **Cavalier (London International Hotel)** Cromwell Road, SW7. Tel. 370 4200.

A **Elizabeth Suite** 59-67 Gresham Street, EC2. Tel. 606 7344. Lunch only. Closed Saturdays and Sundays.

A **Empress** 15 Berkeley Street, W1. Tel. 629 6126. Closed Saturdays evenings.

A **Four Seasons (Inn on the Park)** Hamilton Place, Park Lane, W1. Tel. 499 0888.

A **Grill Room (Dorchester Hotel)** Park Lane, W1. Tel. 629 8888.

A **International (London Hilton)** 22 Park Lane, W1. Tel. 493 8000 Ext; 42.

A **Ivy** 1-5 West Street, W2. Tel. 836 4751. Closed Saturday evenings and Sundays.

A **Manners** 72-73 Wilton Road, Victoria, SW1. Tel. 834 7301.

A **Viceroy Colonial House** Mark Lane, EC3. Tel. 626 4654. Lunch only. Closed Saturdays and Sundays.

A **Vintage Room (Inn on the Park)** Hamilton Place, Park Lane, W1. Tel. 499 0888.

B **Abbots** 3 Blenheim Terrace, off Abbey Road, NW8. Tel. 328 0973. Dinner only. Closed Sundays.

B **Avocado** 22 Chartwood Street, SW1. Tel. 828 3303. Closed Saturday lunchtime and Sundays.

B **Bruno One** 7 Park Walk, SW10. Tel. 352 3546. Weekdays lunch only.

B **Bumbles** 16 Buckingham Palace Road, SW1. Tel. 828 2903. Closed Saturdays and Sundays.

B **Cock and Lion** 61 Wigmore Street, W1. Tel. 935 8727. Closed Saturday lunchtime and Sundays.

B **Falstaff** 12 Philpot Lane, EC3. Tel. 283 5959. Lunch only. Closed Saturdays and Sundays.

B **Frederick's** Camden Passage N1. Tel. 359 2888. Closed Sundays.

B **Grumbles** 35 Churton Street, SW1. Tel. 834 0149. Lunch only. Closed Sundays.

B **King's Head and Eight Bells** 50 Cheyne Walk, SW3. Tel. 352 1820. Closed Saturday lunchtime and Sundays.

B **Knights** 171 Knightsbridge, SW7. Tel. 589 0824. Closed Sundays.

B **Land's** 113 Walton Street, Chelsea, SW3. Tel. 584 7585. Dinner only. Closed Sundays.

B **Little Venice (Clarendon Court Hotel)** Edgware Road, W9. Tel. 289 2111. Closed Saturday lunchtime and Sundays.

B **Marquis** 121a Mount Street, W1. Tel. 499 1256. Closed Sundays.

B **Marynka** 232-234 Brompton Road, SW3. Tel. 589 6753. Closed Saturdays.

B **Mr Fogg** 66 Regent Street, W1. Tel. 930 2373. Closed Sundays afternoons.

B **Paesana, La** 30 Uxbridge Street, W8. Tel. 229 4332.

B **Palmerston** 49 Bishopsgate, EC2. Tel. 588 6317. Lunch only. Closed Saturdays and Sundays.

B **Patricia's** 9 Park Walk, SW10. Tel. 352 7782. Dinner only.

B **Phoenix** 37 Cavendish Square, W1. Tel. 629 1700. Lunch only. Closed Sundays.

B **Pill Box** Westminster Bridge Road, SE1. Tel. 928 3250. Closed Saturday evenings and Sundays.

B **Post House** Haverstock Hill, NW3. Tel. 794 81 21. Open 11 a.m. to 11 p.m.

B **Princess (Alexandra National Hotel)** 330 Seven Sisters Road, Finsbury Park, N4. Tel. 800 8090.

B **Provence** 80 Heath Street, NW3. Tel. 435 4111. Open 6 p.m. to midnight. Dinner only.

B **Sands** 30 New Bond Street, W1. Tel. 629 4946. Open 10 1.m. to 1 a.m.

B **Sans-Souci** 68 Royal Hospital Road, SW3. Tel. 352 6045. Closed Sundays.

B **Simpsons** 38½ Cornhill, EC3. Tel. 626 8901. Lunch only. Closed Sundays.

B **S.P.Q.R.** 87 Dean Street, W1. Tel. 734 6487. Closed Sundays.

B **Stag** 4 Russia Court, Russia Row, Cheapside, EC2. Tel. 606 4103. Lunch only. Closed Saturdays and Sundays.

B **Strand Corner House** Trafalgar Square, WC2. Tel. 930 7373. **VM.**

B **Top of the Tower** G.P.O. Tower, Maple Street, W1. Tel. 636 3000.

B **White Lion** 15 St. Giles High Street, WC2. Tel. 836 8956. Closed Sundays.

B **World's End One** 1a Langton Street, SW10. Tel. 352 0352. Dinner only: also lunch on Sundays.

C **Abingdon** Church House, Great Smith Street, SW1. Tel. 222 4587. Lunch only. Closed Saturdays and Sundays.

C **Alexandra National Coffee Shop (Alexandra National Hotel)** 330 Seven Sisters Road, Finsbury Park, N4. Tel. 800 8090. Open 7 a.m. to 12.30 a.m.

C **Angel** 101 Bermondsey Wall, East Rotherhithe, SE16. Tel. 237 3608. Closed Saturday lunchtime and Sundays.

C **Baker and Oven** 10 Paddington Street, W1.   Tel. 935 5072.
Closed Sundays.

C **Barley Mow** 50 Long Lane, Smithfield, EC1.   Tel. 606 6591.
Lunch only.

C **Casa Cominetti** 129 Rushey Green, SE6.   Tel. 697 2314.
Closed Sunday evenings.

C **Chiltern** Baker Street Station, NW1.   Tel. 935 0428.   Lunch
only.

C **Clowns** 31 Dover Street, W1.   Tel. 629 5134.   Closed weekends.

C **Dukes** 55 Duke Street, W1.   Tel. 499 5000.   Closed Sunday
lunchtime.

C **Hansom Cab** 84-86 Earls Court Road, W8.   Tel. 937 6356.
Lunch only.

C **Kardomah** 162 Tottenham Court Road, W1.   Tel. 387 8802.

C **London Zoo and Zoological Society** Regent's Park, NW1.
Tel. 722 3333.   Lunch only.

C **Maison Lyons** Marble Arch, W1.   Tel. 262 3434 (6 restaurants
and self-service counters).

C **Nag's Head** 10 James Street, WC2.   Tel. 836 4678.   Closed
Sundays.

C **Quality Inns** 5-6 Argyll Street, W1.   Tel. 437 5997.   **VM.**
128 Baker Street, W1.   Tel. 486 9769.   **VM.**

1-2 Coventry Street, W1.   Tel. 437 0756.

22 Leicester Square, WC2.   Tel. 930 6823.   **VM.**

141 Oxford Street, W1.   Tel. 437 2713.   **VM.**

192 Oxford Street, W1.   Tel. 580 1504.   **VM.**

539 Oxford Street, W1.   Tel. 629 3162.

310 Regent Street, W1.   Tel. 580 1079.   **VM.**

75 Strand, WC2.   Tel. 240 1487.   **VM.**

191 Victoria Street, SW1.   Tel. 834 0206.   **VM.**

C **Richoux** 86 Brompton Road, SW3 1ER.   Tel. 584 8300.

C **Romano Santi** 50 Greek Street W1.   Tel. 437 2350.   **VM.**

C **St Stephen's** 10 Bridge Street, SW1.   Tel. 930 2541.   Closed
Sunday evenings.

C **Upstairs (Basil Street Hotel)** Basil Street Knightsbridge,
SW3.   Tel. 730 3411.   Closed Sundays.

C **White House Coffee Shop** Albany Street, Regent's Park,
NW1.   Tel. 387 1200.

C **Melting Pot (Central Park Hotel)** Queensborough Terrace, W2, Tel. 229 2424. Closed Sundays.

C **Ranelagh** 39 Ranelagh Grove, SW1. Tel. 730 2572.

Armenian cooking

B **Ararat** 249 Camden High Street, NW1. Tel. 267 0319. Closed Mondays.

B **Armenian** 20 Kensington Church Street, W8. Tel. 937 5828. Closed Sundays.

Balinese cooking

B **Bali** 101 Edgware Road, W2. Tel. 723 3303.

Ceylonese cooking

C **Sri Lanka** 19 Childs Street, SW5. Tel. 373 4116.

Chinese cooking

B **Fu Tong** 29 Kensington High Street, W8. Tel. 937 1293.

B **Lotus House** 61-69 Edgware Road, W2. Tel. 262 4109.

B **Manchurian** 42 Baker Street, W1. Tel. 935 0331.

C **Chop Suey House** 37 Heath Street, Hampstead, NW3. Tel. 435 4142.

C **Choy's** 45 Fifth Street, W1. Tel. 437 7109.

C **Chinese Lantern** 4 Thackeray Street, W8. Tel. 937 4981. Dinner only.

C **Sailing Junk** 59 Marloes Road, W8. Tel. 937 2589. Dinner only. **VM.**

Canton specialties;

B **Cathay** 4-6 Glasshouse Street, Piccadilly Circus, W1. Tel. 734 3697. **VM.**

B **China Garden** 66 Brewer Street, W1. Tel. 437 6500. Closed Sundays. **VM.**

B **Shangri-La** 233 Brompton Road, SW3 2DA. Tel. 584 3658.

B **Sun Ya** 57 Brewer Street, W1. Tel. 437 3211. **VM.**

C **Choy's** 172 King's Road, SW3. Tel. 352 9085.

C **Tai Wah** 84 Brewer Street, W1. Tel. 437 1777.

Peking specialties:

A **Mr Chow** 151 Knightsbridge SW1. Tel. 589 7347.

B **Dumpling Inn** 15A Gerrard Street, W1. Tel. 437 2567. **VM.**

B **Gallery Rendezvous** 53-55 Beak Street, W1. Tel. 734 0445. **VM.**

B **Good Earth** 316-138 King's Road SW3. Tel. 352 7755.

B **Lee Yuan** 40 Earls Court Road, W8, 6J. Tel. 937 7047.

B **Soho Rendezvous** 21 Romilly Street, W1. Tel. 437 1486. **VM .**

Shanghai specialties;

B **Chelsea Rendezvous** 4 Sydney Street, SW3. Tel. 352 9515.

British cooking

A **Baron of Beef** Gutter Lane, Gresham Street, EC2. Tel. 606 6961. Closed weekends.

A **Cotillion** Bucklersbury House, Walbrook, EC4. Tel. 248 4735. Lunch only. Closed weekends.

A **Father Thames** Cadogan Pier, Chelsea Embankment, SW3. Tel. 402 4725.

A **Hungry Horse** 196 Fulham Road, SW10. Tel. 352 7757.

A **Hunting Lodge** 16 Lower Regent Street, SW1. Tel. 930 4222. Closed Sundays.

A **Kettners** 29 Romilly Street, W1. Tel. 437 6437. British and French cooking.

A **Lockets** Marsham Court, Marsham Street, SW1. Tel. 834 9552. Closed weekends.

A **Overton's** 4, 5, 6, Victoria Buildings, SW1. Tel. 834 3774. Closed Sundays. French and British cooking.

A **Rib Room (Carlton Tower)** Cadogan Place, SW1. Tel. 235 5411. Roast beef a specialty.

A **Scott's** 20 Mount Street, W1. Tel. 629 5248. Closed Sunday lunchtime.

B **Alleyn's Head** Park Hall Road. Dulwich, SE21. Tel. 670 6540.

B **Belgravia** 8444 9 William Street, SW1. Tel. 235 8444.

B **Blue Boar Inn** 7-9 Leicester Square, WC2. Tel. 437 3189. Dinner only.

B **Britannia** 31 Belgrave Road, SW1. Tel. 828 7914. Closed Sundays.

B **Bun Penny** 225 Brompton Road, SW3. Tel. 589 8578.

B **Chanterelle** 119 Old Brompton Road, SW7. Tel. 373 7390.

B **Charles Dickens (Dickens Restaurant)** 264 Strand, WC2. Tel. 405 4484.

B **Daisy** 40 King's Road, SW3. Tel. 584 7346. **VM**

B **Essex Rib Roast** Dunster House, Mark Lane, EC3. Tel. 623 8581. Lunch only. Closed Sundays.

B **Flanagans** 19 Exhibition Road, SW7. Tel. 584 8359.
11 Kensington High Street, W8. Tel. 937 7262. **VM.**
3 Leicester Place, Leicester Square, WC2. Tel. 437 5164. **VM**
37 Martins Lane, WC2. Tel. 836 5358. **VM.**

B **Garden** 9 Henrietta Street, WC2. Tel. 240 0088. Closed Sundays.

B **George Inn** 77 Borough High Street, SE1. Tel. 407 2056. Closed Fridays.

B **Maggie Jones's** 6 Old Court Place, W8. Tel. 937 6462. Closed Sundays.

B **Massey's Chop House** 38 Beauchamp Place, SW3. Tel. 589 4856. Closed Sundays.
65 South Audley Street, W1. Tel. 493 8988.

B **Mayflower** 117 Rotherhithe Street, SE16. Tel. 237 4088. Closed Saturday lunchtime and Sundays.

B **Old Swan** 116 Battersea Church Road, SW11. Tel. 28 7152. Closed Saturday lunchtime and Sundays.

B **Paramount Grill** 14-15 Irving Street, WC2. Tel. 930 0744.

B **Peter Evan's English Kitchen** 1 Knightly Street, W1. Tel. 734 7460. Closed Sundays.

B **Princes Room (Tower Hotel)** St. Katherine's Way, E1. Tel. 481 2575. French and British cooking.

B **Printer's Devil** 98 Fetter Lane, EC4. Tel. 242 2239.

B **Saddle and Sirloin** Chesterfield House, Rood Lane, EC3. Tel. 626 6818. Lunch only. Closed weekends.

B **Shepherd's** 50 Hertford Street, W1. Tel. 499 3017. Closed Sundays.

B **Stone's Chop House** Panton Street, SW1. Tel. 930 0037. Closed Sundays.

B **Tiddy Dols Eating House** 2/6 Hertford Street, W1. Tel. 499 2357. Dinner only.

B **Volunteer** 245-247 Baker Street, NW1. Tel. 935 6356. Closed Sundays.

C **Antelope** 22 Eaton Terrace, SW1. Tel. 730 7781. Dinner only. Closed Sundays.

C **Crispin's** 7 Windmill Row. Kennington, SE11. Tel. 735 5455. Dinner only. French and British cooking.

C **Gilbert and Sullivan** John Adam Street, WC2. Tel. 839 2580. Closed Sundays.

C **Hampstead** 8444 70 Heath Street, NW3. Tel. 435 8444.

C **Maze Coffee House (Royal Garden Hotel)** Kensington High Street, W8. Tel. 937 8000.

C **Samuel Pepys at Brooks Wharf** 48 Upper Thames Street, EC4. Tel. 248 3048.

C **Sherlock Holmes** 10 Northumberland Street, WC2. Tel. 930 2644. Closed Sundays.

French cooking

A **Andrea's** 8-9 Blacklands Terrace, SW3. Tel. 584 2919.

A **Artiste Assoiffé** 122 Kensington Park Road, W11. Tel. 727 4714. Closed Sundays.

A **Au Jardin des Gourmets** 5 Greek Street, Soho Square, W1. Tel. 437 1816. Closed Sundays.

A **Barracuda** 1d Baker Street, W1. Tel. 486 3728.

A **Bressan (Le)** 14 Wrights Lane, W8. Tel. 937 8525. Closed Sundays.

A **Brompton Grill** 243 Brompton Road, SW3. Tel. 589 8005.

A **Chez Noel** 7 Beauchamp Place, SW3. Tel. 589 4109. Closed Sundays.

A **Coq d'Or** Stratton Street, W1. Tel. 629 7807. Closed Sundays.

A **Coq Hardi, Le** 353 Kensington High Street, W8. Tel. 603 6951. Closed Sundays.

A **Ecu de France, A l'** 111 Jermyn Street, SW1. Tel. 930 2837. Closed Saturdays and Sundays lunchtime.

A **Fontaine (La)** Grosvenor House, Park Lane, W1. Tel. 499 6411.

A **Geneviève** 13-14 Thayer Street, Marylebone High Street, W1. Tel. 486 2244. Closed Sundays.

A **Grand Véfour** 20 Chesham Place, SW1. Tel. 235 6040.

A **Lafayette** 32 King Street, St. James's, SW1. Tel. 930 1131. Closed Sundays.

A **Maison Prunier** 72 St. James's Street, SW1. Tel. 493 1373.
Seafood a specialty.

A **Mirabelle** 56 Curzon Street, W1. Tel. 499 4636. Closed
Sundays.

A **Petit Montmartre (Le)** 15 Marylebone Lane, W1. Tel. 935
9226.

A **Quaglino's** Bury Street, St. James's, SW1. Tel. 930 6767.
Floor show and dancing.

A **Relais du Café Royal** 68 Regent Street, W1. Tel. 930 6611.

A **Stable** 123 Cromwell Road, SW7. Tel. 370 1203. Closed
Sundays.

A **White House (White House Hotel)** Albany Street, NW1. Tel.
387 1200. Closed Sundays.

B **Artiste Affamé** 243 Old Brompton Road, SW5. Tel. 373 1659.
Dinner only. Closed Sundays.

B **Au Bon Accueil** 27 Elystan Street, SW3. Tel. 589 3718. Closed
Sundays.

B **Au Fin Bec** 100 Draycott Avenue, SW3. Tel. 584 3600. Closed
Sundays. **VM.**

B **Au Savarin** 8 Charlotte Street, W1. Tel. 636 7134. Closed
Sundays.

B **Bistingo (Le)** 117 Queensway, W2. Tel. 727 07 43.

B **Boulestin** 25 Southampton Street, WC2. Tel. 836 7061. Closed
Saturdays and Sundays.

B **Carrosse (Le)** 19 Elystan Road, SW3. Tel. 584 5248. Dinner
only. Closed Sundays.

B **Casse-croûte** 1 Cale Street, SW3. Tel. 352 6174. Closed
Monday lunchtime.

B **Chanterelle** 119 Old Brompton Road, SW7. Tel. 373 7390.

B **Chateaubriand** 48 Belsize Lane, Hampstead, NW3. Tel. 435
4882 .Dinner only.

B **Chef (Le)** 41 Connaught Street, W2. Tel. 262 5945.

B **Chez Cleo** 11-13 Harrington Gardens, SW7. Tel. 370 1479.

B **Chez Solange** 35 Cranbourne Street, WC2. Tel. 836 5886.
Closed Sundays.

B **Cochon Noir, Le** 26 Motcomb Street, SW1. Tel. 235 5346.
Closed Sundays.

B **Didier** 5 Warwick Place, W9. Tel. 286 7484. Closed Sundays·
VM.

B **Elysée** 13 Percy Street, W1. Tel. 636 4804.

B **Escargot Bienvenu, L'** 48 Greek Street, W1. Tel. 437 4460.
Closed Saturdays and Sundays.

B **Etoile, L'** 30 Charlotte Street, W1. Tel. 636 7189. Closed
Saturdays and Sundays.

B **Gargouille de Notre Dame** 130 Regent's Park Road, Primrose
Hill, NW1. Tel. 586 4338. Dinner only. Closed Sundays.

B **Grand Veneur (Le)** 10 Troy Court, Phillimore Gardens, W8.
Tel. 937 4541.

B **Marcel** 14 Sloane Street, Knightsbridge, SW1. Tel. 235 4912.
Closed Sundays. Provençal cooking.

B **Matelot (Le)** 49 Elizabeth Street, SW1. Tel. 730 1038. Closed
Sundays lunchtime.

B **Pomme d'Amour, La** 128 Holldan Park Avenue, W11. Tel.
229 8532. Closed Sundays. **VM.**

B **Rôtisserie Normande (Portman Hotel)** 22 Portman Square,
W1. Tel. 486 5844.

B **Toque Blanche, La** 21 Abingdon Road, W8. Tel. 937 5832.
Closed Sundays.

C **Bistingo (Le)** 65 Fleet Street, EC4. Tel. 353 4436.

C **Crispin's** 219 Kennington Road, SE11. Tel. 735 5455. Dinner
only. French and British cooking.

C **Elegant Bistro** 272 Brompton Road, SW3. Tel. 584 1668.
Dinner only.

C **Other Bistro** 27 Motcomb Street, SW1. Tel. 235 1668.

C **Suzettes** 34 Sussex Place, W2. Tel. 723 1199.

German cooking

B **Berlin Room** 44-46 Knightsbridge, SW1. Tel. 235 7121.

C **Schmidt's** 33-44 Charlotte Street, W1. Tel. 636 0723.

Greek cooking

A **Grecian Taverna** 27 Percy Street, W1. Tel. 636 8914. **VM.**

B **Number 10** 10 Lancashire Court, New Bond Street, W1.
Tel. 493 5545.

B **Anemos Greek Kebab House** 34 Charlotte Street, W1. Tel.
636 2289.

Hungarian cooking

B **Gay Hussar** 2 Greek Street, W1. Tel. 437 0973. Closed Sundays.

B **Hungarian Csarda** 77 Dean Street, W1. Tel. 437 1261.

B **Mignon Hungarian** 2 Queensway, W2. Tel. 229 0093. Closed Mondays.

Indian cooking

B **Gaylord** 79-81 Mortimer Street, W1. Tel. 580 3615. **VM.**

B **Mumtaz** 56 Edgware Road, W2. Tel. 723 3243.

B **Shezan** 16-22 Cheval Place, SW7. Tel. 589 7918. Closed Sundays.

B **Tandoori** 153 Fulham Road, SW3. Tel. 589 7749. Dinner only: also lunch on Saturdays and Sundays.

B **Tandoori of Mayfair** 37A Curzon Street, W1. Tel. 629 0600. Closed Sundays.

B **Veeraswamy's** 99-101 Regent's Street, W1. Tel. 734 1041.

C **Ashoka** 22 Cranbourne Street, WC2. Tel. 836 5936.

C **Jamshid** 6 Glendower Place, SW7. Tel. 589 8045. **VM.**

C **Khyber Pass** 21 Bute Street, SW7. Tel. 589 7311.

C **Shafi** 18 Garrard Street, W1. Tel. 437 2354. **VM.**

Italian cooking

A **Angelo (Da)** 42 Albemarle Street, W1. Tel. 499 1776. Closed Sundays.

A **Barracuda** 1d Baker Street, W1. Tel. 486 3728.

A **Campana** 31 Marylebone High Street, W1. Tel. 935 5307. Closed Sundays.

A **Gennaro's** 44 Dean Street, W1. Tel. 437 3950. Closed Sundays

A **Leoni's Quo Vadis** 26-29 Dean Street, W1. Tel. 437 9585.

A **Cantina Marchigiana** 13 Beauchamp Place, SW3. Tel. 584 4810.

A **Tiberio** 22 Queen Street, W1. Tel. 629 3561.

A **Trinacria** 20 Frith Street, W1. Tel. 437 6688.

B **Alpino** 29 Leicester Square, WC2. Tel. 839 2939.

B **Arlecchino** 8 Hillgate Street, W8. Tel. 229 2027.

B **Balta, La** 200 Haverstock Hill, NW3. Tel. 794 4126.

B **Bellavista** 132 Cromwell Road, SW7. Tel. 373 0200.

B **Biagi's** 39 Upper Berkeley Street, W1. Tel. 723 0394.

B **Canaletto** 451 Edgware Road, W2. Tel. 262 7027. Closed Mondays.

B **Casina Rossa, La** 169 South Lambeth Road, SW8. Tel. 735 6388. Closed Sundays.

B **Chez Ciccio** 38c Kensington Church Street, W8. Tel. 937 2005.

B **Corretto** 45 Kensington High Street, W8. Tel. 937 6471.

B **Dei Pescatori** 55-57 Charlotte Street, W1. Tel. 580 3289.

B **Dolce Vita (La)** 10 Frith Street, W1. Tel. **437** 2774.

B **Don Luigi** 33c Kings Road, SW3. Tel. 730 3023.

B **Fontana, La** 89 Pimlico Road, SW1. Tel. 730 66 30. Closed Sundays.

B **Giovanni's** 10 Goodwins Court, off St. Martin's Lane, WC2. Tel. 240 2877.

B **Gondoliere** 3 Gloucester Road, SW7. Tel. 584 8062.

B **Mamma Rose** 27 Uxbridge Street, W8. Tel. 727 8800. Closed Sundays.

B **Osteria di Londra** 13 Heddon Street, W1. Tel. 437 6529.

B **Piazza Piccadilly** 196 Piccadilly, W1. Tel. 734 7744.

B **Piccola Venezia** 39 Thurloe Place, South Kensington, SW7. Tel. 589 3883.

B **Rossetti** 23 Queen's Grove, NW8. Tel. 722 7141.

B **San Marino** 26 Sussex Place, W2. Tel. 723 8395.

B **Santa Croce** 112 Cheyne Walk, SW10. Tel. 352 7534.

B **Terrazza** 19 Romilly Street, W1. Tel. 734 2504.

B **Terrazza-Est** 125 Chancery Lane, WC2. Tel. 242 2601. Closed Sundays.

B **Trattoo** 2 Abingdon Road, W8. Tel. 937 4448.

B **Venezia** 21 Great Chapel Street, W1. Tel. 437 6505. Closed Sundays.

C **Bertorelli** 70-72 Queensway, W2. Tel. 229 3160.

C **Casalinga, La** 64 St. John's Wood, NW8. Tel. 722 5959.

C **Dino's** 117 Gloucester Road, SW7. Tel. 373 3678.

C **Dino's** 16 Kensington Church Street, W8. Tel. 937 3896.

C **Hostaria Romana** 70 Dean Street, W1. Tel. 734 2869. **VM.**

C **Osteria San Lorenzo** 22 Beauchamp Place, SW3. Tel. 584 1074. Closed Sundays.

C **Palio di Siena, II** 133 Earls Court Road, SW5. Tel. 373 4487.

C **Spaghetti House** 79 Knightsbridge, SW1. Tel. 235 8141. Closed Sundays.

C **Verbanella** 30 Beauchamp Place, SW3. Tel. 854 1107. Closed Sundays.

Japanese cooking

A **Mikado** 110 George Street, W1. Tel. 935 8320. Closed Sundays

B **Akiko Japanese** 5 Cathedral Place, St. Paul's Shopping Centre, EC4. Tel. 236 4120. Closed weekends.

B **Hokkai** 61 Brewer Street, W1. Tel. 734 5826.

Jewish cooking

Isow's 10 Brewer Street, W1. Tel. 437 7618.

Mexican cooking

B **Cucaracha, La** 12-13 Greek Street, W1. Tel. 734 2253. Closed Sundays.

Oriental cooking

A **Omar Khayyam** 50 Cannon Street, EC4. Tel. 248 7363. Dancing.

B **Petra** 9 Seymour Place, W1. Tel. 402 9930.

Polynesian cooking

B **Beachcomber (May Fair Hotel)** Berkeley Street, W1. Tel. 629 7777. Dinner only. Dancing.

Russian cooking

A **Nikita's** 65 Ifield Road, SW10. Tel. 352 6326. Dinner only. Closed Mondays.

C **Luba's Bistro** 6 Yeomans Row, SW3. Tel. 589 2950. Closed Sundays.

Scandinavian cooking

B **Oslo Court** Prince Albert Road, Regent's Park, NW1. Tel. 722 8795. Closed Mondays.

B **Dania** 293-5 Railton Road, SE24. Tel. 274 9163. Closed Sundays.

B **Norway Food Centre** 166 Brompton Road, SW3. Tel. 584 6062. **VM.** Closed Sundays.

Fish and seafood

A **Cunningham's** 17B Curzon Street, W1. Tel. 499 7595.

A **Overton's** 5 St. James's Street, SW1. Tel. 839 3774. Closed Sundays.

A **Wilton's** 27 Bury Street, SW1. Tel. 930 8391. Closed Sundays.

B **Bentley's** 11-15 Swallow Street, W1. Tel. 734 6120.

B **Fisherman's Wharf** 73 Baker Street, W1. Tel. 935 0471.

B **Garner's Grilled Sole** 27 Wardour Street, W1. Tel. 437 1287.

B **Izaak Walton** 7 Park Walk, Fulham Road, SW10. Tel. 352 3546.

B **Old Caledonia** Victoria Embankment, WC2. Tel. 240 2750.

B **Poissonnerie** 82 Sloane Avenue, SW3. Tel. 589 2457.

B **Staggers of Pimlico** 44 Hugh Street, Pimlico, SW1. Tel. 834 4104. Closed Sundays. **VM.**

B **Wheeler's** 19 Old Compton Street, W1. Tel. 437 2706. Closed Sundays.

B **Wheeler's Alcove** 17 Kensington High Street, W8. Tel. 937 1443. Closed Sundays.

B **Wheeler's Antoine** 40 Charlotte Street, W1. Tel. 636 2817.

B **Wheeler's City** 19 Great Tower Street, EC3. Tel. 626 3685. Closed weekends.

B **Wheeler's George and Dragon** 256 Brompton Road, SW3. Tel. 584 2626.

C **Geale's Fish Restaurant** 2 Farmer Street, W8. Tel. 727 7699. Closed Sundays.

Spanish cooking

B **Casa Pepe** 52 Dean Street, W1. Tel. 437 3916.

B **Martinez** 25 Swallow Street, W1. Tel. 734 5066.

Steak houses

A **Guinea Grill** 30 Bruton Place, W1. Tel. 629 3064. Closed Sundays.

B **Aberdeen Angus** Centre Heights, 149 Finchley Road, NW3. Tel. 722 2232.

B **Aberdeen Steak House** 170 Victoria Street, SW1. Tel. 834 9880.

B **George** 1 Rushey Green, Catford, SE6. Tel. 698 1773. Closed Sundays.

C **Steak House (Lincoln Hotel)** 117-125 Cromwell Road, SW7. Tel. 370 4444.

C **Venture Inn** 232 Camden High Street, NW1. Tel. 485 9543.

C **White Bear Inn** Piccadilly Circus, W1. Tel. 930 7901.

C **Comedy** 38 Panton Street, SW1. Tel. 930 4017.

C **Ducks and Drakes** 112 Queensway, W2. Tel. 229 1474.

C **Pig and Whistle** 14 Little Chester Street, SW1. Tel. 235 4207.

C **Portman Arms** 21 Balcombe Street, NW1. Tel. 723 0352.

C **Riverside** Upper Thames Street, EC4. Tel. 236 2888.

C **Shelley's** 10 Stafford Street, W1. Tel. 499 1174.

Grill rooms

B **Barrie Grill** De Vere Gardens, W8. Tel. 937 8121.

B **Bulldog Chophouse (Royal Garden Hotel)** Kensington High Street, W8. Tel. 937 8000. Closed Sundays.

B **Gore** 189 Queen's Gate, SW7. Tel. 584 6616.

B **Grill Room (Strand Corner House)** Trafalgar Square, WC2. Tel. 930 7373.

B **Rustums le Gourmet** 312 King's Road, SW3. Tel. 352 4483.

B **Vine** 3 Piccadilly Place, W1. Tel. 734 5789.

C **Charcos** 19 Panton Street, SW1. Tel. 839 1955.

C **Grill and Griddle** 219-222 Piccadilly, W1. Tel. 839 7133.

There are also many steak houses belonging to the *Angus, Garner's* and *London Steak House* groups.

Swiss cooking

B **Swiss Centre** 2 New Coventry Street, W1. Tel. 734 1291. 4 restaurants.

Thai cooking

A **Siam** 12 St Albans Grove, Kensington, W8. Tel. 937 8765. Floor show.

Turkish cooking

A **Gallipoli** 7-8 Bishopgate Churchyard, EC2.   Tel. 588 1922.
Dancing and floor show.

B **Nibub Lokanta** 112-114 Edgware Road, W2.   Tel. 262 6636.

Vietnamese cooking

C **Nguyen Vietnamese** 1 Palace Gate, W8.   Tel. 589 4778.   **VM**.

SOME LONDON PUBS

The public house or "pub" is of course a characteristic feature
of British life, and particularly of London life, and visitors from
abroad will want to look in at one of the typical London pubs
and sample the beer (which is available in a much wider range
than on the Continent).   We give below a selection of some of
London's best-known pubs, many of which have historical
associations.   They are given in alphabetical order (from "This
Month in London", published by the British Tourist Authority).
The name given at the end of each entry is that of the owners
(usually a brewing firm): "free house" means that the pub is
not tied to any particular firm of brewers.

Bull and Bush, North End Road, Hampstead NW3.   Made
famous by the old music-hall song "Down at the old Bull and
Bush".   Ind Coope.

City Arms, West Ferry Road, E14. An East End pub patronised
by dockers.   Watney.

Coal Hole, Strand, WC2.   A 17th century pub in the heart
of the theatre district.   Ind Coope.

Dirty Dick's, 202 Bishopsgate, EC2.   A typical City pub dating
from the 18th century, with an atmosphere of its own.   Free
house.

Duke of Cumberland, New King's Road, SW6.   A Victorian-
style pub named after Queen Victoria's uncle.   Young and Co.

George Inn, Borough High St, SE1.   An old inn dating from
1677, mentioned in Dickens's "Little Dorrit".   Whitbread.

Hoop and Grapes, 47 Aldgate St, EC3.   The oldest pub in the
City, with a ghost which haunts the cellars.   Bass Charrington.

Magpie and Stump, 18 Old Bailey, EC4.   Formerly frequented
by those who came here to watch public executions.   Bass Charrington.

Mayflower, 117 Rotherhithe St, EC16. A Tudor-style pub. The Pilgrim Fathers left from here in 1620 to found New England. Bass Charrington.

Nag's Head, 10 James St, Covent Garden, WC2. Patronised by opera-goers. Whitbread.

Pied Bull, 1 Liverpool Road, Islington. N1. Sir Walter Raleigh stayed here and may have introduced the use of tobacco in this old inn. Bass Charrington.

Prospect of Whitby, 57 Wapping Wall, E1. A historic old pub overlooking the Port of London. St George's Taverns.

Samuel Pepys at Brooke Wharf, Upper Thames St, EC4. A pub with the authentic atmosphere of the 17th century. Bass Charrington.

The Anchor, Bankside, SE1. Near Southwark Bridge and the Globe Theatre. Anchor Taverns.

The Escape, Mabledon Place, WC1. Decorated with mementos of second world war escapes. Whitbread.

Sherlock Holmes, Northumberland Avenue, WC2. Decorated in period style, complete with the head of the Hound of the Baskervilles. Whitbread.

Waterman's Arms, 1 Glengarnock Avenue, E14 (Isle of Dogs). A famous East End pub. Ind Coope.

The Underwriter, St Mary Axe, EC3. A City pub, decorated with bottles and casks suspended from the ceiling. Scottish and Newcastle.

Tiger Tavern, 1-2 Tower Hill, EC3. Near the Tower of London, on the site of an earlier establishment patronised by Peter the Great. Bass Charrington.

Trafalgar, 200 King's Road. A fashionable pub: jazz music.

Ye Olde Cheshire Cheese, Fleet St, EC4. A famous old inn frequented by journalists. Good cooking. Closes at 9 p.m.: closed on Saturday afternoons and Sundays. Free house.

Ye Olde Cock Tavern, 22 Fleet St, EC4. Charles Dickens's favourite inn. Literary atmosphere. Truman.

DANCING

A short selection of places where you can dance:

Café de Paris, 3 Coventry St, W1 (tel. 437 2036). From 3 to 5.45 for tea, from 7.30 in the evening (to 11.30, midnight or 1 a.m. according to the day).

Empire Ballroom, Leicester Square, WC2 (tel. 437 1446). Much the same times.

Hammersmith Palais, Shepherds Bush Road, W6 (tel. 748 2812). From 8 p.m. Tea 3 to 5.45 on Saturdays and Sundays.

Lyceum, Wellington St, WC2. Closed Fridays.

Tiffany's, 22 Shaftesbury Avenue, W1 (tel. 437 5012).

OTHER EVENING ENTERTAINMENTS IN LONDON

Folk singing

Bunjie's Folk Cellar, 27 Lichfield St, WC2. Every evening at 8.

The Enterprise, Chalk Farm Road, NW3. Sundays at 7.30.

Folk Cellar, Cecil Sharp House, 2 Regent's Park Road, NW1. Saturdays at 8.

Haystack, Union Building, Malet St, WC1. Fridays at 8.

Nashville Room, 171 North End Road, W14. Every evening at 7.30.

Phoebus Awake, The Rising Sun, Rushey Green, Catford, SE6. Tuesdays 8 to 11.

Troubadour, 265 Old Brompton Road, SW5. Saturdays 10.30 to 2 a.m.

Jazz clubs

100 Club, 100 Oxford St, W1. From 7.30.

Ronnie Scott's, 47 Frith St, W1. From 8.30 to 3 a.m. Closed Sundays.

Torrington Music, 4 Lodge Lane, Finchley, N12. From 8.30.

Discotheques

There are dozens of these, some of them having only an ephemeral existence, others becoming fashionable for a time and then giving place to new ones.

Anthea's Fouberts Place, W1. From 9 to 3 a.m.

Marquee, 90 Wardour St, W1. From 7.15 to 11.

Saddle Room, 1a Hamilton Mews, Park Lane, W1. From 9 to 4 a.m. Closed Sundays.

Night clubs

To secure admission you must be a member or be accompanied by a member of the club.

Astor, Berkeley Square, W1 (tel. 499 2366).

Eve Club, 189 Regent St, W1 (tel. 734 0557).

Gargoyle, 69 Dean St (tel. 437 3278).

Murray's Cabaret Club, 16 Beak St, W1 (tel. 437 4623).

Restaurants with dancing

Celebrity, 13 Clifford St, W1 (tel. 493 0855). Closed Sundays.

Latin Quarter, 13-17 Wardour St, W1 (tel. 437 6001). Closed Sundays.

Omar Khayyam, 50 Cannon St, EC4 (tel. 248 2660). Also open at lunchtime.

007 Night Spot, Hilton Hotel, Park Lane, W1 (tel. 493 8000). Closed Sundays.

Quaglino's, Bury St, SW1 (tel. 930 6767). Also open at lunchtime. Closed Sundays.

Showboat, Trafalgar Square, WC2 (tel. 930 2781). Closed Sundays.

Villa dei Cesari, 135 Grosvenor Road, SW1 (tel. 828 7453). Closed Mondays.

Historical banquets

Medieval Feestes, Trafalgar Square, WC2 (same as Showboat) (tel. 930 7243). At 7.45. Closed Sundays.

Elizabethan Rooms, 190 Queen's Gate, SW7 (tel. 584 6616). At 8.

II. THE SOUTH-EAST

SURREY

Hotel	Tel.	Rooms	Notes	
Bagshot				
C **Cricketers'**	3196	17	G	
Camberley				
C **Camberley Motel** .	63773	15	G	CH
C **Frimley Hall**	28321	69	G	CH NP
D **Cambridge**	5127	14	G	CH NP
Charlwood, nr. Horley				
C **Russ Hill** .... Norwood Hill	255	104	G	CH NP
D **Barfield Farm** Norwood Hill	545	6	G	CH UL
Churt				
B **Frensham Pond** Frensham	3175	7	G	CH NP
D **Pride of the Valley Inn** Hindhead	5799	11	G	CH
Dorking				
B **Burford Bridge**	4561	30	G	CH NP
B **White Horse**	81138	36	G	CH NP
C **Punch Bowl Motor Hotel**	81935	29	G	CH NP
D **Star and Garter** ...	2820	10	G	
East Horsley				
B **Thatchers**	4291	22	G	CH NP
Egham				
C **Angiers**	3886	12		CH
C **Great Fosters**	3822	23	G	CH NP
Epsom				
C **Drift Bridge** Burgh Heath	52163	29	G	CH NP
C **Linden House**	21447	35	G	CH

D Epsom Downs	21639	19	G	CH NP		
D White House	22472	11	G	CH		

Ewell

C Nonsuch Park	22472	11	G	CH		

Farnham

C Nonsuch Park ...01-393 2505		14	G	CH		
C Bishop's Table	5545	20	G			
C Bush	5237	50	G	CH NP		

Guildford

B Angel	64555	24	G	CH NP		
C Clavadel	2064	18	G	CH		
C White Horse	64511	23	G	CH NP		
D Waverley	60070	15	G			

Haslemere

C Georgian	51555	21	G	CH		
C Lythe Hill	4131	6	G	CH		
D White Horse	2103	8	G			

Hindhead

C Devil's Punch Bowl	5718	15	G	NP		

Horley

B Skylane Motor Hotel	6971	15	G	CH NP		
C Chequers	3006	78	GCWCH NP			

Reigate

C Bridge House Motel	46801	26	G	CH NP		

Staines

C Pack Horse	54221	19	G	CH NP		

Weybridge

C Oatlands Park	47242	144	G	CH NP UL		
C Ship	48364	16	G	CH NP		

Woking

C Mayford Manor ...	62695	12	G			
D Wheatsheaf	3047	24	G	CH		

KENT

Ashford

D Croft	22140	15	G		CH	
D George	25512	13	G		CH	

Bickley

C Bickley Manor	01-467 3851	26	G		CH NP	

Broadstairs

B Castle Keep	Thanet 63434	19	G		CH NP	
C Castlemere	Thanet 61566	44	G		CH	

Canterbury

C Abbot's Barton	60341	33	G		CH NP	
C Chaucer	64427	47	G		CH	
C County	66266	40	G		NP	
C Slatters	63271	30	G		CH NP	
D Ersham Lodge	63174	12	G		CH	UL
D Highfield	62772	13	G		CH	
D Pilgrims	64531	10	G		CH	UL
D Queen's Head	62373	7	G		CH	
D Red House	63578	25	G	CW	CH	UL

Cranbrook

C George	3348	11	G			
C Willesley	3234	16	G		CH	

Deal

C Queen's	217i	61	G		CH NP	
D Black Horse	4074	13	G		CH	

Dover

C Castle Guest House 10 Castle Hill Road	4074	6	G		CH	UL
C Central 50-51 Biggin Street	721	17	G		CH NP	
C White Cliffs Sea Front	633	66	G		CH NP	

D **Dover Stage** Sea Front	2112	42				NP	
D **East Cliff** Marine Parade	2299	22	G	CW			
D **St James** Harold Street	1085	17	G	CW		NP	
D **Webb's** 163-165 Folkestone Road	1897	20	G		CH		
D **Whitfield House** Kearsney	2236	9	G		CH		

Faversham

D **Ship**	2179	14	G				

Folkestone

C **Burlington** Earls Avenue	55301	50	G		CH	NP	
C **Grand** The Leas ..	54616	21	G		CH	NP	
C **Princes** Bouverie Road West	52850	70				NP	
C **Salisbury** The Leas	52102	46		CW			
D **Ambassador** The Leas	52140	43		CW		NP	
D **Arundel** 3 Clifton Road	52442	13		CW			UL
D **Barrelle** 14/15 Marine Parade	51387	26	G				
D **Clifton** The Leas ..	53191	58	G			NP	
D **Esplanade** Sandgate Road	53540	36		CW	CH	NP	
D **Garden House** Sandgate Road	52278	67	G				UL
D **Highcliffe** Clifton Gardens ...	55408	45		CW			
D **Joydon** 62 Bouverie Road ..	54167	12	G	CW			UL
D **Laburnham** 23-24 Westbourne Gardens	51146	36	G	CW			UL

D Lismore
   Trinity Crescent ...   52717   31   G
D Lyndhurst
   Sandgate Road   51941   85   G   NP
D Shannon
   59-61 Cheriton Road   52138   21   G CW   UL

Gravesend

C Tollgate Motel   ...   2768   62   G   CH NP
D Clarendon Royal   ..   63151   28   G   CH NP

Hawkhurst

C Tudor Arms   2312   10   G   CH
D Royal Oak   2184   7   G

Hollingbourne

B Great Danes   381   79   CH NP

Hythe

C Imperial   67441   81   G   CH NP

Maidstone

C Royal Star   55721   41   G   CH NP
C Veglios Motel   55459   28   G   NP

Margate and Cliftonville

D Bicken Hall   21967   53   G CW   NP
D Endcliffe ....   Thanet
                  21829   58   G CW   NP
D Hereward ....   Thanet
                  23244   66   CW CH NP

Penshurst

C Leicester Arms   551   7   G

Ramsgate

C Viking Ship Motel
   (Pegwell Bay 2 mls SW) Thanet
                  52493   23   G
D Abbeygail ....   Thanet
                  54154   9   CW   UL
D Beverley ....   Thanet
                  51514   37   G

D	**San Clu**	Thanet 52345	54	G			NP
D	**Sycamore**	Thanet 53453	21	G		CH	

Rochester

C	**Royal Victoria and Bull**	Medway 46266	29	G		CH	NP
D	**King's Head**	Medway 42709	14	G			

Sandwich

C	**Bell**	2360	27	G		CH	NP

Sevenoaks

C	**Royal Oak**	52161	22	G			

Tonbridge

C	**Rose and Crown** ..	4977	32	G			NP

Tunbridge Wells

C	**Beacon**	24252	11	G		CH	
C	**Calverley**	26455	43	G		CH	NP
C	**Royal Well Inn**	23414	16	G			
C	**Spa**	20331	100	G		CH	NP
C	**Wellington**	20286	58	G		CH	NP
D	**Swan**	27590	13	G		CH	

West Malling

C	**Hunting Lodge** ...	3306	10	G		CH	
D	**Swan**	3000	10	G			

SUSSEX

Alfriston

C	**Deans Place**	248	42	G	CW	CH		
C	**Star Inn**	495	34	G		CH		
D	**Riverdale Guest House**	397		G	CW		NP	UL

Arundel

C	**Norfolk Arms**	882242	12	G		CH	
D	**Bridge**	882242	12	G		CH	

Battle

				G	CW	CH	NP	UL
C	Beauport Park	Hastings 51222	20	G		CH		
D	George	2844	18	G				

Bexhill-on-Sea

				G	CW	CH	NP	UL
C	Granville	5437	59	G		CH	NP	
D	Dunselma	2148	11		CW			UL
D	L'Avenir	4708	10					
D	Southlands Court .	628	24	G		CH		

Bognor Regis

				G	CW	CH	NP	UL
C	Black Mill House ..	21945	22	G		CH		UL
C	Clarehaven	23265	28	G				
C	Royal	4665	33				NP	
C	Royal Norfolk	26222	56	G		CH	NP	
D	Montrose	21089	8	G		CH		UL
D	Pinehurst	5912	11	G				

Brighton and Hove

				G	CW	CH	NP	UL
A	Bedford King's Road	29744	124	G		CH	NP	
B	Metropole King's Road, Brighton	775432	275	G		CH	NP	
B	Royal Crescent Marine Parade	66311	56	G		CH	NP	
C	Brighton Touring 216 Preston Road .	507853	15	G		CH		
C	Clarges Marine Parade	63077	65	G			NP	
C	Dudley Lansdowne Place, Hove	736266	75	G		CH	NP	
C	Grand King's Road	26301	194				NP	
C	Lawns 1 First Avenue, Hove	736277	45				NP	
C	Nevill House Marine Parade	66473	55	G				

C **Norfolk Continental** King's Road	739201	70	G	CH NP	
C **Old Ship** King's Road	29001	155	G	CH NP	
C **Sackville** 189 Kingsway, Hove	736292	48	G	CH NP	
C **Seven** Fourth Avenue, Hove	777977	43	G	CH NP	
D **Carlton** 15 Atlingworth Street	61213	10			UL
D **Cooks** Old Steine	67102	40		CH NP	
D **Crest** 70 Marine Parade .	65010	26		CH	
D **Imperial Centre** ...	73121	80		CH NP	
D **La Porte** 12A Marine Parade	62038	10			UL
D **Tatler** 26 Holland Road ..	736698	13	CW		UL

Chichester

C **Chichester Motel** ..	86351	34	G	CH NP	
C **Dolphin and Anchor**	85121	44	G	CH NP	
D **Bedford**	85766	26			UL

Cooden

B **Cooden Beach**	2281	34	G	CH NP	

Crawley

B **Airport**	29991	100	G	CH NP	
C **George**	24215	71	G	CH NP	
D **Grange**	25560	31	G	CH	

Eastbourne

B **Grand** King Edward's Parade ...	22611	200	G	CH NP	
B **Norfolk** Grand Parade	25652	31		NP	
C **Albion** Marine Parade	20101	80	G	NP	

C	**Alexandra**					
	Grand Parade	20131	35		CW	NP
C	**Burlington**					
	Grand Parade	22724	126	G		NP
C	**Cavendish**					
	Grand Parade	27401	120	G	CH	NP
C	**Eastbourne Motel**					
	Pevensey Bay Road	30461	31	G		NP
C	**Haddon Hall**					
	Devonshire Place . .	29552	62			NP
C	**Lansdowne** King					
	Edward's Parade . .	25174	80	G		NP
C	**Princes**					
	Lascelles Terrace . .	22056	52			NP
C	**Queen's**					
	Marine Parade	22822	120	G	CH	NP
D	**Adelaide**					
	23 Gildredge Road	24989	18			UL
D	**Avondale**					
	77-79 Royal Parade	23510	28		CW	
D	**Cavendish**					
	1 Cavendish Place . .	24284	11			UL
D	**Imperial**					
	Devonshire Place . .	2-525	130	G	CH	NP
D	**St Briac**					
	81 Royal Parade . . .	28929	7	G		UL
D	**Southcroft**					
	15 Southcliffe Avenue	33277	6		CW	UL
D	**Sussex**					
	Cornfield Terrace . .	27681	40		CH	NP

East Grinstead

C	**Ye Olde Felbridge** .	24424	58	G	CH	NP
D	**Crown**	23117	10	G		
D	**Dorset Arms**	21797	12	G		

Hastings and St Leonards-on-Sea

C	**Queen's** Hastings . .	4107	120	G	CH	NP
C	**Royal Victoria**					
	St Leonards-on-Sea	3300	90	G	CH	NP

D **Alexandra**					
St Leonards-on-Sea	602	38		CH	NP
D **Warrior**					
St Leonards-on-Sea	3704	46	G		NP
D **Yelton** Hastings ..	2240	41	G		NP

Herstmonceux

C **White Friars**				
(Boreham Street 3½				
mls E)	2355	17	G CW	CH

Lewes

C **White Hart**	3794	15	G	NP
D **Downside**	2356	7	G	CH

Littlehampton

C **Beach**	7277	35	G	CH NP
D **New Inn**	3112	8	G CW	
D **Stetson**	6081	14	G	

Newhaven

D **Sheffield Arms**	3340	7	G	CH

Pulborough

C **Chequers**	2486	8	G	CH NP

Rye

C **Hope Anchor**	2216	13	G	CH NP
C **Mermaid**	3065	27	G	CH NP
D **George**	2114	20	G	CH

Rye Foreign

B **Rumpels Motel**	Peasmarsh			
	313	12	G	CH

Seaford

C **Newhaven Mercury**				
Motor Inn	5555	70	G	CH NP
D **Seaford Head**	3241	19	G CW	CH

Winchelsea

D **New Inn**	252	7	G CW

Worthing

C **Chatsworth**						
The Steyne	36103	96		CH	NP	
D **Beach** Marine Parade	34001	93	G	CH	NP	
D **Berkeley**						
Marine Parade	31122	95		CH	NP	UL
D **Burlington**						
Marine Parade	34880	25	G	CH	NP	
D **Chesswood**						
56 Holmfield Road .	36027	11	G	CH		UL

HAMPSHIRE

Aldershot

D **Glencoe**	20801	9	G		UL

Basingstoke

D **Cypress**	23608	8	G		UL

Bournemouth

D **Barrington Court**				
1 Poole Road	62866	34	G	CH
D **Bourne Pines**	27304	32	G	
D **Bourne Views**				
55-59 Westhill Road	23854	36	G	CH
D **Bristowe**				
Grange Road	43692	43	G	CH
D **Kelvin Court**				
31 Knyveton Road	23568	45	G	CH
D **Naseby-Nye**				
Byron Road	34079	13	G	

Portsmouth and Southsea

D **Averano**					
65 Granada Road ..	20079	12	G		UL
D **Castle Park**					
14-15 Clarence Parade	26708	32	G		
D **Homeleigh**					
42-44 Festing Gardens	23706	10			UL
D **Ryde View**					
9 Western Parade ..	20865	15	CW	CH	UL

D **St. Ronans**
St. Ronans Road .. 31478 17 G

Southampton

D **Alfa** Ordnance Road 21722 26 G CH
D **Banister**
11 Brighton Road .. 21279 11 G CH UL
D **Blenheim Lodge**
1-5 Blenheim Avenue 57238 38 G CH
D **County** Hulse Road 24236 22 G UL
D **Elizabeth** .... 24327 17 G CH
D **Polygon**
40 The Polygon .... 28162 14 UL
D **Welbeck House**
3 Welbeck Avenue . 58207 6 G CH UL

Winchester

C **Wessex** .... 61611 91 G CH NP
D **Bedfield House** ... 3707 10 G CH

ISLE OF WIGHT

Bembridge

D **Barfield** .... 2294 22 G CW
D **Highbury** .... 2838 6 G UL

Freshwater Bay

D **Saunders** .... 2322 13 G CW

Niton

D **Windcliffe House** .. 215 13 G CW

Sandown

D **Chester Lodge** .... 2773 18 G CW UL
D **Fairlawn** .... 3656 9 G CW UL
D **St Kilda** .... 2307 12 G CW

Seaview

D **Princes Mead** .... 2321 11 G CH

Totland Bay

D **Garrow** Freshwater 3174 19 G CW

Ventnor

D **Channel View**	852230	14		CW	
D **Macrocarpa**	852428	26	G		

CHANNEL ISLANDS

St Helier (Jersey)

B **La Plage**	23474	107	G		CH NP
B **Grand**	22301	138	G		CH NP
C **De France**	21321	305	G		CH NP
C **Revere**	20428	38	G		NP
D **Bay View**	22462	46		CW	
D **Royal**	33356	93	G		CH
D **Mont Millais**	30281	54	G	CW	
D **Savoy**	30012	65			CH
D **Normandie**	21347	63		CW	

St Peter Port (Guernsey)

C **Old Government House**	24921	79	G		CH NP
C **Royal**	23921	80			CH
D **Windhams**	20969	31			
D **Grange Lodge**	25161	35			

Sark

D **Dixcart Hotel**	15	10		CW

Alderney

D **Grand**	227	28		CW CH
D **Royal Connaught** .	277	17		CW

III. THE SOUTH-WEST

This region is well provided with hotels, particularly the seaside resorts in Devon and Cornwall. We list below only a small selection; for a complete list see the British Travel Authority publication "Where to stay: the West Country", updated every year, which is available free of charge from B.T.A. offices.

DEVON

Hotel	Tel.	Rooms	Notes		
Axminster					
C Symonds Down House	3010	10	G	CH	
D Devonia	3280	9	G CW		UL
D George	2209	11	G		
Barnstaple					
C Barnstaple Motel .	5016	60	G	CH NP	
C Imperial	5861	54	G	CH NP	
C North Devon Motel	72166	28	G	CH NP	
C Royal and Fortescue	2289	40	G	CH NP	
D Northcliff	2524	9	G		UL
D Tewesley House ..	73150	6	G		UL
Brixham, Torbay					
B Northcliffe	2751	65	G CW	NP	
D Beverley Court ...	3149	12	G CW CH		
Budleigh Salterton					
B Rolle	2188	34	G	CH	
C Rosemullion	2288	62	G	NP	
D Nattore Lodge	2736	20	G	CH	UL
D Park House	3303	11	G CW CH		
Chagford					
B Easton Court	3469	10	G CW		
C Mill End	2282	21	G CW CH		
C Gidleigh Park	2225	18	G CW CH		
D Thornworthy House	3297	8	G CW CH		
D Greenacres	3471	16	G CW		
Combe Martin					
C White Gates Motel	3511	19	G	CH	
D Channel Vista	3514	8	G CW		UL
Dartmouth					
C Raleigh	2360	48			
C Royal Castle	2397	23		CH	
D Gunfield	2896	16	G CW		

Exeter

C	**Countess Wear Motel**						
	398 Topsham Road	Topsham					
		3165	16	G	CW		
C	**Devon Motel**						
	Exeter Bypass	59268	27	G		CH	NP
C	**Imperial** St. David's	72750	30	G		CH	NP
C	**Rougemont**						
	Queen Street	54982	59	G		CH	NP
C	**Royal Clarence**						
	Cathedral Yard	58464	65			CH	NP
D	**Denmark Court**						
	40 Denmark Road .	58028	17	G			
D	**Exeter Crest Motel**						
	Exeter Bypass	8665	57	G		CH	HP
D	**Gledhills**						
	32 Alphington Road	71439	13	G		CH	UL

Exmouth

C	**Devoncourt**	2277	62	G		CH	NP
D	**Cranford**	3514	16	G		CH	
D	**Grand**	3278	40	G			NP
D	**Imperial**	2296	57	G		CH	NP

Ilfracombe

C	**Candar** Ariadne Road	3481	76	G			NP
C	**Imperial** Wilder Road	2536	103	G			NP
D	**Cliffe Hydro**						
	Hillsborough Road	3606	34	G	CW		
D	**Westbourne**						
	Wilder Road	2120	48		CW		UL

Moretonhampstead

D	**Elmfield**	327	6	G	CW		
D	**White Hart**	406	19	G		CH	

Paignton, Torbay

C	**Redcliffe**	56224	74	G		CH	NP
D	**Alta Vista**	59580	30	G	CW		UL
D	**Coverdale**	56967	13		CW		

D **Palace**	55121	59	G		CH NP	

Plymouth

B **Holiday Inn** Armada Way	62866	224	G		CH NP	
B **Mayflower Post House** The Hoe	62828	104	G		CH NP	
C **Duke of Cornwall** Millbay Road	66256	72			NP	
D **Astor** Elliott Street	68916	50			NP	
D **Dunheven** 33 Beaumont Road .	69040	12	G		CH	
D **Strathmore** The Hoe	62101	52	G		NP	
D **St Rita** Alma Road	67024	28	G			

Salcombe

C **Castle Point**	2167	22	G CW			
C **Great Gate**	2108	32	G CW			
C **Marine**	2251	55	G		CH NP	

Sidmouth

B **Belmont**	2555	50			CH NP	
B **Victoria**	2651	62	G		CH NP	
C **Redlands**	4341	24	G CW	CH		UL
D **Fortfield**	2403	57	G CW	CH NP		

Tavistock

D **Bedford**	3221	31	G			

Teignmouth

D **Beach**	4694	19	G			
D **Belvedere**	4561	11	G CW			UL
D **Glendaragh**	2881	21	G CW			UL
D **Hillslay**	3873	11	G CW			UL
D **London**	2776	23	G		CH NP	

Thurlestone

B **Thurlestone**	382	75	G		NP	
C **Links**	204	38	G CW		NP	

Torquay, Torbay

B **Imperial** Park Hill Road	24301	165	G		CH	NP	
B **New Grand** Paignton Road	25234	120	G		CH	NP	
C **Belgrave** Sea Front	24818	70	G	CW	CH	NP	
C **Foxlands** Babbacombe	38072	47	G			NP	
C **Livermead Cliff** Sea Front	22881	54	G		CH	NP	
C **Livermead House** Sea Front	24361	77	G		CH	NP	
C **Osborne** Meadfoot Beach ..	22232	120	G	CW	CH	NP	
C **Palace** Babbacombe Road .	22271	138	G		CH	NP	
C **Rosetor** Chestnut Avenue ..	25735	115	G			NP	
C **Toorak** Chestnut Avenue ..	27135	90	G		CH	NP	
C **Windsor** Abbey Road	23757	48	G	CW	CH	NP	
D **Alpine** Warren Road	27612	22	G		CH	NP	
D **Chelston House** Chelston Road	65200	16	G	CW			
D **Chelston Tower** Rawlyn Road	67351	27	G				
D **Conway Court** Warren Road	25363	32		CW	CH		
D **Dean Prior** St Mark's Road ...	23927	29	G	CW	CH		UL
D **Derwent** Belgrave Road	23452	114	G	CW		NP	UL
D **Glencross** 25 Avenue Road ..	27517	14	G	CW			UL

Yelverton

B **Moorland Links** ..	2245	29	G		CH		

CORNWALL

Bude

B	Strand	3222	40	G		CH	NP	
C	Falcon	2005	49	G	CW	CH	NP	
D	Burn Court	2872	32	G				

Carbis Bay

C	Carbis Bay St Ives	5311	32	G	CW			
D	Cottage St Ives	6351	60	G	CW	CH		UL
D	Hendra's St Ives	5030	40	G	CW		NP	
D	St Uny St Ives	5011	34	G	CW			

Carlyon Bay

B	Carlyon Bay	Par 2304	77	G		CH	NP	
C	Cliff Head	Par 2125	54	G	CW		NP	

Falmouth

C	Bay Cliff Road	312094	38	G	CW	CH	NP	
C	Falmouth Seafront	312671	75	G		CH	NP	
C	Royal Duchy Cliffe Road	313042	41	G			NP	
D	Crill House (Budock)	312994	11	G		CH		
D	Green Lawns	312734	20	G		CH		
D	Pendower	312108	29	G		CH		

Land's End

C	Land's End	Sennen 271	43	G		CH		

Lizard

D	Housel Bay	417	35	G	CW			

Luve

C	Boscarn	2923	26	G			NP	
D	Hannafore	2166	42	G				

Mullion

C	Polurrian	421	58	G	CW		NP	
D	Hencath House	537	8	G	CW			UL
D	Trevelyan	378	7	G	CW			UL

Newquay

B Glendorgal	4937	36	G CW			
C Bristol	2257	115	G			NP
C Edgcumbe	2061	88	G CW CH		NP
C Headland	2211	110	G CW		NP
D Bay	2988	120	G		NP
D Beachcroft	3022	73	G CW		NP
D Great Western	2010	49	G CW		NP
D Kilbirnie	5155	72	G	CH	NP
D St Rumons	2978	89	G CW		NP
D Trebarwith	2288	52	G CW		NP

Padstow

C Treglos (Constantine Bay) ..	St Merryn				
	727	36	G CW CH	
D Dinas	326	28	G CW	
D Metropole	486	44	G	

Penzance

B Mounts Bay	2693	17	G			
C Higher Faugan (Newlyn)	2076	20	G		NP	
C Queen's	2371	53	G	CH	NP	
D Carlton	2081	14	CW			UL
D Pentrea	2711	10	G CW			UL
D Smugglers (Newlyn Harbour) .	4207	19	G CW		NP	
D Union	2318	28	G	CH		
D Willows	3744	6	G	CH		UL

Perranporth

C Ponsmere	2225	110	G		NP
D Cellar Cove	2110	16	G CW		

St Austell

D Duporth Farm Hotel and Country Club .. (Duporth Bay)	2873	17	G CW LC

D **White Hart**	2100	18	G			
D **Woodlands**	2807	11	G		CH	UL

St Ives

D **Chy-An-Drea**	5076	37	G CW CH	
D **Chy-Morvah**	3614	30	G CW	
D **Garrack**	6199	20	G CW	
D **Portminster**	5221	50	G	CH NP
D **St Ives Bay**	5106	54	G CW	CH NP

St Mawes

B **Tresanton**	544	29	G CW CH

Scilly, Isle of

B **Atlantic**	Scillonia 417	35		CW	NP
C **Island**	Scillonia 883	30		CW CH	
D **Godolphin**	Scillonia 316	29		CW	
D **Tregarthen's**	Scillonia 540	31	G CW		

Tintagel

D **Bossiney House** ...	240	21	G CW

Truro

C **Brookdale**	3513	58	G		NP
C **Carlton**	2450	26	G	CH	
D **Culroy**	3280	20	G		
D **St George's**	2554	10	G		UL

SOMERSET

Bath

A **Cliffe** (Limpley Stoke)	Limpley Stoke 3226	8	G		
B **Francis** Queen Square	24257	70	G	CH NP	
B **Priory** Weston Road	21887	8	CW CH		
C **Pratt's** South Parade	60441	54		CH NP	

C Royal Crescent
15/16 Royal Crescent	24803	31	G		CH		UL

C Royal York
George Street	61451	55	G		CH NP	

D Cleveland
55/59 Pulteney Street	25139	60	G				UL

D Limpley Stoke
L. Stoke	3333	33		G CW	

D St Monica's
53 Pulteney Street ..	4092	23	G		CH

Bridgwater

C Bristol	8197	10			CH
D Royal Clarence	2150	25	G		CH

Clevedon

C Highcliffe	3250	22	G		CH
C Walton Park	4253	37	G		CH
D Albion	2558	12	G		

Frome

C Mendip Motel	3223	40	G		CH NP
C Portway	3508	22	G		CH NP

Glastonbury

D Copper Beech	2297	20	G	

Highbridge

C George	Burnham-on-Sea			
	3248	10	G	

Holford

C Alfoxton Park	211	14	G	

Ilchester

D Ivelchester	220	7	G	

Ilminster

C Horton Cross Motel	2144	23	G		CH NP

Long Ashton

C Bristol Motel	2109	36	G		CH NP

Long Sutton

D Devonshire Arms ..	271	7	G		CH NP

Minehead

C	York	2037	20	G	CW	
D	Northfield	2864	33	G		CH

Taunton

B	Castle	2671	52	G		CH NP
C	County	87651	75	G		CH NP
D	Corner House	2665	24	G		

Wells

C	Crown	3457	10	G		CH
C	Swan	8877	26	G		CH
D	Red Lion	2616	21	G		CH

Weston-super-Mare

C	Grand Atlantic ...	26543	80	G		CH NP
C	Grand Central	21878	51		CW	NP
D	Albert	21363	77	G		NP UL
D	Cabot	21205	40	G	CW	NP
D	Royal	23601	37	G		CH NP
D	Salisbury	21321	78			CH

Yeovil

C	Manor	3116	28	G		CH NP
C	Three Choughs ...	4886	38	G		NP

DORSET

Charmouth

C	Coach and Horses .	321	17	G CW		CH NP
D	Fernhill	492	35	G		CH

Dorchester

C	Antelope	3001	21	G		CH
C	King's Arms	3998	28			CH NP

Ferndown

C	Coach House Motel	71222	32	G		CH

Lyme Regis

D	Buena Vista	2494	20	G CW		
D	High Cliff	2300	16	G CW		CH

D **Mariners**	2753	16	G	CW		
D **Three Cups**	2732	16	G	CW	CH	
D **Tudor House**	2472	17	G	CW		

Poole

C **Dolphin**	3612	60	G		CH NP	
C **Sandbanks**	Canford Cliffs 77377	120	G		CH NP	
D **Sandhills**	Canford Cliffs 77721	10	G	CW		UL
D **Sheldon Lodge**	Bournemouth 61186	14	G			UL

Portland

C **Pennsylvania Castle**	3361	13	G		CH	

Shaftesbury

C **Grosvenor**	2282	48	G		NP	

Sherborne

C **Post House**	3191	60	G		CH NP	
D **Half Moon**	2017	17	G		CH	

Studland Bay

B **Knoll House**	Studland 251	106	G	CW	CH NP	

Swanage

B **Grosvenor**	2292	130	G	CW	CH NP	
C **Corrie**	3104	34	G		CH NP	
D **Isles**	2170	34	G	CW		
D **Pines**	2166	42	G		CH	
D **York**	2704	24	G	CW		UL

Weymouth

D **Gloucester**	6404	53			CH NP	
D **Ingleton**	5804	13	G		CH NP	
D **Royal**	2777	66			CH NP	

GLOUCESTERSHIRE

Alveston

B **Ship Post House** ...	Thornbury 2521	74	G		CH NP	

Berkeley

D Berkeley Arms	291	12	G	CH	

Bibury

C Bibury Court	337	17	G	CH	

Bristol

B Unicorn Prince Street	94811	195	G	CH NP	
C College Close College Road, Clifton	38991	34	G	NP	
C Grand Broad Street	21645	193	G	NP	
C Grand Spa Clifton	21645	67	G	NP	
C Hawthorns Woodland Road, Clifton	38432	168	G	NP	
C Royal College Green, Clifton	23591	139		CH NP	
D Birkdale Redland .	33635	24	G	CH	
D Dunraven Upper Belgrave Road	37475	35	G	CH	UL

Cheltenham Spa

B Queen's	54724	77	G	CH NP	
C Carlton	54453	48	G	NP	
C Majestic	25353	60	G	NP	
C Savoy	27788	59	G	CH NP	
D Cotswold Grange ..	55119	9	G	CH	UL
D Ivy Dene	21726	6	G	CH	UL
D Lansdown	22700	12			

Chipping Campden

C Cotswold House ..	Campden 330	28	G	CH	
C Noel Arms	Campden 317	21	G	CH	
D King's Arms	Campden 256	17		CW	
D Seymour House ...	Campden 429	21	G		

Cirencester

D Fleece	2680	22	G	CH	

D	King's Head	3321	52	G	CH
D	Stratton House	3836	32	G	CH

Gloucester

C	New Country	24977	37		CH NP
D	New Inn	22177	12		CH NP

Moreton-in-Marsh

C	Manor House	501	50	G	CH
D	Redesdale Arms ...	308	15	G	CH
D	White Hart Royal .	731	18	G	

Stow-on-the-Wold

C	Fosse Manor	30354	18	G	
C	Stow Lodge	30485	21	G CW	CH
D	Talbot	30631	16	G	
D	Unicorn	30257	16	G	CH

Stroud

C	Bear of Rodborough	Amberley 3522	32	G	CH NP
C	Moor Court	Amberley 3512	22	G	CH

Tetbury

C	Close	272	13	G	CH

Tewkesbury

D	Royal Hop Pole ...	3236	26	G	CH NP

Upton St Leonards

C	Tara	Gloucester 66225	13	G	CH

Winchcombe

B	Langley	602316	11	G CW	CH
C	George	331	16	G	

WILTSHIRE

Amesbury

D	Antrobus Arms	3163	20	G	CH
D	George	2108	25	G	

Bradford-on-Avon
D Swan .... 2224 14 G

Castle Combe
C Manor House .... 206 34 G CH

Chippenham
B Bell House (Sutton   Seagry
   Benger) 336 17
C Angel Motel ...... 2615 52 G CH NP

Mere
D Old Ship .... 258 15 G NP

Salisbury
C King's Arms ...... 27629 16 G
C Rose and Crown
   (Harnham) .... 27908 28 CH NP
C White Hart .... 27476 69 G CH NP
D Cathedral .... 22993 33 CH NP
C County .... 6088 32 G NP
D Red Lion .... 22788 53 G NP

Swindon
B Post House ...... 24601 103 G CH NP
C Goddard Arms Hotel
   and Motel .... 27198 44 G CH NP

Warminster
D Bath Arms .... 2484 14 G CH
D Old Bell .... 2097 14 G CH

IV. EAST ANGLIA

The counties of Norfolk, Suffolk, Essex, Cambridge and Huntingdon.

ESSEX
Braintree
C White Hart .... 21041 33 G CH

Brentwood
B	Moat House	225252	40	G		CH	
C	Lion and Lamb	6427	9	G		CH	

Burnham-on-Crouch
D	Old White Hart ...	2106	15				

Chelmsford
D	County	58854	39	G			NP

Clacton-on-Sea
C	Royal	21215	51	G		CH	NP
D	Waverley Hall	22716	50	G	CW		
D	Westcliff	24741	43	G		CH	

Colchester
C	George	78494	36	G		CH	NP
C	Red Lion	77986	40	G		CH	NP
C	Mark Tey	210158	106	G		CH	NP

Dedham
B	Maison Talbooth ..	2367	10	G		CH	
C	Dedham Vale	2273	12	G	CW	CH	

Epping
B	Bell Post House	01-375 3137	60	G		CH	NP
C	Epping Forest Motel	01-375 3134	28	G		CH	NP

Frinton-on-Sea
C	Frinton Lodge	4391	27	G		CH	NP
C	Grand	4321	41	G	CW		NP

Harlow
B	Saxon Motor Inn ..	22441	100	G		CH	NP

Harwich
D	Cliff	3345	32	G			
D	Phoenix	2071	10	G			

Hornchurch
B	Fairlane Motor Inn	46789	147	G		CH	NP

Maldon
C Blue Boar   2681   25   G

North Stifford
B North Stifford
   Motor Hotel   71451   32   G   CH NP

Purfleet
C Royal   5432   25   G   CH

Saffron Walden
C Saffron   2676   18   G   CH

Southend-on-Sea and Westcliff-on-Sea
B Airport ....   546344 125 G   CH NP
C Queen's   4417   47   G   NP
C West Cliff   45247   83   NP
D Overcliff   44401   100 G   CH
D White Friars 46790   30   G   CH

Thorrington
C Silver Springs Motel   Great Bentley
                         366   27   G CW CH

CAMBRIDGESHIRE

Cambridge
B Garden House   63421   58   G   CH NP
C Blue Boar   63121   47   G   CH NP
C Royal Cambridge ..   51631   91   G   CH NP
C University Arms ... 51241   125 G   CH NP
D Somerset   54007   13   G   CH   UL
D Station   53846   15   G

Ely
D Lamb.............   2204   24   G   CH NP

Wisbech
D Glendon   4812   18   G
D White Lion   4813   25   G   NP

HUNTINGDONSHIRE

Alconbury

D Alconbury Motel ..	Abbots Ripton					
	342	35	G		CH	

Brampton

C Brampton	Buckden					
	434	17	G		CH	

Huntingdon

C George	3096	21	G			
C Old Bridge	2681	23	G		CH NP	

Norman Cross

C Peterborough Crest	Peterborough					
Motel	240209	40	G		CH NP	

Peterborough

C Bull	62192	125	G		NP	

St Ives

D Golden	3159	20	G			

St Neots

D Cross Keys	2368	14	G			

NORFOLK

Blakeney

C Manor .... Cley 241		22	G			

Cromer

C Cliftonville	2543	51		CW	CH NP	
C Colne House	2013	43	G	CW	CH NP	
C Hôtel de Paris	3141	60	G		CH NP	
D Cliff House	2445	26	G			
D Grange	2419	40	G			UL

East Dereham

C Phoenix	2276	27	G		CH NP	

Great Yarmouth

C Carlton	55234	103	G		CH NP	
C Star	2294	42	G		CH NP	
D Palm Court	2908	48	G			UL

D	Royal	2698	59	G		NP

Hunstanton

D	Golden Lion	2688	30	G		
D	Le Strange Arms	2810	30	G		NP
D	Lodge	2896	16	G		

King's Lynn

C	Duke's Head	4996	76	G	CH	NP
C	Stuart House	2196	17	G	CH	

Norwich

B	Nelson	28612	36	G	CH	NP
B	Post House	56431	120	G	CH	NP
C	Castle	24283	79			NP
C	Maid's Head	28821	85	G	CH	NP
D	Royal	28434	68			NP
D	Town House	35212	18	G	CH	

Sheringham

D	Burlington	2224	41	G		NP

Thetford

C	Bell	4455	42	G	CH	NP

SUFFOLK

Aldeburgh

C	Brudenell	2071	45	G	CH	NP
D	Uplands	2420	17	G	CH	

Bury St Edmunds

C	Suffolk	3995	41	G	CH	NP
D	Angel	3926	50	G	CH	NP

Felixstowe

C	De Novo	2809	28	G	CH	NP
C	Orwell	5511	64	G	CH	NP
D	Waverley	2811	28	G		

Ipswich

B	Post House	212313	121	G	CH	NP
C	Belstead Brook	52380	24	G	CH	

C	Crown and Anchor	58506	50		NP
C	Great White Horse	56558	54		NP

Lavenham

B	Swan	477	42	G	CH

Long Melford

C	Bull	494	25	G	CH

Lowestoft

D	Hatfield	5337	37	G	NP

Mildenhall

D	Bell	712134	20	G	CH
D	Bird in Hand	3247	40	G	CH

Newmarket

C	Bedford	3175	12	G	CH
C	Rutland Arms	3016	52	G	NP

Southwold

D	Swan	2186	52	G	CH NP

Sudbury

C	Four Swans	2793	18	G	CH

Woodbridge

C	Melton Grange	3439	28	G	CH
C	Seckford Hall	2678	18	G	CH

V. EAST MIDLANDS

The counties of Lincoln, Nottingham, Derby, Leicester, Northampton and Rutland.

LINCOLN

Boston

C	New England	5255	11		CH

Cleethorpes

C	Kingsway	62836	65	G	CH NP

Gainsborough

D	White Hart	2018	20	G	

Grantham

C **Angel and Royal** ...	5816	32	G	CH NP	

Grimsby

C **Humber Royal**	5295	57	G	CH NP	
C **Grimsby Crest Motel**	59771	134	G	CH NP UL	

Lincoln

B **Eastgate**	20341	61	G	CH NP	
C **White Hart**	26222	59	G	CH NP	
D **Annelsey**	27548	21	G	CH NP	

Scunthorpe

C **Royal**	68181	30	G	CH	

Skegness

C **Crown**	3084	27	G		
D **Links**	3605	21	G		

Stamford

C **George**	2102	54	G	CH NP	

Woodhall Spa

C **Golf**	52434	54	G	NP	
C **Petwood**	52411	35	G	NP	

NOTTINGHAMSHIRE

Barnby Moor

C **Ye Olde Bell**	Ranskill 335	66	G	CH NP	

Newark-on-Trent

C **Robin Hood**	3858	22	G	CH	
D **Clinton Arms**	4471	21	G	NP	

Nottingham

A **George** George Street	45641	65	G	NP	
B **Albany** St James's Street ...	40131	162		CH NP	
B **Bridgford** Trent Bridge	88661	90	G	CH NP	
C **County** Theatre Square	46321	34		NP	

C **Flying Horse** Poultry	52831	58	G	CH NP	
C **Strathdon**					
Derby Road	48501	54		CH NP	
C **Victoria**					
Milton Street	48221	111	G	CH NP	

Pattishall

C **Cornhill Manor** ...	203	16	G	CH	

Ruddington

C **Nottingham Knight**	Nottingham 211171	7	G	CH	

Southwell

C **Saracen's Head** ...	3143	23	G	CH	

Sutton-on-Trent

D **Old England**	216	10	G	CH	

DERBYSHIRE

Ashbourne

D **Green Man**	2017	11	G	CH	

Bakewell

D **Milford House**	2130	11	G		UL
D **Rutland Arms**	2812	28	G	NP	

Bamford

D **Marquis of Granby** ..	206	10	G	CH	

Buxton

C **Lee Wood**	2003	40	G	CH	
C **Palace**	2001	139	G	CH NP	
D **Old Hall**	2481	45		NP	
D **Westminster**	3929	17	G		

Chesterfield

C **Portland**	4502	22	G	CH	
C **Station**	71141	60	G	CH NP	

Derby

B **Pennine**	41741	100	G	CH NP	
C **Clarendon**	44466	46		NP	
C **Crest Motel**	54933	95	G	CH NP	

D York	42716	41	G	CC NP	

Matlock

C New Bath	3275	60	G	CH NP	

Newton Solney

C Newton Park	Repton 3568	25	G	CH NP	

Sandiacre

B Post House	3800	103	G	CH NP	

LEICESTERSHIRE

Ashby-de-la-Zouch

C Royal	2833	29	G	CH NP	
D Holywell House ...	2005	8	G		

Leicester

B Holiday Inn	51161	198	G	CH NP	
B Post House	51311	183	G	CH NP	
C Abbey Motor Hotel	50666	72	G	CH NP	
C Belmont	24177	56	G	CH NP	
C Grand	56222	142	G	NP	
C Leicester Forest East Motel	Kirby Muxloe 4661	31	G	CH NP	
C Midland	22097	74	G	NP	
D Croft	703220	27	G	CH	UL

Loughborough

C King's Head	4893	30	G	NP	

Market Harborough

C Angel	3123	18	G		

Melton Mowbray

C Harboro'	2529	8	G	CH NP	
D George	2112	22	G	CH	

Wigston Fields, nr Leicester

C Wigston Stage Motel	886161	64	G	CH NP	

NORTHAMPTONSHIRE

Corby

C Strathclyde	3441	40	G	CH NP	
D Raven	2313	14	G	CH	

Crick, nr Rugby

B Albany Inn	701	96	G	CH NP	

Kettering

C George	2705	51	G		NP
D Royal	2003	40	G	CH NP	

Northampton

C Angel	34295	42		CH NP	
C Grand	34416	52	G	CH NP	
C Westone (Westone Favell)					
....	42131	61	G	CH NP	
D Plough	38401	29	G	CH NP	

Sywell

C Sywell Airport Motel	Northampton				
	41594	29	G	CH NP	

Wellingborough

C Hind	2827	32	G	CH	

RUTLAND

Oakham

D George	2284	10	G	

Uppingham

C Falcon	3535	23	G	

VI. YORKSHIRE &
NORTHUMBERLAND-DURHAM

YORKSHIRE

Barnsley

C Royal	3658	17	G	CH	
D Queen's	4192	38		CH NP	

Bawtry

C Crown	Doncaster 710341	43	G	CH NP	

Beverley

C Beverley Arms	885241	58	G	CH NP	

Bolton Abbey

C Devonshire Arms ..	265	11	G	CH	

Bradford

B Victoria	28706	58	G	CH NP	
C Alexandra	27122	45	G	NP	
D Maple Hill	44061	12	G	CH	UL

Bridlington

C Expanse	5347	47	G	CH NP	
D Monarch	4447	41	G	CH	

Doncaster

C Danum	62261	70	G	NP	
C Doncaster Acorn ..	61371	47	G	CH NP	
D Elephant	62140	36	G	NP	

Driffield

C Wold House	Nafferton 242	5	G	NP	
D Bell	3342	17	G	CH	

Halifax

C Swan	54227	46	G	CH NP	

Harrogate

B Crown	67755	113	G	CH NP	
B Majestic	68792	158	G	CH NP	
B Old Swan	4051	142	G	CH NP	
C Cairn	4005	144	G	NP	
C Granby	3046	109		NP	
C Prospect	5071	63	G	CH NP	
D Grange	66054	80	G	NP	
D Studley	68407	24	G		

Haworth

D	Old White Lion ...	2313	7	G	CH

Huddersfield

C	George	25444	56	G	CH NP

Hull

C	Dorchester House .	43276	50	G	CH NP
C	Hull Centre	26462	125		CH NP
C	Crest Motel	645212	54	G	CH NP
D	Marlborough	36339	21	G	CH NP
D	Newland Park	42733	45	G	CH NP

Leeds

A	Queen's	31323	198	G	CG NP	
B	Metropole	20841	109	G	CH NP	
B	Post House	2952	120	G	CH NP	
C	Leeds Crest Motel .	826201	100	G	CH NP	
C	Great Northern ...	30431	46		CH NP	
C	Merrion	39191	120	G	CH NP	
C	Parkway	672551	47	G	CH NP	
D	Aragon	26914	10	G	CH	
D	Clock	621259	16	G		UL
D	Croft	621726	9	G		UL
D	Guildford	20915	25		CH NP	

Middlesbrough, Teesside

C	Linthorpe	89287	10	G	CH	
C	Middlesbrough Crest Motel	87651	53	G	CH NP	
D	Cambridge	86775	11	G	CH	
D	Chadwick	45340	6	G		UL
A	Blue Bell Motor Inn	53168	60	G	CH NP	

Northallerton

C	Golden Lion	2404	28	G	CH NP

Ossett

B	Wakefield Albany Inn		96	G	CH NP

Oulton, nr Leeds

C Leeds Crest Motel .	Rothwell 6201	40	G		CH	NP

Richmond

C King's Head	2311	23	G

Ripon

D Unicorn	2202	20	G

Scarborough

C Crown	3491	82	G			NP
C Grand	5371	205				NP
D Crescent	60929	26			CH	
D Cumberland	61826	100	G	CW		NP
D Norbreck	65895	68	G	CW		NP
D Prince of Wales ...	66601	108	G			NP
D Royal	64333	144	G			NP
D St Nicholas	64101	200	G			NP
D Southlands	61447	69	G			NP

Scotch Corner

C Scotch Corner	Richmond 2943	45	G		CH	NP

Selby

D Londesborough Arms	2885	16	G

Sheffield	78822	70	G		CH	NP
B Grosvenor House ..	20041	102	G		CH	NP
B Hallam Tower	66031	136	G		CH	NP
C Kenwood	53347	71	G			NP
C Rutland	65215	112	G		CH	NP
D Glennmore	50494	25	G		CH	UL

Skipton

D Midland	2781	13	G		CH

South Milford, nr. Leeds

C Selby Fork Motor Hotel	2711	119	G		CH	NP

Thirsk

D Golden Fleece	23108	20	G

Thornaby, Teesside

B Post House		140	G	CH NP	
C Golden Eagle	Stockton 62511	57	G	NP	

Wakefield

C Cesar's	72111	68	G	CH NP	

Wentbridge, nr. Pontefract

C Excelsior Motor Lodge	711	71	G	

Whitby

C Royal	2234	88		NP	
D Beach Villa	3130	32	G CW		
D Metropole	3366	13	G	CH	

York

B Royal Station	53681	118	G	CH NP	
B Post House	67921	104	G	CH NP	
B Viking	59822	106		CH NP	
C Abbey Park	25481	63	G	CH NP	
C Dean Court	25081	26		CH NP	
D Blakeney	53220	17	G	CH	UL
D Chase	67171	55	G	CH NP	
D Granby Lodge	53291	53	G	CH	
D White Swan	28851	30		CH NP	
D York Motel	67151	19	G	CH	

NORTHUMBERLAND

Berwick-on-Tweed

C King's Arms	7588	30	G	CH NP	
C Turret House	7344	13	G	CH NP	

Hexham

C Royal	2270	16	G	NP	
D Beaumont	2331	20		NP	

Newcastle-upon-Tyne

A Gosforth Park ..089426-4111		101	G	CH NP	
B Imperial	815511	69	G	CH NP	
B Swallow	25025	83	G	CH NP	

C	Avon	814961	64	G	CH	NP
C	County	22471	99	G		NP
C	Northumbria	814961	100	G		NP
C	Cairn	811358	53	G	CH	NP

Otterburn

C	Otterburn Tower ...	673	14	G		
C	Percy Arms	261	35	G	CH	NP

Wall

D	Hadrian	Humshaugh 232	8	G		

DURHAM

Barnard Castle

D	King's Head	3356	20	G		NP

Billingham, Teesside

B	Billingham Arms ..	552104	61	G	CH	NP

Bishop Auckland

D	Queen's Head	3477	8	G	CH	

Bowburn

C	Bowburn Hall	Coxhoe 311	20	G	CH	NP

Chester-le-Street

C	Lambton Arms ...	3265	10	G	CH	NP

Darlington

B	King's Head	67612	72	G	CH	NP
C	Imperial	67571	39	G		NP
C	North Eastern	4373	25	G	CH	NP

Durham

C	Ramside Hall	5282	12			
C	Royal County	2418	47	G		NP
C	Three Tuns	4326	16	G		NP
C	Crest Motel, Meadowfield	780524	90	G	CH	NP

Gateshead-on-Tyne

B	Five Bridges	71105	105	G	CH	NP

C	Springfield	74121	33	G	CH NP

Peterlee

C	Noseman	2161	26	G	CH NP

South Shields

C	New Crown	3472	12	G	CH NP
C	Sea	2889	18	G	CH NP

Stockton, Teesside

A	Swallow	53168	126	G	CH NP

Sunderland

B	Seaburn	Whitburn 2041	61	G	CH NP
C	Mowbray Park	78221	60	G	CH NP
C	Roker	71786	41	G	CH NP

Washington

B	Post House	462264	145	G	CH NP

VII. NORTH-WEST OF LONDON

The area between London and Oxford, in the upper Thames valley.

BEDFORDSHIRE

Bedford

B	County	55131	70		CH NP
C	Swan	52074	71	G	NP

Dunstable

C	Old Palace Lodge .	62201	14	G	CH
D	Highwayman	61999	12	G	CH

Leighton Buzzard

D	Swan	2148	17	G	CH

Luton

B	Esso Motor Hotel .	55911	99	G	CH NP
C	Red Lion	27337	45	G	NP

C	Luton Crest Motel	55955	100	G		CH NP

Woburn

D	Woburn	643	6	G		

BERKSHIRE

Abingdon

C	Upper Reaches ...	4311	20	G		CH
D	Crown and Thistle .	87	22			CH

Ascot

B	Berystede	21424	92	G		CH NP

Bray-on-Thames

B	Monkey Island ...	Maidenhead				
		28318	27	G		CH NP

Hurley

A	Ye Olde Bell	244	9	G		CH

Maidenhead

B	Esso Motor Hotel .	23444	195	G		CH NP
C	Bear	25183	12			CH
C	Skindles	25115	31	G		CH NP
C	Thames	28721	29	G		
D	Riviera	25425	36	G		CH NP

Newbury

C	Chequers	3666	63	G		CH NP
D	Bacon Arms	408	11	G		CH

Pangbourne

B	Copper Inn	2244	11	G	*Cà*	
D	George Hotel and Motel	2237	18	G		

Reading

B	Post House		121	G		CH NP
C	George	53445	65	G		CH NP
C	Great Western	53255	52	G		NP
D	Calcot	27346	14	G		CH

Streatley-on-Thames

C	Swan	2498	27	G	CH

Windsor

B	Castle	51011	61	G	CH NP
C	Harte and Garter	63426	46	G	CH NP
C	Old House	61354	39	G	CH NP
D	Royal Adelaide	63916	37	G	CH

Wokingham

C	Bush	West Forest 4467	9	G

BUCKINGHAMSHIRE

Amersham

C	Crown	3344	18	G	CH
C	Ken House	6368	27	G	

Aylesbury

C	Bell	2141	17		CH

Beaconsfield

C	Bell House	85522	52	G	CH NP
C	Royal White Hart	71211	41	G	CH NP

Buckingham

C	White Hart	2131	19	G	CH

Burnham

B	Burnham Beeches	3333	18	G	CH NP
B	Grovefield	3131	8	G	CH

Gerrards Cross

C	Ethorpe	82039	40	G	CH NP

High Wycombe

C	Falcon	20126	11	G	CH

Marlow

B	Compleat Angler	4444	39	G	CH NP

Slough

C	Royal	23024	25	G	NP

HERTFORDSHIRE

Baldock

C	Ye Olde George and Dragon	2207	24	G	

Bishop's Stortford

C	Dane House	2289	18	G	CH
C	Foxley	4679	17	G	CH
D	George	4042	20	G	

Boreham Wood

C	Thatched Barn	01-953 4121	10	G	CH NP	
D	York House	01-953 4864	6	G	CH	UL

Harpenden

B	Glen Eagle	60271	43	G	CH NP
D	Harpenden Arms	2095	6	G	CH

Hatfield

C	Comet	65411	47	G	CH NP
C	Hatfield Lodge	64588	25	G	CH
C	Salisbury	62220	18	G	
D	Stonehouse	62114	20	G	CH

Hemel Hempstead

B	Post House	51122	91	G	NP

Hertford

C	Salisbury Arms	3091	10	G	CH

Hertingfordbury

B	White Horse Inn	01-433 6791	30	G	CH

Hitchin

C	Sun	2092	24	G	CH NP

Letchworth

B	Letchworth Hall	3747	19	G	CH
C	Broadway	5651	30	G	CH NP

St Albans

C	Noke	54252	8	G	CH
C	Sopwell House	64477	17	G	CH NP

C	**St Michael's Manor**	64444	23	G	CH NP	
D	**Black Lion**	51786	10	G	CH NP	
D	**Great Red Lion** ...	61411	17	G		

South Mimms

C	**Esso Motor Hotel** .	2261	63	G	CH	

Stevenage

B	**Roebuck Post House**	4171	40	G	CH	
C	**Cromwell**	55542	30	G	CH NP	

Watford

C	**Caledonian**	29212	87	G	CH NP	

Welwyn

C	**Health Lodge Motel**	5101	21	G	CH	

OXFORDSHIRE

Aston Rowant

C	**Lambert Arms Hotel and Motel**	Kingston Blount				
		51496	11	G	CH	

Banbury

C	**Whately Hall**	3451	78	G	CH NP	
D	**Cromwell Lodge** ...	3697	32	G		UL
D	**Crown**	3797	16	G	CH	
D	**White Lion**	4358	29	G	CH NP	

Burford

C	**Bay Tree**	3137	23	G	CH	
C	**Bull**	2220	13	G	CH	
C	**Winter's Tale**	3176	9	G	CH	
D	**Corner House**	3151	10	G CW		
D	**Cotswold Gateway** .	2148	13	G	CH	

Dorchester-on-Thames

C	**George**	Warborough				
		404	22	G		
D	**White Hart**	Warborough				
		501	14	G	CH	

Henley-on-Thames

C	Imperial	2295	18			
C	Red Lion	2161	28	G	CH	
C	Sydney House	3412	9	G	CH	
D	Little White Hart ..	4145	20	G	CH	

Horton-cum-Studley

C	Studley Priory	Stanton St. John				
		203	18	G	CH	

Long Handborough, nr. Oxford

C	Blenheim Motel ..	Freeland					
		881096	6	G	CW	CH	

Newbridge

C	Rose Revived Inn ..	Standlake				
		221	7	G	CH	

Oxford

B	Randolph	47481	114	G	CH	NP
C	Eastgate	48244	51	G	CH	NP
C	Excelsior Motor Lodge	54301	101	G	CH	
C	Oxford Motel	59933	100	G	CH	NP
C	Royal Oxford	48432	26		CH	NP
D	Isis	48894	36	G		
D	Old Parsonage	54843	37	G		UL

Thame

C	Spread Eagle	2917	18	G	CH	NP
D	Black Horse	2886	7	G	CH	

Weston-on-the-Green, nr. Oxford

C	Weston Manor ...	Bletchington				
		260	17	G	CH	

Woodstock

C	Bear	811511	22	G	CH	

VIII. WEST MIDLANDS

The very heart of England, extending from the Shakespeare country to the Welsh border and taking in the counties of Warwickshire, Staffordshire, Worcestershire, Herefordshire and Shropshire.

WARWICKSHIRE

Alcester

C	Cherrytrees Garden Motel	2505	22	G	CH	

Birmingham

A	Plough and Harrow	021-454 1131	44	G	CH NP	
B	Albany	021-643 8171	254	G	CH NP	
B	Midland	021-643 2601	120	G	CH NP	
B	Royal Angus	021-236 4211	140	G	CH NP	
C	Apollo Motor Hotel	021-455 0271	60	G	CH NP	
C	Cobden	021-454 6621	178	G	NP UL	
C	Market	021-643 1134	50		CH NP	
C	Norfolk	021-454 0870	166	G	NP UL	
C	Strathallan	021-455 9777	162	G	CH NP	
D	Bristol Court	021-472 0413	26	G	NP UL	
D	Imperial Centre	021-643 6751	100		CH NP	
B	Magnum	021-643 2747	193		CH NP	

Coventry

B	Post House	Allesley 2151	200	G	CH NP	
C	Allesley	Allesley 3272	49	G	CH NP	
C	Coventry Crest Motel	303398	68		CH NP	
C	Hylands	21486	28	G	CH	
C	Leofric	21371	101		CH NP	
D	Godiva Guest House	58585	108	G	CH	UL

Elmdon

B	Excelsior	021-743 8141	141	G	CH NP	

Kenilworth

A	Avonside	56563	48	G	CH NP	
C	Abbey	51455	23	G	CH	
C	Chesford Grange	52371	34		NP	

| C De Montfort | 55944 | 104 | G | CH NP |
| D Nite Lite | 53594 | 12 | | CH |

Leamington Spa

C Angel	23683	13	G	CH
C Clarendon	22201	50	G	CH NP
C Guy's	25151	34	G	CH
C Manor House	23251	55	G	CH NP
C Regent	27231	85	G	CH NP
D Crown	26421	22	G	CH
D Falstaff	21219	31	G	CH

Meriden, nr. Coventry

| C Manor | 735 | 32 | G | CH NP |

Nuneaton

| C Nuneaton Crest Motel | 5335 | 47 | G | CH NP |

Rugby

| C Grand | 2002 | 33 | G | CH NP |
| C Three Horseshoes | 4585 | 23 | G | CH |

Stratford-upon-Avon

B Welcombe	3611	92	G	CH NP
B Alveston Manor	4581	129	G	CH NP
C Arden	3874	58	G	CH NP
C Grosvenor House	3415	31	G	CH
C Haytor	3420	21	G	CH
C Red Horse	3211	60	G	CH NP
C Shakespeare	3631	70	G	CH NP
C Swan's Nest	66761	80	G	CH NP
C White Swan	3606	60		CH NP
D Anray	2586	9	G		UL
D Argos	4321	8			UL
D Beeches	3006	13	G	CH	UL

Sutton Colafield

| C Belfry | Curdworth | | | |
| | 301 | 60 | G | CH NP |

C Penns Hall	Ashfield				
	3111	73	G		CH NP
Warwick					
C Woolpack	41684	28	G		
D Crown	42087	12	G	CH	
D Lord Leycester	41481	46	G	CH NP	
D Warwick Arms	42759	45	G	CH NP	

STAFFORDSHIRE

Burton-on-Trent

C Midland	2723	15	G	CH	
C Stanhope Arms	7954	20	G	CH	

Great Haywood

C Coach and Horses .	Weston				
	324	41	G		CH NP

Hanley

C Grand	Stoke				
	22361	96	G		CH NP

Lichfield

C Angel Croft	3147	14	G		
C George	3061	35	G		

Newcastle-under-Lyme

B Post House	57264	104	G		CH NP

Stafford

C Tillington Hall	53531	27	G		CH NP
D Vine	51071	24	G		

Walsall

C County	32323	52	G		CH NP
C George	23125	58	G		CH NP
C Walsall Crest Motel	33555	106	G		CH NP

Wolverhampton

C Fox	21680	29	G		CH NP
C Mount	752055	47	G		CH NP
C Victoria	20641	103	G		CH NP
D Castlecroft	61264	26	G	CH	
D Connaught	24433	104	G		CH NP

D	Park Hall	35756	21	G	CH NP	
D	Ravensholt	24140	24	G		

WORCESTERSHIRE

Broadway

B	Lygon Arms	2255	68	G	CH NP	
C	Broadway	2401	18	G	CH	
D	Swan	2278	10	G	CH	

Bromsgrove

C	Perry Hall	31976	31	G	CH

Evesham

C	Crown	6137	14	G	CH

Malvern, Great

C	Abbey	3325	112	G	CH NP	
D	Foley Arms	3397	29	G	CH NP	
D	Gold Hill	4000	20	G	CH	
D	Mount Pleasant ...	61837	16		NP	

Malvern Wells

C	Cottage in the Wood	3487	20	G	CH
D	Essington	61177	11	G	CH

Pershore

C	Angel Inn	2046	15	G	CH

Stourbridge

D	Bell	5641	20	G	
D	Talbot	4350	20	G	

Worcester

B	Giffard	27155	101		CH NP	
C	Diglis	27978	15	G	CH	
C	Star	24308	32	G	NP	
D	Loch Ryan	23721	00		CH	UL
D	Ye Olde Talbot	23573	13		CH	

HEREFORDSHIRE

Hereford

C Castle Pool	3609	31	G		
C Green Dragon	2506	78	G	CH NP	
D Booth Hall	2898	10	G		
D Graftonbury	6243	60	G		UL

Leominster

D Royal Oak	2610	22	G		
D Talbot	2121	16	G	CH	

Ross-on-Wye

D Chase	3161	44	G	NP
D Chasedale	2423	20	G	
D Royal	2769	28	G	

Symonds Yat (East)

D Garth Cottage	364	7	G CW	
D Royal	238	24	G	CH

Symonds Yat (West)

C Old Court	367	22	G	
D Paddocks	246	31	G CW	

SHROPSHIRE

Atcham

C Mytton and	Cross Houses			
Mermaid	220	8	G	CH

Bridgnorth

C Falcon	3134	14	G	
C Parlors Hall	2604	12	G	CH

Church Stretton

C Longmynd	2244	60	G
D Denehurst	2825	24	G

Ludlow

C Feathers	2919	30	G	CH NP
D Angel	2531	16	G	CH
D Overton Grange ..	2810	19	G	CH

Northwood, nr. Wem

D	Woodlands Country House	Loppington 268	8	G	

Shrewsbury

C	Lion	53107	60	G	CH NP
C	Prince Rupert	52461	66		CH NP
D	Abbey Gardens	56538	20	G	
D	Beauchamp	3230	25	G	CH
D	Lord Hill	52601	26	G	CH NP

Wellington

C	Buckatree Hall	2226	9G		CH
D	Swan	3781	10	G	CH

Whitchurch

D	Dodington Lodge	2539	11	G	CH

IX. WALES

ISLE OF ANGLESEY

Amlwch

C	Dinorben Arms	358	14	G	CH

Beaumaris

C	Bulkeley Arms	415	40	G	CH
D	Ye Olde Bull's Head	329	15	G	

Holyhead

D	County	2059	10	G	

Menai Bridge

D	Anglesey Arms	305	19	G	

Trearddur Bay

C	Trearddur Bay	301	37	G	NP
D	Beach	332	28	G	CH

CAERNARVONSHIRE

Aberdaron

D	Ty Newydd	207	16	G CW	

Abersoch

C **Craig-y-Mor**	2666	8	G CW CH		
C **Porth Tocyn**	2966	24	G CW		
D **Harbour**	2406	24	G CW CH		

Bangor

C **British**	3178	33	G	CH NP	
C **Waverley**	2017	15	G	CH	

Betws-y-Coed

C **Royal Oak**	219	29	G CW CH		
D **Glan Aber**	325	22	G CW		

Caernarvon

C **Prince of Wales** ...	3367	19	G		
C **Royal**	3184	68	G	CH NP	

Conwy

D **Castle**	2235	26	G	CH	
D **Erskine**	3415	10	G		

Criccieth

C **Caerwylan**	2547	34	G CW		
C **Lion**	2460	40	G		
D **George IV**	2168	47	G CW		

Llanberis

D **Royal Victoria**	253	90	G CW CH		

Llandudno

C **Craigside Hydro** ...	49228	145	G CW CH		
C **Grand**	76245	153		NP	
C **Imperial**	77466	116	G	NP	
D **County**	76700	80	G	CH NP	
D **Empire**	77260	36	G CW CH		
D **Hydro**	77241	92	G	CH NP	
D **Marine**	77521	81	G	NP	
D **Osborne**	77087	27	G CW	NP	

Porthmadog

C **Royal Sportsman** ..	2015	22	G		

BRECONSHIRE

Brecon

C Penoyre House	2528	25	G		NP
D Castle of Brecon ...	2942	18	G	CH	

Crickhowell

C Mountain	244	7	G CW		
D Bear	408	8	G		

CARDIGANSHIRE

Aberystwyth

C Belle Vue Royal ...	7558	50	G	CH	NP
C Conrah Country ..	7941	12	G	CH	
D Seabank	7617	28		CH	
D Swn-y-Don	2647	29	G		

Llandyssul

D Blaendyffryn Hall .	2375	8	G	CH	

Llechryd

D Castle Malgwyn ...	382	27	G		

New Quay

D Black Lion	209	10	G		NP
D New Quay	282	11		CH	

CARMARTHENSHIRE

Carmarthen

C Ivy Bush Royal	5111	100	G	CH	NP
D Boars Head	6043	10	G		

Llandeilo

D King's Head	2388	11	G	CH	

Llandovery

D Ystrad House	216	7	G CW		

Llanelly

D Stepney	2155	34	G		NP

DENBIGHSHIRE

Chirk

C Hand	2479	9	G	CH

Colwyn Bay

C Colwyn Bay	30345	57	G		NP
C Rhos Abbey	44512	24	G	
D Meadowcroft	48375	30		
D Norfolk	2128	34	G	

Denbigh

D Bull	2072	13	G	CH

Llangollen

C Bryn Howel	2331	36	G	CH	
D Bryn Derwen	3183	19	G		
D Chain Bridge	2215	25	G	CH	NP
D Hand	2303	60	G		NP
D Royal	2202	35	G	CH	

Rhos-on-Sea

D Mount Royal	Colwyn Bay 48429	40	G	
D Mount Steward ...	Colwyn Bay 34269	85		

Ruthin

C Ruthin Castle	2664	64	G	CH	NP
D Castle	2479	22	G	CH	

Wrexham

C Crest Motel	53431	50		CH	NP

FLINTSHIRE

Hawarden

D Glynne Arms	3235	7	G

Northophall

C Chequers	581	20	G	CH

Overton-on-Dee

D White Horse Inn ...	265	5	G	CH

Prestatyn

D	**Grand**	4670	29	G	CH NP
D	**Royal Victoria**	3244	27	G	CH NP

Rhyl

D	**Marina**	2371	19	G	CH NP
D	**Westminster**	2241	54	G	– NP

GLAMORGAN

Barry

C	**Water's Edge**	3392	39	G	CH NP

Bishopston

B	**Ocean Meadows** ...	2288	12	G	

Bridgend

C	**Dunraven Arms** ...	3880	37	G	

Cardiff

B	**Angel** Castle Street	32633	111	G	CH NP
B	**Beverley** 75 Cathedral Road	21432	19	G	CH NP
B	**Park** Park Street ..	23471	98		CH NP
B	**Post House** Church Road		150	G	CH NP
C	**Grand** Westgate Street	26626	45		CH NP
C	**Queen's** StMa ry Street	30601	44		NP
C	**Royal** St Mary Street	23321	72		NP
D	**Central** St Mary Street	25749	85		CH NP
D	**Y Westfa** 46 Marlborough Road	36088	14		CH UL

Cowbridge

C	**Bear**	2169	15	G	CH

Merthyr Tydfil

D	**New Inn**	3756	17		CH

Mumbles

C	**Osborne** (Langland Bay)	Swansea 66274	45	G	CH NP

D **Brynfield** (Langland Bay)	Swansea 66208	18	G CW	

Neath

C **Castle**	3581	36		CH NP

Porthcawl

B **Seabank**	2261	81	G	CH NP
C **Esplanade**	2201	83	G	NP
D **Westward Ho**	3335	16	G	

Port Talbot

C **Twelve Knights** (Margam)	2381	12	G	CH
D **Grand**	2830	21	G	NP

Southerndown

D **Little West**	395	16	G	

Swansea

B **Dolphin**	50011	62		CH NP
B **Dragon**	51074	116	G	CH NP
D **Grand**	50541	35		NP

MERIONETH

Aberdovey

C **Dovey**	217	14		CW
C **Penhelig Arms**	215	13	G	
C **Trefeddian**	213	47	G CW	

Bala

C **Bala Lakeside Motel**	344	12	G CW CH	
C **White Lion Royal** ..	314	26	G	
D **Plas Coch**	309	9	G	CH

Barmouth

D **Min-y-Mor**	555	59	G CW	

Bontddu

C **Bontddu Hall**	209	29	G CW	

Dolgellau

D **Golden Lion Royal** .	579	30	G CW	

Harlech

D St Davids	366	70	G		NP

Pennal

C Llugwy	228	10	G CW		
D Riverside	285	7	G		NP

Penrhyndeudraeth

C Portmeirion	228	78	G CW		NP

MONMOUTHSHIRE

Abergavenny

C Angel	2613	31	G	CH

Caerleon

C Priory	241	9	G	CH

Castleton

B Wentloog Castle Motel	226	55	G	CH	NP

Chepstow

D Castle View	3565	13	G	UL
D George	2365	18	G	

Llandogo

D Old Farmhouse	St Briavels 303	28	G	CH	

Monmouth

D Beaufort Arms	2411	26	G	CH
D King's Head	2177	28	G	
D White Swan	2045	20	G CW	CH

Newport

C Queen's	62992	42		CH	NP
C Westgate	66244	68	G	CH	NP
D King's Head	63211	42	G		NP

Tintern

C Beaufort	202	28	G	CH
C Royal George	205	11	G	

Tredegar

C Castle	2330	23	G	CH	

MONTGOMERYSHIRE

Llangurig

D Black Lion	233	10	G		

Machynlleth

D White Lion	2048	20	G		
D Wynnstay	2003	30	G		

Newtown

D Bear	6977	42	G	CH	
D Elephant and Castle	271	27	G	CH	

Welshpool

D Garth Derwen	Trewern				
	238	9	G		UL
D Royal Oak	2217	23	G		

PEMBROKESAIRE

Broadhaven

D Glenmore	366	7	G		UL

Clynderwen

D Nantyffin Motel ..	329	15	G	CH	

Fishguard

D Fishguard Bay	3323	44	G	CH NP	

Haverfordwest

C Mariner's	3353	31	G	CH NP	
D Pembroke House ..	3652	23	G	CH NP	

Kilgetty

D Crossroads Motel ..	Saundersfoot				
	3285	21	G		
D Manian Lodge	Saundersfoot				
	3273	18	G CW		

Milford Haven

D Lansdowne House .	2480	12	G		UL
D Lord Nelson	3265	26	G	CH NP	

Pembroke

C Lion	2736	33	G		
C Old King's Arms .	2539	16	G	CH NP	
D Corston	Castle Martin				
	220	15	G	CH	UL
D Royal Edinburgh ..	2974	12	G	NP	

Roch

D Roch Gate Motel ..	Camrose				
	308	23	G	CH	

St. David's

D Glan-y-Mor	203	13	G		UL
D Old Cross	387	16	G CW		
D Warpool Court	300	25	G CW		
D Whitesand Bay	403	31	G CW		

Saundersfoot

D St Brides	2304	55	G	CH NP	
D Sundowner Motel ..	2290	20	G		

Tenby

C Atlantic	288*a*	48	C*a*W		
C Belgrave	2377	45	G	CH NP	
C Imperial	2328	50	G	NP	
C Park House	2528	40	G	CH	
C Royal Gatehouse ..	2255	80	G	NP	
D Cliffe-Norton	2333	49	CW		
D Cobourg	2009	30	G CW		
D Norton	2460	14	G		

RADNORSHIRE

Doldowlod

C Vulcan Arms Hotel	Rhayader			
	438	10	G	

Glasbury-on-Wye

C Maesllwch Arms ..	226	13	G	CH

Knighton

D Red Lion Inn ...	231	6	G	

Llandrindod Wells

C **Glen Usk**	2085	88	G	CW	
C **Metropole**	2247	138	G		CH NP
C **Rock Park**	2021	65	G		CH
D **Commodore**	2288	43	G		
D **Hampton**	2585	29	G		

Rhayader

D **Lion Royal**	202	20	G	

X. NORTH-WEST AND LAKE DISTRICT

The counties of Cheshire, Lancashire, Westmoreland and Cumberland.

CHESSHIRE

Alderley Edge

C **De Trafford Arms** .	3881	33	G	CH NP
C **Edge**	3033	29	G	CH

Altrincham

C **George and Dragon**	061-928 1504	13	G	
C **Portofino** 061-928 1511		10	G	
C **Woodlands** (Timperley) ..	061-928 8631	49	G	CH NP

Backford Cross

B **Wirral Mercury Motor Inn** ...	014-455 551	101	G	CH NP

Beeston

C **Wild Boar Motor Lodge Inn**	086-96 550	30	G	CH NP

Birkenhead

C **Central**	051-647 6347	38		CH NP

Bollington

C **Belgrave**	3246	30	G	CH NP

Bowdon

C	Alpine	061-928 6191	15	G	CH NP
C	Bowdon	061-928 7121	44	G	CH NP

Broxton

C	Travel Inn	202	16	G	CH

Bucklow Hill

B	Swan Motor Hotel .	830295	48	G	CH NP

Chester

B	Blossoms St John Street	23186	76	G	CH NP
B	Grosvenor Eastgate Street	24024	100	G	CH NP
C	Chester Curzon Wrexham Road ...	24464	56	G	CH NP
C	Queen City Road ..	28341	84 ·	G	CH NP
C	Riverside 22 City Walls	26580	20	G	
C	Rowton Hall Whitchurch Road ..	35262	27	G	NP
D	Dene Hoole Road .	21165	50	G	CH
D	Oaklands Hoole Road	22156	20	G	CH
D	Ye Olde King's Head Lower Bridge Street	24855	9	G	CH

Christleton

C	Abbots Well Motor Inn Chester	35021	40	G	CH NP

Congleton

C	Lion and Swan	3115	13	G	

Crewe

C	Crewe Arms	3204	35	G	CH NP
C	Royal	2509	35	G	NP

Handforth

B	Belfry	061-437 4321	100	G	CH NP

Knutsford

C	Royal George	4151	24		CH NP
D	Heatherfield	3428	14	G	UL

Nantwich
C **Alvaston Hall** .... 64341 12 G CH
C **Crown** .... 65283 16 G CH

Northwich
D **Woodpecker** ..... 2029 11 G CH

Parkgate
C **Ship** .... Neston
3931 19 G CH

Stepping Hill
C **Belgrade** .... 3851 165 G CH NP

Stockport
C **Alma Lodge** ...061-483 4431 43 G CH NP

LANCASHIRE

Barrow-in-Furness
D **Duke of Edinburgh** . 21039 27 G CW CH NP

Barton
C **Barton Grange** .... Broughton
2551 40 G CH NP

Birtle
B **Normandie** .... Bury
3869 17 G CH NP

Blackburn
B **Saxon Inn Motor**
Hotel .... 64441 100 G CH NP
C **White Bull** .... 52551 40 G NP

Blackpool
C **Claremont** .... 29122 200 G CH NP
C **Cliffs** .... 52551 168 G NP
C **Clifton** .... 21481 87 CH NP
C **Norbreck Castle** ... 52341 327 G CH NP
C **Savoy** .... 52561 143 G CH NP
D **Chequers** .... 51967 55 G CH NP
D **Headlands** .... 41179 54 G CH
D **Kimberley** .... 41184 16 G NP
D **Welbeck** .... 51116 43 G CW
D **York** .... 51465 37 G

Bolton

C **Pack Horse**	27261	87	G	CH	NP
C **Bolton Crest Motel**	651511	100	G	CH	NP

Burnley

B **Keirby**	27611	48	G	CH	NP

Fleetwood

D **North Euston**	3375	58	G	CH	NP

Heysham

D **Carr-Crath**	51175	10	G		UL

Kirkby

C **Golden Eagle**	051-546 4355	47	G	CH	NP
C **Crest Motel** .	051-546 7531	50	G	CH	NP

Liverpool

B **St George's** Lime Street	2522	157		CH	NP
C **Lord Nelson** Nelson Street	051-706 4362	66	G	CH	NP
C **Shaftesbury** 28 Mt Pleasant	051-709 4421	76			NP
C **Stork** Queen Square	051-709 1231	70	G		NP
D **Royal** Bath Street . .	051-928 3576	24	G		NP
B **Adelphi** Ranelagh Place	051-709 7200	275	G	CH	NP

Manchester

B **Grand** Aytoun Street	061-236 9559	137		CH	NP
B **Piccadilly** Piccadilly Plaza	061-236 8414	257	G	CH	NP
B **Queen's** 1 Portland Street	061-236 5612	92			NP
C **Mitre** Cathedral Gates	061-834 4128	24			NP

C **Willow Bank**
340-342 Wilm-
slow Road ... 061-224 2309 72 G   CH NP

D **Brookfield**
Oxford Place . 061-224 1409 41 G   CH NP

D **Darwen** 132 Pa-
latine Road . 061-445 4588 14 G   CH

D **Simpson's**
Withington
Road .... 061-226 2235 38 G CW   NP

A **Midland**
Peter Street .. 061-236 3333 315 G   CH NP

Manchester Airport

B **Belfry** ...... 061-437 4321 100 G   CH NP

B **Excelsior**
(Wythenshawe) .061-437 5811 255 G   NP

Morecambe

C **Headway** .... 2525 50 G

C **Midland** .... 2591 40 G   CH NP

D **Elms** .... 1501 40 G   NP

D **Mayfair** .... 1836 46 G

Preston

C **Bull and Royal** .... 56223 51 G   CH NP

Rochdale

C **Wellington** .... 43654 26 G   CH NP

St Helens

C **Fleece** .... 26546 87 G   CH NP

D **Royal Raven** ...... 22509 11 G   CH NP

Southport

B **Prince of Wales** ... 4131 90 G   NP

C **Brunswick** .... 55558 50 G   CH NP

C **Clifton** .... 3131 64 G   CH NP

D **Glenwood** .... 255992 16 G   CH

Warrington

C **Hill Cliffe Hydro**
(Appleton) .... 63638 15 G

C	**Patten Arms**	32826	46	G		CH	NP
D	**Birchdale** (Appleton)	63662	22	G		CH	

Wigan

C	**Brockett Arms**	46283	24	G		CH	NP

WESTMORELAND

Ambleside

C	**Rothay Manor**	2331	9	G	CW		
D	**Kirkstone Foot** ...	2232	17	G	CW		
D	**Low Wood**	3338	141	G	CW		
D	**Wateredge**	2323	20	G	CW		

Appleby

C	**Tufton Arms**	593	28	G		CH	
D	**Garbridge**	571	12	G	CW	CH	

Bowness

D	**Knoll**	Windermere 3756	12	G		CH	

Crooklands

B	**Crooklands**	432	15	G		CH	NP

Grasmere

C	**Gold Rill**	276	23	G		CH	
C	**Red Lion**	456	38	G	CW	CH	
C	**Swan**	223	35	G	CW		
D	**Hollens**	309	17	G	CW	CH	
D	**Prince of Wales** ...	344	81	G	CW		NP

Heversham

C	**Blue Bell**	3159	16	G		CH	

Kendal

C	**County**	22461	12	G			NP
C	**Woolpack**	20640	29	G			NP
D	**Kendal**	24103	49	G			NP

Langdale, Great

D	**Pillar**	656	25	G		CH	UL

Ullswater

C	Leaming House ...	Pooley Bridge					
		444	17	G		CH	
C	Rampsbeck	Pooley Bridge					
		442	20		CW	CH	
D	Brackenrigg	Pooley Bridge					
		206	29	G	CW		
D	Glenridding	Glenridding					
		228	33	G		CH	

Windermere

B	Old England	2444	90	G		CH	NP
C	Beech Hill	2137	37	G		CH	
C	Burnside	2211	37	G		CH	NP
D	Belsfield	2448	69	G		CH	NP
D	Elleray	3120	13	G			
D	Grey Walls	3741	20	G			
D	Hydro	2226	99	G	CW		NP
D	Royal	3045	28	G	CW		
D	Wild Boar	3178	36	G			

CUMBERLAND

Bassenthwaite

C	Armathwaite Hall	256	33	G			
C	Castle Inn	401	18	G		CH	
D	Pheasant Inn	234	20	G			

Borrowdale

B	Lodore Swiss	285	73	G	CW	CH	NP
C	Grange	251	9	G	CW	CH	
C	Scafell	208	22	G	CW	CH	

Braithwaite

C	Ivy House	338	14	G	CW	CH	

Buttermere

D	Bridge	252	24	G	CW		

Carlisle

C	Carrow House	23977	12	G		CH	
C	County and Station	25386	68	G		CH	NP

C	Crown and Mitre ..	25491	76	G		CH NP
C	Hilltop Motor Hotel	29255	77	G		CH NP
C	Crest Motel	31201	100			CH NP
D	Central	20256	69	G		NP
D	Pinegrove	24828	11	G		
D	Red Lion	21503	69	G		NP

Cockermouth

C	Moota Motel	Aspatria				
		681	47	G		CH
D	Trout	3591	17	G		NP

Eskdale

| D | Bower House Inn .. | 244 | 12 | G | | CH |

Grange-in-Borrowdale

| D | Green Bank ...... | Borrowdale | | | | |
| | | 215 | 10 | G | | UL |

Keswick

C	Derwentwater	72538	54	G CW		NP
C	Keswick	72020	76	G CW	CH	NP
C	Queen's	72054	36	G CW		NP
C	Skiddaw	72071	52	G		CH NP
D	Chaucer House	72318	36	G CW		
D	County	72341	23	G		
D	Royal Oak	72965	65	G		.

Penrith

C	George	2696	36	G		CH NP
D	Glen Cottage	2221	7	G		
D	Hussar	4444	34	G		NP

ISLE OF MAN

Castletown

| C | Golf Links ...... | 2201 | 66 | G | | CH NP |

Douglas

B	Palace	4521	100	G		CH NP
C	Fort Anne	4267	61	G		CH
D	Castle Mona	4355	105	G		CH NP

D Sefton	21775	107	G	CH NP
D Metropole	4881	94		CH
D Williers	5465	130	G	NP

Port St Mary

C Balqueen Hydro ..	3112	145	G	CH NP

Ramsey

C Grand Island	2455	61	G	CH

XI. SOUTHERN SCOTLAND

The Borders and the Lowlands, including Glasgow,
Edinburgh and Perth.

AYRSHIRE

Ayr

C Caledonian	69331	134	G	CH NP
D Ayrshire & Galloway	62626	26		NP
D Berkeley	63658	12	G	
D County	63368	32		CH NP
D Marine Court	65261	21	G	CH

Kilmarnock

D Broomhill	2371	10	G	
D Ross	21400	19		CH NP

Largs

D Mackerston	3264	50	G CW		UL
D Marine and Curlinghall	4551	77	G	CH NP

Prestwick

C Carlton	77418	9	G	CH NP
C Queen's	70501	27	G	NP
D Towans	77831	57	G	CH NP

Troon

C Craiglea	83	21	G	CH
C Marine	980	68	G	NP

C	Sun Court	1066	20	G		CH	

BERWICKSHIRE

Carfraemill

D	Carfraemill	Oxton 200	11	G		CH	

Chirnside

D	Chirnside Country House	219	12	G			

Cockburnspath

D	Cockburnspath	217	6	G		CH	

Coldstream

D	Newcastle Arms ..	2376	7	G			

Lauder

D	Black Bull	208	16	G		CH	

BUTE

Arran, Isle of

D	Bay	224	20	G	CW		UL
D	Belvedere	197	8		CW		UL
D	Blackrock House ..	212	7				UL
D	Blackwaterfoot	Shiskine 202	17	G			
D	Douglas	5	49	G			
D	Ennismor	65	25	G			UL
D	Gwyder Lodge	177	25	G	CW		UL
D	Kinloch	Shiskine 286	41	G		CH	
D	St Elmo	29	21	G	CW		UL

Bute, Isle of

C	Glenburn	500	97	G	CW	CH	NP
D	Marine House	551	34	G	CW		
D	St Blanes	224	156	G		CH	

CLACKMANNANSHIRE

Dollar

C	Dollarbeg Guest House	2420	43	G	CW	CH	NP	UL

DUMFRIESSHIRE

Dumfries

B	Cairndale	4111	46	G	CH	NP
C	County	5401	45	G		NP
D	King's Arms	4247	50	G	CH	NP
D	Station	4316	28	G	CH	NP

Gretna

C	Royal Stewart Motel	210	14	G	CH

Gretna Green

D	Gretna Hall	257	48		
D	Lover's Leap Motel	297	24	G	CH

Lockerbie

D	Bluebell	2309	12	G	CH
D	Dryfesdale	2427	14	G	CH
D	Lockerbie House ..	2610	20	G	
D	Townhead	2298	10	G	CH NP

Moffat

D	Balmoral	288	18	G	
D	Buccleuch Arms ...	3	18	G	
D	Moffat House	39	15	G	CH

Thornhill

D	Buccleuch and Queensberry	215	10	G

DUNBARTONSHIRE

Arrochar

C	Arrochar	222	56	G	CH NP
D	Ardmay House ...	242	23	G	CH NP

Balloch

C	Loch Lomond	041-258 2269	74	G	NP

Bearsden

C	Burnbrae ...	041-942 5951	16	G	CH

Clydebank

C	Radnor	041-952 3427	12	G	CH NP
D	Boulevard	2381	13	G	CH NP

Cumbernauld

C	Golden Eagle	25631	45	G	CH NP

Dumbarton

D	Dumbuck	3818	16	G	CH NP

Duntocher

C	Maltings	6221	27	G	CH NP
D	Erskine Bridge Motel	2333	18	G	CH

Helensburgh

C	Cairndhu	3388	17	G	CH NP
C	Commodore	2966	29	G	NP

Milngavie

C	Black Bull .	041-956 1658	21	G	CH NP

Tarbet

D	Tarbet	Arrochar 228	60	G	CH NP

EAST LOTHIAN

Dunbar

C	Bayswell	2225	15	G	
C	St George	2213	9	G	
D	Bellevue	2322	47	G CW	

Gullane

B	Greywalls	2144	25	G CW	
C	Mallard	3288	21	G	
C	Queen's	2275	32	G	

Haddington

C	George	3372	10	G	

North Berwick

C	Marine	2406	86	G	CH NP

C **Royal Hunting Lodge**	2401	43			CH	NP
D **Blenheim House** ..	2385	12	G			
D **Golf**	2202	18	G		CH	
D **Point Garry**	2380	16	G		CH	
Westerdunes	2366	30		CW		

FIFE

Aberdour

C **Woodside**	328	14	G		CH

Dunfermline

D **Brucefield**	22199	9	G	

Elie

C **Marine**	555	56	G	CW	CH	NP

Glenrothes

C **Golden Acorn**	2292	24	G	CH	NP
C **Rothes Arms**	3701	16	G	CH	NP

Kirkcaldy

C **Ambassadeur**	65483	10	G	CH	NP
C **Station**	62461	36		CH	NP
D **Ollerton**	4286	10	G	CH	

Leven

D **Caledonian**	2273	20	G		NP

St Andrews

C **Ruffiets**	2594	19	G	CW		
C **Russacks**	4321	64	G	CW	CH	NP
C **Scores**	2451	35			CH	NP
D **Cross Keys**	3646	20	G			
D **Imperial**	387	50		CW		NP
D **St Andrews**	2611	30			CH	NP
D **Star**	3698	22				
B **Old Course**	4371	80	G		CH	NP

KINROSS-SHIRE

Kinross

C **Green**	3467	46	G		NP

D **Bridgend**	3413	15	G		CH

KIRKCUDBRIGHTSHIRE

Castle Douglas ......
C **Douglas Arms**	2231	29	G		CH
D **Ernespie House** ...	2188	16	G		CH
D **Imperial**	2086	15	G		CH
D **King's Arms**	2097	13	G		CH

Dalry
D **Lochinvar**	210	18	G		

Gatehouse-of-Fleet
C **Cally**	341	61	G		CH NP
C **Murray Arms**	207	23	G	CW	NP

Kirkcudbright
D **Mayfield**	523	30	G		CH NP UL
D **Royal**	551	22	G		
D **Selkirk Arms**	402	25	G		

New Galloway
D **Cross Keys**	218	8	G		
D **Kenmure Arms** ...	240	18	G		CH

LANARKSHIRE

Bothwell
D **Silvertrees**	2311	27	G	CW	CH NP

Burnside
C **Burnside** ...	041-634 1276	16	G		CH

Coatbridge
C **Coatbridge**	24392	22	G		CH NP

East Kilbride
B **Bruce**	29771	65	G		CH NP
C **Stuart**	21161	29	G		CH NP

Glasgow
B **Beacons** 7 Park Terrace C3 ..	041-332 9438	28			CH NP

B **Clydesdale Bath**
152 Bath Street   041-332 7416   30   NP

B **Ivanhoe**
125 Buchanan
Street ..... 041-332 7284   71   NP

B **Royal Stuart**
Clyde Street . 041-248 4261   110   G   CH NP

B **White House**
11-13 Cleveden
Crescent W2 . 041-339 9375   32   G   CH NP UL

C **Bellahouston**
517 Paisley Road
West .... 041-427 3146   46   G   CH NP

C **Blythswood**
320 Argyle Street
C2 .... 041-221 4133   46   CH NP

C **Crookston**
90 Crookston
Road SW2 ... 041-882 6142   22   G   CH NP

C **Glassford**
80-90 Glassford
Street C1 .... 041-552 4851   48   CH NP

C **Kenilworth**
5 Queen Street C1 041-221 5151   38   CH NP

C **Shawlands**
30 Shawlands
Square S1 ... 041-632 9226   20   G   CH NP

D **Apsley**
903 Sauchiehall
Street C2 .... 041-334 3510   23   CH NP UL

D **Dorchester**
931 Sauchiehall
Street C3 .... 041-339 6876   44   NP

D **Marie Stuart**
46-48 Queen
Mary Avenue S2 041-423 6363   25   G   CH   UL

D **Western**
4 Burnbank
Terrace NW . 041-332 8387   30   G   CH

B **Central** Gordon
Street C1 .... 041-221 9680   235   CH NP

B **North British**
40 George Square
C2 .... 041-332 6711   78   CH NP

B **St Enoch**
St. Enoch Square
C1 .... 041-221 7033   155   G   CH NP

Glasgow Airport

B **Excelsior**
Glasgow Airport 041-887 1212 316   G   CH NP

C **Airport** (Renfrew) .   3771   132   G   CH NP

Hamilton

C **Commercial**   23182   24   G   NP

Lanark

C **Cartland Bridge** ...   3776   15   G   CH

Motherwell

C **Garrion**   64561   57   G   CH NP

Mount Vernon

D **Golden Gate** 041-778 5541   17   G   CH NP

MIDLOTHIAN

Dalkeith

D **Motel Derry** . 031-663 3234   16   G   CH   UL

Edinburgh

B **Caledonian**
Princes Street 031-225 2433   196   G   CH NP

B **North British**
Princes Street 031-556 2414   211   G   CH NP

B **Clydesdale**
Palace 3 Castle
Street ...... 031-225 6222   38   NP

B **Esso Motor**
Hotel Queens-
ferry Road ... 031-332 2442   120   G   CH NP

B **George**
19 George Street 031-225 1251   87   NP

B¹ **Roxburghe**
Charlotte Square 031-225 3921 75 CH NP

B **Royal British**
20 Princes Street 031-556 4901 66 CH NP

C **Barnton** Queen-
ferry Road ... 031-336 2291 50 G CH NP

C **Carlton** North
Bridge ...... 031-556 7277 92 CH NP

C **Ellersly House**
Ellersly Road 031-337 6888 60 G NP

C **Fox Covert**
187 Clermiston
Road .... 031-334 3391 50 G CH NP

C **Gordon**
7-9 Royal Circus 031-225 3000 26 G

C **Howard**
32-36 Great
King Street .. 031-556 1393 26 G CH NP

C **Lady Nairne**
Willowbrae
Road .... 031-661 3396 25 G CH NP

C **Learmonth**
Learmonth
Terrace ..... 031-332 1795 216 G CH NP

C **Mount Royal**
53 Princes Street 031-225 7161 50 CH NP

C **Scotia** 9 Great
King Street .. 031-556 3266 47 CH NP

D **Abercromby**
32-34 Aber-
cromby Place 031-556 1063 32 NP

D **Adelphi** Cock-
burn Street .. 031-225 1520 85 NP

D **Claremont**
Claremont
Crescent .... 031-556 3289 10 G CH

D **County**
8-10 Abercromby
Place .... 031-556 2333 60 G CH NP

D	**Doric** 22 Minto Street	031-667 3489	28	G
D	**Dorlin** 24 St John's Road	031-334 1034	24	G
D	**Green's** 24 Eglinton Crescent	031-337 6311	46	CW
D	**Grosvenor** Centre Grosvenor Street	031-226 6001	165	CH NP
D	**Murrayfield** 18 Corstorphine Road	031-337 2207	31	G NP
D	**Nelson** Nelson Street	031-556 4344	18	CH
D	**Old Waverley** Princes Street	031-556 4648	87	NP
D	**Ritz** 14-18 Grosvenor Street ..	031-337 7743	39	CH NP
D	**Sighthill** Calder Road .	031-443 5151	10	G

Lasswade

C	**Melville Castle** ...	3317	17	G CH

Newbridge

C	**Norton**	Ratho 275	10	G

PEEBLESSHIRE

Eddleston

C	**Black Barony**	202	38	G NP
C	**Cringletie House** ..	233	12	G

Innerleithen

D	**Traquair Arms**	229	9	G

Peebles

C	**Park**	2451	24	G NP
C	**Peebles Hydro**	3102	162	G CH NP
C	**Tontine**	3392	34	G VH

| D Green Tree .... | 3082 | 16 | | | CH NP | |
| D Venlaw Castle .... | 2384 | 12 | G | | CH | |

PERTHSHIRE

Aberfoyle

C Covenanter's Inn ..	347	38	G		CH NP	
D Forest Hills	Kinlochard					
	217	37	G		CH NP	

Auchterarder

| A Gleneagles .... | 2231 | 210 | G CW | CH NP | |

Blair Atholl

| D Atholl Arms ...... | 205 | 28 | G | | CH | |

Blairgowrie

C Kinloch House	237	11	G			
D Angus	2838	84	G		CH	
D Queen's	2217	30	G			

Callander

C Roman Camp	30003	15	G CW			
D Dreadnought	30184	70	G CW		NP	
D Pinewood	30111	16	G CW CH			

Crianlarich

| D Crianlarich ...... | 202 | 25 | G CW | | | |

Crieff

C Drummond Arms ..	2151	41	G		CH NP	
C Strathearn Hydro ..	2401	204	G		NP UL	
D Kingarth	2060	13	G CW		UL	
D Leven House	2529	14	G		UL	

Doune

| C Deanston House ... | 248 | 23 | G CW | | NP | |

Dunblane

| C Dunblane Hydro ... | 2551 | 142 | G | | NP | |
| D Stirling Arms ..,... | 2156 | 8 | G | | CH | |

Dunkeld

B	Cardney House	Butterstone					
		222	10	G		CH	
C	Dunkeld House	243	23	G	CW	CH	
D	Royal Dunkeld ...	322	32	G		CH	
D	Taybank	340	10	G			

Glenshee

D	Spittal of Glenshee .	215	25	G		CH	

Invergowrie

C	Greystane House ..	425	7	G			

Kenmore

C	Kenmore	205	37	G			

Killiecrankie

D	Killiecrankie	220	10	G	CW		

Killin

D	Bridge of Lochay ..	272	17	G	CW		
D	Killin	296	32	G	CW	CH	

Kinloch Rannoch

C	Loch Rannoch	310	45	G			

Lochearnhead

D	Lochearnhead	237	52	G	CW		

Perth

C	Isle of Skye	22962	41	G		CH	
C	Royal George	24455	43	G		CH	NP
D	Queen's	25471	54	G		CH	NP
D	Salutation	22166	81			CH	NP
D	Tay Motel	22804	20			CH	NP
D	Station	24241	52	G			NP

Pitlochry

C	Atholl Palace	66	100	G	CW		NP
C	Fisher's	284	66	G		CH	NP
C	Green Park	37	46	G		CH	
C	Pitlochry Hydro ...	480	70	G	CW		NP

D **Burnside**		203	14	G CW		UL
D **Moulin**		196	23	G		
D **Pine Trees**		121	28	G CW		
D **Scotland's**		185	52	G	NP	

St Fillans

C **Four Seasons**		276	18	G	CH NP
D **Drummond Arms** ..		212	40	G CW	

Trossachs

C **Trossachs**		232	77	G	CH NP
D **Loch Achray**		229	34	G CW CH	

Tyndrum

D **Auchreoch House** **Motel**		219	14	G CW CH	

RENFREWSHIRE

Giffnock

C **Macdonald** ..	041-638 2225	57	G	CH NP	
C **Redhurst**	041-638 6465	16	G	CH NP	

Gourock

C **Bay**	31244	39		CH NP
C **Gantock**	33731	63	G	CH NP
D **Cloch**	32038	16		CH NP
D **Firth**	32202	13		CH
D **Queen's**	31424	21	G	CH

Greenock

C **Tontine**	23316	25	G	CH NP

Paisley

C **Rockfield** .	041-889 6182	9	G	CH NP
C **Silver Thread**	041-887 2196	12	G	CH NP
C **Watermill** ...	041-889 3201	30	G	CH NP

Renfrew

B **Excelsior Glasgow** **Airport**	041-887 1212	316	G	CH NP
B **Normandy** ..	041-886 4100	142	G	CH NP

C	Airport	3771	132	G		CH NP

ROXBURGHSHIRE

Jedburgh
D	Kenmore Bank	2369	6	G	CW		UL

Kelso
C	Ednam House	2168	29	G		

Melrose
C	George and Abbotsford	2308	22	G		NP
C	Waverley Castle	2244	68	G		

St Boswell's
C	Dryburgh Abbey	2261	31	G		

SELKIRKSHIRE

Galashiels
C	Douglas	2189	39	G		NP

Selkirk
D	Heatherliehill	3200	9	G CW	

STIRLINGSHIRE

Bridge of Allan
C	Royal	2284	31	G		CH NP
D	Allan Water	2293	55	G		CH NP

Drymen
C	Buchanan Arms	588	22	G		CH NP
C	Winnock	245	20	G		CH

Falkirk
C	Clydesdale Metropolitan	22531	33	G		CH NP

Grangemouth
C	Leapark	2331	36	G		CH NP

Stirling
C	Golden Lion	5351	57	G		CH NP
D	Garfield	3730	10	G		CH

D Station	2017	25	G		NP

Strathblane

C Kirkhouse Inn	Blanefield				
	621	19	G	CH	NP

WEST LOTHIAN

Bathgate

C Golden Circle	53771	50	G	CH	NP
D Dreadnought	53193	15		CH	NP

South Queensferry

C Forth Bridges Motel	611	98	G	CH	NP
C Hawes Inn	215	5	G		

Uphall

C Houston House	Broxburn			
	3831	19	G	

WIGTOWNSHIRE

Newton Stewart

C Galloway Arms ...	282	25	G	CH	
D Belhotel	294	24	G	CH	
D Cree Bridge House .	372	25	G CW		

Portpatrick

C Portpatrick	333	63	G CW		NP
D Melvin Lodge	238	14	G CW		
D Mount Stewart	291	10	G		
D Roslin	241	13	G		

Stranraer

C George	2487	30		CH	NP
C Lochnaw Castle ...	Leswalt				
	227	6	G	CH	NP
D Buck's Head	2064	16	G		
D North West Castle	2644	29	G	CH	NP

Wigtown

D Craignount	2291	6	G		UL

XII. NORTHERN SCOTLAND
(THE HIGHLANDS)

ABERDEENSHIRE

Aberdeen

C **Amatola** 448 Great Western Road	38724	30	G	CH	NP
C **Caledonian** 10-14 Union Terrace	29233	61	G	CH	
C **Imperial** Stirling Street	29101	134	G	CH	NP
C **Marcliffe** Queen's Terrace	51281	42	G		
C **Tree Tops** Springfield Road ...	33377	51	G	CH	NP
D **Central** 93-95 Crown Street	23685	18	G	CH	
D **Clifton** Bon-Accord Square	28552	35	G		NP
D **Dee Motel** Garthdee Road	38622	44	G	CH	NP
D **Douglas** Market Street	22255	109	G	CH	NP
D **George** 2-4 Bon-Accord Terrace	27366	48		CH	NP
D **Gloucester** 102 Union Street	29095	88		CH	NP
D **Lang Stracht** Lang Stracht	38712	34	G	CH	NP
D **Northern** Kittybrewster	43342	34		CH	NP
D **Atholl** 54 King's Gate	34781	23	G		NP
D **Station** 22 Guild Street	27214	63	G	CH	NP

Ballater

C **Craigendarroch** ...	217	34	G		CH		
D **Darroch Learg**	443	25	G	CW	CH		UL

D Invercauld Arms ...	417	25	G		
D Loirston					
D Loirston	413	40	G	CW	CH
D Tullich Lodge	406	11	G		

Braemar

D Braemar Lodge ..	617	11	G	CW	
D Fife Arms	644	72	G		NP
D Invercauld Arms ...	605	59	G	CW	NP

Cruden Bay

C Red House	216	16	G		CH

Cults, nr. Aberdeen

C Royal Darroch		67	G		CH NP

Ellon

C Craighall	666	26	G		CH
D Buchan	208	10	G		NP
D New Inn	425	11	G		CH

Fraserburgh

C Castle	2966	25	G	CW	CH
D Alexandra	2249	29	G		CH NP

Huntly

D Gordon Arms	2536	14	G		CH

Peterhead

D Palace	2243	24	G		NP

ANGUS

Broughty Ferry

C Ballinard	Dundee 79289	20	G	
D Woodlands	Dundee 79548	20	G	CH NP

Carnoustie

C Bruce	2364	41	G	CH
D Earlston	2352	20	G	

Dundee

C Invercarse	69231	28	G	CH NP	
C Queen's	22515	54	G	CH NP	
C Royal Clydesdale	24074	82		CH NP	
D Tay Centre	21641	100		CH NP	
D Angus	26874	56	G	CH	

Forfar

D Jarman's	2018	12	G		
D Royal	2691	19	G	CH	

Montrose

D Madeira	54	12		CH	
D Park	1415	36	G	CH NP	

ARGYLL

Ardrishaig

D Royal	239	20	G	CH	

Arduaine by Oban

C Loch Melfort Motor	Kilmelford				
Inn	233	28	G CW	CH	

Ballachulish

C Ballachulish	239	35	G	CH	

Campbeltown

D Ardshiel	2133	14	G		
D Argyll Arms	2408	48	G	CH	

Dunoon

C Cowal House	103	38	G CW	CH	UL
D Glenmorag	227	91	G		
D McColl's	764	60	G	CH NP	
D Selborne	761	87	G CW		

Glencoe

D King's House	259	22			

Inveraray

D Argyll Arms	2113	27	G		

D George	2111	19	G			
Iona, Isle of						
D Argyll	234	20		CW		UL
D St Columba	204	30		CW		UL
Islay, Isle of						
D Port Charlotte	219	16	G CW			
D Port Askaig	245	10	G		CH	
D Islay, Port Ellen ...	60	21	G		CH	
Jura, Isle of						
D Jura (Craighouse) .	43	16	G		CH	
Loch Awe						
D Loch Awe	261	73	G			NP
Lochgilphead						
D Kilmory Castle	301	19	G		CH	
Mull, Isle of						
C Isle of Mull	Craignure					
(Craignure)	351	62		CW CH NP		
C Western Isles	Tobermory					
(Tobermory)	2012	50	G CW			NP
D Glenforsa (Salen) ..	Aros					
	77	14	G		CH	
D Mishnish	Tobermory					
(Tobermory)	2009	15	G		CH	
D Argyll Arms	Fionnphort					
(Bunessan)	240	13	G			
North Connell						
C Loch Nell Arms ...	408	13	G			
Oban						
C Caledonian	3133	64	G CW			NP
C King's Arms	2336	32	G			
C Labcaster	2587	28	G			
C Marine	2211	39	G CW CH NP			
C Park	2306	92	G			NP
D Alexandra	2381	62	G CW			NP

D **Balmoral**	2731	18			CH	
D **Columba**	2183	57	G	CW		NP
D **Royal**	3021	126		CW	CH	NP
D **Great Western**	3101	81	G	CW	CH	NP

Port Appin

D **Airds**	Appin 236	17	G	CW

Portsonachan by Dalmally

C **Portsonachan**	Kilchrenan 236	23	G

Strontian by Fort William

C **Ben View**	33	13	G	
D **Loch Sunart**	31	10	G	CW

Tarbert

D **Columba** (Loch Fyne)	241	14	G		NP
D **Tarbert**	264	20	G	
D **West Loch** (West Loch)	283	6	G	

Taynuilt

B **Netherlon**	243	18	G
D **Polfearn**	251	13	G
D **Taynuilt**	226	24	G

Tiree, Isle of

D **Scaronish**	8	17	G

BANFF

Banff

C **Fife Arms**	2427	25	G
D **Crown**	2455	15	

Craigellachie

C **Craigellachie**	204	31	G	CW
D **Cullen Bay**	432	20	G	

Cullen

D **Waverley**	210	9	G

40

Dufftown

D Parkmore House ..	410	10	G	CH	

Keith

D Ashley Lodge	2335	10	G	CH	

Tomintoul

D Gordon Arms	206	35	G		

CAITHNESS

John o'Groats

D John o'Groats ...	203	27	G		

Thurso

D Royal	3191	83	G CW		NP
D Pentland	3202	37		CH	NP

Wick

D MacKay's	2323	19	G		
D Station	2475	60	G		

INVERNESS

Aviemore

B Post House	771	103	G	CH NP
C Badenoch	261	81	G	CH NP
C Coylumbridge	661	133	G	CH NP
C Strathspey	681	90	G	CH NP
D Aviemore Chalets Motel	618	80	G	CH
D Cairngorm	233	27	G	CH

Beauly

D Chrialdon	336	12	G CW		UL

Cannich

D Glen Affric	214	18	G		

Carrbridge

C Carrbridge	202	49	G		

Drummadrochit

C Drummadrochit	218	29	G	CH NP

D **Glenurquhart Lodge**	342	30	G	CW	CH		

Fort Augustus

D **Inchnacardoch**	258	22	G		

Fort William

B **Croit Anna**	2268	90	G		NP	
C **Alexandra**	2241	44	G		NP	
C **Milton**	2331	44	G			
D **Clan Macduff Motel**	2341	50	G	CW		
D **Grand**	2928	35	G			
D **Highland Hotel and Motel Court**	2291	59	G		NP	
D **Imperial**	2040	37	G		CH	
D **Milton Motor Inn** ..	2334	60	G	CW		UL
D **Nevis Bank**	2595	20	G		CH	

Harris, Isle of

D **Harris** (Tarbert) ...	Harris 4	23	G	

Invergarry

C **Invergarry**	206	16	G	CW
D **Glengarry Castle** ..	254	30	G	CW

Invermoriston

C **Glenmoriston Arms**	Glenmoriston 206	15	G	CW

Inverness

C **Caledonian** Church Street	35181	120	G	CH NP	
C **Cumming's** Church Street	32531	35	G	CH	
C **Glen Mhor** Nessbank	34308	28	G	NP	
C **Royal Stuart Motor Hotel** Perth Road ..	33506	111	G	CH NP	
D **Columba** 7 New Walk	31391	54	G	CH NP	
D **Douglas** Union Street	34671	88		CW CH NP	
D **Haughdale** Ness Bank	33065	41	G	CH NP	

D **Muirtown Motel**					
11 Clachnacarry Rd	34806	40	G		
D **Royal** Academy Street	30665	45	G		CH NP
D **Station** Academy Street	31926	61	G		CH NP

Kingussie

D **Duke of Gordon** ...	302	72		CW	NP
D **Star**	431	26	G		CH NP

Mallaig

D **Marine**	2217	25	G		CH
D **West Highland** ...	2210	30	G CW		

Newtonmore

D **Balavil Arms**	220	30	G		
D **Carigh Mor**	210	30	G		CH
D **Truim**	206	35	G		CH

Skye, Isle of

D **Royal, Portree**	225	28	G		CH
D **Coolins Hills, Portree**	003	29	G		CH NP
D **Uig, Uig**	205	25	G CW		CH NP
D **Sligachan, Sligachan**	204	26	G CW		
D **Skeabost House, Portee**	202	25	G CW		NP
D **Broadford, Broadford**	205	30	G		

Spean Bridge

D **Spean Bridge**	250	25			CH

Uist, Isle of

C **Lochmaddy**	331	15	G		CH

KINCARDINE

Banchory

C **Raemoir**	2622	24	G		CH
C **Tor-na-Coille**	2242	27	G		NP
D **Banchory Lodge** ...	2553	23	G		

Nigg
D **Gay Gordon Motel** Aberdeen
50112 10 G CH
Stonehaven
C **Commodore** ...... 2936 40 G CH NP
D **Braemar** .... 2415 16 CW UL
D **Royal** .... 2755 18 G

MORAY
Elgin
D **Gordon Arms** ..... 2646 25 G CH NP
D **Laichmoray** ...... 2558 25 G
Findhorn
D **Culbin Sands** ..... 252 20 G
Fochabers
D **Gordon Arms** ..... 220 17 G CH
Forres
C **Cluny Hill** .... 2288 68 G CW CH NP
Grantown-on-Spey
C **Palace** .... 206 44 G
D **Ben Mhor** .... 56 24 G
D **Craiglyne** .... 97 57 G CH NP
D **Grant Arms** ...... 26 49 G CW NP
D **Rosehall** .... 211 10 G CH

NAIRN
Auldearn
D **Lion** .... 3204 29 G
Nairn
B **Newton** .... 3144 60 G CW CH NP
C **Golf View** .... 2301 58 G CW CH NP
C **Royal Marine** ..... 3381 46 G CW CH NP
D **Highland** .... 3141 65 G CW
D **Washington** ...... 3351 22 CW CH
D **Windsor** .... 3108 48 G CW

ROSS AND CROMARTY

Achnasheen

D Ledgowan	252	25	G				

Dingwall

D National	2166	37	G				
D Royal	2130	16	G				

Gairloch

C Gairloch Motor Inn	2131	20	G CW			
D Gairloch	2002	53	G CW		NP	

Kyle of Lochalsh

D Retreat	4308	14	G CW			UL
D Lochalsh	4202	48	G CW CH NP			

Lewis, Isle of

C Royal	Stornoway 2109	17		CH		
D Hebridean	Stornoway 2268	7				UL
D Crown	Stornoway 781	25		CH		

Poolewe

D Pool House	272	22	G CW			

Strathpeffer

C Ben Wyvis	323	92	G CW		NP	
C Highland	457	100	G CW CH NP		
D Richmond	100	18	G			
D Strathpeffer	200	37	G	CH		

Torridon

C Loch Torridon	242	28	G CW			

Ullapool

D Caledonian	2306	47	G		NP	
D Morefield	2141	30	G			
D Royal	2181	56	G	CH NP		

SUTHERLAND

Bonar Bridge
D Caledonian	Ardgay					
	214	26	G		CH	

Brora
D Links	225	31	G CW		

Dornoch
C Burghfield	212	50	G CW		
D Dornoch	351	93	G CW		
D Royal Golf	283	45	G CW		NP

Golspie
D Golf Links	287	25	G		
D Sutherland Arms ..	287	19	G	CH	NP

Inchnadamph
D Inchnadamph	Assynt			
	202	33	G	

Kinlochbervie
C Garbet	275	24	G CW	

Lairg
C Aultnagar	Invershin				
	245	29	G CW		
D Sutherland Arms ..	2291	38	G CW		NP

Lochinver
D Culag	209	45	G CW	NP

Scourie
D Scourie	6	22	CW	

Tongue
D Ben Loyal	216	20	G	CH	
D Tongue	206	20	G CW	CH	

ORKNEY

Kirkwall
C Ayre	2197	32	G	CH	NP
D Kirkwall	232	42		CH	NP
D Queen's	2200	8		CH	

Stenness

D **Standing Stones** ... Stromness

                                        449   21   G

SHETLAND

Lerwick

C **Lerwick**   1166   26   G   CH

D **Grand**   18   22

Sumburgh

D **Sumburgh**   208   17   G CW

INDEX

This Index is in three parts:
I. London and suburbs;
II. England and Wales;
III. Scotland.
Italic figures in brackets refer to the list of hotels.

I. LONDON

Hotels: p. 1121

A

Adelphi 149
Admiralty 139
Admiralty Arch 139
Albert Hall 171
Albert Memorial 171
Aldgate 190
All Hallows Church 195
All Souls Church 163
Apsley House 170

B

Baden-Powell House 225
Baker St 165
Bank of England 186
Bankside 202
Banqueting House 140
Barking 232
Barnabas House 160
Bayswater Road 165
BBC 163
Bedford Square 161, 163
Berkeley Square 158
Bethlem Hospital 200

Bethnal Green 190, 231
Big Ben 141
Billingsgate Market 196
Birdcage Walk 139
Blackfriars Station 185
Bloomsbury 160
Board of Trade 147
Bond St 158
Borough Road 201
Bowater House 170
Bridgewater House 153
British Museum 161, 203
British Theatre Museum 173
Bromfield Museum 225
Brompton Oratory 172
Brompton Road 170
Buckingham Palace 138
Burlington Arcade 158
Burlington House 158

C

Campden Hill 172
Cannon St Station 197
Canvey Island 232
Carlton Gardens 139
Carnaby St 160
Cenotaph 140
Charing Cross 150
Charterhouse School 180
Cheapside 185
Chelsea 173
Chelsea Hospital 174
Chelsea Old Church 173
Cheshire Cheese Tavern 175
Chingford 242
Chiswick House 225
Christ Church 181
City 175
Clarence House 153

Cleopatra's Needle 148
Clerkenwell 179
College of Arms 185
Commonwealth Institute 172
Coram's Fields 161
County Hall 199
Courtauld Institute 162
Covent Garden 150
Coventry St 160
Crayford 232
Crosby Hall 173
Crown Jewels 194
Croydon 235
Cuming Museum 225
Customs House 196

D

Dagenham 232
Dartford 232
Darwin Museum 225
Dean St 160
Dean's Yard 147
Design Centre 151
Dickens House 162
Discovery'' 148
Docks 230
Dover House 140
Downing St 140
Dr Johnson's House 175, 226
Drury Lane Theatre 150
Dulwich College Gallery 225, 234
Dutch Garden 167

E

Earls Court 173
East End 231
East Ham 232

Edgware 241
Edgware Road 164
Elephant and Castle 201
Eltham Palace 234
Epping 242
Erith 232
Euston Road 162
Euston Station 162

F

Fenchurch St Station 190
Fenton House 225
Fishmongers' Hall 197
Fleet St 175
Foreign Office 140
Forty Hall 226
Frith St 160

G

Geffrye Museum 190, 226
General Post Office 181
Geological Museum 172
George Inn 202
Goldsmiths' Hall 226
Gough Square 175
Gravesend 232
Gray's Inn 179
Green Park 153
Greenwich 232
Grosvenor Square 158
Guildhall 186
Guy's Hospital 201

H

Ham House 236
Hampstead 241
Hampton Court 236
Hanover Square 159

Harley St 163
Harrow 240
Haymarket 151
Hayward Gallery 226
Hertford House 164
Highgate 242
Holborn 175
Holborn Viadudt 179
Holland Park 172
Holy Sepulchre Church 180
Horse Guards 139
Houses of Parliament 140
Hyde Park 166

I

Imperial College 171
Imperial War Museum 200
Isle of Dogs 231
ITA Gallery 226

J

Jewish Museum 226

K

Kempton Park 236
Kensington Gardens 167
Kensington Palace 167
Ken Wood 242
Kew Gardens 235
Kew Palace 236
King's Cross Station 163
Knightsbridge 170

L

Lambeth Palace 199
Lancaster House 153

Law Courts 178
Leicester Square 160
Leighton House 173
Limehouse 518
Lincoln's Inn 178
Little Britain 180
Liverpool St Station 187
London Bridge 197
London Bridge Station 202
London Stone 197
Ludgate Hill 181

M

Madame Tussaud's 165
Mall 138
Manchester Square 164
Mansion House 187
Marble Arch 164
Marlborough House 152
Marylebone 163
Mayfair 155
Mint 195
Mitre Court 175
Monument 196
Mortlake 235
Museum of London 226

N

National Army Museum 226
National Central Library 163
National Film Archive 226
National Film Theatre 199
National Gallery 151, 209
National Maritime Museum 233
National Portrait Gallery 151, 216

National Postal Museum 226
Natural History Museum 171
Nelson Column 150
Norfolk House 155
Notre-Dame-de-France Church 160

O

Old Bailey 181
Old Vic Theatre 201
Olympia 173
Orleans House Gallery 226
Oxford Circus 163
Oxford St 163

P

Paddington Station 165
Pall Mall 151
Parliament 140
Parliament Square 144
Percival David Foundation 162
Petticoat Lane 231
Pharmaceutical Soc. Museum 227
Piccadilly 155
Piccadilly Circus 154
Planetarium 175
Pool of London 195
Poplar 232, 518
Port of London 228
Portobello Road 165
Post Office Tower 163
Poultry 186
Public Record Office 178
Putney 235

Q

Queen Elizabeth Hall 199
Queen's Gallery 138
Queen Victoria St 185

R

RAF Memorial 148
Ranelagh Gardens 174
Regent's Park 165
Regent St 159
Richmond Park 236
Rickmansworth 241
Roman wall 191
Rotherhithe 232
Royal Academy 158
Royal Albert Hall 171
Royal College of Music 227
Royal Coll. of Surgeons 227
Royal Exchange 187
Royal Festival Hall 199
Royal Mews 138
Runnymede 238
Russell Square 161

S

St Andrew by the Wardrobe 185
St Andrew Undershaft 198
St Anne's Church 160
St Bartholomew the Great 180
St Bartholomew's Hospital 180
St Benet's Church 198
St Bride's Church 175
St Clement Danes 149
St Dunstan in the West 176
St Ethelburga's Church 198
St George's, Bloomsbury 161
St George's Cathedral 201

St George's, Hanover Square 159
St George's Hospital 170
St Helen's Church 198
St James Garlickhythe 198
St James's Palace 152
St James's Park 138
St James's, Piccadilly 155
St John of Jerusalem, Priory 179
St Lawrence Jewry 186
St Magnus the Martyr 197
St Margaret Lothbury 198
St Margaret's, Westminster 147
St Martin in the Fields 151
St Martin's, Ludgate 181
St Marylebone 165
St Mary le Bow 185
St Mary le Strand 149
St Mary's, Lambeth 200
St Nicholas Cole Abbey 185
St Olave's Church 190
St Pancras Station 162
St Patrick's Church 160
St Paul's Cathedral 181
St Paul's, Covent Garden 150
St Peter's Church 164
St Stephen's, Walbrook 198
St Swithun's Church 197
St Thomas's Hospital 199
St Vedast's Church 198
Science Museum 171
Scotland Yard 147
Serpentine 166
Serpentine Gallery 227
Shaftesbury Avenue 160
Shell Centre 199
Smithfield Market 179
Soane Museum 178, 216
Soho 159
Soho Square 160
Somerset House 148

Southend 232
South London Art Gallery 227
Southwark Cathedral 201
Staple Inn 179
Stepney 231
Strand 148
Stratford Place 164
Syon House 235

T

Tate Gallery 147, 217
Temple 176
Temple Bar 176
Thurrock 232
Tilbury 231
Tottenham 242
Tower Bridge 195
Tower Hill 190
Tower of London 191
Trafalgar Square 150
Treasury 140
Trinity House 196
Twickenham 236

U

University of London 161
University College 163
Uxbridge 241

V

Valence House Museum 227
Victoria and Albert Museum 172, 221
Victoria Embankment 148
Victoria Station 139
Victoria St 147

W

Wallace Collection 164, 219
Waltham Abbey 242
Waltham Cross 242
Wapping 231
War Office 140
Waterloo Bridge 148
Waterloo Place 152
Waterloo Station 201
Warford 241
Wellington Arch 170
Wellington Museum 170
Welsh Church 198
Wembley 240
Wesley's House 227
West End 154
West Ham 232

Westminster Abbey 144
Westminster Bridge 148
Westminster Cathedral 139
Westminster Hall 141
Westminster School 147
Whitechapel 231
Whitechapel Art Gallery 170
Whitehall 139
Wimbledon 236
Windsor 238
Woolwich 232, 234

Z

Zoo 166

II. ENGLAND AND WALES

A

Abbey Dore 864
Abbot's Langley 655
Abbotsbury 393
Aber 898
Aberdaron 887 *(1213)*
Aberdovey 877 *(1218)*
Aberfan 864
Abergavenny 863 *(1219)*
Abergele 893
Aberystwyth 873 *(1215)*
Abingdon-on-Thames 688 *(1203)*
Abinger Hammer 330
Ab Kettleby 627
Adel 802
Adlington 643
Alcester 701 *(1208)*
Alciston 300
Aldborough 746
Aldeburgh 531 *(1191)*

Alderney, Is. 369 *(1174)*
Aldershot 375 *(1172)*
Alfriston 311 *(1167)*
Alkborough 745
Allesley 668
Allington 281
Alnwick 761
Alston 831
Althorp 602
Alton 342
Altrincham 799 *(1222)*
Alveston 718 *(1184)*
Amberley 326
Ambleside 841 *(1227)*
Amersham 674 *(1204)*
Amesbury 385 *(1186)*
Ammanford 866
Ampthill 600
Anglesey, Is. 882
Appleby (Cumbria) 830 *(1227)*
Appleby (Leics) 645
Appledore 452
Arbury 669

Arundel 325 *(1167)*
Ascot 374 *(1203)*
Ascott House 600
Ashbourne 637 *(1194)*
Ashburton 422
Ashby-de-la-Zouch 645 *(1195)*
Ashby St Legers 644
Ashdown Forest 298
Ashford 282 *(1164)*
Ashford-in-the-Water 636
Ashmansworth 490
Ash-next-Sandwich 267
Ashopton 804
Ashridge Park 655
Ashtead 319
Ashton Keynes 734
Astbury 794
Astley Hall 825
Aston 667
Atherstone 645
Attingham Park 651
Attleborough 566
Audley End 561
Aust 718
Austerfield 744
Avebury 493
Axbridge 467
Axminster 405 *(1175)*
Aycliffe 749
Aylesbury 656 *(1204)*
Aylesford 291
Aynhoe Park 657
Ayot St Lawrence 739
Aysgarth 829
Ayton 783

B

Bacton 535
Badbury Rings 397
Bagshot 374 *(1162)*
Bainbridge 829

Bakewell 634 *(1194)*
Bala 880 *(1218)*
Balcombe 313
Baldock 611, 740 *(1205)*
Bamburgh 761
Banbury 657 *(1206)*
Bangor 881 *(1214)*
Bardsey Is. 887
Barfreston 267
Barmouth 878 *(1218)*
Barnard Castle 831 *(1201)*
Barnet 738
Barnstaple 444 *(1175)*
Barrington Court 463
Barrow-in-Furness 839 *(1224)*
Barry 857 *(1217)*
Barton-in-the-Clay 611
Barton-on-Sea 354
Barton-upon-Humber 745, 779
Basing 377
Basingstoke 376 *(1172)*
Baslow 635
Bath 506 *(1181)*
Battle 300 *(1168)*
Battlefield 654
Bawdeswell 576
Beachley 731
Beachy Head 310
Beaconsfield 674 *(1204)*
Beaminster 404
Beaulieu Abbey 353
Beaumaris 882 *(1213)*
Beccles 565
Beddgelert 889
Bedford 612 *(1202)*
Beeleigh Abbey 523
Beer 398
Belper 631
Belton 580
Belvoir Castle 580, 620
Bembridge 361 «*1173*»
Bentley 342

Bere Regis 395
Berkeley 717 «*1185*»
Berkhamsted 655
Berrington Castle 721
Berwick-upon-Tweed 762 *(1200)*
Bethesda 881
Betws-y-Coed 881 *(1214)*
Beverley 775 *(1197)*
Bewdley 721
Bexhill-on-Sea 304 *(1168)*
Bibury 733 *(1185)*
Bicester 657
Bicknoller 462
Bideford 452
Bignor 325
Billinge 814
Billingshurst 324
Bilston 670
Birchington 270
Birkenhead 814 *(1222)*
Birmingham 664 *(1208)*
Bishop Auckland 748 *(1201)*
Bishop's Castle 871
Bishop's Stortford 560 *(1205)*
Blackburn 825 *(1224)*
Blackpool 826 *(1224)*
Blaise 718
Blakeney 536 *(1190)*
Blenheim 691
Bletchingley 312
Bletsoe 613
Blickling Hall 574
Blisworth 644
Blithfield Hall 650
Blundeston 533
Blyth 761
Bodelwyddan 893
Bodiam 302
Bodmin 434
Bognor Regis 327 *(1168)*
Bolney 313

Bolsover 636
Bolton 823 *(1225)*
Bolton Abbey 788 *(1197)*
Bonchurch 359
Bootle 813
Borden 255
Boreham 523
Borough Green 280
Boscastle 455
Boscobel House 670
Boston 594 *(1192)*
Bosworth 645
Bottesford 627
Boughton 256
Boughton Place 282
Bourne 590
Bournemouth 388 *(1172)*
Bowes 830
Boxgrove 336
Box Hill 319
Boxley 281
Brackley 658
Bradford 825 *(1197)*
Bradford-on-Avon 511 *(1187)*
Bradgate Park 619
Brading 361
Bradsole 278
Bradwell 641
Bradwell-on-Sea 523
Bramall Hall 643
Bramber 321
Brampton 833 *(1190)*
Brancaster 537
Brandon 565
Branxton 763
Brassington 638
Braunton 445
Bray 483 *(1203)*
Breamore 387
Brecon 865 *(1215)*
Brede 303
Breedon-on-the-Hill 646
Brendon 447

Brent Tor 432
Brenzett 288
Bridekirk 840
Bridgend 857 *(1217)*
Bridgnorth 650 *(1212)*
Bridgwater 465 *(1182)*
Bridlington 779 *(1197)*
Bridport 397
Brigg 592
Brightlingsea 528
Brighton 314 *(1168)*
Brinkburn 748
Bristol 495 *(1185)*
Britford 387
Brixham 419 *(1175)*
Brixworth 602
Broadheath 706
Broadstairs 271 *(1164)*
Broadway 700 *(1211)*
Brockenhurst 353
Brockhampton 722
Brocklesbury Park 779
Bromfield 720
Bromley 293 *(1139)*
Brompton 783
Bromsgrove 709 *(1211)*
Bromyard 722
Brookland 288
Brough 830
Broughton 601
Broughton Castle 658
Broughton-in-Furness 839
Bryn Celli Ddu 883
Buckden 740
Buckfast Abbey 423
Buckland Abbey 432
Bucklers Hard 353
Bude 454 *'(1179)*
Builth Wells 872
Bungay 564
Burford 710 *(1206)*
Burghley House 578
Burnham (Norfolk) 537

Burnham-on-Crouch 523 *(1188)*
Burnley 826 *(1225)*
Burton Agnes Hall 780
Burton Lazars 627
Burton-upon-Stuthers 744
Burton-upon-Trent 673 *(1210)*
Bury 823
Bury St Edmunds 563 *(1191)*
Buttermere 841 *(1228)*
Buxton 636 *(1194)*
Byland Abbey 785

C

Cadbury Camp 505
Cadbury Castle 416
Cader Idris 877
Caernarvon 885 *(1214)*
Caerphilly 856
Caerwent 731
Caister-on-Sea 534
Calder Bridge 840
Caldey Is. 867
Caldicot Castle 731
Calne 494
Camber Castle 290
Camberley 375 *(1162)*
Cambridge 542 *(1189)*
Camborne 438
Camelford 454
Cannock 649
Canterbury 256 *(1164)*
Canvey Is. 519
Capel Curig 881
Cardiff 853 *(1217)*
Cardigan 875
Carew 867
Carhampton 463
Carisbrooke 357
Carlisle 831 *(1228)*

Carmarthen 861 *(1215)*
Carter Bar 840
Cartmel 838
Castell Coch 856
Castell Collen 872
Castle Acre 574
Castle Ashby House 603
Castle Bromwich 669
Castle Howard 780
Castle Rising 538
Castleton 639 *(1219)*
Castletown (IOM) 847
  (1229)
Caversham Park 487
Cawsand 428
Cerne Abbas 402
Chacombe 658
Chadwick Manor 709
Chalfont St Giles 674
Chanctonbury Ring 322
Channel Is. 362
Chapel-en-le-Frith 639
Chard 404
Charing 282
Charlecote Park 697
Charmouth 398 *(1193)*
Charnwood Forest 621
Chartham 282
Chastleton House 699
Chatham 253
Chatsworth House 635
Chawton 342
Cheddar 467
Chedworth 711
Chelmsford 521 *(1188)*
Cheltenham 711 *(1185)*
Chepstow 731 *(1219)*
Chequers 656
Chesham 655
Chester 814 *(1223)*
Chesterfield 635 *(1194)*
Chester-le-Street 755
  (1201)
Chestfield 269

Chichester 332 *(1169)*
Chiddingstone 297
Chideock 397
Chilham 282
Chillingham Castle 764
Chillington Hall 670
Chippenham 494 *(1187)*
Chipping Campden 700
  (1185)
Chipping Norton 699
Chipping Ongar 560
Chipping Sodbury 734
Chirk 879 *(1216)*
Chislehurst 293
Chorley 825
Christchurch 388
Christ's Hospital 320
Church Stretton 720
  (1212)
Chysauster 439
Cilgerran 875
Cirencester 732 *(1185)*
Cissbury Ring 322
Clacton-on-Sea 528 *(1188)*
Claughton 828
Claverley 651
Cleethorpes 592 *(1192)*
Cleeve Abbey 451
Cleobury Mortimer 721
Clevedon 466 *(1182)*
Cliffe 252
Clifford 865
Clifton 503
Cliftonville 270
Clipstone 626
Clitheroe 826
Cliveden House 484
Clopton House 697
Clouds Hill 393
Clovelly 453
Clumber Park 625
Clun 871
Clymping 323
Clynnog Fawr 887

Coalville 645
Cobham 244
Cockermouth 840 *(1229)*
Codicote 739
Coggeshall 561
Coity 857
Cokethorpe 710
Colchester 524 *(1188)*
Coleford 730
Cole Orton 646
Coleshill 674
Colly Weston 615
Colwich 650
Colwyn Bay 893 *(1216)*
Combe Martin 446 *(1175)*
Combermere Abbey 822
Compton 329
Compton Wynyates 658, 691
Congleton 794 *(1223)*
Congresbury 466
Conisbrough 745
Coniston 842
Constantine 443
Conwy 894 *(1214)*
Cookham 484
Cooling 252
Corbridge 748
Corby 615 *(1196)*
Corfe Castle 394
Corsham 495
Corwen 880
Cotehele House 429
Cotswolds 699
Coughton Court 701
Coulsdon 306
Coventry 661 *(1208)*
Cowbridge 857 *(1217)*
Cowdray Castle 331
Cowes 356
Cowfold 321
Cowhoe 754
Coxwold 785
Cranbrook 302 *(1164)*

Craswall Abbey 865
Crawley 318 *(1169)*
Crediton 444
Creech Grange 394
Crewe 794 *(1223)*
Crewkerne 404
Criccieth 8889 *(1214)*
Crich 632
Crickhowell 864 *(1215)*
Cricklade 734
Croft Castle 721
Cromer 535 *(1190)*
Croscombe 475
Crowan 443
Crowborough 297
Crowcombe 462
Crowhurst 307
Crowland Abbey 593
Crowle 744
Croxton Kerrial 620
Croydon 305 *(1139)*
Cuckfield 313
Cullercoats 760
Cuxton 245
Cwmhir Abbey 872

D

Dalton 838
Danbury 522
Darenth 280
Darlington 748 *(1201)*
Dartford 244
Darlton 742
Dartmoor 422
Dartmouth 419 *(1175)*
Dawlish 417
Deal 274 *(1164)*
Dean Forest 730
Dean Prior 423
Dedham 530 *(1188)*
Deene Park 615
Deerhurst 719

Deganwy Castle 894
Denbigh 892 *(1216)*
Derby 628 *(1194)*
Derwentwater 843
Devil's Ditch 562
Devizes 494
Devonport 426
Dewsbury 803
Dicker 308
Dinis Mawddwy 877
Dinton 414
Disley 641
Ditchling 314
Dodderhill 709
Doddington 255
Dolaucothi 866
Dolgellau 877 *(1218)*
Dolmelynllyn 878
Doncaster 744 *(1197)*
Dorchester 391 *(1183)*
Dorchester-on-Thames 689 *(1206)*
Dorking 320 *(1162)*
Douai 489
Douglas (IOM) 846 *(1229)*
Dovedale 638
Dover 275 *(1164)*
Drayton Bassett 645
Droitwich 709
Dronfield 806
Druid 880
Ducklington 710
Duddington 615
Dudley 671
Duffield 631
Dunchurch 668
Dungeness 287
Dunham 742
Dunmow 561
Dunstable 598 *(1202)*
Dunster 450
Dunstonburgh Castle 761
Dunwich 532
Durham 749 *(1201)*

Dymchurch 285
Dyserth 893

E

Earith 741
Earls Barton 602
Easby Abbey 831
East Blatchington 310
Eastbourne 309 *(1169)*
East Cowes 356
Eastdean 310
East Dereham 575 *(1190)*
East Grinstead 307 *(1170)*
East Knoyle 415
Eastling 255
East Lulworth 395
Eastnor 707
Easton 491
Easton-on-the-Hill 615
Eastry 268
Eastwood 632
Eaton Hall 822
Eaton Socon 613
Ebbsfleet 272
Ecton 602
Edale 640
Eddystone Lighthouse 429
Edgehill 697
Egglestone Abbey 831
Egham 374 *(1162)*
Egremont 840
Elan Valley 872
Ellastone 637
Ellesmere 814
Elstow 612
Elstree 489
Ely 553 *(1190)*
Embleton 761
Empingham 627
Englefield 488
Ennerdale 840

Epping Forest 242, 560 *(1188)*
Epsom 319 *(1162)*
Epworth 744
Eridge 297
Esher 328
Eton 477
Evesham 701 *(1211)*
Ewell 267, 319 *(1163)*
Ewloe Green 891
Exeter 406 *(1176)*
Exmoor 446
Exmouth 413 *(1176)*
Eyam 634
Eye 574
Eynsham 710
Eythorne 267

F

Fairford 735
Fakenham 540
Falmouth 436 *(1179)*
Fareham 340
Faringdon 689, 735
Farleigh Hungerford 512
Farnborough 375
Farne Is. 761
Farnham 341 *(1163)*
Farningham 279
Farnley Hall 786
Farringford 358
Faversham 255 *(1165)*
Felixstowe 530 *(1191)*
Felpham 327
Fenny Bentley 637
Fens 559
Ffestiniog 889
Field Place 320
Filey 781
Filleigh 450
Filton 718
Findon 322

Fishbourne 336
Fishguard 870 *(1220)*
Flamborough Head 780
Flaxley Abbey 730
Fleetwood 826 *(1225)*
Flint 891
Folkestone 282 *(1165)*
Fonthill Gifford 415
Forde Abbey 404
Fordingbridge 387
Fordwich 270
Forest Row 308
Formby 813
Fotheringhay 615
Fountains Abbey 792
Fowey 435
Framlingham 531
Frimley 374
Frome 512 *(1182)*
Froxfield 491
Furness Abbey 838

G

Gainsborough 743 *(1192)*
Garsdon 735
Gateshead 755 *(1201)*
Gatton 312
Gatwick 313
Gawsworth 642
Geddington 615
Gilling Castle 785
Glasbury-on-Wye 865 *(1221)*
Glastonbury 469 *(1182)*
Glossop 639
Gloucester 712 *(1186)*
Glyndebourne 300
Goathland 783
Godalming 329
Godmanchester 741
Godshill 360
Godstone 307

Goodnestone 256
Goodrich 728
Goodwood Park 331
Gorhambury 610
Goring 323
Goring-on-Thames 689
Gosport 338
Grain, Isle of 252
Grange-over-Sands 838
Grantham 579 *(1193)*
Grasmere 843 *(1227)*
Graveney 256
Great Brington 644
Great Hampden 676
Great Malvern 707 *(1211)*
Great Yarmouth 533 *(1190)*
Greensted 560
Greta Bridge 830
Grime's Graves 565
Grimsby 592, 779 *(1193)*
Grosnez Castle 368
Guernsey, Is. 363
Guestling Green 291
Guildford 328 *(1163)*
Guilsfield 876
Guisborough Priory 782
Gunwalloe 442
Gweek 443

H

Hackness 781
Haddon Hall 634
Hadley 738
Hadrian's Wall 759
Hailes Abbey 712
Hailsham 308
Halifax 824 *(1197)*
Halling 245
Halton 826
Hansworth 668
Hanley 672 *(1210)*

Hardham 325
Hardwick Hall 624
Harewood House 786
Harlech 890 *(1219)*
Harleston 564
Harlow 560 *(1188)*
Harlyn Bay 458
Harnham 387
Harpenden 610 *(1205)*
Harrogate 788 *(1197)*
Hartland 453
Hartlebury 708
Hartlepool 747
Hartlip 253
Hartwell House 656
Harwich 529 *(1188)*
Haslemere 331 *(1163)*
Hastings 301 *(1170)*
Hatfield 738 *(1205)*
Hatfield Forest 560
Hathersage 641
Haverfordwest 868 *(1220)*
Hawarden 822 *(1216)*
Hawkshead 842
Haworth 787 *(1198)*
Haxey 744
Hayes 293
Hayfield 639
Hayle 438
Hay-on-Wye 865
Heacham 537
Heathrow 477
Hedon 779
Helmsley 784
Helston 441
Hembury 423
Hemel Hempstead 655 *(1205)*
Henley 485 *(1207)*
Henley-in-Arden 697
Henllan 892
Hereford 722 *(1212)*
Herm, Is. 366
Hern 270

Herne Bay 269
Hernhill 256
Herstmonceux 308 *(1171)*
Hertford 738 *(1205)*
Hever 297
Hexham 834 *(1200)*
Heysham 828 *(1225)*
Higham 252
Higham Ferrers 614
Highclere 490
Highcliffe 354, 388
High Halstow 252
High Ongar 560
Highworth 690
High Wycombe 675 *(1204)*
Hitchin 611 *(1205)*
Hoghton Tower 825
Holbeach 592
Holkham 536
Holland-on-Sea 528
Holyhead 883 *(1213)*
Holywell 891
Honiton 405
Hoo 252
Hope 640
Hornby 828
Horncastle 581
Horsey 535
Horsham 320
Horton 463 *(1207)*
Horton Court 733
Horton Kirby 280
Houghton-le-Spring 754
Hove 316
Huddersfield 799 *(1198)*
Hughenden Manor 675
Hull 776 *(1198)*
Hungerford 490
Hunstanton 537 *(1191)*
Huntingdon 740 *(1190)*
Hurley 484 *(1203)*
Hurst Castle 354
Hythe 285 *(1166)*

I

Icklesham 291
Ightham Mote 281
Ilchester 403 *(1192)*
Ilfracombe 445 *(1176)*
Ilkley 786
Instow 452
Ipswich 530 *(1191)*
Isfield 299
Isham 614
Ivinghoe 598
Iwade 254
Ixworth 564

J

Jarrow 759
Jersey, Is. 366
Jervaulx Abbey 793
Jethou, Is. 366
Jordans 674

K

Kedleston Hall 631
Keighley 787
Kendal 829 *(1227)*
Kenilworth 660 *(1208)*
Kenton 417
Keswick 843 *(1229)*
Kettering 614 *(1196)*
Kidderminster 708
Kilhampton 454
Killingworth 760
Kilpeck 864
Kimbolton 614
Kimmeridge 395
King's Lynn 538 *(1191)*
Kingston-upon-Thames 328 *(1142)*
Kingswear 419

Kington 871
Kirby Hall 615
Kirkby Lonsdale 828
Kirkdale 784
Kirkham Priory 780
Kirkstone Pass 837
Kit's Coty House 281
Knaresborough 789
Knebworth 739
Knighton 871 *(1212)*
Knole House 294
Knowle 664
Knutsford 794 *(1223)*
Kynance Cove 442

L

Lacock 494
La Hougue Bie 368
Lake District 835
Lambershurst 300
Lamberton 763
Lampeter 875
Lancaster 827
Lancing 318
Landewednack 443
Land's End 439 *(1179)*
Lanercost Priory 833
Langport 469
Lanhydrock House 434
Lastingham 784
Launceston 434
Lavenham 565 *(1192)*
Layer Marney 524
Lea 871
Leamington 660 *(1209)*
Leatherhead 319
Ledbury 708
Leeds 800 *(1198)*
Leeds Castle 282
Leek 642
Leicester 616 *(1195)*

Leighton Buzzard 600 *(1202)*
Leominster 721 *(1212)*
Letchworth 611 *(1205)*
Levens Hall 828
Lewes 299 *(1171)*
Lewtrenchard 433
Lichfield 646 *(1210)*
Lincoln 581 *(1193)*
Lindisfarne 762
Lingfield 307
Liskeard 433
Little Brington 644
Littlehampton 323 *(1171)*
Little Horsted 298
Little Moreton Hall 794
Little Petherick 457
Little Walsingham 540
Liverpool 807 *(1225)*
Lizard 441 *(1179)*
Llanaber 878
Llanaelhaearn 887
Llanbeblig 887
Llanberis 888 *(1214)*
Llandaff 854
Llanddewi Brefi 875
Llandeilo 866 *(1215)*
Llanderfel 880
Llandinabo 727
Llandovery 865 *(1215)*
Llandrindod Wells 872 *(1222)*
Llandudno 894 *(1214)*
Llanelly 861 *(1215)*
Llanfair P.G. 883
Llangollen 879 *(1216)*
Llangurig 872 *(1220)*
Llanidloes 877
Llanrhaiadr 892
Llanrwst 897
Llanstephan 862
Llanthony Abbey 863
Llantwit Major 857
Llanystumdwy 889

Llawhaden 875
Long Crendon 676
Longford Castle 387
Longleat House 513
Long Melford 565 *(1192)*
Long Sutton 592 *(1182)*
Loose 281
Lostwithiel 434
Loughborough 620 *(1195)*
Louth 591, 779
Lower Halstow 254
Lowestoft 532 *(1192)*
Luddesdown 245
Luddington 696
Ludlow 720 *(1212)*
Lullington 311
Lulworth Cove 395
Lundy, Is. 452
Luton 610 *(1202)*
Luton Hoo 610
Lutterworth 644
Lydd 287
Lydford 431
Lyme Regis 398 *(1183)*
Lymington 353
Lymm 799
Lympne 285
Lympstone 414
Lyndhurst 353
Lynmouth 447
Lynton 447
Lytham St Annes 826

M

Mabe 443
Mablethorpe 595
Macclesfield 642
Machynlleth 878 *(1220)*
Maiden Castle 391
Maidenhead 483 *(1203)*
Maidstone 281 *(1166)*
Maldon 522 *(1189)*

Malham 787
Malmesbury 734
Malton 780
Malvern 707 *(1211)*
Man, Isle of 845
Manaccan 443
Manchester 795 *(1225)*
Manorbier 867
Mansfield 624
Maresfield 308
Margam 858
Margate 270 *(1166)*
Market Harborough 616 *(1195)*
Marlborough 491
Marlow 484 *(1204)*
Marsden Bay 759
Marston Moor 789
Mary Tavy 432
Masham 793
Matlock 633 *(1195)*
Mawgan 443
Mawnan 438
Meare 471
Measham 645
Meavy 432
Medmenham 485
Melksham 512
Melton 531
Melton Mowbray 620 *(1195)*
Menai Bridge 882 *(1213)*
Meopham 281
Mere 415 *(1187)*
Merevale Abbey 645
Meriden 668 *(1209)*
Mersea Is. 528
Merstham 312
Merthyr Tydfil 864 *(1217)*
Mickleton 700
Middleham 793
Middlesbrough 746 *(1198)*
Mildenhall 564 *(1192)*

Milford 329, 330
Milford Haven 868 *(1220)*
Milford-on-Sea 354
Millom 839
Milton Abbas 391
Minchinhampton 733
Minehead 448 *(1183)*
Minster 254, 272
Mitcham 319
Mold 891
Monkton 272
Monkwearmouth 747
Monmouth 728 *(1219)*
Montacute 402
Montgomery 876
Mont Orgueil Castle 368
Morecambe 828 *(1226)*
Moreton-in-Marsh 700
  (1186)
Morley 631
Morpeth 760
Mortehoe 445
Morwenstow 454
Moseley Old Hall 649
Mottistone 359
Moulsford 689
Muchelney 469
Much Wenlock 651
Mullion Cove 442 *(1179)*
Mumbles 860 *(1217)*

N

Nantwich 822 *(1224)*
Narberth 875
Naseby 602
Nately Scures 376
Neath 858 *(1218)*
Nether Broughton 627
Netley Abbey 353
Nevern 875
Neville's Cross 749

Newark-on-Trent 742
  (1193)
New Brighton 814
Newbury 489 *(1203)*
Newby Hall 793
Newcastle-under-Lyme 671
  (1210)
Newcastle-upon-Tyne 756
  (1200)
Newenden 303
New Forest 353
Newhaven 311 *(1171)*
Newington 253
Newlyn 439
Newmarket 562 *(1192)*
Newport (Dyfed) 875
Newport (Gwent) 851
  (1219)
Newport (IOW) 357
Newquay 458 *(1180)*
New Radnor 871
New Romney 286
Newstead Abbey 624
Newtimber 314
Newton Abbot 417
Newtown (IOW) 358
Newtown (Powys) 876
  (1220)
Ninfield 308
Niton 359 *(1173)*
Norfolk Broads 573
Norham 763
Norman Cross 577, 742
  (1190)
Northallerton 746 *(1109)*
Northampton 601 *(1196)*
Northiam 303
Northleach 711
North Luffenham 620
North Petherton 465
North Shields 760
North Walsham 575
Northwich 799 *(1224)*
Norwich 566 *(1191)*

Nostell Priory 803
Nottingham 622 *(1193)*
Nuneaton 669 *(1209)*
Nunney 513
Nutfield 312

O

Oakham 620 *(1196)*
Odiham 376
Offa's Dyke 871
Ogofau 866
Okehampton 431
Oldbury 280
Oldham 799
Old Romney 287
Old Sarum 385
Old Soar Manor 280
Ollerton 626
Olney 603
Onchan 848
Ore 291
Orford 531
Ormesby Hall 747
Ormskirk 813
Orpington 294
Ortford 295
Oswestry 879
Otham 282
Otley 786
Otterburn 748 *(1201)*
Otterden Place 282
Ottery St Mary 399
Oundle 614
Owletts 245
Oxford 676 *(1207)*

P

Packwood House 697
Padstow 457 *(1180)*
Paignton 418 *(1176)*

Painswick 733
Pangbourne 689 *(1203)*
Parham Park 327
Pateley Bridge 789
Patrington 779
Patterdale 837
Peel (IOM) 847
Pembroke 867 *(1221)*
Penarth 857
Pendennis 436
Penjerrick 436
Penmaenmawr 897
Penmon 883
Penrhyn 882
Penrith 830 *(1229)*
Penryn 436
Pensarn 893
Penshurst 296 *(1166)*
Pentridge 390
Penzance 438 *(1180)*
Pepperbox 386
Perranporth 459 *(1180)*
Pershore 701 *(1211)*
Peterborough 589 *(1190)*
Petersfield 337
Petworth 330
Pevensey 304
Pickering 783
Piddinghoe 299
Plas-yn-Rhiw 887
Plaxtol 280
Plymouth 424 *(1177)*
Plympton 423
Pocklington 775
Polegate 309
Polesden Lacey 320
Pont Aberglaslyn 889
Pontypridd 864
Poole 395 *(1184)*
Porlock 447
Portchester 340
Port Erin 847
Porthcawl 858 *(1218)*
Porthmadog 889 *(1214)*

Port Isaac 455
Portishead 504
Portland, Isle of 392 *(1184)*
Portsmouth 337 *(1172)*
Port Sunlight 814
Port Talbot 858 *(1218)*
Powderham 417
Powis Castle 876
Poynings 314
Poynton 643
Prestbury 642
Presteigne 871
Preston 825 *(1226)*
Princes Risborough 675
Princetown Prison 432
Prittlewell 517
Pulborough 324 *(1171)*
Puttenham 341
Pwllheli 887
Pyecombe 314

Q

Quantock Hills 462
Quarr Abbey 356

R

Raby Castle 831
Raglan 863
Ragley Hall 701
Rainham 253
Rame Head 429
Ramsey (Hunts) 590
Ramsey (IOM) 848 *(1230)*
Ramsgate 271 *(1166)*
Raunds 614
Ravenglass 839
Ravenscar 781
Ravenstone 645
Reading 486 *(1203)*

Reculver 269
Redhill-Reigate 312 *(1163)*
Redmire 829
Redruth 438
Rhayader 872 *(1222)*
Rhiwaedog 880
Rhondda 864
Rhuddlan Castle 893
Rhyl 893 *(1217)*
Ribchester 825
Richborough 272
Richmond 831 *(1199)*
Rievaulx Abbey 784
Ripèley (Notts) 632
Ripley (Surrey) 328
Ripley (Yorks) 789
Ripon 789 *(1199)*
Robertsbridge 300
Robin Hood's Bay 781
Rochdale 824 *(1226)*
Roche Abbey 745
Rochester 245 *(1167)*
Rochford 517
Rockingham 615
Rolvenden 303
Romney Marsh 286
Romsey 377
Rosedale Abbey 784
Roseland 435
Ross-on-Wye 727 *(1212)*
Rothbury 748
Rotherham 745
Rothley Temple 621
Rottingdean 316
Rowsley 633
Royston 541
Ruabon 879
Rufford 813
Rufford Abbey 626
Rugby 668 *(1209)*
Rugeley 650
Runswick 782
Rushton 615
Rushton Marsh 642

Ruthin 891 *(1216)*
Rydal 842
Ryde (IOW) 355
Rye 288 *(1171)*

S

Saffron Walden 562 *(1189)*
Salcombe 421 *(1177)*
Salisbury 378 *(1187)*
Salisbury Hall 604
Saltburn 782
Saltergate 783
Saltfleet 595
Saltwood Castle 285
Salvington 322
Sandbach 794
Sanderstead 306
Sandown 360 *(1173)*
Sandringham 538
Sandwich 273 *(1176)*
Sark, Is. 369 *(1174)*
Sawston Hall 562
Scarborough 781 *(1199)*
Scawby 745
Scilly Is. 439 *(1181)*
Scrivelsby 581
Scrooby 743
Scunthorpe 744 *(1193)*
Seaford 310 *(1171)*
Seale 341
Sedbergh 829
Sedgefield 754
Sedgemoor 465
Sedlescombe Street 302
Selby 765 *(1199)*
Selling 256
Selsdon 306
Selsey Bill 336
Selworthy 448
Sennen Cove 440
Serlby Hall 743
Sevenoaks 294 *(1167)*

Seven Sisters 310
Severn Bridge 731
Shaftesbury 400 *(1184)*
Shanklin (IOW) 360
Shap 830
Sharpness 717
Sheerness 254
Sheffield 804 *(1199)*
Shefford 613
Shepton Mallet 475
Sherborne 401 *(1184)*
Shere 330
Sheringham 536 *(1191)*
Sherwood Forest 621
Shifnal 671
Sholden 274
Shoreham-by-Sea 316
Shottery 696
Shrewsbury 652 *(1213)*
Sible Hedingham 553
Sidmouth 399 *(1177)*
Silbury Hill 493
Silchester 488
Silloth 841
Silverstone 657
Sinnington 784
Sithney 443
Sittingbourne 254
Sizergh Castle 829
Skegness 595 *(1193)*
Skipton 787 *(1199)*
Sleaford 580
Slindon 327
Slinfold 324
Slough 477 *(1204)*
Snettisham 537
Snowdon 888
Sole Street 245
Solva 868
Somersby 581
Somerton 581
Sompting 322
Sonning 485
Southampton 349 *(1173)*

Southchurch 748
Southease 299
Southend-on-Sea 517
  (1189)
South Molton 450
Southport 813 *(1226)*
Southsea 338
South Shields 759 *(1202)*
Southwell 626 *(1194)*
Southwick 316
Southwold 532 *(1192)*
Spalding 593
Speen 490
Spilsby 595
Springfield 523
Stafford 649 *(1210)*
Staines 373 *(1163)*
Staithes 782
Stalybridge 799
Stamford 577 *(1193)*
Stanford Hall 669
Stanton Harcourt 710
Stapleford Park 620
Stevenage 739 *(1206)*
Steventon 688
Steyning 321
Stilton 616, 741
Stockbridge 377
Stockport 643 *(1224)*
Stockton-on-Tees 747
  (1202)
Stogursey 462
Stoke 252
Stoke Bruerne 644
Stoke-on-Trent 672
Stoke Poges 477
Stokesay Castle 720
Stoke-sub-Hamdon 403
Stone 244
Stonecross 300
Stone Cross 746
Stonehenge 385
Stoneleigh Abbey 664
Stoney Middleton 634

Storrington 327
Stourhead 415
Stow-on-the Wold 699
  (1186)
Stowe School 657
Stowmarket 564
Strata Florida Abbey 873
Stratford-on-Avon 691
  (1209)
Stratford St Mary 529
Stroud 733 *(1186)*
Studland 396
Studley 701
Stuntney 559
Sudbury 566 *(1192)*
Sulgrave Manor 658
Sunderland 747 *(1202)*
Sutton-at-Hone 279
Sutton Coldfield 668
  (1209)
Sutton (Dover) 274
Sutton Place 328
Swaffham 576
Swalecliffe 269
Swanage 394 *(1184)*
Swansea 858 *(1218)*
Swanton Morley 576
Swimbridge 450
Swindon 690 *(1187)*
Swineshead 580
Symonds Yat 728 *(1212)*

St

St Agnes 459
St Albans 604 *(1205)*
St Asaph 892
St Audries 463
St Austell 435 *(1180)*
St Clears 866
St Davids 868 *(1221)*
St Dogmaels 875
St Eval 813

St Helens 813 *(1226)*
St Helier 366 *(1174)*
St Ippolitts 611
St Ives (Cornwall) 440 *(1181)*
St Ives (Hunts) 741 *(1190)*
St Mary-in-the Marsh 286
St Mary's Bay 286
St Mary's Cray 294
St Mawes 436 *(1181)*
St Michael's Mount 441
St Neots 740 *(1190)*
St Osyth 528
St Peter Port 363 *(1174)*
St Peter's 271
St Tudy 456

T

Talley Abbey 866
Tamworth 645
Tandridge 307
Tangley Manor 330
Tankerton 269
Tarring 322
Tattershall 580
Taunton 460 *(1183)*
Tavistock 432 *(1177)*
Teignmouth 417 *(1177)*
Tenbury Wells 721
Tenby 866 *(1221)*
Tenterden 303
Tesson 368
Tewkesbury 718 *(1186)*
Teynham 255
Thame 676 *(1207)*
Thanet, Isle of 272
Thaxted 561
Theddlethorpe 595
Thetford 565 *(1191)*
Thirsk 746 *(1199)*
Thoresby House 626
Thorington Hall 566

Thornbury 718
Thornton Abbey 779
Thornton-le-Dale 783
Throwley 255
Tichborne 342
Tideswell 634
Tintagel 455 *(1181)*
Tintern Abbey 730 *(1219)*
Tintinhull 404
Tiptree 524
Tisbury 415
Titchfield 340
Tiverton 450
Tolpuddle 395
Tonbridge 296 *(1167)*
Tong 671
Topsham 413
Torquay 418 *(1178)*
Totnes 418
Towcester 644
Towyn 877
Tresco, Is. 439
Tretower 864
Tring 656
Troutbeck 837
Trowbridge 512
Truro 436 *(1181)*
Tunbridge Wells 297 *(1167)*
Tunstall 828
Turton Tower 823
Tuxford 742
Twineham 313
Tynemouth 760

U

Uckfield 298
Ullswater 837 *(1228)*
Ulverston 838
Upchurch 255
Upnor 252
Uppingham 619 *(1196)*
Upton House 658

Usk 863
Uttoxeter 672

V

Valle Crucis Abbey 880
Ventnor (IOW) 359 *(1174)*
Veryan 435
Vyne, The 376

W

Waddesdon Manor 657
Wadebridge 456
Wainfleet 594
Wakefield 803 *(1200)*
Walberswick 532
Waldershare 267
Wall 649 *(1201)*
Wallasey 814
Wallingford 689
Wallsend 759
Walmer 274
Waltham Abbey 242
Waltham Cross 541
Waltham-on-the-Wolds 620
Walton-on-the-Naze 529
Wanborough 341
Wantage 688
Wareham 394
Warkworth 761
Warmington 614
Warminster 514 *(1187)*
Warrington 813 *(1226)*
Warwick 658 *(1210)*
Wash, The 592
Washford 463
Washington 321 *(1202)*
Wastwater 839
Watchet 463
Watford 655 *(1206)*
Waverley 342

Wednesbury 670
Welbeck Abbey 625
Wellingborough 602 *(1196)*
Wellington (Salop) 650
  (1213)
Wellington (Somerset) 460
Wells 471 *(1183)*
Wells-next-the-Sea 536
Welshpool 876 *(1220)*
Welwyn Garden City 738
  (1206)
Wendover 656
Wendron 443
Wenhaston 532
Wentworth Woodhouse 745
West Bromwich 669
Westbury-on-Trym 718
Westdean 310
West Humble 319
West Malling 281 *(1167)*
Weston-in-Gordano 504
Weston Park 671
Weston-super-Mare 466
  (1183)
Westward Ho 453
West Wycombe 675
Weybridge 373 *(1163)*
Weymouth 391 *(1184)*
Whaley Bridge 641
Whalley 826
Whatstandwell 632
Whippingham 356
Whipsnade 598
Whitby 782 *(1200)*
Whitchurch (Hants) 490
Whitchurch (Salop) 822
Whitehaven 840
Whitley Abbey 664
Whitley Bay 760
Whitstable-Tankerton 268
Wicken 559
Widecombe 422
Wight, Isle of 355
Wightwick Manor 670

Wilberhope Manor 720
Williton 462
Wilmcote 696
Wilmington 300
Wilton 400
Wimborne Minster 396
Winchcombe 711 *(1186)*
Winchelsea 290 *(1171)*
Winchester 342 *(1173)*
Windermere 836 *(1228)*
Windsor 478 *(1204)*
Wingfield 632
Wingham 267
Winscombe 468
Winslow 656
Winster 633
Wirksworth 632
Wisbech 596 *(1189)*
Wisley 328
Wiston 321
Withernsea 779
Witney 710
Woburn Abbey 600 *(1203)*
Wokingham 487 *(1204)*
Wolverhampton 670 *(1210)*
Woodchester 733
Woodhall Spa 580 *(1193)*
Woodlands 889
Woodnesborough 274
Woodstock 691 *(1207)*

Wookey Hole 467
Wool 393
Wooler 763
Woolsthorpe Manor 579
Wootton Hall 637
Worcester 702 *(1211)*
Workington 840
Worksop 625
Worthing 322 *(1172)*
Wortley 803
Wothorpe 615
Wrexham 879 *(1216)*
Wrotham 280
Wroxeter 651
Wylam-on-Tyne 748
Wymondham 566

Y

Yarm 747
Yarmouth (IOW) 358
Yarmouth (Norfolk) 533
Yeovil 402 *(1183)*
York 765 *(1200)*

Z

Zennor 440

III. SCOTLAND

A

Abbotsford 938
Aberdeen 1009 *(1245)*
Abercairney 998
Aberdour 950 *(1234)*
Aberfeldy 997
Aberfoyle 996 *(1240)*
Abergeldie Castle 1003
Aberlady 902
Abernethy 956

Aboyne 1003
Achfary 1038
Achnasheen 1035 *(1254)*
Achvarasdale 1042
Affleck Castle 1006
Ailsa Craig 979
Alford 1025
Allardice Castle 1007
Alloa 954
Alloway 977
Alness 936
Altnacealgach 1037

Altnaharra 1039
Alyth 1008
Annan 966
Anstruther 953
Applecross 1035
Arbigland 967
Arbroath 1006
Ardgour 1030
Ardnamurchan 1030
7904 signes
Ardrishaig 988 *(1247)*
Ardrossan 975
Ardvreck Castle 1037
Argyll 983
Arisaig 1030
Arran, Is. 976 *(1231)*
Arrochar 985 *(1232)*
Ashiesteel 942
Auchindown Castle 1024
Auchterarder 948 *(1240)*
Auchtermuchty 954
Auldearn 1021 *(1253)*
Aviemore 1017 *(1250)*
Ayr 977 *(1230)*

B

Balcomie Castle 953
Ballachulish 1031 *(1247)*
Ballantrae 979
Ballater 1003 *(1245)*
Balloch 984 *(1232)*
Balmacara 1028
Balmoral 1002
Balquhain Castle 1026
Balquhidder 997
Balvenie Castle 1024
Banchory 1003 *(1252)*
Banff 1023 *(1249)*
Bannockburn 944, 947
Barra, Is. 995
Barra Castle 1026
Bealach nàm Ba 1035

Bearsden 996 *(1233)*
Beauly 1033 *(1250)*
Ben Nevis 1029
Berriedale 1039
Bettyhill 1042
Biggar 930
Birsay 1044
Blackford 948
Black Isle 1033
Blackness Castle 943
Bladnoch 969
Blair Atholl 1016 *(1240)*
Blairgowrie 1000 *(1240)*
Blantyre 957
Boat of Garten 1025
Bonar Bridge 1037 *(1255)*
Bo'ness 943
Bonhill 984
Borthwick Castle 957
Bowhill 933
Braemar 1002 *(1246)*
Brander, Pass 986
Branxholm 933
Brechin 1008
Bridge of Allan 947 *(1243)*
Bridge of Feugh 1004
Brig o' Doon 977
Broadford 993
Brodick 976
Brora 1039 *(1255)*
Broughty Ferry 1006 *(1246)*
Buckhaven 952
Burleigh Castle 956
Burnswark 931
Burntisland 950
Bute, Is. 974 *(1231)*

C

Cadzow Castle 957
Caerlaverock Castle 967
Cairngorm 1017

Cairnryan 980
Caledonian Canal 1027
Callander 997 *(1240)*
Callanish 995
Cambuskenneth Abbey 947
Campbell, Castle 954
Campbeltown 988 *(1247)*
Cannich 1033 *(1250)*
Canonbie 934
Cardoness Castle 968
Cardross 984
Carnoustie 1006 *(1246)*
Carrbridge 1017 *(1250)*
Carter Bar 940
Castlebay 995
Castle Douglas 967 *(1235)*
Castletown 1041
Catrine 971
Cawdor Castle 1021
Chatelherault 957
Clachnaharry 1020
Clava, Stones 1020
Clovenfords 942
Clydebank 983 *(1223)*
Clyne 1039
Coldingham 901
Coll, Is. 991
Colonsay, Is. 992
Comrie 998
Connel Ferry 1032
Conon Bridge 1043
Corra Castle 957
Corrie 976
Coupar Angus 1008
Cowdenbeath 956
Craigellachie 1024
Craigenputtock 970
Craigmillar Castle 902, 934
Crail 953
Cramond 928
Crask 1039
Crathes Castle 1004
Crathie 1003
Creagan 1013

Crianlarich 986 *(1240)*
Crieff 998 *(1240)*
Cromarty 1033
Crossraguel Abbey 979
Cuillin Hills 993
Cullen 1023 *(1249)*
Culloden 1020
Culross 950
Culzean Castle 979
Cumnock 971
Cupar 954

D

Dalbeattie 967
Dalhousie Castle 932
Dalkeith 943 *(1237)*
Dalmally 986
Dalmellington 968
Dalmeny 949
Dalry 976 *(1235)*
Dalwhinnie 1016
Denholm 933
Devil's Elbow 1002
Dingwall 1034 *(1254)*
Dinnet 1003
Dirrie More 1034
Dollar 954 *(1232)*
Dornoch 1038 *(1255)*
Doune 997 *(1240)*
Dounreay 1041
Drum Castle 1004
Drumlanrig Castle 970
Drumnadrochit 1027
  (1250)
Drumochter Pass 1016
Dryburgh Abbey 936
Dryhope Tower 933
Duart Castle 990
Dufftown 1024 *(1250)*
Dumbarton 983 *(1233)*
Dumfries 966 *(1232)*
Dunbar 901 *(1233)*

Dunbeath 1040
Dunblane 948 *(1240)*
Duncansby Head 1040
Dundee 1004 *(1247)*
Dundonnell 1036
Dundrennan Abbey 968
Dunfermline 949 *(1234)*
Dunkeld 1015 *(1241)*
Dunnet Head 1041
Dunnottar Castle 1007
Dunollie Castle 987
Dunoon 985 *(1247)*
Dunrobin Castle 1039
Duns 935
Dunscore 970
Dunstaffnage Castle 987
Duntreath Castle 996
Dunure 977
Dunvegan Castle 994
Dupplin Castle 1000
Durness 1042
Duror 1013

E

Ecclefechan 931
Eday, Is. 1046
Edderton 1037
Edinburgh 903 *(1237)*
Ednam 939
Eglinton Castle 976
Eilean Donan Castle 1028
Elcho Castle 1000
Elgin 1021 *(1253)*
Elie and Earlsferry 952
  (1234)
Ellisland 967
Ellon 1024 *(1246)*
Elphin 1037
Elphinstone 902
Eyemouth 901
Eynhallow, Is. 1046

F

Fair Isle 1046
Fairlie 975
Falkirk 943 *(1243)*
Falkland Palace 954
Fatlips Castle 933
Fawside Castle 902
Ferniehirst Castle 939
Fettercairn 1009
Findhorn 1021 *(1253)*
Findlater Castle 1023
Fingal's Cave 991
Floors Castle 939
Fochabers 1022 *(1253)*
Forbes, Castle 1025
Forfar 1008 *(1247)*
Forres 1021 *(1253)*
Forss 1041
Fort Augustus 1028
  (1251)
Forth Bridges 949
Fortrose 1033
Fort William 1029 *(1251)*
Foula, Is. 1046
Fowlis Wester 998
Fraserburgh 1023 *(1246)*
Fyvie Castle 1026

G

Gairloch 1036 *(1254)*
Galashiels 932 *(1243)*
Ganavan 987
Garelochhead 984
Garlieston 969
Gatehouse of Fleet 968
  (1235)
Gifford 935
Girvan 979
Glamis 1008
Glasgow 957 *(1235)*
Glen Affric 1033

Glencaple 967
Glencoe 1032 *(1247)*
Gleneagles 948
Glen Etive 1032
Glenfinnan 1030
Glenluce 969
Glenshee 1002 *(1241)*
Glen Shiel 1028
Golspie 1039 *(1255)*
Gourock 974 *(1242)*
Grangemouth 943 *(1243)*
Granton 902
Grantown-on-Spey 1024
   (1253)
Great Glen 1027
Greenloaning 948
Greenock 974 *(1242)*
Gretna Green 932 *(1232)*
Gullane 902

H

Haddington 902 *(1233)*
Hamilton 957 *(1237)*
Handa, Is. 1038
Harlaw 1026
Harris, Is. 995 *(1251)*
Hawick 933
Hebrides, Is. 989
Helensburgh 984 *(1233)*
Helmsdale 1039
Hermitage Castle 934
Hill of Fearn 1037
Hoddam Castle 931
Hopetoun House 943
Hoy, Is. 1045
Huna 1041
Hunter House 963
Hunter's Quay 985
Huntingtower Castle 1000
Huntly 1025 *(1246)*
Huntly Castle 1004

I

Inchcolm, Is. 950
Inchmahome Priory 996
Inchnadamph 1037 *(1255)*
Ingliston 928
Innerleithen 942 *(1239)*
Innerpeffray 998
Inveraray 985 *(1247)*
Invergarry 1028 *(1251)*
Invergordon 1037
Inverkeithing 950, 956
Inverlochy Castle 1029
Invermoriston 1027 *(1251)*
Inverness 1018 *(1251)*
Invershin 1037
Inverurie 1025
Iona, Is. 990 *(1248)*
Irvine 976
Islay, Is. 991 *(1248)*

J

Jarlshof 1047
Jedburgh 939 *(1243)*
John o' Groats 1040
   (1250)
Jura, Is. 992 *(1248)*

K

Kames Castle 975
Keith 1024 *(1250)*
Kelso 938 *(1243)*
Kenmore 997 *(1241)*
Kenmure Castle 968
Kilchurn Castle 986
Kildrummy Castle 1025
Killiecrankie, Pass 1015
   (1241)
Killin 997 *(1241)*
Kilmarnock 972 *(1230)*

Kilwinning 976
Kincardine 944
Kincardine O'Neil 1003
Kincraig 1017
Kinfauns Castle 1000
Kinghorn 951
Kingshouse 1032
Kingussie 1016 *(1252)*
Kinlochewe 1035
Kinlochleven 1013
Kinloch Rannoch 1015 *(1241)*
Kinnaird 1004
Kinneil House 943
Kinross 956 *(1234)*
Kirkcaldy 951 *(1234)*
Kirkconnel 931, 971
Kirkcowan 969
Kirkcudbright 968 *(1235)*
Kirkhope 933
Kirhoswald 979
Kirkwall 1044 *(1255)*
Kirriemuir 1008
Kyleakin 993
Kyle of Lochalsh 1028 *(1254)*
Kylesku 1038

L

Laide 1036
Lairg 1038 *(1255)*
Lamington 930
Lamlash 976
Lanark 957 *(1237)*
Langholm 934
Largo 952
Largs 975 *(1230)*
Laurencekirk 1009
Laxford Bridge 1038
Leadhills 970
Leith 902, 926
Lendalfoot 979

Lerwick 1046 *(1256)*
Leuchars 954
Leven 952 *(1234)*
Lewis, Is. 995 *(1254)*
Lincluden Abbey 966
Linlithgow 943
Lismore, Is. 1013
Little Clyde 930
Loch Awe 985 *(1248)*
Loch Broom 1035
Loch Carron 1035
Lochearnhead 997 *(1241)*
Loch Etive 986
Loch Ewe 1036
Lochgilphead 988 *(1248)*
Loch Hope 1042
Lochinch Castle 970
Lochinver 1037 *(1255)*
Loch Katrine 996
Loch Leven (Argyll) 1031
Loch Leven (Kinross) 956
Loch Lomond 984
Lochmaben 931
Loch Maree 1036
Loch Ness 1027
Lochranza 976
Loch Shiel 1030
Loch Tay 997
Lockerbie 931 *(1232)*
Lossiemouth 1022
Loudon Castle 974
Lunan 1007
Lundin Links 952
Luss 984
Lybster 1040
Lyne 942

M

Macduff 1023
Machrihanish 988
Maeshowe 1045
Maidens 979

Mallaig 1030 *(1252)*
Mauchline 971
May, Is. 953
Maybole 979
Meigle 1008
Melrose 937 *(1243)*
Melvich 1042
Methil 952
Mey, Castle of 1041
Milnathort 956
Milngavie 996 *(1233)*
Moffat 930 *(1232)*
Moniaive 970
Montrose 1007 *(1247)*
Monzie Castle 998
Morar 1030
Morton Castle 970
Morven 1030
Mossgiel 971
Mosspaul 934
Mote of Urr 967
Moy Hall 1017
Muir of Ord 1033
Mull, Is. 990 *(1248)*
Musselburgh 902

N

Nairn 1021 *(1253)*
Neidpath Castle 941
Newbattle 935
New Galloway 968 *(1235)*
Newhaven 927
New Lanark 957
Newstead 932
Newton Don 939
Newtonmore 1016 *(1252)*
Newton Stewart 969 *(1244)*
Ninemileburn 930
Nisbet House 935
North Berwick 901 *(1233)*
North Queensferry 949

O

Oban 987 *(1248)*
Ochtertyre 998
Ogilvie Castle 948
Oldmeldrum 1026
Orkney Is. 1044
Ormiston 935
Oronsay, Is. 992
Oykell Bridge 1037

P

Paisley 963 *(1242)*
Peebles 941 *(1239)*
Penicuik 941
Perth 999 *(1241)*
Peterhead 1023 *(1246)*
Pierowall 1046
Pitlochry 1015 *(1241)*
Pitmedden 1024
Pittenweem 953
Plockton 1035
Pluscarden Priory 1022
Poolewe 1036 *(1254)*
Port Appin 1013 *(1249)*
Portincross Castle 975
Portmahomack 1037
Portobello 927
Portpatrick 980 *(1244)*
Portree 994
Portsoy 1023
Port William 970
Prestonpans 902
Prestwick 977 *(1230)*

R

Reay 1042
Renfrew 974 *(1242)*
Renton 984
Rosemarkie 1033

Roslin 941
Rosyth 956
Rothesay 975
Rousay, Is. 1046
Roxburgh 939

S

Sanday, Is. 1046
Sanquhar 975
Sauchie 944
Scalloway 1047
Scapa Flow 1045
Scone Palace 1000
Scourie 1038 *(1255)*
Scrabster 1041
Selkirk 932 *(1243)*
Sheriffmuir 948
Shetland Is.
Shieldaig 1035
Skara Brae 1044
Skiag Bridge 1037
Skibo Castle 1038
Skye, Is. 992 *(1252)*
Sligachan 993
Sma' Glen 998
Smailholm Tower 939
Smoo Cave 1042
Sorn 971
Southend 988
South Queensferry 949
   (1244)
Spean Bridge 1029 *(1252)*
Staffa, Is. 991
Staffin 994
Stenness 1045 *(1256)*
Stirling 944 *(1243)*
Stobs 934
Stonehaven 1007 *(1253)*
Stornoway 995
Stow 932
Stranraer 980 *(1244)*
Strathpeffer 1034 *(1254)*

Strathyre 997
Stroma, Is.
Strome Ferry 1035
Stromness 1044
Stronsay, Is. 1046
Sumburgh 1047 *(1256)*
Sweetheart Abbey 967
Sweno's Stone 1021

St

St Andrews 953 *(1234)*
St Boswells 935 *(1243)*
St Fillans 998 *(1242)*
St Margaret's Hope 1045
St Monance 952

T

Tain 1037
Tarbert 988 *(1249)*
Tarbet 984 *(1233)*
Tay Bridge 954
Terpersie Castle 1025
Thirlestane 933
Thornhill 970 *(1232)*
Threave Castle 967
Thurso 1041 *(1250)*
Tiree, Is. 991 *(1249)*
Tobermory 990
Tomintoul 1025 *(1250)*
Tongue 1042 *(1255)*
Torridon 1036 *(1254)*
Torwoodlee 932
Tranent 902
Traquair House 942
Troon 977 *(1230)*
Trossachs 996 *(1242)*
Turnberry 979
Turriff 1026
Tyndrum 986 *(1242)*
Tynninghame 901

U

Uist, Is. 995 *(1252)*
Ullapool 1035 *(1254)*
Urquhart, Castle 1027

W

Wanlockhead 970
Wemyss Bay 974

Westray, Is. 1046
Whithorn 969
Wick 1040 *(1250)*
Wigtown 969 *(1244)*
Wrath, Cape 1042

Y

Yester Castle 935

This Encyclopedia-Guide has been set, printed and bound
by Nagel Publishers in Geneva (Switzerland)

Legal Deposit N° 760

Printed in Switzerland

Great Britain
Grande-Bretagne
Großbritannien

Central London .... II–V

Central Liverpool .... VI–VII

Central Manchester....... VIII–IX

Birmingham .... X–XI

Glasgow .... XII–XIII

Edinburgh .... XIV–XV

CARTOGRAPHIE NAGEL

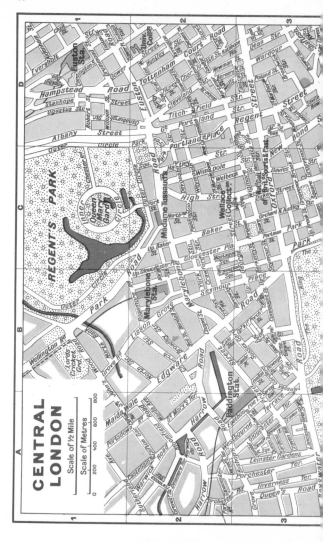

CENTRAL LONDON

Scale of ½ Mile

Scale of Metres

0   200   400   600   800

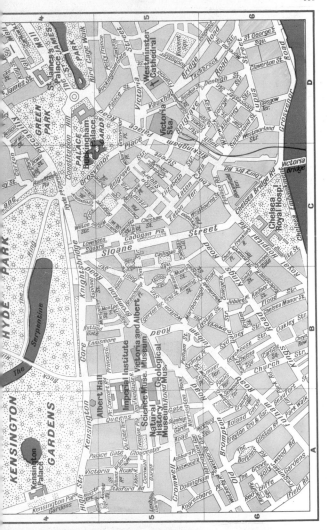

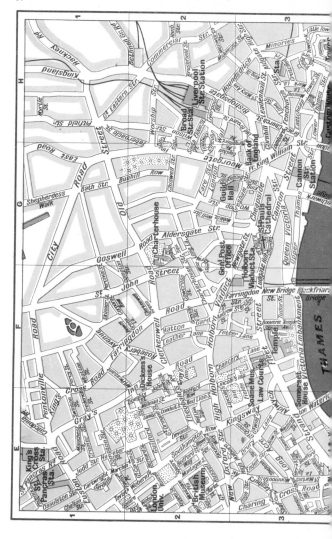

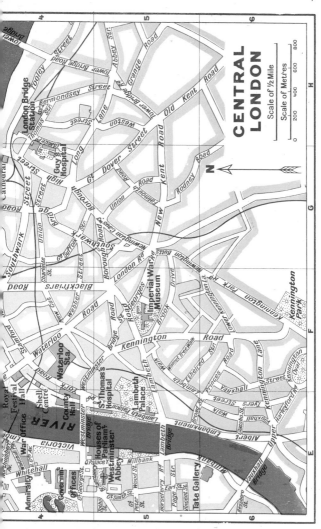

CENTRAL LONDON

Scale of ½ Mile

Scale of Metres

0   200   400   600   800

N

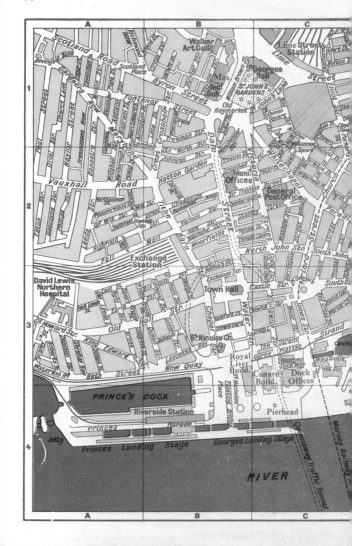

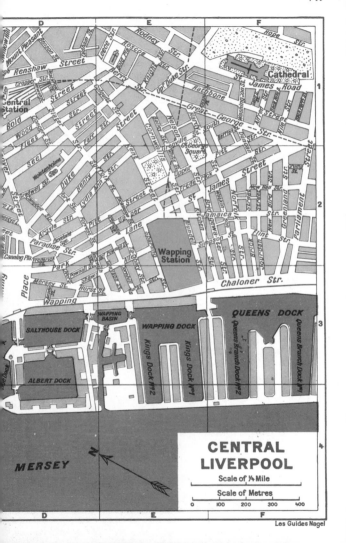

CENTRAL
LIVERPOOL

Scale of ¼ Mile

Scale of Metres

0   100   200   300   400

Les Guides Nagel

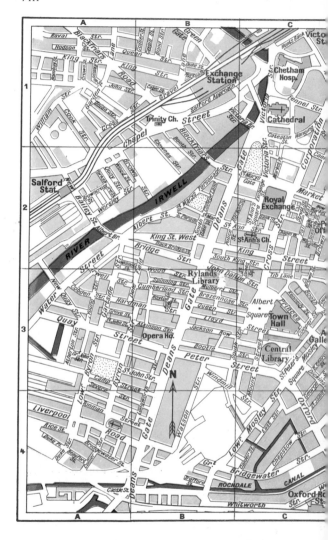

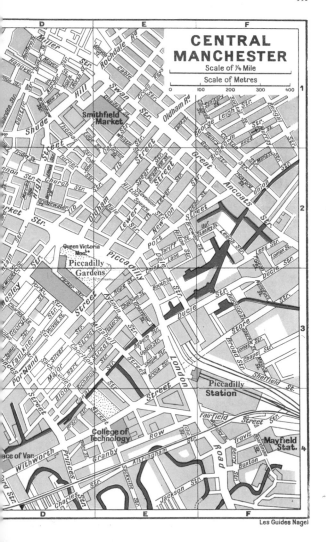

CENTRAL
MANCHESTER

Scale of ¼ Mile

Scale of Metres

0   100   200   300   400

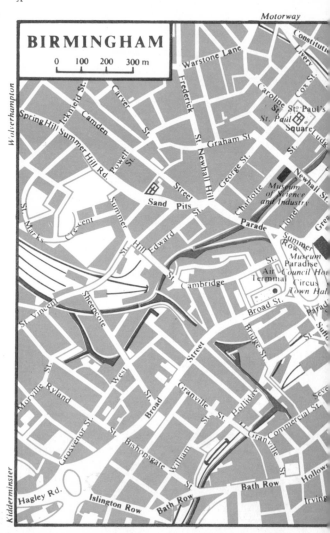

BIRMINGHAM

0   100   200   300 m

Motorway

Constituti...
Livery

Warstone Lane

Frederick

Carver

Caroline St.
Cox St.

Camden

Spring Hill Icknield St.

Summer Hill Rd.

Powell

St.

St. Paul's
St. Paul
Square

Ludg...

Graham St.

George St.

Newhall St.

Charlotte

Museum
of Science
and Industry

Street

Newhall Hill

Sand Pits

Summer Hill

Parade

Lionel

Gre...

St.

St. Hill Edward

Cambridge

Summer
Row
Museum
Paradise
Council Ho...
Circus
Town Hall

St.
Air
Terminal

St. Vincent

Sheepcote

Broad St.

Parad...

St. Marks

Crescent

Bridge St.

Suff...

Morville Ryland

West

St.

Granville

St.

St.

Broad

Crosvenor St.

Bishopsgate

Holliday

Granville

Commercial St.

Seve...

Wilham

St.

Hagley Rd.

Islington Row

Bath Row

Bath Row

Hollow...

Irving...

Wolverhampton

Kidderminster

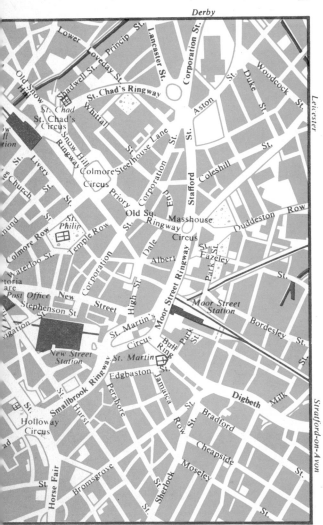

Leicester

Stratford-on-Avon

Worcester

Lower Loveday St.
Princip St.
Lancaster St.
Corporation St.
Woodcock St.
Duke St.
Aston St.
Old Snow Hill
Shadwell St.
St. Chad's Ringway
Whittall St.
St. Chad
St. Chad's Circus
Snow Hill Ringway
Steelhouse Lane
St.
St.
Coleshill St.
Livery St.
Colmore Circus
Priory
Corporation St.
Stafford St.
Duddeston Row
'm tion
es Church
St.
und
St. Philip
Temple Row
Old Sq.
Masshouse Circus
Ringway
St. Fazeley St.
Colmore Row
St.
Dale
Albert
Park
Waitloo St.
Corporation
High St.
Moor Street Ringway
toria are
Post Office
New
Street
St.
Moor Street Station
Bordesley St.
Stephenson St.
vigation
St. Martin's Circus
Park St.
St.
New Street Station
Bull Ring
St. Martin
Digbeth
Milk
Smallbrook Ringway
Edgbaston St.
Jamaica Row
St.
St.
Bradford
St.
Holloway Circus
St. Hurst
Pershore St.
St.
Cheapside
ad
Horse Fair
Bromsgrove
Sherlock
Moseley
St.
St.

GLASGOW

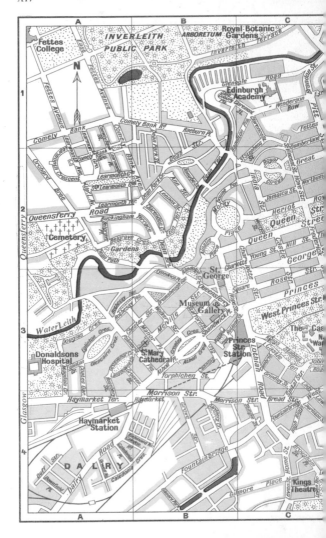

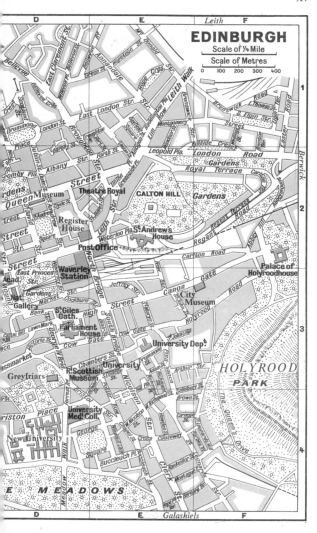

XV

EDINBURGH

Scale of ¼ Mile

Scale of Metres

0   100   200   300   400

Leith

Leith Walk

Berwick

McDonald

East Claremont Str.

Bellevue

East London Str.

Annandale

Hopetoun

Green Side

Greenside Cres.

Brunswick Street

Brunswick Road

S. Elgin Str.

Thomas Str.

Easter Road

London St.

Drummond

Dublin St.

Forth Str.

Broughton

Elm Row

Montgomery Str.

Hillside Cres.

London   Road

Leopold Pla.

Gardens

Royal   Terrace

Romby Pla.

Albany   Str.

Queen   Street

Museum

Theatre Royal

CALTON HILL

Gardens

Regent Terrace

Abbey Hill

Register House

Union

S. Andrew
Square

S. Andrews
House

Waterloo Pla.

Regent Road

Post Office

Carlton Road

East Princes
Str.

Waverley
Station

Jeffrey Str.

Canon   Gate

Holyrood Road

Palace of
Holyroodhouse

Acad.

Nat.
Gallery

Market

Bank

Cockburn Str.

Cow Gate

City
Museum

Castle Hill

S. Giles
Cath.

High   Street

South Bridge

St. Johns Hill

HOLYROOD

Lawn Mark.

Parliament
House

George IV Br.

Victoria Str.

Cow   Gate

Chambers Str.

Drummond Str.

University Dept.

Nicolson

Arthur Str.

Salisbury Str.

PARK

The Queen's Drive

assmarket

Greyfriars

R. Scottish
Museum

University

Bristo St.

Nicolson   Str.

Brown Str.

riston

Place

University
Med. Coll.

George   Square

Lothian

Buccleuch Pl.

Clerk   Str.

Rankeillor Str.

Montague Str.

New University

Meadow   Walk

MEADOWS

Galashiels

D   E   F

1

2

3

4

Gedruckt in der Schweiz – Imprimé en Suisse
Printed in Switzerland